PENGUIN POPU

POCKET SPI

C000045951

POCKET
SPELLING
DICTIONARY

SECOND EDITION

MARKET HOUSE BOOKS

PENGUIN BOOKS

PENGUIN BOOKS

Published by the Penguin Group
Penguin Books Ltd, 80 Strand, London WC2R 0RL, England
Penguin Putnam Inc., 375 Hudson Street, New York, New York 10014, USA
Penguin Books Australia Ltd, 250 Camberwell Road, Camberwell, Victoria 3124, Australia
Penguin Books Canada Ltd, 10 Alcorn Avenue, Toronto, Ontario, Canada M4V 3B2
Penguin Books India (P) Ltd, 11 Community Centre, Panchsheel Park, New Delhi – 110 017, India
Penguin Books (NZ) Ltd, Cnr Rosedale and Airborne Roads, Albany, Auckland, New Zealand
Penguin Books (South Africa) (Pty) Ltd, 24 Sturdee Avenue, Rosebank 2196, South Africa

Penguin Books Ltd, Registered Offices: 80 Strand, London WC2R 0RL, England

www.penguin.com

First published as *The Penguin Spelling Dictionary* 1990
Second edition 1999
Reissued under the present title 2001
2

Typeset in Linotype Stone
Typeset by Market House Books Ltd
Printed in England by Clays Ltd, St Ives plc

CONTENTS

PREFACE TO THE FIRST EDITION

English is a difficult language to spell correctly – and not only for the foreigner. Native speakers, too, find it hard. The problem is that modern English is such a rich and resourceful language, derived from so many sources, that its spelling does not obey simple rules. Although much of the language *is* regular, in the sense that it does obey rules, there are very large numbers of exceptions to the common patterns. While the only safe way to be sure of a spelling is to look it up in this dictionary, the basic rules are given on the following pages.

The *Pocket Spelling Dictionary* is divided into three sections: the main spelling list; a list of first names; and a list of biographical names.

Spelling list

This, the largest section, contains normal vocabulary words, place names, some trademarks, and biblical and mythological names not included in the names lists (see below). Unhyphenated two-word compounds (e.g. phrasal verbs and nouns) are usually not listed, as each element will have its own entry. Exceptions include compounds with irregular inflections (see below) and some eponymous terms (terms derived from the name of a person), in which both elements are included as an aid to the sense.

Centred dots within a word indicate the points at which it can be hyphenated. These divisions are phonetic, rather than etymological, and correspond to syllabification breaks; note, however, that when syllabification breaks are not acceptable as hyphenation points they are not shown. Monosyllabic words should never be hyphenated, nor – if possible – should people's names.

Inflections (changes in the form of a word to indicate changes in grammatical function) are included if they are irregular. In general, regular inflections are not included. For rules on the formation of regular and irregular inflections, see under **The Rules of Spelling** on the following pages.

US spellings and British variant spellings are included after the preferred spelling of the word; they also have their own entries, with an appropriate gloss, if they are widely separated alphabetically from the preferred spelling.

Short glosses are provided for unfamiliar words and to avoid confusion between similarly spelt or pronounced words. Most of the proper names in this section are also glossed.

A few common misspellings are included in the list. These words are bracketed and the correct spelling indicated.

First names

This section comprises a comprehensive list of English first names, together with their spelling variants. It does not include the more obscure biblical and mythological names (many of which are listed in the main section of the dictionary) or the names of monarchs and other rulers that are unfamiliar or foreign (many of these are listed under the biographical names).

Biographical names

This section includes the names of people from all countries, past and present, who have achieved fame in some sphere of human activity. Monarchs are generally not included if their names appear in the first names list. Biographical names are listed in alphabetical order of the surname, followed by first names and any titles; the less familiar names of a subject are bracketed. Variant spellings and pseudonyms are also listed, and similar names are glossed to avoid confusion.

PREFACE TO THE SECOND EDITION

The response to the first edition of the *Pocket Spelling Dictionary*, published in 1990, has been so encouraging that the publishers have decided to produce a revised edition.

Although most standard spellings have not changed over the past ten years, geographical references have been updated to account for such events as the collapse of the Soviet Union, the renaming of Zaïre, and local government reorganization in the UK. We have added a number of new words, reflecting changes in areas as diverse as politics, popular culture, and medicine. We have also included terms that have become more widespread, such as database and organophosphate.

The biographical appendix has been expanded to include major figures who have risen to prominence during the past decade.

Our aim has been to ensure that the *Pocket Spelling Dictionary* continues to be an up-to-date, useful, and comprehensive book.

THE RULES OF SPELLING

Nouns

Regular inflections

Regular plurals are formed by adding -s; for nouns ending in -s, -x, -z, -ch, or -sh, add -es.

Irregular inflections

1. Nouns of Latin origin ending in -a, especially in scientific or technical usage, usually have the plural ending -ae (e.g. **alga/algae; nebula/nebulae**).

   Such nouns ending in -ma usually have the plural ending -mata (e.g. **stoma/stomata**).

2. Nouns ending in -f either form regular plurals (e.g. **chief/chiefs**) or have the plural ending -ves (e.g. **calf/calves**).

   Most nouns ending in -fe form regular plurals (e.g. **safe/safes**) but a few have the plural ending -ves (e.g. **wife/wives**).

3. Nouns ending in -i usually form regular plurals but a few have the plural ending -ies (e.g. **chilli/chillies**).

4. Nouns ending in -is either form regular plurals (e.g. **iris/irises**) or have the plural ending -es (e.g. **basis/bases**). Some scientific and technical nouns have the plural ending -ides (e.g. **apsis/apsides**).

5. Most nouns ending in -o either form regular plurals (e.g. **albino/albinos**) or have the plural ending -oes (e.g. **tomato/tomatoes**). Nouns of Italian origin have the plural form -i, either as the only plural or as an alternative (e.g. **graffito/graffiti; virtuoso/virtuosos** or **virtuosi**).

6. Some nouns of Greek origin ending in -on have the plural ending -a (e.g. **criterion/criteria**).

7. Nouns of Latin origin ending in -um, especially in scientific or technical usage, have the plural ending -a (e.g. **bacterium/bacteria; stratum/strata**).

8. Many nouns of Latin origin ending in -us, especially in scientific or technical usage, have the preferred or alternative plural ending -i (e.g. **fungus/fungi; stylus/styli** or **styluses**). A few such nouns have the plural ending -era or -ora (e.g. **genus/genera; corpus/corpora**).

9. Most nouns ending in -x form regular plurals (e.g. **tax/taxes**) but a few, usually in scientific or technical usage, have the plural ending -ces (e.g. **appendix/appendices**).

   Such nouns ending in -ex have the plural ending -ices (e.g. **index/indices**).

Such nouns ending in *-nx* have the plural ending *-nges* (e.g. **meninx/ meninges**).

10. Nouns ending in *-y* preceded by a vowel form regular plurals (e.g. **donkey/donkeys**). Nouns ending in *-y* preceded by a consonant or *-qu-* have the plural ending *-ies* (e.g. **family/families; colloquy/colloquies**). Note that proper names ending *-y* form regular plurals, irrespective of the preceding letter (e.g. **Sally/Sallys**).

11. In phrasal nouns and most other hyphenated nouns, the final element is pluralized (e.g. **lay-by/lay-bys**), but in some hyphenated and multiword nouns the noun element may be pluralized irrespective of its position (e.g. **looker-on/lookers-on; court martial/court martials** *or* **courts martial**).

    Note, however, that this does not apply to nouns ending in *-ful* (e.g. **spoonful/spoonfuls**; *not* **spoonsful**).

12. Some nouns, especially animals, have the same singular and plural forms (e.g. **sheep/sheep; fish/fish** *or* **fishes**).

13. Abbreviations and numerals usually have the plural ending *-s* (e.g. **MPs; 1920s**).

Suffixes

Many nouns are formed by adding suffixes to the corresponding verb or adjective. A few general rules apply.

1. *-ation*

    For words ending in *-l* preceded by a single vowel, the *-l* is doubled (e.g. **cancel/cancellation**).

2. *-er* and *-or*

    Either of these suffixes may be added to form nouns meaning the 'doer' of the corresponding verb, but the *-er* forms greatly outnumber the *-or* forms. For some verbs, both forms exist; in these cases the following rules may apply:

    (a) the *-or* form is used for objects and the *-er* form for people (e.g. **resister**, person who resists; **resistor**, electrical component).

    (b) the *-or* form is preferred in legal or scientific contexts (e.g. **bailer**, one who bails; **bailor**, transferrer of goods by bailment).

3. *-ment*

(a) For words ending in *-dge*, the preferred form is to drop the *-e* (e.g. **judge/judgment**).

(b) For words ending in *-ll*, the terminal *-l* is dropped (e.g. **install/instalment**).

(c) For words of more than one syllable ending in *-y* preceded by a consonant, the *-y* is changed to *-i* (e.g. **merry/merriment**).

4. *-ness*

    For words of more than one syllable preceded by a consonant, the *-y* is changed to *-i* (e.g. **happy/happiness**).

Adjectives

Regular Inflections

Regular comparatives and superlatives, for adjectives of one or two syllables, are formed by adding *-er* and *-est*, respectively.

For adjectives ending in *-e*, the *-e* is dropped before adding *-er* or *-est* (e.g. **nice/nicer, nicest; free/freer, freest**).

Adjectives of three or more syllables are preceded by *more* and *most* to form the comparative and superlative respectively.

Irregular Inflections

1. For adjectives ending in *-y* preceded by a consonant, the comparative and superlative are formed by dropping the *-y* and adding *-ier* and *-iest* respectively (e.g. **tidy/tidier, tidiest**).

2. For monosyllabic adjectives ending in a consonant preceded by a single vowel, the comparative and superlative are formed by doubling the terminal consonant before adding *-er* and *-est* respectively (e.g. **hot/hotter, hottest**).

Suffixes

-able and *-ible*

The great majority of these adjectives have the ending *-able*; they are derived from native English verbs and nouns. Certain verbs and nouns of Latin origin, however, take the suffix *-ible*; some common examples are **accessible, comprehensible, convertible, divisible, eligible, perceptible, permissible, tangible**. Some can end in either *-able* or *-ible* (e.g. **collectable/collectible, discussible/discussable**).

For adjectives ending in *-able*, the following rules generally apply, although there are exceptions:

(a) For verbs and nouns ending in *-e*, the *-e* is dropped before adding *-able* unless it is preceded by *-c-* or *-g-* (e.g. **noticeable, changeable**) or when its retention aids pronunciation (e.g. **blameable, saleable**).

(b) For words ending in *-y* preceded by a consonant, the *-y* is changed to *-i* before adding *-able* (e.g. **justifiable**).

(c) For verbs ending in *-l* preceded by a single vowel, the *-l* is doubled before adding *-able* (e.g. **distil/distillable**).

Verbs

Regular Inflections

1. The third person singular is formed by adding *-s* or, for verbs ending in *-s*, *-x*, *-z*, *-ch*, or *-sh*, by adding *-es*.

2. The present participle is formed by adding *-ing*.

3. The past tense and past participle are formed by adding *-ed*.

4. For verbs ending in *-e* preceded by a consonant, the *-e* is dropped before adding *-ing* or *-ed* (compare **Irregular inflections** 3 and 4).

Irregular Inflections

1. For verbs ending in *-y* preceded by a consonant, the past tense and past participle are formed by dropping the *-y* and adding *-ied* (e.g. **marry/married**).

2. In monosyllabic verbs ending in a consonant preceded by a single vowel, the terminal consonant is doubled when inflecting (e.g. **pat/patting, patted**).

    With some exceptions, this rule also applies to verbs of more than one syllable, notably when:

    (a) the terminal consonant is *-l* (e.g. **marvel/marvelling, marvelled**); note that in American English the *-l* is not doubled.

    (b) the stress is on the last syllable (e.g. **refer/referring, referred**).

3. For verbs ending in *-e* preceded by a vowel, the *-e* is dropped before adding *-ed* but retained before *-ing* (e.g. **hoe/hoeing, hoed**).

4. For a few verbs ending in *-e* preceded by a consonant, the *-e* is dropped before adding *-ed* but retained before *-ing*, usually to avoid confusion with very similar words (e.g. **singe/singeing, singed**).

5. For verbs ending in *-ac-* or *-ic*, the present participle is formed by adding *-king* and the past tense and participle by adding *-ked* (e.g. **traffic/trafficking, trafficked**).

Suffixes

1. *-ize* and *-ise*

    Most of these verbs have the preferred ending *-ize*, with *-ise* as an acceptable variant in British English (but not in American English); the same applies to the derived nouns (e.g. **specialize/specialization**). Exceptions include **advertise, compromise, improvise, supervise**; for these verbs *-ise* is the only acceptable ending in British and American English.

2. *-yse* and *-yze*

    -yse is the only acceptable form in British English; *-yze* is the US spelling (e.g. **catalyse/***US* **catalyze; paralyse/***US* **paralyze**).

Adverbs

Many adverbs are formed by adding *-ly* to the corresponding adjectives or nouns. Note:

1. For adjectives or nouns ending in *-e*, the *-e* is usually, but not always, retained (e.g. **pale/palely; rude/rudely**). Exceptions include **true/truly, whole/wholly**.

2. For adjectives or nouns ending in *-l*, the *-l* is retained (e.g. **eventual/eventually**).

3. For adjectives ending in *-ll*, the penultimate *-l* is dropped before adding *-ly* (e.g. **full/fully**).

4. For adjectives or nouns ending in *-y*, the adverb is formed by dropping the *-y* and adding *-ily* (e.g. **merry/merrily**).

Common spelling problems

1. *-cede* or *-ceed*

    There is no general rule here: the usual ending is *-cede* (e.g. **concede, precede**); the only verbs ending in *-ceed* are **exceed, proceed,** and **succeed**. Note particularly the spelling of **supersede**.

2. *-ei-* or *-ie-*

    The rule 'i before e except after c' works fairly well when the sound is pronounced 'ee' (e.g. **niece, siege**; but **receipt, receive**). Exceptions include **seize, weir, weird**.

    When the sound is pronounced 'ai' (as in paid), the spelling is *-ei-* (e.g. **deign, neighbour, weigh**).

3. *Difficult words*

    A few words cause many people problems because they follow no rules:

accommodate	exaggerate	phenomenon
anomalous	forty	pursue
business	gauge	surprise
commemorate	harass	threshold
desiccate	inoculate	withhold
ecstasy	necessary	
embarrass	parallel	

A

aa rock
Aachen German city
Aal·borg (or Ål·) Danish port
aalii shrub
aard·vark
aard·wolf (plural ·wolves)
Aar·gau Swiss canton
Aar·hus (or År·) Danish port
aba·ca fibre
aback
ab·ac·ti·nal zoology term
aba·cus (plural ·ci or ·cuses)
Aba·dan Iranian port
Abad·don the devil
abaft nautical term
aba·lo·ne mollusc
ab·am·pere electrical unit
aban·don
aban·doned
aban·doned·ly
aban·donee legal term
aban·don·ment
abase
abase·ment
abash
abash·ed·ly
abat·able
abate
abate·ment
aba·tis (or ab·at·tis) fortifications term
aba·tor legal term
ab·at·toir
ab·ax·ial away from the axis; compare adaxial
ab·ba·cy (plural ·cies)
Abbasid dynasty of caliphs
ab·ba·tial
abbé French abbot
ab·bess
Abbe·vill·ian archaeological period
ab·bey
ab·bot
ab·bre·vi·ate
ab·bre·via·tion
ab·bre·via·tor
(abcess) incorrect spelling of abscess
ab·cou·lomb electrical unit

ab·di·cable
ab·di·cate
ab·di·ca·tion
ab·dica·tive
ab·di·ca·tor
ab·do·men
ab·domi·nal
ab·domi·nal·ly
ab·du·cens nerve
ab·du·cent anatomy term
ab·duct
ab·duc·tion
abeam nautical term
abece·dar·ian learner
abed
abele poplar
Abelian maths term
abel·mosk plant
Ab·eo·ku·ta Nigerian town
Ab·er·dare Welsh town
Ab·er·deen
Ab·er·do·nian
ab·er·nethy biscuit
ab·er·rance (or ·ran·cy)
ab·er·rant
ab·er·ra·tion
Ab·er·yst·wyth
abet (abet·ting, abet·ted)
abet·ment
abet·ter (or esp. in legal contexts ·tor)
abey·ance
abey·ant
ab·far·ad electrical unit
ab·hen·ry (plural ·ries) electrical unit
ab·hor (·hor·ring, ·horred)
ab·hor·rence
ab·hor·rent
ab·hor·rer
abid·ance
abide (abid·ing, abode or abid·ed)
abid·er
abid·ing
abid·ing·ly
Abid·jan Côte d'Ivoire port
abi·et·ic acid
abi·gail maid
Abi·lene Texan city
abil·ity (plural ·ities)

Ab·ing·don
ab ini·tio Latin from the start
abio·gen·esis biological theory
abio·genet·ic
abiog·enist
abio·sis absence of life
abiot·ic
ab·ir·ri·tant relieving irritation
ab·ir·ri·tate
ab·ject
ab·jec·tion
ab·ju·ra·tion
ab·jure renounce; compare adjure
ab·jur·er
Ab·khaz (plural ·khaz) Georgian people
Ab·kha·zia Georgian republic
ab·late
ab·la·tion
ab·la·tive grammar term
ab·la·tor heat shield
ab·laut linguistics term
ablaze
able
able-bodied
abloom
ab·lu·tion
ab·lu·tion·ary
ably
ab·ne·gate
ab·ne·ga·tion
ab·ne·ga·tor
ab·nor·mal
ab·nor·mal·ity (plural ·ities)
ab·nor·mal·ly
aboard
abode
ab·ohm electrical unit
aboi·deau (plural ·deaus or ·deaux) Canadian dyke
abol·ish
abol·ish·er
abol·ish·ment
abo·li·tion
abo·li·tion·ary
abo·li·tion·ism

abo·li·tion·ist
abo·ma·sum ruminant's
stomach
abomi·nable
abomi·nably
abomi·nate
abomi·na·tion
abomi·na·tor
ab·oral zoology term
Abo·rigi·nal
abo·rigi·nal
Abo·rigi·ne native
Australian
abo·rigi·ne an original
inhabitant
abort
abor·ti·cide
abor·ti·fa·cient inducing
abortion
abor·tion
abor·tion·al
abor·tion·ist
abor·tive
Abou·kir battle site
abou·lia *variant spelling of*
abulia
abound
about
about-turn (*or esp. US*
about-face)
above
ab·ra·ca·dab·ra
abra·dant
abrade
abrad·er
abran·chi·ate (*or ·chial*)
zoology term
abra·sion
abra·sive
abrax·as magic charm
ab·re·act psychology term
ab·re·ac·tion
ab·re·ac·tive
abreast
abridg·able (*or abridge·*)
abridge
abridg·er
abridg·ment (*or abridge·*)
abroad
ab·ro·gate
ab·ro·ga·tion
ab·ro·ga·tor
ab·rupt
ab·rup·tion breaking off
ab·rupt·ness

Abruz·zi Italian region
ab·scess
ab·scise to separate
ab·scis·sa (*plural ·sas or*
·sae) maths term
ab·scis·sion shedding of
plant parts
ab·scond
ab·scond·er
ab·seil mountaineering term
ab·sence
ab·sent
ab·sen·tee
ab·sen·tee·ism
ab·sent·er
ab·sen·te reo *Latin* the
defendant being absent
absent-minded
absent-minded·ness
ab·sinthe (*or ·sinth*)
ab·sit omen *Latin* may the
foreboding not be realized
ab·so·lute
ab·so·lute·ly
ab·so·lu·tion
ab·so·lut·ism
ab·solu·tory
ab·solv·able
ab·solve
ab·solv·er
ab·sorb take into or
permeate; *compare* adsorb
ab·sorb·abil·ity
ab·sorb·able
ab·sorb·ance physics term
ab·sorb·ed·ly
ab·sor·be·fa·cient inducing
absorption
ab·sorb·en·cy
ab·sorb·ent
ab·sorb·er
ab·sorb·ing
ab·sorb·ing·ly
ab·sorp·tance physics term
ab·sorp·tion
ab·sorp·tive
ab·sorp·tiv·ity physics term
ab·squatu·late decamp
ab·stain
ab·stain·er
ab·ste·mi·ous
ab·sten·tion
ab·sten·tious
ab·ster·gent cleansing
ab·sti·nence

ab·sti·nent
ab·stract
ab·stract·ed·ly
ab·stract·ed·ness
ab·strac·tion
ab·strac·tion·ism theory of
abstract art
ab·strac·tive
ab·stric·tion biology term
ab·struse
ab·struse·ness
ab·surd
ab·surd·ity (*or ·ness; plural*
·ities *or* ·nesses)
Abu Dha·bi sheikdom
Abu·ja Nigerian capital
abu·lia (*or abou·*) loss of
willpower
abu·lic
abun·dance
abun·dant
abuse
abus·er
Abu Sim·bel Egyptian
temple
abu·sive
abu·sive·ness
abut (abut·ting, abut·ted)
abu·ti·lon shrub
abut·ment (*or abut·tal*)
abut·tals legal term
abut·ter owner of adjoining
property
abuzz
ab·volt electrical unit
ab·watt electrical unit
Aby·dos ancient Egyptian
town
abysm *Archaic* abyss
abys·mal immeasurable;
very bad
abys·mal·ly
abyss
abys·sal of ocean depths
Ab·ys·sinia *former name of*
Ethiopia
Ab·ys·sin·ian
aca·cia
aca·deme
aca·demia
aca·dem·ic
aca·dem·ical·ly
aca·dem·icals academic
dress
acad·emi·cian

aca·demi·cism (*or*
  acad·emism)
  conventionalism
acad·emy (*plural* ·emies)
Aca·dia Canadian region;
  compare Arcadia
Aca·dian of Acadia; *compare*
  Accadian
aca·jou mahogany
ac·an·tha·ceous botany
  term
acan·thine
acan·tho·cepha·lan
  wormlike animal
acan·thoid spiny
ac·an·thop·ter·yg·ian fish
acan·thous thornlike
acan·thus (*plural* ·thuses or
  ·thi) plant; architectural
  ornament
a cap·pel·la musical term
Aca·pul·co Mexican port
aca·ria·sis tick or mite
  infestation
aca·rid (*or* acari·dan) tick or
  mite
aca·roid
aca·rol·ogy
acar·pel·lous lacking carpels
acar·pous producing no
  fruit
aca·rus mite
acata·lec·tic verse form
acau·dal (*or* ·date) having
  no tail
acau·les·cent having no
  stem
Ac·cad *variant spelling of*
  Akkad
Ac·cad·ian *variant spelling of*
  Akkadian; *compare*
  Acadian
ac·cede
ac·ced·ence
ac·ced·er
ac·cel·era·able
ac·cel·er·an·do (*plural* ·dos)
  musical term
ac·cel·er·ant
ac·cel·er·ate
ac·cel·era·tion
ac·cel·era·tive (*or* ·tory)
ac·cel·era·tor
ac·cel·er·om·eter
ac·cent

ac·cen·tor bird
ac·cen·tual rhythmical
ac·cen·tu·ate
ac·cen·tua·tion
ac·cept
ac·cept·abil·ity (*or*
  ·able·ness)
ac·cept·able
ac·cept·ably
ac·cept·ance
ac·cept·ant
ac·cep·ta·tion
ac·cept·ed·ly
ac·cep·ter (*or esp. in legal
  contexts, chemistry, and
  electronics* ·tor)
ac·cess
ac·ces·sa·ry (*plural* ·ries)
  variant spelling of accessory
ac·ces·sibil·ity
ac·ces·sible
ac·ces·sibly
ac·ces·sion
ac·ces·sion·al
ac·ces·so·rial
ac·ces·so·ri·ly
ac·ces·so·ri·ness
ac·ces·so·ry (*or in legal
  contexts* ·sa·ry; *plural* ·ries)
ac·ciac·ca·tu·ra (*plural* ·ras
  or ·re) musical term
ac·ci·dence linguistics term
ac·ci·dent
ac·ci·den·tal
ac·ci·den·tal·ly
ac·ci·die apathy
ac·cipi·ter hawk
ac·cipi·tral (*or* ·trine)
ac·claim
ac·cla·ma·tion
ac·clama·tory
ac·cli·ma·tiz·able (*or*
  ·ma·tis·able, ·mat·able)
ac·cli·ma·tiza·tion (*or*
  ·ma·ti·sa·tion, ·ma·tion)
ac·cli·ma·tize (*or* ·ma·tise,
  ·mate)
ac·cli·ma·tiz·er (*or* ·tis·er)
ac·clivi·tous (*or* ·cli·vous)
ac·cliv·ity (*plural* ·ities)
  upward slope
ac·co·lade
ac·com·mo·date
ac·com·mo·dat·ing
ac·com·mo·dat·ing·ly

ac·com·mo·da·tion
ac·com·mo·da·tive
(accomodate) *incorrect
  spelling of* accommodate
ac·com·pa·ni·er
ac·com·pa·ni·ment
ac·com·pa·nist (*or esp. US*
  ·pa·ny·ist)
ac·com·pa·ny (·nies,
  ·ny·ing, ·nied)
ac·com·plice
ac·com·plish
ac·com·plish·able
ac·com·plish·er
ac·com·plish·ment
ac·cord
ac·cord·able
ac·cord·ance
ac·cord·ant
ac·cord·er
ac·cord·ing
ac·cord·ing·ly
ac·cor·di·on
ac·cor·di·on·ist
ac·cost
ac·cost·able
ac·count
ac·count·abil·ity
ac·count·able
ac·count·ably
ac·count·an·cy
ac·count·ant
ac·count·ing
ac·cou·ple·ment supporting
  beam
ac·cou·tre (*US* ·ter)
ac·cou·tre·ment (*US* ·ter·)
Ac·cra Ghanaian capital
ac·cred·it
ac·credi·ta·tion
ac·cres·cent botany term
ac·crete
ac·cre·tion
ac·cre·tive (*or*
  ac·cre·tion·ary)
Ac·cring·ton
ac·cru·al (*or* ·ment)
ac·crue (·cru·ing, ·crued)
ac·cul·tur·ate
ac·cul·tura·tion
ac·cum·ben·cy
ac·cum·bent botany term
ac·cu·mu·lable
ac·cu·mu·late
ac·cu·mu·la·tion

ac·cu·mu·la·tive
ac·cu·mu·la·tor
ac·cu·ra·cy (*plural* ·cies)
ac·cu·rate
ac·cu·rate·ly
ac·curs·ed
ac·cus·al
ac·cu·sa·tion
ac·cu·sa·ti·val
ac·cu·sa·tive grammar term
ac·cu·sa·to·rial (*or* ·tory)
ac·cuse
ac·cused
ac·cus·er
ac·cus·ing·ly
ac·cus·tom
ac·cus·tomed
Ac·cu·tron (*Trademark*)
watch
ace
acedia apathy
acel·lu·lar
acen·tric
acepha·lous headless
ac·er·ate *variant of* acerose
ac·er·bate embitter
acer·bic
acer·bity (*plural* ·bities)
ac·er·ose (*or* ·ous, ·ate)
needle-shaped
acer·vate growing in
clusters
aces·cence (*or* ·cen·cy)
aces·cent turning sour
ac·etabu·lum (*plural* ·la)
cavity in hipbone
ac·etal chemical
compound
ac·et·al·de·hyde
ac·et·am·ide (*or* ·id)
ac·et·ani·lide (*or* ·lid)
ac·etate
acetic acid
aceti·fi·ca·tion
aceti·fi·er
aceti·fy (·fies, ·fy·ing, ·fied)
convert into vinegar
ac·etom·eter
ac·etone
ac·etous (*or* ·etose)
resembling vinegar
acetum vinegar
ac·etyl
acety·late
acety·la·tion

acetyl·cho·line biochemical
compound
acety·lene
acety·len·ic
acety·lide
ac·etyl·sali·cyl·ic acid
chemical name for
aspirin
acey-deucy backgammon
Achaea (*or* Achaia) region
of Greece
Achae·an (*or* Achaian)
Achaemenid member of
Persian dynasty
Acha·tes loyal friend
ache
ach·ing·ly
achene (*or* akene) botany
term
achenial (*or* akenial)
Acher·nar star
Ach·er·on mythological
river
Acheu·lian (*or* ·lean)
archaeological period
achiev·able
achieve
achieve·ment
achiev·er
Ach·il·lean
Achilles
ach·la·myd·eous lacking
petals and sepals
achlor·hy·dria lacking
stomach acid
achon·drite meteorite
achon·drit·ic
achon·dro·pla·sia skeletal
disorder
achon·dro·plas·tic
ach·ro·mat type of lens
ach·ro·mat·ic
ach·ro·mati·cal·ly
achro·ma·tin part of cell
nucleus
achro·ma·tism (*or* ·tic·ity)
achro·ma·ti·za·tion (*or*
·sa·tion)
achro·ma·tize (*or* ·tise)
remove colour from
achro·ma·tous
a·chro·mic (*or* achro·mous)
colourless
ach·y·fi Welsh expression of
disgust

acicu·la (*plural* ·lae)
needle-shaped structure
acicu·lar
acicu·late (*or* ·lat·ed)
acicu·lum (*plural* ·lums *or*
·la) zoology term
acid
acid-fast
acid-forming
acid·ic
acidi·fi·able
acidi·fi·ca·tion
acidi·fi·er
acidi·fy (·fies, ·fy·ing, ·fied)
aci·dim·eter
acidi·met·ric (*or* ·ri·cal)
aci·di·met·ri·cal·ly
aci·dim·etry
acid·ity (*plural* ·ities)
acid·ness
aci·dom·eter hydrometer
for acids
aci·do·phil (*or* ·phile)
biology term
aci·do·phil·ic (*or*
·dophi·lous)
aci·dophi·lus bacterium
aci·do·sis medical condition
aci·dot·ic
acidu·late make acid
acidu·la·tion
acidu·lous (*or* ·lent)
aci·er·ate change into steel
aci·era·tion
aci·naci·form botany term
acin·ic (*or* aci·nous,
aci·nose)
acini·form
aci·nus (*plural* ·ni) biology
term
Acis mythological character
ack-ack anti-aircraft fire
ackee (*or* akee) fruit
ac·knowl·edge
ac·knowl·edge·able
ac·knowl·edg·er
ac·knowl·edg·ment (*or*
·edge·)
aclin·ic line magnetic
equator
acme peak
acne skin disease
ac·no·dal
ac·node maths term
Acol bridge term

aco•lyte
aco•nite (or •ni•tum)
aco•nit•ic
acorn
acoty•ledon botany term
acoty•ledon•ous
acou•chi (or •chy) rodent
acous•tic (or •ti•cal)
acous•ti•cal•ly
acous•ti•cian
acous•tics
ac•quaint
ac•quaint•ance
ac•quaint•ance•ship
ac•quaint•ed
ac•qui•esce
ac•qui•es•cence
ac•qui•es•cent
ac•quir•able
ac•quire
ac•quire•ment
ac•quir•er
ac•qui•si•tion
ac•quisi•tive
ac•quisi•tive•ness
ac•quit (•quit•ting, •quit•ted)
ac•quit•tal
ac•quit•tance
ac•quit•ter
acre
acre•age
acred having acres of land
acre-foot (plural -feet)
acre-inch
ac•rid
ac•ri•dine chemical compound
acrid•ity (or •ness)
ac•ri•fla•vine antiseptic
Ac•ri•lan (Trademark)
ac•ri•mo•ni•ous
ac•ri•mo•ny (plural •nies)
ac•ro•bat
ac•ro•bat•ic
ac•ro•bati•cal•ly
ac•ro•bat•ics
ac•ro•car•pous botany term
ac•ro•dont zoology term
ac•ro•drome botany term
ac•ro•gen botany term
ac•ro•gen•ic (or acrog•enous)
acro•lein chemical compound

ac•ro•lith type of sculpture
ac•ro•me•gal•ic
ac•ro•mega•ly hormonal disease
acro•mi•on (plural •mia) part of shoulder blade
acrony•chal (or •cal) occurring at sunset
ac•ro•nym
ac•ro•nym•ic (or acrony•mous)
acrop•etal botany term
ac•ro•pho•bia fear of heights
ac•ro•pho•bic
Acropo•lis
ac•ro•spire botany term
across
acros•tic
acros•ti•cal•ly
acro•ter architectural term
acryl•ic
ac•ry•lo•ni•trile
ac•ry•lyl
act
act•abil•ity
act•able
ac•tin protein
ac•ti•nal zoology term
act•ing
ac•tinia (plural •tiniae or •tinias) sea anemone
ac•tin•ic type of radiation
ac•tini•cal•ly
ac•tin•ide (or •non)
ac•tini•form (or ac•ti•noid) star-shaped
ac•tin•ism
ac•tin•ium radioactive element
ac•ti•noid variant of actiniform
ac•tino•lite mineral
ac•ti•no•mere biology term
ac•ti•nom•eter radiation measurer
ac•ti•no•met•ric (or •ri•cal)
ac•ti•nom•etry
ac•ti•no•mor•phic (or •phous) botany term
ac•ti•no•my•cete bacterium
ac•ti•no•my•cin antibiotic
ac•ti•no•my•co•sis bacterial infection
ac•ti•no•my•cot•ic

ac•ti•non variant of actinide
ac•tino•pod protozoan
ac•ti•no•thera•py radiotherapy
ac•ti•no•ura•nium isotope of uranium
ac•ti•no•zo•an marine organism
ac•tion
ac•tion•able
ac•tion•ably
action-packed
Ac•ti•um ancient Greek town
ac•ti•vate
ac•ti•va•tion
ac•ti•va•tor
ac•tive
ac•tive•ly
ac•tive•ness
ac•tiv•ism
ac•tiv•ist
ac•tiv•ity (plural •ities)
ac•to•myo•sin protein
Ac•ton London district
ac•tor
ac•tress
ac•tual
ac•tu•al•ity (plural •ities)
ac•tu•ali•za•tion (or •sa•tion)
ac•tu•al•ize (or •ise)
ac•tu•al•ly
ac•tu•ari•al
ac•tu•ary (plural •aries)
ac•tu•ate
ac•tua•tion
ac•tua•tor
acu•ity
acu•leate (or •leat•ed) pointed
acu•leus (plural •lei) prickle
acu•men
acu•mi•nate pointed
acu•mi•na•tion
acu•mi•nous
acu•punc•ture
acut•ance photography term
acute
acute•ly
acute•ness
acy•clic chemistry term
acyl
ad Slang advertisement

adac·ty·lous without fingers or toes

ad·age

ada·gio (plural ·gios) musical term

ada·mant

ada·man·tine very hard

Ada·ma·wa language group

Ad·am·ite nudist

Ad·ams US mountain

ad·ams·ite tear gas

Ada·na Turkish city

adapt

adapt·abil·ity (or ·able·ness)

adapt·able

adapt·ably

ad·ap·ta·tion

adapt·er one who adapts; compare adaptor

adap·tive

adapt·or electrical device; compare adapter

ad·ax·ial towards the axis; compare abaxial

add

ad·dax antelope

ad·dend number added to

ad·den·dum (plural ·da)

ad·der snake

add·er calculator

ad·dict

ad·dic·tion

ad·dic·tive

Ad·dis Aba·ba Ethiopian capital

ad·di·tion

ad·di·tion·al

ad·di·tion·al·ly

ad·di·tive

ad·dle

ad·dress

ad·dressee

ad·dress·er (or ·dres·sor)

Ad·dres·so·graph (Trademark)

ad·duce

ad·duce·able (or ·duc·ible)

ad·du·cent

ad·duct pull towards

ad·duc·tion

ad·duc·tor muscle

Ad·elaide Australian city

ademp·tion legal term

Aden Yemeni city

ad·enec·to·my (plural ·mies) removal of gland

ad·enine biochemical compound

ad·eni·tis inflammation of a gland

ad·eno·car·ci·no·ma (plural ·mas or ·ma·ta) tumour

ad·eno·hy·phophy·sis part of pituitary gland

ad·enoid resembling a gland

ad·enoi·dal affected by enlarged adenoids

ad·enoid·ec·to·my (plural ·mies)

ad·enoids tonsil tissue

ad·eno·ma (plural ·mas or ·ma·ta) glandular tumour

adeno·sine biochemical compound

ad·eno·vi·rus

adept

ad·equa·cy

ad·equate

à deux French of or for two persons

ad·here

ad·her·ence

ad·her·ent (noun, adj)

ad·he·sion

ad·he·sive

ad·he·sive·ness

ad hoc Latin for a particular purpose

ad ho·mi·nem Latin to the man

adia·bat·ic physics term

adi·aph·or·ism theological term

adi·apho·rist

adi·apho·ris·tic

adi·apho·rous medical term

adieu (plural adieus or adieux) goodbye

ad in·fi·ni·tum Latin without end

ad in·ter·im Latin for the meantime

adi·os Spanish goodbye

adi·po·cere waxy substance

adi·poc·er·ous

adi·pose fatty

adi·pos·ity

Adi·ron·dacks US mountains

adit mine shaft

Adi·va·si Indian people

ad·ja·cen·cy

ad·ja·cent

ad·jec·ti·val

ad·jec·tive

ad·join

ad·join·ing

ad·joint maths term

ad·journ

ad·journ·ment

ad·judge

ad·ju·di·cate

ad·ju·di·ca·tion

ad·ju·di·ca·tive

ad·ju·di·ca·tor

ad·junct

ad·junc·tive

ad·ju·ra·tion

ad·jura·tory

ad·jure appeal to solemnly; compare abjure

ad·jur·er (or ·ju·ror)

ad·just

ad·just·able

ad·just·ment

ad·ju·tan·cy

ad·ju·tant

ad·ju·vant helping; auxiliary

ad lib spontaneously; freely

ad-lib (-libbing, -libbed) improvise

ad-libber

ad·man (plural ·men)

ad·mass people susceptible to advertising

ad·meas·ure

ad·meas·ure·ment

Admetus mythological king

ad·min short for administration

ad·mini·cle legal term

ad·min·is·ter

ad·min·is·trable

ad·min·is·trate

ad·min·is·tra·tion

ad·min·is·tra·tive

ad·min·is·tra·tor (fem ·trix in legal contexts)

ad·mi·rable

ad·mi·rably

ad·mi·ral

ad·mi·ral·ty (plural ·ties)

ad·mi·ra·tion

ad·mire
ad·mirer
ad·mir·ing·ly
ad·mis·sibil·ity (or ·sible·ness)
ad·mis·sible
ad·mis·sion
ad·mis·sive
ad·mit (·mit·ting, ·mit·ted)
ad·mit·tance
ad·mit·ted·ly
ad·mix
ad·mix·ture
ad·mon·ish
ad·mon·ish·er (or ·moni·tor)
ad·mo·ni·tion
ad·moni·tory
ad·nate botany term
ad nau·seam Latin to a disgusting extent
ad·nomi·nal word modifying a noun
ad·noun adjective used as noun
ado
ado·be building term
ado·les·cence
ado·les·cent
Adon·ic type of verse line
Adonis mythological character
adopt
adopt·able
adopt·ed
adop·tee
adopt·er
adop·tion
adop·tion·ism (or ·tian·)
adop·tion·ist (or ·tian·)
adop·tive
ador·able
ador·ably
ado·ra·tion
adore
ador·er
adorn
adorn·ment
ad rem Latin to the point
ad·re·nal gland
adrena·line hormone
ad·ren·er·gic biology term
adre·no·cor·ti·co·troph·ic (US ·trop·ic) stimulating adrenal cortex

Adri·at·ic
adrift
adroit
adroit·ness
ad·sci·ti·tious additional
ad·sorb accumulate on a surface; compare absorb
ad·sorb·abil·ity
ad·sorb·able
ad·sorb·ate
ad·sor·bent
ad·sorp·tion
adu·laria mineral
adu·late
adu·la·tion
adu·la·tor
adu·la·tory
adult
adul·ter·ant
adul·ter·ate
adul·tera·tion
adul·ter·ator
adul·ter·er (fem ·ess)
adul·ter·ine fake
adul·ter·ous
adul·tery (plural ·teries)
adult·hood
ad·um·bral shadowy
ad·um·brate
ad·um·bra·tion
ad·um·bra·tive
Adu·wa Ethiopian town
ad va·lo·rem Latin according to value
ad·vance
ad·vanced
ad·vance·ment
ad·vanc·er
ad·vanc·ing·ly
ad·van·tage
ad·van·ta·geous
ad·van·ta·geous·ness
ad·vec·tion
Ad·vent coming of Christ
ad·vent arrival
Ad·ven·tist
ad·ven·ti·tia anatomy term
ad·ven·ti·tious happening by chance; growing in abnormal position
ad·ven·tive
ad·ven·ture
ad·ven·tur·er (fem ·ess)
ad·ven·tur·ism
ad·ven·tur·ist

ad·ven·tur·ous
ad·verb
ad·ver·bial
ad·ver·sary (plural ·saries)
ad·ver·sa·tive linguistics term
ad·verse
ad·ver·sity (plural ·sities)
ad·vert refer to; Slang advertisement
ad·vert·ence (or ·en·cy)
ad·vert·ent·ly
ad·ver·tise
ad·ver·tise·ment
ad·ver·tis·er
ad·ver·tis·ing
(advertize) incorrect spelling of advertise
ad·vice
ad·vis·abil·ity
ad·vis·able
ad·vise
ad·vised
ad·vis·ed·ly
ad·vise·ment US careful consideration
ad·vis·er (or ·vi·sor)
ad·vi·so·ry
ad·vo·caat
ad·vo·ca·cy (plural ·cies)
ad·vo·cate
ad·vo·ca·tion
ad·vo·ca·tory
Ady·gei (plural ·gei or ·geis) Russian people
ady·na·mia weakness
ady·nam·ic
adze (US adz) tool
Adzhar
Adzha·ria Georgian republic
ad·zuki (or ·su·ki) bean
aecio·spore
aecium (or aecid·ium; plural aecia or ·ia) fungal structure
aedes mosquito
aedile (US also edile) Roman magistrate
Aeëtes mythological king
Aegean
Aegi·na Greek island
Aegir Norse god
aegis (US also egis)
aegro·tat university degree
Aegyptus mythological king

Aeneas mythological prince
Aene·id epic poem
Aeo·lian
aeo·lian harp
Aeol·ic ancient Greek dialect
aeoli·pile model steam turbine
Aeo·lis Greek god
aeon (US **eon**)
aeo·nian (or **eo·**) everlasting
aepy·or·nis extinct bird
aer·ate
aera·tion
aera·tor
aer·en·chy·ma plant tissue
aer·ial relating to air; radio or TV device; compare **ariel**
aeri·al·ist trapeze artist
aerie variant spelling of **eyrie**
aeri·fi·ca·tion
aeri·form gaseous
aeri·fy (·**fies**, ·**fy·ing**, ·**fied**)
aero·bal·lis·tics
aero·bat·ics
aer·obe (or **aero·bium**; plural ·**obes** or ·**bia**)
aero·bic requiring oxygen
aero·bics exercises
aero·bio·sis
aero·bio·tic
aero·bium variant of **aerobe**
aero·do·net·ics study of gliding flight
aero·drome
aero·dy·nam·ic
aero·dy·nami·cal·ly
aero·dy·nam·ics
aero·dyne heavier-than-air machine
aero·em·bo·lism nitrogen in the blood
aero·engine
aero·foil
aero·gel solid foam
aero·gram (or ·**gramme**)
aer·og·ra·phy
aero·lite meteorite
aero·lo·gic (or ·**logi·cal**)
aer·olo·gist
aer·ol·ogy study of the atmosphere
aero·mechan·ic
aero·mechani·cal
aero·mechan·ics

aer·om·eter
aero·met·ric
aer·om·etry branch of physics
aero·naut
aero·nau·ti·cal (or **aero·nau·tic**)
aero·naut·ics
aero·neu·ro·sis
aero·pause region of upper atmosphere
aero·pha·gia swallowing of air
aero·pho·bia
aero·pho·bic afraid of draughts
aero·plane
aero·sol
aero·space
aero·sphere earth's atmosphere
aero·stat lighter-than-air craft
aero·stat·ic (or ·**stati·cal**)
aero·stat·ics
aero·sta·tion
aero·ther·mo·dy·nam·ic
aero·ther·mo·dy·nam·ics
aeru·go verdigris
aeru·gin·ous
aery variant spelling of **eyrie**; poetic airy; insubstantial
Aes·cu·la·pian
Aesculapius Roman god
Aesir Norse gods
aes·the·sia (US **es·**) normal sensitivity
aes·thete (US also **es·**)
aes·thet·ic (or ·**theti·cal**; US also **es·**)
aes·theti·cal·ly (US also **es·**)
aes·the·ti·cian (US also **es·**)
aes·theti·cism (US also **es·**)
aes·thet·ics (US also **es·**)
aes·ti·val (US **es·**) occurring in the summer
aes·ti·vate (US **es·**)
aes·ti·va·tion (US **es·**) biology term
aes·ti·va·tor (US **es·**)
aether former spelling of **ether** (anaesthetic); variant spelling of **ether** (hypothetical medium)

aethe·real rare spelling of **ethereal**
aethe·real·ity rare spelling of **ethereality**
aetio·logi·cal (US **etio·**)
aeti·olo·gist (US **eti·**)
aeti·ol·ogy (US **eti·**) study of causes
Aeto·lia Greek region
afar
afebrile without fever
af·fabil·ity
af·fable
af·fably
af·fair
af·faire French love affair
af·fect have an effect on; compare **effect** (verb)
af·fec·ta·tion
af·fect·ed
af·fect·ed·ly
af·fect·ed·ness
af·fect·ing
af·fect·ing·ly
af·fec·tion
af·fec·tion·al
af·fec·tion·ate
af·fec·tive arousing emotions
af·fec·tiv·ity (or ·**tive·ness**)
af·fen·pin·scher dog
af·fer·ent conducting inwards; compare **efferent**
af·fet·tuo·so musical term
af·fi·ance betroth
af·fi·ant US person who makes an affidavit
af·fi·da·vit
af·fili·ate
af·filia·tion
af·fine maths term
af·fined closely related
af·fini·tive
af·fin·ity (plural ·**ities**)
af·firm
af·firm·able
af·fir·ma·tion
af·firma·tive
af·firm·er (or ·**ant**)
af·fix
af·fix·ture
af·fla·tus creative power
af·flict
af·flic·tion
af·flic·tive

af·flu·ence
af·flu·ent
af·flux flowing towards
af·ford
af·for·est
af·for·esta·tion
af·fran·chise release from
  obligation
af·fran·chise·ment
af·fray
af·freight·ment
af·fri·cate
af·frica·tive phonetics term
af·fright
af·front
af·fu·sion baptism
Af·ghan hound
Af·ghan (*or* ·ghani) people
af·ghan shawl
af·ghani Afghan currency
Af·ghani·stan
afi·cio·na·do (*plural* ·dos)
  supporter
afield
afire
aflame
af·la·tox·in
afloat
aflut·ter
afoot
afore
afore·men·tioned
afore·said
afore·thought
a for·tio·ri *Latin* for a
  stronger reason
afoul
afraid
af·reet Arabian demon
afresh
Af·ri·ca
Af·ri·can
Af·ri·can·ism
Af·ri·kaans language of
  Afrikaners
Af·ri·kan·der (*or* ·can·)
  cattle
Af·ri·ka·ner White South
  African
Af·ri·ka·ner·dom
Afro (*plural* Afros) hairstyle
Afro-American
Afro-Asian
Afro-Asiatic
af·ror·mo·sia wood

aft
af·ter
after·birth
after·body (*plural* ·bodies)
  discarded part of rocket
after·brain
after·burner
after·burning
after·care
after·damp gas in mines
after·deck
after·effect
after·glow
after·heat
after·image
after·life
after·math
after·noon
after·pains
after·piece brief additional
  comic play
af·ters *Slang* dessert
after·sensation
after·shaft type of feather
after·shave
after·shock
after·taste
after·thought
after·wards (*or esp. US*
  ·ward)
after·word postscript
after·world
aga (*or* agha) Turkish title
Aga·dir Moroccan port
again
against
agal·loch tree
aga·ma lizard
Agamemnon mythological
  king
agam·ete biology term
agam·ic biology term
agami·cal·ly
aga·mo·gen·esis biology
  term
aga·mo·genet·ic
aga·mo·geneti·cal·ly
aga·pan·thus lily
Agape Christian love
agape gaping
agar seaweed product
aga·ric mushroom
agari·ca·ceous
Agar·ta·la Indian city
ag·ate

agate·ware
aga·ve plant
age (age·ing *or esp. US*
  ag·ing, aged)
aged (*adj, noun*)
agee *Scot* awry
age·ing (*or esp. US* ag·ing)
age·less
agen·cy (*plural* ·cies)
agen·da (*or* ·dum; *plural*
  ·das *or* ·dums)
agen·esis imperfect
  development
agenet·ic
agent
agen·tial
agen·tive (*or* ·tial)
  linguistics term
agent pro·vo·ca·teur (*plural*
  agents pro·vo·ca·teurs)
ag·era·tum plant
ag·ger Roman earthwork
ag·gior·na·men·to (*plural*
  ·ti) updating Catholic
  church
ag·glom·er·ate
ag·glom·era·tion
ag·glom·era·tive
ag·glu·ti·nabil·ity
ag·glu·ti·nable
ag·glu·ti·nant
ag·glu·ti·nate
ag·glu·ti·na·tion
ag·glu·ti·na·tive
ag·glu·ti·nin antibody
ag·glu·tino·gen
ag·grada·tion
ag·grade geology term
ag·gran·dize (*or* ·dise)
ag·gran·dize·ment (*or*
  ·dise·ment)
ag·gran·diz·er (*or* ·dis·er)
ag·gra·vate
ag·gra·va·tion
ag·gre·gate
ag·gre·ga·tion
ag·gress
ag·gres·sion
ag·gres·sive
ag·gres·sor
ag·grieve
ag·griev·ed·ly
ag·gro *Slang* aggression
aghast
ag·ile

agil·ity
Ag·in·court
ag·ing *variant spelling (esp. US) of* ageing
agio·tage business of currency exchange
agist legal term
agi·tate
agi·ta·tion
agi·ta·to musical term
agi·ta·tor
agit·prop communist propaganda
Aglaia Greek goddess
agleam
ag·let (*or* aiglet) shoelace tag
agley *Scot* awry
aglit·ter
aglow
agma phonetic symbol
ag·mi·nate gathered together
ag·nate having common male ancestor
ag·no·men (*plural* ·nomi·na) ancient Roman's fourth name
ag·nomi·nal
ag·nos·tic
ag·nos·ti·cism
Ag·nus Dei liturgical chant
ago
agog
à gogo *French* as much as one likes
agon (*plural* ago·nes) ancient Greek festival
agon·ic forming no angle
ago·nist
ago·nis·tic
ago·nize (*or* ·nise)
ago·niz·ing·ly (*or* ·nis·)
ago·ny (*plural* ·nies)
ago·ra (*plural* ·rae *or* ·ras) Greek marketplace
ago·ra (*plural* ·rot) Israeli coin
ago·ra·pho·bia
ago·ra·pho·bic
agou·ti (*plural* ·tis *or* ·ties) rodent
Agra Indian city
agraffe fastening

agran·ulo·cy·tosis blood disorder
ag·ra·pha sayings of Christ
agraphia inability to write
agrar·ian
agrari·an·ism
agree (agree·ing, agreed)
agree·able
agree·able·ness
agree·ably
agreed
agree·ment
agres·tal growing as a weed
agres·tic rural
ag·ri·busi·ness
ag·ri·cul·tur·al
ag·ri·cul·ture
ag·ri·cul·tur·ist (*or* ·tur·al·ist)
ag·ri·mo·ny (*plural* ·nies) plant
ag·ro·bio·logi·cal
ag·ro·bi·olo·gist
ag·ro·bi·ol·ogy
ag·ro·logi·cal
agrol·ogy study of soils
ag·ro·nom·ic (*or* ·nomi·cal)
ag·ro·nom·ics land economics
agrono·mist
agrono·my science of cultivation
ag·ros·tol·ogy study of grasses
aground
ag·ryp·not·ic of insomnia
Aguas·ca·lien·tes Mexican state
ague malaria
ague·weed
Agul·has South African headland
ah
aha
ahead
ahem
Ah·meda·bad (*or* ·mada·) Indian city
Ah·med·na·gar (*or* ·mad·) Indian city
ahoy
Ah·waz (*or* ·vaz) Iranian town
ai (*plural* ais) animal
aid help

aide assistant
aide-de-camp (*plural* aides-)
aide-mémoire (*plural* aides-)
aid·er
AIDS (*or* Aids)
aigrette (*or* aigret) feather on hat
aiguille mountain peak
aiguil·lette military ornament
aikido self-defence
ail
ailan·thus (*plural* ·thuses) tree
ailer·on
ail·ing
ail·ment
ailu·ro·phile cat lover
ailu·ro·philia
ailu·ro·phobe fearer of cats
ailu·ro·phobia
aim
aim·less
aim·less·ness
ain *Scot* own
ain't *Nonstandard* am not, is not, has not, have not, are not
Ainu (*plural* Ainus *or* Ainu) Japanese people
aïoli garlic mayonnaise
Aïr Saharan region
air
air·borne
air·brick
air·brush
air·burst
air·bus
air-conditioned
air-conditioner
air-conditioning
air-cool
air·craft (*plural* ·craft)
air·craft·man (*or* ·crafts·; *plural* ·men)
air·craft·woman (*or* ·crafts·; *plural* ·women)
air·crew
Air·drie Scottish town
air·drop (·drop·ping, ·dropped) delivery by parachute
air-dry (-dries, -dry·ing, -dried)

Aire·dale Yorkshire district; terrier
air·field
air·flow
air·foil
air·frame part of aircraft
air·glow
air·head military term
airi·ly
airi·ness
air·ing
air·intake
air·less
air·less·ness
air·lift
air·line
air·lin·er
air·lock
air·man (*plural* **·men**)
air·plane *US* aeroplane
air·port
air·screw propeller
air·ship
air·sick
air·sick·ness
air·space
air·speed
air·stream
air·strip
air·tight
air·waves
air·way
air·woman (*plural* **·women**)
air·worthi·ness
air·worthy
airy (**airi·er, airi·est**)
airy-fairy
aisle
Aisne French river
ait *Dialect* islet
aitch letter H
aitch·bone cut of beef
Aix-en-Provence French city
Ajac·cio Corsican port
ajar
Ajax mythological character
Aj·mer Indian city
Ake·la cub-scout leader
akha·ra Indian gymnasium
akim·bo
akin
Ak·kad (*or* **Ac·cad**) Babylonian city
Ak·ka·dian (*or* **Ac·ca·**)

Ak·mo·la *former name of* Astana
Ak·tyu·binsk Kazakh city
à la *French* in the style of
ala (*plural* **alae**) winglike structure
Ala·bama
Ala·bam·ian
ala·bas·ter
à la carte
alack
alacka·day
alac·ri·tous
alac·rity
Aladdin
Ala·go·as Brazilian state
Alai Central Asian mountain range
ala·meda *US* tree-lined promenade
Ala·mo
à la mode fashionable
ala·mode silk
ala·nine amino acid
alan·nah Irish term of endearment
alap Indian music
alar of wings
alarm
alarmed
alarm·ing
alarm·ing·ly
alarm·ism
alarm·ist
alar·um *Archaic* alarm
alary of wings
alas
Alas·ka
Alas·kan
alate winged
al·ba·core fish
Alba Lon·ga ancient city
Al·ba·nia
Al·ba·nian
Al·ba·ny US city; Canadian river; Australian port
al·ba·ta alloy
al·ba·tross
al·be·do (*plural* **·dos**) physics term
al·be·it
Al·bert lake in Uganda and the Democratic Republic of Congo
Al·ber·ta Canadian province

al·bert·ite variety of bitumen
al·bes·cence
al·bes·cent becoming white
Al·bi·gen·ses medieval heretics
Al·bi·gen·sian
al·bin·ic (*or* **·bin·is·tic**)
al·bi·nism
al·bi·no (*plural* **·nos**)
Al·bi·on *Archaic* Britain
al·bite mineral
al·bit·ic
Ål·borg *variant spelling of* Aalborg
al·bum
al·bu·men white of egg; *compare* albumin
al·bu·menize (*or* **·menise**)
al·bu·min a protein; *compare* albumen
al·bu·mi·nate
al·bu·mi·noid
al·bu·mi·nous
al·bu·mi·nu·ria urine containing albumin
Al·bu·quer·que US city
al·bur·num sapwood
Al·bu·ry Australian city
Al·ca·ic verse form
al·caide Spanish commander
al·cal·de Spanish mayor
Al·ca·traz US island
al·ca·zar Moorish palace
Alcestis mythological queen
al·chem·ic (*or* **·chemi·cal, ·chem·is·tic**)
al·che·mist
al·che·mize (*or* **·mise**)
al·che·my (*plural* **·mies**)
al·che·rin·ga Aboriginal golden age
Al·chevsk Ukrainian city
al·ci·dine ornithology term
al·co·hol
al·co·hol·ic
al·co·hol·ic·ity
al·co·hol·ism
al·co·holi·za·tion (*or* **·sa·tion**)
al·co·hol·ize (*or* **·ise**)
al·co·hol·om·eter
al·co·pop
Al·co·ran Koran

al·cove
Alcyone (or Halcyone) mythological character
Al·dab·ra Indian Ocean islands
Al·deba·ran star
al·de·hyde
al den·te *Italian* cooked until still firm
al·der
al·der·man (*plural* ·men)
al·der·man·ic
Al·der·mas·ton
Al·der·ney Channel Island
Al·der·shot
al·dol chemical compound
al·dose sugar
al·dos·terone hormone
ald·ox·ime chemical compound
al·drin insecticide
ale
alea·to·ry dependent on chance
ale·cost plant
alee nautical term
al·egar malt vinegar
ale·house
Ale·man·ni Germanic people
Al·eman·nic
alem·bic
alem·bi·cat·ed excessively refined
aleph Hebrew letter
aleph·null (or ·zero) maths term
Alep·po Syrian city
alert
alert·ness
Ales·san·dria Italian town
alethic logic term
aleu·rone (or ·ron) plant protein
al·evin young fish
ale·wife fish
al·ex·an·ders plant
Al·ex·an·dria Egyptian port
Al·ex·an·drian
Al·ex·an·drine type of verse
al·ex·an·drite gemstone
alexia word blindness
alex·in immunology term
al·fal·fa
al·fila·ria (or ·fil·eria) plant

al·fres·co
al·gae (*sing.* alga)
al·gal
al·gar·ro·ba (or ·ga·ro·ba) tree
al·ge·bra
al·ge·bra·ic (or ·brai·cal)
al·ge·brai·cal·ly
al·ge·bra·ist
Al·ge·ci·ras Spanish port
Al·ge·ria
Al·ge·rian (or ·rine)
algerine fabric
al·gi·cide
al·gid chilly
Al·giers Algerian capital
al·gin biochemical compound
al·gi·nate
al·gin·ic acid
al·goid resembling algae
Al·gol star; computer language
al·go·lag·nia sexual perversion
al·go·lag·nic
al·go·lag·nist
al·golo·gist
al·gol·ogy study of algae
al·gom·eter
al·gom·etry
Al·gon·quian (or ·kian)
Al·gon·quin (or ·kin; *plural* ·quins, ·quin or ·kins, ·kin) American Indian
al·go·pho·bia fear of pain
al·gor chill
al·go·rism counting system
al·go·ris·mic
al·go·rithm maths term
al·go·rith·mic
al·go·rith·mi·cal·ly
Al·ham·bra Spanish citadel
Al·ham·bresque
Al Hasa Saudi Arabian province
Al Hu·fuf (or Ho·fuf) Saudi Arabian town
ali·as (*plural* ·ases)
Ali Baba
ali·bi (*plural* ·bis)
Ali·can·te Spanish town
ali·cy·clic chemistry term
ali·dade (or ·dad) surveying instrument

al·ien
al·ien·abil·ity
al·ien·able
al·ien·age
al·ien·ate
al·iena·tion
al·iena·tor
al·ienee legal term
al·ien·ism
al·ien·ist *US* psychiatrist
al·ien·or legal term
ali·form wing-shaped
Ali·garh Indian city
alight (alight·ing, alight·ed or alit)
align
align·ment
alike
ali·ment
ali·men·ta·ry
ali·men·ta·tion
ali·men·ta·tive
ali·mo·ny
aline *rare spelling of* align
ali·ped having winglike limbs
ali·phat·ic chemistry term
ali·quant maths term
ali·quot maths term
aliun·de from another source
alive
aliza·rin dye
al·ka·hest (or ·ca·) alchemical solvent
al·ka·li (*plural* ·lis or ·lies)
al·kal·ic
al·ka·li·fy (·fies, ·fy·ing, ·fied)
al·ka·lim·eter
al·ka·li·met·ric
al·ka·lim·etry
al·ka·line
al·ka·lin·ity
al·ka·liz·able (or ·lis·able)
al·ka·lize (or ·lise)
al·ka·loid plant compound
al·ka·lo·sis medical condition
al·kane chemistry term
al·ka·net plant
al·kene chemistry term
al·kyd
al·kyl
al·kyla·tion chemistry term

al·kyne chemistry term
all
Allah
Al·laha·bad Indian city
al·lan·ite mineral
al·lan·to·ic
al·lan·toid
al·lan·toi·dal
al·lan·to·is (*plural* ·ides)
  embryology term
al·lar·gan·do musical term
al·lay
(alledge) *incorrect spelling of*
  allege
al·le·ga·tion
al·lege
al·leged
al·leg·ed·ly
al·le·giance
al·le·gori·cal (*or* ·gor·ic)
al·le·gori·cal·ly
al·le·go·rist
al·le·gori·za·tion (*or*
  ·sa·tion)
al·le·go·rize (*or* ·rise)
al·le·go·ry (*plural* ·ries)
al·le·gret·to (*plural* ·tos)
  musical term
al·le·gro (*plural* ·gros)
al·lele (*or* al·le·lo·morph)
  genetics term
al·lel·ic
al·lel·ism
al·le·luia (*or* hal·le·lu·jah;
  note Handel's Hallelujah
  Chorus)
alle·mande musical term
Al·len Irish bog
Al·len·town US city
Al·lep·pey Indian port
al·ler·gen allergy-causing
  substance
al·ler·gen·ic
al·ler·gic
al·ler·gist allergy specialist
al·ler·gy (*plural* ·gies)
al·le·thrin insecticide
al·le·vi·ate
al·le·via·tion
al·le·via·tive
al·le·via·tor
al·ley narrow lane; *compare*
  ally
alley·way
All·hal·lows

All·hal·low·tide
all·heal plant
al·lia·ceous of allium
al·li·ance
al·lied
Al·lier French river
Al·lies in World War II
al·lies *plural of* ally
al·li·ga·tor
all-important
all-inclusive
al·lit·er·ate
al·lit·era·tion
al·lit·era·tive
al·lium onion genus
Al·loa Scottish town
al·lo·cate
al·lo·ca·tion
al·loch·tho·nous geology
  term
al·lo·cu·tion formal speech
al·lo·dial
al·lo·dium (*or* al·lod; *plural*
  ·dia *or* ·lods) legal term
al·loga·mous
al·loga·my biology term
al·lo·graph signature
  written for another
al·lo·graph·ic
al·lom·er·ism chemistry
  term
al·lom·er·ous
al·lo·met·ric
al·lom·etry biology term
al·lo·morph
al·lo·mor·phic
al·lo·mor·phism chemistry
  term
al·lo·nym assumed name
al·lo·path (*or* ·lopa·thist)
  medical practitioner
al·lo·path·ic
al·lo·pathi·cal·ly
al·lopa·thy
al·lo·pat·ric biology term
al·lo·pat·ri·cal·ly
al·lo·phane mineral
al·lo·phone linguistics term
al·lo·phon·ic
al·lo·plasm biology term
al·lo·plas·mic
al·lo·pu·ri·nol anti-gout
  drug
al·lot (·lot·ting, ·lot·ted)
al·lot·ment

al·lo·trope chemistry term
al·lo·trop·ic
al·lo·tropi·cal·ly
al·lot·ro·py (*or* ·pism)
al·lot·tee
al·low
al·low·able
al·low·ance
Al·lo·way Scottish village
al·low·ed·ly
al·loy
all-round
all-rounder
all·seed plant
all·spice
all-star (*adj*)
all-time (*adj*)
al·lude refer; *compare* elude;
  illude
al·lure
al·lure·ment
al·lur·er
al·lur·ing
al·lu·sion reference; *compare*
  illusion
al·lu·sive
al·lu·sive·ness
al·lu·vial
al·lu·vion overflow
al·lu·vium (*plural* ·viums *or*
  ·via) soil; *compare*
  eluvium
ally (*verb* allies, ally·ing,
  allied; *noun, plural* allies)
  friend; *compare* alley
al·lyl
Alma-Ata Kazakh city
Al·ma·da Portuguese city
Al·ma·gest astronomy
  treatise
alma ma·ter *Latin* one's
  school or university
al·ma·nac
al·ma·nack almanac;
  *Archaic except in proper
  names, as* Whitaker's
  Almanack
al·man·dine gemstone
Al Marj Libyan town
al·me·mar platform in
  synagogue
Al·mería Spanish port
al·mighti·ly
al·mighti·ness
Al·mighty God

al·mighty
Al·mo·hades Muslim group
al·mond
al·mon·er
al·mon·ry
Al·mo·ra·vides Muslim group
al·most
alms
alms·house
al·mu·can·tar astronomy term
al·muce monk's cape
Al·ni·co (*Trademark*)
aloe (*plural* aloes) plant
aloes purgative drug
alo·etic
aloe ve·ra
aloft
alo·ha Hawaiian greeting
alo·in chemical compound
alone
along
along·shore
along·side
aloof
aloof·ness
alo·pecia
aloud
alow nautical term
alp
al·paca
alpen·glow
alpen·horn *variant of* alphorn
alpen·stock
Alpes-de-Haute-Pro·vence French department
Alpes Ma·ri·times French department
al·pes·trine
al·pha
al·pha·bet
al·pha·beti·cal (*or* ·bet·ic)
al·pha·beti·cal·ly
al·pha·beti·za·tion (*or* ·sa·tion)
al·pha·bet·ize (*or* ·ise)
al·pha·bet·iz·er (*or* ·is·er)
Al·pha Cen·tau·ri constellation
al·pha·nu·mer·ic (*or* al·pha·mer·ic)
al·pha·nu·meri·cal·ly (*or* al·pha·meri·cal·ly)

alp·horn (*or* alpen·horn)
al·pho·sis absence of skin pigmentation
Al·pine of the Alps
al·pine of mountains
al·pin·ism
al·pin·ist
Alps
al·ready
al·right *variant spelling of* all right, *regarded by some as* nonstandard
Al·sace French region
Alsace-Lorraine French region
Al·sa·tia *ancient name of* Alsace
Al·sa·tian
al·sike plant
also
also-ran
alt high in pitch
Al·tai Asian mountains
Al·ta·ic language group
Al·tair star
al·tar table in church; *compare* alter
altar·piece
alt·azi·muth astronomical instrument
al·ter to change; *compare* altar
al·ter·abil·ity
al·ter·able
al·tera·tion
al·tera·tive therapeutic drug
al·ter·cate
al·ter·ca·tion
al·ter ego
al·ter·nant
al·ter·nate
al·ter·nate·ly
al·ter·na·tion
al·ter·na·tive
al·ter·na·tive·ly
al·ter·na·tor
al·thaea (*US* ·thea) plant
Al·thing Icelandic parliament
alt·horn brass instrument
al·though
al·time·ter
al·ti·met·ri·cal
al·tim·etry
Al·ti·pla·no Andean plateau

al·tis·si·mo musical term
al·ti·tude
al·ti·tu·di·nal
alto (*plural* altos)
alto·cu·mu·lus (*plural* ·li) cloud
al·to·geth·er entirely; *note* all together all at the same time
Al·to·na German port
al·to re·lie·vo (*or* ri·; *plural* ·vos) sculpture term
al·to·stra·tus (*plural* ·ti) cloud
al·tri·cial ornithology term
Al·trin·cham English town
al·tru·ism
al·tru·ist
al·tru·is·tic
al·tru·is·ti·cal·ly
alu·del chemical vessel
alu·la (*plural* ·lae) tuft of feathers
alum
alu·mi·na aluminium oxide
alu·mi·nate
alu·mi·nif·er·ous
alu·min·ium (*US* ·min·um)
alu·mi·nize (*or* ·nise)
alu·mi·nos·ity
alu·mi·no·ther·my chemical process
alu·mi·nous resembling aluminium
alu·mi·num *US spelling of* aluminium
alum·nus (*fem* ·na; *plural* ·ni, *fem* ·nae) *US* former student
alum·root
Alun·dum (*Trademark*)
alu·nite mineral
al·veo·lar
al·veo·late
al·veo·la·tion
al·veo·lus (*plural* ·li) anatomy term
al·vine anatomy term
al·ways
alys·sum plant
Alzheimer's dis·ease
am
ama·da·vat *variant of* avadavat
ama·dou fungal substance

Ama·ga·sa·ki Japanese city
amah Eastern nurse
amal·gam
amal·gam·ate
amal·gama·tion
(amalgum) *incorrect spelling
of* amalgam
ama·ni·ta fungus
amanu·en·sis (*plural* ·ses)
ama·ranth plant
ama·ran·tha·ceous
ama·ran·thine
ama·relle cherry
Ama·ril·lo US city
ama·ryl·li·da·ceous
Ama·ryl·lis *Poetic*
   shepherdess
ama·ryl·lis plant
amass
amass·er
ama·teur
ama·teur·ish
ama·teur·ish·ness
ama·teur·ism
Amati violin
ama·tol explosive
   substance
ama·tory (*or* ·to·rial)
amau·ro·sis blindness
amau·rot·ic
amaut Eskimo woman's
   hood
amaze
amaze·ment
amaz·ing
amaz·ing·ly
Ama·zon South American
   river; female warrior
ama·zon aggressive female
Ama·zo·nas Brazilian state
Ama·zo·nian
ama·zon·ite gemstone
Am·ba·la Indian city
am·ba·ry (*or* ·ri; *plural* ·ries
   or ·ris) plant; fibre
am·bas·sa·dor
am·bas·sa·dor·ial
am·bas·sa·dor·ship
am·bas·sa·dress
am·ber
amber·gris substance from
   sperm whale
amber·jack fish
am·ber·oid (*or* am·broid)
   synthetic amber

am·bi·dex·ter·ity (*or*
   ·dex·trous·ness)
am·bi·dex·trous
am·bi·ence (*or* ·ance)
am·bi·ent
am·bi·gu·ity (*plural* ·ities)
am·bigu·ous
am·bigu·ous·ness
am·bit
am·bi·tion
am·bi·tious
am·biva·lence (*or* ·len·cy)
am·biva·lent
am·bi·ver·sion
am·bi·vert psychology term
am·ble
am·bler
am·blygo·nite mineral
am·blyo·pia impaired
   vision
am·bly·op·ic
ambo (*plural* ambos)
   pulpit
am·bo·cep·tor immune
   substance
Am·boi·na Indonesian
   island
am·boy·na (*or* ·boi·) wood
am·bro·sia
am·bro·sial (*or* ·sian)
am·bro·type photography
   term
am·bry (*or* aum·; *plural*
   ·bries) cupboard
ambs·ace lowest throw at
   dice
am·bu·lac·ral
am·bu·lac·rum (*plural* ·ra)
   band on starfish
am·bu·lance
am·bu·lant
am·bu·late
am·bu·la·tion
am·bu·la·tory (*plural*
   ·tories)
am·bus·cade ambush
am·bush
ameba *US spelling of*
   amoeba
ame·lio·rant
ame·lio·rate
ame·lio·ra·tion
ame·lio·ra·tive
ame·lio·ra·tor
amen

ame·nabil·ity (*or*
   ·nable·ness)
ame·nable
ame·nably
amend change; *compare*
   emend
amend·able
amenda·tory *US* corrective
amend·er
amend·ment
amends
amen·ity (*plural* ·ities)
amen·or·rhoea (*US* ·rhea)
Amen-Ra Egyptian god
ament mentally deficient
   person
am·ent (*or* am·en·tum;
   plural ·ents *or* ·ta) catkin
amen·tia mental deficiency
Ameri·ca
Ameri·can
Ameri·ca·na
Ameri·can·ism
Ameri·cani·za·tion (*or*
   ·sa·tion)
Ameri·can·ize (*or* ·ise)
Ameri·can·iz·er (*or* ·is·er)
am·eri·cium radioactive
   element
Am·er·in·dian North
   American Indian
Am·er·in·dic
am·ethyst
am·ethys·tine
am·etro·pia eye disorder
Am·ha·ra Ethiopian
   province
Am·har·ic Ethiopian
   language
ami·abil·ity (*or* ·able·ness)
ami·able
ami·ably
ami·an·thine (*or* ·thoid,
   ·thoid·al)
ami·an·thus variety of
   asbestos
ami·cabil·ity (*or*
   ·cable·ness)
ami·cable
ami·cably
am·ice part of priest's
   vestment
ami·cus cu·riae *Latin* friend
   of the court
amid

am·ide chemical compound
amid·ic
Ami·dol (*Trademark*) photographic developer
amid·ships
amidst
Ami·ens French city
ami·go (*plural* ·gos)
amine organic base; *compare* ammine
ami·no acid
ami·no·ben·zo·ic acid
ami·no·phenol
ami·no·py·rine
amir Afghan ruler
amiss
ami·to·sis form of cell division
ami·tot·ic
ami·toti·cal·ly
am·ity (*plural* ·ities)
Am·man Jordanian capital
am·meter
am·mine ammonia compound; *compare* amine
ammo *short for* ammunition
am·mo·coete zoology term
am·mo·nal explosive compound
am·mo·nate
am·mo·nia
am·mo·ni·ac gum resin
am·mo·nia·cal
am·mo·ni·ate
am·mo·nia·tion
am·mon·ic
am·moni·cal
am·moni·fi·ca·tion
am·moni·fy (·fies, ·fy·ing, ·fied)
am·mo·nite fossil
am·mo·nit·ic
am·mo·nium
am·mu·ni·tion
am·ne·sia
am·ne·si·ac (*or* am·ne·sic)
am·nes·ty (*noun, plural* ·ties; *verb* ·ties, ·ty·ing, ·tied)
am·nio·cen·tesis
am·ni·on (*plural* ·ni·ons *or* ·nia) fetal membrane
am·ni·ot·ic
amoe·ba (*US* ame·; *plural* ·bae *or* ·bas)

am·oebaean (*or* ·oebean; *US* am·ebean) verse form
am·oebia·sis (*US* am·ebia·; *plural* ·ses) parasitic infection
amoe·bic (*US* ame·)
amoe·bo·cyte (*US* ame·)
amoe·boid (*US* ame·)
amok (*or* amuck)
among (*or* amongst)
amon·til·la·do (*plural* ·dos) sherry
amor·al morally neutral; *compare* immoral
amo·ral·ity
amor·al·ly
amo·ret·to (*or* ·ri·no; *plural* ·ret·ti *or* ·ri·ni) cupid
amo·rist
amo·ro·so musical term
amo·rous
amo·rous·ness
amor pa·triae *Latin* love of one's country
amor·phism
amor·phous
amor·tiz·able (*or* ·tis·able)
amor·ti·za·tion (*or* ·sa·tion)
amor·tize (*or* ·tise)
amor·tize·ment (*or* ·tise·ment)
amount
amour love affair
amour-propre self-respect
Amoy Chinese port
amp
am·pe·lop·sis vine
am·per·age
am·pere
ampere-hour
ampere-turn
am·per·sand the character &
am·pheta·mine
am·phi·ar·thro·sis (*plural* ·ses) anatomy term
am·phi·as·ter biology term
am·phib·ian
am·phi·bi·ot·ic zoology term
am·phibi·ous
am·phi·blas·tu·la sponge larva
am·phi·bole mineral

am·phi·bol·ic (*or* ·phibo·lous)
am·phibo·lite rock
am·phibo·logi·cal
am·phi·bol·ogy (*or* am·phibo·ly; *plural* ·ogies *or* ·lies) ambiguity
am·phi·brach metrical foot
am·phi·brach·ic
am·phi·chro·ic (*or* am·phi·chro·mat·ic) producing two colours
am·phi·coe·lous zoology term
am·phic·ty·on ancient Greek religious councillor
am·phic·ty·on·ic
am·phic·tyo·ny (*plural* ·nies)
am·phi·dip·loid biology term
am·phi·gor·ic
am·phi·go·ry (*or* ·gou·ri; *plural* ·ries *or* ·ris) nonsense writing
am·phima·cer metrical foot
am·phi·mix·is (*plural* ·mixes) sexual reproduction
am·phi·ox·us (*plural* ·oxi *or* ·ox·uses) aquatic organism
am·phi·pod aquatic organism
am·phip·ro·sty·lar
am·phip·ro·style architectural term
am·phis·bae·na (*plural* ·nae *or* ·nas) worm lizard
am·phis·bae·nic
am·phi·sty·lar architectural term
am·phi·thea·tre (*US* ·ter)
am·phi·thecium (*plural* ·thecia) botany term
am·phit·ri·cha bacteria
am·phit·ri·chous
Amphitrite Greek goddess
am·phit·ro·pous botany term
Amphitryon mythological character
am·pho·ra (*plural* ·rae *or* ·ras)
am·pho·ter·ic chemistry term

am·ple
am·plexi·caul botany term
am·pli·fi·able
am·pli·fi·ca·tion
am·pli·fi·er
am·pli·fy (·fies, ·fy·ing, ·fied)
am·pli·tude
am·ply
am·poule (or esp. US ·pule) container for injectable liquids
am·pul·la (plural ·lae) flask
am·pul·la·ceous (or ·ceal)
am·pul·lar (or ·lary)
am·pu·tate
am·pu·ta·tion
am·pu·tee
Am·ra·va·ti Indian town
am·ri·ta (or ·ree·) Hindu concept
Am·rit·sar Indian city
Am·ster·dam
amuck variant spelling of amok
amu·let
Amur Asian river
amuse
amuse·ment
amus·ing
amus·ing·ly
amyg·da·la (plural ·lae) anatomy term
amyg·da·late of almonds
amyg·dale geology term
amyg·da·lin almond extract
amyg·da·line relating to tonsils or almonds
amyg·da·loid rock
amyg·da·loi·dal
amyl
amy·la·ceous starchy
am·yl·ase enzyme
am·yl·ene chemical compound
amy·loid starchlike protein
amy·loly·sis biology term
amy·lo·pec·tin component of starch
amy·lop·sin enzyme
am·yl·ose component of starch
amy·lum starch
Amy·tal (Trademark) drug
an

ana·bae·na plant
ana·ban·tid fish
Ana·bap·tist Protestant sect
ana·bas fish
anaba·sis (plural ·ses) military expedition
ana·bat·ic
ana·bio·sis resuscitation
ana·bleps (plural ·bleps) fish
ana·bol·ic
anabo·lism
anabo·lite
anabo·lit·ic
ana·branch
ana·car·dia·ceous botany term
anacho·rism geographical misplacement
ana·chron·ic out of date order
anach·ro·nism
anach·ro·nis·tic
anach·ro·nis·ti·cal·ly
ana·cli·nal geology term
ana·cli·sis
ana·clit·ic psychology term
ana·co·lu·thia lack of grammatical sequence
ana·co·lu·thic
ana·co·lu·thon (plural ·tha)
ana·con·da
ana·cous·tic soundless
ana·cru·sis (plural ·ses) linguistics term
ana·crus·tic
ana·dem garland
ana·di·plo·sis rhetorical term
anad·ro·mous migrating up river; compare catadromous
anaemia (US anemia)
anaemic (US anemic)
an·aer·obe (or ·aero·bium; plural ·aer·obes or ·aero·bia)
an·aero·bic not requiring oxygen
an·aero·bi·cal·ly
an·aes·the·sia (US ·es·)
an·aes·thet·ic (US ·es·)
an·aes·thet·ics (US an·es·the·si·ology)
anaes·the·tist (US an·es·the·si·olo·gist)

doctor specializing in anaesthetics; compare anesthetist
anaes·the·ti·za·tion (or ·sa·tion; US anes·the·ti·za·tion)
anaes·the·tize (or ·tise; US anes·the·tize)
ana·glyph stereoscopic picture
ana·glyph·ic (or ·glyphi·cal, ·glyp·tic, ·glyp·ti·cal)
Ana·glyp·ta (Trademark) wallpaper
ana·go·ge (or ·gy) allegorical interpretation
ana·gog·ic (or ·gogi·cal)
ana·gogi·cal·ly
ana·gram
ana·gram·mat·ic (or ·mati·cal)
ana·gram·mati·cal·ly
ana·gram·ma·tism
ana·gram·ma·tist
ana·gram·ma·tize (or ·tise)
Ana·heim Californian city
anal
(analagous) incorrect spelling of analogous
anal·cite (or ·cine) mineral
ana·lec·tic
ana·lects (or ·lec·ta)
ana·lem·ma (plural ·mas or ·ma·ta) type of sundial
ana·lem·mat·ic
ana·lep·tic restorative drug
an·al·gesia (or ·gia)
an·alge·sic
ana·log US variant spelling of analogue
ana·logi·cal (or ·log·ic)
analo·gist
analo·gize (or ·gise) draw comparisons
analo·gous
ana·logue (US also analog; in the UK the US spelling is often used in computer science and in electronics)
anal·ogy (plural ·ogies)
an·al·pha·bet·ic
an·al·pha·beti·cal·ly
ana·lys·able

analy·sand person
  undergoing psychoanalysis
ana·ly·sa·tion
ana·lyse (*US* ·lyze)
ana·lys·er (*US* ·lyz·)
analy·sis (*plural* ·ses)
ana·lyst analyser; *compare*
  annalist
ana·lyt·ic (*or* ·lyti·cal)
ana·lyti·cal·ly
Anam·bra Nigerian state
an·am·ne·sis (*plural* ·ses)
  recollection
an·am·nes·tic
an·am·nes·ti·cal·ly
ana·mor·phic
ana·mor·phism geology
  term
ana·mor·pho·scope optical
  device
ana·mor·pho·sis (*plural*
  ·ses) distorted image
an·an·drous botany term
Ananias biblical character
an·an·thous flowerless
ana·pest (*or* ·paest) metrical
  foot
ana·pes·tic (*or* ·paes·)
ana·phase biology term
anapho·ra rhetorical device
anapho·ral (*or* ana·phor·ic)
ana·phori·cal·ly
an·aph·ro·disia
an·aph·ro·dis·iac
ana·phy·lac·tic
ana·phy·lac·ti·cal·ly
ana·phy·lax·is type of
  allergy
ana·pla·sia biology term
ana·plas·tic
ana·plas·ty plastic surgery
an·ap·tyc·tic
an·ap·tyx·is (*plural* ·tyxes)
  linguistics term
an·ar·chic (*or* ·chi·cal)
an·ar·chi·cal·ly
an·ar·chism
an·ar·chist
an·ar·chis·tic
an·ar·chy
an·ar·thria loss of speech
an·ar·throus
ana·sar·ca medical term
ana·sar·cous
an·as·tig·mat type of lens

an·as·tig·mat·ic
anas·to·mose
anas·to·mo·sis (*plural* ·ses)
anas·to·mot·ic
anas·tro·phe rhetorical
  device
ana·tase mineral
anath·ema (*plural* ·emas)
anath·ema·ti·za·tion (*or*
  ·sa·tion)
anath·ema·tize (*or* ·tise)
Ana·to·lia part of Turkey
Ana·to·lian
ana·tomi·cal
ana·tomi·cal·ly
anato·mist
anato·mi·za·tion (*or*
  ·sa·tion)
anato·mize (*or* ·mise)
anato·miz·er (*or* ·mis·er)
anato·my (*plural* ·mies)
anat·ro·pous botany term
an·bury (*plural* ·buries)
  animal tumour
an·ces·tor
an·ces·tral
an·ces·tral·ly
an·ces·tress
an·ces·try (*plural* ·tries)
Anchises mythological
  prince
an·chor
An·chor·age Alaskan city
an·chor·age
an·cho·rite (*fem* ·ress)
  recluse; *compare* ankerite
an·cho·veta fish
an·cho·vy (*plural* ·vies *or*
  ·vy)
an·chu·sa plant
an·cien ré·gime (*plural*
  an·ciens ré·gimes) *French*
  pre-Revolutionary France
an·cient
an·cient·ness
an·cil·lary (*plural* ·laries)
an·cipi·tal (*or* ·tous) biology
  term
an·con (*or* ·cone; *plural*
  ·cones) architectural term
An·co·na Italian port
an·co·nal (*or* ·neal)
an·cy·los·to·mia·sis (*or*
  an·ky·, an·chy·)
  hookworm disease

and
An·da·lu·sia Spanish region
an·da·lu·site mineral
an·dan·te musical term
an·dan·ti·no (*plural* ·nos)
  musical term
An·dean
An·der·lecht Belgian town
An·der·son Canadian river
An·des
an·desine mineral
an·desite rock
An·dhra Pra·desh Indian
  state
and·iron
An·di·zhan Uzbek city
An·dor·ra
An·dor·ra La Vel·la capital
  of Andorra
An·dor·ran
And·over
an·dra·dite gemstone
Androcles legendary
  character
an·dro·clin·ium botany
  term
an·droe·cial
an·droe·cium (*plural* ·cia)
  stamens of flower
an·dro·gen hormone
an·dro·gen·ic
an·drog·enous producing
  only male offspring;
  compare androgynous
an·dro·gyne
an·drogy·nous having male
  and female characteristics;
  compare androgenous
an·droid
Andromache mythological
  character
An·drom·eda constellation
An·dros Greek island
an·dro·sphinx (*plural*
  ·sphinxes *or* ·sphinges)
an·dros·ter·one hormone
Andvari mythological
  character
ane *Scot* one
an·ec·dot·age
an·ec·do·tal
an·ec·dote
an·ec·dot·ic
an·ec·dot·ist
an·echo·ic

anemia *US spelling of*
  anaemia
anemic *US spelling of*
  anaemic
anemo·chore botany term
anemo·graph
anemo·graph·ic
anemo·graphi·cal·ly
an·emog·ra·phy recording
  wind measurements
an·emol·ogy
an·emom·eter
an·emo·met·ric
an·emo·met·ri·cal
an·emom·etry
anemo·ne
an·emophi·lous
  wind-pollinated
an·emophi·ly
anemo·scope
anent *Scot* concerning
aner·gic lacking energy
an·er·gy
an·er·oid
an·es·the·sia *US spelling of*
  anaesthesia
an·es·thesi·olo·gist *US*
  anaesthetist
an·es·thesi·ology *US*
  anaesthetics
an·es·the·tist *US* person
  qualified to administer
  anaesthetics, not
  necessarily a doctor;
  compare **anaesthetist**
an·es·trus *US spelling of*
  anoestrus
an·ethole organic
  compound
an·eu·ploid biology term
aneu·rin vitamin
aneu·rysm (*or* **·rism**)
  blood-vessel defect
aneu·rys·mal (*or* **·ris·mal**,
  ·rys·mat·ic, **·ris·mat·ic**)
anew
an·frac·tu·os·ity (*plural*
  ·ities)
an·frac·tu·ous convoluted
An·garsk Russian city
an·ga·ry legal term
an·gel
An·ge·leno (*plural* **·nos**)
  inhabitant of Los
  Angeles

angel·fish (*plural* **·fish** *or*
  ·fishes)
an·gel·ic
an·gel·ica
an·geli·cal
an·gel·ol·ogy
An·ge·lus Roman Catholic
  prayers
an·ger
An·gers French town
An·ge·vin inhabitant of
  Anjou
an·gi·na
an·gi·nal
an·gi·na pec·to·ris
an·gi·nose (*or* **·nous**)
an·gi·ol·ogy branch of
  medicine
an·gio·ma (*plural* **·mas** *or*
  ·ma·ta) tumour
an·gi·oma·tous
an·gio·sperm botany term
an·gio·sper·mous
Ang·kor Cambodian region
An·gle ancient German
  invader
an·gle
an·gler
An·gle·sey
an·gle·site mineral
angle·worm
An·glian of Angles or East
  Anglia
An·gli·can of Church of
  England
An·gli·can·ism
An·gli·cism English idiom
An·gli·cist
an·gli·ci·za·tion (*or*
  ·sa·tion)
an·gli·cize (*or* **·cise**)
an·gli·fy (**·fies**, **·fy·ing**,
  ·fied)
an·gling
Anglo-American
Anglo-Catholic
Anglo-Catholicism
Anglo-Irish
An·glo·ma·nia
An·glo·phile (*or* **·phil**)
An·glo·philia
An·glo·phili·ac (*or*
  ·phil·ic)
An·glo·phobe
An·glo·pho·bia

An·glo·phone native
  English speaker
Anglo-Saxon
An·go·la
An·go·lan
an·go·ra
an·gos·tu·ra bitter-tasting
  bark
An·gos·tu·ra Bit·ters
  (*Trademark*)
an·gri·ly
an·gry (**·gri·er**, **·gri·est**)
angst anxiety
ang·strom unit of length
An·guil·la West Indian
  island
an·guil·li·form eel-shaped
an·guine snakelike
an·guish
an·gu·lar
an·gu·lar·ity (*plural* **·ities**)
an·gu·late
an·gu·la·tion
An·gus Scottish council area
ang·wan·ti·bo (*plural* **·bos**)
  animal
An·halt German region
an·he·dral
an·hin·ga bird
An·hwei Chinese province
an·hy·dride
an·hy·drite
an·hy·drous
ani (*plural* **anis**) bird
Ani·ak·chak Alaskan
  volcano
an·icon·ic
anil shrub
an·ile like an old woman
ani·line organic compound
anil·ity
ani·ma
ani·mad·ver·sion
ani·mad·vert
ani·mal
ani·mal·cu·lar
ani·mal·cule (*or* **·cu·lum**;
  plural **·cules** *or* **·cu·la**)
  microscopic animal
ani·mal·ism
ani·mal·ist
ani·mal·ity
ani·mali·za·tion (*or*
  ·sa·tion)
ani·mal·ize (*or* **·ise**)

ani·mate
ani·ma·tion
ani·ma·tism
ani·ma·to *music term*
ani·ma·tor (*or* ·mat·er)
ani·mé resin
ani·mism
ani·mist
ani·mis·tic
ani·mos·ity (*plural* ·ities)
ani·mus
an·ion *chemistry term*
ani·on·ic
an·ise *plant*
ani·seed
an·isei·ko·nia *visual defect*
an·isei·kon·ic
ani·sette liqueur
ani·so·dac·tyl *zoology term*
ani·so·dac·ty·lous
ani·soga·mous
ani·soga·my *type of sexual reproduction*
ani·sole *chemical compound*
an·isom·er·ous *botany term*
an·iso·met·ric
an·iso·metro·pia *visual disorder*
an·iso·trop·ic
an·isot·ro·py
An·jou *French province*
An·ka·ra *Turkish city*
an·ker·ite *mineral; compare* anchorite
ankh *Egyptian cross*
An·king *Chinese city*
an·kle
ankle·bone
an·klet
an·ky·lo·saur *dinosaur*
an·ky·lose (*or* ·chy·)
an·ky·lo·sis (*or* ·chy·) *immobility of joint*
an·ky·lot·ic (*or* ·chy·)
an·lace *medieval dagger*
an·la·ge (*plural* ·gen *or* ·ges) *biology term*
An·na·ba *Algerian port*
an·na·berg·ite *mineral*
an·nal
an·nal·ist *compiler of annals; compare* analyst
an·nal·is·tic
an·nals

An·nam (*or* Anam) part of Vietnam
An·napo·lis *US city*
An·na·pur·na (*or* Ana·) *Nepalese mountains*
an·nates *pope's revenue*
an·nat·to (*or* anat·; *plural* ·tos) *tree*
an·neal
an·neal·er
Anne·cy *French lake*
an·nelid *worm*
an·neli·dan
an·nex *take over or add on; compare* annexe
an·nexa·tion
an·nexa·tion·al
an·nexa·tion·ism
an·nexa·tion·ist
an·nexe *addition to building; compare* annex
an·ni·hil·able
an·ni·hi·late
an·ni·hi·la·tion
an·ni·hi·la·tive
an·ni·hi·la·tor
an·ni·ver·sa·ry (*plural* ·saries)
anno Domi·ni *Latin year of our Lord*
an·no·tate
an·no·ta·tion
an·no·ta·tive
an·no·ta·tor
an·nounce
an·nounce·ment
an·nounc·er
an·noy
an·noy·ance
an·nual
an·nual·ly
an·nui·tant
an·nu·ity (*plural* ·ities)
an·nul (·nul·ling, ·nulled)
an·nu·lar
an·nu·late ringed
an·nu·la·tion
an·nu·let *architectural moulding*
an·nul·lable
an·nul·ment
an·nu·lose *segmented*
an·nu·lus (*plural* ·li *or* ·luses)

an·nun·ci·ate announce; *compare* enunciate
An·nun·cia·tion *Christian feast*
an·nun·cia·tion announcement
an·nun·cia·tive (*or* ·tory)
an·nun·cia·tor
anoa *cattle*
an·ode
an·od·ic
ano·dize (*or* ·dise)
ano·dyne *painkiller*
an·oes·trus (*US* ·es·)
anoint
anoint·er
anoint·ment
anole *lizard*
anoma·lis·tic
anoma·lis·ti·cal·ly
anoma·lous
anoma·ly (*plural* ·lies)
anom·ic
an·omie (*or* ·omy) *lack of social standards*
anon *Archaic soon*
ano·nym *pseudonym*
ano·nym·ity
anony·mous
anophe·les (*plural* ·les) *mosquito*
ano·rak
ano·rexia ner·vo·sa
ano·rex·ic
an·or·thite *mineral*
an·or·thit·ic
an·or·tho·site *rock*
an·os·mat·ic (*or* an·os·mic)
an·os·mia *inability to smell*
an·oth·er
an·ox·aemia (*US* ·emia) *oxygen deficiency in blood*
an·ox·aemic (*US* ·emic)
an·oxia *lack of oxygen*
an·ox·ic
an·sate *having a handle*
An·schluss *union of Austria with Germany*
an·ser·ine (*or* ·ous) *of geese*
An·shan *Chinese city*
an·swer
an·swer·abil·ity (*or* ·able·ness)
an·swer·able
ant

anta architectural term
An·ta·buse (*Trademark*)
ant·acid
an·tago·nism
an·tago·nist
an·tago·nis·tic
an·tago·nis·ti·cal·ly
an·tago·niz·able (*or*
    ·nis·able)
an·tago·ni·za·tion (*or*
    ·sa·tion)
an·tago·nize (*or* ·nise)
ant·al·ka·li (*plural* ·lis *or*
    ·lies)
ant·al·ka·line
An·ta·na·na·ri·vo
    Madagascan capital
Ant·arc·tic
Ant·arc·ti·ca
An·tar·es star
ante stake in poker; advance
    payment; *compare* anti
ant·eater
ante·bel·lum
ante·cede
ante·ced·ence
ante·ced·ent
an·te·ced·ents
ante·choir part of church
ante·date
ante·di·lu·vian
ante·fix (*plural* ·fixes *or*
    ·fixa) roof ornament
ante·fix·al
ante·lope
ante·me·rid·ian (*adj*)
ante me·ridi·em *Latin*
    before noon
ante-mortem (*adj*) before
    death
ante·na·tal
an·ten·na (*plural* ·nae)
    insect feelers
an·ten·na (*plural* ·nas)
    aerial
an·ten·nule
ante·pen·dium (*plural* ·dia)
    altar covering
ante·penult
ante·penul·ti·mate
ante·ri·or
ante·room
ante·type earlier form
ante·ver·sion
ante·vert tilt forwards

ant·he·li·on (*plural* ·lia)
    meteorology term
ant·he·lix (*or* anti·; *plural*
    ·heli·ces *or* ·he·lixes) ear
    cartilage
an·thel·min·tic (*or* ·thic)
    vermifuge
an·them
an·themi·on (*plural* ·mia)
    Greek design
an·ther
an·ther·idial
an·ther·id·ium (*plural* ·ia)
    botany term
an·thero·zo·id botany term
an·thesis flowering
an·tho·cya·nin (*or* ·cy·an)
    pigment
an·tho·dium (*plural* ·dia)
    botany term
an·tho·logi·cal
an·tholo·gist
an·tholo·gize (*or* ·gise)
an·thol·ogy (*plural* ·ogies)
an·tho·phore botany term
an·tho·taxy botany term
an·tho·zo·an marine
    organism
an·thra·cene chemical
    compound
an·thra·cite coal
an·thra·cit·ic
an·thrac·nose fungal
    disease
an·thra·coid
an·thra·qui·none chemical
    compound
an·thrax (*plural* ·thra·ces)
an·thro·po·cen·tric
an·thro·po·cen·trism
an·thro·po·gen·esis (*or*
    ·geny) study of man's
    origin
an·thro·po·genet·ic (*or*
    ·gen·ic)
an·thro·poid
an·thro·poi·dal
an·thro·po·logi·cal
an·thro·polo·gist
an·thro·pol·ogy
an·thro·po·met·ric (*or*
    ·ri·cal)
an·thro·po·met·ri·cal·ly
an·thro·pome·trist
an·thro·pom·etry

an·thro·po·mor·phic
an·thro·po·mor·phism
an·thro·po·mor·phist
an·thro·po·mor·phize (*or*
    ·phise)
an·thro·po·mor·pho·sis
an·thro·po·mor·phous
an·thro·po·path·ic
an·thro·popa·thy (*or*
    ·thism) attribution of
    human passions to a deity
an·thro·popha·gi (*sing.*
    ·gus) cannibals
an·thro·popha·gic
an·thro·popha·gite
an·thro·popha·gy
    cannibalism
an·thro·po·soph·ic
an·thro·poso·phy
an·thu·rium plant
anti *Slang* opposed to;
    compare ante
anti-aircraft
an·ti·ar tree
anti·bary·on physics term
An·tibes French port
anti·bio·sis
anti·bi·ot·ic
anti·body (*plural* ·bodies)
an·tic
anti·cata·lyst
anti·cath·ode
anti·chlor
anti·chlo·ris·tic
anti·cho·lin·er·gic
    physiology term
anti·cho·lin·es·ter·ase
    enzyme
Anti·christ
an·tici·pant
an·tici·pate
an·tici·pa·tion
an·tici·pa·tive
an·tici·pa·tor
an·tici·pa·to·ri·ly
an·tici·pa·tory
anti·clas·tic maths term
anti·cleri·cal
anti·cli·mac·tic
anti·cli·mac·ti·cal·ly
anti·cli·max
anti·cli·nal
anti·cline geology term
anti·cli·no·rium (*plural*
    ·ria) geology term

anti·clock·wise
anti·co·agu·lant
anti·con·vul·sant
An·ti·cos·ti Canadian island
anti·cy·clone
anti·cy·clon·ic
anti·de·pres·sant
anti·dote
anti·drom·ic biology term
An·tie·tam US battle site
anti·febrile
anti·fer·ro·mag·ne·tism
anti·foul·ing protective paint
anti·freeze
anti·gen
anti·gen·ic
anti·geni·cal·ly
Antigone mythological character
An·ti·gua West Indian island
anti·ha·la·tion photography term
anti·he·ro (plural ·roes)
anti·his·ta·mine
anti·icer
anti·imperi·al·ism
anti·imperi·al·ist
anti·knock petrol additive
anti·lep·ton physics term
An·til·les West Indian islands
anti·log
anti·loga·rithm
anti·loga·rith·mic
an·tilo·gism philosophy term
an·til·ogy (plural ·ogies) contradiction in terms
anti·ma·cas·sar
anti·mag·net·ic
anti·ma·lar·ial
anti·masque grotesque dance
anti·mat·ter
anti·mere biology term
anti·mer·ic
an·tim·er·ism
anti·mis·sile
anti·mo·nar·chic
anti·mo·nar·chist
anti·mo·nial
anti·mo·nic
anti·mo·nous

anti·mo·ny chemical element; compare antinomy
anti·mo·nyl
anti·na·tion·al·ist
anti·na·tion·al·is·tic
anti·neu·tri·no (plural ·nos)
anti·neu·tron
anti·nod·al
anti·node physics term
anti·nom·ic
anti·nomi·cal·ly
an·tino·my (plural ·mies) paradox; compare antimony
anti·nu·cleon
An·ti·och Turkish city
anti·oxi·dant
anti·par·al·lel
anti·par·ticle
anti·pas·to (plural ·ti) Italian hors d'oeuvres
anti·pa·thet·ic (or ·ical)
anti·pa·theti·cal·ly
an·tipa·thy (plural ·thies)
anti·peri·od·ic
anti·peri·stal·sis physiology term
anti·per·son·nel
anti·per·spi·rant
anti·phlo·gis·tic
anti·phon
an·tipho·nal
an·tipho·nal·ly
an·tipho·nary (plural ·naries) collection of biblical passages
an·tipho·ny (plural ·nies) type of choral singing
an·tiph·ra·sis rhetorical device
an·tipo·dal
anti·pode
an·tipo·dean
An·tipo·des Australia and New Zealand
an·tipo·des points diametrically opposite on Earth
anti·pope
anti·prag·mat·ic
anti·prag·ma·tism
anti·pro·ton
anti·psy·chia·try
anti·psy·chot·ic

anti·py·resis
anti·py·ret·ic
anti·py·rine
anti·quar·ian
anti·quary (plural ·quaries)
anti·quate
anti·quat·ed
anti·qua·ted·ness
an·tique
an·tiq·uity (plural ·uities)
anti·ra·chit·ic preventing rickets
anti·racism
anti·racist
anti·repub·li·can
anti·revo·lu·tion·ary
an·tir·rhi·num
anti·scor·bu·tic preventing scurvy
anti·Semite
anti·Semitic
anti·Semitism
anti·sep·sis
anti·sep·tic
anti·sep·ti·cal·ly
anti·serum (plural ·serums or ·sera)
anti·slav·ery
anti·so·cial
anti·spas·mod·ic
anti·stat·ic
an·tis·tro·phe
anti·stroph·ic
anti·sub·ma·rine
anti·tank
an·tith·esis (plural ·ses)
anti·theti·cal (or ·thet·ic)
anti·theti·cal·ly
anti·tox·ic
anti·tox·in
anti·trades winds
an·tit·ra·gus (plural ·gi) part of ear
anti·tus·sive alleviating coughing
anti·type
anti·ven·in
anti·vi·ral
anti·vivi·sec·tion
anti·vivi·sec·tion·ist
anti·world world composed of antimatter
ant·ler
ant·lered
Ant·lia constellation

ant·like
ant·li·on insect
An·to·fa·gas·ta Chilean port
an·to·no·ma·sia figure of
speech
an·to·no·mas·tic
an·to·no·mas·ti·cal·ly
an·to·nym
an·tony·mous
an·tre cavern
An·trim
an·trorse directed upwards
an·trum (plural ·tra)
anatomy term
An·tung Chinese port
Ant·werp
Anubis Egyptian god
anu·ran tailless amphibian
anu·resis inability to urinate
anu·ria inability to form
urine
anu·rous tailless
anus
an·vil
anxi·ety (plural ·eties)
anx·ious
anx·ious·ness
any
An·yang Chinese town
any·body
any·how
any·one
any·thing
any·way
any·where
any·wise
An·zac Australian and New
Zealand Army Corps
An·zio Italian port
aorist linguistics term
aoris·tic
aoris·ti·cal·ly
aor·ta (plural ·tas or ·tae)
aor·tic (or ·tal)
aou·dad sheep
apace
Apache (plural Apaches or
Apache) American Indian
apache gangster
apa·go·ge logic term
apa·gog·ic (or ·gogi·cal)
apa·gogi·cal·ly
ap·an·age variant spelling of
appanage
Apar·ri Philippine port

apart
apart·heid
apart·ment
apa·tet·ic of animal
coloration
apa·thet·ic
apa·theti·cal·ly
apa·thy
apa·tite mineral
ape
apeak
Apel·doorn Dutch town
ape·like
ape·man (plural ·men)
Ap·en·nines
aper·çu French outline or
insight
aperi·ent
aperi·od·ic at irregular
intervals
aperi·odi·cal·ly
aperio·dic·ity
apé·ri·tif drink before meal;
compare aperitive
ape·ri·tive laxative; compare
apéritif
ap·er·ture
ap·ery (plural ·eries)
imitative behaviour
apet·al·ous petal-less
apet·aly
apex (plural apexes or
api·ces)
aphaer·esis (or apher·;
plural ·ses) linguistics term
apha·gia inability to
swallow
apha·nite rock
apha·sia language disorder
apha·sic
ap·he·lian
ap·he·li·on (plural ·lia)
point in planet's orbit
ap·he·lio·trop·ic botany
term
apher·esis variant spelling of
aphaeresis
aph·esis linguistics term
aphet·ic
apheti·cal·ly
aphid
aphidi·ous
aphis (plural aphi·des)
apho·nia (or ·ny) loss of
voice

aphon·ic
apho·rism
apho·rist
apho·ris·tic
apho·rize (or ·rise)
apho·tic without light
aph·ro·di·sia
aph·ro·disi·ac
Aphrodite Greek goddess
aph·tha (plural ·thae) ulcer
aphyl·lous leafless
aphyl·ly
apian of bees
api·ar·ian of beekeeping
apia·rist
api·ary (plural ·aries)
beehive; compare aviary
api·cal
api·cal·ly
api·ces plural of apex
apicu·late
api·cul·tur·al
api·cul·ture
api·cul·tur·ist
apiece
à pied French on foot
Api·ezon (Trademark)
Apis sacred bull
ap·ish
ap·ish·ness
apiv·or·ous bee-eating
apla·cen·tal
ap·la·nat·ic physics term
ap·la·nati·cal·ly
aplano·sphere
aplano·spore
apla·sia congenital absence
of organ
aplas·tic
aplen·ty
ap·lite (or hap·) rock
ap·lit·ic (or hap·)
aplomb
ap·noea (US ·nea) inability
to breath
Apo Philippine mountain
apoca·lypse
apoca·lyp·tic
apoca·lyp·ti·cal·ly
apo·carp
apo·car·pous botany term
apo·chro·mat
apo·chro·mat·ic physics
term
apo·chro·ma·tism

apoco·pate
apoco·pa·tion
apoco·pe linguistics term
apo·crine physiology term
Apoc·ry·pha Old Testament appendix
apoc·ry·phal of doubtful authenticity
apoc·ry·phal·ly
apocy·na·ceous botany term
apo·cyn·thi·on astronomy term
apo·dal without feet
apo·dic·tic (or ·deic·) unquestionably true
apo·dic·ti·cal·ly (or ·deic·)
apodo·sis (plural ·ses) grammar term
apo·en·zyme
apo·gam·ic
apoga·mous
apoga·my type of plant reproduction
apo·gee
apo·geo·trop·ic botany term
apo·liti·cal
apo·liti·cal·ly
Apol·li·naris mineral water
Apollo Greek god
Apol·lo spacecraft
Ap·ol·lo·nian
Apollyon the Devil
apolo·get·ic
apolo·geti·cal·ly
apolo·get·ics branch of theology
apo·lo·gia
apolo·gist
apolo·gize (or ·gise)
apolo·giz·er (or ·gis·er)
apo·logue moral fable
apol·ogy (plural ·ogies)
apo·lune astronomy term
apo·mict
apo·mic·tic
apo·mixis (plural ·mixes) asexual reproduction
apo·mor·phine alkaloid
apo·neu·ro·sis (plural ·ses) anatomy term
apo·neu·rot·ic
apopha·sis rhetorical device

apo·phthegm (or apo·thegm) cryptic remark; compare apothem
apophy·ge architectural term
apophyl·lite mineral
apophy·sate
apophy·sial
apophy·sis (plural ·ses) outgrowth
apo·plec·tic
apo·plexy
aport nautical term
apo·semat·ic zoology term
apo·sio·pe·sis (plural ·ses) rhetorical device
apo·sio·pet·ic
apo·spory botany term
apos·ta·sy (plural ·sies)
apos·tate
apos·ta·tize (or ·tise)
a pos·terio·ri Latin from effect to cause; compare a priori
apos·til marginal note
apos·tle
apos·to·late
ap·os·tol·ic
apos·tro·phe
apo·stroph·ic
apos·tro·phize (or ·phise)
apoth·ecary (plural ·ecaries)
apo·the·cial
apo·the·cium (plural ·cia)
apo·thegm variant spelling of apophthegm
apo·them geometry term; compare apophthegm
apoth·eo·sis (plural ·ses)
apoth·eo·size (or ·sise) glorify
apo·tro·pa·ic preventing evil
ap·pal (US ·pall; ·pal·ling, ·palled)
Ap·pa·la·chia US region
Appa·la·chian
ap·pal·ling
ap·pal·ling·ly
Ap·pa·loo·sa horse
ap·pa·nage (or apa·nage) perquisite
ap·pa·rat·us (plural ·rat·us or ·rat·uses)

ap·par·el (·el·ling, ·elled; US ·el·ing, ·eled)
ap·par·ent
ap·par·ent·ness
ap·pa·ri·tion
ap·pari·tor ecclesiastical court officer
ap·pas·sio·na·to musical term
ap·peal
ap·peal·able
ap·peal·er
ap·peal·ing·ly
ap·pear
ap·pear·ance
ap·peas·able
ap·pease
ap·peas·er
ap·pease·ment
ap·pel fencing term
ap·pel·lant
ap·pel·late
ap·pel·la·tion
ap·pel·la·tive
ap·pel·lee
ap·pend
ap·pend·age
ap·pen·dant
ap·pen·di·cec·to·my (or esp. US ap·pen·dec·to·my; plural ·mies)
ap·pen·di·ci·tis
ap·pen·di·cle small appendage
ap·pen·dicu·lar
ap·pen·dix (plural ·dixes or ·di·ces)
Ap·pen·zell Swiss canton
ap·per·ceive
ap·per·cep·tion psychology term
ap·per·cep·tive
ap·per·tain
ap·pes·tat hunger control centre in brain
ap·pe·tence (or ·ten·cy; plural ·tences or ·ten·cies)
ap·pe·tite
ap·pe·tiz·er (or ·tis·er)
ap·pe·tiz·ing (or ·tis·ing)
ap·plaud
ap·plaud·er
ap·plaud·ing·ly
ap·plause
ap·ple

apple·cart
apple·jack
apple·snits Canadian apple
dish
ap·pli·ance
ap·plic·abil·ity
ap·pli·cable
ap·pli·cably
ap·pli·cant
ap·pli·ca·tion
ap·plica·tive
ap·pli·ca·tor
ap·pli·ca·tory
ap·plied
ap·pli·er
ap·pli·qué (·qué·ing,
·quéd)
ap·ply (·plies, ·ply·ing,
·plied)
ap·pog·gia·tu·ra (*plural* ·ras
or ·re) musical term
ap·point
ap·poin·tee
ap·point·er
ap·point·ment
ap·poin·tor legal term
Ap·po·mat·tox US battle
site
ap·por·tion
ap·por·tion·able
ap·por·tion·er
ap·por·tion·ment
ap·pose
ap·po·site apt; *compare*
opposite
ap·po·si·tion
ap·posi·tive linguistics term
ap·prais·able
ap·prais·al (*or*
·praise·ment)
ap·praise assess; *compare*
apprise
ap·prais·er
ap·prais·ing·ly
ap·prais·ive
ap·pre·ci·able
ap·pre·ci·ate
ap·pre·cia·tion
ap·pre·cia·tive (*or* ·tory)
ap·pre·cia·tive·ness
ap·pre·hend
ap·pre·hen·sibil·ity
ap·pre·hen·sible
ap·pre·hen·sion
ap·pre·hen·sive

ap·pre·hen·sive·ness
ap·pren·tice
ap·pren·tice·ship
ap·pressed pressed closely
against
ap·prise (*or* ·prize) inform;
compare appraise
ap·proach
ap·proach·abil·ity (*or*
·able·ness)
ap·proach·able
ap·pro·bate Scottish legal
term; *US* approve
ap·pro·ba·tion
ap·pro·ba·tive (*or* ·tory)
ap·pro·pri·able
ap·pro·pri·ate
ap·pro·pri·ate·ness
ap·pro·pria·tion
ap·pro·pria·tor
ap·prov·al
ap·prove
ap·proved
ap·proxi·mal situated side
by side
ap·proxi·mate
ap·proxi·mate·ly
ap·proxi·ma·tion
ap·proxi·ma·tive
ap·pulse astronomy term
ap·pul·sive
ap·pur·te·nance
ap·pur·te·nant
apraxia disorder of nervous
system
aprax·ic (*or* aprac·tic)
après-ski
apri·cot
April
a prio·ri *Latin* from cause to
effect; *compare* a posteriori
apri·or·ism
apri·or·ity
apron
ap·ro·pos
apse recess in church
ap·si·dal
ap·sis (*plural* ·si·des) point
in planet's orbit
apt
ap·ter·al architectural term
ap·ter·ous wingless
ap·ter·yg·ial lacking fins or
wings
ap·ter·yx kiwi

ap·ti·tude
apt·ness
Apu·lia Italian region
Apu·ri·mac Peruvian river
apy·re·tic
Aqa·ba (*or* Aka·ba)
Jordanian port
aqua (*plural* aquae *or* aquas)
aqua·cul·ture cultivation of
marine organisms; *compare*
aquiculture
aqua·lung
aqua·marine
aqua·naut
aqua·pho·bia
aqua·plane
aqua re·gia strong acid
aqua·relle
aqua·rel·list water-colour
painter
aqua·rist aquarium curator
aquar·ium (*plural*
aquar·iums *or* aquaria)
Aquar·ius
aquat·ic
aquat·ics
aqua·tint
aqua·vit aromatic spirit
aqua vi·tae *Archaic* brandy
aque·duct
aque·ous
aqui·cul·tur·al
aqui·cul·ture hydroponics;
compare aquaculture
aqui·cul·tur·ist
aqui·fer water-containing
rock
Aqui·la constellation
aqui·legia
aqui·line
Aqui·taine French region
Ara constellation
Arab
ara·besque
Ara·bia
Ara·bian
Ara·bic language
arabi·nose sugar
Ar·ab·ist
ar·able
Ara·by *Archaic* Arabia
Ara·ca·jú Brazilian port
Arachne mythological
character
arach·nid spider

arach·ni·dan

arach·noid membrane covering brain

Arad Romanian city

Ara·gon Spanish region

Ara·go·nese

arago·nite mineral

Ara·guaia Brazilian river

Arak Iranian town

arak *variant spelling of* arrack

Aral·dite (*Trademark*)

ara·lia·ceous botany term

Ara·ma·ic language

Aran Irish islands; type of sweater; *compare* Arran

ara·neid spider

Arapa·ho (*plural* ·hos *or* ·ho) American Indian

ara·pai·ma fish

Ara·rat Turkish mountain

ara·ro·ba tree; medicinal substance

Aras Asian river

Arau·ca·nia Chilean region

Arau·ca·nian

arau·ca·ria tree

Ara·wak·an American Indian language

ar·ba·lest crossbow

ar·bi·ter

ar·bi·trable

ar·bi·trage financial term

ar·bi·tral

ar·bit·ra·ment

ar·bi·trari·ly

ar·bi·trari·ness

ar·bi·trary

ar·bi·trate

ar·bi·tra·tion

ar·bi·tra·tor

ar·bi·tress

ar·bor rotating shaft; *US spelling of* arbour

ar·bora·ceous

ar·bor·eal

ar·bo·reous

ar·bo·res·cence

ar·bo·res·cent

ar·bo·retum (*plural* ·ta *or* ·tums)

ar·bori·cul·ture

ar·bor·ist

ar·bori·za·tion (*or* ·sa·tion)

ar·bor vi·tae tree

ar·bour (*US* ·bor) tree-lined shelter; *compare* arbor

Ar·broath Scottish port

ar·bu·tus (*plural* ·tuses) shrub

arc part of curve; *compare* ark

ar·cade

Ar·ca·dia department of Greece; *compare* Acadia

Ar·ca·dian

Ar·ca·dy (*or* ·dia) rustic paradise

ar·ca·na tarot cards

ar·cane

ar·ca·num (*plural* ·na)

ar·ca·ture small arcade

arch

Ar·chaean (*or esp. US* ·chean) geology term

ar·chaeo·logi·cal (*US also* ·cheo·)

ar·chaeo·logi·cal·ly (*US also* ·cheo·)

ar·chae·olo·gist (*US also* ·che·)

ar·chae·ol·ogy (*US also* ·che·)

ar·chaeo·mag·net·ism (*US also* ·cheo·)

ar·chae·op·ter·yx

ar·chae·or·nis extinct bird

Ar·chaeo·zo·ic (*US also* ·cheo·)

ar·cha·ic

ar·chai·cal·ly

ar·cha·ism

ar·cha·ist

ar·cha·is·tic

ar·cha·is·ti·cal·ly

ar·cha·ize (*or* ·ise)

ar·cha·iz·er (*or* ·is·er)

Arch·an·gel Russian port

arch·angel

arch·angelic

arch·bishop

arch·bishop·ric

arch·deacon

arch·deacon·ry (*plural* ·ries)

arch·dioc·esan

arch·dio·cese

arch·ducal

arch·duchess

arch·duchy (*plural* ·duchies)

arch·duke

arched

ar·che·go·nium (*plural* ·nia) botany term

arch·en·emy (*plural* ·emies)

ar·chen·ter·ic

ar·chen·ter·on embryology term

ar·che·ol·ogy *US variant spelling of* archaeology

arch·er

archer·fish (*plural* ·fish *or* ·fishes)

ar·chery

ar·che·spore (*or* ·spo·rium; *plural* ·spores *or* ·spo·ria) spore-making cell

ar·che·spo·rial

ar·che·typ·al (*or* ·typi·cal)

ar·che·typ·al·ly (*or* ·typi·cal·ly)

ar·che·type

arch·fiend

archi·carp fungal structure

archi·di·aco·nal

archi·di·aco·nate

archi·epis·co·pal

archi·epis·co·pate (*or* ·co·pa·cy)

ar·chil *variant spelling of* orchil

archi·mage great magician

archi·man·drite head of Orthodox monastery

Archi·medean

archi·pelag·ic (*or* ·pe·lagian)

archi·pela·go (*plural* ·gos *or* ·goes)

archi·tect

archi·tec·ton·ic

archi·tec·toni·cal·ly

archi·tec·ton·ics

archi·tec·tur·al

archi·tec·tur·al·ly

archi·tec·ture

archi·trave moulding

ar·chiv·al

ar·chive

archi·vist

archi·volt moulding around arch

arch·ness

ar·cho·plasm (*or* archi·) type of protoplasm

ar·cho·plas·mic
arch·priest
arch·way
arco·graph geometric instrument
Arc·tic North Pole region
arc·tic very cold
Arc·to·gaea (US ·gea) zoogeographical area
Arc·to·gaean (US ·gean)
Arc·tu·rian
Arc·tu·rus star
ar·cu·ate arc-shaped
ar·cua·tion
ar·deb unit of measure
Ar·dèche French department
Arden (Forest of)
ar·den·cy
Ar·dennes W European hills
ar·dent
ar·dour (US ·dor)
ar·du·ous
ar·du·ous·ness
are
area
areal
area·way passageway
ar·eca palm tree
arena
ar·ena·ceous geology term
ar·enico·lous living in sandy places
ar·enite sandstone
ar·enit·ic
aren't are not
ar·eog·ra·phy description of Mars
areo·la (plural ·lae or ·las)
areo·lar (or ·late)
areo·la·tion
Arequi·pa Peruvian city
Ares Greek god
arête mountain ridge
ar·ethu·sa plant
Arez·zo Italian city
ar·ga·li (or ar·gal; plural ·ga·li or ·gals) wild sheep
ar·gent silver
Ar·gen·teuil Parisian suburb
ar·gen·tic
ar·gen·tif·er·ous
Ar·gen·ti·na
Ar·gen·tine of Argentina
ar·gen·tine of silver

Ar·gen·tin·ean
ar·gen·tite mineral
ar·gen·tous
ar·gil potter's clay
ar·gil·la·ceous
ar·gil·lif·er·ous
ar·gil·lite rock
ar·gil·lit·ic
ar·gi·nine amino acid
Argo Jason's ship; constellation
ar·gol deposit in wine vats
Ar·go·lis region of ancient Greece
ar·gon chemical element
Ar·go·naut
Ar·gonne French region
Ar·gos ancient Greek city
ar·go·sy (plural ·sies) large merchant ship
ar·got
ar·got·ic
ar·gu·able
ar·gu·ably
ar·gue (·gu·ing, ·gued)
ar·gu·er
ar·gu·fy (·fies, ·fy·ing, ·fied)
ar·gu·ment
ar·gu·men·ta·tion
ar·gu·men·ta·tive
ar·gu·men·ta·tive·ness
ar·gu·men·tum (plural ·ta) Latin argument
Argus mythological giant
argy-bargy (plural ·bargies)
ar·gyle fabric
Ar·gyll (or ·gyll·shire) former Scottish county
År·hus variant spelling of Aarhus
aria
Arian follower of Arianism; compare Aryan
Ari·an·ism heretical doctrine
arid
arid·ity (or ar·id·ness)
Ariège French department
Ari·el satellite of Uranus
ari·el gazelle; compare aerial
Aries constellation; sign of the zodiac

ari·et·ta (plural ·et·tas, ·et·te or ·ettes) short aria
aright
aril botany term
ar·il·late
ar·il·lode
Ari·ma·thea Palestinian town
ario·so musical term
arise (aris·ing, arose, aris·en)
aris·ta (plural ·tae) bristle
Ar·is·tar·chus moon crater
aris·tate
ar·is·toc·ra·cy (plural ·cies)
aris·to·crat
aris·to·crat·ic
aris·to·crati·cal·ly
Ar·is·to·telian
arith·me·tic (noun)
arith·met·ic (or ·meti·cal; adj)
arith·meti·cal·ly
arith·meti·cian
Ari·zo·na
ark Noah's boat; compare arc
Ar·kan·sas
ar·kose sandstone
Ar·ling·ton US county
arm
ar·ma·da
ar·ma·dil·lo (plural ·los)
Ar·ma·ged·don
Ar·magh
Ar·ma·gnac French brandy
ar·ma·ment
ar·ma·men·tar·ium (plural ·tar·iums or ·taria) doctor's equipment
ar·ma·ture moving electrical part
arm·band
arm·chair
Arm·co (Trademark) safety barrier
armed
Ar·me·nia
Ar·me·nian
Ar·men·tières French town
ar·met medieval helmet
arm·ful
arm·hole
ar·mi·ger heraldic term
ar·mil·lary of bracelets
arm·ing

Ar·mini·an
Ar·mini·an·ism Protestant
   doctrine
ar·mipo·tence
ar·mipo·tent strong in
   battle
ar·mi·stice
arm·less
arm·let
ar·moire cabinet
ar·mo·ri·al
ar·mour (US ·mor)
ar·moured (US ·mored)
ar·mour·er (US ·mor·)
ar·moury (US ·mory; plural
   ·mouries, US ·mories)
arm·pit
arm·rest
arms
ar·mure fabric
army (plural armies)
Arn·hem Dutch city
ar·ni·ca plant
Arno Italian river
ar·oid botany term
aro·ma
aro·mat·ic
aro·mati·cal·ly
aro·ma·tic·ity
aro·ma·ti·za·tion (or
   ·sa·tion)
aro·ma·tize (or ·tise)
arose
around
arous·al
arouse
arous·er
ar·peg·gio (plural ·gios)
ar·que·bus (or har·) early
   musket
ar·rack (or arak) alcoholic
   spirit
ar·raign
ar·raign·er
ar·raign·ment legal term
Ar·ran Scottish island;
   compare Aran
ar·range
ar·range·able
ar·range·ment
ar·rang·er
ar·rant
Ar·ras French town
ar·ras hanging tapestry;
   compare arris

ar·ray
ar·ray·al
ar·rears
ar·rest
ar·rest·able
ar·rest·er
ar·rest·ing
ar·rest·ing·ly
ar·rhyth·mia abnormal
   heartbeat
arrière-pensée (plural
   arrière-pensées) French
   mental reservation
Ar Ri·mal Arabian desert
ar·ris (plural ·ris or ·rises)
   sharp edge; compare arras
ar·ri·val
ar·rive
ar·riv·er
ar·ri·viste ambitious person
ar·ro·ba unit of weight
ar·ro·gance
ar·ro·gant
ar·ro·gate claim without
   justification
ar·ro·ga·tion
ar·roga·tive
ar·ro·ga·tor
ar·ron·disse·ment French
   district
ar·row
arrow·head
arrow·root
arrow·wood
arrow·worm
arro·yo US gully
ars antiqua 13th-century
   music style; compare ars
   nova
arse
ar·senal
ar·senate
ar·senic
ar·seni·cal
ar·senide
ar·seni·ous (or ·sen·ous)
ar·senite
ar·seno·py·rite mineral
ar·sine chemical compound
ar·sis (plural ·ses) prosody
   term
ars nova 14th-century
   music style; compare ars
   antiqua
ar·son

ars·phena·mine drug
arsy-versy Slang backwards
art
Art Deco 1920–40 art style;
   compare Art Nouveau
ar·te·fact (or ·ti·)
ar·tel cooperative in the
   former Soviet Union
Artemis Greek goddess
ar·te·mi·sia plant
ar·te·rial
ar·te·ri·ali·za·tion (or
   ·sa·tion)
ar·te·ri·al·ize (or ·ise)
ar·te·ri·ole subdivision of
   artery
ar·te·rio·sclero·sis
ar·te·rio·sclerot·ic
ar·te·rio·venous
ar·te·ri·tis
ar·tery (plural ·teries)
ar·te·sian
art·ful
art·ful·ly
art·ful·ness
ar·thral·gia joint pain
ar·thral·gic
ar·thrit·ic
ar·thri·tis
arthro·mere zoology term
arthro·mer·ic
arthro·pod
ar·thropo·dous (or ·dal)
arthro·spore
ar·thro·spor·ic (or ·ous)
Ar·thu·rian
ar·ti·choke
ar·ti·cle
ar·ticu·lar
ar·ticu·late
ar·ticu·late·ness (or ·la·cy)
ar·ticu·la·tion
ar·ticu·la·tor
ar·ticu·la·tory
ar·ti·fact variant spelling of
   artefact
ar·ti·fice
ar·tifi·cer
ar·ti·fi·cial
ar·ti·fi·ci·al·ity
ar·til·lery
ar·tillery·man (plural ·men)
arti·ness
ar·tio·dac·tyl zoology term
ar·tio·dac·ty·lous

ar·ti·san
art·ist person skilled in art, etc.
ar·tiste entertainer
ar·tis·tic
ar·tis·ti·cal·ly
art·ist·ry
art·less
art·less·ness
Art Nouveau 1890–1910 art style; *compare* Art Deco
Ar·tois former French province
art·work
arty (arti·er, arti·est)
Aru·ba West Indian island
arum
Aru·na·chal Pra·desh Indian state
Ar·un·del
arun·di·na·ceous resembling a reed
Aru·wi·mi river in the Democratic Republic of Congo
Aryan (*or* Arian) non-Jewish Caucasian; *compare* Arian
Ary·an·ize (*or* ·ise)
aryl chemistry term
ary·te·noid (*or* ·tae·) anatomy term
ary·te·noid·al
as
asa·foeti·da (*or esp. US* ·feti·) resin
Asan·te·he·ne Ghanaian ruler
asa·ra·bac·ca plant
asa·rum dried ginger root
as·bes·tos (*US also* ·tus)
as·bes·to·sis
as·ca·ria·sis
as·ca·rid parasitic worm
as·cend
as·cend·ancy (*or* ·ency, ·ance, ·ence)
as·cend·ant (*or* ·ent)
as·cend·er
As·cen·sion Christian feast; S Atlantic island
as·cen·sion
as·cen·sion·al
As·cen·sion·tide
as·cent upward movement; *compare* assent

as·cer·tain
as·cer·tain·able
as·cer·tain·ment
as·cesis (*plural* ·ceses) self-discipline
as·cet·ic
as·ceti·cal·ly
as·ceti·cism
asci *plural of* ascus
Ascii computer language
as·cid·ian marine animal
as·cid·ium (*plural* ·cidia) botany term
as·ci·tes medical term
as·cit·ic
as·cle·pia·da·ceous botany term
Asclepius Greek god
as·co·carp part of a fungus
as·co·go·nium (*plural* ·nia) fungal reproductive body
as·co·my·cete fungus
as·co·my·cetous
ascor·bic acid
as·co·spore
As·cot Berkshire town; racecourse
as·cot cravat
as·crib·able
as·cribe
as·crip·tion (*or* ad·scrip·)
as·cus (*plural* asci) fungal part
as·dic echo sounder
ase·ity philosophy term
asep·al·ous
asep·sis
asep·tic
asexu·al
asexu·al·ity
asexu·al·ly
As·gard home of Norse gods
ash
ashamed
asham·ed·ly
Ashan·ti Ghanaian region
ash·en
Ashes cricket trophy
ashet *Dialect* dish
Ash·ga·bat *variant spelling of* Ashkhabad
Ash·ke·na·zi (*plural* ·zim) Jew of E European descent
ash·key

Ash·kha·bad capital of Turkmenistan
ash·lar (*or* ·ler)
ash·lar·ing building material
ashore
(ashphalt) *incorrect spelling of* asphalt
ash·plant
ash·ram Hindu religious retreat
Ashtoreth biblical character
ash·tray
ashy (ashi·er, ashi·est)
Asia
Asian
Asi·at·ic
aside
asi·nine
asi·nin·ity
Asir Saudi Arabian region
ask
askance (*or* askant)
ask·er
askew
aslant
asleep
As·ma·ra capital of Eritrea
Asmodeus Jewish demon
As·nières Parisian suburb
aso·cial
aso·cial·ly
asp
as·para·gine amino acid
as·para·gus
as·par·tic acid
as·pect
as·pec·tual linguistics term
as·pen
as·per Turkish coin
as·per·gil·lo·sis (*plural* ·ses)
as·per·gil·lus (*plural* ·li) fungus
as·per·ity (*plural* ·ities)
as·perse
as·pers·er
as·per·sion
as·per·sive
as·per·so·rium (*plural* ·ria) basin for holy water
as·phalt
as·phal·tic
as·phal·tite
as·phal·tum
as·pho·del plant

as·phyxia
as·phyx·ial
as·phyxi·ant
as·phyxi·ate
as·phyxia·tion
as·phyxia·tor
as·pic
as·pi·dis·tra
as·pir·ant
as·pi·rate
as·pi·ra·tion
as·pi·ra·tor
as·pira·tory
as·pire
as·pir·er
as·pi·rin (plural ·rin or ·rins)
as·pir·ing
(asprin) incorrect spelling of
    aspirin
asquint
ass
as·sai musical term; palm
    tree
as·sail
assail·able
as·sail·ant
as·sail·er
assail·ment
As·sam Indian state
As·sa·mese (plural ·mese)
as·sas·sin
as·sas·si·nate
as·sas·si·na·tion
as·sault
as·sault·er
as·say test; compare essay
as·say·able
as·say·er
as·se·gai (or ·sa·; plural
    ·gais) spear
as·sem·blage
as·sem·ble
as·sem·bler
as·sem·bly (plural ·blies)
as·sembly·man (plural
    ·men)
as·sent consent; compare
    ascent
as·sen·ta·tion servile
    agreement
as·sen·tient approving
as·sen·tor
as·sert
as·sert·er (or ·ser·tor)
as·sert·ible

as·ser·tion
as·ser·tive
as·ser·tive·ness
as·sess
as·sess·able
as·sess·ment
as·ses·sor
as·ses·so·rial
as·set
asset-stripper
asset-stripping
as·sev·er·ate declare
    emphatically
as·sev·era·tion
as·sibi·late phonetics term
as·sibi·la·tion
as·si·du·ity (plural ·ities)
as·sidu·ous
as·sidu·ous·ness
as·sign
as·sign·abil·ity
as·sign·able
as·sig·nat former French
    currency
as·sig·na·tion
as·signee legal term
as·sign·er
as·sign·ment
as·sign·or legal term
as·simi·lable
as·simi·late
as·simi·la·tion
as·simi·la·tive (or ·tory)
As·sini·boine Canadian
    river
as·sist
as·sis·tance
as·sis·tant
as·sist·er
as·size
as·sizes
as·so·ci·able
as·so·ci·ate
as·so·cia·tion
as·so·cia·tion·ism
    psychology term
as·so·cia·tive
as·so·nance grammar term
as·so·nant
as·so·nan·tal
as·sort
as·sorta·tive (or ·sort·ive)
as·sort·ed
as·sort·er
as·sort·ment

as·suage
as·suage·ment
as·suag·er
as·sua·sive
as·sum·able
as·sume
as·sumed
as·sum·er
as·sum·ing
As·sump·tion Christian
    feast
as·sump·tion
as·sump·tive
Assur Assyrian god
as·sur·able
as·sur·ance note life
    assurance; compare
    insurance
as·sure
as·sured
as·sur·ed·ly
as·sur·ed·ness
as·sur·er
as·sur·gent curving upwards
(assymetric) incorrect spelling
    of asymmetric
(assymptote) incorrect
    spelling of asymptote
As·syria
As·syr·ian
As·syri·olo·gist
As·syri·ol·ogy
As·ta·na Kazakh capital
Astarte Phoenician goddess
astat·ic unstable
astati·cal·ly
astati·cism
as·ta·tine chemical element
as·ter
as·te·ri·at·ed
    crystallography term
as·ter·isk
as·ter·ism
astern
aster·nal anatomy term
as·ter·oid
as·teroi·dal
as·the·nia (or ·ny)
as·then·ic weak
as·the·no·pia eyestrain
as·the·nop·ic
as·theno·sphere layer of
    atmosphere
asth·ma
asth·mat·ic

asthmati·cal·ly
Asti Italian town
as·tig·mat·ic
as·tig·mati·cal·ly
astig·ma·tism (or astig·mia)
astil·be plant
astir
Asti Spumante wine
As·to·lat Arthurian town
astoma·tous biology term
aston·ish
aston·ish·ing
aston·ish·ing·ly
aston·ish·ment
As·to·ria US port
astound
astound·ed
astound·ing
astound·ing·ly
astrad·dle
as·tra·gal architectural
moulding
astraga·lus anklebone
As·tra·khan Russian city
as·tra·khan fur
as·tral
as·tra·pho·bia (or ·tro·) fear
of thunderstorms
as·tra·pho·bic (or ·tro·)
astray
astride
as·trin·gen·cy (or ·gence)
as·trin·gent
as·tro·bi·ol·ogy
as·tro·bota·ny
as·tro·com·pass
as·tro·cyte cytology term
as·tro·dome
as·tro·dy·nam·ics
as·tro·geol·ogy
as·troid maths term
as·tro·labe astronomers'
instrument
as·trolo·ger (or ·gist)
as·tro·logi·cal
as·tro·logi·cal·ly
as·trol·ogy
as·tro·met·ric (or ·ri·cal)
as·trom·etry branch of
astronomy
as·tro·naut
as·tro·nau·tic (or ·ti·cal)
as·tro·nau·ti·cal·ly
as·tro·nau·tics
as·tro·navi·ga·tion

as·tro·navi·ga·tor
as·trono·mer
as·tro·nomi·cal (or
·nom·ic)
as·tro·nomi·cal·ly
as·trono·my
as·tro·photo·graph·ic
as·tro·pho·tog·ra·phy
as·tro·physi·cal
as·tro·physi·cist
as·tro·phys·ics
as·tro·sphere cytology term
As·tu·ri·as former Spanish
kingdom
as·tute
as·tute·ness
Astyanax mythological
character
asty·lar architectural term
Asun·ción Paraguayan
capital
asun·der
As·wan Egyptian city
aswarm
asyl·lab·ic
asy·lum
asym·met·ric (or ·ri·cal)
asym·met·ri·cal·ly
asym·me·try
asymp·to·mat·ic
asymp·to·mati·cal·ly
as·ymp·tote geometry term
as·ymp·tot·ic (or ·toti·cal)
as·ymp·toti·cal·ly
asyn·chro·nism
asyn·chro·nous
as·yn·det·ic
as·yn·deti·cal·ly
asyn·de·ton (plural ·deta)
grammar term
Asyut (or As·siut) Egyptian
city
at
atac·tic chemistry term
Atalanta mythological
character; compare Atlanta
ata·man (plural ·mans)
Cossack leader
ata·rac·tic (or ·rax·ic)
ata·raxia (or ·raxy) peace of
mind
ata·vism
ata·vist
ata·vis·tic (or ·vic)
ata·vis·ti·cal·ly

ataxia (or ataxy) lack of
muscular coordination
atax·ic (or atac·tic)
At·ba·ra Sudanese town
Ate Greek goddess
ate
at·elec·ta·sis lung collapse
at·el·ier French workshop
Atha·bas·ka Canadian lake
athe·ism
athe·ist
athe·is·tic (or ·ti·cal)
athe·is·ti·cal·ly
ath·el·ing Anglo-Saxon
prince
ath·emat·ic musical term
Athena Greek goddess
Ath·enaeum
ath·enaeum (US also
ath·eneum) institution of
learning
Athe·nian
Ath·ens
ather·man·cy
ather·ma·nous opaque to
radiant heat
ath·ero·ma (plural ·mas or
·ma·ta)
ath·er·oma·tous
ath·ero·scle·ro·sis (plural
·ses)
ath·ero·scle·rot·ic
athirst
ath·lete
ath·let·ic
ath·leti·cal·ly
ath·leti·cism
ath·let·ics
atho·dyd ramjet
at-home social gathering
athwart
athwart·ships
atilt
At·lan·ta US city; compare
Atalanta
At·lan·tean
at·lan·tes architectural term
At·lan·tic
At·lan·tis legendary
continent
At·las mountain range
at·las
Atli legendary king
at·man Hindu self
at·moly·sis (plural ·ses)

at·mom·eter
at·mom·etry
at·mos·phere
at·mos·pher·ic (or ·phèri·cal)
at·mos·pheri·cal·ly
at·mos·pher·ics
at·oll
atom
atom·ic
atomi·cal·ly
ato·mic·ity
at·om·ism
at·om·ist
at·om·is·tic (or ·ti·cal)
at·om·is·ti·cal·ly
atomi·za·tion (or ·sa·tion)
at·om·ize (or ·ise)
at·om·iz·er (or ·is·er)
aton·able (or atone·)
aton·al musical term
aton·al·ism
ato·nal·ity
ato·nal·ly
atone
atone·able variant spelling of atonable
atone·ment
aton·er
aton·ic
ato·nic·ity
ato·ny
atop
atrial
atrio·ven·tricu·lar
atrip nautical term
atrium (plural atria)
atro·cious
atro·cious·ness
atroc·ity (plural ·ities)
atroph·ic
at·ro·phy (noun, plural ·phies; verb ·phies, ·phy·ing, ·phied)
at·ro·pine (or ·pin) alkaloid
atta·boy
at·tach
at·tach·able
at·ta·ché diplomat
at·tach·er
at·tach·ment
at·tack
at·tack·er
at·tain

at·tain·abil·ity (or ·able·ness)
at·tain·able
at·tain·der legal term
at·tain·ment
at·taint
at·tar (or ot·) essential oil
(attachment) incorrect spelling of attachment
at·tempt
at·tempt·able
at·tempt·er
at·tend
at·tend·ance
at·tend·ant
at·tend·er
at·ten·tion
at·ten·tive
at·ten·tive·ness
at·tenu·ant
at·tenu·ate
at·tenua·tion
at·tenua·tor physics term
at·test
at·test·able
at·test·ant (or ·test·er)
at·tes·ta·tion
at·test·or (or ·test·ta·tor) legal term
At·tic of Attica
at·tic
At·ti·ca Greek region
at·ti·cism clear expression
at·tire
at·ti·tude
at·ti·tu·di·nal
at·ti·tu·di·nize (or ·nise)
at·ti·tu·di·niz·er (or ·nis·er)
at·torn
at·tor·ney
at·torn·ment
at·tract
at·tract·able
at·tract·ant
at·trac·tion
at·trac·tive
at·trac·tive·ness
at·trac·tor (or ·tract·er)
at·trib·ut·able
at·trib·ute
at·trib·ut·er (or ·tribu·tor)
at·tribu·tion
at·tribu·tive
at·tri·tion
at·tri·tion·al

at·tri·tive
Attu island off Alaska
at·tune
atypi·cal
atypi·cal·ly
aubade ode
Aube French river
auberge French inn
auber·gine
Auber·vil·liers Parisian suburb
aubrie·tia (or aubre·) plant
au·burn
Aubus·son French town
Auck·land New Zealand city; S Pacific islands
au cou·rant French up-to-date
auc·tion
auc·tion·eer
auc·to·rial of an author
auda·cious
auda·cious·ness
audac·ity (plural ·ities)
Aude French department
audibil·ity (or audible·ness)
audible
audi·ence
audile psychology term
audio
audio·gen·ic
audio·logi·cal
audi·olo·gist
audi·ol·ogy
audi·om·eter
audio·met·ric
audio·met·ri·cal·ly
audi·om·etrist
audi·om·etry
audio·phile hi-fi enthusiast
audio·typ·ing
audio·typist
audio·visual
audi·phone hearing aid
audit
audi·tion
audi·tor
audi·to·rium (plural ·riums or ·ria)
audi·tory
au fait French well-informed
au fond French fundamentally
auf Wie·der·seh·en German goodbye

Augean mythological
  stables; very dirty
augend number added
auger boring tool; *compare*
  augur
aught (*or* **ought**) *Archaic*
  anything; zero; *compare*
  ought
augite mineral
au·git·ic
aug·ment
aug·ment·able
aug·men·ta·tion
aug·menta·tive
aug·men·tor (*or* **·ment·er**)
Augs·burg German city
augur predict; *compare*
  auger
augur·al
augu·ry (*plural* **·ries**)
August month
august imposing
Au·gus·ta Sicilian port
Augus·tan of Emperor
  Augustus; literary period
Augus·tin·ian of St
  Augustine
auk
auk·let
au lait *French* with milk
auld lang syne *Scot* old
  times; *compare* **langsyne**
aulic of a royal court
Aulis ancient Greek town
aum·bry *variant spelling of*
  ambry
au na·tu·rel *French* nude or
  raw
aunt
auntie (*or* **aunty**; *plural*
  aunties)
au pair
aura (*plural* **auras** *or* **aurae**)
aural of the ear; *compare*
  oral
aural·ly
aure·ate gilded
aure·ole (*or* **aureo·la**) halo
Aureo·my·cin (*Trademark*)
  antibiotic
aure·us (*plural* **aurei**)
  Roman coin
au re·voir
auric chemistry term
auri·cle anatomical part

auricu·la (*plural* **·lae** *or* **·las**)
  primrose
auricu·lar
auricu·late (*or* **·lat·ed**)
  having ears
aurif·er·ous
Auri·ga constellation
Aurig·na·cian Palaeolithic
  culture
aurist ear specialist
aurochs extinct cattle
Aurora Roman goddess
auro·ra (*plural* **·ras** *or* **·rae**)
auro·ra aus·tra·lis
auro·ra bo·real·is
auro·ral
aur·ous
aurum gold
Ausch·witz
aus·cul·tate
aus·cul·ta·tion
aus·cul·ta·tor
aus·form·ing steel heat
  treatment
aus·pex (*plural* **·pices**)
  Roman soothsayer
aus·pice (*plural* **·pices**)
  omen; guidance
aus·pi·cious
aus·pi·cious·ness
aus·ten·ite metallurgy term
aus·ten·it·ic
aus·tere
aus·tere·ness
aus·ter·ity (*plural* **·ities**)
Aus·ter·litz battle site
aus·tral of the south
Aus·tral·asia
Aus·tral·asian
Aus·tralia
Aus·tral·ian
Aus·tral·ia·na
Aus·trali·an·ism
Aus·trali·an·ize (*or* **·ise**)
Aus·tra·loid
aus·tra·lo·pithe·cine fossil
  man
Aus·tra·lo·pithe·cus genus
  of fossil men
Aus·tral·orp domestic fowl
Aus·tria
Aus·trian
Austro-Asiatic
Aus·tro·nesia S Pacific
  islands

Aus·tro·nesian
auta·coid body secretion
autar·chic (*or* **·chi·cal**)
autar·chy (*plural* **·chies**)
  unrestricted rule; *compare*
  autarky
autar·kic (*or* **·ki·cal**, **·chic**,
  ·chi·cal)
autar·ky (*or* **·chy**; *plural*
  ·kies *or* **·chies**) economic
  self-sufficiency; *compare*
  autarchy
aut·eco·logi·cal
aut·ecol·ogy
auteur film director
authen·tic
authen·ti·cal·ly
authen·ti·cate
authen·ti·ca·tion
au·then·ti·ca·tor
au·then·tic·ity
author
author·ess
autho·rial
authori·tar·ian
authori·tari·an·ism
authori·ta·tive
authori·ta·tive·ness
author·ity (*plural* **·ities**)
authori·za·tion (*or*
  ·sa·tion)
author·ize (*or* **·ise**)
author·iz·er (*or* **·is·er**)
author·ship
autism
autis·tic
auto (*plural* **autos**) *Slang*
  motor car
auto·anti·body (*plural*
  ·bodies)
auto·bahn
auto·bi·og·ra·pher
auto·bio·graphi·cal
auto·bi·og·ra·phy (*plural*
  ·phies)
auto·cade *US* motorcade
auto·ca·taly·sis (*plural* **·ses**)
  chemistry term
auto·chang·er
  record-changing device
autoch·thon (*plural* **·thons**
  or **·tho·nes**) earliest known
  inhabitant
autoch·thon·ism (*or*
  ·tho·ny)

autoch·tho·nous (*or* ·tho·nal)
auto·clave
auto·cor·re·la·tion
autoc·ra·cy (*plural* ·cies)
auto·crat
auto·crat·ic
auto·crati·cal·ly
auto·cross
auto·cue
auto-da-fé (*plural* autos-da-fé) ceremony of Spanish Inquisition
auto·di·dact self-taught person
autoe·cious botany term
autoe·cism
autoga·mous (*or* auto·gam·ic)
autoga·my biology term
auto·gen·esis (*or* autog·eny)
auto·genet·ic
autog·enous
auto·gi·ro (*or* ·gy·; *plural* ·ros)
auto·graft
auto·graph
auto·graph·ic
auto·graphi·cal·ly
autog·ra·phy
auto·hyp·no·sis
auto·hyp·not·ic
auto·hyp·noti·cal·ly
autoi·cous botany term
auto·im·mune
auto·im·mun·ity
auto·ioni·za·tion (*or* ·sa·tion)
auto·ki·net·ic
Autoly·cus moon crater
Autolycus mythological character
auto·lyse (*US* ·lyze)
auto·ly·sin
autoly·sis self-destruction of cells
auto·lyt·ic
auto·mat
automa·ta *plural of* automaton
auto·mate
auto·mat·ic
auto·mati·cal·ly
auto·ma·tion
automa·tism

automa·tist
automa·tize (*or* ·tise)
automa·ton (*plural* ·tons *or* ·ta)
automa·tous
auto·mo·bile
auto·mo·bil·ist
auto·mo·tive
auto·nom·ic
auto·nomi·cal·ly
autono·mist
autono·mous
autono·my (*plural* ·mies)
auto·phyte botany term
auto·phyt·ic
auto·phyti·cal·ly
auto·pi·lot
auto·pis·ta Spanish motorway
auto·plas·tic
auto·plas·ty transplantation from own body
autop·sy (*plural* ·sies)
auto·put Yugoslav motorway
auto·radio·graph
auto·radio·graph·ic
auto·ra·di·og·ra·phy
auto·ro·ta·tion
auto·so·mal
auto·some type of chromosome
auto·sta·bil·ity
auto·stra·da Italian motorway
auto·sug·ges·tion
auto·sug·ges·tive
auto·tim·er
auto·tom·ic
autoto·mize (*or* ·mise)
autoto·my (*plural* ·mies) shedding of body part
auto·tox·ic
auto·tox·in
auto·trans·form·er
auto·troph·ic biology term
auto·type
auto·typ·ic
auto·typy
autoxi·da·tion chemistry term
autumn
autum·nal
autun·ite mineral
Auvergne French region

auxa·nom·eter
aux·esis biology term
aux·ilia·ry (*plural* ·ries)
aux·in hormone
auxo·chrome chemistry term
ava·da·vat (*or* ama·) bird
avail
avail·abil·ity
avail·able
avail·ably
ava·lanche
Ava·lon Arthurian paradise
avant-garde
Avar former European people
ava·rice
ava·ri·cious
avast nautical interjection
ava·tar manifestation of Hindu deity
ave *Latin* welcome; farewell
Ave·bury Wiltshire village; Neolithic stone circle
Ave·lla·ne·da Argentine city
avenge
aveng·er
av·ens (*plural* ·ens) plant
Av·en·tine Roman hill
aven·tu·rine (*or* aven·tu·rin, avan·tu·rine) dark glass
av·enue
aver (aver·ring, averred)
av·er·age
aver·ment
averse
aver·sion
aver·sive
avert
avert·ible (*or* ·able)
Aves·ta Zoroastrian scriptures
Aves·tan
Avey·ron French department
avian of birds
aviary (*plural* aviaries) place for keeping birds; *compare* apiary
avi·ate
avia·tion
avia·tor
avia·trix (*or* ·tress)
avi·cul·ture bird-rearing

avi·cul·tur·ist
avid
avi·din a protein
avid·ity
avid·ness
Avie·more Scottish resort
avi·fau·na
avi·fau·nal
Avi·gnon French city
avi·on·ic
avi·on·ics
aviru·lent
avita·mino·sis (*plural* ·ses)
avi·zan·dum Scottish legal
  term
avo·ca·do (*plural* ·dos)
avo·cet (*or* ·set) bird
avoid
avoid·able
avoid·ance
avoid·er
av·oir·du·pois system of
  weights
Avon English river and
  former county
avow
avow·able
avow·al
avowed
avow·er
avul·sion
avun·cu·lar
avun·cu·late
await
awake (awak·ing, awoke *or*
  awaked, awok·en *or*
  awaked)
awak·en
award
award·able
awardee
award·er
aware
aware·ness
awash
away
awe

aweath·er nautical term
aweigh
awe-inspiring
awe·some
awe·some·ness
awe-stricken (*or*
  awe-struck)
aw·ful
aw·ful·ly
aw·ful·ness
awhile
awk·ward
awk·ward·ness
awl
awl·wort plant
awn plant bristle
awn·ing
awoke
awry
axe (*US* ax)
axel ice-skating jump;
  compare axil; axle
axen·ic uncontaminated
ax·ial
axil angle between leaf and
  stem; *compare* axel;
  axle
ax·ile attached to an axis
ax·il·la (*plural* ·lae) armpit
ax·il·lary (*plural* ·laries) of
  armpit; feather
axio·logi·cal
axi·olo·gist
axi·ol·ogy study of values
axi·om
axio·mat·ic (*or* ·mati·cal)
axio·mati·cal·ly
Axis Nazi alliance
axis (*plural* axes)
axle mechanical part;
  compare axel; axil
axle·tree carriage axle
Ax·min·ster Devon town;
  carpet
axo·lotl salamander
axon part of nerve cell
ax·seed plant

ay (*or* aye) *Archaic* always;
  compare aye
ayah maid
aya·huas·ca plant
ayatollah
Ay·cliffe English town
aye (*or* ay) *Archaic or dialect*
  yes; *compare* ay
aye-aye animal
Ayles·bury
Ay·ma·ra (*plural* ·ras *or* ·ra)
  South American Indian
Ayr Scottish port
Ayr·shire cattle
Ayur·veda Hindu medical
  treatise
Ayut·tha·ya Thai city
azalea
azan Islamic call to prayer
aza·thio·prine drug
Az·bine Saharan region
azeda·rach medicinal bark
azeo·trope chemistry term
azeo·trop·ic
Azer·bai·jan Central Asian
  country; region of Iran
Azer·bai·ja·ni (*plural* ·ni *or*
  ·nis)
az·ide
azi·muth astronomy term
azi·muth·al
az·ine
azo·ben·zene
azo·ic without life
az·ole chemical compound
Azores Atlantic islands
azo·ote *Obsolete* nitrogen
azo·tae·mia (*US* ·te·)
  uraemia
azo·tae·mic (*US* ·te·)
az·oth mercury
azot·ic of nitrogen
azo·to·bac·ter bacterium
Az·tec
az·ure
az·ur·ite mineral
azy·gous

B

Ba soul in Egyptian
  mythology
baa (baa·ing, baaed)

Baal Semitic god
Baal·bek Lebanese town
baba cake

ba·bas·su palm tree
bab·bitt line with alloy
Bab·bitt met·al

bab·ble

bab·bler

babe

Ba·bel biblical tower

ba·biche rawhide thongs

babi·ru·sa wild pig

ba·boon

(babtize) *incorrect spelling of* baptize

ba·bul acacia tree

baby (*noun, plural* babies; *verb* babies, ba·by·ing, ba·bied)

ba·by·hood

ba·by·ish

Baby·lon city

Baby·lo·nia kingdom

Baby·lo·nian

baby's-breath (*or* babies'-) plant

baby-sit (-sitting, -sat)

baby-sitter

baby-snatch·er

bac·ca·lau·re·ate

bac·ca·rat

bac·cate berry-like

Bac·chae priestesses of Bacchus

bac·cha·nal

bac·cha·na·lia

bac·cha·na·lian

bac·chant (*fem* ·chan·te; *plural* ·chants *or* ·chan·tes, *fem* ·chan·tes) drunken reveller

Bac·chic

bac·chius (*plural* ·chii) metrical foot

Bacchus god of wine

bac·cif·er·ous

bac·ci·form

bac·civ·or·ous

bac·cy *Slang* tobacco

bach·elor

bachelor's-buttons plant

ba·cil·lary (*or* ·lar)

ba·cil·li·form

ba·cil·lus (*plural* ·li) rod-shaped bacterium

baci·tra·cin antibiotic

back

back·ache

back·bencher

back·bend

back·bite (·bit·ing, bit, bit·ten *or* bit)

back·board

back·bone

back·breaker

back·breaking

back·chat

back·cloth (*or* ·drop)

back·comb

back·cross genetics term

back·date

back·door

back·er

back·fill archaeology term

back·fire

back·gam·mon

back·ground

back·hand

back·hand·ed

back·handed·ly

back·handed·ness

back·hand·er

back·ing

back·lash

back·less

back·list

back·log

back·most

back-pedal (-pedalling, -pedalled; *US* -pedaling, -pedaled)

back·saw

Backs Cambridge college grounds

back·scratch·er

back·side

back·sight

back-slapping

back·slide (·slid·ing, ·slid, ·slid *or* ·slid·den)

back·slid·er

back·space

back·spin

back·stage

back·stairs

back·stay nautical term

back·stitch

back·stop

back·street

back·stroke

back·swept

back·track

back-up (*noun*)

back·veld South African rural area

back·ward (*adj*)

back·warda·tion stock exchange term

back·ward·ness

back·wards (*US* ·ward; *adv*)

back·wash

back·water

back·woods·man (*plural* ·men)

Ba·co·lod Philippine town

ba·con

ba·con·er pig

bac·te·rae·mia (*US* ·re·) bacteria in the blood

bac·te·ria *plural of* bacterium

bac·te·rial

bac·te·ri·cid·al

bac·te·ri·cide

bac·te·rin vaccine

bac·te·rio·logi·cal

bac·te·ri·olo·gist

bac·te·ri·ol·ogy

bac·te·ri·oly·sis disintegration of bacteria

bac·te·rio·lyt·ic

bac·te·rio·phage virus that destroys bacteria

bac·te·rio·phag·ic

bac·te·rio·opha·gous

bac·te·rio·sta·sis

bac·te·rio·stat·ic

bac·te·rio·stati·cal·ly

bac·te·rium (*plural* ·ria)

bac·ter·oid

Bac·tria ancient Asian country

Bac·trian

ba·cu·li·form rod-shaped

bacu·lum (*plural* ·la *or* ·lums)

bad (worse, worst)

Ba·da·joz Spanish city

Ba·da·lo·na Spanish port

bad·der·locks seaweed

bad·dy (*or* ·die; *plural* ·dies)

bade

Ba·den former German state; Swiss spa

Baden-Baden German spa

Baden-Wurttem·berg German state

badge

badg·er

badi·nage

bad·lands
bad·ly
bad·man (*plural* ·men)
bad·min·ton
bad·mouth
bad·ness
Bae·de·ker travel guidebook
bael tree
Baf·fin Canadian island and bay
baf·fle
baf·fle·ment
baf·fler
bag (bag·ging, bagged)
Ba·gan·da (*plural* ·da or ·das) African people
ba·gasse sugar-cane pulp
baga·telle
ba·gel (or bei·) bread roll
bag·gage
bag·gi·ly
bag·gi·ness
bag·ging
bag·gy (·gier, ·gi·est)
bagh Indian garden
Bagh·dad (or Bag·dad)
bag·man (*plural* ·men)
bag·pipe
ba·guette (or ·guet)
bag·wig 18th-century wig
bag·worm
Ba·hai
Ba·ha·ism religion
Ba·ha·ist
Ba·ha·mas
Ba·ha·mian
Ba·hia Brazilian town
Ba·hía Blan·ca Argentine port
Bah·rain (or ·rein)
Bah·rai·ni (or ·rei·)
baht Thai currency
ba·hu·vri·hi linguistics term
Bai·kal Russian lake
bail (*noun*) security for prisoner; part of wicket; *compare* bale
bail (or bale; *verb*) remove water from boat
bail·able
bailee legal term
bail·er (or bal·) one who bails water
bai·ley castle wall
Bailey bridge

bailie *Scot* magistrate
bail·iff
baili·wick legal term
bail·ment legal term
bail·or legal term
bails·man (*plural* ·men) one who stands bail
bain·ite component of steel
bain-marie (*plural* bains-marie) cooking utensil
Bai·ram Muslim festival
Bai·riki capital of Kiribati
bairn
bait enticement; to torment; *compare* bate
baize
bake
bake·house
Ba·ke·lite (*Trademark*)
bak·er
bak·ery (*plural* ·eries)
Bake·well English town; tart
bak·la·va cake
bak·sheesh
Baku capital of Azerbaijan
Bala Welsh lake
Balaam biblical character
Bala·cla·va helmet
Bala·kla·va (or ·cla·) Ukrainian port
bala·lai·ka
bal·ance
bal·ance·able
bal·anc·er
bal·as gemstone
bala·ta tree
Ba·la·ton Hungarian lake
Bal·boa Panamanian port
bal·boa Panamanian currency
bal·brig·gan fabric
bal·co·nied
bal·co·ny (*plural* ·nies)
bald
bal·da·chin brocade
Balder Norse god
bal·der·dash
bald·headed
bald·ing
bald·money plant
bald·ness
bald·pate
bal·dric sash for sword

bale (*noun*) block of hay; *compare* bail
bale (*verb*) make bales; jump from aircraft; *variant spelling of* bail
Bal·ear·ic Is·lands
ba·leen whalebone
bale·ful
bale·ful·ly
bale·ful·ness
bal·er agricultural machine; *variant spelling of* bailer
Bali Indonesian island
bali·bun·tal straw hat
Ba·lik·pa·pan Indonesian city
Ba·li·nese (*plural* ·nese)
balk (or baulk) stop short; avoid; timber beam; *compare* baulk
Bal·kan
Bal·kani·za·tion (or ·sa·tion)
balk·er (or baulk·)
balky (or baulky; balki·er or baulki·er, balki·est or baulki·est)
ball
bal·lad
bal·lade verse form
bal·lad·eer
bal·lad·ry
Bal·la·rat Australian town
bal·last
bal·le·ri·na
bal·let
bal·let·ic
bal·leto·mane
bal·leto·ma·nia
ball·flower architectural ornament
bal·lis·ta (*plural* ·tae) ancient catapult
bal·lis·tic
bal·lis·ti·cal·ly
bal·lis·tics
bal·locks *variant spelling of* bollocks
bal·lo·net gas compartment in balloon
bal·loon
bal·loon·ist
bal·lot (·lot·ing, ·lot·ed)
bal·lotte·ment medical term

ball·park
ball·point
ball·room
bal·ly slang term
bal·ly·hoo
balm
bal·ma·caan overcoat
balmi·ly
balmi·ness
Bal·mor·al Scottish castle;
  flat cap
balmy (balmi·er, balmi·est)
  soft and soothing; variant
  spelling (esp. US) of barmy
bal·ne·al
bal·neo·logi·cal
bal·ne·olo·gist
bal·ne·ol·ogy study of
  therapeutic baths
ba·lo·ney (or bo·)
bal·sa wood
bal·sam
bal·sam·ic
bal·sam·if·er·ous
bal·sa·mi·na·ceous
Balt person from Baltic
  States
Bal·tic
Bal·ti·more
Ba·lu·chi (or ·lo·; plural
  ·chis or ·chi) Muslim
  people
Ba·lu·chi·stan region of
  Asia
bal·us·ter
bal·us·trade
Ba·ma·ko capital of Mali
Bam·ba·ra (plural ·ra or
  ·ras) African people
Bam·berg German town
bam·bi·no (plural ·nos or
  ·ni)
bam·boo (plural ·boos)
bam·boo·zle
bam·boo·zle·ment
bam·boo·zler
ban (ban·ning, banned)
ba·nal
ba·nal·ity
ba·na·na
Ban·at plain in E Europe
ba·nau·sic utilitarian
Ban·bury
banc legal term
band

band·age
ban·dan·na (or ban·dana)
Ban·dar Seri Beg·a·wan
  capital of Brunei
band·box
ban·deau (plural ·deaux)
  headband
ban·de·ril·la bullfighter's
  dart
ban·de·ril·lero (plural
  ·leros) bullfighter's
  assistant
ban·de·role (or ·de·rol,
  ·ne·rol) flag
ban·di·coot
ban·dit (plural ·dits or
  ·dit·ti)
ban·dit·ry
Band·jar·ma·sin (or
  Ban·jer·ma·sin)
  Indonesian port
band·master
ban·do·leer (or ·lier)
  shoulder belt
ban·do·line hairdressing
  substance
ban·dora (or pan·) musical
  instrument
bands·man (plural ·men)
band·spreading radio
  tuning control
band·stand
Ban·dung Indonesian city
band·wagon
band·width
ban·dy (adj ·di·er, ·di·est;
  verb ·dies, ·dy·ing,
  ·died)
bandy-bandy (plural
  ·bandies) snake
bane
bane·berry (plural ·berries)
bane·ful
Banff former Scottish
  county; Canadian town
bang
Ban·ga·lore Indian city
bang·er
Bang·ka Indonesian island
Bang·kok
Bang·la·desh
Bang·la·deshi
ban·gle
Bangor Welsh or Northern
  Irish town

Ban·gui capital of Central
  African Republic
ban·ish
ban·ish·ment
ban·is·ter
ban·jo (plural ·jos or ·joes)
ban·jo·ist
Ban·jul Gambian capital
bank
bank·able
bank·book
bank·er
bank·et gold-bearing rock
bank·ing
bank·roll
bank·rupt
bank·rupt·cy (plural ·cies)
bank·sia shrub
banned
ban·ner
ban·ner·ette
ban·ning
(bannister) incorect spelling
  of banister
ban·nock Scottish cake
Ban·nock·burn Scottish
  battle site
banns (or bans) of marriage
ban·quet feast
ban·quette seat
ban·shee
bant Dialect string
ban·tam
bantam·weight
ban·ter
ban·ter·er
Ban·toid language
Ban·tu (plural ·tu or ·tus)
Ban·tu·stan former South
  African Bantu homeland
ban·yan (or ·ian) tree
ban·zai Japanese salutation
bao·bab tree
bap
bap·tism
bap·tis·mal
Bap·tist member of
  Christian sect
bap·tist·ry (or ·tis·tery;
  plural ·ries or ·teries)
bap·tize (or ·tise)
bar (bar·ring, barred)
Barabbas biblical character
bara·thea fabric
barb

Bar·ba·dian
Bar·ba·dos
bar·bar·ian
bar·bar·ian·ism
bar·bar·ic
bar·bari·cal·ly
bar·bar·ism
bar·bar·ity (*plural* ·ities)
bar·ba·rize (*or* ·rise)
bar·ba·rous
bar·ba·rous·ness
Bar·ba·ry N African region
bar·bate
bar·becue (·becu·ing, ·becued)
bar·bel fish; bristle
bar·bell weight
bar·bel·late covered with bristles
bar·ber
bar·ber·ry (*plural* ·ries)
barber·shop
bar·bet bird
bar·bette gun platform
Bar·bi·can area of London
bar·bi·can fortified place
bar·bi·cel
bar·bi·tone (US ·tal)
bar·bi·tu·rate
Bar·bour overcoat
Bar·bu·da West Indian island
bar·bule
bar·ca·role (*or* ·rolle)
Bar·ce·lo·na
bar·chan (*or* ·khan, ·chane, ·kan) sand dune
bard
bard·ic
bar·dola·try
bare uncovered; naked; expose; *compare* bear
bare·back (*or* ·backed)
bare·faced
bare·fac·ed·ness
bare·foot (*or* ·footed)
bare·handed
bare·headed
Ba·reil·ly Indian city
bare·ly
bare·ness
Bar·ents Arctic sea
bar·gain
barge
bar·gee

barge·pole
Bari Italian port
bar·ic of atmospheric pressure
ba·ril·la plant extract
bari·tone
bar·ium
bark dog's cry; outer layer of tree; *compare* barque
bark·er
Bark·ing and Dag·en·ham London borough
bar·ley
barley·corn
barm *Dialect* yeast
bar·maid
bar·man (*plural* ·men)
Bar·mecide (*or* ·mecid·al) illusory
bar mitz·vah
bar·my (*or esp. US* balmy; ·mi·er, ·mi·est) *Slang* crazy; *compare* balmy
barn
bar·na·cle
Bar·na·ul Russian city
barn-brack *Dialect* fruit muffin
Bar·net London borough
bar·ney *Slang* argument
barn·storm
barn·yard
Ba·ro·da Indian city
baro·gram
baro·graph
baro·graphic
ba·rom·eter
baro·met·ric
baro·met·ri·cal·ly
bar·on
bar·on·age
bar·on·ess
bar·on·et
bar·on·et·age
bar·on·et·cy (*plural* ·cies)
ba·rong Philippine knife
ba·ro·nial
baro·ny (*plural* ·nies)
ba·roque
baro·recep·tor
baro·scope
baro·stat
Ba·rot·se (*plural* ·se *or* ·ses) African people

Ba·rot·se·land Zambian region
ba·rouche horse-drawn carriage
barque (*US also* bark) boat; *compare* bark
Bar·quisi·me·to Venezuelan city
bar·rack (*verb*)
bar·racks
bar·ra·cou·ta fish
bar·ra·cu·da (*plural* ·da *or* ·das) fish
bar·rage
bar·ra·mun·da (*or* ·di; *plural* ·das, ·da; *or* ·dis, ·dies, di) fish
bar·ran·ca US ravine
Bar·ran·quil·la Colombian port
bar·ra·tor
bar·ra·trous (*or* bar·retrous)
bar·ra·try (*or* bar·retry) legal term
bar·ré music term
barred
bar·rel (·rel·ling, ·relled; US ·rel·ing, ·reled)
bar·ren
bar·ren·ness
bar·rens US barren land
barren·wort plant
bar·ret cap
bar·rette hair clasp
bar·ri·cade
bar·ri·cad·er
bar·ri·er
bar·ring
bar·ris·ter
bar·room
bar·row
Bar·ry Welsh port
Bar·sac wine
bar·tender
bar·ter
bar·ter·er
bar·ti·zan small turret
Bart·lett pear
bary·cen·tre centre of mass
bar·ye unit
bary·on physics term
bary·sphere
ba·ry·tes mineral
bary·ton bass viol

ba·sal
bas·alt
basalt·ware
bas·cule bridge
base
base·ball
base·board
base·born
Ba·sel (or Basle) Swiss city
base·less
base·line
base·man (plural ·men)
baseball fielder
base·ment
base·ness
Ba·sen·ji dog
ba·ses plural of base or basis
bash
Ba·shan biblical region
bash·ful
bash·ful·ly
bash·ful·ness
bashi·ba·zouk Turkish
soldier
Bash·kir (plural ·kir or ·kirs)
Mongoloid people
ba·sic
ba·si·cal·ly
ba·sic·ity chemistry term
ba·sid·ial
ba·sidio·my·cete fungus
ba·sidio·my·cet·ous
ba·sidio·spore
ba·sidio·spor·ous
ba·sid·ium (plural ·ia)
fungal structure
basi·fixed botany term
basi·fy (·fies, ·fy·ing, ·fied)
make basic
bas·il herb
basi·lar anatomy term
basi·lary
Ba·sil·don Essex town
Ba·sil·ian Eastern monk
ba·sil·ic vein
ba·sili·ca Roman building
ba·sil·i·can (or ·sil·ic)
Ba·si·li·ca·ta Italian region
basi·lisk lizard
ba·sin
basi·net medieval helmet;
compare bassinet
ba·sin·ful
Ba·sing·stoke Hampshire
town

ba·sion anatomy term
ba·sip·etal botany term
ba·sis (plural ·ses)
bask
Baskerville style of type
bas·ket
basket·ball
bas·ket·ry
basket-star starfish
basket·work
Basle variant spelling of Basel
ba·so·phil (or ·phile,
·phil·ic) stained by basic
dyes
Ba·so·tho (plural ·tho or
·thos) African people
Basque Pyrenean people
and language
Bas·ra (or Bas·rah, Bus·ra,
Bus·rah) Iraqi port
bas-relief (or bas·relief)
Bas-Rhin French
department
bass voice; singer
bass (plural bass or basses)
fish
Bas·sein Burmese city
Bas·sen·thwaite
bas·set
Basse-Terre West Indian
island
bas·si·net cradle; compare
basinet
bass·ist double bass player
bas·so (plural ·sos or ·si)
singer
bas·soon
bas·soon·ist
bass·wood
bast plant tissue
bas·tard
bas·tardi·za·tion (or
·sa·tion)
bas·tard·ize (or ·ise)
bas·tard·ry Austral
malicious behaviour
bas·tardy illegitimacy
baste
Bas·tille fortress
bas·ti·na·do (noun, plural
·does; verb ·does, ·do·ing,
·doed) torture
bast·ing
bas·ti·on

bast·naes·ite (or ·nas·ite)
mineral
Ba·su·to·land former name
of Lesotho
bat (bat·ting, bat·ted)
Ba·tan·gas Philippine port
batch
(batchelor) incorrect spelling
of bachelor
bate restrain; Slang rage;
compare bait
ba·teau boat
bat·ed
bat·fish (plural ·fish or
·fishes)
Bath English city; order of
knighthood
bath container; wash in
bath
bathe swim; wash wound,
etc.
bath·er
ba·thet·ic
bath·house
bath·ing
batho·lith (or ·lite) granite
mass
batho·lith·ic (or ·lit·ic)
ba·thom·eter
batho·met·ric
batho·met·ri·cal·ly
ba·thom·etry
ba·thos
bath·robe
bath·room
bath·tub
Bath·urst Australian city;
former name of Banjul
bathy·al of ocean depths
bathy·met·ric
bathy·met·ri·cal·ly
ba·thym·etry
bathy·scaph (or ·scaphe,
·scape)
bathy·sphere
ba·tik (or bat·tik)
fabric-printing process
ba·tiste fabric
Bat·ley West Yorkshire town
bat·man (plural ·men)
ba·ton
Bat·on Rouge US city
ba·tra·chi·an amphibian
bats·man (plural ·men)
bats·man·ship

batt quilt wadding
bat·tal·ion
bat·ted
bat·ten
Bat·ten·burg cake
bat·ter
bat·ter·er
bat·tery (plural ·teries)
bat·ting
bat·tle
battle-axe
bat·tle·dore racket game
battle·field
bat·tle·ment
battle·piece
bat·tler
battle-scarred
battle·ship
bat·tue hunting term
bat·ty (·ti·er, ·ti·est)
Ba·tum (or Ba·tu·mi)
  Georgian city
bat·wing
bat·woman (plural
  ·women)
bau·ble
Bau·chi Nigerian state
baud unit of speed; compare
  bawd
Bau·haus school of arts
bau·hinia plant
baulk billiards term (US
  balk); variant spelling of
  balk
Bau·tzen German city
baux·ite
Ba·varia
Ba·var·ian
baw·bee former Scottish
  coin
bawd brothel keeper;
  compare baud
bawdi·ly
bawdi·ness
bawd·ry
bawdy (bawdi·er,
  bawdi·est)
bawdy·house
bawl
bawl·er
bay
ba·ya·dere Hindu dancing
  girl
Ba·ya·mon Puerto Rican
  city

bay·berry (plural ·berries)
Ba·yeux French town
bayo·net (·net·ing, ·net·ed
  or ·net·ting, ·net·ted)
bayou marshy stream
bay·wood
ba·zaar (or ·zar)
ba·zoo US mouth
ba·zoo·ka
bdel·lium tree
be
beach shore; compare beech
beach·comber
beach·head
Beach-la-Mar Pacific
  language
bea·con
Bea·cons·field English town
bead
beadi·ly
beadi·ness
bead·ing
bea·dle
beady (beadi·er, beadi·est)
bea·gle
beak
beaked
beak·er
beaky
beam
beam-ends
beamy
bean
bean·bag
bean·ery (plural ·eries) US
  cheap restaurant
bean·feast
beanie US close-fitting hat
beano (plural beanos) Slang
  party
bean·pole
beanstalk
bear (bear·ing, bore, borne)
  support; convey; endure;
  compare bare
bear (bear·ing, bore, born)
  give birth to
bear (plural bears or bear)
  animal
bear·able
bear·ably
bear·berry (plural ·berries)
beard
beard·ed
beard·less

bear·er
bear·ish
Bé·ar·naise sauce
bear's-breech (or -breeches)
  plant
bear's-foot plant
bear·skin
beast
beast·ings US spelling of
  beestings
beast·li·ness
beast·ly (·lier, ·liest)
beat (beat·ing, beat,
  beat·en or beat)
beat·able
beat·er
bea·tif·ic
bea·tifi·cal·ly
be·ati·fi·ca·tion
be·ati·fy (·fies, ·fy·ing,
  ·fied)
be·ati·tude
beat·nik
beau (plural beaus or beaux)
Beau·fort meteorological
  scale
beau·jo·lais (or Beau·) wine
beau monde fashionable
  society
Beau·mont Texan city
Beaune French city; wine
beaut Slang good
beau·te·ous
beau·ti·cian
beau·ti·fi·ca·tion
beau·ti·ful
beau·ti·ful·ly
beau·ti·fy (·fies, ·fy·ing,
  ·fied)
beau·ty (plural ·ties)
Beau·vais French town
beaux-arts fine art
bea·ver
Beaver·board (Trademark)
be·bee·rine alkaloid
Beb·ing·ton English town
be·bop jazz
be·calmed
be·came
be·cause
bec·ca·fi·co (plural ·cos)
  bird
bé·cha·mel sauce
bêche-de-mer marine
  organism

Bechua·na·land *former
name of* Botswana
beck
beck·et nautical term
beck·on
beck·on·er
be·cloud
be·come (·com·ing, ·came,
·come)
be·com·ing·ly
bed (bed·ding, bed·ded)
be·daub
be·daz·zle
be·daz·zle·ment
bed·bug
bed·dable
bed·ded
bed·der
bed·ding
be·deck
be·dev·il (·il·ling, ·illed; *US*
·il·ing, ·iled)
be·dev·il·ment
be·dew
bed·fellow
Bed·ford
Bed·ford·shire
be·dim (·dim·ming,
·dimmed)
bed·lam
Bed·ling·ton terrier
Bedou·in (*or* Bedu·in; *plural*
·ins *or* ·in)
bed·pan
bed·plate
bed·post
be·drag·gle
bed·rail
bed·rid·den
bed·rock
bed·roll
bed·room
bed·side
bed·sitter (*or* ·sit)
bed·sore
bed·spread
bed·stead
bed·straw plant
bed·time
bed·warmer
bee
bee·bread
beech tree; *compare* beach
beech·nut
bee-eater

beef (*plural* beeves) cattle
beef (*plural* beefs) cut of
meat; complaint
beef·bur·ger
beef·cake
beef·eater
beefi·ness
beef·steak
beef·wood
beefy (beefi·er, beefi·est)
bee·hive
bee·keeper
bee·line
Beelzebub the Devil
been
beep
beep·er
beer
beeri·ness
Beer·she·ba Israeli town
beery (beeri·er, beeri·est)
beest·ings (*or* biest·ings; *US
also* beast·ings) cow's first
milk
bees·wax
bees·wing crust in port
beet
beet·fly (*plural* ·flies)
bee·tle
beet·root
bee·zer *Slang* fellow
be·fall (·fal·ling, ·fell,
·fall·en)
be·fit (·fit·ting, ·fit·ted)
be·fit·ting·ly
be·fog (·fog·ging, ·fogged)
be·fool
be·fore
before·hand
be·foul
be·foul·er
be·foul·ment
be·friend
be·fud·dle
beg (beg·ging, begged)
be·gan
be·get (·get·ting, ·got *or*
·gat, ·got·ten *or* ·got)
be·get·ter
beg·gar
beg·gar·li·ness
beg·gar·ly
beggar·weed
beg·gary
begged

beg·ging
be·gin (gin·ning, ·gan,
·gun)
be·gin·ner
be·gird surround
be·gone
be·gonia
be·gor·ra Irish exclamation
be·got
be·got·ten
be·grime
be·grudge
be·grudg·ing·ly
be·guile (·guil·ing, ·guiled)
be·guile·ment
be·guil·er
be·guil·ing·ly
be·guine dance
be·gum (*or* ·gam) Muslim
woman ruler
be·gun
be·half
be·have
be·hav·iour (*US* ·ior)
be·hav·iour·al (*US* ·ior·)
be·hav·iour·ism (*US* ·ior·)
be·hav·iour·ist (*US* ·ior·)
be·hav·iour·is·tic (*US*
·ior·)
be·head
be·held
be·he·moth biblical
monster
be·hest
be·hind
behind·hand
be·hold (·hold·ing, ·held)
be·hold·en
be·hold·er
be·hove (*US* ·hoove)
beige
bei·gel *variant spelling of*
bagel
Bei·jing capital of China
be·ing
Bei·ra Mozambique port
Bei·rut (*or* Bey·routh)
Lebanese capital
be·jew·el (·el·ling, ·elled;
US ·el·ing, ·eled)
bel unit of power
be·la·bour (*US* ·bor)
be·lah tree
Be·la·rus E European
country

Be·la·rus·sia *variant spelling of* Belorussia
be·lat·ed
be·lat·ed·ness
Be·lau Pacific Ocean country
be·lay (·lay·ing, ·layed) make secure
belch
belch·er
be·lea·guer
Be·lém Brazilian port
be·lem·nite fossil
Bel·fast
Bel·fort French department
bel·fry (*plural* ·fries)
Bel·gae Celtic people
Bel·gian
Bel·gium
Bel·grade Yugoslav capital
Bel·gra·via London district
Belial demon
be·lie (·ly·ing, ·lied)
be·lief
be·li·er
be·liev·able
be·lieve
be·liev·er
Belisha traffic beacon
be·lit·tle
be·lit·tle·ment
be·lit·tler
be·lit·tling·ly
Be·lize Central American state
bell
bel·la·don·na
bel·lar·mine jar
Bel·la·trix star
bell·bird
bell·boy
belle beautiful woman
belle époque *French period before World War I*
Bel·leek porcelain
Bellerophon mythological hero
belles-lettres *French literary works*
bel·let·rist
bel·let·ris·tic
bell·hop
bel·li·cose
bel·li·cos·ity
bel·lig·er·ence

bel·lig·er·en·cy
bel·lig·er·ent
Bellona Roman goddess
bel·low
bel·low·er
bel·lows
bell·pull
bell·push
bell-ringer
bell-ringing
bell·wether flock leader
bell·wort plant
bel·ly (*noun, plural* ·lies; *verb* ·lies, ·ly·ing, ·lied)
belly·band part of harness
belly·button
belly-flop (-flopping, -flopped)
bel·ly·ful
Bel·mo·pan Belize capital
Belo Ho·ri·zon·te Brazilian city
be·long
be·long·ings
Be·lo·rus·sia (*or* Bye·) *another name for* Belarus
Be·lo·rus·sian (*or* Bye·)
be·lov·ed
Be·lo·vo (*or* Bye·) Russian city
be·low
Bel Pa·ese cheese
Bel·sen concentration camp
Belshazzar biblical character
belt
Bel·tane Celtic festival
belt·way *US* ring road
be·lu·ga sturgeon
bel·vedere building with view
bema Athenian speaker's platform
Bem·ba (*plural* ·ba *or* ·bas) African people
be·mire
be·moan
be·muse
be·mused
ben *Scot* mountain peak
Bena·dryl (*Trademark*)
Be·na·res Indian city
bench
bench·er a judge
bend (bend·ing, bent)
bend·er

Ben·di·go Australian city
bends decompression sickness
bendy (bendi·er, bendi·est)
be·neath
Ben·edi·ci·te canticle
ben·edi·ci·te blessing
Ben·edic·tine order of monks; liqueur
ben·edic·tion
ben·edic·tory
Ben·edic·tus canticle
ben·efac·tion
ben·efac·tor
ben·efac·tress
be·nef·ic *rare variant of* beneficent
ben·efice
be·nefi·cence
be·nefi·cent
ben·efi·cial
ben·efi·cial·ly
bene·fi·ciary (*plural* ·ciaries)
ben·efit
Bene·lux
Be·ne·ven·to Italian city
be·nevo·lence
be·nevo·lent
Ben·gal
Ben·ga·lese
Ben·ga·li
ben·ga·line fabric
Ben·gha·zi (*or* ·ga·si) Libyan port
be·night·ed
be·nign
be·nig·nan·cy
be·nig·nant
be·nig·nity (*plural* ·nities)
Be·nin African republic
beni·son
ben·ne plant
Ben Ne·vis
ben·ny *Slang* amphetamine tablet
Be·no·ni South African city
bent
ben·thic
ben·thos (*or* ·thon) biology term
ben·ton·ite clay
bent·wood
Be·nue Nigerian state
be·numb

ben·zal·de·hyde
Ben·ze·drine (*Trademark*)
ben·zene chemical
  compound; *compare*
  benzine
ben·zi·dine
ben·zine (*or* ·zin) petrol;
  compare benzene
ben·zo·ate
ben·zo·caine anaesthetic
Ben·zo·drine (*Trademark*)
ben·zo·fu·ran
ben·zo·ic
ben·zo·in gum resin
ben·zol (*or* ·zole)
ben·zo·phe·none
ben·zo·qui·none
ben·zo·yl
ben·zyl
Beo·wulf epic poem
be·queath
be·queath·er
be·quest
Be·rar Indian region
be·rate
Ber·ber Caucasoid Muslim
Ber·bera Somalian port
ber·beri·da·ceous botany
  term
ber·ber·ine alkaloid
ber·ber·is shrub
ber·ceuse lullaby
Berch·tes·ga·den German
  town
be·reave
be·reave·ment
be·reft
be·ret
Be·rez·ni·ki Russian city
berg iceberg; mountain;
  compare burg; burgh
Ber·ga·mo Italian city
ber·ga·mot tree; oil
Ber·gen Norwegian port
berg·schrund crevasse in
  glacier
beri·beri disease
Bering Arctic sea and strait
berk *variant spelling of* burk
Berkeley Californian city
ber·kelium radioactive
  element
Berk·shire
Ber·lin German capital
berm narrow ledge

Ber·mu·da
Bern (*or* Berne) Swiss capital
Ber·nese
ber·ry (*noun, plural* ·ries;
  verb ·ries, ·ry·ing, ·ried)
ber·sa·gliere Italian soldier
ber·seem plant
ber·serk
berth
Ber·wick former Scottish
  county
Berwick-upon-Tweed
  English town
ber·yl mineral
ber·yl·ine
be·ryl·lium chemical
  element
Bes Egyptian god
Be·san·çon French city
be·seech (·seech·ing,
  ·sought)
be·set (·set·ting, ·set)
be·side
be·sides
be·siege
be·sieg·er
be·smear
be·smirch
be·som
be·sot·ted
be·span·gle
be·spat·ter
be·speak (·speak·ing,
  ·spoke, spo·ken *or*
  ·spoke)
be·spec·ta·cled
be·spoke
be·spread
be·sprent sprinkled over
be·sprin·kle
Bes·sa·ra·bia E European
  region
best
bes·tial
bes·ti·al·ity (*plural* ·ities)
bes·ti·al·ize (*or* ·ise)
bes·tial·ly
bes·ti·ary (*plural* ·aries)
be·stir (·stir·ring, ·stirred)
be·stow
be·stow·al (*or* ·ment)
be·stow·er
be·strew (·strew·ing,
  ·strewed, ·strewn *or*
  ·strewed)

be·stride (·strid·ing, ·strode
  or ·strid, ·strid·den *or*
  ·strid)
bet (bet·ting, bet *or* bet·ted)
beta
be·ta·ine alkaloid
be·take (·tak·ing, ·took,
  ·tak·en)
be·ta·tron particle
  accelerator
be·tel plant
Be·tel·geuse (*or* ·geux) star
bête noire (*plural* bêtes
  noires) pet hate
beth Hebrew letter
Betha·ny biblical village
Beth·el biblical town
Beth·le·hem
be·tide
bê·tise folly
be·to·ken
beto·ny (*plural* ·nies) plant
be·took
be·tray
be·tray·al
be·tray·er
be·troth
be·troth·al
be·trothed
bet·ta fish
bet·ter improved
bett·er one who bets
bet·ter·ment
betu·la·ceous botany term
be·tween
be·tween·times
be·twixt
Beu·lah biblical place
beva·tron synchrotron
bev·el (·el·ling, ·elled; *US*
  ·el·ing, ·eled)
bev·er·age
Bev·er·ly Hills Californian
  city
bev·vy (*plural* ·vies) *Dialect*
  alcoholic drink
bevy (*plural* bevies) flock
be·wail
be·wail·er
be·ware
be·wil·der
be·wil·der·ing·ly
be·wil·der·ment
be·witch
be·witch·ing·ly

bey Turkish title
Bey·og·lu district of
Istanbul
be·yond
bez·ant gold coin
bez·el face of tool or gem
be·zique card game
be·zoar hairball
Bha·gal·pur Indian city
Bha·ga·vad-Gita Hindu text
bhang narcotic
Bha·rat *Hindi* India
Bha·ra·ti·ya Indian
Bhat·pa·ra Indian city
bha·van house
Bhav·na·gar Indian port
bhin·di vegetable
Bho·pal Indian port
Bhu·ba·nes·war Indian city
Bhu·tan Asian kingdom
Bhu·tan·ese
Bi·afra Nigerian region
Bia·ly·stok Polish city
bi·an·nual twice a year;
  compare biennial
bi·an·nual·ly
bi·an·nu·late zoology term
Biar·ritz French town
bias (·as·ing, ·ased *or*
  ·as·sing, ·assed)
bi·ath·lon sport
bi·auricu·late (*or* ·lar)
bi·ax·ial
bib (bib·bing, bibbed)
bib·ber
bib·cock tap with nozzle
bi·belot trinket
Bi·ble
bib·li·cal
Bib·li·cist
bib·lio·graph·er (*or*
  ·graph)
bib·lio·graph·ic (*or*
  ·graphi·cal)
bib·li·og·ra·phy (*plural*
  ·phies)
bib·li·ola·try
bib·lio·man·cy
bib·lio·ma·nia
bib·lio·ma·ni·ac
bib·lio·phile (*or* ·phil)
bib·li·ophi·lis·tic
bib·li·oph·ism
bib·lio·pole (*or* ·li·opo·list)
  dealer in rare books

bib·lio·the·ca (*plural* ·cas *or*
  ·cae) library
bibu·lous
bi·cam·er·al
bi·cap·su·lar
bicarb
bi·car·bo·nate
bice blue colour
bi·cen·tenary (*plural*
  ·tenaries)
bi·cepha·lous two-headed
bi·ceps (*plural* ·ceps *or*
  ·cepses)
bi·chlo·ride
bi·cip·i·tal of the biceps
bick·er
bick·er·er
bi·col·lat·er·al
bi·col·our (*or* ·oured; *US* ·or
  or ·ored)
bi·con·cave
bi·con·cav·ity
bi·con·vex
bi·corn (*or* ·cor·nate,
  ·cor·nu·ate)
bi·cus·pid
bi·cus·pi·date
bi·cy·cle
bi·cy·clic (*or* ·cli·cal)
bi·cy·clist (*or* ·cler)
bid (bid·ding; bad, bade, *or*
  bid; bid·den *or* bid)
bi·dar·ka (*or* ·kee) Eskimo
  canoe
bid·dable
bid·der
bid·dy (*plural* ·dies)
bide (bid·ing, bid·ed *or*
  bode, bid·ed)
bi·den·tate
bi·det
Bie·der·mei·er furniture
  and art style
(biege) *incorrect spelling of*
  beige
Biel Swiss town
bield *Dialect* refuge
Bie·le·feld German city
Biel·sko-Bia·ła Polish town
bi·en·nial every two years;
  compare biannual
bi·en·nial·ly
bier coffin support; *compare*
  byre
bier·kel·ler

bi·fa·cial
bi·fari·ous botany term
biff
bif·fin apple
bi·fid divided into two lobes
bi·fid·ity
bi·fi·lar having two parallel
  threads
bi·flag·el·late biology term
bi·fo·cal
bi·fo·cals
bi·fo·li·ate having two
  leaves
bi·fo·lio·late having two
  leaflets
bi·fo·rate having two
  openings
bi·form
Bif·rost Norse mythological
  rainbow
bi·fur·cate forked
bi·fur·ca·tion
big (big·ger, big·gest)
biga·mist
biga·mous
biga·my (*plural* ·mies)
bi·gar·reau cherry
bi·gen·er hybrid organism
bi·gener·ic
big·eye fish
big·ger
big·gest
big·gin close-fitting cap
big·gish
big·head
big·headed
big·headed·ness
big·horn (*plural* ·horns *or*
  ·horn)
bight bay; bend in rope;
  compare bite; byte
big·mouth
big·no·nia shrub
big·no·nia·ceous
big·ot
big·ot·ed
big·ot·ry (*plural* ·ries)
bi·gua·nide biochemical
  compound
big·wig
Bi·har Indian state
Bi·ha·ri
Bi·ja·pur Indian city
bi·jec·tion maths term
bi·jec·tive

bi·jou (*plural* ·joux)
bi·jou·terie jewellery
bi·ju·gate (*or* ·gous) botany term
Bi·ka·ner Indian city
bike
bi·ki·ni
bi·la·bial
bi·la·bi·ate
bil·an·der cargo ship
bi·lat·er·al
bi·lat·er·al·ly
Bil·bao Spanish port
bil·berry (*plural* ·berries)
bil·boes ankle shackles
bile
bile·stone
bilge
bil·har·zia parasite
bil·har·zia·sis
bili·ary
bi·lin·ear
bi·lin·gual
bi·lin·gual·ism
bili·ous
bil·ious·ness
bili·ru·bin bile pigment
bili·ver·din bile pigment
bilk thwart
bilk·er
bill
bil·la·bong
bill·board
bil·let
billet-doux (*plural* billets-doux) love letter
bill·fish (*plural* ·fish *or* ·fishes)
bill·fold
bill·hook
bil·liard
bill·ing
Bil·lings·gate
bil·lion (*plural* ·lions *or* ·lion)
bil·lion·aire
bil·lionth
bil·lon alloy
bil·low
bil·lowi·ness
bil·lowy
bill·poster
bil·ly (*plural* ·lies)
bil·ly·can
bill·yo slang term

bi·lo·bate (*or* ·lobed)
bi·locu·lar (*or* ·late)
Bim native of Barbados
bima·nous two-handed
bim·bo (*plural* ·bos *or* ·boes)
bi·mes·trial lasting two months
bi·me·tal·lic
bi·met·al·lism economic doctrine
bi·mo·lec·u·lar
bi·month·ly (*plural* ·lies)
bi·morph electronics term
bin (bin·ning, binned)
bi·nal twofold
bi·na·ry (*plural* ·ries)
bi·nate occurring in pairs
bin·aural
bind (bind·ing, bound)
bind·er
bind·ery (*plural* ·eries)
bindi-eye plant
bind·weed
bine botany term
binge
bin·gey *Austral* stomach
bin·gle *Austral* minor crash
bin·go
bin·na·cle
binned
bin·ning
bin·ocu·lar (*adj*)
bin·ocu·lars
bi·no·mial
bi·nomi·nal biology term
bint *Slang* girl
bin·tu·rong animal
bi·nu·cle·ar
bi·nu·cle·ate
bio·assay
bio·as·tro·nau·tics
bio·cata·lyst
bio·cata·lyt·ic
bi·oc·el·late biology term
bio·cenol·ogy branch of ecology
bio·chemi·cal
bio·chemi·cal·ly
bio·chem·ist
bio·chem·is·try
bio·cid·al
bio·cide
bio·cli·ma·tol·ogy
bio·cy·cle ecological region
bio·degrad·able

bio·deg·ra·da·tion
bio·di·ver·sity
bio·dy·nam·ic (*or* ·nami·cal)
bio·dy·nam·ics
bio·en·er·get·ics
bio·en·gi·neer
bio·en·gi·neer·ing
bio·feed·back
bio·fla·vo·noid vitamin
bio·gen hypothetical protein
bio·gen·esis
bio·genet·ic (*or* bio·geneti·cal, biog·enous)
bio·geneti·cal·ly
bio·geo·graphi·cal
bio·geog·ra·phy
bi·og·ra·pher
bio·graphi·cal
bi·og·ra·phy (*plural* ·phies)
bio·herm organic rock
bio·logi·cal (*or* ·log·ic)
bio·logi·cal·ly
bi·olo·gist
bi·ol·ogy
bio·lu·mi·nes·cence
bio·lu·mi·nes·cent
bi·oly·sis
bio·lyt·ic
bio·mass ecology term
bi·ome ecology term
bio·met·ric
bio·met·ri·cal·ly
bi·om·etry (*or* bio·met·rics)
bi·on·ic
bi·on·ics
bio·nom·ic
bio·nomi·cal·ly
bio·nom·ics ecology
bi·ono·mist
bio·physi·cal
bio·physi·cist
bio·phys·ics
bio·plasm
bio·plas·mic
bio·poi·esis biology term
bi·op·sy (*plural* ·sies)
bi·op·tic
bio·rhythm
bio·scope
bi·os·co·py (*plural* ·pies)
bio·sphere ecology term
bio·stat·ic

bio·stati·cal·ly
bio·stat·ics
bio·strome fossil-rich rock
bio·syn·the·sis
bio·syn·thet·ic
bio·syn·theti·cal·ly
bio·ta biology term
bio·tech·no·logi·cal
bio·tech·nolo·gist
bio·tech·nol·ogy
bi·ot·ic
bio·tin vitamin
bio·tite mineral
bio·tit·ic
bio·tope ecological area
bio·type biology term
bio·typ·ic
bi·pa·ri·etal
bip·ar·ous
bi·par·ti·san (or ·zan)
bi·par·ti·san·ship (or ·zan·)
bi·par·tite
bi·par·ti·tion
bi·ped
bi·ped·al
bi·pet·al·ous
bi·phen·yl
bi·pin·nate botany term
bi·plane
bi·pod
bi·po·lar
bi·pro·pel·lant
bi·quad·rate maths term
bi·quad·rat·ic
bi·quar·ter·ly
bi·ra·cial
bi·ra·dial
bi·ra·mous divided into two
  parts
birch
bird
bird·bath
bird-brained
bird·cage
bird·house
birdie
bird·like
bird·lime
bird·man (plural ·men)
bird·seed
bird's-eye (adj)
bird's-foot (or bird-; plural
  -foots) plant
bird-watcher
bird-watching

bi·refrin·gence
bi·refrin·gent
bi·reme ship
bi·ret·ta (or ber·ret·ta)
  clerical cap
bi·ria·ni Indian food
Bir·ken·head
Bir·ming·ham
Biro (Trademark; plural
  Biros)
Bi·ro·bi·dzhan Russian city
birr make whirring sound;
  compare bur; burr
birth
birth·day
birth·mark
birth·place
birth·right
birth·root plant
birth·stone
birth·wort plant
Bis·cay (Bay of)
bis·cuit
bise wind
bi·sect
bi·sec·tion
bi·sec·tor
bi·sec·trix (plural ·tri·ces)
  maths term
bi·ser·rate botany term
bi·sex·ual
bi·sexu·al·ism (or ·ity)
bish Slang mistake
Bish·kek capital of
  Kyrgyzstan
bish·op
bishop·bird
bish·op·ric
Bis·kra Algerian town
bis·muth
bis·muth·al
bis·mu·thic
bis·muth·in·ite mineral
bis·muth·ous
bi·son (plural ·son)
bisque colour; soup; sports
  term
Bis·sau (or ·sao) capital of
  Guinea-Bissau
bis·sex·tile of a leap year
bis·ter US spelling of bistre
bis·tort plant
bis·tou·ry (plural ·ries)
  surgical knife

bis·tre (US ·ter) drawing
  pigment
bis·tro (plural ·tros)
  restaurant
bi·sul·cate cleft
bi·sul·phate (US ·fate)
bi·sul·phide (US ·fide)
bi·sul·phite (US ·fite)
bi·sym·met·ric (or ·ri·cal)
bi·sym·met·ri·cal·ly
bi·sym·met·ry
bit
bi·tar·trate
bitch
bitchi·ly
bitchy (bitchi·er,
  bitchi·est)
bite (bit·ing, bit, bit·ten)
  grip with teeth; compare
  bight; byte
Bi·thynia ancient Asian
  country
bit·ing·ly
bit·ing·ness
bit·ser Austral mongrel dog
bit·stock
bitt mooring post
bit·ten
bit·ter
Bit·ter Lakes
bit·ter·ling fish
bit·tern bird
bit·ter·ness
bitter·nut
bit·ters drink
bitter·sweet
bitter·weed
bitter·wood
bit·ty (·ti·er, ·ti·est)
bi·tu·men
bi·tu·mi·ni·za·tion (or
  ·sa·tion)
bi·tu·mi·nize (or ·nise)
bi·tu·mi·nous
bi·va·len·cy
bi·va·lent
bi·valve
bi·val·vu·lar
bivou·ac (·ack·ing, ·acked)
biv·vy (plural ·vies) Slang
  tent
bi·week·ly (plural ·lies)
bi·year·ly
Biysk (or Biisk, Bisk)
  Russian town

bi·zarre

Bi·zer·te (*or* ·ta) Tunisian port

blab (blab·bing, blabbed)

blab·ber

blabber·mouth

black

black·ball

black·berry (*plural* ·berries)

black·bird

black·board

black·buck antelope

Black·burn

black·butt tree

black·cap bird

black·cock male grouse

black·cur·rant

black·damp

black·en

black·fish (*plural* ·fish *or* ·fishes)

black·fly (*plural* ·flies)

Black·foot (*plural* ·feet *or* ·foot) American Indian

black·guard

black·guard·ism

black·guard·ly

black·head

black·heart plant disease

black·hearted

black·ing

black·ish

black·jack

black·leg (·leg·ging, ·legged)

black·list

black·mail

black·mail·er

black·market (*verb*)

black·ness

black·out

black·poll bird

Black·pool

Black·shirt fascist

black·smith

black·snake

black·tail deer

black·thorn

black·top *US* paving material

Black·wood bridge term

black·wood Australian tree

blad·der

blad·der ket·mia plant

bladder·nose seal

bladder·nut

bladder·wort

bladder·wrack

blade

blah silly talk

blain blister

Blair·ite follower of Tony Blair

blam·able (*or* blame·)

blame

blame·ful

blame·ful·ness

blame·less

blame·less·ness

blame·worthi·ness

blame·worthy

blanch make white; *compare* blench

blanc·mange

bland

blan·dish

blan·dish·ment

bland·ness

blank

blan·ket

blank·ly

Blan·tyre-Limbe Malawian city

blare

blar·ney

bla·sé indifferent

blas·pheme

blas·phem·er

blas·phe·mous

blas·phe·my (*plural* ·mies)

blast

blasted

blas·te·ma (*plural* ·mas *or* ·ma·ta) biology term

blas·tem·ic

blast·ing

blas·to·coel (*or* ·coele) embryology term

blas·to·cyst

blas·to·derm (*or* ·disc) embryology term

blas·to·derm·ic

blast·off

blas·to·gen·esis

blas·to·gen·ic (*or* ·genet·ic)

blas·to·mere embryology term

blas·to·mer·ic

blas·to·pore embryology term

blas·to·por·ic (*or* ·al)

blas·to·sphere

blas·tu·la (*plural* ·las *or* ·lae) embryology term

blas·tu·lar

blat *US* bleat

bla·tan·cy

bla·tant

blath·er (*or* bleth·)

blather·skite talkative person

blau·bok (*plural* ·bok *or* ·boks) antelope

Blay·don English town

blaze

blaz·er

bla·zon

bla·zon·ry (*plural* ·ries)

bleach

bleach·able

bleach·er

bleak

bleak·ness

blear

bleari·ness

bleary (bleari·er, bleari·est)

bleat

bleat·er

bleat·ing·ly

bleb blister

bleed (bleed·ing, bled)

bleed·er

bleep

bleep·er

blem·ish

blem·ish·er

blench shy away; *compare* blanch

blench·er

blench·ing·ly

blend combine

blende type of ore

blend·er

Blen·heim German village

blen·ni·oid fish

blen·ny (*plural* ·nies)

blepha·ri·tic

blepha·ri·tis inflammation of eyelids

bles·bok (*or* ·buck; *plural* ·boks, ·bok *or* ·bucks, ·buck) antelope

bless (bless·ing, blessed *or* blest)

bless·ed (*adj*)

bless·ed·ness
blest
blet fruit decay
blew
blew·its edible fungus;
compare bluet
Bli·da Algerian city
blight
blight·er
Blighty *Slang* England
bli·mey
blimp
blimp·ish
blind
blind·age military screen
blind·er
blind·fish (*plural* ·fish or
·fishes)
blind·fold
blind·ing
blind·ly
blind·ness
blind·storey (or ·story)
blind·worm
blini (or blin·is) pancake
blink
blink·er
blink·ers
blink·ing
blintz (or blintze) filled
pancake
blip (blip·ping, blipped)
bliss
bliss·ful
bliss·ful·ly
bliss·ful·ness
blis·ter
blis·ter·ing·ly
blithe
blithe·ness
blith·er·ing
blithe·some
blitz
blitz·krieg
bliz·zard
bloat
bloated
bloat·er
blob (blob·bing, blobbed)
bloc group of nations
block
block·ade
block·ad·er
block·age
block·board

block·bust·er
block·bust·ing
block·er
block·head
block·house
Bloem·fon·tein South
African city
bloke
blond (*fem* blonde)
blond·ness (*fem*
blonde·ness)
blood
blood·curdling
blood·ed
blood·fin
blood·hound
bloodi·ly
bloodi·ness
blood·less
blood·letting
blood·root
blood·shed
blood·shot
blood·stain
blood·stained
blood·stock
blood·stone
blood·sucker
blood·thirsti·ly
blood·thirsti·ness
blood·thirsty (·thirsti·er,
·thirsti·est)
blood·worm
bloody (*adj* bloodi·er,
bloodi·est; *verb* blood·ies,
bloody·ing, blood·ied)
bloody-minded
bloom
bloom·er
bloom·ers
bloom·ery (*plural* ·eries)
ironworks
bloom·ing
Blooms·bury
bloop·er *US* blunder
blos·som
blot (blot·ting, blot·ted)
blotch
blotchi·ly
blotchi·ness
blotchy (blotchi·er,
blotchi·est)
blot·ter
blot·to *Slang* drunkenly
unconscious

blouse
blou·son
blow (blow·ing, blew,
blown)
blow-dry (-dries, -dry·ing,
-dried)
blow·er
blow·fish (*plural* ·fish or
·fishes)
blow·fly (*plural* ·flies)
blow·hard boastful person
blow·hole
blow·lamp
blown
blow·out (*noun*)
blow·pipe
blow·torch
blow-wave
blowy (blowi·er, blowi·est)
blowzi·ly (or blowsi·)
blowzi·ness (or
blowsi·ness)
blowzy (or blowsy;
blowzi·er, blowzi·ier or
blowsi·er, blowsi·est)
blub (blub·bing, blubbed)
blub·ber
blub·bery
bludge *Austral* scrounge
bludg·eon
bludg·eon·er
blue (*adj* blu·er, blu·est;
verb blue·ing or blu·ing,
blued)
Blue·beard
blue·bell
blue·berry (*plural* ·berries)
blue·bill
blue·bird
blue-blooded
blue·bonnet Scottish hat
blue·book government
publication
blue·bottle
blue·fish (*plural* ·fish or
··fishes)
blue·gill fish
blue·grass
blue·ing (or blu·ing)
blue·jacket
blue·ness
blue·nose *US* puritanical
person
blue·print
blues

blue·stocking
blue·stone
bluet plant; *compare* blewits
blue·throat bird
blue·tit
blue·tongue lizard
blu·ey *Austral* blanket
bluff
bluff·er
bluff·ness
blu·ing *variant spelling of* blueing
blu·ish (*or* blue·ish)
blun·der
blun·der·buss
blun·der·er
blun·der·ing·ly
blunge ceramics term
blung·er
blunt
blunt·ness
blur (blur·ring, blurred)
blurb
blur·red·ly
blur·red·ness
blur·ry
blurt
blush
blush·er
blush·ing·ly
blus·ter
blus·ter·er
blus·ter·ing·ly (*or* ·ous·ly)
blus·tery (*or* ·ter·ous)
Blyth English port
B'nai B'rith Jewish society
boa
boar male pig; *compare* boor; bore
board
board·er
board·ing
board·room
board·walk *US* wooden promenade
boar·fish (*plural* ·fish *or* ·fishes)
boar·hound
boar·ish coarse; sensual; *compare* boorish
boar·ish·ness
boast
boast·er
boast·ful
boast·ful·ly

boast·ful·ness
boast·ing·ly
boat
boat·el waterside hotel
boat·er
boat·hook
boat·house
boat·ing
boat·load
boat·man (*plural* ·men)
boat·swain (*or* bo·sun)
bob (bob·bing, bobbed)
bob·bery (*plural* ·beries) pack of dogs
bob·bin
bob·bi·net fabric
bob·ble
bob·by (*plural* ·bies)
bob·cat
bob·float fishing float
bob·let bobsleigh
bobo·link bird
bo·bo·tie curried dish
bob·owler *Dialect* moth
bob·sleigh (*or esp. US* ·sled)
bob·stay
bob·tail
bob·white bird
bo·cage wooded country
boc·cia bowls game
Boche *Slang* German
Bo·chum German city
bock beer
bod *Slang* person
bode
bo·dega wine shop
bodge
bodg·er
bodgie *Austral* unruly man
Bo·dhi·satt·va Buddhist divine
bod·ice
bodi·less
bodi·ly
bod·kin
Bod·lei·an Oxford library
Bod·min
Bo·do·ni style of type
body (*noun, plural* bodies; *verb* bodies, body·ing, bod·ied)
body-centred
body·check
body·guard
body-snatcher

body·work
boehm·ite mineral
Boeo·tia region of ancient Greece
Boeo·tian
Boer Dutch South African
boeuf Bour·gui·gnon beef casserole
bof·fin
bog (bog·ging, bogged)
bo·gan *Canadian* side stream
bo·gey golf term; *compare* bogie
bo·gey (*or* bogy; *plural* ·geys *or* bogies) evil spirit; *compare* bogie
bogey·man (*plural* ·men)
bog·gart *Dialect* poltergeist
bog·gi·ness
bog·gle
bog·gy (·gi·er, ·gi·est)
bo·gie wheeled undercarriage; *compare* bogey
bo·gle *Dialect* bogey
Bog·nor Re·gis
bo·gong moth
Bo·gor Indonesian city
Bo·go·tá Colombian capital
bo·gus
bog·wood
bogy *variant spelling of* bogey
bo·hea China tea
Bo·he·mia
Bo·he·mian
Bo·hol Philippine island
boil
boil·able
boil·er
boiler·maker
boiler·plate
boiler·suit
boil·ing·ly
Bois de Bou·logne Parisian park
Boi·se *US* city
bois·ter·ous
bois·ter·ous·ness
bok·ma·kie·rie bird
bola weapon
Bo·land South African region
bold

bold·face (*adj*)
bold·ness
bole tree trunk; *compare*
  bowl
bo·lec·tion architectural
  term
bo·lero (*plural* ·ros)
bo·letus (*plural* ·letuses *or*
  ·leti*) fungus
bo·lide meteor
boli·var (*plural* ·vars *or*
  ·vares*) Venezuelan
  currency
Bo·livia
Bo·liv·ian
boll
bol·lard
bol·locks (*or* bal·locks)
boll·worm
bolo (*plural* bolos) knife
Bo·lo·gna Italian city
Bo·lo·gnese
bo·lom·eter
bo·lo·met·ric
bo·lo·met·ri·cal·ly
bo·lo·ney *variant spelling of*
  baloney
Bol·she·vik (*plural* ·viks *or*
  ·vi·ki)
Bol·she·vism
Bol·she·vist
Bol·shie (*or* ·shy)
bol·son US desert valley
bol·ster
bol·ster·er
bol·ster·ing·ly
bolt
bolt·er
Bol·ton
bol·to·nia plant
bolt·rope rope on a sail
bo·lus (*plural* ·luses) chewed
  food
Bol·za·no Italian city
bomb
bom·ba·ca·ceous botany
  term
bom·bard
bom·bar·dier
bom·bard·ment
bom·bar·don musical
  instrument
bom·bast
bom·bas·tic
bom·bas·ti·cal·ly

Bom·bay
bom·ba·zine
bom·be dessert
bom·bé furniture style
bomb·er
bom·bora submerged reef
bomb·shell
bomb·sight bomb-aiming
  device
bomb site bomb-destroyed
  area
bom·by·cid moth
bona fide genuine
bona fides good faith
Bon·aire West Indian island
bo·nan·za
Bo·na·part·ism
bona va·can·tia unclaimed
  goods
bon·bon
bonce *Slang* head
bond
bond·age
bond·ed
bond·holder
bond·maid
bond·servant
bonds·man (*plural* ·men)
bone
bone·black
bone·fish (*plural* ·fish *or*
  ·fishes)
bone·head
bone·less
bon·er *Slang* blunder
bone·set plant
bone·set·ter
bone·shaker
bone·yard
bon·fire
bong
bon·go (*plural* ·gos *or* ·goes)
  drum
bon·go (*plural* ·go *or* ·gos)
  antelope
bon·ho·mie
boni·ness
bon·ism
bo·ni·to (*plural* ·tos *or* ·toes)
  fish
bonk·ers
bon mot (*plural* bons mots)
  fitting remark
Bonn former West German
  capital

bon·net
bon·ny (·ni·er, ·ni·est)
bon·sai (*plural* ·sai)
bon·sela African gift
bon·spiel curling match
bon·te·bok (*plural* ·boks *or*
  ·bok) antelope
bo·nus
bony (boni·er, boni·est)
bonze Buddhist priest
boo (boo·ing, booed)
boob
boo·bi·al·la shrub
boo·book owl
boo·by (*plural* ·bies)
booby-trap (*verb*;
  -trap·ping, -trapped)
boo·dle
booed
boo·gie
boogie-woogie
boo·hoo (·hoo·ing, ·hooed)
boo·ing
book
book·binder
book·bindery (*plural*
  ·binderies)
book·bind·ing
book·case
bookie
book·ing
book·ish
book·ish·ness
book·keeper
book·keeping
book·learning
book·let
book·louse insect
book·maker
book·making
book·mark (*or* ·marker)
book·plate
book·rack
book·sell·er
book·shelf (*plural* ·shelves)
book·shop
book·stall
book·stand
book·worm
Bool·ean type of algebra
boom
boom·er
boom·er·ang
boom·slang snake
boon

boon·docks *US* wild country

boon·dog·gle *US* do futile work

boor unpleasant person; *compare* **boar**; **bore**

boor·ish ill-mannered; insensitive; *compare* **boarish**

boor·ish·ness

boost

boost·er

boot

boot·black

boot·ed

bootee

Boö·tes constellation

booth

boot·lace

Boo·tle

boot·leg (**·leg·ging**, **·legged**)

boot·leg·ger

boot·less

boot·lick

boot·lick·er

boot·loader

boot·strap

boo·ty (*plural* **·ties**)

booze

booz·er

boozi·ness

boozy (**boozi·er**, **boozi·est**)

bop (**bop·ping**, **bopped**)

bora north wind

Bora Bora Pacific island

bo·ra·cic

bo·ra·cite mineral

bor·age plant

bo·ragi·na·ceous

bo·rak *Austral* nonsense

bo·rane chemical compound

bo·rate

bo·rax (*plural* **·raxes** or **·ra·ces**)

bo·ra·zon chemical compound

bor·bo·ryg·mus (*plural* **·mi**) stomach rumbling

Bor·deaux French port; wine

Bor·delaise sauce

bor·del·lo (*plural* **·los**)

bor·der

bor·dereau (*plural* **·dereaux**) insurance invoice

bor·der·er

border·land

border·line

Bor·ders Scottish region

bor·dure heraldry term

bore dull person; drill hole; *compare* **boar**; **boor**

bo·real of the north

Boreas Greek god

bore·dom

boree tree

bor·er

bo·ric

bo·ride chemical compound

bor·ing

born given birth to

borne carried

Bor·neo Malaysian island

bor·neol chemical compound

born·ite mineral

Bor·no Nigerian state

Bo·ro·di·no battle site

bo·ron chemical element

bo·ro·nia shrub

bo·ro·sili·cate

bor·ough

bor·row

bor·row·er

bor·stal

bort (*or* **boart**, **bortz**) inferior diamond

bor·zoi (*plural* **·zois**)

bos·cage (*or* **·kage**) thicket

bosch·vark wild pig

bosh

bosk small wood

bos·ket (*or* **·quet**) thicket

Bos·kop prehistoric African race

bosky (**boski·er**, **boski·est**)

Bos·nia-Her·cego·vi·na (*or* **·zego·**) S European country

Bos·nian

bos·om

bos·omy

bos·on physics term

Bos·po·rus (*or* **Bos·pho·rus**) Turkish strait

boss

bos·sa nova dance

bossi·ly

bossi·ness

bossy (**bossi·er**, **bossi·est**)

Bos·ton

bo·sun *variant spelling of* **boatswain**

Bos·worth battle site

bot (*or* **bott**) botfly larva

bo·tani·cal (*or* **·tan·ic**)

bota·nist

bota·nize (*or* **·nise**)

bota·ny (*plural* **·nies**)

bo·tar·go (*plural* **·goes**) fish roe

botch

botch·er

botchi·ly

botchiness

botchy (**botchi·er**, **botchi·est**)

bot·fly (*plural* **·flies**)

both

both·er

both·era·tion

both·er·some

bothy (*plural* **bothies**) *Scot* small shelter

bot·ryoi·dal (*or* **·ry·ose**)

bots horse disease

Bot·swa·na

bot·tle

bottle·brush shrub

bottle·neck

bottle·nose dolphin

bot·tom

bot·tom·less

bottom·most

bot·tom·ry (*plural* **·ries**) legal term

Bot·trop German city

botu·lin toxin

botu·li·nus (*plural* **·nuses**) bacterium

botu·lism

Boua·ké Côte d'Ivoire town

bou·chée vol-au-vent

Bouches-du-Rhone French department

bou·clé knobbly yarn

bou·clée support for billiard cue

bou·doir

bouf·fant

Bou·gain·ville Pacific island

bou·gain·vil·lea (*or* **·laea**) plant

bough

bought

bought•en *Dialect* bought

bou•gie catheter

bouil•la•baisse fish soup

bouil•lon broth

boul•der

boule gem; *compare* **boulle**

boule•vard

boule•var•di•er fashionable man

boule•verse•ment *French* upheaval

boulle (*or* **boule, buhl**) marquetry; *compare* **boule**

Bou•logne

bounce

bounc•er

bounci•ly

bounci•ness

bounc•ing

bouncy (**bounci•er, bounci•est**)

bound

bounda•ry (*plural* •ries)

bound•en

bound•er

bound•less

bound•less•ness

bounds

boun•te•ous

boun•te•ous•ness

boun•ti•ful

boun•ti•ful•ness

boun•ty (*plural* •ties)

bou•quet

bou•quet gar•ni (*plural* **bou•quets gar•nis**)

bour•bon US whiskey

bour•don organ stop

bourg French market town

bour•geois (*fem* •geoise)

bour•geoi•sie

bourn stream

bourne (*or* **bourn**) destination; boundary

Bourne•mouth

bour•rée dance

Bourse French stock exchange

bouse (*or* **bowse**) nautical term

bou•stro•phedon alternately ordered word lines

bout

bou•tique

bou•ton•ni•ere buttonhole flower

bou•zouki

bo•vid

bo•vine

Bov•ril (*Trademark*)

bov•ver *Slang* rowdiness

bow

bowd•ler•ism

bowd•leri•za•tion (*or* •sa•tion)

bowd•ler•ize (*or* •ise)

bow•el

bow•er

bower•bird

Bow•ery New York street and area

bow•fin fish

bow•head whale

bow•ing

bow•knot

bowl basin; wooden ball; *compare* **bole**

bow-legged

bowl•er

bowl•ful

bow•line

bowl•ing

bowls

bow•man (*plural* •men)

bow•saw

bowse *variant spelling of* **bouse**

bow•ser fuel tanker

bow•shot

bow•sprit

bow•string

bow-wow

bow•yer maker of archery bows

box

box•berry (*plural* •berries)

box•board

box•car US closed railway van

box•er

box•ing

box•room

box•wood

boy

boy•ar

boy•cott

boy•friend

boy•hood

boy•ish

boy•ish•ness

boy•la Aboriginal witch doctor

Boyne Irish river

boysen•berry (*plural* •berries)

bra

Bra•bant Belgian province

brace

brace•let

brac•er

bra•chial of the arm

bra•chi•ate

bra•chia•tion

bra•chio•pod marine invertebrate

bra•chio•saur•us

bra•chium (*plural* •chia) armlike part

brachy•cephal•ic (*or* •cepha•lous) broad-headed

brachy•cepha•ly (*or* •lism)

brachy•dac•tylia (*or* •tyl•ism)

brachy•dac•tyl•ic

bra•chylo•gous

bra•chyl•ogy (*plural* •ogies) concise style

bra•chyp•ter•ous short-winged

brachy•ur•an crustacean

brac•ing

brac•ing•ly

brack•en

brack•et

brack•ish

brack•ish•ness

Brack•nell English town

bract

bract•eal

brac•te•ate

brac•teo•late

brac•te•ole

brad small nail

brad•awl

Brad•ford

Bradshaw railway timetable

brady•car•dia abnormally slow heartbeat

brady•car•di•ac

brady•kin•in blood protein

brae *Scot* hill

brag (**brag•ging, bragged**)

Bra•ga Portuguese city

brag·ga·do·cio (*plural* ·cios)
boasting
brag·gart
brag·ger
brag·ging·ly
Brah·ma Hindu god
Brah·man (*or* ·min; *plural*
·mans, ·min, *or* ·mins)
Hindu caste
Brah·ma·na Hindu treatise
Brah·ma·ni (*plural* ·nis)
woman Brahman
Brah·man·ic (*or* ·min·ic)
Brah·man·ism (*or*
·min·ism)
Brah·ma·pu·tra Asian river
Brah·min *variant spelling of*
Brahman
Bra·hui Pakistani language
braid
braid·ed
braid·er
braid·ing
brail nautical term
Braille writing for blind
brain
brain·child (*plural*
·children)
braini·ness
brain·less
brain·less·ness
brain·pan
brain·sick
brain·stem
brain·storm
brain·storm·er
brain·storm·ing
brain·wash
brain·wash·er
brain·wash·ing
brain·wave
brainy (braini·er,
braini·est)
braise cook; *compare* braze
brake
brakes·man (*plural* ·men)
bram·ble
bram·bling bird
Bram·ley apple
bran
branch
bran·chia (*plural* ·chiae)
animal's gill
bran·chial
bran·chi·ate

branch·ing
bran·chio·pod crustacean
brand
Bran·den·burg German city
bran·dish
bran·dish·er
brand·ling earthworm
brand-new
bran·dy (*plural* ·dies)
bran·le dance
brash
brashi·ness state of being
brashy
brash·ly
brash·ness
brashy (brashi·er,
brashi·est) fragmented
Bra·sília Brazilian capital
Bra·şou Romanian city
brass
bras·sard (*or* ·sart) armband
brass·bound
bras·se·rie
bras·si·ca vegetable
bras·si·ca·ceous
brassie (*or* brassy; *plural*
brassies) golf club
bras·siere
brassi·ly
brassi·ness
brassy (brassi·er, brassi·est)
brat
Bra·ti·sla·va capital of
Slovakia
brat·tice mining term
brat·tish·ing architectural
term
brat·wurst sausage
braun·ite mineral
bra·va·do (*plural* ·does *or*
·dos)
brave
brave·ness
brav·ery (*plural* ·eries)
bra·vo (*plural* ·voes *or* ·vos)
bra·vu·ra
braw *Scot* excellent
brawl
brawl·er
brawn
brawni·ly
brawni·ness
brawny (brawni·er,
brawni·est)
braxy sheep disease

bray
bray·er
braze solder metal; *compare*
braise
bra·zen
bra·zen·ness
braz·er one who brazes
bra·zi·er brass worker;
charcoal-burning pot
Bra·zil
bra·zil·ein (*or* ·sil·ein) red
dye
Bra·zil·ian
brazi·lin (*or* brasi·lin)
yellow dye
Braz·za·ville capital of
Congo
breach break; gap; *compare*
breech
bread
bread·board
bread·crumb
bread·fruit (*plural* ·fruits *or*
·fruit)
bread·line
bread·nut
bread·root plant
breadth
bread·winner
break (break·ing, broke,
brok·en)
break·able
break·age
break·away
break·down
break·er
break·fast
break·front
break-in (*noun*)
break·neck
break·out (*noun*)
break·point
break·through (*noun*)
break-up (*noun*)
break·water
bream (*plural* bream)
breast
breast·bone
breast-feed (-feed·ing, -fed)
breast·pin
breast·plate
breast·stroke
breast·work fortification
breath
breatha·lyse

Breatha·lyz·er (or ·lys·er)
(Trademark)
breathe
breath·er
breathi·ly
breathi·ness
breath·ing
breath·less
breath·less·ness
breath·taking
breathy (breathi·er,
breathi·est)
brec·cia rock
brec·ci·at·ed
Brec·on (or Breck·nock)
Welsh town
Brec·on·shire (or
Breck·nock·shire) former
Welsh county
bred
Bre·da Dutch city
bree Scot thin soup
breech part of gun; buttocks
(note breech birth);
compare breach
breech·block
breech·clout loincloth
breeches
breech·ing harness strap
breech·loader
breech-loading
breed (breed·ing, bred)
breed·er
breeze
breezi·ly
breezi·ness
breezy (breezi·er,
breezi·est)
breg·ma (plural ·ma·ta) part
of skull
Bre·men German city
Brem·er·ha·ven German
port
brems·strah·lung physics
term
Bren gun
Bren·ner Pass
Brent London borough
brent (plural brents or
brent) goose
br'er US dialect brother
Bre·scia Italian city
Brest French port
breth·ren
Bret·on of Brittany

breve accent; musical note
bre·vet (·vet·ting, ·vet·ted
or ·vet·ing, ·vet·ed)
military term
brev·et·cy
brevia·ry (plural ·ries)
bre·vier size of type
brevi·ros·trate ornithology
term
brev·ity (plural ·ities)
brew
brew·age
brew·er
brew·ery (plural ·eries)
brew·ing
brew·is Dialect gravy-soaked
bread
bri·ar (or ·er) tobacco pipe;
variant spelling of brier
Briareus Greek giant
briar·root (or brier·)
brib·able (or bribe·able)
bribe
brib·er
brib·ery (plural ·eries)
bric-a-brac
brick
brick·bat
brickie Slang bricklayer
brick·layer
brick·laying
brick·le Dialect brittle
brick·work
brick·yard
bri·cole billiards term
brid·al
bride
bride·groom
brides·maid
bride·well jail
bridge
bridge·able
bridge·board
bridge·head
Bridge·port US port
Bridge·town capital of
Barbados
bridge·work
bridg·ing
Bridg·wa·ter English town
bri·die Scot meat pie
bri·dle
bri·dler
bri·doon horse's bit
Brie cheese

brief
brief·case
brief·ing
brief·ly
bri·er (or ·ar) thorny shrub;
compare briar
bri·ery (or ·ary)
brig
bri·gade
briga·dier
briga·low tree
brig·and
brig·an·dine armour
brig·an·tine ship
bright
bright·en
bright·en·er
bright·ness
Bright·on
brights US headlights
bright·work metal car
trimmings
brill (plural brill or brills)
bril·liance (or ·lian·cy)
bril·liant
bril·lian·tine
brim (brim·ming,
brimmed)
brim·ful (or ·full)
brim·mer
brim·stone
brin·dle
brin·dled
brine
bring (bring·ing, brought)
brini·ness
brink
brink·man·ship
brin·ny (plural ·nies) Austral
a stone
briny (brini·er, brini·est)
bri·oche
brio·lette jewel
bri·quette
bri·sance power of
explosion
Bris·bane
brise-soleil window
protection
brisk
bris·ket
bris·ling fish
bris·tle
bristle-grass
bristle·tail insect

bris·tly

Bris·tol

bris·tols *Slang* breasts

Brit *Slang* Briton

brit young herring

Brit·ain

Bri·tan·nia

Bri·tan·nic

Briti·cism

Brit·ish

Brit·ish·er

Brit·ish·ism

Brit·on

Brit·ta·ny

brit·tle

brit·tle·ness

brittle·star starfish

Brno Czech city

broach raise topic; tap container; *compare* brooch

broach·er

broad

broad·bill bird

broad·brim hat

broad·cast (cast·ing, ·cast or ·cast·ed)

broad·cast·er

broad·cloth

broad·en

broad·leaf (*plural* ·leaves) tobacco plant

broad-leaved denoting nonconiferous trees

broad·loom

broad·ly

broad-minded

broad-minded·ness

Broad·moor

Broads East Anglian lakes

broad·sheet

broad·side

broad·sword

broad·tail Persian lamb

Broad·way

Brob·ding·nag

bro·cade

broca·telle brocade

broc·co·li

broch Scottish tower

bro·ché woven with raised design

bro·chette skewer

bro·chure

brock badger

brock·et deer

brod·dle *Dialect* poke

bro·de·rie an·glaise

Broeder·bond South African Afrikaner society

bro·gan boot

brogue

broil

broil·er

broke

bro·ken

broken-down

broken·hearted

bro·ker

bro·ker·age

brol·ga bird

brol·ly (*plural* ·lies)

bro·mal sedative

bro·mate

brome grass

bro·melia·ceous

bro·meli·ad botany term

brom·eo·sin dye

bro·mic

bro·mide

bro·mid·ic dull

bro·min·ate chemistry term

bro·mina·tion

bro·mine chemical element

bro·mism (*or* bro·min·ism) bromine poisoning

bro·mo·form chemical compound

Broms·grove English town

bron·chi *plural of* bronchus

bron·chia bronchial tubes

bron·chial

bron·chi·ec·ta·sis bronchial disease

bron·chio·lar

bron·chi·ole

bron·chit·ic

bron·chi·tis

bron·cho·pneu·mo·nia

bron·cho·scope

bron·cho·scop·ic

bron·chos·co·pist

bron·chos·co·py

bron·chus (*plural* ·chi)

bron·co (*or* ·cho; *plural* ·cos *or* ·chos) wild pony

bronco·buster

bron·to·sau·rus (*or* ·to·saur)

Bronx New York borough

bronze

bronzy

brooch piece of jewellery; *compare* broach

brood

brood·er

broodi·ness

broody (broodi·er, broodi·est)

brook

brook·able

brook·ite mineral

brook·let

brook·lime trailing plant

Brook·lyn New York borough

brook·weed

broom

broom·corn sorghum

broom·rape plant

broom·stick

brose *Scot* porridge

broth

broth·el

broth·er

brother·hood

brother-in-law (*plural* brothers-)

broth·er·li·ness

broth·er·ly

brough·am carriage

brought

brou·ha·ha

brow

brow·band part of bridle

brow·beat (·beat·ing, ·beat, ·beat·en)

brown

browned-off

Brownie junior Guide

brownie chocolate cake

brown·ing

brown·ish

brown-out *US* power reduction

browse

brows·er

bru·cel·lo·sis

bruc·ine alkaloid

Bruges Belgian city

bru·in

bruise

bruised

bruis·er

bruis·ing

bruit *Archaic* report

bru·mal wintry

brume mist
Brum·ma·gem *Slang*
  Birmingham
Brum·mie *Slang*
  Birmingham native
brum·ous
brunch
Bru·nei Malaysian state
bru·nette
Brunhild (or Brünnhilde)
  legendary queen
Bruns·wick German city
brunt
brush
brush·er
brush·off (*noun*)
brush·up (*noun*)
brush·wood
brush·work
brusque
brusque·ness
Brus·sels
brut denoting dry
  champagne
bru·tal
bru·tal·ity (*plural* ·ities)
bru·tali·za·tion (*or* ·sa·tion)
bru·tal·ize (*or* ·ise)
bru·tal·ly
brute
bru·ti·fy (·fies, ·fy·ing,
  ·fied) brutalize
brut·ish
brut·ish·ness
Bry·ansk Russian city
bryo·logi·cal
bry·olo·gist
bry·ol·ogy study of mosses
bryo·ny (or brio·; *plural*
  ·nies)
bryo·phyte botany term
bryo·phyt·ic
bryo·zoan invertebrate
  animal
Bry·thon·ic language group
bu·bal (or bu·ba·lis)
  antelope
bu·ba·line
bub·ble
bub·bler
bub·bly (·bli·er, ·bli·est)
bubo (*plural* buboes)
  swelling
bu·bon·ic
bu·bono·cele medical term

Bu·ca·ra·man·ga
  Colombian city
buc·cal of the cheek
buc·ca·neer
buc·ci·na·tor muscle
bu·cen·taur Venetian
  barge
Bu·cha·rest Romanian
  capital
Buch·en·wald
  concentration camp
bu·chu shrub
buck
bucka·roo *US* cowboy
buck·bean
buck·board carriage
buck·et
buck·et·ful (*plural* ·fuls)
buck·eye tree
buck·horn
buck·hound
Buck·ing·ham
Buck·ing·ham·shire
buck·jump·er *Austral*
  untamed horse
buck·le
buckler-fern
buck·ling bloater
bucko *Irish* young fellow
buck·ram (ram·ing,
  ·ramed)
buck·saw
buck·shee
buck·shot
buck·skin
buck·thorn
buck·tooth (*plural* ·teeth)
buck·wheat
bu·col·ic
bu·coli·cal·ly
bud (bud·ding, bud·ded)
Bu·da·pest Hungarian
  capital
Bud·dhism
Bud·dhist
bud·ding
bud·dle trough
bud·dleia
bud·dy (*plural* ·dies)
budge
budg·eri·gar
budg·et
budgie
Bue·na·ven·tu·ra
  Colombian port

Bue·nos Aires Argentinian
  capital
buff
Buf·fa·lo port in New York
  State
buf·fa·lo (*plural* ·loes, ·los,
  or ·lo)
buff·er
buf·fet restaurant; sideboard
buf·fet (·fet·ing, ·fet·ed) to
  batter; a blow
buf·fet·er
buffle-head duck
buf·foon
buf·foon·ery
bug (bug·ging, bugged)
buga·boo source of fear
Bu·gan·da Ugandan state
bug·bane plant
bug·bear
bugged
bug·ger
bug·gery
bug·ging
bug·gy (*noun, plural* ·gies;
  adj ·gi·er, ·gi·est)
bu·gle
bu·gler
bugle·weed
bu·gloss
buhl *variant spelling of*
  boulle
buhr·stone (or bur· or
  burr·)
build (build·ing, built)
build·er
build·ing
build·up (*noun*)
built
built-in
built-up
(buisness) *incorrect spelling of*
  business
Bu·jum·bu·ra capital of
  Burundi
Bu·kha·ra (or Bo·) Uzbek
  city
Bu·ko·vi·na (or ·co·) E
  European region
Bu·la·wa·yo Zimbabwean
  city
bul·ba·ceous
bulb·ar
bulb·if·er·ous
bul·bil (or ·bel) small bulb

bulb·ous
bul·bul bird
Bul·garia
Bul·gar·ian
bulge
bulgi·ness
bulg·ing·ly
bulgy
bu·limia insatiable
  hunger
bulk
bulk·head
bulki·ly
bulki·ness
bulky (bulki·er, bulki·est)
bull
bul·la (plural ·lae) seal on
  papal bull; blister
bul·lace damson
bul·late blistered
bull·bat bird
bull·dog
bull·doze
bull·doz·er
bul·let
bul·letin
bullet·proof
bull·fight
bull·fighter
bull·fighting
bull·finch
bull·frog
bull·head fish
bul·lion
bull·ish
bull·necked
bull·ock
bull·pen
bull·ring
bull's-eye
bull·shit
bull·whip
bul·ly (noun, plural ·lies;
  verb ·lies, ·ly·ing, ·lied)
bully·rag (·rag·ging,
  ·ragged)
bul·rush
bul·wark
bum (bum·ming,
  bummed)
bum·bailiff
bum·ble
bumble·bee
bum·bler
bum·boat

bum·ma·lo (plural ·lo)
  Bombay duck
bum·mer
bump
bump·er
bumph (or bumf) Slang
  documents
bumpi·ly
bumpi·ness
bump·kin
bump·tious
bump·tious·ness
bumpy (bumpi·er,
  bumpi·est)
bun
Buna (Trademark) rubber
bunch
bunchi·ness
bunchy (bunchi·er,
  bunchi·est)
bun·combe US variant
  spelling of bunkum
Bund (plural Bunds or
  Bün·de) federation
bund embankment
Bun·da·berg Australian city
Bun·del·khand Indian
  region
Bun·des·rat German federal
  council
Bun·des·tag German
  legislative assembly
bundh Indian strike
bun·dle
bun·dler
bun·du S African wild region
bung
bun·ga·low
bung·hole
bun·gle
bun·gler
bun·gling
bun·ion
bunk
bun·ker
bun·kum (US also ·combe)
bun·ny (plural ·nies)
bun·raku Japanese puppet
  theatre
Bun·sen burn·er
bunt
bunt·al straw
bunt·ing
bunt·line
bunya-bunya tree

bun·yip Australian monster
buoy
buoy·age
buoy·an·cy
buoy·ant
bu·pres·tid beetle
bur (bur·ring, burred) seed
  vessel; compare birr; burr
bu·ran blizzard
Bu·ray·dah (or ·rai·da)
  Saudi Arabian town
Bur·ber·ry (Trademark;
  plural ·ries)
bur·ble
bur·bler
bur·bot (plural ·bots or ·bot)
  fish
bur·den
bur·den·some
bur·dock
bu·reau (plural ·reaus or
  ·reaux)
bu·reau·cra·cy (plural ·cies)
bu·reau·crat
bu·reau·crat·ic
bu·reau·crati·cal·ly
bu·reau·crat·ism
bu·reau·cra·tize (or ·tise)
bu·rette (or esp. US ·ret)
burg fortified town; compare
  berg; burgh
Bur·gas Bulgarian port
bur·gee ship's flag
Bur·gen·land Austrian
  province
bur·geon (or bour·geon)
burg·er hamburger
bur·gess citizen of borough
burgh Scottish town;
  compare berg; burg
burgh·al
burgh·er citizen
bur·glar
bur·glar·ize US burgle
bur·gla·ry (plural ·ries)
bur·gle
bur·go·mas·ter
bur·go·net helmet
bur·grave German governor
Bur·gun·dian
Bur·gun·dy
bur·ial
buri·er
bu·rin chisel
burk (or berk) Slang fool

bur·ka Muslim garment

burke suffocate

Bur·kina Faso African
country

burl small lump

bur·lap fabric

burl·er

bur·lesque (or ·lesk;
·lesqu·ing, ·lesqued or
·lesk·ing, ·lesked)

bur·les·quer (or ·lesk·er)

bur·ley tobacco

bur·li·ness

Bur·ling·ton Canadian and
US cities

bur·ly (·li·er, ·li·est)

Bur·ma

Bur·mese

burn (burn·ing, burnt or
burned)

burn·er

bur·net plant

burn·ing

burn·ing·ly

bur·nish

burn·ish·able

burn·ish·er

Burn·ley Lancashire town

bur·noose (or bur·nous or
bur·nouse) Arab hood

burn·sides US side-whiskers

burnt

bu·roo Dialect dole

burp

burr rough edge; small drill;
dialect characteristic;
compare birr; bur

bur·ra·wang plant

burred

bur·ring

bur·ro (plural ·ros) donkey

bur·row

bur·row·er

bur·ry (·ri·er, ·ri·est) prickly

Bur·sa Turkish city

bur·sa (plural ·sae or ·sas)
medical term; compare
bursar

bur·sal

bur·sar financial official;
compare bursa

bur·sar·ial

bur·sa·ry (plural ·ries)

burse Scot student allowance

bur·ser·aceous botany term

bur·si·form

bur·si·tis

burst (burst·ing, burst)

burst·er

bur·ton hoisting tackle

Burton-upon-Trent

Bu·run·di African republic

bur·weed

Bury town in Greater
Manchester

bury (buries, bury·ing,
bur·ied)

Bur·yat Mongoloid people

Bury St Ed·munds

bus (noun, plural buses or
busses; verb bus·ing or
bus·sing, bused or bussed)

bus·bar electrical conductor

bus·by (plural ·bies)

bu·sera Ugandan drink

bush

bush·baby (plural ·babies)

bush·buck (or bosch·bok;
plural ·bucks, ·buck or
·boks, ·bok) antelope

bush·el (·el·ing, ·elled; US
·el·ing, ·eled) unit; US
mend garment

bush·el·ler (US ·el·er)

bush·hammer

Bu·shi·do samurai code

bushi·ness

bush·ing

Bu·shire Iranian port

Bush·man (plural ·man or
·men) S African people

bush·man (plural ·men)
bush dweller

bush·master snake

bush·pig

bush·ranger

bush·tit bird

Bush·veld

bush·whack

bush·whacker

bushy (bushi·er, bushi·est)

busi·ly

busi·ness trade, etc.;
compare busyness

business·like

business·man (plural ·men)

business·woman (plural
·women)

bus·ing (or bus·sing)

busk

busk·er

bus·kin boot

bust

bus·tard

bust·er

bus·tle

bus·tler

busty (busti·er, busti·est)

bu·suu·ti garment

busy (adj busi·er, busi·est;
verb busies, busy·ing
bus·ied)

busy·body (plural ·bodies)

busy Liz·zie plant

busy·ness state of being
busy; compare business

but

bu·ta·di·ene

bu·tane

bu·ta·nol

bu·ta·none

butch

butch·er

butcher·bird

butcher's-broom shrub

butch·ery (plural ·eries)

bu·tene

but·ler

but·lery (plural ·leries)

butt

butte steep-sided hill

but·ter food

butt·er one that butts

but·ter·bur plant

butter·cup

butter·fat

butter·fingered

butter·fingers

butter·fish (plural ·fish or
·fishes)

butter·fly (plural ·flies)

but·ter·ine artificial butter

But·ter·mere lake

butter·milk

butter·nut

butter·scotch

butter·wort plant

but·tery (plural ·teries)

but·tock

but·ton

button·hole

button·hook

button·mould (US ·mold)

but·ton·wood

but·tress

but·ty (*plural* **·ties**) *Dialect*
   sandwich
bu·tyl
bu·tyra·ceous
bu·tyr·al·de·hyde
bu·tyr·ate
bu·tyr·ic acid
bu·tyr·in
bux·om
bux·om·ness
Bux·ton Derbyshire
   town
buy (buys, buy·ing,
   bought)
buy·er
buzz
buz·zard
buzz·er
bwa·na

by
by-bidder
by-blow
Byd·goszcz Polish city
bye sports term; something
   incidental
by-election (*or*
   bye-election)
Bye·lo·rus·sia *variant*
   spelling of Belorussia
Bye·lo·rus·sian *variant*
   spelling of Belorussian
Bye·lo·vo *variant spelling of*
   Belovo
by·gone
by·law (*or* bye-law)
by-line
by·pass (·pass·ing, ·passed
   or ·past)

by-path
by-product
byre cowshed; *compare*
   bier
byr·nie armour
by·road
By·ron·ic
bys·si·no·sis lung disease
bys·sus (*plural* ·suses *or* ·si)
   zoology term
by·stander
by·street
byte computer term;
   compare bight; bite
By·tom Polish city
by·way
by·word
Byz·an·tine
By·zan·tium

C

cab
ca·bal (·bal·ling, ·balled)
   secret group
ca·bal·le·ro (*plural* ·ros)
ca·ba·na tent
Ca·ba·na·tuan Philippine
   city
caba·ret
cab·bage
cabbage·town city slum
cab·ba·la (*or* ca·ba·la,
   kab·ba·la, ka·ba·la)
   Jewish teaching
cab·ba·lism (*or* caba·,
   kab·ba·, kaba·)
cab·ba·list (*or* caba·,
   kab·ba·, kaba·)
cab·ba·lis·tic (*or* caba·,
   kab·ba·, kaba·)
cab·by (*or* cab·bie; *plural*
   ·bies)
ca·ber
cab·ezon (*or* ·ezone) fish
Ca·bi·mas Venezuelan town
cab·in
Cabi·net government
cabi·net furniture
cabinet-maker
cabinet·work
ca·ble
ca·ble·gram

cable-laid
ca·blet small cable
cable·way
cab·man (*plural* ·men)
cabo·chon polished gem
ca·boo·dle
ca·boose
Cá·bo·ra Bas·sa African
   dam
cabo·tage coastal navigation
ca·bret·ta leather
ca·bril·la fish
cab·ri·ole furniture leg
cab·rio·let horse-drawn
   carriage
ca·cao cocoa tree
cac·cia·to·re (*or* ·ra)
   cookery term
cacha·lot whale
cache
ca·chec·tic weakened
cache·pot flowerpot
   container
ca·chet
ca·chexia (*or* ·chexy)
   weakness
cach·in·nate laugh loudly
cach·in·na·tion
ca·chou lozenge; *variant of*
   catechu; *compare* cashew
ca·chu·cha dance

ca·cique American Indian
   chief
cack-handed
cack·le
cack·ler
caco·demon
caco·dyl chemical
   compound
caco·epy bad pronunciation
caco·ethes uncontrollable
   urge
caco·eth·ic
caco·gen·ics
caco·graph·ic
ca·cog·ra·phy bad
   handwriting
ca·col·ogy bad speech
caco·mis·tle (*or* ·mix·le)
   animalcab
cacophonic
caco·phon·ic
ca·copho·nous
ca·copho·ny (*plural* ·nies)
cac·ta·ceous
cac·tus (*plural* ·tuses *or* ·ti)
ca·cu·mi·nal phonetics
   term
cad
ca·das·ter (*or* ·tre) property
   register
ca·dav·er

ca·dav·er·ic
ca·dav·er·ine chemical
  compound
ca·dav·er·ous
ca·dav·er·ous·ness
cad·die (or ·dy; noun, plural
  ·dies; verb ·dies, ·dy·ing,
  ·died) golf term; compare
  caddy
cad·dis fly
cad·dis (or ·dice) textile
cad·dish
Cad·do·an language group
cad·dy (plural ·dies) tea
  container; compare caddie
cade tree
ca·delle beetle
ca·dence
ca·den·cy (plural ·cies)
  heraldic term
ca·dent
ca·den·za
ca·det
cadge
cadg·er
cadi Muslim judge
Cadillac (Trademark)
Cá·diz Spanish port
cad·mium
ca·dre trained personnel
ca·du·ceus (plural ·cei)
  medical emblem
ca·du·city senility
ca·du·cous biology term
cae·cal (US ce·)
cae·cil·ian amphibian
cae·cum (US ce·; plural ·ca)
  part of intestine
Cae·lian Roman hill
Cae·lum constellation
Caen French city
cae·no·gen·esis (or cai·,
  kai·; US ce· or ke·) biology
  term
cae·no·genet·ic (or cai·,
  kai·; US ce· or ke·)
caeo·ma botany term
Caer·leon Welsh town
Caer·nar·von (or ·fon)
Caer·nar·von·shire (or
  ·fon·shire) former Welsh
  county
Caer·phil·ly
caes·al·pinia·ceous botany
  term

Caesa·rea Israeli port
Cae·sar·ean (or ·ian) of
  Caesar
Cae·sar·ean sec·tion (or
  cae·; US ce·sar·ean
  sec·tion)
Cae·sar·ism autocratic
  government
cae·sium (US ce·)
caes·pi·tose (US ces·)
  growing in tufts
cae·su·ra (plural ·ras or ·rae)
café
caf·eteria
caf·feine (or ·fein)
caf·tan variant spelling of
  kaftan
cage
cage·ling
cag·ey (or cagy; cagi·er,
  cagi·est)
cagi·ly
cagi·ness
Ca·glia·ri Sardinian port
cag·mag Dialect chat
ca·goule
ca·hier French notebook
ca·hoots
Caiaphas biblical character
Cai·cos West Indian islands
Cain biblical character
Cai·no·zo·ic variant spelling
  of Cenozoic
caïque boat
cairn
cairn·gorm quartz
Cairngorm Scottish
  mountains
Cai·ro
cais·son watertight structure
Caith·ness
cai·tiff cowardly person
ca·jole
ca·jol·ery (plural ·eries)
Ca·jun Acadian descendant
caju·put (or caj·eput) shrub
cake
cake·walk
Cala·bar Nigerian port
cala·bash tree
Ca·la·bria Italian region
ca·la·dium plant
Cal·ais
cala·lu Caribbean leaves
cala·man·co fabric

cala·man·der wood
cala·mine lotion
cala·mint plant
cala·mite plant
ca·lami·tous
ca·lam·ity (plural ·ities)
cala·mon·din fruit
cala·mus (plural ·mi) plant;
  cane
cal·an·dria heat-exchanger
  vessel
ca·lash (or ·leche) carriage
cala·thus (plural ·thi) Greek
  symbol
ca·lav·er·ite mineral
cal·ca·neal (or ·nean)
cal·ca·neus (or ·neum;
  plural ·nei) heel bone
cal·car (plural ·caria) spur
cal·car·eous containing
  lime
cal·ca·rif·er·ous
cal·cei·form (or ·ceo·late)
  botany term
cal·ceo·lar·ia plant
cal·ces (plural of calx)
cal·cic containing calcium
cal·ci·cole lime-loving plant
cal·cico·lous
cal·cif·er·ol vitamin
cal·cif·er·ous
cal·cif·ic
cal·ci·fi·ca·tion
cal·ci·fu·gal
cal·ci·fuge acid-loving plant
cal·cifu·gous
cal·ci·fy (·fies, ·fy·ing,
  ·fied)
cal·ci·mine (or
  kal·so·mine) wash for
  walls
cal·ci·na·tion
cal·cine chemistry term
cal·cite mineral
cal·cit·ic
cal·ci·ton·in hormone
cal·cium
calc·sinter rock
cal·cu·la·bil·ity (plural
  ·ities)
cal·cu·lable
cal·cu·late
cal·cu·la·tion
cal·cu·la·tive
cal·cu·la·tor

cal·cu·lous

cal·cu·lus (*plural* ·luses) maths term

cal·cu·lus (*plural* ·li) stone in body

Cal·cut·ta

cal·dar·ium Roman bathroom

cal·de·ra volcanic crater

cal·dron *variant spelling of* cauldron

Cal·edo·nia

Cal·edo·nian

cal·efa·cient

cal·efac·tion

cal·efac·tory (*plural* ·tories)

cal·en·dar dates; *compare* colander

cal·en·der smoothing machine; *compare* colander

cal·ends (*or* kal·ends)

ca·len·du·la plant

cal·en·ture fever

calf (*plural* calves)

calf·skin

Cal·ga·ry Canadian city

Cali Colombian city

cali·brate

cali·bra·tion

cali·bra·tor (*or* ·brat·er)

cali·bre (*US* ·ber)

cali·bred (*US* ·bered)

cali·ces *plural of* calix

ca·li·che geology term

cali·co (*plural* ·coes *or* ·cos)

Cali·cut Indian port

Cali·for·nia

cali·for·nium radioactive element

cali·pash (*or* cal·li·pash) turtle meat

cali·pee turtle meat

cali·per *US spelling of* calliper

ca·liph (*or* ca·lif, ka·lif, kha·lif)

ca·li·phate (*or* ca·li·fate, ka·li·fate)

cali·sa·ya cinchona bark

cal·is·then·ic *variant spelling of* callisthenic

ca·lix (*plural* cali·ces) chalice; *compare* calyx

calk *variant spelling of* caulk

calk (*or* cal·kin) spike on shoe

call

cal·la plant

call·able

cal·lais ornamental stone

cal·lant (*or* ·lan) youth

Ca·llao Peruvian port

call·boy

call·er one who calls

cal·ler *Scot* fresh food

cal·lig·ra·pher (*or* ·phist)

cal·li·graph·ic

cal·li·graphi·cal·ly

cal·lig·ra·phy

call·ing

cal·lio·pe *US* steam organ

cal·li·pash *variant spelling of* calipash

cal·li·per (*US* cali·per)

cal·li·pyg·ian (*or* ·py·gous) having shapely buttocks

cal·lis·then·ic (*or* cal·is·)

cal·lis·then·ics (*or* cal·is·)

Cal·lis·to satellite of Jupiter

cal·los·ity (*plural* ·ities)

cal·lous (*adj*)

cal·lous·ness

cal·low

cal·low·ness

cal·lus (*noun; plural* ·luses)

calm

cal·ma·tive

calm·ness

calo·mel purgative

Cal·or (*Trademark*)

ca·lor·ic

calo·ric·ity (*plural* ·ities)

Calo·rie kilocalorie

calo·rie

calo·rif·ic

calo·rifi·cal·ly

calo·rim·eter

calo·ri·met·ric (*or* ·ri·cal)

calo·ri·met·ri·cal·ly

calo·rim·etry

ca·lotte priest's skullcap

calo·yer Greek Orthodox monk

cal·pac (*or* cal·pack, kal·pak) brimless hat

calque (calqu·ing, calqued) linguistics term

cal·trop (*or* ·trap, ·throp) plant

calu·met peace pipe

ca·lum·ni·ate

ca·lum·nia·tion

ca·lum·ni·ous (*or* ·nia·tory)

cal·um·ny (*plural* ·nies)

calu·tron physics term

Cal·va·dos French department; brandy

cal·varia top of skull

Cal·va·ry Crucifixion site

cal·va·ry (*plural* ·ries) suffering

calve (*verb*)

calves *plural of* calf

Cal·vin·ism

Cal·vin·ist

Cal·vin·is·tic

cal·vi·ties baldness

calx (*plural* calxes *or* cal·ces) oxide

caly·cate having a calyx

caly·cine (*or* ca·lyci·nal) of a calyx

caly·cle (*or* ca·lycu·lus; *plural* ·cles *or* ·li) biology term

Calypso mythological character

ca·lyp·so (*plural* ·sos) song

ca·lyp·tra botany term

ca·lyp·trate

ca·lyp·tro·gen

ca·lyx (*plural* ca·lyxes *or* caly·ces) sepals of plant; *compare* calix

Cam river

cam machinery

Ca·ma·güey Cuban city

ca·mail armour

ca·ma·ra·derie

cama·ril·la Spanish cabal

cam·ass (*or* ·as) plant

cam·ber

Cam·ber·well

cam·bial of cambium

cam·bist foreign-exchange dealer

cam·bist·ry (*plural* ·ries)

cam·bium (*plural* ·biums *or* ·bia) plant tissue

Cam·bo·dia

Cam·bo·dian

cam·bo·gia gum resin

cam·boose lumberjack's cabin

Cam·brai French town
Cam·bria *Latin* Wales
Cam·brian geological
  period
cam·bric fabric
Cam·bridge
Cam·bridge·shire
Cam·den London borough
came
cam·el
cam·el·eer
ca·mel·lia
ca·melo·pard giraffe
Ca·melo·par·dus (*or* ·da·lis)
  constellation
Cam·elot
Cam·em·bert cheese
cameo (*noun, plural* cameos;
  verb cameos, cameo·ing,
  cam·eoed)
cam·era
cam·er·al
cam·era lu·ci·da
camera·man (*plural* ·men)
cam·era ob·scu·ra
camera-ready
cam·er·len·go (*or* ·lin·go;
  plural ·gos) papal treasurer
Cam·eroon
cami·knick·ers
cami·on lorry
ca·mise smock
cami·sole
cam·let cloth
camo·mile (*or* chamo·)
ca·moo·di snake
Ca·mor·ra secret society
camou·flage
camp
Cam·pa·gna Italian plain
cam·paign
cam·paign·er
Cam·pa·nia Italian region
cam·pa·ni·le bell tower
cam·pa·nolo·gist
cam·pa·nol·ogy
cam·panu·la flower
cam·panu·la·ceous
cam·panu·late bell-shaped
Cam·peche Mexican state
camp·er
cam·pes·tral of fields
cam·phene
cam·phire henna
cam·phor

cam·pho·rate
cam·phor·ic
Cam·pi·nas Brazilian city
camp·ing
cam·pi·on
cam·po Brazilian savanna
campo·ree Scout meeting
Cam·pos Brazilian city
cam·pus (*plural* ·puses)
cam·shaft
cam·wood
can (can·ning, canned)
Cana biblical town
Ca·naan biblical region
Ca·naan·ite
Cana·da
Ca·na·dian
Ca·na·di·an·ism
ca·nai·gre plant
ca·naille *French* mob
ca·nal (·nal·ling, ·nalled;
  US ·nal·ing, ·naled)
cana·licu·lar
cana·licu·lus (*plural* ·li)
  small channel
cana·li·za·tion (*or* ·sa·tion)
cana·lize (*or* ·lise)
cana·pé
ca·nard rumour
ca·nary (*plural* ·naries)
Ca·nary Is·lands (*or*
  Ca·naries)
ca·nas·ta card game
can·as·ter tobacco
Ca·nav·er·al US cape
Can·ber·ra
can·can
can·cel (·cel·ling, ·celled;
  US ·cel·ing, ·celed)
can·cel·late (*or* ·lous,
  ·lat·ed) medical term
can·cel·la·tion
can·cel·ler (*US* ·cel·er)
Can·cer sign of zodiac
can·cer disease
can·cer·ous
can·croid
can·de·la unit
can·de·la·brum (*or* ·bra;
  plural ·bra, ·brums, *or*
  ·bras)
can·did
can·di·da·cy (*or* ·da·ture)
can·di·date
can·did·ness

can·died
Can·di·ot Cretan
can·dle
candle·berry (*plural*
  ·berries)
candle·fish (*plural* ·fish *or*
  ·fishes)
candle·light
Candle·mas
candle·nut
candle·pins bowling game
candle·power
can·dler
candle·stick
candle·wick
candle·wood
can·dour (*US* ·dor)
can·dy (*noun, plural* ·dies;
  verb ·dies, ·dy·ing, ·died)
candy·floss
candy-striped
candy·tuft
cane
cane·brake US thicket
ca·nel·la spice
can·er
ca·nes·cent hoary
can·field card game
cangue wooden collar
Ca·nicu·la the star Sirius
ca·nicu·lar of Sirius
ca·nine
can·ing
can·is·ter
can·ker
can·ker·ous
canker·worm
can·na plant
can·na·bic
can·na·bin
can·na·bis
Can·nae battle site
canned
can·nel coal
can·nel·lo·ni (*or* ·ne·lo·ni)
can·ne·lure groove
can·ner
can·nery (*plural* ·neries)
Cannes French town
can·ni·bal
can·ni·bal·ism
can·ni·bal·is·tic
can·ni·bali·za·tion (*or*
  ·sa·tion)
can·ni·bal·ize (*or* ·ise)

can·ni·kin (*or* cana·kin,
cani·kin) small can
can·ni·ly
can·ni·ness
can·ning
Can·nock Staffordshire
town
can·non (*plural* ·nons *or*
·non) artillery; *compare*
canon
can·non·ade
cannon·ball
can·non·eer
can·non·ry (*plural* ·ries)
artillery; *compare* canonry
can·not
can·nu·la (*or* canu·la; *plural*
·las *or* ·lae) surgical tube
can·nu·late (*or* canu·late)
can·ny (·ni·er, ·ni·est)
ca·noe (·noes, ·noe·ing,
·noed)
ca·noe·ist
can·on priest; decree;
compare cannon
can·on·ess
ca·noni·cal
ca·noni·cate office of canon
can·on·ic·ity
can·on·ist
can·oni·za·tion (*or* ·sa·tion)
can·on·ize (*or* ·ise)
can·on·ry (*plural* ·ries)
office of canon; *compare*
cannonry
ca·noo·dle
Ca·no·pus Egyptian port
cano·py (*noun, plural* ·pies;
verb ·pies, ·py·ing, ·pied)
Ca·nos·sa Italian castle
cans *Slang* headphones
cant platitudes; slope
can't cannot
can·ta·bi·le musical term
Can·ta·brian Spanish
mountains
Can·ta·brig·ian of
Cambridge
Can·tal French department;
cheese
can·ta·la plant
can·ta·loupe (*or* ·loup)
can·tan·ker·ous
can·ta·ta
can·ta·trice singer

can·teen
can·ter
Can·ter·bury
can·thari·des (*sing.* ·tha·ris)
medicine
can·thus (*plural* ·thi) corner
of eye
cant·ic
can·ti·cle
can·ti·lena musical term
can·ti·lever
can·til·late
can·til·la·tion
can·ti·na Spanish bar
cant·ing
can·tle saddle part
can·to (*plural* ·tos)
Can·ton Chinese port
can·ton division of
Switzerland
can·ton·al
Can·ton·ese (*plural* ·ese)
can·ton·ment
can·tor religious singer
can·tor·is musical term
can·trip magic spell
can·tus (*plural* ·tus)
medieval church singing
canty *Dialect* lively
can·vas cloth
canvas·back (*plural* ·backs
or ·back) duck
can·vass solicit
can·vass·er
can·yon
can·zo·na musical term
can·zo·ne (*plural* ·ni) song
can·zo·net song
caou·tchouc rubber
cap (cap·ping, capped)
ca·pa·bil·ity (*plural* ·ities)
ca·pable
ca·pably
ca·pa·cious
ca·paci·tance physics term
ca·paci·tate
ca·paci·ta·tion
ca·paci·tive
ca·paci·tor
ca·pac·ity (*plural* ·ities)
cap-a-pie from head to foot
ca·pari·son
cape
cap·elin (*or* cap·lin) fish
Ca·pel·la star

ca·per
cap·er·cail·lie (*or* ·cail·zie)
Ca·per·na·um Israeli town
Cape Roca Portuguese cape
cape·skin
Capet French dynasty
Ca·petian
Cape Verde island country
ca·pi·as legal term
cap·il·la·ceous hairy
cap·il·lar·ity surface tension
ca·pil·lary (*plural* ·laries)
capi·tal
capi·tal·ism
capi·tal·ist
capi·tal·is·tic
capi·tali·za·tion (*or*
·sa·tion)
capi·tal·ize (*or* ·ise)
capi·tal·ly
capi·tate headline
capi·ta·tion
capi·ta·tive
Capi·tol US Congress
building
Capi·to·line Roman hill
ca·pitu·lar
ca·pitu·lary (*plural* ·laries)
ca·pitu·late
ca·pitu·la·tion
ca·pitu·la·tor
ca·pitu·lum (*plural* ·la)
biology term
capo (*plural* capos) guitar
attachment
ca·pon
ca·pon·ize (*or* ·ise)
capo·ral tobacco; *compare*
corporal
ca·pote cloak
Cap·pa·do·cia ancient
Asian region
cap·pa·ri·da·ceous botany
term
capped
cap·per
cap·pie *Scot* ice-cream cone
cap·ping
cap·puc·ci·no (*plural* ·nos)
cap·reo·late botany term
Ca·pri
ca·pric·cio (*plural* ·cios *or*
·ci) musical work
ca·pric·cio·so musical term
ca·price

ca·pri·cious
ca·pri·cious·ness
Cap·ri·corn sign of zodiac
Cap·ri·cor·nus (*plural* ·ni) constellation
cap·ri·fi·ca·tion
cap·ri·fig wild fig
cap·ri·fo·lia·ceous botany term
cap·rine of goats
cap·ri·ole
cap·sai·cin alkaloid
cap·si·cum
cap·sid plant bug
cap·size
cap·stan
cap·stone (*or* cope·)
cap·su·lar
cap·su·late (*or* ·lat·ed)
cap·su·la·tion
cap·sule
cap·sul·ize (*or* ·ise)
cap·tain
cap·tain·cy (*or* ·tain·ship; *plural* ·cies *or* ·ships)
cap·tion
cap·tious
cap·ti·vate
cap·ti·va·tion
cap·ti·va·tor
cap·tive
cap·tiv·ity (*plural* ·ities)
cap·tor
cap·ture
Capua Italian town
ca·puche friar's hood
Capu·chin friar
capu·chin monkey
ca·put (*plural* capi·ta) head; *compare* kaput
capy·ba·ra rodent
car
cara·bao water buffalo
cara·bid beetle
cara·bi·neer (*or* ·nier) *variants of* carbineer
ca·ra·bi·nie·re (*plural* ·ri) Italian policeman
cara·cal lynx
ca·ra·ca·ra bird
Ca·ra·cas Venezuelan capital
cara·cole (*or* ·col) dressage term

cara·cul fur; *variant spelling of* karakul
ca·rafe
cara·geen *variant spelling of* carrageen
ca·ram·ba (*or* ·bo·la) tree; fruit
cara·mel
cara·mel·ize (*or* ·ise)
ca·ran·gid (*or* ·goid) fish
cara·pace
car·at weight; *compare* caret
cara·van (·van·ning, ·vanned)
cara·van·se·rai (*or* ·sa·ry; *plural* ·rais *or* ·ries)
cara·vel (*or* car·vel) ship
cara·way
car·ba·mate
car·bami·dine
car·ban·ion chemistry term
car·ba·zole
car·bene chemistry term
car·bide
car·bine rifle
car·bi·neer (*or* cara·bi·neer, cara·bi·nier) soldier
car·bo·hy·drate
car·bo·lat·ed
car·bol·ic
car·bo·lize (*or* ·lise)
car·bon
car·bo·na·ceous
car·bo·nade beef stew
car·bo·na·do (*noun, plural* ·does *or* ·dos; *verb* ·do·ing, ·doed) grilled meat; industrial diamond
Car·bo·na·ri political society
car·bon·ate
car·bona·tion
car·bon·ic
car·bon·if·er·ous
car·boni·za·tion (*or* ·sa·tion)
car·bon·ize (*or* ·ise)
car·bon·ous
car·bon·yl
Car·bo·run·dum (*Trademark*)
car·box·yl
car·box·yl·ase enzyme
car·box·yl·ate
car·box·yl·ic

car·boy large bottle
car·bun·cle
car·bun·cu·lar
car·bu·ra·tion
car·bu·ret (·ret·ting, ·ret·ted; *US* ·ret·ing, ·ret·ed)
car·bu·ret·tor (*or* ·ter; *US* ·retor)
car·bu·ri·za·tion (*or* ·sa·tion)
car·bu·rize (*or* ·rise)
car·byla·mine
car·cass (*or* ·case)
Car·chem·ish ancient Syrian city
car·cino·gen
car·cino·gen·ic
car·ci·no·ma (*plural* ·mas *or* ·ma·ta)
car·ci·no·ma·toid (*or* ·tous)
car·ci·no·ma·to·sis
card
car·da·mom (*or* ·mum, ·mon) spice
card·board
card-carrying
car·di·ac
car·di·al·gia heart pain
car·di·al·gic
Car·diff
Car·di·gan Welsh bay
car·di·gan
car·di·nal
car·di·nal·ate (*or* ·ship)
car·di·nal·ly
card·ing
car·dio·gram record
car·dio·graph instrument
car·di·og·ra·pher
car·dio·graph·ic (*or* ·graphi·cal)
car·di·og·ra·phy
car·di·oid
car·dio·logi·cal
car·di·olo·gist
car·di·ol·ogy
car·dio·mega·ly heart enlargement
car·dio·vas·cu·lar
car·di·tis
car·doon plant
card·sharp (*or* ·sharper)
car·dua·ceous botany term
care

ca·reen nautical term
ca·reer
ca·reer·ist
care·free
care·ful
care·ful·ly
care·ful·ness
care·less
care·less·ness
ca·ress
ca·ress·er
ca·ress·ing·ly
car·et printing symbol;
   compare carat
care·taker
care·worn
car·fare *US* bus fare
car·fax crossroads
car·go (*plural* ·goes *or* ·gos)
car·hop
Caria ancient Asian region
Car·ib (*plural* ·ibs *or* ·ib)
   American Indian
Car·ib·bean
Car·ib·bees West Indian
   islands
cari·bou (*plural* ·bous *or*
   ·bou)
cari·ca·ture
cari·ca·tur·ist
cari·es (*plural* cari·es) tooth
   decay
ca·ril·lon (·lon·ning,
   ·lonned)
ca·ril·lon·neur
Ca·ri·na constellation
ca·ri·na (*plural* ·nae *or* ·nas)
   keel-shaped part
cari·nate (*or* ·nat·ed)
Ca·rin·thia Austrian
   province
cario·ca dance
cario·gen·ic producing
   tooth decay
cari·ole (*or* car·ri·ole) cart
cari·os·ity (*or* cari·ous·ness)
cari·ous
car·line plant
car·ling (*or* ·line) ship's
   beam
Car·lisle Cumbrian city
Car·low Irish county
Carl·ton English town
car·ma·gnole French
   costume

car·man (*plural* ·men)
Car·mar·then
Car·mar·then·shire Welsh
   county
Car·mel Israeli mountain
Car·mel·ite friar or nun
car·mina·tive
car·mine
car·nage
car·nal
car·nal·ist
car·nal·ity
car·nall·ite mineral
car·nal·ly
car·nas·sial tooth
Car·nat·ic Indian region
car·na·tion
car·nau·ba wax
car·nel·ian *variant spelling of*
   cornelian
car·net travel document;
   customs licence
car·ni·fi·ca·tion
car·ni·fy (·fies, ·fy·ing,
   ·fied) medical term
Car·nio·la Slovenian region
car·ni·val
car·ni·vore
car·nivo·rous
car·no·tite
car·ny (*or* ·ney; ·nies,
   ·ny·ing, ·nied *or* ·neys,
   ·ney·ing, ·neyed) coax
car·ob
ca·roche carriage
car·ol (·ol·ling, ·olled; *US*
   ·ol·ing, ·oled)
car·ol·er
Caro·li·na
Caro·line (*or* Caro·lean) of
   King Charles
Caro·lin·gian Frankish
   dynasty
Caro·lin·ian of Carolina
caro·lus (*plural* ·luses *or* ·li)
   coin
car·om billiards term
caro·tene (*or* ·tin) orange
   pigment
ca·rot·enoid
ca·rot·id artery
ca·rot·id·al
ca·rous·al drinking party;
   compare carousel
ca·rouse

carou·sel *US* merry-go-
   round; *compare* carousal
ca·rous·er
carp
car·pal of the wrist; *compare*
   carpel
Car·pa·thian Moun·tains
car·pel flower part; *compare*
   carpal
car·pel·lary
car·pel·late
Car·pen·ta·ria Australian
   gulf
car·pen·ter
car·pen·try
car·pet
carpet·bag
carpet·bag·ger
car·phol·ogy medical term;
   compare carpology
car·po·go·nial
car·po·go·nium (*plural*
   ·nia) botany term
car·po·logi·cal
car·po·lo·gist
car·pol·ogy branch of
   botany; *compare*
   carpholigy
car·po·meta·car·pus bird
   bone
car·popha·gous feeding on
   fruit
car·po·phore botany term
car·port
car·po·spore
car·pus (*plural* ·pi) wrist
car·rack galleon
car·ra·geen (*or* ·gheen,
   cara·geen) seaweed
Car·ra·ra Italian town
car·re·four crossroads
car·rel (*or* ·rell) library
   cubicle
car·riage
carriage·way
car·rick
car·ri·er
car·ri·on
car·ron·ade cannon
car·rot
car·roty
car·ry (·ries, ·ry·ing,
   ·ried)
carry·all
carry·cot

carse *Scot* low-lying land

car·sey *variant spelling of* carzey

car·sick

car·sick·ness

cart

cart·age

Car·ta·gena Colombian port

carte blanche (*plural* cartes blanches)

car·tel

car·tel·ize

car·teli·za·tion

Car·tesian of Descartes

cart·ful

Car·thage

Car·tha·gin·ian

cart·horse

Car·thu·sian monk

car·ti·lage

car·ti·lagi·nous

cart·load

car·to·gram map

car·tog·ra·pher

car·to·graph·ic

car·to·graphi·cal

car·tog·ra·phy

carto·man·cy fortune-telling

car·ton

car·toon

car·toon·ist

car·touche (or ·touch)

car·tridge

car·tu·lary (or char·; *plural* ·laries) legal records

cart·wheel

car·un·cle fleshy outgrowth

car·un·cu·lar (or ·lous)

car·un·cu·late (or ·lat·ed)

carve

car·vel *variant of* caravel

carvel-built

carv·er

carv·ery (*plural* ·eries)

carv·ing

cary·at·id (*plural* ·ids or ·ati·des)

cary·ati·dal (or ·dean, cary·at·ic, cary·atid·ic)

caryo·phyl·la·ceous botany term

cary·op·sis (*plural* ·ses or ·si·des) botany term

car·zey (or ·sey) *Slang* lavatory

ca·sa·ba (or cas·sa·ba) melon

Casa·blan·ca

cas·bah *variant spelling of* kasbah

cas·cade

cas·ca·ra

cas·ca·ril·la shrub

case

ca·sease enzyme

ca·seate medical term

ca·sea·tion

case·bound

ca·sefy (·sefies, ·sefy·ing, ·sefied) become cheesy

case-harden

ca·sein protein

ca·seino·gen protein

case·mate part of ship

case·ment

ca·seose biochemical compound

ca·seous cheeselike

ca·sern (or ·serne) soldier's billet

Ca·ser·ta Italian town

case·work

cash

cash·able

cash-and-carry

cash-book

cash·ew nut; *compare* cachou

cash·ier

cash·mere

cas·ing

ca·si·no (*plural* ·nos) gaming house; *compare* cassino

cask

cas·ket

Cas·lon style of type

Cas·pian Sea

casque helmet

casqued

cas·sa·reep cassava juice

cas·sa·ta ice cream

cas·sa·tion legal term

cas·sa·va plant

Cas·se·grain·ian telescope

cas·se·role

cas·sette

cas·sia plant

cas·si·mere (or casi·mere) cloth

cas·si·no (or ca·si·no) card game; *compare* casino

Cas·sio·peia constellation

cas·sis liqueur

cas·sit·er·ite mineral

cas·sock priest's garment; *compare* hassock

cas·socked

cas·sou·let French stew

cas·so·wary (*plural* ·waries) bird

cast (·ing, cast)

cas·ta·net

cast·away

caste Hindu class

cas·tel·lan keeper of castle

cas·tel·lat·ed

cas·tel·la·tion

cast·er one who casts; *compare* castor

cas·ter (or ·tor) sugar dispenser; wheel on furniture; *compare* castor

cas·ti·gate

cas·ti·ga·tion

cas·ti·ga·tor

Cas·tile (or Cas·til·la)

Cas·til·ian

cast·ing

cas·tle

cas·tled

cast-off (*adj*)

cast-off (*noun*)

Cas·tor star; mythological character

cas·tor plant oil; beaver secretion; *compare* caster

cas·trate

cas·tra·tion

cas·tra·to (*plural* ·ti or ·tos)

cas·tra·tor

Cas·tries capital of St Lucia

cas·ual

casu·al·ly

casu·al·ty (*plural* ·ties)

casua·ri·na tree

casu·ist

casu·is·tic (or ·ti·cal)

casu·is·ti·cal·ly

casu·ist·ry (*plural* ·ries)

ca·sus bel·li *Latin* occasion of war

cat

ca·taba·sis (*plural* ·ses)
descent
cata·bat·ic
cata·bol·ic (*or* kata·)
cata·boli·cal·ly (*or* kata·)
cata·bo·lism (*or* ka·)
ca·tabo·lite
cata·caus·tic physics term
cata·chre·sis incorrect use
of words
cata·chres·tic (*or* ·ti·cal)
cata·cla·sis (*plural* ·ses)
geology term
cata·clas·tic
cata·cli·nal geology term
cata·clysm
cata·clys·mic (*or* ·mal)
cata·comb
ca·tad·ro·mous migrating
down river; *compare*
anadromous
cata·falque
Cata·lan language or
inhabitant of Catalonia
cata·lase enzyme
cata·lec·tic prosody term
cata·lep·sy medical term
cata·lep·tic
cata·logue (*US* ·log)
cata·logu·er (*or* ·logu·ist; *US*
·log·)
Cata·lo·nia Spanish region
ca·tal·pa tree
cata·lyse (*US* ·lyze)
cata·lys·er (*US* ·lyz·)
ca·taly·sis (*plural* ·ses)
cata·lyst
cata·lyt·ic
cata·ma·ran
cata·menia menstruation
cata·menial
cata·mite homosexual boy
cata·mount (*or*
·mount·ain) animal
Ca·ta·nia Sicilian port
cata·pho·resis chemistry
term
cata·phyll leaf
cata·pla·sia pathology
term
cata·plasm poultice
cata·plas·tic
cata·plexy paralysis
cata·pult
cata·ract

ca·tarrh
ca·tarrh·al (*or* ·ous)
cat·arrh·ine zoology term
ca·tas·tro·phe
cata·stroph·ic
cata·strophi·cal·ly
ca·tas·tro·phism geological
theory
ca·tas·tro·phist
cata·to·nia schizophrenia
cata·ton·ic
Ca·taw·ba (*plural* ·bas *or*
·ba) American Indian
people
cat·bird
cat·boat
cat·call
catch (catch·ing, caught)
catch·er
catch·fly (*plural* ·flies) plant
catchi·ness
catch·ing
catch·ment
catch·penny (*plural*
·pennies)
catch·pole sheriff's officer
catch·up *US variant of*
ketchup
catch·weight
catch·word
catchy (catchi·er,
catchi·est)
cate·cheti·cal (*or*
cat·echet·ic) teaching
method
cat·echeti·cal·ly
cat·echin chemical
compound
cat·echism
cat·echis·mal
cat·echist (*or* cate·chiz·er,
cate·chis·er)
cat·echis·tic (*or* ·ti·cal)
cat·echi·za·tion (*or*
·sa·tion)
cat·echize (*or* ·ise)
cat·echol chemical
compound
cat·echola·mine
cat·echu (*or* ca·chou,
cutch) resin
cat·echu·men convert
cat·ego·rial
cat·egori·cal (*or* ·egor·ic)
cat·egori·cal·ly

cat·ego·ri·za·tion (*or*
·sa·tion)
cat·ego·rize (*or* ·rise)
cat·ego·ry (*plural* ·ries)
ca·tena (*plural* ·tenae)
biblical comments
cat·enane chemistry term
cat·enar·ian
ca·tena·ry (*plural* ·ries)
geometric curve
cat·enate biology term
cat·ena·tion
cat·enoid geometric surface
ca·tenu·late botany term
ca·ter
cat·er·an brigand
ca·ter·er
ca·ter·ing
cat·er·pil·lar
cat·er·waul
cat·fall nautical term
cat·fish (*plural* ·fish *or*
·fishes)
cat·gut
Cath·ar (*plural* ·ars *or* ·ari)
heretical Christian
Cath·ar·ism
ca·thar·sis
ca·thar·tic purgative
ca·thar·ti·cal·ly
Ca·thay *Archaic* China
cat·head nautical term
ca·thec·tic psychology
term
ca·thedra (*plural* ·thedrae)
bishop's throne
ca·thedral
ca·thep·sin enzyme
Cathe·rine wheel firework
cath·eter
cath·eteri·za·tion (*or*
·sa·tion)
cath·eter·ize (*or* ·ise)
ca·thex·is (*plural* ·thexes)
psychiatry term
ca·thod·al
cath·ode
ca·thod·ic (*or* ·thodi·cal)
Catholic religion
catho·lic universal
Ca·tholi·cism
catho·lic·ity
ca·tholi·ci·za·tion (*or*
·sa·tion)
ca·tholi·cize (*or* ·cise)

ca·tholi·con universal
  remedy
cati·on positive ion
cati·on·ic
cat·kin
cat·like
cat·ling surgical knife
cat·mint (or esp. US ·nip)
cat·nap (verb ·nap·ping,
  ·napped)
cat-o'-nine-tails (plural
  -tails)
ca·top·tric (or ·tri·cal)
ca·top·trics branch of optics
cat's-ear plant
cat's-eye
cat's-foot (plural -feet) plant
cat's-paw
cat·sup US variant of
  ketchup
cat·ta·lo (or cata·lo; plural
  ·loes or ·los) cattle
cat·tery (plural ·teries)
cat·ti·ly
cat·ti·ness
cat·tish
cat·tle
cattle·man (plural ·men)
catt·leya orchid
cat·ty (·ti·er, ·ti·est)
cat·walk
Cau·ca·sia
Cau·ca·sian
Cau·ca·soid
Cau·ca·sus mountain range
cau·cus (plural ·cuses)
cau·dad towards the tail
cau·dal of the tail
cau·dal·ly
cau·date (or ·dat·ed)
cau·da·tion
cau·dex (plural ·di·ces or
  ·dexes) stem
cau·dil·lo (plural ·los)
  Spanish leader
cau·dle spiced wine
caught
caul
caul·dron (or cal·dron)
cau·les·cent
cau·li·cle plant stalk
cau·li·flow·er
cau·line
caulk (or calk) fill cracks
caulk·er (or calk·er)

caus·abil·ity
caus·able
caus·al
cau·sal·gia pathology term
cau·sal·ity (plural ·ities)
cau·sal·ly
cau·sa·tion
causa·tive
cause cé·lè·bre (plural
  causes cé·lè·bres)
caus·er
cau·serie informal talk
cause·way
caus·tic
caus·ti·cal·ly
caus·tic·ness (or ·tic·ity)
cau·ter·ant caustic
cau·teri·za·tion (or ·sa·tion)
cau·ter·ize (or ·ise)
cau·tery (plural ·teries)
cau·tion
cau·tion·ary
cau·tious
cau·tious·ness
cav·al·cade
cava·lier
cava·lier·ism
ca·val·la (or ·ly; plural ·la,
  ·las, or ·lies) fish
cav·al·ry (plural ·ries)
cav·al·ry·man (plural ·men)
Cav·an Irish county
cava·ti·na (plural ·ne)
  musical work
cave
ca·veat warning
ca·veat emp·tor Latin let
  the buyer beware
ca·vea·tor legal term
cave·fish (plural ·fish or
  ·fishes)
cave·man (plural ·men)
cav·en·dish tobacco
cav·er
cav·ern
cav·ern·ous
cav·es·son horse's noseband
ca·vet·to (plural ·ti)
  architectural moulding
cavi·ar (or ·are)
cavi·corn hollow-horned
ca·vie Scot hen coop
cav·il (·il·ling, ·illed; US
  ·il·ing, ·iled)
cav·il·ler

cav·ing
cavi·ta·tion
Ca·vi·te Philippine port
cav·ity (plural ·ities)
cavo-relievo (or -rilievo;
  plural cavo-relievos or
  cavi-rilievi) architectural
  term
ca·vort
cavy (plural cavies) rodent
caw
Cawn·pore Indian city
Cax·ton style of type
cay low island or bank
cay·enne
cay·man (or cai·man; plural
  ·mans) crocodile
Cay·man Is·lands
cay·use US small pony
cea·no·thus shrub
Cea·ra Brazilian state
cease
cease·fire
cease·less
ce·cal US spelling of caecal
ce·ci·ty blindness
Cecrops mythological
  character
ce·cum US spelling of
  caecum
ce·dar tree; compare ceder
cede
ced·er one who cedes;
  compare cedar
cedi Ghanaian currency
ce·dil·la
cei·ba tree
cei·lidh Gaelic party
ceil·ing
ceil·om·eter
cela·don porcelain
cel·an·dine
Ce·la·ya Mexican city
Cel·ebes Indonesian
  island
cel·ebrant
cel·ebrate
cel·ebra·tion
cel·ebra·tive
cel·ebra·tor
cel·ebra·tory
ce·leb·rity (plural ·rities)
ce·leri·ac vegetable
ce·ler·ity speed
cel·ery

ce·les·ta (or ·leste) musical
  instrument
ce·les·tial
ce·les·tial·ly
cel·es·tite (or ·tine) mineral
ce·li·ac US spelling of coeliac
celi·ba·cy (plural ·cies)
celi·bate
cell
cel·la (plural ·lae) room in
  temple
cel·lar
cel·lar·age
cel·lar·er monastic official
cel·lar·et bottle stand
Cel·le German city
cel·list
cel·lo (plural ·los)
cel·lo·bi·ose (or cel·lose)
  biochemical compound
cel·loi·din chemical
  compound
cel·lo·phane
cel·lu·lar
cel·lu·lase enzyme
cel·lule
cel·lu·li·tis
Cel·lu·loid (Trademark)
cel·lu·lose
cel·lu·lo·sic
ce·lom US spelling of coelom
ce·lo·mate US spelling of
  coelomate
Celsius temperature scale
celt axe
Celt (or Kelt) people
Celt·ic (or Kelt·ic)
Celti·cist (or Celt·ist,
  Kelti·cist, Kelt·ist)
cem·ba·lo (plural ·los)
  harpsichord
ce·ment
ce·men·ta·tion
ce·ment·er
ce·ment·ite chemical
  compound
ce·men·tum tooth
  substance
cem·etery (plural ·eteries)
cena·cle (or coena·cle)
  supper room
ce·nes·the·sia variant
  spelling of coenesthesia
ce·no·bite variant spelling of
  coenobite

ce·no·gen·esis US spelling of
  caenogenesis
ce·no·genet·ic US spelling of
  caenogenetic
ce·no·spe·cies (plural
  ·spe·cies) biology term
ceno·taph
ceno·taph·ic
ce·no·te well
Ce·no·zo·ic (or Cai·)
  geological era
cense burn incense
cen·ser incense
  container
cen·sor suppressor; to ban;
  compare sensor
cen·sor·able
cen·so·rial
cen·so·ri·ous
cen·so·ri·ous·ness
cen·sor·ship
cen·sual of a census;
  compare sensual
cen·sur·able
cen·sure
cen·sus (plural ·suses)
cent
cen·tal unit
cen·taur
Cen·tau·rus constellation
cen·tau·ry (plural ·ries)
  plant
cen·te·nar·ian
cen·te·nary (plural ·naries)
cen·ten·nial
cen·ter US spelling of centre
cen·tesi·mal hundredth
cen·tesi·mo (plural ·mos)
  monetary unit
cen·ti·are (or cen·tare) unit
cen·ti·grade
cen·ti·gram (or ·gramme)
cen·ti·li·tre (US ·ter)
cen·til·lion (plural ·lions or
  ·lion) 10^{600}
cen·time
cen·ti·me·tre (US ·ter)
cen·ti·pede
centi·poise unit
cent·ner
cen·to (plural ·tos) type of
  poem
cen·tral
cen·tral·ism
cen·tral·ity (plural ·ities)

cen·trali·za·tion (or
  ·sa·tion)
cen·tral·ize (or ·ise)
cen·tral·ly
cen·tre (US ·ter)
centre·board (US center-)
  keel
centre-fire (US center-)
centre·fold (US center-)
centre·piece (US center-)
cen·tric (or ·tri·cal)
cen·tric·ity
cen·trifu·gal
cen·trifu·gal·ly
cen·trifu·ga·tion
cen·tri·fuge
cen·tring (US ·tering)
cen·tri·ole biology term
cen·trip·etal
cen·trip·etal·ly
cen·trist moderate
cen·tro·bar·ic
cen·tro·cli·nal geology term
cen·troid
cen·tro·mere chromosome
  part
cen·tro·mer·ic
cen·tro·some cell part
cen·tro·som·ic
cen·tro·sphere
cen·trum (plural ·trums or
  ·tra) part of vertebra
cen·tum linguistics term
cen·tu·pli·cate
cen·tu·rial
cen·tu·ri·on
cen·tu·ry (plural ·ries)
cep fungus
cepha·lad towards the head
cepha·lal·gia headache
ce·phal·ic
cepha·lin (or kepha·)
  biochemical compound
cepha·li·za·tion (or
  ·sa·tion)
cepha·lo·chor·date zoology
  term
cepha·lom·eter
cepha·lo·met·ric
cepha·lom·etry
Cepha·lo·nia Greek island
cepha·lo·pod mollusc
cepha·lo·po·dan
cepha·lo·pod·ic (or
  ·lopo·dous)

cepha·lo·tho·rac·ic
cepha·lo·tho·rax (*plural*
·raxes *or* ·races)
Ce·pheus constellation
ce·ra·ceous waxy
Ce·ram Indonesian island
ce·ram·ic
ce·ram·ics
cera·mist (*or* ce·rami·cist)
ce·rar·gy·rite mineral
ce·ras·tes (*plural* ·tes) snake
ce·rate ointment
ce·rat·ed ornithology term
ce·rato·dus (*plural* ·duses)
extinct fish
Cerberus mythological dog
cer·cal zoology term
cer·caria (*plural* ·cariae)
larva
cer·car·ial (*or* ·ian)
cer·cis plant
cer·co·pi·thecoid monkey
cer·cus (*plural* ·ci) zoology
term
cere swelling on bird's beak;
compare sere
ce·real crop; *compare* serial
cer·ebel·lar
cer·ebel·lum (*plural* ·lums
or ·la)
cer·ebral
cer·ebral·ly
cer·ebrate
cer·ebra·tion
cer·ebric
cer·ebroid
cer·ebro·side biochemical
compound
cer·ebro·spi·nal
cer·ebro·vas·cu·lar
cer·ebrum (*plural* ·ebrums
or ·ebra)
cere·cloth waxed cloth
Ce·re·di·gi·on Welsh
county
cere·ment burial clothes
cer·emo·nial
cer·emo·ni·al·ism
cer·emo·ni·al·ist
cer·emo·nial·ly
cer·emo·ni·ous
cer·emo·ny (*plural* ·nies)
Ce·res asteroid
Ceres Roman goddess
cer·esin wax

ce·reus cactus
ce·ria chemical compound
ce·ric
ce·rise
ce·rium chemical element
cer·met metal–ceramic
material
cer·nu·ous drooping
cero (*plural* cero *or* ceros)
fish
ce·ro·graph·ic (*or*
·graphi·cal)
ce·rog·ra·phist
ce·rog·ra·phy engraving on
wax
ce·ro·plas·tic
ce·ro·plas·tics
ce·ro·type printing process
ce·rous
cert *Slang* certainty
cer·tain
cer·tain·ly
cer·tain·ty (*plural* ·ties)
cer·ti·fi·able
cer·ti·fi·ably
cer·tifi·cate
cer·tifi·ca·tion
cer·tifi·ca·tory
cer·ti·fy (·fies, ·fy·ing,
·fied)
cer·tio·ra·ri legal term
cer·ti·tude
ce·ru·lean deep blue
ce·ru·men earwax
ce·ru·mi·nous
ce·ruse white lead
ce·rus·site (*or* ·ru·site)
mineral
cer·ve·lat sausage
cer·vi·cal
cer·vi·ci·tis
cer·vid zoology term
cer·vine of deer
cer·vix (*plural* ·vixes *or*
·vi·ces)
ce·sar·ean sec·tion *US
spelling of* Caesarean
section
ce·sium *US spelling of*
caesium
ces·pi·tose *US spelling of*
caespitose
cess
ces·sa·tion
ces·ser legal term

ces·sion act of ceding;
compare session
ces·sion·ary (*plural* ·aries)
legal term
cess·pool (*or* ·pit)
ces·tode tapeworm
ces·toid ribbon-shaped
ce·ta·cean whale
ce·ta·ceous
ce·tane chemical compound
cete group of badgers
ce·teris pa·ri·bus *Latin*
other things being equal
ce·to·logi·cal
ce·tol·o·gist
ce·tol·ogy study of whales
Ce·tus constellation
Ce·vennes mountain range
Cey·lon
Cey·lon·ese
chaba·zite mineral
chab·lis wine
cha-cha (*or* cha-cha-cha)
chac·ma baboon
cha·conne musical term
Chad African republic; lake
Chad·ean
Chad·ic language group
chae·ta (*plural* ·tae) bristle
on worm
chae·tog·nath wormlike
animal
chae·to·pod worm
chafe
chaf·er beetle
chaff
chaff·er (*noun*)
chaf·fer (*verb*) haggle
chaf·finch
chaffy
chaf·ing
Cha·gas' dis·ease
cha·grin
chain
chain·man (*plural* ·men)
chain·plate
chain-react
chain-smoke
chain-stitch
chain-store
chair
chair·borne
chair·man (*plural* ·men)
chair·man·ship
chair·person

chair·woman (*plural* ·women)

chaise carriage

chaise longue (*plural* chaise longues *or* chaises longues)

cha·la·za (*plural* ·zas *or* ·zae) biology term

cha·la·zal

chal·can·lite mineral

chal·cedon·ic

chal·cedo·ny (*plural* ·nies)

chal·cid insect

Chal·cidi·ce Greek peninsula

Chal·cis Greek city

chal·co·cite mineral

chal·cog·ra·pher (*or* ·phist)

chal·co·graph·ic (*or* ·graphi·cal)

chal·cog·ra·phy engraving

chal·co·lith·ic archaeology term

chal·co·py·rite mineral

Chal·dea (*or* ·daea) Babylonian region

Chal·dean (*or* ·daean)

Chal·dee language

chal·dron unit

cha·let

chal·ice goblet; *compare* challis

chali·co·there extinct mammal

chalk

chalk·board *US* blackboard

chalki·ness

chalk·pit

chalky (chalki·er, chalki·est)

chal·lah (*or* hal·lah; *plural* ·lahs *or* ·loth) Jewish bread

chal·lenge

chal·lenge·able

chal·leng·er

chal·lis (*or* ·lie) fabric; *compare* chalice

chal·one internal secretion

cha·lyb·eate containing iron

cha·made military signal

cham·ber

cham·ber·lain

chamber·maid

cham·bray cloth

cha·me·le·on

cha·meleon·ic

cham·fer

cham·fer·er

cham·ois (*plural* ·ois)

Cha·mo·nix French town

champ

cham·pac (*or* ·pak) tree

Cham·pagne French region

cham·pagne wine

cham·paign open country

cham·pers *Slang* champagne

cham·per·tous

cham·per·ty (*plural* ·ties) legal term

cham·pi·gnon mushroom

cham·pi·on

cham·pion·ship

champ·le·vé enamelling process

Champs Ély·sées

chance

chan·cel

chan·cel·lery (*or* ·lo·ry; *plural* ·leries *or* ·lo·ries)

chan·cel·lor

chan·cel·lor·ship

chan·cery (*plural* ·ceries)

chanci·ly

chan·cre pathology term

chan·croid ulcer

chan·croi·dal

chan·crous

chancy (chanci·er, chanci·est)

chan·de·lier

chan·delle aeronautics term

Chan·der·na·gore Indian port

Chan·di·garh Indian city

chan·dler

chan·dlery (*plural* ·dleries)

Chang·chia·kow (*or* ·k'ou) Chinese city

Chang·chow (*or* Ch'ang-chou) Chinese city

Chang·chun (*or* Ch'ang Ch'un) Chinese city

change

change·abil·ity (*or* ·able·ness)

change·able

change·ably

change·ful

change·less

change·less·ness

change·ling

change·over

chang·er

change-ringing

Chang·sha (*or* Ch'ang-sha) Chinese port

Chang·teh (*or* Ch'ang-te) Chinese port

chan·nel (·nel·ling, ·nelled; *US* ·nel·ing, ·neled)

chan·nel·ize (*or* ·ise)

chan·nel·ler (*US* ·nel·er)

chan·son *French* song

chant

chant·er

chan·te·relle mushroom

chan·teuse

chan·tey *US spelling of* shanty

chan·ti·cleer (*or* ·cler) cock

Chan·til·ly French town

chan·try (*plural* ·tries)

chan·ty *variant spelling of* shanty

Chao·an Chinese city

cha·os

cha·ot·ic

cha·oti·cal·ly

chap (chap·ping, chapped)

chapa·rejos cowboy's overalls

chap·ar·ral wooded area

cha·pat·ti (*or* ·pa·ti; *plural* ·ti *or* ·tis) bread

chap·book

chape scabbard mounting

cha·peau (*plural* ·peaux *or* ·peaus) hat

chap·el

chap·er·on (*or* ·one)

chap·er·on·age

chap·fallen (*or* chop·) dejected

chapi·ter architectural term

chap·lain

chap·lain·cy (*plural* ·cies)

chap·let strung beads

chap·let·ed

chap·pal sandal

chapped

chap·pie *Slang* fellow

chap•ping
chaps *short for* chaparejos
chap•stick *US* lip salve
chap•ter
chap•ter•house
char (char•ring, charred)
char (*or* charr; *plural* char,
   chars *or* charr, charrs) fish
chara•banc
chara•cin (*or* •cid) fish
char•ac•ter
char•ac•ter•ful
char•ac•ter•is•tic
char•ac•ter•is•ti•cal•ly
char•ac•teri•za•tion (*or*
   •sa•tion)
char•ac•ter•ize (*or* •ise)
char•ac•ter•less
cha•rade
char•as hashish
char•coal
char•cu•te•rie delicatessen
chard
Cha•rente French river
Charente-Maritime French
   department
charge
charge•abil•ity
charge•able
char•gé d'af•faires (*plural*
   char•gés d'af•faires)
charg•er
Cha•ri African river
chari•ly
chari•ness
Char•ing Cross
Chari-Nile language group
chari•ot
chari•ot•eer
cha•ris•ma (*or* char•ism)
char•is•mat•ic
char•is•mati•cal•ly
chari•table
chari•table•ness
chari•tably
char•ity (*plural* •ities)
cha•ri•va•ri (*or* shiva•ree)
   mock serenade
char•kha (*or* •ka) spinning
   wheel
char•lady (*plural* •ladies)
char•la•tan
char•la•tan•ism (*or* •ry)
char•la•tan•is•tic
Charles•ton *US* city

charles•ton dance
char•lie *Slang* fool
char•lock plant
Char•lotte *US* city
char•lotte pudding
Charlotte Ama•lie capital of
   US Virgin Islands
charm
charm•er
Char•meuse (*Trademark*)
   fabric
Char•mi•nar Indian
   monument
charm•ing
char•nel sepulchral
Char•ol•lais cattle
Charon mythological
   character
char•poy (*or* •pai) bedstead
char•qui dried meat
char•quid
chart
chart•able
char•ter
char•tered
Char•ter•house Carthusian
   monastery
Chart•ism reform
   movement
Chart•ist
char•tist share analyst
Char•tres French city
char•treuse liqueur
char•woman *plural* •women
chary (chari•er, chari•est)
Cha•ryb•dis mythological
   monster
chase
chas•er
chasm
chas•mal (*or* •mic)
chas•sé ballet step
chas•seur French huntsman
chas•sis (*plural* •sis)
chaste
chas•ten
chas•ten•er
chas•tis•able
chas•tise
chas•tise•ment
chas•tity
chasu•ble
chat (chat•ting, chat•ted)
cha•teau (*or* châ•; *plural*
   •teaux *or* •teaus)

chat•elain (*fem* •elaine)
   castle keeper
Chat•ham Kent town;
   Pacific islands
cha•toy•an•cy
cha•toy•ant changing in
   lustre
Chat•ta•noo•ga *US* city
chat•tel
chat•ter
chatter•box
chat•ter•er
chat•ti•ly
chat•ty (•ti•er, •ti•est)
Chau•cerian
chaud•froid sauce
chauf•fer (*or* chau•fer)
   heater
chauf•feur (*fem* •feuse)
chaul•moo•gra tree
chausses medieval garment
chau•vin•ism
chau•vin•ist
chau•vin•is•tic
chau•vin•is•ti•cal•ly
chaw *Dialect* chew tobacco
cha•yo•te plant
cheap inexpensive; *compare*
   cheep
cheap•en
cheap•ness
cheap•skate
cheat
cheat•er
Che•bo•ksa•ry Russian port
Che•chen (*plural* •chens *or*
   •chen) Russian people
Che•che•nia (*or* Chechnya)
   Russian republic
Chech•nya *variant spelling of*
   Chechenia
check pause; pattern; etc.;
   US spelling of cheque
check•able
check•book *US spelling of*
   chequebook
check•er one who checks;
   US spelling of chequer
check•ered *US spelling of*
   chequered
checker•berry (*plural*
   •berries)
checker•bloom plant
checker•board *US*
   draughtboard

check·ers *US* draughts
check-in (*noun*)
check·mate
check·out (*noun*)
check·point
check·up (*noun*)
checky *heraldic term*
Ched·dar
chedd·ite *explosive*
cheek
cheek·bone
cheeki·ly
cheeki·ness
cheek·piece
cheeky (cheeki·er,
  cheeki·est)
cheep *chirp; compare*
  cheap
cheep·er
cheer
cheer·ful
cheer·ful·ly
cheer·ful·ness
cheeri·ly
cheeri·ness
cheerio
cheer·leader
cheer·less
cheer·less·ness
cheers
cheery (cheeri·er,
  cheeri·est)
cheese
cheese·board
cheese·burg·er
cheese·cake
cheese·cloth
cheese·mon·ger
cheese·paring
cheesi·ness
cheesy (cheesi·er,
  cheesi·est)
chee·tah (*or* che·tah)
chef
chef-d'oeuvre (*plural*
  chefs-d'oeuvre) *French*
  masterpiece
Che·kiang *Chinese
  province*
che·la (*plural* ·lae) claws
che·la (*plural* ·las) *Hindu
  disciple*
che·la·ship
che·late *chemistry term*
che·la·tion

che·lic·era (*plural* ·erae)
  spider's claw
che·lic·er·al
che·lic·er·ate
che·lif·er·ous
che·li·form
Chelms·ford
che·loid *variant spelling of*
  keloid
che·lo·nian *tortoise or*
  turtle
chelp *Dialect chatter*
Chel·sea
Chel·ten·ham
Chel·ya·binsk *Russian city*
chemi·cal
chemi·cal·ly
chemi·lu·mi·nes·cence
chemi·lu·mi·nes·cent
che·min de fer *gambling
  game*
che·mise
chemi·sette *underbodice*
chemi·sorb (*or* chemo·)
chemi·sorp·tion
chem·ist
chem·is·try (*plural* ·tries)
Chem·nitz *German city*
chemo·pro·phy·lac·tic
chemo·pro·phy·lax·is
chemo·recep·tor (*or*
  chemo·cep·tor)
chem·os·mo·sis
chem·os·mot·ic
chemo·sphere *layer of
  atmosphere*
chemo·spher·ic
che·mo·stat
chemo·syn·thesis
chemo·syn·thet·ic
chemo·syn·theti·cal·ly
chemo·tac·tic
chemo·tac·ti·cal·ly
chemo·tax·is *biology term*
chemo·thera·pist
chemo·thera·py
chemo·trop·ic
chemo·tropi·cal·ly
che·mot·ro·pism *botany
  term*
chem·pa·duk *tree*
chem·ur·gic (*or* ·gi·cal)
chem·ur·gy *branch of
  chemistry*
Che·nab *Himalayan river*

Cheng·chow (*or
  Cheng-chou*) *Chinese city*
Cheng·teh *Chinese city*
Cheng·tu (*or* Ch'eng-tu)
  Chinese city
che·nille
Chen·nai *Indian name of*
  Madras
che·no·pod *plant*
che·no·po·dia·ceous
cheong·sam *Chinese dress*
cheque (*US* check)
cheque·book (*US* check·)
cheq·uer (*US* check·)
  pattern of squares; *compare*
  checker
chequer·board (*US*
  checker·)
cheq·uered (*US* check·ered)
Cheq·uers *premier's
  country house*
cheq·uers *US draughts game*
Cher *French river*
Cher·bourg *French port*
Che·rem·kho·vo *Russian
  city*
cher·ish
cher·ish·able
cher·ish·er
Cher·nov·tsy *Ukrainian
  city*
cher·no·zem (*or
  tscher·no·sem*) *black soil*
Chero·kee (*plural* ·kees *or*
  ·kee)
che·root
cher·ry (*plural* ·ries)
cher·so·nese *peninsula*
chert *quartz*
Chert·sey *Surrey town*
cherty
cher·ub (*plural* ·ubs *or*
  cheru·bim)
che·ru·bic
che·ru·bi·cal
cher·vil
cher·vo·nets *former Soviet
  coin*
Chesa·peake *US bay*
Chesh·ire
chess
chess·board
ches·sel *cheese mould*
chess·man (*plural* ·men)
chest

chest·ed
Ches·ter
Ches·ter·field Derbyshire town
ches·ter·field sofa
chesti·ly
chesti·ness
chest·nut
chesty (chesti·er, chesti·est)
cheval-de-frise barrier of spikes
cheva·lier
che·vet part of church
Che·vi·ot hills; sheep
che·vi·ot fabric
chev·rette goat skin
chev·ron
chev·ro·tain animal
chew
chew·able
chew·er
chewy (chewi·er, chewi·est)
Chey·enne American Indian; US city
chez *French* at the home of
chi Greek letter
chi·ack *Austral* to tease
chi·an·ti
Chi·apas Mexican state
chia·ro·scur·ism
chia·ro·scu·rist
chia·ro·scu·ro (*plural* ·ros) art term
chi·as·ma (*or* chi·asm; *plural* ·mas, ·ma·ta, *or* ·asms) biology term
chi·as·mal
chi·as·mic
chi·as·mus (*plural* ·mi) rhetoric term
chi·as·tic
chi·as·to·lite mineral
Chi·ba Japanese city
chi·bouk (*or* ·bouque) Turkish pipe
chic
Chi·ca·go
chi·ca·lo·te poppy
chi·cane
chi·can·er
chi·can·ery (*plural* ·eries)
Chich·es·ter
chi·chi

Chi·chi·haerh (*or* Ch'i-ch'i-haerh) Chinese city
chick
chicka·bid·dy
chicka·dee bird
chicka·ree squirrel
Chicka·saw (*plural* ·saws *or* ·saw) American Indian
chick·en
chicken-hearted (*or* -livered)
chicken·pox
chick·pea
chick·weed
Chi·cla·yo Peruvian city
chic·le gum
chi·co shrub
chico·ry (*or* chic·co·ry; *plural* ·ries)
chide (chid·ing; chid·ed *or* chid; chid·ed, chid, *or* chid·den)
chid·er
chief
chief·ly
chief·tain
chiff·chaff bird
chif·fon
chif·fo·nier (*or* ·fon·nier) furniture
chig·etai wild ass
chig·ger larva
chi·gnon
chigoe flea
Chi·hua·hua Mexican state; dog
chil·blain
child (*plural* chil·dren)
child·bed
child·birth
child·hood
child·ish
child·ish·ness
child·less
child·less·ness
child·like
chil·dren *plural of* child
Chile
Chil·ean
chili·ad group of one thousand
chili·ad·al (*or* ·ad·ic)
chili·asm theology term
chili·ast

chili·as·tic
chill
chil·li (*plural* ·lies)
chil·li con car·ne
chil·li·ness
Chil·lon Swiss castle
chil·lum clay pipe
chil·ly (·li·er, ·li·est)
chi·lo·pod invertebrate
Chil·tern Hills; Hundreds
Chi·lung (*or* Chi-lung) Taiwanese port
chi·maera fish; *compare* chimera
Chim·bo·te Peruvian port
chime
chi·mera (*or* ·maera) monster; biology term; *compare* chimaera
chi·mere (*or* chim·er, chim·ar) bishop's gown
chi·meri·cal (*or* ·mer·ic) fanciful
Chim·kent Kazakh city
chim·ney
chimney·piece
chimney·pot
chimp
chim·pan·zee
chin
Chi·na country
chi·na porcelain
china·berry (*plural* ·berries)
China·graph (*Trademark*)
China·man (*plural* ·men)
China·town
china·ware
chinch *US* bedbug
chin·che·rin·chee plant
chin·chil·la
Chin-Chou (*or* Chin·chow) Chinese city
Chin·dit
Chin·dwin Burmese river
chine
chi·né mottled
Chi·nee *Slang* Chinaman
Chi·nese (*plural* ·nese)
Ching (*or* Ch'ing) Chinese dynasty
chink
Chin·kiang (*or* Cheng-chiang) Chinese port
chin·less

chino (*plural* chinos) cloth
chi·noi·serie
Chi·nook (*plural* ·nook or
·nooks) American Indian
chi·nook wind
Chi·nook·an
chin·qua·pin (*or* ·ca·pin,
·ka·pin) tree
chintz
chintzy (chintzi·er,
chintzi·est)
chin·wag (·wag·ging,
·wagged)
chi·ono·doxa plant
Chios Greek island
chip (chip·ping, chipped)
chip·board
chip·munk
chipo·la·ta
chip·per
chip·ping
chip·py (*noun, plural* ·pies;
adj ·pi·er, ·pi·est)
chir·al chemistry term
chi·ral·ity
chirm chirp
chi·rog·ra·pher
chi·ro·graph·ic (*or*
·graphi·cal)
chi·rog·ra·phy calligraphy
chi·ro·man·cy palmistry
Chiron centaur
chi·ropo·dist
chi·ropo·dy
chi·ro·prac·tic
chi·ro·prac·tor
chi·rop·ter bat
chi·rop·ter·an
chirp
chirp·er
chirpi·ly
chirpi·ness
chirpy (chirpi·er,
chirpi·est)
chirr (*or* chirre, churr)
make shrill sound
chir·rup
chir·rup·er
chir·rupy
chis·el (·el·ling, ·elled; *US*
·el·ing, ·eled)
chis·el·ler (*US* ·el·er)
Chi·şi·nău capital of
Moldova
chi·square statistics term

chit
Chi·ta Russian city
chi·tal deer
chi·tar·ro·ne (*plural* ·ni)
lute
chit·chat (·chat·ting,
·chat·ted)
chi·tin biochemical
compound
chi·tin·oid
chi·tin·ous
chi·ton Greek tunic
Chit·ta·gong Bangladeshi
port
chit·ter *US* twitter
chit·ter·lings (*or* chit·lins,
chit·lings) pig intestines
chiv *Slang* knife
chiv·al·ric
chiv·al·rous
chiv·al·ry (*plural* ·ries)
chive (*or* chives)
chivy (*or* chiv·vy; chivies,
chivy·ing, chiv·ied *or*
chiv·vies, ·vy·ing, ·vied)
chlamy·date zoology term
chla·myd·eous botany
term
chla·mydo·spore
chlor·acne skin disease
chlo·ral chemical
compound
chlo·ram·bu·cil drug
chlo·ra·mine chemical
compound
chlo·ram·pheni·col
antibiotic
chlo·rate
chlor·dane (*or* ·dan)
insecticide
chlo·rel·la alga
chlo·ren·chy·ma plant
tissue
chlo·ric
chlo·ride
chlo·rid·ic
chlo·rin·ate
chlo·rina·tion
chlo·rina·tor
chlo·rine (*or* ·rin)
chlo·rite mineral
chlo·rit·ic
chlo·ro·ben·zene
chlo·ro·form
chlo·ro·hy·drin

Chlo·ro·my·ce·tin
(*Trademark*)
chlo·ro·phyll (*or* ·phyl)
chlo·ro·phyl·loid
chlo·ro·phyl·lous
chlo·ro·pic·rin (*or*
chlor·pic·rin) pesticide
chlo·ro·plast
chlo·ro·plast·ic
chlo·ro·prene chemical
compound
chlo·ro·quine drug
chlo·ro·sis disease
chlo·ro·thia·zide
chlo·rot·ic
chlo·rous of chlorine
chlor·proma·zine drug
chlor·pro·pa·mide drug
cho·ano·cyte zoology term
choc-ice
chock
chock-a-block
chock·er *Slang* fed up
chock-full
choco·late
choco·laty
Choc·taw (*plural* ·taws or
·taw) American Indian
Chog·yal Indian ruler
choice
choice·ly
choice·ness
choir choral group; *compare*
quire
choir·boy
choir·master
Choi·seul Pacific island
choke
choke·able
choke·berry (*plural* ·berries)
choke·bore shotgun
choke·cherry (*plural*
·cherries)
chok·er
choky (*or* ·ey)
cho·lecal·cif·er·ol vitamin
chol·an·gi·og·raphy
bile-duct examination
chol·ecys·tec·to·my (*plural*
·mies) removal of gall
bladder
chol·ecys·tog·raphy
gall-bladder examination
chol·er anger
chol·era

chol•er•ic
chol•eroid
cho•les•ter•ol (or •ter•in)
cho•li bodice
cho•line biochemical
  compound
cho•lin•er•gic biology term
cho•lin•es•ter•ase enzyme
chol•la cactus
Cho•lon Vietnamese city
chomp
chon Korean coin
chon•dri•fi•ca•tion
chon•dri•fy (•fies, •fy•ing,
  •fied) change into cartilage
chon•drio•so•mal
chon•drio•some biology
  term
chon•drite meteorite
chon•drit•ic
chon•dro•ma (plural •mas or
  •ma•ta) tumour
chon•dro•ma•tous
chon•drule meteorology
  term
Chong•jin (or Chung•)
  Korean port
Chon•ju Korean city
choose (choos•ing, chose,
  cho•sen)
choos•er
choosi•ly
choosi•ness
choosy (choosi•er,
  choosi•est)
chop (chop•ping, chopped)
cho•pine shoe
chop•logic
chop•per
chop•pi•ly
chop•pi•ness
chop•py (•pi•er, •pi•est)
chop•stick
cho•ra•gus Greek chorus
  leader
cho•ral (adj)
cho•rale (noun)
cho•ral•ly
chord maths and music
  senses; compare cord
chord•al
chor•date animal with
  notochord; compare
  cordate
chord•ing musical term

chordo•phone musical
  instrument
chore
cho•rea neurological
  disorder
cho•real (or cho•re•ic)
cho•reo•dra•ma
cho•reo•graph
cho•reog•ra•pher (or
  •reg•ra•pher)
cho•reo•graph•ic (or
  •regraph•ic)
cho•reo•graphi•cal•ly (or
  •regraphi•)
cho•reog•ra•phy (or
  •reg•ra•phy)
cho•ri•amb (or •am•bus;
  plural •ambs or •am•bi)
  prosody term
cho•ri•am•bic
cho•ric of a chorus
cho•ri•on embryonic
  membrane
cho•ri•on•ic (or cho•rial)
chor•is•ter
Chor•ley Lancashire town
cho•rog•ra•pher
cho•ro•graph•ic (or
  •graphi•cal)
cho•ro•graphi•cal•ly
cho•rog•ra•phy mapping
  regions
cho•roid membrane of
  eyeball
cho•rol•ogy geography term
chor•tle
cho•rus (plural •ruses)
Chor•zow Polish city
chose
cho•sen
Cho•ta Nag•pur Indian
  plateau
Chou Chinese dynasty
chou (plural choux)
  cabbage; compare choux
chough bird
choux pastry; plural of
  chou
chow
chow-chow
chow-der soup
chow mein Chinese food
chre•ma•tis•tic of
  money-making
chres•ard biology term

chrism (or chris•om)
  anointing oil; compare
  chrisom
chris•mal
chris•ma•tory (plural
  •tories) receptacle for
  consecrated oil
chris•om baptismal robe;
  compare chrism
Christ
Chris•ta•del•phian
Christ•church New Zealand
  city; Dorset town
chris•ten
Chris•ten•dom
chris•ten•er
chris•ten•ing
Chris•tian
Chris•tia•nia former name of
  Oslo
Chris•ti•an•ity
Chris•tiani•za•tion (or
  •sa•tion)
Chris•tian•ize (or •ise)
Chris•tian•iz•er (or •is•er)
Chris•tian•ly
Christ•like
Christ•mas
Christ•mas•sy
Christmas•tide
Chris•to•logi•cal
Chris•tol•ogist
Chris•tol•ogy
Christ's-thorn plant
chro•ma physics term
chro•mate
chro•mat•ic
chro•mati•cal•ly
chro•mati•cism
chro•ma•tic•ity physics
  term
chro•mat•ic•ness physics
  term
chro•mat•ics (or
  chro•ma•tol•ogy) science
  of colour
chro•ma•tid chromosome
  part
chro•ma•tin substance of
  chromosomes
chro•ma•tin•ic
chro•ma•tist (or
  chro•ma•tolo•gist)
chro•ma•to•gram
chro•ma•tog•ra•pher

chro·ma·to·graph·ic
chro·ma·to·graphi·cal·ly
chro·ma·tog·ra·phy
  chemical analysis
chro·ma·tol·ogy *variant of*
  chromatics
chro·ma·toly·sis cytology
  term
chro·ma·to·phore zoology
  term
chro·ma·to·phor·ic
chro·ma·toph·or·ous
chrome
chro·mic
chro·mi·nance physics term
chro·mite mineral
chro·mium
chro·mo·gen
chro·mo·gen·ic colour-
  producing
chro·mo·litho·graph
chro·mo·li·thog·ra·pher
chro·mo·litho·graph·ic
chro·mo·li·thog·ra·phy
chro·mo·mere cytology
  term
chro·mo·nema (*plural*
  ·nema·ta) biology term
chro·mo·nemal (*or*
  ·nemat·ic, ·nemic)
chro·mo·phore chemistry
  term
chro·mo·phor·ic (*or* ·ous)
chro·mo·plast part of cell
chro·mo·pro·tein
chro·mo·so·mal
chro·mo·some
chro·mo·sphere layer of
  sun
chro·mo·spher·ic
chro·mous
chro·myl
chro·naxie (*or* ·naxy)
  physiology term
chron·ic
chroni·cal·ly
chro·nic·ity
chroni·cle
chroni·cler
Chroni·cles Old Testament
  book
chrono·bi·ol·ogy
chrono·gram
chrono·gram·mat·ic (*or*
  ·mati·cal)

chrono·graph time recorder
chro·nog·ra·pher
chrono·graph·ic
chrono·logi·cal
chrono·logi·cal·ly
chro·nolo·gist
chro·nol·ogy (*plural* ·ogies)
chro·nom·eter timepiece
chrono·met·ric (*or* ·ri·cal)
chrono·metri·cal·ly
chro·nom·etry
chro·non unit
chrono·scope
chrono·scop·ic
chrysa·lis (*plural* ·lises,
  ·lids, *or* chry·sali·des)
chry·san·themum
chrysa·ro·bin drug
chrys·el·ephan·tine
  statuary term
chryso·ber·yl
chryso·lite gemstone
chryso·lit·ic
chryso·prase gemstone
chryso·tile mineral
chtho·nian (*or* ·nic) of the
  underworld
chub (*plural* chub *or* chubs)
Chubb (*Trademark*) lock
chub·bi·ness
chub·by (·bi·er, ·bi·est)
chuck
chuck·le
chuck·ler
chuck·wal·la lizard
chuck·will's-widow bird
chud·dar Indian shawl
chu·fa sedge
chuff
chuffed
chuf·fy *Scot* chubby
chug (chug·ging, chugged)
chu·kar partridge
Chuk·chi Siberian
  peninsula
chuk·ker (*or* ·ka) polo term
chum (chum·ming,
  chummed)
chum·mi·ly
chum·mi·ness
chum·my (·mi·er, ·mi·est)
chump
chump·ing *Dialect*
  collecting wood
chun·der

chun·der·ous *Austral*
  nauseating
Chung·king (*or*
  Ch'ung-ch'ing) Chinese
  port
chunk
chunki·ly
chunki·ness
chunky (chunki·er,
  chunki·est)
Chun·nel Channel tunnel
chun·ter
church
church·goer
church·going
Church·ill Canadian river
church·man (*plural* ·men)
church·warden
church·woman (*plural*
  ·women)
church·yard
chu·ri·dars Indian trousers
chu·rin·ga Aboriginal
  amulet
churl
churl·ish
churn
churr *variant spelling of* chirr
chute
chut·ney (*or* ·nee)
chut·tie *Austral* chewing
  gum
Chu·vash (*plural* ·vash *or*
  ·vashes) Russian people
chy·la·ceous (*or* chy·lous)
chyle intestinal fluid
chyme digested food
chy·mo·sin rennin
chy·mo·tryp·sin enzyme
chy·mo·tryp·sino·gen
  enzyme precursor
chy·mous
cia·bat·ta Italian bread
ciao Italian greeting
ci·bo·rium (*plural* ·ria)
  communion vessel
ci·ca·da (*or* ci·ca·la; *plural*
  ·das, ·dae *or* ·las, ·le)
cica·tri·cial
cica·tric·le biology term
ci·cat·ri·cose
cica·trix (*plural* ·tri·ces) scar
cica·tri·zant (*or* ·sant)
cica·tri·za·tion (*or* ·sa·tion)
cica·trize (*or* ·trise) heal

cica·triz·er (*or* ·tris·er)
cic·ely plant
cic·ero (*plural* ·eros) unit
cic·ero·ne (*plural* ·nes *or* ·ni*) tourist guide
Cic·ero·nian eloquent
cich·lid fish
cich·loid
ci·der
ci·gar
ciga·rette
ciga·ril·lo (*plural* ·los) cigar
cig·gy (*plural* ·gies) *Slang* cigarette
cilia *plural of* cilium
cili·ary
cili·ate
cili·at·ed
cili·ation
cil·ice haircloth
cilio·late
cil·ium (*plural* cilia) minute hair
cim·ba·lom dulcimer
Cim·bri Germanic people
Cim·brian
Cim·bric
ci·mex (*plural* cimi·ces) bedbug
Cim·me·rian very dark
cinch
cin·cho·na tree bark
cin·choni·dine alkaloid
cin·cho·nine alkaloid
cin·chon·ism poisoning
cin·cho·ni·za·tion (*or* ·sa·tion)
cin·cho·nize (*or* ·nise)
Cin·cin·nati
cinc·ture surround
cin·der
cin·dery
cine film
cin·easte film enthusiast
cin·ema
Cin·ema·scope (*Trademark*)
cin·ema·theque small cinema
cin·emat·ic
cin·emati·cal·ly
cin·ema·graph
cin·ema·tog·ra·pher
cin·ema·graph·ic
cin·ema·tog·ra·phy
cin·eol (*or* ·eole) eucalyptol

Cin·era·ma (*Trademark*)
cin·eraria plant
cin·erar·ium (*plural* ·eraria) place for cremation ashes
cin·erary (*adj*)
cin·era·tor cremation furnace
ci·ner·eous (*or* cin·eri·tious) greyish
cin·erin chemical compound
cin·gu·late (*or* ·lat·ed)
cin·gu·lum (*plural* ·la) anatomical part
cin·na·bar mineral
cin·na·mon
cin·na·mon·ic (*or* ci·nam·ic)
cin·quain poem
cinque five
cinque·foil plant
Cinque Ports
Cin·za·no (*Trademark*)
ci·pher (*or* cy·pher) secret writing; *compare* sypher
cipo·lin marble
cir·ca
cir·ca·dian daily
Cir·cas·sia Russian region
Cir·cas·sian
Circe mythological character
cir·ci·nate botany term
Cir·ci·nus constellation
cir·cle
cir·cler
cir·clet
cir·cuit
cir·cuit·al of a circuit
cir·cui·tous indirect
cir·cui·tous·ly
cir·cuit·ry circuit system
cir·cu·ity (*plural* ·ities)
cir·cu·lar
cir·cu·lar·ity (*or* ·ness)
cir·cu·lari·za·tion (*or* ·sa·tion)
cir·cu·lar·ize (*or* ·ise)
cir·cu·lar·iz·er (*or* ·is·er)
cir·cu·late
cir·cu·la·tion
cir·cu·la·tive
cir·cu·la·tor
cir·cu·la·tory

cir·cum·am·bi·ence (*or* ·en·cy)
cir·cum·am·bi·ent
cir·cum·am·bu·late
cir·cum·am·bu·la·tion
cir·cum·am·bu·la·tor
cir·cum·am·bu·la·tory
cir·cum·ben·di·bus circumlocution
cir·cum·cise
cir·cum·ci·sion
cir·cum·fer·ence
cir·cum·fer·en·tial
cir·cum·flex
cir·cum·flex·ion
cir·cum·flu·ous surrounded by water
cir·cum·fuse
cir·cum·fu·sion
cir·cum·lo·cu·tion
cir·cum·locu·tory
cir·cum·lu·nar
cir·cum·navi·gable
cir·cum·navi·gate
cir·cum·navi·ga·tion
cir·cum·navi·ga·tor
cir·cum·nu·tate botany term
cir·cum·nu·ta·tion
cir·cum·po·lar
cir·cum·scis·sile botany term
cir·cum·scribe
cir·cum·scrip·tion
cir·cum·spect
cir·cum·spec·tion
cir·cum·spec·tive
cir·cum·stance
cir·cum·stan·tial
cir·cum·stan·ti·ality (*plural* ·alities)
cir·cum·stan·tial·ly
cir·cum·stan·ti·ate
cir·cum·stan·tia·tion
cir·cum·val·late surround with fortification
cir·cum·val·la·tion
cir·cum·vent
cir·cum·vent·er (*or* ven·tor)
cir·cum·ven·tion
cir·cum·vo·lu·tion
cir·cum·vo·lu·tory
cir·cus (*plural* ·cuses)
ciré waxed
Ci·ren·ces·ter

cirque mountain feature
cir·rate (or cir·rose,
cir·rous) biology term
cir·rhosed
cir·rho·sis
cir·rhot·ic
cir·ri·pede (or ·ped) marine
animal
cir·ro·cu·mu·lus (plural ·li)
cir·rose (or ·rous)
cir·ro·stra·tus (plural ·ti)
cir·rus (plural ·ri) cloud;
tentacle; compare
schirrhus
cir·soid medical term
cis·al·pine
cis·co (plural ·coes or ·cos)
fish
cis·lu·nar between earth
and moon
cis·mon·tane
cis·soid curve
cist box; compare cyst
cis·ta·ceous botany term
Cis·ter·cian monk
cis·tern
cis·ter·na (plural ·nae)
anatomy term
cis·tron genetics term
cit·able (or cite·able)
cita·del
ci·ta·tion
cite
citha·ra (or kitha·ra)
musical instrument
citi·fy (or city·fy; ·fies,
·fy·ing, ·fied)
citi·zen
citi·zen·ry (plural ·ries)
citi·zen·ship
Ci·tlal·té·petl Mexican
volcano
cit·ral plant oil
cit·rate
cit·re·ous greenish-yellow
cit·ric
cit·ri·cul·ture
cit·rin vitamin
cit·rine gemstone
cit·ron fruit
cit·ron·el·la grass
cit·ron·el·lal plant oil
cit·rul·line amino acid
cit·rus (plural ·ruses)
cit·tern musical instrument

City London's commercial
area
city (plural cities)
civ·et
civ·ic
civi·cal·ly
civ·ics
civ·il
ci·vil·ian
ci·vil·ity (plural ·ities)
civi·li·za·tion (or ·sa·tion)
civi·lize (or ·lise)
civi·liz·er (or ·lis·er)
civ·il·ly
civ·vy (plural ·vies) Slang
civilian
clack
Clack·man·nan·shire
Scottish county
Clac·ton Essex town
Clac·to·nian Palaeolithic
culture
clad (clad·ding, clad)
clade
cla·dis·tic
cla·dis·tics
cla·doc·er·an animal
clad·ode (or clado·phyll)
plant stem
claim
claim·able
claim·ant
claim·er
clair·audi·ence psychology
term
clair-obscure art term
clair·voy·ance
clair·voy·ant
clam (clam·ming,
clammed)
cla·mant noisy
clama·to·rial ornithology
term
clam·bake
clam·ber
clam·mi·ly
clam·mi·ness
clam·my (·mi·er, ·mi·est)
clam·or·ous
clam·our (US ·or)
clamp
clamp·er shoe spike
clan
clan·des·tine
clang

clang·er that which clangs;
mistake
clang·or (or ·our) loud noise
clang·or·ous (or ·our·ous)
clank
clan·nish
clans·man (plural ·men)
clans·woman (plural
·women)
clap (clap·ping, clapped)
clap·board
Clap·ham
clap·per
clapper·board
clap·trap
claque hired applauders
clara·bel·la (or clari·) organ
stop
clar·ence carriage
Clar·en·don village near
Salisbury
clar·en·don typeface
clar·et
clari·fi·ca·tion
clari·fier
clari·fy (·fies, ·fy·ing, ·fied)
clari·net
clari·net·ist (or ·net·tist)
cla·rino musical term
clari·on
clario·net Obsolete clarinet
clar·ity
clarkia plant
cla·ro cigar
clarts Dialect lumps of mud
clary (plural ·claries) plant
clash
clash·er
clasp
clasp·er
class
class-conscious
class-conscious·ness
clas·sic
clas·si·cal
clas·si·cal·ism
clas·si·cal·ity
clas·si·cal·ly
clas·si·cism (or
clas·si·cal·ism)
clas·si·cist (or clas·si·cal·ist)
clas·si·cis·tic
clas·sics
clas·si·fi·able
clas·si·fi·ca·tion

clas·si·fi·ca·tion·al
clas·si·fi·ca·tory
clas·si·fi·er
clas·si·fy (·fies, ·fy·ing, ·fied)
classi·ly
classi·ness
clas·sis (*plural* ·ses) church elders
class·less
class·less·ness
class·mate
class·room
classy (classi·er, classi·est)
clas·tic geology term
clath·rate netlike
clat·ter
clat·tery
clau·di·ca·tion lameness
claus·al
clause
claus·tral *variant spelling of* cloistral
claus·tro·phobe
claus·tro·pho·bia
claus·tro·pho·bic
claus·tro·pho·bi·cal·ly
cla·vate (*or* clavi·form) club-shaped
clav·er *Scot* gossip
clavi·chord
clavi·chord·ist
clavi·cle
clavi·corn beetle
cla·vicu·lar
cla·vier musical instrument
Cla·vi·us moon crater
claw
claw·er
clay
clay·bank *US* brown colour
clay·ey
clay·like
clay·more sword
clay·pan clay layer
clay·stone
clay·to·nia plant
clean
clean·able
clean-cut
clean·er
clean-limbed
clean·li·ness
clean·ly (·li·er, ·li·est)
clean·ness

cleans·able
cleanse
cleans·er
clean-shaven
clear
clear·ance
clear·cole wall whiting
clear-cut
clear-eyed
clear-headed
clear-headed·ness
clear·ing
clear·ness
clear-sighted
clear·way
clear·wing moth
cleat
cleav·able
cleav·age
cleave (cleav·ing; cleaved *or* clove; cleft, cleaved, *or* clo·ven)
cleav·er
cleav·ers goosegrass
cleck *Dialect* gossip
cleek golf club
Clee·thorpes English resort
clef
cleft
cleg horsefly
cleis·toga·mous (*or* ·to·gam·ic)
cleis·toga·my botany term
clem (clem·ming, clemmed) *Dialect* be hungry
clema·tis
clem·en·cy (*plural* ·cies)
clem·ent
clem·en·tine
clench
cleo·me plant
clep·to·ma·nia *variant spelling of* kleptomania
clere·storied (*or* clear·storied)
clere·story (*or* clear·; *plural* ·stories) church windows
cler·gy (*plural* ·gies)
clergy·man (*plural* ·men)
cler·ic
cleri·cal
cleri·cal·ism
cleri·cal·ly
cleri·hew verse

clerk
clerk·dom
clerk·ly
clerk·ship
Clermont-Ferrand French city
cle·ru·chy Athenian colony
cleve·ite mineral
Cleve·land
clev·er
clev·er·ly
clev·er·ness
clev·is coupling device
clew yarn; *compare* clue
cli·ché
cli·ché'd (*or* ·chéd)
Cli·chy Parisian suburb
click
click·er
cli·ent
cli·en·tal of a client
cli·en·tele customers
cliff
cliff·hanger
cliff·hanging
cli·mac·ter·ic critical period
cli·mac·teri·cal
cli·mac·tic (*or* ·ti·cal) of a climax
cli·mate
cli·mat·ic (*or* ·mati·cal *or* ·mat·al)
cli·ma·to·log·ic (*or* ·logi·cal)
cli·ma·tolo·gist
cli·ma·tol·ogy
cli·max
climb
climb·er
clime climate
clin·al of a cline
cli·nan·drium (*plural* ·dria) botany term
clinch
clinch·er
cline ecology term
cling (cling·ing, clung)
cling·er
cling·fish (*plural* ·fish *or* ·fishes)
clingi·ness (*or* cling·ing·ness)
cling·stone peach
clingy
clin·ic

clini·cal
cli·ni·cian
clink
clink·er
clinker-built (or clincher-)
clink·stone
cli·nom·eter surveying instrument
cli·no·met·ric (or ·ri·cal)
cli·nom·etry
cli·no·stat botany term
clin·quant tinsel
clin·to·nia plant
clip (clip·ping, clipped)
clip·board
clip-clop
clip·per
clip·pers
clip·pie Slang bus conductress
clip·ping
clique
cli·quey (or ·quy)
cli·quish
clish·ma·clav·er Scot gossip
cli·tel·lum (plural ·la) part of worm
clit·ic unstressed
clito·ral
clito·ris
cloa·ca (plural ·cae) zoology term
cloa·cal
cloak
cloak·room
clob·ber
cloche
clock
clock·maker
clock·wise
clock·work
clod
clod·dish
clod·dy
clod·hop·per
clod·hop·ping
clog (clog·ging, clogged)
clog·gi·ness
clog·gy (·gi·er, ·gi·est)
cloi·son·né enamel work
clois·ter
clois·tered
clois·tral (or claus·tral)
clomp
clon·al

clone (or clon)
clon·ic medical term
clo·nic·ity
clonk
clo·nus convulsion
clop (clop·ping, clopped)
close
close-down (noun)
close-fisted
close-grained
close-hauled sailing term
close-knit
close·ly
close·ness
clos·er
close-stool
clos·et
close-up (noun)
clos·ing
clos·trid·ial (or ·ian)
clos·trid·ium (plural ·iums or ·ia) bacterium
clo·sure
clot (clot·ting, clot·ted)
cloth
cloth·bound
clothe (cloth·ing, clothed or clad)
clothes
clothes·horse
clothes·line
clothes·press
clo·thi·er
cloth·ing
clo·ture US closure
cloud
cloud·berry (plural ·berries)
cloud·burst
cloud-cuckoo-land
cloudi·ly
cloudi·ness
cloud·less
cloud·let
cloud·scape
cloudy (cloudi·er, cloudi·est)
clough Dialect gorge
clout
clove
clo·ven
clo·ver
clover-leaf (plural ·leaves)
clown
clown·ery
clown·ish

cloy
cloy·ed·ness
cloy·ing·ly
cloy·ing·ness
club (club·bing, clubbed)
club·bable (or ·able)
club·by (·bi·er, ·bi·est)
club-footed
club·haul nautical term
club·house
club·land
club·man (plural ·men)
cluck
clucky Austral pregnant
clue (clu·ing, clued) evidence; compare clew
clue·less
Cluj Romanian city
clum·ber spaniel
clump
clump·ish (or clump·like)
clumpy
clum·si·ly
clum·si·ness
clum·sy (·si·er, ·si·est)
clung
Clu·ni·ac of Cluny
clunk
Clu·ny French town
clu·peid fish
clu·peoid
clus·ter
clus·tery
clutch
clut·ter
Clw·yd former Welsh county
Clyde Scottish river
Clyde·bank Scottish town
Clydes·dale horse
clype Scot tell tales
clyp·eal (or clype·ate)
clyp·eus (plural clypei) part of insect's head
clys·ter enema
cni·dar·ian zoology term
cnido·blast zoology term
Cni·dus ancient Greek city
Cnos·sus variant spelling of Knossos
co·ac·er·vate chemistry term
co·ac·er·va·tion
coach
coach·er

coach·ing
coach·man (*plural* ·men)
coach·work
co·ac·tion
co·ac·tive
co·ac·tiv·ity
co·ad·ju·tant
co·ad·ju·tor bishop's
assistant
co·adu·nate biology term
co·adu·na·tion
co·adu·na·tive
co·agu·lable
co·agu·lant (*or*
co·agu·la·tor)
co·agu·lase enzyme
co·agu·late
co·agu·la·tion
co·agu·la·tive
co·agu·lum (*plural* ·la)
coagulated mass
Coa·hui·la Mexican state
coal
coal·er coal transporter
coa·lesce
coa·les·cence
coa·les·cent
coal·face
coal·field
coal·fish (*plural* ·fish *or*
·fishes)
coa·li·tion
coa·li·tion·al
coa·li·tion·ist (*or* ·er)
coal·man (*plural* ·men)
Coal·port china
coaly
coam·ing nautical term
co·ap·ta·tion joining two
surfaces
co·arc·tate zoology term
co·arc·ta·tion
coarse rough; *compare* corse;
course
coarse·ly
coars·en
coarse·ness
coast
coast·al
coast·er
coast·guard
coast·line
coat
coat·ed
coatee small coat

coa·ti (*or* coati-mundi)
animal
coat·ing
coat·less
coat-tail
co·author
coax
coax·er
co·ax·ial (*or* ·ax·al)
cob
co·balt
co·bal·tic
co·bal·tite (*or* ·tine) mineral
co·bal·tous
cob·ber *Austral* friend
cob·ble
cob·bler
cobble·stone
co·bel·lig·er·ent
co·bia fish
co·ble *Scot* fishing boat
Co·blenz *variant spelling of*
Koblenz
cob·nut
Cobol computer language
co·bra
Co·burg German city
co·burg loaf
cob·web
cob·webbed
cob·web·by
coca shrub
Coca-Cola (*Trademark*)
co·caine (*or* ·cain)
co·cain·ism
co·caini·za·tion (*or*
·sa·tion)
co·cain·ize (*or* ·ise)
coc·cal
coc·ci *plural of* coccus
coc·cid insect
coc·cidi·oi·do·my·co·sis
fungal disease
coc·cidio·sis (*plural* ·ses)
animal disease
coc·cif·er·ous
coc·coid
coc·co·lith geology term
coc·cous (*adj*)
coc·cus (*plural* ·ci)
bacterium
coc·cyg·eal
coc·cyx (*plural* ·cy·ges)
Co·cha·bam·ba Bolivian
city

Co·chin Indian region and
port
cochi·neal
coch·lea (*plural* ·leae) ear
part
coch·lear
coch·leate shell-shaped
cock
cock·ade
cock-a-doodle-doo
cock-a-hoop
Cock·aigne imaginary land
cock-a-leekie soup
cocka·lo·rum self-
important person
cocka·tiel (*or* ·teel) parrot
cocka·too (*plural* ·toos)
parrot
cocka·trice monster
cock·chafer beetle
cock·crow
cock·er
cock·er·el
cock·eye
cock·eyed
cock·fight
cock·horse
cocki·ly
cocki·ness
cock·le
cockle·bur weed
cockle·shell
cock·loft garret
cock·ney
cock·ney·fi·ca·tion (*or* ·ni·)
cock·ney·fy (*or* ·ni·; ·fies,
·fy·ing, ·fied)
cock·ney·ism
cock·pit
cock·roach
cocks·comb (*or* cox·comb)
cocks·foot (*plural* ·foots)
grass
cock·shy throw
cock·spur grass
cock·sure
cock·swain *variant spelling*
of coxswain
cock·tail
cock·up
cocky (cocki·er, cocki·est)
coco (*plural* cocos) *short for*
coconut
co·coa
coco de mer tree

coco·nut
co·coon
co·co·pan mining wagon
co·cotte
co·co·yam vegetable
cod (*noun, plural* cod *or* cods; *verb* cod·ding, cod·ded)
coda
cod·dle
cod·dler
code
co·dec·li·na·tion
co·deine
cod·er
co·dex (*plural* co·di·ces)
cod·fish (*plural* ·fish *or* ·fishes)
codg·er
codi·cil
codi·cil·la·ry
co·di·col·ogy
codi·fi·ca·tion
codi·fi·er
codi·fy (·fies, ·fy·ing, ·fied)
cod·ling (*or* ·lin) apple
co·do·main maths term
co·don genetics term
cod·piece
co·driver
cods·wallop
co·ed
co·edit
co·edi·tion
co·edi·tor
co·edu·ca·tion
co·edu·ca·tion·al
co·edu·ca·tion·al·ly
co·ef·fi·cient
coe·la·canth primitive fish
coe·len·ter·ate animal
coe·len·ter·ic
coe·len·ter·on (*plural* ·tera) zoology term
coe·li·ac (*US* ce·) of the abdomen
coe·lom (*US* ce·) body cavity
coe·lo·mate (*US* ce·)
coe·lo·stat astronomical instrument
coe·nes·the·sia (*or* ·sis, ce·)
coe·nes·thet·ic (*or* ce·)
coe·no·bite (*or* ce·) member of religious order

coe·no·cyte botany term
coe·no·cyt·ic
coe·no·sarc zoology term
coe·nu·rus larva
co·en·zyme
co·equal
co·equali·ty
co·equal·ly
co·erce
co·er·cible
co·er·cion
co·er·cion·ary
co·er·cion·ist
co·er·cive
co·er·cive·ness
co·er·civ·ity physics term
co·es·sen·tial
co·es·sen·tial·ity (*or* ·ness)
co·eter·nity
co·eval contemporary
co·eval·ity
co·eval·ly
co·ex·ist
co·ex·ist·ence
co·ex·ist·ent
co·ex·tend
co·ex·ten·sion
co·ex·ten·sive
coff *Scot* buy
cof·fee
coffee·pot
cof·fer
coffer·dam underwater chamber
cof·fin
cof·fle chained slaves
cog (cog·ging, cogged)
co·gen·cy
co·gent
cogi·tate
cogi·ta·tion
cogi·ta·tive
cogi·ta·tor
Cog·nac French town; brandy
cog·nate
cog·na·tion relatedness
cog·ni·tion perception
cog·ni·tive
cog·ni·zable (*or* ·sable)
cog·ni·zance (*or* ·sance)
cog·ni·zant (*or* ·sant)
cog·nize (*or* ·nise) perceive
cog·no·men Roman family name

co·gno·scen·ti (*or* cono·scen·ti; *sing.* ·te)
co·gon grass
cog·wheel
co·hab·it
co·hab·it·ant (*or* ·it·er)
co·habi·ta·tion
co·heir
co·here
co·her·ence (*or* ·en·cy)
co·her·ent
co·her·er
co·he·sion
co·he·sive
coho (*plural* coho *or* cohos) fish
co·ho·bate redistil
co·hort
co·hosh plant
co·hune palm tree
coif cap
coif·feur (*fem* ·feuse) hairdresser
coif·fure hair style
coign (*or* coigne) *variant spellings of* quoin; *compare* coin
coil
coil·er
Co·im·ba·tore Indian city
Coim·bra Portuguese city
coin currency; *compare* quoin
coin·age
co·in·cide
co·in·ci·dence
co·in·ci·dent
co·in·ci·dent·al
co·in·ci·dent·al·ly
coin·er
coin-op
co·in·sur·ance
co·in·sure
Coin·treau (*Trademark*)
coir coconut fibre
coit *Austral* buttocks
coi·tal
coi·tus (*or* ·tion)
Coke (*Trademark*) Coca-Cola
coke
coku·lo·ris film term
col
cola (*or* kola) tree; nut
col·an·der sieve; *compare* calendar; calender

col·lati·tude
col·can·non cabbage dish
Col·ches·ter
col·chi·cine alkaloid
col·chi·cum plant
Col·chis ancient Asian
  country
col·co·thar rouge
cold
cold-blooded
cold-blooded·ness
cold-drawn metallurgy term
cold-hearted
cold·ish
cold·ness
cold-weld
cole cabbage
co·lec·to·my (plural ·mies)
cole·man·ite mineral
col·eop·ter·an (plural
  ·ter·ans or ·tera) beetle
col·eop·ter·ist
col·eop·ter·ous
col·eop·tile botany term
col·eo·rhi·za (plural ·zae)
  botany term
cole·slaw
co·leus (plural ·uses) plant
col·ey fish; compare coly
col·ic
col·icky
colic·root
colic·weed
Co·li·ma Mexican state and
  city
coli·seum (or col·os·seum)
co·li·tic
co·li·tis (or colo·ni·tis)
col·labo·rate
col·labo·ra·tion
col·labo·ra·tive
col·labo·ra·tor
col·lage
col·la·gen protein
col·la·gen·ic (or ·gen·ous)
col·lag·ist
col·lap·sar black hole
col·lapse
col·laps·ibil·ity
col·laps·ible (or ·able)
col·lar
collar·bone
col·lard cabbage
col·lar·ette
col·late

col·lat·er·al
col·lat·er·al·ly
col·la·tion
col·la·tive
col·la·tor
col·league
col·lect
col·lect·able (or ·ible)
col·lec·ta·nea miscellany
col·lec·tion
col·lec·tive
col·lec·tiv·ism
col·lec·tiv·ist
col·lec·tiv·is·tic
col·lec·tiv·ity (plural ·ities)
col·lec·tivi·za·tion (or
  ·sa·tion)
col·lec·ti·vize (or ·vise)
col·lec·tor
col·lec·to·rate
col·leen Irish girl
col·lege
col·le·gial
col·legian
col·legi·ate
col·legium (plural ·legiums
  or ·legia)
col·lem·bo·lan insect
col·len·chy·ma plant tissue
Colles' frac·ture
col·let jewellery setting
col·lide
col·lie
col·li·er
col·liery (plural ·lieries)
col·li·gate join
col·li·ga·tion
col·li·ga·tive
col·li·mate
col·li·ma·tion
col·li·ma·tor optical device
col·lin·ear
col·lin·ear·ity
col·lin·sia plant
col·li·sion
col·lo·cate
col·lo·ca·tion
col·lo·cu·tor
col·lo·di·on (or ·dium)
  liquid
col·logue (·lo·guing,
  ·logued) conspire
col·loid
col·loi·dal
col·loi·dal·ity

col·lop Dialect meat slice
col·lo·quial
col·lo·qui·al·ism
col·lo·qui·al·ly
col·lo·quium (plural
  ·quiums or ·quia)
col·lo·quy (plural ·quies)
(collossus) incorrect spelling
  of colossus
col·lo·type printing process
col·lo·typ·ic
col·lude
col·lu·sion
col·lu·sive
col·lu·vial
col·lu·vium (plural ·via or
  ·viums) rock fragments
col·ly Dialect soot
col·lyr·ium (plural ·lyria or
  ·lyr·iums) eye lotion
col·ly·wob·bles
colo·bus monkey
colo·cynth plant
co·loga·rithm
cologne perfume
Co·logne German city
Co·lom·bia South American
  republic; compare
  Columbia
Co·lom·bian
Co·lom·bo Sri Lankan
  capital
co·lon
Co·lón Panamanian port
colo·nel
colo·nel·cy (or
  colo·nel·ship)
co·lo·nial
co·lo·ni·al·ism
co·lo·ni·al·ist
co·lo·ni·al·ly
co·lon·ic
colo·nist
colo·ni·tis variant of colitis
colo·niz·able (or ·nis·able)
colo·ni·za·tion (or ·sa·tion)
colo·nize (or ·nise)
colo·niz·er (or ·nis·er)
col·on·nade
col·on·nad·ed
Col·on·say Hebridean
  island
colo·ny (plural ·nies)
colo·phon emblem
co·lopho·ny rosin

col·or *US spelling of* colour
Colo·ra·do
col·or·ant
col·ora·tion
colo·ra·tu·ra (*or* col·ora·ture) musical term
col·or·if·ic
col·or·im·eter
col·ori·met·ric (*or* ·ri·cal)
col·or·im·etry
co·los·sal
Col·os·sal·ly
Col·os·seum Roman amphitheatre
col·os·seum *variant spelling of* coliseum
co·los·sus (*plural* ·si *or* ·suses)
co·los·to·my (*plural* ·mies) artificial colon opening
co·los·tral
co·los·trum first breast milk
co·loto·my (*plural* ·mies)
col·our (*US* col·or)
col·our·able (*US* ·or·)
col·our·ant (*US* ·or·) (colouration) *incorrect spelling of* coloration
colour-blind (*US* color-)
col·oured (*US* ·ored)
colour-fast (*US* color·)
col·our·ful (*US* ·or·)
col·our·ful·ly (*US* ·or·)
col·our·ing (*US* ·or·)
col·our·ist (*US* ·or·)
col·our·is·tic (*US* ·or·)
col·our·ize (·ise; *US* col·or·ize)
col·our·less (*US* ·or·)
colour·man (*US* color·; *plural* ·men) paint dealer
col·oury (*or* ·ory)
col·pi·tis medical term
col·por·teur book pedlar
Colt (*Trademark*) revolver
colt
col·ter *US spelling of* coulter
colt·ish
colts·foot (*plural* ·foots) plant
colu·brid snake
colu·brine of snakes
co·lu·go lemur
Co·lum·ba constellation

col·um·bar·ium (*plural* ·ia) dovecote
Co·lum·bia US river and city; *compare* Colombia
Co·lum·bian
co·lum·bic
Col·um·bine pantomime character
col·um·bine plant
co·lum·bite mineral
co·lum·bium chemical element
Co·lum·bus US city
colu·mel·la (*plural* ·lae) biology term
colu·mel·lar
col·umn
co·lum·nar
col·umned (*or* ·um·nat·ed)
co·lum·nia·tion
col·umn·ist
co·lure circle on sphere
Col·wyn Bay
coly (*plural* colies) bird; *compare* coley
col·za rape plant
coma (*plural* comas) unconsciousness
coma (*plural* comae) cloud round comet
com·al
Co·man·che (*plural* ·ches *or* ·che)
Co·man·chean
co·mate hairy
co·ma·tose
co·matu·lid (*or* ·matu·la; *plural* ·lids *or* ·lae) marine animal
comb
com·bat
com·bat·able
com·bat·ant
com·bat·er
com·bat·ive
combe *variant spelling of* coomb
comb·er
com·bin·able
com·bi·na·tion
com·bi·na·tive (*or* ·to·rial, ·tory)
com·bine
com·bin·er
comb·ing

com·bo (*plural* ·bos) jazz band
com·bust
com·bus·tibil·ity (*or* ·tible·ness)
com·bus·tible
com·bus·tion
com·bus·tor engine part
come (com·ing, came)
come·back
Com·econ former Communist economic association
co·median
co·medic
co·medi·enne
com·edo (*plural* ·edos *or* ·edo·nes) blackhead
come·down
com·edy (*plural* ·edies)
come·ly (·li·er, ·li·est)
come-on (*noun*)
com·er
co·mes·tible
com·et
come·up·pance
com·fit sweet
com·fort
com·fort·able
com·fort·ably
com·fort·er
com·fort·ing
com·fort·less
com·frey plant
com·fy (·fi·er, ·fi·est)
com·ic
comi·cal
comi·cal·ly
Com·in·form former Communist Information Bureau
com·ing
Com·in·tern former international Communist organization
co·mi·tia Roman assembly
com·ity (*plural* ·ities) courtesy
com·ma
com·mand
com·man·dant
com·man·deer
com·mand·er
com·mand·er·ship
com·mand·ing

com·mand·ment
com·man·do (plural ·dos or
·does)
com·mea·sure
com·media dell'arte Italian
comic theatre
comme il faut French as it
should be
com·memo·rate
com·memo·ra·tion
com·memo·ra·tive (or
·tory)
com·memo·ra·tor
com·mence
com·mence·ment
com·mend
com·mend·able
com·mend·ably
com·men·dam Church
office
com·men·da·tion
com·menda·tory
com·men·sal biology term
com·men·sal·ism (or
·sal·ity)
com·men·su·rable
com·men·su·rate
com·men·su·ra·tion
com·ment
com·men·tar·ial
com·men·tary (plural
·taries)
com·men·tate
com·men·ta·tor
com·ment·er
com·merce
com·mer·cial
com·mer·cial·ism
com·mer·cial·ist
com·mer·cial·is·tic
com·mer·ci·al·ity
com·mer·ciali·za·tion (or
·sa·tion)
com·mer·cial·ize (or ·ise)
com·mer·cial·ly
com·mère female compere
com·mi·na·tion
threatening vengeance
com·mina·tory
com·min·gle
com·mi·nute reduce to
fragments
com·mi·nu·tion
com·mis agent
com·mis·er·ate

com·mis·era·tion
com·mis·era·tive
com·mis·era·tor
com·mis·sar
com·mis·sar·ial
com·mis·sari·at
com·mis·sary (plural
·saries)
com·mis·sion
com·mis·sion·aire
com·mis·sion·al (or ·ary)
com·mis·sion·er
com·mis·su·ral
com·mis·sure anatomy
term
com·mit (·mit·ting,
·mit·ted)
com·mit·ment
com·mit·tal
com·mit·tee
committee·man (plural
·men)
com·mit·ter
(committment) incorrect
spelling of commitment
com·mode
com·mo·di·ous
com·mod·ity (plural ·ities)
com·mo·dore
com·mon
com·mon·able legal term
com·mon·age legal term
com·mon·al·ity
commonness
com·mon·al·ty (or ·ity)
ordinary people
com·mon·er
com·mon·ly
com·mon·ness
common·place
Com·mons (House of)
common·weal Archaic
common goods;
commonwealth
Common·wealth of
Nations; republican
England
common·wealth
independent community
com·mo·tion
com·mo·tion·al
com·mu·nal
com·mu·nal·ism
com·mu·nal·ist
com·mu·nal·is·tic

com·mu·nal·ity
commu·nali·za·tion (or
·sa·tion)
com·mu·nal·ize (or ·ise)
Com·mu·nade supporter of
Paris Commune
com·mu·nard member of a
commune
Com·mune Paris
Revolutionary government
com·mune
com·mu·ni·cabil·ity (or
·cable·ness)
com·mu·ni·cable
com·mu·ni·cant
com·mu·ni·cate
com·mu·ni·ca·tion
com·mu·ni·ca·tive
com·mu·ni·ca·tor
com·mu·ni·ca·tory
Com·mun·ion Eucharist
com·mun·ion
com·mun·ion·al
com·mun·ion·ist
com·mu·ni·qué
com·mun·ism
Com·mun·ist political party
com·mun·ist supporter of
communism
com·mu·nis·tic
com·mu·ni·tar·ian
com·mu·nity (plural ·nities)
com·mu·ni·za·tion (or
·sa·tion)
com·mu·nize (or ·nise)
nationalize
com·mut·able
exchangeable
com·mu·tate
com·mu·ta·tion
com·mu·ta·tive involving
substitution
com·mu·ta·tor electrical
device
com·mute
com·mut·er
Como Italian city and lake
Como·ros island country
co·mose hairy
comp Slang compositor
com·pact
com·pact·er
com·pact·ness
com·pan·der sound
transmission

com·pan·ion
com·pan·ion·able
com·pan·ion·ably
com·pan·ion·able
com·pan·ion·ate
com·pan·ion·ship
com·pan·ion·way stairway on ship
com·pa·ny (*plural* ·nies)
com·pa·rabil·ity
com·pa·rable
com·pa·rably
com·para·tive
com·para·tive·ly
com·para·tor
com·pare
com·par·er
com·pari·son
com·part·ment
com·part·men·tal
com·part·men·tali·za·tion (*or* ·sa·tion)
com·part·men·tal·ize (*or* ·ise)
com·part·men·ted
com·pass
com·pass·able
com·pas·sion
com·pas·sion·ate
com·pat·ibil·ity
com·pat·ible
com·pat·ibly
com·pat·ri·ot
com·pat·ri·ot·ic
com·pat·ri·ot·ism
com·peer equal status
com·pel (·pel·ling, ·pelled)
com·pel·ler
com·pen·di·ous
com·pen·dium (*plural* ·diums *or* ·dia)
com·pen·sate
com·pen·sa·tion
com·pen·sa·tive
com·pen·sa·tor
com·pen·sa·tory
com·pere
com·pete
com·pe·tence
com·pe·ten·cy (*plural* ·cies) legal term
com·pe·tent
com·pe·ti·tion
com·peti·tive
com·peti·tor

com·pi·la·tion
com·pile
com·pil·er
com·pla·cen·cy (*or* com·pla·cence; *plural* ·cencies *or* ·cences) self-satisfaction; *compare* complaisance
com·pla·cent
com·plain
com·plain·ant
com·plain·er
com·plaint
com·plai·sance willingness to comply; *compare* complacency
com·plai·sant
com·ple·ment complete; that which completes; *compare* compliment
com·ple·men·tary (*or* ·tal)
com·ple·men·tiz·er grammar term
com·plete
com·plete·ness
com·plet·er
com·ple·tion
com·ple·tive
com·plex
com·plex·ion
com·plex·ity (*plural* ·ities)
com·pli·ance (*or* ·an·cy)
com·pli·ant (*or* ·able)
com·pli·cate
com·pli·cat·ed
com·pli·ca·tion
com·plic·ity (*plural* ·ities)
com·pli·er
com·pli·ment praise; *compare* complement
com·pli·men·tary
com·pline (*or* ·plin) canonical hour
com·ply (·plies, ·ply·ing, ·plied)
com·po (*plural* ·pos) mixture; *Austral* compensation
com·po·nent
com·po·nen·tial
com·po·ny (*or* ·ne) heraldic term
com·port
com·port·ment
com·pose

com·pos·er
com·po·site
com·po·si·tion
com·po·si·tion·al
com·posi·tor
com·pos men·tis *Latin* sane
com·post
com·po·sure
com·pote
com·pound
com·pound·er
com·pra·dor foreign agent
com·pre·hend
com·pre·hen·sibil·ity (*or* ·sible·ness)
com·pre·hen·sible (*or* ·hend·ible)
com·pre·hen·sibly
com·pre·hen·sion
com·pre·hen·sive
com·press
com·press·ibil·ity (*or* ·ible·ness)
com·press·ible
com·pres·sion
com·pres·sion·al
com·pres·sive
com·pres·sor
com·pris·able
com·pris·al
com·prise
com·pro·mise
com·pro·mis·er
Comp·tom·eter (*Trademark*)
comp·trol·ler
com·pul·sion
com·pul·sive
com·pul·so·ry
com·pul·so·ri·ly
com·punc·tion
com·punc·tious
com·put·abil·ity
com·put·able
com·pu·ta·tion
com·pu·ta·tion·al
com·pute
com·put·er
com·put·eri·za·tion (*or* ·sa·tion)
com·put·er·ize (*or* ·ise)
com·rade
com·rade·ship
com·sat *short for* communications satellite

com·stock·ery *US* excessive censorship

Comus Roman god

con (con·ning, conned)

con amo·re musical term

Con·akry capital of Guinea

co·na·tion psychology term

cona·tive linguistics term

co·na·tus (*plural* ·tus) striving

con brio musical term

con·cat·enate

con·cat·ena·tion series of events

con·cave

con·cav·ity (*plural* ·ities)

concavo-concave

concavo-convex

con·ceal

con·ceal·ment

con·cede

con·ced·er

con·ceit

con·ceit·ed

con·ceiv·able

con·ceiv·ably

con·ceive

con·cel·ebrate

con·cel·ebra·tion

(concensus) *incorrect spelling of* consensus

con·cen·trate

con·cen·tra·tion

con·cen·tra·tive

con·cen·tra·tor

con·cen·tre to concentrate

con·cen·tric (*or* ·tri·cal)

con·cen·tri·cal·ly

con·cen·tric·ity

Con·cep·ción Chilean city

con·cept

con·cep·ta·cle botany term

con·cep·tion

con·cep·tion·al

con·cep·tive

con·cep·tual

con·cep·tu·al·ism

con·cep·tu·al·ist

con·cep·tu·al·is·tic

con·cep·tu·ali·za·tion (*or* ·sa·tion)

con·cep·tu·al·ize (*or* ·ise)

con·cern

con·cerned

con·cern·ed·ly

con·cern·ing

con·cert

con·cer·tan·te musical work

con·cert·ed

con·cert·go·er

con·cer·ti·na (·nas, ·na·ing, ·naed)

con·cer·ti·no (*plural* ·ni) musical work

con·cer·tize

con·cer·to (*plural* ·tos *or* ·ti)

con·cer·to gros·so (*plural* ·ti gros·si)

con·ces·sible

con·ces·sion

con·ces·sion·aire (*or* ·er, ·ary; *plural* ·aires, ·ers, *or* ·aries)

con·ces·sion·ary

con·ces·sive

conch (*plural* conchs *or* conches) mollusc

con·cha (*plural* ·chae) shell-shaped part

con·chal

con·chif·er·ous

con·chio·lin protein

con·choid geometric curve

con·choi·dal geology term

con·cho·logi·cal

con·cholo·gist

con·chol·ogy study of shells

con·chy (*plural* ·chies) *Slang* conscientious objector

con·ci·erge

con·cili·ar of ecclesiastical councils

con·cili·ate

con·cili·ation

con·cilia·tive

con·cili·ator

con·cilia·tory (*or* ·tive)

con·cin·nity (*plural* ·nities) harmonious arrangement

con·cin·nous

con·cise

con·ci·sion

con·clave

con·clav·ist

con·clude

con·clu·sion

con·clu·sive

con·coct

con·coct·er (*or* ·coc·tor)

con·coc·tion

con·coc·tive

con·comi·tance

con·comi·tant

Con·cord *US and Australian cities; compare* Concorde

con·cord agreement

con·cord·ance

con·cord·ant

con·cor·dat treaty

Con·corde airliner; *compare* Concord

con·course

con·cres·cence biology term

con·crete

con·cre·tion

con·cre·tion·ary

con·cre·tive

con·creti·za·tion (*or* ·sa·tion)

con·cre·tize (*or* ·tise)

con·cu·bi·nage

con·cu·bine

con·cu·pis·cence

con·cu·pis·cent

con·cur (·cur·ring, ·curred)

con·cur·rence

con·cur·rent

con·cuss

con·cus·sion

con·cus·sive

con·demn

con·demn·able

con·dem·na·tion

con·dem·na·tory

con·demn·er

con·den·sabil·ity (*or* ·sibil·ity)

con·den·sable (*or* ·sible)

con·den·sate

con·den·sa·tion

con·dense

con·dens·er

con·de·scend

con·de·scend·ence legal term

con·de·scend·ing

con·de·scen·sion

con·dign well-deserved

con·di·ment

con·di·tion

con·di·tion·al

con·di·tion·al·ity

con·di·tion·al·ly

con·di·tioned

con·di·tion·er

con·di·tion·ing
con·do·la·tory
con·dole
con·do·lence (or ·dole·ment)
con·dol·er
con·dom
con·do·min·ium (plural ·iums)
con·do·na·tion
con·done
con·don·er
con·dor vulture
con·dot·tiere (plural ·tieri) mercenary
con·duce
con·duc·er
con·duc·ible
con·du·cive
con·duct
con·duct·ance physics term
con·duct·ible
con·duc·tion
con·duc·tive
con·duc·tiv·ity (plural ·ities)
con·duc·tor (fem ·tress)
con·duit
con·du·pli·cate botany term
con·du·pli·ca·tion
con·dy·lar
con·dyle bone projection
con·dy·loid
con·dy·lo·ma (plural ·mas or ·ma·ta) tumour
con·dy·loma·tous
cone
cone·flower
co·ney variant spelling of cony
Co·ney Is·land US resort
con·fab Slang chat
con·fabu·late
con·fabu·la·tion
con·fabu·la·tor
con·fabu·la·tory
con·fect combine ingredients
con·fec·tion
con·fec·tion·ary (plural ·aries) place where confections are made
con·fec·tion·er

con·fec·tion·ery (plural ·eries) sweets
Con·fed·era·cy seceding US states
con·fed·era·cy (plural ·cies)
Con·fed·er·ate
con·fed·er·ate
Con·fed·era·tion original US states
con·fed·era·tion
con·fed·era·tion·ism
con·fed·era·tion·ist
con·fer (·fer·ring, ·ferred)
con·feree (or ·fer·ree)
con·fer·ence
con·fer·en·tial
con·fer·ment (or ·fer·ral)
con·fer·rable
con·fer·rer
con·fer·va (plural ·vae or ·vas) alga
con·fer·val
con·fer·void
con·fess
confessant
con·fess·ed·ly
con·fes·sion
con·fes·sion·al
con·fes·sion·ary
con·fes·sor
con·fet·ti
con·fi·dant (fem ·dante) person in whom one confides
con·fide
con·fi·dence
con·fi·dent self-assured
con·fi·den·tial
con·fi·den·ti·al·ity (or ·tial·ness)
con·fi·den·tial·ly
con·fid·er
con·fid·ing
con·figu·ra·tion
con·figu·ra·tion·al (or ·ra·tive)
con·figu·ra·tion·ism Gestalt psychology
con·figu·ra·tion·ist
con·fin·able (or ·fine·able)
con·fine
con·fine·ment
con·firm
con·firm·and candidate for confirmation

con·fir·ma·tion
con·firma·tory (or ·tive)
con·fis·cable
con·fis·ca·tor
con·fis·ca·tory
Con·fit·eor prayer
con·fi·ture confection
con·fla·gra·tion
con·fla·gra·tive
con·flate combine
con·fla·tion
con·flict
con·flic·tion
con·flic·tive (or ·tory)
con·flu·ence (or con·flux)
con·flu·ent
con·fo·cal
con·form
con·form·abil·ity (or ·able·ness)
con·form·able
con·form·ably
con·for·mal maths term
con·for·ma·tion
con·form·er
con·form·ist
con·form·ity (or ·ance; plural ·ities or ·ances)
con·found
con·found·er
con·fra·ter·nal
con·fra·ter·nity (plural ·nities)
con·frère fellow member
con·front
con·fron·ta·tion (or con·front·ment)
con·front·er
Con·fu·cian
Con·fu·cian·ism
Con·fu·cian·ist
con fuo·co musical term
con·fus·able
con·fuse
con·fus·ed·ly
con·fus·ing
con·fus·ing·ly
con·fu·sion
con·fu·ta·tion
con·fu·ta·tive
con·fute
con·fut·er
con·ga (·ga·ing, ·gaed) dance; compare conger

con·gé dismissal
con·geal
con·geal·ment
con·ge·la·tion
con·ge·ner member of group
con·ge·ner·ic
con·gen·ial
con·ge·ni·al·ity (or con·gen·ial·ness)
con·gen·ial·ly
con·geni·tal present from birth
con·geni·tal·ly
con·ger eel; compare conga
con·ge·ries collection
con·gest
con·gest·ible
con·ges·tion
con·ges·tive
con·gi·us (plural ·gii) unit
con·glo·bate form into ball
con·glo·ba·tion
con·glom·er·ate
con·glom·er·at·ic (or ·it·ic)
con·glom·era·tion
con·glu·ti·nant
con·glu·ti·nate heal together
con·glu·ti·na·tive
Con·go African republic
con·go eel
Con·go·lese
con·gou (or ·go) China tea
con·grats
con·gratu·late
con·gratu·la·tion
con·gratu·la·tor
con·gratu·la·tory
con·gre·gant
con·gre·gate
con·gre·ga·tion
Con·gre·ga·tion·al evangelical church
con·gre·ga·tion·al
Con·gre·ga·tion·al·ism
Con·gre·ga·tion·al·ist
con·gre·ga·tive
con·gre·ga·tor (or ·gre·gant)
Con·gress US legislature
con·gress
Con·gres·sion·al
con·gres·sion·al
Con·gres·sion·al·ist

con·gres·sion·al·ist
Congress·man (plural ·men)
Congress·woman (plural ·women)
con·gru·ence (or ·en·cy; plural ·ences or ·cies)
con·gru·ent
con·gru·ity (plural ·ities)
con·gru·ous
con·ic (or coni·cal)
con·ics
co·nid·ial (or ·ian)
co·nidio·phore
co·nid·ium (plural ·nidia) fungal spore
co·ni·fer
co·nif·er·ous
co·ni·ine (or co·nin, co·nine) alkaloid
co·nium hemlock
con·jec·tur·al
con·jec·ture
con·jec·tur·er
con·join
con·join·ed·ly
con·join·er
con·joint
con·ju·gable
con·ju·gal
con·ju·gal·ly
con·ju·gal·ity
con·ju·gant
con·ju·gate
con·ju·ga·tion
con·ju·ga·tion·al
con·ju·ga·tive
con·ju·ga·tor
con·junct
con·junc·tion
con·junc·tion·al
con·junc·ti·va (plural ·vas or ·vae) eyeball membrane
con·junc·ti·val
con·junc·tive
con·junc·ti·vi·tis
con·junc·tur·al
con·junc·ture
con·jura·tion
con·jure
con·jur·er (or ·or)
conk
conk·er
con moto musical term

Con·nacht Northern Irish province
con·nate
con·natu·ral
Con·naught former name of Connacht
con·nect
con·nect·ible (or ·able)
Con·necti·cut
con·nec·tion (or ·nex·ion)
con·nec·tion·al (or ·nex·ion·al)
con·nec·tive
con·nect·or (or ·er)
conned
Con·ne·ma·ra
con·ning
con·nip·tion US rage
con·niv·ance (or ·ence)
con·nive
con·niv·ent
con·niv·er
con·nois·seur
con·no·ta·tion
con·no·ta·tive (or con·no·tive)
con·note
con·nu·bial
con·nu·bi·al·ity
con·nu·bi·al·ly
co·no·dont fossil tooth
co·noid geometry term
co·noi·dal
con·quer
con·quer·or
con·quest
con·quis·ta·dor (plural ·dors or ·do·res)
con·san·guin·eous (or ·guine)
con·san·guin·ity
con·science
conscience-stricken
con·sci·en·tious
con·sci·en·tious·ness
con·scion·able
con·scious
con·scious·ness
con·script
con·scrip·tion
con·scrip·tion·al
con·scrip·tion·ist
con·se·crate
con·se·cra·tion
con·se·cra·tor

con·se·cra·tory (or ·tive)
con·se·cu·tion sequence of
  events
con·secu·tive
con·sen·sual
con·sen·sus
con·sent
con·sent·er
con·sen·tience
con·sen·tient in agreement
con·se·quence
con·se·quent
con·se·quen·tial
con·se·quen·tial·ly
con·se·quen·ti·al·ity (or
  ·tial·ness)
con·se·quent·ly
con·serv·able
con·serv·an·cy (plural ·cies)
con·ser·va·tion
con·ser·va·tion·al
con·ser·va·tion·ist
con·serva·tism
Con·serva·tive political
  party
con·serva·tive opposed to
  change
con·serva·toire musical
  institution
con·ser·va·tor custodian
con·serva·tory (plural
  ·tories)
con·serve
con·serv·er
Con·sett Durham town
con·sid·er
con·sid·er·able
con·sid·er·ably
con·sid·er·ate
con·sid·era·tion
con·sid·er·er
con·sign
con·sign·able
con·signa·tion
con·signee
con·sign·ment
con·sign·or (or ·er)
con·sist
con·sist·en·cy (or ·ence;
  plural ·cies or ·ences)
con·sist·ent
con·sis·to·rial (or ·rian)
con·sis·tory (plural ·tories)
  diocesan court
con·so·ci·ate

con·so·cia·tion
con·so·cies (plural ·cies)
  ecology term
con·sol·able
con·so·la·tion
con·sola·tory
con·sole
con·sol·er
con·soli·date
con·soli·da·tion
con·soli·da·tor
con·sols government
  securities
con·so·lute chemistry term
con·som·mé
con·so·nance (or ·nan·cy;
  plural ·nances or ·cies)
  agreement
con·so·nant
con·so·nan·tal
con·sort
con·sort·er
con·sor·tial
con·sor·tium (plural ·tia)
con·spe·cif·ic
con·spec·tus overall view
con·spicu·ous
con·spicu·ous·ness
con·spira·cy (plural ·cies)
con·spira·tor
con·spira·to·rial (or
  con·spira·tory)
con·spira·to·rial·ly
con·spira·tress
con·spire
con·sta·ble
con·stabu·lary (plural
  ·laries)
Con·stance European lake
Con·stance (or Kon·stanz)
  German city
con·stan·cy
con·stant
Con·stan·ţa Romanian port
con·stant·an alloy
Con·stan·tine Algerian city
Con·stan·ti·no·ple
con·sta·ta·tion establishing
  truth
con·stel·late form clusters
con·stel·la·tion
con·stel·la·tory
con·ster·nate
con·ster·na·tion
con·sti·pate

con·sti·pat·ed
con·sti·pa·tion
con·stitu·en·cy (plural ·cies)
con·stitu·ent
con·sti·tute
con·sti·tut·er (or ·tu·tor)
con·sti·tu·tion
con·sti·tu·tion·al
con·sti·tu·tion·al·ism
con·sti·tu·tion·al·ist
con·sti·tu·tion·al·ity
con·sti·tu·tion·al·ly
con·sti·tu·tive
con·strain
con·strain·er
con·straint
con·strict
con·stric·tion
con·stric·tive
con·stric·tor
con·struct
con·struct·ible
con·struc·tion
con·struc·tion·al
con·struc·tive
con·struc·tiv·ism art
  movement
con·struc·tiv·ist
con·struc·tor (or ·ter)
con·strue (·stru·ing,
  ·strued)
con·stru·er
con·sub·stan·tia·tion
  Christian doctrine
con·suetude custom
con·suetu·di·nary
con·sul
con·su·lar
con·su·late
con·sult
con·sul·tan·cy (plural ·cies)
con·sult·ant
con·sul·ta·tion
con·sul·ta·tive (or ta·tory,
  con·sul·tive)
con·sult·er (or ·sul·tor)
con·sum·able
con·sume
con·sum·er
con·sum·er·ism
con·sum·mate
con·sum·ma·tion
con·sum·ma·tive (or ·tory)
con·sum·ma·tor
con·sump·tion

con·sump·tive
con·tact
con·tac·tor
con·tac·tual
con·ta·gion
con·ta·gious
con·ta·gious·ness
con·ta·gium (*plural* ·gia) transmission of disease
con·tain
con·tain·er
con·tain·eri·za·tion (*or* ·sa·tion)
con·tain·er·ize (*or* ·ise)
con·tain·ment
con·tami·nant
con·tami·nate
con·tami·na·tion
con·tami·na·tor
con·tan·go (*noun, plural* ·gos; *verb* ·goes, ·go·ing, ·goed) stock-exchange term
conte *French* short story
con·té crayon
con·temn scorn
con·temn·er (*or* ·tem·nor)
con·tem·nible
con·tem·plate
con·tem·pla·tion
con·tem·pla·tive
con·tem·pla·tor
con·tem·po·ra·neity
con·tem·po·ra·neous
con·tem·po·rari·ly
con·tem·po·rary (*plural* ·raries)
con·tem·po·rize (*or* ·rise) synchronize
con·tempt
con·tempt·ibil·ity (*or* ·ible·ness)
con·tempt·ible
con·temp·tu·ous
con·tend
con·tend·er
con·tent
con·tent·ed
con·ten·tion
con·ten·tion·al
con·ten·tious
con·tent·ment
con·ter·mi·nous
con·test
con·test·able

con·test·ant
con·tes·ta·tion
con·test·er
con·text
con·tex·tual
con·tex·tu·al·ize (*or* ·ise)
con·tex·tual·ly
con·tex·tur·al
con·tex·ture weaving
con·ti·gu·ity
con·tigu·ous
con·ti·nence (*or* con·ti·nen·cy)
Con·ti·nent mainland Europe
con·ti·nent large landmass
Con·ti·nen·tal
con·ti·nen·tal
Con·ti·nen·tal·ism
Con·ti·nen·ta·list
con·ti·nen·tal·ity
con·tin·gence
con·tin·gen·cy (*plural* ·cies)
con·tin·gent
con·tinu·able
con·tin·ual
con·tinu·al·ity (*or* ·al·ness)
con·tin·ual·ly
con·tinu·ance
con·tinu·ant
con·tinu·ation
con·tinu·ative linguistics term
con·tinu·ator
con·tinue
con·tinu·er
con·tinu·ing·ly
con·ti·nu·ity (*plural* ·ities)
con·tinuo (*plural* ·tinuos) musical term
con·tinu·ous
con·tin·uum (*plural* ·tinua *or* ·tin·uums)
con·to (*plural* ·tos) Portuguese currency
con·tort
con·tor·tion
con·tor·tion·al
con·tor·tion·ist
con·tor·tion·is·tic
con·tour
contra·band
contra·band·ist
contra·bass musical instrument

contra·bass·ist
contra·bas·soon
contra·bas·soon·ist
contra·cep·tion
contra·cep·tive
con·tract
con·tract·able able to enter contract
con·tract·ibil·ity (*or* ·ible·ness)
con·tract·ible able to be shortened
con·trac·tile
con·trac·til·ity
con·trac·tion
con·trac·tion·al
con·trac·tive
con·trac·tor
con·trac·tual
con·trac·tual·ly
con·trac·ture muscle disorder
contra·dict
contra·dict·able
contra·dict·er (*or* ·dic·tor)
contra·dic·tion
contra·dic·tive (*or* ·tious)
contra·dic·tory
contra·dis·tinc·tion
contra·dis·tinc·tive
contra·dis·tin·guish
con·trail aircraft vapour trail
contra·in·di·cant
contra·in·di·cate
contra·in·di·ca·tion
con·tral·to (*plural* ·tos *or* ·ti)
contra·po·si·tion
con·trap·tion
contra·pun·tal
contra·pun·tal·ly
contra·pun·tist (*or* ·tal·ist)
contra·ri·ety (*plural* ·eties)
con·tra·ri·ly
con·tra·ri·ness
con·tra·ri·wise
con·tra·ry (*plural* ·ries)
con·trast
con·tras·tive
con·trasty
contra·val·la·tion fortifications
contra·vene
contra·ven·er
contra·ven·tion

contra·yer·va plant root
con·tre·danse dance
con·tre·temps (plural ·temps)
con·trib·ute
con·tri·bu·tion
con·tribu·tive
con·tribu·tor
con·tribu·to·rial
con·tribu·tory
con·trite
con·tri·tion
con·triv·ance
con·trive
con·trol (·trol·ling, ·trolled)
con·trol·lable
con·trol·lably
con·trol·ler
con·tro·ver·sial
contro·ver·sial·ism
contro·ver·sial·ist
con·tro·ver·sial·ly
con·tro·ver·sy (plural ·sies)
con·tro·vert deny
contro·vert·er
contro·vert·ible
con·tu·ma·cious obstinate
con·tu·ma·cy (plural ·cies)
con·tu·meli·ous insolent
con·tu·mely (plural ·melies)
con·tuse bruise
con·tu·sion
con·tu·sioned
con·tu·sive
co·nun·drum
con·ur·ba·tion
con·ure parrot
con·va·lesce
con·va·les·cence
con·va·les·cent
con·vec·tion
con·vec·tion·al
con·vec·tive
con·vec·tor
con·ven·able
con·ve·nance French propriety
con·vene
con·ven·er
con·veni·ence
con·veni·ent
con·vent
con·ven·ti·cle secret assembly

con·ven·tion
con·ven·tion·al
con·ven·tion·al·ism
con·ven·tion·al·ist
con·ven·tion·al·ity (plural ·ities)
con·ven·tion·ali·za·tion (or ·sa·tion)
con·ven·tion·al·ize (or ·ise)
con·ven·tion·al·ly
con·ven·tual of a convent
con·verge
con·ver·gence
con·ver·gen·cy
con·ver·gent
con·vers·able
con·ver·sance (or ·san·cy)
con·ver·sant
con·ver·sa·tion
con·ver·sa·tion·al
con·ver·sa·tion·al·ist (or ·tion·ist)
con·ver·sa·tion·al·ly
con·ver·sa·zio·ne (plural ·zio·ni or ·zio·nes) Italian artistic discussion
con·verse
con·vers·er
con·ver·sion
con·ver·sion·al (or ·ary)
con·vert
con·vert·er (or ·ver·tor)
con·vert·ibil·ity (or ·ible·ness)
con·vert·ible
con·verti·plane (or ·verta·, ·verto·)
con·vex
con·vex·ity (plural ·ities)
convexo-concave
convexo-convex
con·vey
con·vey·able
con·vey·ance
con·vey·anc·er
con·vey·anc·ing
con·vey·or (or ·er)
con·vict
con·vict·able (or ·ible)
con·vic·tion
con·vic·tive convincing
con·vince
con·vinc·er
con·vinc·ible
con·vinc·ing

con·viv·ial
con·vivi·al·ity
con·vivi·al·ly
con·vo·ca·tion legislative assembly
con·vo·ca·tion·al
con·vo·ca·tive
con·vo·ca·tor
con·voke summon
con·vok·er
con·vo·lute
con·vo·lut·ed
con·vo·lu·tion
con·volve coil
con·vol·vu·la·ceous
con·vol·vu·lus (plural ·luses or ·li) plant
con·voy
con·vul·sant
con·vulse
con·vul·sion
con·vul·sive
cony (or co·ney; plural conies or ·neys)
coo (coo·ing, cooed)
Cooch Be·har Indian city
cooee (or coo·ey)
cook
cook·able
cook·book
cook·er
cook·ery
cook·house
cookie
cook·ing
cook·out US barbecue
cool
coo·la·bah (or ·li·) tree
cool·ant
cool·er
coolie (or cooly; plural coolies)
cool·ly (adv)
cool·ness
coomb (or combe, coombe) valley
coon
coon·can card game
coon·skin
coon·tie plant
coop
co-op
coop·er barrel-maker
coop·er·age
co·oper·ate (or co-operate)

co·opera·tion (or co-
operation)
co·opera·tive (or co-
operative)
co·opera·tor (or co-
operator)
coop·ery
co·opt (or co-opt)
co·opta·tion (or co-
optation)
co·opta·tive (or co-
optative)
co·option (or co-option)
co·or·di·nal (or co-ordinal)
biology term
co·or·di·nate (or co-
ordinate)
co·or·di·na·tion (or co-
ordina·tion)
co·or·di·na·tor (or co-
ordina·tor)
Coorg former Indian
province
coot
cootch hiding place
cootie US louse
cop (cop·ping, copped)
co·pai·ba (or ·va) resin
co·pal resin
co·palm resin
co·par·cenary (or ·ceny)
joint ownership
co·par·cener
co·part·ner
cope
Co·pen·ha·gen
co·pepod plankton
constituent
co·per horse dealer
Co·per·ni·can
cope·stone
copi·er
co·pilot
cop·ing
co·pi·ous
co·pla·nar
co·pla·nar·ity
co·poly·mer chemistry term
co·poly·meri·za·tion (or
·sa·tion)
co·poly·mer·ize (or ·ise)
cop·per
cop·per·as chemical
compound
copper·head snake

copper·plate
copper·smith
cop·pery
cop·pice variant of copse
cop·ra coconut kernel
cop·ro·la·lia obscene
language
cop·ro·lite fossilized faeces
cop·ro·lit·ic
cop·rophagous
cop·ropha·gy
cop·ro·philia abnormal
interest in faeces
co·prophi·lous growing on
dung
copse (or cop·pice)
Copt
cop·ter short for helicopter
Cop·tic language; Church
copu·la (plural ·las or ·lae)
linking verb; compare
cupola
copu·lar
copu·late
copu·la·tion
copu·la·tive
copy (noun, plural copies;
verb copies, copy·ing,
copied)
copy·book
copy-edit
copy-editor
copy·hold
copy·holder
copy·ist
copy·read US subedit
copy·right
copy·writer
copy·writing
coq au vin chicken dish
coque·li·cot corn poppy
co·quet (·quet·ting,
·quet·ted) to flirt
co·quet·ry (plural ·ries)
co·quette
co·quet·tish
co·quille seafood
co·qui·na limestone
co·qui·to (plural ·tos) tree
cora·cii·form ornithology
term
cora·cle
cora·coid zoology term
cor·al animal; jewellery;
compare corral

cor·al·line (or ·loid)
cor·al·lite fossil coral
coral-root
cor an·glais (plural cors
an·glais) musical
instrument
cor·ban biblical gift
cor·beil (or ·beille)
architectural ornament
cor·bel (·bel·ling, ·belled)
bracket on building
cor·bicu·la (plural ·lae)
pollen basket
cor bli·mey
cord string; anatomical
senses; compare chord
cord·age
cor·date heart-shaped;
compare chordate
cord·ed
Cor·delier Franciscan friar
Cor·deliers French political
club
cor·dial
cor·di·al·ity (plural ·ities)
cor·di·al·ly
cor·di·er·ite mineral
cor·di·form heart-shaped
cor·dil·lera mountain range
Cor·dil·leras American
mountain range
cord·ite explosive
cord·less
Cór·do·ba Argentinian and
Spanish cities
cor·do·ba Nicaraguan
currency
cor·don
cor·don bleu
cor·do·van leather
cords corduroy trousers
cor·du·roy
cord·wood
core
co·reli·gion·ist
co·reop·sis plant
corer
co-respon·den·cy
co-respond·ent adulterer;
compare correspondent
corf (plural corves) wagon
Cor·fam (Trademark)
Cor·fu
cor·gi (plural ·gis)
co·ria·ceous of leather

co·ri·an·der

Cor·inth Greek port; region of ancient Greece

Co·rin·thian

Co·rin·thians New Testament book

co·rium (plural ·ria) layer beneath skin

Cork

cork

cork·age

cork·board

corked

cork·er

cork·ing

cork·screw

cork·wood

corky

corm

cor·mel new corm

cor·mo·phyte botany term

cor·mo·phyt·ic

cor·mo·rant

cor·mous

corn

cor·na·ceous botany term

corn·cob

corn·cockle plant

corn·crake bird

corn·crib US maize store

cor·nea (plural ·neas or ·neae) eye layer

cor·neal

corned

cor·nel plant

cor·nel·ian of cornel

cor·nel·ian (or car·) gemstone

cor·neous horny

cor·ner

corner·stone

cor·net

cor·net·ist (or ·net·tist)

cor·nett (or ·net) old woodwind instrument

corn·field

corn·flakes

corn·flour cooking ingredient

corn·flower plant

corn·husk

cor·nice architectural embellishment

cor·niche coastal road

cor·nicu·late horned

Cor·nish

corn·stalk Austral native Australian

corn·starch US cornflour

cor·nu (plural ·nua) anatomical part

cor·nual

cor·nu·co·pia

cor·nute (or ·nut·ed) hornlike

Corn·wall

corny (corni·er, corni·est)

co·rol·la flower petals

co·rol·la·ceous

cor·ol·lary (plural ·laries)

co·ro·na (plural ·nas or ·nae)

Co·ro·na Aus·tra·lis constellation

Co·ro·na Bo·real·is constellation

co·ro·nach Scot dirge

co·ro·na·graph (or ·no·) optical instrument

coro·nal

coro·nary (plural ·naries) artery; thrombosis

coro·na·tion

coro·ner

coro·ner·ship

coro·net

coro·net·ed

cor·po·ra plural of corpus

cor·po·ral army officer; of the body; compare corporeal; caporal

cor·po·ra·le altar cloth

cor·po·ral·ity

cor·po·ral·ship

cor·po·rate

cor·po·ra·tion

cor·po·ra·tive

cor·po·ra·tor member of corporation

cor·po·real physical; compare corporal

cor·po·real·ly

cor·po·real·ity (or ·ness)

cor·po·reity bodily nature

cor·po·sant atmospheric phenomenon

corps (plural corps) group of people

corpse dead body

cor·pu·lence (or ·len·cy)

cor·pu·lent

cor·pus (plural ·po·ra)

Cor·pus Chris·ti Christian festival

cor·pus·cle

cor·pus·cu·lar

cor·pus de·lic·ti legal term

cor·pus lu·teum (plural cor·po·ra lu·tea) tissue in ovary

cor·pus stria·tum (plural cor·po·ra stria·ta) brain part

cor·pus vile (plural cor·po·ra vilia) Latin worthless body

cor·rade geology term

cor·ral (·ral·ling, ·ralled) animal enclosure; compare coral

cor·ra·sion geology term; compare corrosion

cor·ra·sive

cor·rect

cor·rect·able (or ·ible)

cor·rec·tion

cor·recti·tude

cor·rec·tive

cor·rect·ness

cor·rec·tor

Cor·regi·dor Philippine island

cor·re·late

cor·re·la·tion

cor·rela·tive mutually related

cor·rela·tive·ness (or ·tiv·ity)

cor·re·spond

cor·re·spond·ence

cor·re·spond·ent one who corresponds; compare co-respondent

Cor·rèze French region

cor·ri·da Spanish bullfight

cor·ri·dor

cor·rie hollow in hill

Cor·rie·dale sheep

Cor·ri·en·tes Argentine port

cor·ri·gen·dum (plural ·da)

cor·ri·gibil·ity

cor·ri·gible

cor·robo·rant

cor·robo·rate

cor·robo·ra·tion

cor·robo·ra·tive
cor·robo·ra·tor
cor·robo·ree *Austral* noisy gathering
cor·rod·ant (*or* ·ent)
cor·rode
cor·rod·er
cor·rod·ibil·ity
cor·rod·ible
cor·ro·sion wearing away; *compare* corrasion
cor·ro·sive
cor·ru·gate
cor·ru·gat·ed
cor·ru·ga·tion
cor·ru·ga·tor muscle
cor·rupt
cor·rupt·er (*or* ·rup·tor)
cor·rupt·ibil·ity (*or* ·ible·ness)
cor·rup·tible
cor·rup·tion
cor·rup·tion·ist
cor·rup·tive
cor·sac fox
cor·sage
cor·sair
corse *Archaic* corpse; *compare* coarse; course
corse·let (*or* cors·let)
cor·set
cor·setière (*masc* ·setier)
cor·set·ry
Cor·si·ca
Cor·si·can
cor·tege (*or* ·tège)
Cor·tes Spanish parliament
cor·tex (*plural* ·ti·ces)
cor·ti·cal
cor·ti·cate (*or* ·cat·ed) having rind or bark
cor·ti·ca·tion
cor·ti·co·ster·oid (*or* cor·ti·coid) hormone
cor·ti·co·ster·one
cor·ti·co·tro·phic (*US* ·pic)
cor·ti·co·tro·phin (*US* ·pin) hormone
cor·ti·sol hormone
cor·ti·sone
co·run·dum mineral
Co·run·na *variant of* La Coruña
cor·rus·cate sparkle
cor·us·ca·tion

cor·vée feudal labour
corves *plural of* corf
cor·vette
cor·vine of crows
co·ryda·lis plant
cor·ymb botany term
co·rym·bose (*or* ·bous)
cory·phaeus (*plural* ·phaei) chorus leader
cory·phée ballet dancer
co·ry·za head cold
cos lettuce; *short for* cosine
co·sec *short for* cosecant
co·secant geometry term
co·sech geometry term
co·seis·mal (*or* ·mic)
Co·sen·za Italian city
cosh
cosh·er
co·sig·na·tory
co·si·ly (*US* ·zi·)
co·sine geometry term
co·si·ness
cos·met·ic
cos·meti·cal·ly
cos·me·ti·cian
cos·mic (*or* ·mi·cal)
cos·mine (*or* ·min) zoology term
cos·mo·drome zoology term
cos·mogo·nal
cos·mo·gon·ic (*or* ·goni·cal)
cos·mogo·nist
cos·mogo·ny (*plural* ·nies) origin of universe
cos·mog·ra·phy mapping of universe
cos·moid fish scale
cos·mo·logi·cal (*or* ·log·ic)
cos·molo·gist
cos·mol·ogy study of universe
cos·mo·naut
cos·mopo·lis international city
cos·mo·poli·tan
cos·mo·poli·tan·ism
cos·mopo·lite cosmopolitan plant or animal
cos·mopo·lit·ism
cos·mos
Cos·mo·tron particle accelerator
coss Indian unit

Cos·sack
cos·set
cost (cost·ing, cost)
cos·ta (*plural* ·tae) rib
Cos·ta Bra·va
cos·tal of ribs
co·star (·star·ring, ·starred)
cos·tard apple
Cos·ta Rica
Cos·ta Ri·can
cos·tate
cost-effective
cos·ter·mon·ger
cost·ing
cos·tive constipated
cost·li·ness
cost·ly (·li·er, ·li·est)
cost·mary (*plural* ·maries) plant
cos·toto·my (*plural* ·mies)
cost-plus
cos·tume
cos·tumi·er (*or* ·tum·er)
cosy (*US* cozy; *noun, plural* cosies, *US* cozies; *adj* cosi·er, cosi·est, *US* coz·ier, cozi·est)
cot
co·tan·gent geometry term
cote shelter for doves
Côte d'Azur
Côte d'Ivoire African country
Côte-d'Or French department
co·ten·an·cy
co·ten·ant
co·terie
co·ter·mi·nous
Côtes-du-Nord French department
co·tid·al
co·til·lion dance
co·tin·ga bird
co·to·neas·ter shrub
Coto·paxi volcano in Ecuador
Cots·wold sheep
Cots·wolds hills
cot·ta surplice; *compare* cotter
cot·tage
cot·tag·er
cot·ter securing pin; peasant farmer; *compare* cotta

cot·tier Irish smallholder
cot·ton
cot·ton·ade fabric
cotton·seed (plural ·seeds or ·seed)
cotton·tail US rabbit
cotton·weed
cotton·wood
cot·tony
coty·ledon seed leaf
coty·ledo·nal
coty·ledo·na·ry
coty·ledo·nous (or ·noid)
coty·loid (or ·oi·dal) cup-shaped
cou·cal bird
couch
cou·chant heraldic term
couch·er
cou·chette
couch·ing embroidery; eye surgery
cou·dé telescope
cou·gar
cough
could
couldn't
cou·lee lava
cou·lisse timber
cou·loir gully
cou·lomb unit
cou·lom·eter (or ·lomb·meter)
coul·ter (US col·) plough blade
cou·ma·ric (or cu·)
cou·ma·rin (or cu·)
cou·ma·rone
coun·cil assembly
coun·cil·lor (US ·ci·lor) council member
coun·cil·lor·ship (US ·ci·lor·)
coun·sel (·sel·ling, ·selled; US ·sel·ing, ·seled) advice; advise
coun·sel·lor (US ·sel·or) advisor
count
count·down
coun·te·nance
count·er
counter·act
counter·ac·tion
counter·ac·tive

counter·at·tack
counter·bal·ance
counter·blast
counter·change
counter·charge
counter·check
counter·claim
counter·claim·ant
counter·clockwise US anticlockwise
counter·culture
counter·es·pio·nage
counter·feit
counter·feit·er
counter·foil
counter·glow glow in sky
counter·in·sur·gen·cy
counter·in·tel·li·gence
counter·ir·ri·tant
counter·ir·ri·ta·tion
counter·mand
counter·march
counter·meas·ure
counter·mine
counter·move
counter·of·fen·sive
counter·pane
counter·part
counter·plot (·plot·ting, ·plot·ted)
counter·point
counter·poise
counter·pro·duc·tive
counter·proof printing term
counter·pro·pos·al
Counter-Reformation religious movement
counter·revolu·tion
counter·revo·lu·tion·ary
counter·scarp fortification
counter·shad·ing
counter·shaft
counter·sign
counter·sink (·sink·ing, ·sank, ·sunk)
counter·spy (plural ·spies)
counter·ten·or
counter·type
counter·vail
counter·weigh
counter·weight
counter·word
counter·work
coun·tess

count·less
coun·tri·fy (or ·try·fy; ·fies, ·fy·ing, ·fied)
coun·try (plural ·tries)
country·man (plural ·men)
country·side
country·woman (plural ·women)
coun·ty (plural ·ties)
coup
coup de grâce (plural coups de grâce)
coup d'état (plural coups d'état)
coupe dish; ice-cream
cou·pé car; carriage
cou·ple
cou·pler
cou·plet
cou·pling
cou·pon
cour·age
cou·ra·geous
cou·rante musical work
cour·gette
cou·ri·er messenger; compare currier
cour·lan bird
Cour·land (or Kur·land) Latvian region
course direction, etc.; compare coarse; corse
cours·er
cours·ing hunting
court
Cour·telle (Trademark)
cour·teous
cour·tesan (or ·tezan)
cour·tesy (plural ·tesies)
court·house
cour·ti·er
court·ing
court·ly (·li·er, ·li·est)
court mar·tial (noun, plural court mar·tials or courts mar·tial)
court-martial (verb ·martial·ling, ·martialled; US ·martial·ing, ·martialed)
court·room
court·ship
court·yard
cous·cous spicy dish; compare cuscus

cous·in relation; *compare*
  cozen
cou·teau knife
couth refined
couthie *Scot* friendly
cou·ture
cou·tu·ri·er (*fem* ·ère)
cou·vade primitive custom
co·va·len·cy (*US* ·va·lence)
  chemistry term
co·va·lent
co·vari·ance
cove
cov·en
cov·enant
cov·enan·tal
cov·enan·tee
Cov·enant·er Scottish
  Presbyterian
cov·enan·tee
cov·enant·er (*or* ·enan·tor)
Cov·en·try
cov·er
cov·er·age
cov·er·er
cov·er·ing
cov·er·less
cov·er·let
co·vers maths term
cov·ert
cov·er·ture legal term
cover-up
cov·et
cov·et·er
cov·et·ous
cov·et·ous·ness
cov·ey flock
cov·in conspiracy
cow
cow·age (*or* ·hage) plant
cow·ard
cow·ard·ice
cow·ard·li·ness
cow·ard·ly
cow·bane plant
cow·bell
cow·berry (*plural* ·berries)
cow·bind plant
cow·bird
cow·boy
cow·er
Cowes
cow·fish (*plural* ·fish *or*
  ·fishes)
cow·girl

cow·hand
cow·herb
cow·herd
cow·hide
cow·itch plant
cowl
cow·lick
cowl·ing
cow·man (*plural* ·men)
co-worker
cow·pat
cow·pea plant
cow·pox
cow·ry (*or* ·rie; *plural* ·ries)
  mollusc
cow·shed
cow·slip
cox
coxa (*plural* coxae) hip joint
cox·al
cox·al·gia
cox·al·gic
cox·comb
cox·comb·ry (*plural* ·ries)
cox·swain (*or* cock·)
coy
coy·ness
coy·ote (*plural* ·otes *or* ·ote)
co·yo·til·lo (*plural* ·los)
  shrub
coy·pu (*plural* ·pus *or* ·pu)
co·zen to trick; *compare*
  cousin
coz·en·age
coz·en·er
cozy *US spelling of* cosy
crab (crab·bing, crabbed)
crab-apple
crab·ber fisherman
crab·by (·bi·er, ·bi·est)
crab·stick
crab·wise
crack
crack·brain
crack·brained
cracked
crack·er
cracker·jack
crack·et *Dialect* stool
crack·ing
crack·jaw
crack·le
crack·ling
crack·nel
crack·pot

Cra·cow Polish city
cra·dle
cradle-snatch·er
cradle-song
craft skill; *compare* kraft
crafti·ly
crafti·ness
crafts·man (*plural* ·men)
crafts·man·ship
crafty (crafti·er, crafti·est)
crag
crag·ged *US* craggy
crag·gy (·gi·er, ·gi·est)
Cra·iova Romanian city
crake bird
cram (cram·ming,
  crammed)
cram·bo (*plural* ·boes) word
  game
cram·mer
cramoi·sy crimson
cramp
cram·pon (*or* ·poon)
cran herring measure
cran·age
cran·berry (*plural* ·berries)
crane
cranes·bill
cra·nial
cra·ni·ate having a skull
cra·nio·logi·cal
cra·ni·olo·gist
cra·ni·ol·ogy
cra·ni·om·eter
cra·nio·met·ric (*or* ·ri·cal)
cra·ni·om·etry
cra·ni·oto·my (*plural* ·mies)
cra·nium (*plural* ·niums *or*
  ·nia)
crank
crank·case
cranki·ly
cranki·ness
crank·pin
crank·shaft
cranky (cranki·er,
  cranki·est)
cran·nied
cran·ny (*plural* ·nies)
crap (crap·ping, crapped)
crape *variant spelling of*
  crepe
crap·pie (*plural* ·pies) fish
crap·py *Slang* worthless
craps *US* dice game

crap·shooter
crapu·lence
crapu·lous (or ·lent)
  drunken
cra·que·lure cracks on
  paintings
crash
crash·ing
crash-land
crash-landing
cra·sis (plural ·ses)
  linguistics term
crass
crass·ness (or cras·si·tude)
cras·su·la·ceous botany
  term
cratch fodder rack
crate
cra·ter
cra·ter·ous
craunch Dialect crunch
cra·vat
crave
cra·ven
crav·ing
craw animal stomach
craw·fish variant spelling of
  crayfish
crawl
crawl·er
Craw·ley Sussex town
cray Austral crayfish
cray·fish (or craw·; plural
  ·fish or ·fishes)
cray·on
cray·on·ist
craze
crazed
cra·zi·ly
cra·zi·ness
cra·zy (·zi·er, ·zi·est)
creak noise; compare creek
creaki·ness
creaky (creaki·er,
  creaki·est)
cream
cream·cups flower
cream·er
cream·ery (plural ·eries)
cream-laid (or ·woven) type
  of paper
creamy (creami·er,
  creami·est)
crease·
crease·less

cre·ate
crea·tine (or ·tin)
  biochemical compound
cre·ati·nine biochemical
  compound
crea·tion
crea·tion·al
crea·tion·ism theological
  belief
crea·tive
crea·tive·ly
crea·tiv·ity
crea·tor
crea·tur·al (or ·ture·ly)
crea·ture
crèche
Cré·cy battlefield
cred·al variant spelling of
  creedal
cre·dence
cre·den·dum (plural ·da)
  article of faith
cre·dent Archaic believing
cre·den·tial
cre·den·za sideboard
cred·ibil·ity (or ·ible·ness)
cred·ible
cred·ibly
cred·it
cred·it·able
cred·it·able·ness (or
  ·abil·ity)
cred·it·ably
credi·tor
cre·do (plural ·dos)
cre·du·lity
credu·lous
Cree American Indian
creed
creed·al (or cred·al)
creek inlet; compare creak
creel basket
creep (creep·ing, crept)
creep·er
creepie Scot stool
creepi·ly
creepi·ness
creeps (noun)
creepy (creepi·er,
  creepi·est)
creepy-crawly (plural
  -crawlies)
cre·mate
cre·ma·tion
cre·ma·tion·ism

cre·ma·tion·ist
cre·ma·tor
crema·to·rium (plural
  ·riums or ·ria)
crema·tory (adj)
crème French cream
crème cara·mel
crème de menthe liqueur
Cre·mo·na Italian city
cre·nate (or ·nat·ed)
  scalloped
cre·na·tion (or crena·ture)
cren·el (or ·nelle)
cren·el·late (US ·el·ate)
  supply with battlements;
  indent
cren·el·la·tion (US
  ·ela·tion)
crenu·late (or ·lat·ed)
  notched
crenu·la·tion
creo·dont extinct mammal
Cre·ole people
cre·ole language
creo·lized (or ·lised)
Creon legendary king
cre·opha·gous flesh-eating
cre·opha·gy
creo·sol constituent of
  creosote; compare cresol
creo·sote
creo·sot·ic
crepe (or crape) fabric
crêpe pancake
crepe de Chine fabric
crêpe su·zette (plural crêpes
  su·zettes) orange pancake
crepi·tant
crepi·tate crackle
crepi·ta·tion
crepi·tus medical term
crept
cre·pus·cu·lar active at dusk
cre·scen·do (plural ·dos)
cres·cent
cres·cen·tic
cre·sol disinfectant; compare
  creosol
cress
cres·set
crest
crest·ed
crest·fallen
crest·ing
cre·syl·ic

Cre·ta·ceous geological period
cre·ta·ceous of chalk
Cre·tan
Crete
cre·tic metrical foot
cret·in
cret·in·ism
cret·in·oid
cret·in·ous
cre·tonne fabric
Creuse French region
cre·vasse glacier crack
crev·ice cleft
crew
Crewe Cheshire town
crew·el yarn; *compare* cruel
crew·el·ist
crewel·work
crew-neck (*or* -necked)
crib (crib·bing, cribbed)
crib·bage
cri·bel·lum spider's organ
crib·ri·form (*or* crib·rous) sievelike
crib·work timber framework
crick
crick·et
crick·et·er
cri·coid anatomy term
cried
cri·er
cri·key
crim *Austral* criminal
crime
Cri·mea
Cri·mean
crime pas·sio·nel (*plural* crimes pas·sio·nel)
crimi·nal
crimi·nal·ity (*plural* ·ities)
crimi·nal·ly
crimi·no·logi·cal (*or* ·log·ic)
crimi·nolo·gist
crimi·nol·ogy
crimp
crimp·er
crim·ple crumple
Crimp·lene (*Trademark*)
crim·son
cringe
crin·gle nautical term
cri·nite having hairs
crin·kle

crinkle·root plant
crin·kly
crinkum-crankum twisted object
cri·noid marine organism
crino·line
cri·num plant
cri·ol·lo (*plural* ·los) cocoa
cripes slang expression
crip·ple
crip·pling
cri·sis (*plural* ·ses)
crisp
cris·pate (*or* ·pat·ed) curled
cris·pa·tion
crisp·bread
crisp·er
crisp·ness
crispy (crispi·er, crispi·est)
cris·sal of a crissum
criss·cross
cris·sum (*plural* ·sa) ornithology term
cris·ta (*plural* ·tae) biology term
cris·tate (*or* ·tat·ed) crested
cri·teri·on (*plural* ·teria *or* ·terions)
crit·ic
criti·cal
criti·cal·ly
criti·cism
criti·cize (*or* ·cise)
criti·cizer (*or* ·ciser)
cri·tique
crit·ter *US* creature
croak
croak·er
croaki·ly
croaki·ness
croaky
Cro·at
Croa·tia S European country
Croa·tian
cro·cein dye
cro·chet (·chet·ing, ·cheted) knitting; *compare* crotchet
cro·chet·er
cro·cido·lite asbestos
crock
crock·ery
crock·et architectural ornament
Crock·ford clergy directory

croco·dile
croco·dil·ian
cro·co·ite (*or* ·coi·site) mineral
cro·cus (*plural* ·cuses)
croft
croft·er
crois·sant
Cro-Magnon prehistoric man
crom·bec bird
crom·lech prehistoric structure
Crom·wel·lian
crone
cronk *Austral* unsound
Cronus Titan
cro·ny (*plural* ·nies)
cro·ny·ism
crook
crook·ed
crook·ed·ness
croon
croon·er
crop (crop·ping, cropped)
crop-eared
crop·per
cro·quet (·quet·ing, ·queted) game
cro·quette savoury cake
cro·sier (*or* ·zier) bishop's crook
cross
cross·bar
cross·beam
cross·bill
cross·bones
cross·bow
cross·breed (·breed·ing, ·bred)
cross·check
cross·country
cross·current
cross·cut (·cut·ting, cut)
crosse lacrosse stick
cross·examina·tion
cross·examine
cross·examiner
cross·eye
cross·eyed
cross·fertili·za·tion (*or* ·sa·tion)
cross·fertilize (*or* ·fertilise)
cross·fire
cross·garnet hinge

cross-grained
cross·hatch
cross·head
cross-index
cross·ing
cross·jack sail
cross-legged
cross·let heraldry term
cross·link
cros·sop·te·ryg·ian primitive fish
cross·over
cross·patch
cross·piece
cross-ply (adj)
cross·pollinate
cross·pollina·tion
cross·purposes
cross·question
cross·question·ing
cross·refer
cross·reference
cross·road (or ·roads)
cross·ruff bridge term
cross·section·al
cross·slide
cross·stitch
cross·talk
cross·tree nautical term
cross·walk US pedestrian crossing
cross·wind
cross·wise (or ·ways)
cross·word
cross·wort plant
crotch
crotch·et musical note; compare crochet
crotch·ety Slang irritable
cro·ton shrub
crouch
croup disease
croup (or croupe) horse's hindquarters
crou·pi·er
croup·ous (or croupy)
crouse Dialect saucy
croute toast
crou·ton cookery garnish
crow (crow·ing, crowed or crew)
crow·bar
crow·berry (plural ·berries)
crow·boot Eskimo boot
crowd

crowd·ed
crow·er
crow·foot (plural ·foots) plant
crown
crown·piece bridle part
crown·work
crow's-foot (plural -feet)
crow's-nest
Croy·don
croze barrel recess
cro·zier variant spelling of crosier
cru vineyard
cru·ces plural of crux
cru·cial important
cru·cial·ly
cru·cian fish
cru·ci·ate
cru·ci·ble
cru·ci·fer plant
cru·cif·er·ous
cru·ci·fier
cru·ci·fix
cru·ci·fix·ion
cru·ci·form
cru·ci·fy (·fies, ·fy·ing, ·fied)
cruck roof timber
crud Slang rubbish
crude
crud·ity (or crude·ness; plural ·ities or ·nesses)
cru·el (·el·ler, ·el·lest) unkind; compare crewel
cru·el·ly
cru·el·ty (plural ·ties)
cru·et
cruise sea trip; compare cruse
cruis·er
cruiser·weight
cruise·way
crul·ler cake
crumb
crum·ble
crum·bly (·bli·er, ·bli·est)
crumby (crumbi·er, crumbi·est) full of crumbs; compare crummy
crum·horn musical instrument
crum·my (·mi·er, ·mi·est) Slang inferior; compare crumby

crump to thud
crum·pet
crum·ple
crum·ply
crunch
crunchi·ly
crunchi·ness
crunchy (crunchi·er, crunchi·est)
cru·node maths term
crup·per saddle strap
cru·ra plural of crus
cru·ral
crus (plural cru·ra) lower leg
cru·sade
cru·sad·er
cruse small pot; compare cruise
crush
crush·er
crust
crus·ta·cean
crus·ta·ceous
crus·tal
crust·ed
crusti·ly
crusti·ness
crusty (crusti·er, crusti·est)
crutch
crux (plural cruxes or cru·ces)
crux an·sa·ta ankh
cru·zei·ro (plural ·ros) Brazilian currency
crwth musical instrument
cry (noun, plural cries; verb cries, cry·ing, cried)
cry·baby (plural ·babies)
cryo·bi·olo·gist
cryo·bi·ol·ogy
cryo·gen freezing mixture
cryo·gen·ics
cryo·hy·drate
cryo·lite mineral
cry·om·eter
cry·om·etry
cry·on·ics
cryo·phil·ic
cryo·phyte plant growing on snow
cryo·plank·ton
cryo·scope
cryo·scop·ic
cry·os·co·py
cryo·stat

cryo·sur·gery
cryo·thera·py (or
  cry·mo·thera·py)
cryo·tron electronic device
crypt
cryp·taes·thesia (US ·tes·)
  extrasensory perception
crypt·al of crypts; compare
  cryptic
crypt·analy·sis study of
  codes
crypt·ana·lyst
crypt·ana·lyt·ic
cryp·tic (or ·ti·cal) obscure;
  compare cryptal
cryp·ti·cal·ly
cryp·to·clas·tic geology
  term
cryp·to·crys·tal·line
cryp·to·gam plant
cryp·to·gam·ic (or
  ·toga·mous)
cryp·to·gen·ic of unknown
  origin
cryp·to·gram
cryp·to·graph
cryp·tog·ra·pher (or ·phist)
cryp·to·graph·ic (or
  ·graphi·cal)
cryp·tog·ra·phy (or
  ·tol·ogy) study of codes
cryp·tolo·gist
cryp·to·meria tree
cryp·to·zo·ic living in dark
  places
cryp·to·zo·ite malarial
  parasite
crys·tal
crys·tal·line
crys·tal·lin·ity
crys·tal·lite
crys·tal·lit·ic
crys·tal·lize (or ·tal·ize,
  ·tal·lise, ·tal·ise)
crys·tal·log·ra·pher
crys·tal·lo·graph·ic
crys·tal·log·ra·phy
crys·tal·loid
cte·nid·ium (plural ·ia)
  mollusc's gill
cte·noid comblike
cte·nopho·ran
cteno·phore invertebrate
cub (cub·bing, cubbed)
Cuba

cub·age
Cu·ban
cub·ane chemical
  compound
cu·ba·ture cubic contents
cubbed
cub·bing
cubby·hole
cube
cu·beb plant
cu·bic
cu·bi·cal (adj) of volume
cu·bi·cle (noun) small room
cu·bicu·lum burial chamber
cu·bi·form
cub·ism
cub·ist
cu·bis·tic
cu·bit unit
cu·bi·tal of the forearm
cu·boid
Cu-bop jazz music
cuck·old
cuck·old·ry
cuckoo (plural cuckoos)
cuckoo-pint
cu·cu·li·form ornithology
  term
cu·cul·late hood-shaped
cu·cum·ber
cu·cur·bit plant
cu·cur·bi·ta·ceous
Cú·cu·ta Colombian city
cud
cud·bear lichen
cud·dle
cud·dle·some
cud·dly (·dli·er, ·dli·est)
cud·dy (plural ·dies) cabin
cudg·el (·el·ling, ·elled; US
  ·el·ing, ·eled)
cudg·el·ler (US ·el·er)
cudg·erie tree
cud·weed
cue (cu·ing, cued) signal;
  billiard shaft; compare
  queue
Cuer·na·va·ca Mexican city
cues·ta ridge
cuff
Cuia·bá (or Cu·ya·bá)
  Brazilian port and river
cu·ing
cui·rass armour
cui·ras·sier

cuir-bouilli leather
cui·sine
cuisse armour
culch (or cultch) oyster bed
cul-de-sac (plural
  culs-de-sac or cul-de-sacs)
cu·let armour
cu·lex (plural ·li·ces)
  mosquito
Cu·lia·cán Mexican city
cu·lic·id mosquito
culi·nary
cull
cull·er
cul·let waste glass
cul·lis gutter
Cul·lod·en battlefield
cul·ly (plural ·lies) Slang pal
culm stem
cul·mif·er·ous
cul·mi·nant
cul·mi·nate
cul·mi·na·tion
cu·lottes women's trousers
cul·pa (plural ·pae) fault
cul·pabil·ity
cul·pable
cul·pably
cul·prit
cult
cul·tic
cul·ti·gen plant
cult·ism
cult·ist
cul·ti·vable (or
  cul·ti·vat·able)
cul·ti·var plant
cul·ti·vate
cul·ti·vat·ed
cul·ti·va·tion
cul·ti·va·tor
cul·trate (or ·trat·ed)
  knife-shaped
cul·tur·al
cul·tur·al·ly
cul·ture
cul·tured
cul·tur·ist
cul·ver Archaic dove
cul·ver·in cannon
cul·vert
Cu·ma·ná Venezuelan city
cum·ber
Cum·ber·land former
  English county

Cum·ber·nauld Scottish
  town
cum·ber·some
cum·brance
Cum·bria
Cum·brian
cum·in (or cum·min) herb
cum·mer·bund (or kum·)
cum·shaw tip; gift
cu·mu·late
cu·mu·la·tion
cu·mu·la·tive
cu·mul·et pigeon
cu·mu·li·form cloud-shaped
cu·mu·lo·nim·bus (plural
  ·bi or ·buses) cloud
cu·mu·lo·stra·tus (plural ·ti)
cu·mu·lous (adj)
cu·mu·lus (noun; plural ·li)
cu·neal
cu·neate
cu·nei·form writing
cun·jevoi plant
cun·ni·lin·gus
cun·ning
cunt
cup (cup·ping, cupped)
cup·bearer
cup·board
cup·cake
cu·pel (·pel·ling, ·pelled;
  US ·pel·ing, ·peled)
cu·pel·la·tion metallurgical
  process
cup·ful (plural ·fuls)
Cupid
cu·pid·ity
cu·po·la dome; compare
  copula
cu·po·lat·ed
cup·pa (or ·per) Slang cup of
  tea
cupped
cup·ping
cu·pre·ous
cu·pric
cu·prif·er·ous
cu·prite mineral
cu·pro·nick·el
cu·prous
cu·pu·late (or ·lar) cup-
  shaped
cu·pule
cur
cur·abil·ity

cur·able
Cu·ra·çao Carribean island;
  liqueur
cu·ra·cy (plural ·cies)
cu·ra·re (or ·ri) poison
cu·ra·rine muscle relaxant
cu·ra·ri·za·tion (or ·sa·tion)
cu·ra·rize (or ·rise)
cu·ras·sow bird
cu·rate
cu·ra·tive
cu·ra·tor museum keeper
cu·ra·to·rial
curb restrain; US spelling of
  kerb
curch woman's cap
cur·cu·lio (plural ·lios)
  weevil
cur·cu·ma plant
curd
curdi·ness
cur·dle
cur·dler
curdy
cur·able
cure
cure-all
cu·rette (or ·ret; ·ret·ting,
  ·ret·ted) surgical
  instrument
cur·few
cu·ria (plural ·riae) papal
  court
Cu·ria Re·gis Norman king's
  court
cu·rie unit
cu·rio (plural ·rios)
  collector's item
cu·rio·sa curiosities
cu·ri·os·ity (plural ·ities)
cu·ri·ous
cu·ri·ous·ness
Cu·ri·ti·ba Brazilian city
cu·rium radioactive element
curl
curl·er
curlew
cur·li·cue (or ·ly·)
curli·ness
curl·ing
curl·paper
curly (curli·er, curli·est)
cur·mudg·eon
cur·mudg·eon·ly

cur·rant fruit; compare
  current
cur·ra·jong variant spelling
  of kurrajong
cur·ra·wong bird
cur·ren·cy (plural ·cies)
cur·rent flow; up-to-date;
  compare currant
cur·ri·cle carriage
cur·ricu·lar
cur·ricu·lum (plural ·la or
  ·lums)
cur·ricu·lum vi·tae (plural
  ·la vi·tae)
cur·ri·er leather worker;
  compare courier
cur·ri·ery (plural ·eries)
cur·rish rude
cur·ry (noun, plural ·ries;
  verb ·ries, ·ry·ing, ·ried)
curry·comb
curse
curs·ed (or curst)
cur·sive printing term
cur·sor VDU device
cur·so·rial adapted for
  running
cur·sori·ly
cur·sory hasty
curt
cur·tail
cur·tail·ment
cur·tain
curtain-raiser
cur·ta·na sword
cur·ti·lage enclosed land
curt·ness
curt·sy (or ·sey; noun, plural
  ·sies or ·seys; verb ·sies,
  ·sy·ing, ·sied or ·seys,
  ·sey·ing, ·seyed)
cur·va·ceous
cur·va·ture
curve
cur·vet (·vet·ting or
  ·vet·ing, ·vet·ted or
  ·vet·ed) dressage term
cur·vi·lin·ear (or ·eal)
cur·vi·lin·ear·ity
curvy (curvi·er, curvi·est)
cus·cus marsupial; compare
  couscous
cu·sec unit
Cush biblical character
cush·ion

cush·iony
Cush·it·ic language
cushy *Slang* easy
cus·pate (*or* ·pat·ed, cusped)
cus·pid
cus·pi·date (*or* ·dat·ed, ·pidal)
cus·pi·da·tion architectural term
cus·pi·dor spittoon
cuss
cuss·ed
cuss·ed·ness
cus·tard
cus·to·dial
cus·to·dian
cus·to·dy (*plural* ·dies)
cus·tom
cus·tom·ari·ly
cus·tom·ary
custom-built
cus·tom·er
cus·tom·ize (*or* ·ise)
cus·tos (*plural* cus·to·des) Franciscan
cus·tu·mal customary
cut (cut·ting, cut)
cu·ta·neous
cut·away
cut·back
Cutch *variant spelling of* Kutch
cutch *variant of* catechou
cute
cute·ness
cu·ti·cle
cu·ticu·la (*plural* ·lae) cuticle
cu·ticu·lar (*adj*)
cutie
cu·tin plant substance
cu·tin·ize (*or* ·ise)
cu·tis (*plural* ·tes *or* ·tises) skin
cut·lass
cut·ler
cut·lery
cut·let
cut-price
cut·purse pickpocket
Cut·tack Indian city
cut·ter
cut·throat
cut·ting

cut·tle
cuttle·bone
cuttle·fish (*plural* ·fish *or* ·fishes)
cut·ty *Dialect* short
cut·water
cut·work embroidery
cut·worm caterpillar
cu·vette dish
Cux·ha·ven German port
Cuz·co (*or* Cus·co) Peruvian city
cwm valley
Cwm·bran Welsh town
cyan blue colour
cy·ana·mide (*or* ·mid)
cya·nate
cy·an·ic
cya·ni·da·tion
cya·nide
cya·nine (*or* ·nin) dye
cya·nite mineral
cya·nit·ic
cya·no·co·bala·min vitamin
cy·ano·gen poisonous gas
cya·no·hy·drin
cya·no·sis blueness of skin
cya·not·ic
cy·ano·type blueprint
Cybele Phrygian goddess
cy·ber·café
cy·ber·nate
cy·ber·na·tion
cy·ber·net·ic
cy·ber·neti·cist
cy·ber·net·ics
cy·ber·space
cy·cad plant
cyca·da·ceous
Cyc·la·des Aegean islands
cyc·la·mate
cyc·la·men
cy·cle
cy·clic (*or* ·cli·cal)
cy·cli·cal·ly
cy·clist
cy·clo·al·kane
cy·clo·hex·ane
cy·cloid
cy·cloi·dal
cy·clom·eter
cy·clom·etry

cy·clone
cy·clon·ic (*or* ·cloni·cal, ·clo·nal)
cy·clo·nite explosive
Cy·clo·pean
cy·clo·pedia (*or* ·pae·dia)
cy·clo·pedic (*or* ·pae·dic)
cy·clo·pen·tane
cy·clo·plegia medical term
cy·clo·pro·pane
Cy·clops one-eyed giant
cy·clops crustacean
cy·clo·rama
cy·clo·ram·ic
cy·clo·sis (*plural* ·ses) biological process
cy·clo·sto·mate (*or* ·clo·stoma·tous)
cy·clo·stome primitive vertebrate
cy·clo·style
cy·clo·thy·mia mood swings
cy·clo·thy·mic (*or* ·mi·ac)
cy·clo·tron physics term
cyg·net young swan; *compare* signet
Cyg·nus constellation
cyl·in·der
cy·lin·dri·cal (*or* ·dric)
cy·lin·dri·cal·ly
cyl·in·droid
cyma (*plural* cymae *or* cymas) architectural moulding
cy·mar woman's jacket
cy·ma·tium architectural moulding
cym·bal musical instrument; *compare* symbol
cym·bal·er (*or* ·eer, ·bal·ist)
cym·ba·lo (*plural* ·los) dulcimer
cyme botany term
cy·mene chemical compound
cy·mif·er·ous
cy·mo·gene *US* petroleum distillate
cy·mo·graph *variant spelling of* kymograph
cy·moid like a cyma
cy·mo·phane mineral
cy·mose of a cyme

Cym·ric (*or* **Kym·**) Welsh language
Cym·ry (*or* **Kym·**) Welsh people
cyn·ic
cyni·cal
cyni·cal·ly
cyni·cism
cy·no·sure
cy·pher *variant spelling of* **cipher**
cy·pera·ceous botany term
cy pres legal term
cy·press tree; *compare* Cyprus
Cyp·rian
cy·pri·nid fish
cy·prino·dont fish
cy·pri·noid carplike
Cyp·ri·ot (*or* **·ote**)
cyp·ri·pedium orchid
Cy·prus country; *compare* cypress
cyp·sela (*plural* **·selae**) botany term
Cyr·enai·ca (*or* **Cir·**) Libyan region
Cy·ril·lic Slavonic alphabet

cyst lump; sac; *compare* cist
cys·tec·to·my (*plural* **·mies**) removal of bladder
cys·teine amino acid
cys·tein·ic
cyst·ic
cys·ti·cer·coid larva
cys·ti·cer·cus (*plural* **·ci**) larva
cys·tine amino acid
cys·ti·tis bladder inflammation
cys·to·carp botany term
cys·to·carp·ic
cys·to·cele
cys·toid
cys·to·lith bladder stone
cys·to·scope medical term
cys·to·scop·ic
cys·tos·co·py (*plural* **·pies**)
cys·toto·my (*plural* **·mies**)
cy·tas·ter cytology term
Cyth·era Greek island
cyti·dine biochemical compound
cy·to·chemi·cal
cy·to·chem·is·try

cy·to·chrome biochemical compound
cy·to·gen·esis (*or* **·tog·eny**) origin of cells
cy·to·genet·ics
cy·to·ki·nesis
cy·to·logi·cal
cy·tolo·gist
cy·tol·ogy study of cells
cy·toly·sin
cy·toly·sis
cy·ton nerve-cell body
cy·to·plasm
cy·to·plasm·ic
cy·to·plast
cy·to·sine biochemical compound
cy·to·taxo·nom·ic
cy·to·tax·ono·mist
cy·to·tax·on·omy
Cyzi·cus ancient Greek colony
czar *variant spelling of* **tsar**
czar·das dance
Czech
Czecho·slo·vak
Czecho·slo·va·kia
Czecho·slo·va·kian
Czę·sto·cho·wa Polish city

D

dab (**dab·bing, dabbed**)
dab·ber
dab·ble
dab·bler
dab·chick
da capo musical term
Dac·ca *variant of* **Dhaka**
dace
da·cha (*or* **·tcha**) Russian country house
dachs·hund
da·coit armed robber
da·coity
Da·cron (*Trademark*)
dac·tyl metrical foot; finger
dac·tyl·ic
dac·tyli·cal·ly
dac·tylo·gram *US* fingerprint
dac·tyl·og·ra·phy

dac·ty·lol·ogy (*plural* **·ogies**) sign language
dad
Dada artistic movement
Da·da·ism
Da·da·ist
Da·da·is·tic
Da·da·is·ti·cal·ly
dad·dy (*plural* **·dies**)
dado (*plural* **da·does** *or* **da·dos**) lower part of wall
Daedalus mythological character
dae·mon (*or* **dai·**) spirit; demigod; *compare* demon
dae·mon·ic (*or* **dai·**)
daff *Scot* to frolic; *Slang* daffodil
daf·fo·dil
daffy (**daffi·er, daffi·est**) *Slang* daft

daft
Da·gan Babylonian god
Dag·en·ham
Da·ge·stan (*or* **Da·ghe·stan**) Russian republic
dag·ga narcotic
dag·ger
dagger·board
dag·lock encrusted wool
da·go (*plural* **·gos** *or* **·goes**)
da·go·ba Buddhist shrine
da·guerreo·type
da·guerreo·typ·er (*or* **·ist**)
da·guerreo·typy
dah Morse code sound
dahl·ia
Dah·na Arabian desert
Da·ho·man (*or* **Da·ho·mean**)
Da·ho·mey *former name of* **Benin**

Dáil Ei·reann Irish
parliament
dai·ly (*plural* **·lies**)
dai·mon *variant spelling of*
daemon
dain·ti·ly
dain·ti·ness
dain·ty (*noun, plural* **·ties;**
adj **·ti·er, ·ti·est**)
dai·qui·ri (*plural* **·ris**) drink
dairy (*plural* **dairies**)
dairy·ing
dairy·man (*plural* **·men**)
dais platform
dai·sy (*plural* **·sies**)
daisy·cutter cricket
Da·kar Senegalese capital
Da·ko·ta
Da·ko·tan
dal Indian food
Dalai Lama Tibetan leader
da·la·si Gambian currency
dale
Dales Yorkshire region
dales·man (*plural* **·men**)
Dal·las US city
dal·li·ance
dal·ly (**·lies, ·ly·ing, ·lied**)
Dal·ma·tia Croatian region
Dal·ma·tian
dal·mat·ic tunic
dal·ton unit
dal·ton·ic
dal·ton·ism colour
blindness
dam (**dam·ming, dammed**)
river barrier; female
parent; *compare* **damn**
dam·age
dam·age·abil·ity
dam·age·able
dam·ag·er
dam·ages
Da·man Indian region
Da·man·hûr Egyptian city
Da·ma·ra (*plural* **·ras** *or* **·ra**)
African people
Dama·scene of Damascus
dama·scene decorate metal
Da·mas·cus Syrian capital
dam·ask
dame
Dami·et·ta Egyptian town
dam·mar (*or* **da·mar,**
dam·mer) resin

dammed obstructed;
compare **damned**
dam·ming
damn condemn; *compare*
dam
dam·nabil·ity
dam·nable
dam·nably
dam·na·tion
dam·na·tory
damned condemned;
compare **dammed**
damned·est
dam·ni·fi·ca·tion
dam·ni·fy (**·fies, ·fy·ing,**
·fied) injure
Damocles mythological
character
damp
damp·course
damp·en
damp·en·er
damp·er
damp·ly
damp·ness
dam·sel
damsel·fish (*plural* **·fish** *or*
·fishes)
damsel·fly (*plural* **·flies**)
dam·son
dan buoy; judo grade
Danaë mythological
character
dance
danc·er
danc·ing
dan·de·lion
dan·der
Dan·die Din·mont terrier
dan·di·fi·ca·tion
dan·di·fy (**·fies, ·fy·ing,**
·fied)
dan·di·prat coin
dan·dle fondle
dan·dler
dan·druff (*or* **·driff**)
dan·druffy (*or* **·driffy**)
dan·dy (*plural* **·dies**)
dandy·ish
dandy·ism
Dane
Dane·geld (*or* **·gelt**)
Anglo-Saxon tax
Dane·law (*or* **·lagh**)
England under Danish law

dane·wort shrub
dang damn
dan·ger
dan·ger·ous
dan·ger·ous·ness
dan·gle
dan·gler
danio (*plural* **danios**) fish
Dan·ish
dank
dank·ness
dan·seur (*fem* **·seuse**) French
dancer
Dan·ube
Danu·bian
Dan·zig Gdańsk; pigeon
dap (**dap·ping, dapped**)
daphne shrub
daph·nia flea
Daph·nis mythological
character
dap·per
dap·ple
dapple-grey (*US* **-gray**)
dar·af unit
dar·bies *Slang* handcuffs
Dar·dan (*or* **·da·nian**)
Trojan
Dar·da·nelles
Dar·da·nus mythological
character
Dar·dic language group
dare
dare·devil
dare·devil·ry (*or* **·try**)
dar·er
Dar es Sa·laam Tanzanian
capital
Dar·fur Sudanese
province
darg *Dialect* day's work
dar·ic coin
Dari·en part of Panama
dar·ing
dari·ole cookery mould
Dar·jee·ling Indian town;
tea
dark
dark·en
dark·en·er
dar·kle darken
dark·ly
dark·ness
dark·room
dark·some

darky (*or* darkie, dark·ey; *plural* darkies *or* ·eys)
Dar·ling Australian river
dar·ling
Dar·ling·ton Durham town
Darm·stadt German city
darn
darned
dar·nel grass
darn·er
darn·ing
dart
dart·board
dart·er
Dart·ford Kent town
Dart·moor
Dart·mouth Devon port
darts
Dar·win Australian port
Dar·win·ian
Dar·win·ism
Dar·win·ist
dash
dash·board
da·sheen plant
dash·er
da·shi·ki garment
dash·ing
dash·pot vibration damper
Dasht-i-Lut (*or* -e-) Iranian desert
das·sie animal
das·tard
das·tard·li·ness
das·tard·ly
dasy·ure marsupial
da·ta information; *plural of* datum
data·base
dat·able (*or* date·)
dat·able·ness (*or* date·)
da·ta·ry (*plural* ·ries) Catholic official
date
dat·ed
dat·ed·ness
date·less
date·line
dat·er
dat·ing
da·ti·val
da·tive
dato Philippine chief
da·to·lite mineral

da·tum (*plural* ·ta) fact; *compare* data
da·tu·ra plant
daub smear
daube stew
daub·er
daub·ery (*or* ·ry)
dauby
Dau·gav·pils Latvian city
daugh·ter
daughter-in-law (*plural* daughters-)
daugh·ter·li·ness
daugh·ter·ly
daunt
daunt·er
daunt·ing
daunt·less
dau·phin heir to French throne
Dau·phi·né former French province
dau·phine (*or* ·phin·ess) wife of dauphin
dav·en·port desk
dav·it
daw jackdaw
daw·dle
daw·dler
dawn
Daw·son Canadian town
day
day·book
day·boy
day·break
day·dream
day·dream·er
day·dream·ing
day·dreamy
day·flower
day·light
day·long
day-neutral botany term
day·star sun
day·time
day-to-day
Day·ton US city
Day·to·na Beach US city
day-tripper
daze
daz·zle
dea·con
dea·con·ess
dea·con·ry (*plural* ·ries)
dea·con·ship

de·ac·ti·vate
de·ac·ti·va·tion
de·ac·ti·va·tor
dead
dead·beat
dead·en
dead·en·er
dead·eye nautical term
dead·fall trap
dead·head
dead·light nautical term
dead·line
dead·li·ness
dead·lock
dead·ly (·li·er, ·li·est)
dead·ness
dead-nettle
dead·pan
dead·wood
deaf
deaf-and-dumb
deaf·en
deaf-mute
deaf-muteness (*or* -mutism)
deaf·ness
deal (deal·ing, dealt) take action, etc.; *compare* dele
dea·late (*or* ·lat·ed) wingless
dea·la·tion
deal·er
deal·fish (*plural* ·fish *or* ·fishes)
deal·ing
dealt
de·ami·nate (*or* ·am·in·ize, ·am·in·ise) biochemistry term
de·ami·na·tion (*or* ·ami·ni·za·tion, ·ami·ni·sa·tion)
dean university official, etc.; *compare* dene
dean·ery (*plural* ·eries)
dean·ship
dear
dear·ly
dear·ness
dearth
deary (*or* dearie; *plural* dearies)
death
death·bed
death·blow
death·less
death·li·ness

death·ly
death's-head
death·trap
death·watch
Deau·ville French resort
deb short for debutante
de·ba·cle
de·bag (·bag·ging, ·bagged)
de·bar (·bar·ring, ·barred)
de·bark disembark
de·bar·ka·tion
de·bar·ment
de·base
de·bas·ed·ness
de·base·ment
de·bas·er
de·bat·able (or ·bate·able)
de·bat·ably
de·bate
de·bat·er
de·bauch
debau·chee
de·bauch·er
de·bauch·ery (or ·ment)
de·ben·ture bond
de·bili·tate
de·bili·ta·tion
de·bili·ta·tive
de·bil·ity (plural ·ities)
deb·it
debo·nair (or deb·on·naire)
de·bouch move into larger
    space
de·bouch·ment (or
    ·bou·chure)
De·bre·cen Hungarian city
dé·bride·ment surgical term
de·brief
de·bris (or dé·)
debt
debt·or
de·bug (·bug·ging,
    ·bugged)
de·bunk
de·bunk·er
de·bus (·bus·ing, ·bused or
    ·bus·sing, ·bussed)
    unload; alight
de·but
debu·tante
de·ca·dal
dec·ade
deca·dence (or ·den·cy)
deca·dent
de·caf·fein·ate

deca·gon
de·cago·nal
deca·he·dral
deca·he·dron
de·cal transferred design
de·cal·ci·fi·ca·tion
de·cal·ci·fi·er
de·cal·ci·fy (·fies, ·fy·ing,
    ·fied)
de·cal·co·ma·nia
    transferring designs
de·ca·les·cence physics
    term
de·ca·les·cent
Deca·logue Ten
    Commandments
de·camp
de·camp·ment
de·ca·nal of a dean
dec·ane chemical
    compound
dec·ane·dio·ic acid
de·ca·ni musical term
deca·no·ic acid
de·cant
de·cant·er
de·capi·tate
de·capi·ta·tion
de·capi·ta·tor
deca·pod crustacean
de·capo·dal (or ·dan, ·dous)
de·car·bon·ate
de·car·boni·za·tion (or
    ·sa·tion)
de·car·bon·ize (or ·ise)
de·car·bon·iz·er (or ·is·er)
de·car·boxy·la·tion
dec·are unit
deca·style architectural
    term
deca·syl·lab·ic
deca·syl·lable
de·cath·lete
de·cath·lon
de·cay
Dec·can Indian plateau
de·cease
de·ceased
de·cedent deceased
de·ceit
de·ceit·ful
de·ceit·ful·ly
de·ceiv·able
de·ceiv·able·ness (or
    ·abil·ity)

de·ceive
de·ceiv·er
de·cel·er·ate
de·cel·era·tion
de·cel·era·tor
de·cel·erom·eter
De·cem·ber
De·cem·brist Russian
    revolutionary
de·cena·ry (or
    de·cen·na·ry) of tithing
de·cen·cy (plural ·cies)
de·cen·nial
de·cen·nium (or
    de·cen·na·ry; plural
    ·niums, ·nia, or ·naries)
decade
de·cent
de·cen·tral·ist
de·cen·trali·za·tion (or
    ·sa·tion)
de·cen·tral·ize (or ·ise)
de·cep·tion
de·cep·tive
de·ce·rebrate remove brain
de·ce·rebra·tion
de·cern legal term
deci·are unit
deci·bel
de·cid·able
de·cide
de·cid·ed
de·cid·ed·ly
de·cid·er
de·cidua (plural ·cid·uas or
    ·ciduae) anatomy term
de·cid·ual (or ·cidu·ate)
de·cidu·ous
dec·ile statistics term
de·cil·lion 10^{60}
de·cil·lionth
deci·mal
deci·mali·za·tion (or
    ·sa·tion)
deci·mal·ize (or ·ise)
deci·mate
deci·ma·tion
deci·ma·tor
deci·metre (US ·meter)
de·ci·pher
de·ci·pher·abil·ity
de·ci·pher·able
de·ci·pher·er
de·ci·pher·ment
de·ci·sion

de·ci·sion·al
de·ci·sive
de·ci·sive·ness
deck
deck·house
deck·le (or ·el) frame
deckle-edged
de·claim
de·claim·er
dec·la·ma·tion
de·clama·to·ri·ly
de·clama·tory
de·clar·able
de·clar·ant
dec·la·ra·tion
de·clara·tive
de·clara·tor legal term
de·clara·to·ri·ly
de·clara·tory
de·clare
de·clar·er
de·class
dé·clas·sé (fem ·sée) French having lost status
de·clas·si·fi·able
de·clas·si·fi·ca·tion
de·clas·si·fy (·fies, ·fy·ing, ·fied)
de·clen·sion
de·clen·sion·al
de·clen·sion·al·ly
de·clin·able
dec·li·nate drooping
dec·li·na·tion
de·cli·na·tory
de·cline
de·clin·er
dec·li·nom·eter
de·clivi·tous
de·cliv·ity (plural ·ities) downward slope
de·clutch
de·coct
de·coc·tion
de·code
de·cod·er
de·coke
de·col·late separate
de·col·la·tion
de·col·la·tor
dé·colle·tage low neckline
dé·colle·té
de·colo·nize (or ·nise)
de·col·or·ant

de·col·ori·za·tion (or ·sa·tion, de·col·ora·tion)
de·col·or·ize (or ·ise, de·col·our)
de·com·mis·sion
de·com·pos·abil·ity
de·com·pos·able
de·com·pose
de·com·pos·er
de·com·po·si·tion
de·com·pound type of leaf
de·com·press
de·com·pres·sion
de·com·pres·sive
de·com·pres·sor
de·con·gest·ant
de·con·secrate
de·con·tami·nant
de·con·tami·nate
de·con·tami·na·tion
de·con·tami·na·tive
de·con·tami·na·tor
de·con·trol (·trol·ling, ·trolled)
dé·cor (or de·)
deco·rate
deco·ra·tion
deco·ra·tive
deco·ra·tor
deco·rous
de·cor·ti·cate remove shell
de·cor·ti·ca·tion
de·cor·ti·ca·tor
de·co·rum
de·cou·page decoration
de·cou·pling electronics term
de·coy
de·coy·er
de·crease
de·creas·ing·ly
de·cree (·cree·ing, ·creed)
de·cree·able
de·cree nisi
de·cre·er
dec·re·ment diminution
de·crep·it
de·crepi·tate crackle on heating
de·crepi·ta·tion
de·crepi·tude
de·cres·cence
de·cres·cent decreasing
de·cre·tal papal edict
de·cre·tal·ist

de·cre·tive
dec·re·tory
de·cri·al
de·cri·er
de·cry (·cries, ·cry·ing, ·cried)
de·crypt decode
de·cum·bence (or ·ben·cy)
de·cum·bent lying flat
de·cu·ple increase tenfold
de·cu·ri·on Roman councillor
de·cur·rent botany term
de·curved bent downwards
decu·ry (plural ·ries) ten Roman soldiers
de·cus·sate intersect
de·cus·sa·tion
De·dé·ag·ach Greek port
dedi·cate
dedi·cat·ed
dedi·ca·tee
dedi·ca·tion
dedi·ca·tor
dedi·ca·tory (or ·tive)
de·dif·fer·en·tia·tion
de·duce
de·duc·ibil·ity (or ·ible·ness)
de·duc·ible
de·duct
de·duct·ibil·ity
de·duct·ible
de·duc·tion
de·duc·tive
Dee river
deed
deek Dialect look at
deem consider; compare deme
deem·ster (or demp·) Manx magistrate
deep
deep·en
deep·en·er
deep-freeze (noun)
deep-freeze (verb; -freez·ing, -froze or -freezed, -frozen or -freezed)
deep-fry (-fries, -fry·ing, -fried)
deep-laid
deep·ness
deep-rooted (or -seated)

deer (*plural* deer *or* deers)
deer·grass
deer·hound
deer·skin
deer·stalker
de·escalate
de·escala·tion
de·face
de·face·able
de·face·ment
de·fac·er
de fac·to
(defaecate) *incorrect spelling of* defecate
de·fal·cate *legal term*
de·fal·ca·tion
de·fal·ca·tor
defa·ma·tion
de·fama·to·ri·ly
de·fama·tory
de·fame
de·fam·er
de·fault
de·fault·er
de·fea·sance *annulment*
de·fea·sible
de·feat
de·feat·er
de·feat·ism
de·feat·ist
def·ecate
def·eca·tion
def·eca·tor
de·fect
de·fec·tion
de·fec·tive
de·fec·tor
de·fence (*US* ·fense)
de·fence·less (*US* ·fense·)
de·fence·less·ness (*US* ·fense·)
de·fend
de·fend·able
de·fend·ant
de·fend·er
de·fen·es·tra·tion *throwing from window*
de·fen·sibil·ity (*or* ·sible·ness)
de·fen·sible
de·fen·sibly
de·fen·sive
de·fer (·fer·ring, ·ferred)
def·er·ence
def·er·ent

def·er·en·tial
def·er·en·tial·ly
de·fer·ment (*or* ·fer·ral)
de·fer·rable (*or* ·fer·able)
de·fer·ral
de·ferred
de·fer·rer
de·fi·cient
defi·cit
de·fi·er
defi·lade *military term*
de·file
de·file·ment
de·fil·er
de·fin·able
de·fine
de·fin·er
de·fini·en·dum (*plural* ·da) *thing defined*
de·fini·ens (*plural* ·en·tia) *definition*
defi·nite
defi·nite·ly
defi·nite·ness
defi·ni·tion
defi·ni·tion·al
de·fini·tive
de·fini·tive·ly
de·fini·tude
def·la·grate *burn*
def·la·gra·tion
de·flate
de·fla·tion
de·fla·tion·ary
de·fla·tion·ist
de·fla·tor
de·flect
de·flec·tion (*or* ·flex·ion)
de·flec·tive
de·flec·tor
de·flexed
de·floc·cu·late *disperse*
de·floc·cu·la·tion
de·flo·ra·tion
de·flow·er
de·flow·er·er
de·fo·li·ant
de·fo·li·ate
de·fo·lia·tion
de·fo·lia·tor
de·force *withhold*
de·force·ment
de·for·ciant *legal term*
de·for·est
de·for·esta·tion

de·for·est·er
de·form
de·form·able
de·for·ma·tion
de·formed
de·form·ed·ness
de·form·er
de·form·ity (*plural* ·ities)
de·fraud
de·frau·da·tion
de·fraud·er
de·fraud·ment
de·fray
de·fray·able
de·fray·al (*or* ·ment)
de·fray·er
de·frock
de·frost
de·frost·er
deft
deft·ness
de·funct
de·func·tive
de·fuse
defy (·fies, ·fy·ing, ·fied)
dé·ga·gé *French* casual
de·gas (·gas·ses *or* ·gases, ·gas·sing, ·gassed)
de·gas·ser
de·gauss *demagnetize*
de·gen·era·cy (*plural* ·cies)
de·gen·er·ate
de·gen·er·ate·ness
de·gen·era·tion
de·gen·era·tive
de·glu·ti·nate *extract gluten*
de·glu·ti·na·tion
de·glu·ti·tion *swallowing*
de·gra·dable
deg·ra·da·tion
de·grade
de·grad·ed
de·grad·er
de·grad·ing
de·grease
de·gree
degree-day *unit*
de·gres·sion *decrease*
de·hisce *burst open*
de·his·cence
de·his·cent
de·horn
Deh·ra Dun *Indian city*
de·hu·mani·za·tion (*or* ·sa·tion)

de·hu·man·ize (or ·ise)
de·hu·midi·fi·ca·tion
de·hu·midi·fi·er
de·hu·midi·fy (·fies,
·fy·ing, ·fied)
de·hy·drate
de·hy·dra·tion
de·hy·dra·tor
de·hydro·gen·ase enzyme
de·hydro·gen·ate (or ·ize,
·ise) remove hydrogen
de·hydro·gena·tion
de·hydro·geni·za·tion (or
·sa·tion)
de·hyp·no·tize (or ·ise)
de-ice
de-icer
dei·ci·dal
dei·cide killing a god
deic·tic logic term
deic·ti·cal·ly
de·ific godlike
dei·fi·ca·tion
dei·fi·er
dei·form
dei·fy (·fies, ·fy·ing, ·fied)
deign
deil Scot devil
de·in·dus·tri·ali·za·tion (or
·sa·tion)
de·in·dus·tri·al·ize (or ·ise)
de·ism
de·ist
de·ist·ic (or ·is·ti·cal)
de·ity (plural ·ities)
deix·is linguistics term
déjà vu
de·ject
de·jec·ta body waste
de·ject·ed
de·ject·ed·ness
de·jec·tion
de jure Latin according to
law
dek·ko (plural ·kos) Slang
look
de·laine fabric
de·lami·nate divide into
layers
de·lami·na·tion
(delapidate) incorrect spelling
of dilapidate
de·late denounce
Dela·ware US state
Dela·war·ean

de·lay
de·lay·er
dele (de·leing, de·led)
symbol for deletion;
compare deal
de·lec·table
de·lec·table·ness (or
·tabil·ity)
de·lec·tably
de·lec·ta·tion
del·egable
del·ega·cy (plural ·cies)
committee
del·egate
del·ega·tion
de·lete
del·eteri·ous
de·letion
Delft Dutch town;
earthenware
Del·hi Indian capital
deli short for delicatessen
De·lian of Delos
de·lib·er·ate
de·lib·er·ate·ness
de·lib·era·tion
de·lib·era·tive
de·lib·era·tor
deli·ca·cy (plural ·cies)
deli·cate
deli·ca·tes·sen
de·li·cious
de·lict civil wrong
de·light
de·light·ed
de·light·er
de·light·ful
de·light·ful·ly
de·light·ful·ness
de·lim·it (or ·limi·tate)
de·limi·ta·tion
de·limi·ta·tive
de·lin·eable
de·lin·eate
de·lin·ea·tion
de·lin·ea·tive
de·lin·ea·tor tailor's pattern
de·lin·quen·cy (plural ·cies)
de·lin·quent
deli·quesce chemistry term
deli·ques·cence
deli·ques·cent
de·liri·ant
de·liri·ous
de·liri·ous·ness

de·lir·ium (plural ·lir·iums
or ·liria)
de·lir·ium tre·mens
deli·tes·cence medical term
deli·tes·cent
de·liv·er
de·liv·er·able
de·liv·er·ance
de·liv·er·er
de·liv·ery (plural ·eries)
dell
Del·mar·va US peninsula
de·lo·cali·za·tion (or
·sa·tion)
de·lo·cal·ize (or ·ise)
De·los Greek island
de·louse
Del·phi Greek oracle
Del·phian
Del·phic
del·phin·ium (plural
·phin·iums or ·phinia)
Del·phi·nus constellation
del·ta
del·ta·ic (or del·tic)
del·ti·olo·gist
del·ti·ol·ogy collecting
postcards
del·toid muscle
de·lude
de·lud·er
del·uge
de·lu·sion
de·lu·sion·al
de·lu·sive
de·lu·so·ry
de luxe
delve
delv·er
de·mag·neti·za·tion (or
·sa·tion)
de·mag·net·ize (or ·ise)
de·mag·net·iz·er (or ·is·er)
dema·gog·ic (or ·gogi·cal)
dema·gogi·cal·ly
dema·gogue (US also ·gog)
dema·gogu·ery (or ·ism)
dema·gogy (plural ·gogies)
de·mand
de·mand·able
de·mand·ant
de·mand·er
de·mand·ing
de·man·toid gemstone
de·mar·cate

de·mar·ca·tion (or ·ka·tion)
dé·mar·ca·tor
dé·marche *French*
  diplomatic manoeuvre
de·ma·teri·al·ize (or ·ise)
Dema·vend Iranian volcano
deme biology term; ancient
  local-government unit;
  compare deem
de·mean
de·mean·ing
de·mean·our (*US* ·or)
de·ment
de·ment·ed
de·ment·ed·ness
de·men·tia
Dem·erara Guyanese river
dem·erara sugar
de·mer·it
de·meri·to·ri·ous
de·mer·sal living in deep
  water
de·mesne land
Demeter Greek goddess
demi·bas·ti·on fortification
demi·can·ton
demi·god (*fem* ·god·dess)
demi·john bottle
de·mili·ta·ri·za·tion (or
  ·sa·tion)
de·mili·ta·rize (or ·rise)
demi·lune crescent shape
demi·mon·daine
  unrespectable woman
demi·monde
de·min·er·al·ize (or ·ise)
demi·relief
de·mis·able
de·mise
demi·semi·qua·ver
de·mis·sion giving up office
de·mist
de·mist·er
demi·tasse small coffee cup
demi·urge philosophy term
demi·vierge *French*
  promiscuous virgin
demo (*plural* demos) *Slang*
  demonstration
de·mob (·mob·bing,
  ·mobbed)
de·mo·bi·li·za·tion (or
  ·sa·tion)
de·mo·bi·lize (or ·lise)

de·moc·ra·cy (*plural* ·cies)
Demo·crat political party
  member
demo·crat
Demo·crat·ic
demo·crat·ic
demo·crati·cal·ly
de·moc·ra·ti·za·tion (or
  ·sa·tion)
de·moc·ra·tize (or ·tise)
dé·mo·dé *French* out of
  fashion
de·modu·late
de·modu·la·tion electronics
  term
de·modu·la·tor
De·mo·gor·gon underworld
  god
de·mog·ra·pher (or ·phist)
de·mo·graph·ic (or
  ·graphi·cal)
de·mo·graphi·cal·ly
de·mog·ra·phy
demoi·selle damsel; bird
de·mol·ish
de·mol·ish·er
de·mol·ish·ment
demo·li·tion
demo·li·tion·ist
de·mon devil; *compare*
  daemon
de·mon·eti·za·tion (or
  ·sa·tion)
de·mon·etize (or ·etise)
de·mo·ni·ac (or ·nia·cal)
de·mo·nia·cal·ly
de·mon·ic
de·moni·cal·ly
de·mon·ism
de·mon·ist
de·mon·ize (or ·ise)
de·mon·ola·ter demon
  worshipper
de·mon·ola·try
de·mono·logi·cal
de·mon·olo·gist
de·mon·ol·ogy
de·mon·strabil·ity (or
  ·strable·ness)
de·mon·strable
de·mon·strably
dem·on·strate
dem·on·stra·tion
dem·on·stra·tion·al
de·mon·stra·tion·ist

de·mon·stra·tive
de·mon·stra·tor
de·mor·ali·za·tion (or
  ·sa·tion)
de·mor·al·ize (or ·ise)
de·mor·al·iz·er (or ·is·er)
de·mos nation
de·mote
de·mot·ic of the people
de·mo·tion
de·mot·ist
de·mount
de·mount·able
demp·ster *variant of*
  deemster
de·mul·cent soothing
de·mul·si·fi·ca·tion
de·mul·si·fi·er
de·mul·si·fy (·fies, ·fy·ing,
  ·fied)
de·mur (·mur·ring,
  ·murred)
de·mure
de·mure·ness
de·mur·rable
de·mur·rage
de·mur·ral
de·mur·rer objection
de·mu·tu·al·ize
demy paper size
de·mys·ti·fi·ca·tion
de·mys·ti·fy (·fies, ·fy·ing,
  ·fied)
de·my·tholo·gize (or ·gise)
den (den·ning, denned)
de·nar·ius (*plural* ·narii)
  coin
de·nary based on ten
de·na·tion·ali·za·tion (or
  ·sa·tion)
de·na·tion·al·ize (or ·ise)
de·natu·rali·za·tion (or
  ·sa·tion)
de·natu·ral·ize (or ·ise)
de·na·tur·ant
de·na·tura·tion
de·na·ture (or ·tur·ize,
  ·tur·ise)
de·na·zi·fy (·fies, ·fy·ing,
  ·fied)
Den·bigh·shire Welsh
  county
den·dri·form branching
den·drite part of nerve cell
den·drit·ic (or ·driti·cal)

den·driti·cal·ly
den·dro·chrono·logi·cal
den·dro·chro·nolo·gist
den·dro·chro·nol·ogy study
 of tree rings
den·droid (*or* ·droi·dal)
 treelike
den·dro·logi·cal (*or* ·log·ic,
 ·drolo·gous)
den·drolo·gist
den·drol·ogy
dene wooded valley;
 compare dean
Den·eb star
de·nega·tion
den·gue viral disease
de·ni·able
de·ni·al
de·nico·tin·ize (*or* ·ise)
de·ni·er one who denies
den·ier unit of weight
deni·grate
deni·gra·tion
deni·gra·tor
den·im
de·ni·trate chemistry term
de·ni·tra·tion
de·ni·tri·fi·ca·tion
de·ni·tri·fy (·fies, ·fy·ing,
 ·fied)
deni·zen
Den·mark
denned
den·ning
de·nomi·nable
de·nomi·nate
de·nomi·na·tion
de·nomi·na·tion·al
de·nomi·na·tion·al·ism
de·nomi·na·tion·al·ist
de·nomi·na·tive naming
de·nomi·na·tor
de·not·able
de·no·ta·tion
de·no·ta·tive
de·note
de·note·ment
de·noue·ment
de·nounce
de·nounce·ment
de·nounc·er
dense
dense·ness
den·sim·eter
den·si·met·ric

den·sim·etry
den·si·tom·eter
den·si·to·met·ric
den·si·tom·etry
den·sity (*plural* ·sities)
dent
den·tal
den·ta·lium (*plural* ·liums
 or ·lia) mollusc
den·tate
den·ta·tion state of having
 teeth; *compare* dentition
den·tex fish
den·ti·cle small tooth
den·ticu·late
den·ticu·la·tion
den·ti·form
den·ti·frice
den·til architectural term
den·ti·la·bial
den·ti·lin·gual phonetics
 term
den·tin·al
den·tine (*or* ·tin) tooth
 tissue
den·tist
den·tis·try
den·ti·tion set of teeth;
 compare dentition
den·toid
Den·ton Lancashire town
den·ture
de·nu·cleari·za·tion (*or*
 ·sa·tion)
de·nu·clear·ize (*or* ·ise)
denu·date
denu·da·tion
de·nude
de·nud·er
de·nu·mer·able
de·nun·ci·ate
de·nun·cia·tion
de·nun·cia·tor
de·nun·cia·tory
Den·ver US city
deny (de·nies, de·ny·ing,
 de·nied)
deo·dand legal term
deo·dar tree
de·odor·ant
de·odori·za·tion (*or*
 ·sa·tion)
de·odor·ize (*or* ·ise)
de·odor·iz·er (*or* ·is·er)
de·on·tic logic term

de·on·to·logi·cal
de·on·tolo·gist
de·on·tol·ogy branch of
 ethics
de·oxi·di·za·tion (*or*
 ·sa·tion)
de·oxi·dize (*or* ·dise)
de·oxi·diz·er (*or* ·dis·er)
de·oxy·cor·ti·co·ster·one
 (*or* de·oxy·cor·tone)
 hormone
de·oxy·gen·ate (*or* ·ize, ·ise)
de·oxy·gena·tion
de·oxy·ribo·nu·cle·ic acid
 (*or* des·)
de·oxy·ri·bose (*or* des·) a
 sugar
de·part
de·part·ment
de·part·men·tal
de·part·men·tal·ism
de·part·men·tali·za·tion (*or*
 ·sa·tion)
de·part·ment·al·ize (*or* ·ise)
de·part·men·tal·ly
de·par·ture
de·pas·ture
de·pend
de·pend·abil·ity (*or*
 ·able·ness)
de·pend·able
de·pend·ably
de·pend·ant (*noun*)
de·pend·ence (*US also*
 ·ance)
de·pend·en·cy (*US also*
 ·an·cy; *plural* ·cies)
de·pend·ent (*US also* ·ant;
 adj)
de·per·son·ali·za·tion (*or*
 ·sa·tion)
de·per·son·al·ize (*or* ·ise)
de·pict
de·pict·er (*or* ·pic·tor)
de·pic·tion
de·pic·tive
de·pic·ture
depi·late
depi·la·tion
depi·la·tor
de·pila·tory (*plural* ·tories)
de·plane
de·plet·able
de·plete
de·ple·tion

de·ple·tive (*or* ·tory)
de·plor·able
de·plor·able·ness (*or* ·abil·ity)
de·plor·ably
de·plore
de·plor·er
de·plor·ing·ly
de·ploy
de·ploy·ment
de·plu·ma·tion
de·plume deprive of feathers
de·po·lari·za·tion (*or* ·sa·tion)
de·po·lar·ize (*or* ·ise)
de·po·lar·iz·er (*or* ·is·er)
de·po·liti·cize (*or* ·cise)
de·pone *Scot* testify
de·po·nent linguistics term; deposition maker
de·popu·late
de·popu·la·tion
de·port
de·port·able
de·por·ta·tion
de·por·tee
de·port·ment
de·pos·able
de·pos·al
de·pose
de·pos·er
de·pos·it
de·posi·tary (*plural* ·taries) person; *compare* depository
depo·si·tion
de·posi·tor
de·posi·tory (*plural* ·tories) warehouse; *compare* depositary
de·pot
dep·ra·va·tion corruption; *compare* deprivation
de·prave
de·praved
de·praved·ness
de·prav·er
de·prav·ity (*plural* ·ities)
dep·re·cate protest against; *compare* depreciate
dep·re·ca·tion
dep·re·ca·tive
dep·re·ca·tor
dep·re·ca·to·ri·ly

dep·re·ca·tory
dep·re·ciable
de·pre·ci·ate lose value; *compare* deprecate
de·pre·cia·tion
de·pre·cia·tor
de·pre·cia·tory (*or* ·tive)
dep·re·date plunder
dep·re·da·tion
de·press
de·pres·sant
de·pressed
de·press·ible
de·press·ing
de·pres·sion
de·pres·sive
de·pres·so·mo·tor physiology term
de·pres·sor
de·pres·suri·za·tion (*or* ·sa·tion)
de·pres·sur·ize
de·priv·able
dep·ri·va·tion (*or* de·priv·al) loss; *compare* depravation
de·prive
de·prived
de·priv·er
dep·side chemistry term
depth
depu·rate purify
depu·ra·tion
depu·ra·tive purifying
depu·ra·tor
depu·ta·tion
de·pute
depu·tize (*or* ·tise)
depu·ty (*plural* ·ties)
de·rac·in·ate uproot
de·raci·na·tion
de·rail
de·rail·leur bicycle gear
de·rail·ment
de·range
de·range·ment
de·ra·tion
Der·by
Der·by·shire
de·reg·is·ter
der·elict
der·elic·tion
de·re·strict
de·re·strict·ed
de·re·stric·tion

de·ride
de·rid·er
de ri·gueur
de·ris·ible
de·ri·sion
de·ri·sive (*or* ·sory)
de·ri·sive·ness
de·riv·able
deri·va·tion
deri·va·tion·al
de·riva·tive
de·rive
de·riv·er
der·ma skin
der·mal
der·ma·ti·tis
der·mato·gen plant tissue
derma·to·glyph·ics skin pattern
der·ma·toid
der·ma·to·logi·cal
der·ma·tolo·gist
der·ma·tol·ogy
der·ma·tome surgical instrument
der·ma·tom·ic
der·ma·to·phyte parasitic fungus
der·ma·to·phyt·ic
der·ma·to·phy·to·sis
der·ma·to·plas·tic
der·ma·to·plas·ty skin grafting
der·ma·to·sis (*plural* ·ses) skin disease
der·mic
der·mis skin layer
der·moid
dero·gate disparage
dero·gation
de·roga·tive
de·roga·to·ri·ly
de·roga·to·ri·ness
de·roga·tory
der·rick
der·rière buttocks
derring-do bold action
der·rin·ger (*or* der·in·ger) pistol
der·ris plant
Der·ry Londonderry
der·ry *Austral* grudge
derv diesel oil
der·vish
Der·went river

Derwent·water lake
de·sali·nate (or ·nize, ·nise)
de·sali·na·tion (or
 ·ni·za·tion, ·ni·sa·tion)
de·scale
des·cant
des·cant·er
de·scend
des·cend·able
de·scend·ant (noun)
de·scend·ent (adj)
de·scend·er
de·scend·ible (or ·able)
de·scent
de·school
de·scrib·able
de·scribe
de·scrib·er
de·scri·er
de·scrip·tion
de·scrip·tive
de·scrip·ti·vism
de·scry (·scries, ·scry·ing,
 ·scried)
des·ecrate
des·ecra·tion
des·ecra·tor (or ·ter)
de·seg·re·gate
de·seg·re·ga·tion
de·seg·re·ga·tion·ist
de·sen·si·ti·za·tion (or
 ·sa·tion)
de·sen·si·tize (or ·tise)
de·sen·si·tiz·er (or ·tis·er)
des·ert plantless region;
 compare dessert
de·sert abandon; merit;
 compare dessert
de·sert·ed
de·sert·er
des·ert·ifi·ca·tion
de·ser·tion
de·serve
de·serv·ed·ly
de·serv·ed·ness
de·serv·er
de·serv·ing
de·sexu·ali·za·tion (or
 ·sa·tion)
de·sexu·al·ize (or ·ise)
des·ha·bille variant spelling
 of dishabille
des·ic·cant
des·ic·cate
des·ic·ca·ted

des·ic·ca·tion
des·ic·ca·tive
des·ic·ca·tor
de·sid·er·ate long for
de·sid·era·tion
de·sid·era·tive
de·sid·era·tum (plural ·ta)
 something wanted
de·sign
de·sign·able
des·ig·nate
des·ig·na·tion
des·ig·na·tive (or ·tory)
des·ig·na·tor
de·sign·ed·ly
de·sign·er
de·sign·ing
desi·nence word ending
desi·nent (or ·nen·tial)
de·sir·abil·ity (or
 ·sirable·ness)
de·sir·able
de·sire
de·sir·er
de·sir·ous
de·sist
de·sist·ance (or ·ence)
desk
des·man (plural ·mans)
 animal
des·mid alga
des·mid·ian
des·moid tumour
Des Moines US city
deso·late
deso·lat·er (or ·or)
deso·la·tion
de·sorb chemistry term
de·sorp·tion
des·pair
des·patch variant spelling of
 dispatch
des·pe·ra·do (plural ·does or
 ·dos)
des·per·ate
des·pera·tion
des·pi·cabil·ity (or
 ·cable·ness)
des·pic·able
des·pic·ably
des·pise
de·spis·er
de·spite
de·spoil
de·spoil·er

de·spoil·ment
de·spo·lia·tion
de·spond
de·spond·en·cy (or ·ence)
de·spond·ent
des·pot
des·pot·ic (or ·poti·cal)
des·poti·cal·ly
des·pot·ism
des·pu·mate clarify
des·pu·ma·tion
des·qua·mate
des·qua·ma·tion
Des·sau German city
des·sert sweet; compare
 desert
dessert·spoon
des·sia·tine Russian unit
(dessicate) incorrect spelling
 of desiccate
des·ti·na·tion
des·tine
des·tined
des·ti·ny (plural ·nies)
des·ti·tute
des·ti·tu·tion
de·stroy
de·stroy·able
de·stroy·er
de·struct
de·struc·tibil·ity
de·struct·ible
de·struc·tion
de·struc·tion·ist
de·struc·tive
de·struc·tive·ness (or
 ·tiv·ity)
de·struc·tor furnace
desue·tude state of disuse
des·ul·to·ri·ly
des·ul·to·ri·ness
des·ul·tory
de·tach
de·tach·abil·ity
de·tach·able
de·tached
de·tach·er
de·tach·ment
de·tail
de·tailed
de·tain
de·tain·able
de·tainee
de·tain·er
de·tain·ment

de·tect
de·tect·able (or ·ible)
de·tec·tion
de·tec·tive
de·tec·tor
de·tent locking device
dé·tente easement
de·ten·tion
de·ter (·ter·ring, ·terred)
de·terge cleanse
de·ter·gen·cy (or ·gence)
de·ter·gent
de·terio·rate
de·terio·ra·tion
de·terio·ra·tive
de·ter·ment
de·ter·mi·nable
de·ter·mi·nant
de·ter·mi·nate
de·ter·mi·na·tion
de·ter·mi·na·tive
de·ter·mine
de·ter·mined
de·ter·mined·ly
de·ter·mined·ness
de·ter·min·er
de·ter·min·ism
de·ter·min·ist
de·ter·min·is·tic
de·ter·rence
de·ter·rent
de·ter·sive
de·test
de·test·abil·ity (or
·able·ness)
de·test·able
de·tes·ta·tion
de·test·er
de·throne
de·throne·ment
de·thron·er
deti·nue legal term
Det·mold German city
deto·nate
deto·na·tion
deto·na·tive
deto·na·tor
de·tour
de·toxi·cant
de·toxi·cate
de·toxi·ca·tion
de·toxi·fi·ca·tion
de·toxi·fy (·fies, ·fy·ing,
·fied)
de·tract

de·trac·tion
de·trac·tive (or ·tory)
de·trac·tor
de·train
de·train·ment
de·trib·ali·za·tion (or
·sa·tion)
de·trib·al·ize (or ·ise)
det·ri·ment
det·ri·men·tal
det·ri·men·tal·ly
de·tri·tal
de·tri·tion wearing away
de·tri·tus debris
De·troit US city
de trop French superfluous
de·trude thrust out
de·trun·cate
de·trun·ca·tion
de·tru·sion
de·tu·mes·cence
Deucalion mythological
character
deuce
deu·ced
deus ex machi·na Latin
providential resolver
deu·ter·ago·nist drama
term
deu·tera·nope
deu·tera·no·pia green
blindness
deu·ter·an·op·ic
deu·ter·ide chemistry term
deu·ter·ium hydrogen
isotope
deu·tero·ca·noni·cal
deu·ter·oga·mist
deu·ter·oga·my
deu·ter·on deuterium
nucleus
Deu·ter·ono·my biblical
book
deu·to·plasm (or deu·tero·)
egg yolk
deu·to·plas·mic (or ·tic)
Deut·sche Mark
deut·zia shrub
Deux-Sèvres French city
deva oriental god; compare
diva
de·valua·tion
de·value (or ·valu·ate;
·valu·ing, ·val·ued or
·at·ing, ·ated)

De·va·na·ga·ri Indian script
dev·as·tate
dev·as·ta·tion
dev·as·ta·tive
dev·as·ta·tor
de·vel·op
de·vel·op·able
de·vel·op·er
de·vel·op·ment
de·vel·op·men·tal
de·vel·op·men·tal·ly
de·vi·ance
de·vi·ant
de·vi·ate
de·via·tion
de·via·tion·ism
de·via·tion·ist
de·via·tor
de·via·tory
de·vice contrivance; plan;
compare devise
dev·il (·il·ling, ·illed; US
·il·ing, ·iled)
devil·fish (plural ·fish or
·fishes)
dev·il·ish
dev·il·ish·ness
dev·il·ment
dev·il·ry (plural ·ries)
de·vi·ous
de·vi·ous·ness
de·vis·able
de·vis·al act of devising
de·vise to plan; leave by
will; a gift by will; compare
device
de·vi·see inheritor
de·vis·er (or in legal contexts
·vi·sor) one who devises;
compare divisor
de·vi·tali·za·tion (or
·sa·tion)
de·vi·tal·ize (or ·ise)
de·vit·ri·fi·ca·tion
de·vit·ri·fy (·fies, ·fy·ing,
·fied) chemistry term
de·vo·cal·ize (or ·ise)
de·voice phonetics term
de·void
de·voirs (plural) French
compliments
de·vo·lu·tion
de·vo·lu·tion·ary
de·vo·lu·tion·ist
de·volve

de·volve·ment
Dev·on
De·vo·nian
Dev·on·shire
de·vote
de·vot·ed
de·vot·ed·ness
devo·tee
de·vote·ment
de·vo·tion
de·vo·tion·al
de·vo·tion·al·ity (or ·ness)
de·vour
de·vour·er
de·vour·ing·ly
de·vout
de·vout·ness
dew
de·wan Indian minister
dew·berry (plural ·berries)
dew·claw
dew·drop
dewi·ly
dewi·ness
dew·lap
Dews·bury Yorkshire town
dewy (dewi·er, dew·iest)
dewy-eyed
Dex·edrine (Trademark)
dex·ter
dex·ter·ity
dex·ter·ous (or dex·trous)
dex·ter·ous·ness (or
  dex·trous·ness)
dex·tral
dex·tral·ity
dex·tral·ly
dex·tran biochemical
  compound
dex·trin (or ·trine) adhesive
  gum
dextro·am·pheta·mine
dextro·glu·cose
dextro·gy·rate (or ·gyre)
dextro·ro·ta·tion
dextro·ro·ta·tory (or
  dextro·ro·ta·ry)
dex·trorse (or ·tror·sal)
  spiralling left to right
dex·trose form of glucose
dex·trous
dey Algerian ruler
Dhah·ran Saudi Arabian
  town
dhak tree

Dhaka (or Dac·ca)
  Bangladeshi capital
dhal vegetable
dhar·ma Hindu custom
dhar·na Indian sit-in
Dhau·la·gi·ri Nepalese
  mountain
dho·bi Indian washerman
dho·le animal
dho·ti (or dhoo·ti,
  dhoo·tie, dhu·ti)
  loincloth
dhow boat
dia·base rock
dia·ba·sic
dia·be·tes
dia·bet·ic
dia·ble·rie devilry
dia·bol·ic
dia·boli·cal
dia·boli·cal·ly
dia·boli·cal·ness
diabo·lism
di·abo·list
di·abo·lize (or ·lise)
di·abo·lo (plural ·los) game
dia·caus·tic physics term
di·ac·etyl·mor·phine
dia·chron·ic linguistics
  term
di·acid
dia·cid·ic
di·aco·nal of a deacon
di·aco·nate
dia·crit·ic phonetic symbol
dia·criti·cal
di·ac·tin·ic physics term
di·ac·tin·ism
dia·del·phous botany term
dia·dem
di·ad·ro·mous fan-shaped
di·aer·esis variant spelling of
  dieresis
di·aeret·ic variant spelling of
  dieretic
dia·gen·esis chemistry term
dia·geo·trop·ic
dia·geot·ro·pism response
  to gravity
di·ag·nos·able
di·ag·nose
di·ag·no·sis (plural ·ses)
di·ag·nos·tic
di·ag·nos·ti·cal·ly
di·ag·nos·ti·cian

di·ag·nos·tics
di·ago·nal
di·ago·nal·ly
dia·gram (·gram·ming,
  ·grammed; US ·gram·ing,
  ·gramed)
dia·gram·mat·ic
dia·gram·mati·cal·ly
dia·graph drawing
  instrument
dia·ki·nesis biology term
dial (dial·ling, dialled; US
  dial·ing, dialed)
dia·lect
dia·lec·tal
dia·lec·tic
dia·lec·ti·cal
dia·lec·ti·cal·ly
dia·lec·tics branch of logic
dia·lec·to·logi·cal
dia·lec·tolo·gist
dia·lec·tol·ogy
di·al·lage mineral
dial·ler
di·alo·gism philosophy
  term
di·alo·gist
dia·lo·gis·tic (or ·ti·cal)
di·alo·gize (or ·gise)
dia·logue (US also ·log)
dia·logu·er
dia·lys·abil·ity
dia·lys·able
dia·ly·sa·tion
dia·lyse (US ·lyze)
dia·lys·er (US ·lyz·)
di·aly·sis (plural ·ses)
dia·lyt·ic
dia·lyti·cal·ly
dia·mag·net
dia·mag·net·ic
dia·mag·neti·cal·ly
dia·mag·net·ism
dia·man·té decorated with
  sequins
dia·man·tine of diamonds
di·am·eter
di·am·etral
dia·met·ric (or ·ri·cal)
dia·met·ri·cal·ly
dia·mine chemistry term
dia·mond
diamond·back terrapin
di·an·drous botany term
dia·no·et·ic of thought

dia·noia philosophy term
di·an·thus (*plural* **·thuses**)
  plant
dia·pa·son organ stop
dia·pa·son·al (*or* **·son·ic**)
dia·pause suspended growth
dia·pede·sis medical term
dia·pedet·ic
dia·per
di·apha·nous
di·apha·nous·ness (*or*
  ·nei·ty)
dia·phone linguistics term
dia·phon·ic
di·apho·ny musical term
dia·pho·resis
dia·pho·ret·ic causing
  perspiration
dia·pho·to·trop·ic biology
  term
dia·photo·trop·ism
dia·phragm
dia·phrag·mat·ic
dia·phrag·mati·cal·ly
dia·phys·ial
di·aphy·sis bone shaft
dia·pir geological fold
di·apo·phys·ial
dia·pophy·sis (*plural* **·ses**)
  anatomy term
dia·posi·tive positive
  transparency
di·arch botany term
di·ar·chic (*or* **di·ar·chi·cal**,
  di·ar·chal, dy·)
di·ar·chy (*or* **dy·**; *plural*
  ·chies) two-state
  government
dia·rist
di·ar·rhoea (*US* **·rhea**)
di·ar·rhoeal (*or* **·rhoe·ic**; *US*
  ·rheal *or* **·rhe·ic**)
di·ar·thro·dial
di·ar·thro·sis (*plural* **·ses**)
  movable joint
dia·ry (*plural* **·ries**)
dia·scope projector
Di·as·po·ra Jews'
  dispersion
dia·spore mineral
dia·stal·sis (*plural* **·ses**)
  physiology term
dia·stal·tic
dia·stase enzyme
dia·sta·sic

dia·sta·sis (*plural* **·ses**)
  separation
dia·stat·ic
dia·ste·ma (*plural* **·ma·ta**)
  fissure
di·as·ter biology term
di·as·to·le dilation of heart
di·as·tol·ic
di·as·tral biology term
dia·stroph·ic
di·as·tro·phism movement
  of earth's crust
dia·style architectural term
dia·tes·sa·ron musical term
dia·ther·man·cy (*plural*
  ·cies) heat transmission
dia·ther·man·ous
dia·ther·mic
dia·ther·my (*or* **·mia**)
  medical term
diath·esis (*plural* **·eses**)
  susceptibility to disease
dia·thet·ic
dia·tom alga
dia·to·ma·ceous
dia·tom·ic
di·ato·mic·ity
di·ato·mite rock
dia·ton·ic musical term
dia·toni·cal·ly
dia·toni·cism
dia·tribe
dia·trop·ic
di·at·ro·pism biology term
dia·zine (*or* **·zin**) chemistry
  term
di·azo (*plural* **·azos** *or*
  ·azoes) chemistry term
dia·zole
di·azo·methane
dia·zo·nium
dia·zo·ti·za·tion (*or*
  ·sa·tion)
dia·zo·tize (*or* **·tise**)
dib (**dib·bing, dibbed**)
di·ba·sic
di·ba·sic·ity
dib·ber
dib·ble garden tool
dib·bler
di·bran·chi·ate zoology
  term
di·bro·mide
di·car·box·yl·ic acid
dic·ast Athenian juror

dice
di·cen·tra plant
di·cepha·lism
di·cepha·lous two-headed
di·cer
dicey (**dici·er, dici·est**)
di·cha·sial
di·cha·sium (*plural* **·sia**)
  botany term
di·chla·myd·eous botany
  term
di·chlo·ride
**di·chloro·di·fluoro·
  methane**
**di·chloro·di·phenyl·tri·
  chloro·ethane** DDT
di·choga·mous (*or*
  ·cho·gam·ic)
di·choga·my botany term
di·choto·mist
di·choto·mi·za·tion (*or*
  ·sa·tion)
di·choto·mize (*or* **·mise**)
di·choto·mous (*or*
  ·cho·tom·ic)
di·choto·my (*plural* **·mies**)
di·chro·ic (*or* **di·chro·it·ic**)
di·chro·ism crystallography
  term
di·chro·ite
di·chro·mate chemistry
  term
di·chro·mat·ic having two
  colours
di·chro·mati·cism
  crystallography term
di·chro·ma·tism
di·chro·mic involving two
  colours
di·chro·scope (*or*
  **·chroi·scope,
  ·chroo·scope**) optical
  instrument
di·chro·scop·ic (*or*
  **·chroi·scop·ic,
  ·chroo·scop·ic**)
dick·ens slang term
Dick·en·sian
dick·er *US* barter
dicky (*or* **dick·ey**; *noun,
  plural* **dickies** *or* **dick·eys**;
  adj **dicki·er, dicki·est**)
di·cli·nism
di·cli·nous botany term
di·cli·ny

di·coty·ledon botany term
di·coty·ledon·ous
di·crot·ic (or ·cro·tal)
  having a double pulse
di·cro·tism
dic·ta plural of dictum
Dic·ta·phone (Trademark)
dic·tate
dic·ta·tion
dic·ta·tion·al
dic·ta·tor
dic·ta·tor·ial
dic·ta·tor·ial·ly
dic·ta·tor·ship
dic·ta·tress (or ·trix)
dic·tion
dic·tion·ary (plural ·aries)
Dic·to·graph (Trademark)
dic·tum (plural ·tums or ·ta)
di·cyno·dont extinct reptile
did
Dida·che treatise
di·dac·tic
di·dac·ti·cal·ly
di·dac·ti·cism
di·dac·tics teaching
did·dle
did·geri·doo musical
  instrument
didi·coy (or did·di·coy,
  dida·kai; plural ·coys or
  ·kais) gypsy
didn't
Dido mythological character
didst
di·dym·ium chemistry term
didy·mous in pairs
di·dyna·mous botany term
die (verb; dy·ing, died)
  expire; compare dye
die (noun) tool; Archaic dice;
  compare dye
die·back tree disease
die-cast (-casting, -cast)
di·ecious variant spelling
  (esp. US) of dioecious
die-hard
die-hardism
diel·drin insecticide
di·elec·tric
di·elec·tri·cal·ly
Dien Bien Phu Vietnamese
  battle site
di·en·cephal·ic
di·en·cepha·lon brain part

Di·eppe French port
di·er·esis (or ·aer·; plural
  ·eses) phonetics symbol;
  compare diuresis
di·eret·ic (or ·aeret·) of
  dieresis; compare diuretic
die·sel
diesel-electric
diesel-hydrau·lic
di·esis (plural ·eses) printing
  term
die·stock tool
di·estrus US spelling of
  dioestrus
diet
di·etary
di·et·er
di·etet·ic (or ·eteti·cal)
di·eteti·cal·ly
di·etet·ics
di·ethyl·stil·boes·trol (US
  ·bes·)
di·eti·tian (or ·cian)
dif·fer
dif·fer·ence
dif·fer·ent
dif·fer·en·tia (plural ·tiae)
  logic term
dif·fer·en·ti·abil·ity
dif·fer·en·ti·able
dif·fer·en·tial
dif·fer·en·ti·ate
dif·fer·en·tia·tion
dif·fer·en·tia·tor
dif·fi·cult
dif·fi·cul·ty (plural ·ties)
dif·fi·dence
dif·fi·dent
dif·fract
dif·frac·tion
dif·frac·tive
dif·frac·tom·eter
dif·fuse
dif·fuse·ness
dif·fus·er (or ·fu·sor)
dif·fus·ibil·ity (or
  ·ible·ness)
dif·fus·ible
dif·fu·sion
dif·fu·sive
dif·fu·siv·ity
dig (dig·ging, dug)
diga·mist
di·gam·ma obsolete Greek
  letter

diga·mous
diga·my (plural ·mies)
  second marriage
di·gas·tric jaw muscle
di·gen·esis zoology term
di·genet·ic
di·gest
di·gest·ant
di·gest·er
di·gest·ibil·ity (or
  ·ible·ness)
di·gest·ible
di·ges·tif French digestive
  drink
di·ges·tion
di·ges·tion·al
di·ges·tive (or ·tant)
dig·ger
dig·ging
dig·it
digi·tal
digi·tal·in chemical
  compound
digi·tal·is
digi·tal·ism
digi·tali·za·tion (or
  ·sa·tion)
digi·tal·ize (or ·ise)
digi·tal·ly
digi·tate (or ·tat·ed)
digi·ta·tion
digi·ti·form
digi·ti·grade walking on
  toes
digiti·za·tion (or ·sa·tion)
digi·tize (or ·ise)
digi·tox·in chemical
  compound
digi·tron electronics term
di·glot bilingual
di·glot·tic
dig·ni·fy (·fies, ·fy·ing,
  ·fied)
dig·ni·tary (plural ·taries)
dig·nity (plural ·nities)
di·graph two-letter sound
di·graph·ic
di·gress
di·gress·er
di·gres·sion
di·gres·sion·al
di·gres·sive
di·he·dral
di·he·dron
di·hy·brid

di·hy·brid·ism
Di·jon French city
dik-dik antelope
dike *variant spelling of* dyke
dik·tat decree
di·lapi·date
di·lapi·da·ted
di·lapi·da·tion
di·lapi·da·tor
di·lat·abil·ity (*or*
·able·ness)
di·lat·able
di·la·tan·cy physics term
di·la·tant
di·la·ta·tion
dila·ta·tion·al
di·late
di·la·tion
di·la·tive
dila·tom·eter
dila·to·met·ric
dila·to·met·ri·cal·ly
dila·tom·etry
di·la·tor (*or* ·lat·er,
di·la·ta·tor)
dila·to·ri·ness
di·la·tory
dil·do (*or* ·doe; *plural* ·dos *or*
·does) artificial penis
di·lem·ma
dil·em·mat·ic (*or*
dil·em·mic)
dil·et·tante (*plural* ·tan·tes
or ·tan·ti)
dil·et·tan·tish (*or* ·teish)
dil·et·tan·tism (*or* ·teism)
dili·gence
dili·gent
dill
dil·ly *Slang* remarkable
person
dilly-dally (-dallies,
-dally·ing, -dallied)
dilu·ent
di·lute
di·lu·tee
di·lut·er
di·lu·tion
di·lu·vial (*or* ·vian)
di·lu·vium (*plural* ·via)
geology term
dim (*adj* dim·mer,
dim·mest; *verb* dim·ming,
dimmed)
dime

di·men·hy·dri·nate drug
di·men·sion
di·men·sion·al
di·men·sion·al·ity
di·men·sion·less
di·mer chemistry term
di·mer·cap·rol drug
di·mer·ic
dim·er·ism
dim·er·ous divided into two
dim·eter verse line
di·methyl·sulph·ox·ide
di·met·ric crystallography
term
di·midi·ate halve; divided
in halves
di·midi·ation
di·min·ish
di·min·ish·able
di·min·ish·ment
di·minu·en·do (*plural*
·dos)
dimi·nu·tion
di·minu·tive
dim·is·sory permission to
depart
dim·ity (*plural* ·ities) fabric
dim·ly
dimmed
dim·mer
dim·mest
dim·ming
dim·ness
di·morph
di·mor·phism
di·mor·phous (*or* ·phic)
chemistry term
dim·ple
dim·ply
dim·wit
dim-witted
dim-witted·ness
din (din·ning, dinned)
di·nar currency
dine
din·er
di·ner·ic chemistry term
di·nette
ding
ding·bat *US* unnamed
object
ding·bats *Austral* delirium
tremens
ding-dong
dinge

din·ghy (*or* ·gy, ·gey; *plural*
·ghies, ·gies, *or* ·geys)
din·gi·ly
din·gi·ness
din·gle dell
din·go (*plural* ·goes)
din·gy (·gi·er, ·gi·est)
di·ni·tro·ben·zene
dink *Scot* neat
Din·ka (*plural* ·kas *or* ·ka)
Sudanese people
din·kum
dinky (dinki·er, dinki·est)
dinned
din·ner
din·ning
di·noc·er·as extinct
mammal
di·no·flag·el·late
unicellular organism
di·no·saur
di·no·saur·ian
di·no·there extinct
mammal
dint
di·oc·esan
dio·cese
di·ode
di·oecious (*or esp. US*
·ecious, ·oicious) botany
term
di·oestrus (*US* ·estrus)
biology term
Diomedes mythological
king
Dio·ny·sia ancient Greek
festivals
Dio·nysi·ac
Dio·ny·sian
Dionysus Greek god
di·op·side mineral
di·op·tase mineral
di·op·tom·eter
di·op·tom·etry
di·op·tral
di·op·tre (*US* ·ter) unit
di·op·tric (*or* ·tri·cal)
di·op·tri·cal·ly
di·op·trics
dio·ra·ma display
dio·ram·ic
dio·rite rock
dio·rit·ic
di·ox·an (*or* ·ane) chemical
compound

di·ox·ide
dip (dip·ping, dipped)
di·pep·tide
di·pet·al·ous having two
  petals
di·phase (or ·phas·ic)
  physics term
di·phenyl biphenyl
di·phenyl·amine
di·phos·gene
diph·theria
diph·therial (or ·therit·ic,
  ·ther·ic)
diph·theroid
diph·thong
diph·thon·gal
diph·thongi·za·tion (or
  ·sa·tion)
diph·thong·ize (or ·ise)
di·phy·cer·cal zoology term
di·phy·let·ic descent from
  two ancestors
di·phyl·lous having two
  leaves
diphy·odont dentition
di·plegia paralysis
di·plegic
di·plex electronics term
di·plex·er
dip·lo·blas·tic zoology term
dip·lo·car·di·ac zoology
  term
dip·lo·coc·cal (or ·cic)
dip·lo·coc·cus (plural
  ·coc·ci) bacterium
dip·lo·do·cus (plural ·cuses)
  dinosaur
dip·loë bone
dip·loid biology term
dip·loi·dic
dip·loidy
dip·lo·ma
di·plo·ma·cy (plural ·cies)
dip·lo·mat
dip·lo·mate
dip·lo·mat·ic (or ·mati·cal)
dip·lo·mati·cal·ly
dip·lo·mat·ics study of
  historical documents
di·plo·ma·tist
dip·lont biology term
di·plo·pia double vision
di·plop·ic
dip·lo·pod invertebrate
di·plo·sis biology term

dip·lo·ste·mo·nous botany
  term
dip·lo·tene genetics term
dip·noan lungfish
dipo·dy (plural ·dies)
  metrical unit
di·po·lar
di·pole physics term
dipped
dip·per
dip·ping
dip·py Slang crazy
di·pro·pel·lant
di·proto·dont marsupial
dip·so·ma·nia
dip·so·ma·ni·ac
dip·so·ma·nia·cal
dip·stick
dip·ter·al architectural term
dip·ter·an (or ·on)
  two-winged insect
dip·tero·car·pa·ceous
  botany term
dip·ter·ous two-winged
(diptheria) incorrect spelling
  of diphtheria
(dipthong) incorrect spelling
  of diphthong
dip·tych
dire
di·rect
di·rec·tion
di·rec·tion·al
di·rec·tion·al·ity
di·rec·tion·al·ly
di·rec·tive
di·rect·ly
di·rect·ness
Di·rec·toire French
  Revolutionary government
di·rec·tor
di·rec·to·rate
di·rec·to·rial
di·rec·tor·ship
di·rec·tory (plural ·tories)
di·rec·tress
di·rect·rix (plural ·rixes or
  ·rices) geometry term
dire·ful
dirge
dir·ham Moroccan currency
diri·gibil·ity
di·rig·ible steerable
di·ri·ment invalidating
dirk

dirndl dress or skirt
dirt
dirti·ly
dirti·ness
dirty (adj dirti·er, dirti·est;
  verb dirties, dirty·ing,
  dirt·ied)
Dis Roman god
dis·abil·ity (plural ·ities)
dis·able
dis·able·ment
dis·abus·al
dis·abuse
di·sac·cha·ride (or ·rid)
dis·ac·cord
dis·ac·cred·it
dis·ac·cus·tom
dis·ad·vant·age
dis·ad·van·taged
dis·ad·van·ta·geous
dis·af·fect
dis·af·fect·ed·ly
dis·af·fec·tion
dis·af·fili·ate
dis·af·fili·ation
dis·af·firm
dis·af·fir·mance (or
  ·ma·tion)
dis·af·for·est legal term
dis·af·for·es·ta·tion (or
  dis·af·for·est·ment)
dis·agree (·agree·ing,
  ·agreed)
dis·agree·able
dis·agree·able·ness (or
  ·abil·ity)
dis·agree·ably
dis·agree·ment
dis·al·low
dis·al·low·able
dis·al·low·ance
dis·am·bigu·ate
dis·an·nul (·nul·ling,
  ·nulled)
dis·an·nul·ment
dis·ap·pear
dis·ap·pear·ance
dis·ap·point
dis·ap·point·ed
dis·ap·point·er
dis·ap·point·ing
dis·ap·point·ment
dis·ap·pro·ba·tion
dis·ap·prov·al
dis·ap·prove

dis·ap·prov·er
dis·arm
dis·arma·ment
dis·arm·er
dis·arm·ing
dis·ar·range
dis·ar·range·ment
dis·ar·ray
dis·ar·ticu·late
dis·ar·ticu·la·tion
dis·ar·ticu·la·tor
dis·as·sem·ble
dis·as·sem·bly
dis·as·so·ci·ate
dis·as·so·cia·tion
dis·as·ter
dis·as·trous
dis·avow
dis·avow·al
dis·avow·ed·ly
dis·avow·er
dis·band
dis·band·ment
dis·bar (·bar·ring, ·barred)
dis·bar·ment
dis·be·lief
dis·be·lieve
dis·be·liev·er
dis·be·liev·ing·ly
dis·branch
dis·bud (·bud·ding, ·bud·ded)
dis·bur·den
dis·bur·den·ment
dis·burs·able
dis·burse
dis·burse·ment (or ·burs·al)
dis·burs·er
disc (US disk) circular plate; record; compare disk
dis·calced barefooted
dis·card
dis·card·er
dis·cern
dis·cern·er
dis·cern·ible (or ·able)
dis·cern·ing
dis·cern·ment
dis·charge
dis·charge·able
dis·charg·er
dis·ci·ple
dis·ci·ple·ship
dis·ci·plin·able
dis·ci·pli·nal

dis·ci·pli·nant member of Catholic sect
dis·ci·pli·nar·ian
dis·ci·pli·nary
dis·ci·pline
dis·ci·plin·er
dis·cipu·lar of disciples
dis·claim
dis·claim·er
dis·cla·ma·tion
dis·cli·max ecology term
dis·close
dis·clos·er
dis·clo·sure
dis·co (plural ·cos)
dis·cobo·lus (or ·los; plural ·li) discus thrower
dis·cog·ra·pher
dis·cog·ra·phy (plural ·phies) record catalogue
dis·coid
dis·coi·dal
dis·col·ora·tion
dis·col·our (US ·or)
dis·col·our·ment (US ·or·)
dis·com·bobu·late confuse
dis·com·fit disconcert
dis·com·fit·er
dis·com·fi·ture
dis·com·fort
dis·com·mend
dis·com·mode
dis·com·mo·di·ous
dis·com·mod·ity (plural ·ities) economics term
dis·com·mon legal term
dis·com·pose
dis·com·pos·ed·ly
dis·com·pos·ing·ly
dis·com·po·sure
dis·con·cert
dis·con·cert·ed
dis·con·cert·ing·ly
dis·con·cer·tion (or ·cert·ment)
dis·con·form·ity (plural ·ities)
dis·con·nect
dis·con·nect·ed
dis·con·nect·er
dis·con·nec·tion (or ·nex·ion)
dis·con·nec·tive
dis·con·so·late

dis·con·so·la·tion (or ·late·ness)
dis·con·tent
dis·con·tent·ed
dis·con·tent·ed·ness
dis·con·tent·ment
dis·con·tinu·ance
dis·con·tinua·tion
dis·con·tinue (·tinu·ing, ·tinued)
dis·con·ti·nu·ity (plural ·ities)
dis·con·tinu·ous
dis·co·phile (or ·phil) record collector
dis·cord
dis·cord·ance (or ·an·cy)
dis·cord·ant
dis·co·theque
dis·count
dis·count·able
dis·coun·tenance
dis·count·er
dis·cour·age
dis·cour·age·ment
dis·cour·ag·er
dis·cour·ag·ing·ly
dis·course
dis·cours·er
dis·cour·teous
dis·cour·tesy (plural ·tesies)
dis·cov·er
dis·cov·er·able
dis·cov·er·er
dis·cov·ert legal term
dis·cov·er·ture
dis·cov·ery (plural ·eries)
dis·cred·it
dis·cred·it·able
dis·cred·it·ably
dis·creet tactful; compare discrete
dis·creet·ness
dis·crep·an·cy (plural ·cies)
dis·crep·ant
dis·crete distinct; separate; compare discreet
dis·crete·ness
dis·cre·tion
dis·cre·tion·ari·ly (or ·tion·al·ly)
dis·cre·tion·ary (or ·al)
dis·cri·mi·nant
dis·crimi·nate
dis·crimi·nat·ing

dis·crimi·na·tion
dis·crimi·na·tion·al
dis·crimi·na·tor
dis·crimi·na·to·ri·ly (*or*
  dis·crimi·na·tive·ly)
dis·crimi·na·tory (*or* ·tive)
dis·cur·sive
dis·cus (*plural* ·cuses *or* ·ci)
  disc
dis·cuss debate
dis·cus·sant (*or* ·cuss·er)
dis·cuss·ible (*or* ·able)
dis·cus·sion
dis·cus·sion·al
dis·dain
dis·dain·ful
dis·dain·ful·ly
dis·ease
dis·eased
dis·em·bark
dis·em·bar·ka·tion (*or*
  ·bark·ment)
dis·em·bar·rass
dis·em·bar·rass·ment
dis·em·bod·ied
dis·em·bodi·ment
dis·em·body (·bodies,
  ·body·ing, ·bod·ied)
dis·em·bogue (·bogu·ing,
  ·bogued) discharge
dis·em·bogue·ment
dis·em·bow·el (·el·ling,
  ·elled; *US* ·el·ing, ·eled)
dis·em·bow·el·ment
dis·em·broil
dis·en·able
dis·en·able·ment
dis·en·chant
dis·en·chant·er
dis·en·chant·ment
dis·en·cum·ber
dis·en·cum·ber·ment
dis·en·dow
dis·en·dow·er
dis·en·dow·ment
dis·en·fran·chise
dis·en·fran·chise·ment
dis·en·gage
dis·en·gage·ment
dis·en·tail
dis·en·tail·ment
dis·en·tan·gle
dis·en·tan·gle·ment
dis·en·thral (*or* ·thrall;
  ·thral·ling, ·thralled)

dis·en·thral·ment (*or*
  ·thrall·)
dis·en·ti·tle
dis·en·tomb
dis·en·twine
di·sepa·lous botany term
dis·equi·lib·rium
dis·es·tab·lish
dis·es·tab·lish·ment
dis·es·teem
di·seur (*fem* ·seuse) French
  monologue performer
dis·fa·vour (*US* ·vor)
dis·fea·ture
dis·fea·ture·ment
dis·fig·ure
dis·fig·ure·ment (*or*
  ·ura·tion)
dis·fig·ur·er
dis·fran·chise
dis·fran·chise·ment
dis·gorge
dis·gorge·ment
dis·gorg·er
dis·grace
dis·grace·ful
dis·grace·ful·ly
dis·grac·er
dis·grun·tle
dis·grun·tled
dis·grun·tle·ment
dis·guis·able
dis·guise
dis·guis·er
dis·gust
dis·gust·ed·ly
dis·gust·ing
dish
dis·ha·bille (*or* des·)
  half-dressed
dis·har·mo·ni·ous
dis·har·mo·ny (*plural* ·nies)
dish·cloth
dis·heart·en
dis·heart·en·ment
dished
di·shev·el (·el·ling, ·elled;
  US ·el·ing, ·eled)
di·shev·el·ment
dis·hon·est
dis·hon·es·ty (*plural* ·ties)
dis·hon·our (*US* ·or)
dis·hon·our·able (*US* ·or·)
dis·hon·our·ably (*US* ·or·)
dis·hon·our·er (*US* ·or·)

dish·washer
dish·water
dishy (dishi·er, dishi·est)
dis·il·lu·sion
dis·il·lu·sion·ment
dis·il·lu·sive
dis·in·cen·tive
dis·in·cli·na·tion
dis·in·cline
dis·in·fect
dis·in·fect·ant
dis·in·fec·tion
dis·in·fec·tor
dis·in·fest
dis·in·fes·ta·tion
dis·in·fla·tion
dis·in·genu·ous
dis·in·genu·ous·ness
dis·in·her·it
dis·in·heri·tance
dis·in·te·grable
dis·in·te·grate
dis·in·te·gra·tion
dis·in·te·gra·tive
dis·in·te·gra·tor
dis·in·ter (·ter·ring, ·terred)
dis·in·ter·est
dis·in·ter·est·ed impartial;
  compare uninterested
dis·in·ter·ment
dis·ject break apart
dis·join separate
dis·join·able
dis·joint dislocate
dis·joint·ed
dis·junct
dis·junc·tion (*or* ·ture)
dis·junc·tive
disk computer device; *US*
  spelling of disc
dis·lik·able (*or* ·like·)
dis·like
dis·limn efface
dis·lo·cate
dis·lo·ca·tion
dis·lodge
dis·lodg·ment (*or* ·lodge·)
dis·loy·al
dis·loy·al·ty (*plural* ·ties)
dis·mal
dis·mal·ly
dis·mal·ness
dis·man·tle
dis·man·tle·ment
dis·man·tler

dis·mast
dis·mast·ment
dis·may
dis·mem·ber
dis·mem·ber·er
dis·mem·ber·ment
dis·miss
dis·mis·sal
dis·miss·ible
dis·miss·ive
dis·mount
dis·mount·able
Dis·ney·land
dis·obedi·ence
dis·obedi·ent
dis·obey
dis·obey·er
dis·oblige
dis·oblig·ing
dis·op·era·tion ecology
   term
dis·or·der
dis·or·der·li·ness
dis·or·der·ly
dis·or·gani·za·tion (or
   ·sa·tion)
dis·or·gan·ize (or ·ise)
dis·or·gan·iz·er (or ·is·er)
dis·ori·en·tate (or
   dis·ori·ent)
dis·ori·en·ta·tion
dis·own
dis·own·er
dis·own·ment
dis·par·age
dis·par·age·ment
dis·par·ag·er
dis·par·ate
dis·par·ity (plural ·ities)
dis·pas·sion detachment
dis·pas·sion·ate
dis·pas·sion·ate·ness
dis·patch (or des·)
dis·patcher (or des·)
dis·pel (·pel·ling, ·pelled)
dis·pel·ler
dis·pen·sabil·ity (or
   ·sable·ness)
dis·pen·sable
dis·pen·sa·ry (plural ·ries)
dis·pen·sa·tion
dis·pen·sa·tion·al
dis·pen·sa·tory (plural
   ·tories) drug catalogue
dis·pense

dis·pens·er
di·sper·mous botany term
dis·per·sal
dis·per·sant
dis·perse
dis·pers·er
dis·per·sion
dis·per·sive
dis·per·soid chemistry term
dis·pir·it
dis·pir·it·ed
dis·pir·it·ing
dis·place
dis·place·able
dis·place·ment
dis·plac·er
dis·play
dis·play·er
dis·please
dis·pleas·ure
dis·port
dis·pos·abil·ity (or
   ·able·ness)
dis·pos·able
dis·pos·al
dis·pose
dis·posed
dis·pos·er
dis·po·si·tion
dis·po·si·tion·al
dis·pos·sess
dis·pos·ses·sion
dis·pos·ses·sor
dis·pos·ses·so·ry
dis·praise
dis·prais·er
dis·proof
dis·pro·por·tion
dis·pro·por·tion·able
dis·pro·por·tion·ate
dis·pro·por·tiona·tion
dis·prov·able
dis·prov·al
dis·prove
dis·put·abil·ity (or
   ·able·ness)
dis·put·able
dis·put·ably
dis·pu·tant
dis·pu·ta·tion
dis·pu·ta·tious (or ·tive)
dis·pute
dis·put·er
dis·quali·fi·able
dis·quali·fi·ca·tion

dis·quali·fi·er
dis·quali·fy (·fies, ·fy·ing,
   ·fied)
dis·qui·et
dis·qui·et·ed·ly (or
   dis·qui·et·ly)
dis·qui·et·ed·ness (or
   dis·qui·et·ness)
dis·qui·et·ing
dis·qui·etude
dis·qui·si·tion formal
   discourse
dis·rate reduce to lower
   rank
dis·re·gard
dis·re·gard·er
dis·re·gard·ful
dis·rel·ish
dis·re·pair
dis·repu·tabil·ity (or
   ·table·ness)
dis·repu·table
dis·repu·tably
dis·re·pute
dis·re·spect
dis·re·spect·abil·ity
dis·re·spect·able
dis·re·spect·ful
dis·re·spect·ful·ly
dis·robe
dis·robe·ment
dis·rob·er
dis·rupt
dis·rupt·er (or ·rup·tor)
dis·rup·tion
dis·rup·tive
dis·sat·is·fac·tion
dis·sat·is·fac·tory
dis·sat·is·fy (·fies, ·fy·ing,
   ·fied)
dis·sect
dis·sec·tible
dis·sec·tion
dis·sec·tor
dis·seise (or ·seize) legal
   term
dis·sei·sin (or ·zin)
dis·sei·sor (or ·zor)
dis·sem·blance
dis·sem·ble
dis·sem·bler
dis·semi·nate
dis·semi·na·tion
dis·semi·na·tive
dis·semi·na·tor

dis·semi·nule botany term
dis·sen·sion
dis·sent
dis·sent·er
dis·sen·tience (or ·tien·cy)
dis·sen·tient dissenting
dis·sen·tious argumentative
dis·sepi·ment dividing
  membrane
dis·sepi·men·tal
dis·ser·tate
dis·ser·ta·tion
dis·ser·ta·tion·al
dis·ser·ta·tion·ist
dis·ser·vice
dis·ser·vice·able
dis·sev·er break off
dis·sev·er·ance (or
  ·er·ment, ·era·tion)
dis·si·dence
dis·si·dent
dis·simi·lar
dis·simi·lar·ity (plural ·ities)
dis·simi·late phonetics
  term; compare dissimulate
dis·simi·la·tion
dis·simi·la·tive
dis·simi·la·tory
dis·si·mili·tude
dis·simu·late pretend;
  compare dissimilate
dis·simu·la·tion
dis·simu·la·tive
dis·simu·la·tor
dis·si·pate
dis·si·pat·ed
dis·si·pat·er (or ·pa·tor)
dis·si·pa·tion
dis·si·pa·tive
dis·so·ci·abil·ity (or
  ·able·ness)
dis·so·ci·able
dis·so·ci·ate
dis·so·cia·tion
dis·so·cia·tive
dis·sol·ubil·ity (or
  ·uble·ness)
dis·sol·uble
dis·so·lute
dis·so·lute·ness
dis·so·lu·tion
dis·so·lu·tive
dis·solv·abil·ity (or
  ·able·ness)
dis·solv·able

dis·solve
dis·sol·vent
dis·solv·er
dis·so·nance (or ·nan·cy)
dis·so·nant
dis·suad·able
dis·suade
dis·suad·er
dis·sua·sion
dis·sua·sive
dis·sua·sive·ness
dis·syl·lab·ic (or di·syl·)
dis·syl·la·ble (or di·syl·)
dis·sym·met·ric (or ·ri·cal)
dis·sym·me·try (plural
  ·tries)
dis·taff
dis·tal anatomy term
dis·tal·ly
dis·tance
dis·tant
dis·taste
dis·taste·ful
dis·taste·ful·ly
dis·tem·per
dis·tend
dis·tend·er
dis·ten·si·bil·ity
dis·ten·sible
dis·ten·sion (or ·tion)
dis·tich poem
dis·ti·chal
dis·ti·chous in two rows
dis·til (US dis·till; ·til·ling,
  ·tilled)
dis·till·able
dis·til·late
dis·til·la·tion (or
  dis·till·ment)
dis·til·la·tory
dis·till·er
dis·till·ery (plural ·eries)
dis·tinct
dis·tinc·tion
dis·tinc·tive
dis·tinc·tive·ness
dis·tinct·ness
dis·tin·gué (fem ·guée)
  French distinguished
dis·tin·guish
dis·tin·guish·able
dis·tin·guish·ably
dis·tin·guished
dis·tin·guish·er
dis·tort

dis·tort·ed
dis·tort·er
dis·tor·tion
dis·tor·tion·al
dis·tor·tive
dis·tract
dis·tract·ed
dis·tract·er
dis·tract·ibil·ity
dis·tract·ible
dis·trac·ting
dis·trac·tion
dis·trac·tive
dis·train
dis·train·able
dis·trainee legal term
dis·train·ment
dis·trai·nor (or ·train·er)
dis·traint legal term
dis·trait absent-minded
dis·traught
dis·tress
dis·tressed
dis·tress·ful
dis·tress·ful·ly
dis·tress·ing
dis·trib·ut·able
dis·tribu·tary (plural ·taries)
  stream
dis·trib·ute
dis·tribu·tee legal term
dis·tri·bu·tion
dis·tri·bu·tion·al
dis·tribu·tive
dis·tribu·tor (or ·tribut·er)
dis·trict
dis·trin·gas legal term
dis·trust
dis·trust·er
dis·trust·ful
dis·trust·ful·ly
dis·turb
dis·turb·ance
dis·turbed
dis·turb·er
di·sul·fi·ram drug
di·sul·phate (US ·fate)
di·sul·phide (US ·fide)
di·sul·phu·ric (US ·fu·)
dis·un·ion
dis·unite
dis·unity (plural ·unities)
dis·use
dis·used
dis·util·ity

dobla

dit Morse code sound

dita shrub

ditch

ditch·er

di·theism

di·theist

di·theis·tic

dith·er

dith·er·er

di·thio·nite chemical
compound

dithy·ramb ancient Greek
hymn

dithy·ram·bic

dithy·ram·bi·cal·ly

dit·tan·der plant

dit·ta·ny (*plural* ·nies) plant

dit·to (*noun, plural* ·tos; *verb*
·tos, ·to·ing, ·toed)

dit·to·graph·ic

dit·tog·ra·phy (*plural*
·phies) repetition

dit·ty (*plural* ·ties)

di·uresis increased
urination; *compare* dieresis

di·uret·ic increasing
urination; *compare* dieretic

di·ureti·cal·ly

di·ur·nal of the day

di·ur·nal·ly

div *Slang* stupid person

diva (*plural* divas *or* dive)
prima donna; *compare*
deva

di·va·lency

di·va·lent

di·van

di·vari·cate branching

di·vari·ca·tion

di·vari·ca·tor zoology term

dive (div·ing, dived (*US*
dove))

dive-bomb

div·er

di·verge

di·ver·gence (*or* ·gen·cy;
plural ·gences *or* ·cies)

di·ver·gent

di·vers *Archaic* several

di·verse varied

di·ver·si·fi·abil·ity

di·ver·si·fi·able

di·ver·si·fi·ca·tion

di·ver·si·fi·er

di·ver·si·form

di·ver·si·fy (·fies, ·fy·ing,
·fied)

di·ver·sion

di·ver·sion·al (*or* ·ary)

di·ver·sity

di·vert

di·vert·ed·ly

di·vert·er

di·vert·ible

di·ver·ticu·lar

di·ver·ticu·li·tis

di·ver·ticu·lo·sis

di·ver·ticu·lum (*plural* ·la)
anatomical pouch

di·vert·ing·ly

di·ver·tisse·ment brief
entertainment

di·ver·tive

Dives biblical character

di·vest

di·vest·ible

di·vesti·ture (*or* ·ves·ture,
·vest·ment)

di·vid·able

di·vide

divi·dend

di·vid·er

di·vid·ers measuring
compass

divi-divi (*plural* -divis *or*
-divi) tree

di·vin·able

divi·na·tion

divi·na·tory

di·vine

di·vin·er

di·vin·ing

di·vin·ity (*plural* ·ities)

divi·ni·za·tion (*or* ·sa·tion)

divi·nize (*or* ·nise) deify

di·vis·ibil·ity

di·vi·sible

di·vi·sion

di·vi·sion·al (*or* ·ary)

di·vi·sion·ism

di·vi·sion·ist

di·vi·sive

di·vi·sor maths term;
compare deviser

di·vorce

di·vor·cé (*fem* ·cée)
divorced person

di·vorce·able

di·vorce·ment

di·vorc·er

di·vor·cive

div·ot turf

di·vulge

di·vul·gence (*or*
·vulge·ment)

di·vulg·er

di·vul·sion tearing apart

di·vul·sive

div·vy (*plural* ·vies) *Slang*
dividend

Dixie southern states of
USA

dixie metal pot

Dixie·land jazz

Di·yar·ba·kir (*or* ·bekir)
Turkish city

diz·zi·ly

diz·zi·ness

diz·zy (*adj* ·zi·er, ·zi·est;
verb ·zies, ·zy·ing, ·zied)

Dja·ja *variant spelling of* Jaya

Dja·ja·pu·ra *variant spelling
of* Jajapura

Dja·kar·ta (*or* Ja·) *variant
spelling of* Jakarta

Djam·bi (*or* Jam·) *variant
spelling of* Jambi

Djer·ba Tunisian island

Dji·bou·ti (*or* Ji·) African
republic

djin·ni (*or* ·ny) *variant
spellings of* jinni

Djok·ja·kar·ta *variant
spelling of* Jogjakarta

Dne·pro·dzer·zhinsk
Ukrainian city

Dne·pro·pe·trovsk
Ukrainian city

Dnie·per (*or* Dnepr) E
European river

Dnie·ster (*or* Dnestr) E
European river

do (*verb* does, do·ing, did,
done; *noun, plural* dos *or*
do's)

doab land between rivers

do·able

dob·bin

dob·by (*plural* ·bies) loom
attachment

Do·ber·man pin·scher dog

do·bla coin

Do·bro (*Trademark; plural ·bros*) guitar

Do·bru·ja E European region

dobson·fly (*plural ·flies*)

doc *Slang* doctor

do·cent US lecturer

do·cent·ship

Do·cetism heresy

doc·ile

do·cil·ity

dock

dock·age dock charge

dock·er

dock·et

dock·land

dock·yard

doc·tor

doc·tor·al (*or ·to·rial*)

doc·tor·ate

doc·tri·naire

doc·tri·nair·ism (*or ·nar·ism*)

doc·tri·nal

doc·tri·nal·ity

doc·tri·nar·ian

doc·trine

doc·trin·ism

docu·ment

docu·men·ta·ri·ly

docu·men·tary (*plural ·taries*)

docu·men·ta·tion

dod·der totter, tremble (*verb*); plant (*noun*)

dod·der·er

dod·der·ing

dod·dery

dod·dle

do·deca·gon 12-sided figure

do·de·cago·nal

do·deca·he·dral

do·deca·he·dron 12-faced solid

Do·deca·nese Aegean islands

do·deca·phon·ic musical term

do·deca·phon·ism

do·deca·phon·ist

do·deca·phony

dodge

Dodg·em (*Trademark*)

dodg·er

dodgy (**dodgi·er, dodgi·est**)

dodo (*plural* **dodos** *or* **dodoes**)

dodo·ism

Do·do·ma Tanzanian town

Do·do·na Greek town

doe (*plural* **does** *or* **doe**)

doek African headscarf

doer

does (*present tense of* do; *plural of* doe)

doe·skin

doff

doff·er

dog (**dog·ging, dogged**)

dog·bane plant

dog·berry (*plural ·berries*) shrub

dog·berry·ism officialdom

dog·cart

doge Venetian magistrate

dog-ear

dog-eared

dog·fight

dog·fish (*plural ·fish or ·fishes*)

dog·ged (*adj*)

dog·ged·ness

Dog·ger North Sea sandbank

dog·ger fishing vessel

dog·ger·el (*or* **dog·rel**)

dog·gery (*plural ·geries*) surly behaviour

dog·gish

dog·go *Slang* in hiding

dog·gone US slang term

dog·gy (*adj; ·gi·er, ·gi·est*)

dog·gy (*or ·gie; noun; plural ·gies*)

dog·house

do·gie US motherless calf

dog·leg (·leg·ging, ·legged) bend sharply

dog·leg·ged (*adj*)

dog·ma (*plural ·mas or ·ma·ta*)

dog·man (*plural ·men*) *Austral* crane-driver's assistant

dog·mat·ic (*or ·mati·cal*)

dog·mati·cal·ly

dog·mat·ics

dog·ma·tism

dog·ma·tist

dog·ma·ti·za·tion (*or ·sa·tion*)

dog·ma·tize (*or ·tise*)

dog·ma·tiz·er (*or ·tis·er*)

do-gooder

dogs·body (*plural ·bodies*)

dog's-tail grass

dog-tired

dog·tooth (*plural ·teeth*)

dog·trot

dog·vane wind vane

dog·watch nautical term

dog·wood

doh musical note

Doha capital of Qatar

doi·ly (*or* **doy·ley, doy·ly**; *plural ·lies or ·leys*)

do·ing

doit coin

do-it-yourself

dol unit of pain

do·lab·ri·form (*or ·rate*) hatchet-shaped

Dol·by (*Trademark*) recording system

dol·ce musical term

dol·ce vita *Italian* luxurious life

dol·drums

dole

dole·ful

dole·ful·ly

dole·ful·ness

dol·er·ite rock

dol·er·it·ic

doli·cho·cephal·ic (*or* cepha·lous) long-headed

doli·cho·cepha·lism (*or ·ly*)

do·li·na (*or ·ne*) ground depression

doll

dol·lar

dollar·bird

dollar·fish (*plural ·fish or ·fishes*)

doll·ish

doll·op

dol·ly (*noun, plural ·lies; verb ·ly·ing, ·lied*)

dol·man (*plural ·mans*) robe

dol·mas (*or ·ma*) stuffed vine leaves

dol·men tomb

do·lo·mite mineral

Do·lo·mites mountain range

dolo·mit·ic

dol·or·im·etry pain measurement

do·lo·ro·so musical term

dol·or·ous

dol·our (*US* ·or) grief

dol·phin

dol·phin·ar·ium

dolt

dolt·ish

dom monk's title

do·main

dome

dome·like

domes·day *variant spelling of* doomsday

Domes·day Book (*or* Dooms·)

do·mes·tic

do·mes·ti·cable

do·mes·ti·cal·ly

do·mes·ti·cate

do·mes·ti·ca·tion

do·mes·ti·ca·tive

do·mes·ti·ca·tor

do·mes·ti·city (*plural* ·cities)

domi·cal (*or* do·mic) of a dome

domi·cile

domi·cili·ary

domi·cili·ate

domi·nance

domi·nant

domi·nate

domi·na·tion

domi·na·tive

domi·na·tor

do·mi·nee Afrikaner clergyman

domi·neer

Domi·ni·ca West Indian country

do·mini·cal relating to the Lord

Do·mini·can Republic; friar

domi·nie *Scot* schoolmaster

do·min·ion

do·min·ium (*or* ·ion) legal term

domi·no (*plural* ·noes)

Don Spanish title; Russian river

don (don·ning, donned)

Doña Spanish woman's title

Donar Germanic god

do·nate

do·na·tion

dona·tive gift

do·na·tor

Don·bass (*or* ·bas) Ukrainian industrial region

Don·cas·ter

done

do·nee receiver of gift

Don·egal Irish county

Do·nets Ukrainian river

Do·netsk Ukrainian city

dong

don·jon castle keep

Don Juan legendary seducer

don·key

Don·na Italian woman's title

donned

don·nert *Scot* stunned

don·ning

don·nish

donny·brook rowdy brawl

do·nor

do·nor·ship

don't do not

do·nut *variant spelling (esp. US) of* doughnut

doo·dah

doo·dle

doodle·bug

doo·dler

doom

dooms·day (*or* domes·)

door

door·bell

do·or·die

door·frame

door·jamb

door·keeper

door·man (*plural* ·men)

door·mat

door·nail

door·post

door·sill

door·step

door·stop

door·way

door·yard *US* outside yard

do·pant chemistry term

dope

dopey (*or* dopy; dopi·er, dopi·est)

dopi·ness

Dop·pel·gäng·er ghost

Dop·per Afrikaner churchgoer

dor beetle

Do·ra·do constellation

Dor·ches·ter

Dor·dogne French region and river

Dor·drecht Dutch port

Do·rian ancient Greek

Dor·ic architectural term

Do·ris region of ancient Greece

Dor·king

dorm *Slang* dormitory

dor·man·cy

dor·mant

dor·mer

dor·mie (*or* ·my) golf term

dor·mi·tory (*plural* ·tories)

Dor·mo·bile (*Trademark*)

dor·mouse (*plural* ·mice)

dor·nick (*or* ·neck) cloth

do·roni·cum plant

dorp South African village

dor·sad towards the back

dor·sal of the back

dor·sal·ly

Dor·set

dor·si·grade walking on backs of toes

dor·si·ven·tral having upper and lower surfaces

dor·si·ven·tral·ity

dor·so·ven·tral from back to belly

dor·so·ven·tral·ly

dor·sum (*plural* ·sa) the back

Dort·mund German city

dorty *Scot* sullen

dory (*plural* dories) fish; boat

dos·age

dose

dos·er

do-si-do dance figure

do·sim·eter (*or* dose·meter)

do·si·met·ric

do·si·metri·cian (*or* do·sim·etrist)

do·sim·etry

doss

dos·sal (or ·sel) church
  hanging

dos·ser *Slang* tramp;
  dosshouse

doss·house

dos·si·er

dot (dot·ting, dot·ted)

dot·age

do·tard

do·ta·tion endowment

dote

dot·er

dotted

dot·ted

dot·ter

dot·ter·el (or ·trel)

dot·ti·ly

dot·ti·ness

dot·ting

dot·tle (or ·tel) tobacco in
  pipe

dot·ty (·ti·er, ·ti·est)

Douai French city

Doua·la (or Dua·la)
  Cameroon port

Dou·ay bible

dou·ble

double-acting

double-barrelled (*US*
  -barreled)

double-bass (*adj*)

double-blind

double-breasted

double-check

double-cross

double-dealing

double-decker

double-dotted musical term

double-edged

dou·ble en·ten·dre

double-faced

double-glazing

double-header

double-hung

double-jointed

double-park

double-quick

dou·bler

double-reed

dou·bles tennis

double-space

double-stop (-stopping,
  -stopped)

dou·blet

double·think

dou·ble·ton bridge term

double-tongue (-tonguing,
  ·tongued) musical term

double-tree horizontal bar
  on vehicle

dou·bloon (or do·blon)
  coin

dou·blure lining inside
  book

dou·bly

Doubs French river

doubt

doubt·able

doubt·er

doubt·ful

doubt·ful·ly

doubt·ful·ness

doubt·less

douc monkey

douce *Scot* sedate

dou·ceur bribe

douche

dough

dough·boy *Slang* dumpling

dough·nut (*or esp. US*
  do·nut)

doughti·ly

dough·ty (·ti·er, ·ti·est)
  hardy

doughy (doughi·er,
  doughi·est)

Doug·las Manx town

Dou·kho·bors Russian sect

doum (*or* doom) palm tree

dour sullen; *compare* dower

dou·rine horse disease

dour·ness

Dou·ro Spanish–Portuguese
  river

dou·rou·cou·li monkey

douse (*or* dowse) drench;
  compare dowse

dous·er (*or* dows·)

dove bird; *US past tense of*
  ·dive

dove·cote (*or* ·cot)

dove·kie (*or* ·key) bird

Do·ver

dove·tail

dov·ish

dow·able legal term

dowa·ger

dow·di·ly

dow·di·ness

dow·dy (*noun, plural* ·dies;
  adj ·di·er, ·di·est)

dow·el

dow·er widow's inheritance;
  compare dour

(dowery) *incorrect spelling of*
  dowry

dow·itch·er bird

Dow-Jones av·er·age US
  stock exchange index

down

down·beat

down·bow

down·cast

down·com·er (*or* ·come)
  plumbing term

down·fall

down·fallen

down·grade

down·haul nautical term

down·hearted

down·hearted·ness

down·hill

downi·ness

Down·ing Street

down·market

Down·pat·rick Irish town

down·pipe

down·pour

down·range

down·right

Downs Sussex hills

downs chalk uplands

down·side

down·size

down·spout US drainpipe

Down's syn·drome

down·stage

down·stairs

down·state US S part of
  state

down·stream

down·swing

down·throw

down-to-earth

down·town

down·trod·den (*or* ·trod)

down·turn

down·ward (*adj*)

down·wards (*adv*)

down·wash

down·wind

downy (downi·er,
  downi·est)

dow·ry (*plural* ·ries)

dowse to divine water;
　variant spelling of douse
dows·er
dows·ing
dox·as·tic logic term
doxo·logi·cal
dox·ol·ogy (*plural* ·ogies)
doxy (*plural* doxies)
doy·en (*fem* ·enne)
doze
doz·en
doz·enth
doz·er
dozy (dozi·er, dozi·est)
drab (drab·ber, drab·best)
drab·bet fabric
drab·ble make wet
drab·ly
drab·ness
dra·cae·na plant
drachm fluid dram
drach·ma (*plural* ·mas or
　·mae) Greek currency
Dra·co constellation
dra·cone container towed
　by ship
Dra·co·nian (or ·con·ic)
　harsh
Dra·co·ni·an·ism
dra·con·ic dragon-like
dra·coni·cal·ly
draff husks
draffy
draft sketch; military
　selection; money order; *US
　spelling of* draught
draftee
draft·er
drafts·man (*plural* ·men)
　document drafter; *compare*
　draughtsman
drag (drag·ging, dragged)
dra·gée sweet
drag·gle trail
drag·hound
drag·line
drag·net
dra·go·man (*plural* ·mans or
　·men) interpreter
drag·on
drag·on·ess
drag·on·et fish
dragon·fly (*plural* ·flies)
dragon·head (or
　dragon's-head) plant

drag·on·ish
drag·on·nade persecution
　by dragoons
dragon·root
dra·goon
dra·goon·age
drag·rope
drail weighted hook
drain
drain·able
drain·age
drain·er
drain·pipe
drake
Dra·kens·berg African
　mountain
dram 1/16 ounce; tot;
　compare drachm
dra·ma
Dra·ma·mine (*Trademark*)
dra·mat·ic
dra·mati·cal·ly
dra·mat·ics
dra·ma·tis per·so·nae
　characters in a play
drama·tist
drama·tiz·able (or ·tis·able)
drama·ti·za·tion (or
　·sa·tion)
drama·tize (or ·tise)
drama·tiz·er (or ·tis·er)
drama·turge (or ·tur·gist)
　dramatist
drama·tur·gic (or ·gi·cal)
drama·tur·gy
Drambuie (*Trademark*)
drank
drap·able (or drape·able)
drape
drap·er
dra·per·ied
dra·pery (*plural* ·peries)
drapes *US* curtains
dras·tic
dras·ti·cal·ly
drat
drat·ted
draught (*US* draft) air
　current; drink; load
　pulling; *compare* draft
draught·board (or
　draughts·)
draught·er (*US* draft·)
draughti·ness (*US* drafti·)
draughts game

draughts·man (*US* drafts·;
　plural ·men) plan drafter;
　compare draftsman
draughts·man·ship (*US*
　drafts·)
draughty (*US* drafty;
　draughti·er, draughti·est;
　US drafti·er, drafti·est)
Dra·va European river
Dra·vid·ian language group
draw (draw·ing, drew,
　drawn)
draw·able
draw·back
draw·bar
draw·bridge
drawee
draw·er
drawer·ful
drawers undergarment
draw·ing
draw·knife (or ·shave;
　plural ·knives or ·shaves)
　woodcutting tool
drawl
drawl·er
drawly
drawn
draw·plate extrusion plate
draw·string
draw·tube
dray cart; *compare* drey
dray·horse
dread
dread·ful
dread·fully
dread·ful·ness
dread·nought (or ·naught)
　battleship
dream (dream·ing, dreamt
　or dreamed)
dream·er
dreami·ly
dreami·ness
dream·ing·ly
dream·less
dream·like
dreamy (dreami·er,
　dreami·est)
dreari·ly
dreari·ness
dreary (dreari·er,
　dreari·est)
dredge
dredg·er

dree *Scot* endure

dreg

dreg·gy (·gi·er, ·gi·est)

drench

drench·er

Dren·the Dutch region

Dres·den German city

dress

dres·sage

dressed

dress·er

dressi·ly

dressi·ness

dress·ing

dress·maker

dress·making

dressy (dressi·er, dressi·est)

drew

drey squirrel's nest; *compare* dray

drib·ble

drib·bler

drib·let (*or* ·blet) small amount

dried

dri·er (*adj*)

dri·est

drift

drift·age

drift·er

drift·wood

drifty

drill

drill·able

drill·er

drill·ing

drill·master

drill·stock tool part

dri·ly

drink (drink·ing, drank, drunk)

drink·able

drink·er

drip (drip·ping, dripped)

drip-dry (-dries, -dry·ing, -dried)

drip·ping

drip·py (·pi·er, ·pi·est)

drip·stone

driv·able (*or* drive·)

drive (driv·ing, drove, driv·en)

drive-in

driv·el (·el·ling, ·elled; *US* ·el·ing, ·eled)

driv·el·ler (*US* ·el·er)

driv·en

driv·er

driv·er·less

drive·way

driv·ing

driz·zle

driz·zly

drogue

droit right

droll

droll·ery (*plural* ·eries)

droll·ness

Drôme French department

drom·edary (*plural* ·edaries) camel

drom·ond sailing vessel

drone

dron·go (*plural* ·gos) bird

dron·ish

drool

droop sag; *compare* drupe

droopi·ly

droopi·ness

droopy (droopi·er, droopi·est)

drop (drop·ping, dropped)

drop·let

drop·light

drop·out

drop·per

drop·pings

drop·si·cal

drop·sied

drop·sonde meteorological device

drop·sy fluid in body

drop·wort plant

drosh·ky (*or* dros·ky; *plural* ·kies) carriage

dro·sophi·la (*plural* ·las *or* ·lae) fruit fly

dross

drossi·ness

drossy (drossi·er, drossi·est)

drought (*or* drouth)

droughty

drove

drov·er

drown

drown·er

drowse

drowsi·ly

drowsi·ness

drowsy (drowsi·er, drowsi·est)

drub (drub·bing, drubbed) beat

drub·ber

drudge

drudg·er

drudg·ery (*plural* ·eries)

druf·fen *Dialect* drunk

drug (drug·ging, drugged)

drug·get fabric

drug·gist

drug·store

dru·id (*fem* ·id·ess)

dru·id·ic (*or* ·idi·cal)

dru·id·ism

drum (drum·ming, drummed)

drum·beat

drum·fire

drum·fish (*plural* ·fish *or* ·fishes)

drum·head

drum·lin landform

drum·mer

drum·stick

drunk

drunk·ard

drunk·en

drunk·en·ness

dru·pa·ceous

drupe fruit; *compare* droop

drupe·let (*or* dru·pel) small fruit

Dru·ry Lane

Druse (*or* Druze) religious sect

druse crystals lining cavity

dry (*adj* dri·er, dri·est; *verb* dries, dry·ing, dried)

dry·able

dry·ad (*plural* ·ads *or* ·ades) wood nymph

dry·ad·ic

dry-clean

dry-cleaner

dry-cleaning

dry·er (*noun*)

dry·ness

dryo·pith·ecine extinct ape

dry-salt preserve by salting

dry-stone wall

dual two; *compare* duel

Du·ala (*plural* ·ala *or* ·alas) African people

dual·ism
dual·ist
dual·is·tic
dual·is·ti·cal·ly
dual·ity (*plural* ·ities)
dual-purpose
dub (dub·bing, dubbed)
Du·bai sheikdom
dub·bin (*or* dub·bing)
    leather grease
du·bi·ety (*or* du·bi·os·ity;
    plural ·ties)
du·bi·ous
du·bi·ous·ness
du·bi·table
du·bi·ta·tion doubt
Dub·lin
Du·bon·net (*Trademark*)
Du·brov·nik Croatian port
du·cal
duc·at coin
duce *Italian* leader
duch·ess
duchy (*plural* duchies)
duck
duck·board
duck·er
duck·ling
ducks trousers
duck·weed
ducky (*or* duckie; *plural*
    duckies)
duct
duc·tile
duc·til·ity (*or* ·tile·ness)
dud
dude
du·deen clay pipe
dudg·eon anger
Dud·ley English town
due
duel (duel·ling, duelled; *US*
    duel·ing, dueled) fight;
    compare dual
duel·ler (*or* ·list; *US* ·er *or*
    ·ist)
du·el·lo (*plural* ·los)
    duelling
du·en·na chaperon
duet (*or* du·ette)
duet·tist
duff
duf·fel (*or* ·fle)
duf·fer
dug

du·gong animal
dug·out
dui·ker (*plural* ·kers *or* ·ker)
    antelope
Duis·burg German city
duke
duke·dom
dul·cet
dul·ci·ana organ stop
dul·ci·fy (·fies, ·fying,
    ·fied) sweeten
dul·ci·mer musical
    instrument
du·lia veneration for saints
dull
dull·ard
dull·ness (*or* dul·ness)
dulls·ville boredom
dul·ly in a dull way
du·lo·sis zoology term
dulse seaweed
Du·luth US port
duly appropriately
dumb
Dum·bar·ton Scottish town
dumb·bell
dumb-cane plant
dumb·found (*or* dum·)
dumb·found·er (*or* dum·)
dumb·ness
dumb·struck (*or* ·stricken)
dumb·waiter stand for
    dishes
dum·dum bullet
Dum·fries
dum·my (*noun, plural* ·mies;
    verb ·mies, ·my·ing,
    ·mied)
du·mor·ti·erite mineral
dump
dump·er
dumpi·ness
dump·ling
dumpy (dumpi·er,
    dumpi·est)
Dum·yat Egyptian town
dun (*verb* dun·ning,
    dunned; *adj* dun·ner,
    dun·nest)
Dun·bar Scottish port
dunce
Dun·dalk Irish town
Dun·dee
dunder·head
dune

Dun·edin New Zealand port
Dun·ferm·line
dung
dun·ga·ree fabric
dun·ga·rees overalls
Dun·ge·ness Kent headland
dun·geon
dung·hill
dungy
dun·ite rock
dunk
dunk·er
Dun·kirk French port
Dun Laoghaire Irish port
dun·lin bird
dun·nage cargo-packing
    material
dun·na·kin *Dialect* lavatory
dunned
dun·ner
dun·nest
dun·ning
dun·nite explosive
dun·nock bird
dun·ny *Scot* cellar
Du·noon Scottish town
Dun·si·nane Scottish hill
Dun·sta·ble
dunt *Dialect* a blow
duo (*plural* duos *or* dui)
duo·deci·mal of 12
duo·deci·mo (*plural* ·mos)
    book size
duo·denal
duo·dena·ry
duo·deni·tis
duo·denum (*plural* ·dena *or*
    ·denums)
duo·logue
duo·mo (*plural* ·mos)
    cathedral
duo·tone printing process
dup *Dialect* open
dup·abil·ity
dup·able
dupe
dup·er
dup·ery
du·ple musical term
du·plet chemistry term
du·plex
du·plex·ity
du·pli·cabil·ity
du·pli·cable
du·pli·cate

du·pli·ca·tion
du·pli·ca·tive
du·pli·ca·tor
du·plic·ity (*plural* ·ities)
du·pon·dius coin
du·rabil·ity (*or* ·rable·ness)
du·rable
Du·ralu·min (*Trademark*) aluminium alloy
dura ma·ter membrane round brain
du·ra·men wood
du·rance imprisonment
Du·ran·go Mexican state
du·ra·tion
du·ra·tion·al
du·ra·tive linguistics term
Dur·ban South African port
dur·bar African court
du·ress
Du·rex (*Trademark*) condom
Dur·ham
du·rian (*or* ·ri·on) fruit
dur·ing
dur·mast tree
duro (*plural* duros) coin
Du·roc US pig
dur·ra (*or* dou·ra, dou·rah) grass
durst *past tense of* dare
du·rum wheat
Du·shan·be Tadzhik capital
dusk
duski·ness
dusky (duski·er, duski·est)
Düs·sel·dorf German city
dust
dust·bin
dust·cart
dust·er
dusti·ly
dusti·ness
dust·man (*plural* ·men)
dust·pan
dust·sheet
dust-up *Slang* fight
dusty (dusti·er, dusti·est)
Dutch
Dutch·man (*plural* ·men)
du·teous *Archaic* dutiful
du·ti·abil·ity
du·ti·able
du·ti·ful
du·ti·ful·ly
du·ti·ful·ness

duty (*plural* duties)
duty-free
du·vet
du·vetyn (*or* ·vetine, ·vetyne) fabric
dux *Scot* best pupil
dvan·dva compound word
dwale deadly nightshade
dwarf (*plural* dwarfs *or* dwarves)
dwarf·ish
dwarf·ish·ness
dwarf·ism
dwell (dwell·ing, dwelt *or* dwelled)
dwell·er
dwell·ing
dwin·dle
dy·able (*or* dye·able)
dyad maths term
dy·ad·ic twofold
Dyak (*plural* Dyaks *or* Dyak) Malaysian people
dy·ar·chic (*or* ·chi·cal, ·chal) *variant spelling of* diarchic
dy·ar·chy (*plural* ·chies) *variant spelling of* diarchy
dyb·buk (*plural* ·buks *or* ·buk·kim) Hebrew spirit
dye (dye·ing, dyed) colour; *compare* die
dye·ing colouring; *compare* dying
dye·line blueprint
dy·er
dyer's-greenweed
dyer's-weed
dye·stuff
dye·wood
Dyf·ed former Welsh county
dy·ing expiring; *compare* dyeing
dyke (*or* dike)
dy·nam·eter
dy·nam·ic
dy·nami·cal·ly
dy·nam·ics
dy·na·mism philosophical theory
dy·na·mist
dy·na·mis·tic

dy·na·mite
dy·na·mit·er (*or* ·mit·ist)
dy·na·mit·ic
dy·na·mo (*plural* ·mos)
dy·na·mo·elec·tric (*or* ·tri·cal)
dy·na·mom·eter
dy·na·mo·met·ric (*or* ·ri·cal)
dy·na·mom·etry
dy·na·mo·tor
dyn·ast ruler
dy·nas·tic (*or* ·ti·cal)
dyn·as·ty (*plural* ·ties)
dy·na·tron type of oscillator
dyne unit
dy·node electrode
dys·en·ter·ic
dys·en·tery
dys·func·tion
dys·gen·ic
dys·gen·ics reducing quality of race
dys·graphia impaired writing ability
dys·lexia impaired reading ability
dys·lex·ic (*or* ·lec·tic)
dys·men·or·rhoea (*US* ·rhea)
dys·men·or·rhoeal (*US* ·rheal)
dys·pep·sia (*or* ·sy) indigestion
dys·pep·tic (*or* ·ti·cal)
dys·pha·gia difficulty in swallowing
dys·phag·ic
dys·pha·sia impaired speech
dys·pha·sic
dys·phe·mism substitution of offensive word
dys·pho·nia impaired speech
dys·phon·ic
dys·pho·ria uneasy feeling
dys·phor·ic
dys·pla·sia abnormal organ development
dys·plas·tic
dysp·noea (*US* ·nea) difficulty in breathing
dysp·noeal (*or* ·noe·ic; *US* ·neal *or* ·ne·ic)

dys·pro·sium chemical
  element
dys·tel·eol·ogy philosophy
  term
dys·thy·mia neurotic
  condition
dys·thy·mic

dys·to·pia worst possible
  place
dys·troph·ic
dys·tro·phy (*or* ·**phia**)
  wasting of tissues
dys·uria painful urination
dys·uric

dy·tis·cid beetle
Dyu·la (*plural* ·**la** *or* ·**las**)
  African people
Dzer·zhinsk Russian city
Dzong·ka Asian language
Dzun·ga·ria (*or* **Zun·**)
  Chinese region

E

each
eager keen; *compare* **eagre**
eager·ness
eagle
eagle-eyed
eagle·stone
eaglet
eagle·wood
eagre (*or* **eager**) tidal bore;
  compare **eager**
eal·dor·man Anglo-Saxon
  official
Ealing
ear
ear·ache
ear·bash *Austral* talk
ear·drop
ear·drum
eared
ear·flap
ear·ful
ear·ing nautical term
earl
ear·lap
earl·dom
ear·li·ness
ear·ly (·**li·er**, ·**li·est**)
Ear·ly Bird satellite
ear·mark
ear·muff
earn
earn·er
ear·nest
ear·nest·ness
earn·ings
ear·phone
ear·piece
ear·plug
ear·ring
ear·shot
ear·splitting
earth

earth·born
earth·bound
earth·en
earthen·ware
earthi·ly
earthi·ness
earth·light *variant of*
  earthshine
earth·li·ness
earth·ling
earth·ly (·**li·er**, ·**li·est**)
earth·nut
earth·quake
earth·rise
earth·shaking
earth·shine (*or* ·**light**)
  earth's reflected light
earth·star fungus
earth·wards (*or esp. US*
  ·**ward**)
earth·work
earth·worm
earthy (**earthi·er**,
  earthi·est)
ear·wax
ear·wig
ease
ease·ful
ease·ful·ness
easel
ease·ment
eas·er
easi·ly
easi·ness
east
East An·glia
East An·glian
East Ber·lin
East Ber·lin·er
east·bound
East·bourne
East·er

Easter-ledges plant
east·er·ly (*plural* ·**lies**)
east·ern
east·ern·er
east·ern·most
East·er·tide
East Ger·man
East Ger·ma·ny
East In·dian
East In·dies
east·ing nautical term
East Kil·bride Scottish town
East·leigh Hampshire town
east-northeast
east-southeast
east·ward (*adj*)
east·ward·ly
east·wards (*adv*)
easy (**easi·er**, **easi·est**)
easy-going
eat (**eat·ing**, **ate**, **eat·en**)
eat·able
eat·age *Dialect* grazing
  rights
eat·en
eat·er
eau de Co·logne
eau de Ja·velle bleaching
  solution
eau de nil greenish colour
eau de vie brandy
eaves
eaves·drop (·**drop·ping**,
  ·**dropped**)
eaves·drop·per
ebb
Ebbw Vale
ebon ebony
eb·on·ite rubber
eb·on·ize (*or* ·**ise**)
eb·ony (*plural* ·**onies**)
Ebora·cum *Latin* York

ebrac·te·ate

ebul·lience (or ·lien·cy)

ebul·lient

ebul·li·os·co·py chemistry term

ebul·li·tion boiling

ebur·na·tion bone condition

ecad ecology term

écar·té card game

Ec·bata·na Iranian city

ec·bol·ic medi term

ec·cen·tric

ec·cen·tri·cal·ly

ec·cen·tri·city (plural ·cities)

ec·chy·mo·sis (plural ·ses) skin condition

Ec·cles English town; cake

ec·cle·sia (plural ·siae) church congregation

ec·cle·si·arch sacristan

Ec·cle·si·as·tes Old Testament book

ec·cle·si·as·tic

ec·cle·si·as·ti·cal

ec·cle·si·as·ti·cal.ly

ec·cle·si·as·ti·cism

Ec·cle·si·as·ti·cus book of Apocrypha

ec·cle·si·ola·ter

ec·cle·si·ola·try ecclesiastical obsession

ec·cle·sio·logi·cal (or ·log·ic)

ec·cle·si·olo·gist

ec·cle·si·ol·ogy study of Church

ec·crine

ec·crin·ol·ogy study of glands

ec·dys·ial

ec·dysi·ast striptease artist

ec·dy·sis (plural ·ses) moulting

ec·dy·sone hormone

ecesis ecology term

ec·hard biology term

eche·lon

ech·eve·ria plant

echid·na (plural ·nas or ·nae) spiny anteater

echi·nate (or ·nat·ed) having bristles

echi·no·coc·cus tapeworm

echi·no·derm marine animal

echi·no·der·mal (or ·ma·tous)

echi·noid marine animal

echi·nus (plural ·ni) sea urchin

echo (noun, plural echoes; verb echoes, echo·ing, ech·oed)

echo·ic

echo·ism linguistics term

echo·la·lia psychiatric term

echo·la·lic

echo·location

echo·prac·tic

echo·praxia (or ·prax·is) psychiatric term

echo·virus

éclair

ec·lamp·sia pregnancy condition

ec·lamp·tic

éclat acclaim

ec·lec·tic selecting the best

ec·lec·ti·cism

eclipse

eclips·er

eclip·sis linguistics term

eclip·tic astronomy term

eclip·ti·cal·ly

ec·lo·gite rock

ec·logue poem

eclo·sion emergence of insect

eco·cide environmental destruction

eco·friend·ly

eco·logi·cal (or ·log·ic)

eco·logi·cal·ly

ecolo·gist

ecol·ogy

econo·met·ric (or ·ri·cal)

econo·me·tri·cian (or ·met·rist)

econo·met·rics economics

eco·nom·ic

eco·nomi·cal

eco·nomi·cal·ly

eco·nom·ics

econo·mist

econo·mi·za·tion (or ·sa·tion)

econo·mize (or ·mise)

econo·miz·er (or ·mis·er)

econo·my (plural ·mies)

écor·ché anatomical figure

eco·spe·cies

eco·spe·cif·ic

eco·sphere

écoss·aise dance

eco·sys·tem

eco·ter·ror·ism

eco·ter·ror·ist

eco·ton·al

eco·tone ecology term

eco·type

eco·typ·ic

eco·typi·cal·ly

écra·seur surgical device

ecru yellowish colour

ec·sta·sy (plural ·sies)

ec·stat·ic

ec·stati·cal·ly

ec·stat·ics

ec·thy·ma skin condition

ec·to·blast biology term

ec·to·blas·tic

ec·to·derm (or exo·derm) embryo part

ec·to·der·mal (or ·mic)

ec·to·en·zyme

ec·to·gen·esis

ec·tog·enous (or ·to·gen·ic) biology term

ec·to·mere embryology term

ec·to·mer·ic

ec·to·morph

ec·to·mor·phic thin

ec·to·morphy

ec·to·para·site

ec·to·para·sit·ic

ec·to·phyte parasitic plant

ec·to·pia congenital displacement

ec·top·ic in abnormal position; compare entopic

ec·to·plasm

ecto·plas·mic

ec·to·proct animal

ec·to·sarc amoeba ectoplasm

ecto·sar·cous

ec·ty·pal

ec·type copy

Ecua·dor

Ecua·do·rian (or ·ran)

ecu·men·ic

ecu·meni·cal (or oecu·)

ecu·meni·cal·ism (or ·cism)
Christian unity
ecu·meni·cal·ly
écu·rie motor-racing team
ec·ze·ma
ec·zema·tous
eda·cious greedy
eda·cious·ness
edac·ity
Edam
edaph·ic of soil
edaphi·cal·ly
Edda Norse poems
eddo plant
eddy (noun, plural eddies;
verb eddies, eddy·ing,
eddied)
Ed·dy·stone rocks;
lighthouse
Ede Dutch city
edel·weiss
ede·ma US spelling of
oedema
edema·tous US spelling of
oedematous
Eden biblical garden
eden·tate zoology term
eden·tu·lous (or ·late)
toothless
edge
Edge·hill English battle
site
edg·er
edge·ways
edgi·ly
edgi·ness
edg·ing
edgy (edgi·er, edgi·est)
edh runic character
ed·ibil·ity (or ·ible·ness)
ed·ible
edict
edic·tal
edi·fi·ca·tion
edifi·ca·tory
edi·fice
edi·fi·cial
edi·fi·er
edi·fy (·fies, ·fy·ing, ·fied)
edi·fy·ing·ly
edile US variant spelling of
oedile
Ed·in·burgh
edit
edi·tion

edi·tio prin·ceps (plural
edi·tio·nes prin·ci·pes)
Latin first edition
edi·tor
edi·to·rial
edi·to·ri·al·ist
edi·to·ri·ali·za·tion (or
·sa·tion)
edi·to·ri·al·ize (or ·ise)
edi·to·ri·al·iz·er (or ·is·er)
edi·to·ri·al·ly
edi·tor·ship
Ed·mon·ton Canadian city
Edom biblical people
edu·cabil·ity (or
educat·abil·ity)
edu·cable (or ·cat·able)
edu·cate
edu·cat·ed
edu·ca·tion
edu·ca·tion·al
edu·ca·tion·al·ist (or
·tion·ist)
edu·ca·tion·al·ly
edu·ca·tive
edu·ca·tor
edu·ca·tory
educe logic term
educ·ible
educt chemistry term
educ·tion
educ·tive
edul·co·rate wash
edul·co·ra·tion
Ed·ward·ian
eel
eel·grass
eel-like
eel·pout fish
eel·worm
e'er ever; compare ere
eerie (eeri·er, eeri·est)
weird; compare eyrie
eeri·ly
eeri·ness
eff
ef·fable expressible
ef·face
ef·face·able
ef·face·ment
ef·fac·er
ef·fect (noun) result; (verb)
cause; compare affect
ef·fect·er
ef·fect·ible

ef·fec·tive
ef·fec·tive·ly
ef·fec·tive·ness
ef·fec·tor physiology term
ef·fects
ef·fec·tual
ef·fec·tu·al·ity (or ·al·ness)
ef·fec·tu·al·ly
ef·fec·tu·ate bring about
ef·fec·tu·ation
ef·femi·na·cy (or
·nate·ness)
ef·femi·nate
ef·fen·di (plural ·dis)
Turkish title
ef·fer·ence
ef·fer·ent conducting
outwards; compare afferent
ef·fer·vesce
ef·fer·ves·cence
ef·fer·ves·cent
ef·fer·ves·cible
ef·fer·ves·cing·ly
ef·fete weak
ef·fi·ca·cious
ef·fi·ca·cy (or ·cious·ness)
ef·fi·cien·cy (plural ·cies)
ef·fi·cient
ef·fig·ial
ef·fi·gy (plural ·gies)
ef·flo·resce
ef·flo·res·cence
ef·flo·res·cent
ef·flu·ence (or ef·flux)
ef·flu·ent
ef·flu·vial
ef·flu·vium (plural ·via or
·viums) bad smell
ef·flux variant of effluence
ef·fort
ef·fort·ful
ef·fort·less
ef·fort·less·ness
ef·fron·tery (plural ·teries)
ef·ful·gence
ef·ful·gent radiant
ef·fuse spread out
ef·fu·si·om·eter physics
apparatus
ef·fu·sion
ef·fu·sive
ef·fu·sive·ness
Efik (plural Efik or Efiks)
African people
eft newt

egad

egali·tar·ian

egali·tari·an·ism

Egeria female adviser

egest excrete

eges·ta

eges·tion

eges·tive

egg

egg·beater

eg·ger (or ·gar) moth

egg·head

egg·nog (or egg-noggin)

egg·plant US aubergine

egg·shell

eggy

Eg·ham Surrey town

egis US variant spelling of aegis

eg·lan·tine plant

Eg·mont extinct volcano

ego (plural egos)

ego·cen·tric

ego·cen·tric·ity

ego·cen·trism

ego·ism self-interest; compare egotism

ego·ist

ego·is·tic (or ·ti·cal)

ego·ma·nia

ego·ma·ni·ac

ego·ma·nia·cal

ego·tism self-centredness; compare egoism

ego·tist

ego·tis·tic (or ·ti·cal)

ego·tis·ti·cal·ly

egre·gious bad

egre·gious·ness

egress

egres·sion

egret bird

Egypt

Egyp·tian

Egyp·to·logi·cal

Egyp·tolo·gist

Egyp·tol·ogy

eh

eider

eider·down

eidet·ic psychology term

eideti·cal·ly

eido·lon (plural ·la or ·lons) apparition

Eiffel Tower

eigen·func·tion physics term

Eiger Swiss mountain

eight

eight·een

eight·een·mo (plural ·mos)

eight·eenth

eight·fold

eighth

eighti·eth

eight·some

eight·vo (plural ·vos)

eighty (plural eighties)

Eilat Israeli port

Eind·ho·ven Dutch city

ein·korn wheat

Ein·stein·ian

ein·stein·ium radioactive element

Eire

eireni·con (or ireni·) philosophy term

eise·gesis (plural ·geses) text interpretation

Eisen·ach German city

eistedd·fod (plural ·fods or ·fodau)

eistedd·fod·ic

ei·ther

ejacu·late

ejacu·la·tion

ejacu·la·tive

ejacu·la·tor

ejacu·la·tory

eject

ejec·ta volcanic material

ejec·tion

ejec·tive phonetics term

ejec·tor

eke

ekis·ti·cal (or ·tic)

ekis·tics human settlements

elabo·rate

elabo·rate·ness

elabo·ra·tion

elabo·ra·tive

elabo·ra·tor

el·aeop·tene variant spelling of eleoptene

El Ala·mein Egyptian battle site

Elam ancient kingdom

Elam·ite (or ·it·ic)

élan style

eland antelope

élan vital philosophy term

ela·pid snake

elapse

elas·mo·branch fish

elas·mo·saur reptile

elas·tance physics term

elas·tic

elas·ti·cal·ly

elas·ti·cate

elas·ti·ca·tion

elas·tici·ty

elas·ti·cize (or ·cise)

elas·tin protein

elas·to·mer rubbery material

elas·to·mer·ic

Elas·to·plast (Trademark)

elate

elat·ed

elat·ed·ness

ela·ter biology term

elat·er·id beetle

elat·er·in purgative

elat·er·ite bitumen

ela·terium purgative

ela·tion

ela·tive linguistics term

Elba Italian island

Elbe European river

el·bow

elbow·room

El·brus Russian mountain

el·der

elder·berry (plural ·berries)

el·der·li·ness

el·der·ly

el·der·ship

eld·est

El Do·ra·do legendary city

el·dritch (or ·drich) unearthly

Ele·at·ic

Ele·ati·cism philosophy term

ele·cam·pane plant

elect

elect·able

elec·tion

elec·tion·eer

elec·tion·eer·er

elec·tion·eer·ing

elec·tive

elec·tiv·ity (or ·tive·ness)

elec·tor

elec·tor·al

elec·tor·ate
elec·tor·ship
Electra mythological
   character
elec·tret physics term
elec·tric
elec·tri·cal
elec·tri·cal·ly
elec·tri·cian
elec·tric·ity
elec·tri·fi·able
elec·tri·fi·ca·tion
elec·tri·fi·er
elec·tri·fy (·fies, ·fy·ing,
   ·fied)
elec·tro (*plural* ·tros)
elec·tro·acous·tic (*or* ·ti·cal)
elec·tro·acous·tics
elec·tro·analy·sis
elec·tro·ana·lytic (*or*
   ·lyti·cal)
elec·tro·car·dio·gram
elec·tro·car·dio·graph
elec·tro·car·dio·graph·ic (*or*
   ·graphi·cal)
elec·tro·car·di·og·ra·phy
elec·tro·chemi·cal
elec·tro·chem·ist
elec·tro·chem·is·try
elec·tro·con·vul·sive
elec·tro·cor·ti·co·gram
   record of brainwaves
elec·tro·cute
elec·tro·cu·tion
elec·trode
elec·tro·de·pos·it
elec·tro·depo·si·tion
   chemistry term
elec·tro·di·aly·sis
elec·tro·dy·nam·ic (*or*
   ·nami·cal)
elec·tro·dy·nam·ics
elec·tro·dy·na·mom·eter
elec·tro·en·cepha·lo·gram
elec·tro·en·cepha·lo·graph
elec·tro·en·cepha·lo-
   graph·ic
elec·tro·en·cepha·lo-
   graphi·cal·ly
elec·tro·en·cepha·log·ra·
   phy
elec·tro·form form by
   electrolysis
elec·tro·graph printing
   term

elec·tro·graph·ic
elec·tro·graphi·cal·ly
elec·trog·ra·phy
elec·tro·jet physics term
elec·tro·ki·net·ic
elec·tro·ki·net·ics
elec·tro·lu·mi·nes·cence
elec·tro·lu·mi·nes·cent
elec·tro·ly·sa·tion (*US*
   ·za·tion)
elec·tro·lyse (*US* ·lyze)
elec·tro·lys·er (*US* ·lyz·er)
elec·troly·sis
elec·tro·lyte
elec·tro·lyt·ic (*or* ·lyti·cal)
elec·tro·mag·net
elec·tro·mag·net·ic
elec·tro·mag·neti·cal·ly
elec·tro·mag·ne·tism
elec·tro·me·chani·cal
elec·tro·mer·ism chemistry
   term
elec·tro·met·al·lur·gi·cal
elec·tro·me·tal·lur·gist
elec·tro·met·al·lur·gy
elec·trom·eter
elec·tro·met·ric (*or* ·ri·cal)
elec·trom·etry
elec·tro·mo·tive current-
   producing
elec·tron
elec·tro·nega·tive
elec·tro·nega·tiv·ity
elec·tron·ic
elec·troni·cal·ly
elec·tron·ics
elec·tron·volt unit
elec·tro·phil·ic chemistry
   term
elec·tro·phone musical
   term
elec·tro·phon·ic
elec·tro·pho·resis physics
   term
elec·tro·pho·ret·ic
elec·tropho·rus physics
   apparatus
elec·tro·physio·logi·cal
elec·tro·physi·olo·gist
elec·tro·physi·ol·ogy
elec·tro·plate
elec·tro·plat·er
elec·tro·po·si·tive
elec·tro·scope
elec·tro·scop·ic

elec·tro·stat·ic
elec·tro·stati·cal·ly
elec·tro·stat·ics
elec·tro·stric·tion physics
   term
elec·tro·sur·gery
elec·tro·sur·gi·cal
elec·tro·thera·peu·tic (*or*
   ·ti·cal)
elec·tro·thera·peu·tics
elec·tro·thera·pist
elec·tro·thera·py
elec·tro·ther·mal
elec·tro·ton·ic
elec·troto·nus physiology
   term
elec·tro·type printing term
elec·tro·typ·er
elec·tro·va·len·cy (*or*
   ·lence) chemistry term
elec·tro·va·lent
elec·trum alloy
elec·tu·ary (*plural* ·aries)
   medical term
el·eemosy·nary dependent
   on charity
el·egance (*or* el·egan·cy;
   plural ·egances *or* ·cies)
el·egant
el·egi·ac
el·egist
el·egize (*or* ·egise)
el·egy (*plural* ·egies)
el·ement
el·ement·al
el·emen·ta·ri·ness
el·emen·ta·ry
el·emi (*plural* ·emis) resin
elen·chus (*plural* ·chi) logic
   term
elenc·tic
el·eop·tene (*or* ·aeop·)
   chemistry term
el·ephant (*plural* ·ephants
   or ·ephant)
el·ephan·ti·as·ic
el·ephan·tia·sis disease
el·ephan·tine
el·ephan·toid
elephant's-ear plant
elephant's-foot (*or*
   elephant-) plant
Eleu·sin·ian
Eleu·sis Greek town
el·evate

el·evat·ed
el·eva·tion
el·eva·tor
elev·en
eleven-plus
elev·en·ses
elev·enth
el·evon aircraft control
    surface
elf (plural elves)
El Fai·yum (or Al Fai·yum)
    Egyptian city
elfin
elf·ish (or elv·)
elf·lock
Elgin Scottish town; marbles
El Giza Egyptian city
Elia Greek department
elic·it evoke; compare illicit
elic·it·able
elici·ta·tion
elici·tor
elide linguistics term
elid·ible
eli·gibil·ity
eli·gible
eli·gibly
elimi·nable
elimi·nant
elimi·nate
elimi·na·tion
elimi·na·tive (or ·tory)
elimi·na·tor
Elis ancient Olympic Games
    site
eli·sion linguistics term
elite (or élite)
elit·ism
elit·ist
elix·ir
Eliza·bethan
elk
elk·hound
ell unit of length
Elles·mere Canadian Island
el·lipse flattened circle
el·lip·sis (plural ·ses)
    missing words
el·lip·soid
el·lip·soi·dal
el·lip·tic
el·lip·ti·cal
el·lip·ti·cal·ly
el·lip·ti·cal·ness
el·lip·ti·city

elm
El Man·su·ra (or Al
    Man·su·rah) Egyptian
    city
El Min·ya Egyptian port
El Mis·ti Peruvian volcano
El Obeid Sudanese city
elo·cu·tion
elo·cu·tion·ary
elo·cu·tion·ist
elon·gate
elon·ga·tion
elon·ga·tive
elope
elope·ment
elop·er
elo·quence
elo·quent
elo·quent·ness
El Paso Texan city
El Sal·va·dor
else·where
El·si·nore
elu·ant variant spelling of
    eluent
elu·ci·date
elu·ci·da·tion
elu·ci·da·tive (or ·da·tory)
elu·ci·da·tor
elude escape from; compare
    allude; illude
elud·er
elu·ate chemistry term
elu·ent (or ·ant)
elu·sion
elu·sive evasive; compare
    illusive
elu·sive·ness
elute chemistry term
elu·tri·ant
elu·tri·ate
elu·tria·tion
elu·tria·tor
elu·vial
elu·via·tion
elu·vium (plural ·via) rock
    particles; compare
    alluvium
el·ver eel
elves plural of elf
elv·ish variant spelling of
    elfish
Ely
Ély·sée Parisian palace
Ely·sian

Ely·sium mythological
    heaven
ely·troid (or ·trous)
ely·tron (or ·trum; plural
    ·tra) beetle's wing
em printer's measure;
    compare en
ema·ci·ate
ema·cia·ted
ema·cia·tion
ema·nate
ema·na·tion
ema·na·tion·al
ema·na·tive
ema·na·tor
ema·na·tory
eman·ci·pate
eman·ci·pa·tion
eman·ci·pa·tion·ist
eman·ci·pa·tive
eman·ci·pa·tor
eman·ci·pa·tory
emar·gi·nate (or ·nat·ed)
    notched
emar·gi·na·tion
emas·cu·late
emas·cu·la·tion
emas·cu·la·tive (or ·tory)
emas·cu·la·tor
em·balm
em·balm·er
em·balm·ment
em·bank
em·bank·ment
(embarass) incorrect spelling
    of embarrass
em·bar·go (noun, plural
    ·goes; verb ·goes, ·go·ing,
    ·goed)
em·bark
em·bar·ka·tion
em·bark·ment
em·bar·rass
em·bar·rass·ing
em·bar·rass·ment
em·bas·sy (plural ·sies)
em·bat·tle
em·bay
em·bay·ment bay-shaped
em·bed (·bed·ding,
    ·bed·ded)
em·bed·ment
em·bel·lish
em·bel·lish·er
em·bel·lish·ment

em·ber
em·bez·zle
em·bez·zle·ment
em·bez·zler
em·bit·ter
em·bit·ter·er
em·bit·ter·ment
em·bla·zon
em·bla·zon·ment
em·bla·zon·ry
em·blem
em·blem·at·ic (or ·ati·cal)
em·blem·ati·cal·ly
em·blema·tize (or ·tise,
·blem·ize, ·blem·ise)
em·ble·ments legal term
em·bodi·ment (or im·)
em·body (·bod·ies,
·body·ing, ·bod·ied)
em·bold·en
em·bo·lec·to·my (plural
·mies)
em·bol·ic
em·bo·lism
em·bo·lis·mic
em·bo·lus (plural ·li)
material blocking blood
vessel
em·bo·ly (plural ·lies)
embryology term
em·bon·point French
plumpness
em·boss
em·boss·er
em·boss·ment
em·bou·chure (plural
·chures)
em·bow architecture term
em·bow·el
em·bow·er
em·bow·ment
em·brace
em·brace·able
em·brace·ment
em·brac·er
em·brac·ery Obsolete jury
bribing
em·branch·ment
em·bra·sure fortification
em·bra·sured
em·brec·to·my (plural
·mies)
em·bro·cate
em·bro·ca·tion
em·broi·der

em·broi·der·er
em·broi·dery (plural
·deries)
em·broil
em·broil·er
em·broil·ment
em·bry·ec·to·my (plural
·mies)
em·brue variant spelling of
imbrue
em·bryo (plural ·bryos)
em·bryo·gen·ic
em·bry·og·eny
development of embryo
em·bry·oid
em·bryo·logi·cal (or
·log·ic)
em·bry·olo·gist
em·bry·ol·ogy
em·bry·on·ic (or ·bryo·nal)
em·bry·oni·cal·ly
em·bus (·bus·ing, ·bused or
·bus·sing, ·bussed)
emend improve text;
compare amend
emend·able
emen·da·tion
emen·da·tor
emen·da·tory
em·er·ald
emerge
emer·gence
emer·gen·cy (plural ·cies)
emer·gent
emeri·tus
emersed botany term
emer·sion emerging;
compare immersion
em·ery mineral
em·esis vomiting
emet·ic
emeti·cal·ly
em·etine (or ·etin) alkaloid
emi·grant
emi·grate leave country;
compare immigrate
emi·gra·tion
emi·gra·tion·al
emi·gra·tive
émi·gré French emigrant
Emilia-Romagna Italian
region
Emi·nence (or ·nen·cy;
plural ·nences or
·nen·cies) cardinal's title

emi·nence (or ·nen·cy;
plural ·nences or
·nen·cies) superiority
émi·nence grise (plural
emi·nences grises) French
powerful person
emi·nent distinguished;
compare immanent;
imminent
emir (or emeer) Islamic
ruler
emir·ate (or emeer·)
em·is·sary (plural ·saries)
emis·sion
emis·sive
emis·siv·ity physics term
emit (emit·ting,
emit·ted)
emit·ter
Em·men Dutch city
em·mena·gog·ic
em·mena·gogue medical
term
Em·men·thal (or ·tal,
·thal·er, ·tal·er) cheese
em·mer wheat
em·met Dialect ant
em·me·tro·pia perfect
vision
em·me·trop·ic
Emmy television award
emol·lience
emol·lient soothing
emolu·ment salary
emote
emot·er
emo·tion
emo·tion·al
emo·tion·al·ism
emo·tion·al·ist
emo·tion·al·is·tic
emo·tion·al·ity
emo·tion·ali·za·tion (or
·sa·tion)
emo·tion·al·ize (or ·ise)
emo·tion·al·ly
emo·tive
emo·tive·ness (or ·tiv·ity)
emo·ti·vism
em·pale less common spelling
of impale
em·pan·el (US im·; ·el·ling,
·elled, US ·el·ing, ·eled)
em·pan·el·ment (US im·)
em·path·ic (or ·pa·thet·ic)

em·pathi·cal·ly (*or*
  ·pa·theti·cal·ly)
em·pa·thize (*or* ·thise)
em·pa·thy
em·pen·nage aircraft tail
em·per·or
em·per·or·ship
em·pery power
em·pha·sis (*plural* ·ses)
em·pha·size (*or* ·sise)
em·phat·ic
em·phati·cal·ly
em·phati·cal·ness
em·phy·sema lung
  condition
em·phy·sema·tous
em·pire
em·pir·ic
em·piri·cal
em·piri·cal·ly
em·piri·cal·ness
em·piri·cism
em·piri·cist
em·place
em·place·ment
em·plane
em·ploy
em·ploy·abil·ity
em·ploy·able
em·ployee
em·ploy·er
em·ploy·ment
em·poi·son
em·po·rium (*plural* ·riums
  or ·ria)
em·pov·er·ish *less common
  spelling of* impoverish
em·pow·er
em·pow·er·ment
em·press
empt *Dialect* empty
emp·ti·able
emp·ti·ly
emp·ti·ness
emp·ty (*adj* ·ti·er, ·ti·est;
  verb ·ties, ·ty·ing, ·tied)
empty-handed
empty-headed
em·py·ema pus
  accumulation
em·py·emic
em·py·real
em·py·rean heavens
em·py·reu·ma burning
  smell

emu
emu·late
emu·la·tion
emu·la·tive
emu·la·tor
emu·lous competitive
emu·lous·ness
emul·si·fi·able (*or*
  emul·sible)
emul·si·fi·ca·tion
emul·si·fi·er
emul·si·fy (·fies, ·fy·ing,
  ·fied)
emul·sion
emul·sive
emul·soid chemistry term
emunc·tory (*plural* ·tories)
  excretory organ
en half an em; *compare* em
en·able
en·abler
en·act
en·ac·tion
en·ac·tive
en·act·ment
en·ac·tor
en·ac·tory
enam·el (·el·ling, ·elled; *US*
  ·el·ing, ·eled)
enam·el·ler (*US* ·el·er)
enam·el·list (*US* ·el·ist)
enam·el·work
en·am·our (*US* ·or)
en·am·oured (*US* ·ored)
en·antio·morph crystal
  form
en·antio·mor·phic
en·antio·morph·ism
en·ar·thro·dial
en·ar·thro·sis (*plural* ·ses)
  ball-and-socket joint
enate of the mother
enat·ic
en bloc *French* in a block
en·cae·nia festival
en·cage
en·camp
en·camp·ment
en·cap·su·late
en·cap·su·la·tion
en·case (*or* in·)
en·case·ment (*or* in·)
en·cash
en·cash·able
en·cash·ment

en·caus·tic ceramics term
en·caus·ti·cal·ly
en·ceinte pregnant
Enceladus mythological
  giant
en·cephal·ic of the brain
en·cepha·lin (*or* ·kepha·)
  brain chemical
en·cepha·li·tic
en·cepha·li·tis
en·cepha·lo·gram
en·cepha·lo·graph
en·cepha·lo·graphi·cal
en·cepha·log·ra·phy
en·cepha·lo·ma (*plural*
  ·mas *or* ·ma·ta) tumour
en·cepha·lo·my·eli·tic
en·cepha·lo·my·eli·tis
en·cepha·lon (*plural* ·la)
  brain
en·cepha·lous
en·chain
en·chain·ment
en·chant
en·chant·er
en·chant·ing
en·chant·ment
en·chant·ress
en·chase engrave
en·chi·la·da Mexican food
en·chon·dro·ma (*plural*
  ·mas *or* ·ma·ta) tumour
en·chon·droma·tous
en·cho·rial (*or* ·ric) of a
  particular country
en·ci·pher
en·ci·pher·er
en·ci·pher·ment
en·cir·cle
en·cir·cle·ment
en·clasp
en·clave
en·clit·ic linguistics term
en·cliti·cal·ly
en·clos·able (*or* in·)
en·close
en·clos·er
en·clo·sure
en·code
en·code·ment
en·cod·er
en·co·mi·ast writer of
  eulogies
en·co·mi·as·tic (*or* ·ti·cal)
en·co·mi·as·ti·cal·ly

en·co·mium (*plural* ·miums
  or ·mia)
en·com·pass
en·com·pass·ment
en·core
en·coun·ter
en·coun·ter·er
en·cour·age
en·cour·age·ment
en·cour·ag·er
en·cour·ag·ing·ly
en·cri·nite fossil
en·croach
en·croach·er
en·croach·ing·ly
en·croach·ment
en·crust (*or* in·)
en·crust·ant (*or* in·)
en·crus·ta·tion (*or* in·)
en·cul·tu·ra·tion
en·cul·tu·ra·tive
en·cum·ber (*or* in·)
en·cum·ber·ing·ly (*or* in·)
en·cum·brance (*or* in·)
en·cum·branc·er legal term
en·cyc·lic
en·cyc·li·cal letter from
  pope
en·cy·clo·pedia (*or*
  ·pae·dia)
en·cy·clo·pedic (*or*
  ·pae·dic)
en·cy·clo·pedi·cal·ly (*or*
  ·pae·di·)
en·cy·clo·pedism (*or*
  ·pae·dism)
en·cy·clo·pedist (*or*
  ·pae·dist)
en·cyst biology term
en·cyst·ment (*or* ·ta·tion)
end
en·dam·age
en·dam·age·ment
en·da·moeba (*US* ·meba;
  plural ·moebae *or*
  ·moebas, *US* ·mebas)
en·dan·ger
en·dan·ger·ment
end·arch botany term
end·blown music term
end·brain
en·dear
en·dear·ing
en·dear·ing·ly
en·dear·ment

en·deav·our (*US* ·or)
en·deav·our·er (*US* ·or·)
en·dem·ic (*noun*) localized
  disease; *compare* epidemic
en·dem·ic (*or* ·demi·al,
  ·demi·cal; *adj*)
en·demi·cal·ly
en·de·mism (*or* ·mic·ity)
end·er
en·der·mic absorbed
  through skin
end·game
end·ing
en·dive
end·less
end·less·ness
end·long
end·most
endo·blast embryology term
endo·blas·tic
endo·car·dial (*or* ·di·ac)
endo·car·di·tic
endo·car·di·tis
endo·car·dium (*plural* ·dia)
  heart membrane
endo·carp part of fruit
endo·car·pal (*or* ·pic)
endo·cen·tric linguistics
  term
endo·cra·nium (*plural* ·nia)
  anatomy term
endo·crin·al
endo·crine ductless; *compare*
  exocrine
endo·crin·ic
endo·crino·log·ic (*or* ·ic·al)
endo·cri·nolo·gist
endo·cri·nol·ogy study of
  hormones
en·doc·ri·nous
endo·derm (*or* ento·) part
  of embryo
endo·der·mal (*or* ento·)
endo·der·mic (*or* ento·)
endo·derm·is botany term
endo·don·tia
endo·don·tic
endo·don·tics dentistry
  term
endo·don·tist
endo·don·tol·ogy
endo·en·zyme
endo·er·gic
  energy-absorbing; *compare*
  exoergic

en·doga·mous (*or*
  endo·gam·ic)
en·doga·my
en·dog·enous developing in
  an organism
en·dog·eny
endo·lymph fluid in ear
endo·lym·phat·ic
endo·metrial
endo·metrio·sis
endo·metrium (*plural*
  ·metria) womb lining
endo·morph
endo·mor·phic heavily
  built
endo·mor·phism geology
  term
endo·mor·phy
endo·neu·rium anatomy
  term
endo·para·site
endo·para·sit·ic
endo·pep·ti·dase enzyme
endo·phyte (*or* ento·)
  parasitic plant
endo·phyt·ic (*or* ento·)
endo·plasm biology term
endo·plas·mic
en·dor·phin brain chemical
en·dors·able (*or* in·)
en·dorse (*or* in·)
en·dor·see (*or* in·)
en·dorse·ment (*or* in·)
en·dors·er (*or* ·dor·sor, in·)
endo·scope medical
  instrument
endo·scop·ic
en·dos·co·pist
en·dos·co·py
endo·skel·etal
endo·skel·eton
endo·mo·sis biology term
en·dos·mot·ic
en·dos·moti·cal·ly
endo·some cell nucleus part
endo·sperm seed tissue
endo·sper·mic
endo·spore
en·dos·por·ous
en·dos·teal
en·dos·teum (*plural* ·tea)
  anatomy term
en·dos·to·sis (*plural* ·ses)
  physiology term
endo·thecial

endo·thecium (*plural*
·thecia) botany term
endo·thelial
endo·theli·oid
endo·thelio·ma (*plural*
·mata) tumour
endo·thelium (*plural*
·thelia) anatomy term
endo·ther·mic (*or* ·mal)
heat-absorbing; *compare*
exothermic
endo·ther·mi·cal·ly
endo·ther·mism
endo·tox·ic
endo·tox·in
en·dow
en·dow·er
en·dow·ment
end·paper part of book
end·plate
end·play bridge term
en·due (*or* in·; ·dues,
·du·ing, ·dued) endow
en·dur·abil·ity (*or*
·dur·able·ness)
en·dur·able
en·dur·ance
en·dure
en·dur·ing
en·dur·ing·ly
end·ways
Endymion mythological
character
en·ema (*plural* ·emas *or*
·ema·ta)
en·emy (*plural* ·emies)
en·er·get·ic
en·er·geti·cal·ly
en·er·geti·cist
en·er·get·ics
en·er·gid biology term
en·er·gize (*or* ·gise)
en·er·giz·er (*or* ·gis·er)
en·er·gu·men possessed
person
en·er·gy (*plural* ·gies)
en·er·vate weaken; *compare*
innervate; innovate
en·er·va·tion
en·er·va·tive
en·er·va·tor
en·face
en face *French* facing
forwards
en·face·ment

en fa·mille *French*
informally
en·fant ter·ri·ble (*plural*
en·fants ter·ri·bles) *French*
indiscreet person
en·fee·ble
en·fee·ble·ment
en·fee·bler
en·feoff legal term
en·feoff·ment
En·field London borough;
rifle
en·fi·lade military term
en·fleu·rage *French*
perfume-making
en·fold (*or* in·)
en·fold·er (*or* in·)
en·fold·ment (*or* in·)
en·force
en·force·abil·ity
en·force·able
en·forc·ed·ly
en·force·ment
en·forc·er
en·fran·chise
en·fran·chise·ment
en·fran·chis·er
En·ga·dine Swiss region
en·gage
en·gagé *French* committed
en·gaged
en·gage·ment
en·gag·er
en·gag·ing
en·gag·ing·ly
en·gag·ing·ness
en garde *French* on guard
en·gen·der
en·gen·der·er
en·gen·der·ment
en·gine
en·gi·neer
en·gi·neer·ing
en·gine·ry (*plural* ·ries)
en·gla·cial
Eng·land
Eng·lish
Eng·lish·ism
English·man (*plural* ·men)
English·woman (*plural*
·women)
en·glut devour
en·gorge
en·gorge·ment
en·graft (*or* in·)

en·graf·ta·tion (*or*
en·graft·ment, in·)
en·grail indent coin
en·grail·ment
en·grain *variant spelling of*
ingrain
en·grained *variant spelling of*
ingrained
en·gram psychology term
en·gram·mic (*or*
·gram·at·ic)
en·grave
en·grav·er
en·grav·ing
en·gross
en·gross·ed·ly
en·gross·er
en·gross·ing·ly
en·gross·ment
en·gulf (*or* in·)
en·gulf·ment
en·hance
en·hance·ment
en·hanc·er
en·hanc·ive
en·har·mon·ic
en·har·moni·cal·ly
enig·ma
en·ig·mat·ic (*or*
·mati·cal)
en·ig·mati·cal·ly
Eni·we·tok Pacific atoll
en·jamb·ment (*or* ·jambe·)
poetry term
en·join
en·join·er
en·join·ment
en·joy
en·joy·able
en·joy·ably
en·joy·er
en·joy·ment
en·kepha·lin *variant spelling*
of encephalin
en·kin·dle
en·kin·dler
en·lace
en·lace·ment
en·large
en·large·able
en·large·ment
en·larg·er
en·light·en
en·light·en·er
en·light·en·ing·ly

En·light·en·ment 18th-century movement
en·light·en·ment
en·list
en·list·er
en·list·ment
en·liv·en
en·liv·en·er
en·liv·en·ing·ly
en·liv·en·ment
en masse *French* in a mass
en·mesh (*or* in·, im·)
en·mity (*plural* ·mities)
en·nage printing term
en·nead group of nine
en·nead·ic
en·nea·gon
en·nea·he·dral
en·nea·he·dron (*plural* ·drons *or* ·dra)
En·nis Irish town
En·nis·kil·len (*or* In·nis·kil·ling) Northern Irish town
en·no·ble
en·no·ble·ment
en·no·bler
en·no·bling·ly
en·nui apathy
enol chemistry term
enol·ogy *US spelling of* aenology
enor·mity (*plural* ·mities)
enor·mous
eno·sis union of Greece and Cyprus
enough
enounce enunciate
en pas·sant *French* in passing
en·phy·tot·ic botany term
en·plane
en·quire (*or esp. US* in·) ask; *compare* inquire
en·quir·er (*or esp. US* in·)
en·quiry (*or esp. US* in·; *plural* ·quiries)
en·rage
en·rag·ed·ly
en·rage·ment
en rap·port *French* in sympathy
en·rap·ture
en·rich
en·rich·er

en·rich·ment
en·robe
en·rob·er
en·rol (*US* ·roll; ·rol·ling, ·rolled)
en·rol·lee
en·rol·ler
en·rol·ment (*US* ·roll·)
en·root
en route *French* on the way
ens metaphysics term
en·san·guine stain with blood
En·schede Dutch city
en·sconce
en·sem·ble
en·shrine (*or* in·)
en·shrine·ment
en·shroud
en·si·form sword-shaped
en·sign
en·sign·ship (*or* ·cy; *plural* ·ships *or* ·cies)
en·si·labil·ity
en·si·lage
en·sile store in silo
en·slave
en·slave·ment
en·slav·er
en·snare (*or* in·)
en·snare·ment
en·snar·er
en·soul (*or* in·)
en·sphere (*or* in·)
en·sta·tite mineral
en·sue (·su·ing, ·sued)
en·su·ing·ly
en suite forming a unit
en·sure make sure; *compare* insure
en·sur·er
en·swathe
en·tab·la·ture
en·ta·ble·ment platform
en·tail
en·tail·er
en·tail·ment
en·ta·moeba (*or* en·da·; *US* ·meba; *plural* ·moebae *or* ·moebas, *US* ·mebas) amoeba
en·tan·gle
en·tan·gle·ment
en·tan·gler
en·ta·sia

en·ta·sis (*plural* ·ses) architectural term
En·teb·be Ugandan town
en·tel·echy (*plural* ·echies) philosophy term
en·tel·lus monkey
en·tente cor·diale *French* friendly relations
en·ter
en·ter·able
en·ter·al·ly
en·ter·er
en·ter·ic (*or* ·al) intestinal
en·teri·tis
en·tero·gas·trone hormone
en·tero·ki·nase enzyme
en·ter·on (*plural* ·tera) digestive tract
en·ter·os·to·my (*plural* ·mies)
en·ter·ot·omy (*plural* ·omies)
en·tero·vi·rus (*plural* ·ruses)
en·ter·prise
en·ter·pris·er
en·ter·pris·ing
en·ter·tain
en·ter·tain·er
en·ter·tain·ing
en·ter·tain·ing·ly
en·ter·tain·ment
en·thal·py physics term
en·thet·ic medical term
en·thral (*US* ·thrall; ·thral·ling, ·thralled)
en·thrall·er
en·thral·ling·ly
en·thral·ment (*US* ·thrall·)
en·throne
en·throne·ment
en·thuse
en·thu·si·asm
en·thu·si·ast
en·thu·si·as·tic
en·thu·si·as·ti·cal·ly
en·thy·memat·ic (*or* ·ical)
en·thy·meme logic term
en·tice
en·tice·ment
en·tic·er
en·tic·ing·ly
en·tic·ing·ness
en·tire
en·tire·ly
en·tire·ness

en·tirety (*plural* ·tireties)
en·ti·tle
en·ti·tle·ment
en·tity (*plural* ·tities)
ento·blast embryology term
ento·blas·tic
ento·derm *variant of* endoderm
ento·der·mal (*or* ·mic)
en·tomb
en·tomb·ment
en·tom·ic of insects
ento·mo·logi·cal (*or* ·log·ic)
ento·molo·gist
ento·mo·lo·gize (*or* ·gise)
ento·mol·ogy study of insects; *compare* etymology
ento·mopha·gous
ento·mophi·lous insect-pollinated
ento·mophi·ly
ento·mos·tra·can crustacean
ento·mos·tra·cous
ento·phyte *variant of* endophyte
ento·phyt·ic *variant of* endophytic
en·top·ic in normal position; *compare* ectopic
en·tou·rage
ento·zo·ic living inside an animal
ento·zo·on (*or* ·an; *plural* ·zoa)
en·tr'acte *French* interval between acts
en·trails
en·train board a train
en·train·ment
en·tram·mel (·mel·ling, ·melled; *US* ·mel·ing, ·meled) obstruct
en·trance
en·trance·ment
en·tranc·ing·ly
en·trant
en·trap (·trap·ping, ·trapped)
en·trap·ment
en·trap·per
en·treat
en·treat·ing·ly
en·treat·ment

en·treaty (*plural* ·treaties)
en·tre·chat ballet movement
en·tre·côte
en·trée
en·tre·mets (*plural* ·mets) dessert
en·trench
en·trench·er
en·trench·ment
en·tre nous *French* between ourselves
en·tre·pôt trading centre
en·tre·pre·neur
en·tre·pre·neur·ial
en·tre·pre·neur·ship
en·tre·sol *French* between floors
en·tro·py (*plural* ·pies) physics term
en·trust
en·trust·ment
en·try (*plural* ·tries)
en·twine
en·twine·ment
enu·cleate remove nucleus
enu·clea·tion
enu·clea·tor
Enu·gu Nigerian city
enu·mer·able countable; *compare* innumerable
enu·mer·ate
enu·mera·tion
enu·mera·tive
enu·mera·tor
enun·ci·abil·ity
enun·ci·able
enun·ci·ate articulate; *compare* annunciate
enun·cia·tion
enun·cia·tive (*or* ·tory)
enun·cia·tor
en·ure *variant spelling of* inure
enu·resis bedwetting
enu·ret·ic
en·vel·op (*verb*)
en·velope (*noun*)
en·vel·op·ment
en·ven·om
en·ven·omed
en·vi·able
en·vi·able·ness
en·vi·ably
en·vi·er

en·vi·ous
en·vi·ous·ness
en·vi·ron (*verb*) encircle
en·vi·ron·ment
en·vi·ron·men·tal
en·vi·ron·men·tal·ism
en·vi·ron·men·tal·ist
en·vi·ron·men·tal·ly
en·vi·rons (*noun*) vicinity
en·vis·age
en·vis·age·ment
en·vi·sion
en·voy
en·vy (*noun, plural* ·vies; *verb* ·vies, ·vy·ing, ·vied)
en·vy·ing·ly
en·wind (·wind·ing, ·wound)
en·womb
en·wrap (*or* ·in; ·wrap·ping, ·wrapped)
en·wreath
en·zo·ot·ic veterinary term
en·zo·oti·cal·ly
en·zy·mat·ic (*or* ·zy·mic)
en·zyme catalyst
en·zy·mo·logi·cal
en·zy·molo·gist
en·zy·mol·ogy
en·zy·moly·sis (*or* ·mo·sis)
en·zy·mo·lyt·ic
eobi·ont biology term
Eocene geological period
Eogene geological period
eohip·pus fossil horse
eolith stone tool
Eolith·ic Stone Age period
eon *US spelling of* aeon
eonism psychiatry term
Eos Greek goddess
eosin (*or* eosine) dye
eosin·ic
eosino·phil blood cell
eosino·phil·ic (*or* eosi·nophi·lous)
Eozo·ic geological period
epact astronomy term
ep·arch Eastern bishop
ep·ar·chial
ep·ar·chy (*or* ·chate; *plural* ·chies *or* ·chates)
ep·aulet (*or* ·aulette)
épée sword
épée·ist

epei·ric (or epei·ro·gen·ic, epei·ro·genet·ic) of continental drift

ep·ei·rog·eny (or epi·rog·eny, ep·ei·ro·gen·esis)

ep·en·cephal·ic

ep·en·cepha·lon (plural ·la) part of brain

epen·thesis (plural ·theses) linguistics term

ep·en·thet·ic

epergne table ornament

ep·ex·egesis (plural ·egeses) linguistics term

ep·ex·eget·ic (or ·egeti·cal)

ep·ex·egeti·cal·ly

ephah Hebrew unit

ephebe Greek youth

ephed·rine (or ·rin) alkaloid

ephem·era (plural ·eras or ·erae) short-lived insect; compare emphemeron

ephem·er·al

ephem·er·al·ity (or ·al·ness)

ephem·er·id mayfly

ephem·er·is (plural eph·emer·ides) astronomical table

ephem·er·on (plural ·era or ·er·ons) transitory thing; compare ephemera

Ephesian

Eph·esus ancient Greek city

ephod vestment

eph·or Greek magistrate

epi·blast embryology term

epi·blas·tic

epi·bol·ic

epibo·ly (plural ·lies) embryology term

epic

epi·ca·lyx (plural ·lyxes or ·ly·ces) botany term

epi·can·thus (plural ·thi) anatomy term

epi·car·di·ac (or ·dial)

epi·car·dium (plural ·dia) anatomy term

epi·carp (or exo·) botany term

epi·cene

epi·cen·ism

epi·cen·tral

epi·cen·tre (US ·ter)

epi·clesis theology term

epi·con·ti·nen·tal

epi·cot·yl botany term

epi·cri·sis medical term

epi·crit·ic anatomy term

epi·cure

Epi·cu·rean of Epicurus

epi·cu·rean devoted to pleasure

Epi·cu·rean·ism

epi·cur·ism (or ·cu·rean·ism)

epi·cy·cle

epi·cy·clic (or ·cli·cal)

epi·cy·cloid geometric curve

epi·cy·cloid·al

Epi·daur·us Greek port

epi·deic·tic (or ·dic·tic) rhetorical term

epi·dem·ic widespread disease; compare endemic

epi·demi·cal

epi·demio·logi·cal

epi·demi·olo·gist

epi·demi·ol·ogy

epi·der·mal (or ·mic, ·moid)

epi·der·mis

epi·dia·scope projector

epi·didy·mal

epi·di·dy·mis (plural ·dymi·des) anatomy term

epi·dote mineral

epi·dot·ic

epi·dur·al anaesthetic

epi·fo·cal geology term

epi·gas·tric (or ·trial)

epi·gas·trium (plural ·tria) abdominal part

epi·geal (or ·gean, ·geous) botany term

epi·gene formed at earth's surface

epi·gen·esis biology theory

epi·gen·esist (or epig·enist)

epi·genet·ic

epi·geneti·cal·ly

epig·enous

epi·glot·tal (or ·tic)

epi·glot·tis (plural ·tises or ·ti·des) anatomy term

epi·gone (or ·gon) imitator

epi·gram saying

epi·gram·mat·ic

epi·gram·mati·cal·ly

epi·gram·ma·tism

epi·gram·ma·tist

epi·gram·ma·tize (or ·tise)

epi·graph inscription

epig·ra·pher

epi·graph·ic (or ·graphi·cal)

epi·graphi·cal·ly

epig·ra·phist

epig·ra·phy

epigy·nous botany term

epigy·ny

epi·lep·sy

epi·lep·tic

epi·lep·ti·cal·ly

epi·lep·toid (or ·lep·ti·form)

epi·lim·ni·on lake water

epilo·gist

epi·logue

epi·mere embryology term

epi·mor·phic

epi·mor·pho·sis zoology term

epi·my·sium (plural ·sia) anatomy term

epi·nas·tic

epi·nas·ty (plural ·ties) botany term

epi·neph·rine US adrenaline

epi·neu·rial

epi·neu·rium anatomy term

epi·phan·ic

Epipha·ny Christian festival

epipha·ny (plural ·nies) manifestation

epi·phenom·enal

epi·phenom·enal·ism philosophy term

epi·phenom·enal·ist

epi·phenom·enon (plural ·ena)

epi·phragm shell

epi·phys·eal (or ·ial)

epiphy·sis (plural ·ses) anatomy term

epi·phyte botany term

epi·phyt·ic (or ·phyti·cal)

epi·phyti·cal·ly

epi·phy·tot·ic

epi·ro·gen·ic (or ·genet·ic) variants of epeirogenic

epi·rog·eny variant spelling of epeirogeny

Epi·rus Greek region
epis·co·pa·cy (*plural* ·cies) church government
epis·co·pal
epis·co·pa·lian
epis·co·pa·lian·ism
epis·co·pal·ism
epis·co·pal·ly
epis·co·pate
epi·scope projector
epi·semat·ic zoology term
epi·si·oto·my (*plural* ·mies) medical term
epi·sode
epi·sod·ic (*or* ·sodi·cal)
epi·sodi·cal·ly
epi·some
epi·spas·tic producing a blister
epi·sta·sis medical term
epi·stat·ic
epi·stax·is nosebleed
ep·is·tem·ic relating to knowledge
epis·temo·logi·cal
epis·temol·o·gist
epis·temol·ogy
epi·ster·num (*plural* ·na) breastbone part
epis·tle
epis·tler (*or* ·to·ler, ·to·list)
epis·to·lary (*or* epi·stol·ic, epis·to·la·tory)
epis·to·ler
epis·tro·phe rhetorical term
epi·style architectural term
epi·taph inscription
epi·taph·ic
epi·taph·ist
epita·sis drama term
epi·tax·ial
epi·taxy (*or* ·tax·is) crystal growth
epi·tha·lam·ic
epi·tha·la·mium (*or* ·mi·on; *plural* ·mia) nuptial ode
epi·thelial (*or* ·theli·oid)
epi·thelio·ma (*plural* ·mas *or* ·ma·ta) tumour
epi·theli·oma·tous
epi·thelium (*plural* ·thelia) tissue
epi·thet
epi·thet·ic (*or* theti·cal)

epito·me typical example
epi·tom·ic (*or* ·tomi·cal)
epito·mist
epito·mi·za·tion (*or* ·sa·tion)
epito·mize (*or* ·mise)
epito·miz·er (*or* ·mis·er)
epi·zo·ic zoology term
epi·zo·ism
epi·zo·ite
epi·zo·on (*plural* ·zoa) animal parasite
epi·zo·ot·ic veterinary term
epi·zo·oti·cal·ly
ep·och
ep·och·al
epoch-making
ep·ode prosody term
epo·nym something named after a person
epony·mous (*or* epo·nym·ic)
epony·my
épo·pée (*or* epo·poeia) poem
epos body of poetry
epox·ide
epoxy
Ep·ping
Ep·si·lon astronomy term
ep·si·lon Greek letter
Ep·som
epyl·li·on (*plural* ·lia) poem
eq·uabil·ity (*or* ·uable·ness)
eq·uable
eq·uably
equal (equal·ling, equalled; *US* equal·ing, equaled)
equal-area cartography term
equali·tar·ian
equali·tari·an·ism
equali·ty (*plural* ·ties)
equali·za·tion (*or* ·sa·tion)
equal·ize (*or* ·ise)
equal·iz·er (*or* ·is·er)
equal·ly
equa·nim·ity
equani·mous
equat·abil·ity
equat·able
equate
equa·tion
equa·tion·al
equa·tor
equa·to·rial

Equa·to·rial Guinea African republic
eq·uer·ry (*plural* ·ries)
eques·trian
eques·tri·an·ism
eques·tri·enne
equi·an·gu·lar
equi·dis·tance
equi·dis·tant
equi·lat·eral
equili·brant
equili·brate
equi·li·bra·tion
equi·li·bra·tor
equili·brist
equili·bris·tic
equi·lib·rium (*plural* ·riums *or* ·ria)
equi·mo·lecu·lar
equine
equin·ity
equi·noc·tial
equi·nox
equip (equip·ping, equipped)
equi·page carriage
equi·par·ti·tion physics term
equip·ment
equi·poise equilibrium
equi·pol·lence (*or* ·len·cy)
equi·pol·lent equal in effect
equi·pon·der·ance (*or* ·ancy)
equi·pon·der·ant
equi·pon·der·ate counterbalance
equi·po·tent
equi·po·ten·tial physics term
equi·po·ten·ti·al·ity
equip·per
equi·setum (*plural* ·setums *or* ·seta) plant
equi·table
equi·table·ness
equi·tably
equi·tant botany term
equi·ta·tion horsemanship
equi·tes Roman cavalry
equi·ty (*plural* ·ties)
equiva·lence
equi·va·len·cy (*or* ·va·lence) chemistry term

equiva·lent
equivo·cal
equivo·cal·ity (or ·ca·cy)
equivo·cal·ly
equivo·cate
equivo·cat·ing·ly
equivo·ca·tion
equivo·ca·tory
equi·voque (or ·voke)
   pun
Equul·eus constellation
era
era·di·ate radiate
era·dia·tion
eradi·cable
eradi·cant
eradi·cate
eradi·ca·tion
eradi·ca·tive
eradi·ca·tor
eras·able
erase
eras·er
era·sion
Eras·ti·an·ism state
   supremacy over church
eras·ure
Er·bil (or Ir·bil, Ar·bil) Iraqi
   city
er·bium chemical element
ere Poetic before; compare
   e'er
Erebus Greek god
Erech·theum (or ·thei·on)
   Athenian temple
erect
erect·able
erect·er (or erec·tor)
erec·tile
erec·til·ity
erec·tion
erect·ness
erec·tor (or ·ter)
er·emite hermit
er·emit·ic (or ·emiti·cal)
er·emit·ism
erep·sin enzyme
er·ethism medical term
er·ethis·mic (or ·ethis·tic,
   ·ethit·ic)
Er·furt German city
erg unit
er·ga·toc·ra·cy (plural ·cies)
   government by workers
ergo Latin therefore

er·go·graph muscle-
   measuring instrument
er·gom·eter dynamometer
er·go·nom·ic
er·go·nom·ics
er·gono·mist
er·gos·terol biochemical
   compound
er·got crop disease
er·got·ism human disease
eri·ca shrub
eri·ca·ceous
Erida·nus constellation
Erie Canadian lake
erig·er·on plant
Erin Archaic Ireland
eri·na·ceous of hedgehogs
Eris Greek goddess
er·is·tic logic term
er·is·ti·cal
Eri·trea
Eri·trean
erk Slang aircraftsman
Er·lang unit
erl·king malevolent
   spirit
er·mine (plural ·mines or
   ·mine)
erne eagle
Er·nie computer lottery
erode
erod·ent
ero·genei·ty
erog·enous (or ero·gen·ic)
Eros
erose uneven
ero·sion
ero·sion·al
ero·sive
ero·sive·ness
ero·tema (or ·teme, ·tesis)
   rhetorical question
ero·temat·ic (or ·tet·ic)
erot·ic (or eroti·cal)
eroti·ca
eroti·cal·ly
eroti·cism (or ero·tism)
ero·to·gen·ic variant of
   erogenous
erot·ol·ogy
ero·to·ma·nia
ero·to·ma·ni·ac
err
er·ran·cy (plural ·cies)
er·rand

er·rant
er·rant·ry (plural ·tries)
er·ra·ta plural of erratum
er·rat·ic
er·rati·cal·ly
er·rati·cism
er·ra·tum (plural ·ta)
   printing error
er·rhine causing nasal
   secretion
Er Rif Moroccan region
er·ro·neous
er·ro·neous·ness
er·ror
er·satz artificial
Erse Gaelic
erst·while
eru·bes·cence redness
eru·bes·cent
eruct (or eruc·tate) belch
eruc·ta·tion
eruc·ta·tive
eru·dite
eru·di·tion (or
   eru·dite·ness)
erum·pent bursting out
erupt break out; compare
   irrupt
erupt·ible
erup·tion
erup·tion·al
erup·tive
erup·tiv·ity (or ·tive·ness)
Ery·man·thus Greek
   mountain
eryn·go (or erin·; plural
   ·goes or ·gos) plant
ery·sip·elas skin disease
ery·si·pela·tous
ery·sip·eloid
ery·thema skin redness
ery·themat·ic (or
   ·thema·tous, ·themic)
eryth·rism abnormal
   redness
ery·thris·mal
eryth·rite mineral
eryth·ri·tol (or ·rite) drug
eryth·ro·blast marrow cell
eryth·ro·blas·tic
eryth·ro·blas·to·sis blood
   disease
eryth·ro·cyte blood cell
eryth·ro·cyt·ic
eryth·ro·cy·tom·eter

eryth·ro·cy·tom·etry

eryth·ro·my·cin antibiotic

eryth·ro·poi·esis red blood cell formation

eryth·ro·poi·et·ic

Er·zu·rum Turkish city

Es·bjerg Danish port

es·ca·drille aircraft squadron; *compare* espadrille

es·ca·lade scaling walls

es·ca·lad·er

es·ca·late

es·ca·la·tion

es·ca·la·tor

es·cal·lo·nia shrub

es·cal·lope scallop

es·ca·lope veal slice

es·cap·able

es·ca·pade

es·cape

es·capee

es·cape·ment

es·cap·er

es·cap·ism

es·cap·ist

es·ca·po·lo·gist

es·ca·pol·ogy

es·carp fortification

es·carp·ment steep slope

escha·lot shallot

es·char scab

es·cha·rot·ic

es·cha·to·logi·cal

es·cha·tolo·gist

es·cha·tol·ogy theology

es·cheat legal term

es·chew avoid

es·chew·al

es·chew·er

es·co·lar (*plural* ·lars *or* ·lar) fish

Es·co·rial Spanish village

es·cort

es·cri·toire

es·crow legal term

es·cu·do (*plural* ·dos) Portuguese currency

es·cu·lent edible

es·cutch·eon heraldry term

es·cutch·eoned

Es·dra·elon Israeli plain

es·em·plas·tic unifying

es·er·ine alkaloid

Es·fa·han *variant spelling of* Isfahan

Esher

es·ker (*or* ·kar) glacial deposit

Eskil·stu·na Swedish city

Es·ki·mo (*plural* ·mos *or* ·mo)

Es·ki·moan

Es·ki·moid

Es·ki·sehir Turkish city

esopha·gus *US spelling of* oesophagus

eso·ter·ic abstruse; *compare* exoteric

eso·teri·cal·ly

eso·teri·cism

es·pa·drille canvas shoe; *compare* escadrille

es·pal·ier wall-trained tree

es·par·to (*plural* ·tos) grass

es·pe·cial

es·pe·cial·ly

Es·pe·ran·to artificial language

es·pial

espi·er

es·pio·nage

Es·pí·ri·to San·to Brazilian state

Es·pí·ri·tu San·to Pacific island

es·pla·nade

es·pous·al

es·pouse

es·pous·er

es·pres·so (*plural* ·sos) coffee

es·prit liveliness

es·prit de corps group pride

espy (espies, espy·ing, espied)

es·quire

es·say composition; attempt; *compare* assay

es·say·ist

Es·sen German city

es·sence

Es·sene Jewish sect

es·sen·tial

es·sen·tial·ism philosophical doctrine

es·sen·tial·ist

es·sen·tial·ity (*or* ·ness)

es·sen·tial·ly

Es·sequi·bo South American river

Es·sex

Es·sonne French department

es·tab·lish

es·tab·lish·er

es·tab·lish·ment

es·tab·lish·men·tar·ian

es·tab·lish·men·tar·ian·ism

es·ta·mi·net French café

es·tan·cia ranch

es·tate

es·teem

es·ter chemistry term

es·ter·ase enzyme

es·teri·fi·ca·tion

es·teri·fy (·fies, ·fy·ing, ·fied)

es·ti·mable

es·ti·mable·ness

es·ti·mate

es·ti·ma·tion

es·ti·ma·tive

es·ti·ma·tor

estipu·late (*or* ex·stipu·) botany term

es·thete *US variant spelling of* aesthete

es·thetic *US variant spelling of* aesthetic

es·ti·val *US spelling of* aestival

es·ti·vate *US spelling of* aestivate

Es·to·nia

Es·to·nian

es·top (·top·ping, ·topped) legal term

es·top·page

es·top·pel

es·to·vers legal term

es·trade dais

es·tra·di·ol *US spelling of* oestradiol

es·tra·gon tarragon

es·trange

es·tranged

es·trange·ment

es·trang·er

es·tray

es·treat legal term

Es·tre·ma·du·ra Spanish region

es·tri·ol *US spelling of* oestriol

es·tro·gen *US spelling of* oestrogen

es·trone *US spelling of* oestrone

es·trous *US spelling of* oestrous

es·trus *US spelling of* oestrus

es·tu·ar·ial

es·tua·rine

es·tu·ary (*plural* ·aries*)

esu·ri·ence (*or* ·en·cy*)

esu·ri·ent greedy

eta Greek letter

etae·rio (*plural* ·rios*) botany term

éta·gère *French* ornament stand

eta·lon physics device

eta·mine (*or* ·min*) fabric

et cet·era and so on

et·cet·eras (*plural noun*) extra things

etch

etch·ant etching acid

etch·er

etch·ing

eter·nal

eter·nal·ity (*or* ·ness*)

eter·nali·za·tion (*or* eter·ni·, ·sa·tion*)

eter·nal·ize (*or* eter·nize, ·ise*)

eter·nal·ly

eter·nity (*plural* ·nities*)

ete·sian meteorology term

ethane

ethane·di·ol

etha·nol

eth·ene *variant of* ethylene

ether anaesthetic

ether (*or* aether*) hypothetical medium

ethe·real

ethe·real·ity (*or* ·ness*)

ethe·reali·za·tion (*or* ·sa·tion*)

ethe·real·ize (*or* ·ise*)

ethe·real·ly

ether·ic

etheri·fi·ca·tion

etheri·fy (·fies, ·fy·ing, ·fied*)

etheri·za·tion (*or* ·sa·tion*)

ether·ize (*or* ·ise*)

ether·iz·er (*or* ·is·er*)

eth·ic

ethi·cal

ethi·cal·ly

ethi·cal·ness (*or* ·cali·ty*)

ethi·cist

ethi·cize (*or* ·cise*)

eth·ics

Ethio·pia

Ethio·pian

Ethio·pic

eth·moid facial bone

eth·moi·dal

eth·narch Roman ruler

eth·nar·chy (*plural* ·chies*)

eth·nic (*or* ·ni·cal*)

eth·ni·cal·ly

eth·no·bota·ny botanical folklore

eth·no·cen·tric

eth·no·cen·tri·cal·ly

eth·no·cen·tric·ity

eth·no·cen·trism belief in group's superiority

eth·no·gen·ic

eth·nog·enist

eth·nog·eny origin of races

eth·nog·ra·pher

eth·no·graph·ic (*or* ·graphi·cal*)

eth·no·graphi·cal·ly

eth·nog·ra·phy anthropology term

eth·no·log·ic (*or* ·logi·cal*)

eth·nol·ogist

eth·nol·ogy study of races; *compare* ethology

etho·log·ic (*or* ·logi·cal*)

etho·logi·cal·ly

etholo·gist

ethol·ogy study of animal behaviour; *compare* ethnology

etho·none chemical compound

ethos

eth·ox·ide

eth·oxy·ethane

ethyl

eth·yl·ate

eth·yla·tion

eth·yl·ene (*or* eth·ene*)

eth·yl·enic

ethyl·ic

ethyne chemical compound

etio·late

etio·la·tion

eti·ol·ogy *US spelling of* aetiology

eti·quette

Etna

Eton

Eto·nian

Etru·ria ancient Italian country

Etrus·can (*or* Etru·rian*)

étude musical composition

étui needle case

ety·mo·logi·cal (*or* ·log·ic*)

ety·molo·gist

ety·mol·ogy (*plural* ·ogies*) study of words; *compare* entomology

ety·mon (*plural* ·mons *or* ·ma*) original word form

Etzel legendary king

eubac·te·ria (*sing.* ·rium*)

Euboea Greek island

Euboean

eucaine anaesthetic

euca·lyp·tol (*or* ·tole*) essential oil

euca·lyp·tus (*or* ·lypt; *plural* ·tuses, ·ti *or* ·lypts*)

eucha·ris plant

Eucha·rist sacrament

Eucha·ris·tic (*or* ·ti·cal*)

Eucha·ris·ti·cal·ly

euchlo·rine (*or* ·rin*) explosive gas

euchre *US* card game

euchro·mat·ic

euchro·ma·tin chromosome part

Euclid·ean (*or* ·ian*)

eudemon benevolent spirit

eudemo·nia (*or* eudaemo·*) happiness

eudemon·ic (*or* eudaemon·*)

eudemon·ics (*or* eudaemon·*)

eudemon·ism (*or* eudaemon·*)

eudemon·is·ti·cal·ly (*or* eudaemon·*)

eudi·om·eter chemistry term

eudio·met·ric (*or* ·ri·cal*)

eudio·met·ri·cal·ly
eudi·om·etry
eugen·ic (*or* eugeni·cal)
eugeni·cal·ly
eugeni·cist
eugen·ics
eugenol essential oil
euglena protozoan
euhe·mer·ism study of
   myths
euhe·mer·ist
euhe·mer·is·tic
euhe·mer·is·ti·cal·ly
euhe·mer·ize (*or* ·ise)
eula·chon (*or* ·chan; *plural*
   ·chons, ·chon *or* ·chans,
   ·chan) fish
eulo·gia holy bread
eulo·gist (*or* ·giz·er, ·gis·er)
eulo·gis·tic (*or* ·ti·cal)
eulo·gis·ti·cal·ly
eulo·gize (*or* ·gise)
eulogy (*plural* eulogies)
Eumeni·des Greek Furies
eunuch
euony·mus (*or* evony·) tree
eupa·to·rium plant
eupat·rid Greek landowner
eupep·sia (*or* ·sy) good
   digestion
eupep·tic
euphau·si·id crustacean
euphemism inoffensive
   word; *compare* euphuism
euphemist
euphemis·tic (*or* ·ti·cal)
euphemis·ti·cal·ly
euphemize (*or* euphemise)
euphemiz·er (*or*
   euphemis·er)
euphon·ic (*or* euphoni·cal)
euphoni·cal·ly
eupho·ni·ous
eupho·ni·ous·ly
eupho·ni·ous·ness
eupho·nium musical
   instrument
eupho·nize (*or* ·nise)
eupho·ny (*plural* ·nies)
   pleasing sound
euphor·bia plant
euphor·bia·ceous
eupho·ria elation
eupho·ri·ant
euphor·ic

euphori·cal·ly
eupho·tic ecology term
euphra·sy (*plural* ·sies)
   plant
Euphra·tes Asian river
euphroe (*or* uphroe)
   nautical term
Euphrosyne Greek goddess
euphuism prose style;
   compare euphemism
euphu·ist
euphu·is·tic (*or* ·ti·cal)
euphu·is·ti·cal·ly
euplas·tic healing quickly
euploid biology term
eup·noea (*US* ·nea) normal
   breathing
eup·noe·ic (*US* ·ne·)
Eura·sia
Eura·sian
Eur·at·om European Atomic
   Energy Commission
Eure French department
Eure-et-Loir French
   department
eureka
eurhyth·mic (*or* ·mi·cal)
eurhyth·mics
eurhyth·my
euri·pus (*plural* ·pi) channel
euro currency unit
Euroc·ly·don biblical wind
Euro·com·mun·ism
Euro·crat EU administrator
Euro·dol·lar
Euro·mar·ket (*or* ·mart)
Eu·ro·pa satellite of Jupiter
Europa mythological
   character
Europe
Euro·pean
Euro·pean·ism
Euro·peani·za·tion (*or*
   ·sa·tion)
Euro·pean·ize (*or* ·ise)
Euro·phile
euro·pium chemical
   element
Euro·poort Dutch port
Euro·scep·tic
Euro·vis·ion broadcasting
   network
Eurus mythological wind
Eurydice dryad
euryp·ter·id extinct animal

eury·ther·mal (*or* ·mic,
   ·mous) ecology term
eury·trop·ic ecology term
euspo·ran·gi·ate botany
   term
Eusta·chian tube anatomy
   term
eusta·sy
eustat·ic geology term
eustati·cal·ly
eutec·tic (*or* ·toid) physics
   term
Euterpe Greek Muse
eutha·na·sia
euthen·ics environmental
   study
euthen·ist
euthe·rian zoology term
eutroph·ic ecology term
eutrophi·ca·tion
eux·enite mineral
evacu·ant
evacu·ate
evacu·ation
evacu·ative
evacu·ator
evac·uee
evad·able (*or* ·ible)
evade
evad·er
evad·ing·ly
evagi·nate turn inside out
evagi·na·tion
evalu·ate
evalu·ation
evalu·ative
evalu·ator
eva·nesce fade gradually
eva·nes·cence
eva·nes·cent
evan·gel gospel
evan·geli·cal
evan·geli·cal·ism
evan·geli·cal·ly
evan·gelism
evan·gelist
evan·gelis·tic
evan·gelis·ti·cal·ly
evan·geli·za·tion (*or*
   ·sa·tion)
evan·gelize (*or* ·gelise)
evan·geliz·er (*or* ·gelis·er)
Ev·ans·ville US city
evapo·rabil·ity
evapo·rable

evapo·rate
evapo·ra·tion
evapo·ra·tive
evapo·ra·tor
evapo·rim·eter (or ·rom·)
evapo·rite rock
evapo·tran·spi·ra·tion
eva·sion
eva·sive
eva·sive·ness
eve
evec·tion astronomy term
evec·tion·al
even
even-handed
even-handed·ness
eve·ning
even·ness
evens betting term
even·song
event
even-tempered
event·ful
event·ful·ly
event·ful·ness
even·tide
even·tual
even·tu·al·ity (plural ·ities)
even·tu·al·ly
even·tu·ate result in
even·tua·tion
ever
Ev·er·est
Ever·glades Florida region
ever·green
ever·lasting
ever·lasting·ness
ever·more
ever·sible
ever·sion
evert turn inside out
evert·or muscle
every
every·body
every·day
Every·man medieval play
every·one
every·thing
every·where
Eve·sham
evict
evic·tion
evic·tor
evi·dence
evi·dent

evi·den·tial
evi·den·tial·ly
evi·dent·ly
evil
evil·doer
evil·doing
evil·ly
evil-minded
evil-minded·ness
evil·ness
evince
evin·cible
evin·cive
evis·cer·ate disembowel
evis·cera·tion
evis·cera·tor
evo·cable
evo·ca·tion
evoca·tive
evoca·tive·ness
evo·ca·tor biology term
evoke
evok·er
evo·lute geometry term
evo·lu·tion
evo·lu·tion·ary (or ·al)
evo·lu·tion·ism
evo·lu·tion·ist
evo·lu·tion·is·tic
evolv·able
evolve
evolve·ment
evolv·er
evony·mus variant spelling
    of euonymus
ev·zone Greek soldier
ewe
ewe-neck
ewer
ex
ex·ac·er·bate aggravate
ex·ac·er·bat·ing·ly
ex·ac·er·ba·tion
ex·act
ex·act·able
ex·act·ing
ex·act·ing·ness
ex·ac·tion
ex·acti·tude
ex·act·ly
ex·act·ness
ex·ac·tor (or ·ter)
ex·ag·ger·ate
ex·ag·ger·at·ed
ex·ag·ger·at·ed·ly

ex·ag·ger·at·ing·ly
ex·ag·gera·tion
ex·ag·gera·tive (or ·tory)
ex·ag·gera·tor
ex·alt
ex·al·ta·tion
ex·alt·ed
ex·alt·ed·ly
ex·alt·ed·ness
ex·alt·er
exam
exa·men examination of
    conscience
ex·am·in·able
ex·ami·na·tion
ex·ami·na·tion·al
ex·am·ine
ex·ami·nee
ex·am·in·er
ex·am·ple
ex·ani·mate
ex·ani·ma·tion
ex·an·thema (or ·them;
    plural ·thema·ta, ·themas,
    or ·thems) rash
ex·an·thema·tous (or
    ·themat·ic)
exa·rate entomology term
ex·arch Eastern bishop;
    botany term
ex·arch·al
ex·arch·ate (or ·ar·chy;
    plural ·ates or ·chies)
ex·as·per·ate
ex·as·per·at·ed·ly
ex·as·per·at·er
ex·as·per·at·ing·ly
ex·as·pera·tion
Ex·cali·bur magic sword
ex ca·thedra Latin with
    authority
ex·cau·date tailless
ex·ca·vate
ex·ca·va·tion
ex·ca·va·tor
ex·ceed
ex·ceed·able
ex·ceed·er
ex·ceed·ing·ly
ex·cel (·cel·ling, ·celled)
ex·cel·lence
Ex·cel·len·cy (or ·lence;
    plural ·cies or ·lences) title
ex·cel·lent
ex·cel·si·or

ex·cept
ex·cept·able
ex·cept·ing
ex·cep·tion
ex·cep·tion·able
  objectionable
ex·cep·tion·able·ness
ex·cep·tion·al very good
ex·cep·tion·al·ity
excep·tion·al·ly
ex·cep·tion·al·ness
ex·cep·tive
ex·cerpt book extract;
  compare exert; exsert
ex·cerpt·er (or ·cerp·tor)
ex·cerpt·ible
ex·cerp·tion
ex·cess
ex·ces·sive
ex·ces·sive·ly
ex·ces·sive·ness
ex·change
ex·change·abil·ity
ex·change·able
ex·chang·er
Ex·cheq·uer Treasury
ex·cipi·ent medical term
ex·cis·able
ex·cise
ex·cise·man (plural ·men)
ex·ci·sion
ex·cit·abil·ity (or
  ·able·ness)
ex·cit·able
ex·cit·ant
ex·ci·ta·tion
ex·cita·tive (or ·tory)
ex·cite
ex·cit·ed
ex·cit·ed·ly
ex·cit·ed·ness
ex·cite·ment
ex·cit·er oscillator
ex·cit·ing
ex·cit·ing·ly
ex·ci·ton chemistry term
ex·ci·tor nerve
ex·claim
ex·claim·er
ex·cla·ma·tion
ex·cla·ma·tion·al
ex·clama·to·ri·ly
ex·clama·tory
ex·claus·tra·tion release of
  nun or monk

ex·clave
ex·clo·sure
ex·clud·abil·ity
ex·clud·able (or ·ible)
ex·clude
ex·clud·er
ex·clu·sion
ex·clu·sion·ary
ex·clu·sion·ist
ex·clu·sive
ex·clu·sive·ness (or ·sivi·ty)
ex·cogi·tate devise
ex·cog·ita·tion
ex·cogi·ta·tive
ex·cogi·ta·tor
ex·com·muni·cable
ex·com·muni·cate
ex·com·mu·ni·ca·tion
ex·com·mu·ni·ca·tive (or
  ·tory)
ex·com·mu·ni·ca·tor
ex·co·ri·ate
ex·co·ria·tion
ex·cre·ment
ex·cre·men·tal (or ·ti·tious)
ex·cres·cence
ex·cres·cen·cy (plural ·cies)
ex·cres·cent
ex·cre·ta
ex·cre·tal
ex·crete
ex·cret·er
ex·cre·tion
ex·cre·tive
ex·cre·tory
ex·cru·ci·ate
ex·cru·ci·at·ing
ex·cru·ci·at·ing·ly
ex·cru·cia·tion
ex·cul·pable
ex·cul·pate vindicate
ex·cul·pa·tion
ex·cul·pa·tory
ex·cur·rent flowing
  outwards
ex·cur·sion
ex·cur·sion·ist
ex·cur·sive
ex·cur·sive·ness
ex·cur·sus (plural ·suses or
  ·sus) digression
ex·cus·able
ex·cus·able·ness
ex·cus·ably
ex·cusa·tory

ex·cuse
ex-directory (adj)
ex·eat leave of absence
ex·ecrable
ex·ecrable·ness
ex·ecrate loathe
ex·ecra·tion
ex·ecra·tive (or ·tory)
ex·ecut·able
ex·ecu·tant
ex·ecute
ex·ecut·er one who executes
  something; compare
  executor
ex·ecu·tion
ex·ecu·tion·er
ex·ecu·tive
ex·ecu·tor trustee of will;
  compare executer
ex·ecu·to·rial
ex·ecu·tor·ship
ex·ecu·tory legal term
ex·ecu·trix (plural ·tri·ces or
  ·trixes) female executor
ex·edra continuous bench
ex·egesis (plural ·egeses)
  Bible interpretation
ex·egete (or ·egetist)
ex·eget·ic (or ·egeti·cal)
ex·egeti·cal·ly
ex·eget·ics
ex·em·plar
ex·em·pla·ri·ly
ex·em·pla·ri·ness
ex·em·pla·ry
ex·em·pli·fi·able
ex·em·pli·fi·ca·tion
ex·em·pli·fi·ca·tive
ex·em·pli·fi·er
ex·em·pli·fy (·fies, ·fy·ing,
  ·fied)
ex·em·pli gra·tia Latin for
  the sake of example
ex·em·plum (plural ·pla)
  example
ex·empt
ex·empt·ible
ex·emp·tion
ex·en·ter·ate remove
  surgically
ex·en·tera·tion
ex·equa·tur official
  authorization
ex·equies funeral rites
ex·er·cis·able

ex·er·cise train; use; *compare* exorcise
ex·er·cis·er
ex·er·gual
ex·ergue date on coin
ex·ert make effort; *compare* excerpt; exsert
ex·er·tion
ex·er·tive
Ex·eter
ex·eunt *Latin* they leave
ex·fo·li·ate
ex·fo·lia·tion
ex·fo·lia·tive
ex gra·tia *Latin* gratuitous
ex·hal·able
ex·hal·ant
ex·ha·la·tion
ex·hale
ex·haust
ex·haust·er
ex·haust·ibil·ity
ex·haust·ible
ex·haus·tion
ex·haus·tive
ex·haust·ive·ness
ex·hib·it
ex·hi·bi·tion
ex·hi·bi·tion·er scholarship student
ex·hi·bi·tion·ism
ex·hi·bi·tion·ist
ex·hi·bi·tion·is·tic
ex·hibi·tive illustrative
ex·hibi·tor (*or* ·hib·it·er)
ex·hibi·tory
ex·hil·ar·ant
ex·hila·rate
ex·hil·arat·ing·ly
ex·hila·ra·tion
ex·hila·ra·tive (*or* ·tory)
ex·hila·ra·tor
ex·hort
ex·hor·ta·tion
ex·hor·ta·tive (*or* ·tory)
ex·hort·er
ex·hu·ma·tion
ex·hume
ex·hum·er
exi·gen·cy (*or* exi·gence; *plural* ·cies *or* ·gences)
exi·gent urgent
exi·gible required
exi·gu·ity (*or* ex·igu·ous·ness)

ex·igu·ous meagre
ex·ile
ex·il·ic (*or* ·ian)
ex·ist
ex·ist·ence
ex·ist·ent
ex·is·ten·tial
ex·is·ten·tial·ism
ex·is·ten·tial·ist
ex·is·ten·tial·ly
exit
exi·tance physics term
ex li·bris *Latin* from the library of
Ex·moor
exo·bi·olo·gist
exo·bi·ol·ogy astrobiology
exo·cen·tric linguistics term
exo·crine having a duct; *compare* endocrine
exo·derm *variant of* ectoderm
exo·don·tics dentistry
exo·don·tist
Exo·dus Old Testament book
exo·dus
exo·en·zyme
exo·er·gic energy-emitting; *compare* endoergic
ex of·fi·cio *Latin* by right of office
ex·oga·mous (*or* exo·gam·ic)
ex·oga·my marrying into another tribe
ex·og·enous
ex·on·er·ate
ex·on·era·tion
ex·on·era·tive
ex·on·era·tor
exo·nym foreigner's version of placename
exo·pep·ti·dase enzyme
exo·oph·thal·mic
ex·oph·thal·mos (*or* ·mus, ·mia) protrusion of eyeball
exo·rabil·ity
exo·rable moved by pleading
ex·or·bi·tance
ex·or·bi·tant
ex·or·cise (*or* ·cize) expel evil spirit; *compare* exercise

ex·or·cis·er (*or* ·ciz·er)
ex·or·cism
ex·or·cist
ex·or·dial
ex·or·dium (*plural* ·diums *or* ·dia) beginning of speech
exo·skel·etal
exo·skel·eton
ex·os·mo·sis biology term
ex·os·mot·ic (*or* ex·os·mic)
exo·sphere atmospheric layer
exo·spore botany term
exo·spor·ous
ex·os·to·sis (*plural* ·ses) outgrowth from bone
exo·ter·ic comprehensible; *compare* esoteric
exo·teri·cal·ly
exo·teri·cism
exo·ther·mic (*or* ·mal) heat-emitting; *compare* endothermic
exo·ther·mi·cal·ly (*or* ·ther·mal·ly)
ex·ot·ic
ex·oti·ca
ex·oti·cal·ly
ex·oti·cism
ex·ot·ic·ness
exo·tox·ic
exo·tox·in
ex·pand
ex·pand·able (*or* ·ible)
ex·pand·er
ex·panse
ex·pan·sibil·ity
ex·pan·sible
ex·pan·sile
ex·pan·sion
ex·pan·sion·ary
ex·pan·sion·ism
ex·pan·sion·ist
ex·pan·sion·is·tic
ex·pan·sive
ex·pan·sive·ness
ex par·te legal term
ex·pa·ti·ate enlarge upon; *compare* expiate
ex·pa·tia·tion
ex·pa·tia·tor
ex·pat·ri·ate
ex·pat·ria·tion
ex·pect

ex·pect·able
ex·pec·tan·cy (or ·tance;
 plural ·cies or ·tances)
ex·pec·tant
ex·pec·ta·tion
ex·pec·ta·tive
ex·pec·to·rant
ex·pec·to·rate
ex·pec·to·ra·tion spitting
ex·pec·to·ra·tor
ex·pedi·en·cy (or ·ence;
 plural ·cies or ·ences)
ex·pedi·ent
ex·pedi·en·tial
ex·pedite
ex·pedit·er (or ·pedi·tor)
ex·pedi·tion
ex·pedi·tion·ary
ex·pedi·tious
ex·pedi·tious·ness
ex·pel (·pel·ling, ·pelled)
ex·pel·lable
ex·pel·lant (or ·lent)
ex·pel·lee
ex·pel·ler
ex·pend
ex·pend·abil·ity
ex·pend·able
ex·pend·er
ex·pendi·ture
ex·pense
ex·pen·sive
ex·pen·sive·ness
ex·peri·ence
ex·peri·en·tial
ex·peri·ment
ex·peri·men·tal
ex·peri·men·tal·ism
ex·peri·men·tal·ist
ex·peri·men·tal·ly
ex·peri·men·ta·tion
ex·peri·ment·er
ex·pert
ex·per·tise
ex·pert·ness
ex·pi·able
ex·pi·ate atone; compare
 expatiate
ex·pia·tion
ex·pia·tor
ex·pia·tory
ex·pi·ra·tion
ex·pira·tory of exhalation
ex·pire
ex·pir·er

ex·pi·ry (plural ·ries)
ex·plain
ex·plain·able
ex·plain·er
ex·pla·na·tion
ex·plana·to·ri·ly
ex·plana·tory (or ·tive)
ex·plant biology term
ex·plan·ta·tion
ex·ple·tive swear word
ex·pli·cable
ex·pli·cate explain
ex·pli·ca·tion
ex·pli·ca·tive (or ·tory)
ex·pli·ca·tor
ex·plic·it
ex·plic·it·ness
ex·plode
ex·plod·er
ex·ploit
ex·ploit·able (or
 ·ploita·tive)
ex·ploi·ta·tion
ex·plo·ra·tion
ex·plora·tory (or ·tive)
ex·plore
ex·plor·er
ex·plo·sion
ex·plo·sive
ex·plo·sive·ness
ex·po·nent
ex·po·nen·tial maths term
ex·po·nen·tial·ly
ex·pon·ible needing
 explanation
ex·port
ex·port·abil·ity
ex·port·able
ex·por·ta·tion
ex·port·er
ex·pos·able
ex·pos·al
ex·pose
ex·po·sé exposure of
 scandal
ex·posed
ex·pos·ed·ness
ex·pos·er
ex·po·si·tion
ex·po·si·tion·al
ex·posi·tor expounder
ex·posi·to·ri·ly (or ·tive·ly)
ex·posi·tory (or ·tive)
ex post fac·to Latin
 retrospective

ex·pos·tu·late dissuade
ex·pos·tu·lat·ing·ly
ex·pos·tu·la·tion
ex·pos·tu·la·tor
ex·pos·tu·la·tory (or ·tive)
ex·po·sure
ex·pound
ex·pound·er
ex·press
ex·press·age conveyance by
 express
ex·press·er
ex·press·ible
ex·pres·sion
ex·pres·sion·al
ex·pres·sion·ism
ex·pres·sion·ist
ex·pres·sion·is·tic
ex·pres·sion·less
ex·pres·sive
ex·pres·sive·ness
ex·pres·siv·ity
(expresso) incorrect spelling of
 espresso
ex·press·way US motorway
ex·pro·pri·able
ex·pro·pri·ate
ex·pro·pria·tion
ex·pro·pria·tor
ex·pul·sion
ex·pul·sive
ex·punc·tion
ex·punge
ex·pung·er
ex·pur·gate
ex·pur·ga·tion
ex·pur·ga·tor
ex·pur·ga·tory (or ·to·rial)
ex·quis·ite
ex·quis·ite·ness
ex·san·gui·nate drain blood
 from
ex·san·guin·ation
ex·san·guine (or ·gui·nous)
ex·san·guin·ity
ex·scind (or ·sect) cut off
ex·sect cut out
ex·sec·tion
ex·sert protrude; compare
 excerpt; exert
ex·ser·tile
ex·ser·tion
ex·sic·cate dry
ex·sic·ca·tion
ex·sic·ca·tive

ex·sic·ca·tor
ex·stipu·late (or
  es·tipu·late) botany term
(extasy) incorrect spelling of
  ecstasy
ex·stro·phy medical term
ex·tant surviving
ex·tem·po·ra·neous (or
  ·po·rary)
ex·tem·po·ra·neous·ness
ex·tem·po·rari·ly
ex·tem·po·rari·ness
ex·tem·po·re impromptu
ex·tem·po·ri·za·tion (or
  ·sa·tion)
ex·tem·po·rize (or ·rise)
ex·tem·po·riz·er (or ·ris·er)
ex·tend
ex·tend·ed·ness
ex·tend·er
ex·tend·ibil·ity (or
  ·abil·ity)
ex·tend·ible (or ·able)
ex·ten·sibil·ity (or
  ·sible·ness)
ex·ten·sible (or ·sile)
ex·ten·sion
ex·ten·sion·al
ex·ten·sion·al·ity (or ·ism)
ex·ten·sity psychology term
ex·ten·sive
ex·ten·sive·ness
ex·ten·som·eter (or ·sim·)
  physics term
ex·ten·sor muscle
ex·tent
ex·tenu·ate
ex·tenu·at·ing·ly
ex·tenu·ation
ex·tenu·ator
ex·tenu·atory
ex·te·ri·or
ex·te·ri·ori·za·tion (or
  ·sa·tion)
ex·te·ri·or·ize (or ·ise)
  medical term
ex·ter·mi·nable
ex·ter·mi·nate
ex·ter·mi·na·tion
ex·ter·mi·na·tive (or ·tory)
ex·ter·mi·na·tor
ex·tern (or ·terne) US
  nonresident hospital
  doctor
ex·ter·nal

ex·ter·nal·ism
ex·ter·nal·ist
ex·ter·nal·ity (plural
  ·ities)
ex·ter·nali·za·tion (or
  ·sa·tion)
ex·ter·nal·ize (or ·ise)
ex·ter·nal·ly
ex·tero·cep·tive
ex·tero·cep·tor biology
  term
ex·ter·ri·to·rial
ex·ter·ri·to·ri·al·ity
ex·tinct
ex·tinc·tion
ex·tinc·tive
ex·tine (or ·ine) botany
  term
ex·tin·guish
ex·tin·guish·able
ex·tin·guish·ant
ex·tin·guish·er
ex·tin·guish·ment
ex·tir·pate destroy
ex·tir·pa·tion
ex·tir·pa·tive
ex·tir·pa·tor
ex·tol (US ·toll; ·tol·ling,
  ·tolled)
ex·tol·ler
ex·tol·ling·ly
ex·tol·ment
ex·tort
ex·tort·er
ex·tor·tion
ex·tor·tion·able
ex·tor·tion·ary
ex·tor·tion·ate
ex·tor·tion·ist (or ·er)
ex·tor·tive
ex·tra
extra·ca·noni·cal outside
  scripture
extra·cel·lu·lar
ex·tract
ex·tract·abil·ity (or
  ·ibil·ity)
ex·tract·able (or ·ible)
ex·trac·tion
ex·trac·tive
ex·trac·tor
extra·cur·ricu·lar
extra·dit·able
extra·dite
extra·di·tion

extra·dos (plural ·dos or
  ·doses) architecture term
extra·ga·lac·tic
extra·ju·di·cial
extra·mari·tal
extra·mun·dane outside the
  world
extra·mu·ral
extra·neous
extra·neous·ness
extra·nu·clear
extraor·di·nari·ly
extraor·di·nari·ness
ex·traor·di·nary
ex·trapo·late
ex·trapo·la·tion
ex·trapo·la·tive (or ·tory)
ex·trapo·la·tor
extra·po·si·tion
extra·sen·so·ry
extra·ter·res·trial
extra·ter·ri·to·rial (or
  ex·ter·)
extra·ter·ri·to·ri·al·ity
extra·uter·ine
ex·trava·gance
ex·trava·gant
ex·trava·gan·za
ex·trava·gate Archaic roam
ex·trava·ga·tion
ex·trava·sate exude
ex·trava·sa·tion
extra·vas·cu·lar
extra·vehicu·lar outside a
  spacecraft
extra·vert variant spelling of
  extrovert
ex·treme
ex·treme·ly
ex·treme·ness
ex·trem·ism
ex·trem·ist
ex·trem·ity (plural ·ities)
ex·tri·cable
ex·tri·cate
ex·tri·ca·tion
ex·trin·sic not contained
  within; compare intrinsic
ex·trin·si·cal·ly
(extrodinary) incorrect
  spelling of extraordinary
ex·trorse (or ·tror·sal)
  turned outwards
extro·ver·sion (or extra·)
extro·ver·sive (or extra·)

extro·vert (*or* extra·)
extro·vert·ed (*or* extra·)
ex·trude
ex·tru·sion
ex·tru·sive
exu·ber·ance (*or* ·ancy)
exu·ber·ant
exu·ber·ate
exu·da·tion
exu·da·tive
ex·ude
ex·ult
ex·ult·ant
ex·ul·ta·tion
ex·ult·ing·ly
ex·ur·bia US outside suburbs
exu·viae shed skin
exu·vial
exu·vi·ate
exu·via·tion
ex-works excluding delivery
cost

eyas nestling hawk
eye (eye·ing *or* ey·ing,
eyed)
eye·ball
eye·bath
eye·bolt
eye·bright plant
eye·brow
eye-catcher
eye-catching
eye·cup
eyed
eye·dropper
eye·ful
eye·glass
eye·glasses US spectacles
eye·hole
eye·ing (*or* ey·ing)
eye·lash
eye·less
eye·let
eye·let·eer

eye·lid
eye·liner
eye-opener
eye·piece
eye·shade
eye·shot
eye·sight
eye·sore
eye·spot
eye·stalk
eye·strain
eye·tooth (*plural* ·teeth)
eye·wash
eye·witness
eyra animal
Eyre Canadian lake;
Australian peninsula
ey·rie (*or* aerie, aery; *plural*
ey·ries *or* aeries) eagle's
nest; *compare* eerie
ey·rir (*plural* aurar)
Icelandic coin

F

fa (*or* fah) musical note
fab
fa·ba·ceous botany term
Fa·bian
Fa·bi·an·ism
fa·ble
fa·bled
fa·bler
fab·ric
fab·ri·cate
fab·ri·ca·tion
fab·ri·ca·tive
fab·ri·ca·tor
Fab·ri·koid (*Trademark*)
waterproof fabric
fabu·list teller of fables
fabu·lous
fabu·lous·ness
fa·çade (*or* ·cade)
face
face·able
face·bar wrestling hold
face-centred (US -centered)
crystallography term
face-harden metallurgy
term
face·less
face·less·ness

face-lift
face-off ice hockey term
face·plate lathe part
fac·er
face-saving
fac·et (*verb* ·et·ing, ·et·ed *or*
·et·ting, ·et·ted)
fa·cetiae witty sayings
fa·cetious
fa·cetious·ness
fa·cia *variant spelling of*
fascia
fa·cial
fa·cial·ly
fa·cies (*plural* ·cies)
appearance; *compare*
fasces; fascia
fac·ile
fac·ile·ly
fac·ile·ness
fa·cili·tate
fa·cili·ta·tion
fa·cili·ta·tive
fa·cili·ta·tor
fa·cil·ity (*plural* ·ities)
fac·ing
fac·simi·le (·le·ing, ·led)
fact

fact·ful
fac·tice rubbery material
fac·tion
fac·tion·al
fac·tion·al·ism
fac·tion·al·ist
fac·tious factional; *compare*
factitious
fac·tious·ness
fac·ti·tious contrived;
compare factious; fictitious
fac·ti·tious·ness
fac·ti·tive linguistics term
fac·tor
fac·tor·abil·ity
fac·tor·able
fac·tor·age commission
paid to factor
fac·torial
fac·to·ri·al·ly
fac·tor·ing business term
fac·tori·za·tion (*or* ·sa·tion)
fac·tor·ize (*or* ·ise)
fac·tor·ship
fac·to·ry (*plural* ·ries)
fac·to·tum
fac·tual
fac·tu·al·ism

fac·tu·al·ist
fac·tu·al·is·tic
fac·tu·al·ly
fac·tu·al·ness (or ·ity)
facu·la (plural ·lae) sun
  spot
facu·lar
fac·ul·ta·tive optional
fac·ul·ty (plural ·ties)
fad
fad·able
fad·di·ness
fad·dish
fad·dism
fad·dist
fad·dy (·di·er, ·di·est)
fade
fad·ed
fad·ed·ness
fade-in
fade·less
fade-out
fad·er
fadge Dialect agree
fad·ing
fae·cal (US fe·)
fae·ces (US fe·)
Fa·en·za Italian city
fae·rie (or ·ry; plural ·ries)
  Archaic fairyland
Fae·roes (or Fa·roes) North
  Atlantic islands
Faero·ese (or Faro·; plural
  ·ese)
faff Slang fuss
fag (fag·ging, fagged)
fa·ga·ceous botany term
fagged
fag·ging
fag·got (or esp. US fag·ot)
fag·got·ing (or esp. US
  fag·ot·) needlework term
fah variant spelling of fa
fahl·band rock
Fahr·en·heit temperature
  scale
faï·ence (or faï·) pottery
fail
fail·ing
faille fabric
fail-safe
fail·ure
fain
fai·ne·ance (or ·an·cy)
fai·né·ant (or ·ne·) idle

faint pale; collapse; compare
  feint
faint·er
faint·ing
faint·ing·ly
faint·ish
faint·ly
faint·ness
faints variant spelling of
  feints
fair just; not dark; event;
  compare fare
Fair·banks Alaskan city
fair·ground
fair·ing
fair·ish
fair·lead (or ·leader)
  nautical term
fair·ly
fair-minded
fair-minded·ness
fair·ness
fair-spoken
fair·way
fair-weather (adj)
fairy (plural fairies)
fairy·land
fairy-like
fait ac·com·pli (plural faits
  accomplis) French
  something done
faith
faith·ful
faith·ful·ly
faith·ful·ness
faith·less
faith·less·ness
Faiza·bad Afghan city;
  variant spelling of Fyzabad
fake
fak·er one who fakes
fa·kir (or ·qir, ·keer) holy
  man
fa-la refrain
Fa·lange Spanish Fascist
  movement
Fa·lang·ism
Fa·lan·gist
fal·ba·la gathered frill
fal·cate (or ·ci·form)
  sickle-shaped
fal·chion sword
fal·con
fal·con·er
fal·con·et small falcon

fal·coni·form
fal·con·ry
fal·deral (or fal·derol,
  fol·derol) trifle
fald·stool bishop's seat
Fa·lerii ancient Italian city
Fa·lis·can language
Fal·kirk Scottish town
Falk·land Is·lands
fall (fall·ing, fell, fall·en)
fal·la·cious
fal·la·cious·ness
fal·la·cy (plural ·cies)
fal·lal ornament
fal·lal·ery
fall·en
fall·er
fall·fish (plural ·fish, ·fishes)
fal·libil·ity (or ·lible·ness)
fal·lible
fal·li·bly
Fal·lo·pian tube anatomy
  term
fall·out
fal·low
fal·low·ness
Fal·mouth Cornish port
false
false-card bridge term
false·hood
false·ly
false·ness
fal·set·to (plural ·tos)
false·work framework
fal·sies false breasts
fal·si·fi·able
fal·si·fi·ca·tion
fal·si·fi·er
fal·si·fy (·fies, ·fy·ing, ·fied)
fal·sity (plural ·sities)
falt·boat collapsible boat
fal·ter
fal·ter·er
fal·ter·ing·ly
Fa·lun Swedish city
Fa·ma·gu·sta Cypriot port
fame
fa·mil·ial
fa·mil·iar
fa·mili·ar·ity (plural ·ities)
fa·mil·iari·za·tion (or
  ·sa·tion)
fa·mil·iar·ize (or ·ise)
fa·mil·iar·iz·er (or ·is·er)
fa·mili·ar·ness

Fami·list member of sect
fa·mille Chinese porcelain
fami·ly (plural ·lies)
fam·ine
fam·ish
fam·ish·ment
fa·mous
fa·mous·ness
famu·lus (plural ·li)
  sorcerer's attendant
fan (fan·ning, fanned)
Fana·ga·lo (or ·ka·lo)
  African language
fa·nat·ic
fa·nati·cal
fa·nati·cal·ly
fa·nati·cism
fa·nati·cize (or ·cise)
fan·cied
fan·ci·er
fan·ci·ful
fan·ci·ful·ly
fan·ci·ful·ness
fan·ci·ly
fan·ci·ness
fan·cy (adj ·ci·er, ·ci·est;
  noun, plural ·cies; verb
  ·cies, ·cy·ing, ·cied)
fancy-free
fancy·work
fan·dan·gle ornament
fan·dan·go (plural ·gos)
  dance
fan·fare
fang
fanged
fan·go mud from thermal
  springs
fan·ion surveyor's flag
fan·jet jet engine
fan·kle Scot entangle
fan·light
fanned
fan·ner
fan·ning
fan·ny (plural ·nies) Slang
  female genitals
fan·on vestment
fan·tail
fan-tailed
fan-tan game
fan·ta·sia
fan·ta·size (or ·sise)
fan·tast visionary
fan·tas·tic (or ·ti·cal)

fan·ta·sy (or phan·; noun,
  plural ·sies; verb ·sies,
  ·sy·ing, ·sied)
Fan·ti (plural ·tis or ·ti)
  Ghanaian people
fan·toc·ci·ni marionettes
far (far·ther or fur·ther,
  far·thest or fur·thest)
far·ad unit
fara·day unit
fa·rad·ic physics term
fara·dism medical use of
  electricity
fara·di·za·tion (or ·sa·tion)
fara·dize (or ·dise)
fara·diz·er (or ·dis·er)
far·an·dole dance
far·away
farce
far·ceur (fem ·ceuse) farce
  writer
far·ci stuffed
far·ci·cal
far·ci·cal·ity (or ·ness)
far·ci·cal·ly
far·cy (plural ·cies) animal
  disease
far·del bundle
fare payment; food; to
  manage; compare fair
Fare·ham Hampshire town
far·er
fare·well
far-fetched
far-flung
fa·ri·na flour
fari·na·ceous containing
  starch
fari·nose flourlike
farl (or farle) cake
farm
farm·able
farm·er
farm·house
farm·ing
farm·land
farm·stead
farm·yard
Farn·bor·ough Hampshire
  town
far·nesol chemical
  compound
far·ness
Farn·ham Surrey town
faro card game

Fa·roes variant spelling of
  Faeroes
Faro·ese variant spelling of
  Faeroese
far-off
fa·rouche sullen
far·ragi·nous
far·ra·go (plural ·goes)
  hotchpotch
far-reaching
far·ri·er
far·ri·ery (plural ·eries)
far·row
far-seeing
far-sighted
far-sighted·ly
far-sighted·ness
fart
far·ther (or fur·) more
  distant; compare further
farther·most
far·thest (or fur·)
far·thing
far·thin·gale hoop under
  skirt
fart·lek sports term
fas·ces (plural noun; sing.
  ·cies) Roman insignia;
  compare facies
fas·cia (or fa·cia; plural
  ·ciae) flat surface; fibrous
  tissue; compare facies
fas·cial (or fa·cial)
fas·ci·ate (or ·at·ed)
fas·cia·tion botany term
fas·ci·cle bundle
fas·ci·cled
fas·cicu·lar (or ·late)
fas·cicu·la·tion
fas·ci·cule instalment
fas·ci·cu·lus (plural ·li)
fas·ci·nate
fas·ci·nat·ed·ly
fas·ci·nat·ing
fas·ci·na·tion
fas·ci·na·tive
fas·cine bundle of sticks
fas·cism
fas·cist
fa·scis·tic
fa·scis·ti·cal·ly
fash Scot worry
fash·ion
fash·ion·able
fash·ion·ably

fash·ion·able·ness
fash·ion·er
Fa·sho·da Sudanese town
fast
fast·back car
fast-breeder nuclear reactor
fas·ten
fas·ten·er
fas·ten·ing
fast·er
fas·tidi·ous
fas·tidi·ous·ness
fas·tigi·ate (or ·at·ed)
   biology term
fast·ness
fat (fat·ter, fat·test)
fa·tal
fa·tal·ism
fa·tal·ist
fa·tal·is·tic
fa·tal·is·ti·cal·ly
fa·tal·ity (plural ·ities)
fa·tal·ly
fat·back pork fat
fate
fat·ed
fate·ful
fate·ful·ly
fate·ful·ness
Fates Greek goddesses
fat·head
fa·ther
father·hood
father-in-law (plural
   fathers-)
father·land
fa·ther·less
father-like
fa·ther·li·ness
fa·ther·ly
fath·om
fath·om·able
fath·om·er
Fa·thom·eter (Trademark)
fath·om·less
fa·tid·ic (or ·tidi·cal)
   prophetic
fati·gabil·ity (·gable·ness)
fa·tig·able
fa·tigue (·tigu·ing, ·tigued)
fat·ling fattened young
   animal
fat·ness
Fat·shan Chinese city
fat·so (plural ·sos or ·soes)

fat-soluble
fat·ted
fat·ten
fat·ten·able
fat·ten·er
fat·ti·ly
fat·ti·ness
fat·tish
fat·ty (adj ·ti·er, ·ti·est;
   noun, plural ·ties)
fa·tui·tous fatuous; compare
   fortuitous
fa·tu·ity (plural ·ities)
fatu·ous
fatu·ous·ness
fau·bourg French suburb
fau·cal (or ·cial)
fau·ces (plural ·ces)
   anatomy term
fau·cet US tap
faugh exclamation
fault
fault-finder
fault-finding
faulti·ly
faulti·ness
fault·less
fault·less·ness
faulty (faulti·er, faulti·est)
faun Roman deity; compare
   fawn
fau·na (plural ·nas or ·nae)
   animals
fau·nal
Faust (or Faustus) legendary
   magician
Faust·ian
faute de mieux French
   lacking better
fau·teuil armchair
Fauv·ism art movement
Fauv·ist
faux pas (plural faux pas)
fa·veo·late honeycombed
fa·vo·nian of the west wind
fa·vour (US ·vor)
fa·vour·able (US ·vor)
fa·vour·ably (US ·vor)
fa·vour·able·ness (US ·vor·)
fa·vour·er (US ·vor·)
fa·vour·ing·ly (US ·vor·)
fa·vour·ite (US ·vor·)
fa·vour·it·ism (US ·vor·)
Fav·rile glass
fa·vus skin disease

fawn animal; colour; cringe;
   compare faun
fawn·er
fawn·ing·ly
fax facsimile transmission
fay fairy; compare fey
fay·al·ite mineral
faze US disconcert
fe·al·ty (plural ·ties) feudal
   loyalty
fear
fear·er
fear·ful
fear·ful·ly
fear·ful·ness
fear·less
fear·less·ness
fear·nought (or ·naught)
   fabric
fear·some
fear·some·ly
fear·some·ness
fea·sibil·ity (or ·sible·ness)
fea·sible
fea·sibly
feast
feast·er
feat exploit; compare feet
feath·er
feather·bed (·bedding,
   ·bedded)
feather·bedding
   overmanning
feather·brain
feather·brained
feather·edge
feath·er·ing
feather·stitch
feather·veined
feather·weight
feath·ery
fea·ture
feature-length (adj)
fea·ture·less
fea·ture·less·ness
feaze nautical term
fe·bric·ity
feb·ri·fa·cient
fe·brif·ic (or ·brif·er·ous)
fe·brifu·gal
feb·ri·fuge fever-reducing
   drug
fe·brile feverish
fe·bril·ity
Feb·ru·ary (plural ·aries)

fe·cal *US spelling of* faecal

fe·ces *US spelling of* faeces

fe·cit *Latin* made it

feck·less

feck·less·ness

fecu·la (*plural* ·lae) starch

fecu·lence

fecu·lent filthy

fe·cund fertile

fe·cun·date

fe·cun·da·tion

fe·cun·da·tor

fe·cun·da·tory

fe·cun·dity

fed

fe·da·yee (*plural* ·yeen) Arab commando

fed·er·al

fed·er·al·ly

fed·er·al·ism

fed·er·al·ist

fed·er·al·is·tic

fed·er·ali·za·tion (*or* ·sa·tion)

fed·er·al·ize (*or* ·ise)

fed·er·ate

fed·era·tion

fed·era·tive

fe·do·ra hat

fee (fee·ing, feed)

fee·ble

feeble-minded

feeble-minded·ly

feeble-minded·ness

fee·ble·ness

feed (feed·ing, fed)

feed·able

feed·back

feed·bag

feed·er

feed·lot

feel (feel·ing, felt)

feel·er

feel·ing

feet *plural of* foot; *compare* feat

feeze *Dialect* beat

feign

feign·er

feign·ing·ly

feint mock action; printing term; *compare* faint

feints (*or* faints) whisky residue

feis·ty

feld·spar (*or* fel·spar) mineral

feld·spath·ic (*or* fel·)

feld·spath·ose (*or* fel·)

fe·li·cif·ic making happy

fe·lici·tate

fe·lici·ta·tion

fe·lici·ta·tor

fe·lici·tous apt

fe·lici·tous·ness

fe·lic·ity (*plural* ·ities)

fe·lid animal

fe·line

fe·lin·ity (*or* ·line·ness)

fell

fell·able

fel·lah (*plural* ·lahs, ·la·hin, *or* ·la·heen) Arab peasant

fel·la·tio oral sex

fell·er

fell·monger animal skin dealer

fel·loe (*or* ·ly; *plural* ·loes *or* ·lies) wheel segment

fel·low

fel·low·ship

felo de se (*plural* fe·lo·nes de se *or* fe·los de se) suicide

fel·on

fe·lo·ni·ous

fe·lo·ni·ous·ness

fel·on·ry (*plural* ·ries)

felo·ny (*plural* ·nies)

fel·site (*or* ·stone) rock

fel·sit·ic

felt

felt·ing

fe·luc·ca boat

fel·wort plant

fe·male

fe·male·ness

feme woman (*in legal contexts*)

femi·nine

femi·nine·ly

femi·nin·ity

femi·nism

femi·nist

femi·ni·za·tion (*or* ·sa·tion)

femi·nize (*or* ·nise)

femme de cham·bre (*plural* femmes de cham·bre) chambermaid

femme fa·tale (*plural* femmes fa·tales) seductive woman

femo·ral of the thigh

fe·mur (*plural* ·murs *or* femo·ra) thigh bone

fen

fence

fenc·er

fenc·ing

fend

fend·er

fend·ered

fen·es·tel·la (*plural* ·lae) wall niche

fe·nes·tra (*plural* ·trae) biology term

fe·nes·tral

fe·nes·trat·ed (*or* ·trate) having windows

fen·es·tra·tion

Fe·nian Irish revolutionary

fen·nec fox

fen·nel

fennel·flower

fen·ny marshy

Fenrir (*or* Fenris, Fenriswolf) mythological wolf

Fens

fenu·greek plant

feoff *variant spelling of* fief

fe·ral (*or* ·rine) wild

fer·bam fungicide

fer-de-lance snake

fer·etory (*plural* ·etories) shrine

Fer·ga·na Asian region

fe·ria (*plural* ·rias *or* ·riae) weekday

fe·rial

fe·rine *variant of* feral

fer·ity wildness

Fer·man·agh Northern Irish county

fer·ma·ta (*plural* ·tas *or* ·te) musical term

fer·ment undergo fermentation; *compare* foment

fer·ment·abil·ity

fer·ment·able

fer·men·ta·tion

fer·menta·tive

fer·menta·tive·ness

fer·ment·er

fer·mi unit

fer·mi·on particle

fer·mium radioactive
element

fern

fern·ery (plural ·eries)

ferny

fe·ro·cious

fe·roc·ity (or ·ro·cious·ness)

Fer·ra·ra Italian city

fer·rate chemistry term

fer·reous containing iron

fer·ret

fer·ret·ing silk tape

fer·ret·er

fer·rety

fer·ri·age

fer·ric chemistry term

fer·ri·cy·an·ic acid

fer·ri·cya·nide

fer·rif·er·ous producing iron

fer·ri·mag·net·ic

fer·ri·mag·net·ism

Ferris wheel fairground
wheel

fer·rite ceramic

fer·ri·tin protein

fer·ro·cene chemical
compound

fer·ro·chro·mium (or
fer·ro·chrome)

fer·ro·con·crete

fer·ro·cy·an·ic acid

fer·ro·cya·nide

fer·ro·elec·tric

fer·ro·elec·tri·cal·ly

fer·ro·elec·tric·ity

fer·ro·mag·ne·sian

fer·ro·mag·net·ic

fer·ro·mag·net·ism

fer·ro·man·ga·nese

fer·ro·sili·con

fer·ro·type photography
term

fer·rous

fer·ru·gi·nous containing
iron

fer·rule (or fer·ule) metal
cap; compare ferule

fer·ry (noun, plural ·ries; verb
·ries, ·ry·ing, ·ried)

fer·tile

fer·til·ity (or ·tile·ness)

fer·ti·liz·able (or ·lis·able)

fer·ti·li·za·tion (or ·sa·tion)

fer·ti·lize (or ·lise)

fer·ti·liz·er (or ·lis·er)

feru·la (plural ·las or ·lae)
plant

feru·la·ceous

fer·ule flat cane; compare
ferrule

fer·ven·cy

fer·vent (or ·vid)

fer·vent·ly (or ·vid·ly)

fer·vid variant of fervent

fer·vour (US ·vor)

fes·cue grass

fesse (or fess) heraldry term

fes·tal festive

fes·ter

fes·ti·na·tion quickening of
gait

fes·ti·val

fes·tive

fes·tive·ly

fes·tive·ness

fes·tiv·ity (plural ·ities)

fes·toon

fes·toon·ery

fest·schrift (plural
·schrift·en or ·schrifts)
commemorative writings

feta cheese

fe·tal (or foe·)

fe·ta·tion (or foe·)
pregnancy

fetch

fetch·er

fetch·ing

fête (or fete)

fe·tial (plural fe·tia·les)
Roman herald

fet·ich variant spelling of
fetish

fe·ti·cid·al (or foe·)

fe·ti·cide (or foe·)
destruction of fetus

fet·id (or foet·)
foul-smelling

fe·tipa·rous (or foe·) of
marsupial birth

fet·ish (or ·ich)

fet·ish·ism (or ·ich·)

fet·ish·ist (or ·ich·)

fet·lock (or fetter·) part of
horse's leg

fe·tor (or foe·) stench

fet·ter

fet·ter·er

fet·ter·less

fet·tle

fet·tling refractory material

fet·tu·ci·ne (or ·tuc·ci·,
tu·ci·ni) pasta

fe·tus (or foe·; plural ·tuses)

feud

feu·dal

feu·dal·ism

feu·dal·ist

feu·dal·is·tic

feu·dal·ity (plural ·ities)

feu·dali·za·tion (or
·sa·tion)

feu·dal·ize (or ·ise)

feu·da·tory

feud·ist

feuil·le·ton review section
of paper

feuil·le·ton·ism

feuil·le·ton·ist

feuil·le·ton·is·tic

fe·ver

fe·vered

fe·ver·few plant

fe·ver·ish (or ·ous)

fe·ver·ish·ness

fever·wort plant

few

few·ness

fey whimsical; compare fay

fez (plural fez·zes)

Fez·zan Libyan region

fezzed

fia·cre carriage

fi·an·cé (fem ·cée)

Fi·an·na Fail Irish political
party

fi·as·co (plural ·cos or
·coes)

Fiat (Trademark)

fiat decree

fib (fibbed, fib·bing)

fib·ber

fi·bre (US ·ber)

fibre·board (US fiber·)

fi·bred (US ·bered)

fibre·fill (US fiber·)

fibre·glass (US fiber·)

fibre·optic (adj; US fiber-)

fibre optics (noun; US fiber
optics)

fibre·scope (US fiber·)

fi·bri·form

fi·bril (*or* **·bril·la**; *plural*
  ·brils *or* **·bril·lae**) small
  fibre
fi·bri·lar (*or* **·bril·lar,**
  ·bril·lose)
fi·bril·la·tion muscle
  twitching
fi·bril·li·form
fi·brin blood-clotting
  protein
fi·brino·gen
fi·brino·gen·ic (*or* **·ous**)
fi·brino·geni·cal·ly
fi·bri·noly·sin enzyme
fi·bri·noly·sis
fi·bri·no·lyt·ic
fi·brin·ous
fi·bro·blast tissue cell
fi·bro·blas·tic
fi·bro·cement
fi·broid
fi·bro·in protein
fi·bro·ma (*plural* **·ma·ta** *or*
  ·mas) tumour
fi·broma·tous
fi·bro·sis
fi·bro·si·tis
fi·brot·ic
fi·brous
fi·brous·ness
fi·bro·vas·cu·lar botany
  term
fibu·la (*plural* **·lae** *or* **·las**)
  leg bone
fibu·lar
fiche *short for* **microfiche**
fichu scarf
fick·le
fick·le·ness
fic·tile moulded from clay
fic·tion
fic·tion·al
fic·tion·ali·za·tion (*or*
  ·sa·tion)
fic·tion·al·ize (*or* **·ise**)
fic·tion·al·ly
fic·tion·ist (*or* **fic·tion·eer**)
fic·ti·tious not genuine;
  compare **factitious**
fic·ti·tious·ness
fic·tive of fiction
fid nautical term
fid·dle
fiddle-de-dee
fiddle-faddle

fiddle·head (*or* **·neck**)
  nautical term
fid·dler
fiddle·stick violin bow
fiddle·sticks nonsense
fiddle·wood
fid·dling
fid·dly (**·dli·er, ·dli·est**)
fid·ei·com·mis·sary (*plural*
  ·saries) legal term
fid·ei·com·mis·sum (*plural*
  ·sa)
fi·deism
fi·deist
fi·deis·tic
fi·del·ity (*plural* **·ities**)
fidg·et
fidg·et·ing·ly
fidg·ety
fi·du·cial
fi·du·ci·ary trustee
fie exclamation
fief (*or* **feoff**) property
  granted to vassal
field
field·er
field·fare bird
field-holler African-
  American singing style
field·mouse
field·piece gun
fields·man (*plural* **·men**)
field·stone
field·work
fiend
fiend·ish
fiend·ish·ness
fierce
fierce·ly
fierce·ness
fi·eri fa·ci·as legal term
fiery
Fie·so·le Italian town
fi·es·ta
Fife Scottish region
fife
fif·er
fif·teen
fif·teenth
fifth
fif·ti·eth
fif·ty (*plural* **·ties**)
fifty-fifty
fig
fight (**fight·ing, fought**)

fight·er
fighter-bomber
fight·ing
fig·ment
figu·ral
figu·rant (*fem* **·rante**)
  dancer
fig·ur·ate musical term
fig·ura·tion
fig·ura·tive
fig·ura·tive·ly
fig·ura·tive·ness
fig·ure
fig·ured
figure-ground psychology
  term
figure·head
fig·ur·er
figu·rine statuette
fig·wort
Fiji
Fi·jian
fil *variant of* **fils**
fila·gree *variant spelling of*
  filigree
fila·ment
fila·men·tary (*or* **·tous**)
fi·lar of thread
fi·laria (*plural* **·lariae**)
  worm
fi·lar·ial (*or* **·ian**)
fila·ria·sis
fila·ture silk spinning
fil·bert nut
filch
filch·er
file
file·card
file·fish (*plural* **·fish** *or*
  ·fishes)
fil·er
fi·let lace; meat fillet
fi·let mi·gnon (*plural* **fi·lets
  mi·gnons**) beef cut
fil·ial
fil·ial·ly
fil·ial·ness
fili·ate legal term
fili·ation lineage
fili·beg (*or* **fil·li·, phili·**)
  kilt
fili·bus·ter
fili·bus·ter·er
fili·bus·ter·ism
fili·cid·al

fili·cide killing son or
daughter

fili·form threadlike

fili·gree (or fila·, filla·;
·gree·ing, ·greed)

fil·ings

Fili·pi·no (plural ·nos)
inhabitant of Philippines

fill

filla·gree variant spelling of
filigree

filled

fill·er

fil·let

fill·ing

fil·lip

fil·lis·ter (or fil·is·ter,
fil·les·ter) wood plane

fil·ly (plural ·lies)

film

film·ic

filmi·ly

filmi·ness

fil·mog·ra·phy (plural
·phies)

film·set (·setting, ·set)

film·setter

film·setting

filmy (filmi·er, filmi·est)

filo thin pastry

filo·plume feather

fi·lose threadlike

filo·selle thread

fils (or fil; plural fils) Middle
Eastern coin

fil·ter separating device;
compare philtre

fil·ter·abil·ity (or
·able·ness)

fil·ter·able (or fil·trable)

filter-tipped

filth

filthi·ly

filthi·ness

filthy (filthi·er, filthi·est)

fil·trat·able variant of
filterable

fil·trate

fil·tra·tion

fi·lum (plural ·la) anatomy
term

fim·ble plant

fim·bria (plural ·briae)
anatomy term

fim·brial

fim·bri·ate (or ·bri·at·ed,
·bril·late) fringed

fim·bria·tion

fin (fin·ning, finned)

fin·able (or fine·)

fi·na·gle use trickery

fi·na·gler

fi·nal

fi·na·le

fi·nal·ism philosophical
doctrine

fi·nal·ist

fi·nal·ity (plural ·ities)

fi·na·li·za·tion (or ·sa·tion)

fi·nal·ize (or ·ise)

fi·nal·ly

fi·nals

fi·nance

fi·nan·cial

fi·nan·cial·ly

fi·nan·ci·er

fin·back whale

finch

find (find·ing, found)

find·able

find·er

fin de siè·cle French end of
19th century

find·ing

fine

fine·able variant spelling of
finable

fine-cut

fine-draw (-drawing, -drew,
-drawn)

Fine Gael Irish political
party

fine-grain

fine-grained

fine·ly

fine·ness

fin·ery (plural ·eries)

fine·spun

fi·nesse

fine-tooth (or -toothed)
comb

fin·foot (plural ·foots) bird

Fin·gal's Cave

fin·ger

finger·board

fin·gered

fin·ger·er

fin·ger·ing

fin·ger·ling young fish

finger·mark

finger·nail

finger·print

finger·stall

finger·tip

Fin·go (plural ·go or ·gos)
African people

fi·nial

fi·ni·aled

fin·icky (or ·ick·ing)

fin·ing clarifying liquid

fin·is the end

fin·ish

fin·ish·er

Fin·is·tère French
department

Fin·is·terre Spanish
headland

fi·nite

fi·nite·ly

fi·nite·ness

fink Slang blackleg

Fin·land

Finn

fin·nan had·dock (or
Fin·nan had·die)

finned

fin·ner whale

Finn·ic language group

fin·ning

Finn·ish

Finn·mark Norwegian
county

Finno-Ugric (or -Ugrian)
language group

fin·ny (·ni·er, ·ni·est)

fino sherry

fi·nochio (or ·noc·chio)
fennel

Fin·ster·aar·horn Swiss
mountain

fiord variant spelling of fjord

fio·rin grass

fip·ple mouthpiece

fir

fire

fire·able

fire-and-brimstone

fire·arm

fire·back

fire·ball

fire·bird

fire·boat

fire·bomb

fire·box

fire·brand

fire·brat insect
fire·break
fire·brick
fire·bug arsonist
fire·cracker
fire·crest bird
fire·damp
fire·dog
fire·drake dragon
fire·eater
fire·eating
fire·extinguish·er
fire·fly (plural ·flies) beetle
fire·guard
fire·man (plural ·men)
fire·pan
fire·place
fire·proof
fir·er
fire·side
fire·stone
fire·thorn
fire·trap
fire·warden
fire·water whisky
fire·weed
fire·wood
fire·work
fir·ing
fir·kin barrel
firm
fir·ma·ment
fir·ma·men·tal
fir·mer chisel
firm·ness
firm·ware computer term
first
first·born
first-class (adj)
first-foot (or ·footer)
first-footing
first-hand
first·ling first offspring
first-nighter
first-rate
firth (or frith)
fis·cal
fish (plural fish or fishes)
fish·able
fish·bolt
fish·bowl
fish·er
fisher·man (plural ·men)
fish·ery (plural ·eries)
fish-eye camera lens

fish·finger
fish·gig pole for impaling
    fish
fish-hook
fishi·ly
fishi·ness
fish·ing
fish·monger
fish·net
fish·plate metal joint
fish·tail dance step
fish·wife (plural ·wives)
fishy (fishi·er, fishi·est)
fis·sile physics term
fis·sil·ity
fis·sion
fis·sion·abil·ity
fis·sion·able
fis·si·pal·mate ornithology
    term
fis·sipa·rous reproducing by
    fission
fis·si·ped (or ·sip·edal)
    zoology term
fis·si·ros·tral ornithology
    term
fis·sure
fist
fist·ic of boxing
fisti·cuffs
fist·mele archery term
fis·tu·la (plural ·las or ·lae)
    medical term
fis·tu·lous (or ·lar, ·late)
fit (verb fit·ting, fit·ted; adj
    fit·ter, fit·test)
fitch (or fitch·et) polecat
fit·ful
fit·ful·ly
fit·ful·ness
fit·ment
fit·ness
fit·table
fit·ted
fit·ter
fit·ting
fit·ting·ly
fit·ting·ness
five
five-finger plant
five·fold
five·penny
five·pins
fiv·er
fives ball game

five-star (adj)
fix
fix·able
fix·ate
fixa·tion
fixa·tive
fixed
fix·ed·ly
fix·ed·ness
fix·er
fix·ity (plural ·ities) stability
fix·ture
fiz·gig
fizz
fizz·er
fizzi·ness
fiz·zle
fizzy (fizzi·er, fizzi·est)
fjeld (or field) rocky plateau
fjord (or fiord)
flab
flab·ber·gast
flab·bi·ly
flab·bi·ness
flab·by (·bi·er, ·bi·est)
fla·bel·late (or ·bel·li·form)
    fan-shaped
fla·bel·lum (plural ·la)
flac·cid
flac·cid·ity (or ·ness)
flac·on bottle
flag (flag·ging, flagged)
flag·el·lant (or ·la·tor)
fla·gel·lar
flag·el·late
flag·el·lat·ed
flag·el·la·tion
fla·gel·li·form
fla·gel·lum (plural ·la or
    ·lums) whiplike part
flageo·let musical
    instrument
flagged
flag·ger
flag·ging
flag·gy (·gi·er, ·gi·est) limp
fla·gi·tious wicked
flag·man (plural ·men)
flag·on
flag·pole
fla·gran·cy (or ·grance)
fla·grant
fla·gran·te de·lic·to
    red-handed

flag·ship
flag·staff (plural ·staffs or ·staves)
flag·stone
flag-waver
flag-waving
flail
flair talent; compare flare
flak (or flack)
flake
flak·er
flaki·ly
flaki·ness
flaky (flaki·er, flaki·est)
flam (flam·ming, flammed) Dialect deceive
flam·bé (or ·bée) cookery term
flam·beau (plural ·beaux or ·beaus) torch
Flam·bor·ough Head English promontory
flam·boy·ance (or ·an·cy)
flam·boy·ant
flame
flame-like
fla·men (plural ·mens or fla·mi·nes) Roman priest
fla·men·co (plural ·cos)
flame-of-the-forest tree
flame·out
flame·proof
flam·er
flame-thrower
flam·ing
fla·min·go (plural ·gos or ·goes)
flam·mabil·ity
flam·mable
flamy (flami·er, flami·est)
flan
Flan·ders
flâne·rie idleness
flâ·neur
flange
flang·er
flank
flank·er
flan·nel (·nel·ling, ·nelled; US ·nel·ing, ·neled)
flan·nel·ette
flan·nel·ly
flap (flap·ping, flapped)
flap·doodle Slang nonsense
flap·jack

flap·per
flare flame; widen; compare flair
flare-up (noun)
flash
flash·back
flash·board
flash·bulb
flash·cube
flash·er
flashi·ly
flashi·ness
flash·ing
flash·light
flash·over electric discharge
flashy (flashi·er, flashi·est)
flask
flask·et basket
flat (flat·ter, flat·test)
flat·boat
flat·fish (plural ·fish or ·fishes)
flat·foot
flat-footed
flat-footed·ly
flat-footed·ness
flat·head (plural ·head or ·heads) fish
flat·iron
flat·let
flat·mate
flat·ness
flat·ten
flat·ten·er
flat·ter
flat·ter·able
flat·ter·er
flat·ter·ing
flat·ter·ing·ly
flat·tery (plural ·teries)
flat·ting metallurgy term
flat·tish
flat·top US aircraft carrier
flatu·lence (or ·len·cy)
flatu·lent
fla·tus (plural ·tuses)
flat·ways
flat·worm
flaunch (or flaunch·ing) slope round chimney
flaunt
flaunt·er
flaunt·ing·ly
flaunty (flaunti·er, flaunti·est)

flau·tist (US flut·ist)
fla·ves·cent turning yellow
fla·vin (or ·vine) pigment
fla·vone plant pigment
fla·vo·pro·tein enzyme
fla·vo·pur·pu·rin dye
fla·vor·ous
fla·vour (US ·vor)
fla·vour·er (US ·vor·)
fla·vour·ful (US ·vor·)
fla·vour·ing (US ·vor·)
fla·vour·less (US ·vor·)
fla·vour·some (US ·vor·)
flaw
flaw·less
flaw·less·ness
flawy squally
flax
flax·en (or flaxy)
flax·seed
flay
flay·er
flea
flea·bag
flea·bane plant
flea·bite
flea-bitten
fleam lancet
flea·pit
flea·wort plant
flèche spire
flé·chette missile
fleck
flec·tion variant spelling (esp. US) of flexion
fled
fledge
fledg·ling (or fledge·)
fledgy (fledgi·er, fledgi·est) feathered
flee (flee·ing, fled)
fleece
fleeci·ly
fleeci·ness
fleecy (fleeci·er, fleeci·est)
fle·er one who flees
fleer sneer
fleet
fleet·ing
fleet·ness
Fleet·wood Lancashire port
Flem·ing native of Flanders
Flem·ish
flense (or flench, flinch) strip blubber from whale

flens·er (or flench·, flinch·)
flesh
flesh·er Scot butcher
fleshi·ness
flesh·ings tights
flesh·li·ness
flesh·ly (·li·er, ·li·est)
flesh·pots
fleshy (fleshi·er, fleshi·est)
fletch
fletch·er arrow maker
Fletch·er·ism chewing food thoroughly
fletch·ings arrow feathers
fleur-de-lis (or ·lys; plural fleurs-de-lis or ·lys)
fleu·rette (or ·ret) ornament
fleur·on ornament
fleu·ry variant of flory
flew
flews bloodhound's lip
flex
flexi·bil·ity (or ·ible·ness)
flex·ible
flex·ibly
flex·ile
flex·ion (or esp. US flection)
flex·ion·al
flexi·time
flex·or muscle
flexu·ous (or ·ose) having many bends
flex·ur·al
flex·ure
fley Dialect be afraid
flib·ber·ti·gib·bet
flick
flick·er
flick·er·ing·ly
flick·ery
fli·er (or fly·)
flies
flight
flighti·ly
flighti·ness
flight·less
flighty (flighti·er, flighti·est)
flim·flam (·flam·ming, ·flammed)
flim·si·ly
flim·si·ness
flim·sy (·si·er, ·si·est)
flinch
flinch·er

flinch·ing·ly
fling (fling·ing, flung)
fling·er
Flint Welsh town
flint quartz
flinti·ly
flinti·ness
flint·lock firearm
Flint·shire Welsh county
flinty (flinti·er, flinti·est)
flip (flip·ping, flipped)
flip-flop (-flopping, -flopped)
flip·pan·cy
flip·pant
flip·per
flip·ping
flirt
flir·ta·tion
flir·ta·tious
flir·ta·tious·ness
flirt·er
flirt·ing·ly
flit (flit·ting, flit·ted)
flitch pork
flite (or flyte) Scot scold
flit·ter
flitter·mouse (plural ·mice) Dialect bat
fliv·ver old car
float
float·abil·ity
float·able
float·age variant spelling of flotage
floata·tion variant spelling of flotation
float·er
float·ing
floaty (floati·er, floati·est) light
floc variant of floccule
floc·cose tufted
floc·cu·lant anticoagulant; compare flocculent
floc·cu·late aggregate
floc·cu·la·tion
floc·cule (or floc·cu·lus, flock, floc) mass of particles
floc·cu·lence (or ·len·cy)
floc·cu·lent fleecy; compare flocculent
floc·cu·lus (plural ·li) marking on sun

floc·cus (plural ·ci) down
flock
flocky
Flod·den battlefield
floe ice; compare flow
flog (flog·ging, flogged)
flog·ger
flog·ging
flong printing term
flood
flood·able
flood·er
flood·gate
flood·light (·light·ing, ·lit)
floor
floor·age
floor·board
floor·ing
floo·zy (or ·zie, ·sy; plural ·zies or ·sies)
flop (flop·ping, flopped)
flop·pi·ly
flop·pi·ness
flop·py (·pi·er, ·pi·est)
Flora Roman goddess
flo·ra (plural ·ras or ·rae) plant life
flo·ral
flo·ral·ly
Flor·ence Italian city
Flor·en·tine
flo·res·cence flowering; compare fluorescence
flo·ret
Flo·ria·nópo·lis Brazilian port
flo·ri·at·ed (or ·reated) architectural term
flo·ri·bun·da rose
flo·ri·cul·tur·al
flo·ri·cul·ture
flo·ri·cul·tur·ist
flor·id
Flori·da
flo·rid·ity (or ·ness)
flo·ri·gen hormone
flo·ri·legium (plural ·legia) book about flowers
flor·in
flo·rist
flo·ris·tic
flo·ris·ti·cal·ly
flo·ris·tics branch of botany
flo·ru·it Latin flourished

flo·ry (or fleu·) heraldic
term

flos fer·ri mineral

floss

flossy (flossi·er, flossi·est)

flo·tage (or float·age)

flo·ta·tion (or floata·tion)

flo·til·la

flot·sam

flounce

flounc·ing

floun·der (plural ·der or
·ders) fish; to struggle;
compare founder

flour

flour·ish

flour·ish·er

floury

flout

flout·er

flout·ing·ly

flow liquid movement;
compare floe

flow·age

flow·er

flow·er·age

flower-bed

flow·ered

flow·er·er

flow·er·et

flow·eri·ness

flow·er·ing

flow·er·less

flower-like

flower-of-an-hour plant

flower-pot

flow·ery

flown

flu illness; compare flue

fluc·tu·ant

fluc·tu·ate

fluc·tua·tion

flue pipe; compare flu

flued

flu·en·cy

flu·ent

fluff

fluffi·ly

fluffi·ness

fluffy (fluffi·er,
fluffi·est)

flu·gel·horn musical
instrument

flu·id

flu·id·al

fluid·extract
pharmaceutical term

flu·id·ic

flu·id·ics

flu·id·ity (or ·ness)

flu·idi·za·tion (or ·sa·tion)

flu·id·ize (or ·ise)

flu·id·iz·er (or ·is·er)

flu·id·ly (or flu·id·al·ly)

fluke

fluki·ness

fluky (or fluk·ey; fluki·er,
fluki·est)

flume ravine

flum·mery (plural ·meries)

flum·mox

flung

flunk Slang fail

flunky (or flunk·ey; plural
flunkies or ·eys) servant

flu·or variant of fluorspar

fluo·rene chemical
compound; compare
fluorine

fluo·resce

fluo·res·cein (or ·ceine)
chemical compound

fluo·res·cence radiation
emission; compare
florescence

fluo·res·cent

flu·or·ic of fluorine

fluori·date

fluori·da·tion

fluo·ride

fluo·rim·eter variant of
fluorometer

fluori·nate treat with
fluorine

fluori·na·tion

fluo·rine (or ·rin) chemical
element; compare
fluorene

fluo·ro·car·bon

fluo·rom·eter (or ·rim·)

fluo·ro·met·ric (or ·ri·)

fluo·rom·etry (or ·rim·)

fluoro·scope X-ray
instrument

fluoro·scop·ic

fluoro·scopi·cal·ly

fluor·os·co·py

fluo·ro·sis

flu·or·spar (or flu·or)
mineral

flur·ry (noun, plural ·ries;
verb ·ries, ·ry·ing, ·ried)

flush

flush·er

Flush·ing Dutch port

flus·ter

flute

flut·ed

flut·er

flut·ing

flut·ist US flautist

flut·ter

flut·ter·er

flut·ter·ing·ly

flut·tery

fluty (fluti·er, fluti·est)

flu·vial (or ·via·tile) of a
river

flu·vio·ma·rine of sea and
river

flux

flux·ion change

flux·ion·al (or ·ary)

flux·meter

fly (noun, plural flies; verb
flies, fly·ing, flew, flown)

fly·able

fly·away

fly·back physics term

fly·blow (·blow·ing, ·blew,
·blown)

fly·boat

fly·book angler's fly case

fly·by (plural ·bys)

fly-by-night

fly·catcher

fly·er variant spelling of flier

fly-fish

fly-fisher

fly-fishing

fly·ing

fly·leaf (plural ·leaves)

fly·over

fly·paper

fly·past

Flysch Alpine rock

fly·speck

flyte variant spelling of flite

fly·trap

fly·weight

fly·wheel

foal

foam

foam·flower

foami·ly

foami·ness

foam·like

foamy (foami·er, foami·est)

fob (fob·bing; fobbed)

fo·cal

fo·cali·za·tion (or ·sa·tion)

fo·cal·ize (or ·ise) focus

fo·cal·ly

fo'c's'le (or fo'c'sle) variant spellings of forecastle

fo·cus (noun, plural ·cuses or ·ci; verb ·cuses, ·cus·ing, ·cused)

fo·cus·able

fo·cus·er

fod·der

foe

foehn variant spelling of föhn

foe·man

foe·tal variant spelling of fetal

foe·ta·tion variant spelling of fetation

foe·ti·cide variant spelling of feticide

foet·id variant spelling of fetid

foe·tipa·rous variant spelling of fetiparous

foe·tor variant spelling of fetor

foe·tus variant spelling of fetus

fog (fog·ging, fogged)

fog·bound

fog·bow light in fog

fog·dog white spot in fog

fogged

Fog·gia Italian city

fog·gi·ly

fog·gi·ness

fog·ging

fog·gy (·gi·er, ·gi·est)

fog·horn

fogy (or fo·gey; plural fogies or ·geys)

fo·gy·ish (or ·gey·)

föhn (or foehn) wind

foi·ble

foil

foil·able

foils·man (plural ·men)

Fo·ism Chinese Buddhism

foi·son plentiful supply

Fo·ist

foist

fola·cin folic acid

fold

fold·able

fold·away

fold·boat

fold·ed

fold·er

fol·derol variant spelling of falderal

fold·ing

fold·out printing term

fo·lia·ceous

fo·li·age

fo·li·ar of leaves

fo·li·ate

fo·li·at·ed

fo·lia·tion

fo·lic acid vitamin

fo·lio (noun, plural ·lios; verb ·lios, ·lio·ing, ·lioed)

fo·lio·late botany term

fo·li·ose leafy

fo·lium (plural ·lia) geometrical curve

folk

Folke·stone

folk·ish

folk·lore

folk·lor·ic

folk·lor·ist

folk·lor·is·tic

folk·moot medieval assembly

folk·rock

folk·si·ness

folk·sy (·si·er, ·si·est)

folk·ways sociology term

fol·li·cle

fol·licu·lar

fol·licu·late (or ·lat·ed)

fol·licu·lin hormone

fol·low

fol·low·able

fol·low·er

fol·low·ing

follow-on (noun)

follow-through (noun)

follow-up (noun)

fol·ly (plural ·lies)

Fol·som man early man

Fo·mal·haut star

fo·ment instigate; compare ferment

fo·men·ta·tion

fo·ment·er

fond

fon·dant

fon·dle

fon·dler

fon·dling·ly

fond·ness

fon·due cookery term

font baptismal bowl; variant spelling (esp. US) of fount

Fon·taine·bleau French town

font·al

fon·ta·nelle (or ·nel) anatomy term

Foo·chow (or Fu-chou) Chinese port

food

food·stuff

fool

fool·ery (plural ·eries)

fool·har·di·ness

fool·hardy (·hardi·er, hardi·est)

fool·ish

fool·ish·ness

fool·proof

fools·cap

fool's-parsley

foot (plural feet)

foot·age

foot-and-mouth disease

foot·ball

foot·ball·er

foot·board

foot·boy

foot·bridge

foot-candle unit

foot·er

foot·fall

foot·gear

foot·hill

foot·hold

footie variant spelling of footy

foot·ing

foot-lambert unit

foot·le potter

foot·lights

foot·ling trivial

foot·loose

foot·man (plural ·men)

foot·mark
foot·note
foot·pace platform before altar
foot·pad highwayman
foot·path
foot·plate
foot-pound unit
foot-poundal unit
foot·print
foot·rest
foot·rope
foots dregs
foot·sie
foot·slog (·slog·ging, ·slogged)
foot·sore
foot·stalk
foot·stall base of column
foot·step
foot·stool
foot-ton unit
foot·wall geology term
foot·way
foot·wear
foot·work
foot·worn
footy (or footie) *Slang* football
foo yong (or foo yoong, foo yung, fu yung) Chinese omelette
foo·zle bungle golf shot
foo·zler
fop
fop·pery (*plural* ·peries)
fop·pish
fop·pish·ness
for
for·age
for·ag·er
fo·ra·men (*plural* ·rami·na or ·ra·mens) hole in bone
fo·rami·nal
fora·mini·fer protozoan
fo·rami·nif·er·al (or ·ous)
for·as·much as
for·ay
for·ay·er
for·bade (or ·bad)
for·bear (·bear·ing, ·bore, ·borne) to refrain; *variant spelling of* forebear
for·bear·ance

for·bear·er
for·bear·ing·ly
for·bid (·bid·ding, ·bade or ·bad, ·bid·den or ·bid)
for·bid·dance
for·bid·den
for·bid·der
for·bid·ding·ly
for·bore
for·borne
for·by *Scot* besides
force
force·able
forced
forc·ed·ly
forc·ed·ness
force-feed (-feeding, -fed)
force·ful
force·ful·ly
force·ful·ness
force ma·jeure
force·meat
for·ceps (*plural* ·ceps or ·ci·pes)
forc·er
for·cible
for·cible·ness (or ·cibil·ity)
for·cibly
forc·ing·ly
ford
ford·able
fore
fore-and-aft (*adj*)
fore-and-after vessel
fore·arm
fore·bear (or for·) ancestor; *compare* forbear
fore·bode
fore·bod·er
fore·bod·ing
fore·brain
fore·cast (·cast·ing, ·cast or ·cast·ed)
fore·cast·er
fore·cas·tle (or fo'c's'le, fo'c'sle)
fore·clos·able
fore·close
fore·clo·sure
fore·course boat's sail
fore·court
fore·deck
fore·doom
fore·father
fore·finger

fore·foot (*plural* ·feet)
fore·front
fore·gather *variant spelling of* forgather
fore·go (·goes, ·go·ing, ·went, ·gone) precede; *variant spelling of* forgo
fore·go·er
fore·going
fore·gone
fore·gone·ness
fore·ground
fore·gut
fore·hand
fore·handed
fore·head
fore·hock bacon
for·eign
for·eign·er
for·eign·ism
for·eign·ness
fore·judge prejudge; *variant spelling of* forjudge
fore·judg·ment (or ·judg·)
fore·know (·know·ing, ·knew, ·known)
fore·know·able
fore·know·ing·ly
fore·knowl·edge
fore·land
fore·leg
fore·limb
fore·lock
fore·man (*plural* ·men)
fore·man·ship
fore·mast
fore·most
fore·name
fore·named
fore·noon
fo·ren·sic of the law; *compare* forensics
fo·ren·si·cal·ity
fo·ren·si·cal·ly
fo·ren·sics debating; *compare* forensic
fore·or·dain
fore·or·dain·ment (or ·di·na·tion)
fore·part
fore·paw
fore·peak nautical term
fore·play
fore·quar·ter
fore·reach nautical term

fore·run (·run·ning, ·ran,
·run)
fore·run·ner
fore·sail
fore·see (·see·ing, ·saw,
·seen)
fore·see·able
fore·seen
fore·seer
fore·shad·ow
fore·shad·ow·er
fore·shank
fore·sheet nautical term
fore·shock US minor
earthquake
fore·shore
fore·short·en
fore·side
fore·sight
fore·sighted
fore·sighted·ness
fore·skin
for·est
for·est·al (or fo·res·tial)
fore·stall
fore·stall·er
fore·stal·ment
for·esta·tion
fore·stay nautical term
forestay·sail
for·est·ed
for·est·er
forest-like
for·est·ry
fore·taste
fore·tell (·tell·ing, ·told)
fore·tell·er
fore·thought
fore·thought·ful
fore·time the past
fore·to·ken foreshadow
fore·told
fore·tooth (plural ·teeth)
fore·top platform on
foremast
fore·topgal·lant nautical
term
fore·topmast
fore·topsail
fore·tri·an·gle nautical term
for·ever
for·ever·more
fore·warn
fore·warn·er
fore·warn·ing·ly

fore·went
fore·wind
fore·wing
fore·word
fore·yard nautical term
for·feit
for·feit·able
for·feit·er
for·fei·ture
for·fend US protect; Archaic
prevent
for·fi·cate forked
for·gath·er (or fore·)
assemble
for·gave
forge
forge·able
forg·er
for·gery (plural ·geries)
for·get (·get·ting, ·got,
·got·ten)
for·get·ful
for·get·ful·ly
for·get·ful·ness
forget-me-not
for·get·table
for·get·ter
forg·ing
for·giv·able
for·giv·ably
for·give (·giv·ing, ·gave,
·giv·en)
for·give·ness
for·giv·er
for·giv·ing·ly
for·giv·ing·ness
for·go (or fore·; ·goes,
·go·ing, ·went, ·gone)
give up; compare forego
for·go·er (or fore·)
for·got
for·got·ten
for·judge (or fore·) legal
term; compare forejudge
for·judg·ment (or fore·)
fork
forked
fork·ed·ly
fork·ed·ness
fork·ful
fork-lift truck
For·lì Italian city
for·lorn
form shape, etc.; US spelling
of forme

form·able
for·mal
for·mal·de·hyde
for·ma·lin (or for·mol)
for·mal·ism
for·mal·ist
for·mal·is·tic
for·mal·ity (plural ·ities)
for·mali·za·tion (or
·sa·tion)
for·mal·ize (or ·ise)
for·mal·iz·er (or ·is·er)
for·mal·ly in a formal way;
compare formerly
for·mal·ness
for·mant acoustics term
for·mat (·mat·ting,
·mat·ted)
for·mate chemistry term
for·ma·tion
for·ma·tion·al
forma·tive
forma·tive·ly
forma·tive·ness
forme (US form) printing
term; compare form
for·mer
for·mer·ly in the past;
compare formally
for·mic of ants; acid
For·mi·ca (Trademark)
for·mi·cary (or ·car·ium;
plural ·caries or ·caria) ant
hill
for·mi·ca·tion skin
sensation
for·mi·dabil·ity (or
·dable·ness)
for·mi·dable
for·mi·dably
form·less
form·less·ness
for·mol variant of formalin
For·mo·sa former name of
Taiwan
for·mu·la (plural ·las or ·lae)
for·mu·laic
for·mu·lari·za·tion (or
·sa·tion)
for·mu·lar·ize (or ·ise)
for·mu·lar·iz·er (or ·is·er)
for·mu·lary (plural ·laries)
for·mu·late
for·mu·la·tion
for·mu·la·tor

for·mu·lism
for·mu·list
form·work concrete mould
for·myl chemistry term
For·nax constellation
for·nenst *Scot* situated
    against
for·ni·cal of a fornix
for·ni·cate
for·ni·ca·tion
for·ni·ca·tor
for·nix (*plural* ·ni·ces) body
    structure
for·sake (·sak·ing, ·sook,
    ·sak·en)
for·sak·en
for·sak·en·ness
for·sak·er
for·sook
for·sooth
for·ster·ite mineral
for·swear (·swear·ing,
    ·swore, ·sworn)
for·swear·er
for·sworn
for·sythia
fort
For·ta·leza Brazilian port
for·ta·lice small fort
Fort-de-France Martinican
    capital
forte strength
for·te musical term
forte-piano musical term
forte-piano piano
Forth Scottish river
forth forward; *compare*
    fourth
forth·com·ing
forth·com·ing·ness
forth·right
forth·right·ness
forth·with
for·ti·eth
for·ti·fi·able
for·ti·fi·ca·tion
for·ti·fi·er
for·ti·fy (·fies, ·fy·ing,
    ·fied)
for·tis (*plural* ·tes) phonetics
    term
for·tis·si·mo (*plural* ·mos or
    ·mi)
for·ti·tude

for·ti·tu·di·nous
Fort Knox
fort·night
fort·night·ly
Fortran computer language
for·tress
for·tui·tism philosophy
    term
for·tui·tist
for·tui·tous unplanned;
    compare fatuitous
for·tui·tous·ness
for·tu·ity (*plural* ·ities)
Fortuna Roman goddess
for·tu·nate
for·tu·nate·ly
for·tu·nate·ness
for·tune
fortune-hunter
fortune-teller
fortune-telling
for·ty (*plural* ·ties)
forty-niner prospector
fo·rum (*plural* ·rums or ·ra)
for·ward (*adj*)
for·ward·er (*noun*)
for·ward·ness
for·wards (*adv*)
for·went
for·zan·do musical term
fos·sa (*plural* ·sae)
    anatomical depression
fosse (*or* foss) ditch
fos·sette bone depression
fos·sil
fos·sil·if·er·ous
fos·sil·iz·able (*or* ·is·able)
fos·sili·za·tion (*or* ·sa·tion)
fos·sil·ize (*or* ·ise)
fos·so·rial used for
    burrowing
fos·ter
fos·ter·age
fos·ter·er
fos·ter·ing·ly
fos·ter·ling foster child
fou·droy·ant sudden
fou·et·té ballet step
fought
foul bad; *compare* fowl
fou·lard fabric
foul·ly
foul-mouthed
Foul·ness Essex island
foul·ness

found
foun·da·tion
foun·da·tion·al
foun·da·tion·ary
found·er one who founds;
    to sink; *compare* flounder
found·ing
found·ling
found·ry (*plural* ·ries)
fount fountain; source
fount (*or esp. US* font)
    printing term
foun·tain
fountain-head
four
four-ball golfing term
four·chette anatomy
    term
four-colour (*US* -color)
    photography term
four-dimension·al
Four·drini·er paper-making
    machine
four·fold
four-handed
Fou·ri·er·ism social system
Fou·ri·er·ist (*or* ·ite)
Fou·ri·er·is·tic
four-in-hand carriage
four-leaf (*or* -leaved) clover
four·pence
four·penny
four-poster
four·ra·gère ornamental
    cord
four·score
four·some
four·square
four-stroke en·gine
four·teen
four·teenth
fourth 4th; *compare* forth
four-way (*adj*)
four-wheel drive
fo·vea (*plural* ·veae)
    anatomy term
fo·veal
fo·veate (*or* ·veat·ed)
fo·veo·la (*plural* ·lae) small
    fovea
fo·veo·lar
fo·veo·late (*or* ·lat·ed)
Fowey Cornish village
fowl chicken; *compare* foul
fowl·er bird hunter

Fow·liang (or Fou-liang)
Chinese city
fowl·ing
fox (plural foxes or fox)
fox·fire glow
fox·glove
fox·hole
fox·hound
fox·hunter
fox·hunting
foxi·ly
foxi·ness
fox·ing part of shoe
fox·like
fox·tail grass
fox·trot (·trot·ting,
·trot·ted)
foxy (foxi·er, foxi·est)
foy·er
Fra monk's title
fra·cas (plural ·cas; US
·cases) uproar
frac·tion
frac·tion·al (or ·ary)
frac·tion·al·ly
frac·tion·ate
frac·tiona·tion
frac·tiona·tor
frac·tioni·za·tion (or
·sa·tion)
frac·tion·ize (or ·ise)
frac·tious
frac·to·cu·mu·lus (plural ·li)
frac·to·stra·tus (plural ·ti)
frac·tura·ble
frac·tur·al
frac·ture
frae Scot from
frae·num (or fre·; plural ·na)
fold
frag (frag·ging, fragged) US
military slang term
frag·ile
frag·ile·ly
fra·gil·ity (or ·gile·ness)
frag·ment
frag·men·tal
frag·men·tal·ly
frag·men·tari·ly
frag·men·tari·ness
frag·men·tary
frag·men·ta·tion
fra·grance (or ·gran·cy;
plural ·grances or
·gran·cies)

fra·grant
frail
frail·ly
frail·ness
frail·ty (plural ·ties)
fraise tool; neck ruff;
rampart
Frak·tur typeface
fram·able (or frame·)
fram·boe·sia (US ·be·)
disease
fram·boise liqueur
frame
frame·less
fram·er
frame-up
frame·work
fram·ing
franc
France
Franche-Comté French
region
fran·chise
fran·chise·ment
Fran·cis·can
fran·cium chemical element
fran·co·lin partridge
Fran·co·nian language
group
Fran·co·phile (or ·phil)
Fran·co·phobe
Fran·co·pho·bia
Fran·co·phone native
French speaker
frang·er Austral condom
fran·gibil·ity (or
·gible·ness)
fran·gible breakable
fran·gi·pane almond pastry
fran·gi·pani (plural ·panis
or ·pani) shrub
Frang·lais French with
English words
frank
frank·able
frank·al·moign legal term
Frankenstein
frank·er
Frank·furt
frank·fur·ter
frank·in·cense
Frank·ish
Frank·lin Canadian district
frank·lin medieval
landowner

frank·lin·ite mineral
frank·ness
frank·pledge medieval
tithing system
fran·tic
fran·ti·cal·ly (or fran·tic·ly)
frap (frap·ping, frapped)
nautical term
frap·pé French chilled
frass insect excrement
fratchy quarrelsome
fra·ter friar
fra·ter·nal
fra·ter·nal·ly
fra·ter·nal·ism
fra·ter·nity (plural ·nities)
frat·er·ni·za·tion (or
·sa·tion)
frat·er·nize (or ·nise)
frat·er·niz·er (or ·nis·er)
frat·ri·cid·al
frat·ri·cide
Frau (plural Frau·en or
Fraus) German woman;
Mrs
fraud
fraudu·lence (or ·len·cy)
fraudu·lent
fraught
Fräu·lein (plural ·lein or
·leins) German young
woman; Miss
fraxi·nel·la plant
fray
fra·zil ice spikes
fraz·zle
freak
freaki·ly
freaki·ness
freak·ish
freak·ish·ness
freaky (freaki·er,
freaki·est)
freck·le
freck·led (or ·ly)
Fred·er·iks·berg Danish city
free (adj fre·er, fre·est; verb
free·ing, freed)
free·bie Slang free gift
free·board
free·boot
free·booter
free·born
freed·man (plural ·men)
free·dom

freed·woman (*plural* ·women)
free-floater uncommitted person
free-floating
free-for-all
free-handed
free-hearted
free·hold
free·holder
free·lance
free·lancer
free-liver
free-living
free·load *US* be a sponger
free·ly
free·man (*plural* ·men)
free·martin female twin calf
Free·mason member of secret order
free·mason stonemason
Free·masonic
free·masonic
Free·masonry
free·masonry
free-range
free·sheet free newspaper
free·sia
free-spoken
free-standing
free·stone
free·style
free-swimmer
free-swimming
free·thinker
free·thinking
Free·town capital of Sierra Leone
free-trader
free·way
free·wheel
free·wheeling
freez·able
freeze (freez·ing, froze, fro·zen)
freeze-dry (-dries, -drying, -dried)
freez·er
freeze-up
freez·ing
Frei·burg German city
freight
freight·age
freight·er
freight·liner

Fre·man·tle Australian port
fremi·tus (*plural* ·tus) medical term
Fre·mont *US* city
French
Frenchi·fy (·fies, ·fy·ing, ·fied)
French·man (*plural* ·men)
French·woman (*plural* ·women)
fre·net·ic
fre·neti·cal·ly
frenu·lum (*plural* ·la) zoology term
fre·num *variant spelling of* fraenum
fren·zied
fren·zy (*noun, plural* ·zies; *verb* ·zies, ·zy·ing, ·zied)
Fre·on (*Trademark*)
fre·quen·cy (*plural* ·cies) physics and statistics term
fre·quen·cy (*or* fre·quence) frequent occurrence
fre·quent
fre·quent·able
fre·quen·ta·tion
fre·quen·ta·tive linguistics term
fre·quent·er
fre·quent·ly
fres·co (*plural* ·coes *or* ·cos)
fresh
fresh·en
fresh·en·er
fresh·er (*or* ·man; *plural* ·ers *or* ·men)
fresh·et river overflowing
fresh·man *variant of* fresher
fresh·ness
fresh·water (*adj*)
fres·nel unit
Fres·no *US* city
fret (fret·ting, fret·ted)
fret·board
fret·ful
fret·ful·ly
fret·ful·ness
fret·less
fret·ted
fret·work
Freud·ian
Freud·ian·ism
Frey Norse god
Freya Norse goddess

fri·abil·ity (*or* ·able·ness)
fri·able
fri·ar
friar-bird
fri·ary (*plural* ·aries)
frib·ble fritter away
frib·bler
Fri·bourg Swiss town
fric·an·deau (*or* ·do; *plural* ·deaus, deaux, *or* ·does) cookery term
fric·as·see (·see·ing, ·seed) cookery term
frica·tive phonetics term
fric·tion
fric·tion·al
Fri·day
fridge
fried
friend
friend·less
friend·less·ness
friend·li·ly
friend·li·ness
friend·ly (·li·er, ·li·est)
friend·ship
fri·er *variant spelling of* fryer
fries
Frie·sian cattle; *variant spelling of* Frisian
Fries·land Dutch province
frieze decorative strip
frig (frig·ging, frigged)
frig·ate
frig·ging
fright
fright·en
fright·en·able
fright·en·er
fright·en·ing
fright·en·ing·ly
fright·ful
fright·ful·ly
frig·id
Frig·id·aire (*Trademark*)
fri·gid·ity (*or* frig·id·ness)
fri·jol (*plural* ·joles) French bean
frill
frilled
frilli·ness
frilly (frilli·er, frilli·est)
fringe
frin·gil·line (*or* ·lid) ornithology term

fringy
frip·pery (*plural* ·peries)
frip·pet *frivolous woman*
Fris·bee (*Trademark*)
Fris·co *Slang* San Francisco
fri·sé *fabric*
fri·sette (*or* ·zette) *fringe*
fri·seur *French hairdresser*
Fri·sian (*or* Frie·) *language;
of Friesland*
Fri·sian Is·lands
frisk
frisk·er
frisk·et *printing term*
friski·ly
friski·ness
frisky (friski·er, friski·est)
fris·son *shiver*
frit (*or* fritt; frit·ting,
frit·ted) *glassy material*
frith *variant of* firth
fri·til·lary (*plural* ·laries)
butterfly; plant
fritt *variant spelling of* frit
frit·ter
frit·ter·er
Friu·li *European region*
Friu·lian
Friuli-Venezia Giu·lia
Italian region
friv·ol (·ol·ling, ·olled)
fri·vol·ity (*plural* ·ities)
friv·ol·er
frivo·lous
frivo·lous·ness
fri·zette *variant spelling of*
frisette
frizz
frizz·er
friz·zi·ness (*or* ·zli·ness)
friz·zle
friz·zler
friz·zy (*or* ·zly; ·zi·er, ·zi·est
or ·zli·er, ·zli·est)
fro *from; compare* froe
frock
frock·ing *coarse material*
froe (*or* frow) *tool; compare*
fro
frog (frog·ging, frogged)
frog-bit *plant*
frog-fish (*plural* ·fish *or*
·fishes)
frogged
frog·ging

frog·gy
frog-hopper *insect*
frog·man (*plural* ·men)
frog·march
frog·mouth *bird*
frog·spawn
frol·ic (·ick·ing, ·icked)
frol·ick·er
frol·ic·some (*or* frol·icky)
from
fro·men·ty *variant of*
frumenty
frond
Fronde *French rebellion*
frond·ed
fron·des·cence *botany
term*
fron·des·cent (*or* fron·dose,
fron·dous)
Fron·deur *French rebel*
frons (*plural* fron·tes)
entomology term
front
front·age
front·al
fron·tal·ity
fron·tal·ly
front-bencher
fron·tier
fron·tiers·man (*plural*
·men)
fron·tis·piece
front·let *forehead
decoration*
fron·to·gen·esis
meteorology term
fron·toly·sis *meteorology
term*
front-runner
front·wards (*or esp. US*
·ward)
frost
frost·bite
frost·bitten
frost·ed
frosti·ly
frosti·ness
frost·ing
frost·work
frosty (frosti·er, frosti·est)
froth
frothi·ly
frothi·ness
frothy (frothi·er, frothi·est)
frott·age *rubbing*

frou-frou *swishing sound*
frow *variant spelling of* froe
fro·ward *obstinate*
frown
frown·er
frown·ing·ly
frowst
frows·ty *stale*
frowzi·ness (*or* frowsi·)
frowzy (*or* frowsy;
frowzi·er, frowzi·est *or*
frowsi·er, frows·iest)
shabby
froze
fro·zen
fro·zen·ness
fruc·tif·er·ous *fruit-bearing*
fruc·ti·fi·ca·tion
fruc·ti·fi·er
fruc·ti·fy (·fies, ·fy·ing,
·fied)
fruc·tose *sugar*
fruc·tu·ous
fru·gal
fru·gal·ly
fru·gal·ity (*or* ·ness)
fru·giv·or·ous *fruit-eating*
fruit
fruit·age
frui·tar·ian
fruit·cake
fruit·er *fruit grower*
fruit·er·er *fruit seller*
fruit·ful
fruit·ful·ly
fruit·ful·ness
fruiti·ness
frui·tion
fruit·less
fruit·less·ness
fruity (fruiti·er, fruiti·est)
fru·men·ta·ceous
resembling wheat
fru·men·ty (*or* fro·, fur·)
porridge
frump
frump·ish (*or* frumpy)
frump·ish·ness (*or*
frumpi·ness)
Frun·ze *former name of*
Bishkek
frus·trate
frus·trat·er
frus·tra·tion
frus·tule *botany term*

frus·tum (*plural* ·tums *or*
·ta) geometric solid
fru·tes·cence
fru·tes·cent (*or* ·ti·cose)
shrublike
fry (*noun, plural* fries; *verb*
fries, fry·ing, fried)
fry·er (*or* fri·)
fry·ing
Fu-chou *variant spelling of*
Foochow
fuch·sia shrub
fuch·sin (*or* ·sine) dye
fuck
fuck·er
fuck·ing
fu·coid
fu·coid·al (*or* fu·cous)
fu·cus (*plural* ·ci *or* ·cuses)
seaweed
fud·dle
fuddy-duddy (*plural*
-duddies)
fudge
Fueh·rer *variant spelling of*
Führer
fuel (fuel·ling, fuelled; *US*
fuel·ing, fueled)
fuel·ler (*US* fuel·er)
fug
fu·ga·cious fleeting
fu·gac·ity
fu·gal of a fugue
fu·gal·ly
fu·ga·to musical term
fu·gi·tive
fu·gi·tive·ly
fugle·man (*plural* ·men)
one used as example
fugue
fu·guist
Füh·rer (*or* Fueh·) German
leader
Fuji (*or* Fujiyama, Fuji-san)
Japanese mountain
Fu·kien Chinese province
Fu·kuo·ka Japanese city
Fu·ku·shi·ma Japanese
city
Fula (*or* Fu·lah; *plural* Fula
or Fulas *or* Fu·lah, Fu·lahs)
African people
Fu·la·ni language
ful·crum (*plural* ·crums *or*
·cra)

ful·fil (*US* ·fill; ·fil·ling,
·filled)
ful·fil·ler
ful·fil·ment (*US* ·fill·)
ful·gent (*or* ·gid)
resplendent
ful·gu·rant
ful·gu·rate flash like
lightning
ful·gu·rat·ing painful
ful·gu·ra·tion surgical
procedure
ful·gu·rite mineral
ful·gu·rous
Ful·ham
fu·ligi·nous smoky
full
full·back
full-blooded
full-blown
full-bodied
full·er
full-faced
full-frontal (*adj*)
full-length
full-mouthed
full·ness
full-rigged
full-sailed
full-scale
full-time (*adj*)
full-timer
ful·ly
fully-fledged
ful·mar bird
ful·mi·nant sudden
ful·mi·nate
ful·mi·na·tion
ful·mi·na·tor
ful·mi·na·tory
ful·min·ic acid
ful·some
ful·some·ly
ful·some·ness
ful·vous tawny
fu·mar·ic acid
fu·ma·role volcano vent
fu·ma·rol·ic
fu·ma·to·rium (*or* ·tory;
plural ·riums, ·ria, *or*
·tories) fumigation
chamber
fu·ma·tory of fumigation;
compare fumitory
fum·ble

fum·bler
fum·bling·ly
fum·bling·ness
fume
fume·less
fum·er
fu·mi·gant
fu·mi·gate
fu·mi·ga·tion
fu·mi·ga·tor
fum·ing
fu·mi·tory (*plural* ·tories)
plant; *compare* fumatory
fumy (fumi·er, fumi·est)
fun (fun·ning, funned)
Fu·na·fu·ti capital of Tuvalu
fu·nam·bu·lism
fu·nam·bu·list tightrope
walker
Fun·chal capital of Madeira
func·tion
func·tion·al
func·tion·al·ism
func·tion·al·ist
func·tion·al·ly
func·tion·ary (*plural* ·aries)
fund
fun·da·ment
fun·da·men·tal
fun·da·men·tal·ism
fun·da·men·tal·ist
fun·da·men·tal·is·tic
fun·da·men·tal·ity (*or*
·ness)
fun·da·men·tal·ly
fund·ed
fun·di mechanic
fun·dic
fun·dus (*plural* ·di) anatomy
term
Fun·dy Canadian bay
fu·ner·al
fu·ner·ary
fu·nereal
fun·fair
fun·gal
fun·gi *plural of* fungus
fun·gibil·ity
fun·gible legal term
fun·gic
fun·gi·cid·al
fun·gi·cide
fun·gi·form
fun·gi·stat
fun·gi·stat·ic

fun·goid

fun·gous (*adj*)

fun·gus (*noun; plural* ·gi or ·guses)

fu·ni·cle botany term

fu·nicu·lar

fu·nicu·late

fu·nicu·lus (*plural* ·li) anatomy term

funk

funk·er

funky (funki·er, funki·est)

fun·nel (·nel·ling, ·nelled; *US* ·nel·ing, ·neled)

fun·ni·ly

fun·ni·ness

fun·ny (·ni·er, ·ni·est)

fur (fur·ring, furred)

fur·al·de·hyde

fu·ran (*or* fur·fu·ran) chemical compound

fur·below ornamental trim

fur·bish

fur·bish·er

fur·cate fork

fur·cat·ed

fur·ca·tion

fur·cu·la (*or* ·lum; *plural* ·lae *or* ·la) forklike organ

fur·fur (*plural* ·fures) scaling of skin

fur·fu·ra·ceous of bran

fur·fur·al·de·hyde

fur·fu·ran *variant of* furan

fu·rio·so musical term

fu·ri·ous

fu·ri·ous·ness

furl

furl·able

furl·er

fur·long unit

fur·lough *US* leave

fur·men·ty *variant of* frumenty

fur·nace

Fur·ness Cumbrian peninsula

fur·nish

fur·nish·er

fur·nish·ings

fur·ni·ture

fu·ro·re (*or esp. US* fu·ror)

fur·phy (*plural* ·phies) *Austral* rumour

furred

fur·ri·er fur dealer; more furry

fur·ri·ery (*plural* ·eries)

fur·ri·ly

fur·ri·ness

fur·ring

fur·row

fur·row·er

fur·rowy

fur·ry (·ri·er, ·ri·est)

fur·ther additional; *variant of* farther

fur·ther·ance

fur·ther·er

further·more

further·most

fur·thest

fur·tive

fur·tive·ly

fur·tive·ness

fu·run·cle boil

fu·run·cu·lar (*or* ·lous)

fu·run·cu·lo·sis skin condition

fury (*plural* furies)

furze gorse

furzy

fu·sain charcoal

fus·cous brownish

fuse

fu·see (*or* ·zee) clock part; match

fu·sel oil

fu·selage

(fushia) *incorrect spelling of* fuchsia

Fu·shun Chinese city

fu·sibil·ity (*or* fusible·ness)

fu·sible

fu·sibly

fu·si·form spindle-shaped

fu·sil musket

fu·sile (*or* ·sil) easily melted

fu·si·lier

fu·sil·lade rapid gunfire

fu·sion

fu·sion·ism

fu·sion·ist

fuss

fuss·er

fussi·ly

fussi·ness

fuss·pot

fussy (fussi·er, fussi·est)

fus·ta·nel·la (*or* ·nelle) Greek skirt

fus·tian fabric

fus·tic tree

fus·ti·ly

fus·ti·ness

fus·ty (·ti·er, ·ti·est)

fu·thark (*or* ·tharc, ·thork, ·thorc) phonetic alphabet

fu·tile

fu·tile·ly

fu·tili·tar·ian

fu·tili·tari·an·ism

fu·til·ity (*plural* ·ities)

fut·tock part of boat

fu·ture

fu·tur·ism

fu·tur·ist

fu·tur·is·tic

fu·tur·is·ti·cal·ly

fu·tur·ity (*plural* ·ities)

fu·tur·olo·gist

fu·tur·ol·ogy

fu yung *variant of* foo yong

fu·zee *variant spelling of* fusee

fuzz

fuzzi·ly

fuzzi·ness

fuzzy (fuzzi·er, fuzzi·est)

fyke *US* fishing net

Fylde region of Lancashire

fyrd Anglo-Saxon militia

Fyza·bad (*or* Faiza·) Indian city; *compare* Faizabad

G

Ga (or **Gã**; plural **Ga, Gas** or **Gã, Gãs**) African people

gab (**gab·bing, gabbed**)

gab·ar·dine variant spelling of **gaberdine**

gab·ber

gab·ble

gab·bler

gab·bro (plural **·bros**) rock

gab·bro·ic (or **·it·ic**)

gab·by (**·bi·er, ·bi·est**) talkative

ga·belle French salt tax

gab·er·dine fabric

gab·er·dine (or **·ar·**) cloak

Ga·bès Tunisian port

gab·fest US gathering

ga·bi·on stone-filled cylinder

ga·bi·on·ade (or **·on·nade**)

ga·ble

ga·bled

ga·blet small gable

Ga·bon

Gabo·nese

Gabo·ro·ne Botswanan capital

gaby (plural **gabies**) simpleton

gad (**gad·ding, gad·ded**)

gad·about

gad·der

gad·fly (plural **·flies**)

gadg·et

gadg·eteer lover of gadgetry

gadg·et·ry

gadg·ety

Gad·hel·ic Gaelic language

ga·did fish

ga·doid

gado·lin·ic

gado·lin·ite mineral

gado·lin·ium chemical element

ga·droon (or **go·**) decorative moulding

ga·drooned (or **go·**)

gad·wall (plural **·walls** or **·wall**) duck

Gael Gaelic speaker

Gael·ic

gaff angling pole; nautical boom; Slang home

gaffe blunder

gaf·fer

gaff-rigged

gaff-sail

gaff-topsail

gag (**gag·ging, gagged**)

gaga Slang senile

Ga·gau·zi Russian language

gage pledge; greengage; US spelling of **gauge**

gagged

gag·ger

gag·ging

gag·gle

gahn·ite mineral

gai·ety (plural **·eties**)

gail·lar·dia plant

gai·ly

gain

gain·able

gain·er

gain·ful

gain·ful·ly

gain·ful·ness

gain·li·ness

gain·ly

gain·say (**·say·ing, ·said**)

gain·say·er

gait walk

gait·er

gal Slang girl; unit

gala

ga·lac·ta·gogue inducing milk secretion

ga·lac·tic

gal·ac·tom·eter

gal·ac·tom·etry

ga·lac·to·poi·esis milk production

ga·lac·to·poi·etic

ga·lac·tose sugar

ga·la·go (plural **·gos**) bushbaby

ga·lah bird

Galahad

ga·lan·gal plant

gal·an·tine glazed pressed meat

Ga·lá·pa·gos Is·lands

Gala·shiels Scottish town

Ga·la·ta Turkish port

Galatea mythological character

gala·tea fabric

Ga·laţi Romanian port

Ga·la·tia ancient Asian region

Ga·la·tians New Testament book

Gal·axy solar system

gal·axy (plural **·axies**) any star system; distinguished gathering

gal·ba·num gum resin

gale

ga·lea (plural **·leae**) helmet-shaped structure

ga·leate (or **·leat·ed**)

ga·lei·form

ga·lena (or **·lenite**) mineral

Ga·len·ic of Galen's medical system

ga·leni·cal pharmacology term

Ga·len·ism

Ga·len·ist

ga·lère French undesirable people

Ga·li·bi (plural **·bi** or **·bis**) American Indian

Ga·li·cia European region

Ga·li·cian

Gali·lean of Galilee; of Galileo

Gali·lee Israeli region

gali·lee church porch

gal·in·gale (or **ga·lan·gal**) plant

gali·ot (or **gal·li·ot**) small galley

gali·pot (or **gal·li·pot**) pine resin

gall

Gal·la (plural **·las** or **·la**) African people

gal·lant

gal·lant·ness

gal·lant·ry (plural **·ries**)

gall blad·der

Gal·le Sri Lankan port

gal·leass (or ·li·ass) warship
gal·leon
gal·ler·ied
gal·lery (plural ·leries)
gal·ley
gall·fly (plural ·flies)
gal·li·am·bic verse metre
gal·liard dance
Gal·lic of France or Gaul
gal·lic chemistry term; of galls
Gal·li·can
Gal·li·can·ism French Catholic movement
Gal·lice Latin in French
Gal·li·cism
Gal·li·ci·za·tion (or ·sa·tion)
Gal·li·cize (or ·cise)
Gal·li·ciz·er (or ·cis·er)
gal·li·gas·kins men's breeches
gal·li·mau·fry (plural ·fries) US hotchpotch
gal·li·na·cean
gal·li·na·ceous ornithology term
gall·ing
gal·li·nule bird
gal·li·ot variant spelling of galiot
Gal·lipo·li Turkish port
gal·li·pot earthenware pot; variant spelling of galipot
gal·lium chemical element
gal·li·vant (or gali·vant, gala·vant)
gal·li·wasp lizard
gall·nut (or gall-apple)
gal·lo·glass (or ·low·) Irish military retainer
gal·lon
gal·lon·age
gal·loon decorative cord
gal·lop horse's gait; compare galop
gal·lop·er
gal·lous chemistry term
Gal·lo·way Scottish area
gal·lows (plural ·lowses or ·lows)
gall·stone
gal·luses Dialect braces
ga·loot US clumsy person

gal·op dance; compare gallop
ga·lore
ga·loshes (or go·)
ga·lumph
gal·van·ic (or ·vani·cal)
gal·vani·cal·ly
gal·va·nism
gal·va·ni·za·tion (or ·sa·tion)
gal·va·nize (or ·nise)
gal·va·niz·er (or ·nis·er)
gal·va·nom·eter
gal·va·no·met·ric (or ·ri·cal)
gal·va·nom·etry
gal·va·no·scope
gal·va·no·scop·ic
gal·va·nos·co·py
gal·va·no·trop·ic
gal·va·not·ro·pism botany term
gal·vo (plural ·vos) short for galvanometer
Gal·way Irish county
Gal·we·gian
gal·yak (or ·yac) fur
gam school of whales
gam·ba·do (plural ·dos or ·does) leather stirrup
gam·beson medieval garment
Gam·bia
Gam·bian
gam·bier (or ·bir) astringent
Gam·bier Is·lands
gam·bit
gam·ble bet; compare gambol
gam·bler
gam·bling
gam·boge gum resin
gam·bo·gian
gam·bol (·bol·ling, ·bolled; US ·bol·ing, ·boled) frolic; compare gamble
gam·brel horse's hock; type of roof
game
game·cock
game·keeper
game·keeping
gam·elan oriental orchestra
game·ly
game·ness

games·man (plural ·men)
games·man·ship
game·some merry
game·ster
ga·met·al (or ·ic)
gam·etan·gial
gam·etan·gium (plural ·gia)
gam·ete reproductive cell
ga·meto·cyte
gam·eto·gen·esis (or ·etog·eny)
gam·eto·gen·ic (or ·etog·enous)
ga·meto·phore plant part
ga·meto·phor·ic
ga·meto·phyte plant producing gametes
gam·eto·phyt·ic
gam·ey variant spelling of gamy
gam·ic biology term
gam·in street urchin
ga·mine boyish girl
gami·ness
gam·ing
gam·ma Greek letter
gam·ma·di·on (plural ·dia) swastika
gam·mer Dialect old woman
gam·mon
gam·mon·er Slang deceiver
gam·my (·mi·er, ·mi·est) Slang lame
gamo·gen·esis biology term
gamo·genet·ic (or ·geneti·cal)
gamo·pet·al·ous botany term
gamo·phyl·lous
gamo·sep·al·ous
gamp umbrella
gam·ut
gamy (or gam·ey; gami·er, gami·est)
gan (gan·ning, ganned) Dialect to go
Gan·da (plural ·das or ·da) African people
gan·der
Gan·dhian
Gan·dhi·ism (or ·dhism)
Gand·zha Azerbaijani city
ga·nef US opportunist
gang

gang·bang

ganged

gang·er labourers' foreman

Gan·ges Indian river

gang·land

gan·glial (or gan·gli·ar)

gan·gling (or ·gly)

gan·gli·on (plural ·glia or ·gli·ons) nerve tissue; cyst

gan·gli·on·ic (or ·at·ed)

gang·plank (or ·way)

gan·grene

gan·gre·nous

gang·ster

Gang·tok Indian city

gangue (or gang) worthless ore

gang·way

gan·is·ter (or gan·nis·) rock

gan·ja cannabis

gan·net

gan·oid zoology term

gan·sey Dialect pullover

gant·let rail track; variant spelling of gauntlet

gant·line nautical term

gan·try (or gaun·; plural ·tries)

Gany·mede satellite of Jupiter

Ganymede mythological character

gaol variant spelling of jail

gaol·er variant spelling of jailer

gap (gap·ping, gapped)

gape

gap·er

gapes fowl disease

gape·worm

gap·ing·ly

gapped

gap·ping grammar term

gar (plural gar or gars) fish

gar·age

Gara·mond typeface

garb

gar·bage

gar·ble

gar·bler

garb·less

gar·board nautical term

gar·çon French waiter

Gard French department

Gar·da Italian lake

gar·den

gar·den·er

gar·denia

gar·den·ing

gar·fish (plural ·fish or ·fishes)

gar·ga·ney duck

gar·gan·tuan

gar·get cattle disease

gar·gety

gar·gle

gar·gler

gar·goyle

gar·goyled

gar·ial variant of gavial

gari·bal·di blouse; biscuit

gar·ish

gar·ish·ness

gar·land

gar·lic

gar·licky

gar·ment

gar·ner

gar·net

gar·ni·er·ite mineral

gar·nish

gar·nishee (·nishee·ing, ·nisheed) legal term

gar·nish·er

gar·nish·ment legal notice

gar·ni·ture decoration

Ga·ronne French river

ga·rotte variant spelling of garrotte

gar·pike fish

gar·ret

gar·ri·son

gar·rotte (or gar·rote, ga·rotte) execution

gar·rott·er (or gar·rot·er, ga·rott·er)

gar·ru·lous

gar·ru·lous·ness (or gar·ru·lity)

gar·rya shrub

gar·ter

garth cloistered courtyard

Gary US port

gas (noun, plural gases or gas·ses; verb gases or gas·ses, gas·sing, gassed)

gas·bag

Gas·con of Gascony

gas·con·ade boastful talk

Gas·co·ny

gas·eous

gas·eous·ness

gases (or gas·ses)

gash

gas·holder

gasi·fi·able

gasi·fi·ca·tion

gasi·fi·er

gasi·form

gasi·fy (·fies, ·fy·ing, ·fied)

gas·ket

gas·kin part of horse's thigh

gas·light

gas·man (plural ·men)

gas·olier (or ·elier) fitting for gaslights

gaso·line (or ·lene) US petrol

gaso·lin·ic

gas·om·eter

gaso·met·ric (or ·ri·cal)

gas·ometry

gasp

Gas·pé Canadian peninsula

gasp·er

gasp·ing·ly

gassed

gas·ser

gas·si·ness

gas·sing

gas·sy (·si·er, ·si·est)

(gasteropod) incorrect spelling of gastropod

gas·tight

gas·tight·ness

gas·tral·gia stomach pain

gas·tral·gic

gas·trec·to·my (plural ·mies)

gas·tric

gas·trin hormone

gas·trit·ic

gas·tri·tis

gas·tro·en·ter·ic

gas·tro·en·terit·ic

gas·tro·en·teri·tis

gas·tro·en·te·rolo·gist

gas·tro·en·ter·ol·ogy (or gas·trol·ogy)

gas·tro·en·ter·os·to·my (plural ·mies) operation

gas·tro·in·tes·ti·nal

gas·tro·lith stomach stone

gas·trol·ogy variant of gastroenterology

gas·tro·nome (*or* ·trono·mer, ·trono·mist)

gas·tro·nom·ic (*or* ·nomi·cal)

gas·tro·nomi·cal·ly

gas·trono·mist

gas·trono·my cooking

gas·tro·pod mollusc

gas·tropo·dan

gas·tropo·dous

gas·tro·scope medical instrument

gas·tro·scop·ic

gas·tros·co·pist

gas·tros·co·py

gas·tros·to·my (*plural* ·mies) artificial stomach opening

gas·tro·to·my (*plural* ·mies) stomach operation

gas·tro·trich aquatic animal

gastro·vas·cu·lar

gas·tru·la (*plural* ·las *or* ·lae) embryology term

gas·tru·lar

gas·tru·la·tion

gas·works

gate

gâ·teau (*or* ga·; *plural* ·teaux)

gate-crash

gate-crasher

gated

gate·fold folded oversize page

gate·house

gate·keeper

gate-leg (*or* -legged) table

gate·post

Gates·head

gate·way

Gath biblical city

gath·er

gath·er·able

gath·er·er

gath·er·ing

Gatling gun

gauche

gauche·ly

gauche·ness

gau·cherie

gau·cho (*plural* ·chos) cowboy

gaud trinket

gaud·ery (*plural* ·eries)

gaudi·ly

gaudi·ness

gaudy (gaudi·er, gaudi·est)

gauf·fer *variant spelling of* goffer

gauge (*US also* gage) measure; *compare* gage

gauge·able (*US also* gage·)

gauge·ably (*US also* gage·)

gaug·er (*US also* gag·)

Gau·ha·ti Indian city

Gaul Roman province

Gau·lei·ter German governor

Gaul·ish

Gaull·ism policies of de Gaulle

Gaull·ist

gaul·theria shrub

gaunt

gaunt·let (*or* gant·)

gaunt·ness

gaun·try *variant spelling of* gantry

gaur cattle

gauss (*plural* gauss) unit

gauss·meter

Gau·teng South African province

gauze

gauzi·ly

gauzi·ness

gauzy (gauzi·er, gauzi·est)

ga·vage forced feeding

gave

gav·el hammer

gäv·el·kind land tenure

ga·vial (*or* ghar·ial, gar·ial) crocodile

Gäv·le Swedish port

ga·votte (*or* ·vot)

gawk

gawki·ly (*or* gawk·ish·)

gawki·ness (*or* gawk·ish·)

gawky (*or* gawk·ish; gawki·er, gawki·est)

gawp

gay

Gay Gor·dons dance

Gaza Palestinian city in Israel

gaze

ga·zebo (*plural* ·zebos *or* ·zeboes)

gaze·hound

ga·zelle (*plural* ·zelles *or* ·zelle)

gaz·er

ga·zette

gaz·et·teer

Ga·zi·an·tep Turkish city

gaz·pa·cho soup

ga·zump

ga·zump·er

Gdańsk Polish port

Gdy·nia Polish port

gean cherry

ge·anti·cli·nal

ge·anti·cline geology term

gear

gear·box

gear·ing

gear·shift *US* gear lever

gear·wheel

gecko (*plural* geckos *or* geckoes)

ge·dact (*or* ·deckt) organ pipe

gee (gee·ing, geed)

gee-gee

geek sideshow performer

Gee·long Australian port

gee·pound unit

geese

geest German heathland

gee·zer *Slang* old man; *compare* geyser

ge·gen·schein glow in sky

Ge·hen·na place of torment

geh·len·ite mineral

Geiger count·er

gei·sha (*plural* ·sha *or* ·shas)

gel (gel·ling, gelled) jelly-like substance; form gel; *variant spelling of* jell

ge·la·da baboon

ge·län·de·sprung ski jump

gela·tin (*or* ·tine)

ge·lati·ni·za·tion (*or* ·sa·tion)

ge·lati·nize (*or* ·nise)

ge·lati·niz·er (*or* ·nis·er)

ge·lati·noid

ge·lati·nous

ge·la·tion freezing

geld (geld·ing, geld·ed *or* gelt)

Gel·der·land (*or* Guel·) Dutch province

gel·id very cold

ge·lid·ity (*or* **·ness**)
gel·ig·nite
gelled
gel·ling
gel·se·mium (*plural* **·miums** *or* **·mia**) shrub
Gel·sen·kir·chen German city
gelt *Slang* money
gem (**gem·ming, gemmed**)
gemi·nate in pairs
gemi·na·tion
Gemi·ni constellation; sign of zodiac
gem·ma (*plural* **·mae**) plant structure
gem·ma·ceous
gem·mate
gem·ma·tion
gemmed
gem·ming
gem·mipa·rous reproducing by gemmae
gem·mu·la·tion
gem·mule reproductive body
gemo·logi·cal (*or* **gem·mo·**)
gem·olo·gist (*or* **gem·molo·**)
gem·ol·ogy (*or* **gem·mol·**) study of gems
ge·mot Anglo-Saxon assembly
gems·bok (*or* **·buck**; *plural* **·bok, ·boks** *or* **·buck, ·bucks**) antelope
gem·stone
ge·müt·lich *German* cosy
gen *Slang* information
ge·nappe worsted
gen·darme
gen·dar·me·rie (*or* **·ry**)
gen·der
gene
ge·nea·logi·cal (*or* **·log·ic**)
ge·nealo·gist
ge·neal·ogy (*plural* **·ogies**)
gen·era *plural of* **genus**
gen·er·able able to be generated
gen·er·al
gen·er·al·is·si·mo (*plural* **·mos**)
gen·er·al·ist
gen·er·al·ity (*plural* **·ities**)

gen·er·ali·za·tion (*or* **·sa·tion**)
gen·er·al·ize (*or* **·ise**)
gen·er·al·iz·er (*or* **·is·er**)
gen·er·al·ly
gen·er·al·ness
gen·er·al·ship
gen·er·ate
gen·era·tion
gen·era·tive
gen·era·tor
gen·era·trix (*plural* **·tri·ces**) geometry term
ge·ner·ic (*or* **·neri·cal**)
ge·neri·cal·ly
gen·er·os·ity (*plural* **·ities**)
gen·er·ous
gen·er·ous·ness
Gen·esis Old Testament book
gen·esis (*plural* **·eses**) beginning
gen·et (*or* **ge·nette**) catlike animal; *variant spelling of* **jennet**
ge·net·ic (*or* **·neti·cal**)
ge·neti·cal·ly
ge·neti·cist
ge·net·ics
Ge·neva
Ge·nevan (*or* **Gen·evese**; *plural* **·evans** *or* **·evese**)
gen·ial cheerful
ge·nial of the chin
ge·ni·al·ity (*or* **gen·ial·ness**)
ge·ni·al·ly
gen·ic of a gene
ge·nicu·late bending sharply
ge·nicu·la·tion
ge·nie (*plural* **ge·nies** *or* **ge·nii**)
geni·pap (*or* **gen·ip**) fruit
geni·tal
geni·tal·ic
geni·tals (*or* **·ta·lia**)
geni·ti·val
geni·tive grammar term
geni·tor biological father
genito·uri·nary
ge·ni·us (*plural* **ge·ni·uses**)
ge·ni·zah synagogue storeroom
Genoa Italian city
genoa yacht sail

geno·cid·al
geno·cide
Geno·ese (*or* **·vese**; *plural* **·ese** *or* **·vese**)
ge·nome (*or* **·nom**) genetics term
geno·type genetics term
geno·typ·ic (*or* **·typi·cal**)
geno·ty·pic·ity
gen·re
gens (*plural* **gen·tes**) Roman aristocratic family
gent
gen·teel
gen·teel·ly
gen·teel·ness
gen·tian plant
gen·tia·na·ceous
gen·tian·el·la plant
Gen·tile not Jewish
gen·tile grammar term
gen·til·ity (*plural* **·ities**)
gen·tle
gentle·folk
gentle·man (*plural* **·men**)
gen·tleman-at-arms (*plural* **·tlemen-**)
gentle·man·li·ness
gentle·man·ly
gen·tle·ness
gentle·woman (*plural* **·women**)
gen·tly
gen·tri·fi·ca·tion
gen·tri·fy (**·fies, ·fy·ing, ·fied**)
gen·try
genu (*plural* **genua**) knee
genu·flect
genu·flec·tion (*or* **·flex·ion**)
genu·flec·tor
genu·ine
genu·ine·ly
genu·ine·ness
ge·nus (*plural* **gen·era** *or* **ge·nuses**)
geo·cen·tric
geo·cen·tri·cal·ly
geo·chemi·cal
geo·chem·ist
geo·chem·is·try
geo·chrono·logi·cal
geo·chro·nol·ogy
ge·ode rock cavity
geo·des·ic

ge·od·esist
geod·esy (or geo·det·ics)
  measurement of earth
geo·det·ic
ge·od·ic
geo·dy·nam·ic
geo·dy·nami·cist
geo·dy·nam·ics
ge·og·nos·tic
ge·og·no·sy study of earth's
  structure
ge·og·ra·pher
geo·graphi·cal (or
  ·graph·ic)
geo·graphi·cal·ly
ge·og·ra·phy (plural ·phies)
ge·oid shape of earth
geo·logi·cal (or ·log·ic)
geo·logi·cal·ly
ge·olo·gist (or ·ger)
ge·olo·gize (or ·gise)
ge·ol·ogy
geo·mag·net·ic
geo·mag·ne·tism
geo·man·cer
geo·man·cy prophecy
geo·man·tic
geo·mechan·ics
ge·om·eter (or
  ge·om·etri·cian)
geo·met·ric (or ·ri·cal)
geo·met·ri·cal·ly
ge·om·etrid moth
ge·om·etrize (or ·etrise)
ge·om·etry
geo·mor·phic of earth's
  surface
geo·mor·pho·logi·cal (or
  ·log·ic)
geo·mor·pho·logi·cal·ly
geo·mor·pholo·gy (or
  ·phog·eny)
ge·opha·gist
ge·opha·gous
ge·opha·gy (or geo·pha·gia,
  ge·opha·gism) eating soil
geo·physi·cal
geo·physi·cist
geo·phys·ics
geo·phyte botany term
geo·phyt·ic
geo·po·liti·cal
geo·poli·ti·cian
geo·poli·tics
geo·pon·ic

geo·pon·ics agricultural
  science
Geor·die Tynesider
George·town capital of
  Guyana
geor·gette fabric
Geor·gia US state; Central
  Asian country
Geor·gian
geor·gic poem
geo·sci·ence
geo·stat·ic
geo·stat·ics geology term
geo·strat·egy
geo·stroph·ic meteorology
  term
geo·syn·chro·nous
geo·syn·cli·nal
geo·syn·cline geology term
geo·tac·tic
geo·tac·ti·cal·ly
geo·tax·is biology term
geo·tec·ton·ic of earth's
  crust
geo·ther·mal (or ·mic)
geo·trop·ic
geo·tropi·cal·ly
ge·ot·ro·pism botany term
ge·rah Hebrew weight
ge·ra·nia·ceous botany
  term
ge·ra·nial chemistry term
ge·ra·ni·ol chemical
  compound
ge·ra·nium
gera·to·log·ic
gera·tol·ogy study of elderly
ger·bil (or ·bille, jer·bil)
ger·ent manager
ger·enuk antelope
ger·fal·con variant spelling of
  gyrfalcon
geri·at·ric
geria·tri·cian (or
  geri·at·rist)
geri·at·rics
germ
ger·man of close
  relationship; compare
  germen
Ger·man
ger·man·der plant
ger·mane relevant
ger·mane·ly
ger·mane·ness

Ger·man·ic of Germany
ger·man·ic chemistry term
Ger·man·ism
ger·man·ite mineral
ger·ma·nium chemical
  element
Ger·mani·za·tion (or
  ·sa·tion)
Ger·man·ize (or ·ise)
Ger·man·iz·er (or ·is·er)
Ger·mano·phile (or ·phil)
Ger·mano·philia
Ger·mano·phobe
Ger·mano·pho·bia
ger·man·ous chemistry
  term
Ger·ma·ny
ger·men (plural ·mens or
  ·mi·na) biology term;
  compare german
ger·mi·cid·al
ger·mi·cide
ger·mi·nable (or ·na·tive)
ger·mi·nal embryonic
ger·mi·nal·ly
ger·mi·nant
ger·mi·nate
ger·mi·na·tion
ger·mi·na·tor
Ger·mis·ton South African
  city
ger·on·toc·ra·cy (plural
  ·cies) government by old
  men
ge·ron·to·crat·ic
ger·on·to·logi·cal
ger·on·tolo·gist
ger·on·tol·ogy study of
  ageing
ger·ry·man·der
ger·und grammar term
ge·run·dial
ge·run·di·val
ge·run·dive grammar term
ges·so (plural ·soes) white
  plaster
ge·stalt (plural ·stalts or
  ·stal·ten) overall structure
Ge·sta·po
ges·tate
ges·ta·tion
ges·ta·tion·al (or ·tive)
ges·ta·to·ry
ges·ticu·late
ges·ticu·la·tion

ges·ticu·la·tive
ges·ticu·la·tor
ges·tur·al
ges·ture
ges·tur·er
get (get·ting, got)
get·able (or get·table)
get-at-able
get·away (noun)
Geth·sema·ne
get-out (noun)
get·ter
get-together
Get·tys·burg US town
get-up (noun)
geum plant
gew·gaw showy trinket
gey·ser hot spring; water
   heater; compare geezer
gey·ser·ite mineral
Ge·zi·ra Sudanese region
Gha·na
Gha·na·ian (or Gha·nian)
ghar·ial variant of gavial
ghar·ry (or ·ri; plural ·ries)
   Indian vehicle
ghast·li·ness
ghast·ly (·li·er, ·li·est)
ghat steps to river
Ghats Indian mountains
gha·zi Muslim fighter
ghee butter
Ghent Belgian port
gher·kin pickled cucumber;
   compare jerkin
ghet·to (plural ·tos or ·toes)
Ghib·el·line political
   faction
Ghib·el·lin·ism
ghib·li (or gib·) hot wind
ghil·lie laced shoe; variant
   spelling of gillie
ghost
ghost-like
ghost·li·ness
ghost·ly (·li·er, ·li·est)
ghost·write (·writ·ing,
   ·wrote, ·writ·ten)
ghost·writ·er
ghoul
ghoul·ish
gi·ant
gi·ant·ess
gi·ant·ism variant of
   gigantism

giaour non-Muslim
gib (gib·bing, gibbed)
gib·ber
gib·ber·el·lin plant
   hormone
gib·ber·ish
gib·bet
gib·bing
gib·bon
gib·bous (or ·bose)
gib·bous·ness
gibbs·ite mineral
gibe (or jibe) taunt; compare
   gybe
Gib·eon Palestinian town
gib·er (or jib·)
gib·ing·ly (or jib·)
gib·lets
gib·li variant spelling of
   ghibli
Gi·bral·tar
Gi·bral·tar·ian
Gib·son Australian desert;
   US cocktail
gid sheep disease
gid·di·ly
gid·di·ness
gid·dy (adj ·di·er, ·di·est;
   verb ·dies, ·dy·ing, ·died)
giddy-up
gidgee (or gidjee) tree
gie Scot give
gift
gift·ed
gift·ed·ness
gift·wrap (·wrap·ing,
   ·wrapped)
gig (gig·ging, gigged)
gi·ga·hertz (plural ·hertz)
   physics term
gi·gan·tesque
gi·gan·tic
gi·gan·ti·cal·ly
gi·gan·tic·ness
gi·gan·tism (or gi·ant·ism)
gi·gan·toma·chy battle of
   giants
gig·gle
gig·gler
gig·gly
gigo·lo (plural ·los)
gi·got leg of mutton
gigue music
Gi·jón Spanish port
gil·bert unit

Gil·ber·tian of W. S. Gilbert
Gil·bert Is·lands former
   name of Kiribati
gild (gild·ing, gild·ed or
   gilt) cover with gold;
   compare guild
gild·er one who gilds;
   variant spelling of guilder
gild·ing
Gil·ead mountain region;
   biblical character
gi·let bodice
gil·gai Austral water hole
Gilgamesh legendary king
gill
gilled
gil·lie (or ghil·lie, gil·ly;
   plural ·lies) huntsman's
   attendant; compare
   ghillie
Gil·ling·ham towns in Kent
   and Dorset
gil·lion one thousand
   million
gill-less
gil·ly·flower (or ·li·)
Gil·son·ite (Trademark)
   asphalt
gilt covered in gold; gilding
   substance; pig; compare
   guilt
gilt-edged
gilt-head fish
gim·bals suspension device
gim·crack
gim·let
gim·mal mechanical joint
gim·me Slang give me
gim·mick
gim·mick·ry
gim·micky
gimp (or guimpe) fabric
   trimming
gin (gin·ning, ginned)
gin·ger
ginger·bread
gin·ger·li·ness
gin·ger·ly
gin·gery
ging·ham
gin·gi·li (or ·gel·li, ·gel·ly)
   sesame oil
gin·gi·va (plural ·vae) gum
gin·gi·val
gin·gi·vi·tis

gin·gly·mus (*plural* ·mi) anatomy term

gink *Slang* man or boy

 gink·go (*or* ging·ko; *plural* ·goes *or* ·koes) tree

gin·nel *Dialect* passageway

gin·seng

gip·py (*plural* ·pies) *Slang* an Egyptian; gipsy

gip·sy (*or* gyp·; *plural* ·sies)

gipsy·wort

gi·raffe (*plural* ·raffes *or* ·raffe)

gir·an·dole (*or* gi·ran·do·la) candle-holder

gira·sol (*or* giro·sol, gira·sole) opal

gird (gird·ing, gird·ed *or* girt)

gird·er

gir·dle

gir·dler

girl

girl·friend

girl·hood

girlie

girl·ish

girl·ish·ness

giro (*plural* ·ros) credit transfer; *compare* gyro

gi·ron (*or* gy·) heraldic term

Gi·ronde French river

Gi·ron·dism

Gi·ron·dist French revolutionary

gi·ron·ny (*or* gy·) heraldic term

girt

girth

gi·sarme battle-axe

Gis·borne New Zealand port

gist

git

git·tern ancient guitar

giu·sto musical term

giv·able (*or* give·able)

give (giv·ing, gave, giv·en)

give·away (*noun*)

giv·en

giv·er

giz·mo

giz·zard

gla·bel·la (*plural* ·lae) anatomy term

gla·bel·lar

gla·brous (*or* ·brate) smooth-skinned

gla·brous·ness

gla·cé (·cé·ing, ·céed)

gla·cial

gla·ci·al·ist

gla·ci·al·ly

gla·ci·ate

gla·cia·tion

glaci·er

glacio·logi·cal (*or* ·log·ic)

glaci·olo·gist (*or* gla·ci·al·ist)

glaci·ol·ogy

glac·is (*plural* ·ises *or* ·is) slope

glad (glad·der, glad·dest)

glad·den

glad·den·er

glade

gladi·ate sword-shaped

gladia·tor

gladia·to·rial

gladio·lus (*plural* ·li *or* ·luses)

glad·ly

glad·ness

glad·some

Glago·lit·ic Slavic alphabet

glair bookbinding glaze

glairi·ness

glairy (*or* glair·eous)

Gla·mor·gan

glam·ori·za·tion (*or* ·sa·tion)

glam·or·ize (*or* ·ise; *US also* ·our·)

glam·or·iz·er (*or* ·is·er)

glam·or·ous (*or* ·our·)

glam·or·ous·ness (*or* ·our·)

glam·our (*US also* glam·or)

glance

glanc·ing·ly

gland

glan·dered

glan·der·ous

glan·ders disease

glan·du·lar (*or* ·lous)

glan·dule small gland

glans (*plural* glan·des) anatomy term

glare

glar·ing

glar·ing·ly

glar·ing·ness

glary

Glas·gow

glass

glass-blower

glass-blowing

glasses

glass·house

glassi·ly

glass·ine book covering

glassi·ness

glass·like

glass-maker

glass-making

glass·man (*plural* ·men)

glass·ware

glass·work

glass-worker

glass·works

glass·wort plant

glassy (glassi·er, glassi·est)

Glas·ton·bury

Glas·we·gian of Glasgow

Glauce mythological character

glau·co·ma eye disease

glau·co·ma·tous

glau·co·nite mineral

glau·co·nit·ic

glau·cous waxy

glaze

glaz·er

gla·zi·er

gla·zi·ery

glaz·ing

gleam

gleam·ing·ly

glean

glean·able

glean·er

glean·ings

glebe clergyman's benefice

glee

glee·ful

glee·ful·ly

glee·ful·ness

gleet medical term

gleety

glen

Glen·coe Scottish massacre

Glen·dale US city

glen·gar·ry (*plural* ·ries) Scottish cap

gle·noid anatomy term

Glen·roth·es Scottish town

gley soil

glia·din (*or* ·dine) protein
glib (glib·ber, glib·best)
glib·ness
glide
glid·er
glid·ing
glid·ing·ly
glim *Slang* lamp
glim·mer
glim·mer·ing
glimpse
glimps·er
glint
glio·ma (*plural* ·ma·ta *or* ·mas) tumour
glio·ma·tous
glis·sade ballet step
glis·sad·er
glis·san·do (*plural* ·di) musical term
glis·ten
glis·ten·ing·ly
glis·ter glitter
glit·ter
glit·ter·ing
glit·tery
Gli·wi·ce Polish city
gloam·ing dusk
gloat
gloat·er
gloat·ing·ly
glob
glob·al
glo·bal·ize
glob·al·ly
glo·bate (*or* ·bat·ed)
globe
globe·flower
globe·trotter
globe·trotting
glo·big·eri·na (*plural* ·nas *or* ·nae) tiny animal
glo·bin protein
glo·boid
glo·bose (*or* ·bous) spherical
glo·bosi·ty (*or* ·bose·ness)
globu·lar (*or* ·lous)
glob·ule
globu·lif·er·ous
globu·lin protein
glo·chidi·ate
glo·chid·ium (*plural* ·chidia) biology term
glock·en·spiel
glogg alcoholic drink

glom·er·ate
glom·era·tion cluster
glo·meru·lar
glo·meru·late
glom·er·ule
glo·meru·lus (*plural* ·li) anatomy term
gloom
gloom·ful
gloomi·ly
gloomi·ness
gloomy (gloomi·er, gloomi·est)
Glo·ria hymn
glo·ria fabric
glo·ri·fi·able
glo·ri·fi·ca·tion
glo·ri·fi·er
glo·ri·fy (·fies, ·fy·ing, ·fied)
glo·ri·ous
glo·ri·ous·ness
glo·ry (*noun, plural* ·ries; *verb* ·ries, ·ry·ing, ·ried)
glory-of-the-snow plant
gloss
glos·sa (*plural* ·sae *or* ·sas) tongue
glos·sal
glos·sar·ial
glos·sa·rist
glos·sa·ry (*plural* ·ries)
glos·sa·tor gloss writer
glos·sec·to·my (*plural* ·mies) removal of tongue
gloss·eme linguistics term
gloss·er
glossi·ly
glossi·ness
glos·sit·ic
glos·si·tis inflammation of tongue
glos·sog·ra·pher
glos·sog·ra·phy
glos·so·la·lia gift of tongues
glossy (*adj* glossi·er, glossi·est; *noun, plural* glossies)
glot·tal
glot·tic
glot·tide·an
glot·tis (*plural* ·tises *or* ·ti·des)
glot·to·chro·nol·ogy branch of linguistics

Glouces·ter
Glouces·ter·shire
glove
glov·er
glow
glow·er
glow·er·ing·ly
glow-worm
glox·inia plant
glu·ca·gon hormone
glu·ci·num (*or* ·cin·ium) beryllium
glu·co·cor·ti·cord biochemistry term
glu·co·gen·esis biochemistry term
glu·co·genet·ic
glu·co·neo·gen·esis
glu·co·pro·tein *variant of* glycoprotein
glu·cose
glu·cos·ic
glu·co·sid·al (*or* ·ic)
glu·co·side
glu·co·su·ria *variant of* glycosuria
glue (glu·ing, glued)
glu·er
gluey (glui·er, glui·est)
glum (glum·mer, glum·mest)
glu·ma·ceous
glume botany term
glum·ness
glu·on hypothetical physics particle
glut (glut·ting, glut·ted)
glu·ta·mate
glu·ta·mine amino acid
glu·ta·thi·one biochemical compound
glu·teal (*or* ·taeal)
glu·telin protein
glu·ten protein
glu·tenous of gluten; *compare* glutinous
glu·teus (*or* ·taeus; *plural* ·tei *or* ·taei) buttock muscle
glu·ti·nous sticky; *compare* glutenous
glu·ti·nous·ness (*or* ·nos·ity)
glut·ton
glut·ton·ous

glut·tony (*plural* ·tonies)
gly·cer·ic of glycerol
glyc·er·ide chemical compound
glyc·er·in (*or* ·ine)
glyc·er·ol syrupy liquid
glyc·er·yl chemistry term
gly·cine amino acid
gly·co·gen biochemical compound
gly·co·gen·esis
gly·co·genet·ic
gly·co·gen·ic
gly·col antifreeze
gly·col·ic (*or* ·col·lic)
gly·coly·sis breakdown of glucose
gly·co·pro·tein (*or* glu·co·)
gly·co·side biochemical compound
gly·co·sid·ic
gly·co·su·ria (*or* glu·) sugar in urine
gly·co·su·ric (*or* glu·)
glyph groove on frieze
glyph·ic
glypho·graph
gly·phog·ra·pher
glypho·graph·ic (*or* ·graphi·cal)
gly·phog·ra·phy printing process
glyp·tic
glyp·tics engraving gems
glyp·to·dont extinct mammal
glyp·tog·ra·pher
glyp·to·graph·ic (*or* ·graphi·cal)
glyp·tog·ra·phy engraving gems
gnarl
gnarled (*or* gnarly)
gnash
gnash·ing·ly
gnat
gnat·catcher bird
gnath·ic (*or* ·al) of the jaw
gna·thi·on anatomy term
gna·thite zoology term
gna·thon·ic deceitfully flattering
gnaw (gnaw·ing, gnawed, gnawed *or* gnawn)
gnaw·able

gnaw·er
gneiss rock
gneiss·ic (*or* ·oid, ·ose)
gnoc·chi dumplings
gnome
gno·mic (*or* ·mi·cal) of aphorisms
gno·mi·cal·ly
gnom·ish
gno·mon part of sundial
gno·mon·ic
gno·moni·cal·ly
gno·sis (*plural* ·ses) spiritual knowledge
gnos·tic (*or* ·ti·cal)
Gnos·ti·cism
Gnos·ti·cize (*or* ·cise)
gno·to·bi·oti·cal·ly
gno·to·bi·ot·ics biology term
gnu (*plural* gnus *or* gnu)
go (*verb* goes, go·ing, went, gone; *noun, plural* goes)
Goa Indian district
goa gazelle
goad
go-ahead (*noun, adj*)
goal
goalie
goal·keeper
goal·keeping
goal·less
goal·mouth
go·an·na lizard
goat
goatee beard
goat·eed
goat·herd
goat·ish
goats·beard (*or* goat's-) plant
goat·skin
goat's-rue plant
goat·sucker bird
gob (gob·bing, gobbed)
gob·bet
gob·ble
gob·ble·de·gook (*or* ·dy·)
gob·bler
Go·belin tapestry
go-between
Gobi desert; *compare* goby
Go·bian
go·bi·oid zoology term
gob·let

gob·lin
gobo (*plural* gobos *or* goboes) microphone shield
gob·stopper
gobu·lar·ity (*or* ·ness)
goby (*plural* goby *or* gobies) fish; *compare* Gobi
god
god·child (*plural* ·children)
god·damn
god·daughter
god·dess
go·detia plant
god·father
god·fearing
god·forsaken
god·head
god·hood
god·less
god·less·ness
god·like
god·li·ness
god·ly (·li·er, ·li·est)
god·mother
go·down warehouse
god·parent
go·droon *variant spelling of* gadroon
god·send
god·son
God·speed
Godt·haab capital of Greenland
god·wit bird
goer
goe·thite (*or* gö·) mineral
gof·fer (*or* gauf·) to crimp; *compare* gopher
Gog biblical character
go-getter
gog·gle
goggle-box
goggle-eyed
gog·gles
Goiâ·nia Brazilian city
Goi·ás Brazilian state
Goi·del Gaelic-speaking Celt
Goi·del·ic (*or* Goi·dhel·ic, Ga·dhel·ic)
go·ing
goi·tre (*US* ·ter) thyroid swelling
goi·trous

go-kart
Gol·con·da ruined Indian town
gold
gold-beater
gold-beating
gold-crest bird
gold-dig·ger
gold-digging
gold·en
golden·eye (*plural* ·eyes or ·eye) duck
golden·rod plant
golden·seal plant
gold·eye (*plural* ·eyes or ·eye) fish
gold·finch
gold·fish (*plural* ·fish or ·fishes)
goldi·locks plant
gold-miner
gold-mining
gold-of-pleasure plant
gold-plate (*verb*)
gold·smith
gold·thread plant
go·lem resurrected being
golf
golf·er
gol·li·ard medieval scholar
gol·li·ard·ery
Goliath
gol·li·wog (*or* ·wogg)
gol·lop to eat greedily
gol·lop·er
gol·ly (*plural* ·lies)
go·loshes *variant spelling of* galoshes
gom·broon pottery
Go·mel Belarus city
Go·mor·rah
gom·pho·sis (*plural* ·ses) anatomy term
go·mu·ti palm tree
gon·ad sex organ
gon·ad·al (*or* go·na·dial, go·nad·ic)
gon·ado·troph·ic (*US* ·trop·ic)
gon·ado·tro·phin (*US* ·tro·pin) hormone
Gond tribal Indian
Gon·dar Ethiopian city
Gon·di Gond language
gon·do·la

gon·do·lier
Gond·wa·na·land ancient continent
gone
gon·er *Slang* one beyond help; *compare* gonna
gon·fa·lon (*or* ·non) banner
gon·fa·lon·ier magistrate
gong
Gon·go·rism literary style
go·nia·tite fossil
go·nid·ial (*or* ·nid·ic)
go·nid·ium (*plural* ·ia) botany term
go·ni·om·eter angle measurer
go·nio·met·ric (*or* ·ri·cal)
go·ni·om·etry
go·ni·on (*plural* ·nia) anatomy term
gonk toy
gon·na *Slang* going to; *compare* goner
gono·coc·cal (*or* ·cic)
gono·coc·coid
gono·coc·cus (*plural* ·coc·ci) bacterium
gono·cyte
gono·phore biology term
gono·phor·ic (*or* go·nopho·rous)
gono·pore zoology term
gon·or·rhoea (*US* ·rhea)
gon·or·rhoeal (*or* ·rhoe·ic; *US* ·rheal *or* ·rhe·ic)
goo
goo·ber peanut
good (bet·ter, best)
good·bye
good-for-nothing
good-humoured
good-humoured·ly
good·ish
good·li·ness
good-looking
good·ly (·li·er, ·li·est)
good·man (*plural* ·men) *Archaic* husband
good-natured
good-natured·ly
good·ness
good-night
goods
good-sized
good·wife (*plural* ·wives)

Good·win Sands
goody (*plural* goodies)
goody-goody (*plural* -goodies)
goo·ey (gooi·er, gooi·est)
goof
goofi·ly
goofi·ness
goofy (goofi·er, goofi·est)
goog·ly (*plural* ·lies) cricket term
goo·gol large number
goo·gol·plex large number
Goole Humberside port
goon
goop *US* rude person
goos·an·der duck
goose (*plural* geese)
goose·berry (*plural* ·berries)
goose·foot (*plural* ·foots) plant
goose·gog *Dialect* gooseberry
goose·grass
goose·neck nautical term
goose-step (-stepping, -stepped)
goosi·ness
goosy (*or* goos·ey; goosi·er, goosi·est)
go·pak dance
go·pher animal; *compare* goffer
Go·rakh·pur Indian city
go·ral antelope
Gor·bals Glaswegian suburb
gor·cock male grouse
gore
go·reng pi·sang Malaysian dish
gorge
gorge·able
gor·geous
gor·geous·ness
gorg·er
gor·ger·in architectural term
Gor·gon mythological monster
gor·go·nian coral
Gor·gon·zo·la cheese
go·ril·la ape; *compare* guerrilla
go·ril·lian (*or* ·line)
go·ril·loid

gori·ly

gori·ness

Gor·ki (or ·ky) former name of Nizhni Novgorod

Gor·lov·ka Ukrainian city

gor·mand·ize (or ·ise) eat greedily; compare gourmandise

gor·mand·iz·er (or is·er)

gorm·less

Gorno-Altai Russian region

Gorno-Badakh·shan Tadzhik region

gorse

Gor·sedd bardic institution

gory (gori·er, gori·est)

gosh

gos·hawk

Go·shen biblical region

gos·ling

go-slow

Gos·pel New Testament book

gos·pel truth; doctrine

gos·pel·ler (US ·pel·er)

Gos·plan former Soviet commission

gos·po·din (plural ·po·da) Russian title of address

Gos·port

gos·sa·mer

gos·sip

gos·sip·er

gos·sip·ing·ly

gossip·monger

gos·sipy

gos·soon Irish servant

gos·ter Dialect laugh

got

Gö·teborg (or Goth·en·burg) Swedish port

Goth Germanic people

Goth·ic

Gothi·cal·ly

Gothi·cism

Got·land Swedish island

got·ten

Göt·tin·gen German city

gouache art term

Gou·da cheese

gouge

goug·er

gou·lash

gou·ra·mi (plural ·mi or ·mis) fish

gourd

gour·mand (or gor·) greedy person; compare gourmet

gour·man·dise love of food; compare gormandize

gour·mand·ism

gour·met epicure; compare gourmand

gout

gouti·ness

gout·weed

gouty

gov·ern

gov·ern·abil·ity (or ·able·ness)

gov·ern·able

gov·ern·ance

gov·er·ness

gov·ern·ment

gov·ern·men·tal

gov·er·nor

gov·er·nor·ship

gow·an Scot daisy

Gower Welsh peninsula

gown

grab (grab·bing, grabbed)

grab·ber

grab·ble grope

grab·bler

gra·ben trough of land

grace

grace-and-favour

grace·ful

grace·ful·ly

grace·ful·ness

grace·less

Graces Greek goddesses

grac·ile slender

gra·cil·ity (or grac·ile·ness)

gra·cious

gra·cious·ness

grack·le bird

grad Slang graduate

grad·abil·ity (or ·able·ness)

grad·able

gra·date to cause to change

gra·da·tion

gra·da·tion·al

grade

grad·er

gra·di·ent

gra·din (or ·dine) step or ledge

grad·ual

gradu·al·ism

gradu·al·ist

gradu·al·is·tic

gradu·al·ly

gradu·al·ness

gradu·and person about to graduate

gradu·ate

gradua·tion

gradua·tor

gra·dus (plural ·dus·es) book of musical exercises

Grae·cism (or esp. US Gre·)

Grae·cize (or esp. US Gre·)

Graeco-Roman (or esp. US Greco·)

graf·fi·ti (sing. ·to)

graft

graft·er

graft·ing

Grail legendary bowl

grain

grain·er

graini·ness

grain·ing

grainy (graini·er, graini·est)

gral·la·to·rial ornithology term

gram plant

gram (or gramme) unit

gra·ma pasture grass

grama-rye magic

gra·mer·cy Archaic thanks

grami·ci·din antibiotic

gra·min·eous (or ·mina·ceous) of grasses

grami·nivo·rous grass-eating

gram·mar

gram·mar·ian

gram·mati·cal

gram·mati·cal·ly

gram·ma·tolo·gist

gram·ma·tol·ogy study of writing systems

gramme variant spelling of gram

gram-molecu·lar (or ·molar)

Gram-negative bacteriology term

gramo·phone

Gram·pian Scottish
  mountains and region
Gram-positive bacteriology
  term
gram·pus (*plural* **·puses**)
  dolphin
Gra·na·da Spanish city
grana·dil·la fruit
grana·ry (*plural* **·ries**)
grand
grand·aunt *variant of*
  great-aunt
grand·child (*plural*
  ·children)
Grand Cou·lee US dam
grand·dad
grand·daughter
gran·dee
gran·deur
grand·father
gran·dilo·quence
gran·dilo·quent
gran·di·ose
gran·di·ose·ly
gran·di·os·ity
grandio·so musical term
grand·ma (*or* **·mama**)
grand mal epilepsy
grand·master
grand·mother
grand·nephew *variant of*
  great-nephew
grand·niece *variant of*
  great-niece
grand·pa (*or* **·papa**)
grand·parent
grand·son
grand·stand
grange
grang·er·ism
grang·eri·za·tion (*or*
  ·sa·tion)
grang·er·ize (*or* **·ise**)
  illustrate with borrowed
  pictures
grang·er·iz·er (*or* **·is·er**)
gran·ite
granite·ware
gra·nit·ic (*or* **gran·it·oid**)
gran·it·ite type of granite
grani·vore
gra·nivo·rous grain-eating
gran·ny (*or* **·nie**; *plural*
  ·nies)
grano·dio·rite rock

grano·lith paving material
grano·lith·ic
grano·phyre rock
grano·phyr·ic
grant
Gran·ta River Cam
grant·able
grantee legal term
grant·er
grant-in-aid (*plural* **grants-**)
gran·tor
gran tur·is·mo touring car
granu·lar
granu·lar·ity
granu·late
granu·la·tion
granu·la·tive
granu·la·tor (*or* **·lat·er**)
gran·ule
granu·lite rock
granu·lit·ic
granu·lo·cyte
granu·lo·cyt·ic
granu·lo·ma (*plural* **·mas** *or*
  ·ma·ta) tumour
granu·loma·tous
grape
grape·fruit (*plural* **·fruit** *or*
  ·fruits)
grapes veterinary term
grape·shot
grape·vine
grap·ey (*or* **grapy**)
graph
graph·eme linguistics term
gra·phemi·cal·ly
graph·ic (*or* **graphi·cal**)
graphi·cal·ly
graphi·cal·ness (*or*
  graph·ic·ness)
graph·ics
graph·ite
gra·phit·ic
graphi·ti·za·tion (*or*
  ·sa·tion)
graphi·tize (*or* **·tise**) convert
  into graphite
grapho·log·ic (*or* **·logi·cal**)
graph·olo·gist
graph·ol·ogy study of
  handwriting
grapho·mo·tor
grap·nel
grap·pa grape spirit
grap·ple

grap·pler
grap·pling
grap·to·lite fossil
grapy *variant spelling of*
  grapey
Gras·mere Cumbrian
  village
grasp
grasp·able
grasp·er
grasp·ing
grass
grass·finch
grass·hook sickle
grass·hopper
grassi·ness
grass·land
grass·quit bird
grassy (**grassi·er**, **grassi·est**)
grate
grate·ful
grate·ful·ly
grate·ful·ness
grat·er
grati·cule grid
grati·fi·ca·tion
grati·fi·er
grati·fy (**·fies**, **·fy·ing**, **·fied**)
grati·fy·ing·ly
gra·tin cookery term
grat·ing
grat·ing·ly
gra·tis free
grati·tude
gra·tui·tous
gra·tu·ity (*plural* **·ities**)
Grau·bün·den Swiss canton
grau·pel hail
grav unit
gra·va·men (*plural*
  ·vami·na) legal term
grave burial place; accent;
  serious; engrave
gra·ve musical term
grav·el (**·el·ling**, **·elled**; *US*
  ·el·ing, **·eled**)
grav·el·ish
grav·el·ly
grav·en
grave·ly
grave·ness
grav·er engraving tool
Graves wine
Graves·end
grave·stone

Gra·vett·ian Palaeolithic culture

grave·yard

grav·id pregnant

gra·vid·ity (*or* **·ness**)

gra·vim·eter

gravi·met·ric (*or* **·ri·cal**)

gra·vim·etry

gra·vi·tas

gravi·tate

gravi·tat·er

gravi·ta·tion

gravi·ta·tion·al

gravi·ta·tion·al·ly

gravi·ta·tive

gravi·ton physics term

grav·ity (*plural* **·ities**)

gra·vure printing method

gra·vy (*plural* **·vies**)

gray US spelling of **grey**; unit

gray·back US spelling of **greyback**

gray·beard US spelling of **greybeard**

gray·ling (*plural* **·ling** *or* **·lings**) fish

gray·wacke US spelling of **greywacke**

graze

graz·er animal

gra·zi·er farmer

graz·ing

grease

grease·paint

greas·er

grease·wood (*or* **·bush**)

greasi·ly

greasi·ness

greasy (**greasi·er, greasi·est**)

great

great-aunt (*or* **grand·**)

great·coat

great·est

great·ly

great-nephew (*or* **grand·**)

great·ness

great-niece (*or* **grand·**)

Greats course at Oxford University

great-uncle (*or* **grand·**)

greave armour

greaves tallow residue

grebe

Gre·cian

Gre·cism *variant spelling* (*esp. US) of* **Graecism**

Gre·cize *variant spelling* (*esp. US) of* **Graecize**

Greco-Roman *variant spelling* (*esp. US) of* **Graeco-Roman**

Greece

greed

greedi·ly

greedi·ness

greedy (**greedi·er, greedi·est**)

Greek

green

green·back US currency note

green·bottle fly

green·brier

green·ery (*plural* **·eries**)

green·finch

green·fly (*plural* **·flies**)

green·gage

green·grocer

green·grocery (*plural* **·groceries**)

green·head male mallard

green·heart tree

green·horn

green·house

green·ing cooking apple

green·ish

Green·land

Green·land·er

green·let bird

green·ling fish

green·ness

Green·ock Scottish port

green·ock·ite mineral

green·room

green·sand

Greens·boro US city

green·shank bird

green·stick fracture

green·stone

green·stuff

green·sward turf

Green·wich

green·wood

greet

greet·er

greet·ing

grega·rine zoology term

gre·gari·ous

gre·gari·ous·ness

Gre·go·rian

greige undyed

grei·sen rock

gre·mi·al bishop's cloth

grem·lin

Gre·na·da West Indian state

gre·nade

grena·dier

grena·dine fabric; syrup

Grena·dines West Indian islands

Grendel legendary monster

Gre·no·ble French city

gres·so·rial (*or* **·ri·ous**) ornithology term

Gret·na Green

grew

grey (US **gray**) colour; *compare* **gray**

grey·back (US **gray·**) animal

grey·beard (US **gray·**)

grey·hen female black grouse

grey·hound

grey·ish (US **gray·**)

grey·lag goose

grey·ness (US **gray·**)

grey-state undyed

grey·wacke (US **gray·**) rock

grib·ble wood-boring animal

grid

grid·dle

griddle·cake

gride grate

grid·iron

grief

griev·ance

grieve

griev·er

griev·ing

griev·ous

griev·ous·ness

griffe architectural ornament

grif·fin (*or* **grif·fon, gryph·on**) winged monster

grif·fon dog; vulture; *variant spelling of* **griffin**

grig

gri·gri (*or* **gris-gris, gree-gree**; *plural* **·gris** *or* **·grees**) talisman

grill cooking senses; *compare*
  grille
gril·lage building term
grille (*or* grill) metal screen;
  compare grill
grilled
grill·er
grill·room
grilse (*plural* grilses *or*
  grilse) salmon
grim (grim·mer,
  grim·mest)
gri·mace
gri·mac·er
gri·mac·ing·ly
Gri·mal·di moon crater
gri·mal·kin old cat
grime
grim·ness
Grims·by
grimy (grim·ier, grim·iest)
grin (grin·ning, grinned)
grind (grind·ing, ground)
grin·de·lia plant
Grin·del·wald Swiss valley
grind·er
grind·ery (*plural* ·eries)
grind·stone
grin·go (*plural* ·gos)
grin·ner
grip (grip·ping, gripped)
gripe
grip·er complainer; *compare*
  gripper
grip·ing·ly
grippe influenza
grip·per one that grips;
  compare griper
grip·ping
grip·ping·ly
gri·saille painting term
gris·eous greyish
gri·sette French girl
gris·kin pork cut
gris·li·ness
gris·ly (·li·er, ·li·est)
  gruesome; *compare* gristly;
  grizzly
gri·son animal
grist
gris·tle
gris·tli·ness
gris·tly having gristle;
  compare grisly; grizzly
grist·mill

grit (grit·ting, grit·ted)
grith place of safety
grits coarsely ground grain
grit·ti·ly
grit·ti·ness
grit·ty (·ti·er, ·ti·est)
griv·et monkey
griz·zle become grey; *Slang*
  whine
griz·zled
griz·zler
griz·zly (*adj* ·zli·er, ·zli·est;
  noun, plural ·zlies)
  grey-haired; bear; *compare*
  grisly; gristly
groan
groan·er
groan·ing·ly
groat old coin
groats crushed grain
gro·cer
gro·cery (*plural* ·ceries)
grock·le *Dialect* tourist
Grod·no Belarussian city
grog
grog·gi·ly
grog·gi·ness
grog·gy (·gi·er, ·gi·est)
grog·ram fabric
groin abdominal region;
  vault; *compare* groyne
Gro·li·er bookbinding style
grom·met (*or* grum·)
grom·well plant
Gro·ning·en Dutch
  province
groom
groom·er
groom·ing
grooms·man (*plural* ·men)
groove
groovy (groovi·er,
  groovi·est)
grope
grop·er
grop·ing·ly
gros·beak bird
gro·schen (*plural* ·schen)
  Austrian coin
gros·grain fabric
gross
gross·ness
gros·su·lar·ite gemstone
grot grotto
gro·tesque

gro·tesque·ly
gro·tesque·ness
gro·tes·query (*or* ·querie;
  plural ·queries)
grot·to (*plural* ·toes *or* ·tos)
grouch
grouchi·ly
grouchi·ness
grouchy (grouch·ier,
  grouch·iest)
ground
ground·age anchorage fee
ground·ing
ground·less
ground·ling
ground·mass
ground·nut
ground·sel
ground·sheet
ground·sill joist
grounds·man (*plural* ·men)
ground·speed
ground·work
group
group·er (*plural* ·er *or* ·ers)
  fish
groupie
group·ing
grouse (*plural* grouse *or*
  grouses)
grous·er complainer
grout
grout·er
grouts coffee grounds
grouty (grouti·er,
  grouti·est) *Dialect* muddy
grove
grov·el (·el·ling, ·elled; *US*
  ·el·ing, ·eled)
grov·el·ler (*US* ·el·er)
grov·el·ling·ly (*US*
  ·el·ing·ly)
grow (grow·ing, grew,
  grown)
grow·able
grow·er
growl
growl·er
grown
grown-up
growth
groyne jetty; *compare* groin
Groz·ny Russian (Chechen)
  city
grub (grub·bing, grubbed)

grub·ber
grub·bi·ly
grub·bi·ness
grub·by (grub·bi·er,
grub·bi·est)
grudge
grudg·er
grudg·ing
grudg·ing·ly
gru·el
gru·el·ling (US ·el·ing)
grue·some (or grew·)
gruff
gruff·ish
gruff·ness
gru·gru palm tree
grum·ble
grum·bler
grum·bling·ly
grum·bly
grum·met variant spelling of
grommet
gru·mous (or ·mose) botany
term
grump
grumpi·ly (or grump·ish·ly)
grumpi·ness (or
grump·ish·ness)
grumpy (or grump·ish;
grumpi·er, grumpi·est)
Grun·dy narrow-minded
critical person
grun·ion fish
grunt
grunt·er
grunt·ing·ly
grun·tled contented
Grus constellation
Gru·yère cheese
gryph·on variant spelling of
griffin
grys·bok antelope
gua·ca·mo·le (or ·cha·)
avocado dish
gua·co (plural ·cos) plant
Gua·dal·ca·nal Pacific
island
Gua·dal·qui·vir Spanish
river
Gua·de·loupe
(guage) incorrect spelling of
gauge
guaia·col medicinal liquid
guaia·cum (or guaio·) tree
or resin

Guam Pacific island
guan bird
Gua·na·ba·ra former
Brazilian state
gua·na·co (plural ·cos)
animal
Gua·na·jua·to Mexican
state
gua·nase enzyme
guani·dine (or ·din)
biochemical compound
gua·nine biochemical
compound
gua·no (plural ·nos) bird
excrement
gua·no·sine biochemical
compound
Guan·ta·na·mo Cuban city
Gua·ra·ni (plural ·ni or ·nis)
Paraguayan people
gua·ra·ni (plural ·ni or ·nis)
currency
guar·an·tee (·tee·ing, ·teed)
guar·an·tor
guar·an·ty (plural ·ties)
legal term
guard
guard·able
guar·dant (or gar·) heraldic
term
guard·ed
guard·ed·ly
guard·ed·ness
guard·er
guard·house
guard·ian
guardi·an·ship
guard·rail
guard·room
Guards regiment
guards·man (plural ·men)
Gua·te·ma·la
gua·va fruit
Gua·ya·quil Ecuadorian
port
gua·yu·le shrub
gub·bins
gu·ber·na·to·rial of a
governor
guck slimy substance
gudg·eon fish
guelder-rose
Guelph (or Guelf) political
faction
Guelph·ic (or Guelf·)

Guelph·ism (or Guelf·)
gue·non monkey
guer·don reward
Guer·ni·ca Spanish town
Guern·sey Channel island
guern·sey sweater
Guer·rero Mexican state
guer·ril·la (or gue·ril·la)
fighter; compare gorilla
guer·ril·la·ism (or gue·)
guess
guess·able
guess·er
guess·ti·mate
guess·work
guest
guest·house
guff Slang ridiculous talk
guf·faw
Gui·ana South American
region
Guia·nese (or Gui·an·an)
guid·able
guid·ance
guide
guide·line
guide·post
guid·er
guid·ing
guid·ing·ly
gui·don flag
Gui·enne (or Guy·enne)
former French province
guild (or gild) organization;
compare gild
guil·der (or gild·er,
gul·den; plural ·ders, ·der
or ·dens, ·den) currency;
compare gilder
Guild·ford
guild·hall (or gild·)
guilds·man (or gilds·; plural
·men)
guile
guile·ful
guile·ful·ly
guile·ful·ness
guile·less
guil·lemot
guil·loche architectural
border
guil·lo·tine
guil·lo·tin·er
guilt guiltiness; remorse;
compare gilt

guilti·ly
guilti·ness
guilt·less
guilty (guilti·er, guilti·est)
guimpe blouse; *variant spelling of* gimp
Guinea African republic
guinea coin
Guinea-Bissau African republic
Guin·ean
guinea pig
Guinevere *legendary queen*
gui·pure lace
guise
gui·tar
guitar·fish (*plural* ·fish *or* ·fishes)
gui·tar·ist
Gu·ja·rat (*or* ·je·) Indian state
Gu·ja·ra·ti (*or* ·je·)
Guj·ran·wa·la Pakistani city
Gu·lag former Soviet administrative department
gu·lar of the throat
gulch *US* ravine
gul·den *variant of* guilder
gules heraldic term
gulf
gulf·weed
gull
Gul·lah (*plural* ·lahs *or* ·lah) African-American people
gul·let
gul·li·bil·ity (*or* ·la·)
gul·lible (*or* ·lable)
gul·li·bly (*or* ·la·)
gull·wing
gul·ly (*noun, plural* ·lies; *verb* ·lies, ·ly·ing, ·lied)
gulp
gulp·er
gulp·ing·ly
gum (gum·ming, gummed)
Gum·bo French patois
gum·bo (*or* gom·; *plural* ·bos) thick stew
gum·boil
gum·boot
gum·bo·til clay
gum·drop
gum·ma (*plural* ·mas *or* ·ma·ta) tumour
gum·ma·tous

gum·mi·ly
gum·mi·ness
gum·mite mineral
gum·mo·sis plant disease
gum·my (·mi·er, ·mi·est)
gump·tion
gum·shield
gum·shoe
gum·tree
gun (gun·ning, gunned)
gun·boat
gun·cotton
gun·fight
gun·fighter
gun·fire
gun·flint
gunge
gun·gy
gunk *Slang* slimy substance
gun·lock
gun·man (*plural* ·men)
gun·metal
gunned
gun·nel fish; *variant spelling of* gunwale
gun·ner
gun·nery
gun·ning
gun·ny (*plural* ·nies) *US* fabric
gun·paper
gun·play
gun·point
gun·powder
gun·runner
gun·running
gun·shot
gun·shy
gun·slinger
gun·smith
gun·smithing
gun·stock
Gun·tur Indian city
gun·wale (*or* gun·nel) nautical term
gun·yah *Austral* bush hut
Guo·min·dang *variant spelling of* Kuomintang
gup·py (*plural* ·pies) fish
Gur language
gurd·wa·ra Sikh place of worship
gur·gi·ta·tion surging movement
gur·gle

gur·gling·ly
gur·jun tree
Gur·kha (*plural* ·khas *or* ·kha)
Gur·kha·li language
Gur·mu·khi Punjabi script
gur·nard (*or* gur·net; *plural* ·nard, ·nards *or* ·net, ·nets) fish
guru (*plural* gurus)
gush
gush·er
gush·ing·ly
gushy
gus·set
gust
gus·ta·tion tasting
gus·ta·tory (*or* ·tive)
gusti·ly
gusti·ness
gus·to
gusty (gusti·er, gusti·est)
gut (gut·ting, gut·ted)
gut·bucket jazz
gut·less
gutsy (gutsi·er, gutsi·est)
gut·ta (*plural* ·tae) drop
gutta-percha
gut·tate (*or* ·tat·ed) biology term
gut·ted
gut·ter
gut·ter·ing
gutter·snipe
gut·ting
gut·tur·al
gut·tur·ali·za·tion (*or* ·sa·tion)
gut·tur·al·ize (*or* ·ise)
gut·tur·al·ly
gut·tur·al·ness (*or* ·ity, ·ism)
gut·ty (*plural* ·ties) *Irish* urchin
guv *Slang* governor
guy
Guy·ana South American republic
Guya·nese (*or* Guy·an·an)
Guy·enne *variant spelling of* Guienne
guy·ot submerged mountain
guz·zle
guz·zler
Gwa·li·or Indian city

Gwe·lo Zimbabwean town
Gwent former Welsh county
Gwyn·edd Welsh county
gwyni·ad fish
gybe (or jibe) nautical term; compare gibe
gym
gym·kha·na
gym·na·si·arch Greek magistrate
gym·na·si·ast
gym·na·sium (plural ·siums or ·sia)
gym·nast
gym·nas·tic
gym·nas·ti·cal·ly
gym·nas·tics
gym·noso·phist Indian ascetic
gym·no·sperm conifer
gym·no·sper·mous
gym·slip
gy·nae·ceum (plural ·cea) women's apartments; compare gynoecium
gy·nae·cium variant spelling of gynoecium
gy·nae·coc·ra·cy (US ·ne· plural ·cies) government by women

gy·nae·co·crat·ic (US ·ne·)
gy·nae·coid (US ·ne·)
gy·nae·co·logi·cal (or ·log·ic; US ·ne·)
gy·nae·co·logi·cal·ly (US ·ne·)
gy·nae·colo·gist (US ·ne·)
gy·nae·col·ogy (US ·ne·)
gy·nae·co·mas·tia (US ·ne·) male breast development
gy·nan·dro·morph biology term
gy·nan·dro·mor·phic (or ·phous)
gy·nan·dro·morph·ism (or ·mor·phy)
gy·nan·drous botany term
gy·nan·dry (or ·drism)
gy·narch·ic
gyn·ar·chy (plural ·chies) gynaecocracy
gy·noe·cium (or ·nae·; US ·ne·; plural ·cia) part of flower; compare gynaeceum
gy·no·phore botany term
gy·no·phor·ic
gyp Slang pain

gyp·se·ous
gyp·sif·er·ous
gyp·sophi·la plant
gyp·sum
gyp·sy variant spelling of gipsy
gy·ral rotating
gy·rate
gy·ra·tion
gy·ra·tor
gy·ra·tory
gyre circular movement
gyr·fal·con (or ger·)
gyro (plural gyros) gyrocompass; gyroscope; compare giro
gy·ro·com·pass
gy·ro·mag·net·ic
gy·ro·plane
gy·ro·scope (or ·stat)
gy·ro·scop·ic
gy·ro·scop·ics
gy·rose botany term
gy·ro·sta·bi·liz·er (or ·lis·er)
gy·ro·stat·ic of rotating bodies
gy·ro·stat·ics
gy·rus (plural gyri) anatomy term
gyve Archaic fetter

H

ha (or hah) exclamation
haaf fishing ground
Haar·lem Dutch city; compare Harlem
haar fog
Habakkuk prophet
Ha·ba·na Spanish Havana
ha·ba·nera dance
ha·beas cor·pus
hab·er·dash·er
hab·er·dash·ery
hab·er·geon (or hau·ber·geon) coat of mail
hab·ile skilful
ha·bili·ment dress
ha·bili·tate
ha·bili·ta·tion
ha·bili·ta·tor

hab·it
hab·it·abil·ity (or ·able·ness)
hab·it·able
hab·it·ably
hab·it·ant
habi·tat
habi·ta·tion
habi·ta·tion·al
hab·it·ed
ha·bitu·al
ha·bitu·al·ly
ha·bitu·al·ness
ha·bitu·ate
ha·bitu·a·tion
habi·tude
habi·tu·di·nal
ha·bitué
habi·tus (plural ·tus) physical state

Habsburg (or Hapsburg) royal dynasty
habu snake
há·ček phonetic symbol
ha·chure shading
haci·en·da
hack
hacka·more US rope halter
hack·berry (plural ·berries)
hack·but (or hag·) gun
hack·but·eer (or hag·)
hack·er
hack·ing
hack·le
hack·ler
hack·les
Hack·ney London borough
hack·ney carriage; make banal
hack·neyed

hack·ney·ism

hack·saw

had

ha·dal of ocean depths

hada·way *Dialect* hurry

had·dock

hade geology term

Ha·de·an

Ha·des underworld

Ha·dhra·maut Arabian plateau

Had·ith Mohammedan tradition

hadj *variant spelling of* hajj

hadj·i *variant spelling of* hajji

hadn't

had·ron elementary particle

had·ron·ic

had·ro·saur (*or* ·saur·us)

hadst *Archaic* had

hae *Scot* have

haec·ce·ity (*plural* ·ities) philosophy term

Haeck·elian of Haeckel

haem (*US* heme) organic pigment

haema·chrome *variant spelling of* haemochrome

haema·cy·tom·eter (*US* hema·)

hae·mag·glu·tin·ate (*US* he·)

hae·mag·glu·ti·nin (*US* he·) antibody

haema·gogue (*US* hema·gogue *or* ·gog)

hae·mal (*US* he·)

haema·tein (*US* hema·) biological stain

haema·tem·esis (*US* hema·)

hae·mat·ic (*US* he·)

haema·tin (*US* hema·) dark pigment

haema·tin·ic (*US* hema·) medicinal drug

haema·tite (*US* hema·) mineral

haema·tit·ic (*US* hema·)

hae·mato·blast (*US* he·)

hae·mato·blas·tic (*US* he·)

haema·to·cele (*US* hema·)

haema·to·crit (*US* hema·) medical term

haema·to·cry·al (*US* hema·) zoology term

haema·to·gen·esis (*US* hema·)

haema·to·gen·ic (*US* hema·)

haema·tog·enous (*US* hema·)

haema·toid (*or* hae·moid; *US* hema·* or* he·)

haema·to·log·ic (*or* ·logi·cal; *US* hema·)

haema·tolo·gist (*US* hema·)

haema·tol·ogy (*US* hema·)

haema·toly·sis *variant of* haemolysis

haema·to·ma (*US* hema·; *plural* ·mas *or* ·mata) blood tumour

haema·to·poi·esis (*or* haemo·poi·esis; *US* hema· *or* hemo·)

haema·to·poi·et·ic (*or* haemo·poi·et·ic; *US* hema· *or* hemo·)

haema·to·sis (*US* hema·)

haema·to·ther·mal (*US* hema·) warm-blooded

haema·toxy·lin (*US* hema·) dye

haema·toxy·lon tree

haema·to·zo·on (*US* hema·; *plural* ·zoa)

haema·tu·ria (*US* hema·)

haema·tu·ric

hae·mic (*US* he·)

hae·min (*US* he·)

haemo·chrome (*or* haema·; *US* hemo· *or* hema·)

haemo·coel (*US* hemo·) zoology term

haemo·cya·nin (*US* hemo·)

haemo·cyte (*US* hemo·)

haemo·cy·tom·eter (*US* hemo·)

haemo·di·aly·sis (*US* hemo·)

haemo·flag·el·late (*US* hemo·) protozoan

haemo·glo·bin (*US* hemo·)

haemo·glo·bi·nu·ria (*US* hemo·)

hae·moid *variant of* haematoid

haemo·ly·sin (*US* hemo·)

hae·moly·sis (*or* haema·toly·sis; *US* he· *or* hema·; *plural* ·ses)

haemo·lyt·ic (*US* hemo·)

haemo·phile (*US* hemo·)

haemo·philia (*US* hemo·)

haemo·phili·ac (*US* hemo·)

haemo·phil·ic (*US* hemo·)

haemo·poi·esis *variant of* haematopoiesis

haemo·poi·et·ic *variant of* haematopoietic

haem·op·ty·sis (*US* hem·) coughing blood

haem·or·rhage (*US* hem·)

haem·or·rhag·ic (*US* hem·)

haem·or·rhoid (*US* hem·)

haem·or·rhoi·dal (*US* hem·)

haem·or·rhoid·ec·to·my (*US* hem·; *plural* ·mies)

haemo·sta·sis (*or* ·sia; *US* hemo·)

haemo·stat (*US* hemo·)

haemo·stat·ic (*US* hemo·)

hae·re·mai Maori welcome

hae·res *variant spelling of* heres

Ha·erh·pin *variant spelling of* Harbin

ha·fiz Islamic title

haf·nium chemical element

haft

Haf·ta·rah (*or* Haph·ta·rah; *plural* ·ta·roth *or* ·ta·rahs) biblical reading

haft·er

hag

Hagar biblical character

hag·but *variant spelling of* hackbut

Ha·gen German city

Hagen legendary character

hag·fish (*plural* ·fish *or* ·fishes)

Hag·ga·dah (*or* ·da; *plural* ·dahs, ·das, *or* ·doth) Jewish literature

hag·gad·ic (*or* ·gadi·cal)

hag·ga·dist

hag·ga·dist·ic

Haggai biblical prophet

hag·gard

hag·gard·ness

hag·gis

hag·gish
hag·gish·ness
hag·gle
hag·gler
hagi·archy (*plural* ·archies)
 government by saints
hagi·oc·ra·cy (*plural* ·cies)
Hagi·og·ra·pha Old
 Testament section
hagi·og·ra·pher (*or* ·phist)
hagi·o·graph·ic (*or*
 ·graphi·cal)
hagi·og·ra·phy (*plural*
 ·phies)
hagi·ola·ter
hagi·ola·trous
hagi·ola·try veneration of
 saints
hagi·o·log·ic (*or* ·logi·cal)
hagi·olo·gist
hagi·ol·ogy (*plural* ·ogies)
 writings about saints
hagi·o·scope architectural
 term
hagi·o·scop·ic
hag·like
Hague
hah *variant spelling of* ha
ha-ha (*or* haw-haw) sunken
 fence
Hai·da (*plural* ·da *or* ·das)
 American Indian
Hai·dan
Hai·duk (*or* Hey·duck,
 Hei·duc) brigand
Hai·fa Israeli port
haik (*or* haick) Arabian
 garment
hai·ku (*or* hok·ku; *plural*
 ·ku) Japanese verse
hail frozen rain; greet;
 compare hale
hail·er
hail·stone
hail·storm
Hai·nan (*or* Hai·nan Tao)
 Chinese island
Hai·naut (*or* ·nault) Belgian
 province
Hai·phong Vietnamese port
hair
hair·ball
hair·brush
hair·cloth
hair·cut

hair·do (*plural* ·dos)
hair·dresser
hair·dressing
hair·grip
hair·if plant
hairi·ness
hair·less
hair·like
hair·line
hair·net
hair·piece
hair·pin
hair·raising
hair's-breadth
hair·splitter
hair·splitting
hair·spring
hair·streak butterfly
hair·style
hair·stylist
hair·tail fish
hair·weaving
hair·worm
hairy (hairi·er, hairi·est)
Hai·ti
Hai·tian
hajj (*or* hadj; *plural* hajjes *or*
 hadjes) Muslim pilgrimage
haj·ji (*or* hadji, haji)
hake (*plural* hake *or* hakes)
ha·kea shrub
ha·kim (*or* ·keem) Muslim
 judge or physician
Ha·ko·da·te Japanese port
Ha·la·fian Neolithic culture
Ha·la·kah (*or* ·cha) Jewish
 literature
Ha·lak·ic (*or* ·lach·ic)
hal·al (*or* hall·al) Muslim
 custom
ha·la·tion photography
 term
ha·la·vah *variant of* halvah
hal·berd (*or* ·bert)
hal·ber·dier
hal·cy·on
Halcyone *variant of* Alcyone
hale healthy; to haul;
 compare hail
Ha·lea·ka·la Hawaiian
 volcano
hale·ness
ha·ler (*plural* ·lers *or* ·leru)
 Czech coin
Hales·ow·en English town

half (*plural* halves)
half·back
half·baked
half·beak fish
half·caste
half·day
half·hearted
half·hearted·ly
half·hearted·ness
half·life
half·light
half·mast
half·naked
half·open
half·penny (*plural* ·pennies
 or ·pence)
half·penny·worth
half·price
half·shut
half·time
half·tone
half·way
half·wit
half·witted
half·witted·ly
half·witted·ness
hali·but (*plural* ·but *or*
 ·buts)
Ha·liç Turkish Golden Horn
Hali·car·nas·si·an
Hali·car·nas·sus ancient
 Greek city
hal·ide (*or* ·id) chemical
 compound
hali·dom *Archaic* holy thing
Hali·fax Canadian port;
 British town
hal·ite mineral
hali·to·sis
hall
hal·lah *variant spelling of*
 challah
hall·al *variant spelling of*
 halal
Hal·lel Jewish chant
hal·le·lu·jah *variant of*
 alleluia
hal·liard *variant spelling of*
 halyard
hall·mark
hal·lo *variant spelling of*
 halloo *or* hello
hal·loo (*or* ·lo; *noun, plural*
 ·loos *or* ·los; *verb* ·loos,
 ·loo·ing, ·looed; *or* ·los,

•loing, •loed) shout;
compare hello
hal•low
hal•lowed
hal•lowed•ness
Hal•low•e'en (*or*
Hal•low•een)
hal•low•er
Hal•low•mas (*or* •mass)
Hall•statt archaeology term
Hall•statt•ian
hal•lu•ci•nate
hal•lu•ci•na•tion
hal•lu•ci•na•tion•al (*or*
•na•tive)
hal•lu•ci•na•tor
hal•lu•ci•na•tory
hal•lu•cino•gen drug
hal•lu•ci•no•gen•ic
hal•lu•ci•no•sis mental
disorder
hal•lux (*plural* •luces) first
digit on foot
hall•way
halm *variant spelling of*
haulm
hal•ma
Hal•ma•he•ra Indonesian
island
halo (*noun, plural* haloes *or*
halos; *verb* haloes *or*
halos, halo•ing, haloed)
ha•lo•bi•ont salt-water
organism
halo•gen
halo•gen•ate
halo•gen•a•tion
halo•gen•oid
ha•log•enous
hal•oid
halo-like
halo•phyte plant
halo•phyt•ic
halo•phyt•ism
halo•thane
halt
Hal•tem•price Hull suburb
hal•ter
hal•tere zoology term
halter-like
halt•ing
halt•ing•ness
hal•vah (*or* hal•va,
ha•la•vah) sweetmeat
halve

hal•yard (*or* hal•liard)
ham (ham•ming, hammed)
Hama Syrian city
Hama•dān (*or* Ham•edān)
Iranian city
hama•dry•ad nymph
hama•dry•as baboon
ha•mal (*or* ham•mal,
ha•maul) Oriental servant
Ha•ma•ma•tsu Japanese city
hama•meli•da•ceous
botany term
ha•mate hook-shaped
Ham•ble•to•nian horse
Ham•burg
ham•burg•er
hame harness attachment
Ham•elin (*or* Ha•meln)
German town
Ham•ers•ley Australian
mountain range
Ham•il•ton Canadian port
Ham•il•to•ni•an maths term
Ham•ite African people
Ham•it•ic
ham•let
ham•mer
ham•mer•er
hammer•head animal
hammer•headed
ham•mer•less
hammer-like
Ham•mer•smith
hammer•toe
ham•mock
hammock-like
Ham•mond US city
ham•my (ham•mi•er,
ham•mi•est)
ham•per
ham•pered•ness
ham•per•er
Hamp•shire
Hamp•stead
Hamp•ton US city
ham•shack•le fetter a horse
ham•ster
ham•string (•string•ing,
•strung)
hamu•lar
hamu•lus (*plural* •li)
hooklike projection
ham•za (*or* •zah) Arabic
phonetic sign
Han Chinese dynasty; river

hana•per wickerwork basket
hance (*or* haunch)
architectural term
hand
hand•bag
hand•ball
hand•baller
hand•barrow
hand•bell
hand•bill
hand•book
hand•brake
hand•breadth
hand•cart
hand•clasp
hand•craft
hand•cuff
hand•fast *Archaic* agreement
hand•fasting
hand•feed (•feed•ing, •fed)
hand•ful
hand•grip
hand•gun
hand•hold
handi•cap (•cap•ping,
•capped)
handi•cap•per
handi•craft
handi•crafts•man (*plural*
•men)
handi•ly
handi•ness
handi•work
hand•ker•chief
han•dle
han•dle•able
handle•bar
han•dled
han•dle•less
han•dler
hand•less
hand•like
han•dling
hand•made
hand•maiden (*or* •maid)
hand-me-down
hand-out (*noun*)
hand•rail
hand•saw
hand•sel (*or* han•) *Dialect*
new year gift
hand•set
hand•shake
hand•some good-looking;
compare hansom

hand·some·ly

hand·some·ness

hand·spike lever

hand·spring

hand·stand

hand·stroke bell-ringing term

hand·writing

hand·written

handy (handi·er, handi·est)

handy·man (plural ·men)

hang (hang·ing, hung or hanged)

hang·ar aircraft shed; compare hanger

hang·bird

Hang·chow (or Hang-chou) Chinese port

hang·dog

hanged killed; compare hung

hang·er support; one that hangs; compare hangar

hanger-on (plural hangers-on)

hang·man (plural ·men)

hang·nail

hang·over

hang-up (noun)

hank

hank·er

(hankerchief) incorrect spelling of handkerchief

hank·er·er

Han·kow (or Han-k'ou) former Chinese city

hanky (or hankie; plural hankies)

hanky-panky

Ha·noi Vietnamese capital

Hano·ver

Hano·verian

Han·sard parliamentary report

Hanse (or Han·sa) medieval guild

Han·seat·ic

han·sel variant spelling of handsel

han·som cab; compare handsome

Ha·nuk·kah Jewish festival

Hanu·man monkey god

hanu·man monkey

Han·yang former Chinese city

hap (hap·ping, happed) Archaic happen; luck

ha·pax le·go·menon (plural ha·pax le·go·mena) nonce word

ha'·penny (plural ·pennies)

hap·haz·ard

hap·haz·ard·ness

Haph·ta·rah variant spelling of Haftarah

hap·less

hap·less·ness

hap·lite variant spelling of aplite

hap·lit·ic variant spelling of aplitic

hap·log·ra·phy (plural ·phies) omission of letter in writing

hap·loid biology term

hap·loidy

hap·lo·log·ic

hap·lol·ogy (plural ·ogies) omission of syllable in speech

hap·lo·sis biology term

hap·ly

ha'·p'orth

hap·pen

hap·pen·ing

hap·pen·stance

hap·pi·ly

hap·pi·ness

hap·py (·pi·er, ·pi·est)

happy-go-lucky

Hapsburg variant spelling of Habsburg

hap·ten (or ·tene) medical term

hap·ter·on botany term

hap·tic of touch

hap·to·trop·ism botany term

ha·ra·ki·ri (or ha·ri·ka·ri) Japanese suicide

ha·ram·bee African chant

ha·rangue

ha·rangu·er

Ha·rap·pa Pakistani city

Ha·rap·pan

Ha·rar (or Har·rar) Ethiopian city

Ha·rare Zimbabwean capital

har·ass

har·ass·er

har·ass·ing·ly

har·ass·ment

Har·bin (or Ha-erh-pin) Chinese city

har·bin·ger

har·bour (US ·bor)

har·bour·age (US ·bor·)

har·bour·er (US ·bor·)

har·bour·less (US ·bor·)

hard

hard·back

hard·bake almond toffee

hard·board

hard·en

hard·ened

hard·en·er

hard·en·ing

hard·hack plant

hard·headed

hard·headed·ly

hard·headed·ness

hard·heads plant

hard·hearted

hard·hearted·ly

hard·hearted·ness

har·di·hood

har·di·ly

har·di·ness

hard·ly

hard·ness

hard·pan clay layer

hards (or hurds) coarse fibres

hard·ship

hard·tack

hard·top

hard·ware

hard·wood

har·dy (·di·er, ·di·est)

hare

hare·bell

hare·brained

hare·like

hare·lip

hare·lipped

har·em (or ·eem)

Har·gei·sa Somalian city

hari·cot

(haridan) incorrect spelling of harridan

Ha·ri·jan Indian untouchable

ha·ri·ka·ri *variant spelling of*
   harakiri
Ha·rin·gey London borough
hark
hark·en *US variant spelling of*
   hearken
harl *variant spelling of* herl
Har·lem New York district;
   compare Haarlem
har·lequin
har·lequin·ade
Har·ley Street
har·lot
har·lot·ry
Har·low Essex town
harm
har·mat·tan Saharan wind
harm·er
harm·ful
harm·ful·ly
harm·ful·ness
harm·less
harm·less·ness
har·mon·ic
har·moni·ca
har·moni·cal·ly
har·mon·ics
har·mo·ni·ous
har·mo·nist
har·mo·nis·tic
har·mo·nis·ti·cal·ly
har·mo·nium
har·mo·niz·able
har·mo·ni·za·tion
har·mo·nize (*or* ·nise)
har·mo·niz·er
har·mo·ny (*plural* ·nies)
har·mo·tome
har·ness
har·ness·er
har·ness·less
harness-like
Har·ney US mountain
harp
harp·er
harp·ings (*or* ·ins) nautical
   term
har·poon
har·poon·er
har·poon-like
harp·si·chord
harp·si·chord·ist
har·py (*plural* ·pies)
har·que·bus *variant spelling
   of* arquebus

Har·rar Ethiopian city
(harrass) *incorrect spelling of*
   harass
har·ri·dan
har·ri·er
Har·ris Scottish island
Har·ris·burg US city
Har·ro·gate Yorkshire town
Har·ro·vian
Har·row London borough
har·row tool
har·row·er
har·row·ing
har·row·ment
har·rumph
har·ry (·ries, ·ry·ing, ·ried)
harsh
harsh·ly
harsh·ness
hars·let *variant spelling of*
   haslet
hart (*plural* hart *or* harts)
har·tal
har·te·beest (*or* hart·beest)
   antelope
Hart·ford US port
Har·tle·pool
harts·horn
harum-scarum
ha·rus·pex (*plural*
   ha·rus·pi·ces) Roman
   priest
ha·rus·pi·cal
ha·rus·pi·cy
Har·vard
har·vest
har·vest·er
har·vest·ing
har·vest·less
harvest·man (*plural* ·men)
Har·wich Essex port
Har·ya·na Indian state
Harz German mountain
   range
has
Ha·sa Saudi Arabian
   province
has-been
hash
Hash·e·mite descendant of
   Mohammed
hash·ish
Ha·sid·ic (*or* Has·sid·ic)
Hasi·dim (*or* Has·si·dim)
   Jewish sect

Has·id·ism (*or* Has·sid·ism)
hask *Dialect* cough
has·let (*or* hars·) meat loaf
hasn't
hasp
has·sle
has·sock kneeling cushion;
   compare cassock
hast
has·tate botany term
haste
haste·ful
haste·ful·ly
has·ten
has·ten·er
hasti·ly
hasti·ness
Hast·ings
has·ty (·ti·er, ·ti·est)
hat (hat·ting, hat·ted)
hat·able *variant spelling of*
   hateable
hat·band
hat-box
hatch
hatch·able
hatch·back
hatch·el (·el·ling, ·elled;
   US ·el·ing, ·eled) comb
   flax
hatch·el·ler (US ·el·er)
hatch·er
hatch·ery (*plural* ·eries)
hatch·et
hatchet-like
hatch·ing
hatch·ment heraldic term
hatch·way
hate
hate·able (*or* hat·)
hate·ful
hate·ful·ly
hate·ful·ness
hater
Hat·field Hertfordshire
   town
hath
Hath·or Egyptian goddess
Ha·thor·ic
hat·less
hat·like
hat·pin
ha·tred
hat·ter
Hat·ter·as US cape

hau·ber·geon *variant spelling of* habergeon
hau·berk coat of mail
haugh *Dialect* flat valley base
haugh·ti·ly
haugh·ti·ness
haugh·ty (·ti·er, ·ti·est)
haul
haul·age
haul·er (*or* ·ier)
haulm (*or* halm) plant stem
haunch
haunched
haunt
haunt·ed
haunt·er
haunt·ing
Hau·ra·ki New Zealand gulf
Hau·sa (*plural* ·sas *or* ·sa) African people
haus·frau
haus·tel·late
haus·tel·lum (*plural* ·la) entomology term
haus·to·ri·al
haus·to·rium (*plural* ·ria) plant organ
haut·boy strawberry
haute cou·ture
haute cui·sine
hau·teur
Ha·vana Cuban capital
Hav·ant Hampshire town
have (has, hav·ing, had)
have·lock protective cap cover
ha·ven
ha·ven·less
have-not (*noun*)
haven't
ha·ver dither
Ha·ver·ing London borough
hav·er·sack
Ha·ver·sian anatomy term
hav·er·sine maths term
hav·il·dar Indian NCO
hav·ing
hav·oc (·ock·ing, ·ocked)
hav·ock·er
haw
Ha·waii
Ha·wai·ian
Hawes English lake
haw·finch

Haw·ick Scottish town
hawk
hawk·bit plant
hawk·er
hawk·ing
hawk·ish
hawk·like
hawks·bill turtle
hawk·weed
Ha·worth Yorkshire village
hawse nautical term
hawse·hole
hawse·pipe
haws·er
haw·thorn
hay
hay·box
hay·cock pile of hay
hay·fork
hay·maker
hay·making
hay·mow
hay·rack
hay·rick
hay·seed
hay·stack
hay·ward *Obsolete* parish officer
hay·wire
haz·ard
haz·ard·able
haz·ard-free
haz·ard·ous
haz·ard·ous·ness
haze
ha·zel
hazel·hen
hazel·nut
haz·er nautical term
ha·zi·ly
ha·zi·ness
hazy (ha·zi·er, ha·zi·est)
he
head
head·ache
head·achy
head·band
head·board
head·cheese US brawn
head·dress
head·ed
head·er
head·fast mooring rope
head·first
head·gear

head-hunt
head-hunter
head-hunting
headi·ly
headi·ness
head·ing
head·less
head·light (*or* ·lamp)
head·like
head·line
head·lin·er
head·lock
head·long
head·man (*plural* ·men)
head·master (*fem* ·mistress)
head·master·ship (*fem* ·mistress·)
head·most
head-on
head·phones
head·piece
head·pin
head·quarters
head·race
head·rail billiards term
head·reach nautical term
head·rest
head·room
head·sail
head·scarf (*plural* ·scarves)
head·set
head·ship
head·shrinker
heads·man (*plural* ·men) executioner
head·spring
head·square
head·stall
head·stand
head·stock part of machine tool
head·stone
head·stream
head·strong
head·strong·ness
head·wards (*or esp. US* ·ward)
head·waters
head·way
head·wind
head·word
head·work
head·worker
heady (head·ier, head·iest)
heal cure; *compare* heel

heal·able
heal·er
heal·ing·ly
health
health·ful
health·ful·ly
health·ful·ness
healthi·ly
healthi·ness
healthy (health·ier,
 health·iest)
heap
heap·er
heap·ing
hear (hear·ing, heard)
hear·able
hear·er
heark·en (*US also* hark·)
heark·en·er
hear·say
hearse
heart
heart·ache
heart·beat
heart·break
heart·breaker
heart·breaking
heart·breaking·ly
heart·broken
heart·broken·ly
heart·broken·ness
heart·burn
heart·en
heart·en·ing·ly
heart·felt
hearth
hearth·stone
hearti·ly
hearti·ness
heart·land
heart·less
heart·less·ness
heart·rending
hearts·ease wild pansy
heart·sick
heart·sickness
heart·some
heart·some·ly
heart·some·ness
heart·strings
heart·wood
heart·worm
hearty (heart·ier,
 hearti·est)
heat

heat·ed
heat·ed·ly
heat·ed·ness
heat·er
heath
heath·berry (*plural* ·berries)
hea·then (*plural* ·thens *or*
 ·then)
hea·then·dom
hea·then·ish
hea·then·ish·ness
hea·then·ism
hea·then·ize
hea·then·ness
heath·er
heath·ered
heath·ery
heath·fowl
heath·like
heathy
heat·ing
heat·less
heat·stroke
heaume medieval helmet
heave (heav·ing, heaved *or*
 hove)
heav·en
heav·en·li·ness
heav·en·ly
heav·en·ward (*adj*)
heav·en·wards (*adv*)
heav·er
heaves horse disease
heavi·ly
heavi·ness
heavy (*adj* heavi·er,
 heavi·est; *noun, plural*
 heavies)
heavy-handed
heavy-handed·ly
heavy-handed·ness
heavy·weight
heb·do·mad *Obsolete* seven
heb·doma·dal (*or* ·da·ry)
 weekly
heb·doma·dal·ly
Hebe Greek goddess
he·be·phre·nia
 schizophrenia
he·be·phren·ic
heb·etate blunt
heb·eta·tion
he·bet·ic of puberty
heb·e·tude lethargy
heb·etu·di·nous

He·bra·ic (*or* ·brai·cal)
He·bra·i·cal·ly
He·bra·ism
He·bra·ist
He·bra·is·tic
He·bra·is·ti·cal·ly
He·bra·i·za·tion
He·bra·ize
He·bra·iz·er
He·brew
Heb·ri·dean
Heb·ri·des
Heb·ron Jordanian city
Heca·te (*or* Heka·te) Greek
 goddess
heca·tomb sacrifice
heck
heck·el·phone oboe
heck·le
heck·ler
hec·tare
hec·tic
hec·ti·cal·ly
hec·to·coty·lus zoology
 term
hec·to·gram
hec·to·graph copying
 process
hec·to·graph·ic
hec·to·graphi·cal·ly
hec·tog·ra·phy
hec·tor
Hec·u·ba mythological
 character
he'd
hed·dle part of loom
hedge
hedge·hog
hedge·hop (·hop·ping,
 ·hopped)
hedge·hop·per
hedg·er
hedge·row
hedgy
He·djaz Saudi Arabian
 region
he·don·ics branch of
 psychology
he·don·ism
he·don·ist
heebie-jeebies
heed
heed·er
heed·ful

heed·ful·ly
heed·ful·ness
heed·less
heed·less·ly
heed·less·ness
hee·haw
heel part of foot; *compare* heal
heel·ball
heeled
heel·er
heel·less
heel·piece
heel·post
heel·tap
Heer·len Dutch city
heft
heft·er
hefti·ly
hefti·ness
hefty (hefti·er, hefti·est)
He·geli·an
He·geli·an·ism school of philosophy
heg·emon·ic
he·gemo·ny
Hegi·ra (*or* Heji·ra) flight of Mohammed
he·gu·men (*or* ·menos) Eastern Church leader
heh exclamation
Hei·del·berg German city
Hei·duc *variant spelling of* Haiduk
heif·er
heigh-ho
height tallness; *compare* hight
height·en
height·en·er
Hei·lung·kiang Chinese province
Heim·dall (*or* Heim·dal, Heim·dallr) Norse god
hei·nous
hei·nous·ness
heir
heir·dom
heir·ess
heir·less
heir·loom
heir·ship
heist
heist·er
hei·ti·ki Maori ornament

He·jaz (*or* Hi·jaz) Saudi Arabian province
Heji·ra *variant spelling of* Hegira
Heka·te *variant spelling of* Hecate
Hek·la Icelandic volcano
Hel (*or* Hela) Norse goddess
held
Hel·ena US city
Hel·go·land *variant spelling of* Heligoland
he·li·a·cal astronomy term; *compare* helical
he·li·an·thus (*plural* ·thuses) sunflower
heli·cal spiral; *compare* heliacal
heli·cal·ly
heli·ces *plural of* helix
heli·chrysum plant
heli·cline spiral ramp
heli·co·graph
heli·coid
heli·coi·dal·ly
heli·con tuba
Heli·con Greek mountain
heli·cop·ter
Heli·go·land (*or* Hel·go·) North Sea island
helio·cen·tric
helio·cen·tri·cal·ly
helio·cen·tric·i·ty (*or* helio·cen·tri·cism)
Helio·chrome (*Trademark*)
helio·chro·mic
helio·graph
he·li·og·ra·pher
helio·graph·ic
heliog·ra·phy
helio·gra·vure printing term
he·li·ola·ter
he·li·ola·trous
he·li·ola·try sun worship
he·lio·lith·ic
he·li·om·eter telescope
helio·met·ric
helio·met·ri·cal·ly
he·li·om·etry
He·li·opo·lis ancient Egyptian city
Helios sun god
helio·stat
helio·stat·ic

helio·tac·tic
helio·tax·is biology term
helio·thera·py
helio·trope plant
helio·trop·ic growing towards sunlight
helio·trop·i·cal·ly
he·li·ot·ro·pism
helio·type printing process
helio·typ·ic
helio·zo·an biology term
heli·port
he·lium chemical element
he·lix (*plural* heli·ces *or* he·lixes)
hell
he'll he will; he shall
Hel·ladic archaeology term
Hel·las ancient Greece
hell·bender
hell·bent
hell·box
hell·cat
hell-diver bird
Hel·le mythological character
hel·le·bore plant
hel·le·bor·ine orchid
Hel·len legendary king
Hel·lene (*or* Hel·le·nian) Greek
Hel·len·ic
Hel·leni·cal·ly
Hel·len·ism
Hel·len·ist
Hel·len·is·tic
Hel·len·is·ti·cal·ly
Hel·leni·za·tion (*or* ·sa·tion)
Hel·len·ize (*or* ·ise)
Hel·len·iz·er (*or* ·is·er)
hel·ler (*plural* ·ler) German coin
hell·ery wild behaviour
Hel·les Turkish cape
Hel·les·pont Dardanelles
hell·fire
hell·gram·mite insect larva
hell·hole
hell·hound
hel·lion
hell·ish
hell·ish·ness

hel·lo (or hal·lo, hul·lo;
  plural ·los)
helm
Hel·mand Asian river
hel·met
hel·met·ed
helmet-like
hel·minth parasitic worm
hel·min·thia·sis
hel·min·thic
hel·min·thoid
hel·min·tho·logi·cal
hel·min·tholo·gist
hel·min·thol·ogy
helm·less
helms·man (plural ·men)
Helot ancient Greek class
helot serf
hel·ot·ism
hel·ot·ry
help
help·able
help·er
help·ful
help·ful·ly
help·ful·ness
help·ing
help·less
help·less·ness
help·mate
help·meet Archaic helpmate
Hel·sin·ki
helter-skelter
helve tool handle
Hel·vel·lyn English
  mountain
Hel·ve·tia Switzerland
Hel·ve·tian
Hel·vet·ic
Hel·vetii Celtic tribe
hem (hem·ming, hemmed)
hema· (or hemato·) US
  spelling of words beginning
  with haemo· or
  haemato·
he·mal US spelling of
  haemal
he·man (plural -men)
heme US spelling of haem
Hem·el Hemp·stead
hem·ely·tron (or hemi·;
  plural ·tra) zoology term
hem·era·lo·pia day
  blindness
hem·era·lop·ic

hemi·al·gia pain on one
  side
hemi·an·ops·ia sight defect
he·mic US spelling of haemic
hemi·cel·lu·lose
hemi·chor·date zoology
  term
hemi·cy·cle
hemi·cy·clic
hemi·demi·semi·qua·ver
hemi·ely·tron variant
  spelling of hemelytron
hemi·he·dral
  crystallography term
hemi·hy·drate
hemi·hy·drat·ed
hemi·mor·phic
  crystallography term
hemi·mor·phism (or ·phy)
hemi·mor·phite mineral
he·min US spelling of
  haemin
hemio·la musical term
hemi·ol·ic
hemi·para·site
hemi·plegia
hemi·ple·gic
hemi·pode (or ·pod) bird
he·mip·ter·an (or ·on)
  insect
he·mip·ter·ous
hemi·sphere
hemi·spher·ic (or
  ·spheri·cal)
hemi·spher·oid
hemi·spher·oi·dal
hemi·stich half line of verse
hemi·ter·pene chemistry
  term
hemi·trope chemistry term
hemi·trop·ic
hemi·tro·pism (or
  he·mit·ro·py)
hem·line
hem·lock
hem·mer
hemo· US spelling of words
  beginning with haemo·
hemp
hemp·en
hem·stitch
hem·stitch·er
hen
hen·bane plant
hen·bit plant

hence
hence·forth
hence·forward
hench·man (plural ·men)
hen·coop
hen·deca·gon
hen·de·cago·nal
hen·deca·he·dron
hen·deca·syl·lab·ic
hen·deca·syl·la·ble
hen·dia·dys rhetorical
  device
hen·equen (or hen·equin,
  heni·quen) fibre
henge archaeology term
Heng-yang Chinese city
hen·house
Hen·ley Oxfordshire town
hen·na
hen·nery (plural ·neries)
  poultry house
heno·theism worship of
  one deity
heno·theist
heno·theis·tic
hen·peck
hen·pecked
hen·ry (plural ·ry, ·ries, or
  ·rys) unit
hent Archaic seize
hep
hepa·rin biochemical
  substance
he·pat·ic of liver
he·pati·ca plant
hepa·ti·tis
hep·cat
Hephaestus (or Hephaistos)
  Greek god
hep·tad
hep·ta·deca·no·ic acid
hep·ta·gon
hep·tago·nal
hep·ta·he·dral
hep·ta·he·dron
hep·tam·er·ous
hep·tam·eter type of verse
  line
hep·ta·met·ri·cal
hep·tane chemical
  compound
hep·tan·gu·lar
hep·tarch
hep·tar·chic
hep·tar·chy (plural ·chies)

hep·ta·stich
Hep·ta·teuch Old
 Testament books
hep·tava·lent
hep·tose
her
Hera (or Here) Greek
 goddess
Hera·clea ancient Greek
 colony
Hera·clean
Heracles (or Herakles)
 variants of Hercules
Hera·cli·dan
Hera·clid (or ·klid)
 descendant of Hercules
her·ald
he·ral·dic
he·ral·di·cal·ly
her·ald·ist
her·ald·ry
He·rat Afghan city
herb
her·ba·ceous
herb·age
herb·al
herb·al·ist
her·bar·ial
her·bar·ium (plural ·iums or
 ·ia)
her·bi·cid·al
herbi·cide
her·bi·vore
her·bivo·rous
her·bivo·rous·ness
herb·like
herby (herbi·er, herbi·est)
Her·cego·vi·na (or ·zego·)
 region of Bosnia-
 Hercegovina
Her·cu·la·neum ancient
 Italian city
her·cu·lean
Her·cu·les constellation
Hercules (or Heracles,
 Herakles) mythological
 hero
Her·cyn·ian geology term
herd
herd·er
her·dic US small carriage
herds·man (plural ·men)
Herd·wick sheep
here
here·abouts

here·after
here·at
here·by
he·redes plural of heres
he·redi·tabil·ity
he·redi·table
he·redi·tably
her·edita·ment legal term
he·redi·tari·an·ism
 psychology term
he·redi·tari·ly
he·redi·tari·ness
he·redi·tary
he·redi·tist
he·red·ity (plural ·ities)
Her·eford
here·in
here·in·after
here·in·before
here·into
here·of
here·on
He·rero (plural ·rero or
 ·reros) African people
he·res (or hae·; plural
 ·redes) heir
he·resi·arch heretical leader
her·esy (plural ·esies)
her·etic
he·reti·cal
he·reti·cal·ly
here·to
here·to·fore
here·under
here·unto
here·upon
here·with
heri·ot medieval death duty
her·it·abil·ity
her·it·able
her·it·ably
her·it·age
heri·tor (fem ·tress)
herl (or harl) angling term
herm
her·maph·ro·dite
her·maph·ro·dit·ic
her·maph·ro·diti·cal·ly
her·maph·ro·dit·ism
Hermaphroditus
 mythological character
her·meneu·tic
her·meneu·ti·cal·ly
her·meneu·tics
her·meneu·tist

Hermes Greek god
Her·mes asteroid
her·met·ic air-tight; compare
 hermitic
her·meti·cal·ly
her·mit
her·mit·age
Her·mit·ian maths term
her·mit·ic hermit-like;
 compare hermetic
her·miti·cal·ly
her·mit·like
Her·mon mountain
Her·mou·po·lis Greek port
hern Dialect heron
her·nia
her·nial
her·ni·at·ed
her·ni·or·rha·phy (plural
 ·phies) hernia surgery
Hero mythological character
hero (plural heroes)
Herodias mother of Salome
he·ro·ic
he·roi·cal·ly
he·ro·ics
hero·in drug
hero·ine heroic female
hero·ism
her·on
her·on·ry (plural ·ries)
her·pes
her·pes sim·plex
her·pes zos·ter
her·pet·ic
her·pe·to·log·ic (or
 ·logi·cal)
her·pe·to·logi·cal·ly
her·pe·tolo·gist
her·pe·tol·ogy study of
 reptiles
Herr (plural Her·ren)
 German title of address
her·ring (plural ·rings or
 ·ring)
herring·bone
hers of her
her·self
Herst·mon·ceux (or Hurst·)
Hert·ford
Hert·ford·shire
hertz (plural hertz) unit
Hertz·ian physics term
Hertzsprung-Russell
 diagram

Her·zego·vi·na *variant
  spelling of* **Hercegovina**
he's he is; he has
Hesi·od·ic of Hesiod
Hesione mythological
  princess
hesi·tan·cy
hesi·tant
hesi·tant·ly
hesi·tate
hesi·tat·er
hesi·tat·ing·ly
hesi·ta·tion
hesi·ta·tive
Hes·per·ia western land
Hes·pe·rian
Hesperides mythological
  characters
Hes·per·id·ian (*or* ·ean)
hes·peri·din biochemical
  compound
hes·per·id·ium botany term
Hes·per·us evening star
Hesse German state
Hes·sian of Hesse
hes·sian fibre
hes·site mineral
hes·so·nite gemstone
hest behest
Hestia Greek goddess
Hesy·chast Greek Orthodox
  mystic
Hesy·chast·ic
het *Archaic* heated
he·tae·ra (*or* ·tai·; *plural*
  ·tae·rae *or* ·tai·rai) Greek
  prostitute
he·tae·ric (*or* ·tai·)
he·tae·rism (*or* ·tai·)
he·tae·rist (*or* ·tai·)
he·tae·ris·tic (*or* ·tai·)
hetero·cer·cal zoology term
hetero·chro·mat·ic
hetero·chro·ma·tin
hetero·chro·ma·tism
hetero·chro·mo·some
hetero·chro·mous
hetero·clite grammar term
hetero·clit·ic
hetero·cy·clic
hetero·dac·tyl ornithology
  term
hetero·dont zoology term
hetero·dox
hetero·doxy

hetero·dyne electronics
  term
het·er·oecious botany term
het·er·oecism
hetero·gam·ete
heteroga·mous
het·er·oga·my botany term
hetero·geneity
hetero·geneous of different
  parts; *compare*
  heterogenous
hetero·gen·esis
hetero·genet·ic
hetero·genetical·ly
hetero·gen·ous of different
  origin; *compare*
  heterogeneous
heter·ogeny
het·er·ogo·nous
heter·ogo·ny biology term
hetero·graft
hetero·graph·ic
het·er·og·ra·phy grammar
  term
het·er·ogy·nous
hetero·leci·thal
het·er·olo·gous
het·er·ol·ogy
het·er·oly·sis
hetero·lyt·ic
het·er·om·er·ous
hetero·mor·phic
hetero·mor·phism
het·er·ono·mous
het·er·ono·my
hetero·nym grammar term
het·er·ony·mous
Hetero·ousian Christian
  sect
het·er·opho·ny musical
  term
hetero·phyl·lous
hetero·phyl·ly
hetero·phyte
hetero·plas·tic
hetero·plas·ty (*plural* ·ties)
  surgical transplant
hetero·po·lar
hetero·po·larity
het·er·op·ter·ous zoology
  term
hetero·scedas·tic·ity
  statistics term
hetero·sex·ism
hetero·sex·ist

hetero·sex·ual
hetero·sexu·al·ity
hetero·sex·ual·ly
hetero·sis
het·er·os·po·rous
het·er·os·po·ry
hetero·sty·lous
hetero·sty·ly botany term
hetero·tac·tic
hetero·tax·is
hetero·thal·lic botany term
hetero·to·pia (*or*
  het·er·oto·py)
  displacement of body part
hetero·top·ic
hetero·troph·ic biology
  term
hetero·typ·ic (*or* ·typi·cal)
  biology term
hetero·zy·go·sis
hetero·zy·gote
hetero·zy·gous genetics
  term
heth (*or* **cheth**) Hebrew
  letter
het·man (*plural* ·men)
  Cossack leader
heu·land·ite mineral
heu·ris·tic
heu·ris·ti·cal·ly
hew (**hew·ing**, **hewed**,
  hewed *or* **hewn**) cut;
  compare **hue**
hew·er
hex *US* bewitch
hexa·chloro·cyclo·hex·ane
hexa·chloro·ethane
hexa·chloro·phene
hexa·chord musical term
hexa·co·sa·no·ic acid
hex·ad six
hexa·decane
hexa·deci·mal
hex·adic
hexa·em·er·ic
hexa·em·er·on (*or*
  ·hem·er·on) the Creation
hexa·gon
hex·ago·nal
hex·ag·o·nal·ly
hexa·gram
hexa·gram·moid
hexa·he·dral
hexa·he·dron
hexa·hy·drate

hexa·hy·drat·ed
hex·am·er·ism
hex·am·er·ous (or ·eral)
hex·am·eter
hexa·methylene·tetramine
hexa·met·ric
hex·ane
hex·an·gu·lar
hexa·no·ic acid
hexa·pla Old Testament edition
hexa·plar (or ·plar·ic)
hexa·pod insect
hexa·pod·ic
hex·apo·dy (plural ·dies) verse form
hexa·stich (or hex·as·ti·chon) six-line poem
hexa·stich·ic
hexa·style architecture term
Hexa·teuch Old Testament books
Hexa·teu·chal
hexa·va·lent
hex·one chemical compound
hexo·san biochemical compound
hex·ose sugar
hex·yl
hexyl·resor·cin·ol
hey exclamation
hey·day
Hey·duck variant spelling of Haiduk
Hey·sham Lancashire port
Hey·wood English town
Hezekiah biblical character
hi
Hia·leah US city
hia·tal
hia·tus (plural ·tuses or ·tus)
hi·ba·chi brazier
hi·ber·nacu·lum (or ·nac·le; plural ·ula or ·les)
hi·ber·nal
hi·ber·nate
hi·ber·na·tion
hi·ber·na·tor
Hi·ber·nia Ireland
Hi·ber·nian
Hi·ber·ni·an·ism
Hi·ber·ni·cism
hi·bis·cus

hic·cup (·cup·ing, ·cuped or ·cup·ping, ·cupped)
hick
hick·ey US gadget
hicko·ry (plural ·ries)
hid
hid·able
hi·dal·go (plural ·gos) Spanish nobleman
Hi·dal·go Mexican state
hid·den
hid·den·ite gemstone
hid·den·ness
hide (hid·ing, hid, hid·den or hid)
hide-and-seek
hide·away
hide·bound
hide·less
hid·eous
hid·eous·ly
hid·eous·ness (or hid·eos·ity)
hid·er
hid·ing
hi·dro·sis sweating
hi·drot·ic
hie (hie·ing or hy·ing, hied) hurry
hie·land Scot easily tricked
hi·emal of winter
hi·era·co·sphinx (plural ·sphinxes or ·sphin·ges)
hi·er·arch
hi·er·ar·chal
hi·er·ar·chi·cal
hi·er·ar·chi·cal·ly
hi·er·arch·ism
hi·er·ar·chy (plural ·chies)
hi·er·at·ic of priests
hi·er·ati·cal·ly
hi·er·oc·ra·cy (plural ·cies)
hi·ero·crat·ic
hi·ero·dule Greek slave
hi·ero·du·lic
hi·ero·glyph
hi·ero·glyph·ic
hi·ero·glyphi·cal·ly
hi·ero·glyph·ics
hi·ero·glyph·ist
hi·ero·gram sacred symbol
hi·ero·log·ic
hi·er·olo·gist
hi·er·ol·ogy (plural ·ogies) sacred literature

hi·ero·phant ancient Greek priest
hi·ero·phant·ic
hi·ero·phan·ti·cal·ly
hi·fa·lu·tin variant spelling of highfalutin
hi-fi
hig·gle
higgledy-piggle·dy
high
high·ball
high·bind·er US gangster
high·born
high·boy US tallboy
high·brow
high·chair
high·fa·lu·tin (or hi·)
high-flier (or -flyer)
high-flown
high-handed
high-handed·ly
high-handed·ness
high·jack less common spelling of hijack
high·jack·er less common spelling of hijacker
High·land of Scottish Highlands
high·land
high·land·er
High·lander
High·lands
high·life
high·light
high·ly
highly-strung
high-minded
high-minded·ness
high·ness high condition
High·ness title for royalty
high-rise
high·road
high-spirit·ed
high-spirit·ed·ness
hight Archaic named; compare height
high·tail
high-tech (or hi·)
High·veld South African region
high·way
highway·man (plural ·men)
High Wy·combe
hi·jack (or high·)
hi·jack·er (or high·)

Hi·jaz *variant spelling of* Hejaz

hike

hik·er

hi·lar anatomy term

hi·lari·ous

hi·lari·ous·ness

hi·lar·ity

hill

Hil·la Iraqi town

hill·bil·ly (*plural* ·lies)

hill·er

hill·fort

Hil·ling·don London borough

hill·ock

hill·ocked (*or* ·ocky)

hill·side

hilly (hilli·er, hilli·est)

hilt

hi·lum (*plural* ·la) botany term

hi·lus (*plural* ·li) anatomy term

Hil·ver·sum Dutch city

him

Hi·ma·chal Pra·desh Indian state

Hima·la·yan

Hima·la·yas

hi·mati·on (*plural* ·matia) Greek cloak

Hi·meji Japanese city

Hims *variant of* Homs

him·self

Him·yar·ite Arabian people

Him·yar·it·ic language group

hin Hebrew unit

Hi·na·ya·na Buddhism

Hi·na·ya·nist

Hi·na·ya·nis·tic

Hinck·ley English town

hind (*adj* hind·er, hind·most *or* hinder·most; *noun, plural* hinds *or* hind)

hind·brain

hin·der obstruct

hind·er at the rear

hin·der·er

hin·der·ing·ly

hind·gut

Hin·di language; *compare* Hindu

hind·most (*or* hinder·most)

Hin·doo *former spelling of* Hindu

Hin·doo·ism *former spelling of* Hinduism

hind·quarter

hin·drance

hind·sight

Hin·du (*plural* ·dus) people; *compare* Hindi

Hin·du·ism

Hin·du Kush Asian mountains

Hin·du·stan

Hin·du·sta·ni

hinge

hinge·like

hing·er

hin·ny (*noun, plural* ·nies; *verb* ·nies, ·ny·ing, ·nied)

hint

hint·er

hinter·land

hip

hip·bone

hip·less

hip·like

hip·parch ancient Greek cavalry commander

Hip·par·chus moon crater

hip·pe·as·trum plant

hipped

hip·pie (*or* ·py; *plural* ·pies)

hip·po (*plural* ·pos)

hippo·campal

hippo·campus (*plural* ·campi)

hip·po·cras wine

Hip·po·crat·ic of Hippocrates

Hip·po·crene ancient Greek spring

Hip·po·crenian

hippo·drome

hip·po·griff mythological monster

Hippolyta (*or* Hippolyte) Amazonian queen

Hippolytus son of Theseus

Hippomenes mythological character

hippo·pota·mus (*plural* ·muses *or* ·mi)

Hip·po Re·gius ancient African city

hip·py *variant spelling of* hippie

hip·sters trousers

hir·able (*or* hire·)

hi·ra·ga·na Japanese writing

Hi·ram biblical character

hir·cine lascivious

hire

hire·ling

hir·er

Hi·ro·shi·ma

hir·sute

hir·sute·ness

hiru·din anticoagulant

hi·run·dine of swallows

his

His·pania Iberia

His·pan·ic

His·pani·cism

His·pani·cist

His·pani·ci·za·tion (*or* ·sa·tion)

His·pani·cize (*or* ·cise)

His·panio·la West Indian island

his·pid bristly

his·pid·ity

hiss

hiss·er

hist

his·tami·nase enzyme

his·ta·mine

his·ta·min·ic

his·ti·dine amino acid

his·tio·cyte

his·tio·cyt·ic

his·to·chemi·cal

his·to·chem·is·try

his·to·gen plant tissue

his·to·gen·esis (*or* his·tog·eny)

his·to·genet·ic (*or* ·gen·ic)

his·to·geneti·cal·ly (*or* ·geni·cal·ly)

his·to·gram

his·toid

his·to·logi·cal (his·to·log·ic)

his·to·logi·cal·ly

his·tolo·gist

his·tol·ogy study of tissues

his·toly·sis

his·to·lyt·ic

his·to·lyti·cal·ly

his·tone protein

his·to·patho·logi·cal
his·to·pa·thol·ogy
his·to·plas·mo·sis
his·to·rian
his·tori·at·ed decorated
his·tor·ic
his·tori·cal
his·tori·cal·ly
his·tor·i·cal·ness
his·tori·cism
his·tori·cist
his·to·ric·ity
his·to·ri·og·ra·pher
his·to·rio·graph·ic
his·to·ri·og·ra·phy
his·to·ry (plural ·ries)
his·tri·on·ic (or ·oni·cal)
his·tri·oni·cal·ly
histrionics
hit (hit·ting, hit)
hitch
hitch·er
hitch·hike
hitch·hik·er
hi-tech variant spelling of
  high-tech
hith·er
hither·most
hither·to
Hit·ler·ism
hit·ter
Hit·tite
hive
hive·like
hives nettle rash
ho exclamation; compare
  hoe
ho·act·zin variant spelling of
  hoatzin
hoar
hoard store; compare horde
hoard·er
hoard·ing
hoar·frost
hoar·hound variant spelling
  of horehound
hoari·ly
hoari·ness
hoarse grating; compare
  horse
hoarse·ly
hoars·en
hoarse·ness
hoary (hoari·er, hoari·est)
hoatch·ing Scot infested

ho·at·zin (or ·act·) bird
hoax
hoax·er
hob (hob·bing, hobbed)
Ho·bart Tasmanian capital
Hobbes·ian
Hob·bism political
  philosophy
Hob·bist
hob·ble
hobble-dehoy
hob·bler
hob·by (plural ·bies)
hobby·horse
hob·byist
hob·goblin
hob·like
hob·nail
hob·nailed
hob·nob (·nob·bing,
  ·nobbed)
hobo (plural hobos or
  hoboes) vagrant
hobo·ism
Ho·bo·ken Belgian city
hobson-jobson folk
  etymology
Hoch·hei·mer wine
hock
hock·er
hock·ey
Hock·tide former festival
ho·cus (·cus·ing, cused, or
  ·cus·sing, ·cussed)
hocus-pocus (-pocusing,
  -pocused or -pocussing,
  -pocussed)
hod
hod·den coarse cloth
hod·din
Ho·dei·da Yemeni port
hodge·podge US
  hotchpotch
hod·man (plural ·men)
ho·dom·eter variant of
  odometer
hodo·scope
hoe (hoe·ing, hoed)
  gardening tool; compare ho
hoe·down dance
Hoek van Hol·land Hook of
  Holland
hoe·like
hoer
Ho·fei Chinese city

hog (hog·ging, hogged)
ho·gan American Indian
  dwelling
Ho·garth·ian
hog·back narrow ridge
hog·fish plural ·fish or
  ·fishes
hogged
hog·ger
hog·ging
hog·gish
hog·gish·ly
hog·gish·ness
hog·like
Hog·ma·nay
hog·nose snake
hog·nut
hogs·head
hog·tie (·ty·ing, ·tied) US
  tie limbs
hog·wash
hog·weed
hoick
hoi·den variant spelling of
  hoyden
hoi pol·loi
hoist
hoist·er
hoity-toity
hoke overact
hokey cokey song and
  dance
ho·key-pokey hocus-pocus
Hok·kai·do Japanese island
hok·ku variant spelling of
  haiku
ho·kum
Hol·arc·tic zoogeographical
  term
hold (hold·ing, held)
hold·able
hold·all
hold·er
hold·er·ship
hold·fast
hold·ing
hole
holey
holi·day
ho·li·ly
Ho·li·ness pope's title
ho·li·ness
ho·lism
ho·lis·tic
ho·lis·ti·cal·ly

hol·la *variant of* hollo
hol·land cloth
Hol·land
hol·lan·daise sauce
Hol·land·er
Hol·lands Dutch gin
hol·ler *Slang* shout
hol·lo (*or* ·la; *plural* ·los *or*
·las) shout
hol·low
hol·low·ly
hol·low·ness
hol·ly (*plural* ·lies)
hol·ly·hock
Hol·ly·wood
holm *Dialect* river island
hol·mic
hol·mium chemical
element
holo·blas·tic
holo·blas·ti·cal·ly
holo·caust
hol·o·caus·tal (*or* ·caus·tic)
Holo·cene geological period
holo·crine physiology term
holo·en·zyme
holo·gram handwritten
document
holo·graph
three-dimensional image
holo·graph·ic
hol·o·graphi·cal·ly
ho·log·ra·phy
holo·he·dral
holo·he·drism
holo·mor·phic
holo·phras·tic
holo·phyte
holo·phyt·ic
holo·plank·ton
holo·thu·rian zoology term
holo·type
holo·typ·ic
holo·zo·ic
hol·pen *Archaic* helped
Hol·stein German region;
cattle
hol·ster
hol·stered
holt *Archaic* woodland
holus-bolus *Slang* all at once
holy (*adj* ho·li·er, ho·li·est;
noun, plural holies)
Holy·head
ho·ly·stone

holy·tide
hom (*or* homa) sacred plant
hom·age
hom·bre *US* man
hom·burg hat
home
home·bred
home·coming
home·land
home·less
home·less·ness
home·like
home·li·ness
home·ly (·li·er, ·li·est)
unpretentious; *US* ugly;
compare homy
home·mak·ing
homeo·mor·phic (*or*
homoeo·)
homeo·mor·phism (*or*
homoeo·)
homeo·path·ic (*or*
homoeo·)
homeo·pathi·cal·ly (*or*
homoeo·)
homeopa·thist (*or*
homoepa·)
homeopa·thy (*or*
homoeopa·)
homeo·sta·sis (*or*
homoeo·)
homeo·stat·ic (*or*
homoeo·)
homeo·typ·ic (*or* ·typi·cal,
homoeo·) biology term
home·own·er
home·own·er·ship
hom·er
Ho·merian
Ho·mer·ic
Ho·meri·cal·ly
home·sick
home·sick·ness
home·spun
home·stead
home·stead·er
home·ward (*adj*)
home·wards (*adv*)
home·work
homey *variant spelling of*
homy
homey·ness *variant spelling*
of hominess
homi·ci·dal
homi·ci·dal·ly

homi·cide
homi·let·ic (*or*
homi·leti·cal*)
homi·leti·cal·ly
homi·let·ics art of
preaching sermons
homi·list
homi·ly (*plural* ·lies)
homi·ness (*or* homey·ness)
hom·ing
homi·nid
homi·noid
homi·ny *US* ground maize
homo (*plural* homos) *Slang*
homosexual
homo·cen·tric
homo·cen·tri·cal·ly
homo·cer·cal zoology term
homo·chro·mat·ic
homo·chro·ma·tism
homo·chro·mous
homo·cy·clic
homo·dont
homoeo· *variant spelling of*
words beginning homeo·
homo·erotic
homo·eroti·cism
homo·ero·tism
ho·moga·mous
ho·moga·my botany term
ho·mog·enate
homo·genei·ty
homo·geneous uniform;
compare homogenous
homo·geneous·ness
ho·mog·eni·za·tion (*or*
·sa·tion)
ho·mog·enize·(*or* ·enise)
ho·mog·eniz·er (*or* ·enis·er)
ho·mog·enous similar
through common
ancestry; *compare*
homogeneous
ho·mog·eny
ho·mogo·nous
ho·mog·ony botany term
homo·graft
homo·graph
homo·graph·ic
ho·moio·ther·mic
warm-blooded
ho·moio·ther·my
Ho·moi·ou·sian
Ho·moi·ou·si·an·ism
Christian sect

ho·mo·log *US variant spelling*
of homologue
ho·mo·lo·gate ratify
ho·mo·lo·ga·tion
ho·mo·logi·cal homologous
ho·mo·logi·cal·ly
ho·mo·lo·gize (*or* ·gise)
ho·mo·lo·giz·er (*or* ·gis·er)
ho·mo·lo·gous
ho·mo·lo·graph·ic
ho·mo·logue (*US also* ·log)
ho·mol·ogy (*plural* ·ogies)
ho·mo·lo·sine cartography
term
ho·moly·sis
homo·lyt·ic
homo·mor·phic (*or* ·phous)
homo·mor·phism
homo·nym
homo·nym·ic
homo·nym·ity
Homo·ou·sian
Homo·ou·si·an·ism
Christian sect
homo·phile
homo·phone
homo·phon·ic
homo·phoni·cal·ly
ho·mopho·nous
ho·mopho·ny linguistics
term
homo·phyl·lic
ho·mophy·ly biology term
homo·plas·tic
homo·plas·ti·cal·ly
homo·plas·ty
homo·po·lar chemistry
term
homo·po·lar·ity
ho·mop·ter·ous
entomology term
ho·mor·gan·ic linguistics
term
Homo sa·pi·ens
homo·scedas·tic·ity
statistics term
homo·sex·ual
homo·sex·ual·ity
homo·sex·ual·ly
ho·mos·po·rous botany
term
ho·mos·po·ry
homo·taxi·al·ly
homo·tax·ic
homo·tax·is

homo·thal·lic
homo·thal·lism botany
term
homo·zy·go·sis
homo·zy·gote
homo·zy·got·ic
homo·zy·gous genetics
term
Homs (*or* Hims, Hums)
Syrian city
ho·mun·cu·lar
ho·mun·cu·lus (*plural* ·li)
miniature man
homy (*or* homey; homi·er,
homi·est) cosy; *compare*
homely
ho·nan fabric
Honda (*Trademark*)
Hon·do *variant of* Honshu
Hon·du·ran
Hon·du·ras
hone
hon·est
hon·est·ly
hon·est·ness
hon·es·ty (*plural* ·ties)
hone·wort plant
hon·ey
honey·bee
honey·bunch
honey·comb
honey·dew
hon·ey·dewed
honey-eater bird
hon·eyed (*or* ·ied)
hon·eyed·ly (*or* ·ied·)
honey-like
honey·moon
honey·moon·er
honey·sucker bird
honey·suckle
hong Chinese factory
Hong Kong
Ho·nia·ra capital of
Solomon Islands
hon·ied *variant spelling of*
honeyed
Honi·ton lace
honk
honk·er
honky (*plural* honkies) *US*
slang white man
honky-tonk
Hono·lu·lu
hon·or *US spelling of* honour

hono·rar·ium (*plural*
·rar·iums *or* ·raria)
hon·or·ary
hon·or·if·ic
hon·or·ifi·cal·ly
hon·our (*US* ·or)
Hon·our·able title of respect
hon·our·able (*US* ·or·)
hon·our·able·ness (*US* ·or·)
hon·our·ably (*US* ·or·)
hon·our·er (*US* ·or·)
hon·our·less (*US* ·or·)
Hon·shu (*or* Hon·do)
hooch
hood
hood·ed
hoodie crow
hood·less
hood·like
hood·lum
hood·lum·ism
hoo·doo (*plural* ·doos)
hoo·doo·ism
hood·wink
hood·wink·er
hoo·ey
hoof (*plural* hoofs *or*
hooves)
hoof·bound veterinary
term
hoofed
hoof·er
hoof·less
hoof·like
Hoogh·ly Indian river
hoo-ha
hook
hook·ah oriental pipe
hooked
hook·ed·ness
hook·er
hook·less
hook·like
hook·nose
hook·nosed
hook·worm
hooky (*or* hookey)
hoo·li·gan
hoo·li·gan·ism
hoop
hooped
hoop·er
hoop·la
hoop·like
hoo·poe bird

hoo·rah (or ·ray) variants of
hurrah
hoose·gow US jail
hoot
hoot·en·an·ny (or
hoot·nan·ny; plural ·nies)
US folksinging
hoot·er
Hoo·ver (Trademark)
hoo·ver (verb)
hooves
hop (hop·ping, hopped)
hope
hope·ful
hope·ful·ly
hope·ful·ness
Ho·peh Chinese province
hope·less
hope·less·ly
hope·less·ness
hop·er
hop·head Slang drug addict
Hopi (plural Hopis or Hopi)
American Indian
hop·lite Greek soldier
hop·lit·ic
hop·lol·ogist
hop·lol·ogy study of
weapons
hop·per
hop·ping
hop·ple hobble
hop·pler
Hop·pus foot unit
hop·sack
hop·scotch
hora dance
Horae Roman goddesses
ho·ral hourly
ho·ra·ry Archaic hourly
Ho·ra·tian of the poet
Horace
Horatius legendary Roman
hero
horde mob; compare hoard
hor·dein protein
Ho·reb biblical mountain
hore·hound (or hoar·) plant
ho·ri·zon
ho·ri·zon·less
hori·zon·tal
hori·zon·tal·ly
hori·zon·tal·ness
hor·me psychology term
hor·mic

hor·mo·nal
hor·mone
Hor·muz (or Or·muz)
Iranian island
horn
horn·beam
horn·bill
horn·blende mineral
horn·blen·dic
horn·book
horned
horn·ed·ness
hor·net
horn·fels rock
horni·ly
horni·ness
horn·less
horn·like
horn·pipe
horn-rimmed
horn·stone
horns·wog·gle Slang cheat
horn·tail insect
horn·wort plant
horny (horni·er, horni·est)
horo·loge timepiece
horo·log·ic
ho·rol·o·gist (or
ho·rolo·ger)
horo·lo·gium (plural ·gia)
clock tower
ho·rol·ogy
horo·scope
horo·scop·ic
ho·ros·co·py (plural ·pies)
hor·ren·dous
hor·ri·ble
hor·ri·ble·ness
hor·ri·bly
hor·rid
hor·rid·ness
hor·rif·ic
hor·rifi·cal·ly
hor·ri·fi·ca·tion
hor·ri·fy (·fies, ·fy·ing,
·fied)
hor·ri·fy·ing·ly
hor·ripi·la·tion gooseflesh
hor·ror
horror-stricken (or -struck)
hors de com·bat French
injured
hors d'oeu·vre (plural hors
d'oeu·vre or hors
d'oeu·vres)

horse animal; compare
hoarse
horse·back
horse·box
horse·flesh
horse·fly (plural ·flies)
horse·hair
horse·hide
horse·leech
horse·less
horse·like
horse·man (plural ·men)
horse·man·ship
horse·mint
horse·play
horse·power (plural
horse·power) unit
horse·radish
horse·shoe (·shoe·ing,
·shoed)
horse·tail plant
horse·weed
horse·whip (·whip·ping,
·whipped)
horse·whip·per
horse·woman (plural
·women)
horsi·ly
horsi·ness
horst ridge
horsy (or horsey; horsi·er,
horsi·est)
hor·ta·to·ri·ly
hor·ta·tory (or ·tive) urging
hor·ti·cul·tur·al
hor·ti·cul·tur·al·ly
hor·ti·cul·ture
hor·ti·cul·tur·ist
hor·tus sic·cus collection of
dried plants
Horus Egyptian god
ho·san·na
hose
Hosea biblical character
ho·sier
ho·siery
hos·pice
hos·pi·table
hos·pi·table·ness
hos·pi·tably
hos·pi·tal
hos·pi·tal·ity
hos·pi·tali·za·tion (or
·sa·tion)
hos·pi·tal·ize (or ·ise)

Hos·pi·tal·ler religious
   knight
hos·pi·tal·ler (US ·tal·er)
   hospital worker
hos·pit·ium (plural ·ia)
   travellers' refuge
hos·po·dar Ottoman ruler
host
hos·ta plant
hos·tage
hos·tel
hos·tel·ler (US ·tel·er)
hos·tel·ling (US ·tel·ing)
hos·tel·ry (plural ·ries)
host·ess
hos·tile
hos·tile·ly
hos·til·ity (plural ·ities)
host·ler variant of ostler
hot (adj hot·ter, hot·test;
   verb hot·ting, hot·ted)
hot·bed
hot-blooded
hot-blooded·ness
hotch·pot legal term
hotch·potch (US
   hodge·podge)
ho·tel
ho·tel·ier
hot·foot
hot·head
hot-headed
hot-headed·ly
hot-headed·ness
hot·house
Ho·tien (or Ho-t'ien,
   Kho·tan) Chinese oasis
hot·ly
hot·ness
hot·plate
hot·pot
hot·spur impetuous person
Hot·ten·tot (plural ·tot or
   ·tots)
hot·tish
Hou·dan fowl
hough hock
Houghton-le-Spring
   Tyneside town
hou·mous (or ·mus) variant
   of hummus
hound
hound·er
Houns·low
hour

hour·glass
hou·ri (plural ·ris) Muslim
   nymph
hour·ly
house
house·boat
house·bound
house·boy
house·break·er
house·break·ing
house·carl medieval servant
house·coat
house·fath·er
house·fly (plural ·flies)
house·hold
house·holder
house·holder·ship
house·keeper
house·keeping
hou·sel Archaic Eucharist
house·leek
house·less
house·line nautical term
house·maid
house·man (plural ·men)
house·master
house·mistress
house·moth·er
house-proud
house·room
house·top
house·wife (plural ·wives)
house·wife·li·ness
house·wife·ly
house·wif·ery
house·work
house·worker
housey-housey
hous·ing
Hou·ston Texan port
hous·to·nia plant
hout·ing fish
hove
Hove Sussex town
hov·el (·el·ling, ·elled; US
   ·el·ing, ·eled)
hov·er
hover·craft
hov·er·er
hov·er·ing·ly
hover·port
hover·train
how
how·be·it
how·dah seat on elephant

how·dy US hello
howe'er
how·ever
howf Scot public house
how·itz·er
howl
How·land Pacific island
howl·er
how·let owl
howl·ing
How·rah Indian city
how·so·ever
how·tow·die Scottish
   chicken dish
hoy
hoya plant
hoy·den (or hoi·)
hoy·den·ish (or hoi·)
hoy·den·ish·ness (or hoi·)
Hoy·lake English town
Hsi variant spelling of Si
Hsian variant spelling of Sian
Hsiang variant spelling of
   Siang
Hsin-hai-lien variant spelling
   of Sinhailien
Hsi·ning variant spelling of
   Sining
Hsü-chou variant spelling of
   Süchow
Huai-nan Chinese city
Huang Hai variant spelling of
   Hwang Hai
Huang Ho variant spelling of
   Hwang Ho
hub
hubble-bubble
hub·bub
hub·by (plural ·bies)
hub·cap
Hub·li Indian city
hu·bris (or hy·bris)
hu·bris·tic
hucka·back fabric
huck·le
huckle·berry (plural
   ·berries)
huck·le·bone Archaic
   anklebone
huck·ster
huck·ster·ism
Hud·ders·field
hud·dle
hud·dler
hu·di·bras·tic mock-heroic

Hud·son Canadian bay; US river

hue colour; *compare* hew

hued

huff

huffi·ly

huffi·ness

huff·ish

huffy (huffi·er, huffi·est)

hug (hug·ging, hugged)

huge

huge·ly

huge·ness

hug·gable

hug·ger

hug·ger·mug·ger

Hu·guenot

Hu·guenot·ic

Hu·guenot·ism

huh exclamation

Hu·he·hot (*or* Hu-ho-hao-t'e) Chinese town

hula (*or* hula-hula) Hawaiian dance

hulk

hulk·ing

hull

Hull English port; Canadian city

hul·la·ba·loo (*or* ·bal·loo; *plural* ·loos)

hull·er

hull-less

hul·lo *variant spelling of* hello

hum (hum·ming, hummed)

hu·man

hu·mane

hu·mane·ly

hu·mane·ness

hu·man·ism

hu·man·ist

hu·man·ist·ic

hu·mani·tar·ian

hu·mani·tari·an·ism

hu·mani·tari·an·ist

hu·man·ity (*plural* ·ities)

hu·mani·za·tion (*or* ·sa·tion)

hu·man·ize (*or* ·ise)

hu·man·iz·er (*or* ·is·er)

human·kind

hu·man-like

hu·man·ly

hu·man·ness

hu·man·oid

Hum·ber

Humber·side

hum·ble

hum·ble·bee

hum·ble·ness

hum·bler

hum·bling·ly

hum·bly

Hum·boldt cur·rent

hum·bug (·bug·ging, ·bugged)

hum·bug·ger

hum·bug·gery

hum·ding·er

hum·drum

hum·drum·ness

hu·mec·tant

hu·mer·al

hu·mer·us (*plural* ·meri) arm bone; *compare* humorous

hu·mic

hu·mid

hu·midi·fi·ca·tion

hu·midi·fi·er

hu·midi·fy (·fies, ·fy·ing, ·fied)

hu·midi·stat

hu·mid·ity

hu·mid·ness

hu·mi·dor tobacco container

hu·mili·ate

hu·mili·at·ing·ly

hu·milia·tion

hu·mil·ia·tive

hu·mil·ia·tor

hu·mil·ia·tory

hu·mil·ity (*plural* ·ities)

hummed

hum·mel *Scot* hornless

hum·mer

hum·ming

humming·bird

hum·mock

hum·mocky

hum·mus (*or* hou·mus, ·mous) Middle Eastern food

hu·mor *US spelling of* humour

hu·mor·al of body fluids

hu·mor·esque

hu·mor·ist

hu·mor·is·tic

hu·mor·ous funny; *compare* humerus

hu·mor·ous·ness

hu·mour (*US* ·mor)

hu·mour·ful (*US* ·mor·)

hu·mour·less (*US* ·mor·)

hu·mour·less·ness (*US* ·mor·)

hu·mour·some (*US* ·mor·)

hump

hump·back

hump·backed

humph

humpi·ness

hump·like

hump·ty (*plural* ·ties) padded seat

humpy (humpi·er, humpi·est)

Hums *variant of* Homs

hu·mus

Hun

Hu·nan Chinese province

hunch

hunch·back

hunch·backed

hun·dred (*plural* ·dreds *or* ·dred)

hun·dredth

hundred·weight (*plural* ·weights *or* ·weight)

hung suspended; *compare* hanged

Hun·gar·ian

Hun·ga·ry

hun·ger

Hung·nam North Korean port

hun·gri·ly

hun·gri·ness

hun·gry (·gri·er, ·gri·est)

hunk

hunk·ers *Dialect* haunches

hunky-dory

Hun·like

Hun·nish

Hun·nish·ly

Hun·nish·ness

hunt

hunt·ed

hunt·er

hunt·ing

Hun·ting·don
Cambridgeshire town
Hun·ting·don·shire former
English county
hunts·man (*plural* ·men)
Hunts·ville US city
Huon Tasmanian river
Hu·peh (*or* ·pei) Chinese
province
hup·pah Jewish wedding
ceremony
hur·dle
hur·dler
hurds *variant of* hards
hurdy-gurdy (*plural*
-gurdies)
hurl
hurl·er
hur·ley hurling stick
hurl·ing
hurly-burly (*plural* -burlies)
Hu·ron (*plural* ·rons *or* ·ron)
American Indian
Hu·ron (Lake)
hur·rah (*or* hoo·ray,
hoo·rah)
hur·ri·cane
hur·ried
hur·ried·ly
hur·ried·ness
hur·ry (*verb* ·ries, ·ry·ing,
·ried; *noun, plural* ·ries)
hur·ry·ing·ly
hurst *Archaic* wood
Hurst·mon·ceux *variant
spelling of*
Herstmonceux
hurt (hurt·ing, hurt)
hur·ter
hurt·ful
hurt·ful·ly
hurt·ful·ness
hurt·le
hus·band
hus·band·er
hus·band·less
husband·man (*plural* ·men)
hus·band·ry
hush
husha·by
husk
husk·er
huski·ly
huski·ness
husk·like

husky (*adj* huski·er,
huski·est; *noun, plural*
huskies)
huss dogfish
hus·sar
Huss·ism (*or* Huss·it·ism)
Huss·ite heretical Christian
hus·sy (*plural* ·sies)
hus·tings
hus·tle
hus·tler
hut
hutch
hut·like
hut·ment
Hu·tu (*plural* ·tu *or* ·tus)
African people
huz·zah *Archaic* hurrah
hwan *variant of* won
Hwang Hai (*or* Huang Hai)
Chinese sea
Hwang Ho (*or* Huang Ho)
Chinese river
hwyl poetic fervour
hya·cinth
hya·cin·thine
Hyacinthus mythological
character
Hya·des (*or* Hy·ads) star
cluster
hy·aena *variant spelling of*
hyena
hya·lin biochemical
substance
hya·line translucent
hya·lite variety of opal
hya·loid transparent
hya·lu·ron·ic acid
hya·lu·roni·dase enzyme
hy·brid
hy·brid·ism
hy·brid·ity
hy·brid·iz·able (*or* ·is·able)
hy·bridi·za·tion (*or*
·sa·tion)
hy·brid·ize (*or* ·ise)
hy·brid·iz·er (*or* ·is·er)
hy·bris *variant spelling of*
hubris
hy·dan·to·in crystalline
substance
hy·da·thode botany term
hy·da·tid tapeworm cyst
Hyde English town
Hy·dera·bad

hyd·no·car·pate
hyd·no·car·pic acid
hy·dra (*plural* ·dras *or*
·drae) marine animal
Hy·dra mythological
character
hy·drac·id acid without
oxygen
hy·dran·gea
hy·drant
hy·dranth zoology term
hy·drar·gy·ric
hy·drar·gy·rum mercury
hy·dras·tine biochemical
compound
hy·dras·ti·nine biochemical
compound
hy·dras·tis plant
hy·drate
hy·drat·ed
hy·dra·tion
hy·dra·tor
hy·drau·lic
hy·drau·li·cal·ly
hy·drau·lics
hy·dra·zine
hy·dra·zo·ic acid
hy·dria ancient Greek jar
hy·dric
hy·dride
hy·dri·od·ic
hy·dro (*plural* ·dros)
hydro·bro·mic
hydro·car·bon
hydro·cele pathology term
hydro·cel·lu·lose
hydro·cephal·ic
hydro·cepha·lus (*or*
·cephaly)
hydro·chlo·ric
hydro·chlo·ride
hydro·cor·al (*or*
·cor·al·line) zoology term
hydro·cor·ti·sone
hydro·cy·an·ic
hydro·dy·nam·ic
hydro·dy·nami·cal·ly
hydro·dy·nam·ics
hydro·elec·tric
hydro·elec·tric·ity
hydro·flu·or·ic
hydro·foil
hydro·gen
hydro·gen·ate
hydro·gena·tion

hydro·gena·tor
hydro·geni·za·tion (or ·sa·tion)
hydro·gen·ize (or ·ise)
hydro·gen·oly·sis
hy·drog·enous
hydro·graph
hy·drog·ra·pher
hydro·graph·ic (or ·graphi·cal)
hydro·graphi·cal·ly
hy·drog·ra·phy mapping oceans and rivers
hy·droid
hydro·ki·net·ic (or ·neti·cal)
hydro·ki·net·ics
hydro·log·ic (or ·logi·cal)
hydro·logi·cal·ly
hy·drolo·gist
hy·drol·ogy
hydro·lys·able (US ·lyz·)
hy·droly·sate
hydro·ly·sa·tion (US ·za·tion)
hydro·lyse (US ·lyze)
hydro·lys·er (US ·lyz·er)
hy·droly·sis
hydro·lyte
hydro·lyt·ic
hydro·mag·net·ics
hydro·manc·er
hydro·man·cy divination by water
hydro·man·tic
hydro·mechani·cal
hydro·mechan·ics
hydro·medu·sa (plural ·sas or ·sae) zoology term
hydro·medu·san
hydro·mel mead
hydro·met·al·lur·gi·cal
hydro·met·al·lur·gy
hydro·meteor
hydro·meteoro·logi·cal
hydro·meteor·ol·ogy
hy·drom·eter
hydro·met·ric (or ·met·ri·cal)
hy·drom·etry
hydro·path·ic (or ·pathi·cal)
hy·dropa·thist (or hydro·path)
hy·dropa·thy water cure

hydro·phane variety of opal
hydro·phil·ic
hy·drophi·lous botany term
hy·drophi·ly
hydro·pho·bia
hydro·pho·bic
hydro·phone underwater microphone
hydro·phyte
hydro·plane
hydro·poni·cal·ly
hydro·pon·ics
hydro·pow·er
hydro·scope
hydro·ski hydrofoil on seaplane
hydro·sphere
hydro·stat
hydro·stat·ic
hydro·stat·ics
hydro·sul·phide (US ·fide)
hydro·thera·peu·tic
hydro·thera·pist
hydro·thera·py
hydro·trop·ic growing towards water
hy·drous
hy·drox·ide
hy·droxy chemistry term
hy·droxyl
hydro·zoan zoology term
Hy·drus constellation
hy·ena (or ·aena)
hy·eto·graph rainfall chart
hy·eto·graph·ic (or ·graphi·cal)
hy·eto·graphi·cal·ly
hy·etog·ra·phy
Hygeia Greek goddess
hy·giene
hy·gien·ic
hy·gieni·cal·ly
hy·gien·ics
hy·gien·ist
hygro·graph
hy·grom·eter humidity measurer
hygro·met·ric
hygro·met·ri·cal·ly
hy·grom·etry
hygro·phi·lous botany term
hygro·scope
hygro·scop·ic
hygro·scopi·cal·ly

Hyk·sos (plural ·sos) Asian nomad
hyla tree frog
hy·lo·zo·ism philosophical doctrine
hy·lo·zo·ist
Hymen god of marriage
hy·men anatomical membrane
hy·men·al of the hymen
hy·meneal of marriage
hy·menium (plural ·menia) fungal tissue
hy·menop·ter·an (plural ·ter·ans or ·tera) insect
hymn
hym·nal
hym·nic
hym·nist (or hym·no·dist)
hym·no·dy
hym·nolo·gist
hym·nol·ogy
hy·oid bone
hy·os·cine
hy·os·cya·mine
hype
hyper·ac·id (adj)
hyper·acid·ity
hyper·ac·tive
hyper·ac·tiv·ity
hyper·aemia (US ·emia) pathology term
hyper·aemic (US ·emic)
hyper·aes·the·sia (US ·es·) increased sensitivity
hyper·aes·thet·ic (US ·es·)
hyper·bar·ic of high pressure
hyper·ba·ton reversed word order
hyper·bo·la (plural ·las or ·lae) geometrical curve
hyper·bo·le exaggeration
hyper·bol·ic (or ·boli·cal)
hyper·bo·lize (or ·lise) exaggerate
hyper·bo·loid
Hyper·bo·rean mythological character
hyper·bo·rean of extreme north
hyper·charge
hyper·criti·cal
hyper·criti·cal·ly
hyper·criti·cism

hyper·du·lia veneration for Virgin Mary
hyper·du·lic (or hyper·du·li·cal)
hyper·gly·cae·mia (US ·cemia) excess blood sugar
hyper·gly·cae·mic (US ·cemic)
hyper·gol·ic spontaneously flammable
hyper·icum plant
hyper·in·fla·tion
hyper·in·su·lin·ism
Hyperion Greek god
hyper·ki·nesia (or ·nesis)
hyper·ki·net·ic
hyper·mar·ket
hyper·meter verse line
hyper·met·ric (or ·metri·cal)
hyper·metro·pia (US hyper·opia) long-sightedness
hyper·metrop·ic
hy·perm·ne·sia psychology term
hyper·on elementary particle
hyper·opia US hypermetropia
hyper·plasia enlargement of body part
hyper·plas·tic
hy·perp·noea (US ·nea) increased breathing rate
hyper·py·rexia high fever
hyper·sen·si·tive
hyper·sen·si·tiv·ity
hyper·sen·si·tize (or ·tise) photography term
hyper·son·ic
hyper·space
hyper·spa·tial
hyper·ten·sion
hyper·ten·sive
hyper·ther·mia (or ·ther·my)
hyper·thy·roid
hyper·thy·roid·ism
hyper·ton·ic
hyper·troph·ic
hyper·tro·phy (noun, plural ·phies; verb ·phies, ·phy·ing, ·phied)
hyper·ven·ti·la·tion

hyper·vita·mi·no·sis
hy·pha (plural ·phae) part of fungus
hy·phen
hy·phen·ate
hy·phena·tion
hyp·na·gog·ic psychology term
hyp·noid
hyp·nol·ogy study of sleep
hyp·no·pae·dia
hyp·no·sis (plural ·ses)
hyp·no·thera·py
hyp·not·ic
hyp·noti·cal·ly
hyp·no·tism
hyp·no·tist
hyp·no·tize (or ·tise)
hypo (plural hypos) photographic fixer; syringe
hypo·acid·ity
hypo·caust Roman heating system
hypo·cen·tre (US ·ter)
hypo·chlor·ite
hypo·chlor·ous
hypo·chon·dria
hypo·chon·dri·ac
hypo·chon·dria·cal·ly
hypo·chon·drium (plural ·dria) anatomy term
hy·poco·rism pet name
hy·poc·ri·sy (plural ·sies)
hypo·crite
hypo·criti·cal
hypo·criti·cal·ly
hypo·cy·cloid geometric curve
hypo·cy·cloi·dal
hypo·der·mic
hypo·der·mis biology term
Hy·po·do·rian musical term
hypo·gas·tric
hypo·gas·trium (plural ·tria) anatomy term
hypo·geal (or ·geous) botany term
hypo·gene geology term
hy·pog·enous botany term
hypo·gen·ic
hypo·geum (plural ·gea) burial vault
hypo·glos·sal anatomy term
hypo·gly·cae·mia (US ·cemia) low blood sugar

hypo·gly·caem·ic (US ·cemic)
hy·poid
hypo·lim·nion bottom layer in lake
hypo·ma·nia
hypo·man·ic
hypo·nas·tic
hypo·nas·ty botany term
hypo·phys·eal
hy·pophy·sis (plural ·ses) pituitary gland
hypo·plasia (or ·plas·ty)
hypo·sen·si·tize (or ·tise)
hypo·stat·ic
hypos·ta·sis (plural ·ses)
hy·pos·ta·tize (or ·tise)
hypo·style architectural term
hypo·ten·sion
hypo·ten·sive
hy·pot·enuse
hypo·thala·mus (plural ·mi)
hy·poth·ecate legal term
hy·poth·eca·tion
hy·poth·eca·tor
hypo·ther·mia
hy·poth·esis (plural ·eses)
hy·poth·esize (or ·esise)
hypo·theti·cal
hypo·theti·cal·ly
hypo·thy·roid
hypo·thy·roid·ism
hypo·ton·ic
hy·poxia oxygen deficiency
hy·pox·ic
hyp·so·met·ric (or ·ri·cal)
hyp·som·etry altitude measurement
hy·rax animal
hy·son Chinese tea
hys·sop herb
hys·ter·ec·to·my (plural ·mies)
hys·te·re·sis physics term
hys·te·ria
hys·ter·ic
hys·teri·cal
hys·teri·cal·ly
hys·ter·ics
hys·tero·gen·ic
hys·ter·oid (or ·teroi·dal)
hys·ter·oto·my (plural ·mies) incision into uterus
hys·tri·co·morph rodent

I

iamb
iamb (or iam·bus; *plural*
  iambs, iam·bi, *or*
  iam·buses) metrical foot
iam·bic
iam·bi·cal·ly
Iap·etus satellite of Saturn
iat·ric (or ·ri·cal) of
  medicine
iat·ro·gen·ic
iat·ro·genic·ity
Iba·dan Nigerian city
Iba·gué Colombian city
I-beam girder
Iberia
Iberian
ibex (*plural* ibexes, ibi·ces,
  or ibex) goat
Ibibio (*plural* Ibibio *or*
  Ibibios) Nigerian
  people
ibis (*plural* ibises *or* ibis)
  bird
Ibi·za (or Ivi·za) Spanish
  island
Ibo (or Igbo; *plural* Ibos, Ibo
  or Igbos, Igbo) African
  people
Icaria Greek island
Icar·ian
Icarus mythological
  character
ice
ice·berg
ice·blink
ice·bound
ice·box
ice·breaker
ice·cap
ice cream
ice·fall
Ice·land
Ice·land·er
Ice·land·ic
Iceni ancient British tribe
Ichang (or I-ch'ang)
  Chinese port
I Ching Chinese book of
  divination
Ichi·no·mi·ya Japanese
  town

ich·neu·mon mongoose;
  insect
ich·nite (or ·no·lite) fossil
  footprint
ich·no·graph·ic (or
  ·graphi·cal)
ich·no·graphi·cal·ly
ich·nog·ra·phy ground-plan
  drawing
ich·no·logi·cal
ich·nol·ogy study of fossil
  footprints
ichor
ichor·ous
ich·thy·ic of fishes
ich·thy·oid (or ·oid·al)
ich·thyo·log·ic (or ·logi·cal)
ich·thyo·logi·cal·ly
ich·thy·olo·gist
ich·thy·ol·ogy
ich·thy·opha·gous
ich·thy·opha·gy
ich·thy·or·nis extinct
  bird
ich·thyo·saur (or ·saur·us;
  plural ·saurs, ·saur·uses, *or*
  ·sau·ri)
ich·thyo·sis skin disease
ich·thy·ot·ic
ici·cle
ici·cled
ici·ly
ici·ness
ic·ing
icon (or ikon)
icon·ic (or iconi·cal)
icono·clasm
icono·clast
icono·clas·tic
icono·clas·ti·cal·ly
ico·nog·ra·pher
icono·graph·ic (or
  ·graphi·cal)
ico·nog·ra·phy (*plural*
  ·phies)
ico·nola·ter
ico·nola·trous
ico·nola·try
icono·logi·cal
ico·nolo·gist
ico·nol·ogy

icono·mat·ic representing
  sounds with pictures
icono·mati·cism
icono·scope
ico·sa·he·dral
ico·sa·he·dron (*plural*
  ·drons *or* ·dra)
ic·ter·ic
ic·ter·us jaundice
ic·tus (*plural* ·tuses *or* ·tus)
  poetry term
icy (ici·er, ici·est)
I'd I had; I would
id
Ida Cretan mountain
Ida·ho
ide fish
idea
ideal
ideal·ism
ideal·ist
ideal·is·tic
ideal·is·ti·cal·ly
ideal·ity (*plural* ·ities)
ideali·za·tion (or ·sa·tion)
ideal·ize (or ·ise)
ideal·iz·er (or ·is·er)
ideal·ly
ideate imagine
idea·tion
idea·tion·al
idea·tive
idea·tum (*plural* ·ta)
  philosophy term
idée fixe (*plural* idées fixes)
idem·po·tent maths term
iden·tic diplomacy term
iden·ti·cal
iden·ti·cal·ly
iden·ti·cal·ness
iden·ti·fi·able
iden·ti·fi·able·ness
iden·ti·fi·ca·tion
iden·ti·fi·er
iden·ti·fy (·fies, ·fy·ing,
  ·fied)
Iden·ti·kit (*Trademark*)
iden·tity (*plural* ·tities)
ideo·gram (or ·graph)
  symbol
id·eog·ra·phy

idio·logi·cal (*or* ·logic)
idio·logi·cal·ly
ideol·ogist (*or* ideo·logue)
ideol·ogy (*plural* ·ogies)
ideo·mo·tor physiology
  term
ides day in Roman calendar
idio·blast plant cell
idio·blas·tic
idio·cy (*plural* ·cies)
idio·graph·ic
idio·lect individual's
  language
idio·lect·al (*or* ·ic)
idi·om
idio·mat·ic (*or* ·mati·cal)
idio·mati·cal·ly
idio·mor·phic mineralogy
  term
idio·mor·phi·cal·ly
idio·mor·phism
idio·path·ic
idio·opa·thy (*plural* ·thies)
  disease of unknown cause
idio·phone musical
  instrument
idio·phon·ic
idio·syn·cra·sy (*plural* ·sies)
idio·syn·crat·ic
idio·syn·crati·cal·ly
idi·ot
idi·ot·ic
idi·oti·cal·ly
idle lazy; *compare* idol
idle·ness
idler
idly
idol image; *compare* idle
idola·ter (*fem* ·tress)
idola·trize (*or* ·trise)
idola·triz·er (*or* ·tris·er)
idola·trous
idola·try
idoli·za·tion (*or* ·sa·tion)
idol·ize (*or* ·ise)
idol·iz·er (*or* ·is·er)
idyll (*or* idyl)
idyl·lic
idyl·li·cal·ly
idyl·list
if
Ife Nigerian town
Igbo *variant spelling of* Ibo
ig·loo (*or* iglu; *plural* ·loos *or*
  iglus)

ig·ne·ous geology term
ig·nes·cent giving off sparks
ig·nit·abil·ity (*or* ·ibil·ity)
ig·nit·able (*or* ·ible)
ig·nite
ig·nit·er
ig·ni·tion
ig·ni·tron physics term
ig·no·bil·ity (*or* ·ble·ness)
ig·no·ble
ig·no·bly
ig·no·mini·ous
ig·no·miny (*plural* ·minies)
ig·nor·able
ig·no·ra·mus (*plural*
  ·muses)
ig·no·rance
ig·no·rant
ig·no·ra·tio elen·chi logic
  term
ig·nore
ig·nor·er
Igraine (*or* Ygerne) King
  Arthur's mother
Igua·çú (*or* Iguas·sú) South
  American river
igua·na lizard
igua·nian
iguano·don dinosaur
ih·ram Muslim pilgrim's
  robes
IJs·sel·meer (*or* Ys·) Dutch
  lake
ikeba·na Japanese flower
  arranging
ikon *variant spelling of* icon
il·eac (*or* ·eal) of ileum;
  compare iliac
Île-de-France
il·ei·tis intestinal disorder
il·eos·to·my (*plural* ·mies)
  abdominal operation
Ilesha Nigerian town
il·eum small intestine;
  compare ilium
il·eus intestinal obstruction
ilex tree
ili·ac of ilium; *compare* ileac
Ili·ad
Ili·ad·ic
Il·ium Troy
il·ium (*plural* ·ia) hip bone;
  compare ileum
ilk
Il·kes·ton Derbyshire town

I'll I will; I shall
ill
ill-advised
ill-assorted
il·la·tive linguistics term
Il·la·war·ra Australian
  district
ill-bred
ill-breed·ing
ill-considered
Ille-et-Vilaine French
  department
il·legal
il·legal·ity (*plural* ·ities)
il·legali·za·tion (*or* ·sa·tion)
il·legal·ize (*or* ·ise)
il·legal·ly
il·leg·ibil·ity (*or* ·ible·ness)
il·leg·ible
il·leg·ibly
il·legiti·ma·cy (*or*
  ·mate·ness)
il·legiti·mate
il·legiti·mate·ly
ill-fated
ill-favoured (*US* -favored)
ill-gotten
il·lib·er·al
il·lib·er·al·ity (*or* ·ness,
  ·ism)
il·lic·it illegal; *compare*
  elicit
il·lim·it·abil·ity (*or*
  ·able·ness)
il·lim·it·able
Il·li·nois
Il·li·nois·an (*or* ·noian,
  ·nois·ian)
il·liq·uid
il·lit·era·cy (*plural* ·cies)
il·lit·er·ate
ill-mannered
ill-natured
ill·ness
il·locu·tion philosophy
  term
il·lo·cu·tion·ary
il·logi·cal
il·logi·cal·ity (*or* ·ness)
il·logi·cal·ly
ill-omened
ill-starred
ill-timed
ill-treat
ill-treatment

il·lude deceive; *compare* allude; elude
il·lume
il·lu·mi·nance
il·lu·mi·nant
il·lu·mi·nate
il·lu·mi·na·ti (*sing.* ·to) enlightened people
il·lu·mi·na·tion
il·lu·mi·na·tive
il·lu·mi·na·tor
il·lu·mine
il·lu·mi·nism belief in enlightenment
il·lu·mi·nist
ill-use (*verb*)
ill-use (*or* -usage)
il·lu·sion delusion; *compare* allusion
il·lu·sion·ary (*or* ·al)
il·lu·sion·ism
il·lu·sion·ist
il·lu·sion·is·tic
il·lu·sive illusory; *compare* elusive
il·lu·so·ri·ly
il·lu·so·ri·ness
il·lu·sory
il·lus·trat·able
il·lus·trate
il·lus·tra·tion
il·lus·tra·tion·al
il·lus·tra·tive
il·lus·tra·tor
il·lus·tri·ous
il·lu·via·tion
Il·lyria Adriatic region
Il·lyr·ian
il·men·ite mineral
Iloi·lo Philippine port
Ilor·in Nigerian city
I'm
(imaculate) *incorrect spelling of* immaculate
im·age
im·age·ry (*plural* ·ries)
im·agi·nable
im·agi·nably
im·agi·nal of an image or imago
im·agi·nari·ly
im·agi·nary
im·agi·na·tion
im·agi·na·tive
im·ag·ine

im·ag·in·er
im·ag·ism poetic movement
im·ag·ist
im·ag·is·tic
im·ag·is·ti·cal·ly
ima·go (*plural* ·gos, ·goes, or ·gi·nes) adult insect; psychiatry term
imam (*or* imaum) Islamic priest
imam·ate
ima·ret Turkish hospice
im·bal·ance
im·becile
im·becil·ity (*plural* ·ities)
im·bed *less common spelling of* embed
im·bibe
im·bib·er
im·bi·bi·tion
im·bri·cate (*or* ·cat·ed)
im·bri·ca·tion
im·bro·glio (*plural* ·glios)
im·brue (*or* em·; ·bru·ing, ·brued) to stain; *compare* imbue
im·bue (·bu·ing, ·bued) instil; *compare* imbrue
im·id·az·ole
im·ide chemistry term
im·id·ic
(imigrate) *incorrect spelling of* immigrate
imine chemistry term
imi·tabil·ity (*or* ·table·ness)
imi·table
imi·tate
imi·ta·tion
imi·ta·tion·al
imi·ta·tive
imi·ta·tor
im·macu·la·cy (*or* ·late·ness)
im·macu·late
im·ma·nence (*or* ·nen·cy)
im·ma·nent existing within; *compare* eminent; imminent
im·ma·nent·ism religious belief
im·ma·terial
im·ma·teri·al·ism
im·ma·teri·al·ist
im·ma·terial·ity (*or* ·teri·al·ness)

im·ma·teri·al·ize (*or* ·ise)
im·ma·ture
im·ma·tu·rity (*or* ·ture·ness)
im·meas·ur·abil·ity (*or* ·able·ness)
im·meas·ur·able
im·meas·ur·ably
im·media·cy (*or* im·medi·ate·ness)
im·medi·ate
im·medi·ate·ly
im·medi·cable
im·memo·ri·able
im·memo·rial
im·memo·ri·al·ly
im·mense
im·mense·ly
im·men·si·ty (*plural* ·ties)
im·men·su·rable
im·merse
im·mers·ible
im·mer·sion immersing; *compare* emersion
im·mer·sion·ism Christian doctrine
im·mer·sion·ist
im·methodi·cal
im·methodi·cal·ly
im·mi·grant
im·mi·grate enter country; *compare* emigrate
im·mi·gra·tion
im·mi·gra·tory
im·mi·gra·tor
im·mi·nence
im·mi·nent impending; *compare* eminent; immanent
Im·ming·ham Humberside port
im·mis·cibil·ity
im·mis·cible
im·mis·cibly
im·mo·bile
im·mo·bil·ism political policy
im·mo·bil·ity
im·mo·bi·li·za·tion (*or* ·sa·tion)
im·mo·bi·lize (*or* ·lise)
im·mo·bi·liz·er (*or* ·lis·er)
im·mo·der·ate
im·mo·der·ate·ly

im·mod·era·tion (*or*
·er·ate·ness)
im·mod·est
im·mod·es·ty
im·mo·late sacrifice
im·mo·la·tion
im·mo·la·tor
im·mor·al morally bad;
compare amoral
im·mor·al·ist
im·mor·al·ity (*plural* ·ities)
im·mor·al·ly
im·mor·tal
im·mor·tal·ity
im·mor·tali·za·tion (*or*
·sa·tion)
im·mor·tal·ize (*or* ·ise)
im·mor·tal·iz·er (*or* ·is·er)
im·mor·tal·ly
im·mor·telle everlasting
flower
im·mo·tile
im·mo·til·ity
im·mov·abil·ity (*or*
·mov·able·ness)
im·mov·able (*or in legal
contexts* ·move·)
im·mov·ably
im·mune
im·mu·nity (*plural* ·nities)
im·mu·ni·za·tion (*or*
·sa·tion)
im·mu·nize (*or* ·nise)
im·mu·niz·er (*or* ·nis·er)
im·mu·no·as·say
im·mu·no·chem·is·try
im·mu·no·com·pro·mised
im·mu·no·genet·ic (*or*
·geneti·cal)
im·mu·no·genet·ics
im·mu·no·gen·ic
im·mu·no·geni·cal·ly
im·mu·no·globu·lin
im·mu·no·log·ic (*or*
·logi·cal)
im·mu·no·logi·cal·ly
im·mu·nolo·gist
im·mu·nol·ogy
im·mu·no·reac·tion
im·mu·no·sup·pres·sion
im·mu·no·sup·pres·sive
im·mu·no·thera·py
im·mure
im·mu·tabil·ity (*or*
·table·ness)

im·mu·table
im·mu·tably
Imo Nigerian state
imp
im·pact
im·pact·ed
im·pac·tion
im·pair
im·pair·er
im·pair·ment
im·pa·la (*plural* ·las *or* ·la)
antelope
im·pale
im·pale·ment
im·pal·er
im·pal·pa·bil·ity
im·pal·pable
im·pal·pably
im·pa·na·tion Christian
ritual
im·pan·el *US spelling of*
empanel
im·pari·pin·nate botany
term
im·pari·syl·la·bic
im·par·ity (*plural* ·ities)
disparity
im·part
im·par·ta·tion (*or*
·part·ment)
im·part·er
im·par·tial
im·par·ti·al·ity (*or* ·ness)
im·par·tial·ly
im·part·ibil·ity
im·part·ible legal term
im·pass·abil·ity (*or*
·able·ness)
im·pass·able
im·pass·ably
im·passe
im·pas·sion
im·pas·sioned
im·pas·sioned·ly
im·pas·sive
im·pas·sive·ness (*or*
·siv·ity)
im·pas·ta·tion
im·paste paint thickly
im·pas·to paint applied
thickly
im·pa·tience
im·pa·ti·ens (*plural* ·ens)
plant
im·pa·tient

im·peach
im·peach·abil·ity
im·peach·able
im·peach·er
im·peach·ment
im·pearl
im·pec·cabil·ity
im·pec·cable
im·pec·cably
im·pec·cant sinless
im·pecu·ni·ous
im·pecu·ni·ous·ness (*or*
·os·ity)
im·ped·ance physics term
im·pede
im·ped·er
im·pedi·ment
im·pedi·men·ta impeding
objects
im·pedi·men·tal (*or* ·tary)
im·ped·ing·ly
im·pel (·pel·ling, ·pelled)
im·pel·lent
im·pel·ler
im·pend
im·pend·ence (*or* ·en·cy)
im·pend·ing
im·pen·etrabil·ity
im·pen·etrable
im·pen·etrably
im·peni·tence (*or* ·ten·cy,
·tent·ness)
im·peni·tent
im·pera·tive
im·pera·tor
im·per·cep·tibil·ity (*or*
·tible·ness)
im·per·cep·tible
im·per·cep·tibly
im·per·cep·tion
im·per·cep·tive
im·per·cep·tiv·ity (*or*
·tive·ness)
im·per·cipi·ent
im·per·cipi·ence
im·per·fect
im·per·fec·tion
im·per·fec·tive
im·per·fo·rate
im·per·fo·ra·tion
im·perial
im·peri·al·ism
im·peri·al·ist
im·peri·al·is·tic
im·peri·al·is·ti·cal·ly

im·peri·al·ly
im·per·il (·il·ling, ·illed; US also ·il·ing, ·iled)
im·peri·ous
im·per·ish·abil·ity (or ·able·ness)
im·per·ish·able
im·perium (plural ·peria) ancient Roman supreme power
im·per·ma·nence (or ·nen·cy)
im·per·ma·nent
im·per·meabil·ity (or ·meable·ness)
im·per·meable
im·per·mis·sibil·ity
im·per·mis·sible
im·per·son·al
im·per·son·al·ity
im·per·son·ali·za·tion (or ·sa·tion)
im·per·son·al·ize (or ·ise)
im·per·son·al·ly
im·per·son·ate
im·per·sona·tion
im·per·sona·tor
im·per·ti·nence (or ·nen·cy)
im·per·ti·nent
im·per·turb·abil·ity (or ·able·ness)
im·per·turb·able
im·per·turb·ably
im·per·tur·ba·tion
im·per·vi·ous
im·petigi·nous
im·peti·go skin disease
im·petrate obtain by prayer
im·petra·tion
im·petra·tive
im·petra·tor
im·petu·os·ity (or ·ous·ness)
im·petu·ous
im·petus (plural ·petuses)
Im·phal Indian city
impi (plural impi or impies) Bantu warrior group
im·pi·ety (plural ·eties)
im·pinge
im·pinge·ment
im·ping·er
im·pi·ous
imp·ish

im·plac·abil·ity (or ·able·ness)
im·plac·able
im·plac·ably
im·plant
im·plan·ta·tion
im·plant·er
im·plau·sibil·ity (or ·sible·ness)
im·plau·sible
im·plau·sibly
im·plead prosecute
im·plead·able
im·plead·er
im·ple·ment tool; to carry out
im·ple·men·tal
im·ple·men·ta·tion
im·ple·ment·er (or ·or)
im·pli·cate
im·pli·ca·tion
im·plica·tive
im·plic·it
im·plic·it·ness (or ·plic·ity)
(impliment) incorrect spelling of implement
im·plode
im·plo·ra·tion
im·plo·ra·tory
im·plore
im·plor·er
im·plor·ing·ly
im·plo·sion
im·plo·sive phonetics term
im·ply (·plies, ·ply·ing, ·plied)
im·poli·cy (plural ·cies)
im·po·lite
im·po·lite·ness
im·poli·tic
im·poli·tic·ly
im·pon·dera·bilia
im·pon·der·abil·ity (or ·able·ness)
im·pon·der·able
im·pon·der·ably
im·po·nent
im·port
im·port·able
im·por·tance
im·por·tant
im·por·ta·tion
im·port·er
im·por·tu·nate
im·por·tune

im·por·tun·er
im·por·tu·nity (plural ·nities)
im·pos·able
im·pose
im·pos·er
im·pos·ing
im·pos·ing·ly
im·po·si·tion
im·pos·sibil·ity (plural ·ities)
im·pos·sible
im·pos·sibly
im·post customs duty
im·pos·tor (or ·post·er)
im·pos·trous (or ·tur·ous)
im·pos·ture
im·po·tence (or ·ten·cy, ·tent·ness)
im·po·tent
im·pound
im·pound·age (or ·ment)
im·pound·er
im·pov·er·ish
im·pov·er·ish·er
im·pov·er·ish·ment
im·prac·ti·cabil·ity (or ·cable·ness)
im·prac·ti·cable not feasible
im·prac·ti·cably
im·prac·ti·cal not practical
im·prac·ti·cal·ity (or ·ness)
im·prac·ti·cal·ly
im·pre·cate
im·pre·ca·tion
im·pre·ca·tory
im·pre·cise
im·pre·ci·sion (or ·cise·ness)
im·preg·nabil·ity (or ·nable·ness)
im·preg·nable (or im·preg·na·table)
im·preg·nate
im·preg·na·tion
im·preg·na·tor
im·pre·sa (or im·prese) emblem
im·pre·sa·rio (plural ·rios)
im·pre·scrip·tibil·ity
im·pre·scrip·tible legal term
im·press
im·press·er

im·press·ible
im·pres·sion
im·pres·sion·abil·ity (*or* ·able·ness)
im·pres·sion·able
im·pres·sion·al
im·pres·sion·al·ly
im·pres·sion·ism
im·pres·sion·ist
im·pres·sion·is·tic
im·pres·sive
im·pres·sive·ness
im·press·ment conscription
im·prest
im·pri·ma·tur sanction
im·print
im·print·er
im·print·ing
im·pris·on
im·pris·on·er
im·pris·on·ment
im·prob·abil·ity (*or* ·able·ness)
im·prob·able
im·pro·bity (*plural* ·bities)
im·promp·tu
im·prop·er
im·pro·pri·ate transfer to laity
im·pro·pria·tion
im·pro·pria·tor
im·pro·pri·ety (*plural* ·eties)
im·prov·abil·ity (*or* ·able·ness)
im·prov·able
im·prove
im·prove·ment
im·prov·er
im·provi·dence
im·provi·dent
im·prov·ing·ly
im·provi·sa·tion
im·provi·sa·tion·al
im·pro·vise
im·pro·vis·er
im·pru·dence
im·pru·dent unwise; *compare* impudent
im·pu·dence (*or* ·den·cy)
im·pu·dent impertinent; *compare* imprudent
im·pugn
im·pug·na·tion (*or* ·pugn·ment)
im·pugn·er

im·pu·is·sance
im·pu·is·sant
im·pulse
im·pul·sion
im·pul·sive
im·pul·sive·ness
im·pu·nity (*plural* ·nities)
im·pure
im·pu·rity (*plural* ·rities)
im·put·abil·ity (*or* ·able·ness)
im·put·able
im·pu·ta·tion
im·pu·ta·tive
im·pute
im·put·er
in
in·abil·ity (*plural* ·ities)
in ab·sen·tia *Latin* in the absence of
in·ac·ces·sibil·ity (*or* ·sible·ness)
in·ac·ces·sible
in·ac·ces·sibly
in·ac·cu·ra·cy (*plural* ·cies)
in·ac·cu·rate
in·ac·tion
in·ac·ti·vate
in·ac·ti·va·tion
in·ac·tive
in·ac·tiv·ity (*or* ·tive·ness)
in·ad·equa·cy (*plural* ·cies)
in·ad·equate
in·ad·mis·sibil·ity
in·ad·mis·si·ble
in·ad·mis·sibly
in·ad·vert·ence (*or* ·en·cy)
in·ad·vert·ent
in·ad·vis·abil·ity (*or* ·able·ness)
in·ad·vis·able
in·ad·vis·ably
in·al·ien·abil·ity (*or* ·able·ness)
in·al·ien·able
in·al·ien·ably
in·al·ter·abil·ity (*or* ·able·ness)
in·al·ter·able
in·al·ter·ably
in·amo·ra·ta (*masc* ·to; *plural* ·tas *or* ·tos) lover
in·ane
in·ani·mate
ina·ni·tion

in·ani·mate·ness (*or* ·ma·tion)
in·an·ity (*plural* ·ities)
in·ap·pli·cabil·ity (*or* ·cable·ness)
in·ap·pli·cable
in·ap·po·site
in·ap·pre·ciable
in·ap·pre·cia·tive
in·ap·pre·hen·sive
in·ap·proach·abil·ity
in·ap·proach·able
in·ap·pro·pri·ate
in·ap·pro·pri·ate·ness
in·apt inappropriate; *compare* inept
in·ap·ti·tude (*or* ·apt·ness)
in·arch botany term
in·ar·ticu·late
in·ar·tis·tic
in·ar·tis·ti·cal·ly
in·as·much
in·at·ten·tion (*or* ·tive·ness)
in·at·ten·tive
in·audibil·ity (*or* ·audible·ness)
in·audible
in·audibly
in·augu·ral
in·augu·rate
in·augu·ra·tion
in·augu·ra·tor
in·augu·ra·tory
in·aus·pi·cious
in·board
in·born
in·bound
in·bred
in·breed (·breed·ing, ·bred)
Inca (*plural* Inca *or* Incas)
In·caic
in·cal·cu·labil·ity (*or* ·lable·ness)
in·cal·cu·lable
in·cal·cu·lably
in·ca·les·cence
in·ca·les·cent chemistry term
in cam·era *Latin* in private
In·can
in·can·desce
in·can·des·cence (*or* ·cen·cy)
in·can·des·cent
in·can·ta·tion

in•can•ta•tion•al (*or* •ta•tory)
in•ca•pabil•ity (*plural* •ities)
in•ca•pable
in•ca•pably
in•ca•paci•tate
in•ca•paci•ta•tion
in•ca•pac•ity (*plural* •ities)
in•cap•su•late *less common spelling of* encapsulate
in•car•cer•ate
in•car•cera•tion
in•car•cera•tor
in•car•di•nate
in•car•di•na•tion
in•car•nate
in•car•na•tion
in•cau•tious
in•cau•tious•ness (*or* •cau•tion)
in•cen•dia•rism
in•cen•di•ary (*plural* •aries)
in•cense
in•cen•so•ry (*plural* •ries) incense-burner
in•cen•tive
in•cept
in•cep•tion
in•cep•tive
in•cept•or
in•cer•ti•tude
in•ces•san•cy (*or* •sant•ness)
in•ces•sant
in•cest
in•ces•tu•ous
inch
inch•meal inch by inch
in•cho•ate
in•choa•tion
in•choa•tive
In•chon (*or* •cheon) South Korean port
inch•worm
in•ci•dence
in•ci•dent
in•ci•den•tal
in•ci•den•tal•ly
in•cin•er•ate
in•cin•era•tion
in•cin•era•tor
in•cipi•ence (*or* •en•cy)
in•cipi•ent
in•ci•pit *Latin* here begins
in•cise
in•ci•sion

in•ci•sive
in•ci•sor
in•ci•sur•al
in•ci•sure
in•ci•ta•tion
in•cite
in•cite•ment
in•cit•er
in•cit•ing•ly
in•ci•vil•ity (*plural* •ities)
in•clem•en•cy (*or* •ent•ness)
in•clem•ent
in•clin•able
in•cli•na•tion
in•cli•na•tion•al
in•cline
in•clin•er
in•cli•nom•eter
in•close *less common spelling of* enclose
in•clos•ure *less common spelling of* enclosure
in•clud•able (*or* •ible)
in•clude
in•clu•sion
in•clu•sive
in•co•er•cible
in•cog•ni•to (*fem* •ta; *plural* •tos *or* •tas)
in•cog•ni•zance
in•cog•ni•zant
in•co•her•ence (*or* •en•cy, •ent•ness)
in•co•her•ent
in•com•bus•tibil•ity (*or* •tible•ness)
in•com•bus•tible
in•com•bus•tibly
in•come
in•com•ing
in•com•men•su•rabil•ity (*or* •rable•ness)
in•com•men•su•rable
in•com•men•su•rably
in•com•men•su•rate
in•com•mode
in•com•mo•di•ous
in•com•mod•ity (*plural* •ities)
in•com•mu•ni•cabil•ity (*or* •cable•ness)
in•com•mu•ni•cable
in•com•mu•ni•cably
in•com•mu•ni•ca•do
in•com•mu•ni•ca•tive

in•com•mut•abil•ity (*or* •able•ness)
in•com•mut•able
in•com•mut•ably
in•com•pa•rabil•ity (*or* •rable•ness)
in•com•pa•rable
in•com•pa•rably
in•com•pat•ibil•ity (*or* •ible•ness)
in•com•pat•ible
in•com•pat•ibly
in•com•pe•tence (*or* •ten•cy)
in•com•pe•tent
in•com•plete
in•com•plete•ness (*or* •ple•tion)
in•com•pli•ance (*or* •an•cy)
in•com•pli•ant
in•com•pre•hen•sibil•ity (*or* •sible•ness)
in•com•pre•hen•sible
in•com•pre•hen•sibly
in•com•pre•hen•sion
in•com•pre•hen•sive
in•com•press•ibil•ity (*or* •ible•ness)
in•com•press•ible
in•com•press•ibly
in•com•put•abil•ity
in•com•put•able
in•con•ceiv•abil•ity (*or* •able•ness)
in•con•ceiv•able
in•con•ceiv•ably
in•con•clu•sive
in•con•den•sabil•ity (*or* •sibil•)
in•con•den•sable (*or* •sible)
in•con•form•ity
in•con•gru•ity (*plural* •ities)
in•con•gru•ous (*or* •ent)
in•con•gru•ous•ness (*or* •gru•ence)
in•con•sequence (*or* •sequent•ness)
in•con•sequen•tial (*or* •sequent)
in•con•sequen•ti•al•ity (*or* •tial•ness)
in•con•sequen•tial•ly
in•con•sid•er•able
in•con•sid•er•ate
in•con•sid•era•tion

in·con·sist·en·cy (*plural* ·cies)
in·con·sist·ent
in·con·sol·abil·ity (*or* ·able·ness)
in·con·sol·able
in·con·sol·ably
in·con·so·nance
in·con·so·nant
in·con·spicu·ous
in·con·stan·cy (*plural* ·cies)
in·con·stant
in·con·sum·able
in·con·sum·ably
in·con·test·abil·ity (*or* ·able·ness)
in·con·test·able
in·con·test·ably
in·con·ti·nence (*or* ·nen·cy)
in·con·ti·nent
in·con·tro·vert·ibil·ity (*or* ·ible·ness)
in·con·tro·vert·ible
in·con·tro·vert·ibly
in·con·ven·ience
in·con·ven·ient
in·con·vert·ibil·ity (*or* ·ible·ness)
in·con·vert·ible
in·con·vert·ibly
in·con·vin·cibil·ity (*or* ·cible·ness)
in·con·vin·cible
in·co·ordi·nate
in·co·ordi·na·tion
in·cor·po·rable
in·cor·po·rate
in·cor·po·rat·ed
in·cor·po·ra·tion
in·cor·po·ra·tive
in·cor·po·ra·tor
in·cor·po·real
in·cor·po·real·ly
in·cor·po·reity (*or* ·real·ity)
in·cor·rect
in·cor·rect·ness
in·cor·ri·gibil·ity (*or* ·gible·ness)
in·cor·ri·gible
in·cor·ri·gibly
in·cor·rupt
in·cor·rupt·ibil·ity (*or* ·ible·ness)
in·cor·rupt·ible
in·cor·rupt·ibly

in·cras·sate (*or* ·sat·ed) thickened
in·cras·sa·tion
in·creas·able
in·crease
in·creas·ing·ly
in·creas·er
in·cred·ibil·ity (*or* ·ible·ness)
in·cred·ible
in·cred·ibly
in·cre·du·lity
in·credu·lous
in·cre·ment
in·cre·men·tal
in·cres·cent
in·cre·tion secretion into bloodstream
in·cre·tion·ary (*or* ·tory)
in·crimi·nate
in·crimi·na·tion
in·crimi·na·tor
in·crimi·na·tory
in·cross inbreed
in·crust *variant spelling of* encrust
in·cu·bate
in·cu·ba·tion
in·cu·ba·tion·al
in·cu·ba·tive (*or* ·tory)
in·cu·ba·tor
in·cu·bus (*plural* ·bi *or* ·buses) male demon
in·cu·date (*or* ·dal) of incus
in·cul·cate
in·cul·ca·tion
in·cul·ca·tor
in·cul·pabil·ity (*or* ·pable·ness)
in·cul·pable
in·cul·pate
in·cul·pa·tion
in·cul·pa·tive (*or* in·cul·pa·to·ry)
in·cum·ben·cy (*plural* ·cies)
in·cum·bent
in·cu·nabu·la (*sing.* ·lum) early books
in·cu·nabu·lar
in·cur (·cur·ring, ·curred)
in·cur·abil·ity (*or* ·able·ness)
in·cur·able not curable; *compare* incurrable
in·cu·ri·os·ity (*or* ·ous·ness)

in·cu·ri·ous
in·cur·rable liable to incur; *compare* incurable
in·cur·rence
in·cur·rent
in·cur·sion
in·cur·sive
in·cur·vate
in·cur·va·tion
in·cur·va·ture
in·curve
in·cus (*plural* ·cu·des) ear bone
in·cuse design on coin
Ind India
in·da·mine chemical compound
in·debt·ed
in·debt·ed·ness
in·de·cen·cy (*plural* ·cies)
in·de·cent
in·de·cidu·ous
in·de·ci·pher·abil·ity (*or* ·able·ness)
in·de·ci·pher·able
in·de·ci·sion
in·de·ci·sive
in·de·clin·able
in·deco·rous
in·de·co·rum
in·deed
in·de·fati·gabil·ity (*or* ·gable·ness)
in·de·fati·gable
in·de·fati·gably
in·de·fea·sibil·ity (*or* ·sible·ness)
in·de·fea·sible
in·de·fea·sibly
in·de·fen·sibil·ity (*or* ·sible·ness)
in·de·fen·sible
in·de·fin·able
in·de·fin·ably
in·defi·nite
in·de·his·cence
in·de·his·cent botany term
in·del·ibil·ity (*or* ·ible·ness)
in·del·ible
in·del·ibly
in·deli·ca·cy (*plural* ·cies)
in·deli·cate
in·dem·ni·fi·ca·tion
in·dem·ni·fi·er

in·dem·ni·fy (·fies, ·fy·ing,
  ·fied)
in·dem·ni·ty (*plural* ·nities)
in·de·mon·stra·ble
in·dene chemical
  compound
in·dent
in·den·ta·tion
in·dent·er (*or* den·tor)
in·den·tion indentation
in·den·ture
in·den·ture·ship
in·de·pend·ence
in·de·pend·en·cy (*plural*
  ·cies)
in·de·pend·ent
in·de·scrib·abil·ity (*or*
  ·able·ness)
in·de·scrib·able
in·de·scrib·ably
in·de·struct·ibil·ity (*or*
  ·ible·ness)
in·de·struct·ible
in·de·struct·ibly
in·de·ter·mi·nable
in·de·ter·mi·na·cy (*or*
  ·na·tion, ·nate·ness)
in·de·ter·mi·nate
in·de·ter·min·ism
  philosophy term
in·de·ter·min·ist
in·de·ter·min·is·tic
in·dex (*plural* ·dexes *or esp.*
  in mathematical contexts
  ·di·ces)
in·dex·er
in·dexi·cal
index-linked
In·dia
In·dian
In·di·ana US state
In·di·an·apo·lis US city
In·dic language group
in·di·can chemical
  compound
in·di·cant
in·di·cat·able
in·di·cate
in·di·ca·tion
in·dica·tive
in·di·ca·tor
in·dica·tory
in·di·ces *plural of* index
in·di·cia (*sing.* ·cium)
  distinguishing markings

in·di·cial
in·dict accuse; *compare*
  indite
in·dict·able
in·dictee
in·dict·er (*or* ·dic·tor)
in·dict·ment
In·dies
in·dif·fer·ence
in·dif·fer·ent
in·dif·fer·ent·ism
  indifference to religion
in·dif·fer·ent·ist
in·di·gence
in·di·gene (*or* ·gen) a native
in·dig·enous
in·dig·enous·ness (*or*
  in·di·gen·ity)
in·di·gent
in·di·gest·ibil·ity (*or*
  ·ible·ness)
in·di·gest·ible
in·di·ges·tion
in·di·ges·tive
in·dign undeserving
in·dig·nant
in·dig·na·tion
in·dig·nity (*plural* ·nities)
in·di·go (*plural* ·gos *or*
  ·goes)
in·di·goid
in·di·got·ic
in·di·rect
in·di·rec·tion
in·di·rect·ness
in·dis·cern·ible
in·dis·cern·ibly
in·dis·ci·pline
in·dis·creet tactless
in·dis·crete undivided
in·dis·cre·tion
in·dis·cre·tion·ary
in·dis·crimi·nate
in·dis·crimi·na·tion
in·dis·crimi·na·tive
in·dis·pen·sabil·ity (*or*
  ·sable·ness)
in·dis·pen·sable
in·dis·pen·sably
in·dis·pose
in·dis·posed
in·dis·po·si·tion
in·dis·put·abil·ity (*or*
  ·able·ness)
in·dis·put·able

in·dis·put·ably
in·dis·sol·ubil·ity (*or*
  ·uble·ness)
in·dis·sol·uble
in·dis·sol·ubly
in·dis·tinct
in·dis·tinc·tive
in·dis·tin·guish·abil·ity (*or*
  ·able·ness)
in·dis·tin·guish·able
in·dis·tin·guish·ably
in·dite *Archaic* write;
  compare indict
in·dium chemical element
in·di·vid·ual
in·di·vidu·al·ism
in·di·vidu·al·ist
in·di·vidu·al·is·tic
in·di·vidu·al·is·ti·cal·ly
in·di·vidu·al·ity (*plural*
  ·ities)
in·di·vidu·ali·za·tion (*or*
  ·sa·tion)
in·di·vidu·al·ize (*or* ·ise)
in·di·vidu·al·iz·er (*or* ·is·er)
in·di·vidu·al·ly
in·di·vidu·ate
in·di·vidu·ation
in·di·vidu·a·tor
in·di·vis·ibil·ity (*or*
  ·ible·ness)
in·di·vis·ible
in·di·vis·ibly
Indo·china (*or* Indo-China)
Indo·chinese (*or*
  Indo-Chinese)
in·do·cile
in·do·cil·ity
in·doc·tri·nate
in·doc·tri·na·tion
in·doc·tri·na·tor
Indo-European
in·dole (*or* ·dol) chemical
  compound
in·dole·acetic acid
in·dole·bu·tyr·ic acid
in·do·lence
in·do·lent
In·dolo·gist
In·dol·ogy
in·do·metha·cin
in·domi·tabil·ity (*or*
  ·table·ness)
in·domi·table
in·domi·tably

In·do·nesia
In·do·nesian
in·door (*adj*)
in·doors (*adv*)
Indo-Pacific
in·do·phenol
In·dore Indian city
in·dorse *variant spelling of*
endorse
in·dox·yl chemical
compound
in·draught (*US* ·draft)
in·drawn
Indre French department
Indre-et-Loire French
department
in·dris (*or* ·dri) animal
in·du·bi·tabil·ity (*or*
·table·ness)
in·du·bi·table
in·du·bi·tably
in·duce
in·duce·ment
in·duc·er
in·duc·ible
in·duct
in·duct·ance electrical
property
in·duc·tee *US* military
conscript
(inducter) *incorrect spelling of*
inductor
in·duc·tile not pliant
in·duc·til·ity
in·duc·tion
in·duc·tion·al
in·duc·tive
in·duc·tor
in·dulge
in·dul·gence
in·dul·gent
in·dulg·er
in·dulg·ing·ly
in·du·line (*or* ·lin) dye
in·dult Catholic
dispensation
in·du·pli·cate (*or* ·cat·ed)
in·du·pli·ca·tion
in·du·rate
in·du·ra·tion
in·du·ra·tive
In·dus Asian river
in·du·sial
in·du·sium (*plural* ·sia)
membrane

in·dus·trial
in·dus·tri·al·ism
in·dus·tri·al·ist
in·dus·tri·ali·za·tion (*or*
·sa·tion)
in·dus·tri·al·ize (*or* ·ise)
in·dus·tri·al·ly
in·dus·tri·ous
in·dus·try (*plural* ·tries)
in·dwell (·dwell·ing,
·dwelt)
in·earth bury
in·ebri·ant
in·ebri·ate
in·ebri·at·ed
in·ebria·tion
in·ebri·ety
in·ed·ibil·ity
in·ed·ible
in·ed·it·ed
in·edu·cabil·ity
in·edu·cable
in·ef·fabil·ity (*or*
·fable·ness)
in·ef·fable
in·ef·fably
in·ef·face·abil·ity
in·ef·face·able
in·ef·fec·tive
in·ef·fec·tual
in·ef·fec·tu·al·ity (*or* ·ness)
in·ef·fec·tual·ly
in·ef·fi·ca·cious
in·ef·fi·ca·cy (*or*
·ca·cious·ness)
in·ef·fi·cien·cy
in·ef·fi·cient
in·elas·tic
in·elas·tic·al·ly
in·elas·tic·ity
in·el·egance (*or* ·egan·cy)
in·el·egant
in·eli·gibil·ity (*or*
·gible·ness)
in·eli·gible
in·elo·quence
in·elo·quent
in·eluc·tabil·ity
in·eluc·table
in·eluc·tably
in·ept incompetent; *compare*
inapt
in·epti·tude
in·equal·ity (*plural* ·ities)
in·equi·table

in·equi·tably
in·equi·ty (*plural* ·ties)
in·eradi·cable
in·eradi·cably
in·ert
in·er·tia
in·er·tial
in·es·cap·able
in·es·cap·ably
in·es·cutch·eon heraldic
term
in esse *Latin* actually
existing
in·es·sen·tial
in·es·sen·ti·al·ity
in·es·sive linguistics term
in·es·ti·mabil·ity (*or*
·mable·ness)
in·es·ti·mable
in·es·ti·mably
in·evi·tabil·ity (*or*
·table·ness)
in·evi·table
in·evi·tably
in·ex·act
in·ex·acti·tude
in·ex·cus·abil·ity (*or*
·able·ness)
in·ex·cus·able
in·ex·cus·ably
in·ex·haust·ibil·ity (*or*
·ible·ness)
in·ex·haust·ible
in·ex·haust·ibly
in·ex·ist·ence (*or* ·en·cy)
in·ex·ist·ent
in·exo·rabil·ity (*or*
·rable·ness)
in·exo·rable
in·exo·rably
in·ex·pe·di·ence (*or* ·en·cy)
in·ex·pe·di·ent
in·ex·pen·sive
in·ex·pe·ri·ence
in·ex·pe·ri·enced
in·ex·pert
in·ex·pi·able
in·ex·pi·ably
in·ex·pli·cabil·ity (*or*
·cable·ness)
in·ex·pli·cable
in·ex·pli·cably
in·ex·plic·it
in·ex·press·ibil·ity (*or*
·ible·ness)

in·ex·press·ible
in·ex·press·ibly
in·ex·pres·sive
in·ex·ten·sibil·ity
in·ex·ten·sible
in·ex·tin·guish·able
in·ex·tir·pable
in ex·tre·mis *Latin* in
  extremity
in·ex·tri·cabil·ity (*or*
  ·cable·ness)
in·ex·tri·cable
in·ex·tri·cably
in·fal·libil·ity (*or*
  ·lible·ness)
in·fal·lible
in·fal·libly
in·fam·ize (*or* ·ise) make
  infamous
in·fa·mous
in·fa·my (*plural* ·mies)
in·fan·cy (*plural* ·cies)
in·fant
in·fan·ta Spanish princess
in·fan·te Spanish prince
in·fan·ti·cid·al
in·fan·ti·cide
in·fan·tile
in·fan·ti·lism
in·fan·til·ity
in·fan·try (*plural* ·tries)
in·fantry·man (*plural* ·men)
in·farct dead tissue
in·farct·ed
in·farc·tion
in·fare *Dialect* wedding
  reception
in·fatu·ate
in·fatu·at·ed
in·fatu·at·ed·ly
in·fatu·ation
in·fect
in·fec·tion
in·fec·tious
in·fec·tious·ness
in·fec·tive
in·fec·tive·ness (*or* ·tiv·ity)
in·fec·tor (*or* ·fect·er)
in·fe·cund
in·fe·cun·dity
in·fe·lici·tous
in·fe·lic·ity (*plural* ·ities)
in·fer (·fer·ring, ·ferred)
in·fer·able (*or* ·ible, ·rable,
  ·rible)

in·fer·ence
in·fer·en·tial
in·fe·ri·or
in·fe·ri·or·ity
in·fer·nal
in·fer·nal·ity
in·fer·nal·ly
in·fer·no (*plural* ·nos)
in·ferred
in·fer·rer
in·fer·ring
in·fer·tile
in·fer·til·ity
in·fest
in·fes·ta·tion
in·fest·er
in·fi·del
in·fi·del·ity (*plural* ·ities)
in·field
in·fielder
in·fighter
in·fighting
in·fil·trate
in·fil·tra·tion
in·fil·tra·tive
in·fil·tra·tor
in·fi·nite
in·fi·nite·ly
in·fini·tesi·mal
in·fini·tesi·mal·ly
in·fini·ti·val
in·fini·tive
in·fini·tude
in·fin·ity (*plural* ·ities)
in·firm
in·fir·ma·ry (*plural* ·ries)
in·fir·mity (*plural* ·mities)
in·fix
in·fix·ion
in·flame
in·flam·er
in·flam·ing·ly
in·flam·mabil·ity (*or*
  ·mable·ness)
in·flam·mable
in·flam·ma·tion
in·flam·ma·to·ri·ly
in·flam·ma·tory
in·flat·able
in·flate
in·flat·ed·ly
in·flat·er (*or* ·fla·tor)
in·fla·tion
in·fla·tion·ary
in·fla·tion·ism

in·fla·tion·ist
in·flect
in·flect·ed·ness
in·flec·tion (*or* ·flex·ion)
in·flec·tion·al (*or* ·flex·ion·)
in·flec·tive
in·flec·tor
in·flexed botany term
in·flex·ibil·ity (*or*
  ·ible·ness)
in·flex·ible
in·flex·ibly
in·flex·ion variant spelling of
  inflection
in·flict
in·flict·er (*or* ·flic·tor)
in·flic·tion
in·flic·tive
in·flo·res·cence
in·flo·res·cent
in·flow
in·flu·ence
in·flu·ence·able
in·flu·enc·er
in·flu·ent flowing in
in·flu·en·tial
in·flu·en·tial·ly
in·flu·en·za
in·flu·en·zal
in·flux
info *Slang* information
in·fold variant spelling of
  enfold
(inforce) incorrect spelling of
  enforce
in·form
in·for·mal
in·for·mal·ity (*plural* ·ities)
in·for·mal·ly
in·form·ant
in·for·ma·tion
in·for·ma·tion·al
in·forma·tive (*or* ·tory)
in·forma·tive·ly
in·form·ed·ly
in·form·er
in·form·ing·ly
infra·cos·tal anatomy term
in·fract violate
in·frac·tion
in·frac·tor
in·fra dig
infra·lap·sar·ian theology
  term
infra·lap·sari·an·ism

in·fran·gibil·ity (or ·gible·ness)
in·fran·gible
infra·red
infra·son·ic
infra·soni·cal·ly
infra·sound
infra·struc·ture
in·fre·quen·cy (or ·quence)
in·fre·quent
in·fringe
in·fringe·ment
in·fring·er
in·fu·lae (sing. ·la) ribbons on bishop's mitre
in·fun·dibu·lar (or ·late)
in·fun·dibu·li·form
in·fun·dibu·lum (plural ·la) anatomical part
in·furi·ate
in·furi·at·ing·ly
in·furia·tion
in·fus·cate (or ·cat·ed) tinged with brown
in·fuse
in·fus·er
in·fu·sibil·ity (or ·sible·ness)
in·fu·sible
in·fu·sion
in·fu·sion·ism theology term
in·fu·sion·ist
in·fu·sive
in·fu·so·rial
in·gath·er
in·gen·ious skilful; compare ingenuous
in·gé·nue naive girl
in·genu·ity (plural ·ities)
in·genu·ous naive; compare ingenious
in·gest
in·ges·ta (plural) food
in·gest·ible
in·ges·tion
in·ges·tive
in·gle
ingle·nook
in·glo·ri·ous
in·go·ing
in·got
in·graft variant spelling of engraft
in·grain (or en·)

in·grained (or en·)
in·grain·ed·ly (or en·)
in·grain·ed·ness (or en·)
in·grate
in·gra·ti·ate
in·gra·ti·at·ing (or in·gra·tia·tory)
in·gra·tia·tion
in·grati·tude
in·gra·ves·cence
in·gra·ves·cent becoming worse
in·gre·di·ent
in·gress
in·gres·sion
in·gres·sive
in·group
in·grow·ing
in·grown
in·growth
in·gui·nal of the groin
in·gur·gi·tate to gorge
in·gur·gi·ta·tion
In·gush (plural ·gushes or ·gush) Russian people
in·hab·it
in·hab·it·abil·ity
in·hab·it·able
in·hab·it·an·cy (or ·ance)
in·hab·it·ant
in·habi·ta·tion
in·hal·ant
in·ha·la·tion
in·ha·la·tor device aiding breathing
in·hale
in·hal·er
in·har·mon·ic
in·har·mo·ni·ous
in·har·mo·ny
in·haul (or ·haul·er) nautical term
in·here
in·her·ence (or ·en·cy)
in·her·ent
in·her·it
in·her·it·abil·ity (or ·able·ness)
in·her·it·able
in·her·it·ance
in·heri·tor (fem ·tress or ·trix; plural ·tors, ·tresses, or ·tri·ces)
in·he·sion inherence
in·hib·it

in·hib·it·able
in·hib·it·er (or ·hibi·tor)
in·hi·bi·tion
in·hibi·tive (or ·tory)
in·hibi·tor
in·hos·pi·table
in·hos·pi·tably
in·hos·pi·tal·ity
in·house
in·hu·man
in·hu·mane
in·hu·man·ity (plural ·ities)
in·hu·ma·tion
in·hume inter
in·hum·er
in·imi·cal
in·imi·cal·ly
in·imi·cal·ness (or ·ity)
in·imi·tabil·ity (or ·table·ness)
in·imi·table
in·imi·tably
ini·on anatomy term
in·iqui·tous
in·iquity (plural ·iquities)
ini·tial (·tial·ling, ·tialled; US ·tial·ing, ·tialed)
ini·tial·er (or ·tial·ler)
ini·tiali·za·tion (or ·sa·tion)
ini·tial·ize (or ·ise) computer term
ini·tial·ly
ini·ti·ate
ini·tia·tion
ini·tia·tive
ini·tia·tor
ini·tia·tory
ini·tia·tress (or ·trix)
in·ject
in·ject·able
in·jec·tion
in·jec·tive
in·jec·tor
in·ju·di·cious
In·jun US American Indian
in·junc·tion
in·junc·tive
in·jur·able
in·jure
in·jur·er
in·ju·ri·ous
in·ju·ry (plural ·ries)
in·jus·tice
ink
ink·berry (plural ·berries)

ink·blot
ink-cap fungus
In·ker·man Crimean battle
ink·horn
inki·ness
in·kle linen tape
ink·ling
ink·stand
ink·well
inky (inki·er, inki·est)
in·laid
in·land
in·land·er
in-law
in·lay (·lay·ing, ·laid)
in·lay·er
in·let (·let·ting, ·let)
in·li·er geology term
in loco pa·ren·tis
in·mate
in me·mo·ri·am
in·mi·grant immigrant
in·most
inn
in·nards
in·nate
in·ner
inner·most
in·ner·vate supply with
   nerves; *compare* enervate;
   innovate
in·ner·va·tion
in·nerve stimulate
in·ning baseball term
in·nings (*plural* ·nings)
inn·keeper
in·no·cence
in·no·cent
(innoculate) *incorrect spelling
   of* inoculate
in·nocu·ous
in·nomi·nate
in nomi·ne musical term
in·no·vate introduce new
   ideas; *compare* enervate;
   innervate
in·no·va·tion
in·no·va·tion·al
in·no·va·tion·ist
in·no·va·tive (*or* ·tory)
in·no·va·tor
in·nox·ious harmless
Inns·bruck Austrian city
in·nu·en·do (*plural* ·dos *or*
   ·does)

In·nu·it (*or* Inu·it; *plural* ·it
   or ·its) Eskimo
in·nu·mer·abil·ity (*or*
   ·able·ness)
in·nu·mer·able (*or* ·ous)
in·nu·mer·ably
in·nu·mer·ate
in·nu·tri·tion
in·nu·tri·tious
in·ob·serv·ance
in·ob·serv·ant
in·ocu·labil·ity
in·ocu·lable
in·ocu·late
in·ocu·la·tion
in·ocu·la·tive
in·ocu·la·tor
in·ocu·lum (*or* ·lant; *plural*
   ·la *or* ·lants)
in·odor·ous
in·of·fen·sive
in·of·fi·cious contrary to
   moral duty
in·op·er·abil·ity (*or*
   ·able·ness)
in·op·er·able
in·op·era·tive
in·op·por·tune
in·op·por·tune·ness (*or*
   ·tun·ity)
in·or·di·na·cy (*or*
   ·nate·ness)
in·or·di·nate
in·or·gan·ic
in·or·gani·cal·ly
in·os·cu·late
in·os·cu·la·tion
ino·si·tol chemical
   compound
ino·trop·ic physiology term
in·pa·tient
in per·pe·tuum
in pos·se *Latin* possible
in·put (·put·ting, ·put)
in·qi·lab Indian revolution
in·quest
in·qui·et
in·qui·etude
in·qui·line biology
   term
in·qui·lin·ism (*or* ·ity)
in·qui·li·nous
in·quire formally
   investigate; *US spelling of*
   enquire

in·quir·er
in·quiry (*plural* ·quiries)
   formal investigation; *US
   spelling of* enquiry
in·qui·si·tion
in·qui·si·tion·al
in·qui·si·tion·ist
in·quisi·tive
in·quisi·tive·ness
in·quisi·tor
in·quisi·to·rial
in·quisi·to·rial·ly
in re legal term
in rem legal term
in·road
in·rush
in·sali·vate
in·sali·va·tion
in·sa·lu·bri·ous
in·sa·lu·bri·ty
in·sane
in·sani·tari·ness (*or*
   ·ta·tion)
in·sani·tary
in·san·ity (*plural* ·ities)
in·sa·tiabil·ity (*or*
   ·tiable·ness, ·ti·ate·ness)
in·sa·tiable (*or* ·ti·ate)
in·sa·tiably (*or* ·ti·ate·ly)
in·scape person's
   nature
in·scrib·able
in·scribe
in·scrib·er
in·scrip·tion
in·scrip·tion·al
in·scrip·tive
in·scru·tabil·ity (*or*
   ·table·ness)
in·scru·table
in·sect
in·sec·tar·ium (*or* ·tary;
   plural ·tar·iums, ·tar·ia, *or*
   ·taries)
in·sec·tean (*or* ·tan, ·tile)
in·sec·ti·cid·al
in·sec·ti·cide
in·sec·ti·vore
in·sec·tivo·rous
in·secure
in·secu·rity (*plural* ·rities)
in·sel·berg rocky hill
in·semi·nate
in·semi·na·tion
in·semi·na·tor

in·sen·sate
in·sen·sibil·ity (or
 ·sible·ness)
in·sen·sible
in·sen·sibly
in·sen·si·tive
in·sen·si·tiv·ity
in·sen·ti·ence (or ·en·cy)
in·sen·ti·ent
in·sepa·rabil·ity (or
 ·rable·ness)
in·sepa·rable
in·sepa·rably
in·sert
in·sert·able
in·sert·er
in·ser·tion
in·ser·tion·al
in·ses·so·rial ornithology
 term
in·set (·set·ting, ·set)
in·set·ter
in·shore
in·side
in·sid·er
in·sidi·ous
in·sight
in·sight·ful
in·sig·nia (plural ·nias or
 ·nia)
in·sig·nifi·cance (or
 ·can·cy)
in·sig·nifi·cant
in·sin·cere
in·sin·cere·ly
in·sin·cer·ity (plural ·ities)
in·sinu·ate
in·sinu·a·tion
in·sinua·tive (or ·tory)
in·sinua·tor
in·sip·id
in·si·pid·ity (or ·ness)
in·sist
in·sist·ence (or ·en·cy)
in·sist·ent
in·sist·er
in situ
in·so·bri·ety
in so far (US in·so·far)
in·so·late expose to sun;
 compare insulate
in·so·la·tion
in·sole
in·so·lence
in·so·lent

in·sol·ubil·ity (or
 ·uble·ness)
in·sol·uble
in·sol·ubly
in·solv·abil·ity
in·solv·able
in·sol·ven·cy
in·sol·vent
in·som·nia
in·som·ni·ac
in·som·ni·ous
in·so·much
in·sou·ci·ance
in·sou·ci·ant
in·span (·span·ning,
 ·spanned) harness
in·spect
in·spect·able
in·spec·tion
in·spec·tion·al
in·spec·tive
in·spec·tor
in·spec·to·ral (or ·rial)
in·spec·tor·ate
in·spec·tor·ship
in·spir·able
in·spi·ra·tion
in·spi·ra·tion·al
in·spira·tive
in·spira·tory
in·spire
in·spir·er
in·spir·ing
in·spir·it
in·spir·it·er
in·spir·it·ing·ly
in·spir·it·ment
in·stabil·ity (plural ·ities)
in·stall (or ·stal; ·stall·ing,
 ·stalled or ·stal·ling,
 ·stalled)
in·stal·la·tion
in·stall·er
in·stal·ment (US ·stall·)
in·stance
in·stant
in·stan·ta·neous
in·stan·ta·neous·ness (or
 ·neity)
in·stan·ter without delay
in·stan·ti·ate represent by
 example
in·stant·ly
in·star zoology term
in·state

in·state·ment
in·stead
in·step
in·sti·gate
in·sti·ga·tion
in·sti·ga·tive
in·sti·ga·tor
in·stil (or ·still; ·stil·ling,
 ·stilled or ·still·ing,
 ·stilled)
in·stil·la·tion
in·stil·ler
in·stil·ment (or ·still·)
in·stinct
in·stinc·tive (or ·tual)
in·sti·tute
in·sti·tu·tion
in·sti·tu·tion·al
in·sti·tu·tion·al·ism
in·sti·tu·tion·al·ist
in·sti·tu·tion·ali·za·tion (or
 ·sa·tion)
in·sti·tu·tion·al·ize (or ·ise)
in·sti·tu·tion·ary
in·sti·tu·tive
in·sti·tu·tor (or ·tut·er)
in·struct
in·struct·ible
in·struc·tion
in·struc·tion·al
in·struc·tive
in·struc·tor
in·struc·tor·ship
in·struc·tress
in·stru·ment
in·stru·men·tal
in·stru·men·tal·ism
 philosophy term
in·stru·men·tal·ist
in·stru·men·tal·ity
in·stru·men·tal·ly
in·stru·men·ta·tion
in·sub·or·di·nate
in·sub·or·di·na·tion
in·sub·stan·tial
in·sub·stan·ti·al·ity
in·sub·stan·tial·ly
in·suf·fer·able
in·suf·fer·ably
in·suf·fi·cien·cy (or
 ·cience)
in·suf·fi·cient
in·suf·flate
in·suf·fla·tion
in·suf·fla·tor

in·su·la (*plural* ·lae)
anatomy term
in·sul·ant
in·su·lar
in·su·lar·ity (*or* ·ism)
in·su·late isolate; *compare*
insolate
in·su·la·tion
in·su·la·tor
in·su·lin hormone; *compare*
inulin
in·sult
in·sult·er
in·su·per·abil·ity (*or*
·able·ness)
in·su·per·able
in·su·per·ably
in·sup·port·able
in·sup·port·ably
in·sup·press·ible
in·sur·abil·ity
in·sur·able
in·sur·ance financial
protection; *insurance*
against death is life
assurance
in·sure protect against loss;
compare ensure
in·sured
in·sur·er
in·sur·gence
in·sur·gen·cy (*plural* ·cies)
in·sur·gent
in·sur·mount·abil·ity (*or*
·able·ness)
in·sur·mount·able
in·sur·mount·ably
in·sur·rec·tion
in·sur·rec·tion·al
in·sur·rec·tion·ary
in·sur·rec·tion·ism
in·sur·rec·tion·ist
in·sus·cep·tibil·ity
in·sus·cep·tible
in·swing cricket term
in·swinger
in·tact
in·tag·li·at·ed
in·tag·lio (*plural* ·lios *or* ·li)
engraving
in·take
in·tan·gibil·ity (*or*
·gible·ness)
in·tan·gible
in·tan·gibly

in·tar·sia mosaic of wood
in·te·ger
in·te·gral
in·te·gral·ly
in·te·grand maths term
in·te·grant part of
whole
in·te·grate
in·te·gra·tion
in·te·gra·tion·ist
in·te·gra·tive
in·te·gra·tor
in·teg·rity
in·tegu·ment
in·tegu·men·tary (*or*
·men·tal)
in·tel·lect
in·tel·lec·tion thought
in·tel·lec·tive
in·tel·lec·tual
in·tel·lec·tu·al·ism
in·tel·lec·tu·al·ist
in·tel·lec·tu·al·is·tic
in·tel·lec·tu·al·is·ti·cal·ly
in·tel·lec·tu·al·ity (*or* ·ness)
in·tel·lec·tu·ali·za·tion (*or*
·sa·tion)
in·tel·lec·tu·al·ize (*or* ·ise)
in·tel·lec·tu·al·iz·er (*or*
·is·er)
in·tel·lec·tu·al·ly
in·tel·li·gence
in·tel·li·gent
in·tel·li·gent·sia
in·tel·li·gibil·ity (*or*
·gible·ness)
in·tel·li·gi·ble
in·tel·li·gibly
In·tel·sat communications
satellite
in·tem·per·ance
in·tem·per·ate
in·tend
in·tend·ance French public
department
in·tend·an·cy
in·tend·ant provincial
official
in·tend·ed
in·tend·er
in·tend·ment legal term
in·ten·er·ate make tender
in·tense
in·ten·si·fi·ca·tion
in·ten·si·fi·er

in·ten·si·fy (·fies, ·fy·ing,
·fied)
in·ten·sion logic term;
compare intention
in·ten·sion·al
in·ten·sity (*plural* ·sities)
in·ten·sive
in·tent
in·ten·tion purpose;
compare intension
in·ten·tion·al
in·ten·tion·al·ity
in·ten·tion·al·ly
in·tent·ly
in·ter (·ter·ring, ·terred)
inter·act
inter·ac·tion
inter·ac·tion·al
inter·ac·tive
inter·ac·tiv·ity
in·ter alia *Latin* among
other things
in·ter ali·os *Latin* among
other people
inter·atom·ic
inter·bed·ded
inter·brain
inter·breed (·breed·ing,
·bred)
inter·ca·lari·ly
inter·ca·lary
inter·ca·late
inter·ca·la·tion
inter·ca·la·tive
inter·cede
inter·ced·er
inter·cel·lu·lar
inter·cept
inter·cep·tion
inter·cep·tive
inter·cep·tor (*or* ·cept·er)
inter·ces·sion
inter·ces·sion·al (*or*
inter·ces·sory)
inter·ces·sor
inter·ces·so·ri·al
inter·change
inter·change·abil·ity (*or*
·able·ness)
inter·change·able
inter·change·ably
inter·city
inter·clavi·cle
inter·cla·vicu·lar
inter·col·legi·ate

inter·co·lum·nar
inter·co·lum·nia·tion
inter·com
inter·com·mu·ni·cabil·ity
inter·com·mu·ni·cable
inter·com·mu·ni·cate
inter·com·mu·ni·ca·tion
inter·com·mu·ni·ca·tive
inter·com·mu·ni·ca·tor
inter·com·mun·ion
inter·con·nect
inter·con·nec·tion
inter·con·ti·nen·tal
inter·cos·tal anatomy term
inter·course
inter·crop (·crop·ping,
·cropped)
inter·cross crossbreed
inter·cur·rence
inter·cur·rent
inter·denomi·na·tion·al
inter·denomi·na·tion·al-
ism
inter·den·tal
inter·de·part·men·tal
inter·de·pend·ence (or
·en·cy)
inter·de·pend·ent
inter·dict
inter·dic·tion
inter·dic·tive (or ·tory)
inter·dic·tor
inter·dis·ci·pli·nary
in·ter·est
in·ter·est·ed
in·ter·est·ed·ly
in·ter·est·ing
inter·face
inter·fa·cial
inter·fa·cial·ly
inter·fac·ing
inter·fere
inter·fer·ence
inter·feren·tial
inter·fer·er
inter·fer·ing
inter·fer·om·eter physics
instrument
inter·fero·met·ric
inter·fero·met·ri·cal·ly
inter·fer·om·etry
inter·fer·on biochemical
substance
inter·fer·tile
inter·fer·til·ity

inter·file
inter·flu·ent flowing
together
inter·fluve land between
rivers
inter·flu·vial
inter·fuse
inter·fu·sion
inter·ga·lac·tic
inter·gla·cial
inter·gov·ern·men·tal
inter·gra·da·tion
inter·gra·da·tion·al
inter·grade
inter·gra·di·ent
inter·group
in·ter·im
in·te·ri·or
inter·ject
inter·jec·tion
inter·jec·tion·al (or
·tion·ary, ·tur·al)
inter·jec·tor
inter·jec·tory
inter·lace
inter·lace·ment
In·ter·la·ken Swiss town
inter·lami·nar
inter·lami·nate
inter·lami·na·tion
inter·lard
inter·lay (·lay·ing, ·laid)
inter·leaf (noun; plural
·leaves)
inter·leave (verb)
inter·line
inter·lin·ear (or ·eal)
inter·lin·eate
inter·line·ation
inter·lin·er
Inter·lin·gua language
inter·lin·ing
inter·link
inter·lock
inter·lock·er
inter·lo·cu·tion
inter·locu·tor
inter·locu·to·ri·ly
inter·locu·tory
inter·locu·tress (or ·trice,
·trix)
inter·lope
inter·lop·er
inter·lude
inter·lu·nar

inter·lu·na·tion period of
moon's invisibility
inter·mar·riage
inter·mar·ry (·ries, ·ry·ing,
·ried)
inter·media·cy
inter·medi·ary (plural
·aries)
inter·medi·ate
inter·media·tor
in·ter·ment burial; compare
internment
inter·mez·zo (plural ·zos or
·zi)
inter·mi·gra·tion
in·ter·mi·nable
in·ter·mi·nable·ness (or
·nabil·ity)
in·ter·mi·nably
inter·min·gle
inter·mis·sion
inter·mis·sive
inter·mit (·mit·ting,
·mit·ted)
inter·mit·tence (or ·ten·cy)
inter·mit·tent sporadic;
compare intromittent
inter·mit·tor
inter·mix
inter·mix·able
inter·mix·ture
inter·mo·lecu·lar
in·tern
in·ter·nal
in·ter·nal·ity (or ·ness)
in·ter·nali·za·tion (or
·sa·tion)
in·ter·nal·ize (or ·ise)
in·ter·nal·ly
inter·na·tion·al
inter·na·tion·al·ism
inter·na·tion·al·ist
inter·na·tion·al·ity
inter·na·tion·ali·za·tion (or
·sa·tion)
inter·na·tion·al·ize (or ·ise)
inter·na·tion·al·ly
inter·necine
in·ternee
In·ter·net
inter·neu·rone (or ·ron)
in·tern·ist
in·tern·ment confinement;
compare interment
inter·nod·al

inter·node part of plant
stem

in·tern·ship

inter·nun·cial

inter·nun·cio (*plural* ·cios)
papal ambassador

intero·cep·tive

intero·cep·tor physiology
term

inter·os·cu·late biology
term

inter·os·cu·la·tion

inter·page

inter·pel·lant

inter·pel·late question in
parliament; *compare*
interpolate

in·ter·pel·la·tion

in·ter·pel·la·tor

inter·pen·etrable

inter·pen·etrant

inter·pen·etrate

inter·pen·etra·tion

inter·pen·etra·tive

inter·per·son·al

inter·phase

inter·phone

inter·plan·etary

inter·play

inter·plead (·plead·ing,
·plead·ed, ·plead *or* ·pled)
legal term

inter·plead·er

Inter·pol

in·ter·po·late insert;
compare interpellate

in·ter·po·lat·er (*or* ·la·tor)

in·ter·po·la·tion

in·ter·po·la·tive

inter·pos·able

inter·pos·al

inter·pose

inter·pos·er

inter·po·si·tion

in·ter·pret

in·ter·pret·abil·ity (*or*
·able·ness)

in·ter·pret·able

in·ter·pre·ta·tion

in·ter·pre·ta·tion·al

in·ter·pre·ta·tive

in·ter·pret·er

in·ter·pre·tive

inter·ra·cial

inter·ra·cial·ly

inter·ra·di·al

inter·reg·nal

inter·reg·num (*plural*
·nums *or* ·na)

inter·re·late

inter·re·la·tion

inter·re·la·tion·ship

inter·rex (*plural* ·re·ges)
interim ruler

in·ter·ro·bang (*or*
·tera·bang) punctuation
mark

in·ter·ro·gate

in·ter·ro·gat·ing·ly

in·ter·ro·ga·tion

in·ter·ro·ga·tion·al

in·ter·rogative

in·ter·ro·ga·tor

in·ter·roga·to·ri·ly

in·ter·roga·tory (*plural*
·tories)

in·ter·rupt

in·ter·rupt·er (*or* ·rup·tor)

in·ter·rupt·ible

in·ter·rup·tion

in·ter·rup·tive

inter·scho·las·tic

inter·sect

inter·sec·tion

inter·sec·tion·al

inter·sex

inter·sex·ual

inter·sexu·al·ity (*or* ·ism)

inter·sexu·al·ly

inter·space

inter·spa·tial

inter·sperse

inter·sper·sion (*or* ·sal)

inter·sta·dial interglacial

inter·state

inter·stel·lar

in·ter·stice

in·ter·sti·tial

inter·strati·fi·ca·tion

inter·strati·fy (·fies, ·fy·ing,
·fied) geology term

inter·tex·ture

inter·tid·al

inter·trib·al

inter·tri·go (*plural* ·gos)
chafed skin

inter·tropi·cal

inter·twine

in·ter·val

inter·vene

inter·ven·er (*or* ·ve·nor)

inter·ven·tion

inter·ven·tion·al

inter·ven·tion·ism

inter·ven·tion·ist

inter·view

inter·viewee

inter·view·er

in·ter vivos legal term

inter·vo·cal·ic between
vowels

inter·vo·cali·cal·ly

inter·weave (·weav·ing,
·wove *or* ·weaved, ·woven
or ·weaved)

inter·weav·er

inter·wind (·wind·ing,
·wound)

inter·woven

in·tes·ta·cy

in·tes·tate

in·tes·ti·nal

in·tes·tine

in·ti·ma (*plural* ·mae)
anatomy term

in·ti·ma·cy (*plural* ·cies)

in·ti·mal

in·ti·mate

in·ti·ma·tion

in·timi·date

in·timi·da·tion

in·timi·da·tor

in·tinc·tion part of
Communion

in·tine botany term

into

in·tol·er·abil·ity (*or*
·able·ness)

in·tol·er·able

in·tol·er·ably

in·tol·er·ance

in·tol·er·ant

in·to·nate

in·to·na·tion

in·to·na·tion·al

in·tone

in·ton·er

in·tor·sion botany term

in toto *Latin* entirely

in·toxi·cable

in·toxi·cant

in·toxi·cate

in·toxi·cat·ing·ly

in·toxi·ca·tion

in·toxi·ca·tive

in·toxi·ca·tor
intra-atomic
intra·car·di·ac
intra·cel·lu·lar
intra·cos·tal anatomy term
intra·cra·nial
in·trac·tabil·ity (or
·table·ness)
in·trac·table
in·trac·tably
intra·cu·ta·neous
intra·der·mal (or ·mic)
in·tra·dos (plural ·dos or
·doses) inner curve of arch
intra·mo·lecu·lar
intra·mu·ral
intra·mus·cu·lar
in·tran·si·gence (or
·gen·cy)
in·tran·si·gent
in·tran·si·gent·ist
in·tran·si·tive
intra·nu·clear
intra·state
intra·tel·lu·ric
intra·uter·ine
in·trava·sa·tion
intra·venous
(intravert) incorrect spelling
of introvert
in·treat Archaic entreat
in·trench less common
spelling of entrench
in·trep·id
in·tre·pid·ity (or
·trep·id·ness)
in·tri·ca·cy (plural ·cies)
in·tri·cate
in·tri·cate·ness
in·trigue (·trigu·ing,
·trigued)
in·tri·guer
intrigu·ing
in·trin·sic (or ·si·cal)
in·trin·si·cal·ly
in·tro (plural ·tros)
intro·duce
intro·duc·er
intro·duc·ible
intro·duc·tion
intro·duc·to·ri·ly
intro·duc·tory
in·tro·gres·sion
in·troit prayer
in·troi·tal

intro·ject
intro·jec·tion psychology
term
intro·jec·tive
intro·mis·sion insertion
intro·mit·tent insertable;
compare intermittent
in·trorse turned inwards
intro·spect
intro·spec·tion
intro·spec·tion·al
intro·spec·tion·ist
intro·spec·tive
intro·ver·sion
intro·ver·sive (or ·tive)
intro·vert
in·trude
in·trud·er
in·trud·ing·ly
in·tru·sion
in·tru·sion·al
in·tru·sive
in·trust less common spelling
of entrust
in·tu·bate
in·tu·ba·tion
in·tu·it
in·tu·it·able
in·tu·ition
in·tu·ition·al
in·tu·ition·ism (or
·tion·al·ism)
in·tu·ition·ist (or
tion·al·ist)
in·tui·tive
in·tui·tiv·ism
in·tui·tiv·ist
in·tu·mesce
in·tu·mes·cence (or
·cen·cy)
in·tu·mes·cent
in·tus·sus·cept
in·tus·sus·cep·tion medical
and biology term
in·tus·sus·cep·tive
in·twine less common
spelling of entwine
inu·lin plant compound;
compare insulin
in·unc·tion
in·un·dant (or ·da·tory)
in·un·date
in·un·da·tion
in·un·da·tor
in·ure (or en·)

in·ur·ed·ness (or en·)
in·urn
in ut·ero Latin in the womb
in·utile
in·util·ity
in va·cuo Latin in a vacuum
in·vad·able
in·vade
in·vad·er
in·vagi·nable
in·vagi·nate
in·vagi·na·tion
in·va·lid disabled person
in·val·id not valid
in·vali·date
in·vali·da·tion
in·vali·da·tor
in·va·lid·ism being an
invalid
in·va·lid·ity (or
·val·id·ness) being not
valid
in·valu·able
in·valu·ably
In·var (Trademark)
in·vari·abil·ity (or
·able·ness)
in·vari·able
in·vari·ably
in·vari·ance (or ·an·cy)
in·vari·ant
in·va·sion
in·va·sive
in·vec·tive
in·veigh rail against
in·veigh·er
in·vei·gle cajole
in·vei·gle·ment
in·vei·gler
in·vent
in·vent·ible (or ·able)
in·ven·tion
in·ven·tion·al
in·ven·tive
in·ven·tive·ness
in·ven·tor
in·ven·to·ri·able
in·ven·to·ri·al
in·ven·tory (noun, plural
·tories; verb ·tories,
·tory·ing, ·toried)
in·ve·rac·ity (plural ·ities)
In·ver·car·gill New Zealand
city
In·ver·ness

in·verse
in·ver·sion
in·ver·sive
in·vert
in·vert·ase enzyme
in·ver·te·bra·cy (or
·tebrate·ness)
in·ver·te·bral
in·ver·tebrate
in·vert·er (or ·ver·tor)
in·vert·ibil·ity
in·vert·ible
in·vest
in·vest·able (or ·ible)
in·ves·ti·gable
in·ves·ti·gate
in·ves·ti·ga·tion
in·ves·ti·ga·tion·al
in·ves·ti·ga·tive (or ·ga·tory)
in·ves·ti·ga·tor
in·ves·ti·tive
in·ves·ti·ture
in·vest·ment
in·ves·tor
in·vet·era·cy (or
·er·ate·ness)
in·vet·er·ate
in·vi·abil·ity (or ·able·ness)
in·vi·able
in·vidi·ous
in·vigi·late
in·vigi·la·tion
in·vigi·la·tor
in·vig·or·ate
in·vig·or·at·ing·ly
in·vig·ora·tion
in·vig·ora·tive
in·vig·ora·tor
in·vin·cibil·ity (or
·cible·ness)
in·vin·cible
in·vin·cibly
in·vio·labil·ity (or
·lable·ness)
in·vio·lable
in·vio·lably
in·vio·la·cy (or ·late·ness)
in·vio·late
in·vis·ibil·ity (or ·ible·ness)
in·vis·ible
in·vis·ibly
in·vi·ta·tion
in·vi·ta·tory
in·vite
in·vit·er

in·vit·ing
in vi·tro outside the body
in vivo within the body
in·vo·cable
in·vo·ca·tion
in·vo·ca·tion·al
in·voca·tory
in·voice
in·voke
in·vok·er
in·volu·cel (or ·cel·lum;
plural ·cels or ·cel·la)
botany term
in·volu·cel·ate (or ·at·ed)
in·vo·lu·cral
in·vo·lu·crate
in·vo·lu·cre (or ·crum;
plural ·cres or ·cra) botany
term
in·vol·un·tari·ly
in·vol·un·tari·ness
in·vol·un·tary
in·vo·lute (or lut·ed)
in·vo·lu·tion
in·vo·lu·tion·al
in·volve
in·volved
in·volve·ment
in·volv·er
in·vul·ner·abil·ity (or
·able·ness)
in·vul·ner·able
in·vul·ner·ably
in·vul·tua·tion making
images for witchcraft
in·ward (adj)
in·ward·ly
in·wards (adv)
in·weave (·weav·ing, ·wove
or ·weaved, ·wo·ven or
·weaved)
in·wrought
Io satellite of Jupiter
iodate chemistry term
ioda·tion
iod·ic chemistry term
iodide
iodine
iodism iodine poisoning
iodi·za·tion (or ·sa·tion)
iodize (or iodise)
iodiz·er (or iodis·)
iodo·form antiseptic
iodo·met·ric (or ·ri·cal)
iodo·met·ri·cal·ly

iodom·etry chemistry
term
iodop·sin retinal pigment
iodous chemistry term
ion
Io·na Scottish island
Ionia Aegean region
Ionian
Ion·ic architecture term
ion·ic of ions
ioni·za·tion (or ·sa·tion)
ion·ize (or ·ise)
ionone plant extract
iono·pause
iono·sphere
iono·spher·ic
ion·to·pho·resis
biochemical technique
iota
iota·cism
IOU (plural IOUs)
Iowa
ip·ecac (or ·ecacu·an·ha)
purgative
Ipoh Malaysian city
ipo·moea plant
ipso facto
Ips·wich
ira·cund easily angered
Irá·kli·on Cretan port
Iran
Ira·nian
Iraq
Ira·qi
iras·cibil·ity (or ·cible·ness)
iras·cible
iras·cibly
irate
Ir·bid Jordanian town
ire
Ire·land
iren·ic (or ireni·cal)
conciliatory
ireni·cal·ly
iren·ics branch of theology
iri·da·ceous botany term
iri·dec·to·my (plural ·mies)
eye surgery
iri·des·cence
iri·des·cent
irid·ic
irid·ium chemical element
iri·doto·my (plural ·mies)
eye surgery
iris (plural irises) flowers

iris (*plural* iri·des *or* irises)
  part of eye
Irish
Irish·ism
Irish·man (*plural* ·men)
Irish·woman (*plural*
  ·women)
irit·ic
iri·tis eye disease
irk
irk·some
Ir·ku·tsk Russian city
iron
iron·bark tree
iron·bound unyielding
iron·clad
iron·er
iron·ic (*or* ironi·cal)
ironi·cal·ly
iron·ing
iro·nist
iro·nize indulge in irony
iron·monger
iron·mongery
Ironsides Cromwell's
  cavalry
iron·stone
iron·ware
iron·wood
iron·work
iro·ny (*plural* ·nies) sarcasm
irony containing iron
Iro·quoi·an
Iro·quois (*plural* ·quois)
  American Indian
ir·ra·di·ance
ir·ra·di·ant
ir·ra·di·ate
ir·ra·dia·tion
ir·ra·dia·tive
ir·ra·dia·tor
ir·ra·tion·al
ir·ra·tion·al·ity (*or* ·ism)
ir·ra·tion·al·ly
Ir·ra·wad·dy Burmese river
ir·re·claim·abil·ity (*or*
  ·able·ness)
ir·re·claim·able
ir·re·claim·ably
ir·rec·on·cil·abil·ity (*or*
  ·able·ness)
ir·rec·on·cil·able
ir·rec·on·cil·ably
ir·re·cov·er·able
ir·re·cov·er·ably

ir·re·cu·sable unable to be
  rejected
ir·re·deem·abil·ity (*or*
  ·able·ness)
ir·re·deem·able
ir·re·deem·ably
ir·re·den·tism
ir·re·den·tist territorial
  claimant
ir·re·duc·ibil·ity (*or*
  ·ible·ness)
ir·re·duc·ible
ir·re·duc·ibly
ir·ref·ra·gabil·ity (*or*
  ·gable·ness)
ir·ref·ra·gable indisputable
ir·ref·ra·gably
ir·re·fran·gibil·ity (*or*
  ·gible·ness)
ir·re·fran·gible inviolable
ir·refu·tabil·ity (*or*
  ·table·ness)
ir·refu·table
ir·refu·tably
ir·regu·lar
ir·regu·lar·ity (*plural* ·ities)
ir·rela·tive unrelated
ir·rel·evance (*or* ·evan·cy;
  plural ·evances *or* ·cies)
ir·rel·evant
ir·re·liev·able
ir·re·li·gion
ir·re·li·gion·ist
ir·re·li·gious
ir·re·medi·able
ir·re·medi·ably
ir·re·mis·sibil·ity (*or*
  ·sible·ness)
ir·re·mis·sible
ir·re·mis·sibly
ir·re·mov·abil·ity (*or*
  ·able·ness)
ir·re·mov·able
ir·re·mov·ably
ir·repa·rabil·ity (*or*
  ·rable·ness)
ir·repa·rable
ir·repa·rably
ir·re·place·able
ir·re·plevi·able (*or* ·sable)
  legal term
ir·re·press·ibil·ity (*or*
  ·ible·ness)
ir·re·press·ible
ir·re·press·ibly

ir·re·proach·abil·ity (*or*
  ·able·ness)
ir·re·proach·able
ir·re·proach·ably
ir·re·sist·ibil·ity (*or*
  ·ible·ness)
ir·re·sist·ible
ir·re·sist·ibly
ir·re·so·lubil·ity
ir·re·so·luble
ir·re·so·lute
ir·re·so·lu·tion
ir·re·solv·abil·ity (*or*
  ·able·ness)
ir·re·solv·able
ir·re·spec·tive
ir·re·spir·able
ir·re·spon·sibil·ity (*or*
  ·sible·ness)
ir·re·spon·sible
ir·re·spon·sibly
ir·re·spon·sive
ir·re·ten·tive
ir·re·triev·abil·ity (*or*
  ·able·ness)
ir·re·triev·able
ir·re·triev·ably
ir·rev·er·ence
ir·rev·er·ent (*or* ·eren·tial)
ir·re·vers·ibil·ity (*or*
  ·ible·ness)
ir·re·vers·ible
ir·re·vers·ibly
ir·revo·cabil·ity (*or*
  ·cable·ness)
ir·revo·cable
ir·revo·cably
(irridescent) *incorrect spelling
of* iridescent
ir·ri·gable
ir·ri·gate
ir·ri·ga·tion
ir·ri·ga·tion·al
ir·ri·ga·tive
ir·ri·ga·tor
ir·ri·tabil·ity
ir·ri·table
ir·ri·tably
ir·ri·tant
ir·ri·tate
ir·ri·ta·tion
ir·ri·ta·tive
ir·ri·ta·tor
ir·rupt enter or increase
  suddenly; *compare* erupt

ir·rup·tion
ir·rup·tive
Ir·tysh (or Ir·tish) Asian
river
Ir·vine Scottish town
is
isa·go·ge
isa·gog·ic
isa·gog·ics introductory
studies
is·al·lo·bar line on map
Isar European river
isa·tin (or ·tine)
isa·tin·ic
Iscariot biblical character
is·chae·mia (US ·che·)
inadequate blood supply
is·chaem·ic (US ·chem·)
Is·chia Mediterranean island
is·chial
is·chium (plural ·chia) hip
bone
is·en·trop·ic physics term
Isère French river
Is·fa·han (or Es·) Iranian
city
Ishmael biblical character
isin·glass
Isis Thames at Oxford;
Egyptian goddess
Is·ken·de·run Turkish port
Is·lam
Is·lama·bad Pakistani
capital
Is·lam·ic
Is·lam·ist
Is·lam·ize
is·land
is·land·er
Is·lay Scottish island
isle
Isle of Wight
is·let
Is·ling·ton
ism
Is·mai·li Muslim sect
Is·mai·lia Egyptian city
isn't
iso·ag·glu·ti·na·tion
iso·ag·glu·ti·na·tive
iso·ag·glu·ti·nin
iso·anti·gen
iso·bar
iso·bar·ic
iso·bar·ism

iso·bath line on map
iso·bath·ic
iso·cheim (or ·chime) line
on map
iso·chei·mal (or ·menal,
·chi·mal)
iso·chor (or ·chore) line on
graph
iso·chor·ic
iso·chro·mat·ic
isoch·ro·nal (or ·nous)
isoch·ro·nize (or ·nise)
isoch·ro·ous of uniform
colour
iso·cli·nal (or ·clin·ic)
iso·cline geology term
isoc·ra·cy (plural ·cies)
political equality
iso·crat·ic
iso·cya·nide
iso·dia·met·ric
iso·dia·phere physics term
iso·di·mor·phism chemistry
term
iso·di·mor·phous (or ·phic)
iso·dy·nam·ic
iso·elec·tric
iso·elec·tron·ic
iso·gam·ete biology term
iso·ga·met·ic
isoga·mous
isoga·my
isog·enous genetically
uniform
isog·eny
iso·geo·therm
iso·geo·ther·mal (or ·mic)
iso·gloss linguistics term
iso·glos·sal
iso·glot·tic
iso·gon maths term
iso·gon·ic (or isogo·nal)
iso·hel line on map
iso·hy·et line on map
iso·labil·ity
iso·lable
iso·late
iso·la·tion
iso·la·tion·ism
iso·la·tion·ist
iso·la·tive
iso·la·tor
iso·leci·thal biology term
iso·leu·cine amino acid
iso·lex linguistics term

iso·line isopleth
isolo·gous chemistry term
iso·logue
iso·mag·net·ic
iso·mer
iso·mer·ic
isom·er·ism
isom·eri·za·tion (or
·sa·tion)
isom·er·ize (or ·ise)
isom·er·ous
iso·met·ric
iso·met·ri·cal
iso·met·rics exercises
iso·metro·pia physiology
term
isom·etry maths term
iso·morph
iso·mor·phic (or ·phous)
iso·mor·phism
iso·nia·zid medicinal drug
isono·my equality before
the law
iso·octane chemical
compound
iso·phone linguistics term
iso·pi·es·tic having equal
atmospheric pressure
iso·pi·es·ti·cal·ly
iso·pleth line on map
iso·pod crustacean
isopo·dan (or ·dous)
iso·prene chemical
compound
iso·pro·pyl
iso·rhyth·mic musical term
isos·celes geometry term
iso·seis·mal
is·os·mot·ic
iso·spon·dy·lous zoology
term
isos·ta·sy (plural ·sies)
geological theory
iso·stat·ic
iso·ster·ic chemistry term
iso·tac·tic
isoth·er·al
iso·there line on map
iso·therm
iso·ther·mal
iso·tone chemistry term
iso·ton·ic
iso·to·nic·ity
iso·tope
iso·top·ic

iso·topi·cal·ly
isoto·py
iso·tron physics apparatus
iso·trop·ic
iso·tropi·cal·ly
isot·ro·pous
isot·ro·py
Is·ra·el
Is·rae·li (plural ·lis or ·li)
Is·rael·ite
Is·ra·fil Islamic archangel
is·su·able
is·su·ance
is·su·ant
is·sue (·su·ing, ·sued)
is·su·er
Is·sus battle
Is·tan·bul
isth·mi·an
isth·moid
isth·mus (plural ·muses or
·mi)
is·tle (or ix·) fibre
Is·tria Adriatic peninsula
Is·trian

it
ita·colu·mite sandstone
Ital·ian
Ital·ian·ate
Ital·ian·esque
Ital·ian·ism
Ital·ian·ize
Ital·ic language
ital·ic type or print
Itali·cism
itali·ci·za·tion (or ·sa·tion)
itali·cize (or ·cise)
Ita·ly
itch
itchi·ness
itch·ing
itchy (itchi·er, itchi·est)
item
itemi·za·tion (or ·sa·tion)
item·ize (or ·ise)
it·er·ant
it·er·ate
it·era·tion (or ·er·ance)
it·era·tive
Itha·ca Greek island

Itha·can
ithy·phal·lic poetry term
itin·er·an·cy (or ·era·cy;
plural ·cies)
itin·er·ant
itin·er·ary (plural ·aries)
itin·er·ate travel about
itin·era·tion
it'll it will; it shall
its of it
it's it is
it·self
Iva·no·vo Russian city
I've I have
ivied
ivo·ry (plural ·ries)
ivy (plural ivies)
Iwo Jima Pacific island
ixia plant
ix·tle variant spelling of
istle
izard chamois
Izhevsk Russian city
Iz·mir Turkish port
Iz·mit Turkish town

J

jab (jab·bing, jabbed)
Jab·al·pur (or Jub·bul·pore)
Indian city
jabbed
jab·ber
jab·ber·er
jab·ber·wocky nonsense
verse
jab·bing
jabi·ru bird
jabo·ran·di shrub
ja·bot frill
jaca·mar bird
ja·ça·na bird
jaca·ran·da tree
ja·cinth gemstone
jack
jack·al
jacka·napes
jack·ass
jack·boot
jack·daw
jack·eroo (or jacka·roo;
plural ·roos) Austral trainee
sheep-station manager

jack·et
jack·et·ed
jack·fish (plural ·fish or
·fishes)
jack·fruit
jack·hammer
jack·knife (plural ·knives)
jack·pot
jacks game
jack·shaft
jack·smelt (plural ·smelts or
·smelt) fish
jack·snipe (plural ·snipe or
·snipes) bird
Jack·son US city
Jack·son·ville US port
jack·stay nautical term
jack·straws game
Jaco·bean of James I
Ja·co·bian maths term
Jaco·bin French radical
Jaco·bin·ic (or ·bini·cal)
Jaco·bin·ism
Jaco·bite of James II
Jaco·bit·ic

Jaco·bit·ism
ja·co·bus (plural ·buses)
coin
jaco·net fabric
Jac·quard fabric; loom
jac·ti·ta·tion boasting
Ja·cuzzi (Trademark)
jade
jad·ed
jade·ite mineral
jae·ger marksman; bird
Jael biblical character
Jaf·fa Israeli port
Jaff·na Sri Lankan port
jag (jag·ging, jagged)
jag·ged
jag·ged·ly
jag·ged·ness
jag·gery (or ·gary, ·ghery)
date sugar
jag·ging
jag·gy (·gi·er, ·gi·est)
jagu·ar
ja·gua·ron·di (or ·run·;
plural ·dis) feline

jai alai Spanish game
jail (*or* gaol)
jail•bird (*or* gaol•)
jail•break (*or* gaol•)
jail•er (*or* •or, gaol•er)
jail•house
Jain (*or* Jai•na) Hindu
Jain•ism
Jain•ist
Jai•pur Indian city
Ja•ja•pu•ra (*or* Dja•)
  Indonesian port
Ja•kar•ta (*or* Dja•)
  Indonesian capital
jal•ap (*or* •op) purgative
ja•lap•ic
Ja•lis•co Mexican state
ja•lopy (*or* •lop•py; *plural*
  •lopies *or* •lop•pies)
jalou•sie shutter
jam (jam•ming, jammed)
  crowd; preserve; *compare*
  jamb
Ja•mai•ca
Ja•mai•can
jamb (*or* jambe) part of
  frame; *compare* jam
jam•ba•laya Creole dish
jam•bart (*or* jam•beau,
  jam•ber; *plural* •barts,
  •beaux, *or* •bers)
  armour
Jam•bi (*or* Djam•)
  Indonesian port
jam•bo•ree
jammed
jam•mer
jam•ming
Jam•mu Indian city
jam•my (•mi•er, •mi•est)
Jam•na•gar Indian city
jam•pan sedan chair
Jam•shed•pur Indian city
Jamshid (*or* Jamshyd)
  mythological king
Ja•na•ta Indian political
  party
jan•gle
jan•gler
Ja•nicu•lum Roman hill
jan•is•sary (*or* jani•zary;
  plural •saries *or* •zaries)
  Turkish guard
jani•tor (*fem* •tress)
jani•to•ri•al

Jan•sen•ism Catholic
  doctrine
Jan•sen•ist
Jan•sen•is•tic (*or* •ti•cal)
Janu•ary (*plural* •aries)
Janus Roman god
Ja•pan
ja•pan (•pan•ning,
  •panned) lacquer
Japa•nese
jape
jap•er
jap•ery
Japheth biblical character
jap•ing•ly
ja•poni•ca shrub
Ja•pu•rá South American
  river
jar (jar•ring, jarred)
jar•di•nière plant holder
jar•ful
jar•gon language
jar•gon (*or* •goon) gemstone
jar•goni•za•tion (*or*
  •sa•tion)
jar•gon•ize (*or* •ise)
jarl Scandinavian chieftain
jaro•site mineral
jarp (*or* jaup) *Dialect* to
  smash
jar•rah tree
jarred
jar•ring
jar•ring•ly
Jar•row English port
jar•vey (*or* •vie) coachman
jas•mine
jas•pé variegated
jas•per
Jat (*plural* Jat *or* Jats)
  Indo-European people
jato (*plural* •tos) jet-assisted
  takeoff
jaun•dice
jaunt
jaun•ti•ly
jaun•ty (•ti•er, •ti•est)
Java
Java•nese (*or* Ja•van)
jave•lin
jaw
Ja•wan Indian soldier
jaw•bone
jaw•breaker
jay

Jaya (*or* Dja•ja) Indonesian
  mountain
jay•walk
jay•walk•er
jay•walk•ing
jazz
jazzi•ly
jazzi•ness
jazzy (jazzi•er, jazzi•est)
jeal•ous
jeal•ous•ly
jeal•ousy (*plural* •ousies)
jeans
jeb•el (*or* djeb•) Arab hill
Jeb•el Musa Moroccan
  mountain
Jed•da *variant spelling of*
  Jidda
jeep
jeer
jeer•er
jeer•ing•ly
je•had *variant spelling of*
  jihad
Je•hol Chinese region
Je•ho•vah
Je•ho•vian (*or* •vic)
je•ju•nal
je•june naive
je•june•ly
je•june•ness (*or* je•jun•ity)
je•ju•num small intestine
Jekyll and Hyde
jell (*or* gel; jel•ling, jelled *or*
  gel•ling, gelled) congeal;
  compare gel
jel•laba (*or* •lab•ah) cloak
jel•lied
jel•li•fi•ca•tion
jel•li•fy (•fies, •fy•ing, •fied)
jello *US* jelly
jel•ly (*noun, plural* •lies; *verb*
  •lies, •ly•ing, •lied)
jelly•bean
jelly•fish (*plural* •fish *or*
  •fishes)
jem•my (*noun, plural* •mies;
  verb •mies, •my•ing,
  •mied)
jen•net (*or* gen•et, gen•net)
  female donkey; *compare*
  genet
jen•ny (*plural* •nies)
  machine; female animal
jeop•ard•ize (*or* •ise)

jeop·ardy

je·quir·ity (or ·quer·; plural ·ties) plant

jer·bil variant spelling of gerbil

jer·boa

jer·emi·ad lamentation

Je·rez Spanish town

Jeri·cho

je·rid javelin

jerk

jerk·er

jerki·ly

jer·kin jacket; compare gherkin

jerky (jerki·er, jerki·est)

jero·bo·am wine bottle

Jer·ry (plural ·ries) Slang German

jer·ry (plural ·ries) Slang chamber pot

jerry-build (-building, -built)

Jer·sey island; cattle

jer·sey garment

Je·ru·sa·lem

jess falconry term

jes·sa·mine Archaic jasmine

jest

jes·ter

Jesu

Jesu·it

Jesu·it·ic (or ·iti·cal)

Jesu·it·ism (or ·it·ry)

Jesus

jet (jet·ting, jet·ted)

jeté ballet step

jet·liner

jet·port

jet-propelled

jet·sam (or ·som)

jet·setter

jet·ti·ness

jet·ti·son

jet·ton gambling token

jet·ty (plural ·ties)

Jew

jew·el (·ell·ing, ·elled; US ·el·ing, ·eled)

jewel·fish (plural ·fish or ·fishes)

jew·el·ler (US ·el·er)

jew·el·lery (US ·el·ry)

Jew·ess

jew·fish (plural ·fish or ·fishes)

Jew·ish

Jew·ish·ness

Jew·ry (plural ·ries)

jew's-ear fungus

jew's-harp

Jezebel biblical character

jezebel shameless woman

Jhan·si Indian city

jib (jib·bing, jibbed)

jib·ber

jib·bons Dialect spring onions

jibe variant spelling of gibe or gybe

jib-headed

Ji·bou·ti variant spelling of Djibouti

Jid·da (or ·dah, Jed·) Saudi Arabian port

jif·fy (or jiff; plural jif·fies or jiffs)

jig (jig·ging, jigged)

jig·ger

jig·gered

jigger-mast

jiggery-pokery

jig·ging

jig·gle

jig·gly

jig·saw

ji·had (or je·) Islamic holy war

jil·lion large number

jil·lionth

jilt

jilt·er

jin·gle

jin·gler

jin·gly (·gli·er, ·gli·est)

jin·go (plural ·goes)

jin·go·ism

jin·go·ist

jin·go·is·tic

jin·go·is·ti·cal·ly

Jin·ja Ugandan town

jink

jinks high spirits; compare jinx

jin·ni (or ·nee, djin·ni, djin·ny; plural jinn or djinn) Muslim spirit

jinx bad luck; compare jinks

ji·pi·ja·pa plant

jit·ter

jitter·bug (·bug·ging, ·bugged)

jit·tery

jive

Joab biblical character

Job biblical character

job (job·bing, jobbed)

job·ber

job·bery corruption

job·bing

Job·cen·tre

job·less

job·less·ness

Jocasta mother of Oedipus

Jock Slang Scot

jock·ey

jock·strap

jo·cose

jo·cose·ly

jo·cose·ness (or jo·cos·ity)

jocu·lar

jocu·lar·ity

joc·und

jo·cun·dity (or joc·und·ness)

Jodh·pur Indian city

jodh·purs riding trousers

Jodo Buddhist sect

joey Austral young kangaroo

jog (jog·ging, jogged)

jog·ger

jog·gle

jog·gler

Jog·ja·kar·ta variant spelling of Yokyakarta

jog-trot (-trot·ting, -trot·ted)

jo·han·nes (or ·an·; plural ·nes) Portuguese coin

Jo·han·nes·burg

John Dory fish

john·ny (plural ·nies) Slang man; condom

John o'Groats

John·so·nian of Samuel Johnson

Jo·hore Malaysian state

joie de vivre

join

join·der legal term

join·er

join·ery

joint

joint·ed

joint·er
joint·ly
joint·ress legal term
join·ture legal term
joint·worm
joist
jo·joba tree; oil
joke
jok·er
jok·ey (or joky; joki·er, joki·est)
jok·ing·ly
jol·li·fi·ca·tion
jol·li·fy (·fies, ·fy·ing, ·fied)
jol·lity (plural ·lities)
jol·ly (adj ·li·er, ·li·est; verb ·lies, ·ly·ing, ·lied)
Jolo Philippine island
jolt
jolt·er
jolt·ing·ly
jolty
Jön·kö·ping Swedish city
jon·nock Dialect genuine
jon·quil
Jop·pa biblical Jaffa
Jor·dan
Jor·da·nian
jo·rum drinking bowl
Jos Nigerian city
josh US tease
joss Chinese deity
jos·tle
jos·tler
jot (jot·ting, jot·ted)
jot·ter
joual Canadian French dialect
joule unit of energy
jounce jolt
jour·nal
jour·nal·ese
jour·nal·ism
jour·nal·ist
jour·nal·is·tic
jour·nal·is·ti·cal·ly
jour·nali·za·tion (or ·sa·tion)
jour·nal·ize (or ·ise) record in journal
jour·nal·iz·er (or ·is·er)
jour·ney
jour·ney·er
journey·man (plural ·men) craftsman

journo (plural journos) Austral journalist
joust
joust·er
Jove Roman god
jo·vial
jo·vi·al·ity (or ·ness)
jo·vi·al·ly
Jo·vian
jowl
joy
joy·ful
joy·ful·ly
joy·ful·ness
joy·less
joy·less·ness
joy·ous
joy·ous·ness
joy·pop (·pop·ping, ·popped) Slang take drugs
joy·ride (·riding, ·rode, ·ridden)
joy·rider
Juan de Fuca US–Canadian strait
juba African-American dance
Ju·bal biblical character
Jub·bul·pore variant spelling of Jabalpur
jube church gallery
ju·bi·lance (or ·lan·cy)
ju·bi·lant
ju·bi·late
ju·bi·la·tion
ju·bi·lee
Ju·daea (or ·dea)
Ju·daean (or ·dean)
Ju·da·ic (or ·dai·cal)
Ju·dai·ca Jewish literature
Ju·da·ism
Ju·da·ist
Ju·da·is·tic
Ju·dai·za·tion (or ·sa·tion)
Ju·da·ize (or ·ise)
Ju·da·iz·er (or ·is·er)
Judas traitor
ju·das peephole
jud·der
judge
judge·able
judg·er
judge·ship
judg·ing·ly
judg·ment (or judge·)

judg·men·tal (or judge·)
ju·di·cable
ju·di·ca·tive
ju·di·ca·tor judge
ju·di·ca·to·rial
ju·di·ca·tory
ju·di·ca·ture
ju·di·cial
ju·di·cial·ly
ju·di·ci·ary (plural ·aries)
ju·di·cious
ju·di·cious·ly
ju·di·cious·ness
judo
ju·do·gi judo costume
ju·do·ist
ju·do·ka judo expert
Judy (or judy; plural Judies or judies) Slang girl
jug (jug·ging, jugged)
ju·gal cheekbone
ju·gate botany term
jug·ful (plural ·fuls)
jugged
Jug·ger·naut Hindu idol
jug·ger·naut vehicle; destructive force
jug·ging
jug·gins silly fellow
jug·gle
jug·gler
jug·glery
jug·gling
ju·glan·da·ceous botany term
Ju·go·sla·via variant spelling of Yugoslavia
jugu·lar
ju·gum biology term
juice
juici·ly
juici·ness
juicy (juici·er, juici·est)
ju·jit·su (or ju·jut·su, jiu·)
juju African fetish
ju·ju·ism
ju·ju·ist
ju·jube plant; sweet
juke·box
ju·lep drink
Jul·ian of Julius Caesar
ju·li·enne cookery term
Jul·lun·dur Indian city
July (plural Julies)
jum·ble

jum·bler
jum·bly (·bli·er, ·bli·est)
jum·bo (*plural* ·bos)
jum·buck *Austral* sheep
Jum·na Indian river
jump
jump·able
jump·er
jumpi·ly
jumpi·ness
jump-off (*noun*)
jump-start
jumpy (jumpi·er,
jumpi·est)
jun·ca·ceous botany term
jun·co (*plural* ·cos) bird
junc·tion
junc·tion·al
junc·ture
Jun·diaí Brazilian city
June
Ju·neau Alaskan capital
Jung·frau Swiss mountain
Jung·ian psychiatry term
jun·gle
jun·gly (·gli·er, ·gli·est)
jun·ior
ju·ni·per
junk
Jun·ker Prussian landowner
jun·ket
jun·ket·er (*or* ·ket·ter,
·ke·teer)
junkie (*or* junky; *plural*
junkies)
junk·yard
Juno Roman goddess;
asteroid

Ju·no·esque
jun·ta
Ju·pi·ter planet
Jupiter Roman god
ju·pon garment
Jura European mountains;
Scottish island
jura *plural of* jus
ju·ral of the law
Ju·ras·sic geological period
ju·rat legal term
ju·ra·tory
ju·rel fish
ju·ridi·cal (*or* ·rid·ic)
ju·ris·con·sult legal advisor
ju·ris·dic·tion
ju·ris·dic·tion·al
ju·ris·dic·tion·al·ly
ju·ris·dic·tive
ju·ris·pru·dence
ju·ris·pru·dent
ju·ris·pru·den·tial
ju·ris·pru·den·tial·ly
ju·rist
ju·ris·tic (*or* ·ti·cal)
ju·ror
Ju·ruá South American river
jury (*plural* juries)
jury·man (*plural* ·men)
jury-rigged nautical term
jury·woman (*plural*
·women)
jus (*plural* jura) legal right
jus ci·vi·le civil law
jus di·vi·num divine law
jus na·tu·ra·le natural law
jus·sive grammar term
jus soli legal term

just
jus·tice
jus·tice·ship
jus·ti·ci·abil·ity
jus·ti·ci·able subject to
jurisdiction
jus·ti·ci·ar medieval legal
officer
jus·ti·ci·ar·ship
jus·ti·ci·ary (*plural* ·aries)
jus·ti·fi·abil·ity (*or*
·able·ness)
jus·ti·fi·able
jus·ti·fi·ably
jus·ti·fi·ca·tion
jus·ti·fi·ca·tory (*or* ·tive)
jus·ti·fi·er
jus·ti·fy (·fies, ·fy·ing, ·fied)
jus·ti·fy·ing·ly
jus·tle jostle
just·ly
just·ness
jut (jut·ting, jut·ted)
Jute Germanic tribe
jute fibre
Jut·ish
Jut·land Danish peninsula
Jut·land·er
jut·ted
jut·ting
ju·venes·cence youth
ju·venes·cent
ju·venile
ju·venilia
ju·venil·ity (*plural* ·ities)
jux·ta·pose
jux·ta·po·si·tion
jux·ta·po·si·tion·al

K

kab·ba·la (*or* ka·ba·la)
variant spellings of
cabbala
ka·ba·ra·go·ya lizard
Ka·bardino-Balkar Russian
republic
ka·bu·ki Japanese drama
Ka·bul Afghan capital
Ka·byle (*plural* ·byles *or*
·byle) Berber people
ka·chang pu·teh Malaysian
dish

ka·chi·na American Indian
spirit
Kad·dish (*plural*
kad·di·shim) Jewish
prayer
Ka·di·yev·ka *former name of*
Stakhanov
Ka·du·na Nigerian state
Kaf·fir (*plural* ·firs *or* ·fir)
kaf·fir sorghum
Kaf·ir (*plural* ·irs *or* ·ir)
Afghan people

kaf·tan (*or* caf·)
Ka·gera African river
Ka·go·shi·ma Japanese port
kai·ak *variant spelling of*
kayak
Kai·feng Chinese city
kail *variant spelling of* kale
kai·nite mineral
kai·no·gen·esis *variant
spelling of* caenogenesis
Kai·ser
kai·ser·dom (*or* ·ism)

Kai·sers·lau·tern German
city
kaka parrot
ka·ka·po (*plural* **·pos**) parrot
ka·kemo·no (*plural* **·nos**)
Japanese wall hanging
kaki (*plural* **kakis**) fruit
kala-azar disease
Ka·la·ha·ri African desert
Kala·ma·zoo US city
Ka·lat (*or* **Khe·**) Pakistani
region
kale (*or* **kail**) cabbage
ka·lei·do·scope
ka·lei·do·scop·ic
ka·lei·do·scopi·cal·ly
kal·ends *variant spelling of*
calends
kale·yard (*or* **kail·**) *Scot*
vegetable garden
Kal·goor·lie Australian city
Kali Hindu goddess
kali plant
kal·ian hookah
ka·lif (*or* **kha·**) *variant
spellings of* caliph
Ka·li·nin *former name of*
Tver
Ka·li·nin·grad Russian port
kal·mia shrub
Kal·muck (*or* **·myk**; *plural*
·mucks, **·muck** *or* **·myks**,
·myk) Mongoloid people
ka·long fruit bat
kal·so·mine *variant spelling
of* calcimine
Ka·lu·ga Russian city
Kama Russian river; Hindu
god
kama·cite alloy
Kama·ku·ra Japanese city
ka·ma·la tree
Ka·ma·su·tra Hindu text
Kam·chat·ka Russian
peninsula
kame mound
Kamensk-Uralski Russian
city
Ka·met Indian mountain
kami (*plural* **kami**) Japanese
spirit
ka·mi·ka·ze
Kam·pa·la Ugandan capital
kam·pong Malaysian village
Kampuchea

Kampuchean
kana Japanese writing
kana·my·cin antibiotic
Ka·nan·ga city in the
Democratic Republic of
Congo
Ka·na·ra (*or* **Ca·**) Indian
region
Ka·na·rese (*or* **Ca·**; *plural*
·rese)
Kana·za·wa Japanese port
Kan·chi·pu·ram Indian
city
Kan·da·har Afghan city
Kan·dy Sri Lankan city
kan·ga (*or* **khan·**) African
garment
kan·ga·roo (*plural* **·roos**)
Kang·chen·jun·ga (*or*
Kan·chen·) Himalayan
mountain
Kan·na·da Indian language
Kano Nigerian state
Kan·pur Indian city
Kan·sas
Kan·su Chinese province
kan·tar unit of weight
Kant·ian
Kant·ian·ism (*or* **Kant·ism**)
philosophy
Kao·hsiung (*or* **Kao-hsiung**)
Chinese port
kao·li·ang sorghum
kao·lin (*or* **·line**)
kao·lin·ic
kao·lin·ite mineral
kaon physics particle
ka·pell·meis·ter (*plural* **·ter**)
ka·pok
kap·pa Greek letter
ka·put *Slang* not
functioning; *compare*
caput
kara·bi·ner mountaineering
clip
Karachai-Cherkess Russian
region
Ka·ra·chi Pakistani city
Ka·ra·gan·da Kazakh city
Kara·ite Jewish sect
Kara-Kalpak Uzbek republic
Ka·ra·ko·ram mountain
range
Ka·ra·ko·rum Mongolian
city

kara·kul (*or* **cara·**) sheep;
compare caracul
ka·ra·te
Kar·ba·la (*or* **Ker·be·**) Iraqi
town
Ka·relia Russian republic
Ka·relian
Ka·ren (*plural* **·rens** *or* **·ren**)
Thai language and people
Ka·ri·ba African lake and
dam
Karl-Marx-Stadt *former
name of* Chemnitz
Karls·ruhe German city
kar·ma destiny
kar·mic
Kar·na·taka Indian state
Ka·roo (*or* **Kar·roo**) South
African plateau
ka·roo (*or* **kar·roo**; *plural*
·roos) plateau
ka·ross African garment
kar·ri tree
karst limestone scenery
karst·ic
karyo·gam·ic
kary·oga·my biology term
karyo·ki·nesis
karyo·ki·net·ic
karyo·lymph
kary·oly·sis
karyo·lyt·ic
karyo·plasm
karyo·plas·mic (*or* **·mat·ic**)
karyo·some
karyo·type
karyo·typ·ic (*or* **·typi·cal**)
Ka·sai African river
kas·bah (*or* **cas·**)
ka·sher *variant spelling of*
kosher
Kash·gar Chinese city
Kash·mir
Kash·miri (*plural* **·miris** *or*
·miri)
Kash·mir·ian
Kas·sa·la Sudanese city
Kas·sel German city
kat (*or* **khat**) narcotic
kata·bat·ic meteorology
term
ka·ta·ka·na Japanese
writing
Ka·tan·ga *former name of*
Shaba

Kat·an·gese

Ka·thia·war Indian peninsula

Kat·mai Alaskan volcano

Kat·man·du (or Kath·) Nepalese capital

Ka·to·wi·ce Polish city

Kat·si·na Nigerian city

Kat·te·gat Scandinavian strait

ka·ty·did insect

Ka·uai Hawaiian island

Kau·nas Lithuanian city

kau·ri (or ·ry; plural ·ris or ·ries) tree

kava drink

Ka·wa·sa·ki Japanese port

kay·ak (or kai·) canoe

Kay·seri Turkish city

ka·za·chok dance

Ka·zakh (or ·zak; plural ·zakhs or ·zaks)

Ka·zakh·stan Central Asian country

Ka·zan Russian city

Kaz·bek Georgian volcano

ka·zoo (plural ·zoos) musical instrument

ke·bab

keck retch

Ked·ah Malaysian state

ked·dah variant spelling of kheda

kedge nautical term

ked·geree

Ke·di·ri Indonesian city

keek Scot peep

keel

keel·haul

keel·son (or kel·)

keen

keen·ness

keep (keep·ing, kept)

keep·er

keep·net

keep·sake

kees·hond (plural ·honds or ·honden) dog

Kee·wa·tin Canadian district

keg

Keigh·ley Yorkshire town

keis·ter (or kees·) US buttocks

keit·loa rhinoceros

Ke·lan·tan Malaysian state

ke·loid (or che·) scar tissue

ke·loi·dal (or che·)

kelp seaweed

kel·pie (or ·py; plural ·pies) sheepdog

kel·son variant spelling of keelson

Kelt variant spelling of Celt

kelt salmon

kel·ter (or esp. US kil·)

Kelt·ic variant spelling of Celtic

kel·vin unit

Ke·mero·vo Russian city

kempt tidy

ken (ken·ning, kenned or kent)

ke·naf fibre

Ken·dal Cumbrian town

ken·do Japanese sport

Ken·il·worth Warwickshire town

kenned (or kent)

ken·nel (·nel·ling, ·nelled; US ·nel·ing, ·neled)

ke·no (or kee·no, ki·no, qui·no) US game

ke·no·sis theology term

ke·not·ic

Ken·sing·ton

ken·speckle Scot easily recognized

Kent

ken·te fabric

Kent·ish

kent·ledge ship's ballast

Ken·tuck·ian

Ken·tucky

Ken·ya

Ken·yan

Keos Greek island

kep Dialect to catch

kepi (plural kepis) military cap

kept

Kera·la Indian state

kera·tin protein

ke·rat·ini·za·tion (or ·sa·tion)

ke·rat·in·ize (or ·ise)

kera·ti·tis eye disease

kera·tog·enous

kera·toid horny

kera·to·plas·tic

kera·to·plas·ty (plural ·ties) eye surgery

kera·tose zoology term

kera·to·sis skin condition

kerb (US curb) pavement edge; compare curb

Ker·be·la variant spelling of Karbala

kerb·ing (US curb·)

kerb·stone (US curb·)

Kerch Ukrainian port

ker·chief

ker·chiefed

kerf saw cut

ker·fuf·fle

Ker·gue·len Is·lands

Ker·man Iranian city

Ker·man·shah Iranian city

ker·mes insect; dye

ker·mis Dutch carnival

kern (or kerne) printing term

ker·nel

ker·nite mineral

kero·sene (or ·sine)

Ker·ry Irish county

Ker·ry (plural ·ries) cattle

ker·sey woollen cloth

ker·sey·mere woollen cloth

Kes·te·ven Lincolnshire region

kes·trel

Kes·wick

ketch sailing vessel

ketch·up (US also catch·up, cat·sup)

ke·tene toxic gas

keto chemistry term

ke·tone

ke·ton·ic

ke·to·nu·ria

ke·tose sugar

ke·to·sis medical term

ke·tox·ime

Ket·ter·ing Northamptonshire town

ket·tle

kettle·drum

kettle·drummer

kettle·ful

kev·el nautical term

Kew

kex plant

key

key·board

key·hole
Keynes·ian·ism economic
  theory
key·note
key·stone
key·stroke
key·way
Kha·ba·rovsk Russian port
khad·dar (or kha·di) Indian
  cloth
Kha·kass Russian region
kha·ki (plural ·kis)
Khal·kha Mongolian
  language
kham·sin (or kam·seen,
  ·sin) wind
khan
khan·ate
khan·ga variant spelling of
  kanga
kha·rif Indian crop
Khar·kov Ukrainian city
Khar·toum (or ·tum)
khat variant spelling of kat
kha·yal Indian music
kheda (or khed·ah,
  ked·dah) elephant
  enclosure
khe·dive viceroy of Egypt
Kher·son Ukrainian port
Khmer Cambodian people
Khmer·ian
Kho·dzhent Tadzhik city
Khoi·khoi language group
Khoi·san language
Kho·tan variant of Hotien
Khul·na Bangladeshi city
khus·khus grass
Khy·ber Pass
ki·aat tree
ki·ang wild ass
Kiang·si Chinese province
Kiang·su Chinese province
Kiao·chow Chinese territory
kib·ble
kib·butz (plural ·but·zim)
kib·butz·nik
kibe chilblain
kib·itz US interfere
kib·lah (or ·la) direction of
  Mecca
ki·bosh
kick
kick·able
kick·back

kick·er
kick·off
kick·shaw trinket
kick·sorter physics
  apparatus
kick·stand
kick-start
kid (kid·ding, kid·ded)
kid·der
Kid·der·min·ster
kid·ding
kid·dle device for catching
  fish
Kid·dush Jewish blessing
kid·dy (or ·die; plural ·dies)
kid·nap (·nap·ping,
  ·napped; US ·nap·ing,
  ·naped)
kid·nap·per (US ·nap·er)
kid·ney
kid·skin
Kiel German port
Kiel·ce Polish city
kier bleaching vat
kie·sel·guhr soft rock
kie·ser·ite mineral
Kiev
kif (or kaif, keef, kef, kief)
  marijuana
Ki·ga·li capital of Rwanda
ki·koi cloth
kiku·mon Japanese emblem
Ki·ku·yu (plural ·yus or ·yu)
  African people
Kil·dare
Kili·man·ja·ro
Kil·ken·ny
kill
Kil·lar·ney
kill·deer (plural ·deer or
  ·deers) bird
kill·er
kil·lick (or ·lock) anchor
Kil·lie·cran·kie Scottish
  battle site
kil·li·fish (plural ·fish or
  ·fishes)
kill·ing
kill·ing·ly
kill-joy
Kil·mar·nock
kiln
kilo (plural kilos)
kilo·calo·rie
kilo·cycle

kilo·gram (or ·gramme)
kilo·hertz
kilo·metre (US ·meter)
kilo·met·ric (or ·ri·cal)
kilo·ton
kilo·volt
kilo·watt
kilowatt-hour
kilt
kilt·ed
kil·ter variant spelling (esp.
  US) of kelter
Kim·ber·ley South African
  city
kim·ber·lite rock
ki·mo·no (plural ·nos)
ki·mo·noed
kin
Kina·ba·lu Malaysian
  mountain
kin·aes·the·sia (or ·sis; US
  ·es·) physiology term
kin·aes·thet·ic (US ·es·)
ki·nase biochemical agent
Kin·car·dine (or
  Kin·car·dine·shire)
  former Scottish county
kin·cob fabric
kind
kin·der·gar·ten
kin·der·gar·ten·er
kind-hearted
kind-hearted·ly
kind-hearted·ness
kin·dle
kin·dler
kind·less Archaic heartless
kind·li·ness
kind·ling
kind·ly (·li·er, ·li·est)
kind·ness
kin·dred
kin·dred·ness (or
  kin·dred·ship)
kine cattle
kin·emat·ic
kin·emati·cal·ly
kin·emat·ics branch of
  physics
ki·nesics study of body
  language
ki·net·ic
ki·neti·cal·ly
ki·net·ics branch of
  mechanics

ki·neto·nu·cle·us
ki·neto·plast
king
king·bird
king·bolt
king·cup
king·dom
king·fish (*plural* ·fish *or* ·fishes)
king·fisher
king·let
king·li·ness
king·ly
king·maker
king-of-arms (*plural* kings-)
king·pin
king·ship
king-size (*or* -sized)
King's Lynn
King·ston Jamaican capital; Canadian port
Kingston upon Thames
Kings·town capital of St Vincent and the Grenadines
King·wa·na African language
king·wood
ki·nin protein
kink
kin·ka·jou animal
kinki·ly
kinki·ness
kinky (kinki·er, kinki·est)
kin·ni·kin·nick (*or* ·ki·nic) mixture for smoking
kino resin
Kin·ross former Scottish county
kins·folk
Kin·sha·sa capital of the Democratic Republic of Congo
kin·ship
kins·man (*plural* ·men)
kins·woman (*plural* ·women)
ki·osk
kip (kip·ping, kipped)
kip·per
Kir·ghiz (*or* ·giz; *plural* ·ghiz *or* ·giz) *variant spelling of* Kyrgyz
Kir·ghi·zia (*or* ·gi·) *variant spelling of* Kyrgyzstan

Ki·ri·ba·ti island republic
kiri·gami paper cutting
Ki·rin Chinese province
kirk
Kirk·by Merseyside town
Kirk·cal·dy Scottish port
Kirk·cud·bright Scottish county
kirk·man (*plural* ·men) *Scot* church member
Kirk·patrick Antarctic mountain
Kir·kuk Iraqi city
Kirk·wall Scottish town
Kir·man Persian carpet
Ki·rov Russian city
Ki·ro·va·bad *former name of* Gandzha
Ki·ro·vo·grad Ukrainian city
Kirsch (*or* Kirsch·was·ser) cherry brandy
Ki·run·di African language
Kis·an·ga·ni city in the Democratic Republic of Congo
kish graphite
Ki·shi·nev *Russian name of* Chişinău
kis·met
kiss
kiss·able
kis·sel Russian dessert
kiss·er
kiss·ing
kist *Dialect* large coffer
kit (kit·ting, kit·ted)
Ki·ta·kyu·shu Japanese port
kit·bag
kitch·en
Kitch·ener Canadian town
kitch·en·ette (*or* ·et)
kitchen·ware
kite
kith
kitsch
kit·ten
kit·ten·ish
kit·ten·ish·ness
kit·ti·wake
kit·tle *Scot* capricious
kit·ty (*plural* ·ties)
Kit·we Zambian city
kiva underground room
Ki·wa·nis US organization

kiwi (*plural* kiwis)
Klai·pe·da Lithuanian port
klang·far·be musical term
Klans·man (*plural* ·men) Ku Klux Klan member
klax·on
Kleen·ex (*Trademark; plural* ·ex *or* ·exes)
klepht Greek brigand
kleph·tic
klep·to·ma·nia (*or* clep·)
klep·to·ma·ni·ac (*or* clep·)
klip·spring·er antelope
Klon·dike Canadian region
kloof mountain pass
klys·tron electronics apparatus
knack
knack·er
knack·ery
knack·wurst (*or* knock·) sausage
knag knot in wood
knap (knap·ping, knapped) *Dialect* hill crest; to hit
knap·per
knap·sack
knap·weed
knar *variant spelling of* knur
knave
knav·ery (*plural* ·eries)
knav·ish
knav·ish·ness
knaw·el plant
knead
knead·er
knee (knee·ing, kneed)
knee·cap (·cap·ping, ·capped)
knee-deep
knee·hole
kneel (kneel·ing, knelt *or* kneeled)
kneel·er
knee·pad
knee·pan kneecap
knees-up
knell
knelt
Knes·set Israeli parliament
knew
Knickerbocker US New Yorker
knick·er·bock·ers

knick•ers

knick•knack (or nick•nack)

knick•point

knife (plural knives)

knif•er

knife•rest

knight

knight-errant (plural knights-)

knight-errantry

knight•head nautical term

knight•hood

knight•li•ness

knight•ly

knish dumpling

knit (knit•ting, knit•ted or knit)

knit•table

knit•ter

knit•ting

knit•wear

knob (knob•bing, knobbed) projection; compare nob

knob•bly (•bli•er, •bli•est)

knob•by (•bi•er, •bi•est)

knob•ker•rie stick

knock

knock•down (adj)

knock•er

knock-kneed

knock-on

knock•out

knoll

Knos•sos (or Cnos•sus) Cretan city

knot (knot•ting, knot•ted)

knot•grass

knot•hole

knot•ted

knot•ter

knot•ti•ly

knot•ti•ness

knot•ting

knot•ty (•ti•er, •ti•est)

knot•weed

knout whip

know (know•ing, knew, known)

know•able

know•er

know-how

know•ing

know•ing•ly

know•ing•ness

knowl•edge

knowl•edge•able (or •edg•able)

knowl•edge•ably

known

Knox•ville US city

knuck•le

knuckle•bone

knuckle-duster

knuckle•head

knuck•ly

knur (or knurr, knar) knot in wood

knurl (or nurl) ridge

knurled

KO (verb KO's, KO'ing, KO'ed; noun, plural KO's)

koa tree

koa•la

koan Buddhist riddle

kob antelope

Kobe Japanese port

Ko•blenz (or Co•) German city

kob•old mythological spirit

Ko•chi Japanese port

Kodak (Trademark)

Ko•di•ak bear; Alaskan island

Ko•dok Sudanese town

kof•ta Indian food

koft•gar Indian goldsmith

Ko•hi•ma Indian city

Kohi•noor (or •nor, •nur) diamond

kohl cosmetic

kohl•ra•bi (plural •bies) cabbage

Ko•hou•tek comet

koi•ne common language

Ko•kand Uzbek city

ko•kanee salmon

Koko Nor (or Kuka Nor) Chinese lake

kola variant spelling of cola

Kol•ha•pur Indian city

ko•lin•sky (plural •skies) mink

kol•khoz (or •khos, •koz) collective farm

Kol Ni•dre Jewish prayer

kolo (plural kolos) dance

Ko•lom•na Russian city

Ko•lo•ni•a capital of Micronesia

Ko•ly•ma Russian river

Ko•ma•ti African river

ko•mat•ik Eskimo sledge

Komi (plural •mi or •mis) Finnish people

Kom•mu•narsk former name of Alchevsk

Ko•mo•do Indonesian island

Kom•so•mol former Soviet association

Kom•so•molsk Russian city

Kon•go (plural •gos or •go) African people

kon•go•ni animal

ko•ni•ol•ogy (or co•)

Kon•stanz variant spelling of Constance

Kon•ya (or Konia) Turkish city

koo•doo variant spelling of kudu

kook US eccentric person

kooka•bur•ra

kooky (or kookie; kooki•er, kooki•est) US crazy

Koo•te•nay (or •nai) US river

kop hill

ko•peck (or •pek, co•peck) Russian coin

Ko•peisk (or •peysk) Russian city

kop•je (or •pie) hill

Ko•ran

Ko•ran•ic

Kor•do•fan Sudanese province

Ko•rea

Ko•rean

kor•ma food

Kor•or capital of Belau

ko•ru•na Czech coin

Kos Greek island

kos (plural kos) Indian unit of distance

Kos•ci•us•ko Australian mountain

ko•sher (or ka•)

Ko•ši•ce Czech city

Kosovo-Metohi•ja region in Serbia

Ko•stro•ma Russian city

Kota (or Ko·tah) Indian city

koto (plural kotos) musical instrument

kou·li·bia·ca (or cou·) food

kou·mis (or ·miss) variant spellings of kumiss

Kov·rov Russian city

kow·hai tree

Kow·loon part of Hong Kong

kow·tow

kow·tow·er

Ko·zhi·kode Indian port

Kra Thai isthmus

kraal (or craal) African village

kraft wrapping paper; compare craft

krait snake

Kra·ka·toa (or ·tau) Indonesian island

kra·ken sea monster

Kra·ma·torsk Ukrainian city

kra·meria shrub

Kras·no·dar Russian city

Kras·no·yarsk Russian city

Kre·feld German city

Kre·men·chug Ukrainian city

Krem·lin

krieg·spiel war game

krill (plural krill)

krim·mer (or crim·) lambswool

Krio African language

kris knife

Krish·na

Krish·naism

Kriss Krin·gle US Santa Claus

Kris·tian·sand Norwegian port

Kris·tian·stad Swedish town

kro·mes·ky savoury dish

kró·na (plural ·nur) Icelandic or Swedish coin

kro·ne (plural ·ner) Danish or Norwegian coin

Kron·stadt Russian port

kroon (plural kroons or krooni) Estonian coin

Kru·gers·dorp South African city

kryp·ton

Kua·la Lum·pur

Ku·ching Malaysian port

ku·dos prestige

kudu (or koo·doo) antelope

kud·zu plant

Ku·fic (or Cu·) Arabic script

Kui·by·shev (or Kuy·) former name of Samara

Ku Klux Klan

Ku Klux·er (or Ku Klux Klan·ner)

kuk·ri (plural ·ris) Gurkha knife

kula Pacific island ceremony

ku·lak wealthy Russian peasant

Ku·ma·mo·to Japanese city

Ku·masi Ghanaian city

kum·ba·loi worry beads

ku·miss (or kou·miss, kou·mis, kou·myss) drink

küm·mel German liqueur

kum·quat (or cum·) fruit

kung fu

Kun·gur Chinese mountain

Kun·lun (or Kuen·, Kwen·) Chinese mountains

Kun·ming (or K'un·ming) Chinese city

kunz·ite gemstone

Kuo·min·tang (or Guo·min·dang) political party

Ku·ra Asian river

Kurd Turkic people

Kurd·ish

Kur·di·stan (or Kur·destan, Kor·destan)

Kure Japanese port

Kur·gan Russian city

Ku·ril Is·lands

kur·ra·jong (or cur·) tree

kur·saal building at health resort

Kursk Russian city

kur·to·sis statistics term

Kus·ko·kwim Alaskan river

Ku·tai·si Georgian city

Kutch (or Cutch) former Indian state

Ku·wait

Ku·wai·ti

Kuz·netsk Ba·sin Russian region

kvass (or kvas, quass) drink

Kwa language group

kwa·cha Zambian currency

Kwa·ja·lein Pacific atoll

Kwa·ki·utl (plural ·utl or ·utls) American Indian

Kwang·chow·an Chinese region

Kwang·ju Korean city

Kwangsi-Chuang Chinese region

Kwang·tung Chinese province

kwan·za Angolan currency

kwashi·or·kor protein deficiency

Kwa·Zu·lu/Na·tal South African province

Kwei·chow (or Kuei·chou) Chinese province

Kwei·lin (or Kuei·lin) Chinese city

Kwei·yang (or Kuei·yang) Chinese city

kwe·la African music

ky·ani·za·tion (or ·sa·tion)

ky·an·ize (or ·ise) treat timber

kyat Burmese currency

kyle Scot narrow strait

ky·lix (or cy·lix; plural ·li·kes) drinking vessel

ky·loe cattle

ky·mo·graph (or cy·) medical instrument

ky·mo·graph·ic (or cy·)

Kyo·to (or Kio·) Japanese city

ky·pho·sis (plural ·ses) spinal curvature

ky·phot·ic

Kyr·gyz (plural ·gyz)

Kyr·gyz·stan Central Asian country

Kyrie elei·son

kyu judo grade

Kyu·shu (or Kiu·) Japanese island

L

laa·ger (or la·) African camp; compare lager
lab
laba·rum (plural ·ra) Christian banner
lab·da·num (or la·) plant resin
la·bel (·bel·ling, ·belled; US ·bel·ing, ·beled)
la·bel·ler (US ·bel·er)
la·bel·loid
la·bel·lum (plural ·la) biology term
la·bia plural of labium
la·bial
la·bi·al·ism
la·bi·al·ity
la·bi·ali·za·tion (or ·sa·tion)
la·bi·al·ize (or ·ise)
la·bial·ly
la·bi·ate plant
la·bile
la·bil·ity
la·bio·den·tal
la·bio·na·sal
la·bio·velar
la·bium (plural ·bia)
lab·lab bean
la·bora·tory (plural ·tories)
La·bor Australian political party
la·bor US spelling of labour
la·bo·ri·ous
la·bo·ri·ous·ly
la·bo·ri·ous·ness
La·bour British political party
la·bour (US ·bor)
la·boured (US ·bored)
la·boured·ly (US ·bored·)
la·bour·er (US ·bor·)
la·bour·ism (US ·bor·)
la·bour·ist (US ·bor·)
La·bour·ite Labour Party supporter
Lab·ra·dor Canadian peninsula; dog
lab·ra·dor·ite mineral
la·bret lip ornament
lab·roid (or ·rid) fish

la·brum (plural ·bra) lip
La·buan Malaysian island
la·bur·num
Laby·rinth mythological maze
laby·rinth
laby·rin·thi·cal·ly
laby·rin·thine (or ·thian, ·thic)
lac resin; variant spelling of lakh
lac·co·lith (or ·lite) geology term
lac·co·lith·ic (or ·lit·ic)
lace
Lac·edae·mon Sparta
Lac·edae·mo·nian
lac·er
lac·er·abil·ity
lac·er·able
lac·er·ant distressing
lac·er·ate
lac·era·tion
lac·era·tive
La·cer·ta constellation
lac·er·til·ian lizard
lace-up (adj, noun)
lace·wing insect
(lacey) incorrect spelling of lacy
lach·es (sing.) legal term
lach·ry·mal variant spelling of lacrimal
lach·ry·ma·tory (plural ·tories) vessel; variant spelling of lacrimatory
lach·ry·mose
lach·ry·mose·ly
lach·ry·mos·ity
laci·ly
laci·ness
lac·ing
la·cini·ate (or ·cinia·ted) jagged
la·cinia·tion
lack
lacka·dai·si·cal
lacka·dai·si·cal·ly
lacka·dai·si·cal·ness
lack·ey
lack·lustre (US ·luster)

La·co·nia ancient Greek country
La·co·nian
la·con·ic (or ·coni·cal) of few words
la·coni·cal·ly
La Co·ru·ña (or Co·run·na) Spanish port
lac·quer
lac·quer·er
lac·ri·mal (or lach·ry·, lac·ry·)
lac·ri·ma·tion
lac·ri·ma·tor (or lach·ry·, lac·ry·) substance causing tear flow
lac·ri·ma·tory (or lach·ry·, lac·ry·; adj) of tears; compare lachrymatory
la·crosse
lac·tal·bu·min
lac·tam chemical group
lac·ta·ry of milk
lac·tase enzyme
lac·tate
lac·ta·tion
lac·ta·tion·al
lac·ta·tion·al·ly
lac·teal
lac·teal·ly
lac·tes·cence
lac·tes·cent
lac·tic
lac·tif·er·ous
lac·to·ba·cil·lus (plural ·li)
lac·to·gen·ic
lac·tom·eter
lac·tone chemical compound
lac·ton·ic
lac·to·pro·tein
lac·to·scope
lac·tose milk sugar
la·cu·na (plural ·nae or ·nas)
la·cu·nar (plural ·nars or ·nar·ia) ceiling panel; of lacunae
la·cu·nose (or ·nal, ·nary)
lacu·nos·ity
la·cus·trine
lacy (laci·er, laci·est)

lad
lad·der
lad·die
lad·dish
lade (lad·ing, lad·ed,
 lad·en or lad·ed) load
 cargo; compare laid
lad·er
la·di·da (or lah-di-dah)
la·dies plural of lady
la·dies' man
lad·ing cargo
La·di·no language
la·di·no (plural ·nos) clover
la·dle
ladle·ful
la·dler
lady (plural la·dies)
lady·bird
la·dy·fy (or ·di·; ·fy·ing,
 ·fied)
lady-in-waiting (plural
 ladies-)
lady-killer
lady·like
lady·love
la·dy·ship
lady's maid (plural la·dies'
 maids)
La·dy·smith South African
 city
lady's-slipper orchid
lady's-smock plant
Laertes mythological
 character
lae·vo·ro·ta·tion (US le·)
lae·vo·ro·ta·tory (or
 ·ro·ta·ry; US le·)
laevu·lin (US levu·)
laevu·lose (US levu·) a sugar
lag (lag·ging, lagged)
lag·an (or li·gan) wreckage
la·gena bottle
la·ger beer; compare laager
lag·gard
lag·gard·ly
lag·gard·ness
lagged
lag·ging
la·gniappe (or ·gnappe) US
 small gift
lago·morph type of
 mammal
lago·mor·phic (or ·phous)
la·goon

La·gos Nigerian port
lah musical note
lah-di-dah variant spelling of
 la-di-da
Lahn·da language
La·hore Pakistani city
Lah·ti Finnish town
laic (or lai·cal) secular
lai·cal·ly
lai·cism
lai·ci·za·tion (or ·sa·tion)
lai·cize (or ·cise)
laid past tense and past
 participle of lay; compare
 lade; lain
laik Dialect to play
lain past participle of lie;
 compare laid
lair
laird
lairy (lairi·er, lairi·est)
 Austral gaudy
lais·sez faire (or lais·ser
 faire)
laissez-faireism (or laisser-)
lais·sez pas·ser
la·ity
lake
Lake·land the Lake District
lak·er lake cargo boat
lakh (or lac) 100 000 Indian
 rupees
Lak·shad·weep Indian
 islands
laky (laki·er, laki·est)
 reddish
Lala Indian form of address
la·lang grass
Lal·lans (or ·lan) Scottish
 dialect
lal·la·tion speech defect
lal·ly·gag (·gag·ging,
 ·gagged) US loiter
lam (lam·ming, lammed)
lama Tibetan priest;
 compare llama
La·ma·ism form of
 Buddhism
La·ma·ist
La·ma·is·tic
La·marck·ian
La·marck·ism theory of
 evolution
la·ma·sery (plural ·series)
lamb

lam·baste (or ·bast) Slang
 beat severely
lamb·da Greek letter
lamb·da·cism phonetics
 term
lamb·doid (or ·doi·dal)
lam·ben·cy
lam·bent
lam·bert unit of
 illumination
Lam·beth
lamb·kin
lam·bre·quin ornamental
 hanging
lamb·skin
lamé fabric
lame
la·mel·la (plural ·lae or ·las)
 thin layer
la·mel·lar (or lam·el·late,
 la·mel·lose)
lam·el·lat·ed
lam·el·la·tion
la·mel·li·branch mollusc
la·mel·li·bran·chi·ate
la·mel·li·corn beetle
la·mel·li·form
la·mel·li·ros·tral (or ·trate)
 zoology term
lam·el·los·ity
lame·ly
lame·ness
la·ment
lam·en·table
lam·en·table·ness
lam·en·tably
la·men·ta·tion
La·men·ta·tions biblical
 book
la·ment·ed
la·ment·er
la·mia (plural ·mias or
 ·miae) mythological
 monster
lami·na (plural ·nae or ·nas)
 thin plate
lami·nable
lami·nar (or ·nose)
lami·naria seaweed
lami·nate
lami·nat·ed
lami·na·tion
lami·na·tor
lami·ni·tis horse disease
Lam·mas religious feast

lam·mer·gei·er (or ·gey·er)
vulture
lamp
lam·pas animal disease;
fabric
lamp·black
Lam·pedu·sa
Mediterranean island
lam·pern lamprey
lam·pion oil lamp
lamp·lighter
lam·poon
lam·poon·er (or ·ist)
lam·poon·ery
lamp·post
lam·prey
lam·pro·phyre rock
La·nai Hawaiian island
la·nai veranda
Lan·ark Scottish town
la·nate (or ·nose) woolly
Lan·ca·shire
Lan·cas·ter
Lan·cas·trian
lance
lance·let tiny animal
lan·ceo·late tapering
lanc·er
lan·cers dance
lan·cet surgical knife
lan·cet·ed architectural
term
lance·wood
Lan·chow (or Lan·chou)
Chinese city
lan·cin·ate
lan·ci·na·tion
Land (plural Län·der)
German state
land
land·am·mann Swiss
official
lan·dau
lan·dau·let (or ·lette)
land·ed
Landes French region
Lan·des·haupt·mann
Austrian governor
land·fall
land·form
land·grave German ruler
land·gra·vine landgrave's
wife
land·ing
land·lady (plural ·ladies)

land·locked
land·lop·er Scot vagrant
land·lord
land·lub·ber
land·mark
land·mass
land·owner
land·owner·ship
land·owning
land·race pig breed
land·scape
land·scap·ist
Land's End
land·shark land profiteer
land·side part of plough
lands·knecht a mercenary
land·slide
lands·man (plural ·men)
Land·tag German assembly
land·ward
lane
lang Scot long
lang·lauf cross-country
skiing
lang·läuf·er
lan·gouste spiny lobster
lang·syne Scot long ago;
compare auld lang syne
lan·guage
langue linguistics term
langue de chat biscuit
Langue·doc French region
langue d'oc language
lan·guid
lan·guid·ness
lan·guish
lan·guish·er
lan·guish·ment
lan·guor weariness; compare
langur
lan·guor·ous
lan·guor·ous·ness
lan·gur monkey; compare
languor
lan·iard variant spelling of
lanyard
la·ni·ary (plural ·aries)
tooth
la·nif·er·ous (or ·nig·)
wool-bearing
lank
lanki·ly
lanki·ness
lank·ly
lank·ness

lanky (lanki·er, lanki·est)
lan·ner falcon
lan·ner·et male lanner
lano·lat·ed
lano·lin (or ·line)
Lan·sing US city
lans·que·net gambling
game
lan·ta·na shrub
lan·tern
lan·tha·nide (or ·non)
chemistry term
lan·tha·num chemical
element
la·nu·go (plural ·gos) fine
hair
lan·yard (or ·iard)
Lao (plural Lao or Laos)
Asian people
Laoag Philippine city
Laocoon mythological
priest
La·odi·cea ancient Greek
city
La·odi·cean
la·odi·cean indifferent
Laoigh·is Irish county
Laos
Lao·tian
lap (lap·ping, lapped)
lapa·rot·omy (plural
·omies) abdominal surgery
La Paz Bolivian capital
lap·board
lap·chart
la·pel
la·pelled
lapi·dar·ian
lapi·dary (plural ·daries)
lapi·date to stone
lapi·da·tion
la·pidi·fy (·fy·ing, ·fied)
change into stone
la·pil·lus (plural ·li) piece of
lava
lap·is lazu·li
Lap·land
Lap·land·er
Lapp
lapped
lap·per
lap·pet
lap·pet·ed
lap·ping
Lapp·ish

laps·able (*or* ·ible)
lapse
laps·er
lap·strake nautical term
lap·sus (*plural* ·sus) error
lap·wing
lar·board
lar·cenist (*or* ·cener)
lar·cenous
lar·ceny (*plural* ·cenies)
larch
lard
lar·der
lar·don (*or* ·doon) strip of fat
lardy
lares Roman gods
large
large·ly
large-minded
larg·en
large·ness
large-scale
lar·gess (*or* ·gesse)
lar·ghet·to (*plural* ·tos) music term
larg·ish
lar·go (*plural* ·gos)
lari·at lasso
lar·ine of gulls
Lá·ri·sa (*or* La·ris·sa) Greek city
lark
lark·er
lark·ish·ness
lark·some
lark·spur
lar·nax terracotta coffin
La Ro·chelle French port
lar·ri·gan leather boot
lar·ri·kin *Austral* hooligan
lar·rup *Dialect* to beat
lar·va (*plural* ·vae) preadult animal; *compare* lava
lar·val
lar·vi·cid·al
lar·vi·cide
lar·yn·geal (*or* la·ryn·gal)
la·ryn·ges *plural of* larynx
lar·yn·git·ic
lar·yn·gi·tis
la·ryn·go·logi·cal (*or* ·log·ic)
lar·yn·golo·gist
lar·yn·gol·ogy

la·ryn·go·scope
la·ryn·go·scop·ic
la·ryn·gos·co·pist
la·ryn·gos·co·py
lar·yn·got·omy (*plural* ·omies)
lar·ynx (*plural* la·ryn·ges *or* lar·ynxes)
la·sa·gne (*or* ·gna)
La Salle Canadian city
las·car (*or* lash·kar) East Indian sailor
Las·caux French cave
las·civi·ous
las·civi·ous·ly
las·civi·ous·ness
lase act as laser
la·ser
lash
lash·er
lash·ing
Lashio Burmese town
lash·kar *variant spelling of* las·car
lash-up (*noun*)
las·ket nautical term
Las Pal·mas
La Spe·zia Italian port
lass
Las·sa fe·ver
las·sie
las·si·tude
las·so (*noun, plural* ·sos *or* ·soes; *verb* ·sos *or* ·soes, ·so·ing, ·soed)
las·so·er
last
last·er
last·ing
last·ing·ly
last·ly
Las Ve·gas
Lata·kia Syrian port
latch
latch·et *Archaic* shoelace
latch·key
late
late-comer
la·teen nautical term
lateen-rigged
(lateish) *incorrect spelling of* latish
late·ly
la·ten·cy
late·ness

la·tent
lat·er
lat·er·al
lat·er·al·ly
Lat·er·an Roman palace
lat·er·ite clay
lat·er·it·ic
lat·ero·ver·sion
lat·est
la·tex (*plural* ·texes *or* lati·ces)
lath (*plural* laths) wood strip
lathe machine
lath·er
lath·ery
la·thi Indian stick
lati·cif·er·ous botany term
lati·meria fish
Lat·in
Lat·in·ate
Lat·in·ism
Lat·in·ist
La·tin·ity
Lat·ini·za·tion (*or* ·sa·tion)
Lat·in·ize (*or* ·ise)
Lat·in·iz·er (*or* ·is·er)
La·ti·no (*plural* ·nos) *US* Latin American
lat·ish
lati·tude
lati·tu·di·nal
lati·tu·di·nal·ly
lati·tu·di·nar·ian
lati·tu·di·nari·an·ism
La·tium Italian region
la·tria Catholic worship
la·trine
lats (*plural* latu, *or* lati) Latvian currency
lat·ten sheet metal
lat·ter
latter-day
lat·ter·ly
latter·most
lat·tice
lat·ticed
Lat·via
Lat·vian
laud
laud·abil·ity (*or* ·able·ness)
laud·able
laud·ably
lau·da·num
lau·da·tion praise

lauda·tory (*or* ·tive)
laud·er
laugh
laugh·able
laugh·able·ness
laugh·ably
laugh·er
laugh·ing·ly
laugh·ter
launch
launch·er
laun·der
laun·der·er
Laun·der·ette (*Trademark*)
laun·dress
Laun·dro·mat (*Trademark*)
laun·dry (*plural* ·dries)
laundry·man (*plural* ·men)
laundry·woman (*plural*
·women)
lau·ra·ceous botany term
Laura·sia ancient continent
lau·reate
lau·reate·ship
lau·rea·tion
lau·rel (·rel·ling, ·relled; *US*
·rel·ing, ·reled)
Lau·ren·tian of St Lawrence
river; *compare* Lawrentian
lau·rus·ti·nus shrub
Lau·sanne
lav *short for* lavatory
lava molten rock; *compare*
larva
lava·bo (*plural* ·boes *or* ·bos)
lav·age medical procedure
La·val Canadian city
la·va·tion washing
la·va·tion·al
lava·tory (*plural* ·tories)
lav·en·der
la·ver seaweed; font
lav·er·ock *Dialect* skylark
lav·ish
lav·ish·er
lav·ish·ly
lav·ish·ness
law
law-abiding
law-breaker
law-breaking
law·ful
law·ful·ly
law·ful·ness
law·giver

law·giving
law·less
law·less·ly
law·less·ness
law·man (*plural* ·men)
lawn
lawny
law·ren·cium chemical
element
Law·ren·tian of D. H.
Lawrence; *compare*
Laurentian
law·suit
law·yer
lax
laxa·tion defecation
laxa·tive
lax·ity (*or* lax·ness)
lax·ly
lay (lay·ing, laid)
lay·about
lay-by
lay·er
lay·er·ing
lay·ette
lay·ing
lay·man (*plural* ·men)
lay·shaft
lay·woman (*plural* ·women)
laz·ar leper
laza·ret·to (*or* ·ret, ·rette;
plural ·tos, ·rets, ·rettes)
ship's locker; leper hospital
laze
la·zi·ly
la·zi·ness
lazu·lite mineral
lazu·rite lapis lazuli
lazy (la·zi·er, la·zi·est)
lazy·bones
L-dopa
lea meadow; unit of length;
compare lee; ley
leach percolate; *compare*
leech
leach·er
lead (lead·ing, led) guide
lead (lead·ing, lead·ed)
metal
lead·en
lead·en·ly
lead·en·ness
lead·er

lead·er·ship
lead-in (*noun*)
lead·ing
leads·man (*plural* ·men)
lead·wort shrub
leady
leaf (*plural* leaves)
leaf·age
leaf-climber
leaf-cutter ant
leaf-hopper insect
leafi·ness
leaf·let
leaf·stalk
leafy (leafi·er, leafi·est)
league (leagu·ing, leagued)
leak hole; escape; *compare*
leek
leak·age
leak·er
leaki·ness
leaky (leaki·er, leaki·est)
leal *Scot* loyal
Leam·ing·ton
lean (lean·ing, leant *or*
leaned)
Leander mythological
character
lean·ness
leant
lean-to (*plural* ·tos)
leap (leap·ing, leapt *or*
leaped)
leap·er
leap-frog (·frog·ging,
·frogged)
leapt
learn (learning, learnt *or*
learned)
learn·able
learn·ed wise
learn·ed·ly
learn·ed·ness
learn·er
learn·ing
learnt
leary *variant spelling of* leery
leas·able
lease
lease·back property
transaction
lease·hold
lease·holder
leas·er
leash

least
least·ways
leat trench
leath·er
leather·back turtle
Leath·er·ette (*Trademark*)
Leath·er·head Surrey town
leather·head bird
leath·eri·ness
leather·jacket fish; insect
leath·ern
leather·neck *Slang* US
    marine
leather·wood
leath·ery
leave (leav·ing, left)
leaved with leaves
leav·en
leav·en·ing
leav·er
leaves *plural of* leaf *or* leave;
    present tense of leave
leave-taking
leav·ing
Leba·nese
Leba·non
leb·en curdled milk
Le·bens·raum *German*
    territory
leb·ku·chen (*plural* ·chen)
    biscuit
Lech European river
lech lust
lech·er
lech·er·ous
lech·ery (*plural* ·eries)
leci·thin biochemical
    compound
le·cithi·nase enzyme
lec·tern
lec·tion variant reading
lec·tion·ary (*plural* ·aries)
    book of church readings
lec·tor lecturer
lec·tor·ate (*or* ·ship)
lec·ture
lec·tur·er
lec·ture·ship
lecy·thus (*plural* ·thi) Greek
    vase
led
Leda mythological
    character
le·der·ho·sen leather shorts
ledge

ledged
ledg·er
ledg·er line (*or* leg·) musical
    term
ledgy
lee sheltered side; *compare*
    lea; ley
lee·board
leech bloodsucker; *compare*
    leach
leech (*or* leach) nautical
    term; *compare* leach
Leeds
leek vegetable; *compare*
    leak
leer
leer·ing·ly
leery (*or* leary; leeri·er,
    leeri·est *or* leari·er,
    leari·est)
lees sediment
leet manorial court
lee·ward
Lee·ward Is·lands
lee·way
left
left-hand (*adj*)
left-handed
left-handed·ly
left-handed·ness
left-hander
left·ism
left·ist
left·over
left·wards
left-winger
lefty (*plural* lefties)
leg (leg·ging, legged)
lega·cy (*plural* ·cies)
le·gal
le·gal·ese legal jargon
le·gal·ism
le·gal·ist
le·gal·is·tic
le·gal·is·ti·cal·ly
le·gal·ity (*plural* ·ities)
le·gali·za·tion (*or* ·sa·tion)
le·gal·ize (*or* ·ise)
le·gal·ly
leg·ate envoy
lega·tee recipient of legacy
leg·ate·ship
lega·tine
le·ga·tion
le·ga·tion·ary

le·ga·to (*plural* ·tos) music
    term
lega·tor bequeather
lega·to·rial
leg·end
leg·end·ary (*adj*)
leg·end·ry (*noun*)
leg·er·demain
leg·er·demain·ist
leg·er line *variant spelling of*
    ledger line
legged *past tense of* leg
leg·ged having legs
leg·gi·ness
leg·ginged
leg·gings
leg·gy (·gi·er, ·gi·est)
Leg·horn Livorno; domestic
    fowl
leg·horn straw hat
leg·ibil·ity (*or* ·ible·ness)
leg·ible
leg·ibly
le·gion
le·gion·ary (*plural* ·aries)
le·gion·naire
leg·is·late
leg·is·la·tion
leg·is·la·tive
leg·is·la·tor
leg·is·la·to·rial
leg·is·la·tress
leg·is·la·ture
le·gist legal expert
le·git *Slang* legitimate
le·giti·ma·cy (*or*
    ·mate·ness)
le·giti·mate
le·giti·mate·ly
le·giti·ma·tion
le·giti·ma·ti·za·tion (*or*
    ·sa·tion) legitimization
le·giti·ma·tize (*or* ·tise)
    legitimize
le·giti·mism
le·giti·mist supporter of
    legitimate ruler
le·giti·mis·tic
le·giti·mi·za·tion (*or*
    ·sa·tion)
le·giti·mize (*or* ·mise)
leg·less
leg·man (*plural* ·men) US
    newspaper reporter
leg·room

leg·ume pod
le·gu·min protein
le·gu·mi·nous botany term
leg·work
Le Ha·vre French port
lei Hawaiian garland
Leices·ter
Leices·ter·shire
Lei·den (or Ley·) Dutch city
Leigh English town
Lein·ster Irish province
Leip·zig German city
leish·ma·nia protozoan
leish·mania·sis (or
·ma·nio·sis) infection
leis·ter fishing spear
lei·sure
lei·sured
lei·sure·li·ness
lei·sure·ly
Leith Scottish port
leit·mo·tiv (or ·tif)
Lei·trim Irish county
lek Albanian currency
Le Mans French city
lem·ma (plural ·mas or
·ma·ta) logic term
lem·ming
lem·nis·cate maths term
lem·nis·cus (plural ·nis·ci)
anatomy term
Lem·nos (or Lím·) Greek
island
lem·on
lem·on·ade
lem·ony
lem·pi·ra Honduran
currency
le·mur
lemu·roid (or ·rine)
Lena Russian river
lend (lend·ing, lent)
lend·er
lend-lease
length
length·en
length·en·er
lengthi·ly
lengthi·ness
length·ways (or ·wise)
lengthy (lengthi·er,
lengthi·est)
le·ni·en·cy (or ·ni·ence)
le·ni·ent
le·ni·ent·ly

Le·ni·na·bad former name of
Khodzhent
Le·ni·na·kan Armenian city
Le·nin·grad
Len·in·ism political theory
Len·in·ist (or ·ite)
le·nis (plural le·nes)
linguistics term
leni·tive soothing pain
len·ity (plural ·ities)
leno (plural lenos) fabric
weave
lens
Lent
lent
len·ta·men·te musical term
Len·ten of Lent
len·tic ecology term
len·ti·cel botany term
len·ti·cel·late
len·ticu·lar (or ·ti·form)
len·ti·form
len·tigi·nous (or ·nose)
len·ti·go (plural ·tigi·nes)
freckle
len·til
len·tis·si·mo music term
len·to (plural ·tos) music
term
Leo constellation
León cities in Spain,
Mexico, and Nicaragua
Leo·nid (plural Leo·nids or
Le·oni·des) meteor shower
leo·nine
leop·ard
leop·ard·ess
leopard's-bane plant
leo·tard
lep·er
le·pido·lite mineral
lepi·dop·ter·an (plural
·ter·ans or ·tera)
lepi·dop·ter·ist
lepi·dop·ter·ous
lepi·do·si·ren fish
lepi·dote biology term
lepo·rid hare
lepo·rine of hares
lep·re·chaun
lep·ro·sar·ium (plural ·ia)
leper hospital
lep·rose
lep·ro·sy
lep·rous

lep·rous·ness
lep·to·cepha·lus (plural ·li)
eel larva
lep·ton (plural ·ta) Greek
currency
lep·ton (plural ·tons)
physics particle
lep·to·phyl·lous botany
term
lep·tor·rhine zoology term
lep·to·some slender person
lep·to·so·mic (or ·mat·ic)
lep·to·spi·ro·sis disease
lep·to·tene biology term
le·quear ceiling panel
Ler·wick Scottish town
Les·bian of Lesbos
les·bian female homosexual
les·bi·an·ism
Les·bos Greek island
Les Cayes Haitian port
lese-majesty (or
lèse-majesté)
le·sion
Le·so·tho African kingdom
less
less·see one to whom lease is
granted
les·see·ship
less·en
less·er less great; compare
lessor
les·son
les·sor one who grants lease;
compare lesser
lest
let (let·ting, let)
le·thal
le·thal·ity
le·thal·ly
le·thar·gic (or ·gi·cal)
le·thar·gi·cal·ly
leth·ar·gy (plural ·gies)
Leth·bridge Canadian city
Le·the mythological river
Leto mother of Apollo
let's
Lett a Latvian
let·ter
let·tered
let·ter·er
letter·head
let·ter·ing
letter·press
let·ter·set

let·ting
Let·tish Latvian
let·tuce
leu·cine (or ·cin) amino acid
leu·cite mineral
leu·cit·ic
leu·co·crat·ic geology term
leu·co·cyte (US ·ko·)
leu·co·cyt·ic (US ·ko·)
leu·co·cy·to·sis (US ·ko·)
leu·co·cy·tot·ic (US ·ko·)
leu·co·der·ma (US ·ko·)
  unpigmented skin
leu·co·der·mal (or ·mic; US
  ·ko·)
leu·co·ma corneal scar
leu·co·maine biochemical
  compound
leu·co·penia (US ·ko·)
leu·co·penic (US ·ko·)
leu·co·plast (or ·plas·tid)
  structure in plant cell
leu·co·poi·esis (US ·ko·)
leu·co·poi·et·ic (US ·ko·)
leu·cor·rhoea (US
  ·kor·rhea) vaginal
  discharge
leu·cor·rhoeal (US
  ·kor·rheal)
leu·cot·omy brain surgery
leu·kae·mia (US ·ke·mia)
leuko US spelling of some
  words beginning with leuco·
lev (plural leva) Bulgarian
  currency
Le·val·loi·sian (or ·lois)
  Palaeolithic culture
Le·vant Middle Eastern
  region
le·vant leather
le·vant·er wind
Le·van·tine of Levant
le·van·tine silk cloth
le·va·tor
levee
lev·el (·el·ling, ·elled; US
  ·el·ing, ·eled)
level-headed
level-headed·ly
level-headed·ness
Lev·el·ler radical
  Parliamentarian
lev·el·ler (US ·el·er)
lev·el·ly
Le·ven Scottish loch

lev·er
lev·er·age
lev·er·et young hare
Le·ver·ku·sen German town
levi·able
le·via·than biblical monster
levi·er
levi·gate grind into powder
levi·ga·tion
levi·ga·tor
levi·rate marrying brother's
  widow
Le·vis (Trademark) jeans
levi·tate
levi·ta·tion
levi·ta·tor
Le·vite priest
Le·viti·cal (or Le·vit·ic)
Le·viti·cus biblical book
lev·ity (plural ·ities)
le·vo·ro·ta·tion US spelling
  of laevorotation
le·vo·ro·ta·tory US spelling
  of laevorotatory
levu·lin US spelling of
  laevulin
levu·lose US spelling of
  laevulose
levy (verb levies, levy·ing,
  levied; noun, plural levies)
lewd
lewd·ly
lewd·ness
Lew·es Sussex town
Lew·is Scottish island
lew·is (or lew·is·son) lifting
  device
Lewi·sham
lew·is·ite war gas
lex (plural leges) body of
  laws
lex·eme linguistics term
lexi·cal
lexi·cal·ity
lexi·cal·ly
lexi·cog·ra·pher
lexi·co·graph·ic (or
  ·graphi·cal)
lexi·co·graphi·cal·ly
lexi·cog·ra·phy
lexi·co·logi·cal
lexi·co·logi·cal·ly
lexi·colo·gist
lexi·col·ogy
lexi·con

lexi·co·sta·tis·tics
lexi·gra·phy
Lex·ing·ton US city
lex·is vocabulary
lex loci law of the place
ley prehistoric track;
  compare lea; lee
Ley·den variant spelling of
  Leiden
Ley·te Philippine island
Lha·sa Tibetan capital
li unit of length
lia·bil·ity (plural ·ities)
lia·ble
li·aise
liai·son
lia·na (or li·ane) plant
lia·noid
Liao·ning Chinese province
Liao·tung (or ·dong)
  Chinese peninsula
Liao·yang Chinese city
liar
Li·ard Canadian river
li·ard coin
Lias rock series
lias blue limestone
Li·as·sic
lib Slang liberation
li·ba·tion
li·ba·tion·al (or ·ary)
li·bec·cio (or ·chio)
  Corsican wind
li·bel (·bel·ling, ·belled; US
  ·bel·ing, ·beled)
li·bel·lant (US ·bel·ant)
li·bel·lee (US ·bel·ee)
li·bel·ler (or li·bel·ist; US
  ·bel·er or ·bel·ist)
li·bel·lous (US ·bel·ous)
Lib·er·al political party
lib·er·al progressive;
  abundant
lib·er·al·ism
lib·er·al·ist
lib·er·al·is·tic
lib·er·al·ity (plural ·ities)
lib·er·ali·za·tion (or
  ·sa·tion)
lib·er·al·ize (or ·ise)
lib·er·al·iz·er (or ·is·er)
lib·er·al·ly
lib·er·al·ness
lib·er·ate
lib·era·tion

lib·era·tor (*fem* ·tress)
Li·beria
Li·berian
lib·er·tar·ian freethinker;
  compare libertine
lib·er·tari·an·ism
li·ber·ti·cid·al
li·ber·ti·cide destruction of
  freedom
lib·er·tine dissolute person;
  compare libertarian
lib·er·tin·ism (*or* ·age)
lib·er·ty (*plural* ·ties)
li·bidi·nal
li·bidi·nous
li·bi·do (*plural* ·dos)
Li·bra constellation; sign of
  zodiac
Lib·ran
li·brar·ian
li·brar·ian·ship
li·brary (*plural* ·braries)
li·brate waver
li·bra·tion
li·bra·tion·al
li·bra·tory
li·bret·tist
li·bret·to (*plural* ·tos *or* ·ti)
Li·breville Gabonese capital
li·bri·form botany term
Lib·rium (*Trademark*)
Libya
Liby·an
lice
li·cence (*US* ·cense) a
  permit
li·cens·able
li·cense to grant licence; *US*
  spelling of licence
li·cen·see
li·cens·er (*or* ·cen·sor)
li·cen·ti·ate licence holder;
  compare licentious
li·cen·ti·ate·ship
li·cen·tia·tion
li·cen·tious promiscuous;
  compare licentiate
li·cen·tious·ness
li·chee (*or* ·chi) *variant*
  spelling of litchi
li·chen
li·chen·in chemical
  compound
li·chen·oid
li·chen·ol·ogy

li·chen·ous (*or* ·ose)
Lich·field Staffordshire city
lich gate (*or* lych gate)
lic·it lawful
lick
lick·er
lick·er·ish *Archaic* lustful;
  compare liquorice
lickety-split *US* very quickly
lick·ing
lick·spit·tle
lico·rice *US spelling of*
  liquorice
lic·tor Roman official
lid
lid·ded
lid·less
lido (*plural* lidos)
lie (ly·ing, lied) tell
  untruth; *compare* lye
lie (ly·ing, lay, lain) recline;
  compare lye
Lieb·frau·milch (*or*
  ·frau·en·milch) wine
Liech·ten·stein
lied (*plural* lied·er) song
lief *Archaic* willingly
Li·ège Belgian city
liege owed allegiance
liege·man (*plural* ·men)
lien legal term
lien·al
li·en·ter·ic
li·en·tery medical term
li·erne architectural term
Li·etu·va Lithuania
lieu
lieu·ten·an·cy
lieu·ten·ant
life (*plural* lives)
life·blood
life·boat
life·guard
life·less
life·less·ly
life·less·ness
life·like
life·line
life·long for life; *compare*
  livelong
lif·er
life-saver
life-saving
life-size (*or* -sized)
life·time

Lif·fey Irish river
lift
lift·able
lift·boy
lift·er
lift-off
liga·ment
liga·men·tous (*or* ·tal,
  ·ta·ry)
li·gan *variant spelling of*
  lagan
lig·and chemistry term
li·gate constrict with
  ligature
li·ga·tion
liga·tive
liga·ture
li·ger animal
light (light·ing, light·ed *or*
  lit)
light·en
light·en·er
light·en·ing making lighter;
  compare lightning
light·er
light·er·age
lighter·man (*plural* ·men)
light-fast
light-fingered
light-footed
light-headed
light-headed·ly
light-headed·ness
light-hearted
light-hearted·ly
light-hearted·ness
light·house
light·ing
light·ish
light·ly
light·ness
light·ning light flash;
  compare lightening
light·ship
light·some
light·weight
lign·al·oes tree
lig·ne·ous
lig·ni·fi·ca·tion
lig·ni·form
lig·ni·fy (·fies, ·fy·ing,
  ·fied) make woody
lig·nin plant tissue
lig·nite brown coal
lig·nit·ic

lig·no·caine anaesthetic
lig·no·cel·lu·lose
lig·num vi·tae wood
lig·ro·in chemical compound
ligu·la (*plural* ·lae *or* ·las) part of insect's lip
ligu·lar
ligu·late
lig·ule plant part
ligu·loid
lig·ure biblical gem
Li·gu·ria Italian region
Li·gu·ri·an
lik·able (*or* like·)
lik·able·ness (*or* like·)
Li·ka·si city in the Democratic Republic of Congo
like
like·li·hood (*or* ·ness)
like·ly (·li·er, ·li·est)
like-minded
like-minded·ly
like-minded·ness
lik·en
like·ness
like·wise
lik·ing
li·lac
lilia·ceous
lil·ied
Lilith biblical demon
Lille French city
Lil·li·pu·tian tiny person
lilly-pilly tree
Lilo (*Trademark; plural* Lilos)
Li·long·we Malawian capital
lilt
lilting
lily (*plural* lilies)
lily-livered
Lima Peruvian capital
lima bean
lima·cine of slugs
li·ma·çon maths term
Li·mas·sol Cypriot port
limb
lim·bate botany term
lim·ber
lim·bic anatomy term
limb·less
lim·bo (*plural* ·bos)

Lim·burg (*or* ·bourg) Belgian or Dutch province
Lim·burg·er cheese
lim·bus (*plural* ·bi) anatomy term
lime
lime·ade
lime·kiln
lime·light
li·men (*plural* ·mens *or* limi·na) psychology term
Lim·er·ick Irish port and county
lim·er·ick comic verse
li·mes (*plural* limi·tes) boundary of Roman empire
lime·stone
lime·water
lim·ey *US* Briton; *compare* limy
li·mico·line ornithology term
li·mico·lous living in mud
limi·nal psychology term
limi·ness
lim·it
lim·it·able
limi·tar·ian
limi·tary
limi·ta·tion
lim·it·ed
lim·it·er
lim·it·less
lim·it·less·ly
lim·it·less·ness
limi·trophe near a frontier
limn to draw
lim·ner
lim·net·ic ecology term
lim·no·logi·cal (*or* ·log·ic)
lim·no·lo·gist
lim·nol·ogy study of lakes
Lím·nos *variant spelling of* Lemnos
Li·moges French city
limo·nene chemical compound
li·mo·nite mineral
Li·mou·sin French region
lim·ou·sine car
limp
limp·er
lim·pet
lim·pid

lim·pid·ity (*or* ·ness)
limp·ing·ly
limp·kin bird
limp·ness
Lim·po·po African river
limu·lus (*plural* ·li) crab
limy (limi·er, limi·est) of lime; *compare* limey
lin·able (*or* line·)
lin·age (*or* line·) number of lines; *compare* lineage
lin·alo·ol (*or* ·alol)
linch·pin pin for wheel; *compare* lynch
Lin·coln
Lin·coln·shire
lin·crus·ta embossed wallpaper
linc·tus (*plural* ·tuses)
lin·dane pesticide
lin·den
Lin·dis·farne
line (lin·ing, lined)
lin·eage descent from ancestor; *variant spelling of* linage
lin·eal
lin·eal·ly directly; *compare* linearly
linea·ment facial feature; *compare* liniment
linea·men·tal
lin·ear
lin·ear·ity
lin·ear·ly in a line; *compare* lineally
lin·eate (*or* ·eat·ed)
lin·ea·tion
line·caster
line-engrav·er
line-engrav·ing
line·man (*plural* ·men) *US* footballer; rail worker; *compare* linesman
lin·en fabric; *compare* linin
lineo·late (*or* ·lat·ed)
line-out
lin·er
lines·man (*plural* ·men) sporting official; rail worker; *compare* lineman
line-up (*noun*)
ling heather
ling (*plural* ling *or* lings) fish

ling·cod (*plural* ·cod *or* ·cods) fish

lin·ger

lin·ger·er

lin·gerie

lin·ger·ing·ly

lin·go (*plural* ·goes)

lin·gua (*plural* ·guae) the tongue

lin·gua fran·ca (*plural* lin·gua fran·cas *or* lin·guae fran·cae) common language

lin·gual

lin·gual·ly

lin·gui·form

lin·gui·ni pasta

lin·guist

lin·guis·tic

lin·guis·ti·cal·ly

lin·guis·tics

lin·gu·late (*or* ·lat·ed)

lin·hay *Dialect* farm building

lini·ment topical medicine; *compare* lineament

li·nin biology term; *compare* linen

lin·ing

link

link·able

link·age

link·boy torch carrier

link·man (*plural* ·men) broadcaster

Lin·kö·ping Swedish city

link·up (*noun*)

link·work

Lin·lith·gow Scottish town

linn *Scot* waterfall

Lin·nean (*or* ·naean) of Linnaeus; *note* Linnean Society

lin·net

Lin·nhe Scottish loch

lino (*plural* linos)

li·no·cut

li·no·leate

li·no·leum

Li·no·type (*Trademark*)

Li·no·typ·er (*or* ·ist)

lin·sang animal

lin·seed

linsey-woolsey fabric

lin·stock

lint

lin·tel

lin·telled (*US* ·teled)

lint·er

lint·white *Scot* linnet

linty

Linz Austrian port

lion

li·on·ess

lion·fish (*plural* ·fish *or* ·fishes)

lion-hearted

li·oni·za·tion (*or* ·sa·tion)

li·on·ize (*or* ·ise)

li·on·iz·er (*or* ·is·er)

lip (lip·ping, lipped)

li·pase enzyme

Li·petsk Russian city

li·pid

lip·oid fatty

lip·oi·dal

li·poly·sis

lipo·lyt·ic

li·po·ma (*plural* ·mas *or* ·mata) tumour

li·poma·tous

lipo·phil·ic (*or* lipo·trop·ic) chemistry term

lipo·pro·tein

Lip·pe German river

Lip·pi·zan·er horse

lip·py (·pi·er, ·pi·est) *US* insolent

lip-read (-reading, -read)

lip-reader

lip·stick

li·quate separate by melting

li·qua·tion

liq·ue·fa·cient

liq·ue·fac·tion (*or* ·ui·)

liq·ue·fac·tive (*or* ·ui·)

liq·ue·fi·able (*or* ·ui·)

liq·ue·fi·er (*or* ·ui·)

liq·ue·fy (*or* ·ui·; ·fies, ·fy·ing, ·fied)

li·quesce

li·ques·cence (*or* ·cen·cy)

li·ques·cent

li·queur

liq·uid

liq·uid·am·bar balsam

liq·ui·date

liq·ui·da·tion

liq·ui·da·tor

li·quid·ity

liq·uid·ize (*or* ·ise)

liq·uid·iz·er (*or* ·is·er)

liq·ui·fy *variant spelling of* liquefy

liq·uor

liquo·rice (*US* lico·) confectionery; *compare* lickerish

lira (*plural* lire *or* liras)

lirio·den·dron (*plural* ·drons *or* ·dra) tree

liri·pipe (*or* ·poop) tip of graduate's hood

Lis·bon

lisle

lisp

lis pen·dens legal term

lisp·er

lis·som (*or* ·some)

lis·som·ness (*or* ·some·)

list

list·able

list·ed

lis·tel architectural term

lis·ten

lis·ten·er

lis·ter plough

lis·teri·osis food poisoning

list·ing

list·less

list·less·ness

lit

lita·ny (*plural* ·nies)

li·tchi (*or* ·chee, ·chi, ly·chee; *plural* ·tchis, ·chees, ·chis, *or* ·chees)

lit·era·cy

lit·er·al of words or letters; *compare* littoral

lit·er·al·ism

lit·er·al·ist

lit·er·al·is·tic

lit·er·al·is·ti·cal·ly

lit·er·al·ly

lit·er·al·ness (*or* ·ity)

lit·er·ari·ly

lit·er·ari·ness

lit·er·ary

lit·er·ate

lit·era·ti scholarly people

lit·era·tim letter for letter

lit·era·tion

lit·era·tor *variant of* littérateur

lit·era·ture
lith·arge lead compound
lithe
lithe·ly
lithe·ness
lithe·some
lithia lithium compound
li·thia·sis medical term
lith·ic of stone
lith·ium
li·tho (*plural* ·thos)
  lithograph
litho·graph
li·thog·ra·pher
litho·graph·ic (*or*
  ·graphi·cal)
litho·graphi·cal·ly
li·thog·ra·phy
lith·oid (*or* li·thoi·dal)
litho·log·ic (*or* ·logi·cal)
litho·logi·cal·ly
li·tholo·gist
li·thol·ogy study of rocks
litho·marge kaolin
litho·meteor
litho·phyte
litho·phyt·ic
litho·pone pigment
litho·sol soil
litho·sphere
litho·tom·ic (*or* ·tomi·cal)
li·thoto·mist
li·thoto·my (*plural* ·mies)
  removal of bladder stone
li·thot·rity (*plural* ·rities)
  crushing of bladder stone
Lithua·nia
Lithua·nian
liti·gable
liti·gant
liti·gate
liti·ga·tion
liti·ga·tor
li·ti·gious
lit·mus
li·to·tes (*plural* ·tes)
  understatement
li·tre (*US* ·ter)
lit·ter
lit·té·ra·teur (*or* lit·era·tor)
  professional writer
litter·bug
lit·tle
lit·to·ral of the shore;
  compare literal

li·tur·gi·cal (*or* ·gic)
li·tur·gi·cal·ly
li·tur·gics study of liturgies
lit·ur·gism
lit·ur·gist
lit·ur·gis·tic
lit·ur·gy (*plural* ·gies)
liv·abil·ity (*or* live·)
liv·able (*or* live·)
liv·able·ness (*or* live·)
live
live·able *variant spelling of*
  livable
live·li·hood
live·li·ness
live·long very long; entire;
  compare lifelong
live·ly (·li·er, ·li·est)
liv·en
liv·en·er
liv·er
liv·er·ied
liv·er·ish
liv·er·ish·ness
Liv·er·pool
Liv·er·pud·lian
liver·wort plant
liver·wurst sausage
liv·ery (*plural* ·eries)
liv·ery·man (*plural* ·men)
live·stock
live·trap (·trap·ping,
  ·trapped)
live·ware computer workers
liv·id
liv·id·ly
liv·id·ness (*or* li·vid·ity)
liv·ing
Li·vo·nia former Russian
  province; US city
Li·vo·nian
Li·vor·no Italian port
lix·ivi·ate chemistry term
lix·ivia·tion
lix·iv·ium (*plural* ·iums *or*
  ·ivia) alkaline solution
liz·ard
Lju·blja·na Slovenian
  capital
lla·ma animal; *compare*
  lama
Llan·daff Cardiff suburb
Llan·dud·no Welsh town
Llan·elli (*or* ·elly) Welsh
  town

lla·no (*plural* ·nos) grassland
Lla·no Es·ta·ca·do Texan
  region
Lloyd's underwriters
lo exclamation
loach
load burden, etc.; *compare*
  lode
load·ed
load·er
load·ing
load·star *variant spelling of*
  lodestar
load·stone *variant spelling of*
  lodestone
loaf (*plural* loaves)
loaf·er
loam
loami·ness
loamy (loami·er, loami·est)
loan
loan·able
loan·er
loath (*or* loth) reluctant
loathe to hate
loath·er
loath·ing
loath·ly
loath·some
loath·some·ness
loaves *plural of* loaf
lob (lob·bing, lobbed)
lo·bar
lo·bate (*or* ·bat·ed)
lobbed
lob·bing
lob·by (*noun, plural* ·bies;
  verb ·bies, ·by·ing, ·bied)
lob·by·er
lob·by·ism
lob·by·ist
lobe
lo·bec·to·my (*plural* ·mies)
lo·belia
lo·beline alkaloid
Lo·bi·to Angolan port
lob·lol·ly (*plural* ·lies) tree
lo·boto·my (*plural* ·mies)
lob·scouse sailor's stew
lob·ster (*plural* ·sters *or*
  ·ster)
lobu·lar (*or* ·late, ·lat·ed,
  ·lose)
lobu·la·tion
lob·ule

lo•cal

lo•cale (*noun*)

lo•cal•ism

lo•cal•ist

lo•cal•is•tic

lo•cal•ity (*plural* •ities)

lo•cal•iz•able (*or* •is•able)

lo•cali•za•tion (*or* •sa•tion)

lo•cal•ize (*or* •ise)

lo•cal•iz•er (*or* •is•er)

lo•cal•ly

lo•cat•able

lo•cate

lo•cat•er

lo•ca•tion

loca•tive

loch

lochia vaginal discharge

loch•ial

loci *plural of* locus

lock

lock•able

lock•age canal locks

lock•er

lock•et

lock•jaw

lock•nut

lock•out (*noun*)

lock•smith

lock•smithery (*or* •smithing)

lock•up (*noun*)

loco (*plural* locos) *Slang* locomotive; *US* insane

lo•co•ism cattle disease

lo•co•man (*plural* •men) engine driver

lo•co•mo•tion

lo•co•mo•tive

lo•co•mo•tor of locomotion

lo•co•weed

locu•lar (*or* •late) biology term

locu•la•tion

loc•ule (*or* locu•lus; *plural* •ules *or* •li) biology term

lo•cum *short for* locum tenens

lo•cum te•nens (*plural* lo•cum te•nen•tes) professional stand-in

lo•cus (*plural* loci)

lo•cust

lo•cu•tion

Lod Israeli town

lode ore deposit; *compare* load

lo•den wool

lode•star (*or* load•)

lode•stone (*or* load•)

lodge

lodge•able

lodg•er

lodg•ing

lodg•ings

lodg•ment (*or* lodge•)

lodi•cule botany term

Łódź Polish city

lo•ess soil

lo•ess•ial (*or* •al)

Lo•fo•ten Is•lands

loft

loft•er golf club

lofti•ly

lofti•ness

lofty (lofti•er, lofti•est)

log (log•ging, logged)

Lo•gan Canadian mountain

logan•berry (*plural* •berries)

lo•ga•nia•ceous botany

lop-eared

lop•er

lo•pho•branch fish

lopho•bran•chi•ate

lo•pho•phor•ate

lo•pho•phore zoology term

lop•ing

loga•oedic verse form

loga•rithm

loga•rith•mic (*or* •mi•cal)

loga•rith•mi•cal•ly

log•book

loge theatre box

logged

log•ger

log•ger•head

log•gia (*plural* •gias *or* •gie) roofed gallery; *compare* logia

log•ging

logia *plural of* logion; *compare* loggia

log•ic

logi•cal

logi•cal•ity (*or* •ness)

logi•cal•ly

lo•gi•cian

logi•cism

logi•on (*plural* logia) saying of Christ

lo•gis•tic

lo•gis•ti•cal

lo•gis•ti•cal•ly

log•is•ti•cian

lo•gis•tics

log•log maths term

logo (*plural* logos)

logo•gram (*or* •graph)

logo•gram•mat•ic (*or* •graph•ic, •graphi•cal)

logo•gram•mati•cal•ly (*or* •graphi•cal•ly)

lo•gog•ra•pher

lo•gog•ra•phy

logo•griph word puzzle

logo•griph•ic

lo•goma•chist

lo•goma•chy (*plural* •chies) word argument

logo•paedic (*US* •pedic)

logo•paedics (*US* •pedics) speech therapy

log•or•rhoea (*US* •rhea) talkativeness

Log•os second person of Trinity

log•os reason

logo•type printing term

lo•go•typy

log•wood

logy (logi•er, logi•est) *US* dull or listless

Lohengrin legendary character

loin

loin•cloth

Loire French river

Loire-Atlantique French department

Loi•ret French department

Loir-et-Cher French department

loi•ter

loi•ter•er

loi•ter•ing•ly

Loki Norse god

loll

Lol•lard

Lol•lardy (*or* •lard•ry, •lard•ism)

loll•er

loll•ing•ly

lol·li·pop
lol·lop
lol·ly (*plural* ·lies)
Lom·bard
Lom·bar·dic
Lom·bok Indonesian island
Lomé capital of Togo
lo·ment (*or* ·men·tum;
plural ·ments *or* ·men·ta)
plant pod
lo·men·ta·ceous
Lo·mond Scottish lake
Lon·don
Lon·don·der·ry
Lon·don·er
Lon·dri·na Brazilian city
lone
lone·li·ness
lone·ly (·li·er, ·li·est)
lone·ness
lon·er
lone·some
lone·some·ly
lone·some·ness
long
lon·gan fruit
lon·ga·nim·ity patience
lon·gani·mous
long·boat
long·bow
long·cloth
long-distance (*adj*)
long-drawn-out
lon·geron part of aircraft
lon·gev·ity
lon·gevous
Long·ford Irish county
long-haired
long-hand
long-headed shrewd
long·horn cattle
lon·gi·corn beetle
long·ing
long·ing·ly
long·ish
lon·gi·tude
lon·gi·tu·di·nal
long johns underpants
long-lived
long-range (*adj*)
long·ship
long·shore
long·shore·man (*plural*
·men)

long-sighted
long-sighted·ly
long-sighted·ness
long·spur bird
long-standing
long-suffer·ance
long-suffer·ing
long-term
long·time (*adj*)
Lon·gueuil Canadian city
lon·gueur *French* boredom
long·ways (*US* ·wise)
long-winded
long-winded·ly
long-winded·ness
Long·year·byen Norwegian
village
lo·nic·era honeysuckle
loo (*plural* loos)
loo·by (*plural* ·bies) fool
loo·fah (*US also* ·fa, luf·fa)
look
look-alike
look·er
looker-on (*plural* lookers-)
look-in (*noun*)
look·out
loom
loom-state undyed
loon
looni·ness
loony (*or* looney; *adj*
looni·er, looni·est; *noun,*
plural loonies)
loop
loop·er caterpillar
loop·hole
loopi·ness
loopy (loopi·er, loopi·est)
loose
loose·box
loose-jointed
loose-leaf (*adj*)
loose·ly
loos·en
loos·en·er
loose·ness
loose-strife plant
loose-tongued
loos·ish
loot
loot·er
lop (lop·ping, lopped)
lope
lopped

lop·per
lop·ping
lop-sided
lop·sided·ly
lop·sided·ness
lo·qua·cious
lo·quac·ity (*or*
lo·qua·cious·ness)
lo·quat fruit
lo·qui·tur *Latin* he or she
speaks
lor exclamation
lo·ran navigation system
Lord God
lord nobleman
lord·li·ness
lord·ling
lord·ly (·li·er, ·li·est)
lor·do·sis spinal curvature
lor·dot·ic
lord·ship
lordy exclamation
lore knowledge; zoology
term; *compare* law
Lo·relei siren
lor·gnette
lor·gnon
lo·ri·ca (*plural* ·cae) shell
lori·cate (*or* ·cat·ed)
lori·keet parrot
lori·mer (*or* ·ner)
metalworker
lo·ris (*plural* ·ris) animal
lorn forsaken
Lor·raine
lor·ry (*plural* ·ries) vehicle
lory (*plural* lories) parrot
los·able
Los An·ge·les
lose (los·ing, lost)
lo·sel *Dialect* worthless
person
los·er
los·ing
loss
los·sy dissipating energy
lost
lot (lot·ting, lot·ted)
lota (*or* lo·tah) water
container
Lot-et-Garonne French
department
loth *variant spelling of* loath
Lo·thario (*plural* ·tharios)
libertine

Lo·thian former Scottish region
lo·tic ecology term
lo·tion
lot·ted
lot·tery (plural ·teries)
lot·ting
lot·to
lo·tus (or lo·tos)
lotus-eater
louche shifty
loud
loud·en
loud-hailer
loud·ish
loud·ly
loud·mouth
loud·ness
loud·speaker
lough
Lough·bor·ough Leicestershire town
lou·is (or lou·is d'or; plural lou·is or lou·is d'or) coin
Lou·is·burg (or ·bourg) Canadian fortress
Loui·si·ana
Lou·is·ville US port
lounge
loung·er
loupe magnifying glass
lour (or low·er) look menacing
Lourdes French town
lour·ing·ly (or low·er·)
louse (plural lice)
louse·wort
lousi·ly
lousi·ness
lousy (lousi·er, lousi·est)
lout
Louth Irish county
lout·ish
lout·ish·ly
lout·ish·ness
Lou·vain Belgian town
lou·var fish
Lou·vre French museum
lou·vre (US ·ver) slat
lou·vred (US ·vered)
lov·abil·ity (or love·)
lov·able (or love·)
lov·ably (or love·)
lov·age plant
lov·at fabric

love
love·bird
love·less
love·li·ness
love·lock
love·lorn
love·ly (adj ·li·er, ·li·est; noun, plural ·lies)
love·making
lov·er
love·sick
love·sick·ness
lov·ey
lovey-dovey
lov·ing
lov·ing·ly
lov·ing·ness
low
low·an bird
low·born (or ·bred)
low·boy US table with drawers
low·bred
low·brow
low·brow·ism
low·down (noun)
low·down (adj)
low·er less high; variant spelling of lour
low·er·able
low·er·ing·ly variant spelling of louringly
lower·most
low·est
Lowes·toft
low-key (or -keyed)
Low·land of Lowlands
low·land flat ground
Low·land·er
low·land·er
Low·lands Scottish region
low·li·ness
low·ly (·li·er, ·li·est)
low-minded
low·ness
low-pitched
low-rise (adj)
low-spirit·ed
lox smoked salmon
loxo·drom·ic (or ·dromi·cal)
loxo·dromi·cal·ly
loxo·drom·ics (or lox·od·ro·my) navigation technique

loy·al
loy·al·ism
Loy·al·ist Northern Irish Protestant
loy·al·ist
loy·al·ly
loy·al·ty (plural ·ties)
Lo·yang Chinese city
loz·enge
loz·engy heraldic term
Lo·zère French department
Lozi Zambian language
Lu·an·da Angolan capital
Luba (plural Luba) African people
lub·ber clumsy person
Lub·bock Texan city
Lü·beck German port
Lu·blin Polish city
lub·ri·cant
lu·bri·cate
lu·bri·ca·tion
lu·bri·ca·tion·al
lu·bri·ca·tive
lu·bri·ca·tor
lu·bric·ity lewdness
lu·bri·cous (or ·cious)
Lu·bum·ba·shi city in the Democratic Republic of Congo
lu·carne dormer window
lu·cen·cy
lu·cent
Lu·cerne Swiss town
lu·cerne plant
lu·cid
lu·cid·ity (or ·cid·ness)
Lu·ci·fer
lu·cif·er·in biochemical compound
Lucina Roman goddess
luck
lucki·ly
lucki·ness
luck·less
luck·less·ness
Luck·now Indian city
lucky (lucki·er, lucki·est)
luc·ra·tive
lu·cra·tive·ly
lu·cre
lu·cu·brate to study
lu·cu·bra·tion
lu·cu·bra·tor
Lud·dite

Lu·dhia·na Indian city

lu·di·crous

Lud·low Shropshire town

ludo

Lud·wigs·ha·fen German city

luff nautical term

luf·fa US variant spelling of loofah

Luft·waf·fe German Air Force

lug (lug·ging, lugged)

Lu·gan·da African language

Lu·gansk Ukrainian city

luge toboggan

Lu·ger (Trademark)

lug·gage

lugged

lug·ger

lug·ging

lug·sail

lu·gu·bri·ous

lug·worm

luke·warm

lull

lulla·by (noun, plural ·bies; verb ·bies, ·by·ing, ·bied)

lull·ing·ly

lulu US wonderful person or thing

lum·ba·go

lum·bar of loin

lum·ber timber; move awkwardly

lum·ber·er

lum·ber·ing

lum·ber·ing·ly

lumber·jack

lumber·jacket

lumber·yard

lum·bri·cal

lum·bri·ca·lis muscle

lum·bri·coid wormlike

lu·men (plural ·mens) unit

lu·men (plural ·mina) anatomical duct

lu·men·al (or ·min·)

lu·mi·nance

lu·mi·nary (plural ·naries)

lu·mi·nesce

lu·mi·nes·cence

lu·mi·nes·cent

lu·mi·nos·ity (plural ·ities)

lu·mi·nous

lu·mi·nous·ly

lu·mis·te·rol biochemical compound

lum·me exclamation

lum·mox clumsy person

lump

lump·en stupid

lum·pen·pro·le·tari·at

lum·per US stevedore

lump·fish (plural ·fish or ·fishes)

lumpi·ly

lumpi·ness

lump·ish

lumpy (lumpi·er, lumpi·est)

Luna Roman goddess

luna moth; compare lunar

lu·na·cy (plural ·cies)

lu·nar of the moon; compare luna

lu·nate (or ·nat·ed)

lu·na·tic (or lu·nati·cal)

lu·na·tion lunar month

lunch

lunch·eon

lunch·eon·ette US café

lunch·er

Lund Swedish city

Lun·dy island

lune maths term

Lü·ne·burg German city

lu·nette

lung

lunge

lung·er

lung·fish (plural ·fish or ·fishes)

lung·ful

lun·gi (or ·gee) Indian cloth

lung·worm

lung·wort plant

lu·ni·so·lar

lu·ni·tid·al

lu·nu·la (or ·nule; plural ·lae or ·nules)

lu·nu·late (or ·lat·ed)

luny (adj luni·er, luni·est; noun, plural lunies)

Lu·per·ca·lia (plural ·lia or ·lias) Roman festival

lu·pin (US ·pine) plant

lu·pine wolflike; US spelling of lupin

lu·pu·lin sedative

Lu·pus constellation

lu·pus skin disease

lur (or lure; plural lures) musical horn

lurch

lurch·er

lurch·ing·ly

lur·dan stupid

lure

lur·er

Lu·rex (Trademark)

lu·rid

lu·rid·ness

lur·ing·ly

lurk

lurk·er

lurk·ing·ly

Lu·sa·ka Zambian capital

Lu·sa·tia German region

Lu·sa·tian

lus·cious

lus·cious·ness

lush

lush·ly

lush·ness

Lü·shun Chinese port

Lu·si·ta·nia ship

lust

lus·ter US spelling of lustre

lust·ful

lust·ful·ly

lust·ful·ness

lusti·ly

lusti·ness

lus·tral

lus·trate purify

lus·tra·tion

lus·tra·tive

lus·tre (US ·ter)

lus·tre·less (US ·ter·)

lustre·ware (US luster·)

lus·trous

lus·trum (plural ·trums or ·tra) five years

lusty (lusti·er, lusti·est)

lute

lu·teal biology term

lu·tein·iz·ing hor·mone

lu·tenist lute player

lu·teo·lin plant compound

lu·teous greenish-yellow

Lu·tetia Latin Paris

lu·tetium (or ·tecium) chemical element

Lu·ther·an

Lu·ther·an·ism

Lu·ther·ism
lu·thern dormer window
Lu·tine bell
Lu·ton
lux (*plural* lux) unit
lux·ate dislocate
luxa·tion
Lux·em·bourg
Lux·or Egyptian town
lux·ulia·nite (*or*
·ul·lia·nite) granite
luxu·ri·ance
luxu·ri·ant
luxu·ri·ate
luxu·ria·tion
luxu·ri·ous
luxu·ry (*plural* ·ries)
Lu·zon Philippine island
Ly·all·pur Pakistani city
ly·can·thrope werewolf
ly·can·thro·py
ly·cée (*plural* ·cées) French
school
Ly·ceum Athenian school
ly·ceum public building
ly·chee *variant spelling of*
litchi
lych gate *variant spelling of*
lich gate
lych·nis plant
ly·co·pod club moss
ly·co·po·dium type of club
moss
lydd·ite explosive
Lydia ancient Asian region
Lyd·ian

lye alkaline solution;
compare lie
ly·ing
lying-in (*plural* lyings-in)
lyke-wake vigil over corpse
Lyme Re·gis
Lym·ing·ton Hampshire
town
lymph
lym·phad·eni·tis
lym·phan·gial
lym·phan·git·ic
lym·phan·gi·tis (*plural*
·gi·des)
lym·phat·ic
lym·phati·cal·ly
lym·pho·blast blood cell
lym·pho·blas·tic
lym·pho·cyte blood cell
lym·pho·cyt·ic
lym·pho·cy·to·sis
lym·pho·cy·tot·ic
lym·phoid
lym·pho·ma (*plural* ·ma·ta
or ·mas) tumour
lym·pho·ma·toid
lym·pho·poi·esis (*plural*
·eses)
lym·pho·poi·et·ic
lyn·cean resembling a lynx
lynch kill; *compare*
linchpin
lynch·er
lynch·ing
lynx (*plural* lynxes *or* lynx)
Lyon French city

Lyon·nais former French
province
ly·on·naise cookery term
Ly·on·nesse legendary place
lyo·phil·ic
ly·ophi·lize (*or* ·lise)
freeze-dry
lyo·pho·bic
Lyra constellation
ly·rate (*or* rat·ed)
lyre
lyre·bird
lyr·ic
lyri·cal
lyri·cal·ly
lyri·cism
lyri·cist
lyr·ist
lyse biology term
ly·ser·gic acid
ly·sim·eter
ly·sin substance that
destroys cells
ly·sine amino acid
ly·sis (*plural* ·ses) biology
term
Ly·sol (*Trademark*)
ly·so·so·mal
ly·so·some cell particle
ly·so·zyme enzyme
Lyth·am St. Anne's
lyth·ra·ceous botany
term
lyt·ic biology term
lyt·ta (*plural* ·tas *or* ·tae)
zoology term

M

ma *Slang* mother
Ma'am title of address for
royalty
maar (*plural* maars *or*
maare) volcanic crater
Maas·tricht (*or* Maes·)
Dutch city
Mab fairy queen
ma·bela ground corn
mac
ma·ca·bre
ma·ca·co (*plural* ·cos)
lemur; *compare* macaque
mac·ad·am road surface

maca·da·mia tree
mac·ad·ami·za·tion (*or*
·sa·tion)
mac·ad·am·ize (*or* ·ise)
mac·ad·am·iz·er (*or* ·is·er)
Ma·cao Chinese city
ma·caque monkey; *compare*
macaco
maca·ro·ni (*plural* ·nis)
pasta
maca·ro·ni (*plural* ·nies)
dandy
maca·ron·ic type of verse
maca·roni·cal·ly

maca·roon
Ma·cas·sar *variant spelling of*
Makassar
ma·caw
Mac·ca·bean
Mac·ca·bees Apocryphal
book
mac·ca·boy (*or* ·co·boy,
·ca·baw) snuff
Mac·cles·field
mace
mace·bearer
ma·cedoine diced
vegetables

Mac·edon (*or* **·edo·nia**) former kingdom

Mac·edo·nia S European country; division of Greece

Mac·edo·nian

Ma·ceió Brazilian port

mac·er macebearer

mac·er·ate

mac·er·at·er (*or* **·era·tor**)

mac·era·tion

mac·era·tive

ma·chan tiger-hunting platform

ma·chete

Machia·vel·lian (*or* **·vel·ian**)

ma·chico·late fortifications term

ma·chico·la·tion

ma·chin·abil·ity

ma·chin·able (*or* **·chine·**)

machi·nate

machi·na·tion

machi·na·tor

ma·chine

machine-gun (*verb*; **-gunning, -gunned**)

ma·chin·ery (*plural* **·eries**)

ma·chin·ist

ma·chis·mo

Mach·meter physics term

Mach num·ber physics term

macho

ma·chree *Irish* my dear

Ma·chu Pic·chu Incan city

Ma·cí·as Ngue·ma Guinean island

Mac·kay Australian port

Mac·ken·zie Canadian district or river

macke·rel (*plural* **·rel** *or* **·rels**)

Macki·naw coat

mack·in·tosh (*or* **mac·in·**)

mack·le (*or* **mac·ule**) printing term; *compare* **macle**

Maclaurin's se·ries maths term

ma·cle mineral; *compare* **mackle**

Mâ·con French city; wine

mac·ra·mé

mac·ren·cepha·ly (*or* **·lia**) abnormally large brain

macro·bi·ot·ic

macro·cephal·ic (*or* **mega·**, **mega·lo·**)

macro·cepha·ly (*or* **mega·**, **mega·lo·**) abnormally large head

macro·cli·mate

macro·cli·mat·ic

macro·cli·mati·cal·ly

macro·cosm

macro·cos·mic

macro·cos·mi·cal·ly

macro·cyst

macro·cyte blood cell

macro·cyt·ic

macro·cy·to·sis

macro·eco·nom·ic

macro·eco·nom·ics

macro·evo·lu·tion

macro·evo·lu·tion·ary

macro·gam·ete (*or* **mega·**)

macro·graph

macro·graph·ic

macro·mo·lecu·lar

macro·mol·ecule

mac·ron phonetic symbol

macro·nu·cleus (*plural* **·clei**)

macro·nu·tri·ent

macro·phage cell

macro·phag·ic

macro·phys·ics

mac·rop·ter·ous having large wings

macro·scop·ic (*or* **·scopi·cal**)

macro·scopi·cal·ly

macro·spo·ran·gium (*plural* **·gia**) botany term

macro·spore

ma·cru·ral (*or* **·roid, ·rous**)

ma·cru·ran crustacean

macu·la (*or* **mac·ule**; *plural* **·lae** *or* **·ules**) anatomy term

macu·la lu·tea (*plural* **macu·lae lu·teae**) spot on retina

macu·lar

macu·la·tion

mac·ule *variant of* **mackle** *or* **macula**

mad (**mad·der, mad·dest**)

Mada·gas·can

Mada·gas·car

mad·am term of address; conceited girl; brothel keeper

mad·ame (*plural* **mes·dames**) *French* lady; Mrs

mad·cap

mad·den

mad·den·ing

mad·der plant; dye; more mad

mad·dest

mad·ding *Archaic* mad or maddening

made

Ma·dei·ra

mad·eleine cake

mad·emoi·selle (*plural* **mes·de·moi·selles**)

mad·house

Madh·ya Pra·desh Indian state

Madi·son US city and avenue

mad·ly

mad·man (*plural* **·men**)

mad·ness

Ma·don·na Virgin Mary

Ma·dras Indian port

mad·ras fabric

mad·re·por·al (*or* **·por·ic, ·por·it·ic, ·po·rian**)

mad·re·pore coral

Ma·drid

madri·gal

madri·gal·esque

madri·gal·ian

madri·gal·ist

madri·lène consommé

ma·dro·ña (*or* **·ño, ·ne**; *plural* **·ñas, ·ños,** *or* **·nes**) tree

Ma·du·ra Indonesian island

Ma·du·rai Indian city

Ma·du·rese of Madura

ma·du·ro cigar

mad·woman (*plural* **·women**)

mad·wort plant

Ma·eba·shi Japanese city

Mael·strom Norwegian whirlpool

mael·strom whirlpool; confusion

mae·nad (*or* **me·nad**)

mae·nad·ic

maes·to·so musical term

maes·tro (plural ·tros or ·tri)

Maf·eking South African town

Ma·fia (or Maf·fia)

ma·fio·so (plural ·sos or ·si)

mag

maga·zine

mag·da·len reformed prostitute

Mag·da·lena Colombian river

Mag·da·lenian Palaeolithic culture

Mag·de·burg German city

Ma·gel·lan strait

ma·gen·ta

mag·got fly larva; compare magot

mag·goti·ness

mag·goty

Ma·ghreb (or ·ghrib)

Ma·ghre·bi (or ·ghri·)

Magi (sing. Magus) biblical wise men

magi plural of magus

ma·gian

mag·ic (·ick·ing, ·icked)

magi·cal

magi·cal·ly

ma·gi·cian

ma·gilp variant spelling of megilp

Ma·gi·not line

mag·is·te·rial

mag·is·te·rial·ly

mag·is·tery (plural ·teries) alchemical substance

mag·is·tra·cy (or ·ture; plural ·cies or ·tures)

mag·is·tral pharmacology term

mag·is·tral·ly (or mag·is·trati·cal·ly)

mag·is·trate

mag·is·trate·ship

mag·is·tra·ture variant of magistracy

Mag·le·mo·sian (or ·sean) Mesolithic culture

mag·ma (plural ·mas or ·ma·ta) molten rock

mag·mat·ic

mag·ma·tism

Mag·na Car·ta (or Char·ta)

mag·na·nim·ity (plural ·ities)

mag·nani·mous

mag·nani·mous·ness

mag·nate

mag·ne·sia magnesium oxide

mag·ne·sian (or ·ne·sic, ·ne·sial)

mag·ne·site mineral

mag·ne·sium

mag·net

mag·net·ic

mag·neti·cal·ly

mag·net·ics

mag·net·ism

mag·net·ite mineral

mag·net·it·ic

mag·net·iz·able (or ·is·able)

mag·neti·za·tion (or ·sa·tion)

mag·net·ize (or ·ise)

mag·net·iz·er (or ·is·er)

mag·ne·to (plural ·tos)

mag·ne·to·chemi·cal

mag·ne·to·chem·is·try

mag·ne·to·elec·tric (or ·tri·cal)

mag·ne·to·elec·tric·ity

mag·ne·to·graph

mag·ne·to·hy·dro·dy·nam·ic

mag·ne·to·hy·dro·dy·nam·ics

mag·ne·tom·eter

mag·ne·to·met·ric

mag·ne·tom·etry

mag·ne·to·mo·tive

mag·ne·ton physics unit; compare magnetron

mag·ne·to·sphere

mag·ne·to·stric·tion

mag·ne·to·stric·tive

mag·ne·tron microwave generator; compare magneton

mag·ni·fi·able

Mag·nifi·cat canticle

mag·ni·fi·ca·tion

mag·nifi·cence

mag·nifi·cent

mag·nifi·co (plural ·coes) grandee

mag·ni·fi·er

mag·ni·fy (·fies, ·fy·ing, ·fied)

mag·nilo·quence

mag·nilo·quent

Mag·ni·to·gorsk Russian city

mag·ni·tude

mag·ni·tu·di·nous

mag·no·lia

mag·no·lia·ceous

mag·num (plural ·nums) wine bottle

mag·num opus

mag·nus hitchknot

Magog biblical character

ma·got oriental figurine; compare maggot

mag·pie

mag·uey fibre

Magus (sing. of Magi)

magus (plural magi) Zoroastrian priest; sorcerer

Mag·yar Hungarian

Ma·ha·bha·ra·ta (or ·tam, ·tum) Indian poem

Ma·hal·la el Ku·bra Egyptian city

Ma·ha·na·di Indian river

ma·ha·ra·jah (or ·ja)

ma·ha·ra·ni (or ·nee) maharajah's wife

Ma·ha·rash·tra Indian state

ma·ha·ri·shi Hindu teacher

ma·hat·ma Brahman sage

Ma·ha·ya·na Buddhist school

Mahé Seychelles island

Ma·hi·can (or Mo·; plural ·cans or ·can) American Indian

mah·jong (or mah·jongg)

mahl·stick variant spelling of maulstick

ma·hoga·ny (plural ·nies)

Ma·hom·etan Muslim

ma·ho·nia shrub

ma·hout elephant keeper

Mah·rat·ta variant spelling of Maratha

mah·seer fish

Maia mythological character

maid

mai·dan meeting place

maid·en young girl

maiden·hair fern

Maid·en·head S English town

maid·en·head virginity

maid·en·hood

maid·en·li·ness

maid·en·ly

maid·servant

Maid·stone Kent town

maieu·tic (or ·ti·cal) philosophy term

Mai·kop Russian city

mail

mail·able

mail·bag

mail·box

mail·coach

mail·er

mail·sack

mail·shot

maim

maim·er

main

main·brace

Maine US state

Maine-et-Loire French department

Main·land Scottish island

main·land

main·line (adj, verb)

main·ly

main·mast

main·sail

main·sheet

main·spring

main·stay

main·stream

main·tain

main·tain·able

main·tain·er

main·te·nance

main·top

main·topmast

main·top·sail

Mainz German port

ma·ioli·ca variant spelling of majolica

mai·son·ette (or ·son·nette)

maî·tre d'hô·tel (plural maî·tres d'hô·tel)

maize cereal; compare maze

ma·jes·tic (or ·ti·cal)

ma·jes·ti·cal·ly

Maj·es·ty (plural ·ties) title for royalty

maj·es·ty dignity

ma·joli·ca (or ·ioli·) pottery

ma·jor

Ma·jor·ca

major-domo (plural -domos)

ma·jor·ette

ma·jor·ity (plural ·ities)

Ma·juro capital of the Marshall Islands

ma·jus·cu·lar

ma·jus·cule printing term

Ma·ka·lu Himalayan mountain range

Ma·kas·ar (or ·kas·sar, ·cas·sar) Indonesian port

make (mak·ing, made)

make-believe (noun)

make·fast

mak·er

make·shift

make-up (noun)

make·weight (noun)

Ma·ke·yev·ka Ukrainian city

Ma·khach·ka·la Russian port

mak·ing

mako (plural makos) shark; tree

Ma·kur·di Nigerian port

Mala·bar Indian region

Ma·la·bo capital of Equatorial Guinea

mal·ab·sorp·tion

Ma·lac·ca Malaysian state

ma·lac·ca walking stick

mala·chite mineral

mala·co·logi·cal

mala·colo·gist

mala·col·ogy study of molluscs

mala·coph·yl·lous having fleshy leaves

mala·cop·te·ryg·ian fish

mala·cos·tra·can crustacean

mala·cos·tra·cous

mal·ad·dress awkwardness

mal·ad·just·ed

mal·ad·just·ment

mal·ad·min·is·ter

mal·ad·min·is·tra·tion

mal·ad·min·is·tra·tor

mala·droit

mala·droit·ness

mala·dy (plural ·dies)

mala fide Latin in bad faith

Má·la·ga Spanish port; wine

Mala·gasy Madagascan language

ma·la·gueña dance

ma·laise

mala·mute (or mal·emute) Eskimo dog

mal·an·ders (or mal·lan·, mal·len·) horse disease

Ma·lang Indonesian city

mala·pert saucy

mala·prop·ian

mala·prop·ism

mal·ap·ro·pos

ma·lar of the cheek

ma·laria

ma·lar·ial (or ·lar·ian, ·lari·ous)

ma·lar·key (or ·ky)

mal·as·simi·la·tion

mal·ate chemistry term

Mala·thi·on (Trademark)

Ma·la·tya Turkish city

Ma·la·wi

Ma·la·wian

Ma·lay

Ma·laya

Mala·ya·lam (or ·laam) language

Ma·lay·an

Ma·lay·sia

Ma·lay·sian

mal·con·tent

mal de mer French sea sickness

Mal·dives

Mal·div·ian (or ·di·van)

male

Malé capital of the Maldives

ma·leate chemistry term

mal·edict

mal·edic·tion

mal·edic·tive (or ·tory)

mal·efac·tion

mal·efac·tor (fem ·tress)

ma·lef·ic

ma·lefi·cence

ma·lefi·cent

ma·leic acid

male·ness

ma·levo·lence

ma·levo·lent

mal·fea·sance illegal act

mal·fea·sant

mal·for·ma·tion
mal·formed
mal·func·tion
mal·gré lui *French* in spite
  of himself
Mali African republic
Malian
mal·ic acid
mal·ice
ma·li·cious
ma·li·cious·ness
ma·lign
ma·lig·nan·cy (*plural* ·cies)
ma·lig·nant
ma·lign·er
ma·lig·nity (*plural* ·nities)
mal·im·print·ed
mal·im·print·ing
ma·lines fabric
ma·lin·ger
ma·lin·ger·er
Ma·lin·ke (*or* ·nin·ke; *plural*
  ·ke *or* ·kes) African people
mali·son curse
mall
mal·lam (*or* mal·am)
  Islamic scholar
mal·lard (*plural* ·lard *or*
  ·lards)
mal·le·abil·ity (*or*
  ·able·ness)
mal·le·able
mal·lee tree
mal·le·muck bird
mal·leo·lar
mal·leo·lus (*plural* ·li) ankle
  bone
mal·let
mal·le·us (*plural* ·lei) ear
  bone
mal·low
malm limestone
Malmö Swedish port
malm·sey wine
mal·nour·ished
mal·nu·tri·tion
mal·oc·clud·ed
mal·oc·clu·sion dentistry
  term
mal·odor·ous
ma·lo·nic acid
mal·pighia·ceous botany
  term
Mal·pigh·ian anatomy term
mal·posed

mal·po·si·tion
mal·prac·tice
mal·prac·ti·tion·er
malt
Mal·ta
malt·ase enzyme
malt·ed
Mal·tese (*plural* ·tese)
mal·tha mineral tar
Mal·thu·sian
Mal·thu·si·an·ism
  population theory
malti·ness
malt·ing
malt·ose sugar
mal·treat
mal·treat·er
mal·treat·ment
malt·ster
malty (malti·er, malti·est)
mal·va·ceous botany term
mal·va·sia wine
Mal·vern
mal·voi·sie wine
mam *Slang* mother
mama (*or* mam·ma)
  mother; *compare* mamma
mam·ba snake
mam·bo (*plural* ·bos) dance
mam·elon hillock
Mam·eluke (*or* Mama·luke)
  Egyptian ruler
ma·mey (*or* mam·mee)
  fruit; *compare* mammy
ma·mil·la (*US* mam·mil·;
  plural ·lae) nipple
ma·mil·lary (*US* mam·mil·)
ma·mil·late (*or* ·lat·ed; *US*
  mam·mil·)
mam·ma (*plural* ·mae)
  breast; *compare* mama
mam·ma *variant spelling of*
  mama
mam·mal
mam·ma·lian
mam·ma·logi·cal
mam·malo·gist
mam·mal·ogy
mam·ma·ry
mam·mee *variant spelling of*
  mamey
mam·mif·er·ous
mam·mil·la *US spelling of*
  mamilla
mam·mock *Dialect* shred

mam·mo·gram
mam·mog·ra·phy
mam·mon
mam·mon·ism
mam·mon·ist (*or* ·ite)
mam·mon·is·tic
mam·moth
mam·my (*or* ·mie; *plural*
  ·mies) mother; *compare*
  mamey
Man (Isle of)
man (*noun, plural* men; *verb*
  man·ning, manned)
mana power; *compare*
  manna
mana·cle
Ma·na·do *variant spelling of*
  Menado
man·age
man·age·abil·ity (*or*
  ·able·ness)
man·age·able
man·age·ably
man·age·ment
man·ag·er
man·ag·er·ess
mana·gerial
mana·geri·al·ly
man·ag·ing
Ma·na·gua Nicaraguan
  capital
mana·kin bird; *compare*
  manikin; mannequin
Ma·na·ma capital of
  Bahrain
ma·ña·na *Spanish* tomorrow
Ma·nas·sas *US* town
man-at-arms (*plural* men-)
mana·tee sea mammal
mana·toid
Ma·naus (*or* Ma·náos)
  Brazilian port
Manche French department
Man·ches·ter
man·chi·neel tree
Man·chu (*plural* ·chus *or*
  ·chu) Chinese dynasty
Man·chu·ria
Man·chu·rian
man·ci·ple steward
Man·cu·nian native of
  Manchester
Man·daean
Man·dae·an·ism Iraqi sect
Man·da·lay Burmese city

man·da·mus (*plural* ·muses)
legal term

Man·da·rin language

man·da·rin official; fruit;
duck

man·da·tary *variant spelling
of* mandatory (*noun*)

man·date

man·da·to·ri·ly

man·da·tory obligatory

man·da·tory (*or* ·tary; *plural*
·tories *or* ·taries) mandate
holder

Man·de (*plural* ·de *or* ·des)
language group

man·di Indian market

man·di·ble

man·dibu·lar

man·dir Hindu temple

man·do·la mandolin

man·do·lin (*or* ·line)

man·do·lin·ist

man·dor·la art term

man·drake (*or*
man·drago·ra)

man·drel (*or* ·dril) spindle

man·drill monkey

man·du·cate eat or chew

mane

man-eater

maned

ma·nège (*or* ·nege) riding
school; compare ménage

ma·nes Roman deities

ma·neu·ver *US spelling of*
manoeuvre

man·ful

man·ful·ly

man·ful·ness

man·ga·bey monkey

Man·ga·lore Indian port

man·ga·nate

man·ga·nese

man·gan·ic

Man·gan·in (*Trademark*)

man·ga·nite mineral

man·ga·nous

mange skin disease

man·gel-wur·zel (*or* ·gold-)

man·ger

mange-tout pea

man·gi·ly

man·gi·ness

man·gle

man·gler

man·go (*plural* ·goes *or*
·gos)

man·go·nel war engine

man·go·steen fruit

man·grove

man·gy (*or* ·gey; ·gi·er,
·gi·est)

man·handle

Man·hat·tan

man·hole

man·hood

man-hour

man·hunt

man·hunter

ma·nia

ma·ni·ac

ma·nia·cal

ma·nia·cal·ly

man·ic

manic-depres·sive

Mani·chae·ism (*or* ·che·)
religion

Mani·chee

ma·ni·cot·ti stuffed noodles

mani·cure

mani·cur·ist

mani·fest

mani·fest·able

mani·fes·ta·tion

mani·fes·ta·tion·al

mani·fes·to (*plural* ·toes *or*
·tos)

mani·fold

mani·fold·er

mani·kin (*or* mana·kin,
man·ni·kin) dwarf;
compare manakin;
mannequin

Ma·nila Philippine port

ma·nil·la African currency

ma·nille card trump

mani·oc (*or* manio·ca)
plant

mani·ple

ma·nipu·labil·ity

ma·nipu·lar

ma·nipu·lat·able (*or*
·lable)

ma·nipu·late

ma·nipu·la·tion

ma·nipu·la·tive

ma·nipu·la·tor

ma·nipu·la·tory

Ma·ni·pur Indian region

Ma·ni·sa Turkish city

Mani·to·ba Canadian
province

mani·tou (*or* ·tu; *plural*
·tous, tou, *or* ·tus, ·tu)
American Indian spirit

Mani·tou·lin Canadian
island

Mani·za·les Colombian city

man·kind

manky (manki·er,
manki·est) *Scot* dirty

man·like

man·li·ness

man·ly (·li·er, ·li·est)

man-made

man·na celestial food;
compare mana

manned

man·ne·quin model;
compare manakin;
manikin

man·ner

man·nered

man·ner·ism

man·ner·ist

man·ner·is·tic (*or* ·ti·cal)

man·ner·is·ti·cal·ly

man·ner·less

man·ner·less·ness

man·ner·li·ness

man·ner·ly

Mann·heim German city

man·nish

man·nish·ness

man·nit·ic

man·ni·tol plant compound

man·nose sugar

ma·noeu·vrabil·ity (*US*
·neu·)

ma·noeu·vrable (*US* ·neu·)

ma·noeu·vre (*US* ·neu·ver)

ma·noeu·vrer (*US*
·neu·ver·er)

man-of-war (*plural* men-)

ma·nom·eter

mano·met·ric (*or* ·ri·cal)

mano·met·ri·cal·ly

ma·nom·etry

man·or

ma·no·rial

man·power

man·qué unfulfilled

man·rope ship railing

man·sard roof

manse

man·servant (*plural*
men·servants)

Mans·field Nottinghamshire
town

man·sion

man-sized

man·slaughter

man·sue·tude gentleness

man·ta fish; fabric

man·teau (*plural* ·teaus *or*
·teaux) cloak

man·tel (*or* ·tle) frame
round fireplace; *compare*
mantle

man·tel·et woman's mantle

man·tel·let·ta vestment

mantel·piece

mantel·shelf (*plural*
·shelves)

mantel·tree lintel over
fireplace

man·tic of prophecy

man·ti·cal·ly

man·til·la Spanish scarf

man·tis (*plural* ·tises *or* ·tes)

man·tis·sa maths term

man·tle cloak; *compare*
mantel

man·tling

man·tra Hindu psalm

man·trap

Man·tua Italian city

man·tua gown

manu·al

manu·al·ly

ma·nu·brial

ma·nu·brium (*plural* ·bria
or ·briums) zoology term

manu·fac·tory (*plural*
·tories)

manu·fac·tur·able

manu·fac·tur·al

manu·fac·ture

manu·fac·tur·er

manu·fac·tur·ing

ma·nu·ka tree

Ma·nu·kau New Zealand
city

manu·mis·sion

manu·mit (·mit·ting,
·mit·ted) free from slavery

ma·nure

ma·nur·er

ma·nus (*plural* ·nus) hand

manu·script

Manx

Manx·man (*plural* ·men)

many

many·plies cow's stomach

many-sided

many-sided·ness

man·za·nil·la sherry

Mao·ism

Mao·ist

Mao·ri (*plural* ·ris *or* ·ri)

map (map·ping, mapped)

ma·ple

map·pable

Ma·pu·to capital of
Mozambique

ma·quette sculptor's model

Ma·quis French Resistance

ma·quis (*plural* ·quis)
shrubby vegetation

mar (mar·ring, marred)

mara rodent

mara·bou stork

mara·bout Muslim holy
man

ma·ra·bun·ta wasp

ma·raca percussion
instrument

Mara·cai·bo Venezuelan
port and lake

Ma·ra·cay Venezuelan city

mar·ag·ing steel

Ma·ra·nhão Brazilian state

ma·ras·ca cherry tree

mara·schi·no (*plural* ·nos)
liqueur; cherry

ma·ras·mic

ma·ras·mus

Ma·ra·tha (*or* Mah·rat·ta)
Indian people

Ma·ra·thi (*or* Mah·rat·ti)

Mara·thon Greek plain

mara·thon race

ma·raud

ma·raud·er

mara·vedi (*plural* ·vedis)
coin

mar·ble

mar·bled

mar·bler

mar·bling

mar·bly

Mar·burg German city

marc brandy

mar·ca·site mineral

mar·ca·siti·cal

mar·cel (·cel·ling, ·celled)
hair style

mar·ces·cence

mar·ces·cent botany term

March month; *compare*
Marche

march

Marche former French
province; *compare* March

march·er

Marches border country

mar·che·sa (*plural* ·se) wife
of marchese

mar·che·se (*plural* ·si)
Italian nobleman

mar·chion·ess wife of
marquis or marquess

Mar del Pla·ta Argentine
city

Mar·di Gras Shrove Tuesday

mardy *Dialect* spoilt or
irritable

mare (*plural* mares) female
horse

mare (*plural* ma·ria) lunar
plain

mare clau·sum legal term

mare li·be·rum legal term

ma·rem·ma (*plural* ·me)
marsh

mare's-tail cloud; plant

marg (*or* marge) *short for*
margarine

mar·gar·ic (*or* ·it·ic) of pearl

mar·ga·rine (*or* ·rin)

mar·ga·ri·ta cocktail

mar·ga·rite mineral;
compare marguerite

Mar·gate

Mar·gaux wine

mar·gay animal

mar·gin

mar·gin·al

mar·gi·na·lia

mar·gin·al·ity

mar·gin·al·ly

mar·gin·ate

mar·gina·tion

mar·gra·vate

mar·grave German
nobleman

mar·gra·vine wife of ·
margrave

mar·gue·rite flower; *compare*
margarite

mari·achi Mexican street
musicians

Mar·ian of the Virgin Mary

Ma·ria·nao Cuban city

Ma·ri·bor Slovenian city

mari·cul·ture

mari·gold

ma·ri·jua·na (or ·hua·)

ma·rim·ba percussion
instrument

ma·ri·na

mari·nade (noun, verb)

mari·nate (verb)

mari·na·tion

Ma·rin·du·que Philippine
island

ma·rine

Mari·ner US space probe

mari·ner seaman

Mari·ola·try (or Mary·)
veneration of Virgin Mary

Mari·ol·ogy (or Mary·)

mari·on·ette

mari·po·sa plant

Mar·ist member of Christian
sect

mar·it·age feudal right

mari·tal

mari·time

Mari·time Alps; Provinces

Mari·tim·er

Ma·ri·u·pol Ukrainian city

mar·jo·ram

mark

mark·down (noun)

marked

mark·ed·ly

mark·ed·ness

mark·er

mar·ket

mar·ket·abil·ity (or
·able·ness)

mar·ket·able

mar·ket·ably

mar·ket·er

mar·ket·ing

market·place

mar·khor (or ·khoor; plural
·khors, ·khor or ·khoors,
·khoor) goat

mark·ing

mark·ka (plural ·kaa)
Finnish currency

marks·man (plural ·men)

marks·man·ship

marks·woman (plural
·women)

mark·up (noun)

marl

mar·la·cious (or marly)

Marl·bor·ough

mar·lin (plural ·lin or ·lins)
fish

mar·line (or ·lin, ·ling)
nautical rope

mar·line·spike (or ·lin·,
·ling·)

mar·lite (or marl·stone)

marly

mar·ma·lade

Mar·ma·ra (or ·mo·)
Turkish sea

Mar·mite (Trademark) food

mar·mite cooking pot

mar·mo·real (or ·rean) of
marble

mar·mo·set

mar·mot animal

Marne French river

maro·cain fabric

Maro·nite Syrian Christian

ma·roon

ma·rooned

maro·quin leather

Marprelate tracts

marque brand of car

mar·quee

mar·quess British nobleman

mar·quess·ate

mar·que·try (or ·que·te·rie;
plural ·tries or ·ries)

mar·quis (plural ·quises or
·quis) foreign nobleman

mar·quis·ate

mar·quise gemstone; wife of
marquis

mar·qui·sette fabric

Mar·ra·kech (or ·kesh)
Moroccan city

mar·ram grass

Mar·ra·no (plural ·nos)
Iberian Jew

marred

mar·rer

mar·riage

mar·riage·abil·ity (or
·able·ness)

mar·riage·able

mar·ried

mar·ri·er

mar·ring

mar·ron chestnut

mar·ron gla·cé (plural
mar·rons gla·cés) glazed
chestnut

mar·row

marrow·bone

marrow·fat pea

mar·ry (·ries, ·ry·ing, ·ried)

Mars

Mar·sa·la Sicilian port; wine

Mar·seil·laise French
national anthem

Mar·seille (or ·seilles)
French port

mar·seille (or ·seilles) fabric

marsh

mar·shal (·shal·ling,
·shalled; US ·shal·ing,
·shaled)

mar·shal·cy (or ·shal·ship)

Mar·shall Is·lands Pacific
Ocean country

mar·shal·ler (US ·shal·er)

Mar·shal·sea former prison

marshi·ness

marsh·land

marsh·mal·low sweet

marsh mal·low plant

marshy (marshi·er,
marshi·est)

mar·su·pial

mar·su·pia·lian (or
·su·pian)

mar·su·pium (plural ·pia)
pouch

mart

mar·ta·gon lily

mar·tel·la·to (or ·lan·do)
music term

Mar·tel·lo tower

mar·ten (plural ·tens or
·ten) mammal; compare
martin

mar·ten·site metallurgy
term

mar·ten·sit·ic

mar·tial

mar·tial·ism

mar·tial·ist

mar·tial·ly

Mar·tian

mar·tin bird; compare
marten

mar·ti·net

mar·ti·net·ish
mar·ti·net·ism
mar·tin·gale
Mar·ti·ni (*Trademark*)
  vermouth
mar·ti·ni (*plural* ·nis)
  cocktail
Mar·ti·ni·can
Mar·ti·nique
Mar·tin·mas
mart·let heraldic swallow
mar·tyr
mar·tyr·dom
mar·tyr·ize (*or* ·ise)
mar·tyri·za·tion (*or*
  ·sa·tion)
mar·tyro·logi·cal (*or*
  ·log·ic)
mar·tyr·olo·gist
mar·tyr·ol·ogy (*plural*
  ·ogies)
mar·tyry (*plural* ·tyries)
  martyr's shrine
mar·vel (·vel·ling, ·velled;
  US ·vel·ing, ·veled)
mar·vel·lous (*US* ·vel·ous)
mar·vel·ment
Marx·ian
Marxi·an·ism
Marx·ism
Marxism-Leninism
Marx·ist
Marxist-Leninist
Mary·land
mar·zi·pan
Ma·sai (*plural* ·sais *or* ·sai)
  African people
Ma·san Korean port
Mas·ba·te Philippine
  island
mas·cara
mas·cle heraldic term
mas·con lunar region
mas·cot
mas·cu·line
mas·cu·lin·ity (*or*
  ·line·ness)
mas·cu·li·ni·za·tion (*or*
  ·sa·tion)
mas·cu·lin·ize (*or* ·ise)
ma·ser microwave laser;
  compare mazer
Ma·se·ru capital of Lesotho
mash
mash·er

Mash·had (*or* Me·shed)
  Iranian city
mashie (*or* mashy; *plural*
  mashies) golf club
mas·jid (*or* mus·) mosque
mask face covering, etc.;
  variant spelling of masque
mas·ka·nonge (*or* ·ki·)
  variants of muskellunge
masked
mask·er
maso·chism
maso·chist
maso·chis·tic
Ma·son freemason
ma·son stone worker
Mason-Dixon Line
Ma·son·ic
ma·son·ic
ma·soni·cal·ly
ma·son·ry (*plural* ·ries)
Ma·so·ra (*or* Ma·so·rah,
  Mas·so·ra, Mas·so·rah)
  Hebrew text
Maso·rete (*or* Mas·so·rete,
  Maso·rite) Hebrew scholar
masque (*or* mask)
  entertainment; *compare*
  mask
mas·quer (*or* mask·er)
mas·quer·ade
mas·quer·ad·er
Mass church service
mass
Mas·sa·chu·set (*or* ·setts;
  plural ·sets, ·set, *or* ·setts)
  American Indian
Mas·sa·chu·setts *US* state
mas·sa·cre
mas·sa·crer
mas·sage
mas·sag·er (*or* ·ist)
mas·sa·sau·ga snake
mas·sé billiards stroke
mass·edly
mas·se·ter muscle
mas·se·ter·ic
mas·seur (*fem* ·seuse)
mas·si·cot mineral
mas·sif landform; *compare*
  massive
Mas·sif Cen·tral French
  plateau
mas·sive huge; *compare*
  massif

mas·sive·ness (*or* ·siv·ity)
Mas·so·ra (*or* ·rah) *variant
  spellings of* Masora
mas·so·thera·peu·tic
mas·so·thera·pist
mas·so·thera·py massage
mass-produce
mass-produc·er
mass-pro·duc·tion
massy (massi·er, massi·est)
  massive
mast
mas·ta·ba (*or* ·bah) pyramid
  prototype
mas·tec·to·my (*plural*
  ·mies)
mas·ter
master-at-arms (*plural*
  masters-)
mas·ter·dom
mas·ter·ful
mas·ter·ful·ly
mas·ter·ful·ness
mas·ter·hood
mas·ter·li·ness
mas·ter·ly
master·mind
master·piece
mas·ter·ship
master·stroke
master·work
mas·tery (*plural* ·teries)
mast·head
mas·tic resin
mas·ti·cable chewable
mas·ti·cate
mas·ti·ca·tion
mas·ti·ca·tor
mas·ti·ca·tory (*plural*
  ·tories)
mas·tiff
mas·ti·gopho·ran (*or*
  ·go·phore) protozoan
mas·ti·tis breast
  inflammation
mas·to·don extinct
  elephant
mas·toid ear bone
mas·toid·ec·to·my (*plural*
  ·mies)
mas·toid·itis ear
  inflammation
mas·tur·bate
mas·tur·ba·tion
mas·tur·ba·tor

Ma·su·ria Polish region
Ma·su·rian
mat (mat·ting, mat·ted)
floor covering; tangle;
compare matte
mat (*or* matt, matte;
mat·ting, mat·ted)
lacking gloss; *compare*
matte
Mata·be·le (*plural* ·les *or* ·le)
African people
Mata·be·le·land
Ma·ta·di port in the
Democratic Republic of
Congo
mata·dor
Mata·mo·ros Mexican port
Mata·pan Greek cape
match
match·board
match·box
match·less
match·less·ness
match·maker
match·mark
match·stick
match·wood
mate
maté (*or* mate) tea
matelas·sé embossed
mate·lot (*or* ·lo, ·low) *Slang*
sailor
mat·elote (*or* ·elotte) fish
stew
ma·ter *Slang* mother
ma·ter·fa·mili·as
ma·terial
ma·teri·al·ism
ma·teri·al·ist
ma·teri·al·is·tic
ma·teri·al·ity (*plural* ·ities)
ma·teri·ali·za·tion (*or*
·sa·tion)
ma·teri·al·ize (*or* ·ise)
ma·teri·al·iz·er (*or* ·is·er)
ma·teri·al·ly
ma·teria medi·ca study of
drugs
ma·teri·el (*or* ·téri·)
materials and equipment
ma·ter·nal
ma·ter·nal·ism
ma·ter·nal·is·tic
ma·ter·nal·ly
ma·ter·nity

matey (mati·er, mati·est)
matey·ness (*or* mati·ness)
math·emati·cal (*or*
·emat·ic)
math·emati·cal·ly
math·ema·ti·cian
math·emat·ics
Ma·thu·ra Indian city
mati·er
mati·est
Ma·til·da *Austral* bushman's
swag
mat·in (*or* mat·tin,
mat·in·al) of matins
mati·née
mati·ness *variant spelling of*
mateyness
mat·ins (*or* mat·tins)
Mat·lock Derbyshire town
Mato Gros·so (*or* Mat·to
Gros·so) Brazilian plateau
ma·tri·arch
ma·tri·ar·chal (*or* ·chic)
ma·tri·ar·chate
ma·tri·ar·chy (*plural* ·chies)
ma·tri·ces *plural of* matrix
mat·ri·cid·al
mat·ri·cide
mat·ri·cli·nous (*or*
mat·ro·cli·nous,
mat·ro·cli·nal) biology
term
ma·tricu·lant
ma·tricu·late
ma·tricu·la·tion
ma·tricu·la·tor
mat·ri·lin·eal
mat·ri·lin·eal·ly
mat·ri·lo·cal living with
wife's family
mat·ri·lo·cal·ity
mat·ri·mo·nial
mat·ri·mo·nial·ly
mat·ri·mo·ny (*plural* ·nies)
ma·trix (*plural* ·tri·ces)
mat·ro·cli·nous (*or* ·nal)
variants of matriclinous
ma·tron
ma·tron·age
ma·tron·al
ma·tron·li·ness
ma·tron·ly
mat·ro·nym·ic *variant
spelling of* metronymic
Ma·tsu·ya·ma Japanese port

matt *variant spelling of* mat
mat·ta·more subterranean
storehouse
matte smelting material;
variant spelling of mat
mat·ted
mat·ter
Mat·ter·horn
matter-of-fact (*adj*)
mat·ting
mat·tock agricultural tool
mat·tress
matu·rate
matu·ra·tion
matu·ra·tion·al
ma·tura·tive
ma·ture
ma·tur·ity
ma·tu·ti·nal of morning
(maty) *incorrect spelling of*
matey
mat·zo (*or* ·zoh; *plural* ·zos,
·zohs, *or* ·zoth) Jewish
biscuit
mat·zoon (*or* mad·)
fermented milk
maud plaid shawl
maud·lin
maud·lin·ism
maud·lin·ness
maul
maul·er
maul·stick (*or* mahl·)
artist's stick
Mau Mau (*plural* Mau Maus
or Mau Mau) Kenyan
terrorist
Mau·na Kea Hawaiian
volcano
Mau·na Loa Hawaiian
volcano
maund unit of weight
maun·der behave aimlessly
maun·der·er
Maun·dy money; Thursday
Mau·rist French monk
Mau·ri·ta·nia African
republic
Mau·ri·ta·nian
Mau·ri·tian
Mau·ri·tius island state
Mau·ser (*Trademark*) gun
mau·so·lean
mau·so·leum (*plural* ·leums
or ·lea)

mauve

mav·er·ick

ma·vis *Dialect* thrush

ma·vour·neen Irish term of endearment

maw

mawk·ish

mawk·ish·ness

maw·sie *Scot* jersey

maxi (*plural* maxis) long garment

max·il·la (*plural* ·lae) upper jaw

max·il·lar (*or* ·lary)

max·il·li·ped (*or* ·pede) zoology term

max·il·li·ped·ary

max·im

maxi·ma (*plural of* maximum)

maxi·mal

Maxi·mal·ist Russian revolutionary

maxi·mal·ist activist

maxi·mal·ly

maxi·min maths term

maxi·mi·za·tion (*or* ·sa·tion)

max·im·ize (*or* ·ise)

maxi·miz·er (*or* ·mis·er)

maxi·mum (*plural* ·mums *or* ·ma)

maxi·mus bell-ringing term

maxi·sin·gle

ma·xixe dance

max·well unit

May

may (might)

Maya (*plural* Maya *or* Mayas) American Indian

maya Hindu concept

Ma·yan

may·be (*adv*)

May·day signal

May Day 1 May

Ma·yenne French department

May·fair

May·flower ship

may·flower plant

may·fly (*plural* ·flies)

may·hem (*or* mai·)

May·ing May Day celebration

mayn't may not

Mayo Irish county

Ma·yon Philippine volcano

may·on·naise

mayor

mayor·al

mayor·al·ty (*plural* ·ties)

mayor·ess

mayor·ship

may·pole

may·weed

Ma·zat·lán Mexican port

Maz·da·ism (*or* Maz·deism) religion

maze confusing network; *compare* maize

ma·zer (*or* ·zard, maz·zard) bowl; *compare* maser

ma·zi·ly

ma·zi·ness

ma·zu·ma *US* money

ma·zur·ka (*or* ·zour·)

mazy (·zi·er, ·zi·est) perplexing

maz·zard (*or* ma·zard) *variants of* mazer

Mba·ba·ne capital of Swaziland

Mbu·ji·ma·yi city in the Democratic Republic of Congo

McCar·thy·ism anticommunism

McCoy *Slang* genuine thing

McNaughten Rules (*or* McNaghten Rules)

me pronoun; *variant spelling of* mi

mea cul·pa *Latin* my fault

mead drink; *compare* meed

mead·ow

meadow·lark

meadow·sweet

mea·gre (*US* ·ger)

meal

meal·worm

mealy (meali·er, meali·est)

mealy-mouthed

mean (mean·ing, meant) intend; miserly; midpoint; *compare* mien

me·ander

me·ander·er

me·ander·ing·ly

me·androus

mean·ing

mean·ing·ful

mean·ing·ful·ly

mean·ing·ful·ness

mean·ing·less

mean·ing·less·ness

mean·ness

means (*plural* means) method

meant

mean·time

mean·while

meany (*plural* meanies) *Slang* miserly person

mea·sled

mea·sles

mea·sly (·sli·er, ·sli·est)

meas·ur·abil·ity (*or* ·able·ness)

meas·ur·able

meas·ur·ably

meas·ure

meas·ured

meas·ured·ly

meas·ure·less

meas·ure·ment

meas·ur·er

meas·ur·ing

meat

meat·ball

Meath Irish county

meati·ly

meati·ness

mea·tus (*plural* ·tuses *or* ·tus) anatomy term

meaty (meati·er, meati·est)

Mec·ca

Mec·ca·no (*Trademark*)

me·chan·ic

me·chani·cal

me·chani·cal·ly

mecha·ni·cian

me·chan·ics

mecha·nism

mecha·nist

mecha·nis·tic

mecha·nis·ti·cal·ly

mecha·ni·za·tion (*or* ·sa·tion)

mecha·nize (*or* ·nise)

mecha·niz·er (*or* ·nis·er)

mecha·no·thera·py

Mech·elen (*or* ·lin) Belgian city

meck *Dialect* small coin

Meck·len·burg German
region

me·co·nium

Med *short for*
Mediterranean

med·al (*verb* ·al·ling, ·alled;
US ·al·ing, ·aled) award;
compare meddle

me·dal·lic

me·dal·lion

me·dal·lion·ist

med·al·list (*US* ·al·ist)

Me·dan Indonesian city

med·dle interfere; *compare*
medal

med·dler interferer; *compare*
medlar

med·dle·some

med·dle·some·ness

med·dling·ly

Mede inhabitant of Media

Medea mythological
princess

Me·del·lín Colombian city

Me·dia ancient country

me·dia *plural of* medium,
*esp. in communications
sense*

me·dia (*plural* ·diae)
anatomy and phonetics
term

me·dia·cy

me·di·aeval *variant spelling
of* medieval

me·dial

me·dial·ly

Me·dian of Medes or Media

me·dian

me·di·ant music term

me·di·as·ti·nal

me·di·as·ti·num (*plural* ·na)
anatomy term

me·di·ate

me·dia·tion

me·dia·tive (*or* ·tory,
·to·rial)

me·dia·ti·za·tion (*or*
·sa·tion)

me·dia·tize (*or* ·tise) annex
a state

me·dia·tor

me·dia·to·ri·al·ly

me·dia·trix (*or* ·trice)

med·ic *Slang* doctor; *US
spelling of* medick

medi·cable

medi·ca·bly

Medi·caid US health
assistance

medi·cal

medi·cal·ly

me·dica·ment

medi·ca·men·tal (*or* ·tary)

Medi·care US health
insurance

medi·cate

medi·ca·tion

medi·ca·tive

me·dici·nal

me·dici·nal·ly

medi·cine

med·ick (*US* ·ic) plant;
compare medic

medi·co (*plural* ·cos)

me·di·eval (*or* ·aeval)

me·di·eval·ism (*or* ·aeval·)

me·di·eval·ist (*or* ·aeval·)

me·di·eval·is·tic (*or* ·aeval·)

me·di·eval·ly (*or* ·aeval·)

Me·di·na Saudi Arabian city

me·dio·cre

me·di·oc·rity (*plural* ·rities)

medi·tate

medi·tat·ing·ly

medi·ta·tion

medi·ta·tive

medi·ta·tive·ness

medi·ta·tor

Medi·ter·ra·nean

me·dium (*plural* ·dia *or*
·diums)

med·lar fruit; *compare*
meddler

med·ley

Mé·doc French region; wine

me·dul·la (*plural* ·las *or*
·lae)

me·dul·lary (*or* ·lar)

med·ul·lat·ed

Medusa mythological
character

me·du·sa (*plural* ·sas *or* ·sae)
jellyfish

me·du·san

me·du·soid

Med·way

mee Malaysian noodles

meed *Archaic* reward;
compare mead

meek

meek·ly

meek·ness

meer·kat mongoose

meer·schaum

Mee·rut Indian city

meet (meet·ing, met) come
together; *compare* mete

meet (*adj*) *Archaic* fitting;
compare mete

meet·er

meet·ing

mega·cephal·ic *variant of*
macrocephalic

mega·cepha·ly *variant of*
macrocephaly

mega·cy·cle

mega·death

mega·ga·mete *variant of*
macrogamete

mega·lith

mega·lith·ic

mega·lo·blast blood cell

mega·lo·blast·ic

mega·lo·car·dia abnormally
large heart

mega·lo·cephal·ic *variant of*
macrocephalic

mega·lo·cepha·ly *variant of*
macrocephaly

mega·lo·ma·nia

mega·lo·ma·ni·ac

mega·lo·ma·nia·cal

mega·lopo·lis

mega·lo·poli·tan

mega·lo·saur dinosaur

mega·phone

mega·phon·ic

mega·phoni·cal·ly

mega·pode bird

Mega·ra Greek town

mega·ron (*plural* ·ra) room

mega·spore botany term

mega·spor·ic

mega·spo·ro·phyll

me·gass (*or* ·gasse) paper

mega·there (*or* ·ther·ium;
plural ·theres *or* ·ther·ia)
extinct sloth

mega·ton

mega·volt

mega·watt

me·gil·lah (*plural* ·lahs *or*
·loth) Hebrew scroll

me·gilp (*or* ma·)
oil-painting medium

meg·ohm

me·grim *Archaic* migraine

Mei·ji period in Japanese history

meio·sis (*plural* ·ses) cell division; rhetorical device; *compare* miosis

mei·ot·ic

mei·oti·cal·ly

Meis·sen German town

Meis·ter·sing·er (*plural* ·er *or* ·ers)

Mek·nès Moroccan city

Me·kong Asian river

mel honey

mela·leu·ca shrub

mela·mine

mel·an·cho·lia

mel·an·cho·li·ac

mel·an·chol·ic

mel·an·choli·cal·ly

mel·an·choli·ly

mel·an·choli·ness

mel·an·choly (*plural* ·cholies)

Mela·nesia

Mela·nesian

mé·lange *French* mixture

me·lan·ic

mela·nin pigment

mela·nism dark pigmentation; *variant of* melanosis

mela·nis·tic

mela·nite gemstone

mela·no·cyte melanin cell

mela·noid

mela·no·ma (*plural* ·mas *or* ·ma·ta) tumour

mela·no·sis (*or* ·nism) skin disease

mela·nos·ity

mela·not·ic

mela·nous

mela·phyre rock

mela·to·nin hormone

Melba sauce; toast

Mel·bourne

Mel·bur·nian

Mel·chite Eastern Church member

meld

me·lee (*or* mê·lée)

me·lia·ceous botany term

mel·ic to be sung

meli·lot plant

meli·nite explosive

me·lio·rate ameliorate

me·lio·ra·tion

me·lio·rism

me·lis·ma (*plural* ·ma·ta *or* ·mas) musical term

mel·is·mat·ic

Me·li·to·pol Ukrainian city

mel·lif·er·ous (*or* ·lif·ic) producing honey

mel·lif·lu·ous (*or* ·lu·ent) sweet-sounding

mel·lif·lu·ous·ness (*or* ·lu·ence)

mel·lo·phone brass instrument

mel·low

mel·low·ness

me·lo·deon accordion

me·lod·ic

me·lodi·cal·ly

me·lo·dious

me·lo·di·ous·ness

melo·dist

melo·dize (*or* ·dise)

melo·diz·er (*or* ·dis·er)

melo·dra·ma

melo·dra·mat·ic

melo·dra·mati·cal·ly

melo·drama·tist

melo·drama·tize (*or* ·tise)

melo·dy (*plural* ·dies)

mel·oid beetle

mel·on

Me·los Greek island

melt (melt·ing, melt·ed, melt·ed *or* mol·ten)

melt·abil·ity

melt·able

melt·age

melt·down

melt·er

melt·ing·ly

mel·ton fabric

Mel·ton Mow·bray

melt·water

Mem·ber an MP

mem·ber

mem·ber·ship

mem·brane

mem·bra·nous (*or* ·bra·na·ceous)

me·men·to (*plural* ·tos *or* ·toes)

me·men·to mori

memo (*plural* memos)

mem·oir

memo·ra·bilia (*sing.* ·rabi·le)

memo·rabil·ity (*or* ·rable·ness)

memo·rable

memo·rably

memo·ran·dum (*plural* ·dums *or* ·da)

me·mo·rial

me·mo·ri·al·ist

me·mo·ri·ali·za·tion (*or* ·sa·tion)

me·mo·ri·al·ize (*or* ·ise)

me·mo·ri·al·iz·er (*or* ·is·er)

memo·riz·able (*or* ·ris·able)

memo·ri·za·tion (*or* ·sa·tion)

memo·rize (*or* ·rise)

memo·riz·er (*or* ·ris·er)

memo·ry (*plural* ·ries)

Mem·phis

Mem·phre·ma·gog North American lake

mem·sa·hib

men

men·ace

men·ac·er

men·ac·ing·ly

me·nad *variant spelling of* maenad

mena·di·one vitamin

Me·na·do (*or* Ma·) Indonesian port

mé·nage household; *compare* manège

mé·nage à trois (*plural* mé·nage à trois)

me·nag·erie

Menai Strait

Me·nam Thai river

mena·qui·none vitamin

men·ar·che start of menstruation

men·ar·cheal (*or* ·chial)

mend

mend·able

men·da·cious

men·da·cious·ness

men·dac·ity (*plural* ·ities) untruthfulness; *compare* mendicancy

men·de·levium chemical
element

Men·de·lian

Men·del·ism (or
·de·li·an·ism) science of
heredity

mend·er

men·di·can·cy (or
men·dic·ity) begging;
compare mendacity

men·di·cant

mend·ing

Men·dips

Men·do·za Argentine city

Menelaus mythological king

men·folk

men·ha·den (*plural* ·den)
fish

men·hir Bronze Age stone

me·nial

me·nial·ly

me·nin·geal

me·nin·ges (*sing.* me·ninx)
brain membranes

men·in·git·ic

men·in·gi·tis

me·nis·coid

me·nis·cus (*plural* ·ci or
·cuses)

meni·sper·ma·ceous botany
term

meno musical term

me·nol·ogy (*plural* ·ogies)
ecclesiastical calendar

meno·pau·sal (or ·sic)

meno·pause

me·no·rah Jewish
candelabrum

men·or·rha·gia excessive
menstruation

men·or·rhag·ic

Men·sa constellation

men·ses (*plural* ·ses)
menstruation

Men·she·vik Russian
socialist

mens rea legal term

men·strual

men·stru·ate

men·strua·tion

men·struous

men·struum (*plural*
·struums or ·strua) solvent

men·sur·able

men·su·ral

men·su·ra·tion measuring;
compare menstruation

men·su·ra·tion·al

men·su·ra·tive

mens·wear

men·tal

men·tal·ism philosophy
term

men·tal·is·tic

men·tal·is·ti·cal·ly

men·tal·ity (*plural* ·ities)

men·tal·ly

men·tha·ceous botany
term

men·thol

men·tho·la·ted

men·tion

men·tion·able

men·tion·er

Men·ton French town

men·tor

men·to·rial

menu

meow (or miaou, miaow)

mepa·crine drug

Meph·is·to·phelean (or
·phelian)

Mephistopheles (or
Mephisto)

me·phit·ic (or ·phiti·cal)
poisonous

me·phiti·cal·ly

me·phi·tis foul stench

me·pro·ba·mate
tranquillizer

mer·bro·min antiseptic

mer·can·tile

mer·can·til·ism

mer·can·til·ist

mer·cap·tan chemical
compound

mer·cap·tide chemical
compound

mer·cap·to·pu·rine drug

mer·ce·nari·ly

mer·ce·nari·ness

mer·ce·nary (*plural* ·naries)

mer·cer

mer·ceri·za·tion (or
·sa·tion)

mer·cer·ize (or ·ise)

mer·chan·dise

mer·chan·dis·er

mer·chant

mer·chant·able

mer·chant·man (*plural*
·men) ship

Mer·cia Anglo-Saxon
kingdom

Mer·cian

mer·ci·ful

mer·ci·ful·ly

mer·ci·ful·ness

mer·ci·less

mer·ci·less·ness

mer·cu·rate treat with
mercury

mer·cu·ra·tion

mer·cu·rial

mer·cu·ri·al·ism mercury
poisoning

mer·cu·ri·ali·za·tion (or
·sa·tion)

mer·cu·ri·al·ize (or ·ise)

mer·cu·rial·ly

mer·cu·ri·al·ness (or
·ri·al·ity)

mer·cu·ric

Mer·cu·ro·chrome
(*Trademark*)

mer·cu·rous

Mer·cu·ry planet

Mercury Roman god

mer·cu·ry (or ·ries)

mer·cy (*plural* ·cies)

mere

mere·ly

me·ren·gue dance

mer·etri·cious insincere;
compare meritorious

mer·gan·ser (*plural* ·sers or
·ser) duck

merge

mer·gence

mer·ger

me·rid·ian

me·ridio·nal

me·ringue

me·ri·no (*plural* ·nos)

Meri·on·eth·shire former
Welsh county

me·ri·stem plant tissue

meri·ste·mat·ic

me·ris·tic biology term

mer·it

mer·it·ed·ly

mer·it·less

meri·toc·ra·cy (*plural* ·cies)

meri·to·ri·ous praiseworthy;
compare meretricious

mer·kin pubic wig

merle *Scot* blackbird

mer·lin falcon

mer·lon part of battlement

mer·maid

mer·man (*plural* ·men)

mero·blas·tic biology term

mero·blas·ti·cal·ly

mero·crine physiology term

Meroë ancient Sudanese city

mero·plank·ton

Mero·vin·gian Frankish
dynasty

mero·zo·ite biology term

mer·ri·ly

mer·ri·ment

mer·ri·ness

mer·ry (·ri·er, ·ri·est)

merry-go-round

merry·maker

merry·making

merry·thought wishbone

Merse Scottish area

Mer·se·burg German city

Mer·sey

Mer·sey·side

Mer·sin Turkish port

Mer·thyr Tyd·fil

Mer·ton London borough

mesa tableland

mé·sal·li·ance *French*
unsuitable marriage;
compare misalliance

mes·arch botany term

Mesa Verde Colorado
plateau

mes·cal cactus; alcohol

mes·ca·line (*or* ·lin) drug

mes·dames *plural of*
madame

mes·de·moi·selles *plural of*
mademoiselle

mes·em·bry·an·themum
plant

mes·en·cephal·ic

mes·en·cepha·lon part of
brain

mes·en·chy·mal (*or*
·chyma·tous)

mes·en·chyme embryology
term

mes·en·ter·ic

mes·en·teri·tis

mes·en·ter·on (*plural* ·tera)
zoology term

mes·en·ter·on·ic

mes·en·tery (*plural* ·teries)

mesh

Meshach biblical character

Me·shed *variant spelling of*
Mashhad

meshy

me·sial anatomy term

me·sial·ly

me·sic ecology term; of a
meson

mesi·cal·ly

me·sity·lene chemical
compound

mes·mer·ic

mes·meri·cal·ly

mes·mer·ism

mes·mer·ist

mes·meri·za·tion (*or*
sa·tion)

mes·mer·ize (*or* ·ise)

mes·mer·iz·er (*or* ·is·er)

mesne legal term

meso·ben·thos

meso·blast embryonic tissue

meso·carp botany term

meso·ce·phal·ic

meso·ceph·aly

meso·crat·ic geology term

meso·derm

meso·der·mal (*or* ·mic)

meso·gas·tric

meso·gas·trium

meso·glea (*or* ·gloea)

me·sog·na·thism (*or* ·thy)

me·sog·na·thous

Meso·lith·ic archaeological
period

meso·morph

meso·mor·phic of muscular
build

meso·mor·phism

meso·mor·phous

meso·mor·phy

me·son elementary particle

meso·neph·ric

meso·neph·ros

meso·pause meteorology
term

meso·phyll

meso·phyl·lic (*or* ·lous)

meso·phyte

meso·phyt·ic

Meso·po·ta·mia

Meso·po·ta·mian

meso·sphere

meso·spher·ic

meso·thelial

meso·thelium

meso·tho·raç·ic

meso·tho·rax (*plural* ·raxes
or ·races)

Meso·zo·ic geological
period

mes·quite (*or* ·quit) tree

mess

mes·sage

mes·sa·line fabric

Mes·sene ancient Greek city

mes·sen·ger

Mes·senia Greek region

Mes·si·ah

mes·si·an·ic (*or* Mes·)

mes·sieurs *plural of*
monsieur

messi·ly

Mes·si·na Sicilian port

messi·ness

mess·mate

Messrs *plural of* Mr

mes·suage legal term

messy (messi·er, messi·est)

mes·ter *Dialect* master

mes·ti·zo (*fem* ·za; *plural*
·zos *or* ·zoes, ·zas) one of
mixed parentage

mes·tra·nol synthetic
hormone

met

Meta Colombian river

meta·bol·ic

meta·boli·cal·ly

me·tabo·lism

me·tabo·lite

me·tabo·liz·abil·ity (*or*
·lis·abil·ity)

me·tabo·liz·able (*or*
·lis·able)

me·tabo·lize (*or* ·lise)

meta·car·pal

meta·car·pus (*plural* ·pi)
hand bones; *compare*
metatarsus

meta·cen·tre (*US* ·ter)
physics term

meta·cen·tric

meta·chro·mat·ic

meta·chro·ma·tism

meta·cin·nab·a·rite
mercury ore

meta·female genetics term

meta·ga·lac·tic

meta·gal·axy (plural ·axies)

met·age official measuring of goods

meta·gen·esis

meta·ge·net·ic (or ·gen·ic)

meta·geneti·cal·ly

me·tag·na·thism

me·tag·na·thous

met·al (verb ·al·ling, ·alled; US ·al·ing, ·aled) substance; compare mettle

meta·lan·guage

me·tal·lic

me·tal·li·cal·ly

met·al·lif·er·ous

met·al·line of metals

met·al·list (US ·al·ist)

met·al·li·za·tion (or ·sa·tion; US met·ali·za·tion)

met·al·lize (or ·lise; US ·al·ize)

me·tal·lo·cene chemical compound

met·al·log·ra·pher (or ·phist)

me·tal·lo·graph·ic

me·tal·lo·graphi·cal·ly

met·al·log·ra·phy

met·al·loid

met·al·loi·dal

met·al·lur·gic (or ·gi·cal)

met·al·lur·gi·cal·ly

met·al·lur·gist

met·al·lur·gy

metal·work

metal·worker

metal·working

meta·male genetics term

meta·math·emati·cal

meta·math·ema·ti·cian

meta·math·emat·ics

meta·mer chemistry term

me·tam·er·al

meta·mere zoology term

meta·mer·ic

meta·meri·cal·ly

me·tam·er·ism

meta·mor·phic (or ·phous)

meta·mor·phism geology term

meta·mor·phose

meta·mor·pho·sis (plural ·ses)

meta·neph·ros

meta·phase biology term

meta·phor

meta·phor·ic (or ·phori·cal)

meta·phori·cal·ly

meta·phori·cal·ness

meta·phos·phate

meta·phrase literal translation

meta·phrast

meta·phras·tic (or ·ti·cal)

meta·phras·ti·cal·ly

meta·phys·ic

Meta·physi·cal denoting poetic group

meta·physi·cal of metaphysics

meta·physi·cal·ly

meta·phy·si·cian (or ·physi·cist)

meta·phys·ics

meta·pla·sia

meta·plasm

meta·plas·mic

meta·psy·cho·logi·cal

meta·psy·chol·ogy

meta·so·ma·tism (or ·ma·to·sis) geology term

meta·sta·bil·ity

meta·sta·ble

me·tas·ta·sis (plural ·ses) medical term

me·tas·ta·size (or ·sise)

meta·stat·ic

meta·stati·cal·ly

meta·tar·sal

meta·tar·sus (plural ·si) foot bones; compare meta carpus

meta·theo·ry study of philosophy

meta·therian marsupial

me·tath·esis (plural ·eses) linguistics term

me·tath·esize (or ·esise)

meta·thet·ic (or ·theti·cal)

meta·tho·rac·ic

meta·tho·rax (plural ·raxes or ·races)

meta·xy·lem

meta·zo·an

meta·zo·ic

mete allot; compare meet

met·em·piri·cal (or ·pir·ic)

met·em·piri·cist

met·em·pir·ics

me·tem·psy·cho·sis (plural ·ses)

met·en·cephal·ic

met·en·cepha·lon (plural ·lons or ·la) embryology term

me·teor

me·teor·ic

me·teori·cal·ly

me·teor·ite

me·teor·it·ic

me·teoro·graph

me·teoro·graph·ic (or ·graphi·cal)

me·teor·oid

me·teoro·logi·cal (or ·log·ic)

me·teoro·logi·cal·ly

me·teor·olo·gist

me·teor·ol·ogy study of weather; compare metrology

me·ter instrument; US spelling of metre

met·es·trus US spelling of metoestrus

meth·ac·ry·late

metha·done (or ·don) drug

met·haemo·glo·bin (US ·hemo·)

me·thane

metha·nol

me·thinks

me·thio·nine amino acid

meth·od

me·thodi·cal (or ·thod·ic)

me·thodi·cal·ly

me·thodi·cal·ness

Meth·od·ism

Meth·od·ist

Meth·od·is·ti·cal·ly

meth·odi·za·tion (or ·sa·tion)

meth·od·ize (or ·ise)

meth·od·iz·er (or ·is·er)

meth·odo·logi·cal

meth·odo·logi·cal·ly

meth·od·olo·gist

meth·od·ol·ogy (plural ·ogies)

metho·trex·ate drug

me·thought

meth·ox·ide
Me·thu·se·lah
me·thyl
meth·yl·al chemical
  compound
me·thyla·mine
meth·yl·ate
meth·yla·tion
meth·yla·tor
me·thyl·do·pa
meth·yl·ene
me·thyl·ic
me·thyl·naph·tha·lene
met·ic ancient Greek alien
me·ticu·lous
me·ticu·lous·ness (or
  ·los·ity)
mé·ti·er profession
Mé·tis (or ·tif; plural ·tis or
  ·tifs) one of mixed
  parentage
met·oes·trus (US ·es·)
me·tol chemical compound
Me·ton·ic cy·cle
meto·nym
meto·nymi·cal (or ·nym·ic)
me·tony·my (plural ·mies)
  linguistics term
met·ope architectural term
me·top·ic of the forehead
me·tral·gia womb pain
me·tre (US ·ter) unit; verse
  rhythm; compare meter
met·ric
met·ri·cal
met·ri·cal·ly
met·ri·cate
met·ri·ca·tion
met·rics use of poetic metre
met·ri·fi·er
met·ri·fy (·fies, ·fy·ing,
  ·fied)
met·rist
me·tri·tis inflammation of
  womb
met·ro (or mét·; plural ·ros)
met·ro·logi·cal
me·trolo·gist
me·trol·ogy (plural ·ogies)
  study of measurement;
  compare meteorology
met·ro·ni·da·zole
met·ro·nome
met·ro·nom·ic of a
  metronome

met·ro·nym·ic (or mat·)
  maternal name
me·tropo·lis (plural ·lises)
met·ro·poli·tan
met·ro·poli·tan·ism
me·tror·rha·gia abnormal
  bleeding from womb
met·tle courage; compare
  metal
met·tle·some
Metz French city
meu plant
meu·nière cookery term
Meurthe-et-Moselle French
  department
Meuse European river
mew
mewl
mewl·er
mews (plural mews)
Mexi·cali Mexican city
Mexi·can
Mexi·co
me·zereon shrub
me·zereum (or ·zereon)
  drug
Me·zières French town
me·zu·zah (plural ·zahs or
  ·zoth)
mez·za·nine
mez·zo (plural ·zos) musical
  term
mezzo-relievo (or ·rilievo;
  plural -relievos or -rilievos)
mezzo-soprano (plural
  -sopranos)
mez·zo·tint
mi (or me) musical term
Mi·ami
miaou (or miaow) variant
  spellings of meow
mi·as·ma (plural ·ma·ta or
  ·mas)
mi·as·mal (or ·mat·ic,
  ·mati·cal, ·mic)
mica
mi·ca·ceous
Mi·caw·ber feckless person
Mi·caw·ber·ish
mice
mi·cel·lar
mi·celle (or ·cell, ·cel·la)
Mich·ael·mas
Michi·gan
Michi·gan·der

Michi·gan·ite
Mi·choa·cán Mexican state
mick·ery pool in river bed
mick·ey (or micky; as in
  take the mickey)
Mick·ey Finn
mick·le Dialect much
Mic·mac (plural ·macs or
  ·mac) American Indian
micro·analy·sis (plural ·ses)
micro·ana·lyst
micro·ana·lyt·ic (or
  ·lyti·cal)
micro·bal·ance
micro·baro·graph
mi·crobe
mi·cro·bial (or ·bic, ·bian)
micro·bio·logi·cal (or
  ·log·ic)
micro·bi·olo·gist
micro·bi·ol·ogy
micro·cephal·ic
micro·cepha·lous
micro·cepha·ly abnormally
  small skull
micro·chemi·cal
micro·chem·is·try
micro·chip
micro·cir·cuit
micro·cir·cuit·ry
micro·cli·mate
micro·cli·mat·ic
micro·cli·mati·cal·ly
micro·cli·ma·to·log·ic (or
  ·logi·cal)
micro·cli·ma·tolo·gist
micro·cli·ma·tol·ogy
micro·cline mineral
micro·coc·cus (plural
  ·coc·ci)
micro·com·put·er
micro·copy (plural ·copies)
  reduced photographic
  copy
micro·cosm (or ·cos·mos)
micro·cos·mic (or
  ·cos·mi·cal)
micro·crys·tal·line
micro·cyte blood cell
micro·cyt·ic
micro·detec·tor
micro·dont (or ·don·tous)
micro·dot
micro·eco·nom·ic
micro·eco·nom·ics

micro·elec·tron·ic
micro·elec·tron·ics
micro·fiche
micro·film
micro·gam·ete
micro·graph
mi·crog·ra·pher
micro·graph·ic
micro·graphi·cal·ly
mi·crog·ra·phy
micro·groove
micro·habi·tat
micro·light
micro·lith
micro·meteor·ite
micro·meteor·ol·ogy
mi·crom·eter measuring
   instrument
micro·metre (US ·meter)
   unit of length
micro·met·ric (or ·ri·cal)
mi·crom·etry
micro·minia·turi·za·tion
   (or ·sa·tion)
mi·cron (plural ·crons or
   ·cra) unit of length
Micro·nesia
Micro·nesian
micro·nu·cleus (plural ·clei)
micro·nu·tri·ent
micro·or·gan·ism
micro·palae·on·to·logi·cal
   (or ·log·ic; US ·pale·)
micro·palae·on·tolo·gist
   (US ·pale·)
micro·palae·on·tol·ogy (US
   ·pale·)
micro·para·site
micro·para·sit·ic
micro·phone
micro·phon·ic
micro·pho·to·graph
micro·pho·to·graph·ic
micro·pho·tog·ra·phy
micro·physi·cal
micro·phys·ics
micro·phyte microscopic
   plant
micro·phyt·ic
micro·print
micro·pro·ces·sor
micro·py·lar
micro·pyle biology term
micro·py·rom·eter
micro·read·er

micro·scope
micro·scop·ic (or
   ·scopi·cal)
micro·scopi·cal·ly
mi·cros·co·pist
mi·cros·co·py
micro·sec·ond
micro·seism
micro·seis·mic (or ·mi·cal)
micro·so·mal (or ·so·mial,
   ·so·mic)
micro·some biology term
micro·spo·ran·gium (plural
   ·gia)
micro·spore
micro·spor·ic (or ·spo·rous)
micro·sporo·phyll
micro·stoma·tous (or
   mi·cros·to·mous) having
   small mouth
micro·struc·ture
micro·tome cutting
   instrument
micro·tom·ic (or
   ·tomi·cal)
mi·croto·mist
mi·croto·my (plural ·mies)
micro·ton·al
micro·to·nal·ity
micro·tone musical term
micro·wave
mi·crurgy microscopy
   technique
mic·tu·rate
mic·tu·ri·tion
mid Archaic amid
mid- prefix denoting middle
mid·air
Midas legendary king
mid·brain
mid·day
Mid·del·burg Dutch city
mid·den
mid·dle
middle-aged
middle·brow
middle·browism
middle-class (adj)
middle-distance (adj)
middle·man (plural ·men)
Mid·dles·brough
Mid·dle·ton English town
middle·weight
mid·dling

mid·dy (plural ·dies)
   midshipman
mid·field
Mid·gard Norse
   mythological place
midge
midg·et
Mid Gla·mor·gan former
   Welsh county
mid·gut
Mid·heav·en astrology term
Midi S France
midi skirt length
Mid·ian biblical character
Midi·an·ite
midi·nette Parisian salesgirl
mid·iron golf club
mid·land inland region
Mid·lands central England
mid·line
Mid·lo·thian Scottish
   council area
mid·most
mid·night
mid·off
mid·on
mid·point
mid·rash (plural ·ra·shim)
   Jewish biblical
   commentaries
mid·rib leaf vein
mid·riff
mid·sec·tion
mid·ship
mid·ship·man (plural ·men)
mid·ships
midst
mid·sum·mer
mid·term
mid·town US town centre
mid·way
mid·week
Mid·west (or Mid·dle West)
   US region
Mid·west·ern
Mid·west·ern·er
mid·wicket
mid·wife (plural ·wives)
mid·wife·ry
mid·win·ter
mid·year
mien bearing; compare
   mean
miff Slang take offence
mif·fi·ness

mif·fy (·fi·er, ·fi·est)
might
mighti·ly
mighti·ness
mighty (mighti·er,
  mighti·est)
mi·gnon *French* dainty
mi·gnon·ette plant
mi·graine
mi·grain·ous
mi·grant
mi·grate
mi·gra·tion
mi·gra·tion·al
mi·gra·tor
mi·gra·tory
mih·rab niche in mosque
mi·ka·do (*plural* ·dos)
mike *Slang* microphone
mil unit of length
mi·la·dy (or ·la·di; *plural*
  ·dies)
mil·age *variant spelling of*
  mileage
Mi·lan
Mil·an·ese (*plural* ·ese)
milch
mild
mil·dew
mil·dewy
mild·ness
mile
mile·age (or mil·age)
mile·om·eter (or
  mi·lom·eter)
mile·post
mil·er
Mi·lesian
mile·stone
Mi·letus old Asian city
mil·foil plant
mili·aria heat rash
mil·iary
mi·lieu (*plural* ·lieus or
  ·lieux)
mili·tan·cy (or ·tant·ness)
mili·tant
mili·tari·ly
mili·ta·rism
mili·ta·rist
mili·ta·ris·tic
mili·ta·ris·ti·cal·ly
mili·ta·ri·za·tion (or
  ·sa·tion)
mili·ta·rize (or ·rise)

mili·tary (*plural* ·taries)
mili·tate
mili·ta·tion
mi·li·tia
mi·li·tia·man (*plural* ·men)
mil·ium (*plural* milia) skin
  nodule
milk
milk·er
milk·fish (*plural* ·fish or
  ·fishes)
milki·ly
milki·ness
milk·maid
milk·man (*plural* ·men)
milko *Austral* milkman
milk·sop
milk·weed
milk·wort
milky (milki·er, milki·est)
Milky Way
mill
mill·able
mill·board
mill·dam
milled
mille·feuille pastry
mille·fleurs textile design
mil·le·nar·ian (or ·nary)
mil·le·nari·an·ism
  Christian belief
mil·le·nary (*plural* ·naries)
  a thousand; *compare*
  millinery
mil·len·nial
mil·len·ni·al·ist
mil·len·nium (*plural*
  ·niums or ·nia)
mil·le·pede *variant spelling
  of* millipede
mil·le·pore coral-like
  organism
mil·ler
mil·ler·ite mineral
mil·lesi·mal denoting a
  thousandth
mil·let
mil·li·ard thousand million
mil·liary denoting Roman
  mile
mil·li·bar
mil·lieme Tunisian coin
mil·li·gram (or ·gramme)
mil·li·li·tre (*US* ·ter)
mil·li·metre (*US* ·meter)

mil·line unit of advertising
  copy
mil·li·ner
mil·li·nery hat making;
  compare millenary
mill·ing
mil·lion (*plural* ·lions or
  ·lion)
mil·lion·aire (or
  ·lion·naire)
mil·lion·air·ess
mil·lionth
mil·li·pede (or ·le·pede,
  ·le·ped)
mil·li·sec·ond
mill·pond
mill·race
mill·run
mill·stone
mill·stream
mill·wheel
mill·wright
mi·lord
mi·lom·eter *variant spelling
  of* mileometer
milque·toast *US* timid
  person
milt
mil·ter
Mil·ton·ic (or ·to·nian) of
  John Milton
Mil·ton Keynes
Mil·wau·kee US port
mim *Dialect* prim
Mi·mas satellite of Saturn
mime
Mimeo·graph (*Trademark*)
mim·er
mi·mesis
mi·met·ic
mi·meti·cal·ly
mim·etite mineral
mim·ic (·ick·ing, ·icked)
mim·ick·er
mim·ic·ry (*plural* ·ries)
miminy-pimeny *variant of*
  niminy-piminy
Mimir Norse giant
mi·mo·sa
mimo·sa·ceous
Min Chinese dialect
mina (*plural* minae or
  minas) ancient unit
mina *variant spelling of*
  myna

min·able (*or* mine·able)
mi·na·cious threatening
mi·nac·ity
Mina Has·san Tani
  Moroccan port
mina·ret
mina·ret·ed
Mi·nas Ge·rais Brazilian
  state
mina·to·ri·ly (*or* ·ri·al·ly)
mina·tory (*or* ·to·rial)
mince
mince·meat
minc·er
Minch Atlantic channel
minc·ing
minc·ing·ly
mind
Min·dan·ao Philippine
  island
mind·ed
Min·del glaciation period
mind·er
mind·ful
mind·ful·ly
mind·ful·ness
mind·less
mind·less·ness
mind-reader
mind-reading
mine
mine·field
mine·lay·er
min·er one who mines;
  compare minor
min·er·al
min·er·ali·za·tion (*or*
  ·sa·tion)
min·er·al·ize (*or* ·ise)
min·er·al·iz·er (*or* ·is·er)
min·er·alo·cor·ti·coid
  hormone
min·er·al·ogi·cal (*or* ·og·ic)
min·er·alo·gist
min·er·al·ogy
min·estro·ne
mine·sweeper
mine·sweeping
Ming
min·gle
Min·gre·lian (*or* Min·grel)
  Georgian people
min·gy (·gi·er, ·gi·est)
mini (*plural* minis)
minia·ture

minia·tur·ist
minia·turi·za·tion (*or*
  ·sa·tion)
minia·tur·ize (*or* ·ise)
mi·ni·bar
mini·bus
mini·cab
mini·com·put·er
mini·dress
mini·fi·ca·tion
mini·fy (·fies, ·fy·ing, ·fied)
min·im
mini·ma (*plural of*
  minimum)
mini·mal
Mini·mal·ist Russian
  revolutionary
mini·mal·ist advocate of
  minimal policy
mini·mal·ly
mini·max maths term
mini·mi·za·tion (*or*
  ·sa·tion)
mini·mize (*or* ·mise)
mini·miz·er (*or* ·mis·er)
mini·mum (*plural* ·mums *or*
  ·ma)
mini·mus youngest
min·ing
min·ion
mini·pill
(miniscule) *incorrect spelling
  of* minuscule
mini·skirt
mini·skirted
min·is·ter
min·is·terial
min·is·terial·ly
min·is·te·rium (*plural* ·ria)
  Lutheran ministers
min·is·trant
min·is·tra·tive
min·is·tra·tion
min·is·try (*plural* ·tries)
Mini·track (*Trademark*)
(miniture) *incorrect spelling
  of* miniature
min·ium red lead
mini·ver fur
mini·vet bird
mink
minke whale
Min·na Nigerian city
Min·ne·apo·lis
min·neo·la hybrid fruit

min·ne·sing·er German
  minstrel
Min·ne·so·ta
Min·ne·so·tan
min·now (*plural* ·nows *or*
  ·now)
Mi·no·an of Cretan culture
mi·nor lesser; *compare*
  miner
Mi·nor·ca
Mi·nor·can
Mi·no·rite friar
mi·nor·ity (*plural* ·ities)
Minos legendary king
Minotaur legendary
  monster
Minsk Belarussian capital
min·ster
min·strel
min·strel·sy (*plural* ·sies)
mint
mint·age
mint·er
Min·ton porcelain
minty (minti·er, minti·est)
minu·end maths term
minu·et
mi·nus
mi·nus·cu·lar
mi·nus·cule
min·ute 60 seconds
mi·nute very small
min·ute·ly every minute
mi·nute·ly in great detail
Min·ute·man (*plural* ·men)
mi·nute·ness
min·utes record of
  proceedings
mi·nu·tiae (*sing.* ·tia)
  trifling details
minx
minx·ish
Mio·cene geological period
mio·sis (*or* myo·)
  constriction of pupil;
  compare meiosis
mi·ot·ic (*or* my·)
Mi·que·lon French island
mi·ra·bi·le dic·tu *Latin*
  wonderful to relate
Mira Ceti star
mi·ra·cid·ial
mi·ra·cid·ium (*plural* ·iia)
  fluke larva
mira·cle

mi·rac·u·lous

mira·dor balcony or turret

mi·rage

Mi·ran·da satellite of
Uranus

mire

mire·poix vegetable
mixture

mir·ky *variant spelling of*
murky

mir·ror

mirth

mirth·ful

mirth·ful·ly

mirth·ful·ness

mirth·less

mirth·less·ness

miry

mis·ad·ven·ture

mis·ad·vise

mis·align·ment

mis·al·li·ance unsuitable
alliance; *compare*
mésalliance

mis·an·thrope (*or*
·thro·pist)

mis·an·throp·ic (*or*
·thropi·cal)

mis·an·thropi·cal·ly

mis·an·thro·pist *variant of*
misanthrope

mis·an·thro·py

mis·ap·pli·ca·tion

mis·ap·ply (·plies, ·ply·ing,
·plied)

mis·ap·pre·hend

mis·ap·pre·hend·ing·ly

mis·ap·pre·hen·sion

mis·ap·pre·hen·sive

mis·ap·pro·pri·ate

mis·ap·pro·pria·tion

mis·be·come (·com·ing,
·came) be unsuitable for

mis·be·got·ten

mis·be·have

mis·be·hav·er

mis·be·hav·iour (*US* ·ior)

mis·be·lief

mis·cal·cu·late

mis·cal·cu·la·tion

mis·call

mis·car·riage

mis·car·ry (·ries, ·ry·ing,
·ried)

mis·cast (·cast·ing, ·cast)

mis·ce·gena·tion
interbreeding

mis·ce·genet·ic

mis·cel·la·nea (*plural*)

mis·cel·la·neous

mis·cel·la·nist

mis·cel·la·ny (*plural* ·nies)

mis·chance

mis·chief

mis·chie·vous

mis·chiev·ous·ness

misch met·al

mis·cibil·ity

mis·cible capable of mixing;
compare missable

mis·con·ceive

mis·con·ceiv·er

mis·con·cep·tion

mis·con·duct

mis·con·struc·tion

mis·con·strue (·stru·ing,
·strued)

mis·copy (·copies,
·copy·ing, ·cop·ied)

mis·count

mis·cre·ance (*or* ·an·cy)

mis·cre·ant wrongdoer

mis·cre·ate create badly

mis·crea·tion

mis·cue (·cu·ing, ·cued)

mis·date

mis·deal (·deal·ing, ·dealt)

mis·deal·er

mis·deed

mis·de·mean·ant

mis·de·mean·our (*US* ·or)

mis·di·rect

mis·di·rec·tion

mis·doubt

mise legal term

mise en scène scenery

mi·ser

mis·er·able

mis·er·able·ness

mis·er·ably

mi·sère call in solo whist

Mis·erere 51st psalm

mis·erere misericord

mis·eri·cord (*or* ·corde) part
of church

mis·er·li·ness

mi·ser·ly

mis·ery (*plural* ·eries)

mis·fea·sance legal term

mis·file

mis·fire

mis·fit (·fit·ting, ·fit·ted)

mis·for·tune

mis·give (·giv·ing, ·gave,
·giv·en)

mis·giv·ing

mis·gov·ern

mis·gov·ern·ment

mis·gov·er·nor

mis·guid·ance

mis·guide

mis·guid·ed

mis·guid·er

mis·han·dle

mis·hap

mis·hear (·hear·ing,
·heard)

mis·hit (·hit·ting, ·hit)

mish·mash

Mish·nah (*or* ·na) Jewish
precepts

Mish·na·ic

mis·in·form

mis·in·form·ant (*or*
·form·er)

mis·in·for·ma·tion

mis·in·ter·pret

mis·in·ter·pre·ta·tion

mis·in·ter·pret·er

mis·join·der legal term

mis·judge

mis·judg·er

mis·judg·ment (*or* ·judge·)

Mis·kolc Hungarian city

mis·lay (·lay·ing, ·laid)

mis·lay·er

mis·lead (·lead·ing, ·led)

mis·lead·er

mis·man·age

mis·man·age·ment

mis·man·ag·er

mis·match

mis·no·mer

mi·soga·mist marriage hater

mi·soga·my

mi·sogy·nist woman hater

mi·sogy·nous

mi·sogy·ny

mi·solo·gist

mi·sol·ogy hatred of
reasoning

miso·neism hatred of
anything new

miso·neist

miso·neis·tic

mis·pick·el mineral
mis·place
mis·place·ment
mis·play
mis·plead (·plead·ing,
·plead·ed, ·plead, or
·pled)
mis·plead·ing
mis·print
mis·pri·sion concealment of
treason
mis·prize (or ·prise)
undervalue
mis·pro·nounce
mis·pro·nun·cia·tion
mis·pro·por·tion
mis·quo·ta·tion
mis·quote
mis·read (·read·ing, ·read)
mis·re·mem·ber
mis·re·port
mis·rep·re·sent
mis·rep·re·sen·ta·tion
mis·rep·re·sen·ta·tive
mis·rep·re·sent·er
mis·rule
Miss title of address
miss
miss·able able to be missed;
compare miscible
mis·sal prayer book
mis·sel thrush *variant
spelling of* mistle thrush
mis·shape (·shap·ing,
·shaped or ·shap·en)
mis·sile
mis·sile·ry (or ·sil·ry)
mis·sing
mis·sion
mis·sion·ary (*plural* ·aries)
mis·sion·er
mis·sis
miss·ish
Mis·sis·sau·ga Canadian
town
Mis·sis·sip·pi
Mis·sis·sip·pian
mis·sive
Mis·souri
Mis·sou·rian
mis·spell (·spell·ing, ·spelt
or ·spelled)
mis·spend (·spend·ing,
·spent)
mis·state

mis·state·ment
mis·sup·pose
missy (*plural* missies)
mist
mis·tak·able (or ·take·)
mis·tak·ably (or ·take·)
mis·take (·tak·ing, ·took or
·tak·en)
mis·tal *Scot* cowshed
Mis·tas·si·ni Canadian lake
mis·teach (·teach·ing,
·taught)
mis·ter
mis·ti·gris joker in poker
misti·ly
mis·time
misti·ness
mis·tle thrush (or mis·sel
thrush)
mis·tle·toe
mis·took
mis·tral wind; *compare*
mistrial
mis·treat
mis·treat·ment
mis·tress
mis·tri·al void trial; *compare*
mistral
mis·trust
mis·trust·er
mis·trust·ful
mis·trust·ful·ly
mis·trust·ful·ness
mis·trust·ing·ly
misty (misti·er, misti·est)
mis·under·stand
(·stand·ing, ·stood)
mis·us·age
mis·use
mis·us·er
mitch *Dialect* play truant
mite
mi·ter *US spelling of* mitre
Mith·ra·ic
Mith·ra·ism (or ·rai·cism)
Mith·ra·ist
Mith·ras (or ·ra) Persian god
mith·ri·dat·ic
mith·ri·da·tism immunity
to poison
miti·cid·al
miti·cide mite-killer
miti·gable
miti·gate
miti·gat·ing

miti·ga·tion
miti·ga·tive (or ·tory)
miti·ga·tor
mi·tis malleable iron
mi·to·chon·drial
mi·to·chon·drion (*plural*
·dria) biology term
mi·to·sis (*plural* ·ses) cell
division
mi·tot·ic
mi·toti·cal·ly
mi·trail·leuse machine gun
mi·tral
mi·tre (*US* ·ter)
mitre·wort (*US* miter·)
plant
mitt
mit·ten
mit·ti·mus (*plural* ·muses)
legal term
mitz·vah (*plural* ·vahs or
·voth)
mix
mix·abil·ity
mix·able
mixed
mix·er
mix·ing
mixo·lyd·ian music term
Mix·tec (*plural* ·tecs or ·tec)
American Indian
mix·ture
mix-up (*noun*)
Mi·zar star
Mi·zo·ram Indian state
miz·zen (or miz·en)
nautical term
miz·zen·mast (or miz·en·)
miz·zle *Dialect* drizzle
m'lud
mne·mon·ic memory aid
mne·moni·cal·ly
mne·mon·ics
Mnemosyne Greek goddess
mo (*plural* mos) *Slang*
moment
moa extinct bird
Moab biblical kingdom
Mo·ab·ite
moan
moan·er
moan·ing·ly
moat ditch; *compare* mote
mob (mob·bing, mobbed)
mob·ber

mob·cap
Mo·bile US port
mo·bile
mo·bil·ity
mo·bi·liz·able (or ·lis·able)
mo·bi·li·za·tion (or
·sa·tion)
mo·bi·lize (or ·lise)
mob·oc·ra·cy (plural ·cies)
mobo·crat
mobo·crat·ic (or ·crati·cal)
mob·ster
Mo·bu·tu former name of
Albert
moc·ca·sin
Mo·cha Yemeni port
mo·cha coffee
mock
mock·able
mock·er
mock·ery (plural ·eries)
mock-heroic
mock-heroical·ly
mocking·bird
mock·ing·ly
mock-up (noun)
mod
mod·al
mo·dal·ity
mo·dal·ly
mode
mod·el (·el·ling, ·elled; US
·el·ing, ·eled)
mod·el·ler (US ·el·er)
mo·dem computer term
Mo·dena Italian city
mod·er·ate
mod·er·ate·ly
mod·er·ate·ness
mod·era·tion
mod·era·to music term
mod·era·tor
mod·era·tor·ship
mod·ern
mo·derne architectural style
mod·ern·ism
mod·ern·ist
mod·ern·is·tic
mod·ern·is·ti·cal·ly
mo·der·nity (plural ·nities)
mod·erni·za·tion (or
·sa·tion)
mod·ern·ize (or ·ise)
mod·ern·iz·er (or ·is·er)
mod·ern·ness

mod·est
mod·est·ly
mod·es·ty (plural ·ties)
modge Dialect to botch
modi·cum
modi·fi·abil·ity (or
·able·ness)
modi·fi·able
modi·fi·ca·tion
modi·fi·ca·tory (or ·tive)
modi·fi·er
modi·fy (·fies, ·fy·ing,
·fied)
mo·dil·lion architectural
ornament
mo·dio·lus (plural ·li)
anatomy term
mod·ish
mod·ish·ness
mo·diste (plural ·distes)
fashionable dressmaker
modu·la·bil·ity
modu·lar
modu·late
modu·la·tion
modu·la·tive (or ·tory)
modu·la·tor
mod·ule
modu·lus (plural ·li) physics
term
mo·dus op·eran·di (plural
modi op·eran·di) method
of working
mo·dus vi·ven·di (plural
modi vi·ven·di) practical
compromise
mo·fette opening in
volcano
mog Slang cat
Moga·dishu (or ·discio)
Somali capital
Moga·don (Trademark) drug
Moga·dor Moroccan port
mog·gy (or ·gie; plural ·gies)
Slang cat
Mo·gi·lev (or ·hi·)
Belarussian city
Mo·gul Muslim ruler
mo·gul important person
mo·hair
Mo·ham·med·an Muslim
Mo·ha·ve (or ·ja·; plural ·ves
or ·ve) American Indian
Mo·ha·ve Des·ert (or
Mo·ja·ve Des·ert)

Mo·hawk (plural ·hawks or
·hawk) American Indian
Mo·hi·can variant spelling of
Mahican
Mo·hock ruffian
Mo·hole geological project
moi·der Dialect to bother
moi·dore coin
moi·ety (plural ·eties) half
moire (noun) fabric
moi·ré (adj) having watered
pattern
moist
mois·ten
moist·en·er
moist·ness
mois·ture
mois·tur·ize (or ·ise)
mois·tur·iz·er (or ·is·er)
Mo·ja·ve variant spelling of
Mohave
moke Slang donkey
Mok·po South Korean
port
mola (plural mola or molas)
fish
mo·lal
mo·lal·ity (plural ·ities)
chemistry term
mo·lar tooth; chemistry
term
mo·lar·ity
mo·las·ses
mold US spelling of mould
Mol·da·via
Mol·da·vian
mol·da·vite glass
mold·er US spelling of
moulder
Mol·do·va E European
country
mole
mo·lecu·lar
mol·ecule
mole·hill
mole·skin
mo·lest
mo·les·ta·tion
mo·lest·er
mo·line heraldic term
Mo·li·se Italian region
moll
mol·li·fi·able
mol·li·fi·ca·tion
mol·li·fi·er

mol·li·fy (·fies, ·fy·ing,
·fied)
mol·li·fy·ing·ly
mol·lusc (*US* ·lusk)
mol·lus·can (*US* ·kan)
mol·lus·coid (*or* ·coi·dal)
zoology term
mol·ly (*plural* ·lies) fish
molly·coddle
molly·coddler
Molly Maguire Irish secret
society member
Mo·loch Semitic god
mo·loch lizard
Mo·lo·kai Hawaiian island
molt *US spelling of* moult
mol·ten
mol·to musical term
Mo·luc·cas Indonesian
islands
moly (*plural* molies)
mythological herb; flower
mo·lyb·date
mo·lyb·de·nite mineral
mo·lyb·de·nous
mo·lyb·de·num chemical
element
mo·lyb·dic
mo·lyb·dous
mom *US* mother
Mom·ba·sa Kenyan port
mo·ment
mo·men·tari·ly
mo·men·tary
mo·men·tous
mo·men·tum (*plural* ·ta *or*
·tums)
Momus Greek god
mona monkey
Mona·can
mona·chal monastic
mona·chism
Mona·co
mon·ad (*plural* ·ads *or*
mona·des)
mona·del·phous botany
term
mo·nad·ic (*or* ·nadi·cal)
mon·ad·ism (*or* ·ad·ol·ogy)
philosophy
mon·ad·is·tic
mo·nad·nock hill
mon·ad·ol·ogy *variant of*
monadism
Mona·ghan Irish county

mon·al (*or* ·aul) pheasant
mo·nan·drous botany term
mo·nan·dry
mo·nan·thous botany term
mon·arch
mo·nar·chal (*or* ·chi·al)
mo·nar·chic (*or* ·chi·cal)
mon·ar·chism
mon·ar·chist
mon·ar·chis·tic
mon·ar·chy (*plural* ·chies)
mo·nar·da plant
mon·as·te·rial
mon·as·tery (*plural* ·teries)
mo·nas·tic (*or* ·ti·cal)
mo·nas·ti·cal·ly
mo·nas·ti·cism
mon·atom·ic (*or* mono·)
mon·aural
mona·zite mineral
Mönchen-Gladbach
German city
Mon·day
mondi·al of the world
Mon·egasque citizen of
Monaco
Monel metal (*Trademark*)
mon·etar·ism
mon·etar·ist
mon·etary
mon·eti·za·tion (*or*
·sa·tion)
mon·etize (*or* ·etise)
mon·ey (*plural* ·eys *or* ·ies)
money·changer
mon·eyed (*or* mon·ied)
money·lender
money·lending
money·maker
money·making
money·spinner
money·wort
mon·ger
mon·ger·ing
mon·go *or* goe; *plural* ·gos
or ·goes) Mongolian
currency
Mon·gol
Mon·go·lia
Mon·go·lian
Mon·gol·ic
mon·go·lism *former name of*
Down's syndrome
Mon·gol·oid
mon·goose (*plural* ·gooses)

mon·grel
mon·grel·ism (*or* ·ness)
mon·greli·za·tion (*or*
·sa·tion)
mon·grel·ize (*or* ·ise)
mon·grel·ly
moni·ker (*or* mon·ick·er)
Slang nickname
mo·nili·form
mon·ism
mon·ist
mo·nis·tic
mo·nis·ti·cal·ly
mo·ni·tion warning
moni·tor
moni·to·rial
moni·tor·ship
moni·tory (*or* ·to·rial)
warning
moni·tress
monk
mon·key
monkey·pot tree
monk·fish (*plural* ·fish *or*
·fishes)
Mon-Khmer language
monk·hood being a monk
monk·ish
monks·hood plant
Mon·mouth
Mon·mouth·shire Welsh
county
mono (*plural* monos)
mono·ac·id (*or* mon·ac·id,
mono·acid·ic,
mona·cid·ic)
mono·atom·ic *variant of*
monatomic
mono·ba·sic
mono·carp botany term
mono·car·pel·lary
mono·car·pic (*or* ·pous)
Mo·noc·er·os constellation
mono·cha·sial
mono·cha·sium (*plural* ·sia)
botany term
mono·chlo·ride
mono·chord acoustic
instrument
mono·chro·mat (*or* ·mate)
mono·chro·mat·ic (*or*
mono·chro·ic)
mono·chro·mati·cal·ly
mono·chro·ma·tism visual
defect

mono‑chrome
mono‑chro‑mic (or ‑mi‑cal)
mono‑chrom‑ist
mono‑cle
mono‑cli‑nal
mono‑cline geology term
mono‑clin‑ic
    crystallography term
mono‑cli‑nism botany term
mono‑cli‑nous
mono‑coque car or aircraft
    body
mono‑coty‑ledon botany
    term
mono‑coty‑ledon‑ous
mo‑noc‑ra‑cy (plural ‑cies)
mono‑crat
mono‑crat‑ic
mo‑nocu‑lar
mono‑cul‑ture
mono‑cy‑clic
mono‑cyte blood cell
mono‑cyt‑ic
mo‑nod‑ic (or ‑nodi‑cal)
mono‑dist
mono‑dra‑ma
mono‑dra‑mat‑ic
mono‑dy (plural ‑dies)
mo‑noecious (or ‑necious,
    ‑noi‑cous) botany term
mono‑fila‑ment (or ‑fil)
mo‑noga‑mist
mo‑noga‑mis‑tic
mo‑noga‑mous
mo‑noga‑my having one
    spouse; compare
    monogyny
mono‑gen‑esis biology term
mono‑genet‑ic
mono‑gen‑ic genetics term
mo‑nog‑enous
mo‑nog‑eny
mono‑gram
mono‑gram‑matic
mono‑grammed
mono‑graph
mo‑nog‑ra‑pher
mono‑graph‑ic
mono‑graphi‑cal‑ly
mo‑nogy‑nist
mo‑nogy‑nous
mo‑nogy‑ny having one
    female partner; compare
    monogamy
mono‑hull

mono‑hy‑brid
mono‑hy‑drate
mono‑hy‑droxy
mo‑nola‑ter (or ‑trist)
mo‑nola‑trous
mo‑nola‑try worship of one
    god
mono‑lay‑er
mono‑lin‑gual
mono‑lith
mono‑lith‑ic
mono‑lithi‑cal‑ly
mono‑log‑ic (or ‑logi‑cal)
mono‑log‑ist
mono‑logue (US also ‑log)
mo‑nol‑ogy
mono‑ma‑nia
mono‑ma‑ni‑ac
mono‑ma‑nia‑cal
mono‑mark
mono‑mer chemistry term
mono‑mer‑ic
mo‑nom‑er‑ous botany
    term
mono‑me‑tal‑lic
mono‑met‑al‑lism
mono‑met‑al‑list
mo‑nom‑eter verse line
mono‑met‑ri‑cal (or
    ‑met‑ric)
mo‑no‑mial
mono‑mo‑lecu‑lar
mono‑mor‑phic (or ‑phous)
mono‑mor‑phism
mono‑nu‑clear
mono‑nu‑cleo‑sis
mono‑pet‑al‑ous
mo‑nopha‑gous
mo‑nopha‑gy
mono‑pho‑bia
mono‑pho‑bic
mono‑phon‑ic
mo‑nopho‑ny
mon‑oph‑thong
mon‑oph‑thon‑gal
mono‑phy‑let‑ic genetics
    term
mono‑phyl‑lous botany
    term
mono‑plane
mono‑plegia
mono‑plegic
mono‑po‑dial
mono‑po‑dium (plural ‑dia)
    botany term

mo‑nopo‑lism
mo‑nopo‑list
mo‑nopo‑lis‑tic
mo‑nopo‑lis‑ti‑cal‑ly
mo‑nopo‑li‑za‑tion (or
    ‑sa‑tion)
mo‑nopo‑lize (or ‑lise)
mo‑nopo‑liz‑er (or ‑lis‑er)
Mo‑nopo‑ly (Trademark)
    game
mo‑nopo‑ly (plural ‑lies)
mono‑pro‑pel‑lant
mo‑nop‑so‑nis‑tic
mo‑nop‑so‑ny (plural ‑nies)
    economics term
mon‑op‑te‑ros (or ‑ron;
    plural ‑roi or ‑ra)
    architectural term
mono‑rail
mono‑sac‑cha‑ride
mono‑semy having only
    one meaning
mono‑sepa‑lous
mono‑so‑dium glu‑ta‑mate
mono‑some chromosome
mono‑so‑mic
mono‑sper‑mous (or
    ‑sper‑mal)
mono‑stich single‑line
    poem
mono‑stich‑ic
mono‑stich‑ous botany
    term
mono‑stome (or
    mo‑nos‑to‑mous) having
    one mouth
mo‑nos‑tro‑phe poem
mono‑stroph‑ic
mono‑sty‑lous botany
    term
mono‑syl‑lab‑ic
mono‑syl‑labi‑cal‑ly
mono‑syl‑la‑bism
mono‑syl‑la‑ble
mono‑theism
mono‑theist
mono‑theis‑tic
mono‑theis‑ti‑cal‑ly
mono‑tint
mono‑tone
mono‑ton‑ic
mo‑noto‑nous
mo‑noto‑ny (plural ‑nies)
mono‑trema‑tous
mono‑treme mammal

mo·no·tri·chous (*or*
 ·trich·ic) bacteriology
 term
Mono·type (*Trademark*)
 typesetting machine
mono·type
mono·typ·ic
mono·va·lence (*or* ·len·cy)
mono·va·lent
mon·ox·ide
Mon·ro·via Liberian capital
Mons Belgian town
mons (*plural* mon·tes)
 anatomy term
Mon·sei·gneur (*plural*
 Mes·sei·gneurs) French
 title
mon·sieur (*plural*
 mes·sieurs) French
 gentleman; Mr
Mon·sig·nor (*plural* ·nors *or*
 ·nori) ecclesiastical title
mon·soon
mon·ster
mon·strance receptacle for
 consecrated Host
mon·stros·ity (*plural* ·ities)
mon·strous
mon·strous·ness
mon·tage
Mon·ta·gnard (*plural*
 ·gnards *or* ·gnard)
 mountain people
Mon·tana
mon·tane of mountainous
 regions
Mon·tau·ban French city
Mont Blanc
mont·bre·tia plant
mon·te gambling game
Mon·te Car·lo
Mon·te·go Bay Jamaican
 port
mon·teith bowl for cooling
 wineglasses
Mon·te·ne·grin
Mon·te·ne·gro Yugoslav
 republic
Mon·te·rey Californian city
mon·te·ro (*plural* ·ros)
 hunting cap
Mon·ter·rey Mexican city
Montessori meth·od
Mon·te·vi·deo Uruguayan
 capital

mont·gol·fier hot-air
 balloon
Mont·gom·ery US city
month
month·ly (*plural* ·lies)
mon·ti·cule small hill
Mont·mar·tre
Mont·par·nasse
Mont·pel·lier
Mon·treal
Mon·treuil Parisian suburb
monu·ment
monu·men·tal
monu·men·tal·ly
monu·men·tal·ity
Mon·za Italian city
mon·zo·nite rock
mon·zo·nit·ic
moo
mooch
mooch·er
mood
moodi·ly
moodi·ness
moody (moodi·er,
 moodi·est)
Moog syn·the·siz·er
 (*Trademark*)
moo·lah *Slang* money
mool·vie (*or* ·vi) Muslim
 learned man
moon
moon·beam
moon·calf (*plural* ·calves)
moon·eye fish
moon-faced
moon·fish (*plural* ·fishes *or*
 ·fish)
moon·flower
mooni·ly
mooni·ness
moon·less
moon·light
moon·lighter
moon·light·ing
moon·lit
moon·quake
moon·raker sail
moon·rise
moon·scape
moon·seed
moon·set
moon·shine
moon·shiner *US* whisky
 smuggler

moon·shot
moon·stone
moon·struck (*or* ·stricken)
moon·wort
moony (mooni·er,
 mooni·est)
Moor African Muslim
moor open ground; attach
 boat; *compare* more
moor·age
moor·cock
moor·fowl
moor·hen
moor·ing
moor·ings
Moor·ish
moor·land
moor·wort shrub
moose (*plural* moose)
moot
moot·er
mop (mop·ping, mopped)
mope
moped *past tense of* mope
mo·ped motorcycle
mop·er
mop·ing·ly
mo·poke owl
mopped
mop·pet
mop·ping
mo·quette fabric
mor humus
mora (*plural* morae *or*
 moras) prosody term
mo·ra·ceous botany term
Mo·ra·da·bad Indian city
mo·rain·al (*or* ·ic)
mo·raine glacier debris;
 compare murrain
mor·al
mo·rale confidence
mor·al·ism
mor·al·ist
mor·al·is·tic
mor·al·is·ti·cal·ly
mo·ral·ity (*plural* ·ities)
mor·ali·za·tion (*or* ·sa·tion)
mor·al·ize (*or* ·ise)
mor·al·iz·er (*or* ·is·er)
mor·al·iz·ing·ly (*or*
 ·is·ing·ly)
mor·al·ly
Mor·ar Scottish loch
mo·rass

mora·to·rium (*plural* ·ria *or* ·riums)
mora·tory
Mo·ra·va Czech river
Mo·ra·via
Mo·ra·vian
Mo·ra·vi·an·ism religious movement
Mor·ay Scottish council area
mo·ray (*plural* ·rays) eel
mor·bid
mor·bid·ity
mor·bid·ness
mor·bif·ic causing disease
mor·bifi·cal·ly
Mor·bi·han French department
mor·bil·li measles
mor·ceau (*plural* ·ceaux) *French* morsel
mor·cha Indian demonstration
mor·da·cious sarcastic
mor·dac·ity (*or* ·da·cious·ness)
mor·dan·cy
mor·dant sarcastic; dye fixer
mor·dent musical ornament
Mord·vin (*plural* ·vin *or* ·vins) Finnish people
Mor·dvin·ian
more *comparative of* much; *compare* moor
More·cambe Lancashire town
mo·reen fabric
more·ish (*or* mor·ish)
mo·rel edible fungus
Mo·relia Mexican city
mo·rel·lo (*plural* ·los) cherry
Mo·relos Mexican state
more·over
mo·res customs
Mo·res·co *variant spelling of* Morisco
Mo·resque Moorish
Mor·gan horse
mor·ga·nat·ic
mor·ga·nati·cal·ly
mor·gan·ite gemstone
Morgan le Fay legendary character
morgue
mori·bund
mori·bun·dity

mo·ri·on helmet
Mo·ris·co (*or* ·res·; *plural* ·coes *or* ·cos) Spanish Moor
mor·ish *variant spelling of* moreish
Mor·mon
Mor·mon·ism
morn morning; *compare* mourn
mor·nay cookery term
morn·ing
morning-glory (*plural* ·glories)
Moro (*plural* Moros *or* Moro) Muslim people
Mo·roc·can
Mo·roc·co
mo·roc·co leather
mor·on
Mo·ro·ni capital of Comoro Islands
mo·ron·ic
mo·roni·cal·ly
mo·ron·ism (*or* ·ity)
mo·rose
mo·rose·ly
mo·rose·ness
morph linguistics term
mor·phal·lax·is (*plural* ·laxes) zoology term
mor·pheme grammatical unit
mor·phem·ic
mor·phemi·cal·ly
Morpheus Greek god
mor·phine (*or* ·phia)
mor·phin·ism
mor·pho·gen·esis
mor·pho·genet·ic (*or* ·gen·ic)
mor·pho·log·ic (*or* ·logi·cal)
mor·pho·logi·cal·ly
mor·pholo·gist
mor·phol·ogy
mor·pho·pho·neme linguistics term
mor·pho·phonemic
mor·pho·pho·nemics
mor·pho·sis (*plural* ·ses) biology term
mor·ris dance
mor·ro (*plural* ·ros) hill
mor·row

Mors Roman god
Morse code
morse cloak fastening
mor·sel
mort hunting term
mor·tal
mor·tal·ity (*plural* ·ities)
mor·tal·ly
mor·tar
mortar·board
mort·gage
mort·gage·able
mort·ga·gee
mort·gag·or (*or* ·er)
mor·tice *variant spelling of* mortise
mor·ti·cian *US* undertaker
mor·ti·fi·ca·tion
mor·ti·fi·er
mor·ti·fy (·fies, ·fy·ing, ·fied)
mor·ti·fy·ing·ly
mor·tise (*or* ·tice)
mor·tis·er
mort·main legal term
mor·tu·ary (*plural* ·aries)
moru·la (*plural* ·las *or* ·lae) biology term
moru·lar
mor·wong fish
Mo·sa·ic (*or* ·sai·cal) of Moses
mo·sa·ic (·ick·ing, ·icked)
mo·sai·cist
mos·cha·tel plant
Mos·cow
Mo·selle European river; wine
mo·sey
Mos·lem *variant spelling of* Muslim
Mo·so·tho (*plural* ·tho *or* ·thos) African people
mosque
mos·qui·to (*plural* ·toes *or* ·tos)
moss
moss·back *US* conservative
moss·bunk·er fish
Mos·si (*plural* ·sis *or* ·si) African people
mos·sie bird
mossi·ness
mos·so musical term
moss·trooper

mossy (mossi·er, mossi·est)
most
most·ly
Mosul Iraqi city
mote tiny speck; *compare*
    moat
mo·tel
mo·tet
moth
moth·ball
moth-eaten
moth·er
moth·er·hood
mother-in-law (*plural*
    mothers-)
mother·land
moth·er·less
moth·er·li·ness
moth·er·ly
mother-of-pearl
mother·wort plant
moth·proof
mothy (mothi·er,
    mothi·est)
mo·tif theme; *compare*
    motive
mo·tile
mo·til·ity
mo·tion
mo·tion·er
mo·tion·less
mo·tion·less·ness
mo·ti·vate
mo·ti·va·tion
mo·ti·va·tion·al
mo·ti·va·tive
mo·tive reason; causing
    motion; *compare* motif
mo·tive·less
mo·tive·less·ness
mo·tiv·ity
mot juste (*plural* mots
    justes)
mot·ley
mot·mot bird
mo·to·cross motorcycle race
mo·to·neu·ron nerve cell
mo·tor
motor·bike
motor·boat
motor·bus
motor·cade
motor·car
motor·coach
motor·cycle

motor·cyclist
mo·tor·ist
mo·tori·za·tion (*or* ·sa·tion)
mo·tor·ize (*or* ·ise)
motor·man (*plural* ·men)
motor·way
motte castle mound
mott·le
mot·to (*plural* ·toes *or* ·tos)
mouf·lon (*or* mouf·flon)
    wild sheep
mouil·lé phonetics term
mould (US mold)
mould·abil·ity (US mold·)
mould·able (US mold·)
mould·board (US mold·)
    curved blade of plough
mould·er (US mold·)
    crumble; one who moulds
mouldi·ness (US moldi·)
mould·ing (US mold·)
mould·warp *Dialect* mole
mouldy (US moldy;
    mouldi·er, mouldi·est, US
    moldi·er, moldi·est)
mou·lin glacier shift
Moul·mein (*or* Maul·main)
    Burmese port
moult (US molt)
moult·er (US molt·)
mound
mount
mount·able
moun·tain
moun·tain·eer
moun·tain·eer·ing
moun·tain·ous
mountain-top
moun·tebank
moun·tebank·ery
mount·ed
mount·er
Mountie Canadian
    policeman
mount·ing
Mount Rush·more
mourn grieve; *compare*
    morn
mourn·er
mourn·ful
mourn·ful·ly
mourn·ful·ness
mourn·ing
mouse (*plural* mice)
mous·er

mouse·tail plant
mouse·trap
mousi·ness
mous·ing nautical term
mous·sa·ka (*or* mou·sa·)
mousse
mousse·line fabric; cookery
    term
mous·tache (US mus·)
mousy (*or* mous·ey;
    mousi·er, mousi·est)
mouth
mouth·brooder (*or*
    ·breeder) fish
(mouthe) *incorrect spelling of*
    mouth (*verb*)
mouth·er
mouth·ful (*plural* ·fuls)
mouth·part
mouth·piece
mouth-to-mouth
mouth·wash
mouth·water·ing
mou·ton processed
    sheepskin
mov·abil·ity (*or* ·able·ness)
mov·able (*or in legal contexts*
    move·)
mov·ably
move (mov·ing, moved)
move·ables legal term
move·ment
mov·er
movie
Movie·tone (*Trademark*)
mov·ing
mov·ing·ly
Mo·vio·la (*Trademark*)
mow (mow·ing, mowed,
    mowed *or* mown)
mow·burnt agricultural
    term
mow·er
moxa medicinal substance
moxie US courage
Mo·zam·bi·can
Mo·zam·bique (*or*
    Mo·çam·)
moz·za·rel·la cheese
moz·zet·ta (*or* mo·zet·ta)
    clerical cape
Mpu·ma·lan·ga South
    African province
Mr (*plural* Messrs)
Mrs

Ms
much (more, most)
much·ness
mu·cic acid
mu·cid mouldy
mu·ci·lage
mu·ci·lagi·nous
mu·cin biochemical
  compound
mu·cin·ous
muck
muck·er
mucki·ly
mucki·ness
muck·le *Scot* much
muck·rake
muck·rak·er
muck·worm
mucky (mucki·er,
  mucki·est)
mu·coid (*or* ·coi·dal)
mu·co·mem·bra·nous
mu·co·poly·sac·cha·ride
mu·co·pro·tein
mu·co·pu·ru·lent
mu·co·sa (*plural* ·sae)
  mucous membrane
mu·cos·ity
mu·cous (*or* ·cose; *adj*)
mu·cro (*plural* mu·cro·nes)
  biology term
mu·cro·nate (*or* ·nat·ed)
mu·cro·na·tion
mu·cus (*noun*)
mud (mud·ding,
  mud·ded)
mud·cat fish
mud·died
mud·di·ly
mud·di·ness
mud·dle
mud·dled·ness
muddle·headed
muddle·headed·ness
mud·dle·ment
mud·dler
mud·dling·ly
mud·dy (*adj* ·di·er, ·di·est;
  verb ·dies, ·dy·ing, ·died)
mud·fish (*plural* ·fish *or*
  ·fishes)
mud·guard
mu·dir governor
mud·lark
mud·pack

mu·dra Hindu dance
  movement
mud·skipper fish
mud·slinger
mud·slinging
mud·stone
muen·ster cheese
mues·li
mu·ez·zin mosque official
muff
muf·fin
muf·fle
muf·fler
Muf·ti (*plural* ·tis) Muslim
  legal adviser
muf·ti (*plural* ·tis) civilian
  dress
Mu·fu·li·ra Zambian town
mug (mug·ging, mugged)
mug·ger street robber
mug·ger (*or* ·gar, ·gur)
  crocodile
mug·gi·ly
mug·gi·ness
mug·gins
mug·gy (·gi·er, ·gi·est)
mug·wort
mug·wump politically
  neutral person
Mu·ham·mad·an Muslim
Mühl·hau·sen German city
muk·luk Eskimo boot
mu·lat·to (*plural* ·tos *or*
  ·toes)
mul·berry (*plural* ·berries)
mulch soil enricher
mulct cheat
mule
mu·leta matador's cape
mu·leteer mule driver
mul·ey (*or* mul·ley)
  hornless cattle
mul·ga tree
Mül·heim an der Ruhr
  German city
mu·li·eb·rity womanhood
mul·ish
mul·ish·ness
Mull Scottish island
mull
mul·lah (*or* mul·la) Muslim
  leader
mul·lein (*or* ·len) plant
mul·ler
mul·let

mul·ley *variant spelling of*
  muley
mul·li·gan stew
mul·li·ga·taw·ny
mul·li·on
mul·li·oned
mul·lite mineral
mul·lock *Dialect* mess
mullo·way fish
Mul·tan Pakistani city
mul·tan·gu·lar (*or*
  multi·an·)
mul·teity manifoldness
multi·birth
multi·cel·lu·lar
multi·chan·nel
multi·cide mass murder
multi·col·lin·ear·ity
  statistics term
multi·col·oured (*US* ·ored)
multi·di·rec·tion·al
multi·dis·ci·pli·nary
multi·fac·et·ed
multi·fac·to·rial
multi·fari·ous
multi·fid (*or* mul·tifi·dous)
multi·foil looped design
multi·fold
multi·fo·li·ate
multi·form
multi·for·mity
multi·gravi·da obstetrics
  term
multi·hull
multi·lami·nar
multi·lat·er·al
multi·lin·gual
multi·media
multi·mil·lion·aire
multi·na·tion·al
multi·no·mial
multi·nu·clear (*or* ·cleate)
mul·tipa·ra (*plural* ·rae)
  obstetrics term
multi·par·ity
mul·tipa·rous
multi·par·tite
multi·plane multi-winged
  aircraft
multi·ple
multiple·choice
multiple·poind·ing Scottish
  legal term
multi·plet physics term
multi·plex electronics term

multi·plex·er
multi·pli·able
multi·pli·cand number
multiplied
multi·pli·cate manifold
multi·pli·ca·tion
multi·pli·ca·tion·al
multi·pli·ca·tive
multi·plic·ity (*plural* ·ities)
multi·pli·er
multi·ply (·plies, ·ply·ing,
·plied)
multi·pro·gram·ming
multi·pur·pose
multi·racial
multi·role
multi·screen
multi·stage
multi·sto·rey
multi·tude
multi·tu·di·nous
multi·va·len·cy
multi·va·lent
multi·vi·bra·tor
mul·ture miller's fee
mum mother; silent
mum (*or* mumm;
mum·ming, mummed)
act in mummer's play
Mum·bai *Indian name of*
Bombay
mum·ble
mum·bler
mum·bling·ly
mum·bo jum·bo (*plural*
mum·bo jum·bos)
mum·chance dumbstruck
mum·mer
mum·mery (*plural* ·meries)
mum·mi·fi·ca·tion
mum·mi·fy (·fies, ·fy·ing,
·fied)
mum·my (*plural* ·mies)
mumps
munch
munch·er
mun·dane
mun·dane·ness
mung bean
munga *Austral* food
mun·go (*or* mon·go,
mon·goe; *plural* ·gos *or*
·goes) fabric
Mu·nich
mu·nici·pal

mu·nici·pal·ity (*plural*
·ities)
mu·nici·pali·za·tion (*or*
·sa·tion)
mu·nici·pal·ize (*or* ·ise)
mu·nici·pal·ly
mu·nifi·cence (*or*
·cent·ness)
mu·nifi·cent
mu·ni·ment means of
defence
mu·ni·ments title deeds
mu·ni·tion
Mun·ster Irish province
Mün·ster German city
munt·jac (*or* ·jak) deer
muon elementary
particle
mu·ral
mu·ral·ist
mur·der
mur·der·er (*fem* ·ess)
mur·der·ous
mur·der·ous·ness
Mu·reş European river
mu·rex (*plural* mu·ri·ces)
mollusc
mu·ri·cate (*or* ·cat·ed)
biology term
mu·rine of rats and mice
murk (*or* mirk)
murki·ly (*or* mirki·)
murki·ness (*or* mirki·)
murky (*or* mirky; murki·er,
murki·est *or* mirki·er,
mirki·est)
Mur·mansk Russian port
mur·mur
mur·mur·er
mur·mur·ing
mur·mur·ous
mur·phy (*plural* ·phies)
Dialect potato
mur·rain cattle disease;
compare moraine
Mur·ray Australian river
murre guillemot
murre·let bird
mur·rhine (*or* ·rine) Roman
vase material
Mur·rum·bidgee Australian
river
mur·ther *Archaic* murder
mu·sa·ceous botany term
Mus·ca constellation

mus·ca·del (*or* ·delle)
variants of muscatel
mus·ca·dine US grape
mus·ca·rine poisonous
alkaloid
Mus·cat capital of Oman
mus·cat grape
mus·ca·tel (*or* ·del, ·delle)
wine
mus·cid fly
mus·cle
muscle-bound
mus·cle·man (*plural* ·men)
mus·cly
mus·co·va·do (*or* mus·ca·)
raw sugar
Mus·co·vite native of
Moscow
mus·co·vite mineral
Mus·co·vy Russian
principality; duck
mus·cu·lar
mus·cu·lar·ity
mus·cu·la·ture
muse
muse·ful
mus·eol·ogy museum
organization; *compare*
musicology
mus·er
mu·sette bagpipe
mu·seum
mush
mushi·ly
mushi·ness
mush·room
mushy (mushi·er,
mushi·est)
mu·sic
mu·si·cal
mu·si·cale *US* musical
evening
mu·si·cal·ly
mu·si·cal·ness (*or* ·ity)
mu·si·cian
mu·si·cian·ship
mu·si·co·logi·cal
mu·si·colo·gist
mu·si·col·ogy study of
music; *compare*
museology
mus·jid *variant spelling of*
masjid
musk
mus·keg bog

mus·kel·lunge (*or* mas·ka·nonge, ·ki·) fish
mus·ket
mus·ket·eer
mus·ket·ry
muski·ness
musk·melon
musk·rat (*plural* ·rats *or* ·rat)
musky (muski·er, muski·est)
Mus·lim (*or* Mos·lem; *plural* ·lims, ·lim *or* ·lems, ·lem)
Mus·lim·ism (*or* Mos·lem·)
mus·lin
muso *Austral* musician
mus·quash
muss *US* rumple
mus·sel mollusc; *compare* muscle
must
mus·tache *US spelling of* moustache
mus·ta·chio (*plural* ·chi·os)
mus·ta·chi·oed
mus·tang
mus·tard
mus·tee (*or* mes·) person of mixed parentage
mus·te·line of badger family
mus·ter
musth (*or* must) sexual heat in animals
musti·ly
musti·ness
mus·ty (·ti·er, ·ti·est)
mu·tabil·ity (*or* ·table·ness)
mu·table
mu·tably
mu·ta·gen substance causing mutation
mu·ta·gen·ic
mu·tant
mu·tate
mu·ta·tion
mu·ta·tion·al
mu·ta·tis mu·tan·dis
mutch linen cap
mute
mute·ness
mu·ti·cous botany term
mu·ti·late
mu·ti·la·tion
mu·ti·la·tive
mu·ti·la·tor

mu·ti·neer
mu·ti·nous
mu·ti·ny (*noun, plural* ·nies; *verb* ·nies, ·ny·ing, ·nied)
mut·ism
mutt *Slang* fool; cur
mut·ter
mut·ter·er
mut·ter·ing·ly
mut·ton
mutton·chops side whiskers
mut·tony
mu·tu·al
mu·tu·al·ity (*or* ·ness)
mu·tu·al·ize (*or* ·ise)
mu·tu·al·ly
mu·tule architecture term
Mu·zak (*Trademark*)
mu·zhik (*or* mou·jik, mu·jik) Russian peasant
muzz make muzzy
muz·zi·ly
muz·zi·ness
muz·zle
muz·zler
muz·zy (·zi·er, ·zi·est)
my
my·al·gia muscle pain
my·al·gic
mya·lism witchcraft
my·all tree
My·an·mar *official name of* Burma
my·as·thenia muscular weakness
my·as·then·ic
my·celial
my·celium (*plural* ·celia) fungal body
my·celoid
My·cenae ancient Greek city
My·cenaean
my·ceto·ma (*plural* ·mas *or* ·ma·ta) fungal infection
my·ceto·zoan fungus
my·co·bac·te·rium (*plural* ·ria)
my·co·logi·cal (*or* ·log·ic)
my·colo·gist
my·col·ogy study of fungi
my·cor·rhi·za (*or* ·co·rhi·; *plural* ·zae *or* ·zas) botany term
my·cor·rhi·zal (*or* ·co·rhi·)

my·co·sis fungal disease
my·cot·ic
my·dria·sis pupil dilation
myd·ri·at·ic
my·elen·cephal·ic
my·elen·cepha·lon (*plural* ·lons *or* ·la) embryology term
my·elin (*or* ·eline) nerve sheath
my·elin·ic
my·eli·tis
my·eloid
my·elo·ma tumour
my·elo·ma·toid
myia·sis (*plural* ·ses) infestation by fly larvae
my·lo·nite rock
myna (*or* my·nah, mina) bird
Myn·heer Dutch title of address
myo·car·dial
myo·car·dio·graph
myo·car·di·tis
myo·car·dium (*plural* ·dia) heart muscle
myo·gen·ic
myo·glo·bin protein
myo·graph
myo·graph·ic
myo·graphi·cal·ly
my·og·ra·phy
myo·log·ic (*or* ·logi·cal)
my·olo·gist
my·ol·ogy study of muscle diseases
myo·ma (*plural* ·mas *or* ·ma·ta) tumour
my·ope
myo·pia
my·op·ic
my·opi·cal·ly
myo·sin protein
myo·sis *variant spelling of* miosis
myo·so·tis (*or* ·sote) plant
myo·tome anatomy term
myo·to·nia lack of muscle tone
myo·ton·ic
myri·ad
myria·pod invertebrate
myri·apo·dan
myri·apo·dous

my·ri·ca medicinal bark
myr·meco·logi·cal
myr·mecolo·gist
myr·mecol·ogy study of ants
myr·mecopha·gous
myr·meco·phile
myr·mecophi·lous
Myr·mi·don (*plural* mi·dons *or* mido·nes) mythological race
my·roba·lan fruit
myrrh
myr·ta·ceous
myr·tle
my·self
My·sore Indian city
mys·ta·gog·ic (*or* ·gogi·cal)
mys·ta·gogi·cal·ly
mys·ta·gogue mystic teacher
mys·ta·go·gy
mys·teri·ous
mys·teri·ous·ness

mys·tery (*plural* ·teries)
mys·tic
mys·ti·cal
mys·ti·cal·ly
mys·ti·cism
mys·ti·fi·ca·tion
mys·ti·fi·er
mys·ti·fy (·fies, ·fy·ing, ·fied)
mys·ti·fy·ing·ly
mys·tique
myth
mythi·cal
mythi·cal·ly
mythi·cist (*or* ·ciz·er, ·cis·er)
mythi·ci·za·tion (*or* ·sa·tion)
mythi·cize (*or* ·cise)
mytho·logi·cal
my·tholo·gist
my·tholo·gi·za·tion (*or* ·sa·tion)
my·tholo·gize (*or* ·gise)

my·tholo·giz·er (*or* ·gis·er)
my·thol·ogy (*plural* ·ogies)
mytho·ma·nia psychiatric term
mytho·ma·ni·ac
mytho·poeia (*or* ·po·esis) myth making
mytho·poe·ic
mytho·poe·ism
mytho·poe·ist
my·thos (*plural* ·thoi) group of beliefs
(myxamatosis) *incorrect spelling of* myxomatosis
myx·oedema (*US* ·edema) thyroid disease
myx·oedem·ic (*US* ·edem·)
myxo·ma (*plural* ·mas *or* ·ma·ta) tumour
myxo·ma·to·sis
myx·oma·tous
myxo·my·cete fungus
myxo·my·cetous
myxo·vi·rus

N

Naafi (*or* NAAFI)
nab (nab·bing, nabbed)
Na·blus (*or* Nabu·lus) Jordanian town
na·bob
na·bob·ery (*or* ·ism)
Nabonidus biblical character
Naboth biblical character
na·celle part of aircraft
na·cre mother-of-pearl
na·cred
na·cre·ous
Na-Dene (*or* -Déné) language group
na·dir
nae *Scot* no
nae·void (*US* ne·)
nae·vus (*US* ne·; *plural* ·vi) birthmark
nag (nag·ging, nagged)
Naga (*plural* Nagas *or* Naga) Indian people
Na·ga·land
na·ga·na (*or* n'ga·na) animal disease

Na·ga·no Japanese city
Na·ga·ri Indian script
Na·ga·sa·ki Japanese port
nagged
nag·ger
nag·ging
na·gor antelope
Nagorno-Karabakh Azerbaijani autonomous region
Na·go·ya Japanese city
Nag·pur Indian city
Na·huatl (*plural* ·huatl *or* ·huatls) American Indian
Na·hua·tlan
nai·ad (*plural* ·ads *or* ·ades)
na·if *variant spelling of* naive
nail
nail·brush
nail·er
nail·file
nail·head decorative device
nain·sook fabric
nai·ra Nigerian currency
Nairn former Scottish county

Nai·ro·bi
nais·sant heraldry term
na·ive (*or* ·ïve, ·if)
na·ive·ty (*or* ·ive·té, ·ive·té)
Najd *variant spelling of* Nejd
na·ked
na·ked·ness
na·ker kettledrum
Na·khi·che·van Azerbaijani autonomous region
Nal·chik Russian city
Nama (*or* Na·ma·qua; *plural* Nama, Namas *or* ·qua, ·quas) Khoikhoi people
nam·able (*or* name·)
Na·man·gan Uzbek city
namby-pamby (*plural* -pambies)
nam·dah *variant spelling of* numdah
name
name-dropper
name-dropping
name·less
name·ly
name·plate

name·sake
name·tape
Nam·hoi Chinese city
Na·mibia
Na·mib·ian
Na·mur Belgian province
nan (or nanna) Slang
  grandmother
Nan·chang (or Nan-ch'ang)
  Chinese city
Nan·cy French city
nan·cy (plural ·cies)
  effeminate man
Nan·da Devi Himalayan
  mountain
Nan·ga Par·bat Himalayan
  mountain
nan·keen (or ·kin) fabric
Nan·king (or Nan-ching)
  Chinese port
nanna variant of nan
Nan·ning (or Nan-ning)
  Chinese port
nan·ny (plural ·nies)
na·no·metre (US ·meter)
na·no·plank·ton (or
  nan·no·)
na·no·sec·ond
Nan Shan Chinese
  mountain range
Nantes French port
Nan·tuck·et US island
Nan·tung Chinese city
Naoise Irish mythological
  character
nap (nap·ping, napped)
na·palm
nape
naph·tha
naph·tha·lene (or ·line,
  ·lin)
naph·thene
naph·thol
naph·thyl
Na·pier New Zealand port
Na·pier·ian loga·ri·thm
na·pi·form turnip-shaped
nap·kin
Na·ples
na·po·le·on coin
Na·po·leon·ic
nap·pa leather
nappe rock fold
napped
nap·per Slang head

nap·pi·ness
nap·ping
nap·py (noun, plural ·pies;
  adj ·pi·er, ·pi·est)
Nara Japanese city
Na·ra·yan·ganj Bangladeshi
  city
nar·ceine (or ·ceen) alkaloid
nar·cis·sism (or nar·cism)
nar·cis·sist
nar·cis·sis·tic
nar·cis·sus (plural ·si or
  ·suses)
nar·co·analy·sis
nar·co·lep·sy
nar·co·lep·tic
nar·co·sis (plural ·ses)
nar·co·syn·thesis medical
  treatment
nar·cot·ic
nar·coti·cal·ly
nar·co·tism
nar·co·ti·za·tion (or
  ·sa·tion)
nar·co·tize (or ·tise)
nard medicinal plant
nar·es (sing. ·is) nostrils
nar·ghi·le hookah
nar·ial (or ·ine)
nark
Nar·ra·gan·set (or ·sett;
  plural ·set, ·sets or ·sett,
  ·setts) American Indian
nar·rat·able
nar·rate
nar·ra·tion
nar·ra·tive
nar·ra·tor (or ·rat·er)
nar·row
narrow-minded
narrow-minded·ness
nar·row·ness
nar·thex church portico
Nar·vik Norwegian port
nar·whal (or ·wal, ·whale)
  whale
nary Dialect not
na·sal
na·sal·ity
na·sali·za·tion (or ·sa·tion)
na·sal·ize (or ·ise)
na·sal·ly
nas·cence (or ·cen·cy)
nas·cent
Nash·ville US city

na·sial
na·si·on anatomy term
na·so·fron·tal
na·so·pha·ryn·geal
na·so·phar·ynx (plural
  ·pha·ryn·ges or
  ·phar·ynxes)
Nas·sau German region;
  Bahamian capital
nas·tic botany term
nas·ti·ly
nas·ti·ness
na·stur·tium
nas·ty (adj ·ti·er, ·ti·est;
  noun, plural ·ties)
Na·tal Brazilian port; former
  South African province
na·tal of birth
na·tal·ity
na·tant floating
na·ta·tion swimming
na·ta·tion·al
na·ta·tory
na·tes (sing. ·tis) buttocks
na·tion
na·tion·al
na·tion·al·ism
na·tion·al·ist
na·tion·al·is·tic
na·tion·al·ity (plural ·ities)
na·tion·ali·za·tion (or
  ·sa·tion)
na·tion·al·ize (or ·ise)
na·tion·al·ly
na·tion·hood
nation·wide
na·tive
na·tiv·ism
na·tiv·ist
na·tiv·is·tic
Na·tiv·ity Christ's birth
na·tiv·ity (plural ·ities)
  birth or origin
NATO
nat·ro·lite mineral
na·tron mineral
nat·ter
nat·ter·jack toad
nat·ti·ly
nat·ti·ness
nat·ty (·ti·er, ·ti·est)
natu·ral
natu·ral·ism artistic
  movement; compare
  naturism

natu·ral·ist
natu·ral·is·tic
natu·ral·is·ti·cal·ly
natu·rali·za·tion (or
·sa·tion)
natu·ral·ize (or ·ise)
natu·ral·ly
natu·ral·ness
na·ture
na·tur·ism nudism; compare
naturalism
na·tur·ist
na·turo·path
na·turo·path·ic
na·tur·opa·thy nature cure
naught Archaic nothing; US
spelling of nought
naugh·ti·ly
naugh·ti·ness
naugh·ty (·ti·er, ·ti·est)
nau·plius (plural ·plii)
crustacean larva
Nau·ru island republic
Nau·ruan
nau·sea
nau·seate
nau·sea·tion
nau·seous
nau·seous·ness
nautch (or nauch) Indian
dance
nau·ti·cal
nau·ti·cal·ly
nau·ti·loid
nau·ti·lus (plural ·luses or
·li) mollusc
Nava·ho (or ·jo; plural ·ho,
·hos or ·jo, ·jos) American
Indian
na·val of ships; compare
navel
na·val·ly
nav·ar navigation system
nava·rin mutton stew
Na·varre
nave
na·vel umbilicus; compare
naval
navi·cert cargo certificate
na·vicu·lar boat-shaped
navi·gabil·ity (or
·gable·ness)
navi·gable
navi·gably
navi·gate

navi·ga·tion
navi·ga·tion·al
navi·ga·tor
nav·vy (plural ·vies)
labourer
navy (plural navies)
na·wab Indian prince
Nax·os Greek island
nay no; compare neigh
Na·ya·rit Mexican state
Naza·rene inhabitant of
Nazareth; Syrian Christian
Naza·reth
Naza·rite (or Nazi·) Old
Testament ascetic
Naze Essex headland
Nazi (plural Nazis)
Na·zi·fy (·fies, ·fy·ing,
·fied)
Na·zism
Ndja·me·na capital of
Chad
Ndo·la Zambian city
Neagh Northern Irish lake
Ne·an·der·thal
neap tide
Nea·poli·tan
near
near·by
Ne·arc·tic zoogeographical
term
near·ly
near·ness
near·side
near-sighted
near-sighted·ness
neat
neat·en
neath Archaic beneath
neat·ness
neat's-foot oil
neb Dialect projecting part
Ne·bras·ka
nebu·chad·nez·zar wine
bottle
nebu·la (plural ·lae or ·las)
nebu·lar
nebu·li·za·tion (or ·sa·tion)
nebu·lize (or ·lise) atomize
nebu·liz·er (or ·lis·er)
nebu·los·ity (plural ·ities)
nebu·lous
nebu·lous·ness
ne·ces·saries
nec·es·sari·ly

nec·es·sary
ne·ces·si·tar·ian (or
nec·es·sar·ian)
ne·ces·si·tari·an·ism (or
nec·es·sari·an·ism)
philosophy term
ne·ces·si·tate
ne·ces·sita·tion
ne·ces·si·ta·tive
ne·ces·si·tous
ne·ces·sity (plural ·sities)
neck
Neck·ar German river
neck·band
neck·cloth
neck·er
neck·er·chief
neck·lace
neck·line
neck·piece
neck·tie
neck·wear
nec·ro·bio·sis death of cells
nec·ro·bi·ot·ic
ne·crola·try worship of the
dead
nec·ro·logi·cal
ne·crolo·gist
ne·crol·ogy (plural ·ogies)
list of dead people
nec·ro·man·cer
nec·ro·man·cy
nec·ro·man·tic
nec·ro·philia (or
ne·crophi·lism)
nec·ro·phili·ac (or ·phile)
nec·ro·phil·ic
nec·ro·phobe
nec·ro·pho·bia
nec·ro·pho·bic
ne·cropo·lis (plural ·lises or
·leis)
nec·rop·sy (plural ·sies)
ne·crose (verb)
ne·cro·sis
ne·crot·ic
ne·croto·my (plural ·mies)
dissection of corpse
nec·tar
nec·tar·eous (or ·ous)
nec·tar·ine
nec·ta·ry (plural ·ries)
ned·dy (plural ·dies)
née (or nee) indicating
maiden name

need
need·ful
need·ful·ness
needi·ness
nee·dle
needle·cord
needle·craft
needle·fish (*plural* ·fish *or*
·fishes)
needle·ful
needle·point
need·less
need·less·ness
needle·woman (*plural*
·women)
needle·work
need·ments
needn't
needy (needi·er, needi·est)
neep *Dialect* turnip
ne'er
ne'er-do-well
ne·fari·ous
nefari·ous·ness
ne·gate
ne·ga·tion
nega·tive
nega·tive·ness
negative-raising grammar
term
nega·ti·vism
nega·tiv·ist
nega·tiv·is·tic
nega·tiv·ity
ne·ga·tor (*or* ·gat·er)
ne·ga·to·ry
Neg·ev (*or* ·eb) Israeli
desert
ne·glect
ne·glect·er (*or* ·glec·tor)
ne·glect·ful
ne·glect·ful·ly
ne·glect·ful·ness
neg·li·gee (*or* ·gée, ·gé)
neg·li·gence
neg·li·gent
neg·li·gibil·ity (*or*
·gible·ness)
neg·li·gible
neg·li·gibly
ne·go·tiabil·ity
ne·go·tiable
ne·go·ti·ant
ne·go·ti·ate
ne·go·tia·tion

ne·go·tia·tor
Ne·gress
Ne·gril·lo (*plural* ·los *or*
·loes) African Negroid
people
Neg·ri Sem·bi·lan
Malaysian state
Ne·grit·ic of Negroes or
Negritos
Ne·gri·to (*plural* ·tos *or*
·toes) Asian Negroid
people
ne·gri·tude
Ne·gro (*plural* ·groes)
Ne·groid
Ne·gro·ism
Ne·gro·phile (*or* ·phil)
Ne·gro·phobe
Ne·gro·pho·bia
Neg·ro·pont Greek island
Ne·gros Philippine island
ne·gus (*plural* ·guses) spiced
drink
neigh sound of a horse;
compare nay
neigh·bour (*US* ·bor)
neigh·bour·hood (*US*
·bor·)
neigh·bour·ing (*US* ·bor·)
neigh·bour·li·ness (*US*
·bor·)
neigh·bour·ly (*US* ·bor·)
Neis·se Polish river
nei·ther
Nejd (*or* Najd) Saudi
Arabian province
nek mountain pass
nek·ton minute marine
organisms
nek·ton·ic
nel·ly (*plural* ·lies)
Nel·son Lancashire town;
New Zealand port
nel·son wrestling hold
ne·lum·bo (*plural* ·bos)
plant
nema·thel·minth worm
ne·mat·ic chemistry term
nema·to·cyst
nema·to·cys·tic
nema·tode
Nem·bu·tal (*Trademark*)
Ne·mea ancient Greek
valley
Ne·mean

ne·mer·tean (*or*
nem·er·tine) marine
worm
ne·mesia plant
Nemesis Greek goddess
nem·esis (*plural* ·eses)
retribution
(nemonic) *incorrect spelling
of* mnemonic
nene goose
neo·an·throp·ic
neo·ars·phena·mine
Neo·cene geological term
neo·clas·si·cal (*or* ·sic)
neo·clas·si·cism
neo·clas·si·cist
neo·co·lo·nial
neo·co·lo·ni·al·ism
neo·co·lo·ni·al·ist
neo·dym·ium chemical
element
Neo·gaea zoogeographical
area
Neo·gaean
Neo·gene geological term
neo·im·pres·sion·ism
neo·lith
Neo·lith·ic
neo·logi·cal
neo·logi·cal·ly
ne·olo·gism (*or* ne·ol·ogy;
plural ·gisms *or* ·ogies)
ne·olo·gist
ne·olo·gis·tic (*or* ·ti·cal)
ne·olo·gis·ti·cal·ly
ne·olo·gize (*or* ·gise)
ne·ol·ogy *variant of*
neologism
neo·my·cin antibiotic
neon
neo·na·tal
neo·nate newborn child
neo·phyte novice
neo·phyt·ic
neo·plasm tumour
neo·plas·tic
neo·plas·ti·cism style of
painting
neo·plas·ty plastic surgery
Neo-Platonism philosophy
Neo-Platonist
neo·prene synthetic rubber
ne·ot·enous
ne·ot·eny zoology term
neo·ter·ic modern

neoterically 302

neo·teri·cal·ly
Neo·tropi·cal
 zoogeographical term
neo·type
Neo·zo·ic geological term
Ne·pal
Nepa·lese (plural ·lese)
Ne·pali
ne·pen·the
ne·pen·thean
ne·per unit
neph·eline (or ·elite)
 mineral
neph·elin·ite rock
neph·elom·eter chemistry
 apparatus
neph·elom·etry
neph·ew
nepho·gram
nepho·graph
nepho·logi·cal
ne·pholo·gist
ne·phol·ogy study of clouds
nepho·scope
ne·phral·gia kidney pain
ne·phral·gic
ne·phrec·to·my (plural
 ·mies) removal of kidney
ne·phrid·ial
ne·phrid·ium (plural
 ·phridia) excretory organ
neph·rite mineral
ne·phrit·ic of the kidneys
ne·phri·tis
ne·phrol·ogy
neph·ron
ne·phro·sis
ne·phrot·ic
ne·phroto·my (plural ·mies)
ne plus ul·tra Latin the
 perfect state
ne·pot·ic (or ·tis·tic)
nepo·tism
nepo·tist
Nep·tune planet
Neptune Roman god
Nep·tu·nian
nep·tu·nium chemical
 element
ne·ral chemistry term
Ne·reid (plural ·rei·des)
 Greek nymph
ne·reis worm
ne·rit·ic ecology term
nero·li oil

ner·vate having leaf veins
nerve
nerve·less
nerve·less·ness
nerve-racking (or
 -wracking)
nervi·ly
nerv·ine soothing the
 nerves
nervi·ness
nerv·ous
nerv·ous·ness
ner·vure biology term
nervy (nervi·er, nervi·est)
nes·ci·ence ignorance
nes·ci·ent
nesh Dialect timid
Ness Scottish lake
ness promontory
nes·sel·rode pudding
nest
nest·er
nes·tle
nes·tler
nest·ling
Nestor mythological
 character
Nes·to·ri·an·ism theological
 doctrine
net (net·ting, net·ted) mesh
net (or nett; net·ting,
 net·ted) remaining; earn
 as profit
net·ball
neth·er
Neth·er·land·er
Neth·er·lands
nether·most
net·su·ke
nett variant spelling of net
net·ted
net·ting
net·tle
net·tle·some causing
 irritation
net·tly
net·ty Dialect lavatory
net·work
Neu·châ·tel Swiss city and
 lake
Neuf·châ·tel French town;
 cheese
neume (or neum) musical
 symbol
neu·ral

neu·ral·gia
neu·ral·gic
neu·ras·the·nia
neu·ras·then·ic
neu·ras·theni·cal·ly
neu·rec·to·my (plural
 ·mies)
neu·rit·ic
neu·ri·tis
neu·ro·blast embryonic cell
neu·ro·coele embryology
 term
neu·ro·fi·bril
neu·ro·fi·bril·lar
neu·ro·gen·ic
neu·rog·lia nerve tissue
neu·ro·hy·pophy·sis (plural
 ·ses)
neu·ro·lem·ma (or neu·ri·)
 nerve sheath
neu·ro·logi·cal
neu·rolo·gist
neu·rol·ogy
neu·ro·ma (plural ·ma·ta or
 ·mas) tumour
neu·roma·tous
neu·ro·mus·cu·lar
neu·rone (or ·ron) nerve cell
neu·ron·ic
neu·ro·path person with
 nervous disorder
neu·ro·path·ic
neu·ro·pathi·cal·ly
neu·ro·pa·tholo·gist
neu·ro·pa·thol·ogy
neu·ropa·thy disease of
 nervous system
neu·ro·physio·logi·cal
neu·ro·physio·logi·cal·ly
neu·ro·physi·olo·gist
neu·ro·physi·ol·ogy
neu·ro·psy·chi·at·ric
neu·ro·psy·chia·trist
neu·ro·psy·chia·try
neu·rop·ter·an (or ·on;
 plural ·ter·ans or ·tera)
 insect
neu·rop·ter·ous (or ·ter·an)
neu·ro·sci·ence
neu·ro·sis (plural ·ses)
neu·ro·sur·geon
neu·ro·sur·gery
neu·ro·sur·gi·cal
neu·ro·sur·gi·cal·ly
neu·rot·ic

neu·roti·cal·ly

neu·roti·cism

neu·roto·mist

neu·roto·my (*plural* ·mies) nerve surgery

neu·ro·vas·cu·lar

Neuss German city

neu·ter

neu·tral

neu·tral·ism

neu·tral·ist

neu·tral·ity

neu·trali·za·tion (*or* ·sa·tion)

neu·tral·ize (*or* ·ise)

neu·tral·iz·er (*or* ·is·er)

neu·tral·ly

neu·tret·to (*plural* ·tos) physics term

neu·tri·no (*plural* ·nos) elementary particle

neu·tron

neu·tro·phil (*or* ·phile) blood cell

Neva Russian river

Ne·va·da

névé mass of ice

nev·er

never·more

never-never

never·the·less

Ne·vis West Indian island

ne·vus *US spelling of* naevus

new

New·ark English town; US port

new·born

New Bruns·wick

New·burg cookery term

New·bury

New·cas·tle Australian port

New·castle-under-Lyme

New·castle-upon-Tyne

new·comer

new·el

new·fan·gled

New·fie *Slang* inhabitant of Newfoundland

New·found·land

New·found·land·er

New·gate former prison

New·ham London borough

New·ha·ven

new·ish

new·ly

newly·wed

New·mar·ket

new·mar·ket gambling game; riding coat

new·ness

New Or·le·ans

New·port Isle of Wight town; Welsh port

news

news·agent

news·cast *US* news broadcast

news·caster

news·hawk

newsi·ness

news·letter

news·paper

news·paper·man (*plural* ·men)

new·speak

news·print

news·reel

news·stand

news·worthi·ness

news·worthy

newsy (newsi·er, newsi·est)

newt

New·ton Welsh town

new·ton unit

Newton·abbey Northern Irish town

New·to·nian of Isaac Newton

New Zea·land

New Zea·land·er

next

next-door (*adj*)

nex·us (*plural* nex·us *or* nex·uses)

ngaio (*plural* ngaios) tree

ngo·ma African drum

Ngu·ni language

ngwee Zambian coin

nia·cin vitamin

Ni·aga·ra

Nia·mey capital of Niger

nib (nib·bing, nibbed)

nib·ble

nib·bler

nib·lick golf club

Nica·ra·gua

Nica·ra·guan

nic·co·lite mineral

Nice French city

nice

Ni·cene Creed

nice·ness

ni·cety (*plural* ·ceties)

niche

Ni·chrome (*Trademark*)

nic·ish

nick

nick·el (·el·ling, ·elled; *US* ·el·ing, ·eled)

nick·el·ic

nick·el·if·er·ous

nickel·odeon

nick·el·ous

nick·er

nick·nack *variant spelling of* knickknack

nick·name

Nico·bar Indian islands

Nicol prism

Nico·sia Cypriot capital

ni·co·tia·na plant

nico·tina·mide vitamin

nico·tine

nico·tin·ic

nico·tin·ism

nic·ti·tate (*or* nic·tate) to blink

nic·ti·ta·tion (*or* nic·ta·tion)

ni·dal

niddle-noddle nod rapidly

nide *variant of* nye

ni·dico·lous ornithology term

nidi·fi·cate build nest

nidi·fi·ca·tion

ni·difu·gous ornithology term

nidi·fy (·fies, ·fy·ing, ·fied) build nest

nid-nod (-nod·ding, -nod·ded)

ni·dus (*plural* ·di)

niece

ni·el·list

ni·el·lo (*noun, plural* ·li *or* ·los; *verb* ·lo·ing, ·loed) engraving term

Nier·stein·er wine

Nie·tzschean

Nie·tzsche·ism (*or* ·tzschean·ism) philosophy

nieve *Dialect* fist

Niè·vre French department

niff
niffy (niffi•er, niffi•est)
nif•ti•ly
nif•ti•ness
nif•ty (•ti•er, •ti•est)
Ni•ger
Ni•geria
Ni•gerian
nig•gard
nig•gard•li•ness
nig•gard•ly
nig•ger
nig•gle
nig•gler
nig•gling
nig•gly
nigh
night
night•cap
night•club
night•dress
night•fall
night•gown
night•hawk
nightie (or nighty; plural
  nighties)
night•in•gale
night•jar
night•life
night•light
night•long
night•ly
night•mare
night•mar•ish
night•rider
night•shade
night•shirt
night•spot
night•time
night•wear
ni•gres•cence
ni•gres•cent blackish
ni•gro•sine (or •sin)
  pigment
ni•hil Latin nothing
ni•hil•ism
ni•hil•ist
ni•hil•is•tic
ni•hil•ity
Nii•ga•ta Japanese port
Nij•megen Dutch town
Nik•ko Japanese town
Ni•ko•la•yev Ukrainian
  city
nil

nil de•spe•ran•dum Latin
  never despair
Nile
nil•gai (or •ghau; plural •gai,
  •gais, or •ghau, •ghaus)
  antelope
Ni•lot•ic
nim game
nim•ble
nim•ble•ness
nimble•wit US clever person
nim•bly
nim•bo•stra•tus (plural •ti)
nim•bus (plural •bi or
  •buses)
Nîmes French city
niminy-piminy (or
  miminy-)
Nimrod biblical hunter
nin•com•poop
nine
nine•fold
nine•pins
nine•teen
nine•teenth
nine•ti•eth
nine•ty (plural •ties)
Ni•neveh Assyrian capital
Ning•po Chinese port
Ning•sia Hui Chinese
  region
nin•ny (plural •nies)
ni•non fabric
ninth
nio•bic
nio•bite
nio•bium chemical
  element
nio•bous
nip (nip•ping, nipped)
nipa palm tree
Nipi•gon Canadian lake
Nip•is•sing Canadian lake
nip•per
nip•pi•ly
nip•ple
nipple•wort plant
Nip•pon
Nip•pon•ese (plural •ese)
Nip•pur Babylonian city
nip•py (•pi•er, •pi•est)
nir•va•na
nir•va•nic
Niš Yugoslav town
Ni•sha•pur Iranian town

Ni•shi•no•mi•ya Japanese
  city
nisi legal term
nisi pri•us legal term
ni•sus (plural •sus) striving
nit
ni•ter US spelling of nitre
Ni•terói Brazilian port
ni•tid bright
ni•tra•mine
ni•trate
ni•tra•tion
ni•tre (US •ter)
ni•tric containing nitrogen
ni•tride chemical
  compound
ni•trid•ing metallurgy term
ni•tri•fi•able
ni•tri•fi•ca•tion
ni•tri•fy (•fies, •fy•ing,
  •fied)
ni•trile
ni•trite
ni•tro•bac•te•ria (sing.
  •rium)
ni•tro•ben•zene
ni•tro•cel•lu•lose
ni•tro•chlo•ro•form
ni•tro•gen
ni•trog•eni•za•tion (or
  •sa•tion)
ni•trog•en•ize (or •ise)
ni•trog•enous
ni•tro•glyc•er•in (or •ine)
ni•trom•eter
ni•tro•methane
ni•tro•met•ric
ni•tro•par•af•fin
ni•trosa•mine
ni•tro•so (or •syl)
ni•trous
nit•ty (•ti•er, •ti•est)
nitty-gritty
nit•wit
Niue Pacific island
ni•val of snow
ni•va•tion geology term
niv•eous resembling snow
Ni•ver•nais former French
  province
nix (fem nixie) water sprite
nix•er Irish spare-time job
Ni•zam Indian title
ni•zam former Turkish
  soldier

Nizh•ni (*or* •nii) Nov•go•rod
· Russian city
Njord (*or* Njorth) Norse god
no (*plural* noes *or* nos)
No (*or* Noh) Japanese drama
Noa•chian (*or* No•ach•ic) of
Noah
nob *Slang* wealthy person;
cribbage term; *compare*
knob
no-ball
nob•ble
nob•bler
nob•but *Dialect* nothing but
no•belium chemical
element
no•bili•ary
no•bil•ity (*plural* •ities)
no•ble
no•ble•man (*plural* •men)
no•ble•ness
no•blesse oblige *French*
nobility obliges
noble•woman (*plural*
•women)
no•bly
no•body (*plural* •bodies)
no•ci•cep•tive causing pain
nock notch on arrow
noc•tam•bu•lism (*or*
•la•tion)
noc•tam•bu•list
noc•ti•lu•ca (*plural* •cae)
protozoan
noc•ti•lu•cence
noc•ti•lu•cent
noc•tu•id moth
noc•tule bat
noc•turn part of Catholic
matins; *compare* nocturne
noc•tur•nal
noc•tur•nal•ity
noc•tur•nal•ly
noc•turne musical piece;
compare nocturn
nocu•ous
nod (nod•ding, nod•ded)
no•dal
no•dal•ity
nod•dle
nod•dy (*plural* •dies) bird;
fool
node
nodi•cal astronomy term
no•dose (*or* •dous)

no•dos•ity
nodu•lar (*or* •lose, •lous)
nod•ule
no•dus (*plural* •di)
problematic situation
Noel (*or* Noël)
no•esis intellectual
functioning
no•et•ic
nog
nog•gin measure of spirits
nog•ging building term
Noh *variant spelling of* No
noil textile fibres
noise
noise•less
noise•less•ness
noi•sette
noisi•ly
noisi•ness
noi•some offensive
noi•some•ness
noisy (noisi•er, noisi•est)
no•lens vo•lens *Latin*
willing or unwilling
noli-me-tangere warning;
plant
nol•le pros•equi legal term
nolo con•ten•de•re legal
term
noma medical term
no•mad
no•mad•ic
no•madi•cal•ly
no•mad•ism
no•man's-land
nom•arch
nom•ar•chy (*or* nome;
plural •chies *or* nomes)
Greek province
nom•bril heraldic term
nom de guerre (*plural* noms
de guerre) assumed name
nom de plume (*plural* noms
de plume) pen name
nome *variant of* nomarchy
no•men (*plural* nomi•na)
ancient Roman's name
no•men•cla•tor inventor of
names
no•men•cla•ture
nomi•nal
nomi•nal•ism
nomi•nal•ist
nomi•nal•is•tic

nomi•nal•ly
nomi•nate
nomi•na•tion
nomi•na•tive
nomi•na•tor
nomi•nee
no•mism theology term
no•mis•tic
no•moc•ra•cy (*plural* •cies)
government based on law
nomo•gram (*or* •graph)
type of graph
no•mog•ra•pher
nomo•graph•ic
nomo•graphi•cal
no•mo•graphi•cal•ly
no•mog•ra•phy (*plural*
•phies)
no•mo•logi•cal
no•mo•logi•cal•ly
no•molo•gist
no•mol•ogy science of law
nomo•thet•ic (*or* •theti•cal)
giving laws
no•nage
no•na•genar•ian
nona•gon
non-ago•nal
non-aligned
non-ap•pear•ance
non-at•tend•ance
non-at•tribu•tive
nonce
non-cha•lance
non-cha•lant
non-com *Slang*
noncommissioned officer
non-com•bat•ant
non-com•mis•sioned
non-com•mit•tal
non-com•mit•tal•ly
non-com•pli•ance
non com•pos men•tis *Latin*
of unsound mind
non-con•cur•rent
non-con•duc•tor
non-con•form•ism
Non-con•form•ist
dissenting Protestant
non-con•form•ist one who
does not conform
Non-con•form•ity (*or* •ism)
non-con•form•ity
non-con•sti•tu•tion•al
non-con•ta•gious

non·con·tribu·ting
non·con·tribu·tory
non·co·op·era·tion
non·co·op·era·tive
non·co·op·era·tor
non·cor·rod·ing
non·crea·tive
non·de·nomi·na·tion·al
non·de·script
non·dis·junc·tion
non·drink·er
none
non·ed·ible
non·ego philosophy term
non·en·tity (plural ·tities)
non·equiva·lence
nones Roman date;
    canonical hour
non·es·sen·tial
none·such (or non·)
non·et
none·the·less
non·ethi·cal
non·event
non·ex·ist·ence
non·ex·ist·ent
non·ex·plo·sive
non·fac·tual
non·fea·sance legal term
non·fer·rous
non·fic·tion
non·fic·tion·al
non·flam·mable
nong Austral stupid person
non·har·mon·ic
non·iden·ti·cal
non·idio·mat·ic
no·nil·lion 10^{54}
no·nil·lionth
non·in·dus·trial
non·in·fec·tious
non·in·flam·mable
non·inter·ven·tion
non·inter·ven·tion·al
non·inter·ven·tion·ist
non·in·toxi·cat·ing
non·ir·ri·tant
non·join·der legal term
non·judg·men·tal (or
    ·judge·)
non·ju·ror one refusing to
    take oath
non li·cet Latin unlawful
non·ma·lig·nant
non·medi·cal

non·mem·ber
non·met·al
non·met·al·lic
non·op·er·able
non·op·era·tive
non·pa·reil unsurpassed
non·par·ous never having
    given birth
non·par·tici·pat·ing
non·par·ti·san (or ·zan)
non·par·ty
non·plus (noun, plural
    ·pluses; verb ·plusses,
    ·plus·sing, ·plussed; US
    ·pluses, ·plus·ing,
    ·plused)
non·poi·son·ous
non·po·liti·cal
non·pro·duc·tive
non·pro·duc·tive·ness
non·pro·duc·tiv·ity
non·pro·gres·sive
non·pro·lif·era·tion
non·pros (-prosses,
    -prossing, -prossed) legal
    term
non pro·sequi·tur legal
    term
non·rep·re·sen·ta·tion·al
non·resi·dence (or ·den·cy)
non·resi·dent
non·resi·den·tial
non·re·sist·ant
non·re·stric·tive
non·re·turn·able
non·rig·id
non·sched·uled
non·sec·ta·rian
non·sense
non·sen·si·cal
non·sen·si·cal·ly
non·sen·si·cal·ness (or ·ity)
non se·qui·tur
non·slip
non·smok·er
non·spe·cif·ic
non·stand·ard
non·stand·ard·ized (or
    ·ised)
non·start·er
non·sta·tive linguistics term
non·stick
non·stimu·lat·ing
non·stop
non·stra·te·gic

non·striker
non·such variant spelling of
    nonesuch
non·suit
non·swim·mer
non·tech·ni·cal
non·tox·ic
non·typi·cal
non-U
non·un·ion
non·un·ion·ism
non·ver·bal
non·vio·lence
non·vio·lent
non·vot·er
non-White
noo·dle
nook
noon
noon·day
no-one (or no one)
noon·ing US midday break
noon·time (or ·tide)
noose
no·pal cactus
no-par (adj)
nope Slang no
nor
nor·adrena·line
Nor·dic
Nor·folk
no·ria waterwheel
Nori·cum Celtic Alpine
    kingdom
nor·ite rock
nork Austral breast
norm
Nor·ma constellation
nor·mal
nor·mal·ity (or esp. US ·cy)
nor·mali·za·tion (or
    ·sa·tion)
nor·mal·ize (or ·ise)
nor·mal·ly
Nor·man
Nor·man·dy
nor·ma·tive
Norn Norse goddess
Norr·kö·ping Swedish port
Norse
Norse·man (plural ·men)
north
North·al·ler·ton Yorkshire
    town
North·amp·ton

North·amp·ton·shire
north·bound
north·country·man (plural
·men)
north·east
north·easter
north·easter·ly (plural ·lies)
north·eastern
north·eastward
nor·ther·ly (plural ·lies)
north·ern
north·ern·er
north·ern·most
north·ing navigation term
north-northeast
north-northwest
North Pole
North·um·ber·land county
North·um·bria region
North·um·brian
north·ward (adj)
north·wards (adv)
north·west
north·wester
north·wester·ly (plural ·lies)
north·western
north·westward
North·wich Cheshire town
Nor·way
Nor·we·gian
Nor·wich
nose
nose·bag
nose·band
nose·bleed
nose-dive (verb)
nose·gay
nos·ey variant spelling of
nosy
nosh
no-side rugby term
nosi·ly
nosi·ness
nos·ing
no·so·co·mial medical term
no·sog·ra·pher
no·so·graph·ic
no·sog·ra·phy written
description of disease
noso·logi·cal
noso·logi·cal·ly
no·solo·gist
no·sol·ogy classification of
diseases
nos·tal·gia

nos·tal·gic
nos·tal·gi·cal·ly
nos·toc alga
nos·to·log·ic
nos·tol·ogy study of
senility
nos·tril
nos·trum quack medicine
nosy (or nos·ey; nosi·er,
nosi·est)
nosy-parker
not
nota bene Latin note well
no·tabil·ity (plural ·ities)
no·table
no·table·ness
no·tably
no·tar·ial
no·ta·rize (or ·rise)
no·ta·ry (plural ·ries)
no·tate
no·ta·tion
no·ta·tion·al
notch
note
note·book
note·case
not·ed
note·let
note·paper
note·worthi·ly
note·worthi·ness
note·worthy
noth·ing
noth·ing·ness
no·tice
no·tice·abil·ity
no·tice·able
no·tice·ably
no·ti·fi·able
no·ti·fi·ca·tion
no·ti·fi·er
no·ti·fy (·fies, ·fy·ing, ·fied)
no-tillage farming system
not·ing
no·tion
no·tion·al
no·tion·al·ly
no·titia ecclesiastical
register
no·to·chord zoology term
no·to·chord·al
No·to·gaea zoogeographical
term
No·to·gaean

no·to·ri·ety (or
no·to·ri·ous·ness)
no·to·ri·ous
no·tor·nis bird
no·to·ther·ium (plural
·theria) extinct marsupial
no·tour legal term
No·tre Dame
no-trump bridge term
Not·ting·ham
Not·ting·ham·shire
no·tum (plural ·ta)
entomology term
No·tus mythological wind
not·with·stand·ing
Nou·ak·chott capital of
Mauritania
nou·gat
nought (US naught) zero;
compare naught
nou·menon (plural ·mena)
philosophy term
noun
noun·al
nour·ish
nour·ish·er
nour·ish·ing·ly
nour·ish·ment
nous Slang common
sense
nou·veau riche (plural
nou·veaux riches)
nova (plural novae or
novas) star
no·vacu·lite rock
No·va·ra Italian city
Nova Sco·tia
no·va·tion legal term
nov·el
nov·el·ese
nov·el·ette
nov·el·et·tish
nov·el·ist
nov·el·is·tic
nov·eli·za·tion (or ·sa·tion)
nov·el·ize (or ·ise)
nov·el·la (plural ·las or ·le)
nov·el·ty (plural ·ties)
No·vem·ber
no·vena (plural ·venae)
Catholic devotion
Nov·go·rod Russian city
nov·ice
no·vi·ti·ate (or ·ci·ate)
No·vo·caine (Trademark)

No·vo·kuz·netsk Russian
city

No·vo·si·birsk Russian city

now

nowa·days

no·way

Now·el (or ·ell) Archaic Noel

no·where

nowt Dialect nothing

Nox Roman goddess

nox·ious

nox·ious·ness

no·yade execution by
drowning

noy·au (plural ·aux) liqueur

noz·zle

nth

nu·ance

nub

Nuba (plural Nubas or
Nuba) Sudanese people

nub·bin US undeveloped
fruit

nub·ble

nub·bly (or ·by)

nu·becu·la (plural ·lae)
small galaxy

Nu·bia

Nu·bian

nu·bile

nu·bil·ity

nu·cel·lar

nu·cel·lus (plural ·li) botany
term

nu·cha (plural ·chae) nape
of neck

nu·chal

nu·clear

nu·clease enzyme

nu·cleate

nu·clea·tion

nu·clea·tor

nu·clei plural of nucleus

nu·cleic

nu·clein protein

nu·cleo·lar (or ·late, ·lat·ed,
·loid)

nu·cleo·lus (plural ·li) part
of cell nucleus

nu·cleon

nu·cleon·ic

nu·cleoni·cal·ly

nu·cleon·ics branch of
physics

nu·cleo·phile

nu·cleo·phil·ic

nu·cleo·plasm

nu·cleo·plas·mic (or
·mat·ic)

nu·cleo·pro·tein

nu·cleo·side biochemical
compound

nu·cleo·tide biochemical
compound

nu·cleus (plural ·clei or
·cleuses)

nu·clide type of atom

nude

nude·ness

nudge

nudg·er

nu·di·branch mollusc

nu·di·caul (or ·cau·lous)
botany term

nud·ism

nud·ist

nu·dity (plural ·dities)

Nue·vo León Mexican state

nu·ga·tory

nug·gar sailing boat

nug·get

nug·gety

nui·sance

nuke Slang nuclear bomb

Nu·ku'a·lo·fa Tongan
capital

null

nul·lah Indian stream

nulla-nulla Aboriginal club

nul·li·fi·ca·tion

nul·li·fi·ca·tion·ist

nul·li·fid·ian sceptic

nul·li·fi·er

nul·li·fy (·fies, ·fy·ing,
·fied)

nul·lipa·ra (plural ·rae)
obstetrics term

nul·lipa·rous

nul·li·pore seaweed

nul·lity (plural ·lities)

Nu·man·tia ancient Spanish
city

numb

num·bat marsupial

num·ber numeral

numb·er more numb

num·ber·less

number·plate

numb·fish (plural ·fish or
·fishes)

numb·ness

numb·skull variant spelling
of numskull

num·dah (or nam·) Indian
fabric

nu·men (plural ·mi·na)
Roman deity

nu·mer·able

nu·mer·ably

nu·mera·cy

nu·mer·al

nu·mer·ary of numbers;
compare nummary

nu·mer·ate

nu·mera·tion

nu·mera·tive

nu·mera·tor

nu·meri·cal (or ·mer·ic)

nu·meri·cal·ly

nu·mero·logi·cal

nu·mer·ol·ogy divination
by numbers

nu·mer·ous

nu·mer·ous·ness

Nu·midia ancient African
country

Nu·mid·ian

nu·mi·nous awe-inspiring

nu·mis·mat·ic

nu·mis·mat·ics (or
·ma·tol·ogy)

nu·mis·ma·tist (or
·tolo·gist)

num·ma·ry of coins;
compare numerary

num·mu·lar

num·mu·lite fossil

num·mu·lit·ic

num·skull (or numb·)

nun

nuna·tak mountain
peak

Nunc Di·mit·tis canticle

nun·cia·ture

nun·cio (plural ·cios)

nun·cle Dialect uncle

nun·cu·pa·tive legal term

Nun·eaton

nun·hood

nun·like

nun·nery (plural ·neries)

Nupe (plural Nupe or
Nupes) Nigerian people

nup·tial

Nu·rem·berg

Nuri (*plural* Nuris *or* Nuri)
    Indo-European people
Nu·ri·stan Afghan region
nurse
nurse·maid
nurs·ery (*plural* ·ries)
nursery·man (*plural* ·men)
nurs·ing
nurs·ling (*or* nurse·) nursed
    child
nur·tur·able
nur·ture
nur·tur·er
nut (nut·ting, nut·ted)
nu·tant botany term
nu·ta·tion
nu·ta·tion·al
nut·brown
nut·case
nut·cracker
nut·gall
nut·hatch
nut·let
nut·meg
nu·tria coypu fur
nu·tri·ent
nu·tri·ment
nu·tri·tion

nu·tri·tion·al (*or* ·ary)
nu·tri·tion·ist
nu·tri·tious
nu·tri·tious·ness
nu·tri·tive
nut·shell
nut·ted
nut·ter
nut·ti·ly
nut·ti·ness
nut·ting
nut·ty (·ti·er, ·ti·est)
nut·wood
nux vomi·ca
nuz·zle
nya·la (*plural* ·la *or* ·las)
    antelope
Nyan·ja (*plural* ·ja *or* ·jas)
    African people
Ny·asa·land *former name of*
    Malawi
nyc·ta·gi·na·ceous botany
    term
nyc·ta·lo·pia night
    blindness
nyc·ti·nas·tic
nyc·ti·nas·ty botany term
nyc·ti·trop·ic

nyc·tit·ro·pism botany
    term
nyc·to·pho·bia
nyc·to·pho·bic
nye (*or* nide) flock of
    pheasants
ny·lon
nymph
nym·pha (*plural* ·phae)
    anatomy term
nym·phaea·ceous botany
    term
nym·phal (*or* ·phean)
nym·pha·lid butterfly
nymph·et
nymph·like
nym·pho (*plural* ·phos)
nym·pho·lep·sy (*plural*
    ·sies) violent emotion
nym·pho·lept
nym·pho·lep·tic
nym·pho·ma·nia
nym·pho·ma·ni·ac
nym·pho·ma·nia·cal
nys·tag·mic
nys·tag·mus eye condition
nys·ta·tin antibiotic
Nyx Greek goddess

O

O exclamation; *used chiefly
    in religious and poetic
    contexts*
oaf (*plural* oafs)
oaf·ish
oaf·ish·ness
oak
oak·en
Oak·ham Leicestershire
    town
Oak·land US port
oakum fibre
oar
oared
oar·fish (*plural* ·fish *or*
    ·fishes)
oar·lock
oars·man (*plural* ·men)
oars·man·ship
oasis (*plural* oases)
oast
oast·house

oat
oat·cake
oat·en
oath (*plural* oaths)
oat·meal
Oaxa·ca Mexican state
oba African chief
Oban Scottish port
ob·bli·ga·to (*or* ob·li·; *plural*
    ·tos *or* ·ti) musical term
ob·con·ic botany term
ob·cor·date botany term
ob·du·ra·cy (*or* ·rate·ness)
ob·du·rate
obeah *variant of* obi
obedi·ence
obedi·ent
obedi·en·tia·ry (*plural* ·ries)
    holder of monastic office
obei·sance
obei·sant
ob·elis·cal

ob·elisk
ob·elis·koid
ob·elize (*or* ·elise)
ob·elus (*plural* ·eli) text
    symbol
Ober·am·mer·gau German
    village
Ober·hau·sen German city
Ober·land Swiss region
Ober·on satellite of Uranus
Oberon fairy king
obese
obesity (*or* obese·ness)
obey
obey·er
ob·fus·cate
ob·fus·ca·tion
ob·fus·ca·tory
obi (*plural* obis *or* obi)
    Japanese sash
obi (*or* obeah; *plural* obis *or*
    obeahs) witchcraft

obit obituary; memorial
service
obi·ter dic·tum (plural
obi·ter dic·ta) Latin
something said in passing
obi·tu·ar·ist
obi·tu·ary (plural ·aries)
ob·ject
ob·jec·ti·fi·ca·tion
ob·jec·ti·fy (·fies, ·fy·ing,
·fied)
ob·jec·tion
ob·jec·tion·abil·ity (or
·able·ness)
ob·jec·tion·able
ob·jec·tion·ably
ob·jec·tive
ob·jec·tiv·ism
ob·jec·tiv·ist
ob·jec·tiv·is·tic
ob·jec·tiv·is·ti·cal·ly
ob·jec·tiv·ity (or ·tive·ness)
ob·jet d'art (plural ob·jets
d'art)
ob·jet trou·vé (plural ob·jets
trou·vés) French object
considered aesthetically
ob·jur·gate scold
ob·jur·ga·tion
ob·jur·ga·tor
ob·jur·ga·tory (or ·tive)
ob·lan·ceo·late botany term
ob·last Russian
administrative division
ob·late
ob·la·tion
ob·la·tory (or ·tion·al)
ob·li·gable
ob·li·gate
ob·li·ga·tion
ob·li·ga·tion·al
ob·liga·tive
ob·li·ga·to variant spelling of
obbligato
ob·li·ga·tor
ob·liga·to·ri·ly
ob·liga·tory
oblige
ob·li·gee creditor
oblig·er
oblig·ing
ob·li·gor debtor
oblique
oblique·ness
obliqui·tous

obliqui·ty (plural ·ties)
oblit·erate
oblit·era·tion
oblit·era·tive
oblit·era·tor
blivi·on
oblivi·ous
ob·livi·ous·ness
ob·long
ob·lo·quy (plural ·quies)
ob·nox·ious
ob·nox·ious·ness
ob·nu·bil·ate to darken
oboe
obo·ist
obo·lus (or obol; plural ·li or
obols) Greek unit; coin
ob·ovate botany term
ob·ovoid botany term
ob·rep·tion obtaining by
deceit
ob·scene
ob·scen·ity (plural ·ities)
ob·scur·ant
ob·scu·rant·ism
ob·scu·rant·ist
ob·scu·ra·tion
ob·scure
ob·scu·rity (plural ·rities)
ob·se·quent
ob·se·quies (sing. ·quy)
ob·se·qui·ous
ob·se·qui·ous·ness
ob·serv·able
ob·serv·able·ness (or
·abil·ity)
ob·serv·ably
ob·ser·vance
ob·ser·vant
ob·ser·va·tion
ob·ser·va·tion·al
ob·ser·va·tion·al·ly
ob·ser·va·tory (plural
·tories)
ob·serve
ob·serv·er
ob·sess
ob·ses·sion
ob·ses·sion·al
ob·ses·sive
ob·ses·sive·ness
ob·sid·ian
ob·so·lesce
ob·so·les·cence
ob·so·les·cent

ob·so·lete
ob·so·lete·ness
ob·sta·cle
ob·stet·ric (or ·ri·cal)
ob·stet·ri·cal·ly
ob·ste·tri·cian
ob·stet·rics
ob·sti·na·cy (plural ·cies)
ob·sti·nate
ob·sti·pa·tion
ob·strep·er·ous
ob·strep·er·ous·ness
ob·struct
ob·struct·er (or ·struc·tor)
ob·struc·tion
ob·struc·tion·al
ob·struc·tion·ism
ob·struc·tion·ist
ob·struc·tive
ob·struc·tive·ness
ob·stru·ent medical term
ob·tain
ob·tain·abil·ity
ob·tain·able
ob·tain·er
ob·tain·ment
ob·tect entomology
term
ob·trude
ob·trud·er
ob·tru·sion
ob·tru·sive
ob·tru·sive·ness
ob·tund deaden
ob·tu·rate block up
ob·tu·ra·tion
ob·tu·ra·tor
ob·tuse
ob·tuse·ness
ob·verse
ob·ver·sion
ob·vert logic term
ob·vi·ate
ob·via·tion
ob·vi·ous
ob·vi·ous·ly
ob·vi·ous·ness
ob·vo·lute
ob·vo·lu·tion
ob·vo·lu·tive
oca plant
oca·ri·na musical
instrument
oc·ca·sion
oc·ca·sion·al

oc·ca·sion·al·ism
philosophical theory
oc·ca·sion·al·ly
Oc·ci·dent Europe and
America
oc·ci·dent the west
Oc·ci·den·tal (*noun*)
oc·ci·den·tal (*or* Oc·; *adj*)
Oc·ci·den·tal·ism
Oc·ci·den·tal·ist
oc·ci·den·tali·za·tion (*or*
Oc·, ·sa·tion)
oc·ci·den·tal·ize (*or* Oc·,
·ise)
oc·ci·den·tal·ly (*or* Oc·)
oc·cipi·tal
oc·ci·put (*plural* ·puts *or*
·cipi·ta) anatomy term
oc·clude
oc·clud·ent
oc·clu·sal
oc·clu·sion
oc·clu·sive
oc·clu·sive·ness
oc·cult
oc·cul·ta·tion astronomy
term
oc·cult·ism
oc·cult·ist
oc·cu·pan·cy (*plural* ·cies)
oc·cu·pant
oc·cu·pa·tion
oc·cu·pa·tion·al
oc·cu·pi·er
oc·cu·py (·pies, ·py·ing,
·pied)
oc·cur (·cur·ring, ·curred)
oc·cur·rence
oc·cur·rent
ocean
ocean·ar·ium (*plural*
·ar·iums *or* ·aria)
ocean-going
Oceania Pacific islands
Oce·an·ian
Ocean·ic of Oceania
ocean·ic of the ocean
Ocea·nid (*plural* Ocea·nids
or Oceani·des) Greek
nymph
ocean·og·ra·pher
oceano·graph·ic (*or*
·graphi·cal)
oceano·graphi·cal·ly
ocean·og·ra·phy

ocean·ol·ogy
ocel·lar
oc·el·late (*or* ·lated) having
ocelli; *compare* oscillate;
osculate
oc·el·la·tion
ocel·lus (*plural* ·li) simple
eye
oc·elot
och *Scot* exclamation
ocher *US spelling of* ochre
och·loc·ra·cy (*plural* ·cies)
mob rule
och·lo·crat
och·lo·crat·ic
och·lo·pho·bia fear of
crowds
ochre (*US* ocher)
ochre·ous (*or* ochrous,
ochry; *US* ocher·ous *or*
ochery)
ochroid
ock·er *Austral* boorish
person
o'clock
oco·til·lo (*plural* ·los) tree
oc·rea (*or* och·; *plural* ·reae)
sheath
oc·re·ate
oc·ta·chord musical
instrument
oc·tad
oc·tad·ic
oc·ta·gon (*or* ·tan·gle)
oc·tago·nal
oc·tago·nal·ly
oc·ta·he·dral
oc·ta·he·drite
oc·ta·he·dron (*plural* ·drons
or ·dra)
oc·tal number system
oc·tam·er·ous
oc·tam·eter
oc·tane
oc·tan·gu·lar
Oc·tans constellation
oc·tant eighth part of circle
oc·tar·chy (*plural* ·chies)
(octaroon) *incorrect spelling
of* octoroon
oc·ta·va·lent
oc·tave
oc·ta·vo (*plural* ·vos) book
size
oc·ten·nial

oc·ten·nial·ly
oc·tet
oc·til·lion 10^{48}
oc·til·lionth
Oc·to·ber
oc·to·deci·mo (*plural* ·mos)
oc·to·genar·ian (*or*
oc·tog·enary; *plural* ·ians
or ·enaries)
(octogon) *incorrect spelling of*
octagon
(octohedral) *incorrect spelling
of* octahedral
oc·to·pod
oc·to·pus (*plural* ·puses)
oc·to·roon
oc·to·syl·lab·ic
oc·to·syl·la·ble
oc·troi duty on goods
oc·tu·ple
ocu·lar
ocu·lar·ist artificial-eye
maker
ocu·list ophthalmologist
ocu·lo·mo·tor
oda·lisque (*or* ·lisk)
odd
odd·ball
odd·ity (*plural* ·ities)
odd·ly
odd·ment
odd·ness
odd-pinnate botany term
odds-on
ode
Oden·se Danish port
Oder European river
Odes·sa Ukrainian port
odeum (*plural* odea)
(building for musical
performances; *compare*
odium; oidium
Odin (*or* Othin) Norse
god
odi·ous
odi·ous·ness
odium hatred; *compare*
odeum; oidium
odom·eter (*or* ho·dom·) *US*
mileometer
od·on·tal·gia toothache
od·on·tal·gic
odon·to·blast
odon·to·blas·tic
odon·to·glos·sum orchid

odon·to·graph gear-tooth marking aid
odon·to·graph·ic
od·on·tog·ra·phy
odon·toid
odon·to·logi·cal
od·on·tolo·gist
od·on·tol·ogy science of teeth
od·on·topho·ral (or ·toph·or·ous)
odon·to·phore zoology term
odor US spelling of odour
odor·if·er·ous
odor·ous
odor·ous·ness
odour (US odor)
odour·less (US odor·)
Od·ys·sean
Odysseus mythological hero
Od·ys·sey poem
oede·ma (US ede·; plural ·ma·ta)
oedema·tous (or ·tose; US edema·)
oedi·pal (or ·pean)
Oedipus mythological character
oeil·lade suggestive glance
oeno·logi·cal (US eno·)
oenolo·gist (US es·)
oenol·ogy (US enol·) study of wine
oeno·mel drink
Oenone Greek nymph
o'er over
oer·sted unit
oesopha·geal (US esopha·)
oesopha·gus (US esopha·; plural ·gi)
oes·tra·di·ol (US es·) hormone
oes·tri·ol (US es·) hormone
oes·tro·gen (US es·)
oes·tro·gen·ic (US es·)
oes·tro·geni·cal·ly (US es·)
oes·trone (US es·) hormone
oes·trous (adj; US es·)
oes·trus (noun; US es·)
oeuvre work of art
of
off
of·fal
Of·fa·ly Irish county

off·beat
off·centre
off·drive (·driving, ·drove, ·driven)
Of·fen·bach German city
of·fence (US ·fense)
of·fend
of·fend·er
of·fen·sive
of·fen·sive·ness
of·fer
of·fer·er (or ·fe·ror)
of·fer·ing
of·fer·tory (plural ·tories)
off·glide
off·hand
off·handed
off·handed·ly
off·hand·ed·ness
of·fice
of·fic·er
of·fi·cial
of·fi·cial·dom
of·fi·cial·ese
of·fi·cial·ly
of·fi·ci·ant
of·fi·ci·ary (plural ·aries) body of officials
of·fi·ci·ate
of·fi·cia·tion
of·fi·cia·tor
of·fi·cious
of·fi·cious·ness
of·fing
of·fish
off·key (adj)
off·licence
off·line (adj)
off·load
off·peak
off·print
off·putting
off·season (adj)
off·set (·set·ting, ·set)
off·shoot
off·shore
off·side
off·spring
off·stage
off·white
oft
of·ten
Oga·den Ethiopian region
Og·bo·mo·sho Nigerian city
og·do·ad group of eight

ogee architectural moulding
og·ham (or ogam) ancient writing
ogiv·al
ogive architectural term
ogle
ogler
Ogo·oué (or ·we) African river
ogre (fem ogress)
ogre·ish
Ogyg·ian prehistoric
oh
Ohio
ohm
ohm·age
ohm·meter
oid·ium (plural ·ia) fungal spore
oil
oil·bird
oil·can
oil·cloth
oil·cup
oil·er
oil·field
oil·fired
oili·ly
oili·ness
oil·man (plural ·men)
oil·skin
oil·stone
oily (oili·er, oili·est)
oint·ment
Oi·reach·tas Irish parliament
Oita Japanese city
OK (or okay; noun, plural OK's or okays; verb OK'ing, OK'ed or okay·ing, okayed)
oka (or oke) Turkish weight
oka·pi (plural ·pis or ·pi)
okay variant of OK
Oka·ya·ma Japanese city
Okee·cho·bee Florida lake
okey-doke (or -dokey)
Oki·na·wa Japanese island
Ok·la·ho·ma
Okla·ho·man
okra vegetable
okta meteorological unit
old
Old Bai·ley
old·en

Ol·den·burg German city
old·er
old·fangled
old-fashioned
Old·ham English town
oldie
old·ness
old-time
old-timer
Ol·du·vai Tanzanian
  gorge
old·wife (*plural* •wives)
  duck; fish
old-world
olé Spanish exclamation
olea·ceous botany term
oleagi·nous oily
olean·der shrub
oleas·ter shrub
oleate chemistry term
olec·ra·nal
olec·ra·non anatomy term
olefine (*or* olefin)
olefin·ic
oleic acid
oleo·graph
oleo·graph·ic
oleog·ra·phy
oleo·res·in
oleo·res·in·ous
oleum (*plural* olea *or*
  oleums) chemistry term
ol·fac·tion
ol·fac·tory (*plural* •tories)
oliba·num frankincense
olid foul-smelling
oli·garch
oli·gar·chic (*or* •chi·cal)
oli·gar·chi·cal·ly
oli·gar·chy (*plural* •chies)
Oli·go·cene geological
  period
oli·go·chaete worm
oli·go·clase mineral
oli·gopo·lis·tic
oli·gopo·ly (*plural* •lies)
  economics term
oli·gop·so·nis·tic
oli·gop·so·ny (*plural* •nies)
  economics term
oli·go·sac·cha·ride
oli·go·troph·ic ecology
  term
oli·got·ro·phy
oli·gu·ret·ic

oli·gu·ria (*or* •resis) medical
  term
olio (*plural* olios) miscellany
oli·va·ceous
oli·vary
ol·ive
oliv·en·ite mineral
oli·vine mineral
olla cooking pot
olla po·dri·da Spanish stew
ol·ogy (*plural* •ogies) *Slang*
  branch of knowledge
olo·ro·so (*plural* •sos) sherry
Olym·pia
Olym·pi·ad
Olym·pian
Olym·pic
Olym·pus Greek mountain
Om Hindu syllable
oma·dhaun *Irish* fool
Omagh Irish town
Oma·ha US city
Oman Arabian sultanate
Omani
oma·sum (*plural* •sa) cow's
  stomach
Omay·yad (*or* Umay·; *plural*
  •yads *or* •ya·des) caliph
om·bre (*US* •ber) card game
om·buds·man (*plural* •men)
Om·dur·man Sudanese city
omega
ome·lette (*or esp. US*
  ome·let)
omen
omen·tal
omen·tum (*plural* •ta)
  anatomy term
omer Hebrew unit
omi·cron Greek letter
omi·nous
omi·nous·ness
omis·sible
omis·sion
omit (omit·ting, omit·ted)
omit·ter
om·ma·tid·ial
om·ma·tid·ium (*plural*
  •tidia) zoology term
om·mato·phore zoology
  term
om·ma·topho·rous
om·ni·bus (*plural* •buses)
om·ni·com·pe·tence
om·ni·com·pe·tent

om·ni·di·rec·tion·al
om·ni·fari·ous of all sorts
om·nif·ic (*or* om·nifi·cent)
om·nipo·tence
om·nipo·tent
om·ni·pres·ence
om·ni·pres·ent
om·ni·range navigation
  system
om·nis·ci·ence
om·nis·ci·ent
omnium-gather·um
  assortment
om·ni·vore
om·niv·or·ous
omo·pha·gia (*or*
  omoph·agy) eating raw
  food
omo·phag·ic (*or*
  omopha·gous)
Omphale mythological
  queen
om·pha·los sacred object
Omu·ta Japanese city
on
ona·ger (*plural* •gri *or* •gers)
  wild ass
ona·gra·ceous botany term
onan·ism
onan·ist
once
once-over
onco·gene
on·co·gen·ic (*or*
  on·cog·enous)
on·co·logi·cal
on·colo·gist
on·col·ogy study of
  tumours
on·coming
on·cost
on·do·gram
on·do·graph
on·dom·eter
one
Onei·da (*plural* •das *or* •da)
  US city and lake; American
  Indian
onei·ric of dreams
onei·ro·crit·ic
onei·ro·criti·cal
one·ness
one-off
oner *Slang* something
  outstanding

on·er·ous
on·er·ous·ness
one·self
one-sided
one-sidedness
one-step
one-time
one-to-one
one-track
one-upmanship
one-way
on-glide
on·going
on·ion
onion·skin paper
on·iony
Onit·sha Nigerian port
on·looker
on·looking
only
ono·ma·si·ol·ogy
ono·mas·tic
ono·mas·tics study of
    proper names
ono·mato·poeia
ono·mato·poe·ic (or
    ·po·et·ic)
ono·mato·poei·cal·ly (or
    ·po·eti·cal·ly)
on·rush
on·set
on·shore
on·side sports term
on·slaught
on·stage
On·tario
onto
on·to·gen·ic (or
    ·ge·net·ic)
on·to·geni·cal·ly (or
    ·ge·neti·cal·ly)
on·tog·eny (or ·to·gen·esis)
    biology term
on·to·logi·cal
on·to·logi·cal·ly
on·tol·ogy philosophy term
onus (plural onuses)
onus pro·ban·di burden of
    proof
on·ward
on·wards
ony·chopho·ran zoology
    term
ony·mous bearing author's
    name

onyx gemstone; compare
    oryx
oocyte biology term
oodles
oof Slang money
ooga·mous
oog·amy biology term
oogen·esis
ooge·net·ic
oogo·nial
oogo·nium (plural ·nia or
    ·niums) biology term
ooh exclamation
oolite rock
oolit·ic
oologi·cal
oolo·gist
ool·ogy study of birds' eggs
oolong tea
oomi·ak variant spelling of
    umiak
oom·pah
oopho·rec·to·my (plural
    ·mies) removal of ovary
oopho·rit·ic
oopho·ri·tis
oophyte botany term
oophyt·ic
oosperm
oosphere botany term
oospore
oo·spor·ic (or ·ous)
ootheca (plural oothecae)
    zoology term
oothecal
ootid zoology term
ooze
oozi·ly
oozi·ness
oozy (oozi·er, oozi·est)
opac·ity (plural ·ities)
opah fish
opal
opa·lesce
opal·es·cence
opal·es·cent
opal·ine
opaque (opaqu·ing,
    opaqued)
opaque·ness
open
open-and-shut
open·cast
open-ended
open·er

open-eyed
open-faced
open·handed
open·handed·ness
open·hearted
open·hearted·ness
open·ing
open-minded
open-minded·ness
open-mouthed
open·ness
open·work
op·era
op·er·abil·ity
op·er·able
op·er·and maths term
op·er·ant
op·er·ate
op·er·at·ic
op·er·ati·cal·ly
op·er·at·ics
op·era·tion
op·era·tion·al
op·era·tion·al·ism (or
    ·tion·ism) science term
op·era·tion·al·ist·ic
op·era·tion·al·ly
op·era·tive
op·era·tive·ness (or ·tiv·ity)
op·era·tize (or ·tise) make
    into an opera
op·era·tor
oper·cu·lar (or ·late)
oper·cu·lum (plural ·la or
    ·lums) biology term
op·er·et·ta
op·er·et·tist
op·er·on genetics term
ophi·cleide musical
    instrument
ophid·ian
ophio·logi·cal
ophi·olo·gist
ophi·ol·ogy study of snakes
Ophir biblical region
ophite rock
ophit·ic
Ophiu·chus constellation
oph·thal·mia
oph·thal·mic
oph·thal·mi·tis
oph·thal·mo·logi·cal
oph·thal·molo·gist
oph·thal·mol·ogy
oph·thal·mo·scope

oph·thal·mo·scop·ic
oph·thal·mos·co·py
opi·ate
opine
opin·ion
opin·ion·at·ed (*or* opin·iona·tive)
opin·ion·at·ed·ness
opis·tho·branch zoology term
op·is·thog·na·thism
op·is·thog·na·thous
opium
opi·um·ism
Opor·to Portuguese port
opos·sum (*plural* ·sums *or* ·sum)
op·pi·dan urban
op·pi·late to block
op·pi·la·tion
op·po·nen·cy
op·po·nent
op·por·tune
op·por·tune·ness
op·por·tun·ism
op·por·tun·ist
op·por·tun·is·tic
op·por·tu·ni·ty (*plural* ·nities)
op·pos·abil·ity
op·pos·able
op·pos·ably
op·pose
op·pos·er
op·pos·ing·ly
op·po·site on the other side of; *compare* apposite
op·po·site·ness
Op·po·si·tion parliamentary party
op·po·si·tion
op·po·si·tion·al
op·po·si·tion·ist
op·press
op·pres·sing·ly
op·pres·sion
op·pres·sive
op·pres·sive·ness
op·pres·sor
op·pro·bri·ous
op·pro·brium
op·pugn to dispute
op·pug·nant
op·pug·ner
Ops Roman goddess

op·son·ic
op·so·nin
op·so·ni·za·tion (*or* ·sa·tion, ·soni·fi·ca·tion)
op·so·nize (*or* ·nise, ·soni·fy) medical term
opt
op·ta·tive expressing a wish
(opthalmic) *incorrect spelling of* ophthalmic
(opthalmology) *incorrect spelling of* ophthalmology
op·tic
op·ti·cal
op·ti·cal·ly
op·ti·cian
op·tics
op·ti·mal
op·ti·mal·ly
op·ti·mism
op·ti·mist
op·ti·mis·tic (*or* ·ti·cal)
op·ti·mis·ti·cal·ly
op·ti·mi·za·tion (*or* ·sa·tion)
op·ti·mize (*or* ·mise)
op·ti·mum (*plural* ·ma *or* ·mums)
op·tion
op·tion·al
op·tion·al·ly
op·tom·eter
op·to·met·ric
op·tom·etrist ophthalmic optician
op·tom·etry
opu·lence (*or* ·len·cy)
opu·lent
opun·tia plant
opus (*plural* opuses *or* opera)
or
or·ache (*or esp. US* or·ach) plant
ora·cle
oracu·lar
ora·cy
Ora·dea Romanian city
oral of the mouth; *compare* aural
oral·ly
Oran Algerian port
or·ange
or·ange·ade
Or·ange·ism

Orange·man (*plural* ·men) Irish Protestant
or·ang·ery (*plural* ·eries)
orange·wood
orang-utan (*or* -outang)
orate
ora·tion
ora·tor
ora·tori·cal
ora·to·rio (*plural* ·rios)
ora·tory (*plural* ·tories)
orb
or·bicu·lar (*or* ·late, ·lat·ed)
or·bicu·lar·ity
or·bit
or·bit·al
orc whale
Or·cad·ian of the Orkneys
or·cein dye
or·chard
or·ches·tra
or·ches·tral
or·ches·tral·ly
or·ches·trate
or·ches·tra·tion
or·ches·tra·tor
or·ches·tri·na (*or* ·on) musical instrument
or·chid
or·chi·da·ceous
or·chil (*or* ar·) lichen; dye
or·chis orchid
or·chit·ic
or·chi·tis inflammation of testicle
or·ci·nol (*or* or·cin) chemical compound
Or·cus Roman god
or·dain
or·dain·er
or·dain·ment
or·deal
or·der
or·der·er
or·der·li·ness
or·der·ly (*plural* ·lies)
or·di·nal
or·di·nance decree; *compare* ordnance; ordonnance
or·di·nand
or·di·nari·ly
or·di·nari·ness
or·di·nary (*plural* ·naries)
or·di·nate
or·di·na·tion

ord·nance weaponry; *compare* ordinance; ordonnance

or·don·nance systematic arrangement; *compare* ordnance; ordinance

Or·do·vi·cian geological period

or·dure excrement

Or·dzho·ni·ki·dze (*or* Or·jo·) *former name of* Vladikavkas

ore mineral

öre (*plural* öre) Swedish currency

øre (*plural* øre) Danish or Norwegian currency

oread Greek nymph

Örebro Swedish town

orec·tic of desire

orega·no

Or·egon

Oren·burg Russian city

Orestes mythological character

orfe fish

or·fray *variant spelling of* orphrey

or·gan

or·gan·die (*US* ·dy; *plural* ·dies)

or·ga·nelle

or·gan·ic

or·gani·cal·ly

or·gani·cism biological theory

or·gani·cist

or·gani·cis·tic

or·gan·ism

or·gan·is·mal (*or* ·mic)

or·gan·ist

or·gani·za·tion (*or* ·sa·tion)

or·gani·za·tion·al (*or* ·sa·tion·al)

or·gan·ize (*or* ·ise)

or·gan·iz·er (*or* ·is·er)

or·gano·gen·esis

or·gano·genet·ic

or·gano·geneti·cal·ly

or·gano·graph·ic (*or* ·graphi·cal)

or·gan·og·ra·phist

or·gan·og·ra·phy

or·gano·lep·tic

or·gano·logi·cal

or·gan·olo·gist

or·gan·ol·ogy

or·gano·metal·lic

or·ga·non (*or* ·num; *plural* ·na, ·nons, *or* ·nums) philosophy term

or·gano·phos·phate

or·gano·thera·peu·tic

or·gano·thera·py

or·ga·num (*plural* ·na *or* ·nums) music; *variant spelling of* organon

or·gan·za fabric

or·gan·zine silk thread

or·gasm

or·gas·mic (*or* ·tic)

or·geat barley drink

or·gi·as·tic

orgy (*plural* orgies)

ori·bi (*plural* ·bi *or* ·bis) antelope

ori·el window; *compare* oriole

Ori·ent eastern countries

ori·ent the east; *variant of* orientate

Ori·en·tal (*noun*)

ori·en·tal (*or* Ori·; *adj*)

Ori·en·tal·ism

Ori·en·tal·ist

ori·en·tali·za·tion (*or* Ori·, ·sa·tion)

ori·en·tal·ize (*or* Ori·, ·ise)

ori·en·tal·ly (*or* Ori·)

ori·en·tate (*or* ori·ent)

ori·en·ta·tion

ori·en·ta·tion·al

Ori·en·te Cuban province

ori·en·teer·ing

ori·fice

ori·flamme flag

ori·ga·mi paper folding

ori·ga·num marjoram or oregano

ori·gin

origi·nal

origi·nal·ity (*plural* ·ities)

origi·nal·ly

origi·nate

origi·na·tion

origi·na·tor

ori·na·sal phonetics term; *compare* oronasal

Ori·no·co South American river

ori·ole bird; *compare* oriel

Ori·on constellation

Orion mythological character

ori·son prayer

Oris·sa Indian state

Ori·ya (*plural* ·ya) Indian people

Ori·za·ba Mexican city

Ork·ney Is·lands (*or* Ork·neys)

orle heraldic term

Or·lé·ans French city

Or·lon (*Trademark*)

or·lop nautical term

Orly Parisian suburb

or·mer mollusc

or·mo·lu decoration

Or·muz *variant spelling of* Hormuz

or·na·ment

or·na·men·tal

or·na·men·tal·ly

or·na·men·ta·tion

or·nate

or·nate·ness

or·nith·ic of birds

or·ni·thine amino acid

or·ni·this·chian zoology term

or·ni·tho·logi·cal

or·ni·tho·logi·cal·ly

or·ni·tholo·gist

or·ni·thol·ogy

or·ni·tho·man·cy divination from bird behaviour

or·ni·tho·pod dinosaur

or·ni·thop·ter (*or* or·thop·ter) aircraft

or·ni·tho·rhyn·chus platypus

or·ni·thos·co·py divination by bird observation

or·ni·tho·sis

oro·ban·cha·ceous botany term

oro·gen·ic (*or* ·ge·net·ic)

oro·geni·cal·ly (*or* ·geneti·cal·ly)

orog·eny (*or* oro·gen·esis) mountain formation

orog·ra·pher (*or* orolo·gist)

oro·graph·ic (*or* oro·logi·cal)

oro·graphi·cal·ly (*or* oro·logi·cal·ly)

orog·ra·phy (*or* orol·ogy) mapping mountain relief

oro·ide alloy

orom·eter

Oron·tes Asian river

oro·tund resonant; pompous; *compare* rotund

or·phan

or·phan·age

or·phari·on lute

Or·phean

Orpheus

Or·phic

Or·phism ancient Greek religion

or·phrey (*or* ·fray) border on vestment

or·pi·ment mineral

or·pine (*or* ·pin) plant

or·re·ry (*plural* ·ries) model of solar system

or·ris (*or* ·rice) plant

or·ta·nique fruit

or·thi·con electronic device

ortho·cen·tre (*US* ·ter) maths term

ortho·cephal·ic (*or* ·cepha·lous) anatomy term

ortho·cepha·ly

ortho·chro·mat·ic

ortho·chro·ma·tism

ortho·clase mineral

ortho·don·tic

ortho·don·tics (*or* ·don·tia)

or·tho·don·tist

Ortho·dox religion

ortho·dox conforming

ortho·doxy (*plural* ·doxies)

ortho·ep·ic

ortho·epi·cal·ly

ortho·epy correct pronunciation

ortho·gen·esis

ortho·ge·net·ic

ortho·geneti·cal·ly

ortho·gen·ic medical term

ortho·geni·cal·ly

or·thog·na·thism (*or* ·thy)

or·thog·na·thous anatomy term

or·thogo·nal

or·thogo·nal·ly

or·thog·ra·pher (*or* ·phist)

ortho·graph·ic (*or* ·graphi·cal)

ortho·graphi·cal·ly

or·thog·ra·phy (*plural* ·phies)

ortho·hy·dro·gen

ortho·mor·phic

ortho·paedic (*US* ·pedic)

ortho·paedics (*US* ·pedics)

ortho·paedist (*US* ·pedist)

ortho·phos·phate

ortho·psy·chi·at·ric

ortho·psy·chia·trist

ortho·psy·chia·try

or·thop·ter *variant of* ornithopter

or·thop·ter·an (*or* ·on; *plural* ·ans *or* ·tera) insect

or·thop·ter·ous (*or* ·an)

or·thop·tic

or·thop·tics

or·thop·tist

ortho·rhom·bic crystallography term

ortho·scop·ic

or·thos·ti·chous

or·thos·ti·chy (*plural* ·chies) botany term

ortho·trop·ic

or·thot·ro·pism

or·thot·ro·pous botany term

or·to·lan bird

orts *Dialect* scraps

Oru·ro Bolivian city

Or·vie·to Italian town; wine

Or·wel·lian

oryx (*plural* or·yxes *or* oryx) antelope; *compare* onyx

os (*plural* ossa) bone

os (*plural* ora) mouth

Osage (*plural* Osages *or* Osage) American Indian

Osa·ka Japanese port

Os·car film award

os·cil·late fluctuate regularly; *compare* ocellate; osculate

os·cil·la·tion

os·cil·la·tor

os·cil·la·tory

os·cil·lo·gram

os·cil·lo·graph

os·cil·lo·graph·ic

os·cil·log·ra·phy

os·cil·lo·scope

os·cine ornithology term

os·ci·tan·cy (*or* ·tance; *plural* ·tan·cies *or* ·tances)

os·ci·tant drowsy

os·cu·lant biology term

os·cu·lar

os·cu·late kiss; maths term; *compare* ocellate; oscillate

os·cu·la·tion

os·cu·la·tory

os·cu·lum (*plural* ·la) mouthlike part

Osha·wa Canadian city

Oshog·bo Nigerian city

osier willow tree

Osiris Egyptian god

Oslo

Os·man·li of Ottoman Empire

os·mic

os·mi·ous *variant of* osmous

os·mi·rid·ium alloy

os·mium metal

os·mom·eter

os·mo·met·ric

os·mo·met·ri·cal·ly

os·mom·etry

os·mose undergo osmosis

os·mo·sis (*plural* ·ses)

os·mot·ic

os·moti·cal·ly

os·mous (*or* ·mi·ous)

os·mun·da (*or* ·mund) fern

Os·na·brück German city

os·na·burg fabric

os·prey

Ossa Greek mountain

os·sein protein

os·seous bony

Os·setia Georgian and Russian region

Os·set·ic (*or* ·se·tian)

Ossian legendary Irish bard

os·si·cle small bone

os·sicu·lar

os·sif·er·ous

os·si·fi·ca·tion

os·si·fi·er

os·si·frage bird

os·si·fy (·fies, ·fy·ing, ·fied)

os·su·ary (*plural* ·aries) urn for bones

os·teal

os·tei·tic
os·tei·tis
Os·tend Belgian port
os·ten·sibil·ity
os·ten·sible
os·ten·sibly
os·ten·sive
os·ten·sory (plural ·sories) container for Host
os·ten·ta·tion
os·ten·ta·tious
os·teo·ar·thrit·ic
os·teo·ar·thri·tis
os·teo·blast bone cell
os·teo·blas·tic
os·teoc·la·sis medical term
os·teo·clast
os·teo·clas·tic
os·teo·gen·esis
os·teoid
os·teo·logi·cal
os·teo·logi·cal·ly
os·teolo·gist
os·teol·ogy study of bones
os·teo·ma (plural ·ma·ta or ·mas) tumour
os·teo·ma·la·cia
os·teo·ma·la·cial (or ·lac·ic)
os·teo·my·eli·tis
os·teo·path (or ·teopa·thist)
os·teo·path·ic
os·teo·pathi·cal·ly
os·teopa·thy
os·teo·phyte bony outgrowth
os·teo·phyt·ic
os·teo·plas·tic
os·teo·plas·ty (plural ·ties) bone grafting
os·teo·por·o·sis
os·teo·tome surgical instrument
os·teoto·my (plural ·mies)
Os·tia ancient Italian town
os·ti·ary (plural ·aries) Catholic official
os·ti·na·to (plural ·tos) musical term
os·tio·lar
os·ti·ole pore
os·tium (plural ·tia) biology term
ost·ler (or host·ler)
ost·mark former East German currency

os·to·sis formation of bone
os·tra·cism
os·tra·ciz·able (or ·cis·)
os·tra·cize (or ·cise)
os·tra·ciz·er (or ·cis·er)
os·tra·cod tiny animal
os·tra·co·dan (or ·dous)
os·tra·co·derm extinct fish
Os·tra·va Czech city
os·trich (plural ·triches or ·trich)
Os·tro·goth
otal·gia earache
oth·er
other-direct·ed
other·gates Archaic otherwise
oth·er·ness
other·where Archaic elsewhere
other·wise
other·worldli·ness
other·worldly
otic of the ear
oti·ose futile
oti·os·ity (or ·ose·ness)
oti·tis
oto·cyst
oto·cys·tic
oto·la·ryn·go·logi·cal
oto·lar·yn·golo·gist
oto·lar·yn·gol·ogy
oto·lith
oto·lith·ic
oto·logi·cal
otolo·gist
otol·ogy
oto·scope
oto·scop·ic
ot·ta·va octave
Ot·ta·wa
ot·ter (plural ·ters or ·ter)
Ot·to·man (or Oth·man; plural ·mans) Turk; Turkish
ot·to·man (plural ·mans) sofa
oua·ba·in drug
Ouachi·ta (or Washi·ta) US river
Oua·ga·dou·gou capital of Burkina Faso
oua·na·niche salmon
oubli·ette dungeon
ouch

Oudh Indian region
ought should; variant spelling of aught
Ouj·ja (Trademark)
Ouj·da Moroccan city
ounce
our
ours of us
our·selves
Ouse English river
ousel variant spelling of ouzel
oust
out
out·age missing goods
out-and-out
out·back
out·bal·ance
out·bid (·bid·ding, ·bid, ·bid·den or ·bid)
out·bluff
out·board
out·bound
out·brave
out·break
out·breed (·breed·ing, ·bred)
out·build·ing
out·burst
out·cast one cast out
out·caste one with no caste
out·class
out·come
out·crop (·crop·ping, ·cropped)
out·cross
out·cry (noun, plural ·cries; verb ·cries, ·cry·ing, ·cried)
out·date
out·dat·ed
out·dis·tance
out·do (·does, ·do·ing, ·did, ·done)
out·door (adj)
out·doors (adv)
out·er
outer·most
out·face
out·fall
out·field
out·field·er
out·fit (·fit·ting, ·fit·ted)
out·fit·ter
out·flank

out·flow
out·foot
out·fox
out·gas (·gas·ses, ·gas·sing, ·gassed)
out·go (·goes, ·go·ing, ·went, ·gone)
out·go·ing (adj)
out·go·ings
out·group
out·grow (·grow·ing, ·grew, ·grown)
out·growth
out·gun (·gun·ning, ·gunned)
out·haul
out·house
out·ing
out·jockey
out·land·er
out·land·ish
out·last
out·law
out·law·ry (plural ·ries)
out·lay (·lay·ing, ·laid)
out·let
out·li·er
out·line
out·live
out·look
out·ly·ing
out·man (·man·ning, ·manned)
out·ma·noeu·vre (US ·ver)
out·match
out·mod·ed
out·num·ber
out-of-doors
out-of-the-way
out·pa·tient
out·point
out·port
out·post
out·pour
out·pour·ing
out·put (·put·ting, ·put or ·put·ted)
out·rage
out·ra·geous
out·ra·geous·ness
out·rank
ou·tré unconventional
out·reach
out·ride (·rid·ing, ·rode, ·rid·den)

out·rid·er
out·rig·ger
out·right
out·ri·val (·val·ling, ·valled; US ·val·ing, ·valed)
out·run (·run·ning, ·ran, ·run)
out·run·ner
out·rush
out·sell (·sell·ing, ·sold)
out·sert printing term
out·set
out·shine (·shin·ing, ·shone)
out·shoot (·shoot·ing, ·shot)
out·side
out·sid·er
out·size
out·skirts
out·smart
out·sole
out·spo·ken
out·spread (·spread·ing, ·spread)
out·stand (·stand·ing, ·stood)
out·stand·ing (adj)
out·stare
out·sta·tion
out·stay
out·stretch
out·strip (·strip·ping, ·stripped)
out·swing
out·swing·er
out·talk
out·think (·think·ing, ·thought)
out·vote
out·ward (adj)
out·ward·ly
out·wards (adv)
out·wash glacial deposit
out·wear (·wear·ing, ·wore, ·worn)
out·weigh
out·wit (·wit·ting, ·wit·ted)
out·work (·work·ing, ·worked or ·wrought)
out·work·er
ouzel (or ousel) bird
ouzo (plural ouzos) drink
ova plural of ovum

oval
oval·ness (or ·ity)
ovar·ian
ovari·ec·to·my
ovari·oto·my (plural ·mies)
ova·ri·tis
ova·ry (plural ·ries)
ovate
ova·tion
ova·tion·al
oven
oven·bird
oven-ready
oven·ware
over
over·abun·dance
over·achieve
over·act
over·ac·tive
over·age
over·all
over·alls
over·am·bi·tious
over·anx·ious
over·arch
over·arm
over·awe
over·bal·ance
over·bear (·bear·ing, ·bore, ·borne)
over·bear·ing·ly
over·bid (·bid·ding, bid, ·bid·den or ·bid)
over·blown
over·board
over·book
over·boot
over·build (·build·ing, ·built)
over·bur·den
over·call
over·came
over·ca·pac·ity
over·capi·tali·za·tion (or ·sa·tion)
over·capi·tal·ize (or ·ise)
over·cast
over·cau·tious
over·charge
over·check
over·cloud
over·coat
over·come (·com·ing, ·came, ·come)
over·com·pen·sate

over·com·pen·sa·tion
over·com·pen·sa·tory
over·con·fi·dent
over·cook
over·criti·cal
over·criti·cize (*or* ·cise)
over·crop (·crop·ping, ·cropped)
over·crowd
over·crowd·ing
over·cul·ti·vate
over·devel·op
over·devel·op·ment
over·do (·does, ·do·ing, ·did, ·done)
over·dos·age
over·dose
over·draft money
over·draught air current
over·draw (·draw·ing, ·drew, ·drawn)
over·dress
over·drive (·driv·ing, ·drove, ·driv·en)
over·due
over·dye
over·eat (·eat·ing, ·ate, ·eat·en)
over·elabo·rate
over·em·pha·size (*or* ·sise)
over·em·phat·ic
over·en·thu·si·asm
over·en·thu·si·as·tic
over·es·ti·mate
over·es·ti·ma·tion
over·ex·cite
over·ex·pose
over·ex·po·sure
over·feed (·feed·ing, ·fed)
over·fill
over·flight
over·flow (·flow·ing, ·flowed, ·flown)
over·fly (·flies, ·fly·ing, ·flew, ·flown)
over·fold geology term
over·gar·ment
over·gen·er·ous
over·glaze
over·ground
over·grow (·grow·ing, ·grew, ·grown)
over·growth
over·hand

over·hang (·hang·ing, ·hung)
over·haul
over·head
over·heads
over·hear (·hear·ing, ·heard)
over·heat
over·hung
Over·ijs·sel Dutch province
over·in·dulge
over·in·dul·gence
over·in·dul·gent
over·is·sue (·sues, ·su·ing, ·sued)
over·joyed
over·kill
over·land
over·lap (·lap·ping, ·lapped)
over·lay (·lay·ing, ·laid)
over·leaf
over·lie (·ly·ing, ·lay, ·lain)
over·load
over·long
over·look
over·lord
over·ly
over·man (·man·ning, ·manned)
over·man·tel
over·master
over·mat·ter
over·much
over·nice
over·night
over·pass (·pas·sing, ·passed, ·past)
over·pay (·pay·ing, ·paid)
over·pitch
over·play
over·plus excess
over·popu·late
over·popu·la·tion
over·pow·er
over·pow·er·ing
over·print
over·pro·duce
over·pro·duc·tion
over·pro·tect
over·pro·tec·tion
over·pro·tec·tive
over·quali·fied
over·ran
over·rate

over·reach
over·react
over·reac·tion
over·ride (·rid·ing, ·rode, ·rid·den)
over·rid·er
over·riding (*adj*)
over·ripe
over·rode
over·rule
over·run (·run·ning, ·ran, ·run)
over·score cross out
over·seas
over·see (·see·ing, ·saw, ·seen)
over·seer
over·sell (·sell·ing, ·sold)
over·set (·set·ting, ·set) disturb
over·sew (·sew·ing, ·sewed, ·sewn)
over·sexed
over·shad·ow
over·shoe
over·shoot (·shoot·ing, ·shot)
over·side
over·sight
over·sim·pli·fi·ca·tion
over·sim·pli·fy (·fies, ·fy·ing, ·fied)
over·size
over·sized
over·skirt
over·slaugh military term
over·sleep (·sleep·ing, ·slept)
over·soul spiritual essence
over·spend (·spend·ing, ·spent)
over·spill (·spill·ing, ·spilt *or* ·spilled)
over·staff
over·state
over·state·ment
over·stay
over·steer
over·step (·step·ping, ·stepped)
over·strung
over·stuff
over·sub·scribe
overt

over·take (·tak·ing, ·took,
  ·tak·en)
over·task
over·tax
over-the-counter (adj)
over·throw (·throw·ing,
  ·threw, ·thrown)
over·thrust geological
  fault
over·time
over·tire
over·tired
over·tone
over·took
over·top (·top·ping,
  ·topped)
over·trade
over·trick bridge term
over·trump
over·ture
over·turn
over·use
over·view
over·watch
over·ween·ing
over·weigh
over·weight
over·whelm
over·whelm·ing
over·wind (·wind·ing,
  ·wound)
over·win·ter
over·word repeated
  word
over·work
over·write (·writ·ing,
  ·wrote, ·writ·ten)
over·wrought
ovi·du·cal (or ·duc·tal)
ovi·duct
Ovie·do Spanish city
ovif·er·ous
ovi·form egg-shaped
ovine sheeplike
ovi·par·ity
ovipa·rous egg-laying
ovi·pos·it
ovi·po·si·tion
ovi·posi·tor
ovi·sac egg sac

ovoid
ovo·lo (plural ·li)
  architectural term
ovo·tes·tis (plural ·tes)
ovo·vi·vi·par·ity
ovo·vi·vipa·rous
ovu·lar
ovu·late
ovu·la·tion
ovule
ovum (plural ova)
ow exclamation
owe
ow·el·ty (plural ·ties) legal
  term
Ower·ri Nigerian town
ow·ing
owl
owl·et
owl·ish
own
own·er
owner-occupier
own·er·ship
owt Dialect anything
ox (plural oxen)
oxa·late chemistry term
ox·al·ic acid
oxa·lis plant
oxa·zine
ox·blood
ox·bow lake
Ox·bridge
oxen plural of ox
ox·eye plant
Ox·fam
Ox·ford
Ox·ford·shire
ox·heart cherry
ox·hide
oxi·dant
oxi·dase enzyme
oxi·date oxidize
oxi·da·tion
oxi·da·tion·al
oxi·da·tion-reduction
oxi·da·tive
ox·ide
oxi·di·met·ric
oxi·dim·etry

oxi·diz·able chemistry
  term
oxi·di·za·tion (or ·sa·tion)
oxi·dize (or ·dise)
oxi·diz·er (or ·dis·er)
ox·ime chemical compound
ox·lip plant
Oxo·nian
ox·pecker bird
ox·tail
ox·tongue
oxy·acety·lene
oxy·acid
oxy·cephal·ic (or
  ·cepha·lous) anatomy
  term
oxy·cepha·ly
oxy·gen
oxy·gen·ate (or ·ize, ·ise)
oxy·gena·tion
oxy·gen·ic (or ox·yg·enous)
oxy·gen·iz·able (or ·is·able)
oxy·ge·niz·er (or ·is·er)
oxy·hae·mo·glo·bin (US
  ·he·)
oxy·hy·dro·gen
oxy·mo·ron (plural ·mo·ra)
  rhetoric term
oxy·salt
oxy·sul·phide (US ·fide)
oxy·tet·ra·cy·cline
oxy·to·cic
oxy·to·cin hormone
oxy·tone linguistics term
oyer legal term
oyez (or oyes) interjection
Oyo Nigerian state
oys·ter
oyster-catcher
Oz Austral Australia
Oza·lid (Trademark)
ozo·cerite (or ·kerite) wax
ozone
ozon·ic (or ozo·nous)
ozo·nif·er·ous
ozo·ni·za·tion (or ·sa·tion)
ozo·nize (or ·nise)
ozo·niz·er (or ·nis·er)
ozo·noly·sis
ozo·no·sphere ozone layer

P

pa *Slang* father
paca animal
pace
pace·maker
pac·er
pace·setter
pace·way *Austral* racecourse
pa·cha *variant spelling of* pasha
pa·chi·si board game
pachy·derm animal
pachy·der·ma·tous
pachy·tene genetics term
Pa·cif·ic ocean, etc.
pa·cif·ic conciliatory
pa·cifi·cal·ly
paci·fi·ca·tion
paci·fi·er
paci·fism
paci·fist
paci·fy (·fies, ·fy·ing, ·fied)
pack
pack·able
pack·age
pack·ag·er
pack·ag·ing
pack·er
pack·et
pack·horse
pack·ing
pack·saddle
pack·thread
pact
pad (pad·ding, pad·ded)
pa·dang Malaysian field
pa·dauk (*or* ·douk) tree
pad·ding
pad·dle
paddle·fish (*plural* ·fish *or* ·fishes)
pad·dler
pad·dock
Pad·dy (*plural* ·dies) *Slang* Irishman
pad·dy (*plural* ·dies) rice field; temper
pad·dy·whack
pad·emel·on (*or* pad·dy·mel·on) wallaby
pad·lock
pa·dre

pa·dro·ne Italian innkeeper
Pad·ua
padua·soy fabric
paean (*US also* pean) song of praise; *compare* paeon; pean; peon
pae·di·at·ric (*US* pe·)
pae·dia·tri·cian (*US* pe·)
pae·di·at·rics (*US* pe·)
pae·do·gen·esis biology term
pae·do·genet·ic (*or* ·gen·ic)
pae·do·logi·cal (*US* pe·)
pae·dolo·gist (*US* pe·)
pae·dol·ogy (*US* pe·)
pae·do·mor·pho·sis biology term
pae·do·phile (*US* pe·)
pae·do·philia (*US* pe·)
pa·el·la (*plural* ·las)
pae·on metrical foot; *compare* paean; pean; peon
(paeony) *incorrect spelling of* peony
pa·gan
pa·gan·ism
pa·gan·ist
pa·gan·ist·ic
pa·gan·isti·cal·ly
pa·gani·za·tion (*or* ·sa·tion)
pa·gan·ize (*or* ·ise)
pa·gan·iz·er (*or* ·is·er)
page
pag·eant
pag·eant·ry (*plural* ·ries)
page·boy
pagi·nal
pagi·nate
pagi·na·tion
pa·go·da
pa·gu·rian (*or* ·rid) zoology term
Pa·hang Malaysian state
Pa·ha·ri language group
Pah·la·vi Persian language
paid
pai·gle *Dialect* cowslip
Paign·ton
pail bucket; *compare* pale
pail·lette sequin

pain hurt; *compare* pane
pained
pain·ful
pain·ful·ly
pain·ful·ness
pain·killer
pain·less
pain·less·ness
pains·taking
pains·taking·ness
paint
paint·box
paint·brush
paint·er
paint·er·ly
paint·ing
paint·work
painty
pair two similar things; *compare* pare
pair-oar
pai·sa (*plural* ·se) Indian coin
Pais·ley Scottish town
pais·ley fabric; pattern
pa·jam·as *US spelling of* pyjamas
pa·keha non-Maori
Pa·ki·stan
Pa·ki·stani
pal (pal·ling, palled) *Slang* friend; to befriend; *compare* pall
pal·ace
pala·din
palae·an·throp·ic (*US* pale·)
Palae·arc·tic zoogeographical region
palae·eth·no·logi·cal (*US* pale·)
palae·eth·nolo·gist (*US* pale·)
palae·eth·nol·ogy (*US* pale·)
palaeo·an·thro·pol·ogy (*US* paleo·)
palaeo·bo·tani·cal (*or* ·tan·ic; *US* paleo·)
palaeo·bota·nist (*US* paleo·)
palaeo·bota·ny (*US* paleo·)

Palaeo·cene (*US* Paleo·)
geological epoch

palaeo·cli·ma·tol·ogy (*US* paleo·)

palaeo·eth·no·bota·ny (*US* paleo·)

Palaeo·gene (*US* Paleo·) geology term

palaeo·graph·ic (*US* paleo·)

palaeo·graphi·cal (*US* paleo·)

palae·og·ra·phy (*US* paleo·) study of ancient handwriting

palaeo·lith (*US* paleo·)

Palaeo·lith·ic (*US* Paleo·)

palae·on·to·graph·ic (or ·graphi·cal; *US* pale·)

palae·on·tog·ra·phy (*US* pale·) description of fossils

palae·on·to·logi·cal (*US* pale·)

palae·on·tolo·gist (*US* pale·)

palae·on·tol·ogy (*US* pale·)

Palaeo·zo·ic (*US* Paleo·) geological era

palaeo·zoo·logi·cal (*US* paleo·)

palaeo·zo·olo·gist (*US* paleo·)

palaeo·zo·ol·ogy (*US* paleo·)

pal·aes·tra (*plural* ·tras or ·trae)

pal·ais dance

pal·an·quin (or ·keen)

pal·at·abil·ity (or ·able·ness)

pal·at·able

pal·at·ably

pala·tal

pala·tali·za·tion (or ·sa·tion)

pala·tal·ize (or ·ise) phonetics term

pal·ate roof of mouth; *compare* **palette; pallet**

pa·la·tial

pa·la·tial·ly

pa·la·tial·ness

Pa·lati·nate German region

pa·lati·nate territory of palatine prince

Pala·tine of the Palatinate; Roman hill

pala·tine

Pa·lau *former name of* **Belau**

pa·la·ver

pale lacking colour; wooden post; *compare* **pail**

pa·lea (*plural* ·leae) botany term

pa·lea·ceous

pale·face

pale·ly in a pale way; *compare* **paly**

Pa·lem·bang Indonesian port

pale·ness

paleo· *US spelling of words beginning with* **palaeo·**

Pa·ler·mo Sicilian capital

Pal·es·tine

Pal·es·tin·ian

pal·ette (or **pal·let**) artist's board; *compare* **palate; pallet**

pal·ette knife (*plural* **pal·ette knives**)

pal·frey

pal·imp·sest manuscript

pal·in·drome

pal·in·drom·ic

pal·ing

pal·in·gen·esis (*plural* ·eses) theology term

pal·in·genet·ic

palin·geneti·cal·ly

pali·node poem

pali·sade

pal·ish

pall coffin cover; to be boring; *compare* **pal; pawl**

Pal·la·dian architectural term

pal·lad·ic chemistry term

Pal·la·dium statue of Athena

pal·la·dium chemical element

pal·la·dous chemistry term

Pallas Athena; asteroid

pall·bearer

palled *past tense of* **pal** or **pall**

pal·let straw bed; potter's knife; machine part;

variant spelling of **palette**; *compare* **palate**

pal·leti·za·tion (or ·sa·tion)

pal·let·ize (or ·ise)

pal·li·asse (or **pail·lasse**)

pal·li·ate

pal·lia·tion

pal·lia·tive

pal·lia·tor

pal·lid

pal·lium (*plural* ·lia or ·liums) vestment; anatomy term

Pall Mall

pal·lor

pal·ly (·li·er, ·li·est)

palm

Pal·ma Spanish resort; *compare* **Parma**

palm·a·ceous botany term

pal·mar

pal·mate (or ·mat·ed)

pal·ma·tion

palm·er pilgrim

pal·mette archaeological ornament

pal·met·to (*plural* ·tos or ·toes) palm tree

Pal·mi·ra Colombian city

palm·ist

palm·is·try

pal·mi·tate chemistry term

pal·mi·tin chemical compound

palmy (palmi·er, palmi·est)

pal·my·ra palm tree

pa·lo·lo (*plural* ·los) worm

Palo·mar Californian mountain

palo·mi·no (*plural* ·nos) horse

pa·loo·ka *US* clumsy person

palp (or **pal·pus**; *plural* **palps** or **pal·pi**)

pal·pabil·ity (or ·pable·ness)

pal·pable

pal·pably

pal·pate examine medically; of palps; *compare* **palpitate**

pal·pa·tion

pal·pe·bral of the eyelid

pal·pe·brate

pal·pi·tate beat rapidly;
  compare palpate
pal·pi·ta·tion
pal·sied
pal·stave archaeology term
pal·sy (*noun, plural* ·sies;
  verb ·sies, ·sy·ing, ·sied)
pal·ter be insincere
pal·ter·er
pal·tri·ly
pal·tri·ness
pal·try (·tri·er, ·tri·est)
paly heraldic term; *compare*
  palely
paly·no·logi·cal
paly·nolo·gist
paly·nol·ogy study of
  pollen
Pa·mirs Asian mountains
pam·pas
pam·pean
pam·per
pam·per·er
pam·pero (*plural* ·peros)
  wind
pam·phlet
pam·phlet·eer
Pam·phylia ancient Asian
  region
Pam·plo·na Spanish city
Pan Greek god
pan (pan·ning, panned)
pana·cea
pana·cean
pa·nache
pa·na·da thick sauce
Pana·ma
pana·ma
Pana·ma·nian
Pan-Ameri·can
Pan-Ameri·can·ism
Pan-Arab (*or* -Arabic)
Pan-Arabism
pana·tela (*or* pana·tel·la)
Pa·nay Philippine island
pan·cake
pan·chax fish
Pan·chen Lama
pan·chro·mat·ic
pan·chro·ma·tism
pan·cre·as
pan·cre·at·ic
pan·crea·tin
pan·da animal; *compare*
  pander

(pandamonium) *incorrect
  spelling of* pandemonium
pan·da·na·ceous botany
  term
pan·da·nus (*plural* ·nuses)
  plant
Pandarus mythological
  character
Pan·dean of Pan
pan·dect treatise
pan·dem·ic
pan·de·mo·ni·ac (*or*
  ·mon·ic)
pan·de·mo·nium
pan·der gratify weakness;
  pimp; *compare* panda
pan·der·er
pan·dit *less common spelling
  of* pundit *except as Indian
  title, as in* Pandit Nehru
Pandora mythological
  character
pan·dora *variant of* bandora
pan·dour Croatian soldier
pan·dow·dy (*plural* ·dies)
  US fruit pie
pan·du·rate (*or*
  ·du·ri·form) botany term
pan·dy (*plural* ·dies) school
  punishment
pane sheet of glass; *compare*
  pain
pan·egyr·ic praise; *compare*
  paregoric
pan·egyri·cal
pan·egyr·ist
pan·egy·rize (*or* ·rise)
pan·el (·el·ling, ·elled; *US*
  ·el·ing, ·eled)
pan·el·list
pan·et·to·ne spiced bread
pan·ful (*plural* ·fuls)
pang
pan·ga knife
Pan·gaea ancient continent
pan·gen·esis heredity
  theory
pan·genet·ic
pan·geneti·cal·ly
pan·go·lin animal
pan·han·dle
Pan·hel·len·ic
Pan·hel·len·ism
Pan·hel·len·ist
Pan·hel·len·is·tic

pan·ic (·ick·ing, ·icked)
pan·icky
pani·cle botany term
pani·cled
panic-stricken (*or* -struck)
pa·nicu·late (*or* ·lat·ed)
pan·jan·drum
pan·mix·is (*or* ·mixia)
  genetics term
Pan·mun·jom Korean
  village
pan·nage pig pasturage
panne fabric
pan·ni·er
pan·ni·kin
pa·no·cha (*or* pe·nu·che)
  sugar
pano·plied
pano·ply (*plural* ·plies)
pan·op·tic (*or* ·ti·cal)
pan·op·ti·cal·ly
pano·ra·ma
pano·ram·ic
pano·rami·cal·ly
pan·pipes
pan·soph·ic (*or* ·sophi·cal)
pan·sophi·cal·ly
pan·so·phy universal
  knowledge
pan·sy (*plural* ·sies)
pant
pan·ta·lets (*or* ·lettes)
  women's drawers
pan·ta·loon pantomime
  character
pan·ta·loons men's trousers
pan·tech·ni·con
pan·theism
pan·theist
pan·theis·tic (*or* ·ti·cal)
pan·theis·ti·cal·ly
Pan·the·on Roman temple
pan·the·on temple to all
  gods
pan·ther (*plural* ·thers *or*
  ·ther)
panties
pan·ti·hose
pan·tile
pan·ti·soc·ra·cy community
  ruled by all
pan·to (*plural* ·tos) *Slang*
  pantomime
pan·to·graph
pan·tog·ra·pher

pan·to·graph·ic
pan·to·graphi·cal·ly
pan·tog·ra·phy
pan·to·mime
pan·to·mim·ic
pan·to·mim·ist
pan·to·then·ic acid
pan·toum verse form
pan·try (*plural* ·tries)
pants
pant·suit *US* trouser suit
panty·waist *US* childish
person
pan·zer
Pao·ting (*or* Pao-ting)
Chinese city
Pao·tow Chinese city
pap
papa
pa·pa·cy (*plural* ·cies)
pa·pa·in enzyme
pa·pal
pa·pal·ly
pa·pa·vera·ceous botany
term
pa·pa·ver·ine alkaloid
pa·paw (*or* paw·) American
fruit
pa·pa·ya West Indian fruit
Pa·pe·ete Tahitian capital
pa·per
paper·back
paper·bark tree
paper·board
paper·boy
paper·clip
paper-cutter
pa·per·er
paper·girl
paper·hanger
paper·hanging
pa·peri·ness
paper·knife (*plural* ·knives)
paper·weight
paper·work
pa·pery
pap·eterie box for papers
Paph·la·go·nia Roman
province
Pa·phos Cypriot village
papier-mâché
pa·pil·la (*plural* ·lae)
pa·pil·lary (*or* ·late, ·lose)
pap·il·lo·ma (*plural* ·ma·ta
or ·mas) tumour

pap·il·lo·ma·to·sis
pap·il·lo·ma·tous
pap·il·lon dog
pap·il·lote paper frill in
cookery
pa·pist
pa·pis·ti·cal (*or* ·pis·tic)
pa·pist·ry
pa·poose (*or* pap·poose)
American Indian baby
pap·pose (*or* ·pous)
pap·pus (*plural* ·pi) plant
hairs
pap·py (·pi·er, ·pi·est)
mushy
pap·ri·ka
Pa·puan
Pa·pua New Guinea
papu·lar
pap·ule (*or* papu·la; *plural*
·ules *or* ·lae)
papu·lif·er·ous
papy·ra·ceous
papy·rolo·gist
papy·rol·ogy
pa·py·rus (*plural* ·ri *or*
·ruses)
par accepted standard;
compare parr
para (*plural* paras *or* para)
coin
para (*plural* paras)
paratrooper; paragraph
Pará Brazilian state
pa·raba·sis (*pluras* ·ses)
speech of Greek chorus
para·bio·sis (*plural* ·ses)
union of two individuals
para·bi·ot·ic
para·blast biology term
para·blas·tic
para·ble religious story
pa·rabo·la maths term
para·bol·ic of a parabola
para·bol·ic (*or* ·boli·cal) of
parables
para·boli·cal·ly
pa·rabo·list
pa·rabo·li·za·tion (*or*
·sa·tion)
pa·rabo·lize (*or* ·lise)
pa·rabo·loid maths term
pa·rabo·loi·dal
para·brake
pa·ra·ceta·mol

pa·rach·ro·nism error in
dating
para·chute
para·chut·ist
Para·clete Holy Ghost
para·clete mediator
pa·rade
pa·rad·er
para·digm
para·dig·mat·ic
para·dise
para·di·sia·cal (*or* ·disi·ac)
para·dos bank behind
trench
para·dox
para·doxi·cal
para·doxi·cal·ly
para·drop
par·aes·thesia (*US* ·es·;
plural ·thesiae) medical
term
par·aes·thet·ic (*US* ·es·)
par·af·fin (*or* ·fine)
para·form·al·de·hyde (*or*
para·form)
para·gen·esis (*or* ·genesia)
geology term
para·genet·ic
para·geneti·cal·ly
para·go·ge (*or* para·gogue)
linguistics term
para·gog·ic (*or* ·gogi·cal)
para·gogi·cal·ly
para·gon
para·graph
para·graphia psychiatric
term
para·graph·ic (*or*
·graphi·cal)
para·graphi·cal·ly
Para·guay
Para·guay·an
para·hy·dro·gen
Pa·raí·ba Brazilian state
para·keet (*or* par·ra·keet)
para·lan·guage
par·al·de·hyde
para·leip·sis (*or* ·lip·sis;
plural ·ses) rhetorical
device
pa·ra·li·pom·ena
supplementary writings
par·al·lac·tic
par·al·lac·ti·cal·ly
par·al·lax

par·al·lel (·lel·ing, ·leled)
par·al·lel·epi·ped (*or*
·lelo·pi·ped)
par·al·lel·ism
par·al·lel·ist
par·al·lelo·gram
pa·ralo·gism invalid
argument
pa·ralo·gist
pa·ralo·gis·tic
para·ly·sa·tion (*US*
·za·tion)
para·lyse (*US* ·lyze)
para·lys·er (*US* ·lyz·er)
pa·raly·sis (*plural* ·ses)
para·lyt·ic
para·lyti·cal·ly
para·mag·net·ic
para·mag·net·ism
Para·mari·bo capital of
Surinam
para·mat·ta (*or*
par·ra·mat·ta) fabric
para·mecium (*plural*
·mecia) protozoan
para·med·ic
para·medi·cal
para·ment (*plural* ·ments *or*
·men·ta) vestment
pa·ram·eter
para·met·ric (*or* ·ri·cal)
para·mili·tary
par·am·ne·sia
para·mo (*plural* ·mos)
Andean plateau
para·morph mineralogy
term
para·mor·phic (*or* ·phous)
para·mor·phism
para·mount
par·amour
Pa·ra·ná Brazilian state,
river, and city
pa·rang knife
para·noia
para·noi·ac
para·noid
para·nor·mal
para·pet
para·pet·ed
par·aph flourish after
signature
para·pher·na·lia
para·phrase
para·phras·tic

pa·raphy·sis (*plural* ·ses)
botany term
para·plegia
para·plegic
para·po·dium (*plural* ·dia)
zoology term
para·prax·is psychology
term
para·psy·chol·ogy
Para·quat (*Trademark*)
para·sang Persian unit
para·sele·ne (*plural* ·nae)
astronomy term
Pa·ra·shah (*plural* ·shoth)
synagogue reading
para·site
para·sit·ic
para·siti·cal·ly
para·siti·cid·al
para·siti·cide
para·sit·ism
para·si·tize (*or* ·tise)
para·si·to·logi·cal
para·sit·olo·gist
para·sit·ol·ogy
para·sol
pa·ras·ti·chy (*plural* ·chies)
botany term
para·sym·pa·thet·ic
para·syn·the·sis linguistics
term
para·syn·the·ton (*plural* ·ta)
para·tac·tic
para·tac·ti·cal·ly
para·tax·is linguistics term
para·thi·on insecticide
para·thy·roid
para·troop·er
para·troops
para·ty·phoid
para·vane device on
minesweeper
par avion *French* by plane
para·zo·an (*plural* ·zoans *or*
·zoa) zoology term
par·boil
par·buck·le rope sling
par·cel (·cel·ling, ·celled;
US ·cel·ing, ·celed)
par·cenary joint heirship
par·cener
parch
parch·ment
par·close church screen
pard *Archaic* leopard

par·da·lote bird
pard·ner *US* partner
par·don
par·don·able
par·don·ably
par·don·er
pare trim; *compare* pair
par·egor·ic medicine;
compare panegyric
pa·rei·ra medicinal root
pa·ren·chy·ma tissue
par·en·chyma·tous
par·ent
par·ent·age
pa·ren·tal
par·en·ter·al medical term
par·en·ter·ally
pa·ren·thesis (*plural*
·theses)
pa·ren·thesize (*or* ·thesise)
par·en·thet·ic (*or* ·theti·cal)
par·en·theti·cal·ly
par·ent·hood
par·er
par·er·gon (*plural* ·ga)
additional work
pa·resis paralysis
par·es·thesia *US spelling of*
paraesthesia
pa·ret·ic
par ex·cel·lence *French*
beyond comparison
par·fait dessert
par·fleche rawhide
par·get
par·get·ing
par·he·lic (*or* ·he·lia·cal)
par·he·li·on (*plural* ·lia)
astronomy term
pa·ri·ah
Parian marble
pari·es (*plural* pa·ri·etes)
anatomy term
pa·ri·etal
pari-mutuel (*plural*
pari-mutuels *or*
paris-mutuels) betting
system
par·ing
pari pas·su *Latin* legal term
pari·pin·nate botany term
Par·is French capital
Paris mythological character
par·ish
pa·rish·ion·er

Pa·ris·ian
Pa·risi·enne Parisian
  woman
pari·son glass mass
pari·syl·lab·ic
par·ity (*plural* ·ities)
park
par·ka coat
par·kin cake
park·ing
par·kin·son·ism
park·land
park·way
parky (parki·er, parki·est)
par·lance
par·lan·do music term
par·lay US double up in
  betting
par·ley discuss
par·ley·er
par·lia·ment (*or* Par·)
Par·lia·men·tar·ian
  parliamentary supporter in
  Civil War
par·lia·men·tar·ian
par·lia·men·tari·an·ism (*or*
  ·tar·ism)
par·lia·men·ta·ry
par·lour (US ·lor)
par·lous dangerous
Par·ma Italian city; *compare*
  Palma
Par·men·tier cookery term
Par·me·san cheese
Par·nas·sian
Par·nas·sus
pa·ro·chial
pa·ro·chi·al·ism
pa·ro·chi·al·ly
pa·rod·ic (*or* ·rodi·cal)
paro·dy (*noun, plural* ·dies;
  verb ·dies, ·dy·ing, ·died)
pa·roi·cous (*or* ·roe·cious)
  botany term
pa·rol oral
pa·rol·able
pa·role conditional release
pa·rolee
paro·no·ma·sia play on
  words
paro·no·mas·ti·cal·ly
paro·nym linguistics term
paro·nym·ic (*or*
  pa·rony·mous)
Pár·os Greek island

pa·rot·ic near the ear
pa·rot·id gland
paro·ti·tis (*or* pa·roti·di·tis)
  mumps
pa·ro·toid poison gland on
  toad
par·ox·ysm
par·ox·ys·mal (*or* ·mic)
par·quet
par·quet·ry
parr (*plural* parrs *or* parr)
  salmon; *compare* par
par·rel (*or* ·ral) nautical
  term
par·ri·cid·al
par·ri·cide killing of parent;
  compare patricide
par·rot
parrot-fashion
parrot-fish (*plural* ·fish *or*
  ·fishes)
par·ry (*verb* ·ries, ·ry·ing,
  ·ried; *noun, plural* ·ries)
pars·able
parse
par·sec unit
Par·see
Par·see·ism Indian religion
pars·er
par·si·mo·ni·ous
par·si·mo·ny
pars·ley
pars·nip
par·son
par·son·age
part
par·take (·tak·ing, ·took,
  ·tak·en)
par·tak·er
par·tan Scot crab
part·ed
par·terre garden
par·theno·car·pic (*or*
  ·pous)
par·theno·car·py botany
  term
par·theno·genesis
par·theno·genet·ic
par·theno·geneti·cal·ly
Par·the·non Greek temple
Parthenope mythological
  character
Par·thia ancient Asian
  country
Par·thian

par·tial
par·tial·ity (*plural* ·ities)
par·tial·ly
par·tial·ness
part·ible
par·tici·pant
par·tici·pate
par·tici·pa·tion (*or*
  ·tici·pance)
par·tici·pa·tor
par·ti·cipi·al
par·ti·ci·ple
par·ti·cle
parti-coloured (US
  -colored)
par·ticu·lar
par·ticu·lar·ism
par·ticu·lar·ist
par·ticu·lar·is·tic
par·ticu·lar·ity (*plural*
  ·ities)
par·ticu·lari·za·tion (*or*
  ·sa·tion)
par·ticu·lar·ize (*or* ·ise)
par·ticu·lar·iz·er (*or* ·is·er)
par·ticu·late (*adj*)
part·ing
par·ti pris French
  preconceived opinion
par·ti·san (*or* ·zan)
par·ti·san·ship (*or*
  ·zan·ship)
par·ti·ta musical piece
par·tite divided
par·ti·tion
par·ti·tion·er (*or* ·ist)
par·ti·tive
part·let shawl
part·ly
part·ner
part·ner·ship
par·ton physics term
par·took
par·tridge (*plural* ·tridges *or*
  ·tridge)
part-time (*adj*)
part-timer
par·tu·ri·ent of childbirth
par·tu·ri·fa·cient
par·tu·ri·tion
par·ty (*plural* ·ties)
pa·ru·lis (*plural* ·li·des)
  gumboil
pa·rure set of jewels
par·venu (*fem* ·venue)

par·vis (or **·vise**) church
porch
Pasa·dena US city
Pa·sar·ga·dae ancient
Persian city
Pa·say Philippine city
pas·cal unit
pas·chal of Easter
Pas-de-Calais French
department
pas de deux (plural **pas de
deux**) ballet sequence
pash Slang infatuation
Pa·sha Turkish title
pa·sha (or **·cha**) Ottoman
governor
pa·sha·lik (or **·lic**) province
of pasha
Pash·to (or **Push·tu**)
language
paso do·ble (plural **paso
do·bles** or **pasos do·bles**)
dance
pasque·flow·er
pas·quin·ade (or **pas·quil**)
satire
pas·quin·ad·er
pass
pass·able able to be passed;
compare **passible**
pass·ably
pas·sa·ca·glia musical piece
pas·sade dressage term
pas·sage
passage·way
pas·sant heraldic term
pass·book
pas·sé out-of-date
passed past tense of **pass**;
compare **past**
passe·men·terie decorative
trimming
pas·sen·ger
passe-partout picture
mounting
passe·pied dance
passer-by (plural **passers-by**)
pas·ser·ine ornithology
term
pas seul dance sequence
pas·sibil·ity
pas·sible sensitive; compare
passable
pas·si·flo·ra·ceous botany
term

pas·sim Latin throughout
pass·ing
Pas·sion Christ's sufferings
pas·sion
pas·sion·al
pas·sion·ate
pas·sion·ate·ness
passion·flower
pas·sion·less
pas·sion·less·ness
Passion·tide
pas·sive
pas·sive·ness (or **pas·siv·ity**)
pas·siv·ism
pas·siv·ist
pass·key
Pass·over
pass·port
(**passtime**) incorrect spelling of
pastime
pas·sus (plural **·sus** or **·suses**)
part of poem
pass·word
past
pas·ta
paste
paste·board
pas·tel drawing crayon;
compare **pastille**
pas·tel·list (or **·tel·ist**)
pas·tern part of horse's foot
paste-up
pas·teur·ism rabies
treatment
pas·teuri·za·tion (or
·sa·tion)
pas·teur·ize (or **·ise**)
pas·teur·iz·er (or **·is·er**)
pas·tic·cio (plural **·cios**)
pastiche
pas·tiche artistic medley;
compare **postiche**
pas·tille (or **·til**) lozenge;
compare **pastel**
pasti·ly
pas·time
pasti·ness
pas·tis alcoholic drink
pas·tor
pas·to·ral of shepherds or
pastors
pas·to·rale (plural **·rales** or
·ra·li) musical piece
pas·to·ral·ly
pas·tor·ate

pas·tra·mi smoked beef
pas·try (plural **·tries**)
pas·tur·age
pas·ture
(**pasturize**) incorrect spelling
of **pasteurize**
pasty (noun, plural **pasties**;
adj **pasti·er**, **pasti·est**) a
pastry; pale
pat (**pat·ting**, **pat·ted**)
pa·ta·gium (plural **·gia**)
zoology term
Pata·go·nia South American
region
patch
patch·able
patch·er
patchi·ly
patchi·ness
patchou·li (or **pachou·li**,
patchou·ly) perfume
patch·work
patchy (**patchi·er**,
patchi·est)
pate the head
pâté food; compare **pattée**
pâté de foie gras (plural
pâtés de foie gras)
pa·tel·la (plural **·lae**)
kneecap
pa·tel·lar
pa·tel·late
pa·tel·li·form
pat·en (or **·in**, **·ine**) plate for
Eucharist; compare **patten**
pa·ten·cy
pa·tent
pa·tent·able
pa·tentee
pa·tent·ly
pa·ten·tor
pa·ter Slang father
pa·ter·fa·mili·as (plural
pa·tres·fa·mili·as) male
head of family
pa·ter·nal
pa·ter·nal·ism
pa·ter·nal·ist
pa·ter·nal·is·tic
pa·ter·nal·is·ti·cal·ly
pa·ter·nal·ly
pa·ter·nity
Pat·er·nos·ter Lord's Prayer
pat·er·nos·ter rosary beads;
fishing tackle; lift

Pat·er·son US city
path
Pa·than Afghan or Pakistani
 Muslim
pa·thet·ic
pa·thet·i·cal·ly
path·finder
path·finding
patho·gen (or ·gene)
patho·gen·esis (or
 pa·thog·eny)
patho·genet·ic of disease
patho·gen·ic causing
 disease
path·og·no·mon·ic
 indicating disease
path·og·no·moni·cal·ly
path·og·no·my study of
 emotions
patho·logi·cal (or ·log·ic)
patho·logi·cal·ly
pa·tholo·gist
pa·thol·ogy (plural ·ogies)
pa·thos
path·way
Pa·tia·la Indian city
pa·tience
pa·tient
pa·tient·ly
pati·na
pa·tio (plural ·tios)
pa·tis·serie
Pat·mos Greek island
Pat·na Indian city; rice
pat·ois (plural pat·ois)
 dialect
Pa·tras Greek port
pa·trial
pa·tri·arch
pa·tri·ar·chal
pa·tri·ar·chate
pa·tri·ar·chy (plural ·chies)
pa·tri·cian
pa·tri·ci·ate rank of
 patrician
pat·ri·cid·al
pat·ri·cide killing one's
 father; compare parricide
pat·ri·cli·nous (or
 ·ro·cli·nous, ·ro·cli·nal)
 resembling male parent
pat·ri·lin·eal (or ·ear)
pat·ri·lo·cal living with
 husband's family
pat·ri·mo·nial

pat·ri·mo·ny (plural ·nies)
pa·tri·ot
pat·ri·ot·ic
pat·ri·ot·ism
pa·tris·tic (or ·ti·cal)
pa·tris·ti·cal·ly
pa·trol (·trol·ling, ·trolled)
pa·trol·ler
patrol·man (plural ·men)
pa·trol·ogy writings of
 Church Fathers
pa·tron
pat·ron·age
pa·tron·al
pa·tron·ess
pat·ron·ize (or ·ise)
pat·ron·iz·er (or ·is·er)
pat·ron·iz·ing·ly (or
 ·is·ing·ly)
pat·ro·nym·ic
pat·ted
pat·tée type of cross;
 compare pâté
pat·ten wooden clog;
 compare paten
pat·ter
pat·tern
pat·ting
pat·ty (plural ·ties)
patu·lous
paua shellfish
pau·cal linguistics term
pau·city
paul·dron armour plate
Paul·ine of St Paul
pau·low·nia tree
paunch
paunchi·ness
paunchy (paunchi·er,
 paunchi·est)
pau·per
pau·per·ism
pau·per·ize (or ·ise)
pause
paus·er
paus·ing·ly
pav·age paving tax
pa·vane (or pa·van) dance
pave
pavé paved surface
pave·ment
pa·vil·ion
pav·ing
pav·ior (or ·iour) one who
 paves

pav·is (or ·ise) shield
Pav·lo·va meringue cake
pavo·nine of peacocks
paw
pawky (pawki·er,
 pawki·est) Scot drily witty
pawl part of ratchet;
 compare pall
pawn
pawn·age
pawn·broker
pawn·broking
Paw·nee (plural ·nees or
 ·nee) American Indian
pawn·shop
paw·paw variant spelling of
 papaw
pax
pax·wax Dialect ligament
pay (pay·ing, paid)
pay·able
pay·day
payee
pay·er
pay·load
pay·master
pay·ment
pay·nim Archaic heathen
pay·off (noun)
pay·ola US bribe
pay·phone
pay·roll
pea
peace
peace·able
peace·able·ness
peace·ful
peace·ful·ly
peace·ful·ness
peace·maker
peace·time
peach
peachi·ness
peachy (peachi·er,
 peachi·est)
pea·cock (plural ·cocks or
 ·cock)
pea·fowl (plural ·fowls or
 ·fowl)
pea·hen
peak summit; to sicken;
 compare peek; peke
peaked
peaky (peaki·er,
 peaki·est)

peal loud sound; compare
peel

pean heraldic term; US
variant spelling of paean;
compare paeon; peon

pea·nut

pear

pearl jewel; compare purl

pearl·er

pearl·ite steel constituent;
variant spelling of perlite

pearl·it·ic

pearl·ized (or ·ised)

pearly (adj pearli·er,
pearli·est; noun, plural
pearlies)

pear·main apple

peas·ant

peas·ant·ry

pease Dialect pea

pea·shooter

pea·soup·er Slang fog

peat

peaty

peau de soie fabric

peb·ble

pebble-dash

peb·bling

peb·bly

pe·can nut; compare pekan

pec·ca·bil·ity

pec·cable liable to sin

pec·ca·dil·lo (plural ·los or
·loes)

pec·can·cy

pec·cant

pec·ca·ry (plural ·ries or ·ry)
piglike animal

pec·ca·vi (plural ·vis)
confession of guilt

peck

peck·er

peck·ing

peck·ish

pec·tase enzyme

pec·tate

pec·ten (plural ·tens or
·ti·nes) zoology term;
compare pectin

pec·tic of pectin; compare
peptic

pec·tin gelling substance;
compare pecten

pec·ti·nate (or ·nat·ed)
comb-shaped

pec·ti·na·tion

pec·tin·ous

pec·tiz·able (or ·tis·able)

pec·ti·za·tion (or ·sa·tion)

pec·tize (or ·tise) jellify

pec·to·ral

pecu·late embezzle

pecu·la·tion

pecu·la·tor

pe·cu·liar

pe·cu·li·ar·ity (plural ·ities)

pe·cu·ni·ari·ly

pe·cu·ni·ary

peda·gog·ic (or ·gogi·cal)

peda·gogi·cal·ly

peda·gog·ics

peda·gog·ism (or
·gogu·ism)

peda·gogue (or ·gog)

peda·go·gy

ped·al (·al·ling, ·alled; US
·dal·ing, ·daled) foot
lever; operate pedals;
compare peddle

pe·dal of the foot

pe·dal·fer soil

ped·al·ler (US ·al·er) one
who pedals; compare
peddler; pedlar

peda·lo (plural ·los or ·loes)
pedal boat

ped·ant

pe·dan·tic

ped·ant·ry (plural ·ries)

ped·ate biology term

pe·dati·fid botany term

ped·dle sell; compare pedal

ped·dler drugs seller; US
spelling of pedlar

ped·er·ast (or paed·)

ped·er·as·tic (or paed·)

ped·er·as·ty (or paed·)

ped·es·tal

pe·des·trian

pe·des·tria·ni·za·tion (or
·sa·tion)

pe·des·tri·an·ize (or ·ise)

Pedi African people

pe·di·at·rics US spelling of
paediatrics

pedi·cab tricycle cab

pedi·cel flower stalk

pedi·cle small stalk

pe·dicu·lar of lice or
pedicles

pe·dicu·late zoology term

pe·dicu·lo·sis infestation
with lice

pe·dicu·lous

pedi·cure

pedi·form

pedi·gree

pedi·greed

pedi·ment

pedi·ment·al

pedi·palp zoology term

ped·lar (US ped·dler)
hawker; compare
peddler

pedo·cal soil

pe·do·logi·cal

pe·dolo·gist

pe·dol·ogy study of soils

pe·dom·eter

pe·dun·cle flower stalk

pe·dun·cu·lar

pe·dun·cu·late (or ·lat·ed)

pe·dun·cu·la·tion

pee (pee·ing, peed)

Pee·bles former Scottish
county

peek peep; compare peak;
peke

peeka·boo

peel rind; to be shed;
fortified tower; compare
peal

peel·er

peelie-wally Scot unwell

peel·ing

peen part of hammer

peep

peep·er

peep·hole

peep·show

pee·pul (or pi·pal) sacred
tree

peer a noble; an equal; to
look; compare pier

peer·age

peer·ess

peer·less

peeve Slang irritate

peev·ers Scot hopscotch

peev·ish

peev·ish·ness

pee·wee variant spelling of
pewee

pee·wit (or pe·wit) lapwing

peg (peg·ging, pegged)

Pega·sus mythological
  horse; constellation
peg·board
peg·ma·tite rock
peg·ma·tit·ic
peign·oir
pejo·ra·tion
pe·jo·ra·tive
pek·an animal; compare
  pecan
peke Slang Pekingese dog;
  compare peak; peek
Pe·kin duck
Pe·king variant spelling of
  Beijing
Pe·king·ese (or ·kin·) dog;
  of Peking
pe·koe tea
pel·age
Pe·la·gi·an·ism Christian
  doctrine
pe·lag·ic of open sea
pel·ar·go·nium
Pe·lée West Indian
  volcano
pel·er·ine cape
Peleus mythological
  character
pelf Slang money
pel·ham horse's bit
peli·can
Pe·li·on Greek mountain
pe·lisse
pe·lite rock
pe·lit·ic
Pel·la ancient Greek city
pel·la·gra
pel·la·grous
pel·let
pel·li·cle
pel·licu·lar
pel·li·tory (plural ·tories)
  plant
pell-mell
pel·lu·cid
pel·lu·cid·ity (or ·ness)
Pel·man·ism memory
  training
pel·man·ism card game
pel·met
Pelo·pon·nese
Pelo·pon·ne·sian
Pelops mythological
  character
pe·lo·ria botany term

pe·lo·rus (plural ·ruses)
  gyrocompass
pe·lo·ta ball game
Pe·lo·tas Brazilian port
pelt
pel·tast ancient Greek
  soldier
pel·tate botany term
pel·ta·tion
pelt·er
Peltier ef·fect
pelt·ry (plural ·ries) animal
  pelts
pel·vic
pel·vis (plural ·vises or ·ves)
Pem·ba Tanzanian island
Pem·broke
Pem·broke·shire Welsh
  county
pem·mi·can (or pemi·can)
  food
pem·phi·gus skin disease
pen (pen·ning, penned)
  writing tool; write
pen (pen·ning, penned or
  pent) enclosure; enclose
pe·nal
pe·nali·za·tion (or ·sa·tion)
pe·nal·ize (or ·ise)
pen·al·ty (plural ·ties)
pen·ance
Pe·nang Malaysian state
pe·na·tes Roman gods
pence
pen·cel (or ·sel, ·sil) small
  flag; compare pencil
pen·chant
Pen·chi (or ·ki) Chinese city
pen·cil (·cil·ling, ·cilled; US
  ·cil·ing, ·ciled) writing
  tool, etc.; compare pencel
pen·cil·ler (US ·cil·er)
pend
pen·dant necklace
pen·dent dangling
pen·den·te lite legal term
pen·den·tive architectural
  term
pend·ing
pen·dragon leader of
  ancient Britons
pen·du·lous
pen·du·lum
pe·neplain (or ·neplane)
  flat land

pe·ne·pla·na·tion
pen·etrabil·ity
pen·etrable
pen·etra·lia innermost parts
pen·etra·lian
pen·etrance
pen·etrant
pen·etrate
pen·etra·tion
pen·etra·tor
Peng·pu (or Pang-fou)
  Chinese city
pen·guin
peni·cil·late biology term
peni·cil·la·tion
peni·cil·lin antibiotic
peni·cil·lium (plural ·liums
  or ·lia) mould
pe·nile of the penis
pe·nil·li·on (sing. pe·nill)
  Welsh sung poetry
pen·in·su·la
pen·in·su·lar
pe·nis (plural ·nises or ·nes)
peni·tence
peni·tent
peni·ten·tial
peni·ten·tia·ry (plural ·ries)
pen·knife (plural ·knives)
pen·man (plural ·men)
pen·man·ship
pen·na (plural ·nae) feather
pen·nant ship's flag;
  compare pennon
pen·nate (or ·nat·ed)
penned
pen·nies
pen·ni·less
pen·ni·less·ness
Pen·nine
Pen·nines
pen·ning
pen·ni·nite mineral
pen·non long flag; compare
  pennant
Penn·syl·va·nia
Penn·syl·va·nian
pen·nul·ti·mate
pen·ny (plural pen·nies or
  pence)
pen·ny·cress
penny-pincher
penny-pinching
penny·royal plant
penny·weight

penny-wise
penny·wort plant
penny·worth
pe·no·logi·cal (or poe·)
pe·nolo·gist (or poe·)
pe·nol·ogy (or poe·)
Pen·rith Cumbrian town
pen·sile ornithology term
pen·sil·ity (or ·sile·ness)
pen·sion
pen·sion·able
pen·sion·ary (plural ·aries)
pen·sion·er
pen·sive
pen·sive·ness
pen·stock water channel
pent
pen·ta·chlo·ro·phe·nol
pen·ta·cle variant of
  pentagram
pen·tad group of five
pen·ta·dac·tyl
Pen·ta·gon US defence
  headquarters
pen·ta·gon five-sided
  polygon
pen·tago·nal
pen·ta·gram (or ·cle)
  magical symbol
pen·ta·he·dron (plural
  ·drons or ·dra)
pen·tam·er·ous botany
  term
pen·tam·eter verse line
pen·tane organic compound
pen·tan·gu·lar
pen·ta·no·ic acid
pen·ta·prism
pen·ta·quine drug
pen·tar·chi·cal
pen·tar·chy (plural ·chies)
  government by five
pen·ta·stich five-line poem
Pen·ta·teuch Old Testament
  books
pen·tath·lete
pen·tath·lon
pen·ta·ton·ic musical term
pen·ta·va·lent
Pen·tecost
Pen·tecos·tal
pen·tene organic compound
pent·house
pen·ti·men·to (plural ·ti) art
  term

pent·land·ite mineral
pen·to·bar·bi·tone (US ·tal)
pen·tode electronic valve
pen·tom·ic military term
pen·to·san biochemical
  compound
pen·tose sugar
Pen·to·thal (Trademark)
pent·ox·ide
pent·ste·mon (or
  pen·ste·mon) plant
pent-up
pen·tyl chemistry term
pentylene·tetrazol
pe·nu·che variant of
  panocha
pen·ult (or pe·nul·ti·ma)
pe·nul·ti·mate
pe·num·bra (plural ·brae or
  ·bras)
pe·num·bral (or ·brous)
pe·nu·ri·ous
penu·ry
Pen·za Russian city
Pen·zance
peon Indian worker; debtor;
  compare paean; paeon;
  pean
pe·on·age (or pe·on·ism)
peo·ny (plural ·nies)
peo·ple
Peo·ria US port
pep (pep·ping, pepped)
pep·lum (plural ·lums or ·la)
  ruffle
pepo (plural pepos) botany
  term
pep·per
pepper·corn
pepper·grass
pepper·mint
pepper·wort
pep·pery
pep·py (·pi·er, ·pi·est)
pep·sin (or ·sine) enzyme
pep·si·nate
pep·sino·gen enzyme
pep·tic of digestion; compare
  pectic
pep·ti·dase enzyme
pep·tide protein
pep·tiz·able (or ·tis·able)
pep·ti·za·tion (or ·sa·tion)
pep·tize (or ·tise)
pep·tiz·er (or ·tis·er)

pep·tone product of
  digestion
pep·to·ni·za·tion (or
  ·sa·tion)
pep·to·nize (or ·nise)
pep·to·niz·er (or ·nis·er)
Pe·quot (plural ·quot or
  ·quots) American Indian
per
per·acid
pera·cid·ity
per·ad·ven·ture Archaic by
  chance
Pe·raea ancient Palestinian
  region
Pe·rak Malaysian state
per·am·bu·late
per·am·bu·la·tion
per·am·bu·la·tor
per·am·bu·la·tory
per an·num
per·bo·rate chemistry term
per·cale sheet fabric
per·ca·line lining fabric
per capi·ta
per·ceiv·abil·ity
per·ceiv·able
per·ceive
per·ceiv·er
per cent
per·cent·age
per·cen·tile
per·cept object of
  perception
per·cep·tibil·ity (or
  ·tible·ness)
per·cep·tible
per·cep·tibly
per·cep·tion
per·cep·tion·al
per·cep·tive
per·cep·tivi·ty (or
  ·tive·ness)
per·cep·tual
perch (plural (for fish)
  perch or perches)
per·chance
perch·er
Per·cheron horse
per·chlo·rate
per·chlo·ride
per·cipi·ence
per·cipi·ent
per·coid (or ·coi·dean)
  zoology term

per·co·late
per·co·la·tion
per·co·la·tive
per·co·la·tor
per·cuss
per·cus·sion
per·cus·sion·ist
per·cus·sive
per·cus·sor
per·cu·ta·neous
per diem *Latin* every day
per·di·tion
per·egri·nate
per·egri·na·tion
per·egri·na·tor
per·egrine
Pe·rei·ra Colombian city
pe·rei·ra medicinal bark
per·emp·to·ri·ly
per·emp·to·ri·ness
per·emp·tory
pe·ren·nate botany term
pe·ren·na·tion
per·en·nial
per·en·nial·ly
perfect
per·fect·er
per·fect·ibil·ity
per·fect·ible
per·fec·tion
per·fec·tion·ism
per·fec·tion·ist
per·fec·tive
per·fec·to (*plural* ·tos) cigar
per·fer·vid ardent
per·fidi·ous
per·fidi·ous·ness
per·fi·dy (*plural* ·dies)
per·fo·li·ate botany term
per·fo·li·a·tion
per·fo·rable
per·fo·rate
per·fo·ra·tion
per·fo·ra·tive (*or* ·tory)
per·fo·ra·tor
per·force
per·form
per·form·able
per·for·mance
per·for·ma·tive
per·form·er
per·form·ing
per·fume
per·fum·er
per·fum·ery (*plural* ·eries)

per·func·to·ri·ly
per·func·to·ri·ness
per·func·tory
per·fuse
per·fu·sion
per·fu·sive
Per·ga·mum ancient Asian
  city
per·go·la
per·haps
peri (*plural* peris) fairy
peri·anth petals of flower
peri·apt amulet
peri·blem plant tissue
peri·car·dit·ic
peri·car·di·tis
peri·car·dium (*plural* ·dia)
peri·carp botany term
peri·car·pial (*or* ·pic)
peri·chon·drium (*plural*
  ·dria) anatomy term
peri·clase mineral
peri·clas·tic
peri·cli·nal botany term
peri·cline mineral
pe·rico·pe church reading
peri·cra·nial
peri·cra·nium (*plural* ·nia)
peri·cy·cle plant tissue
peri·cy·clic
peri·cyn·thi·on point in
  lunar orbit
peri·derm botany term
peri·derm·al (*or* ·ic)
pe·rid·ium (*plural* ·ridia)
  botany term
peri·dot gemstone
peri·do·tite rock
peri·do·tit·ic
peri·gean (*or* ·geal)
peri·gee point in lunar orbit
peri·gon maths term
Peri·gor·dian Palaeolithic
  culture
pe·rigy·nous botany term
pe·rigy·ny
peri·he·lion (*plural* ·lia)
  point in planet's orbit
per·il
peri·lous
peri·lous·ness
peri·lune point in lunar
  orbit
peri·lymph anatomy term
pe·rim·eter

peri·met·ric (*or* ·ri·cal,
  pe·rim·etral)
peri·met·ri·cal·ly
pe·rim·etry
peri·morph mineralogy
  term
peri·mor·phic (*or* ·phous)
peri·mor·phism
peri·mys·ium anatomy
  term
peri·na·tal
peri·neal
peri·neph·rium (*plural* ·ria)
  anatomy term
peri·neum (*plural* ·nea)
  vaginal area
peri·neu·ri·tic
peri·neu·ri·tis
peri·neu·rium nerve tissue
pe·ri·od
pe·rio·date chemistry term
pe·ri·od·ic
peri·od·ic acid
pe·ri·odi·cal
pe·ri·odi·cal·ly
pe·rio·dic·ity (*plural* ·ities)
perio·don·tal
perio·don·tic
perio·don·ti·cal·ly
perio·don·tics
perio·don·tol·ogy branch
  of dentistry
peri·onych·ium (*plural*
  ·onychia) anatomy term
peri·os·teum (*plural* ·tea)
  bone tissue
peri·os·tit·ic
peri·os·ti·tis
peri·otic around the ear
peri·pa·tet·ic
peri·pa·teti·cal·ly
peri·peteia (*or* ·petia,
  pe·rip·ety) drama term
peri·peteian (*or* ·petian)
pe·riph·er·al
pe·riph·er·al·ly
pe·riph·ery (*plural* ·eries)
pe·riph·ra·sis (*plural* ·ses)
  circumlocution
peri·phras·tic
peri·phras·ti·cal·ly
pe·riphy·ton aquatic
  organisms
pe·rip·teral
pe·rique tobacco

peri·sarc zoology term
peri·sar·cal (or ·cous)
peri·scope
peri·scop·ic
peri·scopi·cal·ly
per·ish
per·ish·abil·ity (or
·able·ness)
per·ish·able
per·ish·er
per·ish·ing
peri·sperm botany term
peri·sperm·al
peri·spo·menon linguistics
term
pe·ris·so·dac·tyl (or ·tyle)
zoology term
pe·ris·so·dac·ty·lous
peri·stal·sis (plural ·ses)
peri·stal·tic
peri·stal·ti·cal·ly
peri·sto·mal (or ·mial)
peri·stome botany term
peri·sty·lar
peri·style colonnade
peri·thecium (plural
·thecia) botany term
peri·to·neal
peri·to·neum (plural ·nea or
·niums)
peri·to·nit·ic
peri·to·ni·tis
peri·track taxiway
pe·rit·ri·cha (sing.
peri·trich) biology term
pe·rit·ri·chous
peri·wig
peri·win·kle
(perjorative) incorrect spelling
of pejorative
per·jure
per·jur·er
per·jury (plural ·juries)
perk
perki·ly
perki·ness
perky (perki·er, perki·est)
Per·lis Malaysian state
per·lite (or pearl·) filler and
soil-conditioner; compare
pearlite
per·lit·ic (or pearl·)
per·lo·cu·tion
per·lo·cu·tion·ary
Perm Russian port

perm
per·ma·frost
perm·al·loy
per·ma·nence
per·ma·nen·cy (plural ·cies)
per·ma·nent
per·man·ga·nate
per·me·abil·ity (plural
·ities)
per·me·able
per·me·ance
per·me·ant
per·me·ate
per·mea·tion
per·mea·tive
per·mea·tor
per men·sem Latin every
month
Per·mian geological period
per·mis·sibil·ity
per·mis·sible
per·mis·sion
per·mis·sive
per·mis·sive·ness
per·mit (·mit·ting,
·mit·ted)
per·mit·ter
per·mit·tiv·ity (plural ·ities)
physics term
per·mu·ta·tion
per·mu·ta·tion·al
per·mute
Per·nam·bu·co Brazilian
state
per·ni·cious
per·ni·cious·ness
per·nick·eti·ness
per·nick·ety
Per·nod (Trademark)
pe·ro·neal of the outer leg
pero·rate
pero·ra·tion
pe·roxi·dase enzyme
per·ox·ide
per·pend (or ·pent) wall
stone
per·pen·dicu·lar
per·pen·dicu·lar·ity
per·pe·trate
per·pe·tra·tion
per·pe·tra·tor
per·pet·ual
per·pet·ual·ly
per·petu·ate
per·petua·tion

per·pe·tu·ity (plural ·ities)
Per·pi·gnan French town
per·plex
per·plex·ity (plural ·ities)
per·qui·site
Per·rier (Trademark)
per·ron flight of steps
per·ry (plural ·ries) pear
wine
per·salt chemical
compound
per se Latin in itself
perse greyish-blue
per·secute
per·secu·tion
per·secu·tive (or ·tory)
per·secu·tor
Per·seid meteor shower
Persephone mythological
character
Per·sepo·lis capital of
ancient Persia
Perseus mythological
character
Per·seus constellation
per·sever·ance
per·se·ver·ant
per·sev·era·tion psychology
term
per·severe
Per·sia
Per·sian
per·si·caria plant
per·si·ennes Persian
blinds
per·si·flage
per·sim·mon fruit
Per·sis ancient Persian
region
per·sist
per·sis·tence (or ·ten·cy)
per·sis·tent
per·sist·er
per·son (plural ·sons)
per·so·na (plural ·nae)
per·son·able
per·son·able·ness
per·son·age
per·so·na gra·ta (plural
per·so·nae gra·tae)
per·son·al
per·son·al·ism
per·son·al·ist
per·son·al·is·tic
per·son·al·ity (plural ·ities)

per·son·ali·za·tion (or
 ·sa·tion)
per·son·al·ize (or ·ise)
per·son·al·ly
per·son·al·ty (plural ·ties)
 personal property
per·so·na non gra·ta (plural
 per·so·nae non gra·tae)
per·son·ate
per·sona·tion
per·sona·tive
per·sona·tor
per·soni·fi·able
per·soni·fi·ca·tion
per·soni·fy (·fies, ·fy·ing,
 ·fied)
per·son·nel
per·spec·tive
Per·spec·tiv·ism
 philosophical doctrine
Per·spex (Trademark)
per·spi·ca·cious perceptive;
 compare perspicuous
per·spi·cac·ity (or
 ·ca·cious·ness)
per·spi·cu·ity (or
 ·spicu·ous·ness)
per·spicu·ous lucid; compare
 perspicacious
per·spi·ra·tion
per·spir·atory
per·spire
per·spir·ing·ly
per·suad·abil·ity (or
 per·sua·si·bil·ity)
per·suad·able (or
 per·sua·sible)
per·suade
per·suad·er
per·sua·sion
per·sua·sive
per·sua·sive·ness
(persue) incorrect spelling of
 pursue
pert
per·tain
Perth
per·ti·na·cious
per·ti·nac·ity (or
 ·na·cious·ness)
per·ti·nence
per·ti·nent
pert·ness
per·turb
per·turb·able

per·turb·ably
per·tur·ba·tion
per·turb·ing·ly
per·tus·sis whooping cough
Peru
Pe·ru·gia Italian city
pe·ruke wig
pe·rus·al
pe·ruse
pe·rus·er
Pe·ru·vian
per·vade
per·vad·er
per·va·sion
per·va·sive
per·va·sive·ness
per·verse
per·verse·ness
per·ver·sion
per·ver·sity (plural ·sities)
per·ver·sive
per·vert
per·vert·ed
per·vert·ed·ly
per·vert·ed·ness
per·vert·er
per·ver·tible
per·vi·ous
per·vi·ous·ness
pes (plural pedes) foot
Pe·sach (or ·sah) Passover
pe·sade dressage term
Pe·sca·ra Italian city
pe·seta Spanish currency
pe·sewa Ghanaian currency
Pesha·war Pakistani city
Pe·shit·ta (or ·shi·to) Syriac
 Bible
pesky (peski·er, peski·est)
peso (plural pesos) coin
pe·soni·fi·er
pes·sa·ry (plural ·ries)
pes·si·mism
pes·si·mist
pes·si·mis·tic (or ·ti·cal)
pes·si·mis·ti·cal·ly
pest
pes·ter
pes·ter·er
pes·ter·ing·ly
pest·hole
pes·ti·cid·al
pes·ti·cide
pes·tif·er·ous
pes·ti·lence

pes·ti·lent
pes·ti·len·tial
pes·tle
pet (pet·ting, petted)
pet·al
pet·al·if·er·ous (or ·al·ous)
pet·al·ine
pet·alled (US ·aled)
petal-like
peta·lod·ic
pet·alo·dy botany term
pet·al·oid
pe·tard
pet·cock valve on steam
 boiler
pe·techia (plural ·techiae)
 red spot on skin
pe·techial
pe·ter
Pe·ter·bor·ough
Pe·ter·lee Durham town
Pe·ter·loo massacre
peter·man (plural ·men)
 Slang safe-breaker
Pe·ters·burg US city;
 compare St Petersburg
pe·ter·sham ribbon
pethi·dine
petio·late (or ·la·ted)
peti·ole leaf stalk
pe·tio·lule
pet·it of lesser importance;
 small; compare petite
pe·tit bour·geois (plural
 pe·tits bour·geois)
pe·tite small and dainty;
 compare petit
pet·ite bour·geoisie
pet·it four (plural pet·its
 fours) small cake
pe·ti·tion
pe·ti·tion·ary
pe·ti·tion·er
pet·it mal epilepsy
pet·it point needlework
 stitch
pe·tits pois French peas
Pet·ra ancient city
pet·rel bird; compare petrol
Pe·tri dish
pet·ri·fac·tion (or
 pet·ri·fi·ca·tion)
pe·tri·fi·er
pet·ri·fy (·fies, ·fy·ing,
 ·fied)

Pe·trine of St Peter

pet·ro·chemi·cal

pet·ro·chem·is·try

pet·ro·dol·lar

pet·ro·glyph prehistoric rock carving

Pet·ro·grad *former name of* Leningrad

pe·trog·ra·pher

pet·ro·graph·ic (or ·graphi·cal)

pet·ro·graphi·cal·ly

pe·trog·ra·phy classification of rocks

pet·rol fuel; *compare* petrel

pet·ro·la·tum petroleum jelly

pe·tro·leum

pe·trol·ic of petroleum

pet·ro·logi·cal

pe·trolo·gist

pe·trol·ogy (*plural* ·ogies) study of rocks

pet·ro·nel firearm

Pe·tro·pav·lovsk Kazakh city

Pe·tró·po·lis Brazilian city

pe·tro·sal anatomy term

pet·rous

Pe·tro·za·vodsk Russian city

pet·ter

pet·ti·coat

pet·ti·fog (·fog·ging, ·fogged)

pet·ti·fog·ger

pet·ti·fog·gery

pet·ti·ly

pet·ting

pet·tish

pet·tish·ness

pet·ti·toes pigs' trotters

pet·ty (·ti·er, ·ti·est)

petu·lance (or ·lan·cy)

petu·lant

pe·tu·nia

pe·tun·tse (or ·tze) mineral

pew

pe·wee (or pee·) bird

pe·wit *variant spelling of* peewit

pew·ter

pew·ter·er

pe·yo·te cactus

pfen·nig (*plural* ·nigs or ·ni·ge) German coin

Pforz·heim German city

Phaedra wife of Theseus

Phaëthon mythological character

phae·ton horse-drawn carriage

phage virus

phag·edae·na (or *esp. US* ·edena) ulcer

phago·cyte

phago·cyt·ic

phago·cy·to·sis

phago·ma·nia compulsive eating

phago·ma·ni·ac

phago·pho·bia

phago·pho·bic

phal·ange *variant of* phalanx

pha·lan·geal anatomy term

pha·lan·ger marsupial

pha·lan·ges *plural of* phalanx

phal·an·stery (*plural* ·steries)

phal·anx (*plural* phal·anxes *or* pha·lan·ges) battle formation; compact group

phal·anx (or ·ange; *plural* pha·lan·ges) finger or toe bone

phala·rope bird

phal·lic

phal·li·cism (or phal·lism)

phal·li·cist (or phal·list)

phal·lus (*plural* ·li *or* ·luses)

phan·ero·crys·tal·line

phan·ero·gam botany term

phan·ero·gam·ic (or ·er·oga·mous)

pha·nero·phyte botany term

Pha·nero·zo·ic biology term

phan·tasm

phan·tas·ma·go·ria (or ·gory)

phan·tas·ma·go·ric (or ·ri·cal)

phan·tas·ma·go·ri·cal·ly

phan·tas·mal (or ·mic)

phan·tom

phar·aoh (or Phar·)

phar·aon·ic (or Phar·)

Phari·sa·ic (or ·sai·cal)

Phari·see

phar·ma·ceu·ti·cal (or ·tic)

phar·ma·ceu·tics

phar·ma·cist (or ·ma·ceu·tist)

phar·ma·co·dy·nam·ic

phar·ma·co·dy·nam·ics

phar·ma·cog·no·sist

phar·ma·cog·nos·tic

phar·ma·cog·no·sy branch of pharmacology

phar·ma·co·logi·cal

phar·ma·colo·gist

phar·ma·col·ogy

phar·ma·co·poeia

phar·ma·co·poe·ial (or ·poe·ic)

phar·ma·co·poe·ist

phar·ma·cy (*plural* ·cies)

Pha·ros Greek lighthouse

phar·yn·geal (or pha·ryn·gal)

phar·yn·gi·tis

phar·yn·go·logi·cal

phar·yn·golo·gist

phar·yn·gol·ogy

pha·ryn·go·scope

pha·ryn·go·scop·ic

phar·yn·gos·co·py

phar·yn·goto·my (*plural* ·mies)

phar·ynx (*plural* pha·ryn·ges *or* phar·ynxes)

phase

pha·sic (or phaseal)

phas·mid insect

phat·ic of conversation

pheas·ant

phel·lem

phel·lo·derm

phel·lo·der·mal

phel·lo·gen

phel·lo·genet·ic (or ·gen·ic)

phe·na·caine anaesthetic

phe·nac·etin analgesic

phena·cite (or ·kite) mineral

phe·nan·threne

phena·zine

phe·net·ic biology term

phe·neti·dine

phen·etole

phen·for·min drug

phe·no·bar·bi·tone (*US* ·tal)

phe·no·copy (*plural
·copies*) biology term
phe·no·cryst geology term
phe·nol
phe·no·late disinfect
phe·nol·ic
phe·no·logi·cal
phe·nolo·gist
phe·nol·ogy study of
phenomena
phenol·phthalein
phe·nom·ena *plural of*
phenomenon
phe·nom·enal
phe·nom·enal·ism
phe·nom·enal·ist
phe·nom·enal·is·ti·cal·ly
phe·nom·enal·ly
phe·nom·eno·logi·cal
phe·nom·enol·ogy
phe·nom·enon (*plural ·ena
or ·enons*)
phe·no·thia·zine
phe·no·type biology term
phe·no·typ·ic (*or ·typi·cal*)
phe·no·typi·cal·ly
phe·nox·ide
phe·nyl
phenyl·alanine
phenyl·keton·uria
phero·mone chemical in
animals
phew
phial
Phi Beta Kap·pa US
academic society
Phila·del·phia
phila·del·phus shrub
Phi·lae Egyptian island
phi·lan·der
phi·lan·der·er
phil·an·throp·ic (*or
·thropi·cal*)
phi·lan·thro·pist (*or
phil·an·thrope*)
phi·lan·thro·py (*plural
·pies*)
phil·an·thropi·cal·ly
phila·tel·ic
phila·teli·cal·ly
phi·lat·ely
phil·har·mon·ic
phil·hel·lene (*or ·len·ist*)
lover of Greece

phil·hel·len·ism
Phi·lip·pi ancient
Macedonian city
phi·lip·pic bitter speech
Phil·ip·pine
Phil·ip·pines
Phil·is·tine
Phil·is·tin·ism
phil·lu·men·ist collector of
matchbox labels
philo·den·dron (*plural
·drons or ·dra*) plant
phi·logy·ny fondness for
women
philo·logi·cal
phi·lolo·gist (*or ·ger*)
phi·lol·ogy
philo·mel (*or ·mela*)
nightingale
Philomela mythological
princess
phi·loso·pher
philo·soph·ic
philo·sophi·cal (*or
·soph·ic*)
philo·sophi·cal·ly
philo·sophi·cal·ness
phi·loso·phi·za·tion (*or
·sa·tion*)
phi·loso·phize (*or ·phise*)
phi·loso·phiz·er (*or
·phis·er*)
phi·loso·phy (*plural ·phies*)
phil·tre (*US ·ter*) love
potion; *compare* filter
phi·mo·sis medical term
phi·phenom·enon (*plural
·ena*) psychology term
phiz *Slang* face
phle·bit·ic
phle·bi·tis
phlebo·scle·ro·sis
phlebo·tom·ic (*or
·tomi·cal*)
phle·boto·mist
phle·boto·mize
phle·boto·my (*plural ·mies*)
incision into vein
phlegm
phleg·mat·ic (*or ·mati·cal*)
phleg·mati·cal·ly
phleg·mati·cal·ness (*or
·mat·ic·ness*)
phlo·em plant tissue
phlo·gis·tic

phlo·gis·ton
phlogo·pite mineral
phlox (*plural phlox or
phloxes*)
phlyc·ten (*or ·te·na; plural
·tens or ·nae*) blister
Phnom Penh (*or Pnom
Penh*) Cambodian capital
pho·bia
pho·bic
Pho·bos satellite of Mars
pho·cine of seals
Pho·cis region of ancient
Greece
pho·co·melia (*or ·com·ely*)
Phoe·be satellite of Saturn
phoe·be bird
Phoebus Apollo
Phoe·ni·cia
Phoe·ni·cian
Phoe·nix US city
phoe·nix legendary bird
phon unit
pho·nate utter speech
pho·na·tion
pho·na·tory
phone
phone-in (*noun*)
pho·neme linguistics term
pho·nemic
pho·nemi·cal·ly
pho·nemics
pho·net·ic
pho·neti·cal·ly
pho·neti·cian
pho·net·ics
pho·net·ist
pho·ney (*or ·ny; adj ·ni·er,
·ni·est; noun, plural ·neys
or ·nies*)
pho·ney·ness (*or ·ni·*)
phon·ic
phoni·cal·ly
phon·ics teaching method
pho·ni·ness *variant spelling
of* phoneyness
pho·no·gram
pho·no·gram·ic (*or
·gram·mic*)
pho·no·graph
pho·nog·ra·pher (*or ·phist*)
pho·nog·ra·phy
pho·no·lite rock
pho·no·lit·ic
pho·no·logi·cal

pho·nolo·gist
pho·nol·ogy (plural ·ogies)
pho·nom·eter
pho·no·met·ric (or ·ri·cal)
pho·non physics term
pho·no·scope
pho·no·tac·tics branch of
linguistics
pho·no·type
pho·no·typ·ic (or ·typi·cal)
pho·no·typ·ist (or ·typ·er)
pho·no·typy phonetic
transcription
pho·ny variant spelling of
phoney
phoo·ey
phos·gene poisonous gas
phos·ge·nite mineral
phos·pha·tase enzyme
phos·phate
phos·phat·ic
phos·pha·tide biochemical
compound
phos·pha·ti·za·tion (or
·sa·tion)
phos·pha·tize (or ·tise)
phos·pha·tu·ria
phos·pha·tu·ric
phos·phene physiology
term; compare phosphine
phos·phide
phos·phine gas; compare
phosphene
phos·phite
phos·pho·crea·tine (or ·tin)
phos·pho·lip·id
phos·pho·pro·tein
phos·phor
phos·pho·rate
phos·pho·resce
phos·pho·res·cence
phos·pho·res·cent
phos·phor·ic
phos·pho·rism
phos·pho·rite mineral
phos·pho·rit·ic
phos·phoro·scope
phos·pho·rous (adj)
phos·pho·rus (noun)
phos·phory·lase enzyme
phot unit
pho·tic of light
pho·to (plural ·tos)
photo·ac·tin·ic
photo·ac·tive

photo·auto·troph·ic
biology term
photo·bath·ic biology term
photo·cath·ode
photo·cell
photo·chemi·cal
photo·chem·ist
photo·chem·is·try
photo·com·pose
photo·com·pos·er
photo·com·po·si·tion
photo·con·duc·tion
photo·con·duc·tiv·ity
photo·con·duc·tor
photo·copi·er
photo·copy (noun, plural
·copies; verb ·copies,
·copy·ing, ·cop·ied)
photo·cur·rent
photo·dis·in·te·gra·tion
photo·dy·nam·ic
photo·dy·nam·ics
photo·elas·tic·ity
photo·elec·tric (or ·tri·cal)
photo·elec·tri·cal·ly
photo·elec·tric·ity
photo·elec·tron
photo·elec·tro·type
photo·emis·sion
photo·emis·sive
photo·en·grave
photo·en·grav·er
photo·en·grav·ing
Photo·fit (Trademark)
photo·flash
photo·flood tungsten lamp
photo·fluo·rog·ra·phy
photo·gen·ic
photo·geni·cal·ly
photo·geol·ogy
photo·gram type of
photograph
photo·gram·met·ric
photo·gram·metrist
photo·gram·metry
photo·graph
pho·tog·ra·pher
photo·graph·ic
photo·graphi·cal·ly
pho·tog·ra·phy
photo·gra·vure
photo·jour·nal·ism
photo·jour·na·list
photo·jour·na·lis·tic
photo·ki·nesis

photo·ki·net·ic
photo·ki·neti·cal·ly
photo·litho·graph
photo·li·thog·ra·pher
photo·li·thog·ra·phy
pho·to·lu·mi·nes·cence
pho·to·lu·mi·nes·cent
pho·toly·sis
photo·lyt·ic
photo·map (·map·ping,
·mapped)
photo·mechani·cal
pho·tom·eter
photo·met·ric
photo·met·ri·cal·ly
pho·tom·etrist
pho·tom·etry
photo·micro·graph
photo·mi·crog·ra·pher
photo·micro·graph·ic
photo·micro·graphi·cal·ly
photo·mi·crog·ra·phy
photo·mon·tage
photo·multi·pli·er
photo·mu·ral
pho·ton
photo·nas·tic
photo·nas·ty botany term
photo·neu·tron
photo·nu·cle·ar
photo·offset
photo·peri·od
photo·peri·od·ic
photo·peri·odi·cal·ly
photo·peri·od·ism biology
term
pho·tophi·lous botany term
pho·tophi·ly
photo·pho·bia
photo·pho·bic
photo·phore
light-producing organ
photo·pia day vision
pho·top·ic
photo·poly·mer
photo·recep·tor
photo·recon·nais·sance
photo·sen·si·tive
photo·sen·si·tiv·ity
photo·sen·si·ti·za·tion (or
·sa·tion)
photo·sen·si·tize (or ·tise)
photo·set (·set·ting, ·set)
photo·set·ter
photo·sphere surface of sun

photo·spher·ic
Photo·stat (*Trademark*)
  machine
photo·stat (*noun, verb*)
  photocopy
photo·stat·ic
photo·syn·the·sis
photo·syn·the·size
photo·syn·thet·ic
photo·syn·theti·cal·ly
photo·tac·tic
photo·tax·is (*or* ·taxy)
  biology term
photo·tele·graph·ic
photo·tele·graphi·cal·ly
photo·teleg·ra·phy
photo·thera·peu·tic
photo·thera·peu·ti·cal·ly
photo·thera·py (*or*
  ·peu·tics)
photo·ther·mic (*or* ·mal)
photo·ther·mi·cal·ly (*or*
  ·mal·ly)
photo·ton·ic
pho·toto·nus botany term
photo·to·pog·ra·phy
photo·tran·sis·tor
photo·trop·ic
pho·tot·ro·pism botany
  term
photo·tube
photo·type
photo·type·set·ting
photo·typ·ic
photo·typi·cal·ly
photo·ty·pog·ra·phy
photo·vol·ta·ic
photo·zin·co·graph
photo·zin·cog·ra·phy
phras·al
phrase
phra·seo·gram symbol
phra·seo·graph phrase
phra·seo·graph·ic
phra·seog·ra·phy
phra·seo·logi·cal
phra·seolo·gist
phra·seol·ogy (*plural* ·ogies)
phras·ing
phra·tric anthropology term
phra·try (*plural* ·tries)
phre·at·ic geography term
phren·ic of the diaphragm
phre·net·ic *obsolete spelling*
  of frenetic

phreno·logi·cal
phre·nolo·gist
phre·nol·ogy study of head
  bumps
Phrygia ancient Asian
  country
Phryg·ian
phtha·lein
phthal·ic acid
phthalo·cya·nine
phthi·ria·sis infestation
  with lice; *compare* pthisis
phthi·sic
phthisi·cal
phthi·sis wasting disease;
  compare phthiriasis
phut
phy·co·logi·cal
phy·colo·gist
phy·col·ogy study of algae
phy·co·my·cete fungus
phy·co·my·cetous
phy·lac·tery (*plural* ·teries)
  case for Hebrew texts
phy·le (*plural* ·lae) ancient
  Greek tribe
phy·let·ic (*or*
  phy·lo·genet·ic) biology
  term
phy·leti·cal·ly (*or*
  phy·lo·geneti·cal·ly)
phyl·lite rock
phyl·lit·ic
phyl·lo·clade (*or* ·clad)
  botany term
phyl·lode botany term
phyl·lo·dial
phyl·loid leaflike
phyl·lome botany term
phyl·lom·ic
phyl·lo·qui·none vitamin
phyl·lo·tax·is (*or* ·taxy;
  plural ·taxes *or* taxies)
phyl·lox·era (*plural* ·erae *or*
  ·eras) vine pest
phy·lo·gen·ic (*or* ·genet·ic)
phy·log·eny (*or*
  ·lo·gen·esis; *plural* ·nies *or*
  ·eses) biology term
phylo·tac·tic
phy·lum (*plural* ·la)
physi·at·ric (*or* ·ri·cal)
physi·at·rics US
  physiotherapy
phys·ic (·ick·ing, ·icked)

physi·cal
physi·cal·ism philosophical
  doctrine
physi·cal·ist
physi·cal·is·tic
physi·cal·ly
physi·cal·ness
phy·si·cian
physi·cist
physi·co·chemi·cal
phys·ics
physio·crat
physio·crat·ic
physi·og·nom·ic (*or*
  ·nomi·cal)
physi·og·nomi·cal·ly
physi·og·no·mist
physi·og·no·my (*plural*
  ·mies)
physi·og·ra·pher
physio·graph·ic (*or*
  ·graphi·cal)
physi·og·ra·phy physical
  geography
physio·logi·cal
physio·logi·cal·ly
physi·olo·gist
physi·ol·ogy
(physionomy) *incorrect*
  spelling of physiognomy
physio·thera·pist
physio·thera·py
phy·sique
phy·so·clis·tous zoology
  term
phy·so·stig·mine (*or* ·min)
  drug
phy·sos·to·mous zoology
  term
phyto·gen·esis (*or*
  phy·tog·eny) botany term
phyto·genet·ic
phyto·geneti·cal·ly
phyto·gen·ic
phyto·geog·ra·pher
phyto·geog·ra·phy
phy·tog·ra·phy
phyto·hor·mone
phy·tol·ogy
phy·ton botany term
phyto·patho·logi·cal
phyto·pa·tholo·gist
phyto·pa·thol·ogy
phy·topha·gous
phy·topha·gy

phyto·plank·ton
phyto·plank·ton·ic
phyto·so·cio·logi·cal
phyto·so·ci·olo·gist
phyto·so·ci·ol·ogy
phyto·tox·in
phyto·tron botanical apparatus
pi (plural pis) Greek letter
Pia·cen·za Italian town
pi·acu·lar making atonement
pi·affe dressage term
pia ma·ter brain membrane
pia·nism
pia·nis·si·mo
pia·nist
pia·nis·tic
pi·ano (plural ·anos)
pi·ano·for·te
Pia·no·la (Trademark)
pi·as·sa·va (or ·ba) palm tree
pi·as·tre (or esp. US ·ter) currency
Piauí Brazilian state
pi·az·za
pi·broch bagpipe music
pica printer's measure; eating dirt; compare pika
pica·dor
Pic·ar·dy French region
pica·resque of type of fiction; compare picturesque
pica·roon (or picka·) adventurer
pica·yune US of little value
Pic·ca·dil·ly
pic·ca·lil·li pickle
pic·ca·nin·ny (or picka·; plural ·nies)
pic·co·lo (plural ·los)
pice (plural pice) coin
pic·eous of pitch
pichi·ci·ego (plural ·egos) animal
pick
picka·back variant of piggyback
pick·able
pick·axe (US ·ax)
pick·er
pick·er·el (plural ·el or ·els) fish

pickerel·weed
pick·et
pick·et·er
pick·et·ing
pick·ings
pick·le
pick·led
pick·ler
pick·lock
pick·me·up
pick·pocket
pick·up (noun)
Pick·wick·ian
picky
pic·nic (·nick·ing, ·nicked)
pic·nick·er
pico·line chemical compound
pico·lin·ic
pi·cot pattern of loops
pico·tee carnation
pic·rate chemistry term
pic·ric acid
pic·rite rock
pic·ro·tox·in
Pict
Pict·ish
pic·to·graph
pic·to·rial
pic·to·rial·ly
pic·ture
pic·tur·esque strikingly pleasing; compare picaresque
pic·tur·esque·ness
pic·ul unit
pid·dle
pid·dling
pid·dock mollusc
pidg·in language; compare pigeon
pie
pie·bald
piece
pièce de ré·sis·tance (plural pièces de ré·sis·tance)
piece·dyed
piece·meal
piec·er
piece·work
pie·crust
pied multi-coloured
pied·à·terre (plural pieds·à·terre)
Pied·mont Italian region

pied·mont at mountain base
pied·mont·ite mineral
pie·eyed
pie·man (plural ·men)
pier landing place; pillar; compare peer
pierc·able
pierce
pierc·er
pierc·ing
pierc·ing·ly
Pi·erian
Pi·eri·des Muses
pi·eri·dine zoology term
Pi·er·rot pantomime clown
pi·età religious painting
Pie·ter·mar·itz·burg South African city
pi·ety (plural ·eties)
pi·ezo·chem·is·try
pi·ezo·elec·tric
pi·ezo·elec·tri·cal·ly
pi·ezo·elec·tric·ity
pi·ezom·eter
pi·ezo·met·ric
pi·ezo·met·ri·cal·ly
pif·fle
pig (pig·ging, pigged)
pi·geon bird; compare pidgin
pigeon·hole
pigeon·toed
pig·face plant
pig·fish (plural ·fish or ·fishes)
pig·gery (plural ·geries)
pig·gin small bucket
pig·gish
pig·gish·ness
pig·gy (noun, plural ·gies; adj ·gi·er, ·gi·est)
piggy·back (or picka·back)
pig·headed
pig·headed·ness
pig·let
pig·like
pig·meat
pig·ment
pig·men·tary
pig·men·ta·tion
pig·ment·ed
pig·my variant spelling of pygmy
pig·nut

pig·skin
pig·stick
pig·stick·er
pig·stick·ing
pig·sty (*plural* ·sties)
pig·swill
pig·tail
pig·tailed
pig·weed
pika animal; *compare* pica
pike
pike·let crumpet
pike·perch (*plural* ·perch *or* ·perches) fish
pik·er
pike·staff
pil·af (*or* ·aff) *variant of* pilau
pi·las·ter
pi·lau (*or* pil·af, pil·aff) rice dish
pilch *Archaic* infant's garment
pil·chard
pile
pi·leate (*or* ·leat·ed) biology term
pile-driver
pi·leous of hair
piles
pi·leum (*plural* ·lea) top of bird's head
pile-up (*noun*)
pi·leus (*plural* ·lei) mushroom cap
pile·wort
pil·fer
pil·fer·age
pil·fer·er
pil·garlic *Dialect* pitiful person
pil·grim
pil·grim·age
pili (*plural* pilis) tree
pi·li *plural of* pilus
pi·lif·er·ous
pili·form
pil·ing
pill
pil·lage
pil·lag·er
pil·lar
pill·box
pil·lion

pil·li·winks instrument of torture
pil·lo·ry (*noun, plural* ·ries; *verb* ·ries, ·ry·ing, ·ried)
pil·low
pillow·case (*or* ·slip)
pi·lo·car·pine (*or* ·pin) drug
pi·lose biology term
pi·lot
pi·lot·age
Pils·ner (*or* Pil·sen·er) beer
Pilt·down man
pilu·lar
pil·ule
pi·lus (*plural* ·li) a hair
pi·men·to (*plural* ·tos) spice
pi·mien·to (*plural* ·tos) sweet pepper
pimp
pim·per·nel
pim·ple
pim·pled
pim·pli·ness
pim·ply (·pli·er, ·pli·est)
pin (pin·ning, pinned)
pi·na·ceous botany term
pina·fore
pi·nas·ter pine tree
pin·ball
pince-nez (*plural* pince-nez)
pin·cer
pin·cers tool
pinch
pinch·beck imitation gold
pinch·cock clamp
pinch·penny (*plural* ·pennies)
pin·cushion
Pin·dar·ic ode
pind·ling *Dialect* peevish
Pin·dus Greek mountain range
pine
pin·eal gland
pine·apple
pi·nene chemical compound
pi·nery (*plural* ·neries)
pi·netum (*plural* ·neta) plantation
pin·feather
pin·fish (*plural* ·fish *or* ·fishes)
pin·fold
ping

ping·er
pin·go (*plural* ·gos) landform
Ping-Pong (*Trademark*) (*or* ping·pong)
pin·guid fatty
pin·guid·ity (*or* ·ness)
pin·head
pin·hole
pin·ion
pin·ite mineral
pink
pink·eye
pinkie (*or* pinky) *US* little finger
pink·ish
pink·root
pinky pinkish; *variant spelling of* pinkie
pin·na (*plural* ·nae *or* ·nas) biology term
pin·nace boat
pin·na·cle
pin·nate (*or* ·nat·ed) feather-like
pin·nati·fid botany term
pin·na·tion
pin·nati·par·tite botany term
pin·nati·ped ornithology term
pin·nati·sect botany term
pinned
pin·ner
pin·ning
pin·ni·ped (*or* ·pedian) zoology term
pin·nu·lar
pin·nule (*or* ·nu·la; *plural* ·nules *or* ·nu·lae)
pin·ny (*plural* ·nies) *Slang* pinafore
pi·noch·le (*or* ·nuch·le, ·noc·le) card game
pi·no·le flour
pin·point
pin·prick
pin·stripe
pint
pin·ta skin disease
pin·ta·dera Neolithic stamp
pin·tail (*plural* ·tails *or* ·tail) duck
pin·tle hinge pin

pin·to (*plural* ·tos) piebald horse

pin-up (*noun*)

pin·wheel

pin·work

pin·worm

pinx·it *Latin* painted (*inscription on painting*)

piny (*or* piney; pini·er, pini·est)

pio·let ice axe

pion physics term

pio·neer

pi·ous

pi·ous·ness

pip (pip·ping, pipped)

pipa toad

pip·age

pi·pal *variant spelling of* peepul

pipe

pipe·clay

pipe·fish (*plural* ·fish *or* ·fishes)

pipe·fitting

pipe·line

pip·er

pip·era·ceous botany term

pi·pera·zine drug

pi·peri·dine organic compound

pip·er·ine alkaloid

pip·ero·nal fragrant compound

pipe·stone

pi·pette

pipe·wort

pip·ing

pipi·strelle bat

pip·it bird

pip·kin small pot

pipped

pip·pin apple

pip·ping

pip·sis·sewa plant

pip·squeak

pi·quan·cy (*or* ·quant·ness)

pi·quant

pique (piqu·ing, piqued)

pi·qué fabric

pi·quet card game

pi·ra·cy (*plural* ·cies)

Pi·rae·us (*or* Pei·) Greek port

pi·ra·nha (*or* ·na)

pi·rate

pi·rat·ic (*or* ·rati·cal)

pi·rati·cal·ly

pirn fishing rod

pi·rog (*plural* ·ro·gi) pie

pi·rogue (*or* pi·ra·gua) canoe

pirou·ette

Pisa

pis al·ler *French* a last resort

pis·ca·ry (*plural* ·ries) fishing place

pis·ca·to·rial (*or* ·tory)

Pi·sces constellation; sign of zodiac

pis·ci·cul·tur·al

pis·ci·cul·ture

pis·ci·cul·tur·ist

pis·ci·na (*plural* ·nae *or* ·nas) basin in church

pis·cine

pis·civo·rous

pi·shogue *Irish* sorcery

pisi·form pealike

pis·mire *Dialect* ant

pi·so·lite rock

piss

pis·ta·chio (*plural* ·chios)

pis·ta·reen coin

piste skiing slope

pis·til flower part; *compare* pistol

pis·til·late

pis·tol (·tol·ling, ·tolled; *US* ·tol·ing, ·toled) gun; *compare* pistil

pis·tole coin

pis·to·leer soldier

pis·ton

pit (pit·ting, pit·ted)

pita fibre; *compare* pitta

pita·pat (·pat·ting, ·pat·ted)

Pit·cairn Pacific island

pitch

pitch-black

pitch·blende mineral

pitch-dark

pitch·er

pitch·fork

pitchi·ness

pitch·om·eter nautical term

pitch·stone

pitchy (pitchi·er, pitchi·est)

pit·eous

pit·eous·ness

pit·fall

pith

pit·head

pith·ecan·thro·pine (*or* ·poid)

pith·ecan·thro·pus (*plural* ·pi) apelike man

pithi·ly

pithi·ness

pi·thos (*plural* ·thoi) oil container

pithy (pithi·er, pithi·est)

piti·able

piti·able·ness

piti·ably

piti·ful

piti·ful·ly

piti·ful·ness

piti·less

piti·less·ness

pit·man (*plural* ·men)

pi·ton mountaineering spike

pit·saw

pit·ta flat bread; *compare* pita

pit·tance

pitter-patter

Pitts·burgh *US* port

pi·tui·tary (*plural* ·taries)

pitu·ri shrub

pity (*noun, plural* pities; *verb* pities, pity·ing, pit·ied)

pity·ing·ly

pity·ria·sis (*plural* ·ses) skin disease

Piu·ra Peruvian city

piv·ot

piv·ot·al

pix *Slang* pictures; *compare* pyx

pix·el component of digitized picture

pix·el·ate video technique

pix·el·a·tion

pixie (*or* pixy; *plural* pixies)

pixi·lat·ed *US* eccentric

pize *Dialect* to hit

piz·za

piz·ze·ria

piz·zi·ca·to (*plural* ·ti *or* ·tos)

plac·abil·ity (*or* ·able·ness)

plac·able easily placated;
  compare placeable
plac·ard
pla·cate
pla·ca·tion
placa·tory (*or* ·tive)
place position; *compare*
  plaice
place·able easily placed;
  compare placable
pla·cebo (*plural* ·cebos *or*
  ·ceboes)
place·ment
pla·cen·ta (*plural* ·tas *or*
  ·tae)
pla·cen·tal (*or* ·tate)
plac·en·ta·tion
plac·er
pla·cet vote of assent
plac·id
pla·cid·ity (*or* ·ness)
plac·ing
plack·et dressmaking term
placo·derm extinct fish
plac·oid platelike
(plad) *incorrect spelling of*
  plaid
pla·fond ceiling; card game
pla·gal musical term
plage astronomy term
pla·gia·rism
pla·gia·rist
pla·gia·ris·tic
pla·gia·rize (*or* ·rise)
pla·gia·riz·er (*or* ·ris·er)
pla·gio·clase mineral
pla·gio·cli·max ecology
  term
pla·gi·ot·ro·pism botany
  term
plague (plagu·ing,
  plagued)
plagu·er
pla·gui·ly
pla·guy (*or* ·guey)
plaice (*plural* plaice *or*
  plaices) fish; *compare*
  place
plaid tartan cloth
plain simple; unattractive;
  treeless region; *compare*
  plane
plain·chant
plain·ish rather plain;
  compare planish

plain-laid describing rope
plain·ness
plains·man (*plural* ·men)
plain·song
plain-spoken
plaint
plain·tiff legal term
plain·tive melancholy
plain·tive·ness
plait braid; *compare* plat
plan (plan·ning, planned)
pla·nar
pla·nar·ian flatworm
pla·na·tion erosion of land
planch·et blank coin
plan·chette board for spirit
  messages
plane aircraft; level; tool;
  tree; *compare* plain
plan·er
plan·et
plan·etar·ium (*plural* ·iums
  or ·taria)
plan·etary (*plural* ·etaries)
plan·etesi·mal small
  planetary body
plan·et·oid asteroid
plan·etoid·al
plan·form silhouette
plan·gen·cy
plan·gent
pla·nim·eter
pla·ni·met·ric (*or* ·ri·cal)
pla·nim·etry
plan·ish to smooth; *compare*
  plainish
plan·ish·er
plani·sphere
plani·spher·ic
plank
plank·ing
plank-sheer nautical term
plank·ton
plank·ton·ic
planned
plan·ner
plan·ning
plano-concave
plano-convex
plano·gam·ete
pla·no·graph·ic
pla·no·graphi·cal·ly
pla·nog·ra·phy printing
  process
pla·nom·eter

pla·no·met·ric
pla·nom·etry
pla·no·sol soil
plant
plant·able
plan·tain weed; cooking
  banana
plan·tar of sole of foot
plan·ta·tion
plant·er
plan·ti·grade zoology
  term
planu·la (*plural* ·lae) larva
planu·lar
plaque
plash
plashy (plashi·er,
  plashi·est)
plasm protoplasm
plas·ma blood fluid; physics
  term
plas·ma·gel jelly-like
  protoplasm
plas·ma·gene
plas·ma·gen·ic
plas·ma·sol fluid
  protoplasm
plas·min enzyme
plas·mo·des·ma (*or* ·desm;
  plural ·des·ma·ta *or*
  ·desms) botany term
plas·mo·dium (*plural* ·dia)
  biology term; malaria
  parasite
plas·mo·lyse (*US* ·lyze)
plas·moly·sis
plas·mo·lyt·ic
plas·mo·lyti·cal·ly
plas·mon biology term
plas·mo·some
Plas·sey Indian battle site
plas·ter
plaster·board
plas·tered
plas·ter·er
plas·ter·ing
plas·tic
plas·ti·cal·ly
Plas·ti·cine (*Trademark*)
plas·tic·ity
plas·ti·ci·za·tion (*or*
  ·sa·tion)
plas·ti·cize (*or* ·cise)
plas·ti·ciz·er (*or* ·cis·er)
plas·tid cell structure

plas·tom·eter plasticity measurer

plas·to·met·ric

plas·tom·etry

plas·tral

plas·tron

plat small plot; *compare* plait

plat·an plane tree; *compare* platen

plat du jour (*plural* plats du jour)

plate

plat·eau (*plural* ·eaus *or* ·eaux)

plat·ed

plate·ful (*plural* ·fuls)

plate·layer

plate·let

plate·mark hallmark

plat·en printing plate; typewriter roller; *compare* platan

plat·er

plat·form

plati·na alloy

plat·ing

pla·tin·ic

plati·nif·er·ous

plat·ini·rid·ium alloy

plati·ni·za·tion (*or* ·sa·tion)

plati·nize (*or* ·nise)

plati·no·cya·nide

plati·noid

plati·no·type photographic process

plati·nous

plati·num

platinum-blond (*fem* -blonde)

plati·tude

plati·tu·di·nize (*or* ·nise)

plati·tu·di·niz·er (*or* ·nis·er)

plati·tu·di·nous

Pla·ton·ic of Plato

pla·ton·ic nonerotic

pla·toni·cal·ly

Pla·to·nism

Pla·to·nize (*or* ·nise)

pla·toon

Platte US river

plat·ter

platy (plati·er, plati·est)

platy (*plural* platy, platys, *or* platies) fish

platy·hel·minth flatworm

platy·hel·min·thic

platy·pus (*plural* ·puses)

plat·yr·rhine (*or* ·rhin·ian) zoology term

plau·dit

plau·sibil·ity (*or* ·sible·ness)

plau·sible

plau·sibly

plau·sive approving

play

pla·ya lake

play·able

play·act

play·actor

play·back

play·bill

play·boy

play·er

play·fellow

play·ful

play·ful·ly

play·ful·ness

play·goer

play·ground

play·group

play·house

play·let

play·mate

play·off (*noun*)

play·pen

play·room

play·school

play·suit

play·thing

play·time

play·wright

pla·za

plea

pleach make hedge

plead (plead·ing, plead·ed, plead *or* pled)

plead·able

plead·er

pleas·able

pleas·ance secluded garden

pleas·ant

pleas·ant·ness

pleas·ant·ry (*plural* ·ries)

please

pleased

pleas·ed·ly

pleas·er

pleas·ing

pleas·ing·ness

pleas·ur·able

pleas·ur·able·ness

pleas·ur·ably

pleas·ure

pleas·ure·ful

pleas·ure·less

pleat

pleat·er

pleb

pleb·by (·bi·er, ·bi·est)

ple·beian

ple·beian·ism

plebi·scite

plec·tog·nath fish

plec·trum (*or* ·tron; *plural* ·tra, ·trums, *or* ·trons)

pledge

pledgee

pledg·er (*or esp. in legal contexts* ·or)

pledg·et bandaging pad

plei·ad talented group

Pleia·des constellation

Pleiades (*sing.* Pleiad) mythological characters

plein-air art term

plei·ot·ro·pism genetics term

Pleis·to·cene geological epoch

ple·na·ri·ly

ple·na·ry

ple·nipo·tent

pleni·po·ten·ti·ary (*plural* ·aries)

pleni·tude abundance

plen·teous

plen·teous·ness

plen·ti·ful

plen·ti·ful·ly

plen·ti·ful·ness

plen·ty (*plural* ·ties)

ple·num (*plural* ·nums *or* ·na)

pleo·chro·ic

ple·och·ro·ism chemistry term

pleo·mor·phic

pleo·mor·phism (*or* ·phy) biology term

pleo·nasm use of superfluous words

pleo·nas·tic

pleo·nas·ti·cal·ly

ple·sio·saur
ples·sor *variant of* **plexor**
pletho·ra
ple·thys·mo·graph
pleu·ra (*plural* **·rae**)
  membrane round lungs;
  plural of **pleuron**
pleu·ral
pleu·ri·sy
pleu·rit·ic
pleu·ro·dont zoology term
pleu·ro·dy·nia pain
  between ribs
pleu·ron (*plural* **·ra**) zoology
  term; *compare* **pleura**
pleu·ro·pneu·mo·nia
pleu·roto·my (*plural* **·mies**)
pleus·ton floating algae
plew (*or* **plue, plu**) beaver
  skin
plexi·form
Plexi·glass (*Trademark*)
plex·or (*or* **ples·sor**) medical
  hammer
plex·us (*plural* **·uses** *or* **·us**)
  network
pli·abil·ity (*or* **able·ness**)
pli·able
pli·an·cy (*or* **·ant·ness**)
pli·ant
pli·ca (*plural* **·cae**) anatomy
  term
pli·cal
pli·cate (*or* **·cat·ed**) pleated
pli·cate·ness
pli·ca·tion (*or* **plica·ture**)
plié ballet posture
pli·er (*or* **ply·**) one who
  plies
pli·ers tool
plight
plight·er
plim·soll (*or* **·sole**)
Plim·soll line
plinth
Plio·cene (*or* **Pleio·cene**)
  geological epoch
plis·sé fabric with wrinkled
  finish
ploat *Dialect* thrash
plod (**plod·ding, plod·ded**)
plod·der
plod·ding·ly
plod·ding·ness
plodge *Dialect* wade

Plo·eş·ti Romanian city
plonk
plonk·er *Slang* idiot
plonko *Austral* alcoholic
plop (**plop·ping, plopped**)
plo·sion phonetics term
plo·sive phonetics term
plot (**plot·ting, plot·ted**)
plot·ter
Plough group of stars
plough (*US* **plow**)
plough·boy (*US* **plow·**)
plough·er (*US* **plow·**)
plough·man (*US* **plow·**;
  plural **·men**)
plough·man·ship (*US*
  plow·)
plough·share (*US* **plow·**)
plough·staff (*US* **plow·**)
Plov·div Bulgarian city
plov·er
plow *US spelling of* **plough**
ploy
pluck
pluck·er
plucki·ly
plucki·ness
plucky (**plucki·er,**
  plucki·est)
plug (**plug·ging, plugged**)
plug·board
plum fruit; *compare* **plumb**
plum·age
plu·mate (*or* **·mose**)
plumb work as plumber;
  experience misery; *compare*
  plum
plumb·able
plum·bagi·na·ceous botany
  term
plum·ba·go (*plural* **·gos**)
  graphite; plant
plum·beous of lead
plumb·er
plumb·ery (*plural* **·eries**)
plum·bic chemistry term
plum·bi·con TV camera
  tube
plum·bif·er·ous
plumb·ing
plum·bism lead poisoning
plum·bous chemistry term
plum·bum lead
plume
plum·met

plum·my (**·mi·er, ·mi·est**)
plump
plump·er
plump·ness
plu·mule
plumy (**plumi·er,**
  plumi·est)
plun·der
plun·der·able
plun·der·age
plun·der·er
plun·der·ous
plunge
plung·er
plunk
plu·per·fect grammar term
plu·ral
plu·ral·ism
plu·ral·ist
plu·ral·ity (*plural* **·ities**)
plu·rali·za·tion (*or* **·sa·tion**)
plu·ral·ize (*or* **·ise**)
plu·ral·iz·er (*or* **·is·er**)
plu·ral·ly
plus
plush
plush·ness
plushy (**plushi·er,**
  plushi·est)
Pluto Greek god
Plu·to planet
plu·toc·ra·cy (*plural* **·cies**)
plu·to·crat
plu·to·crat·ic (*or* **·crati·cal**)
plu·to·crati·cal·ly
plu·ton geology term
Plu·to·nian infernal
plu·ton·ic geology term
plu·to·nium
plu·vial of rain
plu·vi·om·eter
plu·vio·met·ric
plu·vio·met·ri·cal·ly
plu·vi·om·etry
plu·vi·ous (*or* **·ose**)
ply (*verb* **plies, ply·ing,**
  plied; *noun, plural* **plies**)
ply·er *variant spelling of*
  plier
Plym·outh
ply·wood
Plzeň Czech city
pneu·ma philosophy term
pneu·mat·ic
pneu·mati·cal·ly

pneu·mat·ics branch of physics

pneu·ma·tol·ogy branch of theology

pneu·ma·toly·sis geology term

pneu·ma·tom·eter

pneu·ma·tom·etry

pneu·mato·phore biology term

pneu·mo·ba·cil·lus (*plural* ·li)

pneu·mo·coc·cus (*plural* ·coc·ci)

pneu·mo·co·nio·sis

pneu·mo·dy·nam·ics pneumatics

pneu·mo·en·cepha·lo·gram

pneu·mo·gas·tric

pneu·mo·graph

pneu·mo·nec·to·my (*or* pneu·mec·to·my; *plural* ·mies)

pneu·mo·nia

pneu·mon·ic

pneu·mon·it·is

pneu·mo·tho·rax

Po Italian river

po (*plural* pos) chamber pot

poa·ceous botany term

poach

poach·er

poach·ing

po·chard (*plural* ·chards *or* ·chard) duck

pock

pock·et

pock·et·able

pocket·book

pock·et·ful (*plural* ·fuls)

pocket·knife (*plural* ·knives)

pock·mark

poco musical term

po·co·cu·ran·te indifferent

pod (pod·ding, pod·ded)

po·dag·ra gout

po·dag·ral (*or* ·ric, ·ri·cal, ·rous)

pod·dy (*plural* ·dies) *Austral* hand-fed calf

po·des·ta Italian magistrate

podgi·ly

podgi·ness

Pod·go·ri·ca capital of Montenegro

podgy (podgi·er, podgi·est)

po·dia·try *US* chiropody

po·dium (*plural* ·diums *or* ·dia)

Po·dolsk Russian city

podo·phyl·lin medicinal resin

pod·zol (*or* ·sol)

pod·zol·ic (*or* ·sol·ic)

poem

po·esy (*plural* ·esies)

poet

po·et·as·ter inferior poet

po·et·ess

po·et·ic (*or* ·eti·cal)

po·eti·cal·ly

po·eti·cize (*or* po·et·ize, po·eti·cise, po·et·ise)

po·et·ics

poet lau·reate (*plural* poets lau·reate)

po·et·ry

po-faced

pogge fish

po·go·nia orchid

pog·rom

Po·hai inlet of Yellow Sea

poi Hawaiian food

poign·an·cy

poign·ant

poi·ki·lo·ther·mic (*or* ·mal) cold-blooded

poi·ki·lo·ther·mism (*or* ·my)

poi·lu French soldier

poin·cia·na tree

poin·set·tia house plant

point

point-blank

pointe ballet term

point·ed

point·ed·ly

point·ed·ness

Pointe-Noire Congolese port

point·er

poin·til·lism painting technique

poin·til·list

point·ing

point·less

point·less·ness

points·man (*plural* ·men)

point-to-point

poise

poised

poi·son

poi·son·er

poi·son·ous

poi·son·ous·ness

Poi·tiers French town

Poi·tou former French province

poke

poke·berry (*plural* ·berries)

pok·er

poke·weed

poki·ly

poki·ness

poky (poki·er, poki·est)

Po·land

po·lar

po·lar·im·eter

po·lari·met·ric

po·lar·im·etry

Po·la·ris North Star; missile

po·lari·scope

po·lar·ity (*plural* ·ities)

po·lar·iz·able (*or* ·is·able)

po·lari·za·tion (*or* ·sa·tion)

po·lar·ize (*or* ·ise)

po·lar·iz·er (*or* ·is·er)

po·lar·og·ra·phy

Po·lar·oid (*Trademark*)

pol·der reclaimed land

Pole Polish native; star

pole

pole-axe (*US* ·ax)

pole·cat (*plural* ·cats *or* ·cat)

pol·emarch ancient Greek official

po·lem·ic

po·lemi·cal

po·lemi·cal·ly

po·lemi·cist (*or* ·emist)

po·lem·ics

pol·emo·nia·ceous botany term

po·len·ta Italian porridge

pol·er

pole-vault (*verb*)

po·leyn armour

po·lice

police·man (*plural* ·men)

police·woman (*plural* ·women)

poli·cy (*plural* ·cies)

policy·holder

po·lio
po·lio·my·eli·tis
pol·is (*plural* ·eis) Greek
  city-state
Po·lish
pol·ish
pol·ish·er
Pol·it·bu·ro
po·lite
po·lite·ness
poli·tesse *French* formal
  politeness
poli·tic shrewd
po·liti·cal of politics
po·liti·cal·ly
poli·ti·cian
po·liti·cize (*or* ·cise)
poli·tick·ing political
  canvassing
po·liti·co (*plural* ·cos) *Slang*
  politician
poli·tics
pol·ity (*plural* ·ities)
pol·je geography term
pol·ka (*noun, plural* ·kas;
  verb ·kas, ·ka·ing, ·kaed)
poll
pol·lack (*or* ·lock; *plural*
  ·lacks, ·lack *or* ·locks,
  ·lock) fish
pol·lan fish; *compare* pollen
pol·lard
polled
pol·len plant product;
  compare pollan
pol·lex (*plural* ·li·ces)
  thumb
pol·li·cal
pol·li·nate (*or* ·lenate)
pol·li·na·tion (*or*
  ·lena·tion)
pol·li·na·tor (*or* ·lena·tor)
poll·ing
pol·lin·ic of pollen
pol·li·nif·er·ous (*or*
  ·lenif·er·ous)
pol·lin·ium (*plural* ·linia)
pol·lino·sis (*or* ·leno·) hay
  fever
pol·li·wog (*or* ·ly·) *Slang*
  sailor; tadpole
poll·ster
pol·lu·cite mineral
pol·lu·tant
pol·lute

pol·lut·er
pol·lu·tion
Pollux star; mythological
  character
polo
polo·naise
po·lo·nium radioactive
  element
po·lo·ny (*plural* ·nies)
  sausage
Pol·ta·va Ukrainian city
pol·ter·geist
pol·troon
poly (*plural* polys) *Slang*
  polytechnic
polya·del·phous botany
  term
poly·am·ide
poly·an·drous
poly·an·dry
poly·an·thus (*plural*
  ·thuses)
poly·atom·ic
poly·ba·sic
poly·ba·site mineral
poly·car·pel·lary
poly·car·pic (*or* ·pous)
  botany term
poly·carpy
poly·cen·trism political
  theory
poly·chaete worm
poly·chae·tous
poly·cha·sium (*plural* ·sia)
  botany term
poly·chro·mat·ic (*or* ·mic,
  ·mous)
poly·chro·ma·tism
poly·chrome
poly·chro·my
poly·clin·ic hospital
poly·con·ic maths term
poly·coty·ledon
poly·coty·ledon·ous
poly·cy·clic
poly·cy·thae·mia (*US*
  ·themia)
poly·dac·tyl
poly·dac·ty·lous
poly·dem·ic ecology term
poly·dip·sia
poly·dip·sic
poly·em·bry·on·ic
poly·em·bry·ony
poly·es·ter

po·lyga·la plant
poly·ga·la·ceous
po·lyga·mist
po·lyga·mous
po·lyga·my
poly·gene genetics term
poly·gen·ic
poly·gen·esis biology term
poly·genet·ic
poly·geneti·cal·ly
poly·glot
poly·glot·ism (*or*
  ·glot·tism)
poly·gon
poly·go·naceous botany
  term
po·lygo·nal
po·lygo·num plant
poly·graph lie detector
poly·graph·ic
poly·graphi·cal·ly
po·lygy·nist
po·lygy·nous
po·lygy·ny
poly·he·dral
poly·he·dron (*plural* ·drons
  or ·dra)
poly·hy·droxy (*or* ·dric)
poly·iso·prene
poly·math
poly·math·ic
poly·mer
poly·mer·ic
po·lym·er·ism
po·lym·eri·za·tion (*or*
  ·sa·tion)
po·lym·er·ize (*or* ·ise)
po·lym·er·ous
poly·morph
poly·mor·phism
poly·mor·pho·nu·clear
poly·mor·phous (*or* ·phic)
poly·myx·in antibiotic
Poly·nesia
Poly·nesian
poly·neu·ri·tis
Polynices mythological
  character
poly·no·mial
poly·nu·clear (*or* ·cleate)
poly·nu·cleo·tide
po·lyn·ya arctic water
poly·ony·mous having
  several names
pol·yp

poly·pary (*or* ·par·ium; *plural* ·paries *or* ·paria) zoology term
poly·pep·tide
poly·pet·al·ous
poly·pha·gia
pol·ypha·gous
poly·phase
poly·phone linguistics term
poly·phon·ic
poly·phoni·cal·ly
po·lypho·nous
po·lypho·ny (*plural* ·nies) musical term
poly·phy·let·ic biology term
poly·phy·leti·cal·ly
poly·phyo·dont zoology term
poly·ploid genetics term; *compare* polypoid
poly·ploi·dal (*or* ·dic)
poly·ploi·dy
poly·pod many-legged animal
po·lypo·dous
poly·po·dy (*plural* ·dies) fern
poly·poid of a polyp; *compare* polyploid
poly·pro·pyl·ene
poly·pro·to·dont zoology term
pol·yp·tych altarpiece
poly·pus (*plural* ·pi) pathological polyp
poly·rhythm
poly·rhyth·mic
poly·sac·cha·ride (*or* ·rose)
poly·semous
poly·semy ambiguity
poly·sep·al·ous
poly·so·mic genetics term
poly·sty·rene
poly·sul·phide (US ·fide)
poly·syl·lab·ic (*or* ·labi·cal)
poly·syl·labi·cal·ly
poly·syl·la·ble
poly·syl·lo·gism
poly·syn·deton grammar term
poly·syn·the·sis
poly·syn·the·sism
poly·syn·thet·ic
poly·tech·nic

poly·tet·ra·fluo·ro·ethy·lene
poly·theism
poly·theist
poly·theis·tic
poly·theis·ti·cal·ly
poly·thene
poly·to·nal
poly·to·nal·ist
poly·to·nal·ity (*or* ·ism)
poly·troph·ic biology term
poly·typ·ic (*or* ·typi·cal)
poly·un·satu·rat·ed
poly·urethane (*or* ·urethan)
poly·uria
poly·ur·ic
poly·va·len·cy
poly·va·lent
poly·vi·nyl
Polyxena mythological princess
poly·zoan aquatic organism
poly·zo·ar·ium (*plural* ·aria)
poly·zo·ic
pom *short for* pommy
pom·ace pulped apples
po·ma·ceous botany term
po·made hair oil
po·man·der
pome fruit of apple
pom·egran·ate
pom·elo (*plural* ·elos) grapefruit
Pom·era·nia European region
Pom·era·nian
pom·fret liquorice sweet
pomi·cul·ture
pom·if·er·ous
pom·mel part of saddle; *less common spelling of* pummel
pom·my (*plural* ·mies) *Austral* English person
pomo·logi·cal
pom·olo·gist
pom·ol·ogy fruit cultivation
Po·mo·na Roman goddess
pomp
pom·pa·dour hairstyle
pom·pa·no (*plural* ·no *or* ·nos) fish
Pom·peii
Pom·pei·ian
Pom·pey *Slang* Portsmouth

pom-pom cannon
pom·pon (*or* ·pom) globular tuft, flower, etc.
pom·pos·ity (*plural* ·ities)
pomp·ous
pomp·ous·ness
Pon·ce Puerto Rican port
ponce
pon·cho (*plural* ·chos)
pond
pon·der
pon·der·abil·ity
pon·der·able
pon·der·er
pon·der·ous
Pon·di·cher·ry Indian territory
Pon·do·land South African region
pond-skater insect
pond·weed
pone maize bread
pong
pon·gee fabric
pon·gid ape
pon·iard dagger
pons (*plural* pon·tes) anatomy term
pons asi·no·rum geometry theorem
pons Va·ro·lii (*plural* pon·tes Va·ro·lii) part of brain
pont river ferry
Pont·char·train US lake
Pon·te·fract
Pon·tia·nak Indonesian port
Pon·tic of the Black Sea
pon·ti·fex (*plural* ·tifi·ces)
pon·tiff
pon·tifi·cal
pon·tifi·cals bishop's robes
pon·tifi·cate
pon·tine of bridges
pon·to·nier bridge builder
pon·toon
Pon·ty·pool Welsh town
Pon·ty·pridd Welsh town
pony (*plural* ponies)
pony·tail
pooch
pood unit of weight
poo·dle

poof (*or* poove) *Slang*
 homosexual; *compare* pouf
pooh
Pooh-Bah pompous official
pooh-pooh
pool
Poole Dorset port
pools gambling system
poon tree
Poo·na (*or* Pune) Indian city
poop
poor needy; unfortunate;
 compare pore; pour
poor·house
poor·ly
poor·ness
pop (pop·ping, popped)
pop·corn
pope
pope·dom
pop·ery
pop·eyed
pop·gun
pop·in·jay
pop·ish
pop·ish·ness
pop·lar
pop·lin
pop·lit·eal anatomy term
Po·po·ca·té·petl Mexican
 volcano
pop·over
pop·pa·dom (*or* ·dum)
 Indian bread
popped
pop·per
pop·pet
pop·ping
pop·ple
pop·py (*plural* ·pies)
poppy·cock
poppy·head
Pop·si·cle (*Trademark*)
pop·sy (*plural* ·sies)
popu·lace
popu·lar
popu·lar·ity
popu·lari·za·tion (*or*
 ·sa·tion)
popu·lar·ize (*or* ·ise)
popu·lar·iz·er (*or* ·is·er)
popu·late
popu·la·tion
popu·lism
popu·list

Popu·list member of US
 political party
popu·lous
popu·lous·ness
por·bea·gle shark
porce·lain
por·cel·la·neous
porch
por·cine
por·cu·pine
pore examine; small hole;
 compare poor; pour
por·gy (*plural* ·gy *or* ·gies)
 fish
po·rif·er·an a sponge
po·rif·er·ous
Po·ri·rua New Zealand city
po·rism mathematical
 proposition
pork
pork·er
porki·ness
pork·pie
porky (porki·er, porki·est)
por·noc·ra·cy (*plural* ·cies)
 government by prostitutes
por·nog·ra·pher
por·no·graph·ic
por·no·graphi·cal·ly
por·nog·ra·phy
poro·mer·ic chemistry
 term
po·ros·ity (*plural* ·ities)
po·rous
po·rous·ness
por·phy·ria disease
por·phy·rin pigment
por·phy·rit·ic geology term
por·phy·rog·enite prince
por·phy·roid geology term
por·phy·rop·sin pigment
por·phy·ry (*plural* ·ries)
 rock
por·poise (*plural* ·poise *or*
 ·poises)
por·ridge
por·rin·ger dish
Porsena legendary king
port
port·abil·ity (*or* ·able·ness)
port·able
Por·ta·down Northern Irish
 town
por·tage
por·tal

por·ta·men·to (*plural* ·ti)
 musical term
por·ta·tive portable
Port-au-Prince Haitian
 capital
port·cul·lis
porte-cochere covered
 entrance
por·tend
por·tent
por·ten·tous
por·ten·tous·ness
por·ter
por·ter·age
porter·house
port·fire
port·fo·lio (*plural* ·lios)
Port Har·court Nigerian
 port
port·hole
por·ti·co (*plural* ·coes *or*
 ·cos)
por·ti·ère door curtain
por·tion
Port·land
Port·laoise Irish town
port·li·ness
Port Louis capital of
 Mauritius
port·ly (·li·er, ·li·est)
port·man·teau (*plural*
 ·teaus *or* ·teaux)
Port Mores·by capital of
 New Guinea
Pôr·to Ale·gre Brazilian port
Port of Spain capital of
 Trinidad and Tobago
Por·to Novo capital of
 Benin
por·trait
por·trait·ist
por·trai·ture
por·tray
por·tray·able
por·tray·al
por·tray·er
port·ress
Port Said Egyptian port
Port-Salut cheese
Ports·mouth
Port Tal·bot Welsh port
Por·tu·gal
Por·tu·guese (*plural* ·guese)
por·tu·laca plant
por·tu·la·ca·ceous

pose
Poseidon Greek god
pos·er one who poses; problem
po·seur affected person
posh
pos·it postulate; *compare* posset
posi·tif organ keyboard
po·si·tion
po·si·tion·al
posi·tive
posi·tive·ly
posi·tive·ness
posi·tiv·ism
posi·tiv·ist
posi·tiv·is·tic
posi·tiv·is·ti·cal·ly
posi·tron physics term
posi·tro·nium physics term
po·sol·ogy branch of medicine
pos·se
pos·sess
pos·sessed
pos·ses·sion
pos·ses·sive
pos·ses·sive·ness
pos·ses·sor
pos·ses·so·ry
pos·set hot drink; *compare* posit
pos·sibil·ity (*plural* ·ities)
pos·sible
pos·sibly
pos·sum *Slang* opossum; phalanger
post
post·age
post·al
post·ax·ial
post·bag
post·bellum after war
post·box
post·boy
post·card
post·ca·val anatomy term
post chaise
post·code
post·coit·al
post·date
post·di·lu·vial
post·di·lu·vian
post·doc·tor·al
post·er

poste res·tante
pos·teri·or
pos·ter·ity
pos·tern
post·fix add to the end
post·free
post·gla·cial
post·gradu·ate
post·haste
post·hu·mous
post·hyp·not·ic
pos·tiche architectural term; *compare* pastiche
pos·ti·cous posterior
pos·til marginal note
pos·til·ion (*or* ·til·lion)
post·im·pres·sion·ism
post·im·pres·sion·ist
post·ing
post·limi·ny (*or* ·li·min·ium; *plural* ·nies *or* ·minia) legal term
post·lude concluding music
post·man (*plural* ·men)
post·mark
post·master
post·me·rid·ian (*adj*)
post me·rid·iem *Latin* after noon
post·mil·len·nial
post·mod·ern
post·mod·ern·ism
post·mod·ern·ist
post·mor·tem
post·na·tal
post·nup·tial
post·obit legal term
post·op·era·tive
post·paid
post·par·tum after childbirth
post·pon·able
post·pone
post·pone·ment
post·pon·er
post·po·si·tion
post·po·si·tion·al
post·posi·tive
post·pran·dial
post·script
pos·tu·lan·cy (*or* ·lant·ship)
pos·tu·lant
pos·tu·late
pos·tu·la·tion
pos·tu·la·tor

pos·tur·al
pos·ture
pos·tur·er
post·war
posy (*plural* posies)
pot (pot·ting, pot·ted)
pot·abil·ity (*or* ·able·ness)
po·table drinkable
po·tage *French* soup; *compare* pottage
po·ta·mol·ogy study of rivers
pot·ash
po·tas·sic
po·tas·sium
po·ta·tion drinking
po·ta·to (*plural* ·toes)
pot-au-feu French stew
pot·bel·lied
pot·belly (*plural* ·bellies)
pot·boiler
pot·boy (*or* pot·man; *plural* ·boys *or* ·men)
potch *Austral.* inferior opal
po·teen *Irish* illicit whiskey
po·ten·cy (*or* ·tence; *plural* ·ten·cies *or* ·tences)
po·tent
po·ten·tate ruler; *compare* potentiate
po·ten·tial
po·ten·ti·al·ity (*plural* ·ities)
po·ten·tial·ly
po·ten·ti·ate increase effectiveness; *compare* potentate
po·ten·til·la
po·ten·ti·om·eter
po·tent·ness
pot·ful (*plural* ·fuls)
pot·head *Slang* cannabis user
poth·er
pot·herb
pot·hole
pot·holer
pot·hol·ing
pot·hook
pot·house
pot·hunter
po·tiche (*plural* ·tiches) tall vase
po·tion

Potiphar biblical character
pot·latch ceremonial feast
pot·luck
Po·to·mac US river
pot·pie stew pie
pot·pour·ri (plural ·ris)
Pots·dam German city
pot·sherd (or ·shard)
pot·stone
pot·tage thick soup; compare
  potage
pot·ted
pot·ter
pot·ter·er
Pot·teries Staffordshire
  region
pot·tery (plural ·teries)
pot·ting
pot·to (plural ·tos) animal
pot·ty (adj ·ti·er, ·ti·est;
  noun, plural ·ties)
pouch
pouched
pouchy
pouf (or pouffe) cushion
  seat; compare poof
pou·lard (or ·larde) spayed
  hen
poult young chicken
poul·ter·er
poul·tice
poul·try
poultry·man (plural ·men)
pounce
pound
pound·age
pound·al unit
pound·er
pour flow; compare poor;
  pore
pour·boire French tip
pour·er
pour·par·ler French informal
  conference
pour·point doublet
pous·sette country dance
pous·sin spring chicken
pout
pout·er
pout·ing·ly
pov·er·ty
poverty-stricken
pow exclamation
pow·an fish
pow·der

pow·der·er
pow·dery
pow·er
power·boat
pow·er·ful
pow·er·ful·ly
pow·er·ful·ness
power·house
pow·er·less
pow·er·less·ness
pow·wow
Pow·ys Welsh county
pox
poxy
Po·yang Chinese lake
Poz·nań Polish city
poz·zuo·la·na (or ·zo·)
  volcanic ash
prac·ti·cabil·ity (or
  ·cable·ness)
prac·ti·cable
prac·ti·cably
prac·ti·cal
prac·ti·cal·ity (or ·cal·ness)
prac·ti·cal·ly
prac·tice (noun)
prac·tise (US ·tice; verb)
prac·tised (US ·ticed)
prac·ti·tion·er
prae·dial (or pre·) of land
prae·di·al·ity (or pre·)
prae·mu·ni·re legal term
prae·no·men Roman's first
  name
Prae·se·pe star cluster
prae·sid·ium variant spelling
  of presidium
prae·tor (or pre·) Roman
  magistrate
prag·mat·ic
prag·mati·cal·ly
prag·mat·ics (sing.)
prag·ma·tism
prag·ma·tist
prag·ma·tis·tic
Prague
Praia capital of Cape Verde
prai·rie
praise acclaim; compare
  prase
prais·er
praise·worthi·ly
praise·worthi·ness
praise·worthy
pra·line

prall·triller musical term
pram
prance
pranc·er
pranc·ing·ly
pran·dial
prang
prank
prank·ish
prank·ster
prase quartz; compare praise
pra·seo·dym·ium chemical
  element
prat Slang idiot
prate chatter
prat·er
prat·in·cole bird
prat·ing·ly
pra·tique permission to use
  port
Pra·to Italian city
prat·tle
prat·tler
prat·tling·ly
prau variant of proa
prawn
prawn·er
prax·is (plural prax·ises or
  praxes) practice
pray utter prayer; compare
  prey
prayer petition
pray·er one who prays
prayer·ful
prayer·ful·ly
preach
preach·er
preachi·fi·ca·tion
preachi·fy (·fies, ·fy·ing,
  ·fied)
preach·ment
pre·ad·am·ite
pre·ad·ap·ta·tion
pre·ado·les·cence
pre·ado·les·cent
pre·am·ble
pre·am·bu·lar (or ·la·tory,
  ·lary)
pre·am·pli·fi·er
pre·ar·range
pre·ar·ranged
pre·ar·range·ment
pre·ar·rang·er
pre·ax·ial
preb·end

pre·ben·dal
preb·en·dary (*plural* ·daries)
Pre·cam·brian geological
term
pre·can·cel (·cel·ling,
·celled; *US* ·cel·ing,
·celed)
pre·can·cel·la·tion
pre·cari·ous
pre·cari·ous·ness
pre·cast (·cast·ing, ·cast)
preca·tory (*or* ·tive)
pre·cau·tion
pre·cau·tion·ary (*or*
·tion·al)
pre·cau·tious
pre·cede come before;
compare proceed
prec·edence
prec·edent
prec·eden·tial
pre·ced·ing
pre·cen·tor cleric; *compare*
preceptor
pre·cen·to·rial
pre·cept
pre·cep·tive
pre·cep·tor teacher; *compare*
precentor
pre·cep·to·rate
pre·cep·to·rial (*or* ·to·ral)
pre·cep·tor·ship
pre·cep·tress
pre·cess
pre·ces·sion rotation;
motion of equinoxes;
compare procession
pre·ces·sion·al
pre·cinct
pre·ci·os·ity (*plural* ·ities)
affectation
pre·cious
pre·cious·ness
preci·pice
preci·piced
pre·cipi·tance (*or* ·tan·cy)
pre·cipi·tant
pre·cipi·tate
pre·cipi·ta·tion
pre·cipi·ta·tive
pre·cipi·ta·tor
pre·cipi·tin antibody
pre·cipi·tous
pre·cipi·tous·ness
pre·cis (*or* pré·; *plural* ·cis)

pre·cise
pre·cise·ness
pre·ci·sian strict observer
of rules; *compare*
precision
pre·ci·sian·ism
pre·ci·sion accuracy;
compare precisian
pre·ci·sion·ism
pre·ci·sion·ist
pre·clini·cal
pre·clud·able
pre·clude
pre·clu·sion
pre·clu·sive
pre·co·cial ornithology
term
pre·co·cious
pre·co·cious·ness (*or*
pre·coc·ity)
pre·cog·ni·tion
pre·cog·ni·tive
pre·con·ceive
pre·con·cep·tion
pre·con·cert
pre·con·demn
pre·con·di·tion
pre·co·ni·za·tion (*or*
·sa·tion)
pre·co·nize (*or* ·nise)
announce publicly
pre·con·scious
pre·con·scious·ness
pre·con·tract
pre·cook
pre·criti·cal
pre·cur·sor
pre·cur·sory (*or* ·sive)
pre·da·cious (*or* ·ceous)
predatory
pre·da·cious·ness (*or*
·ceous·ness, pre·dac·ity)
pre·date precede
pre·da·tion predatory
action
preda·tor
preda·to·ri·ly
preda·to·ri·ness
preda·tory
pre·de·cease
pre·de·ces·sor
pre·del·la (*plural* ·le) altar
platform; painting
pre·des·ti·nar·ian
pre·des·ti·nari·an·ism

pre·des·ti·nate predestined;
variant of predestine
pre·des·ti·na·tion
pre·des·tine (*or* ·ti·nate)
pre·de·ter·mi·nate
pre·de·ter·mi·na·tion
pre·de·ter·mi·na·tive
pre·de·ter·mine
pre·de·ter·min·er
pre·dial *variant spelling of*
praedial
predi·cabil·ity (*or*
·cable·ness)
predi·cable affirmable
predica·ment
predi·cant of preaching
predi·cate
predi·ca·tion
predi·ca·tive
predi·ca·tory of preaching
pre·dict
pre·dict·abil·ity (*or*
·able·ness)
pre·dict·able
pre·dict·ably
pre·dic·tion
pre·dic·tive
pre·dic·tive·ly
pre·dic·tor
pre·di·gest
pre·di·ges·tion
pre·di·lec·tion
pre·dis·pos·al
pre·dis·pose
pre·dis·po·si·tion
pred·ni·sone drug
pre·domi·nance (*or*
·nan·cy)
pre·domi·nant
pre·domi·nate
pre·domi·na·tion
pre·domi·na·tor
pre-eclamp·sia
pree·mie (*or* pre·mie) *US*
premature baby
pre-eminence
pre-eminent
pre-empt
pre-emption
pre-emptive
pre-emptor
pre-emptory
preen
preen·er
pre-exist

pre·exist·ence
pre·fab
pre·fab·ri·cate
pre·fab·ri·ca·tion
pre·fab·ri·ca·tor
pref·ace
pref·ac·er
prefa·to·ri·ly (or ·ri·al·ly)
prefa·tory (or ·to·rial)
pre·fect
pre·fec·to·rial
pre·fec·tur·al
pre·fec·ture
pre·fer (·fer·ring, ·ferred)
pref·er·abil·ity (or
·able·ness)
pref·er·able
pref·er·ably
pref·er·ence
pref·er·en·tial
pref·er·en·tial·ly
pref·er·en·ti·al·ity
pre·fer·ment
pre·fer·rer
pre·figu·ra·tion
pre·figu·ra·tive
pre·figu·ra·tive·ness
pre·fig·ure
pre·fig·ure·ment
pre·fix
pre·fix·al
pre·flight
pre·form
pre·for·ma·tion
pre·fron·tal anatomy term
pre·gla·cial
preg·nabil·ity
preg·nable
preg·nan·cy (plural ·cies)
preg·nant
pre·heat
pre·hen·sile
pre·hen·sion
pre·his·to·rian
pre·his·tor·ic (or ·tori·cal)
pre·his·tori·cal·ly
pre·his·to·ry (plural ·ries)
pre·homi·nid
pre·ignition
pre·judge
pre·judg·er
pre·judg·ment (or
·judge·ment)
preju·dice
preju·di·cial

prela·cy (plural ·cies)
prel·ate
pre·lat·ic
prela·tism
prela·tist
prela·ture
pre·lect to lecture
pre·lec·tion
pre·lec·tor
pre·lexi·cal grammar term
pre·limi·nari·ly
pre·limi·nary (plural
·naries)
pre·lims front matter of
book; first exams
pre·lit·era·cy
pre·lit·er·ate
prel·ude
pre·lud·er
pre·lu·di·al
pre·lu·sion
pre·lu·sive (or ·so·ry)
pre·mari·tal
prema·ture
prema·tur·ity (or
·ture·ness)
pre·max·il·la (plural ·lae)
bone
pre·max·il·lary
pre·med short for
premedical;
premedication
pre·medi·cal
pre·medi·ca·tion
pre·medi·tate
pre·medi·tat·ed·ly
pre·medi·ta·tion
pre·medi·ta·tive
pre·medi·ta·tor
pre·men·stru·al
prem·ier first in importance
premi·ere first performance
prem·ier·ship
prem·ise state as premiss;
variant spelling of premiss
prem·ises land and
buildings
prem·iss (or ·ise) logical
statement
pre·mium
pre·mo·lar
premo·ni·tion
pre·moni·tory
pre·morse biology term
pre·mu·ni·tion immunity

pre·na·tal
pre·nomi·nal
pre·oc·cu·pa·tion (or
·pan·cy)
pre·oc·cu·py (·pies,
·py·ing, ·pied)
pre·or·dain
pre·or·di·na·tion
prep Slang homework;
preparatory school
pre·pack
pre·pack·age
prepaid
prepa·ra·tion
pre·para·tive
pre·para·to·ri·ly
pre·para·tory
pre·pare
pre·par·ed·ly
pre·par·ed·ness
pre·pay (·pay·ing, ·paid)
pre·pay·able
pre·pay·ment
pre·pense premeditated
pre·pon·der·ance (or
·an·cy)
pre·pon·der·ant
pre·pon·der·ate
pre·pon·der·at·ing·ly
pre·pon·dera·tion
prepo·si·tion
prepo·si·tion·al
pre·posi·tive linguistics
term
pre·posi·tor (or ·pos·tor)
prefect
pre·pos·sess
pre·pos·sess·ing
pre·pos·sess·ing·ness
pre·pos·ses·sion
pre·pos·ter·ous
pre·pos·ter·ous·ness
pre·po·ten·cy
pre·po·tent
pre·puce foreskin
pre·pu·tial
Pre-Raphael·ite
pre·re·cord
pre·requi·site
pre·roga·tive
pre·sa (plural ·se) musical
term
pres·age
pre·sage·ful
pre·sag·er

pres·byo·pia
pres·by·op·ic
pres·by·ter church elder
pres·by·ter·al
pres·byt·er·ate
pres·by·ter·ial
Pres·by·ter·ian Church
pres·by·ter·ian of
  government by presbyters
Pres·by·teri·an·ism
pres·by·teri·an·is·tic
pres·by·tery (*plural* ·teries)
pre·school
pres·ci·ence foreknowledge
pres·ci·ent
pre·scribe give ruling; order
  use of drug; *compare*
  proscribe
pre·scrib·er
pre·script
pre·scrip·tibil·ity
pre·scrip·tible
pre·scrip·tion
pre·scrip·tive
pre·scrip·tiv·ism
pres·ence
pres·ent the time now; in
  existence now
pre·sent gift; to give
pre·sent·able
pre·sent·ably
pre·sent·able·ness (or
  ·abil·ity)
pres·en·ta·tion
pres·en·ta·tion·al
pres·en·ta·tion·ism
  philosophy term
pres·en·ta·tion·ist
pre·senta·tive
pre·senta·tive·ness
present-day (*adj*)
pres·en·tee
pre·sent·er
pre·sen·tient
pre·sen·ti·ment
pres·ent·ly
pre·sent·ment
pre·serv·abil·ity
pre·serv·able
pres·er·va·tion
pre·serva·tive
pre·serve
pre·serv·er
pre·set (·set·ting, ·set)
pre·set·ter

pre·shrunk
pre·side
presi·den·cy (*plural* ·cies)
presi·dent
president-elect
presi·den·tial
pre·sid·er
pre·sidio (*plural* ·sidios)
  military establishment
pre·sid·ium (or prae·; *plural*
  ·iums or ·ia) Communist
  committee
pre·sig·ni·fy (·fies, ·fy·ing,
  ·fied)
press
press·er one that presses;
  compare pressor
press-gang (*verb*)
press·ing
press·ing·ness
press·man (*plural* ·men)
press·mark code on library
  book
pres·sor (*adj*) increasing
  blood pressure; *compare*
  presser
press·room
press-up (*noun*)
press·ure
pres·suri·za·tion (or
  ·sa·tion)
pres·sur·ize (or ·ise)
pres·sur·iz·er (or ·is·er)
press·work
pres·ti·digi·ta·tion
pres·ti·digi·ta·tor
pres·tige
pres·tig·ious
pres·tig·ious·ness
pres·tis·si·mo (*plural* ·mos)
  musical term
pres·to (*plural* ·tos)
Pres·ton Lancashire town
Pres·ton·pans Scottish
  battle site
pre·stress
Prest·wich Scottish town
pre·sum·able
pre·sum·ably
pre·sume
pre·sum·ed·ly
pre·sum·er
pre·sum·ing·ly
pre·sump·tion
pre·sump·tive

pre·sump·tive·ness
pre·sump·tu·ous
pre·sump·tu·ous·ness
pre·sup·pose
pre·sup·po·si·tion
pre·tence (*US* ·tense)
pre·tend
pre·tend·ed·ly
pre·tend·er
pre·ten·sion
pre·ten·tious
pre·ten·tious·ness
pret·er·ite (or ·it) grammar
  term
pret·eri·tion act of omitting
pret·eri·tive grammar term
pre·ter·natu·ral
pre·ter·natu·ral·ism
pre·ter·natu·ral·ness (or
  ·ral·ity)
pre·test
pre·text
Pre·to·ria
pret·ti·fy (·fies, ·fy·ing,
  ·fied)
pret·ti·ly
pret·ti·ness
pret·ty (*adj* ·ti·er, ·ti·est;
  verb ·ties, ·ty·ing, ·tied)
pret·zel biscuit
pre·vail
pre·vail·er
pre·vail·ing
pre·vail·ing·ly
preva·lence (or ·lent·ness)
preva·lent
pre·vari·cate
pre·vari·ca·tion
pre·vari·ca·tor
pre·ve·ni·ent preceding
pre·vent
pre·vent·able
pre·vent·ably
pre·ven·ta·tive *variant of*
  preventive
pre·vent·er
pre·ven·tion
pre·ven·tive (or ·ta·tive)
pre·ven·tive·ness (or
  ·ta·tive·ness)
pre·view (or ·vue)
pre·vi·ous
pre·vi·ous·ly
pre·vi·ous·ness
pre·vi·sion

pre·vo·cal·ic coming before a vowel
pre·war
prey victim; to hunt; victimize; *compare* **pray**
prey·er
Priam mythological king
pri·ap·ic of Priapus
pria·pism medical term
Priapus fertility god
price
price·less
price·less·ness
pricey (*or* **pricy**; **prici·er**, **prici·est**)
prick
prick·er
prick·et
prick·le
prick·li·ness
prick·ly (**·li·er**, **·li·est**)
pricy *variant spelling of* **pricey**
pride
pride·ful
prie-dieu kneeling desk
pri·er (*or* **pry·**) one who pries; *compare* **prior**
priest
priest·craft
priest·ess
priest-hole
priest·hood
priest·li·ness
priest·ly (**·li·er**, **·li·est**)
priest-ridden
prig
prig·gery (*or* **prig·gish·ness**)
prig·gish
prig·gism
prill
prim (*adj* **prim·mer**, **prim·mest**; *verb* **prim·ming, primmed**)
pri·ma bal·leri·na
pri·ma·cy (*plural* **·cies**)
pri·ma don·na (*plural* **pri·ma don·nas**)
pri·mae·val *variant spelling of* **primeval**
pri·ma fa·cie
pri·mal
pri·ma·quine drug
pri·mari·ly
pri·ma·ry (*plural* **·ries**)

pri·mate
pri·ma·tial
pri·ma·tol·ogy branch of zoology
prime
prime·ness
pri·mer introductory text
prim·er one that primes
pri·mero card game
pri·meval (*or* **·mae·val**)
pri·meval·ly
primi·gravi·da (*plural* **·das** *or* **·dae**) obstetrics term
pri·mine botany term
prim·ing
pri·mipa·ra (*or* **uni·**; *plural* **·ras** *or* **·rae**) obstetrics term
primi·par·ity
pri·mipa·rous
primi·tive
primi·tive·ness
primi·tiv·ism
primi·tiv·ist
primi·tiv·is·tic
prim·ness
pri·mo (*plural* **·mos** *or* **·mi**)
pri·mo·geni·tary
pri·mo·geni·tor
pri·mo·geni·ture
pri·mor·dial
pri·mor·dium (*plural* **·dia**)
primp
prim·rose
primu·la
primu·la·ceous
pri·mum mo·bi·le *Latin* prime mover
Pri·mus (*Trademark*) stove
pri·mus presiding bishop
prince
prince·dom
prince·li·ness
prince·ling
prince·ly (**·li·er**, **·li·est**)
prin·cess
Prince·ton US town
prin·ci·pal foremost; head person; *compare* **principle**
prin·ci·pal·ity (*plural* **·ities**)
prin·ci·pal·ly
Prín·ci·pe island
prin·cip·ium (*plural* **·cipia**) fundamental principle
prin·ci·ple standard; *compare* **principal**

prin·ci·pled
prink
prink·er
print
print·abil·ity (*or* **·able·ness**)
print·able
print·er
print·ing
print·maker
print·out
pri·on
pri·or abbot's deputy; *compare* **prier**
pri·or·ate
pri·or·ess
pri·or·ity (*plural* **·ities**)
pri·ory (*plural* **·ories**)
pris·age duty on wine
prise (*or* **prize**) force open; *compare* **prize**
prism
pris·mat·ic
pris·ma·toid geometric solid
pris·ma·toid·al
pris·moid
pris·moid·al
pris·on
pris·on·er
pris·si·ly
pris·si·ness
pris·sy (**·si·er**, **·si·est**)
pris·tine
prithee
pri·va·cy (*plural* **·cies**)
pri·vate
pri·va·teer
pri·va·tion
priva·tive
priv·et
privi·lege
privi·leged
privi·ly
priv·ity (*plural* **·ities**) legal relationship
privy (*noun, plural* **privies**; *adj* **privi·er**, **privi·est**) lavatory; secret
prize award; *variant spelling of* **prise**
prize·fight
prize·fighter
pro (*plural* **pros**)
proa (*or* **prau**) boat
pro·ac·tive

pro·am *professional and amateur*
proba·bil·ism
prob·abil·ist
prob·abil·is·tic
prob·abil·ity *(plural ·ities)*
prob·able
prob·ably
pro·band *person in genealogical study*
pro·bang *surgical instrument*
pro·bate
pro·ba·tion
pro·ba·tion·al *(or ·tion·ary)*
pro·ba·tion·er
pro·ba·tive *(or ·tory)*
probe
probe·able
prob·er
pro·bity
prob·lem
prob·lem·at·ic *(or ·ati·cal)*
prob·lem·ati·cal·ly
pro bono pub·li·co *Latin for the public good*
pro·bos·cid·ean *(or ·ian) zoology term*
pro·bos·cis *(plural ·cises or ·ci·des)*
pro·caine
pro·cam·bial
pro·cam·bium *botany term*
pro·carp *botany term*
pro·ca·thedral *church*
pro·cedur·al
pro·cedure
pro·ceed *carry on; compare* precede
pro·ceed·er
pro·ceed·ing
pro·ceed·ings
pro·ceeds *(noun)*
proc·eleus·mat·ic *prosody term*
pro·cephal·ic *anatomy term*
pro·cess
pro·ces·sion
pro·ces·sion·al
pro·ces·sor
process-server
pro·chro·nism *dating error*
pro·claim
proc·la·ma·tion
pro·clama·tory

pro·clit·ic *linguistics term*
pro·cliv·ity *(plural ·ities)*
Procne *mythological princess*
pro·con·sul
pro·con·su·lar
pro·con·su·late *(or ·sul·ship)*
pro·cras·ti·nate
pro·cras·ti·na·tion
pro·cras·ti·na·tor
pro·creant *(or ·crea·tive)*
pro·cre·ate
pro·crea·tion
pro·crea·tor
Pro·crus·tean
Procrustes *mythological robber*
pro·cryp·tic *zoology term*
pro·cryp·ti·cal·ly
proc·to·logi·cal
proc·tol·o·gist
proc·tol·ogy *branch of medicine*
proc·tor
proc·to·rial
proc·to·scope
proc·to·scop·ic
proc·tos·co·py
pro·cum·bent
pro·cur·able
procu·ra·tion
procu·ra·tor
procu·ra·tor fis·cal *Scottish legal officer*
procu·ra·tory
pro·cure
pro·cure·ment *(or ·cur·ance, ·cur·al)*
pro·cur·er *(fem ·ess)*
prod *(prod·ding, prod·ded)*
prod·der
prodi·gal
prodi·gal·ity *(plural ·ities)*
prodi·gal·ly
pro·di·gious
pro·di·gious·ness
prodi·gy *(plural ·gies)*
pro·dro·mal *(or ·drom·ic)*
pro·drome *symptom of disease*
pro·duce
pro·duc·er
pro·duc·ibil·ity
pro·duc·ible

prod·uct
pro·duc·tion
pro·duc·tion·al
pro·duc·tive
prod·uc·tiv·ity *(or ·tive·ness)*
pro·em *preface*
pro·emial
prof *Slang professor*
profa·na·tion
pro·fana·to·ry
pro·fane
pro·fane·ness
pro·fan·er
pro·fan·ity *(plural ·ities)*
pro·fess
pro·fess·ed·ly
pro·fes·sion
pro·fes·sion·al
pro·fes·sion·al·ism
pro·fes·sion·al·ist
pro·fes·sion·al·ly
pro·fes·sor
prof·es·so·rial
prof·es·sor·iate *(or ·so·rate)*
pro·fes·sor·ship
prof·fer
prof·fer·er
pro·fi·cien·cy *(plural ·cies)*
pro·fi·cient
pro·file
prof·it
prof·it·abil·ity
prof·it·able
prof·it·ably
profi·teer
prof·it·er
pro·fit·er·ole
prof·it·less
profit-sharing
prof·li·ga·cy
prof·li·gate
pro·flu·ent *flowing smoothly*
pro·form *grammar term*
pro for·ma *Latin as prescribed*
pro·found
pro·found·ly
pro·found·ness
pro·fun·dity *(plural ·dities)*
pro·fuse
pro·fuse·ly
pro·fuse·ness
pro·fu·sion

prog (prog·ging, progged)
 Slang prowl
pro·geni·tive
pro·geni·tive·ness
pro·geni·tor
prog·eny (*plural* ·enies)
pro·ges·ta·tion·al before
 pregnancy
pro·ges·ter·one hormone
pro·ges·to·gen (*or*
 pro·ges·tin) synthetic
 progesterone
pro·glot·tis (*or* ·tid; *plural*
 ·glot·ti·des) tapeworm
 segment
prog·na·thism
prog·na·thous (*or* ·nath·ic)
prog·no·sis (*plural* ·ses)
prog·nos·tic
prog·nos·ti·cate
prog·nos·ti·ca·tion
prog·nos·ti·ca·tive
prog·nos·ti·ca·tor
pro·gram US spelling of
 programme
pro·gram (·gram·ming,
 ·grammed) computer term
pro·gram·ma·ble
pro·gram·mat·ic
pro·gramme (US ·gram;
 ·gram·ming, ·grammed;
 US ·gram·ing, ·gramed)
pro·gram·mer
pro·gress
pro·gres·sion
pro·gres·sion·al
Pro·gres·sive political party
pro·gres·sive
pro·gres·sive·ness
pro·gres·siv·ism
pro·gres·siv·ist
pro·hib·it
pro·hib·it·er (*or* ·hibi·tor)
pro·hi·bi·tion
pro·hi·bi·tion·ary
pro·hi·bi·tion·ism
pro·hi·bi·tion·ist
pro·hibi·tive (*or* ·tory)
pro·hibi·tive·ness
proj·ect
pro·jec·tile
pro·jec·tion
pro·jec·tion·al
pro·jec·tion·ist
pro·jec·tive

pro·jec·tor
pro·jet draft treaty
Pro·kop·yevsk Russian city
pro·lac·tin hormone
pro·la·mine plant protein
pro·lapse
pro·late spheroidal
pro·late·ness
prole
pro·leg zoology term
pro·legom·enal
pro·legom·enon (*plural*
 ·ena) critical introduction
pro·lep·sis (*plural* ·ses)
 rhetorical device
pro·lep·tic
pro·lep·ti·cal·ly
pro·letar·ian (*or* ·letary;
 plural ·ians *or* ·letaries)
pro·letar·ian·ism
pro·letar·ian·ness
pro·letari·at
pro·lif·er·ate
pro·lif·era·tion
pro·lif·era·tive
pro·lif·er·ous
pro·lif·ic
pro·lifi·cal·ly
pro·lif·ic·ness (*or*
 ·lifi·ca·cy)
pro·line amino acid
pro·lix long-winded
pro·lix·ity (*or* ·ness)
pro·locu·tor Anglican
 official
pro·logue (US also ·log;
 ·logu·ing, ·logued; US also
 ·log·ing, ·loged)
pro·long
pro·lon·ga·tion
pro·long·er
pro·long·ment
pro·lu·sion preliminary
 essay
pro·lu·so·ry
prom
prom·enade
prom·enad·er
Pro·methean
Prometheus mythological
 character
pro·methium radioactive
 element
promi·nence
promi·nent

promi·nent·ness
promis·cu·ity (*plural* ·ities)
pro·mis·cu·ous
pro·mis·cu·ous·ness
prom·ise
promi·see
prom·is·er (*or in legal
 contexts* promi·sor)
prom·is·ing
prom·is·sory
prom·on·tory (*plural*
 ·tories)
pro·mot·able
pro·mote
pro·mot·er
pro·mo·tion
pro·mo·tion·al
pro·mo·tive
pro·mo·tive·ness
prompt
prompt·book
prompt·er
promp·ti·tude
prompt·ness
prom·ul·gate
prom·ul·ga·tion
prom·ul·ga·tor
pro·my·celium (*plural*
 ·celia) botany term
pro·nate
pro·na·tion
pro·na·tor muscle
prone
prone·ness
pro·neph·ric
pro·neph·ros (*plural* ·roi *or*
 ·ra) zoology term
prong
prong·horn deer
pro·nomi·nal of a pronoun
pro·nomi·nali·za·tion (*or*
 ·sa·tion)
pro·nomi·nal·ize (*or* ·ise)
pro·noun
pro·nounce
pro·nounce·able
pro·nounced
pro·nounc·ed·ly
pro·nounce·ment
pro·nounc·er
pron·to
pro·nu·clear
pro·nu·cleus (*plural* ·clei)
pro·nun·cia·men·to (*plural*
 ·tos) manifesto

pro·nun·cia·tion
pro-oestrus (*US* pro·es·trus)
proof
proof·read (·read·ing, ·read)
proof·reader
prop (prop·ping, propped)
pro·pae·deu·tic preparatory instruction
pro·pae·deu·ti·cal
propa·gabil·ity (or ·gable·ness)
propa·gable
propa·gan·da
propa·gan·dism
propa·gan·dist
propa·gan·dize (or ·dise)
propa·gate
propa·ga·tion
propa·ga·tion·al
propa·ga·tive
propa·ga·tor
propa·gule (or pro·pagu·lum; *plural* ·gules *or* ·la) botany term
pro·pane
pro·pa·roxy·tone grammar term
pro pa·tria *Latin* for one's country
pro·pel (·pel·ling, ·pelled)
pro·pel·lant (or ·lent; *noun*)
pro·pel·lent (*adj*)
pro·pel·ler
pro·pene chemical compound
pro·pen·sity (*plural* ·sities)
prop·er
prop·er·ly
prop·er·ness
prop·er·tied
prop·er·ty (*plural* ·ties)
pro·phage virus
pro·phase biology term
proph·ecy (*plural* ·ecies)
proph·esi·able
proph·esi·er
proph·esy (·esies, ·esy·ing, ·esied)
proph·et (*fem* ·et·ess)
pro·phet·ic
pro·pheti·cal·ly
prophy·lac·tic
prophy·lax·is
pro·pin·quity

pro·pio·nate
pro·pi·on·ic acid
pro·piti·able
pro·pi·ti·ate
pro·pi·tia·tion
pro·pi·tia·tious appeasing; *compare* propitious
pro·pi·tia·tive
pro·pi·tia·tor
pro·pi·tious favourable; *compare* propipiatious
pro·pi·tious·ness
prop·jet
propo·lis substance collected by bees
pro·po·nent
pro·por·tion
pro·por·tion·abil·ity
pro·por·tion·able
pro·por·tion·al
pro·por·tion·al·ity
pro·por·tion·al·ly
pro·por·tion·ate
pro·por·tion·ate·ness
pro·por·tion·ment
pro·po·sable
pro·po·sal
pro·pose
pro·pos·er
propo·si·tion
propo·si·tion·al
pro·posi·tus (*plural* ·ti) legal term
pro·pound
pro·pound·er
pro·prae·tor provincial praetor
pro·prano·lol
pro·pri·etari·ly
pro·pri·etary
pro·pri·etor (*fem* ·etress)
pro·pri·etor·ial
pro·pri·ety (*plural* ·eties)
pro·prio·cep·tive
pro·prio·cep·tor nerve ending
prop·to·sis (*plural* ·ses) medical term
pro·pul·sion
pro·pul·sive (or ·sory)
pro·pyl chemistry term
propy·laeum (or ·lon; *plural* ·laea *or* ·lons, ·la) temple portico
pro·pyl·ene propene

propy·lite geology term
pro rata
pro·rate
pro·ra·tion
pro·ro·ga·tion
pro·rogue
pro·sa·ic
pro·sai·cal·ly
pro·sa·ic·ness
pro·sa·ism (or ·sai·cism) prosaic style
pro·scenium (*plural* ·scenia *or* ·sceniums)
pro·sciut·to Italian ham
pro·scribe prohibit; *compare* prescribe
pro·scrip·tion
pro·scrip·tive
pro·scrip·tive·ness
prose
pro·sec·tor dissector
pros·ecut·able
pros·ecute
pros·ecu·tion
pros·ecu·tor
pros·elyte
pros·elyt·ic
pros·elyt·ism
pros·elyti·za·tion (or ·sa·tion)
pros·elyt·ize (or ·ise)
pros·elyt·iz·er (or ·is·er)
pros·en·cepha·lon (*plural* ·la) anatomy term
pros·en·chy·ma plant tissue
pros·en·chy·ma·tous
Proserpina Roman goddess
prosi·ly
pro·sim·ian zoology term
prosi·ness
pro·sod·ic
proso·dist
proso·dy
proso·po·poeia (or ·peia) rhetorical device
proso·po·poeial (or ·peial)
pros·pect
pro·spec·tive
pro·spec·tor
pro·spec·tus (*plural* ·tuses)
pros·per
pros·per·ity (*plural* ·ities)
pros·per·ous
pros·per·ous·ness

pros·ta·glan·din
hormone-like compound

pros·tate gland; *compare*
prostrate

pros·ta·tec·to·my (*plural*
·mies)

pros·tat·ic

pros·ta·ti·tis

pros·the·sis (*plural* ·ses)
artificial body part;
compare prothesis

pros·thet·ic

pros·theti·cal·ly

pros·thet·ics

pros·tho·don·tics branch of
dentistry

pros·tho·don·tist

pros·ti·tute

pros·ti·tu·tion

pros·ti·tu·tor

pro·sto·mium (*plural* ·mia)
zoology term

pros·trate face down;
compare prostate

pros·tra·tion

pro·style architectural term

prosy (prosi·er, prosi·est)

pro·tac·tin·ium radioactive
element

pro·tago·nism

pro·tago·nist

pro·ta·mine protein

pro·tan·drous botany term

pro·tan·dry

pro·ta·no·pia red blindness

pro·ta·nop·ic

prota·sis (*plural* ·ses)
conditional clause

pro·tea shrub

pro·tean variable

pro·tease enzyme

pro·tect

pro·tec·tion

pro·tec·tion·ism

pro·tec·tion·ist

pro·tec·tive

pro·tec·tive·ness

pro·tec·tor

pro·tec·to·ral

pro·tec·tor·ate

pro·tec·tory (*plural* ·tories)
institution for children

pro·tec·tress

pro·té·gé (*fem* ·gée)

pro·tein

pro·teina·ceous (*or* ·tein·ic,
·tei·nous)

pro·tein·ase enzyme

pro tem (*or* pro tem·po·re)
temporarily

pro·teoly·sis

pro·teo·lyt·ic

pro·teose biochemical
compound

Pro·tero·zo·ic geology term

pro·test

Prot·es·tant religion

pro·test·ant protester

Prot·es·tant·ism

pro·tes·ta·tion

pro·test·er

pro·test·ing·ly

Proteus Greek god

pro·tha·la·mi·on (*or*
·mium; *plural* ·mia)
marriage song

pro·thal·lic (*or* ·lial)

pro·thal·lus (*or* ·lium; *plural*
·li *or* ·lia) botany term

proth·esis linguistics term;
compare prosthesis

pro·thet·ic

pro·theti·cal·ly

pro·thono·tar·ial (*or*
pro·tono·)

pro·tho·no·tary (*or*
proto·no·tary; *plural*
·taries)

pro·tho·rax (*plural* ·raxes *or*
·ra·ces)

pro·throm·bin

pro·tist microscopic
organism

pro·tium isotope of
hydrogen

proto·chor·date zoology
term

proto·col

pro·togy·nous

pro·togy·ny biology term

proto·his·tor·ic

proto·his·to·ry

proto·hu·man

proto·lan·guage

proto·lith·ic of the Stone
Age

proto·mor·phic primitive

pro·ton

proto·nema (*plural*
·ne·ma·ta) botany term

proto·ne·mal (*or* ·nema·tal)

proto·path·ic

pro·topa·thy physiology
term

proto·plasm

proto·plas·mic (*or* ·mal,
·mat·ic)

proto·plast

proto·plas·tic

Proto·semit·ic language

proto·star

proto·stele botany term

proto·stelic

proto·therian zoology term

proto·troph·ic biology term

proto·ty·pal (*or* ·typ·ic,
·typi·cal)

proto·type

pro·tox·ide

proto·xy·lem

proto·zoan (*or* ·zo·on; *plural*
·zoans *or* ·zoa)

proto·zoo·logi·cal

proto·zo·olo·gist

proto·zo·ol·ogy

pro·tract

pro·tract·ed·ly

pro·tract·ed·ness

pro·trac·tile (*or* ·tract·ible)

pro·trac·tion

pro·trac·tive

pro·trac·tor

pro·trud·able

pro·trude

pro·tru·dent

pro·tru·sile

pro·tru·sion

pro·tru·sive

pro·tru·sive·ness

pro·tu·ber·ance (*or* ·an·cy;
plural ·ances *or* ·an·cies)

pro·tu·ber·ant

pro·tyle (*or* ·tyl) chemistry
term

proud

proud·ness

proust·ite mineral

prov·abil·ity

prov·able

prove (prov·ing, proved,
proved *or* prov·en)

prov·enance (*or* ·veni·ence)

Pro·ven·çal of Provence

Pro·ven·çale cookery term

Pro·vence

prov·en·der
prov·en·ly
pro·ven·tricu·lar
pro·ven·tricu·lus (*plural* ·li)
   zoology term
prov·erb
pro·ver·bial
pro·ver·bial·ly
pro·vide
Provi·dence US port
provi·dence
provi·dent
provi·den·tial
provi·den·tial·ly
pro·vid·er
prov·ince
pro·vin·cial
pro·vin·cial·ism
pro·vin·ci·al·ity
pro·virus
pro·vi·sion
pro·vi·sion·al (*or* ·ary)
pro·vi·sion·al·ly
pro·vi·sion·er
pro·vi·sions
pro·vi·so (*plural* ·sos *or* ·soes)
pro·vi·so·ri·ly
pro·vi·sory
pro·vita·min
Pro·vo (*plural* ·vos)
   Provisional IRA member
provo·ca·tion
pro·voca·tive
pro·voca·tive·ness
pro·voke
pro·vok·ing·ly
pro·vo·lo·ne cheese
prov·ost
prow
prow·ess
prowl
prowl·er
Proxi·ma star
proxi·mal anatomy term
proxi·mal·ly
proxi·mate nearest
proxi·mate·ness
proxi·ma·tion
prox·im·ity
proxi·mo next month
proxy (*plural* proxies)
prude
pru·dence
pru·dent

pru·den·tial
pru·dent·ness
prud·ery (*plural* ·eries)
prud·ish
prud·ish·ness
prui·nose botany term
prun·able
prune
pru·nel·la (*or* ·nelle, ·nel·lo) fabric
pru·nelle liqueur
prun·er
pru·ri·ence
pru·ri·ent lewd; *compare* purulent
pru·ri·go skin disease
pru·rit·ic
pru·ri·tus itching
Prus·sia
Prus·sian
prus·si·ate cyanide
prus·sic acid
pry (*verb* pries, pry·ing, pried; *noun, plural* pries)
pry·er *variant spelling of* prier
pryta·neum (*plural* ·nea) ancient Greek town hall
psalm
psalm·ic
psalm·ist
psalm·od·ic
psalmo·dist
psalmo·dy (*plural* ·dies)
Psalms Old Testament book
Psal·ter (*or* psal·) psalm book
psal·ter·ium (*plural* ·teria) cow's stomach
psal·tery (*plural* ·teries) musical instrument
pse·phite rock
pse·phit·ic
psepho·logi·cal
psepho·logi·cal·ly
pse·pholo·gist
pse·phol·ogy study of elections
pseud *Slang* pretentious person
pseud·axis botany term
Pseud·epig·ra·pha Jewish writings
pseu·do *Slang* pretended
pseudo·carp botany term

pseudo·morph geology term
pseudo·mor·phic (*or* ·phous)
pseudo·mor·phism
pseudo·mu·tu·al·ity (*plural* ·ities) psychology term
pseudo·nym
pseudo·nym·ity
pseu·dony·mous
pseudo·po·dium (*plural* ·dia) biology term
pshaw exclamation
psi Greek letter
psilo·cy·bin hallucinogen
psi·lom·elane mineral
psit·ta·cine of parrots
psit·ta·co·sis
Pskov Russian city
pso·as muscle
pso·ra·lea plant
pso·ria·sis skin disease
pso·ri·at·ic
psych *Slang* deduce; prepare
Psyche mythological character
psy·che human mind
psychedelia
psychedel·ic (*or* psycho·)
psychedeli·cal·ly (*or* psycho·deli·)
psy·chi·at·ric
psy·chi·at·ri·cal·ly
psy·chia·trist
psy·chia·try
psy·chic telepathic
psy·chi·cal
psy·cho (*plural* ·chos) *Slang* psychopath
psycho·acous·tics
psycho·ac·tive
psycho·ana·lyse (US ·lyze)
psycho·analy·sis
psycho·ana·lyst
psycho·ana·lyt·ic (*or* ·lyti·cal)
psycho·ana·lyti·cal·ly
psycho·bio·logi·cal
psycho·bi·olo·gist
psycho·bi·ol·ogy
psycho·chemi·cal
psycho·dra·ma
psycho·dra·mat·ic
psycho·dy·nam·ic
psycho·dy·nami·cal·ly

psycho·dy·nam·ics
psycho·gen·esis
psycho·genet·ic
psycho·geneti·cal·ly
psycho·gen·ic
psycho·geni·cal·ly
psy·chog·no·sis
psy·chog·nos·tic
psycho·graph
psycho·graph·ic
psy·chog·ra·phy
psycho·his·to·ry (plural
·ries)
psycho·ki·nesis
psycho·ki·net·ic
psycho·lin·guist
psycho·lin·guis·tic
psycho·lin·guis·tics
psycho·logi·cal
psycho·logi·cal·ly
psy·cholo·gism belief in
psychology
psy·cholo·gist
psy·cholo·gist·ic
psy·cholo·gize (or ·gise)
psy·chol·ogy (plural ·ogies)
psycho·met·ric (or ·ri·cal)
psycho·met·ri·cal·ly
psycho·metri·cian (or
psy·chom·etrist)
psycho·met·rics (or
psy·chom·etry) testing
mental processes
psycho·mo·tor
psycho·neu·ro·sis (plural
·ses)
psycho·neu·rot·ic
psycho·path
psycho·path·ic
psycho·path·ical·ly
psycho·patho·logi·cal
psycho·pa·tholo·gist
psycho·pa·thol·ogy
psy·chopa·thy
psycho·phar·ma·co·logi·cal
psycho·phar·ma·colo·gist
psycho·phar·ma·col·ogy
psycho·physi·cal
psycho·phys·ics
psycho·physio·logi·cal
psycho·physi·olo·gist
psycho·physi·ol·ogy
psycho·sex·ual
psycho·sexu·al·ity
psy·cho·sis (plural ·ses)

psycho·so·cial
psycho·so·mat·ic
psycho·sur·gery
psycho·sur·gi·cal
psycho·tech·ni·cal
psycho·tech·ni·cian
psycho·tech·nics
psycho·thera·peu·tic
psycho·thera·peu·ti·cal·ly
psycho·thera·pist
psycho·thera·py
psycho·trop·ic
psy·chot·ic
psy·choti·cal·ly
psy·choto·mi·met·ic
psy·chrom·eter humidity
meter
psy·chro·phil·ic biology
term
psyl·lid (or ·la) insect
Ptah Egyptian god
ptar·mi·gan (plural ·gans or
·gan) bird
pteri·do·logi·cal
pteri·dolo·gist
pteri·dol·ogy study of ferns
pteri·do·phyte
pteri·do·phyt·ic (or
·dophy·tous)
pteri·do·sperm extinct
plant
ptero·dac·tyl
ptero·pod mollusc
ptero·saur
ptery·goid anatomy term
ptery·la (plural ·lae)
ornithology term
pti·san grape juice
pto·choc·ra·cy (plural ·cies)
government by the poor
Ptol·emae·us moon crater
Ptol·ema·ic
Ptol·ema·ist
pto·maine (or ·main)
chemical compound
pto·sis (plural ·ses) drooping
of eyelid
ptya·lin enzyme
ptya·lism excessive
salivation
pub (pub·bing, pubbed)
pu·ber·ty
pu·beru·lent downy
pu·bes (plural ·bes) pubic
region; plural of pubis

pu·bes·cence
pu·bes·cent
pu·bic
pu·bis (plural ·bes) hip
bone
pub·lic
pub·li·can
pub·li·ca·tion
pub·li·cist
pub·lic·ity
pub·li·cize (or ·cise)
pub·lic·ly
public-spirit·ed
pub·lish
pub·lish·able
pub·lish·er
puc·coon plant
puce
puck
puck·er
puck·ish
puck·ish·ness
pud·ding
pud·dle
pud·dler
pud·dling
pud·dly
pu·den·cy modesty
pu·den·dal
pu·den·dum (plural ·da)
pudgi·ly
pudgi·ness
pudgy (pudgi·er,
pudgi·est)
Pue·bla Mexican city
Pueb·lo (plural ·lo or ·los)
American Indian
pueb·lo (plural ·los) village
pu·er·ile
pu·er·il·ism
pu·er·il·ity (plural ·ities)
pu·er·per·al
pu·er·per·ium period after
childbirth
Puer·to Ri·can
Puer·to Rico
puff
puff·ball
puff·bird
puff·er
puff·ery (plural ·eries)
exaggerated praise
puffi·ly
puf·fin
puffi·ness

puffy (puffi•er, puffi•est)
pug (pug•ging, pugged)
  dog; knead clay
pug•gish
pu•gi•lism
pu•gi•list
pu•gi•lis•tic
pu•gi•lis•ti•cal•ly
pug•na•cious
pug•nac•i•ty (or
  •na•cious•ness)
pug-nosed
puis•ne legal term
pu•is•sance Archaic power;
  showjumping event
pu•is•sant
puke
puk•ka
pul (plural puls or puli)
  Afghan coin
pul•chri•tude
pul•chri•tudi•nous
pule to whimper
pul•er
pull
pul•let
pul•ley
pull-in (noun)
Pull•man (plural •mans) rail
  coach
pull-out (noun)
pull•over
pul•lu•late breed rapidly
pul•lu•la•tion
pul•mo•nary
pul•mo•nate
pul•mon•ic
Pul•motor (Trademark)
pulp
pulpi•ness
pul•pit
pulp•wood
pulpy (pulpi•er, pulpi•est)
pul•que alcoholic drink
pul•sar star
pul•sate
pul•sa•tile
pul•sa•til•ity
pul•sa•tion
pul•sa•tive
pul•sa•tor
pul•sa•tory
pulse
pulse-jet
pul•sim•eter (or •som•)

pul•ver•able
pul•veri•za•tion (or
  •sa•tion)
pul•ver•ize (or •ise)
pul•ver•iz•er (or •is•er)
pul•veru•lence
pul•veru•lent of dust
pul•vil•lus (plural •li)
  zoology term
pul•vi•nate (or •nat•ed)
pul•vi•nus (plural •ni)
  botany term
puma
pum•ice
pu•mi•ceous
pum•mel (or pom•;
  •mel•ling, •melled; US
  •mel•ing, •meled) to
  pound; compare
  pommel
pump
pum•per•nick•el
pump•kin
pumpkin•seed
pun (pun•ning, punned)
punce Dialect kick
punch
punch•ball
punch•board
punch•bowl
punch-drunk
pun•cheon
punch•er
Pun•chi•nel•lo (plural •los or
  •loes) clown
punch-up (noun)
punchy (punchi•er,
  punchi•est)
punc•tate (or •tat•ed)
punc•ta•tion
punc•tilio (plural •tilios)
  etiquette
punc•tili•ous
punc•tili•ous•ness
punc•tu•al
punc•tu•al•ity
punc•tu•al•ly
punc•tu•ate
punc•tua•tion
punc•tua•tor
punc•tum (plural •ta)
  anatomy term
punc•tur•able
punc•ture
punc•tur•er

pun•dit (or pan•) expert;
  learned Hindu; compare
  pandit
pung US sleigh
pun•gen•cy
pun•gent
Pu•nic of Carthage
puni•ness
pun•ish
pun•ish•abil•ity
pun•ish•able
pun•ish•er
pun•ish•ing•ly
pun•ish•ment
pu•ni•tive (or •tory)
pu•ni•tive•ness
Pun•jab
Pun•ja•bi (or Pan•)
punk
pun•ka (or •kah) palm-leaf
  fan
punned
pun•ner
pun•net
pun•ning
pun•ster
punt
punt•er
pun•ty (plural •ties)
  glass-blowing rod
puny (pu•ni•er, pu•ni•est)
pup (pup•ping, pupped)
pupa (plural pupae or
  pupas)
pu•pal
pu•par•ial
pu•par•ium (plural •paria)
pu•pate
pu•pa•tion
pu•pil
pu•pil•lage (US •pil•age)
pu•pil•lary (or •pi•lary)
pu•pipa•rous entomology
  term
pup•pet
pup•pet•eer
pup•pet•ry
pup•ping
Pup•pis constellation
pup•py (plural •pies)
pup•py•hood
pup•py•ish
Pu•ra•na Sanskrit writings
Pur•beck Dorset peninsula;
  marble

pur·blind
pur·chasa·bil·ity
pur·chas·able
pur·chase
pur·chas·er
pur·dah (or pur·da, par·dah)
pure
pure·bred
pu·ree (or puri) Indian bread
pu·rée (·rée·ing, ·réed) pulped food
pure·ly
pure·ness
pur·fle ornamental band
pur·ga·tion
pur·ga·tive
pur·ga·to·rial
pur·ga·tory
purge
purg·er
Puri Indian port
pu·ri·fi·ca·tion
pu·ri·fi·ca·tor Communion cloth
pu·rifi·ca·tory
pu·ri·fi·er
pu·ri·fy (·fies, ·fy·ing, ·fied)
Pu·rim Jewish holiday
pu·rine (or ·rin) biochemical compound
pur·ism
pur·ist
pu·rist·ic
pu·ris·ti·cal·ly
Pu·ri·tan extreme Protestant
pu·ri·tan strictly moral person
pu·ri·tani·cal (or ·tan·ic)
pu·ri·tani·cal·ness
Pu·ri·tan·ism
pu·ri·tan·ism
pu·rity
purl knitting stitch; compare pearl
pur·ler headlong fall
pur·lieu outlying area
pur·lin (or ·line) roof beam
pur·loin
pur·loin·er
pur·ple
pur·ple·ness
pur·plish
pur·port

pur·pose
pur·pose·ful
pur·pose·ful·ly determinedly; compare purposely
pur·pose·ful·ness
pur·pose·less
pur·pose·less·ness
pur·pose·ly intentionally; compare purposefully
pur·pos·ive
pur·pos·ive·ness
pur·pu·ra disease
pur·pure heraldic purple
pur·pu·rin biological dye
purr
purse
purs·er
purs·lane plant
pur·su·ance
pur·su·ant
pur·sue (·su·ing, ·sued)
pur·su·er
pur·suit
pur·sui·vant heraldic officer
pursy short-winded
pu·ru·lence (or ·len·cy)
pu·ru·lent of pus; compare prurient
pur·vey
pur·vey·ance
pur·vey·or
pur·view scope
pus matter from wound; compare puss
Pu·san South Korean port
push
push·chair
push·er
pushi·ly
pushi·ness
push·ing
push·ing·ly
push·ing·ness
push·over
push·pull
push·rod
Push·tu variant of Pashto
push-up US press-up
pushy (pushi·er, pushi·est)
pu·sil·la·nim·ity
pu·sil·lani·mous
puss Slang cat; compare pus
pus·sy (·si·er, ·si·est) full of pus

pussy (or pussy·cat; plural pussies or ·cats)
pussy·foot
pus·tu·lant
pus·tu·lar
pus·tu·late
pus·tu·la·tion
pus·tule
put (put·ting, put) to place, etc.; compare putt
pu·ta·men (plural ·tami·na) botany term
pu·ta·tive
put-down (noun)
put·log (or ·lock) scaffold beam
put-on (noun)
pu·tre·fac·tion
pu·tre·fac·tive (or ·fa·cient)
pu·tre·fi·able
pu·tre·fi·er
pu·tre·fy (·fies, ·fy·ing, ·fied)
pu·tres·cence
pu·tres·cent
pu·tres·cine organic compound
pu·trid
pu·trid·ity (or ·trid·ness)
(putrify) incorrect spelling of putrefy
Putsch German uprising
putt golf stroke; compare put
put·tee (or ·ty; plural ·tees or ·ties) leg cloth
putt·er golf club
put·ter placer
putt·ing golf stroke
put·ting placing
put·to (plural ·ti) boy cupid
put·ty (noun, plural ·ties; verb ·ties, ·ty·ing, ·tied)
putty·root
put-up (adj)
Puy de Dôme French department
puz·zle
puz·zle·ment
puz·zler
puz·zling·ly
pya Burmese coin
py·aemia (US ·emia) blood poisoning

py·aemic (*US* ·emic)
pyc·nid·ium (*plural* ·nidia)
   botany term
pyc·nom·eter density
   measurer
pyc·no·met·ric
Pyd·na ancient Macedonian
   town
pye-dog (*or* pie-)
py·elit·ic
py·eli·tis kidney disease
py·elo·gram
py·elo·graph·ic
py·elog·ra·phy
py·elo·nephri·tis
py·emia *US spelling of*
   pyaemia
py·gid·ial
py·gid·ium (*plural* ·gidia)
   zoology term
Pygmalion mythological
   king
Pyg·my (*or* Pig·; *plural*
   ·mies) African race
pyg·my (*or* pig·; *plural*
   ·mies) dwarf
py·ja·ma (*US* pa·; *adj*)
py·ja·mas (*US* pa·)
pyk·nic squat
py·lon
py·lo·rec·to·my (*plural*
   ·mies)
py·lo·ric
py·lo·rus (*plural* ·ri)
   stomach opening
pyo·der·ma skin disease
pyo·gen·esis
pyo·gen·ic causing pus;
   compare pyrogenic
py·oid
Pyong·yang capital of
   North Korea
py·or·rhoea (*US* ·rhea)
   gum disease
py·or·rhoeal (*or* ·rhoe·ic;
   US ·rheal *or* ·rhe·ic)
pyo·sis pus formation
py·ra·can·tha shrub
pyra·lid moth
pyra·mid
py·rami·dal (*or*
   pyra·midi·cal,
   pyra·mid·ic)
Pyramus legendary
   lover

py·ran chemical
   compound
py·ra·nom·eter solarimeter
py·rar·gy·rite mineral
py·ra·zole chemical
   compound
pyre
py·rene chemical
   compound; botany term
Pyr·enean
Pyr·enees
Py·ré·nées At·lan·tiques
   French department
Py·ré·nées-Orientales
   French department
pyr·enoid protein granule
py·rethrin insecticide
py·rethrum plant
py·ret·ic of fever
Py·rex (*Trademark*)
py·rexia fever
py·rex·ial (*or* ·rex·ic)
pyr·he·li·om·eter
pyr·he·lio·met·ric
pyri·dine chemical
   compound
pyri·dox·al biochemical
   compound
pyri·doxa·mine
pyri·dox·ine
pyri·form pear-shaped
py·rimi·dine biochemical
   compound
py·rite mineral
py·ri·tes (*plural* ·tes)
   mineral
py·rit·ic (*or* ·ti·tous)
pyro·cat·echol (*or* ·echin)
pyro·chemi·cal
pyro·clas·tic geology
   term
pyro·con·duc·tiv·ity
pyro·elec·tric
pyro·elec·tric·ity
pyro·gal·late
pyro·gal·lic
pyro·gal·lol
pyro·gen
pyro·gen·ic (*or*
   py·rog·enous*) causing
   heat or fever; *compare*
   pyogenic
py·rog·nos·tics
py·rog·ra·pher
pyro·graph·ic

py·rog·ra·phy (*plural*
   ·phies) design by burning
pyro·lig·ne·ous (*or* ·lig·nic)
pyro·lit·ic
pyro·lu·site mineral
py·roly·sis chemical
   reaction
pyro·man·cer
pyro·man·cy divination by
   fire
pyro·ma·nia
pyro·ma·ni·ac
pyro·ma·nia·cal
pyro·man·tic
pyro·met·al·lur·gy
py·rom·eter
pyro·met·ric (*or*
   ·met·ri·cal)
pyro·met·ri·cal·ly
py·rom·etry
pyro·mor·phite mineral
py·rone chemical
   compound
py·rope garnet
pyro·phor·ic
pyro·phos·phate
pyro·pho·tom·eter
pyro·pho·tom·etry
pyro·phyl·lite mineral
pyro·sis heartburn
pyro·stat
pyro·stat·ic
pyro·sul·phate (*US* ·fate)
pyro·tech·nic (*or* ·ni·cal)
pyro·tech·nics
py·rox·ene mineral
py·rox·en·ic
py·rox·enite rock
py·roxy·lin constituent of
   plastics
Pyrrha mythological
   character
Pyr·rhic of Pyrrhus
pyr·rhic prosody term
pyr·rho·tite (*or* ·tine)
   mineral
pyr·rhu·loxia bird
pyr·role biochemical
   compound
pyr·rol·ic
pyr·roli·dine
pyr·ru·vic acid
Py·thago·rean
Pythia mythological
   priestess

Pyth·ian
py·thon
py·thon·ess female
 soothsayer

py·thon·ic
pyu·ria medical term
pyx container for Eucharist;
 compare **pix**

pyx·id·ium (*plural* ·idia)
 botany term
pyxie shrub
pyx·is (*plural* **pyxi·des**) box

Q

Qair·wan Tunisian city
Qa·tar Arabian state
Qa·ta·ri
Qeshm (*or* **Qishm**) Iranian
 island
qin·tar (*or* ·**dar**) Albanian
 coin
qua in the capacity of
quack
quack·ery (*plural* ·**eries**)
quack·sal·ver quack doctor
quad quadrangle;
 quadruplet; *compare* **quod**
quad·ra·ge·nar·ian
Quad·ra·gesi·ma
Quad·ra·gesi·mal
quad·ran·gle
quad·ran·gu·lar
quad·rant
quad·ran·tal
quad·ra·phon·ic (*or* ·**ro·**)
quad·ra·phon·ics (*or* ·**ro·**)
quad·rat ecology term
quad·rate cube; bone
quad·rat·ic
quad·rat·ics branch of
 algebra
quad·ra·ture maths term
quad·ren·nial
quad·ren·nial·ly
quad·ren·nium (*plural*
 ·**niums** *or* ·**nia**)
quad·ric maths term
quad·ri·cen·ten·nial
quad·ri·ceps (*plural* ·**cepses**)
 muscle
quad·ri·cipi·tal
quad·ri·fid botany term
quad·ri·ga (*plural* ·**gas** *or*
 ·**gae**) chariot
quad·ri·lat·er·al
quad·rille dance
quad·ril·lion 10²⁴
quad·ril·lionth
quad·ri·no·mial
quad·ri·par·tite

quad·ri·plegia
quad·ri·plegic
quad·ri·sect
quad·ri·sec·tion
quad·ri·va·len·cy (*or*
 ·**lence**)
quad·ri·va·lent
quad·riv·ial having four
 roads meeting
quad·riv·ium medieval
 branch of learning
quad·roon
quad·ru·ma·nous zoology
 term
quad·ru·ped
quad·ru·ped·al
quad·ru·ple
quad·ru·plet
quad·ru·plex fourfold
quad·ru·pli·cate
quad·ru·pli·ca·tion
quad·ru·plic·ity (*plural*
 ·**ities**)
quaes·tor (*or* **ques·**) Roman
 magistrate
quaff
quaff·er
quag·ga (*plural* ·**gas** *or* ·**ga**)
 extinct horse
quag·gy (·**gi·er**, ·**gi·est**)
 marshy
quag·mire
qua·hog clam
quail (*plural* **quails** *or* **quail**)
quaint
quaint·ness
quake
Quak·er
Quak·er·ism
quaki·ly
quaki·ness
quaky (**quaki·er**,
 quaki·est)
qua·le (*plural* ·**lia**)
 philosophy term
quali·fi·able

quali·fi·ca·tion
quali·fi·ca·tory
quali·fied
quali·fi·er
quali·fy (·**fies**, ·**fy·ing**, ·**fied**)
quali·fy·ing·ly
quali·ta·tive
qual·ity (*plural* ·**ities**)
qualm
qualm·ish
quam·ash plant
quan·da·ry (*plural* ·**ries**)
quan·dong (*or* ·**dang**, ·**tong**)
 fruit tree
quango (*plural* **quangos**)
quant punting pole
quan·tal
quan·tic maths term
quan·ti·fi·able
quan·ti·fi·ca·tion
quan·ti·fi·er
quan·ti·fy (·**fies**, ·**fy·ing**,
 ·**fied**)
quan·ti·ta·tive (*or*
 quan·ti·tive)
quan·tity (*plural* ·**tities**)
quan·ti·za·tion (*or* ·**sa·tion**)
quan·tize (*or* ·**tise**)
quan·tum (*plural* ·**ta**)
qua·qua·ver·sal geology
 term
quar·an·tine
quare *Irish* remarkable
quark
quar·rel (·**rel·ling**, ·**relled**;
 US ·**rel·ing**, ·**reled**)
quar·rel·ler (*US* ·**rel·er**)
quar·rel·some
quar·rian bird
quar·ri·er (*or* **quarry·man**;
 plural ·**ers** *or* ·**men**)
quar·ry (*noun, plural* ·**ries**;
 verb ·**ries**, ·**ry·ing**, ·**ried**)
quart
quar·tan every third day
quar·ter

quar·ter·age quarterly
payment
quarter·back
quarter·bound
quarter·deck
quar·tered
quarter·final
quarter·hour
quar·ter·ing
quarter·light window
quar·ter·ly (*plural* ·lies)
quarter·master
quar·tern measure of weight
quar·ters
quarter·saw (·saw·ing,
·sawed, ·sawed *or* ·sawn)
quarter·staff (*plural* ·staves)
quar·tet (*or* ·tette)
quar·tic maths term
quar·tile
quar·to (*plural* ·tos)
quartz
quartz·if·er·ous
quartz·ite
qua·sar
quash
quas·sia tree
qua·ter·cen·te·nary (*plural*
·naries)
Qua·ter·nary geological
period
qua·ter·nary (*plural* ·naries)
of four; fourth
qua·ter·ni·on maths term
qua·ter·ni·ty (*plural* ·ties)
group of four
quat·rain
qua·tre playing card
quatre·foil
quat·tro·cen·to 15th
century
qua·ver
qua·ver·er
qua·ver·ing·ly
qua·very (*or* ·ver·ous)
quay
quay·age
quay·side
quea·si·ly
quea·si·ness
quea·sy (·si·er, ·si·est)
Que·bec
Qué·be·cois (*plural* ·cois)
que·bra·cho (*plural* ·chos)
tree

Quech·ua (*or* Kech·ua;
plural ·uas *or* ·ua)
American Indian
Quech·uan (*or* Kech·)
queen
queen·cake
queen·dom
queen·li·ness
queen·ly (·li·er, ·li·est)
Queens New York borough
Queens·ber·ry rules
Queens·land
queer
queer·ness
quell
quell·er
quel·que·chose
insignificant thing
quench
quench·able
quench·er
que·nelle dumpling
quer·cetin (*or* ·ci·tin)
pigment
quer·cine of the oak
Que·réta·ro Mexican state
que·rist questioner
quern stone hand mill
queru·lous
queru·lous·ness
que·ry (*noun, plural* ·ries;
verb ·ries, ·ry·ing, ·ried)
quest
quest·er
quest·ing·ly
ques·tion
ques·tion·able
ques·tion·able·ness (*or*
·abil·ity)
ques·tion·ably
ques·tion·ary
ques·tion·er
ques·tion·ing
ques·tion·less
ques·tion·naire
Quet·ta Pakistani city
quet·zal bird
Quet·zal·coa·tl Aztec god
queue (queu·ing, queued)
line; pigtail; *compare* cue
Que·zon City Philippine
capital
quib·ble
quib·bler
quib·bling·ly

Qui·beron French peninsula
quiche
quick
quick·en
quick-freeze (-freezing,
-froze, -frozen)
quickie
quick·lime
quick·ly
quick·ness
quick·sand
quick·set hedge
quick·silver
quick·step (·step·ping,
·stepped)
quick-tempered
quick-witted
quick-witted·ness
quid
quid·dity (*plural* ·dities)
quid·nunc gossipmonger
quid pro quo (*plural* quid
pro quos)
qui·es·cence (*or* ·cen·cy)
qui·es·cent
qui·et
qui·et·en
qui·et·ism form of
mysticism
qui·et·ness
qui·etude
qui·etus (*plural* ·etuses)
quiff
quill
quil·lai tree
quill·wort
Quil·mes Argentine city
quilt
quilt·er
quilt·ing
quin
qui·na·ry (*noun, plural* ·ries)
consisting of five
qui·nate composed of five
parts
quince
quin·cen·te·nary (*plural*
·naries)
quin·cun·cial
quin·cunx arrangement of
five
quin·deca·gon 15-sided
figure
quin·deca·plet group of 15
quin·de·cen·nial

Qui Nhong Vietnamese port
quini·dine
qui·nine
quin·ol
quino·line
qui·none
quino·noid (or **quin·oid**)
quin·qua·genar·ian
Quin·qua·gesi·ma
quin·que·fo·li·ate
quin·quen·nial
quin·quen·nial·ly
quin·quen·nium (plural ·nia)
quin·que·par·tite
quin·que·reme ship
quin·que·va·len·cy (or ·lence)
quin·que·va·lent
quin·sy
quint organ stop; piquet term
quin·tain tilting target
quin·tal unit of weight
quin·tan recurring every fourth day
quin·tes·sence
quin·tes·sen·tial
quin·tes·sen·tial·ly
quin·tet (or ·tette)
quin·tic maths term
quin·tile astrology term
quin·til·lion (plural ·lions or ·lion) 10^{30}
quin·til·lionth

quin·tu·ple
quin·tu·plet
quin·tu·pli·cate
quin·tu·pli·ca·tion
quip (·quip·ping, ·quipped)
quip·ster
quire set of paper; compare choir
Quiri·nal Roman hill
Quirinus Roman god
quirk
quirki·ly
quirki·ness
quirky (quirki·er, quirki·est)
quirt whip
quis·ling
quist Dialect wood pigeon
quit (quit·ting, quit·ted or quit)
quitch grass
quit·claim legal term
quite
Qui·to Ecuadorian capital
quits
quit·tance
quit·ter one that quits
quit·tor horse's foot infection
quiv·er
quiv·er·er
quiv·er·ful
quiv·er·ing·ly
quiv·ery

qui vive French attentive
quix·ot·ic (or ·oti·cal)
quix·oti·cal·ly
quixo·tism
quiz (noun, plural quiz·zes; verb quiz·zes, quiz·zing, quizzed)
quiz·master
quiz·zer
quiz·zi·cal
quiz·zi·cal·ity
quiz·zi·cal·ly
quod Slang jail; compare quad
quod erat de·mon·stran·dum Latin which was to be proved
quod·li·bet piece of music
quod·li·beti·cal
quod·li·beti·cal·ly
quoin (or **coign, coigne**) cornerstone
quoit
quoits
quok·ka wallaby
quon·dam former
quor·um
quo·ta
quot·abil·ity
quot·able
quo·ta·tion
quote
quoth Archaic said
quo·tid·ian daily
quo·tient
quo war·ran·to legal term

R

Ra (or **Re**) Egyptian god
Ra·bat Moroccan capital
ra·ba·to (or re·; plural ·tos) collar
rab·bet variant of rebate
rab·bi (or ·bin; plural ·bis or ·bins)
rab·bin·ate office of rabbi
Rab·bin·ic language
rab·bini·cal (or ·bin·ic)
rab·bin·ism
rab·bit note Welsh rabbit (or rarebit)
rab·bit·er

rabbit·fish (plural ·fish or ·fishes)
rab·bit·ry (plural ·ries)
rab·bity
rab·ble
rab·bler
rabble-rouser
rabble-rousing
Rab·elai·sian
rabi Indian crop
rab·id
ra·bid·ity (or rab·id·ness)
ra·bies
rac·coon (or **ra·coon**)

race
race·card
race·course
race·go·er
race·horse
ra·ceme botany term
ra·cemic chemistry term
rac·emism
rac·emi·za·tion (or ·sa·tion)
rac·emize
rac·emose (or ·emous) botany term
rac·er
race·track

ra·chial (or ·chid·ial, rha·)
ra·chis (or rha·; *plural*
  ·chises or ·chi·des) biology
  term
ra·chit·ic
ra·chi·tis rickets
Rach·man·ism exploitation
  of tenants
ra·cial
ra·cial·ly
raci·ly
raci·ness
rac·ing
rac·ism (or ra·cial·ism)
rac·ist (or ra·cial·ist)
rack frame; toothed bar; to
  strain; etc.; *compare* wrack
rack (or wrack) destruction,
  esp. in rack and ruin
rack-and-pinion
rack·er
rack·et disturbance;
  dishonest practice
rack·et (or rac·quet) bat
rack·et·eer
rack·ets game
rack·ety
rack-rent
rack-renter
rac·on·teur
ra·coon *variant spelling of*
  raccoon
rac·quet *variant spelling of*
  racket
racy (raci·er, raci·est)
rad unit
ra·dar
radar·scope
rad·dle
rad·dled
ra·dial
ra·dial·ly
radial-ply
ra·dian unit
ra·di·ance (or ·an·cy; *plural*
  ·ances or ·an·cies)
ra·di·ant
ra·di·ate
ra·dia·tion
ra·dia·tion·al
ra·dia·tive (or ·tory)
ra·dia·tor
radi·cal basic; extreme;
  chemistry term; *compare*
  radicle

radi·cal·ism
radi·cal·is·tic
radi·cal·is·ti·cal·ly
radi·cal·ly
radi·cal·ness
radi·cand maths term
radi·cel tiny root
radi·ces *plural of* radix
radi·cle embryonic plant
  root; *compare* radical
ra·dii *plural of* radius
ra·dio (*noun, plural* ·dios;
  verb ·dios, ·dio·ing,
  ·di·oed)
radio·ac·ti·vate
radio·ac·ti·va·tion
radio·ac·tive
radio·ac·tiv·ity
radio·bio·logi·cal
radio·bi·olo·gist
radio·bi·ol·ogy
radio·car·bon
radio·chemi·cal
radio·chem·ist
radio·chem·is·try
radio·com·mu·ni·ca·tion
radio·el·ement
radio·gen·ic
radio·gram
radio·graph
ra·di·og·ra·pher
radio·graph·ic
ra·di·og·ra·phy
radio·iso·tope
radio·iso·top·ic
radio·lar·ian marine
  organism
radio·lo·ca·tion·al
radio·logi·cal
ra·di·olo·gist
ra·di·ol·ogy
radio·lu·cent
radio·lu·mi·nes·cence
radio·lu·mi·nes·cent
ra·di·oly·sis
ra·di·om·eter
radio·met·ric
ra·di·om·etry
ra·dio·mi·crom·eter
radio·nu·clide
radio·pac·ity (or
  radio-opacity)
radio·paque (or
  radio-opaque) impervious
  to X-rays

radio·phone
radio·phon·ic
radio·phoni·cal·ly
ra·di·opho·ny
radio·scope
radio·scop·ic
radio·scopi·cal·ly
ra·di·os·co·py
radio·sen·si·tive
radio·sen·si·tiv·ity
radio·sonde meteorological
  device
radio·tele·gram
radio·tele·graph
radio·tele·graph·ic
radio·tele·graphi·cal·ly
radio·teleg·ra·phy
radio·telem·etry
radio·tele·phone
radio·tele·phon·ic
radio·telepho·ny
radio·tele·type
radio·thera·peu·tic
radio·thera·peu·ti·cal·ly
radio·thera·pist
radio·thera·py
radio·thermy
radio·tox·ic
rad·ish
ra·dium radioactive element
ra·dius (*plural* ·dii or
  ·di·uses)
ra·dix (*plural* ·di·ces or
  ·dixes) maths or biology
  term
Rad·nor·shire former Welsh
  county
Ra·dom Polish city
ra·dome radar antenna's
  housing
ra·don radioactive element
radu·la (*plural* ·lae) zoology
  term
radu·lar
raff *Dialect* rubbish
raf·fia (or raphia)
raf·fi·nate chemistry term
raf·fi·nose sugar
raff·ish
raff·ish·ness
raf·fle
raf·fler
raf·fle·sia plant
raft
raft·er

rag (rag·ging, ragged)
raga musical term
raga·muf·fin
rag·bag
rage
ragged teased
rag·ged tattered
rag·ged·ness
rag·gedy
raggle-taggle
ragi (or rag·gee, rag·gy)
  cereal
rag·lan
rag·man (plural ·men)
ra·gout stew
rag·tag
rag·time
rag·weed
rag·worm
rag·wort
raid
raid·er
rail
rail·car
rail·er
rail·head
rail·ing
rail·lery (plural ·leries)
rail·road
rail·way
rail·way·man (plural ·men)
rai·ment
rain
rain·band
rain·bird
rain·bow
rain·check
rain·coat
rain·drop
rain·fall
Rai·ni·er US mountain
raini·ly
raini·ness
rain·maker
rain·making
rain·out radioactive fallout
rain·proof
rain·storm
rain·water
rain·wear
rainy (raini·er, raini·est)
rais·able (or raise·)
raise elevate; compare raze
rais·er
rai·sin

rais·ing
rai·siny
rai·son d'être (plural
  rai·sons d'être)
raj
ra·jah (or raja)
Ra·ja·sthan Indian state
Raj·kot Indian city
Raj·put (or ·poot) Indian
  clan
Ra·jya Sa·bha chamber of
  Indian parliament
rake
rake-off (noun)
rak·er
raki (or ra·kee) drink
rak·ish
rak·ish·ly
rak·ish·ness
rale (or râle) medical term
Ra·leigh US city
ral·len·tan·do musical term
ral·li·er
ral·line ornithology term
ral·ly (verb ·lies, ·ly·ing,
  ·lied; noun, plural ·lies)
ral·ly·cross
ram (ram·ming, rammed)
Rama Hindu hero
Ramachandra mythological
  character
Rama·dan (or
  Rhama·dhan, Rama·zan)
  period in Muslim year
Ra·mat Gan Israeli city
ram·ble
ram·bler
ram·bling
Ram·bouil·let sheep
ram·bunc·tious Slang
  boisterous
ram·bu·tan fruit
ram·ekin (or ·equin)
ram·en·ta·ceous
ra·men·tum (plural ·ta) fern
  scale
ramie (or ramee) fibre
rami·fi·ca·tion
rami·form
rami·fy (·fies, ·fy·ing, ·fied)
Ra·mil·lies Belgian battle
  site
ram·jet
rammed
ram·mer

ram·ming
ram·mish (or ram·my)
ra·mose (or ·mous)
  branched
ra·mos·ity
ramp
ram·page
ram·pa·geous
ram·pa·geous·ness
ram·pag·er
ram·pan·cy
ram·pant
ram·part
ram·pi·on plant
Ram·pur Indian city
ram·rod
Rams·gate
ram·shack·le
ram·sons plant
ram·til plant
ramu·lose (or ·lous)
ra·mus (plural rami) biology
  term
ran
rance marble
ranch
ranch·er
ran·che·ro (plural ·ros) US
  rancher
Ran·chi Indian city
ran·cid
ran·cid·ness (or ·ity)
ran·cor·ous
ran·cor·ous·ness
ran·cour (US ·cor)
rand
ran·dan boat
randi·ly
randi·ness
ran·dom
ran·domi·za·tion (or
  ·sa·tion)
ran·dom·ize (or ·ise)
ran·dom·ness
randy (randi·er, randi·est)
rang
range
range·finder
Rang·er senior Guide
rang·er
rangi·ly
rangi·ness
Ran·goon Burmese
  capital
rangy (rangi·er, rangi·est)

rani (or ra·nee) Indian
queen or princess

rank

rank·er

Rankine scale

rank·ing

ran·kle

rank·ness

ran·sack

ran·sack·er

ran·som

ran·som·er

rant

rant·er

rant·ing·ly

ra·nun·cu·la·ceous botany
term

ra·nun·cu·lus (plural ·luses
or ·li) plant

rap (rap·ping, rapped)
strike; compare wrap

ra·pa·cious

ra·pac·ity (or
·pa·cious·ness)

Rapa Nui Easter Island

rape

rape·seed

Rapha·el·esque

ra·phe (plural ·phae) botany
term

raphia variant spelling of
raffia

ra·phide (or ra·phis; plural
raphi·des) botany term

rap·id

ra·pid·ity (or rap·id·ness)

rap·ids

ra·pi·er

rap·ine (noun)

rap·ist

rap·pa·ree Irish soldier

rapped past tense of rap;
compare rapt

rap·pee snuff

rap·pel (·pel·ling, ·pelled)
mountaineering technique

rap·per

rap·ping

rap·port harmony

rap·por·teur preparer of
report

rap·proche·ment

rap·scal·lion

rapt engrossed; compare
rapped

rap·tor bird of prey

rap·to·rial

rap·ture

rap·tur·ous

rap·tur·ous·ness

rara avis (plural ra·rae aves)
Latin unusual person or
thing

rare

rare·bit variant of (Welsh)
rabbit

rar·efac·tion (or
·efi·ca·tion)

rar·efac·tion·al (or
·efac·tive)

rar·efi·able

rar·efi·er

rar·efy (·fies, ·fy·ing, ·fied)

rare·ly

rare·ripe US ripening early

rar·ing

rar·ity (plural ·ities)

Ra·ro·ton·ga Pacific island

ras·bo·ra fish

ras·cal

ras·cal·ity (plural ·ities)

ras·cal·ly

rase variant spelling of raze

rash

rash·er

rash·ness

Rasht (or Resht) Iranian city

ra·so·rial zoology term

rasp

ras·pa·tory (plural ·tories)
surgical instrument

rasp·berry (plural ·berries)

rasp·er

rasp·ing (or raspy)

rasse civet; compare wrasse

Ras·ta·far·ian (or Ras·ta)

ras·ter electronics term

rat (rat·ting, rat·ted)

ra·ta tree

rat·abil·ity (or ·able·ness,
rate·)

rat·able (or rate·)

rat·ably (or rate·)

rata·fia (or ·fee) liqueur;
biscuit

ra·tal ratable value

ra·tan variant spelling of
rattan

rata·tat-tat (or rata·tat)

ra·ta·touille vegetable stew

rat·bag

ratch·et

rate

rate·able variant spelling of
ratable

ra·tel animal

rate·payer

rat·fink

rat·fish (plural ·fish or
·fishes)

rathe (or rath) Archaic
blossoming early

ra·ther

rati·fi·able

rati·fi·ca·tion

rati·fi·er

rati·fy (·fies, ·fy·ing, ·fied)

ra·tine (or ra·teen, rat·teen,
rati·né) cloth

rat·ing

ra·tio (plural ·tios)

ra·ti·oci·nate argue logically

ra·ti·oci·na·tion

ra·ti·oci·na·tor

ra·tion

ra·tion·al using reason

ra·tion·ale basis

ra·tion·al·ism

ra·tion·al·ist

ra·tion·al·is·tic

ra·tion·al·is·ti·cal·ly

ra·tion·al·ity (plural ·ities)

ra·tion·ali·za·tion (or
·sa·tion)

ra·tion·al·ize (or ·ise)

ra·tion·al·iz·er (or ·is·er)

ra·tion·al·ly

ra·tions

Rat·is·bon Regensburg

rat·ite flightless bird

Rat·lam Indian city

rat·line (or ·lin) nautical
term

ra·toon (or rat·toon) new
shoot

rats·bane

rat·tail fish; horse; file

rat·tan (or ra·tan)

rat·ted

rat·ter

rat·ti·ly

rat·ti·ness

rat·ting

rat·tish

rat·tle

rattle·box

rat·tler

rattle·snake

rattle·trap

rat·tling

rat·tly (·tli·er, ·tli·est)

rat·trap

rat·ty (·ti·er, ·ti·est)

rau·cous

rau·cous·ness (or rau·city)

raun·chy (·chi·er, ·chi·est)

rau·wol·fia drug

rav·age

rav·age·ment

rav·ag·er

rave

rav·el (·el·ling, ·elled; US ·el·ing, ·eled)

rave·lin fortification

rav·el·ler (US ·el·er)

rav·el·ly

ra·ven bird

rav·en to plunder

rav·en·er

rav·en·ing

Ra·ven·na Italian city

rav·en·ous

rav·en·ous·ness

rav·er

rave-up

ra·vine

rav·ing

ra·vio·li

rav·ish

rav·ish·er

rav·ish·ing

rav·ish·ment

raw

Ra·wal·pin·di

raw·boned

raw·hide

ra·win·sonde meteorological balloon

raw·ness

ray

ray·less

ray·let

ray·on

raze (or rase) destroy; compare raise

razee ship

raz·er (or ras·) demolisher; compare razor

ra·zoo Austral small sum of money

ra·zor shaver; compare razer

razor·back whale

razor·bill

razor-cut (-cutting, -cut)

razz Slang deride

razz·ma·tazz (or razzle-dazzle)

re concerning

re·ab·sorb

reach

reach·able

reach·er

re·act act in response

re·act act again

re·ac·tance physics term

re·ac·tant

re·ac·tion

re·ac·tion·al

re·ac·tion·ary (plural ·aries)

re·ac·tion·ism

re·ac·ti·vate

re·ac·ti·va·tion

re·ac·tive

re·ac·tiv·ity (or ·tive·ness)

re·ac·tor

read (read·ing, read)

read·abil·ity (or ·able·ness)

read·able

read·ably

re·ad·dress

read·er

read·er·ship

read·ily

readi·ness

Read·ing

re·adjust

re·adjust·able

re·adjust·er

re·adjust·ment

re·admis·sion

re·admit (·admit·ting, ·admit·ted)

re·admit·tance

read-out (noun)

ready (adj readi·er, readi·est; verb readies, ready·ing, readied)

ready-made

ready-mix

ready-to-wear

ready-witted

re·affirm

re·affir·ma·tion (or ·affirm·ance)

re·affor·est (or ·for·est)

re·affor·esta·tion (or ·for·esta·tion)

re·agent

real actual

real (plural reals or rea·les) Spanish coin

real (plural reis) Portuguese coin

re·al·gar mineral

re·align

re·align·ment

re·al·ism

re·al·ist

re·al·is·tic

re·al·is·ti·cal·ly

re·al·ity (plural ·ities)

re·al·iz·able (or ·is·able)

re·al·iz·ably (or ·is·ably)

re·ali·za·tion (or ·sa·tion)

re·al·ize (or ·ise)

re·al·iz·er (or ·is·er)

re·allo·cate

re·allo·ca·tion

re·al·ly

realm

Re·al·po·li·tik German opportunistic politics

re·al·tor US estate agent

re·al·ty real property

ream

ream·er

re·ani·mate

re·ani·ma·tion

reap

reap·able

reap·er

re·appear

re·appear·ance

re·apply (·applies, ·apply·ing, ·applied)

re·appoint

re·appoint·ment

re·appor·tion

re·apprais·al

re·appraise

rear

rear·er

rear·guard

re·arm

rear·most

re·arrange

re·arrange·ment

re·arrang·er

rear·ward (adj)

rear·wards (adv)

rea·son
rea·son·able
rea·son·able·ness (or
 ·abil·ity)
rea·son·ably
rea·soned
rea·son·er
rea·son·ing
re·as·sem·ble
re·assur·ance
re·assure
re·assur·er
re·assur·ing
rea·ta *variant spelling of* riata
re·awak·en
reb *US* Confederate soldier
re·bar·ba·tive
re·bat·able (or ·bate·)
re·bate refund
re·bate (or rab·bet)
 carpentry term
re·bat·er
re·bec (or ·beck) musical
 instrument
re·bel (·bel·ling, ·belled)
re·bel·lion
re·bel·lious
re·bel·lious·ness
re·birth
re·born
re·bound
re·buff
re·build (·build·ing, ·built)
re·buk·able
re·buke
re·buk·er
re·buk·ing·ly
re·bus (*plural* ·buses) picture
 puzzle
re·but (·but·ting, ·but·ted)
re·but·table
re·but·tal
re·but·ter
rec *Slang* recreation ground
re·cal·ci·trance (or ·tran·cy)
re·cal·ci·trant
re·cal·esce
re·ca·les·cence chemistry
 term
re·ca·les·cent
re·call
re·call·able
re·cant
re·can·ta·tion
re·cant·er

re·cap (·cap·ping, ·capped)
re·capi·tali·za·tion (or
 ·sa·tion)
re·capi·tal·ize (or ·ise)
re·ca·pitu·late
re·ca·pitu·la·tion
re·ca·pitu·la·tive (or ·tory)
re·cap·tion legal term
re·cap·ture
re·cast (·cast·ing, ·cast)
rec·ce (·ce·ing, ·ced or
 ·ceed) *Slang* reconnoitre;
 reconnaissance
re·cede withdraw
re·cede restore
re·ceipt
re·ceipt·or
re·ceiv·able
re·ceive
re·ceiv·er
re·ceiv·er·ship
re·cen·sion literary revision
re·cent
re·cent·ness (or ·cen·cy)
re·cept psychology term
re·cep·ta·cle
re·cep·tion
re·cep·tion·ist
re·cep·tive
re·cep·tiv·ity (or ·tive·ness)
re·cep·tor
re·cess
re·ces·sion
re·ces·sion·al
re·ces·sive
re·ces·sive·ness
Rech·abite teetotaller
re·charge
ré·chauf·fé warmed-up food
re·cher·ché exquisite; rare
re·chris·ten
re·cidi·vism
re·cidi·vist
re·cidi·vis·tic (or
 ·cidi·vous)
(recieve) *incorrect spelling of*
 receive
Re·ci·fe Brazilian port
reci·pe
re·cipi·ence
re·cipi·ent
re·cip·ro·cal
re·cip·ro·cal·ity (or ·ness)
re·cip·ro·cal·ly
re·cip·ro·cate

re·cip·ro·ca·tion
re·cip·ro·ca·tive (or ·tory)
re·cip·ro·ca·tor
reci·proc·ity
re·ci·sion cancellation
re·cit·able
re·cit·al
reci·ta·tion
reci·ta·tive (or ·ta·ti·vo)
re·cite
re·cit·er
reck·less
reck·less·ness
Reck·ling·hau·sen German
 city
reck·on
reck·on·er
reck·on·ing
re·claim
re·claim·able
re·claim·ant (or ·er)
rec·la·ma·tion
ré·clame acclaim
re·clin·able
rec·li·nate bent backwards
rec·li·na·tion
re·cline
re·clin·er
re·clothe
re·cluse
re·clu·sion
re·clu·sive
rec·og·ni·tion
rec·og·ni·tion·al (or
 ·ni·tive, ·ni·tory)
rec·og·niz·abil·ity (or ·nis·)
rec·og·niz·able (or ·nis·)
rec·og·niz·ably (or ·nis·)
re·cog·ni·zance (or ·sance)
rec·og·nize (or ·nise)
rec·og·ni·zee (or ·see)
rec·og·niz·er (or ·nis·er or *in
 legal contexts* ·ni·zor,
 ·ni·sor)
re·coil
re·coil·er
re·coil·ing·ly
re·coil·less
rec·ol·lect
rec·ol·lec·tion
rec·ol·lec·tive
re·com·bi·nant
re·com·bi·na·tion
re·com·bine
re·com·mence

re·com·mence·ment
rec·om·mend
rec·om·mend·able
rec·om·men·da·tion
rec·om·menda·tory
rec·om·mend·er
re·com·mit (·mit·ting,
·mit·ted)
re·com·mit·ment (or
·mit·tal)
rec·om·pen·sable
rec·om·pense
rec·om·pens·er
re·com·pose
re·com·po·si·tion
rec·on·cil·abil·ity (or
·able·ness)
rec·on·cil·able
rec·on·cil·ably
rec·on·cile
rec·on·cile·ment
rec·on·cil·er
rec·on·cilia·tion
rec·on·cilia·tory
rec·on·cil·ing·ly
re·con·dite
re·con·dite·ness
re·con·di·tion
re·con·di·tion·er
re·con·nais·sance (or
·nois·sance)
rec·on·noi·tre (US ·ter)
rec·on·noi·trer (US ·ter·er)
re·con·sid·er
re·con·sid·era·tion
re·con·stitu·ent
re·con·sti·tute
re·con·sti·tut·ed
re·con·sti·tu·tion
re·con·struct
re·con·struc·tible
re·con·struc·tion
re·con·struc·tive (or
·tion·al)
re·con·struc·tor
re·con·vene
re·con·ver·sion
re·con·vert
rec·ord (noun)
re·cord (verb)
re·cord·able
record-changer
re·cord·er
re·cord·ing
record-player

re·count relate
re·count count again
re·count·al
re·coup
re·coup·able
re·coup·ment
re·course
re·cov·er regain
re-cover cover again
re·cov·er·abil·ity
re·cov·er·able
re·cov·er·er
re·cov·ery (plural ·eries)
re-create
re-creation new creation
rec·rea·tion enjoyment
rec·rea·tion·al
re-creator
re·cre·ment waste matter
re·cre·men·tal
re·crimi·nate
re·crimi·na·tion
re·crimi·na·tive (or
·tory)
re·crimi·na·tor
re·cru·desce
re·cru·des·cence
re·cruit
re·cruit·able
re·cruit·er
re·cruit·ment
re·crys·tal·li·za·tion (or
·sa·tion)
re·crys·tal·lize (or ·lise)
rec·ta plural of rectum
rec·tal
rec·tan·gle
rec·tan·gu·lar
rec·tan·gu·lar·ity
rec·ti plural of rectus
rec·ti·fi·able
rec·ti·fi·ca·tion
rec·ti·fi·er
rec·ti·fy (·fies, ·fy·ing,
·fied)
rec·ti·lin·ear (or ·eal)
rec·ti·tude
rec·to (plural ·tos)
  right-hand page
rec·to·cele hernia
rec·tor
rec·tor·ate
rec·tor·ial
rec·tor·ship
rec·tory (plural ·tories)

rec·trix (plural ·tri·ces) tail
  feather
rec·tum (plural ·tums or ·ta)
  part of intestine
rec·tus (plural ·ti) muscle
re·cum·bence (or ·ben·cy)
re·cum·bent
re·cu·per·ate
re·cu·pera·tion
re·cu·pera·tive
re·cu·pera·tor
re·cur (·cur·ring, ·curred)
re·cur·rence
re·cur·rent
re·cur·ring·ly
re·cur·sion returning
re·curve
recu·sance (or ·san·cy)
recu·sant insubordinate
re·cy·cle
red (red·der, red·dest)
  colour; variant spelling of
  redd
re·dact prepare for
  publication
re·dac·tion
re·dac·tion·al
re·dac·tor
re·dan fortification
red-blooded
red·breast
red·brick
red·bud tree
red·bug
red·cap
red·coat
red·cur·rant
redd (or red; red·ding, redd
  or red·ded) Dialect to tidy
red·den
red·dish
Red·ditch
red·dle variant spelling of
  ruddle
re·deco·rate
re·deem
re·deem·abil·ity
re·deem·able (or
  re·demp·tible)
re·deem·ably
re·deem·er
re·deem·ing
re·deliv·er
re·deliv·ery
re·demand

re·demand·able

re·demp·tion

re·demp·tion·al (*or* ·tive, ·tory)

re·demp·tion·er emigrant to America

Re·demp·tor·ist Catholic missionary

re·deploy

re·deploy·ment

re·de·sign

re·devel·op

re·devel·op·er

re·devel·op·ment

red·eye

red-faced

red·fin fish

red·fish (*plural* ·fish *or* ·fishes)

red-handed

red·head

red-headed

red-hot

re·dia (*plural* ·diae) zoology term

re·dial (·dial·ling, ·dialled; *US* ·dial·ing, ·dialed)

Re·dif·fu·sion (*Trademark*)

red·in·gote overcoat

red·in·te·grate renew

red·in·te·gra·tion

red·in·te·gra·tive

re·di·rect

re·di·rec·tion

re·dis·count

re·dis·cov·er

re·dis·cov·ery (*plural* ·eries)

re·dis·trib·ute

re·dis·tri·bu·tion

red·neck

red·ness

redo (re·does, ·do·ing, ·did, ·done)

redo·lence (*or* ·len·cy)

redo·lent

re·dou·ble

re·doubt fortification

re·doubt·able

re·doubt·able·ness

re·doubt·ably

re·dound affect

redo·wa folk dance

re·dox chemistry term

red·poll bird

re·draft

re·draw (·drawing, ·drew, ·drawn)

re·dress put right

re·dress dress again

re·dress·able (*or* ·ible)

re·dress·er (*or* ·dres·sor)

red·root plant

red·shank bird

red·skin

red·start bird

re·duce

re·duc·er

re·duc·ibil·ity

re·duc·ible

re·duc·tase enzyme

re·duc·tio ad ab·sur·dum

re·duc·tion

re·duc·tion·al (*or* ·tive)

re·dun·dan·cy (*plural* ·cies)

re·dun·dant

re·du·pli·cate

re·du·pli·ca·tion

re·du·pli·ca·tive

re·du·vi·id insect

red·ware seaweed

red·wing bird

red·wood

re·echo (-echoes, -echoing, -echoed)

reed

reed·buck (*plural* ·bucks *or* ·buck) antelope

reedi·ness

reed·ing moulding

reed·ling bird

re·educate

re·education

reedy (reedi·er, reedi·est)

reef

reef·er

reek

reek·ing·ly

reeky

reel

reel·able

reel·ably

re·elect

re·election

reel·er

re·em·ploy

re·em·ploy·ment

reen (*or* rean) *Dialect* ditch

re·enact

re·enforce enforce again; *compare* reinforce

re·enforce·ment

re·enforc·er

re·enter

re·entrance

re·entrant

re·entry (*plural* -entries)

reeve (reev·ing, reeved *or* rove) nautical term; bird; medieval official

re·examin·able

re·examina·tion

re·examine

re·examin·er

re·export

re·exporta·tion

re·export·er

ref *Slang* referee

re·face

re·fash·ion

re·fec·tion

re·fec·tory (*plural* ·tories)

re·fer (·fer·ring, ·ferred)

ref·er·able (*or* re·fer·rable)

ref·eree (·cree·ing, ·ereed)

ref·er·ence

ref·er·enc·er

ref·er·en·dum (*plural* ·dums *or* ·da)

ref·er·ent

ref·er·en·tial of a reference; *compare* reverential

re·fer·ral

re·fer·rer

re·fill

re·fill·able

re·fin·able

re·fi·nance

re·fine

re·fined

re·fine·ment

re·fin·er

re·fin·ery (*plural* ·eries)

re·fin·ish

re·fin·ish·er

re·fit (·fit·ting, ·fit·ted)

re·flate

re·fla·tion

re·flect

re·flec·tance

re·flect·ing·ly

re·flec·tion (*or* ·flex·ion)

re·flec·tion·al (*or* ·flex·ion·al)

re·flec·tive contemplative; able to reflect; *compare* reflexive

re·flec·tive·ness (*or* ·tiv·ity)

re·flec·tor

re·flet lustre

re·flex

re·flex·ion *variant spelling of* reflection

re·flex·ive grammar term; *compare* reflective

re·flex·ive·ness (*or* ·iv·ity)

re·flex·ol·ogy therapy

re·flux

re·form improve

re-form form again

re·form·able

Ref·or·ma·tion religious movement

ref·or·ma·tion

re-formation

ref·or·ma·tion·al

re·forma·tive

re·forma·tory (*plural* ·tories)

re·formed

re·form·er

re·form·ism

re·form·ist

re·fract

re·fract·able

re·frac·tion

re·frac·tion·al

re·frac·tive

re·frac·tive·ness (*or* ·tiv·ity)

re·frac·tom·eter

re·frac·to·met·ric

re·frac·tom·etry

re·frac·tor

re·frac·to·ri·ly

re·frac·to·ri·ness

re·frac·tory (*plural* ·tories)

re·frain

re·frain·er

re·frain·ment

re·fran·gibil·ity (*or* ·gible·ness)

re·fran·gible

re·freeze (·freez·ing, ·froze, ·fro·zen)

re·fresh (*or* ·fresh·en)

re·fresh·er

re·fresh·ful

re·fresh·ing

re·fresh·ment

re·frig·er·ant

re·frig·er·ate

re·frig·era·tion

re·frig·era·tive (*or* ·tory)

re·frig·era·tor

re·frin·gen·cy (*or* ·gence)

re·frin·gent

re·froze

re·fu·el (·el·ling, ·elled; *US* ·el·ing, ·eled)

ref·uge

refu·gee

refu·gee·ism

re·fu·gium (*plural* ·gia)

re·ful·gence (*or* ·gen·cy)

re·ful·gent shining

re·fund give back money

re-fund replace bond issue

re·fund·able

re·fund·er

re·fur·bish

re·fur·bish·ment

re·fus·able

re·fus·al

re·fuse decline

ref·use rubbish

re·fus·er

refu·tabil·ity

refu·table

refu·ta·tion

re·fute

re·fut·er

re·gain

re·gain·able

re·gain·er

re·gal royal

re·gale amuse

re·gale·ment

re·ga·lia

re·gal·ity (*plural* ·ities)

re·gal·ly

re·gard

re·gard·able

re·gar·dant heraldic term

re·gard·ful

re·gard·ing

re·gard·less

re·gards

re·gat·ta

re·ge·late

re·ge·la·tion physics term

Re·gen·cy historical period

re·gen·cy (*plural* ·cies) rule by regent

re·gen·er·able

re·gen·era·cy

re·gen·er·ate

re·gen·era·tion

re·gen·era·tive

re·gen·era·tor

Re·gens·burg German city

re·gent

re·gent·al

re·gent·ship

reg·gae

Reg·gio di Ca·la·bria Italian port

Reg·gio nell'Emilia Italian city

regi·cid·al

regi·cide

re·gime (*or* ré·gime) administration

regi·men course of treatment

regi·ment

regi·men·tal

regi·men·tals military dress

regi·men·ta·tion

Re·gi·na the queen; Canadian city

re·gion

re·gion·al

re·gion·al·ism

re·gion·al·ist

re·gion·al·ly

reg·is·ter

reg·is·ter·er

reg·is·trable

reg·is·trant

reg·is·trar

reg·is·trar·ship

reg·is·tra·tion

reg·is·tra·tion·al

reg·is·try (*plural* ·tries)

Re·gius pro·fes·sor

reg·let

reg·nal of a sovereign

reg·nant reigning

rego·lith

re·gorge

rego·sol soil

re·grate buy up for profit

re·grat·er

re·gress

re·gres·sion

re·gres·sive

re·gres·sive·ness

re·gres·sor

re·gret (·gret·ting,
·gret·ted)
re·gret·ful
re·gret·ful·ly
re·gret·ful·ness
re·gret·table
re·gret·tably
re·gret·ter
re·group
re·growth
regu·lable
regu·lar
regu·lar·ity (*plural* ·ities)
regu·lari·za·tion (*or*
·sa·tion)
regu·lar·ize (*or* ·ise)
regu·late
regu·la·tion
regu·la·tive (*or* ·tory)
regu·la·tor
regu·line
regu·lus (*plural* ·luses *or* ·li)
impure metal
re·gur·gi·tant
re·gur·gi·tate
re·gur·gi·ta·tion
re·ha·bili·tate
re·ha·bili·ta·tion
re·ha·bili·ta·tive
re·hash
re·hear (·hear·ing, ·heard)
re·hears·al
re·hearse
re·hears·er
re·heat
re·heat·er
re·ho·bo·am wine bottle
re·house
Reich *German* kingdom or
republic
Reichs·mark (*plural* ·marks
or ·mark) currency
Reichs·tag German
assembly
rei·fi·ca·tion
rei·fier
rei·fy (·fies, ·fy·ing, ·fied)
make real
Rei·gate
reign rule; *compare* rein
re·im·burs·able
re·im·burse
re·im·burse·ment
re·im·burs·er
re·im·port

re·im·por·ta·tion
re·im·pose
re·im·po·si·tion
re·im·pres·sion
Reims (*or* Rheims) French
city
rein long strap; *compare*
reign
re·incar·nate
re·incar·na·tion
re·incar·na·tion·ist
rein·deer (*plural* ·deer *or*
·deers)
re·inforce strengthen;
compare re-enforce
re·inforce·ment
re·install
re·in·stal·la·tion
re·instate
re·instate·ment
re·insta·tor
re·insur·ance
re·insure
re·insur·er
re·intro·duce
re·intro·duc·tion
re·invest
re·invest·ment
re·issu·able
re·issue (·issu·ing, ·issued)
re·issu·er
re·it·er·ant
re·it·er·ate
re·it·era·tion
re·it·era·tive
re·ject
re·ject·able
re·ject·er (*or* ·jec·tor)
re·jec·tion
re·jec·tive
re·jig (·jig·ging, ·jigged)
re-equip
re·joice
re·joic·er
re·joic·ing
re·join
re·join·der
re·ju·venate (*or* ·venize,
·venise)
re·ju·vena·tion
re·ju·vena·tor
re·ju·venesce
re·ju·venes·cence
re·ju·venes·cent
re·kin·dle

re·la·bel (·bel·ling, ·belled;
US ·bel·ing, ·beled)
re·lapse
re·laps·er
re·lat·able
re·late
re·lat·ed
re·lat·ed·ness
re·lat·er one that relates;
compare relator
re·la·tion
re·la·tion·al
re·la·tion·ship
rela·tive
rela·tive·ly
rela·tiv·ism
rela·tiv·ist
rela·tiv·is·tic
rela·tiv·is·ti·cal·ly
rela·tiv·ity
re·la·tor legal term; *compare*
relater
re·la·tum (*plural* ·ta) logic
term
re·lax
re·lax·able
re·lax·ant
re·laxa·tion
re·lax·ed·ly
re·lax·er
re·lax·in hormone
re·lay convey
re-lay (-laying, -laid) lay
again
re·lease
re·leas·er
rel·ega·table
rel·egate
rel·ega·tion
re·lent
re·lent·less
re·lent·less·ness
re·let (·let·ting, ·let)
rel·evance (*or* ·evan·cy)
rel·evant
re·li·abil·ity (*or* ·able·ness)
re·li·able
re·li·ably
re·li·ance
re·li·ant
rel·ic object from past
rel·ict biology term; widow
re·lief
re·liev·able
re·lieve

re·liev·er
re·li·gion
re·li·gion·ism
re·ligi·ose
re·ligi·os·ity
re·li·gious
re·li·gious·ness
re·line
re·lin·quish
re·lin·quish·er
re·lin·quish·ment
reli·quary (plural
·quaries)
re·liquiae fossil remains
rel·ish
rel·ish·able
rel·ish·ing·ly
re·liv·able
re·live
re·load
re·lo·cate
re·lo·ca·tion
re·luc·tance (or ·tan·cy)
re·luc·tant
rel·uc·tiv·ity (plural ·ities)
physics term
rely (re·lies, rely·ing,
re·lied)
re·made
re·main
re·main·der
remainder·man (plural
·men) legal term
re·mains
re·make (·mak·ing, ·made)
re·mand
re·mand·ment
rema·nence physics term
re·mark
re·mark·able
re·mark·able·ness (or
·abil·ity)
re·mark·ably
re·mark·er
re·marque (or ·mark) mark
on engraved plate
re·mar·riage
re·mar·ry (·ries, ·ry·ing,
·ried)
re·match
re·medi·able
re·medi·ably
re·medial
re·medial·ly
rem·edi·less

rem·edy (noun, plural ·edies;
verb ·edies, ·edy·ing,
·edied)
re·mem·ber
re·mem·ber·er
re·mem·brance
Re·mem·branc·er
Exchequer official
re·mex (plural remi·ges)
flight feather
re·mig·ial
re·mind
re·mind·er
re·mind·ful
remi·nisce
remi·nis·cence
remi·nis·cent
re·mise legal term
re·miss negligent
re·mis·sibil·ity (or
·sible·ness)
re·mis·sible
re·mis·sion (or ·mit·tal)
re·mis·sive
re·miss·ness
re·mit (·mit·ting, ·mit·ted)
re·mit·table
re·mit·tal
re·mit·tance payment
re·mit·tee
re·mit·tence (or ·ten·cy)
diminution
re·mit·tent
re·mit·ter (or ·tor)
rem·nant
re·mod·el (·el·ling, ·elled)
re·mod·el·ler
re·mon·eti·za·tion (or
·sa·tion)
re·mon·etize (or ·etise)
re·mon·strance
re·mon·strant
re·mon·strate
re·mon·stra·tion
re·mon·stra·tive
re·mon·stra·tor
re·mon·tant
rem·on·toir (or ·toire)
device in clock
remo·ra fish
re·morse
re·morse·ful
re·morse·ful·ly
re·morse·ful·ness
re·morse·less

re·morse·less·ness
re·mote
remote-controlled
re·mote·ness
re·mould (US ·mold)
re·mount
re·mov·abil·ity (or
·able·ness)
re·mov·able
re·mov·ably
re·mov·al
re·mov·al·ist Austral
furniture remover
re·move
re·mov·er
Rem·scheid German city
re·mu·ner·abil·ity
re·mu·ner·able
re·mu·ner·ate
re·mu·nera·tion
re·mu·nera·tive
re·mu·nera·tor
Re·nais·sance historical
period
re·nais·sance (or
·nas·cence) revival
re·nal
re·name
re·nas·cent
Ren·ault (Trademark)
rend (rend·ing, rent)
rend·er (noun)
ren·der (verb)
rend·er·able submittable;
compare rendible
rend·er·er
ren·der·ing
ren·dez·vous (plural ·vous)
rend·ible tearable; compare
renderable
ren·di·tion
ren·dzi·na soil
ren·egade
re·nege (or ·negue)
re·neg·er (or ·negu·er)
re·nego·ti·able
re·nego·ti·ate
re·nego·tia·tion
re·new
re·new·abil·ity
re·new·able
re·new·al
re·new·edly
re·new·er
Ren·frew Scottish town

reni·form kidney-shaped
re·nin kidney enzyme;
  compare rennin
Rennes French city
ren·net
ren·nin milk-coagulating
  enzyme; *compare* renin
Reno US city
re·nounce
re·nounce·ment
re·nounc·er
reno·vate
reno·va·tion
reno·va·tive
reno·va·tor
re·nown
re·nowned
re·nown·edly
rens·selaer·ite mineral
rent
rent·abil·ity
rent·able
rent·al
rente *French* type of
  income
rent·er
rent-free
ren·tier one living on rentes
rent-roll
re·num·ber
re·nun·cia·tion
re·nun·cia·tive (or ·tory)
ren·voi legal term
re·oc·cu·pa·tion
re·oc·cu·py (·pies, ·py·ing,
  ·pied)
re·open
re·or·der
re·or·gani·za·tion (or
  ·sa·tion)
re·or·gan·ize (or ·ise)
re·or·gan·iz·er (or ·is·er)
rep *Slang* representative;
  repertory
rep (or repp) fabric
re·paint
re·pair
re·pair·able able to be
  repaired; *compare*
  reparable
re·pair·er
re·pair·man (*plural* ·men)
re·pand having a wavy
  margin
repa·rabil·ity

repa·rable able to be made
  good; *compare* repairable
repa·rably
repa·ra·tion
re·para·tive (or ·tory)
rep·ar·tee
rep·ar·ti·tion
re·past
re·pat·ri·ate
re·pat·ria·tion
re·pay (·pay·ing, ·paid)
re·pay·able
re·pay·ment
re·peal
re·peal·able
re·peal·er
re·peat
re·peat·abil·ity
re·peat·able
re·peat·ed
re·peat·ed·ly
re·peat·er
rep·echage contest for
  runners-up
re·pel (·pel·ling, ·pelled)
re·pel·lence (or ·len·cy)
re·pel·lent
re·pel·ler
re·pel·ling·ly
re·pel·ling·ness
re·pent
re·pent·ance
re·pent·ant
re·pent·er
re·peo·ple
re·per·cus·sion
re·per·cus·sive
rep·er·toire
rep·er·to·rial
rep·er·tory (*plural* ·tories)
rep·etend repeated digit
ré·pé·ti·teur opera-singer
  coach
rep·eti·tion
rep·eti·tious
rep·eti·tious·ness
re·peti·tive
re·peti·tive·ness
re·phrase
re·pine
re·place
re·place·abil·ity
re·place·able
re·place·ment
re·plac·er

re·plan (·plan·ning,
  ·planned)
re·plant
re·play
re·plen·ish
re·plen·ish·er
re·plen·ish·ment
re·plete
re·plete·ness
re·ple·tion
re·ple·tive
re·plevi·able (or
  ·plev·is·able)
re·plev·in legal term
re·plevy (*verb* ·plevies,
  ·plevy·ing, ·plev·ied;
  noun, plural ·plevies) legal
  term
rep·li·ca
rep·li·cate
rep·li·ca·tion
rep·li·ca·tive
re·pli·er
re·ply (*verb* ·plies, ·ply·ing,
  ·plied; *noun, plural* ·plies)
re·point
re·pone legal term
re·port
re·port·able
re·port·age
re·port·ed·ly
re·port·er
re·pos·al
re·pose
re·pos·ed·ly
re·pose·ful
re·pose·ful·ly
re·pose·ful·ness
re·pos·er
re·pos·it put away
re·po·si·tion
re·posi·tory (*plural* ·tories)
re·pos·sess
re·pos·ses·sion
re·pos·ses·sor
re·pot (·pot·ting, ·pot·ted)
re·pous·sé raised design
repp *variant spelling of* rep
rep·re·hend
rep·re·hend·able
rep·re·hend·er
rep·re·hen·sibil·ity (or
  ·sible·ness)
rep·re·hen·sible
rep·re·hen·sibly

rep·re·hen·sion
rep·re·hen·sive
rep·re·hen·sory
rep·re·sent correspond to
re·present present again
rep·re·sent·abil·ity
rep·re·sent·able
rep·re·sen·ta·tion
rep·re·sen·ta·tion·al
rep·re·sen·ta·tion·al·ism
  philosophy term
rep·re·sen·ta·tion·al·is·tic
rep·re·senta·tive
rep·re·senta·tive·ness
re·press restrain
re·press press again
re·press·er (or ·pres·sor)
re·press·ible
re·pres·sion
re·pres·sive
re·pres·sive·ness
re·priev·able
re·prieve
re·priev·er
rep·ri·mand
rep·ri·mand·er
rep·ri·mand·ing·ly
re·print
re·print·er
re·pris·al
re·prise
re·pro (plural ·pros)
re·proach
re·proach·able
re·proach·ably
re·proach·er
re·proach·ful
re·proach·ful·ly
re·proach·ful·ness
re·proach·ing·ly
rep·ro·ba·cy (or ·bate·ness)
rep·ro·bate
rep·ro·bat·er
rep·ro·ba·tion
rep·ro·ba·tive (or ·tion·ary)
re·pro·duce
re·pro·duc·er
re·pro·duc·ibil·ity
re·pro·duc·ible
re·pro·duc·tion
re·pro·duc·tive
re·pro·duc·tive·ness
rep·ro·graph·ic
re·prog·ra·phy
re·proof rebuke

re·proof renew texture
re·prov·able
re·prov·al
re·prove
re·prov·er
re·prov·ing·ly
re·pro·vi·sion
rep·tant
rep·tile
rep·til·ian
rep·ti·loid
re·pub·lic
Re·pub·li·can political party
re·pub·li·can of a republic
re·pub·li·can·ism
re·pub·li·cani·za·tion (or
  ·sa·tion)
re·pub·li·can·ize (or ·ise)
re·pub·li·ca·tion
re·pub·lish
re·pub·lish·able
re·pub·lish·er
re·pu·di·able
re·pu·di·ate
re·pu·dia·tion
re·pu·dia·tive
re·pu·dia·tor
re·pu·dia·tory
re·pugn oppose
re·pug·nance (or ·nan·cy;
  plural ·nances or
  ·nan·cies)
re·pug·nant
re·pulse
re·puls·er
re·pul·sion
re·pul·sive
re·pul·sive·ness
repu·tabil·ity (or
  ·table·ness)
repu·table
repu·tably
repu·ta·tion
re·pute
re·put·ed
re·put·ed·ly
re·quest
re·quest·er
requi·em
requi·es·cat prayer
re·quir·able
re·quire
re·quire·ment
re·quir·er
requi·site

requi·si·tion
requi·si·tion·ary
requi·si·tion·er (or ·ist)
re·quit·able
re·quit·al
re·quite
re·quite·ment
re·quit·er
re·ra·dia·tion
re·read (·read·ing, ·read)
rere·dos
rere·mouse Dialect bat
re·route (·route·ing or
  ·rout·ing, ·routed)
re·run (·run·ning, ·ran,
  ·run)
re·sal·able (or ·sale·)
re·sale
re·scind
re·scind·able
re·scind·er
re·scind·ment
re·scis·sible rescindable
re·scis·sion
re·scis·sory able to rescind
re·script
res·cu·able
res·cue (·cu·ing, ·cued)
res·cu·er
re·search
re·search·able
re·search·er
re·seat
re·seau (plural ·seaux or
  ·seaus) lace mesh
re·sect remove surgically
re·sec·tion
re·sec·tion·al
res·eda plant
re·sell (·sell·ing, ·sold)
re·sem·blance
re·sem·blant
re·sem·ble
re·sem·bler
re·sent
re·sent·ful
re·sent·ful·ly
re·sent·ful·ness
re·sent·ment
re·ser·pine drug
re·serv·able
re·servable
res·er·va·tion
re·serve set aside, etc.
re·serve serve again

re·served
re·serv·ed·ly
re·serv·ed·ness
re·serv·er
re·serv·ist
res·er·voir
re·set (·set·ting, ·set)
re·set·ter
re·set·tle
re·set·tle·ment
re·shape
re·ship (·ship·ping, ·shipped)
re·ship·ment
Resht *variant spelling of* Rasht
re·shuf·fle
re·side
resi·dence
resi·den·cy (*plural* ·cies)
resi·dent
resi·den·tial
resi·den·tiary (*plural* ·tiaries)
resi·dent·ship
re·sid·er
re·sid·ual
re·sid·u·ary
resi·due
re·sid·uum (*plural* ·sidua)
re·sign *give up*
re-sign *sign again*
res·ig·na·tion
re·signed
re·sign·ed·ly
re·sign·ed·ness
re·sign·er
re·sile *spring back*
re·sile·ment
re·sili·ence (*or* ·en·cy)
re·sili·ent
res·in *gumlike substance; compare* rosin
res·in·ate
res·in·if·er·ous
res·in·oid
res·in·ous
res·in·ous·ness
resi·pis·cence *acknowledgment of error*
re·sist
Re·sist·ance *French organization*
re·sist·ance
re·sist·ant (*or* ·sis·tive)

Re·sis·ten·cia *Argentine city*
re·sist·er *opposer; compare* resistor
re·sist·ibil·ity (*or* ·ible·ness)
re·sist·ible
re·sist·ibly
re·sist·ing·ly
re·sis·tive·ness (*or* ·tiv·ity)
re·sis·tiv·ity *electrical property*
re·sist·less
re·sis·tor *electrical component; compare* resister
re·sit (·sit·ting, ·sat)
res·na·tron *electronic valve*
re·sole
re·sol·ubil·ity (*or* ·uble·ness)
re·sol·uble *resolvable*
re·soluble *able to be dissolved again*
reso·lute
reso·lute·ness
reso·lu·tion
reso·lu·tion·er (*or* ·ist)
re·solv·abil·ity (*or* ·able·ness)
re·solv·able
re·solve
re·solved
re·solv·ed·ness
re·sol·vent
re·solv·er
reso·nance
reso·nant
reso·nate
reso·na·tion
reso·na·tor
re·sorb
re·sorb·ent
res·or·cin·ol *chemical compound*
re·sorp·tion
re·sorp·tive
re·sort *holiday town; to use*
re-sort *sort again*
re·sort·er
re·sound *echo*
re-sound *sound again*
re·sound
re·sound·ing
re·sound·ing·ly
re·source
re·source·ful

re·source·ful·ly
re·source·ful·ness
re·source·less
re·spect
re·spect·abil·ity (*plural* ·ities)
re·spect·able
re·spect·ably
re·spect·er
re·spect·ful
re·spect·ful·ly
re·spect·ful·ness
re·spect·ing
re·spec·tive
re·spec·tive·ly
re·spir·abil·ity
re·spir·able
res·pi·ra·tion
res·pi·ra·tion·al
res·pi·ra·tor
re·spira·tory
re·spire
res·pite
re·splend·ence (*or* ·en·cy)
re·splend·ent
re·spond
re·spond·ence (*or* ·en·cy)
re·spond·ent *legal term*
re·spond·er
re·sponse
re·spons·er (*or* ·spon·sor) *radio receiver*
re·spon·sibil·ity (*plural* ·ities)
re·spon·sible
re·spon·sible·ness
re·spon·sibly
re·spon·sive
re·spon·sive·ly
re·spon·sive·ness
re·spon·so·ry (*plural* ·ries)
re·spray
res pu·bli·ca *Latin the state*
rest
re·state
re·state·ment
res·tau·rant
res·tau·ra·teur
rest·er
rest·ful
rest·ful·ly
rest·ful·ness
rest·harrow *plant*
res·ti·form
rest·ing

res·ti·tu·tion
res·ti·tu·tive (*or* ·tory)
res·tive
res·tive·ly
res·tive·ness
rest·less
rest·less·ly
rest·less·ness
re·stock
re·stor·able
Res·to·ra·tion historical period
res·to·ra·tion
res·to·ra·tion·ism theological belief
re·stora·tive
re·store
re·stor·er
re·strain
re·strain·able
re·strain·ed·ly
re·strain·er
re·strain·ing·ly
re·straint
re·strict
re·strict·ed·ly
re·strict·ed·ness
re·stric·tion
re·stric·tion·ist
re·stric·tive
re·stric·tive·ly
re·stric·tive·ness
re·struc·ture
re·style
re·sult
re·sult·ant
re·sum·able
re·sume restart
ré·su·mé summary
re·sump·tion
re·sump·tive
re·su·pi·nate botany term
re·su·pi·na·tion
re·sur·face
re·surge
re·sur·gence
re·sur·gent
res·ur·rect
Res·ur·rec·tion rising of Christ
res·ur·rec·tion revival
res·ur·rec·tion·al
res·ur·rec·tion·ary
res·ur·rec·tion·ism
res·ur·rec·tion·ist

re·sus·ci·table
re·sus·ci·tate
re·sus·ci·ta·tion
re·sus·ci·ta·tive
re·sus·ci·ta·tor
ret (ret·ting, ret·ted) soak fibre
re·ta·ble altar screen
re·tail
re·tail·er
re·tain
re·tain·abil·ity (*or* ·able·ness)
re·tain·able
re·tain·er
re·tain·ment
re·take (·tak·ing, ·took, ·tak·en)
re·tak·er
re·tali·ate
re·talia·tion
re·talia·tive (*or* ·tory)
re·talia·tor
re·tard
re·tard·ant
re·tard·ate retarded person
re·tar·da·tion (*or* ·tard·ment)
re·tarda·tive (*or* ·tory)
re·tard·ed
re·tard·er
re·tard·ing·ly
retch vomit; *compare* wretch
rete (*plural* re·tia) anatomy term
re·tell (·tell·ing, ·told)
re·tene chemical compound
re·ten·tion
re·ten·tive
re·ten·tive·ly
re·ten·tive·ness
re·ten·tiv·ity
re·think (·think·ing, ·thought)
re·tial of a rete
re·ti·ar·ius (*plural* ·arii) gladiator
reti·cence
reti·cent
reti·cle (*or* ·cule) grid; *compare* reticule
re·ticu·lar
re·ticu·late
re·ticu·la·tion

reti·cule woman's bag; *variant of* reticle
re·ticu·lo·cyte
re·ticu·lo·en·do·the·lial anatomy term
re·ticu·lum (*plural* ·la) network; cow's stomach
reti·na (*plural* ·nas *or* ·nae)
reti·nacu·lar
reti·nacu·lum (*plural* ·la) biology term
reti·nal
reti·nene biochemical compound
reti·nite resin
reti·ni·tis
reti·nol biochemical compound
reti·no·scop·ic
reti·no·scopi·cal·ly
reti·nos·co·pist
reti·nos·co·py ophthalmic procedure
reti·nue
reti·nued
re·tire
re·tire·ment
re·tir·er
re·tir·ing
re·tir·ing·ly
re·tool
re·tor·sion reprisal
re·tort
re·tort·er
re·tor·tion retorting
re·touch
re·touch·able
re·touch·er
re·trace
re·trace·able
re·trace·ment
re·tract
re·tract·abil·ity (*or* ·ibil·)
re·tract·able (*or* ·ible)
re·trac·tile
re·trac·til·ity
re·trac·tion
re·trac·tive
re·trac·tor
re·train
re·tread (·tread·ing, ·tread·ed) remould
re-tread (-tread·ing, -trod, -trod·den *or* -trod) tread again

re·treat
re·treat·al
re·trench
re·trench·able
re·trench·ment
re·tri·al
ret·ri·bu·tion
re·tribu·tive (*or* ·tory)
re·tribu·tive·ly
re·triev·abil·ity
re·triev·able
re·triev·ably
re·triev·al
re·trieve
re·triev·er
ret·ro (*plural* ·ros) *Slang* retrorocket
retro·act
retro·ac·tion
retro·ac·tive
retro·ac·tive·ly
retro·ac·tiv·ity (*or* ·tive·ness)
retro·cede give back
retro·ces·sion (*or* ·ced·ence)
retro·ces·sive (*or* ·ced·ent)
retro·choir space behind altar
retro·fire
retro·fit (·fit·ting, ·fit·ted) equip with extra parts
retro·flex (*or* ·flexed)
retro·flex·ion (*or* ·flec·tion)
retro·gra·da·tion
retro·gra·da·tory
retro·grade
retro·gress
retro·gres·sion
retro·gres·sive
retro·gres·sive·ly
retro·ject throw backwards
retro·len·tal anatomy term
retro·operative
retro·pack
retro·rock·et
re·trorse pointing backwards
retro·spect
retro·spec·tion
retro·spec·tive
retro·spec·tive·ly
retro·spec·tive·ness
re·trous·sé
retro·verse
retro·ver·sion

retro·vert·ed
re·try (·tries, ·try·ing, ·tried)
ret·si·na
re·tune
re·tuner
re·turn
re·turn·abil·ity
re·turn·able
re·turn·er
re·tuse botany term
re·type
re·uni·fi·ca·tion
re·uni·fy (·fies, ·fy·ing, ·fied)
Réu·nion French island
re·union
re·union·ism
re·union·ist
re·union·is·tic
re·unit·able
re·unite
re·unit·er
re·up·hol·ster
re·us·abil·ity (*or* ·able·ness)
re·us·able
re·use
re·uti·li·za·tion (*or* ·sa·tion)
re·uti·lize (*or* ·lise)
rev (rev·ving, revved)
re·val·ori·za·tion (*or* ·sa·tion)
re·val·or·ize (*or* ·ise) revalue
re·valua·tion
re·value (·valu·ing, ·valued)
re·vamp
re·vamp·er
re·vamp·ing
re·vanch·ism foreign policy
re·vanch·ist
re·veal
re·veal·abil·ity
re·veal·able
re·veal·ed·ly
re·veal·er
re·veal·ing
re·veal·ing·ly
re·veal·ment
re·veg·etate grow again
re·veg·eta·tion
re·veil·le
rev·el (·el·ling, ·elled; *US* ·el·ing, ·eled)
rev·ela·tion

rev·ela·tion·al
rev·ela·tion·ist believer in divine revelation
rev·el·ler (*US* ·el·er)
rev·el·ment
rev·el·rous
rev·el·ry (*plural* ·ries)
rev·enant
re·venge
re·venge·ful
re·venge·ful·ly
re·veng·er
re·veng·ing·ly
rev·enue
rev·enued
rev·enu·er *US* revenue officer
re·ver·able
re·ver·ber·ant
re·ver·ber·ate
re·ver·bera·tion
re·ver·bera·tive
re·ver·bera·tor
re·ver·bera·tory (*plural* ·tories)
re·vere
rev·er·ence
rev·er·enc·er
rev·er·end deserving reverence; clergyman
rev·er·ent feeling reverence
rev·er·en·tial showing reverence; *compare* referential
rev·er·en·tial·ly
rev·er·ent·ly
rev·er·ent·ness
rev·er·er
rev·erie (*or* ·ery; *plural* ·eries)
re·vers (*plural* ·vers) lapel
re·ver·sal
re·verse
re·vers·er
re·ver·si board game
re·vers·ibil·ity (*or* ·ible·ness)
re·vers·ible
re·vers·ibly
re·ver·sion
re·ver·sion·ary (*or* ·al)
re·ver·sion·er legal term
re·vert
re·vert·er
re·vert·ible

re·ver·tive
re·vest restore power
re·vet (·vet·ting, ·vet·ted)
  face with stones
re·vet·ment
re·view survey; critical
  opinion; *compare* revue
re·view·able
re·view·al
re·view·er
re·vile
re·vile·ment
re·vil·er
re·vil·ing·ly
re·vis·abil·ity
re·vis·able
re·vis·al
re·vise
re·vis·er (*or* ·or)
re·vi·sion
re·vi·sion·al (*or* ·ary)
re·vi·sion·ism
re·vi·sion·ist
re·vi·so·ry
re·vi·tali·za·tion (*or*
  ·sa·tion)
re·vi·tal·ize (*or* ·ise)
re·viv·abil·ity
re·viv·able
re·viv·ably
re·viv·al
re·viv·al·ism
re·viv·al·ist
re·viv·al·is·tic
re·vive
re·viv·er
re·vivi·fi·ca·tion
re·vivi·fy (·fies, ·fy·ing,
  ·fied)
re·viv·ing·ly
revi·vis·cence revival
revi·vis·cent
revo·cabil·ity (*or*
  ·cable·ness)
revo·cable (*or* re·vok·able)
revo·cably
revo·ca·tion
re·voca·tive (*or*
  revo·ca·tory)
re·voice
re·vok·able *variant spelling*
  of revocable
re·voke
re·vok·er
re·vok·ing·ly

re·volt
re·volt·er
re·volt·ing
re·volt·ing·ly
revo·lute botany term
revo·lu·tion
revo·lu·tion·ari·ly
revo·lu·tion·ary (*plural*
  ·aries)
revo·lu·tion·ist
revo·lu·tion·ize (*or* ·ise)
revo·lu·tion·iz·er (*or* ·is·er)
re·volv·able
re·volve
re·volv·er
re·volv·ing
re·volv·ing·ly
re·vue entertainment;
  compare review
re·vul·sion
re·vul·sion·ary
re·vul·sive
re·ward
re·ward·able
re·ward·er
re·ward·ing
re·wind (·wind·ing,
  ·wound)
re·wind·er
re·wir·able
re·wire
re·word
re·work
re·write (·writ·ing, ·wrote,
  ·writ·ten)
Rex the king
Rey·kja·vik Icelandic capital
Rey·no·sa Mexican city
rhab·do·man·cy water
  divining
rhab·do·man·tist (*or*
  ·man·cer)
rhab·do·myo·ma (*plural*
  ·mas *or* ·ma·ta) tumour
Rhae·tia Roman province
Rhae·tian
Rhae·tic (*or* Rhe·tic)
  geology term
rham·na·ceous botany term
rhap·sod·ic
rhap·sodi·cal·ly
rhap·so·dist
rhap·so·dis·tic
rhap·so·dize (*or* ·dise)
rhap·so·dy (*plural* ·dies)

rhata·ny (*plural* ·nies) shrub
rhea bird
rhe·bok (*or* ree·; *plural*
  ·boks *or* ·bok) antelope
Rheims *variant spelling of*
  Reims
Rhe·mish of Reims
Rhen·ish of the Rhine
rhe·nium chemical element
rheo·base physiology term
rheo·logi·cal
rhe·olo·gist
rhe·ol·ogy branch of
  physics
rhe·om·eter
rheo·met·ric
rhe·om·etry
rheo·stat
rheo·stat·ic
rheo·tac·tic
rheo·tax·is biology term
rheo·trop·ic
rhe·ot·ro·pism botany term
rhe·sus
rhe·tor teacher of rhetoric
rheto·ric
rhe·tori·cal
rhe·tori·cal·ly
rhe·tori·cian
rheum
rheu·mat·ic
rheu·mati·cal·ly
rheu·mat·ics
rheu·ma·tism
rheu·ma·toid (*or* ·toi·dal)
rheu·ma·tolo·gist
rheu·ma·tol·ogy
rheumy
Rheydt German town
rhigo·lene anaesthetic
rhi·nal of the nose
Rhine
Rhine·land
Rhineland-Palati·nate
  German state
rhi·nen·cephal·ic
rhi·nen·cepha·lon (*plural*
  ·lons *or* ·la) anatomy term
rhine·stone
rhi·ni·tis
rhi·no (*plural* ·nos *or* ·no)
rhi·noc·er·os (*plural* ·oses *or*
  ·os)
rhi·no·cerot·ic
rhi·no·logi·cal

rhi·nolo·gist
rhi·nol·ogy branch of medicine
rhi·no·plas·tic
rhi·no·plas·ty plastic surgery of nose
rhi·no·scop·ic
rhi·nos·co·py
rhi·zo·bium (*plural* ·bia) bacterium
rhi·zo·car·pous botany term
rhi·zo·cepha·lan zoology term
rhi·zo·cepha·lous
rhi·zo·gen·ic (*or* ·zo·genet·ic, ·zog·enous)
rhi·zoid rootlike part
rhi·zoi·dal
rhi·zoma·tous
rhi·zome
rhi·zo·morph
rhi·zo·mor·phous
rhi·zo·pod protozoan
rhi·zopo·dan
rhi·zopo·dous
rhi·zo·pus fungus
rhi·zo·sphere
rhi·zoto·my (*plural* ·mies) surgery
rho Greek letter
rho·da·mine dye
Rhode Is·land
Rhodes
Rho·desia
Rho·desian
Rho·dian of Rhodes
rho·dic
rho·di·nal oil
rho·dium chemical element
rho·do·chro·site mineral
rho·do·den·dron
rhodo·lite gemstone
rhodo·nite mineral
rho·dop·sin retinal pigment
rhomb rhombus; *compare* rhumb
rhom·ben·cepha·lon anatomy term
rhom·bic (*or* ·bi·cal)
rhom·bo·he·dral
rhom·bo·he·dron (*plural* ·drons *or* ·dra)
rhom·boid
rhom·boi·dal

rhom·bus (*plural* ·buses *or* ·bi) geometric figure
rhon·chal (*or* ·chial)
rhon·chus (*plural* ·chi) breathing sound
Rhon·dda
Rhône
rho·ta·cism phonetics term
rho·ta·cist
rho·ta·cis·tic
rho·tic
rhu·barb
rhumb navigation term; *compare* rhomb; rum
rhum·ba *variant spelling of* rumba
rhum·ba·tron
rhyme identical-sounding word; verse; *compare* rime
rhyme·ster (*or* rhym·er)
rhyn·cho·cephal·ian zoology term
rhyo·lite rock
rhyo·lit·ic
rhythm
rhyth·mic (*or* ·mi·cal)
rhyth·mi·cal·ly
rhyth·mic·ity
rhyth·mics
rhy·ton (*plural* ·ta) drinking vessel
ria inlet
rial currency
Ri·al·to Venetian island
ri·al·to (*plural* ·tos) market
ria·ta (*or* rea·ta) lasso
rib (rib·bing, ribbed)
rib·ald
rib·ald·ry
rib·and (*or* rib·band) award
Rib·ble English river
rib·bon
ribbon·fish (*plural* ·fish *or* ·fishes)
ribbon·wood
Ri·bei·rão Pré·to Brazilian city
ri·bo·fla·vin (*or* ·vine) vitamin
ri·bo·nu·clease enzyme
ri·bo·nu·cleic acid
ri·bose sugar
ri·bo·so·mal
ri·bo·some part of cell
rib·wort

rice
rice·bird
ric·er *US* sieve
ri·cer·ca·re (*or* ri·cer·car; *plural* ·ca·ri *or* ·cars) musical term
rich
riches
Rich·mond
rich·ness
Richter scale
ri·cin protein
ric·ino·leic acid
rick
rick·eti·ness
rick·ets
rick·ett·sia (*plural* ·siae *or* ·sias) pathogenic microorganism
rick·ett·sial
rick·ety
rick·rack (*or* ric·rac) braid
rick·shaw (*or* ·sha)
rico·chet (·chet·ing, ·chet·ed *or* ·chet·ting, ·chet·ted)
ri·cot·ta cheese
ric·tal
ric·tus (*plural* ·tus *or* ·tuses) gape
rid (rid·ding, rid *or* rid·ded)
rid·able (*or* ride·)
rid·dance
rid·den
rid·der
rid·dle
rid·dler
ride (rid·ing, rode, rid·den)
ride·able *variant spelling of* ridable
rid·er
rid·er·less
ridge
ridge·ling (*or* ridg·ling, rid·gel) veterinary term
ridge·pole (*or* ·tree) roof timber
ridge·way
ridgy
ridi·cule
ridi·cul·er
ri·dicu·lous
ri·dicu·lous·ly
ri·dicu·lous·ness
rid·ing

ri·dot·to (*plural* ·tos)
  musical entertainment
ries·ling wine
Rif (*or* Riff; *plural* Rifs, Riffs,
  Rifis *or* Rif, Riff) Moroccan
  people
rife
rife·ness
riff jazz term
rif·fle
rif·fler
riff·raff
ri·fle
rifle·bird
rifle·man (*plural* ·men)
ri·fler
ri·fle·ry
ri·fling
rift
rig (rig·ging, rigged)
Riga Latvian port
riga·doon (*or* ri·gau·don)
  dance
ri·ga·to·ni pasta
rig·ger
rig·ging
right
right·able
right-angled
right·en
right·eous
right·eous·ly
right·eous·ness
right·er
right·ful
right·ful·ly
right·ful·ness
right-hand (*adj*)
right-handed
right-handed·ness
right-hander
right·ish
right·ism
right·ist
right·ly
right-minded
right-minded·ly
right-minded·ness
right·ness
right·ward (*adj*)
right·wards (*adv*)
right-winger
rig·id
ri·gidi·fy (·fy·ing, ·fied)
ri·gid·ity (*or* ·ness)

rig·id·ly
rig·ma·role (*or* riga·)
ri·gor medical term; *compare*
  rigour
rig·or *US spelling of* rigour
rig·or·ism
rig·or·ist
rig·or·is·tic
rig·or mor·tis
rig·or·ous
rig·or·ous·ly
rig·or·ous·ness
rig·our (*US* ·or) harshness;
  compare rigor
Rig-Veda Hindu poetry
Ri·je·ka Croatian port
Rijks·museum
rile
rill stream; channel
rill (*or* rille) moon valley
ril·let
rim (rim·ming, rimmed)
rime frost; *less common
  spelling of* rhyme
rim-fire
Ri·mi·ni
rimmed
rim·ming
ri·mose botany term
ri·mos·ity
rim·rock
rimy (rimi·er, rimi·est)
rind
rinder·pest
ring (ring·ing, rang, rung)
  produce sound
ring (ring·ing, ringed)
  circular band; to encircle
ring·bolt
ring·bone
ring·dove
ring-dyke
rin·gent botany term
ring·er
ring·git Malaysian
  currency
ring·hals (*plural* ·hals *or*
  ·halses) snake
ring·ing
ring·leader
ring·let
ring·master
ring-necked
ring·side
ring·tail animal

ring-tailed
ring·worm
rink
rins·abil·ity (*or* ·ibil·ity)
rins·able (*or* ·ible)
rinse
rins·er
Rio de Ja·nei·ro
Rio Grande
Rio Gran·de do Nor·te
  Brazilian state
Rio Gran·de do Sul
  Brazilian state
riot
ri·ot·er
ri·ot·ous
ri·ot·ous·ly
ri·ot·ous·ness
rip (rip·ping, ripped)
ri·par·ian of a river bank
rip·cord
ripe
ripe·ly
rip·en
rip·en·er
ripe·ness
ri·pieno (*plural* ·pienos)
  musical term
rip-off (*noun*)
Rip·on
ri·poste (*or* ·post)
rip·pable
ripped
rip·per
rip·ping
rip·ple
rip·pler
rip·plet
rip·pling·ly
rip·ply
rip-roaring
rip·saw
rip·snorter
rip·tide
rise (ris·ing, rose,
  ris·en)
ris·er
ris·ibil·ity (*plural* ·ities)
ris·ible laughable
ris·ibly
ris·ing
risk
risk·er
risk·ily
riski·ness

risky (riski·er, riski·est)
involving risk; *compare*
risqué
Ri·sor·gi·men·to political
movement
ri·sot·to (*plural* ·tos)
ris·qué improper; *compare*
risky
Riss glaciation
ris·sole
ri·tar·dan·do musical term
rite
ri·tenu·to musical term
ri·tor·nel·lo musical term
ritu·al
ritu·al·ism
ritu·al·ist
ritu·al·is·tic
ritu·al·is·ti·cal·ly
ritu·al·ize (*or* ·ise)
ritu·al·ly
ritzy (ritzi·er, ritzi·est)
ri·val (·val·ling, ·valled; *US*
·val·ing ·valed)
ri·val·rous
ri·val·ry (*plural* ·ries)
rive (riv·ing, rived, rived *or*
riv·en)
riv·er
river·bed
river·head
riv·er·ine
River·side *US city*
river·side
riv·et
riv·et·er
Rivi·era
ri·vi·ère necklace
rivu·let
rix-dollar
Ri·yadh Saudi Arabian
capital
ri·yal currency
roach nautical term; *Slang*
cockroach
roach (*plural* roach *or*
roaches) fish
road
road·bed
road·block
road·holding
road·house
road·roller
road·runner bird
road·stead

road·ster
road·way
road·work sports training
road·works road repairs
road·worthi·ness
road·worthy
roam
roam·er
roan
Roa·noke *US island*
roar
roar·er
roar·ing
roast
roast·er
roast·ing
rob (rob·bing, robbed)
roba·lo (*plural* ·los *or* ·lo)
fish
rob·and (*or* rob·bin)
nautical term
rob·ber
rob·bery (*plural* ·beries)
rob·bin variant of roband;
compare robin
rob·bing
robe
rob·in bird; *compare* robbin
ro·binia tree
ro·ble oak
ro·bor·ant fortifying
ro·bot
ro·bot·ics
ro·bot·ism (*or* ·bot·ry)
ro·bust
ro·bust·ness
roc legendary bird; *compare*
rock
ro·caille decorative work
roc·am·bole plant
Roch·dale Lancashire town
Roch·es·ter Kent city; *US*
city
roch·et bishop's surplice
rock hard mass; sway;
compare roc
rocka·bil·ly
rock-and-roll (*or* rock-'n'-
roll)
rock-and-roller (*or*
rock-'n'-roller)
rock-bottom (*adj*)
rock-bound
rock·er
rock·ery (*plural* ·eries)

rock·et
rock·et·eer (*or* ·er) rocket
engineer
rock·et·ry
rock·fish (*plural* ·fish *or*
·fishes)
Rock·ford *US city*
Rockies Rocky Mountains
rocki·ly
rocki·ness
rock·like
rock·ling (*plural* ·lings *or*
·ling) fish
rock·oon exploratory rocket
rock·rose
rock·shaft
rock·weed
rocky (rocki·er, rocki·est)
Rocky Moun·tains
ro·co·co
rod
rode
ro·dent
ro·denti·cide
ro·deo (*plural* ·deos)
rod·like
rodo·mon·tade boastful talk
roe fish ovary or testis; deer;
compare row
roe·buck (*plural* ·bucks *or*
·buck)
roent·gen (*or* rönt·)
radiation unit
roent·geno·gram (*or*
·graph, rönt·) *US* X-ray
photograph
roent·gen·ol·ogy (*or* rönt·)
radiology
ro·ga·tion
roga·tory
rog·er
rogue
ro·guery (*plural* ·gueries)
ro·guish
ro·guish·ly
ro·guish·ness
roil
roily (roili·er, roili·est)
cloudy
rois·ter
roist·er·er
roist·er·ous
role (*or* rôle)
role-playing
roll

roll•away mounted on
rollers
roll•bar
roll•er
rol•lick
rol•lick•ing
rol•lick•some (or •licky)
roll•ing
roll•mop
roll•neck
roll-on (noun, adj)
Rolls Royce (Trademark)
roll-top
roll•way
roly-poly (plural -polies)
Rom (plural Roma) male
gipsy
Ro•ma•gna Italian region
Ro•ma•ic language
ro•maine US cos lettuce
ro•ma•ji alphabet
Ro•man of Rome
ro•man type style
Ro•mance language
ro•mance love affair
Roma•nes Romany language
Ro•man•esque art style
Ro•ma•nia (or Ru•)
Ro•ma•nian (or Ru•)
Ro•man•ism Roman
Catholicism
Ro•man•ist
Ro•man•ize (or •ise)
Ro•ma•no cheese
Romanov Russian dynasty
Ro•mansch (or •mansh)
Swiss language
ro•man•tic
ro•man•ti•cal•ly
ro•man•ti•cism
ro•man•ti•cist
ro•man•ti•ci•za•tion (or
•sa•tion)
ro•man•ti•cize (or •cise)
Roma•ny (or Rom•ma•ny;
plural •nies)
Rome
Romeo (plural Romeos)
romp
romp•er
romp•ers baby garment
romp•ing•ly
ron•deau (plural •deaux)
poem; compare rondo
ron•del (or roun•del) poem

ron•delet poem
ron•do (plural •dos) musical
work; compare rondeau
ron•dure curvature
rone Scot drainpipe
Ro•neo (Trademark; verb
•neos, •neo•ing, •neod;
noun, plural •neos)
rong•geng Malay dance
rönt•gen variant spelling of
roentgen
roo Austral kangaroo
rood
Roo•depoort South African
city
roof (plural roofs)
roof•ing
roof•less
roof•tree
rook
rook•ery (plural •eries)
rookie Slang new recruit
room
room•er
room•ette US rail sleeper
room•ful (plural •fuls)
roomi•ly
roomi•ness
room•mate
roomy (roomi•er,
roomi•est)
roor•back US false report
roose Dialect to praise
roost
roost•er
root
root•age
root•er
rooti•ness
root•le
root•less
root•let
root•like
root•stock
rooty
rop•able (or rope•)
rope
rope•walk
ropi•ly
ropi•ness
ropy (ropi•er, ropi•est)
roque US game
Roque•fort cheese
roque•laure cloak
ro•quet croquet term

ror•qual whale
Rorschach test
rort Austral party
rorty
ros•ace rose window
ro•sa•ceous botany term
ro•sani•line (or •lin) dye
ro•sar•ian rose grower
Ro•sa•rio Argentine port
ro•sar•ium (plural •sar•iums
or •saria) rose garden
ro•sary (plural •saries)
prayer beads; compare
rosery
Ros•com•mon Irish county
rosé wine
rose
ro•seate
Ros•eau capital of Dominica
rose•bay plant
rose•bud
rose•bush
rose•fish (plural •fish or
•fishes)
rose•hip
ro•sel•la parrot
ro•sema•ling decoration
rose•mary (plural •maries)
ro•seo•la skin rash
ro•seo•lar
rose-root plant
ro•sery (plural •series) rose
garden; compare rosary
Ro•set•ta Egyptian town
ro•sette
rose•wood
Rosh Ha•sha•nah (or Rosh
Ha•sha•na) Jewish New
Year
Ro•si•cru•cian
Ro•si•cru•cian•ism
rosi•ly
ros•in type of resin
Ros•in•ante old horse
rosi•ness
rosin•weed
ros•iny
ros•tel•late (or •lar)
ros•tel•lum (plural •la)
biology term
ros•ter
Ros•tock German port
Ros•tov Russian port
ros•tral (or •trate,
•trat•ed)

ros·trum (*plural* ·trums *or* ·tra)

rosy (rosi·er, rosi·est)

rot (rot·ting, rot·ted)

rota

Ro·ta·me·ter (*Trademark*)

Ro·tar·ian

Ro·ta·ry association

ro·ta·ry (*plural* ·ries)

ro·tat·able

ro·tate

ro·ta·tion

ro·ta·tion·al

ro·ta·tive

ro·ta·tor

ro·ta·tory

rote

ro·tenone insecticide

rot·gut

Roth·er·ham Yorkshire town

Rothe·say Scottish town

roti bread

ro·ti·fer minute organism

ro·tif·er·al (*or* ·ous)

ro·tis·serie

rotl (*plural* rotls *or* ar·tal) unit of weight

ro·to·gra·vure printing process

ro·tor

Ro·to·rua New Zealand city

rot·ted

rot·ten

rot·ten·ly

rot·ten·ness

rotten·stone

rot·ter

Rot·ter·dam

rot·ting

Rott·wei·ler dog

ro·tund stout; *compare* orotund

ro·tun·da building

ro·tun·dity (*or* ·tund·ness)

Rou·baix French city

rou·ble (*or* ru·)

rouche *variant spelling of* ruche

roué

Rou·en French city

rouge

rouge et noir card game

rough

rough·age

rough-and-readi·ness

rough-and-ready

rough-and-tumble

rough·cast (cast·ing, ·cast)

rough·cast·er

rough-dry (-dries, -dry·ing, -dried)

rough·en

rough-hew (-hewing, -hewed, -hewed *or* -hewn)

rough·house

rough·ish

rough·ly

rough·neck

rough·ness

rough·rider

rough·shod

rough-spoken

rou·lade

rou·leau (*plural* ·leaux *or* ·leaus)

rou·lette

round

round·about (*noun, adj*)

round-arm cricketing term

round·ed

round·ed·ness

roun·del

roun·de·lay dance

round·er

round·ers

Round·head Parliamentarian

round·house

round·ish

round·ly

round·ness

round-shouldered

rounds·man (*plural* ·men)

round·up (*noun*)

round·worm

roup *Dialect* auction; bird disease

roupy

rouse

rous·edness

rous·er

rous·ing

rous·ing·ly

Rous·sil·lon former French province

roust

roust·about

rout defeat

route road; course

route·march

rout·er

rou·tine

rou·tine·ly

rou·tin·ism

rou·tin·ist

roux (*plural* roux) fat-and-flour paste; *compare* rue

rove

rove-over prosody term

rov·er

row line; propel boat; *compare* roe

ro·wan

row·boat

row·di·ly

row·di·ness (*or* ·dy·ism)

row·dy (·di·er, ·di·est)

row·el (·el·ling, ·elled; *US* ·el·ing, ·eled) spur wheel

row·er

row·lock

roy·al

roy·al·ism

roy·al·ist

roy·al·is·tic

roy·al·ly

roy·al·ty (*plural* ·ties)

roz·zer *Slang* policeman

rub (rub·bing, rubbed)

ru·bái·yát Persian verse form

Rub' al Kha·li Arabian desert

ru·ba·to (*plural* ·tos) musical term

rubbed

rub·ber

rub·ber·ize (*or* ·ise)

rubber·neck *Slang* inquisitive person

rubber-stamp (*verb*)

rub·bery

rub·bing

rub·bish

rub·bishy

rub·ble

rubble·work

rub·bly

rube *US* country bumpkin

ru·befa·cient

ru·befac·tion

ru·befy (·befies, ·befy·ing, ·befied) make red

ru·bel·la German measles;
  compare rubeola
ru·bel·lite gemstone
ru·beo·la measles; *compare*
  rubella
ru·beo·lar
ru·bes·cence
ru·bes·cent
ru·bia·ceous botany term
Ru·bi·con
ru·bi·cund
ru·bi·cun·dity
ru·bid·ic
ru·bid·ium radioactive
  element
ru·bigi·nous (*or* ·nose)
  rust-coloured
ru·bi·ous dark red
ru·bric
ru·bri·cal
ru·bri·cate
ru·bri·ca·tion
ru·bri·ca·tor
ru·bri·cian
ruby (*plural* rubies)
ruche (*or* rouche)
ruch·ing
ruck
ruck·sack
ruck·us (*plural* ·uses) uproar
ruc·tion
ru·da·ceous geology term
rud·beckia plant
rudd (*plural* rudd *or* rudds)
  fish
rud·der
rudder·head
rudder·less
rudder·post
rud·di·ly
rud·di·ness
rud·dle (*or* rad·, red·) red
  dye
rud·dock *Dialect* robin
rud·dy (·di·er, ·di·est)
rude
rude·ly
rude·ness (*or* ru·dery)
ru·deral botany term
Ru·des·heim·er wine
ru·di·ment
ru·di·men·ta·ril·ly (*or*
  ·men·tal·ly)
ru·di·men·ta·ry (*or*
  ·men·tal)

rud·ish
rue (ru·ing, rued) regret;
  plant; *compare* roux
rue·ful
rue·ful·ly
rue·ful·ness
ru·fes·cence
ru·fes·cent
ruff raised collar; bird; cards
  term
ruffe (*or* ruff) fish
ruf·fian
ruf·fi·an·ism
ruf·fi·an·ly
ruf·fle
ruf·fler
ruf·fly
ru·fous
rug
ruga (*plural* rugae) anatomy
  term
Rug·by Warwickshire town
rug·by football
rug·ged
rug·ged·ize (*or* ·ise) make
  durable
rug·ged·ly
rug·ged·ness
rug·ger
ru·gose (*or* ·gous, ·gate)
ru·gos·ity
Ruhr German river
ruin
ru·in·able
ru·ina·tion
ru·in·er
ru·ing
ru·in·ous
Ruis·lip
rul·able
rule
rul·er
rul·ing
rum (rum·mer, rum·mest)
  spirit; *Slang* odd; *compare*
  rhumb
Ru·ma·nia *variant spelling of*
  Romania
rum·ba (*or* rhum·)
rum·ble
rum·bler
rum·bling·ly
rum·bly
rum·bus·tious
rum·bus·tious·ly

rum·bus·tious·ness
Ru·melia part of Ottoman
  empire
ru·men (*plural* ·mens *or*
  ·mi·na) cow's stomach
ru·mi·nant
ru·mi·nate
ru·mi·nat·ing·ly
ru·mi·na·tion
ru·mi·na·tive
ru·mi·na·tor
rum·mage
rum·mag·er
rum·mer drinking glass
rum·my
ru·mour (*US* ·mor)
rump
rum·ple
rum·ply
rum·pus (*plural* ·puses)
run (run·ning, ran, run)
run·about (*noun*)
run·away (*noun, adj*)
runch plant
run·ci·nate botany term
Run·corn Cheshire town
run·dle ladder rung
run·down (*noun*)
run-down (*adj*)
rune
rung
ru·nic
run·nel (*or* ·let)
run·ner
runner-up (*plural*
  runners-up)
run·ning
run·ny (·ni·er, ·ni·est)
Run·ny·mede
run·off (*noun*)
run-of-the-mill
run-on (*noun*)
runt
runti·ness
runt·ish
runt·ish·ness
runty
run-up (*noun*)
run·way
ru·pee
ru·pi·ah (*plural* ·ah *or* ·ahs)
  Indonesian currency
rup·tur·able
rup·ture
ru·ral

ru·ral·ism
ru·ral·ist (or ·ite)
ru·ral·ity
ru·rali·za·tion (or ·sa·tion)
ru·ral·ize (or ·ise)
ru·ral·ly
Ru·ri·ta·nia fictional
    kingdom
Ru·ri·ta·nian
Ruse Bulgarian city
ruse
rush
rush·er
rushi·ness
rushy (rushi·er, rushi·est)
rusk
rus·set
rus·set·ish (or ·sety)
Rus·sia
Rus·sian
Rus·sian·ize (or ·ise)
Russ·ky (or ·ki; plural ·kies
    or ·kis) Slang a Russian
Rus·so·phile (or ·phil)
Rus·so·phobe
Rus·so·pho·bia

Rus·so·pho·bic
rust
rus·tic
rus·ti·cal·ly
rus·ti·cate
rus·ti·ca·tion
rus·ti·ca·tor
rus·tic·ity
rusti·ly
rusti·ness
rus·tle
rus·tler
rus·tling·ly
rust·proof
rusty (rusti·er, rusti·est)
rut (rut·ting, rut·ted)
ru·ta·ba·ga US swede
ru·ta·ceous botany term
Ru·the·nia Ukrainian
    region
Ru·the·nian
ru·then·ic
ru·the·nious
ru·the·nium chemical
    element
ruth·er·ford unit

ruth·ful
ruth·less
ruth·less·ly
ruth·less·ness
ru·ti·lat·ed mineralogy term
ru·tile mineral
Rut·land English county
rut·ted
rut·ti·ly
rut·ti·ness
rut·ting
rut·tish of an animal in rut
rut·tish·ness
rut·ty (·ti·er, ·ti·est) full of
    ruts
Ru·wen·zo·ri African
    mountains
Rwan·da African republic
Rya·zan Russian city
Ry·binsk Russian city
Ry·dal Cumbrian village
rye
rye-brome plant
rye-grass
ryo·kan Japanese inn
ryot Indian peasant

S

Saab (Trademark)
Saar European river
Saar·brück·en German city
Saar·land German state
Saba West Indian island
Sa·ba·dell Spanish town
saba·dil·la plant
Sa·bah Malaysian state
sa·ba·yon dessert
Sab·ba·tar·ian observer of
    Sabbath
Sab·bath seventh day
sab·bath (or ·bat) rest
    period
Sab·bati·cal (or ·bat·ic) of
    the Sabbath
sab·bati·cal (noun)
    academic leave
Sa·bel·lian language
sa·ber US spelling of sabre
sa·bin unit
Sab·ine
sa·ble (plural ·bles or ·ble)
sab·ot

sabo·tage
sabo·teur
sa·bra Israeli-born Jew
sa·bre (US ·ber)
sa·bre·tache (US ·ber·)
    leather case
sabu·los·ity
sabu·lous (or ·lose)
    gritty
sac biological pouch;
    compare sack
saca·ton grass
sac·cate
sac·cha·rase enzyme
sac·cha·rate chemical
    compound
sac·cha·ride sugar
sac·chari·fi·ca·tion
sac·chari·fy (·fies, ·fy·ing,
    ·fied)
sac·cha·rim·eter
sac·cha·rin sugar
sac·cha·rine sugary
sac·cha·rin·ity

sac·cha·ri·za·tion (or
    ·sa·tion)
sac·cha·rize (or ·rise)
sac·cha·roid (or ·roi·dal)
    geology term
sac·cha·rom·eter
sac·cha·rose
sac·cu·late (or ·lat·ed, ·lar)
sac·cu·la·tion
sac·cule (or ·cu·lus)
sac·er·do·tal
sac·er·do·tal·ism
sa·chet
sack bag; to plunder, etc.;
    compare sac
sack·but
sack·cloth
sack·er
sack·ful (plural ·fuls)
sack·ing
sack·like
sa·cral of sacred rites or the
    sacrum
sac·ra·ment

sac·ra·men·tal
sac·ra·men·tal·ism
sac·ra·men·tal·ist
sac·ra·men·tal·ity (or ·ness)
sac·ra·men·tal·ly
Sac·ra·men·tar·ian
   theology term
Sac·ra·men·to US port
sa·crar·ium (plural ·craria)
   church sanctuary
sa·cred
sa·cred·ness
sac·ri·fice
sac·ri·fice·able
sac·ri·fic·er
sac·ri·fi·cial
sac·ri·fi·cial·ly
sac·ri·fic·ing
sac·ri·lege
sac·ri·legious
sac·ri·legious·ness
sac·ri·legist
sac·ris·tan (or sac·rist)
sac·ris·ty (plural ·ties)
sa·cro·ili·ac anatomy term
sac·ro·sanct
sac·ro·sanc·tity (or
   ·sanct·ness)
sa·crum (plural ·cra) bone
sad (sad·der, sad·dest)
sad·den
sad·den·ing
sad·der
sad·dest
sad·dle
saddle·back
saddle·bag
saddle·bill
saddle·bow
saddle·cloth
sad·dler
sad·dlery (plural ·dleries)
saddle·tree saddle frame
Sad·du·cean
Sad·du·cees
sad·iron heavy iron
sad·ism
sad·ist
sa·dis·tic
sa·dis·ti·cal·ly
sad·ly
sad·ness
sado·maso·chism
sado·maso·chist
sado·maso·chis·tic

Sa·do·wa battle site
sa·fa·ri (plural ·ris)
safe
safe-conduct
safe-deposit (or safety-)
safe·guard
safe·keeping
safe·light photography term
safe·ness
safe·ty (plural ·ties)
saf·fian tanned leather
saf·flow·er
saf·fron
Sa·fid Rud Iranian river
saf·ra·nine (or ·nin) dye
saf·role plant oil
sag (sag·ging, sagged)
saga
sa·ga·cious
sa·ga·cious·ness
sa·gac·ity
saga·more American Indian
   chief
sage
sage·brush shrub
sag·gar (or ·ger)
   pottery-firing box
sagged
sag·ging
Sa·git·ta constellation
sag·it·tal
Sag·it·ta·rian
Sag·it·ta·rius
sag·it·tate (or
   sa·git·ti·form)
sago (plural sagos)
Sa·guache US mountain
   range
sa·gua·ro (or ·hua·; plural
   ·ros) cactus
Sa·hap·tin (or ·tan; plural
   ·tins, ·tin or ·tans, ·tan)
   American Indian
Sa·ha·ra
Sa·har·an
Sa·ha·ran·pur Indian town
Sa·hel African region
sa·hib (or ·heb)
said
Sai·da Lebanese port
sai·ga antelope
Sai·gon
sail
sail·able
sail·cloth

sail·er sailing vessel; compare
   sailor
sail·fish (plural ·fish or
   ·fishes)
sail·ing
sail·or seaman; compare
   sailer
sail·or·ly
sail·plane
sain·foin plant
saint
St Al·bans
St An·drews
St Aus·tell Cornish town
St Ber·nard dog
saint·ed
Sainte Foy suburb of
   Quebec
Saint-Émilion wine
St-Étienne French town
St Gall Swiss town
St George's capital of
   Grenada
St He·le·na Atlantic island
St Hel·ens Merseyside town
St Hel·ier Jersey town
saint·hood
St Ives
St John Canadian city
St John's Canadian city;
   Antiguan port
St Kil·da Hebridean island
St Kitts West Indian country
St Law·rence North
   American river
St Leg·er horse race
saint·li·ly
saint·li·ness
St Lou·is US city
St Lu·cia West Indian
   country
saint·ly
St Mo·ritz Swiss resort
St Paul US city
saint·pau·lia plant
St Pe·ters·burg Russian city
St Vitus's dance
Sai·pan Pacific island
Saïs Egyptian city
saithe fish
Sai·va Hindu
Sa·kai Japanese port
sake benefit
sake (or saké, saki) Japanese
   liquor; compare saki

sa·ker falcon

Sa·kha·lin (or ·ghal·ien) Russian island

saki monkey; compare sake

Sak·tas Hindu sect

Sa·kya·mu·ni title of Buddha

sal salt

sa·laam Muslim greeting

sal·able variant spelling (esp. US) of saleable

sa·la·cious

sa·la·cious·ness (or ·lac·ity)

sal·ad

Sala·man·ca Spanish city

sala·man·der amphibian

sala·man·drine

Sa·lam·bria Greek river

sa·la·mi sausage; compare salmi

Sala·mis Greek island

sala·ried

sala·ry (noun, plural ·ries; verb ·ries, ·ry·ing, ·ried)

sal·chow ice-skating jump

sale

sale·abil·ity (or ·able·ness)

sale·able (or esp. US sal·able)

sale·ably

Sa·lem Indian city; US city

sal·ep dried orchid tuber

sal·era·tus sodium bicarbonate

Sa·ler·no Italian port

sale·room

sales·clerk

sales·man (plural ·men)

sales·man·ship

sales·room

sales·woman (plural ·women)

Sal·ford

Sa·lian Frankish

Sal·ic of Frankish law

sal·ic geology term

sali·ca·ceous botany term

sa·li·cin (or ·cine) drug

sa·li·cion·al (or sa·li·cet) organ stop

sali·cor·nia plant

sa·licy·late

sali·cyl·ic acid

sa·li·ence (or ·en·cy)

sa·li·ent

sa·li·en·tian amphibian

sa·li·ent·ness

sa·lif·er·ous containing salt

sali·fi·able

sali·fi·ca·tion

sali·fy (·fies, ·fy·ing, ·fied) mix with salt

sal·im·eter

sali·met·ric

sal·im·etry

sa·lina salt lake

sa·line containing salt

sa·lin·ity

sali·nom·eter

sali·no·met·ric

sali·nom·etry

Salis·bury

Sa·lish (or ·lish·an) language

sa·li·va

sali·vary

sali·vate

sali·va·tion

sal·lee tree

sal·let (or sal·et, sa·lade) helmet

sal·li·er

sal·low

sal·low·ness

sal·ly (noun, plural ·lies; verb ·lies, ·ly·ing, ·lied)

Sal·ly Lunn cake

sal·ma·gun·di salad

sal·ma·naz·ar wine bottle

sal·mi (or ·mis; plural ·mis) French stew; compare salami

salm·on (plural ·ons or ·on)

salmon·berry (plural ·berries)

sal·mo·nel·la (plural ·lae) bacterium

sal·mo·nel·lo·sis

sal·mo·noid

sal·ol chemical compound

sa·lon reception room; beauty establishment, etc.; compare saloon

Sa·lo·ni·ka Greek port

sa·loon large room; pub bar; compare salon

sa·loop aromatic infusion

salo·pette skiing garment

sal·pa (plural ·pas or ·pae) marine organism

sal·pi·con chopped food

sal·pi·form

sal·pi·glos·sis plant

sal·pin·gec·to·my (plural ·mies)

sal·pin·gian

sal·pin·gi·tic

sal·pin·git·is

sal·pinx (plural ·pin·ges) Fallopian tube

sal·si·fy (plural ·fies) vegetable

salt

Sal·ta Argentine city

sal·tant biology term

sal·ta·rel·lo (plural ·li or ·los) dance

sal·ta·tion biology term

sal·ta·to·rial (or sal·ta·tory) adapted for jumping

salt·box

salt·bush

salt·cellar

salt·ed

salt·er

salt·ern saltworks

salt·fish

sal·ti·grade moving by jumps

Sal·til·lo Mexican state

salti·ly

salti·ness

sal·tire (or ·tier) heraldic term

salt·ness

salt·pan

salt·pe·tre (US ·ter)

salt·pot

sal·tus (plural ·tuses) break in sequence

salt·water

salt·works

salt·wort

salty (salti·er, salti·est)

sa·lu·bri·ous

sa·lu·bri·ous·ness (or ·bri·ty)

Sa·lu·ki dog

salu·tari·ly

salu·tari·ness

salu·tary beneficial; compare salutatory

salu·ta·tion

sa·lu·ta·to·ri·ly

sa·lu·ta·tory welcoming; *compare* salutary
sa·lute
sa·lut·er
sal·vabil·ity (*or* ·vable·ness)
salv·able
sal·vably
Sal·va·dor Brazilian port
Sal·va·do·rian
sal·vage rescue; *compare* selvage
sal·vage·able
sal·vag·er
sal·va·tion
sal·va·tion·al
sal·va·tion·ism
sal·va·tion·ist member of evangelical sect
salve
sal·ver tray; *compare* salvor
sal·ver·form botany term
sal·via plant
sal·vo (*plural* ·vos *or* ·voes) gun fire
sal·vo (*plural* ·vos) provisos
sal vola·ti·le
sal·vor one who salvages; *compare* salver
Sal·ween Asian river
Sal·yut Soviet space station
Salz·burg
Salz·git·ter German city
Sa·ma·ra Russian city
sa·ma·ra botany term
Sa·maria Palestinian region
Sa·mari·tan
Sa·mari·tan·ism
sa·mar·ium chemical element
Sa·mar·kand
sa·mar·skite mineral
sam·ba (*plural* ·bas) dance
sam·bar (*or* ·bur; *plural* ·bars, ·bar *or* ·burs, ·bur) deer
same
same·ness
Sa·mian of Samos
sami·sen musical instrument
sam·ite fabric
sa·mi·ti (*or* ·thi) Indian political association
Sam·nite

Sam·ni·um ancient Italian city
Sa·moa Pacific island country
Sa·mo·an
Sa·mos Greek island
Samo·thrace Greek island
samo·var
Samo·yed (*plural* ·yed *or* ·yeds) Siberian people; dog
sam·pan boat
sam·phire plant
sam·ple
sam·pler
sam·pling
Sam·sun Turkish port
samu·rai (*plural* ·rai)
San language group
San'a (*or* Sa·naa) capital of Yemen
San An·to·nian
San An·to·nio US city
sana·to·rium (*US* sani·ta·; *plural* ·riums *or* ·ria)
san·be·ni·to (*plural* ·tos) garment
San Ber·nar·di·no US city
sanc·ti·fi·able
sanc·ti·fi·ca·tion
sanc·ti·fi·er
sanc·ti·fy (·fies, ·fy·ing, ·fied)
sanc·ti·mo·ni·ous
sanc·ti·mo·ni·ous·ness
sanc·ti·mo·ny
sanc·tion
sanc·tion·able
sanc·tion·er
sanc·ti·tude
sanc·tity (*plural* ·tities)
sanc·tu·ary (*plural* ·aries)
sanc·tum (*plural* ·tums *or* ·ta)
Sanc·tus hymn
sand
san·dal
san·dalled (*US* ·daled)
sandal·wood
san·da·rac (*or* ·rach) tree
sand·bag (*verb* ·bag·ging, ·bagged)
sand·bag·ger
sand·bank
sand·blast

sand·blast·er
sand·blind
sand·blindness
sand·box
sand·cast (-casting, -cast)
sand·er
sand·er·ling bird
sand·fly (*plural* ·flies)
sand·grouse
san·dhi (*plural* ·dhis) linguistics term
sand·hog *US* underground worker
Sand·hurst
San Di·ego US port
sandi·ness
sand·man (*plural* ·men)
sand·paper
sand·piper
sand·pit
San·dring·ham
sand·soap
sand·stone
sand·storm
sand·wich
sand·worm
sand·wort
sandy (sandi·er, sandi·est)
sane
sane·ness
San Fernando Trinidadian port
San·for·ize (*or* ·ise; *Trademark*)
San Fran·cis·can
San Fran·cis·co
sang
san·ga·ree spiced drink
sang-froid
San·graal (*or* ·greal) Holy Grail
san·gria drink
san·gui·naria drug; plant
san·gui·nari·ly
san·gui·nari·ness
san·gui·nary
san·guine
san·guine·ness (*or* ·guin·ity)
san·guin·eous
san·guino·len·cy
san·guino·lent containing blood
San·hed·rin Jewish tribunal
sani·cle plant

sa·ni·es discharge from wound

sani·tar·ian of sanitation

san·itari·ly

sani·tari·ness

sani·ta·rium *US spelling of* sanatorium

sani·tary

sani·ta·tion

sani·tize (*or* ·tise)

san·ity

San Jose Californian city

San José Costa Rican capital

San Juan Puerto Rican capital

sank

San Luis Po·to·sí Mexican state

San Mari·nese (*or* Sam·mari·nese)

San Ma·ri·no European republic

sann·ya·si Brahman mendicant

San Sal·va·dor capital of El Salvador

sans-culotte

San Se·bas·tián Spanish port

san·ser·if (*or* sans serif)

san·se·vieria plant

San·skrit

San·skrit·ic

San·skrit·ist

sans serif *variant spelling of* san·ser·if

San Ste·fa·no Turkish village

San·ta Ana El Salvador city; Californian city

San·ta Ca·ta·ri·na Brazilian state

San·ta Cla·ra Cuban city

Santa Claus

San·ta Cruz Argentine province; Bolivian city

San·ta Cruz de Te·ne·rife Tenerife port

San·ta Fe Mexican city; Argentine port

san·ta·la·ceous botany term

San·ta Maria Brazilian city

San·ta Mar·ta Colombian port

San·tan·der Spanish port

San·ta·rém Brazilian port

San·tee US river

San·tia·go Chilean capital

San·tia·go de Cuba Cuban port

San·tia·go del Es·te·ro Argentine city

San·to Do·min·go capital of Dominican Republic

san·toni·ca plant

san·to·nin

San·tos Brazilian port

São Luís (*or* São Luíz) Brazilian port

Saône-et-Loire French department

São Pau·lo Brazilian port

São Tomé e Prín·ci·pe island republic

sap (sap·ping, sapped)

sapa·jou monkey

sa·pele tree

sa·phe·na (*plural* ·nae) vein

sa·phe·nous

(saphire) *incorrect spelling of* sapphire

sap·id palatable

sa·pid·ity (*or* ·ness)

sa·pi·ence (*or* ·en·cy) wisdom

sa·pi·ent

sa·pi·en·tial

sap·in·da·ceous botany term

sap·less

sap·ling

sapo·dil·la fruit

sapo·na·ceous soapy

sa·poni·fi·able

sa·poni·fi·ca·tion

sa·poni·fi·er

sa·poni·fy (·fies, ·fy·ing, ·fied)

sapo·nin plant compound

sapo·nite mineral

sa·po·ta fruit

sapo·ta·ceous

sap·pan·wood (*or* sap·an·)

sapped

sap·per

Sap·phic verse form; of Sappho

sap·phire

sap·phir·ine mineral

sap·pi·ly

sap·pi·ness

sap·ping

Sap·po·ro Japanese city

sap·py (·pi·er, ·pi·est)

sa·prae·mia (*US* ·pre·) blood poisoning

sa·prae·mic (*US* ·pre·)

sap·robe organism inhabiting foul water

sap·ro·bic

sap·ro·gen·ic (*or* ·ous)

sap·ro·genic·ity

sap·ro·lite geological deposit

sap·ro·lit·ic

sap·ro·pel sludge

sap·ro·pel·ic

sa·propha·gous feeding on decaying matter

sap·ro·phyte

sap·ro·phyt·ic

sap·ro·phyti·cal·ly

sap·ro·zo·ic

sap·sa·go cheese

sap·sucker bird

sap·wood

sara·band (*or* ·bande)

Sara·cen

Sara·cen·ic (*or* ·ceni·cal)

Sara·gos·sa Spanish city

Sa·ra·jevo (*or* Se·) Bosnia-Hercegovinan capital

sa·ran resin

Sa·ransk Russian city

Sa·ra·tov Russian city

Sa·ra·wak Malaysian state

sar·casm

sar·cas·tic

sar·cas·ti·cal·ly

sar·co·carp botany term

sar·coid

sar·co·ma (*plural* ·mas *or* ·ma·ta)

sar·co·ma·toid (*or* ·tous)

sar·co·ma·to·sis

sar·copha·gus (*plural* ·gi *or* ·guses)

sar·cous muscular or fleshy

sard gemstone

sar·dine (*plural* ·dine *or* ·dines)

Sar·dinia

Sar·din·ian

Sar·dis (*or* ·**des**) ancient Asian city
sar·di·us biblical gemstone
sar·don·ic
sar·doni·cal·ly
sar·doni·cism
sar·don·yx gemstone
Sar·gas·so sea
sar·gas·so (*plural* ·**sos**) seaweed
sar·gas·sum seaweed
sarge *Slang* sergeant
Sar·go·dha Pakistani city
sari (*plural* ·**ris**)
Sark Channel island
sar·men·tose (*or* ·**tous**, ·**ta·ceous**) botany term
Sar·nia Canadian port
sa·rong
sa·ron·ic
sa·ros cycle of eclipses
sar·panch Indian leader
sar·ra·cenia plant
sar·ra·cenia·ceous
sar·sa·pa·ril·la
sar·sen boulder
Sarthe French department
sar·tor tailor
sar·to·rial
sar·to·rius (*plural* ·**to·rii**) muscle
Sar·um Salisbury
Sa·sebo Japanese port
sash
Sas·katch·ewan
Sas·ka·toon Canadian city
sas·ka·toon fruit
(sarsparilla) *incorrect spelling of* sarsaparilla
sass *US* insolent
sas·sa·by (*plural* ·**bies**) antelope
sas·sa·fras tree; oil
Sas·sa·nid (*plural* ·**sa·nids** *or* ·**sani·dae**) member of Persian dynasty
Sas·sa·ri Sardinian city
Sas·se·nach
sas·si·ly
sas·si·ness
sas·sy (·**si·er**, ·**si·est**) saucy
sas·sy (*or* **sass·wood**, **sas·sy wood**) tree
sa·stru·ga (*or* **zas·tru·**) ridge on snowfield

sat
sa·tai (*or* ·**tay**) Indonesian food
Satan
sa·tang (*plural* ·**tang**) Thai coin
sa·tan·ic (*or* ·**tani·cal**)
sa·tani·cal·ly
sa·tani·cal·ness
Sa·tan·ism
Sa·tan·ist
satch·el
sate
sa·teen imitation satin
sat·el·lite
sat·el·lit·ium astrology term
sa·tem linguistics term
sa·ti·abil·ity (*or* ·**able·ness**)
sa·ti·able
sa·ti·ably
sa·ti·ate
sa·tia·tion
sa·ti·ety
sat·in
sati·net (*or* ·**nette**) imitation satin
satin·wood
sat·iny
sat·ire parody; *compare* satyr
sa·tir·ic
sa·tiri·cal (*or* ·**tir·ic**)
sa·tiri·cal·ly
sa·tiri·cal·ness
sati·rist
sati·ri·za·tion (*or* ·**sa·tion**)
sati·rize (*or* ·**rise**)
sati·riz·er (*or* ·**ris·er**)
sat·is·fac·tion
sat·is·fac·tion·al
sat·is·fac·to·ri·ly
sat·is·fac·to·ri·ness
sat·is·fac·tory
sat·is·fi·able
sat·is·fi·er
sat·is·fy (·**fies**, ·**fy·ing**, ·**fied**)
sat·is·fy·ing·ly
sa·trap Persian governor
sa·trapy (*plural* ·**trapies**)
Sa·tsu·ma Japanese province; porcelain
sat·su·ma fruit
satu·rabil·ity
satu·rable
satu·rant

satu·rate
satu·rat·ed
satu·rat·er (*or* ·**ra·tor**)
satu·ra·tion
Sat·ur·day
Sat·urn planet
Saturn Roman god
Sat·ur·na·lia (*plural* ·**lia** *or* ·**lias**) ancient festival
Sa·tur·nian
sa·tur·ni·id moth
sat·ur·nine
sat·ur·nine·ness (*or* ·**nin·ity**)
sat·ur·nism lead poisoning
sat·ya·gra·hi nonviolent protester
sa·tyr goatlike deity; lustful man; *compare* satire
saty·ria·sis (*or* **sa·tyro·ma·nia**)
sa·tyr·ic (*or* ·**tyri·cal**)
sa·ty·rid butterfly
sauce
sauce·pan
sau·cer
sau·cer·ful (*plural* ·**fuls**)
sau·ci·ly
sau·ci·ness
saucy (·**ci·er**, ·**ci·est**)
Sau·di (*or* **Sau·di Ara·bian**)
Sau·di Ara·bia
sau·er·bra·ten beef dish
sau·er·kraut
sau·ger fish
Sault Ste Ma·rie Canadian city; US city
sau·na
saun·ter
saun·ter·er
sau·rian lizard-like
saur·is·chian dinosaur
sau·ro·pod dinosaur
sau·ro·po·dous
sau·ry (*plural* ·**ries**) fish
sau·sage
sau·té (·**té·ing** *or* ·**tée·ing**, ·**téed**)
Sau·ternes wine
Sava (*or* **Save**) Yugoslav river
sav·able (*or* **save·able**)
sav·able·ness (*or* **save·**)
sav·age
sav·age·ness

sav·age·ry (*plural* ·ries)
Sa·vaii Samoan island
sa·van·na (*or* ·nah)
Sa·van·nah US port
sa·vant (*fem* ·vante) learned person
sa·vate form of boxing
save
save·able *variant spelling of* savable
save-all
sav·eloy
sav·er
sav·in (*or* ·ine) shrub
sav·ing
sav·ings
Sav·iour (*US* ·ior) Christ
sav·iour (*US* ·ior) rescuer
Sa·voie French department
savoir-faire
sa·vor·ous
sa·vory (*plural* ·vories) plant; *US spelling of* savoury
sa·vour (*US* ·vor)
sa·vouri·ness (*US* ·vori·)
sa·vour·ing·ly (*US* ·vor·)
sa·voury (*US* ·vory; *plural* ·vouries)
Sa·voy French region
sa·voy cabbage
Sa·voy·ard of Savoy
sav·vy (·vies, ·vy·ing, ·vied)
saw (saw·ing, sawed, sawed *or* sawn)
saw·bill
saw·bones
saw·der flatter
saw·dust
sawed
saw·er one that saws; *compare* sawyer
saw·fish (*plural* ·fish *or* ·fishes)
saw·fly (*plural* ·flies)
saw·horse
saw·ing
saw·mill
sawn
sawn-off
saw·tooth
saw·yer professional timber sawer; *compare* sawer
sax axe
saxe blue

sax·horn
sax·ico·lous (*or* saxa·tile) biology term
saxi·fra·ga·ceous
saxi·frage
Sax·on
Saxo·ny German state
saxo·ny yarn
Saxo·ny-An·halt German state
saxo·phone
saxo·phon·ic
sax·opho·nist
sax·tuba
say (say·ing, said)
say·er
say-so
say·yid (*or* say·id, said) Muslim title
saz·erac cocktail
scab (scab·bing, scabbed)
scab·bard
scab·bi·ly
scab·bi·ness
scab·ble shape roughly
scab·by (·bi·er, ·bi·est)
sca·bies
sca·bi·et·ic
sca·bi·ous scabby; plant
sca·brous scaly; salacious
scad fish
scads *US* many
Sca·fell Pike Cumbrian mountain
scaf·fold
scaf·fold·er
scaf·fold·ing
scag (scag·ging, scagged) *Dialect* to tear
scaglio·la imitation marble
scal·able
scal·able·ness
scal·ably
scal·age *US* price reduction
sca·lar maths term; *compare* scaler
sca·lare fish
sca·lari·form
scala·wag *variant spelling of* scallywag
scald
scald·fish (*plural* ·fish *or* ·fishes)
scale
scale·board veneer

sca·lene maths term
sca·lenus (*plural* ·leni) muscle
scal·er one that scales; *compare* scalar
scales
scali·ness
scall scalp disease
scal·lion small onion
scal·lop
scal·lop·er
scal·ly·wag (*or* scala·wag)
sca·lop·pi·ne (*or* ·ni) Italian dish
scalp
scal·pel
scal·pel·lic
scalp·er
scalp·ing
scaly (scali·er, scali·est)
scam·mo·ni·ate
scam·mo·ny (*plural* ·nies) plant; medicinal resin
scamp
scamp·er
scam·per·er
scam·pi
scamp·ish
scan (scan·ning, scanned)
scan·dal
scan·dali·za·tion (*or* ·sa·tion)
scan·dal·ize (*or* ·ise)
scan·dal·iz·er (*or* ·is·er)
scandal-monger
scan·dal·ous
scan·dal·ous·ness
Scan·da·roon pigeon
scan·dent climbing
Scan·dian Scandinavian
scan·dic of scandium
Scan·di·na·via
Scan·di·na·vian
scan·dium chemical element
scan·ner
scan·sion
scan·so·rial adapted for climbing
scant
scanti·ly
scanti·ness
scant·ling rafter
scant·ness

scanty (scanti•er, scanti•est)
Scapa Flow naval base
scape biology term
scape•goat
scape•grace
scapho•pod mollusc
scapo•lite mineral
scap•ose botany term
scapu•la (plural •lae or •las) shoulder bone
scapu•lar of scapula; part of monk's habit
scar (scar•ring, scarred)
scar•ab beetle
scara•bae•id (or •baean)
scara•bae•oid (or scara•boid)
scara•bae•us (plural •bae•uses or •baei) scarab
Scar•borough
scarce
scarce•ly
scarce•ment wall ledge
scarce•ness
scar•city (plural •cities)
scare
scare•crow
scare•monger
scar•er
scarf (plural scarfs or scarves)
scarf•skin outer skin layer
scari•fi•ca•tion
scari•fi•ca•tor surgical instrument
scari•fi•er
scari•fy (•fies, •fy•ing, •fied)
scar•ing•ly
scari•ous (or •ose) botany term
scar•la•ti•na scarlet fever
scar•la•ti•nal (or •nous)
scar•let
scarp
scarp•er
scary (scari•er, scari•est)
scat (scat•ting, scat•ted)
scathe
scath•ing
scato•logi•cal (or •log•ic)
sca•tolo•gist
sca•tol•ogy study of excrement
scat•ter

scat•ter•able
scatter•brain
scatter•brained
scat•ter•er
scatter-gun
scat•ter•ing
scat•ti•ly
scat•ti•ness
scat•ty (•ti•er, •ti•est)
scaup duck
scav•enge
scav•en•ger
sce•nario (plural •narios)
sce•nar•ist
scend (or send; scend•ing, scend•ed or send•ing, sent) nautical term
scene
scen•ery (plural •eries)
sce•nic
sce•ni•cal•ly
sce•nog•raph•er
sce•no•graph•ic (or •graphi•cal)
sce•no•graphi•cal•ly
sce•nog•ra•phy depicting in perspective
scent
scented
scent•less
scep•tic (US skep•) doubter; compare septic
scep•ti•cal (US skep•)
scep•ti•cal•ly (US skep•)
scep•ti•cal•ness (US skep•)
scep•ti•cism (US skep•)
scep•tre (US •ter)
scep•tred (US •tered)
Schaer•beek Belgian city
Schaff•hau•sen Swiss town
schap•pe yarn or fabric
schedu•lar
sched•ule
scheel•ite mineral
Scheldt European river
sche•ma (plural •ma•ta)
sche•mat•ic
sche•mati•cal•ly
sche•ma•tism
sche•ma•ti•za•tion (or •sa•tion)
sche•ma•tize (or •tise)
scheme
schem•er
schem•ing

schem•ing•ly
scher•zan•do (plural •di or •dos) musical term
scher•zo (plural •zos or •zi)
schil•ler metallic lustre
schil•ling Austrian currency
schip•per•ke dog
schism
schis•mat•ic (or •mati•cal)
schis•mati•cal•ly
schis•mati•cal•ness
schist rock
schis•tose
schis•tos•ity
schis•to•some blood parasite
schis•to•so•mia•sis
schizo (plural schizos)
schizo•carp botany term
schizo•car•pous (or •pic)
schizo•gen•esis biology term
schizo•genet•ic
schi•zogo•ny zoology term
schiz•oid
schizo•my•cete biology term
schizo•my•cet•ic
schizo•my•cetous
schi•zont zoology term
schizo•phre•nia
schizo•phren•ic
schizo•phy•ceous
schizo•phyte
schizo•phyt•ic
schizo•pod crustacean
schizo•thy•mia psychology term
schizo•thy•mic
schle•miel US clumsy
schlep (schlep•ping, schlepped) US drag
Schleswig-Holstein German state
schlie•ren physics term
schlie•ric
schlock US inferior goods
schmaltz (òr schmalz) sentimentality
schmaltzy
schmooze US chat
schnapps (or schnaps)
schnau•zer dog
schnecke (plural schneck•en) US bread roll

schnit·zel

schnook *US* stupid person

schnor·rer *US* professional
beggar

schnoz·zle *Slang* nose

scho·la can·to·rum (*plural*
schol·ae can·to·rum)
choir

schol·ar

schol·ar·li·ness

schol·ar·ly

schol·ar·ship

scho·las·tic

scho·las·ti·cal

scho·las·ti·cal·ly

scho·las·ti·cate Jesuit's
probation period

scho·las·ti·cism

scho·li·ast

scho·li·as·tic

scho·lium (*plural* ·lia)
marginal note

school

school·boy

school·child (*plural*
·children)

school·girl

school·fellow

school·house

schoolie *Austral*
schoolteacher

school·ing

school·marm

school·marm·ish

school·master

school·master·ship

school·mate

school·mistress

school·mistressy

school·teacher

schoon·er

schorl mineral

schor·la·ceous

schot·tische dance

schuss ski run

schwa (*or* shwa) unstressed
vowel sound

Schwa·ben German region

Schwe·rin German city

Schwyz Swiss town

sci·aenid (*or* ·aenoid) fish

sci·ama·chy (*or* ·oma·, ski·)
fight with imaginary
enemy

sci·at·ic

sci·ati·ca

sci·ence

sci·en·ter legal term

sci·en·tial knowledgeable

sci·en·tif·ic

sci·en·tifi·cal·ly

sci·en·tism

sci·en·tist

sci·en·tis·tic

Sci·en·tolo·gist

Sci·en·tol·ogy religious cult

sci-fi

scili·cet that is

scil·la plant

Scil·lo·nian

Scil·ly Isles (*or* Scil·lies)

scimi·tar (*or* simi·)

scin·coid (*or* ·coid·ian)
skinklike

scin·tig·ra·phy medical
technique

scin·til·la minute amount

scin·til·late

scin·til·lat·ing·ly

scin·til·la·tion

scin·til·la·tor physics term

scin·til·lom·eter

scio·man·cer

scio·man·cy divination
through ghosts

scio·man·tic

sci·on descendant; plant
graft

scir·rhoid

scir·rhos·ity

scir·rhous (*adj*)

scir·rhus (*plural* ·rhi *or*
·rhuses) cancerous growth;
compare cirrus

scis·sel waste metal

scis·sile divisible

scis·sion

scis·sor

scis·sors

sciu·rine of squirrels

sciu·roid

sclaff golf stroke

sclaff·er

scle·ra eyeball covering

scle·ren·chy·ma plant tissue

scle·ren·chyma·tous

scle·rite zoology term

scle·rit·ic

scle·ri·tis (*or* ·ro·ti·tis) eye
inflammation

scle·ro·der·ma skin disease

scle·ro·der·ma·tous

scle·roid

scle·ro·ma (*plural* ·ma·ta)
hard tissue

scle·rom·eter geology
apparatus

sclero·met·ric

scle·ro·phyll botany term

scle·ro·pro·tein

scle·ro·sal

scle·rosed

scle·ro·sis (*plural* ·ses)

scle·rot·ic

scle·ro·ti·oid (*or* ·ro·tial)

scle·ro·tium (*plural* ·tia)
fungal tissue

scle·roto·my (*plural* ·mies)
eye surgery

scle·rous

scoff

scoff·er

scoff·ing·ly

scoff·law *US* habitual
lawbreaker

scold

scold·able

scold·er

scold·ing

scold·ing·ly

scol·ecite mineral

sco·lex (*plural* sco·leces *or*
scoli·ces) tapeworm head

sco·lio·sis (*or* ·lio·ma)
spinal curvature

sco·li·ot·ic

(scollop) *incorrect spelling of*
scallop

scolo·pen·drid centipede

scolo·pen·drine

scom·broid fish

sconce

Scone Scottish site of
coronation stone

scone cake

scoop

scoop·er

scoot

scoot·er

scop Anglo-Saxon minstrel

scope

sco·pola·mine drug

sco·po·line sedative

scopu·la (*plural* ·las *or* ·lae)
zoology term

scopu·late
scor·bu·tic (or ·ti·cal)
  having scurvy
scorch
scorch·er
scorch·ing
score
score·board
score·card
scor·er
sco·ria (plural ·riae) solid
  lava; slag
sco·ria·ceous
sco·ri·fi·ca·tion
sco·ri·fi·er
sco·ri·fy (·fies, ·fy·ing,
  ·fied)
scorn
scorn·er
scorn·ful
scorn·ful·ly
scorn·ful·ness
scorn·ing·ly
scor·pae·nid fish
scor·pae·noid
scor·per (or scau·)
  chisel
Scor·pi·an of Scorpio
Scor·pio sign of zodiac
scor·pi·oid
Scor·pi·on Scorpius
scor·pi·on arachnid
Scor·pius constellation
Scot
Scotch whisky; eggs; broth;
  its use as a synonym for
  Scottish or Scots is
  regarded as incorrect
scotch
sco·ter (plural ·ters or ·ter)
  duck
scot-free
sco·tia architectural
  moulding
Scot·land
sco·to·ma (plural ·mas or
  ·ma·ta) visual defect
sco·toma·tous
sco·to·pia night vision
sco·top·ic
Scots
Scots·man (plural ·men)
Scots·woman (plural
  ·women)
Scot·ti·cism

Scot·tie (or Scot·ty; plural
  ·ties)
Scot·tish
scoun·drel
scoun·drel·ly
scour
scour·er
scourge
scourg·er
scourg·ing·ly
Scouse Liverpudlian
scouse Dialect stew
scout
scout·er
scout·master
scow boat
scowl
scowl·er
scowl·ing·ly
Scrab·ble (Trademark) game
scrab·ble
scrab·bler
scrag (scrag·ging, scragged)
scrag·gi·ly
scrag·gi·ness
scrag·gly (·gli·er, ·gli·est)
  untidy
scrag·gy (·gi·er, ·gi·est)
  scrawny
scram (scram·ming,
  scrammed)
scramb (or scram) Dialect
  scratch
scram·ble
scram·bler
scran Slang food
Scran·ton US city
scrap (scrap·ping,
  scrapped)
scrap·able
scrap·book
scrape
scrap·er
scrap·er·board
scrap·heap
scrap·pi·ly
scrap·pi·ness
scrap·py (·pi·er, ·pi·est)
scratch
scratch·card
scratch·er
scratchi·ly
scratchi·ness
scratchy (scratchi·er,
  scratchi·est)

scrawl
scrawl·er
scrawly
scrawni·ly
scrawni·ness
scrawny (scrawni·er,
  scrawni·est)
screak Dialect screech
scream
scream·er
scree
screech
screech·er
screechy
screed
screen
screen·able
screen·er
screen·ings sifted refuse
screen·play
screw
screw·ball
screw·driver
screw·er
screw·worm
screwy (screwi·er,
  screwi·est)
scrib·al of scribes
scrib·ble
scrib·bler
scrib·bly
scribe
scrib·er tool
scrim fabric
scrim·mage struggle;
  compare scrummage
scrim·mag·er
scrimp
scrimpi·ly
scrimpi·ness
scrimpy (scrimpi·er,
  scrimpi·est)
scrim·shank Slang shirk
  work
scrim·shaw sailors' carving
scrip certificate
script
scrip·to·rium (plural ·riums
  or ·ria)
scrip·tur·al
scrip·ture sacred book
Scrip·tures Bible
script·writer
script·writing
scrive·ner

scro·bicu·late (or ·lat·ed)
biology term
scrod US young cod
scrofu·la
scrofu·lous
scroll
scroll·work
scroop Dialect creak
scrophu·laria·ceous botany
term
scro·tal
scro·tum (plural ·ta or
·tums)
scrouge Dialect to crowd
scrounge
scroung·er
scrub (scrub·bing,
scrubbed)
scrub·ber
scrub·bi·ness
scrub·by (·bi·er, ·bi·est)
scrub·land
scruff
scruffi·ly
scruffi·ness
scruffy (scruffi·er,
scruffi·est)
scrum (scrum·ming,
scrummed)
scrum·mage rugby scrum;
compare scrimmage
scrum·mag·er
scrump Dialect steal apples
scrump·tious
scrump·tious·ness
scrumpy cider
scrunch
scru·ple
scru·pu·lous
scru·pu·lous·ness
scru·ta·tor examiner
scru·ti·neer
scru·ti·nize (or ·nise)
scru·ti·niz·er (or ·nis·er)
scru·ti·niz·ing·ly (or
·nis·ing·ly)
scru·ti·ny (plural ·nies)
scry (scry·ing, scried)
crystal-gaze
scu·ba
scud (scud·ding, scud·ded)
scuff
scuf·fle
scull oar; compare skull
scull·er

scul·lery (plural ·leries)
scul·lion
scul·pin (plural ·pin or
·pins) fish
sculp·sit Latin sculptured
(inscription on sculpture)
sculpt
sculp·tor (fem ·tress)
sculp·tur·al
sculp·tur·al·ly
sculp·ture
sculp·tur·esque
scum (scum·ming,
scummed)
scum·ble art term
scum·mer
scum·my (·mi·er, ·mi·est)
scun·cheon part of door
jamb; compare scutcheon
scunge Austral borrow
scungy (scungi·er,
scungi·est) Austral
miserable
scun·ner Scot aversion
Scun·thorpe
scup fish
scup·per ship's drain
scup·per·nong wine
scurf
scurfy
scur·ril·ity
scur·ril·ous
scur·ri·lous·ness
scur·ry (verb ·ries, ·ry·ing,
·ried; noun, plural ·ries)
scur·vi·ly
scur·vi·ness
scur·vy (·vi·er, ·vi·est)
scut tail
scu·tage feudal payment
Scu·ta·ri Albanian town;
Turkish town
scu·tate biology term
scu·ta·tion
scutch separate fibres
scutch·eon escutcheon;
compare scuncheon
scute zoology term
scu·tel·lar
scu·tel·late
scu·tel·la·tion
scu·tel·lum (plural ·la)
biology term
scu·ti·form shield-shaped
scut·ter

scut·tle
scuttle·butt ship's drinking
fountain
scu·tum (plural ·ta) zoology
term; Roman shield
Scylla sea monster
scy·phi·form cup-shaped
scy·phis·to·ma (plural ·mae
or ·mas) zoology term
scy·pho·zo·an jellyfish
scy·phus (plural ·phi)
drinking cup
scythe
Scythia ancient Asian
region
Scyth·ian
sea
sea·bed
sea·board
sea·borne
sea·coast
sea·cock
sea·dog
sea·farer
sea·faring
sea·food
sea·front
sea·girt
sea·going
sea·gull
seal device; to close; animal;
compare seel
seal·able
sea-lane
seal·ant
sealed-beam
seal·er
seal·ery (plural ·eries)
sea·lion
seal-point Siamese cat
seal·skin
Sealy·ham terrier
seam
sea·man (plural ·men)
sailor; compare semen
sea·man·ly
sea·man·ship
sea·mark
seam·er
seami·ness
seam·less
sea·mount underwater
mountain
seam·stress (or semp·)
seamy (seami·er, seami·est)

Sean·ad Éire·ann Irish
  parliament
se·ance
sea·plane
sea·port
sea·quake
sear scorch; gun part;
  compare seer; sere
search
search·able
search·er
search·ing
search·ing·ly
search·light
sear·ing
sea·scape
sea·shell
sea·shore
sea·sick
sea·sick·ness
sea·side
sea·son
sea·son·able
sea·son·able·ness
sea·son·ably
sea·son·al
sea·son·al·ly
sea·son·al·ness
sea·soned·ly
sea·son·er
sea·son·ing
seat
seat·ed
seat·er
seat·ing
Se·at·tle
sea·wan (or se·wan) shell
  beads
sea·ward (adj)
sea·wards (adv)
sea·ware seaweed
sea·water
sea·way
sea·weed
sea·worthiness
sea·worthy
se·ba·ceous
Se·bas·to·pol variant spelling
  of Sevastopol
se·bif·er·ous biology
  term
seb·or·rhoea (US ·rhea)
seb·or·rhoeal (or ·rhoe·ic;
  US ·rheal or ·rhe·ic)
se·bum oily secretion

sec short for second or
  secant; dry (of wine)
se·cant
seca·teurs
sec·co (plural ·cos) wall
  painting
se·cede withdraw
se·ced·er
se·ces·sion
se·ces·sion·al
se·ces·sion·ism
se·ces·sion·ist
se·clude
se·clud·ed sheltered;
  compare seclusive
se·clud·ed·ness
se·clu·sion
se·clu·sive reclusive;
  compare secluded
se·clu·sive·ness
sec·ond unit of time;
  following first
se·cond transfer
sec·ond·ari·ly
sec·ond·ari·ness
sec·ond·ary (plural ·aries)
second-best (adj)
second-class (adj)
se·conde fencing position
sec·ond·er
second-floor (adj)
second-hand
se·cond·ment
se·con·do (plural ·di) part in
  piano duet
second-rate
second-rater
second-sighted
se·cre·cy (plural ·cies)
se·cret
sec·re·taire writing desk
sec·re·tar·ial
sec·re·tari·at
sec·re·tary (plural ·taries)
sec·retary-general (plural
  sec·re·taries-general)
sec·re·tary·ship
se·crete
se·cre·tin hormone
se·cre·tion
se·cre·tion·ary
se·cre·tive
se·cre·tive·ness
se·cre·tory
sect

sec·tar·ian
sec·tari·an·ism
sec·tary (plural ·taries)
  member of sect
sec·tile easily sliced
sec·til·ity
sec·tion
sec·tion·al
sec·tion·al·ism
sec·tion·al·ist
sec·tion·ali·za·tion (or
  ·sa·tion)
sec·tion·al·ize (or ·ise)
sec·tion·al·ly
sec·tor
sec·tor·al
sec·to·rial
secu·lar
secu·lar·ism
secu·lar·ist
secu·lar·is·tic
secu·lar·ity (plural ·ities)
secu·lari·za·tion (or
  ·sa·tion)
secu·lar·ize (or ·ise)
secu·lar·iz·er (or ·is·er)
se·cund botany term
se·cun·dine botany term
sec·un·dines (plural)
  afterbirth
se·cur·able
se·cure
se·cure·ment
se·cure·ness
se·cur·er
se·cu·rity (plural ·rities)
se·dan
se·date
se·date·ness
se·da·tion
seda·tive
sed·en·tari·ly
sed·en·tari·ness
sed·en·tary
Se·der Jewish meal
sedge
Sedge·moor English battle
  site
sedgy
se·di·lia (sing. ·le) church
  seats
sedi·ment
sedi·men·tari·ly
sedi·men·tary (or ·tal)
sedi·men·ta·tion

sedi·men·tol·ogy
sedi·men·tous
se·di·tion
se·di·tion·ary (*plural* ·aries)
se·di·tious
se·di·tious·ness
se·duce
se·duc·er
se·duc·ible (*or* ·duce·able)
se·duc·ing·ly
se·duc·tion
se·duc·tive
se·duc·tive·ness
se·duc·tress
se·du·lity
sedu·lous
sedu·lous·ness
se·dum plant
see (see·ing, saw, seen)
see·able
See·beck philately term
seed
seed·bed
seed·cake
seed·case
seed·er
seedi·ly
seedi·ness
seed·less
seed·ling
seedy (seedi·er, seedi·est)
see·ing
seek (seek·ing, sought)
seek·er
seel falconry term; *compare*
seal
seem
seem·er
seem·ing
seem·ing·ly
seem·li·ness
seem·ly (·li·er, ·li·est)
seen
seep
seep·age
seer prophet; *compare* sear;
sere
seer·sucker
see·saw
seethe
seeth·ing·ly
Sef·ton area of Merseyside
seg·ment
seg·men·tal
seg·men·tary

seg·men·ta·tion
se·gno (*plural* ·gni) musical
term
Se·go·via Spanish town
seg·re·gable
seg·re·gate
seg·re·ga·tion
seg·re·ga·tion·al
seg·re·ga·tion·ist
seg·re·ga·tive
seg·re·ga·tor
se·gui·dil·la dance
seiche water movement
(seige) *incorrect spelling of*
siege
sei·gneur
sei·gneu·rial
sei·gneury (*plural* ·gneuries)
sei·gnior·age
Seine French river
seine fishing net
Seine-et-Marne French
department
Seine-Maritime French
department
Seine-Saint-Denis French
department
seis·able
seise legal term; *compare*
seize
seis·er
sei·sin legal term
seism earthquake
seis·mic (*or* ·mal, ·mi·cal)
seis·mi·cal·ly
seis·mism
seis·mo·gram
seis·mo·graph
seis·mog·ra·pher
seis·mo·graph·ic
seis·mog·ra·phy
seis·mo·log·ic (*or* ·logi·cal)
seis·molo·gist
seis·mol·ogy
seis·mo·scope
seis·mo·scop·ic
(seive) *incorrect spelling of*
sieve
seiz·able
seize grasp; *compare* seise
seiz·er
seiz·ing
sei·zure
se·jant (*or* ·jeant) heraldic
term

Sejm Polish legislature
Sek·on·di Ghanaian port
se·la·chian zoology term
sela·gi·nel·la moss
Se·lan·gor Malaysian state
sel·dom
se·lect
se·lec·tion
se·lec·tive
se·lec·tive·ness
se·lec·tiv·ity
se·lect·ness
se·lec·tor
sel·enate
se·lenic
se·leni·ous (*or* ·lenous)
sel·enite mineral
se·lenium chemical element
se·leno·graph
se·lenog·ra·pher (*or* ·phist)
se·leno·graph·ic (*or*
·graphi·cal)
se·leno·graphi·cal·ly
se·lenog·ra·phy mapping
moon's surface
se·lenolo·gist
se·lenol·ogy study of
moon
se·leno·mor·phol·ogy
Se·leu·cid (*plural* ·cids *or*
·cidae) member of
Hellenistic dynasty
self (*plural* selves)
self-abasement
self-abnega·tion
self-absorbed
self-absorp·tion
self-abuse
self-action
self-actuali·za·tion
self-addressed
self-aggran·dize·ment
self-analy·sis
self-analyti·cal
self-anneal·ing
self-annihi·la·tion
self-appoint·ed
self-assertion
self-assertive
self-assurance
self-assured
self-aware
self-aware·ness
self-cater·ing
self-centred (*US* -centered)

self-centred•ness (US
-centered•ness)
self-coloured (US -colored)
self-concept
self-confessed
self-confidence
self-confident
self-conscious
self-conscious•ness
self-contained
self-contra•dic•tion
self-contra•dic•tory
self-control
self-controlled
self-deception (or -deceit)
self-deceptive
self-defence
self-denial
self-denying
self-discipline
self-disciplined
self-educat•ed
self-employed
self-efface•ment
self-effacing
self-esteem
self-evident
self-evidence
self-feeder
self-fertile
self-fertili•za•tion (or
•sa•tion)
self-fertilized (or
-fertilised)
self-govern•ment
self-heal plant
self-help
self-hood
self-image
self-import•ance
self-import•ant
self-imposed
self-improve•ment
self-induced
self-induct•ance
self-induction
self-inductive
self-indulgence
self-indulgent
self-inflict•ed
self-inflic•tion
self-interest
self•ish
self-ish•ness
self-justifi•ca•tion

self-justify•ing
self-knowledge
self•less
self•less•ness
self-liquidat•ing
self-loading
self-made
self-opin•ion•at•ed (or
-opinioned)
self-pity
self-pitying
self-pollinat•ed
self-pollina•tion
self-portrait
self-possessed
self-posses•sion
self-preser•va•tion
self-propelled
self-protec•tion
self-raising
self-regard
self-reliance
self-reliant
self-reproach
self-reproach•ful
self-respect
self-respect•ing
self-restraint
self-righteous
self-righteous•ness
self-rule
self-sacrifice
self-sacrific•ing
self•same
self-satisfac•tion
self-satisfied
self-sealing
self-seeker
self-seeking
self-service
self-starter
self-styled
self-sufficiency
self-sufficient (or
-suffic•ing)
self-taught
self-willed
self-winding
Sel•juk (or •ju•kian)
member of Turkish
dynasty
Sel•kirk former Scottish
county
sell (sell•ing, sold)
sell•er

selling-plater type of
racehorse
Sel•lo•tape (Trademark)
sell•out (noun)
Selt•zer mineral water
sel•va forest
sel•vage (or •vedge) edge of
fabric; compare salvage
selves plural of self
se•man•tic
se•man•ti•cal•ly
se•man•ti•cist
se•man•tics
sema•phore
sema•phor•ic (or •phori•cal)
sema•phori•cal•ly
Se•ma•rang (or Sa•)
Indonesian port
se•ma•sio•logi•cal
se•ma•sio•logi•cal•ly
se•ma•si•olo•gist
se•ma•siol•ogy semantics
se•mat•ic zoology term
sema•tol•ogy semantics
sem•blance
semé (or se•mée) heraldry
term
sem•eme linguistics term
se•men ejaculated fluid;
compare seaman
se•mes•ter
se•mes•tral
semi (plural semis)
semi•an•nual
semi•an•nu•al•ly
semi•aquat•ic
semi•ar•id
semi•arid•ity
semi•auto•mat•ic
semi•auto•mati•cal•ly
Semi-Bantu African
language
semi•bold printing term
semi•breve
semi•cen•ten•nial
semi•cir•cle
semi•cir•cu•lar
semi•co•lon
semi•con•duc•tion
semi•con•duc•tor
semi•con•scious
semi•con•scious•ness
semi•de•tached
semi•di•am•eter
semi•di•ur•nal

semi·dome
semi·el·lip·ti·cal
semi·fi·nal
semi·fi·nal·ist
semi·flu·id
semi·flu·id·ic
semi·flu·id·ity
semi·lit·er·ate
semi·lu·nar
semi·month·ly
semi·nal
semi·nal·ity
semi·nal·ly
semi·nar
semi·nar·ial
semi·nar·ian *student at seminary*
semi·nary (*plural* ·naries)
semi·nif·er·ous *transporting semen*
Semi·nole (*plural* ·noles *or* ·nole) *American Indian*
se·mi·ol·ogy (*or* ·mei·)
se·mi·ot·ic (*or* ·mei·)
se·mi·ot·ics (*or* ·mei·) *study of symbols*
Se·mi·pa·la·tinsk *Kazakh city*
semi·pal·mate (*or* ·mat·ed) *zoology term*
semi·para·sit·ic
semi·para·sit·ism
semi·per·meabil·ity
semi·per·meable
semi·porce·lain
semi·precious
semi·pro (*plural* ·pros)
semi·pro·fes·sion·al
semi·qua·ver
Se·mira·mis *legendary queen*
semi·rig·id
semi·skilled
semi·sol·id
Se·mite (*or* Shem·ite)
Se·mit·ic (*or* She·)
Se·mit·ics *study of Semitic languages*
Semi·tist
semi·ton·al·ly
semi·tone
semi·ton·ic
semi·trail·er
semi·tropi·cal
semi·trop·ics

semi·vit·reous
semi·vo·cal (*or* ·cal·ic)
semi·vow·el
semi·week·ly
semi·year·ly
semo·li·na
sem·per fi·de·lis *Latin always faithful*
sem·per pa·ra·tus *Latin always prepared*
sem·pi·ter·nal *everlasting*
sem·pi·ter·nity
sem·pli·ce *musical term*
sem·pre *musical term*
semp·stress *variant spelling of* seamstress
sen (*plural* sen) *Oriental currency*
sen·ar·mon·tite *mineral*
sen·ary *of six*
Sen·ate *senate of USA, ancient Rome, etc.*
sen·ate *legislative body*
sena·tor
sena·to·rial
send (send·ing, sent)
send·able
Sen·dai *Japanese city*
sen·dal *fabric*
send·er
send·off
send-up (*noun*)
Sen·eca (*plural* ·ecas *or* ·eca) *American Indian*
sen·ega *plant*
Sen·egal
Sen·ega·lese
Sen·egam·bia *African region*
se·nes·cence
se·nes·cent
sen·eschal *medieval steward*
sen·hor (*plural* ·hors *or* ·hores) *Portuguese man; Mr*
sen·hora *Portuguese woman; Mrs*
sen·hor·ita *Portuguese young woman; Miss*
se·nile
se·nil·ity
sen·ior
sen·ior·ity (*plural* ·ities)
Sen·lac *battle site*
sen·na
Sen·nar *Sudanese region*

sen·net *fanfare*
sen·nit *braided cordage*
se·ñor (*plural* ·ñors *or* ·ñores) *Spanish man; Mr*
se·ño·ra *Spanish woman; Mrs*
se·ño·ri·ta *Spanish young woman; Miss*
sen·sate (·sat·ed)
sen·sa·tion
sen·sa·tion·al
sen·sa·tion·al·ly
sen·sa·tion·al·ism
sen·sa·tion·al·ist
sen·sa·tion·al·is·tic
sense
sense·less
sense·less·ness
sen·si·bilia *what can be sensed*
sen·sibil·ity (*plural* ·ities)
sen·sible
sen·sible·ness
sen·sibly
sen·sil·lum (*plural* ·la) *zoology term*
sen·si·tive
sen·si·tive·ness
sen·si·tiv·ity (*plural* ·ities)
sen·si·ti·za·tion (*or* ·sa·tion)
sen·si·tize (*or* ·tise)
sen·si·tiz·er (*or* ·tis·er)
sen·si·tom·eter
sen·si·tom·etry
sen·sor *sensing device; compare* censor
sen·so·ri·mo·tor (*or* sen·so·mo·tor) *physiology term*
sen·so·rium *area of brain*
sen·so·ry (*or* ·rial)
sen·sual *gratifying the senses; compare* censual; sensuous
sen·su·al·ism
sen·su·al·ist
sen·su·al·ity (*plural* ·ities)
sen·su·al·ly
sen·su·al·ness
sen·su·ous *pleasing to the senses; compare* sensual
sen·su·ous·ness
sent
sen·tence

sen·ten·tial
sen·ten·tious
sen·ten·tious·ness
sen·tience (or ·tien·cy)
sen·ti·ent
sen·ti·ment
sen·ti·ment·al
sen·ti·men·tal·ism
sen·ti·men·tal·ist
sen·ti·men·tal·ity (plural
·ities)
sen·ti·men·tali·za·tion (or
·sa·tion)
sen·ti·men·tal·ize (or ·ise)
sen·ti·men·tal·ly
sen·ti·nel
sen·try (plural ·tries)
Se·nus·si (or ·nu·si; plural
·sis) member of Muslim
sect
sen·za musical term
Seoul capital of South
Korea
sep·al
se·palled (or ·pal·ous)
se·pa·loid (or ·line)
sepa·rabil·ity (or
·rable·ness)
sepa·rable
sepa·rate
sepa·rate·ness
sepa·ra·tion
sepa·ra·tism
sepa·ra·tist (or
·ra·tion·ist)
sepa·ra·tis·tic
sepa·ra·tive
sepa·ra·tive·ness
sepa·ra·tor
sepa·ra·trix (plural ·trices)
oblique stroke
Se·phar·di (plural ·dim)
Iberian Jew
Se·phar·dic
se·pia
se·pio·lite mineral
se·poy Indian soldier
sep·sis
sept clan
sep·ta plural of septum
sep·tal
sep·tar·ian
sep·tar·ium (plural ·ia)
geology term
sep·tate

sep·ta·va·lent variant
spelling of septivalent
Sep·tem·ber
Sep·tem·brist French
revolutionary
sep·te·nary (plural ·naries)
sep·ten·nial
sep·ten·nium (plural
·niums or ·nia)
sep·tet (or ·tette)
sep·tic putrefying; compare
sceptic
sep·ti·cae·mia (US ·cemia)
sep·ti·cae·mic (US ·cemic)
sep·ti·cal·ly
sep·ti·cid·al botany term
sep·tic·ity
sep·tif·ra·gal botany term
sep·ti·lat·er·al
sep·til·lion (plural ·lion or
·lions) 10^{42}
sep·til·lionth
sep·time fencing position
sep·ti·va·lent (or ·ta·)
sep·tua·genar·ian
Sep·tua·gesi·ma third
Sunday before Lent
Sep·tua·gint Greek Old
Testament
sep·tum (plural ·ta)
sep·tu·ple
sep·tup·let
sep·tu·pli·cate
se·pul·chral
se·pul·chral·ly
se·pul·chre (US ·cher)
sep·ul·ture burial
se·qua·cious in sequence
se·quac·ity
se·quel
se·quela (plural ·quelae)
medical term
se·quence
se·quenc·er electronic
device
se·quent
se·quen·tial
se·quen·ti·al·ity
se·quen·tial·ly
se·ques·ter
se·ques·trable
se·ques·tral
se·ques·trant
se·ques·trate
se·ques·tra·tion

se·ques·tra·tor
se·ques·trum (plural ·tra)
medical term
se·quin
se·quined
se·quoia
ser (or seer) Indian unit
sera plural of serum
sé·rac ice pinnacle
se·ra·glio (plural ·glios)
se·rail harem
Se·rang Indonesian island
ser·aph (plural ·aphs or
·aphim) angel; compare
serif
se·raph·ic (or ·raphi·cal)
Sera·pis Egyptian god
Serb a Serbian
Ser·bia Yugoslav republic
Ser·bian
Serbo-Croat (or -Croa·tian)
language
ser·dab chamber in
Egyptian tomb
sere ecology term; compare
cere; sear; seer
sere (or sear) withered;
compare cere; sear; seer
se·rein tropical rain
ser·enade
ser·enad·er
se·rena·ta cantata
ser·en·dip·ity
se·rene
se·rene·ness
se·ren·ity (plural ·ities)
serf medieval peasant;
compare surf
serf·dom (or ·hood)
serge fabric; compare
surge
ser·gean·cy (or ·geant·ship)
ser·geant
Ser·gi·pe Brazilian state
se·rial story in instalments;
in series; compare cereal
se·rial·ism
se·riali·za·tion (or ·sa·tion)
se·rial·ize (or ·ise)
se·rial·ly
se·ri·ate
se·ria·tim in a series
se·ri·ceous
seri·cin protein in silk
seri·cul·tur·al

seri·cul·ture silkworm rearing

seri·cul·tur·ist

seri·ema bird

se·ries (plural ·ries)

series-wound electrical term

ser·if (or ·iph) printing term; compare seraph

seri·graph silk-screen print

se·rig·ra·phy

ser·in bird

ser·ine amino acid

se·rin·ga rubber tree; compare syringa

se·rio·com·ic (or ·comi·cal)

se·rio·comi·cal·ly

se·ri·ous grave; compare serous

se·ri·ous·ly

se·ri·ous·ness

ser·jeant at law

ser·mon

ser·mon·ic

ser·moni·cal

ser·mon·ize (or ·ise)

ser·mon·iz·er (or ·is·er)

se·ro·log·ic (or ·logi·cal)

se·rolo·gist

se·rol·ogy study of serums

se·ro·sa membrane

se·rosi·ty (or ·rous·ness)

se·roti·nal (or ·nous)

sero·tine bat

sero·to·nin biochemical compound

se·rous of serum; compare serious

ser·ow antelope

ser·pent

ser·pen·tine

ser·pigi·nous

ser·pi·go skin disease

ser·pu·lid worm

ser·ra·nid (or ·noid) fish

ser·rate

ser·rat·ed

ser·ra·tion (or ·ture)

ser·ried

ser·ri·form

ser·ru·late (or ·lat·ed)

ser·ru·la·tion notch

ser·tu·lar·ian zoology term

se·rum (plural ·rums or ·ra)

serv·able (or serve·)

ser·val (plural ·vals or ·val) animal

serv·ant

serve

serv·er

serv·ery (plural ·eries)

ser·vice

ser·vice·abil·ity (or ·able·ness)

ser·vice·able

ser·vice·ably

ser·vice·berry (plural ·berries)

ser·vice·man (plural ·men)

ser·vi·ette

ser·vile

ser·vil·ity (or ·vile·ness)

serv·ing

ser·vi·tor

ser·vi·tude

ser·vo (plural ·vos)

ser·vo·mechani·cal

ser·vo·mecha·nism

ser·vo·mo·tor

sesa·me

sesa·moid bone

Se·so·tho language

ses·qui·al·te·ra organ stop

ses·qui·car·bon·ate

ses·qui·cen·ten·nial

ses·qui·ox·ide

ses·qui·peda·lian (or ·quip·edal) using long words

ses·qui·peda·li·an·ism

ses·sile

ses·sil·ity

ses·sion meeting; compare cession

ses·sion·al

ses·sion·al·ly

ses·terce (or ·ter·tius; plural ·terces or ·tia) Roman coin

ses·ter·tium (plural ·tia) Roman coin

ses·tet six-line verse; compare sextet

ses·ti·na verse form

Ses·tos ancient Turkish town

set (set·ting, set)

seta (plural setae) small bristle

se·ta·ceous

se·tal

set·back

se·ti·form

set·line

set-off printing term

se·tose bristly

set·screw

sett (or set) paving slab; badger's den

set·tee

set·ter

set·ting

set·tle

set·tle·able

set·tle·ment

set·tler (or in legal contexts ·tlor)

set-to (noun, plural -tos)

set-up (noun)

Se·van Armenian lake

Se·vas·to·pol (or ·bas·) Ukrainian port

sev·en

sev·en·fold

sev·en·teen

sev·en·teenth

sev·enth

sev·en·ti·eth

sev·en·ty (plural ·ties)

sev·er

sev·er·able

sev·er·al

sev·er·al·ly

sev·er·al·ty (plural ·ties) separateness

sev·er·ance

se·vere

se·vere·ness

se·ver·ity (plural ·ities)

Sev·ern British river

Se·ville Spanish port

Sèvres porcelain

sew (sew·ing, sewed, sewn or sewed) to stitch; compare sow

sew·age waste matter

sew·er sewage drain; one who sews; compare suer

sew·er·age system of sewers

sew·ing

sewn

sex

sexa·genar·ian

sex·ag·enary (plural ·enaries)

Sexa·gesi·ma second
Sunday before Lent
sexa·gesi·mal of 60
sex·cen·te·nary (plural
·naries)
sex·en·nial
sexi·ly
sexi·ness
sex·ism
sex·ist
sexi·va·lent (or sexa·)
sex·less
sex·less·ness
sex·olo·gist
sex·ol·ogy
sex·par·tite
sex·pot
sext canonical hour
sex·tant
sex·tet (or ·tette) group of
six; compare sestet
sex·tile
sex·til·lion (plural ·lions or
·lion) 10³⁶
sex·til·lionth
sex·to·deci·mo (plural
·mos)
sex·ton
sex·tu·ple
sex·tup·let
sex·tu·pli·cate
sex·ual
sexu·al·ity
sex·ual·ly
sexy (sexi·er, sexi·est)
Sey·chelles
Sfax Tunisian port
sfor·zan·do (or ·za·to)
musical term
sfu·ma·to art term
sgraf·fi·to (plural ·ti) art
term
Sha·ba region of the
Democratic Republic of
Congo
shab·bi·ly
shab·bi·ness
shab·by (·bi·er, ·bi·est)
shack
shack·le
shack·ler
shad (plural shad or shads)
fish
shad·bush
shad·dock fruit

shade
shadi·ly
shadi·ness
shad·ing
sha·doof (or ·duf)
water-raising device
shad·ow
shadow-box
shadow-boxing
shad·ow·er
shad·ow·graph
shad·owi·ness
shad·owy
Shadrach biblical character
shady (shadi·er, shadi·est)
shaft
shaft·ing
shag (shag·ging, shagged)
shag·bark (or shell·bark)
shag·gi·ly
shag·gi·ness
shag·gy (·gi·er, ·gi·est)
sha·green
shah
shah·dom
Shah·ja·han·pur Indian city
shak·able (or shake·)
shake (shak·ing, shook,
shak·en)
shake·down (noun)
shak·er
Shak·ers US sect
Shake·spear·ean (or ·ian)
Shake·spear·ea·na
shake-up (noun)
Shakh·ty Russian city
shaki·ly
shaki·ness
shako (or shacko; plural
shakos or shackos)
military headdress
shaky (shaki·er, shaki·est)
shale
shall (should)
shal·loon fabric
shal·lop boat
shal·lot
shal·low
shal·low·ness
sha·lom Jewish greeting;
compare slalom
shalt
shaly
sham (sham·ming,
shammed)

sham·able (or shame·)
sham·an priest
sham·an·ism
Sha·mash Assyrian god
sham·ble
sham·bles
sham·bol·ic
shame
shame·faced
shame·faced·ness
shame·ful
shame·ful·ly
shame·ful·ness
shame·less
shame·less·ness
sham·mer
sham·my (plural ·mies)
leather
sham·poo (noun, plural
·poos; verb ·poos,
·poo·ing, ·pooed)
sham·poo·er
sham·rock
Shan (plural Shans or Shan)
Mongoloid people
shan·dry·dan cart
shan·dy (plural ·dies)
shan·dy·gaff US shandy
Shang Chinese dynasty
Shang·hai Chinese port
shang·hai (·hais, ·hai·ing,
·haied) kidnap
Shangri-la
shank
Shan·non Irish river
shan·ny (plural ·nies) fish
Shan·si Chinese province
shan't shall not
Shan·tung Chinese
province
shan·tung silk
shan·ty (plural ·ties) hut
shan·ty (or shan·tey,
chan·ty; US chan·tey;
plural ·ties or ·teys) sea
song
shanty·town
shap·able (or shape·)
shape
shape·less
shape·less·ness
shape·li·ness
shape·ly (·li·er, ·li·est)
shap·er
shar·able (or share·)

shard (*or* sherd)

share

share·crop (·crop·ping, ·cropped)

share·crop·per

share·holder

share-out (*noun*)

shar·er

sha·ria (*or* she·) Islamic doctrines

shark

shark·skin

Sha·ron Israeli plain

sharp

sharp·en

sharp·en·er

sharp·er

sharp-eyed

sharp·ish

sharp·ness

sharp·set

sharp·shooter

sharp-sighted

sharp-sighted·ness

sharp-tongued

sharp-witted

sharp-witted·ness

shash·lik (*or* ·lick) kebab

shat·ter

shat·ter·er

shat·ter·ing·ly

shatter·proof

shav·able (*or* shave·)

shave (shav·ing, shaved, shaved *or* shav·en)

shav·er

Sha·vian of G. B. Shaw

shav·ing

shawl

shawm musical instrument

Shaw·nee (*plural* ·nees *or* ·nee) American Indian

she

shea tree

shead·ing Manx region

sheaf (*plural* sheaves)

shear (shear·ing, sheared, sheared *or* shorn) cut; deformation; *compare* sheer

shear·er

shear·legs *variant spelling of* sheerlegs

shear·ling

shears

shear·water bird

sheat·fish (*plural* ·fish *or* ·fishes)

sheath (*noun; plural* sheaths)

sheath·bill

sheathe (*verb*)

sheath·ing

sheave bind in sheaves; grooved wheel

She·ba ancient kingdom

she·bang *Slang* situation

she·been (*or* ·bean) illegal drinking place

She·chem ancient Jordanian town

shed (shed·ding, shed)

she'd she had; she would

shed·able (*or* shed·dable)

shed·der

sheen

sheeny

sheep (*plural* sheep)

sheep·cote

sheep-dip

sheep·dog

sheep·fold

sheep·ish

sheep·ish·ness

sheeps·shank knot

sheeps·head (*plural* ·head *or* ·heads) fish

sheep·shearer

sheep·shearing

sheep·skin

sheep·walk grazing land

sheer steep; transparent; absolutely; deviate; *compare* shear

sheer·legs (*or* shear·) lifting device

Sheer·ness English port

sheer·ness

sheet

sheet·ing

Shef·field

sheik (*or* sheikh)

sheik·dom (*or* sheikh·)

shei·la *Austral* girl

shek·el

shel·duck (*or* ·drake; *plural* ·ducks, ·duck *or* ·drakes, ·drake)

shelf (*plural* shelves)

shell

she'll she will

shel·lac (·lack·ing, ·lacked)

shell·back experienced sailor

shell·fire

shell·fish (*plural* ·fish *or* ·fishes)

shell-less

shell-like

shell·proof

shell-shocked

Shel·ta tinkers' language

shel·ter

shel·ter·er

shel·tie (*or* ·ty; *plural* ·ties) dog; pony

shelve (*verb*)

shelv·er

shelv·ing

She·ma Jewish doctrine

she·moz·zle

Shen·an·do·ah US river; national park

she·nani·gan

Shen·si Chinese province

Shen·yang Chinese city

She·ol abode of the dead

shep·herd

shep·herd·ess

shepherd's-purse

Shep·pey (Isle of)

sher·ardi·za·tion (*or* ·sa·tion)

sher·ard·ize (*or* ·ise)

Sheraton furniture

sher·bet

Sher·brooke Canadian city

sherd *variant spelling of* shard

she·rif (*or* ·reef) Muslim ruler

sher·iff officer

Sher·pa (*plural* ·pas *or* ·pa)

sher·ry (*plural* ·ries)

sher·wa·ni Indian coat

she's she is

Shet·land

shew·bread (*or* show·) biblical bread

Shi·ah Muslim sect

shiai judo contest

shib·bo·leth

shick·er *Austral* alcoholic drink

shied

shield
shield·er
shiel·ing *Scot* hut; pasture
shi·er (*adj*) *variant spelling of*
 shyer
shi·est *variant spelling of*
 shyest
shift
shift·er
shifti·ly
shifti·ness
shift·ing·ly
shift·less
shift·less·ness
shifty (shifti·er, shifti·est)
shi·gel·la bacterium
Shih·chia·chuang (*or*
 ·kia·chwang) Chinese city
shih-tzu dog
Shi·ism
Shi·ite adherent of Shiah
shi·kar (·kar·ring, ·karred)
 hunt game
shi·ka·ri (*or* ·ree; *plural* ·ris
 or ·rees) hunter
Shi·ko·ku Japanese island
shil·lelagh (*or* shil·la·la)
 Irish cudgel
shil·ling
Shil·long Indian city
shilly·shalli·er
shilly·shally (·shallies,
 ·shally·ing, ·shallied)
Shi·loh biblical city
shi·ly *less common spelling of*
 shyly
shim (shim·ming,
 shimmed)
shim·mer
shim·mer·ing·ly
shim·mery
shim·my (*noun, plural*
 ·mies; *verb* ·mies, ·my·ing,
 ·mied) dance
Shi·mo·no·seki Japanese
 port
shin (shin·ning, shinned)
shin·bone
shin·dig (*or* ·dy; *plural* ·digs
 or ·dies)
shine (shin·ing, shone)
shin·er
shin·gle
shin·gler
shin·gles

shin·gly
shini·ness
Shin·to Japanese religion
Shin·to·ism
Shin·to·ist
shin·ty (*US* ·ny; *plural* ·ties
 or ·nies) hockey
shiny (shini·er, shini·est)
ship (ship·ping, shipped)
ship·able
ship·board
ship·builder
ship·building
ship·load
ship·master (*or* ·man; *plural*
 ·masters *or* ·men)
ship·mate
ship·ment
ship·owner
ship·per
ship·ping
ship-rigged
ship·shape
ship·way
ship·worm
ship·wreck
ship·wright
ship·yard
shi·ra·lee *Austral* swagman's
 bundle
Shi·raz Iranian city
Shi·ré African river
shire
shirk
shirk·er
shirr
shirr·ing
shirt
shirti·ly
shirti·ness
shirt·ing
shirt·sleeve
shirt-tail
shirt·waister
shirty (shirti·er, shirti·est)
shit (shit·ting, shit·ted *or*
 shit)
shit·tah (*plural* ·tim *or*
 ·tahs) biblical tree
Shit·tim biblical place
shit·ty
Shiva *variant spelling of* Siva
shive cork
shiv·er
shiv·er·er

shiv·er·ing·ly
shiv·ery
Shi·zuo·ka Japanese city
Shluh (*plural* Shluhs *or*
 Shluh) African people
shoal
shoali·ness
shoaly
shoat (*or* shote) weaned
 piglet
shock
shock·abil·ity
shock·able
shock·er
shock-headed
shock·ing
shock·ing·ness
shock·proof
shod
shod·di·ly
shod·di·ness
shod·dy (·di·er, ·di·est)
shoe (shoe·ing, shod)
 footwear; *compare* shoo
shoe·bill
shoe·black
shoe·horn
shoe·lace
shoe·maker
shoe·making
shoe·shine
shoe·string
shoe·tree
sho·far (*or* ·phar; *plural*
 ·fars, ·phars *or* ·froth,
 ·phroth) Jewish horn
sho·gun Japanese leader
sho·gun·ate
sho·ji (*plural* ·ji *or* ·jis) paper
 screen
Sho·la·pur Indian city
Sho·na (*plural* ·na *or* ·nas)
 African people
shone
shoo (shoos, shoo·ing,
 shooed) chase off; *compare*
 shoe
shook
shoon *Scot* shoes
shoot (shoot·ing, shot)
shoot·er
shoot-out (*noun*)
shop (shop·ping, shopped)
shop·girl
shop·keeper

shop·keeping
shop·lifter
shop·lifting
shop·per
shop·ping
shop·soiled (*US* ·worn)
shop·talk
shop·walker
shop·worn *US* shopsoiled
shor·an radar system
shore
shore·less
shore·line
shore·ward (*adj*)
shore·wards (*adv*)
shor·ing
shorn
short
short·age
short·bread
short·cake
short-change
short-changer
short-circuit (*verb*)
short·coming
short·en
short·en·er
short·en·ing
short·fall
short-haired
short·hand
short-handed
short-handed·ness
short·horn cattle
shortie (*or* shorty; *plural* shorties)
short·ish
short-list (*verb*)
short-lived
short·ly
short·ness
short-range
shorts
short-sighted
short-sighted·ness
short-spoken
short-tempered
short-term (*adj*)
short-waisted
short-winded
shorty *variant spelling of* shortie
Sho·sho·ne (*or* ·ni; *plural* ·nes, ·ne *or* ·nis, ·ni)
    American Indian

Sho·sho·nean (*or* ·nian)
shot
shote *variant spelling of* shoat
shot·gun (·gun·ning, ·gunned)
shot-putter
shott (*or* chott) salt lake
shot·ten recently spawned
should
shoul·der
shouldn't
shouse *Austral* lavatory
shout
shout·er
shove
shov·el (·el·ling, ·elled; *US* ·el·ing, ·eled)
shov·el·er duck; *compare* shoveller
shovel·ful (*plural* ·fuls)
shovel·head shark
shov·el·ler (*US* ·el·er) one who shovels; *compare* shoveler
shovel·nose fish
shov·er
show (show·ing, showed, shown *or* showed)
show·biz
show·boat
show·case
showd *Scot* rock
show·down
show·er
shower·proof
show·ery
show·girl
showi·ly
showi·ness
show·ing
show·jumper
show·jumping
show·man (*plural* ·men)
show·man·ship
shown
show-off (*noun*)
show·piece
show·place
show·room
showy (showi·er, showi·est)
shrank
shrap·nel

shred (shred·ding, shred·ded *or* shred)
shred·der
Shreve·port *US* city
shrew
shrewd
shrewdie *Austral* shrewd person
shrewd·ness
shrew·ish
shrew·ish·ness
Shrews·bury
shriek
shriek·er
shrie·val of a sheriff
shriev·al·ty (*plural* ·ties)
shrift
shrike
shrill
shrill·ness
shrilly
shrimp
shrimp·er
shrine
shrink (shrink·ing, shrank *or* shrunk, shrunk *or* shrunk·en)
shrink·able
shrink·age
shrink·er
shrink·ing·ly
shrink-wrap (-wrapping, -wrapped)
shrive (shriv·ing, shrove *or* shrived, shriv·en *or* shrived)
shriv·el (·el·ling, ·elled; *US* ·el·ing, ·eled)
shriv·er
shroff detector of counterfeit money
Shrop·shire
shroud
shroud-laid
shrove
Shrove·tide
shrub
shrub·bery (*plural* ·beries)
shrub·bi·ness
shrub·by (·bi·er, ·bi·est)
shrug (shrug·ging, shrugged)
shrunk
shrunk·en
shuck

shuck·er
shucks exclamation
shud·der
shud·der·ing·ly
shud·dery
shuf·fle
shuffle·board
shuf·fler
shug·gy (plural ·gies) Dialect swing
shul (or schul; plural shuln or schuln) synagogue
shun (shun·ning, shunned)
shun·nable
shun·ner
shunt
shunt·er
shunt-wound electrical term
shush
shut (shut·ting, shut)
shut·down (noun)
shut·eye
shut-off (noun)
shut·out (noun)
shut·ter
shut·ter·ing
shut·tle
shuttle·cock
shy (adj shy·er, shy·est or shi·er, shi·est; verb shies, shy·ing, shied; noun, plural shies)
shy·er (noun)
Shy·lock heartless creditor
shy·ly
shy·ness
shy·ster
Si (or Hsi) Chinese river
sial part of earth's crust
si·ala·gog·ic (or ·alo·) stimulating salivation
si·ala·gogue (or ·alo·)
si·al·ic
Si·al·kot Pakistani city
sia·loid saliva-like
Siam former name of Thailand
sia·mang ape
Sia·mese (plural ·mese)
Sian (or Hsian) Chinese city
Siang (or Hsiang) Chinese river
Siang·tan Chinese city
sib (or sibb) kin

Si·beria
Si·berian
sibi·lance (or ·lan·cy)
sibi·lant
sibi·late
sibi·la·tion
Si·biu Romanian town
sib·ling
sib·yl prophetess
sib·yl·line (or si·byl·lic)
sic Latin thus; indicates the deliberate inclusion of a questionable word in text
sic·ca·tive drying agent
sice variant spelling of syce
Si·cil·ian
Sici·ly
sick
sick·bay
sick·bed
sick·en
sick·en·er
sick·en·ing
sick·en·ing·ly
sick·le
sickle·bill
sick·li·ness
sick·ly (·li·er, ·li·est)
sick·ness
sic pas·sim Latin thus everywhere; indicates a word in text is the same throughout
Sicy·on ancient Greek city
side
side·band electronics term
side·board
side·boards (or esp. US ·burns)
side·car
side-dress
side·kick
side·light
side·line
side·long
si·dereal of stars
si·der·ite mineral
si·der·it·ic
si·dero·lite meteorite
si·der·osis disease
si·dero·stat astronomical instrument
si·dero·stat·ic
sid·er·ot·ic
side-saddle

side·show
side·slip (·slip·ping, ·slipped)
sides·man (plural ·men)
side-splitting
side·step (·step·ping, ·stepped)
side·step·per
side·stroke
side·swipe
side·swip·er
side·track
side·walk US pavement
side·wall
side·ward (adj)
side·wards (adv)
side·ways
side·wheel
side·wheeler boat
side·winder snake
Sidi-bel-Abbès Algerian city
sid·ing
si·dle
si·dler
Si·don Phoenician city
siè·cle French century
siege
sie·mens (plural ·mens) unit
Si·ena Italian city
si·en·na pigment
si·er·ra
Si·er·ra Leo·ne
Si·er·ra Le·on·ean
Si·er·ra Ma·dre Mexican mountains
si·er·ran
Si·er·ra Ne·va·da US mountains
si·es·ta
sieve
(sieze) incorrect spelling of seize
si·fa·ka animal
sift
sift·er
sift·ings
sigh
sigh·er
sight vision; compare site
sight·able
sight·ed
sight·er
sight·less
sight·less·ness
sight·li·ness

sight·ly (·li·er, ·li·est)
sight-read (-reading, -read)
sight-reader
sight·screen
sight·see (·see·ing, ·saw, ·seen)
sight·seer
sig·la list of symbols
sig·los (plural ·loi) coin
sig·ma Greek letter
sig·mate
sig·ma·tion
sig·moid (or ·moi·dal)
sig·moido·scope medical instrument
sig·moido·scop·ic
sig·moid·os·co·py
sign
sig·nal (·nal·ling, ·nalled; US ·nal·ling, ·naled)
sig·nal·ize (or ·ise)
sig·nal·ler (US ·nal·er)
sig·nal·ly
sig·nal·man (plural ·men)
sig·na·tory (plural ·tories)
sig·na·ture
sign·board
sign·er
sig·net seal on ring; compare cygnet
sig·ni·fi·able
sig·nifi·cance
sig·nifi·cant
sig·nifi·cant·ly
sig·nifi·ca·tion
sig·nifi·ca·tive
sig·nifi·ca·tive·ness
sig·ni·fi·er
sig·ni·fy (·fies, ·fy·ing, ·fied)
si·gnor (plural ·gnors or ·gnori) Italian man; Mr
si·gno·ra (plural ·ras or ·re) Italian woman; Mrs
si·gno·re (plural ·ri) Italian man; Sir
si·gnori·na (plural ·nas or ·ne) Italian young woman; Miss
sign·post
Sigurd Norse hero
sika deer
sike Dialect small stream
Sikh
Sikh·ism

Sik·kim Indian state
Sik·ki·mese
si·lage
Si·las·tic (Trademark)
sild fish
sile Dialect rain
si·lence
si·lenc·er
si·lent
si·lent·ly
si·lent·ness
Silenus Greek satyr
Si·lesia European region
si·lesia fabric
si·lex heat-resistant glass
sil·hou·ette
sili·ca mineral; compare silicon; silicone
sili·cate
si·li·ceous (or ·cious)
si·lic·ic
sili·cide chemical compound
sili·cif·er·ous
si·lici·fi·ca·tion
si·lici·fy (·fies, ·fy·ing, ·fied)
sili·cle (or si·licu·la, sili·cule) botany term
sili·con chemical element; compare silica; silicone
sili·cone polymer; compare silica; silicon
sili·co·sis disease
si·licu·lose
si·li·qua (or ·lique; plural ·li·quae, ·li·quas, or ·liques) botany term
sili·qua·ceous
silk
silka·line (or ·lene) fabric
silk·en
silki·ly
silki·ness
silk·worm
silky (silki·er, silki·est)
sill
sil·la·bub variant spelling of syllabub
sil·li·ly
sil·li·ma·nite mineral
sil·li·ness
sil·ly (adj ·li·er, ·li·est; noun, plural ·lies)
silo (plural silos)

si·lox·ane
silt
sil·ta·tion
silty
Si·lu·res ancient Britons
Si·lu·rian geological period; of Silures
si·lu·rid fish
sil·va variant spelling of sylva
sil·van variant spelling of sylvan
Silvanus (or Sylvanus) Roman god
sil·ver
sil·ver·er
silver·fish (plural ·fish or ·fishes)
sil·veri·ness
sil·ver·ing
silver·point drawing technique
silver·side
silver·smith
silver·ware
silver·weed
sil·very
sil·vi·cul·tur·al
sil·vi·cul·ture tree cultivation
sil·vi·cul·tur·ist
s'il vous plaît French please
sima layer of earth's crust
sima·rou·ba (or ·ru·) tree
sima·rou·ba·ceous (or ·ru·)
Sim·birsk Russian city
Sim·fero·pol Ukrainian city
sim·ian (or simi·ous)
simi·lar
simi·lar·ity (plural ·ities)
simi·lar·ly
simi·le (plural ·les)
si·mili·tude
simi·ous variant of simian
sim·mer
sim·mer·ing·ly
sim·nel cake
si·mo·ni·ac practiser of simony
si·mo·nia·cal
si·mo·nia·cal·ly
si·mon·ist
si·mo·ny
si·moom (or ·moon) wind
simp US simpleton

sim·pa·ti·co
sim·per
sim·per·er
sim·per·ing·ly
sim·ple
simple-minded
simple-minded·ly
simple-minded·ness
sim·ple·ness
sim·ple·ton
sim·plex
sim·pli·ci·den·tate zoology term
sim·plic·ity (*plural* ·ities)
sim·pli·fi·ca·tion
sim·pli·fi·ca·tive
sim·pli·fi·er
sim·pli·fy (·fies, ·fy·ing, ·fied)
sim·plism
sim·plis·tic
sim·plis·ti·cal·ly
Sim·plon Pass
simp·ly
Simp·son Australian desert
simu·la·crum (*plural* ·cra)
simu·lant
simu·lar
simu·late
simu·lated
simu·la·tion
simu·la·tive
simu·la·tor
sim·ul·cast radio–TV broadcast
sim·ul·ta·neous
sim·ul·ta·neous·ly
sim·ul·ta·neous·ness (*or* ·ta·neity)
sin (sin·ning, sinned)
Si·nai Egyptian peninsula
Si·na·it·ic (*or* Si·na·ic)
Si·na·loa Mexican state
sin·an·thro·pus primitive man
sina·pism mustard plaster
Sin·ar·quist Mexican fascist
since
sin·cere
sin·cere·ly
sin·cer·ity (*or* ·cere·ness)
sin·cipi·tal
sin·ci·put (*plural* ·ci·puts *or* ·cipi·ta) part of skull
Sind Pakistani province

Sin·dhi (*plural* ·dhi *or* ·dhis)
sine trigonometry term; *Latin* without
si·necure
si·necur·ism
si·necur·ist
sine die *Latin* without a day fixed
sine qua non *Latin* essential requirement
sin·ew
sin·ewi·ness
sin·ewy
sin·fo·nia (*plural* ·nie) symphony
sin·fo·niet·ta
sin·ful
sin·ful·ly
sin·ful·ness
sing (sing·ing, sang, sung)
sing·able
Sin·ga·pore
Sin·ga·po·rean
singe (singe·ing, singed)
sing·er
sing·ing·ly
sin·gle
single-acting
single-action
single-blind
single-breasted
single-cross
single-decker
single-handed
single-minded
single-minded·ness
single·ness
single-phase
sin·gles tennis match
single-space (*verb*)
single·stick wooden sword
sin·glet
sin·gle·ton
single-track (*adj*)
sin·gly
sing·song
sin·gu·lar
sin·gu·lar·ity (*plural* ·ities)
sin·gu·lari·za·tion (*or* ·sa·tion)
sin·gu·lar·ize (*or* ·ise)
sin·gu·lar·ly
sin·gu·lar·ness
sin·gul·tus hiccup
sinh trigonometry term

Sin·hai·lien (*or* Hsin-hai-lien) Chinese city
Sin·ha·lese (*or* ·gha·; *plural* ·leses *or* ·lese) Sri Lankan
Si·ning (*or* Hsi·ning) Chinese city
sin·is·ter
sin·is·ter·ly
sin·is·ter·ness
sin·is·tral of the left side
sin·is·tral·ly
sin·is·tro·dex·tral
sin·is·tror·sal
sin·is·trorse spiralling right to left
sin·is·trous
Si·nit·ic language group
sink (sink·ing, sank *or* sunk, sunk *or* sunk·en)
sink·able
sink·er
sink·hole
Sinkiang-Uighur Chinese region
sink·ing
sin·less
sin·less·ness
sinned
sin·ner
Sinn Fein
Sinn Fein·er
Sinn Fein·ism
sin·ning
Si·no·logi·cal
Si·nolo·gist
Si·no·logue
Si·nol·ogy study of Chinese
Sino-Tibetan
sin·ter silicaceous deposit
sinu·ate (*or* ·at·ed) botany term
Si·nŭi·ju North Korean port
sinu·os·ity (*or* sinua·tion; *plural* ·ities *or* ·tions)
sinu·ous
sinu·ous·ly
sinu·ous·ness
si·nus (*plural* ·nuses)
si·nusi·tis
si·nus·oid maths term
si·nusoi·dal
Siouan
Sioux (*plural* Sioux)
sip (sip·ping, sipped)

si·phon (*or* sy·)
si·phon·age
si·phon·al (*or* ·ic)
si·pho·no·phore marine animal
si·pho·nopho·rous
si·phono·stele botany term
si·pho·no·stelic
Si·ple Antarctic mountain
sipped
sip·per
sip·pet small piece
sip·ping
sir
sir·dar leader
sire
si·ren
si·renian zoology term
Si·ret European river
Sir·ius star
sir·loin
si·roc·co (*plural* ·cos) wind
sir·rah archaic term of address
sir·ree US exclamation
sir·up US variant spelling of syrup
sir·vente verse form
sis
si·sal
Sisera biblical character
sis·kin bird
sis·sy (*plural* ·sies)
sis·sy·ish
sis·ter
sis·ter·hood
sister-in-law (*plural* sisters-)
sis·ter·li·ness
sis·ter·ly
Sis·tine chapel
sis·troid maths term
sis·trum (*plural* ·tra) musical instrument
Sisy·phean
Sisyphus mythological king
sit (sit·ting, sat)
si·tar musical instrument
si·tar·ist
sit·com
site place; *compare* sight
sit·fast sore on horse
sit-in (*noun*)
si·tol·ogy study of nutrition
si·tos·ter·ol soya-bean extract

sit·ter
sit·ting
situ·ated (*or esp. in legal contexts* ·ate)
situa·tion
situa·tion·al
situ·la (*plural* ·lae) Iron Age container
si·tus (*plural* ·tus) anatomical location
sitz·kreig
sitz·mark skiing term
Siva (*or* Shiva) Hindu god
Si·va·ism
Si·va·ist
Si·vas Turkish city
si·wash Canadian sweater
six
six·ain six-line poem
six·fold
six-footer
six·mo (*plural* ·mos) book size
six·pence
six·penny
sixte fencing position
six·teen
six·teen·mo (*plural* ·mos) book size
six·teenth
sixth
sixth-former
six·ti·eth
six·ty (*plural* ·ties)
siz·able (*or* size·)
siz·able·ness (*or* size·)
siz·ably (*or* size·)
siz·ar maintained student
si·zar·ship
size
sized
siz·er
siz·zle
siz·zler
sjam·bok whip
Ska·gen *variant of* Skaw
Skag·er·rak Scandinavian channel
skald (*or* scald) Scandinavian bard
skat card game
skate (*noun, verb*) sport
skate (*plural* skate *or* skates) fish
skate·board

skate·board·er
skat·er
skat·ing
skat·ole organic compound
Skaw (*or* Ska·gen) Danish cape
skean dagger
ske·dad·dle
skeet clay-pigeon shooting
skeg nautical term
skein
skel·etal
skel·etal·ly
skel·eton
skel·eton·ize (*or* ·ise)
skelf *Dialect* wood splinter
skel·ly (*plural* ·lies) fish
Skel·mers·dale Merseyside town
kelp *Dialect* slap; metal tube
sken (sken·ing, skenned) *Dialect* squint
skep beehive
skep·tic US spelling of sceptic
sker·rick US small fragment
sker·ry (*plural* ·ries) *Scot* small island
sket (sket·ting, sket·ted) *Welsh* splash
sketch
sketch·able
sketch·book
sketch·er
sketchi·ly
sketchi·ness
sketchy (sketchi·er, sketchi·est)
skew
skew·back
skew·bald
skew·er long pin; *compare* skua
skew·ness
skew·whiff
ski (*verb* skis, ski·ing, skied *or* ski'd; *noun, plural* skis)
ski·able
skia·scope eye-examining instrument
ski·as·co·py
ski·bob
ski·bob·ber
ski·bob·bing

skid (skid·ding, skid·ded)

skid·lid *Slang* crash helmet

skid·pan

skid·proof

skid·way *US* platform for logs

skied

ski·er one who skis; *compare* skyer

skiff

skif·fle

ski·ing

ski·jor·er

ski·jor·ing snow sport

skil·ful (*US* skill·)

skil·ful·ly (*US* skill·)

skil·ful·ness (*US* skill·)

skill

skilled

skil·let

skill·ful *US* spelling of skilful

skil·ling coin

skil·lion *Austral* lean-to

skil·ly thin soup

skim (skim·ming, skimmed)

skim·mer

skim·mia shrub

skim·mings

skimp

skimpi·ly

skimpi·ness

skimpy (skimpi·er, skimpi·est)

skin (skin·ning, skinned)

skin-deep

skin-diver

skin·flint

skin·ful

skin·head

skink lizard

skin·less

skinned

skin·ner

skin·ni·ness

skin·ning

skin·ny (·ni·er, ·ni·est)

skint

skin·tight

skip (skip·ping, skipped)

skip·jack (*plural* ·jacks or ·jack) fish

ski·plane

skip·per

skip·pet box for document

skip·ping

skipping-rope

Skip·ton Yorkshire town

skirl *Dialect* play bagpipes

skir·mish

skir·mish·er

skirr move rapidly

skir·ret plant

skirt

skirt·er *Austral* fleece trimmer

skirt·ing

skit

skite *Austral* boast

skit·ter

skit·tish

skit·tish·ly

skit·tish·ness

skit·tle

skive

skiv·er

skiv·vy (*noun, plural* ·vies; *verb* ·vies, ·vy·ing, ·vied)

skoal drinking toast

skoki·aan South African liquor

Skop·je Macedonian capital

(skrimshank) *incorrect spelling of* scrimshank

skua bird; *compare* skewer

skul·dug·gery

skulk

skulk·er

skull head bones; *compare* scull

skull·cap

skunk (*plural* skunk or skunks)

sky (*noun, plural* skies; *verb* skies, sky·ing, skied)

sky·dive (·div·ing, ·dived (*US* dove), dived)

sky·div·er

Skye Scottish island

sky·er one who skies; *compare* skier

sky-high

sky·jack

sky·jack·er

Sky·lab *US* space station

sky·lark

sky·lark·er

sky·light

sky·line

sky·rocket

Sky·ros (*or* Scy·) Greek island

sky·sail

sky·scape

sky·scraper

sky·wards (*or esp. US* ·ward)

sky·writer

sky·writing

slab (slab·bing, slabbed)

slab·ber *Dialect* slobber

slack

slack·en

slack·er

slack·ness

slacks

slag (slag·ging, slagged)

slag·gy

slain

slais·ter *Scot* confused mess

slak·able (*or* slake·)

slake

slak·er

sla·lom skiing race; *compare* shalom

slam (slam·ming, slammed)

slan·der

slan·der·er

slan·der·ous

slan·der·ous·ness

slang

slangi·ly

slangi·ness

slangy

slant

slant·ing

slant·ing·ly (*or* slant·ly)

slant·wise (*or* ·ways)

slap (slap·ping, slapped)

slap-bang

slap·dash

slap-happy (·happier, ·happiest)

slap·jack card game

slap·per

slap·shot ice hockey shot

slap·stick

slap-up (*adj*)

slash

slash·er

slash·ing·ly

slat (slat·ting, slat·ted)

slate

slat·er

slath·er *Slang* large quantity

slati·ness
slat·ing
slat·tern
slat·tern·li·ness
slat·tern·ly
slaty (slati·er, slati·est)
slaugh·ter
slaugh·ter·er
slaughter·house
slaughter·man (*plural* ·men)
slaugh·ter·ous
Slav
slave
slave-drive (-driving, -drove, -driven)
slave-driver
slav·er
slav·er·er
slav·ery
slav·ey servant
Slav·ic *variant of* Slavonic
slav·ish
slav·ish·ly
slav·ish·ness
slav·oc·ra·cy (*plural* ·cies) domination by slaveholders
Sla·vo·nia Croatian region
Sla·vo·nian
Sla·von·ic (*or* Slav·ic) language
Slavo·phile (*or* ·phil)
Sla·vophi·lism
slay (slay·ing, slew, slain) kill; *compare* sleigh
slay·er
sleave tangled thread; *compare* sleeve
slea·zi·ly
slea·zi·ness
slea·zy (·zi·er, ·zi·est)
sled (sled·ding, sled·ded) *variant* (*esp. US*) *of* sledge
sled·der
sledge (*or esp. US* sled)
sledge·hammer
sleek
sleek·ness
sleep (sleep·ing, slept)
sleep·er
sleepi·ly
sleepi·ness
sleep·less
sleep·less·ly

sleep·less·ness
sleep·walk
sleep·walk·er
sleep·walk·ing
sleepy (sleepi·er, sleepi·est)
sleepy·head
sleet
sleety
sleeve covering; *compare* sleave
sleeve·less
sleev·ing wire insulation
sleigh sledge; *compare* slay
sleigh·er
sleight trick; *compare* slight
slen·der
slen·der·ize (*or* ·ise)
slen·der·ness
slept
sleuth
sleuth·hound
slew *past tense of* slay
slew (*US also* slue) twist
slice
slice·able
slic·er
slick
slick·en·side geology term
slick·er
slick·ly
slick·ness
slid
slid·able
slide (slid·ing, slid *or* slid·den)
slide-action
slid·er
slid·ing
sli·er *variant spelling of* slyer
sli·est *variant spelling of* slyest
slight small; snub; *compare* sleight
slight·ing
slight·ing·ly
slight·ly
slight·ness
Sli·go Irish county
sli·ly *variant spelling of* slyly
slim (*adj* slim·mer, slim·mest; *verb* slim·ming, slimmed)
slime
slimi·ly
slimi·ness

slim·mer
slim·ming
slim·ness
slim·sy *US* frail
slimy (slimi·er, slimi·est)
sling (sling·ing, slung)
sling·back
sling·er
sling·shot
slink (slink·ing, slunk)
slinki·ly
slinki·ness
slink·ing·ly
slinky (slinki·er, slinki·est)
slip (slip·ping, slipped)
slip·case
slip·knot
slip·noose
slip-on (*adj, noun*)
slip·over
slip·page
slip·per
slip·pered
slip·peri·ness
slipper·wort
slip·pery
slip·pi·ness
slip·ping·ly
slip·py (·pi·er, ·pi·est)
slip·sheet
slip·shod
slip·shoddi·ness (*or* ·shod·ness)
slip·slop
slip·stream
slip-up (*noun*)
slip·way
slit (slit·ting, slit)
slith·er
slith·ery
slit·ter
sliv·er
sliv·er·er
slivo·vitz plum brandy
slob
slob·ber
slob·ber·er
slob·bery
sloe fruit; *compare* slow
sloe-eyed
slog (slog·ging, slogged)
slo·gan
slo·gan·eer
slog·ger
sloop

sloop-rigged
sloot ditch
slop (slop•ping, slopped)
slope
slop•er
slop•ing
slop•ing•ly
slop•pi•ly
slop•pi•ness
slop•py (•pi•er, •pi•est)
slops
slop•work
slop•worker
slosh
sloshy
slot (slot•ting, slot•ted)
sloth
sloth•ful
sloth•ful•ly
sloth•ful•ness
slot•ter
slouch
slouch•er
slouchi•ly
slouchi•ness
slouch•ing•ly
slouchy
Slough Berkshire town
slough bog; to shed
sloughy
Slo•vak (or •vak•ian)
Slo•vakia E European
    country
slov•en
Slo•vene (or •venian)
Slo•venia SE European
    country
slov•en•li•ness
slov•en•ly
slow not fast, etc.; compare
    sloe
slow•coach
slow•down
slow•ly
slow•ness
slow•poke US slowcoach
slow-witted
slow•worm
slub (slub•bing, slubbed)
    lump in yarn; twist
    fibre
slub•ber•de•gul•lion
    slovenly person
sludge
sludgy

slue (slu•ing, slued) US
    variant spelling of slew
slug (slug•ging, slugged)
sluga•bed
slug•gard
slug•gard•li•ness
slug•gard•ly
slug•ger
slug•gish
slug•gish•ness
sluice
sluice-gate
slum (slum•ming,
    slummed)
slum•ber
slum•ber•er
slum•ber•ing•ly
slum•ber•less
slum•ber•ous
slum•ber•ous•ness
slum•mer
slum•my (•mi•er, •mi•est)
slump
slung
slunk
slur (slur•ring, slurred)
slurp
slur•ry (plural •ries)
slush
slushi•ness
slushy
slut
slut•tish
slut•tish•ness
sly (sly•er, sly•est or sli•er,
    sli•est)
sly•ly (or sli•)
sly•ness
slype passageway in
    cathedral
smack
smack•er
small
small•boy steward's
    assistant
small•holder
small•holding
small•ish
small-minded
small-minded•ly
small-minded•ness
small•ness
small•pox
smalls underwear
small-scale

smalt blue glass; pigment
smalt•ite mineral
smal•to (plural •tos or •ti)
    mosaic pieces
sma•rag•dite mineral
smarm
smarmy (smarmi•er,
    smarmi•est)
smart
smart•en
smartie clever person
smart•ing•ly
smart•ish
smart•ness
smash
smash•able
smash•er
smash•ing
smash-up (noun)
smat•ter
smat•ter•er
smat•ter•ing
smaze US smoky haze
smear
smear•er
smeari•ness
smeary (smeari•er,
    smeari•est)
smec•tic chemistry term
smeg•ma sebum
smell (smell•ing, smelt or
    smelled)
smelli•ness
smelly (smelli•er,
    smelli•est)
smelt (plural smelt or
    smelts) extract metal; fish
smel•ter
smelt•ery (plural •eries)
smew duck
smid•gen (or •gin)
smi•la•ca•ceous botany
    term
smi•lax shrub
smile
smil•er
smil•ing•ly
smil•ing•ness
smirch
smirch•er
smirk
smirk•er
smirk•ing•ly
smit (or smit•tle) Dialect
    infection

smite (smit·ing, smote, smit·ten or smit)
smit·er
smith
smith·er·eens
smith·ery (plural ·eries)
Smith·so·nian US museum
smith·son·ite mineral
smithy (plural smithies)
smit·ten
smock
smock·ing
smog
smog·gy
smok·able (or smoke·)
smoke
smoke·house
smoke·jack spit-turning device
smoke·less
smok·er
smoke·stack
smoki·ly
smoki·ness
smok·ing
smo·ko (or smoke·ho; plural ·kos or ·hos) Austral teabreak
smoky (smoki·er, smoki·est)
smol·der US spelling of smoulder
Smo·lensk Russian city
smolt young salmon
smooch
smoodge Austral smooch
smooth
smooth·able
smooth·bore
smooth·en
smooth·er
smooth-faced
smoothie
smooth·ness
smooth-spoken
smooth-tongued
smor·gas·bord Scandinavian hors d'oeuvres
smote
smoth·er
smoth·ery
smoul·der (US smol·)
smri·ti Hindu literature
smudge

smudgi·ly (or smudg·ed·ly)
smudgi·ness
smudgy (smudgi·er, smudgi·est)
smug (smug·ger, smug·gest)
smug·gle
smug·gler
smug·gling
smug·ly
smug·ness
smut (smut·ting, smut·ted)
smutch smudge
smutchy
smut·ti·ly
smut·ti·ness
smut·ty (·ti·er, ·ti·est)
Smyr·na ancient Asian city
snack
snack·ette snack bar
snaf·fle
sna·fu (·fues, ·fu·ing, ·fued) US chaos; make chaotic
snag (snag·ging, snagged)
snaggle·tooth (plural ·teeth)
snag·gy
snail
snail-like
snake
snake·bite
snake·like
snake·mouth orchid
snake·root
snake·skin
snaki·ly
snaki·ness
snaky (snaki·er, snaki·est)
snap (snap·ping, snapped)
snap·back
snap·dragon
snap·pable
snap·per
snap·pi·ly
snap·pi·ness
snap·ping·ly
snap·py (·pi·er, ·pi·est)
snap·shot
snare
snar·er
snar·ing·ly
snarl
snarl·er
snarl·ing·ly
snarl-up (noun)
snarly

snatch
snatch·er
snatchi·ly
snatchy (snatchi·er, snatchi·est) spasmodic
snath (or snathe) scythe handle
snaz·zi·ly
snaz·zi·ness
snaz·zy (·zi·er, ·zi·est)
sneak
sneak·ers shoes
sneaki·ly
sneaki·ness
sneak·ing
sneak·ing·ly
sneak·ing·ness
sneaky (sneaki·er, sneaki·est)
sneck wall stone; latch
sned (sned·ding, sned·ded) Dialect to prune
sneer
sneer·er
sneer·ing
sneer·ing·ly
sneeze
sneez·er
sneeze·wort
sneezy
snib Scot door fastening
snick
snick·er
snick·et Dialect passageway
snide
snide·ness
sniff
sniff·er
sniffi·ly
sniffi·ness
sniff·ing·ly
snif·fle
snif·fler
snif·fy (·fi·er, ·fi·est)
snif·ter
snig·ger
snig·ger·ing·ly
snig·gle catch eels
snig·gler
snip (snip·ping, snipped)
snipe (plural snipe or snipes) bird; to attack
snipe·fish (plural ·fish or ·fishes)
snip·er

sniper•scope
snip•pet
snip•pi•ly
snip•pi•ness (or •peti•ness)
snip•py (•pi•er, •pi•est)
snips shears
snitch
sniv•el (•el•ling, •elled; US •el•ing, •eled)
sniv•el•ler (US •el•er)
sniv•el•ly
snob
snob•bery
snob•bish
snob•bish•ness (or •bism)
Sno-Cat (Trademark)
snog (snog•ging, snogged)
snood
snook rude gesture
snook (plural snook or snooks) fish
snook•er
snoop
snoop•er
snooper•scope
snoopy
snoot Slang nose
snooti•ly
snooti•ness
snooty (snooti•er, snooti•est)
snooze
snooz•er
snoozy
snore
snor•er
snor•kel
snort
snort•er
snort•ing•ly
snot
snot•ti•ly
snot•ti•ness
snot•ty (noun, plural •ties; adj •ti•er, •ti•est)
snout
snout•ed
snout•like
snow
snow•ball
snow•ball•ing
snow•berry (plural •berries)
snow•bird
snow•blind
snow•blind•ness

snow•blink reflection from snow
snow•bound
snow•cap
snow•capped
Snow•don
Snow•donia
snow•drift
snow•drop
snow•fall
snow•field
snow•flake
snowi•ly
snowi•ness
snow•man (plural •men)
snow•mobile
snow•plough
snow•shed
snow•shoe (•shoe•ing, •shoed)
snow•sho•er
snow•storm
snow-white
snowy (snowi•er, snowi•est)
snub (snub•bing, snubbed)
snub•ber
snub•bing•ly
snub•by
snub-nosed
snuff
snuff•box
snuf•fer
snuffi•ness
snuff•ing•ly
snuf•fle
snuf•fler
snuf•fly
snuffy (snuffi•er, snuffi•est) unpleasant
snug (adj snug•ger, snug•gest; verb snug•ging, snugged)
snug•gery (plural •geries)
snug•gle
snug•ness
snye river channel
so
soak
soak•age
soak•er
soak•ing
soak•ing•ly
so-and-so (plural so-and-sos)

soap
soap•bark
soap•berry (plural •berries)
soap•box
soapi•ly
soapi•ness
soap•less
soapo•lal•lie drink
soap•stone (or •rock)
soap•suds
soap•sudsy
soap•wort
soapy (soapi•er, soapi•est)
soar
soar•er
soar•ing•ly
sob (sob•bing, sobbed)
sob•ber
sob•bing•ly
so•beit Archaic provided that
so•ber
so•ber•ing•ly
so•ber•ness
so•bri•ety
so•bri•quet (or sou•)
soc•age legal term
soc•ag•er
so-called (adj)
soc•cer
So•che (or So-ch'e) Chinese town
So•chi Russian city
so•cia•bil•ity (or •ble•ness)
so•cia•ble
so•cia•bly
so•cial
so•cial•ism
so•cial•ist
so•cial•is•tic
so•cial•is•ti•cal•ly
so•cial•ite
so•ci•al•ity (plural •ities)
so•cial•iz•able (or •is•able)
so•ciali•za•tion (or •sa•tion)
so•cial•ize (or •ise)
so•cial•iz•er (or •is•er)
so•cial•ly
so•cial•ness
so•ci•etal
so•ci•ety (plural •eties)
So•cin•ian
So•cini•an•ism religious doctrine
so•cio•biolo•gy

so·cio·eco·nom·ic
so·cio·eco·nomi·cal·ly
so·cio·lin·guist
so·cio·lin·guis·tic
so·cio·lin·guis·tics
so·cio·logi·cal
so·ci·olo·gist
so·ci·ol·ogy
so·cio·met·ric
so·ci·om·etrist
so·ci·om·etry
so·cio·path
so·ci·o·path·ic
so·ci·opa·thy
so·cio·po·liti·cal
sock
sock·dolo·ger (or ·dola·) US decisive blow
sock·et
sock·eye salmon
so·cle plinth
soc·man (or soke·; plural ·men) tenant
So·crat·ic (or ·crati·cal)
sod (sod·ding, sod·ded)
soda
so·da·lite mineral
so·dal·ity (plural ·ities) Catholic society
so·da·mide chemical compound
sod·den
sod·den·ness
sod·ding
so·dium
Sod·om biblical city
sodo·mite
sodo·mize (or ·mise)
sodo·my
so·ever
sofa
so·far marine locating system
sof·fit architectural term
So·fia Bulgarian capital
soft
sof·ta Muslim student
soft·ball
soft-boiled
sof·ten
sof·ten·er
soft-finned
soft-headed
soft-hearted
soft-hearted·ness

softie variant spelling of softy
soft·ness
soft-pedal (-pedalling, -pedalled; US -pedaling, -pedaled)
soft-soap (verb)
soft-spoken
soft·ware
soft·wood
softy (or softie; plural softies)
sog·gi·ly
sog·gi·ness
sog·gy (·gi·er, ·gi·est)
soh (or so) musical note
Soho
soi-disant French so-called
soi·gné (fem ·gnée) well-groomed
soil
soil·age green fodder
soil·less
soi·ree
so·journ
so·journ·er
soke legal term
sol colloid
sol (plural sols or so·les) Peruvian currency
sol·ace
sol·ac·er
sola·na·ceous botany term
so·lan·der botanical box
so·la·num plant
so·lar
so·lar·im·eter
so·lar·ium (plural ·laria or ·lar·iums)
so·lari·za·tion (or ·sa·tion)
so·lar·ize (or ·ise)
sold
sol·dan Archaic sultan
sol·der
sol·der·able
sol·der·er
sol·dier
sol·dier·li·ness
sol·dier·ly
sol·diery (plural ·dieries)
sole only; underside of foot or shoe; compare soul
sole (plural sole or soles) fish; compare soul
sol·ecism
sol·ecist

sol·ecis·tic (or ·ti·cal)
sole·ly
sol·emn
so·lem·ni·fi·ca·tion
so·lem·ni·fy (·fies, ·fy·ing, ·fied)
so·lem·nity (plural ·nities)
sol·em·ni·za·tion (or ·sa·tion)
sol·em·nize (or ·nise)
sol·em·niz·er (or ·nis·er)
sol·emn·ness (or ·em·ness)
so·leno·don animal
so·lenoid
so·lenoi·dal
So·lent English strait
sol-fa musical system
sol·fa·ta·ra volcanic vent
sol·fa·ta·ric
sol·feg·gio (or ·fège; plural ·feg·gi, feg·gios, or ·fèges) musical term
sol·fe·ri·no reddish-purple
soli musical term
so·lic·it
so·lici·ta·tion
so·lici·tor
So·lici·tor Gen·er·al (plural So·lici·tors Gen·er·al)
so·lici·tor·ship
so·lici·tous
so·lici·tous·ly
so·lici·tous·ness
so·lici·tude
sol·id
soli·da·go (plural ·gos) plant
soli·dar·ity (plural ·ities)
soli·dary united by interests
so·lidi·fi·able
so·lidi·fi·ca·tion
so·lidi·fi·er
so·lidi·fy (·fies, ·fy·ing, ·fied)
so·lid·ity
sol·id·ness
solid-state (adj)
soli·dus (plural ·di) oblique stroke in text
soli·fid·ian religious term
soli·fluc·tion (or ·flux·ion) soil movement
So·li·hull English town
so·lilo·quist (or ·quiz·er, ·quis·er)
so·lilo·quize (or ·quise)

sophomore

so·lilo·quy (*plural* ·quies)
So·ling·en German city
sol·ip·sism
sol·ip·sist
sol·ip·sis·tic
soli·taire game; gem
soli·tari·ly
soli·tari·ness
soli·tary (*plural* ·taries)
soli·tude
soli·tu·di·nous
sol·ler·et part of armour
sol·mi·za·tion (*or* ·sa·tion) musical term
solo (*plural* solos *or* soli)
so·lo·ist
Solo·mon Is·lands
sol·on·chak soil
solo·netz (*or* ·nets) soil
So·lo·thurn Swiss town
sol·stice
sol·sti·tial
sol·ubil·ity (*plural* ·ities)
solu·bil·ize (*or* ·ise)
sol·uble
sol·uble·ness
sol·ubly
so·lum (*plural* ·lums *or* ·la) soil layer
so·lute
so·lu·tion
So·lu·trean Palaeolithic culture
solv·abil·ity (*or* ·able·ness)
solv·able
solv·ate
solva·tion
Solvay pro·cess
solve
sol·ven·cy
sol·vent
solv·er
sol·voly·sis chemistry term
Sol·way Firth
soma (*plural* soma·ta *or* somas) biology term
So·ma·li (*plural* ·lis *or* ·li)
So·ma·lia African republic
So·ma·lian
So·ma·li·land former African region
so·mat·ic of the body
so·mati·cal·ly
so·ma·to·log·ic (*or* ·logi·cal)

so·ma·tolo·gist
so·ma·tol·ogy
so·ma·to·plasm
so·ma·to·plas·tic
so·ma·to·pleu·ral (*or* ·ric)
so·ma·to·pleure embryonic tissue
so·ma·to·type
som·bre (*US* ·ber)
som·bre·ly (*US* ·ber·)
som·bre·ness (*US* ·ber·)
som·brero (*plural* ·breros)
som·brous
some
some·body (*plural* ·bodies)
some·day
some·how
some·one
some·place
som·er·sault (*or* sum·mer·sault)
Som·er·set
some·thing
some·time (*adv, adj*)
some·times
some·way
some·what
some·where
some·wise somehow
so·mi·tal (*or* ·mit·ic)
so·mite embryonic tissue
Somme French river
som·melier wine steward
som·nam·bu·lance
som·nam·bu·lant
som·nam·bu·late
som·nam·bu·la·tion
som·nam·bu·la·tor
som·nam·bu·lism
som·nam·bu·list
som·nam·bu·lis·tic
som·nilo·quy (*plural* ·quies) talking in one's sleep
som·no·lence (*or* ·len·cy)
som·no·lent
son
so·nance
so·nant phonetics term
so·nant·al (*or* ·nan·tic)
so·nar
so·na·ta
sona·ti·na
son·dage archaeological trench

sonde observing device
sone unit
son et lu·mi·ère
song
song·bird
song·ful
song·ful·ly
song·ful·ness
Son·ghai (*plural* ·ghai *or* ·ghais) African people
song·ster (*fem* ·stress)
song·writer
son·ic
so·nif·er·ous
son-in-law (*plural* sons-)
son·net
son·net·eer
son·ny (*plural* ·nies)
so·no·buoy
So·no·ra Mexican state
so·nor·ity
so·no·rous
so·no·rous·ness
Soo·chow (*or* Su-chou) Chinese city
sook *Dialect* coward
soon
soon·er
soot
sooth *Archaic* truth
soothe
sooth·er
sooth·ing
sooth·ing·ly
sooth·say (·say·ing, ·said)
sooth·say·er
sooti·ly
sooti·ness
sooty (sooti·er, sooti·est)
sop (sop·ping, sopped)
soph·ism
soph·ist
soph·ist·er second-year undergraduate
so·phis·tic (*or* ·ti·cal)
so·phis·ti·cal·ly
so·phis·ti·cate
so·phis·ti·cat·ed
so·phis·ti·ca·tion
so·phis·ti·ca·tor
soph·ist·ry (*plural* ·ries)
sopho·more *US* second-year student

So·phy (*or* **So·phi**; *plural* **·phies**) title of Persian kings
so·por stupor
sopo·rif·er·ous
sopo·rif·ic
sopo·rifi·cal·ly
sopped
sop·pi·ly
sop·pi·ness
sop·ping
sop·py (**·pi·er**, **·pi·est**)
so·pra·ni·no (*plural* **·nos**)
so·pra·no (*plural* **·nos** *or* **·ni**)
sora bird
sorb tree
sor·befa·cient causing absorption
sor·bet
sorb·ic acid
sor·bi·tol
Sor·bonne French university
sor·bose sugar
sor·cer·er (*fem* **·ess**)
sor·cer·ous
sor·cery (*plural* **·ceries**)
sor·did
sor·did·ness
sor·di·no (*plural* **·ni**) musical term
sore
so·redium (*plural* **·redia**) botany term
sore·head *US* peevish person
sore·ly
sore·ness
sor·ghum cereal crop
sor·go (*or* **·gho**; *plural* **·gos** *or* **·ghos**) fodder crop
sori *plural of* **sorus**
sori·cine shrewlike
so·ri·tes logic term
so·riti·cal (*or* **·rit·ic**)
sorn *Scot* scrounge hospitality
So·ro·ca·ba Brazilian city
so·ror·ate marriage custom
so·rori·cid·al
so·rori·cide
so·ror·ity (*plural* **·ities**)
so·ro·sis (*plural* **·ses**) botany term
sorp·tion adsorption or absorption
sor·rel

Sor·ren·to Italian port
sor·ri·ly
sor·ri·ness
sor·row
sor·row·er
sor·row·ful
sor·row·ful·ly
sor·row·ful·ness
sor·ry (**·ri·er**, **·ri·est**)
sort
sort·able
sort·er
sor·tie (**·tie·ing**, **·tied**)
sor·ti·lege divination by drawing lots
sor·ti·tion casting lots
so·rus (*plural* **·ri**) spore-producing structure
Sos·no·wiec Polish town
so-so
sos·te·nu·to musical term
sot
so·te·ri·ol·ogy doctrine of salvation
So·thic of Sirius
So·tho (*plural* **·tho** *or* **·thos**) African people
sot·tish
sot·to voce
sou coin
sou·bise onion sauce
sou·brette pert girl
sou·bri·quet *variant spelling of* **sobriquet**
sou·chong tea
Sou·dan *French* Sudan
souf·fle medical term
souf·flé light dish
sough sighing sound
sought
soul spirit; *compare* **sole**
soul-destroy·ing
soul·ful
soul·ful·ly
soul·ful·ness
soul·less
soul·less·ly
soul·less·ness
soul-searching
sound
sound·able
sound·box
sound·er
sound·ing
sound·less

sound·less·ness
sound·ly
sound·ness
sound·post musical term
sound·proof
sound·track
soup
soup·çon *French* slight amount
soup·fin shark
soupy (**soupi·er**, **soupi·est**)
sour
source
sour·dine organ stop
sour·ish
sour·ly
sour·ness
sour·puss
sour·sop fruit
sou·sa·phone
sou·sa·phon·ist
souse
sous·lik (*or* **sus·**) animal
Sousse Tunisian port
sou·tache braid
sou·tane cassock
sout·er *Scot* cobbler
sou·ter·rain underground chamber
south
South·amp·ton
south·bound
South·down sheep
south·east
south·easter
south·easter·ly (*plural* **·lies**)
south·eastern
south·eastern·most
south·eastward (*adj*)
south·eastwards (*adv*)
South·end-on-Sea Essex town
south·er
south·er·li·ness
south·er·ly (*plural* **·lies**)
south·ern
south·ern·er
south·ern·most
southern·wood
south·ing navigation term
south·paw
South Pole
South·port
south-southeast
south-southwest

south•ward (*adj*)
south•wards (*adv*)
South•wark London
  borough
south•west
south•wester strong wind
south•wester•ly (*plural* •lies)
south•western
south•western•most
south•westward (*adj*)
south•westwards (*adv*)
sou•venir
sou'•west•er hat
sov•er•eign
sov•er•eign•ty (*plural* •ties)
So•vetsk Russian town
So•vi•et of the former USSR
so•vi•et a former Soviet
  council
so•vi•et•ism
so•vi•et•ist
so•vi•et•is•tic
so•vi•eti•za•tion (*or*
  •sa•tion)
so•vi•et•ize (*or* •ise)
sov•khoz (*plural* •kho•zy)
  state farm
sov•ran *Poetic* sovereign
sow female pig
sow (sow•ing, sowed, sown
  or sowed) plant seed;
  compare sew
sow•bread plant
sow•er
So•we•to South African
  suburb
sow•ing
sown
soya bean (*US* soy•bean)
soy sauce
So•yuz Russian spacecraft
soz•zled
spa mineral spring; *compare*
  spar
space
space•band printing term
space•bar
space•craft
space•less
space•man (*plural* •men)
space•port
spac•er
space•ship
space•suit
space-time physics term

space•walk
space•woman (*plural*
  •women)
spac•ing
spa•cious roomy; *compare*
  specious
spa•cious•ness
spade
spade•fish (*plural* •fish *or*
  •fishes)
spade•ful (*plural* •fuls)
spad•er
spade•work
spa•di•ceous
spa•dix (*plural* •di•ces)
  botany term
spae *Scot* foretell
spa•ghet•ti
Spain
spake
spall rock splinter
spalla•tion nuclear reaction
spal•peen *Irish* rascal
Spam (*Trademark*)
span (span•ning, spanned)
span•cel (•cel•ling, •celled;
  US •cel•ing, •celed)
  fettering rope
span•drel (*or* •dril)
  architectural term
spang *US* exactly
span•gle
span•gly
Span•iard
span•iel
Span•ish
Spanish-American
spank
spank•er
spank•ing
span•ner
spar (spar•ring, sparred)
  fight; nautical gear;
  mineral; *compare* spa
spar•able small nail
spare
spare•ly
spare•ness
spar•er
spare•rib
sparge sprinkle
spar•id (*or* •oid) fish
spar•ing frugal; *compare*
  sparring
spar•ing•ly

spar•ing•ness
spark
spar•kle
spar•kler
spar•ling (*plural* •lings *or*
  •ling) fish
spar•ring fighting; *compare*
  sparing
spar•row
sparrow-grass *Dialect*
  asparagus
sparrow-hawk
spar•ry geology term
sparse
sparse•ly
sparse•ness (*or* spar•sity)
Spar•ta
Spar•tan
Spar•tan•ism
spar•teine alkaloid
spasm
spas•mod•ic (*or* •modi•cal)
spas•modi•cal•ly
spas•tic
spas•ti•cal•ly
spat *past tense of* spit
spat (spat•ting, spat•ted)
  quarrel
spatch•cock
spate
spa•tha•ceous
spathe botany term
spathed
spath•ic (*or* •ose)
  mineralogy term
spa•tial (*or* •cial)
spa•ti•al•ity
spa•tial•ly
spa•tio•tem•por•al
spat•ter
spatu•la
spatu•lar
spatu•late
spav•in
spav•ined
spawn
spawn•er
spay
speak (speak•ing, spoke,
  spo•ken)
speak•able
speak•easy (*plural* •easies)
speak•er
speak•er•ship
speak•ing

spear
spear·er
spear·head
spear·mint
spear·wort
spec speculation
spe·cial
spe·cial·ism
spe·cial·ist
spe·cial·is·tic
spe·ci·al·ity (US ·ty; plural
·ities) special skill; compare
specialty
spe·ciali·za·tion (or
·sa·tion)
spe·cial·ize (or ·ise)
spe·cial·ly
spe·cial·ness
spe·cial·ty (plural ·ties) legal
term; medical speciality;
US spelling of speciality
spe·cia·tion biology term
spe·cie coin money
spe·cies (plural ·cies)
speci·fi·able
spe·cif·ic
spe·cifi·cal·ly
speci·fi·ca·tion
speci·fi·ca·tive
speci·fic·ity
speci·fi·er
speci·fy (·fies, ·fy·ing,
·fied)
speci·men
spe·ci·os·ity (plural ·ities)
spe·cious deceptively
plausible; compare
spacious
spe·cious·ly
spe·cious·ness
speck
speck·le
specs Slang spectacles
spec·ta·cle
spec·ta·cled
spec·ta·cles
spec·tacu·lar
spec·tacu·lar·ly
spec·ta·tor
spec·tra plural of spectrum
spec·tral
spec·tral·ity (or ·tral·ness)
spec·tral·ly
spec·tre (US ·ter)
spec·tro·bo·lom·eter

spec·tro·bolo·met·ric
spec·tro·graph
spec·tro·graph·ic
spec·tro·graphi·cal·ly
spec·trog·ra·phy
spec·tro·he·lio·graph
spec·tro·he·lio·graph·ic
spec·tro·he·lio·scope
spec·tro·he·lio·scop·ic
spec·trom·eter
spec·tro·met·ric
spec·trom·etry
spec·tro·pho·tom·eter
spec·tro·photo·met·ric
spec·tro·pho·tom·etry
spec·tro·scope
spec·tro·scop·ic (or
·scopi·cal)
spec·tro·scopi·cal·ly
spec·tros·co·pist
spec·tros·co·py
spec·trum (plural ·tra)
specu·lar
specu·late
specu·la·tion
specu·la·tive
specu·la·tive·ly
specu·la·tive·ness
specu·la·tor
specu·lum (plural ·la or
·lums)
sped
speech
speechi·fi·ca·tion
speechi·fi·er
speechi·fy (·fies, ·fy·ing,
·fied)
speech·less
speech·less·ly
speech·less·ness
speed (speed·ing, sped or
speed·ed)
speed·boat
speed·er
speedi·ly
speedi·ness
speedo (plural speedos)
Slang speedometer
speed·om·eter
speed·ster
speed·way
speed·well
Speed·writing (Trademark)
speedy (speedi·er,
speedi·est)

speel Dialect wood splinter;
compare spiel
speiss smelting term
spe·laean (or ·lean) of caves
spe·leo·logi·cal (or ·laeo·)
spe·leolo·gist (or ·laeolo·)
spe·leol·ogy (or ·laeol·)
study of caves
spelk Dialect wood
splinter
spell (spell·ing, spelt or
spelled)
spell·able
spell·bind (·bind·ing,
·bound)
spell·bind·er
spell·bound
spell·er
spell·ing
spelt wheat; past tense of
spell
spel·ter impure zinc
spe·lunk·er cave explorer
spe·lunk·ing
spence Dialect larder
spen·cer short coat; vest
Spen·cer Gulf
spend (spend·ing, spent)
spend·able
spend·er
spend·thrift
Spen·serian of the poet
Spenser
spent
spe·os temple
sperm (plural sperm or
sperms)
sper·ma·ceti waxy
substance
sper·mary (plural ·maries)
sperm-producing organ
sper·ma·the·ca
sper·ma·the·cal
sper·mat·ic
sper·ma·tid immature
sperm
sper·ma·tium (plural ·tia)
sper·mato·cyte
sper·mato·gen·esis
sper·ma·to·genet·ic
sper·mato·go·nial
sper·mato·go·nium (plural
·nia)
sper·ma·topho·ral
sper·mato·phore

sper·ma·to·phyte seed
  plant
sper·ma·to·phyt·ic
sper·ma·tor·rhoea (US
  ·rhea)
sper·ma·to·zo·al (or ·an,
  ·ic)
sper·ma·to·zo·id botany
  term
sper·ma·to·zo·on (plural
  ·zoa)
sper·mic
sper·mi·ci·dal
sper·mi·cide
sperm·ine biochemical
  compound
sper·mio·gen·esis
sper·mio·genet·ic
sper·mo·go·nium (plural
  ·nia)
sper·mo·phile animal
sper·mous
sperry·lite mineral
spes·sar·tite mineral
spew
spew·er
Spey Scottish river
sphag·nous
sphag·num
sphal·er·ite mineral
sphene mineral
sphe·nic wedge-shaped
sphe·no·don lizard
sphe·noid (noun) bone
sphe·noid (or ·noi·dal; adj)
  wedge-shaped
spher·al
sphere
spheri·cal (or spher·ic)
spheri·cal·ly
spheri·cal·ness
sphe·ric·ity
spher·ics (US sfer·ics)
  atmospherics
sphe·roid
sphe·roi·dal
sphe·roi·dic·ity
sphe·rom·eter
spheru·lar
spheru·le tiny sphere
spheru·lite geology term
spheru·lit·ic
sphery Poetic spherelike;
  starlike
sphinc·ter

sphinc·ter·al
sphin·go·my·elin
sphin·go·sine
Sphinx mythological
  monster
sphinx (plural sphinxes or
  sphin·ges) Egyptian statue
sphra·gis·tic
sphra·gis·tics study of
  seals
sphyg·mic of the pulse
sphyg·mo·graph
sphyg·mo·graph·ic
sphyg·mog·ra·phy
sphyg·moid
sphyg·mo·ma·nom·eter
Spi·ca star
spi·ca (plural ·cae or ·cas)
  spiral bandage
spi·cate botany term
spic·ca·to musical term
spice
spice·berry (plural ·berries)
spice·bush
spic·er
spic·ery (plural ·eries)
spici·ly
spici·ness
spick-and-span (or spic-)
spicu·late
spic·ule
spicu·lum (plural ·la)
spicy (spici·er, spici·est)
spi·der
spider·man (plural ·men)
spider·wort
spi·dery
spied
spie·gelei·sen pig iron
spiel Slang glib talk; compare
  speel
spiel·er
spif·fing
spif·fy (·fi·er, ·fi·est) US
  smart
spif·li·cate Slang destroy
spig·nel plant
spig·ot cask stopper
spike
spike·let grass flower
spike·nard plant
spike-rush plant
spiki·ly
spiki·ness
spiky (spiki·er, spiki·est)

spile heavy stake
spill (spill·ing, spilt or
  spilled)
spill·age
spill·er
spil·li·kin (or spili·) thin
  strip
spil·li·kins game
spill·way
spilt
spin (spin·ning, spun)
spi·na bi·fi·da
spin·ach
spi·nal
spi·nal·ly
spin·dle
spin·dling
spin·dly (·dli·er, ·dli·est)
spin·drift (or spoon·) sea
  spray
spin-dry (-dries, -drying,
  -dried)
spin-dryer
spine
spine-chiller
spine-chilling
spi·nel mineral
spine·less
spine·less·ness
spi·nes·cence
spi·nes·cent
spin·et
spi·nif·er·ous (or ·nig·)
spini·fex plant
spini·ness
spin·na·ker racing sail
spin·ner
spin·ner·et zoology term
spin·ney
spin·ning
spin-off
spi·nose
spi·nos·ity
spi·nous
Spi·no·zism philosophical
  system
spin·ster
spin·ster·hood
spin·ster·ish
spin·tha·ri·scope physics
  apparatus
spi·nule
spi·nu·lose
spiny (spini·er, spini·est)
spiny-finned

spira·cle respiratory
aperture
spi·racu·lar
spi·racu·late
spi·raea shrub
spi·ral (·ral·ling, ·ralled; US
·ral·ing, ·ralled)
spi·ral·ly
spi·rant phonetics term
spire
spi·reme cytology term
spi·rif·er·ous
spi·ril·lar
spi·ril·lum (plural ·la)
bacterium
spir·it
spir·it·ed
spir·it·ed·ly
spir·it·ed·ness
spir·it·less
spir·it·less·ness
spi·ri·to·so musical term
spiri·tous variant of
spirituous
spir·itu·al
spir·itu·al·ism
spir·itu·al·ist
spir·itu·al·ity (plural ·ities)
spir·itu·ali·za·tion (or
·sa·tion)
spir·itu·al·ize (or ·ise)
spir·itu·al·iz·er (or ·is·er)
spir·itu·al·ly
spir·itu·al·ness
spir·itu·el (fem ·elle) witty
spir·itu·os·ity (or ·ous·ness)
spir·itu·ous (or spiri·tous)
alcoholic
spir·ket·ting nautical term
spi·ro·chaete bacterium
spi·ro·chae·to·sis
spi·ro·graph medical
apparatus
spi·ro·graph·ic
spi·ro·gy·ra alga
spi·roid
spi·rom·eter
spi·ro·met·ric
spi·rom·etry
spi·ro·no·lac·tone drug
spirt variant spelling of spurt
spiru·la mollusc
spiry
spit (spit·ting, spat or spit)
expectorate

spit (spit·ting, spit·ted)
pointed rod; pierce
spitch·cock
spite
spite·ful
spite·ful·ly
spite·ful·ness
spit·fire
Spit·head
spit·sticker wood-engraving
tool
spit·ter
spit·tle
spittle·bug
spit·toon
spitz dog
spiv
spiv·vy
splake trout
splanch·nic visceral
splash
splash·back
splash·board
splash·down
splash·er
splashi·ly
splashi·ness
splashy (splashi·er,
splashi·est)
splat
splat·ter
splay
splay·foot
splay·footed·ly
spleen
spleen·ish (or spleeny)
spleen·wort
splen·did
splen·did·ness
splen·dif·er·ous
splen·dor·ous (or ·drous)
splen·dour (US ·dor)
sple·nec·to·my (plural
·mies) removal of spleen
sple·net·ic (or ·neti·cal)
peevish
sple·neti·cal·ly
sple·nial of the splenius
splen·ic of the spleen
sple·ni·tis
sple·nius (plural ·nii)
muscle
sple·no·mega·ly
splice
splic·er

spline machine part
splint
splin·ter
splin·tery
Split Croatian port
split (split·ting, split)
split-level
splits gymnastic act
split·ter
split·ting
splodge
splodgy
splotch
splotchy
splurge
splut·ter
splut·ter·er
splut·tery
spode porcelain
spodu·mene mineral
spoil (spoil·ing, spoilt or
spoiled)
spoil·age
spoil·er
spoil-five card game
spoils
spoil·sport
Spo·kane US city
spoke
spo·ken
spoke·shave
spokes·man (plural ·men)
spokes·woman (plural
·women)
spo·li·ate despoil
spo·lia·tion
spo·lia·tory
spon·da·ic (or ·dai·cal)
spon·dee metrical foot
spon·du·lix (or ·licks) Slang
money
spon·dy·li·tis spinal
disorder
sponge
sponge·able
spong·er
spon·gi·ly
spon·gin
spon·gi·ness
spon·gio·blast nerve cell
spon·gio·blas·tic
spon·gy (·gi·er, ·gi·est)
spon·sion sponsorship
spon·son support on boat

spon·sor
spon·so·rial
spon·sor·ship
spon·ta·neity (*plural* ·neities)
spon·ta·neous
spon·ta·neous·ly
spon·ta·neous·ness
spon·toon short pike
spoof
spoof·er
spook
spooki·ly
spooki·ness
spook·ish
spooky (spooki·er, spooki·est)
spool
spoon
spoon·bill
spoon·er·ism
spoon-feed (-feeding, -fed)
spoon·ful (*plural* ·fuls)
spoony (spooni·er, spooni·est) amorous
spoor animal trail; *compare* spore
spoor·er
Spora·des Greek islands
spo·rad·ic (or ·radi·cal)
spo·radi·cal·ly
spo·radi·cal·ness
spo·ran·gial
spo·ran·gium (*plural* ·gia)
spore reproductive body; *compare* spoor
spo·ro·carp
spo·ro·cyst
spo·ro·cyte
spo·ro·gen·esis
spo·rog·enous
spo·ro·go·nial
spo·ro·go·nium (*plural* ·nia)
spo·rogo·ny
spo·ro·phore
spo·ro·phyll (or ·phyl)
spo·ro·phyte
spo·ro·phyt·ic
spo·ro·zo·an
spo·ro·zo·ite
spor·ran
sport
sport·er
sporti·ly
sporti·ness

sport·ing
sport·ing·ly
spor·tive
spor·tive·ly
spor·tive·ness
sports·cast
sports·caster
sports·man (*plural* ·men)
sportsman-like
sports·man·ly
sports·man·ship
sports·wear
sports·woman (*plural* ·women)
sporty (sporti·er, sporti·est)
sporu·late produce spores
sporu·la·tion
spor·ule
spot (spot·ting, spot·ted)
spot·less
spot·less·ness
spot·light (·light·ing, ·lit or ·light·ed)
spot-on
spot·table
spot·ted
spot·ter
spot·ti·ly
spot·ti·ness
spot·ty (·ti·er, ·ti·est)
spot-weld
spot-welder
spous·al marriage ceremony
spouse
spout
spout·er
sprag
sprain
sprang
sprat
sprawl
sprawl·er
sprawl·ing
sprawly
spray
spray·er
spread (spread·ing, spread)
spread·able
spread-eagle
spread·er
sprech·stimme *German* musical term
spree
sprig (sprig·ging, sprigged)
sprig·ger

sprig·gy
spright·li·ness
spright·ly (·li·er, ·li·est)
spring (spring·ing, sprang or sprung, sprung)
spring·board
Spring·bok South African athlete
spring·bok (or ·buck; *plural* ·bok, boks or ·buck, ·bucks) antelope
spring-clean
spring-cleaning
springe snare
spring·er
Spring·field US city
spring·haas (*plural* ·haas, ·ha·se) animal
spring·head
springi·ly
springi·ness
spring·ing
spring·let
Springs South African city
spring·tail
spring·time
spring·wood
springy (springi·er, springi·est)
sprin·kle
sprin·kler
sprin·kling
sprint
sprint·er
sprit nautical term
sprite
sprit·sail
sprock·et
sprout
spruce
spruce·ly
spruce·ness
sprue disease
spru·ik *Austral* speak in public
sprung
spry (spri·er, spri·est)
spry·ly
spry·ness
spud (spud·ding, spud·ded)
spume froth
spu·mes·cence
spu·mes·cent
spu·mo·ne (or ·ni; *plural* ·ni) ice cream

spu·mous (*or* spumy)
spun
spunk
spunki·ly
spunki·ness
spunky (spunki·er, spunki·est)
spur (spur·ring, spurred)
spurge plant
spu·ri·ous
spu·ri·ous·ly
spu·ri·ous·ness
spurn
spurn·er
spur·ri·er spur maker
spur·ry (*or* ·rey; *plural* ·ries) plant
spurt (*or* spirt)
sput·nik Soviet satellite
sput·ter
sput·ter·er
spu·tum (*plural* ·ta)
spy (*noun, plural* spies; *verb* spies, spy·ing, spied)
spy·glass
spy·ing
squab (*plural* squabs *or* squab) young pigeon
squab·ble
squab·bler
squab·by (·bi·er, ·bi·est)
squac·co (*plural* ·cos) heron
squad
squad·die (*or* ·dy; *plural* ·dies) *Slang* soldier
squad·ron
squa·lene biochemical compound
squal·id
squa·lid·ity (*or* squal·id·ness)
squall
squall·er
squal·ly
squal·or
squa·ma (*plural* ·mae) scale
squa·mate
squa·ma·tion
squa·mo·sal bone
squa·mous (*or* ·mose)
squa·mous·ness (*or* ·mose)
squamu·lose covered with small scales
squan·der
squan·der·er

squan·der·ing·ly
square
square·ly
square·ness
squar·er
square-rigger
squar·ish
squar·rose biology term
squash
squash·er
squashi·ly
squashi·ness
squashy (squashi·er, squashi·est)
squat (squat·ting, squat·ted)
squat·ness
squat·ter
squat·toc·ra·cy *Austral* rich farmers
squaw
squawk
squawk·er
squeak
squeak·er
squeaki·ly
squeaki·ness
squeaky
squeal
squeal·er
squeam·ish
squeam·ish·ness
squee·gee (*or* squil·; ·gee·ing, ·geed)
squeez·able
squeeze
squeez·er
squelch
squelch·er
squelch·ing·ly
sque·teague (*plural* ·teague *or* ·teagues) fish
squib (squib·bing, squibbed)
squid (*plural* squid *or* squids)
squif·fy (·fi·er, ·fi·est)
squig·gle
squig·gler
squig·gly
squill plant
squil·la (*plural* ·las *or* ·lae) shrimp
squinch architectural support

squint
squint·er
squinty
squire
squire·ar·chy (*or* squir·ar·chy; *plural* ·chies)
squirm
squirm·er
squirm·ing·ly
squirmy
squir·rel
squirrel·fish (*plural* ·fish *or* ·fishes)
squirt
squirt·er
squish
squishy (squishi·er, squishi·est)
squit *Slang* insignificant person
squiz (*plural* squizzes) *Austral* inquisitive glance
Sri Lan·ka
Sri Lan·kan
Sri·na·gar Indian city
St *abbrev. for* Saint; *all entries preceded by* St *are listed in the section of this dictionary following the entry* saint
stab (stab·bing, stabbed)
Sta·bat Ma·ter hymn
stab·ber
sta·bile arts term
sta·bil·ity (*plural* ·ities)
sta·bi·li·za·tion (*or* ·sa·tion)
sta·bi·lize (*or* ·lise)
sta·bi·li·zer (*or* ·ser)
sta·ble
stable·boy
stable·man (*plural* ·men)
sta·ble·ness
sta·bling
sta·bly
stac·ca·to
stack
stack·er
stac·te biblical spice
stad·dle prop
staddle·stone
stad·hold·er (*or* stadt·) Dutch ruler
sta·di·om·eter
sta·di·um (*plural* ·diums *or* ·dia)

staff (*plural* **staffs**)
  personnel
staff (*plural* **staffs** *or* **staves**)
  pole
staff (*or* **stave**; *plural* **staffs**
  or **staves**) musical term
Staf·fa Scottish island
staff·er *Slang* staff member
staff·man (*plural* **·men**)
Staf·ford
Staf·ford·shire
stag
stage
stage·coach
stage·craft
stage·hand
stage·manage
stag·er
stag·fla·tion economics
  term
stag·gard deer
stag·ger
stagger·bush
stag·ger·er
stag·ger·ing
stag·ger·ing·ly
stag·gers horse disease
stag·hound
stagi·ly
stagi·ness
stag·ing
Sta·gi·ra ancient
  Macedonian city
stag·nan·cy (*or* **·nance**)
stag·nant
stag·nate
stag·na·tion
stagy (stagi·er, stagi·est)
  theatrical
staid sedate; *compare* **stayed**
staid·ness
stain
stain·abil·ity
stain·able
stain·er
Staines Surrey town
stain·less
stair step; *compare* **stare**
stair·case
stair·head
stairs
stair·way
stair·well
stake stick; money; *compare*
  steak

stake·hold·er
stake·out
Stak·han·ov Ukrainian city
sta·lac·ti·form
stal·ac·tite downward
  projection in cave
stal·ac·tit·ic (*or* **·titi·cal**)
sta·lag German prison camp
stal·ag·mite upward
  projection in cave
stal·ag·mit·ic (*or* **·miti·cal**)
stale
stale·ly
stale·mate
stale·ness
Sta·lin·ism
Sta·lin·ist
stalk
stalked
stalk·er
stalki·ly
stalki·ness
stalk·like
stalky (stalki·er, stalki·est)
stall
stall-feed (-feeding, -fed)
stal·lion
stal·wart
stal·wart·ness
Stam·bul (*or* **·boul**) part of
  Istanbul
sta·men (*plural* **sta·mens** *or*
  stami·na)
Stam·ford US city
stami·na
stami·nal
stami·nate having stamens
stami·nif·er·ous
stami·node (*or* **·no·dium**;
  plural **·nodes** *or* **·no·dia**)
  botany term
stami·no·dy
stam·mel fabric
stam·mer
stam·mer·er
stam·mer·ing·ly
stamp
stam·pede
stam·ped·er
stamp·er
stance
stanch (*or* **staunch**) check
  blood flow; *compare*
  staunch
stanch·able (*or* **staunch·**)

stanch·er (*or* **staunch·**)
stan·chion
stand (stand·ing, stood)
stand·ard
standard-bearer
stand·ardi·za·tion (*or*
  ·sa·tion)
stand·ard·ize (*or* **·ise**)
stand·ard·iz·er (*or* **·is·er**)
stand-by (*noun*; *plural* **-bys**)
standee one who stands
stand·er
stand-in (*noun*)
stand·ing
stand·ish inkstand
stand·offish
stand·pipe
stand·point
stand·still
stang *Dialect* throb with
  pain
stan·hope carriage
stank
Stan·ley capital of Falkland
  Islands
Stan·na·ries English district
stan·na·ry (*plural* **·ries**) tin
  mine
stan·nic chemistry term
stan·nif·er·ous
stan·nite mineral
stan·nous chemistry term
stan·za
stan·zaed
stan·za·ic
sta·pedial
sta·pelia plant
sta·pes (*plural* **·pes** *or*
  ·pedes) ear bone
staphy·lo·coc·cal
staphy·lo·coc·cus (*plural*
  ·coc·ci)
staphy·lo·plas·tic
staphy·lo·plas·ty palate
  surgery
staphy·lor·rhaph·ic
staphy·lor·rha·phy repair
  of cleft palate
sta·ple
sta·pler
star (star·ring, starred)
star-apple
Sta·ra Za·go·ra Bulgarian
  city
star·board

starch
starch·er
starchi·ly
starchi·ness
starch-reduced
starchy (starchi·er,
  starchi·est)
star-crossed
star·dom
star·dust
stare look at; compare stair
star·er
star·fish (plural ·fish or
  ·fishes)
star·flower
star·gaze
star·gaz·er
star·gaz·ing
stark
stark·ness
star·less
star·let
star·light
star·like
star·ling
star·lit
star-of-Bethlehem plant
starred
star·ri·ly
star·ri·ness
star·ry (·ri·er, ·ri·est)
starry-eyed
star-spangled
start
start·er
star·tle
star·tler
star·tling
star·tling·ly
star·va·tion
starve
starve·ling
starv·er
starv·ing
star·wort
stash
sta·sis stagnation
stat·able (or state·)
sta·tant heraldic term
state
state·craft
state·hood
State·house US state capitol
state·less
state·less·ness

state·li·ness
state·ly (·li·er, ·li·est)
state·ment
Stat·en Is·land
sta·ter one who states;
  ancient coin; compare
  stator
state·room
States the USA
state·side
states·man (plural ·men)
statesman-like (or
  states·man·ly)
states·man·ship
states·woman (plural
  ·women)
stat·ic
stati·cal
stati·cal·ly
stat·ice plant
stat·ics
sta·tion
sta·tion·ari·ly
sta·tion·ari·ness
sta·tion·ary not moving;
  compare stationery
sta·tion·er
sta·tion·ery writing
  materials; compare
  stationary
station·master
stat·ism state control
stat·ist
sta·tis·tic
sta·tis·ti·cal
sta·tis·ti·cal·ly
stat·is·ti·cian
sta·tis·tics
sta·tive linguistics term
stato·blast zoology term
stato·cyst zoology term
stato·lith biology term
stato·lith·ic
sta·tor part of machine;
  compare stater
stato·scope aircraft
  instrument
statu·ary (plural ·aries)
statue
stat·ued
statu·esque
statu·esque·ly
statu·esque·ness
statu·ette
stat·ure

sta·tus (plural ·tuses)
sta·tus quo
statu·table
stat·ute
statu·to·ri·ly
statu·tory
staunch loyal; variant
  spelling of stanch
staunch·ness
stau·ro·lite mineral
stau·ro·lit·ic
stau·ro·scope
stau·ro·scopi·cal·ly
Sta·vang·er Norwegian
  port
stave (stav·ing, staved or
  stove) wooden strip; to
  crush; variant spelling of
  staff
staves (noun) plural of staff
  or stave
staves·acre plant
Stav·ro·pol Russian city
stay
stayed past tense of stay;
  compare staid
stay·er
stays boned corsets
stay·sail
stead
stead·fast (or sted·)
stead·fast·ness (or sted·)
steadi·ly
steadi·ness
steady (adj steadi·er,
  steadi·est; verb stead·ies,
  steady·ing, stead·ied)
steady·ing·ly
steak meat; compare stake
steak·house
steal (steal·ing, stole,
  sto·len)
steal·er
stealth
stealth·ful
stealthi·ly
stealthi·ness
stealthy (stealthi·er,
  stealthi·est)
steam
steam·boat
steam-boiler
steam-chest
steam-engine
steam·er

steamie *Scot* public
washhouse

steami·ly

steami·ness

steam·roller

steam·ship

steam·shovel

steam·tight

steam·tight·ness

steamy (steami·er,
steami·est)

ste·ap·sin enzyme

stea·rate

stea·aric

stea·rin (*or* ·rine)
biochemical compound

stea·rop·tene

stea·tite mineral

stea·tit·ic

stea·toly·sis digestive
process

stea·to·py·gia (*or* ·ga)
excessively fat buttocks

stea·to·pyg·ic (*or* ·py·gous)

stea·tor·rhoea (*US* ·rhea)

steed

steel alloy; *compare* stele

steel·head (*plural* ·heads *or*
·head) fish

steeli·ness

steel·work

steel·worker

steel·working

steel·works

steely (steeli·er, steeli·est)

steel·yard

steen·bok *variant spelling of*
steinbok

steep

steep·en

steep·er

steep·ish

stee·ple

steeple·chase

steeple·chas·er

steeple·jack

steep·ness

steer guide; bullock; *compare*
stere

steer·able

steer·age

steer·age·way

steer·er

steer·ing

steers·man (*plural* ·men)

steeve nautical term

stego·don (*or* ·dont) extinct
mammal

stego·myia mosquito

stego·saur (*or* ·saur·us)

stein beer mug

stein·bok (*or* steen·; *plural*
·boks *or* ·bok) antelope

ste·lar of a stele; *compare*
stellar

ste·le (*or* ·la; *plural* ·lae *or*
·les) stone slab

stele plant tissue; *compare*
steel

stel·lar of stars; *compare*
stelar

stel·lara·tor physics
apparatus

stel·late (*or* ·lat·ed)

stel·lif·er·ous

stel·li·form

stel·li·fy (·fies, ·fy·ing,
·fied) change into a star

Stel·lite (*Trademark*)

stel·lu·lar

stem (stem·ming,
stemmed)

stem·head

stem·ma family tree

stem·mer

stem·son nautical term

stem·ware stemmed glasses

stem·winder

stench

sten·cil (·cil·ling, ·cilled;
US ·cil·ing, ·ciled)

sten·cil·ler (*US* ·cil·er)

Sten gun

steno (*plural* stenos) *US*
shorthand typist

steno·graph

ste·nog·ra·pher *US*
shorthand typist

steno·graph·ic (*or*
·graphi·cal)

ste·nog·ra·phy

steno·ha·line

steno·pet·al·ous

ste·nopha·gous

steno·phyl·lous

ste·no·sis (*plural* ·ses)

steno·ther·mal

ste·not·ic

steno·trop·ic (*or* ·top·)
ecology term

Steno·type (*Trademark*)

steno·typ·ic

steno·typ·ist

steno·typy form of
shorthand

sten·tor loud person;
microscopic animal

sten·to·rian

step (step·ping, stepped)
motion of foot; stage; etc.;
compare steppe

step·brother

step·child (*plural* ·children)

step·daughter

step·father

stepha·no·tis

step·ladder

step·mother

step-parent

steppe grassy plain; *compare*
step

step·per

Steppes Eurasian grasslands

step·sister

step·son

step·wise

ste·ra·dian unit

ster·co·ra·ceous of dung

ster·co·rico·lous

ster·cu·lia·ceous botany
term

stere unit; *compare* steer

ste·reo (*plural* ·reos)

ste·reo·bate foundation of
building

ste·reo·chem·is·try

ste·reo·chrome

ste·reo·chro·my wall
painting

ste·reo·gram

ste·reo·graph

ste·reo·graph·ic (*or*
·graphi·cal)

ste·reog·ra·phy

ste·reo·iso·mer

ste·reo·isom·er·ism

ste·reo·iso·met·ric

ste·reo·met·ric

ste·reo·met·ri·cal

ste·reom·etry

ste·reo·phon·ic

ste·reo·phoni·cal·ly

ste·reoph·ony

ste·reop·sis stereoscopic
vision

ste·reop·ti·con type of
   projector
ste·reo·scope
ste·reo·scop·ic (or
   ·scopi·cal)
ste·reo·scopi·cal·ly
ste·reos·co·pist
ste·reos·co·py
ste·reo·spe·cif·ic
ste·reo·tac·tic (or ·ti·cal)
ste·reo·tac·ti·cal·ly
ste·reo·tax·is biology term
ste·reot·omy
ste·reo·trop·ic
ste·reot·ro·pism botany
   term
ste·reo·type
ste·reo·typ·er (or ·ist)
ste·reo·typ·ic (or ·typi·cal)
ste·reo·typy
ste·reo·vi·sion
ste·ric (or ·ri·cal) chemistry
   term
ste·ri·cal·ly
ster·ig·ma (plural ·ma·ta)
   botany term
steri·lant
ster·ile
ste·ril·ity
steri·liz·able (or ·lis·able)
steri·li·za·tion (or ·sa·tion)
steri·lize (or ·lise)
steri·liz·er (or ·lis·er)
ster·let fish
ster·ling
stern
ster·nal of the sternum
stern·most
stern·ness
stern·post
stern·son nautical term
ster·num (plural ·na or
   ·nums) breastbone
ster·nu·ta·tion sneezing
ster·nu·ta·tive
ster·nu·ta·tor
ster·nu·ta·tory (plural
   ·tories)
stern·wards (or esp. US
   ·ward)
stern·way
ster·oid
ster·oi·dal
ster·ol biochemical
   compound

ster·tor noisy breathing
ster·to·rous
ster·to·rous·ness
stet (stet·ting, stet·ted)
stetho·scope
stetho·scop·ic
ste·thos·co·py
stet·son
ste·vedore
Ste·ven·age Hertfordshire
   town
Ste·ven·graph (or ·vens·)
   silk picture
stew
stew·ard
stew·ard·ess
stew·ard·ship
stewed
sthen·ic strong
stib·ine poisonous gas
stib·nite mineral
stich line of poetry; compare
   stitch
stich·ic
stichi·cal·ly
sticho·met·ric (or ·ri·cal)
sti·chom·etry
sticho·mythia (or
   sti·chomy·thy) drama
   term
stick (stick·ing, stuck)
stick·er
stick·ful (plural ·fuls)
sticki·ly
sticki·ness
stick·le argue
stickle·back
stick·ler
stick·seed
stick·tight plant
stick-up (noun)
stick·weed
sticky (sticki·er, sticki·est)
sticky·beak Austral
   inquisitive person
stiff
stiff·en
stiff·en·er
stiff·ness
sti·fle
sti·fler
sti·fling
sti·fling·ly
stig·ma (plural ·mas) mark;
   flower part

stig·ma (plural ·ma·ta)
   crucifixion mark
stig·mas·ter·ol biochemical
   compound
stig·mat·ic (or ·mati·cal)
stig·ma·tism
stig·ma·tist
stig·ma·ti·za·tion (or
   ·sa·tion)
stig·ma·tize (or ·tise)
stig·ma·tiz·er (or ·tis·er)
stil·bene
stil·bite mineral
stil·boes·trol (US ·bes·)
stile steps over fence;
   compare style
sti·let·to (noun, plural ·tos;
   verb ·toes, ·toe·ing, ·toed)
still
stil·lage platform
still·birth
still·born
still life (plural still lifes)
   picture
stil·li·cide legal term
still·ness
stilt
stilt·ed
stilt·ed·ness
Stil·ton cheese
stimu·lable
stimu·lant
stimu·late
stimu·lat·ing·ly
stimu·la·tion
stimu·la·tive
stimu·la·tor (or ·lat·er)
stimu·lus (plural ·li)
sting (sting·ing, stung)
sting·er
stin·gi·ly
stin·gi·ness
sting·ing·ly
stin·go beer
sting·ray
stin·gy (·gi·er, ·gi·est)
stink (stink·ing, stank or
   stunk)
stink·er
stink·horn fungus
stink·ing·ly
stink·ing·ness
stink·pot
stink·stone
stink·weed

stink·wood
stint
stint·er
stipe plant stalk
sti·pel small leaflike
  structure; compare stipple
sti·pel·late
sti·pend
sti·pen·di·ary (plural ·aries)
sti·pes (plural stipi·tes)
  zoology term
sti·pi·form (or stipi·ti·)
stipi·tate
stip·ple dot or fleck; compare
  stipel
stip·pler
stip·pling
stipu·lable
stipu·lar
stipu·late
stipu·la·tion
stipu·la·tor
stipu·la·tory
stip·ule leaflike structure
stir (stir·ring, stirred)
stirk heifer
Stir·ling Scottish town
stirps (plural stir·pes) line of
  descendants
stir·rable
stir·rer
stir·ring
stir·ring·ly
stir·rup
stitch needlework link;
  compare stich
stitch·er
stitch·ing
stitch·wort
stithy (plural stithies)
  Dialect forge
sti·ver coin
stoa (plural stoae or stoas)
  covered walk
stoat
stob Dialect stump
sto·chas·tic statistics term
sto·chas·ti·cal·ly
stock
stock·ade
stock·breeder
stock·breeding
stock·broker
stock·bro·ker·age (or
  ·broking)

stock·er
stock·fish (plural ·fish or
  ·fishes)
stock·holder
stock·holding
Stock·holm
stocki·ly
stocki·ness
stocki·net
stock·ing
stock·inged
stock·ish stupid
stock·ist
stock·jobber
stock·jobbery (or ·jobbing)
stock·man (plural ·men)
stock·pile
stock·pil·er
Stock·port English town
stock·pot
stock·room
stocks instrument of
  punishment
stock·still
stock·taking
Stock·ton English town; US
  port
stocky (stocki·er,
  stocki·est)
stock·yard
stodge
stodgi·ly
stodgi·ness
stodgy (stodgi·er,
  stodgi·est)
sto·gy (or sto·gey; plural
  ·gies) US cigar
Sto·ic philosopher
sto·ic self-controlled person
stoi·cal
stoi·cal·ly
stoi·cal·ness
stoi·chio·logi·cal
stoi·chi·ol·ogy branch of
  biology
stoi·chio·met·ric
stoi·chi·om·etry branch of
  chemistry
stoi·cism
stoke
stoke·hold
stoke·hole
Stoke Mandeville
  Buckinghamshire town
stok·er

stokes (or stoke; plural
  stokes) unit
stole long shawl; past tense
  of steal
stol·en
stol·id
sto·lid·ity (or stol·id·ness)
stol·len bread
sto·lon stem
sto·loni·fer·ous
sto·ma (plural ·ma·ta)
stom·ach
stomach·ache
stom·ach·er
sto·mach·ic
sto·machi·cal
stom·achy
sto·ma·tal (or stoma·tous)
sto·mat·ic of the mouth
sto·ma·ti·tic
sto·ma·ti·tis
sto·ma·tol·ogy
stoma·to·plas·ty
stoma·to·pod crustacean
sto·mo·daeal (or ·deal)
sto·mo·daeum (or ·deum)
  embryonic mouth cavity
stomp
stomp·er
ston·able (or stone·)
stone
stone·blind
stone·chat bird
stone·crop plant
stone·cutter
stone·cutting
stoned
stone·fish (plural ·fish or
  ·fishes)
stone·fly (plural ·flies)
stone·ground
Stone·henge
stone·less
stone·lily fossil
stone·mason
stone·mason·ry
ston·er
stone·wall
stone·wall·er
stone·ware
stone·work
stone·worker
stone·wort alga
stoni·ly
stoni·ness

stonk bombard with artillery

stony (or stoney; stoni•er, stoni•est)

stony-broke

stony-hearted

stony-hearted•ness

stood

stooge

stook

stook•er

stool

stoop bend body; compare stoup; stupe

stoop•er

stoop•ing•ly

stop (stop•ping, stopped)

stop•cock

stope mine excavation

stop-gap

stop-go economics term

stop•ing geology term

stop•light

stop•over (noun)

stop•pable

stop•page

stop•per

stop•ping

stops card game

stop•watch

stor•able

stor•age

sto•rax plant; drug

store

store•house

store•keeper

store•keeping

store•room

sto•rey (plural •reys or •ries) level; compare story

sto•reyed multilevelled

sto•ried recorded

stork

storks•bill plant

storm

storm•bound

stormi•ly

stormi•ness

storm•proof

storm-trooper

stormy (stormi•er, stormi•est)

Stor•no•way Scottish port

Stor•ting (or •thing) Norwegian parliament

sto•ry (plural •ries) tale; compare storey

story•book

story•teller

story•telling

stoss geology term

stot (stot•ting, stot•ted) Scot bounce

sto•tin•ka (plural •ki) Bulgarian coin

sto•tious Irish drunk

stot•ter Scot good-looking woman

stound Dialect short period

stoup basin for holy water; drinking mug; compare stoop; stupe

stour Dialect turmoil

Stour•bridge English town

stout

stout•hearted

stout•hearted•ness

stout•ish

stout•ness

stove

stove•pipe

stove•pipes tight trousers

stov•er

stow

stow•age

stow•away

stra•bis•mal (or •mic, •mi•cal)

stra•bis•mus squint

strad•dle

strad•dler

Stradi•var•ius violin

strafe

straf•er

strag•gle

strag•gler

strag•gling•ly

strag•gly (•gli•er, •gli•est)

straight not curved; directly; compare strait

straight•away

straight•edge

straight•en put straight; compare straiten

straight•en•er

straight-faced

straight•forward

straight•forward•ness

straight•ness

strain

strained

strained•ness

strain•er

strain•ing•ly

strait sea channel; difficulty; compare straight

strait•en embarrass financially; compare straighten

strait•jacket (or straight•)

strait-laced (or straight-)

strait•ness

strake metal part of wheel

stra•mo•nium drug

Strand London street

strand

stranded

strange

strange•ness

stran•ger

stran•gle

strangle•hold

stran•gler

stran•gles horse disease

stran•gu•late

stran•gu•la•tion

stran•gu•ry painful urination

Stran•raer Scottish port

strap (strap•ping, strapped)

strap•hanger

strap•hanging

strap•less

strap•pa•do (plural •does) torture

strap•per

strap•ping

Stras•bourg French city

strass imitation gem

stra•ta plural of stratum

strata•gem

stra•tal

stra•tegic (or •tegi•cal)

stra•tegi•cal•ly

stra•tegics military strategy

strat•egist

strat•egy (plural •egies)

Stratford-on-Avon

strath Scot glen

Strath•clyde former Scottish region

strath•spey dance

stra•ticu•late geology term

stra•ticu•la•tion

strati•fi•ca•tion

strati·form
strati·fy (·fies, ·fy·ing,
·fied)
stra·tig·ra·pher (or ·phist)
strati·graph·ic (or
·graphi·cal)
stra·tig·ra·phy study of rock
strata
stra·toc·ra·cy (plural ·cies)
military rule
strato·crat
strato·crat·ic
strato·cu·mu·lus (plural ·li)
strato·pause meteorology
term
strato·sphere
strato·spher·ic (or
·spheri·cal)
stra·tum (plural ·ta or
·tums) layer
stra·tus (plural ·ti) cloud
stra·vaig Scot wander
straw
straw·berry (plural
·berries)
straw·board
straw·flower
strawy
stray
stray·er
strays electronics term
streak
streaked
streak·er
streaki·ly
streaki·ness
streak·ing
streaky (streaki·er,
streaki·est)
stream
stream·er
stream·line
stream·lined
street
street·car
street·light (or ·lamp)
street·walker
street·walking
stre·lit·zia plant
strength
strength·en
strength·en·er
strenu·os·ity (or ·ous·ness)
strenu·ous
strep·to·coc·cal (or ·cic)

strep·to·coc·cus (plural
·coc·ci)
strep·to·ki·nase drug
strep·to·my·cin antibiotic
strep·to·thri·cin antibiotic
stress
stress·ful
stress·ful·ly
stretch
stretch·abil·ity
stretch·able
stretch·er
stretcher-bearer
stretchi·ness
stretchy (stretchi·er,
stretchi·est)
stret·to (plural ·tos or ·ti)
musical term
streu·sel pastry topping
strew (strew·ing, strewed,
strewn or strewed)
strew·er
strewth exclamation
stria (plural striae)
stri·ate (or ·at·ed)
stria·tion
strick textile fibres
strick·en
strick·le
strict
strict·ness
stric·ture
stride (strid·ing, strode,
strid·den)
stri·dence (or ·den·cy)
stri·dent
stri·dor wheezing sound
stridu·late zoology term
stridu·la·tion
stridu·la·tor
stridu·la·tory
stridu·lous (or ·lant)
stridu·lous·ness (or
stridu·lance)
strife
strigi·form ornithology
term
strig·il body scraper
stri·gose biology term
strik·able
strike (strik·ing, struck)
strike·bound
strike·breaker
strike·breaking
strik·er

strik·ing
strik·ing·ness
string (string·ing, strung)
string·board
stringed
strin·gen·cy
strin·gen·do musical term
strin·gent
string·er
string·halt veterinary term
stringi·ly
stringi·ness
string·piece
stringy (stringi·er,
stringi·est)
strip (strip·ping, stripped)
stripe
strip·er
strip·ling lad
strip·per
strip·tease
stripy (stripi·er stripi·est)
strive (striv·ing, strove,
striv·en)
striv·er
strobe lighting
stro·bic spinning
stro·bi·la (plural ·lae) body
of tapeworm
stro·bi·la·ceous
stro·bi·la·tion
stro·bi·lus (or stro·bile;
plural ·li, ·luses or ·biles)
plant cone
stro·bo·scope
stro·bo·scop·ic (or
·scopi·cal)
stro·bo·scopi·cal·ly
strode
stroga·noff
stroke
stroll
stroll·er
stro·ma (plural ·ma·ta)
biology term
stro·mat·ic (or ·ma·tous)
stro·mato·lite rock
stro·mato·lit·ic
Strom·bo·li volcanic island
strong
strong·arm
strong·box
strong·hold
strong·ly
strong·man (plural ·men)

strong-minded
strong-minded·ness
strong·ness
strong·room
strong-willed
stron·gyle (or ·gyl) parasitic worm
strontia strontium compound
stron·ti·an·ite (or stron·tian) mineral
stron·tium chemical element
strop (strop·ping, stropped)
stro·phan·thin drug
stro·phan·thus tree
stro·phe prosody term
stroph·ic (or strophi·cal)
strop·pi·ly
strop·pi·ness
strop·py (·pi·er, ·pi·est)
Stroud English town
stroud fabric
strove
struck
struc·tur·al
struc·tur·al·ism
struc·tur·al·ist
struc·tur·al·ly
struc·ture
struc·ture·less
stru·del
strug·gle
strug·gler
strug·gling·ly
strum (strum·ming, strummed)
stru·ma (plural ·mae) swelling
stru·mat·ic (or stru·mous, stru·mose)
strum·mer
strum·pet
strung
strut (strut·ting, strut·ted)
stru·thi·ous ostrich-like
strut·ter
strut·ting·ly
strych·nic
strych·nine
strych·nin·ism
stub (stub·bing, stubbed)
stub·bi·ly
stub·bi·ness

stub·ble
stub·bled
stub·bly
stub·born
stub·born·ness
stub·by (·bi·er, ·bi·est)
stuc·co (noun, plural ·coes or ·cos; verb ·coes or ·cos, ·co·ing, ·coed)
stuck
stud (stud·ding, stud·ded)
stud·book
stud·ding
studding·sail
stu·dent
stu·dent·ship
stud·horse
stud·ied
stud·ied·ly
stud·ied·ness
stu·dio (plural ·dios)
stu·di·ous
stu·di·ous·ness
stud·work
study (noun, plural studies, verb stud·ies, study·ing, stud·ied)
stuff
stuffed
stuff·er
stuf·fi·ly
stuffi·ness
stuff·ing
stuffy (stuffi·er, stuffi·est)
stull mining prop
stul·ti·fi·ca·tion
stul·ti·fi·er
stul·ti·fy (·fies, ·fy·ing, ·fied)
stum (stum·ming, stummed) wine-making term
stum·ble
stum·bler
stum·bling·ly
stu·mer Slang forgery
stump
stump·er
stumpi·ness
stumpy (stumpi·er, stumpi·est)
stun (stun·ning, stunned)
stung
stunk
stun·ner

stun·ning
stun·ning·ly
stunt
stunt·ed
stunt·ed·ness
stupe medical compress; compare stoop; stoup
stu·pefa·ci·ent (or ·pefac·tive)
stu·pefac·tion
stu·pefi·er
stu·pefy (·pefies, ·pefy·ing, ·pefied)
stu·pefy·ing·ly
stu·pen·dous
stu·pen·dous·ness
stu·pid
stu·pid·ity (plural ·ities)
stu·pid·ness
stu·por
stu·por·ous
stur·di·ly
stur·di·ness
stur·dy (·di·er, ·di·est)
stur·geon
Stur·mer apple
stut·ter
stut·ter·er
stut·ter·ing·ly
Stutt·gart German city
sty (noun, plural sties, verb sties, sty·ing, stied) pig's pen
sty (or stye; plural sties or styes) inflamed eye spot
Styg·ian of the Styx
stylar
style form; elegance; flower part; compare stile
style·book
styl·er
sty·let
sty·li·form
styl·ish
styl·ish·ness
styl·ist
sty·lis·tic
sty·lis·ti·cal·ly
sty·lite recluse
styli·za·tion (or ·sa·tion)
styl·ize (or ·ise)
styl·iz·er (or ·is·er)
sty·lo·bate architectural term
sty·lo·graph

sty·lo·graph·ic (*or* ·graphi·cal)
sty·lo·graphi·cal·ly
sty·log·ra·phy engraving
sty·loid
sty·lo·lite geology term
sty·lo·lit·ic
sty·lo·pize (*or* ·pise) parasitize with stylops
sty·lo·po·dium (*plural* ·dia) botany term
sty·lops (*plural* ·lo·pes) insect
sty·lo·stix·is acupuncture
sty·lus (*plural* ·li *or* ·luses)
sty·mie (*or* ·my; *verb* ·mies, ·mie·ing, ·mied *or* ·mies, ·my·ing, ·mied; *noun, plural* ·mies)
styp·sis
styp·tic
styp·ti·cal
styp·tic·ity
sty·ra·ca·ceous
sty·rax tree
sty·rene organic compound
Styria Austrian province
Styx mythological river
su·abil·ity
su·able
Sua·kin Sudanese port
suave
suave·ly
suav·ity (*or* suave·ness)
sub (sub·bing, subbed)
sub·ac·etate
sub·acid
sub·acid·ity (*or* ·acid·ness)
sub·acute medical term
sub·acute·ly
sub·agent
su·bah Mogul province
sub·al·pine
sub·al·tern
sub·al·ter·nate botany term
sub·al·ter·na·tion
sub·ant·arc·tic
sub·aquat·ic
sub·aque·ous
sub·arc·tic
sub·ar·id
sub·as·sem·bly (*plural* ·blies)
sub·atom·ic
sub·audi·tion

sub·auricu·lar
sub·ax·il·la·ry
sub·base pedestal base
sub·base·ment
sub·bass (*or* ·base) organ stop
sub·cali·bre
sub·car·ti·lagi·nous
sub·ce·les·tial
sub·cep·tion subliminal perception
sub·chlo·ride
sub·class
sub·cla·vian
sub·cli·mac·tic
sub·cli·max
sub·com·mit·tee
sub·con·scious
sub·con·scious·ness
sub·con·ti·nent
sub·con·ti·nen·tal
sub·con·tract
sub·con·trac·tor
sub·con·tra·ry (*plural* ·ries)
sub·cor·tex (*plural* ·tices)
sub·cor·ti·cal
sub·cul·tur·al
sub·cul·ture
sub·cu·ta·neous
sub·dea·con
sub·dea·con·ate
sub·de·lir·ium (*plural* ·lir·iums *or* ·liria)
sub·di·aco·nal
sub·di·aco·nate subdeacon's rank
sub·di·vide
sub·di·vid·er
sub·di·vi·sion
sub·di·vi·sion·al
sub·domi·nant
sub·du·able
sub·du·al
sub·duct
sub·duc·tion
sub·due (·dues, ·du·ing, ·dued)
sub·dued·ly
sub·dued·ness
sub·edit
sub·edi·tor
sub·equa·to·rial
su·ber·in plant substance
su·beri·za·tion (*or* ·sa·tion)
su·ber·ize (*or* ·ise)

su·ber·ose (*or* ·bereous, ·ber·ic) of cork
sub·fami·ly (*plural* ·lies)
sub·floor
sub·fusc drab; academic dress
sub·ge·ner·ic
sub·ge·nus (*plural* ·gen·era *or* ·ge·nuses)
sub·gla·cial
sub·gla·cial·ly
sub·group
sub·head·ing (*or* ·head)
sub·hu·man
sub·in·dex (*plural* ·dices *or* ·dexes)
sub·in·feu·date
sub·in·feu·da·tion
sub·in·feu·da·tory (*plural* ·tories)
sub·ir·ri·gate
sub·ir·ri·ga·tion
su·bi·to musical term
sub·ja·cen·cy
sub·ja·cent
sub·ject
sub·ject·abil·ity
sub·ject·able
sub·jec·ti·fi·ca·tion
sub·jec·ti·fy (·fies, ·fy·ing, ·fied)
sub·jec·tion
sub·jec·tive
sub·jec·tive·ly
sub·jec·tiv·ism
sub·jec·tiv·ist
sub·jec·ti·vis·tic
sub·jec·ti·vis·ti·cal·ly
sub·jec·tiv·ity (*or* ·tive·ness)
subject-raising
sub·join
sub·join·der
sub ju·di·ce
sub·ju·gable
sub·ju·gate
sub·ju·ga·tion
sub·ju·ga·tor
sub·junc·tion
sub·junc·tive
sub·king·dom
sub·lease
sub·les·see
sub·les·sor
sub·let (·let·ting, ·let)

sub·lieu·ten·an·cy
sub·lieu·ten·ant
sub·li·mable
sub·li·mate
sub·li·ma·tion
sub·lime
sub·lime·ly
sub·limi·nal
sub·limi·nal·ly
sub·lim·ity (*plural* ·ities)
sub·lin·gual
sub·lit·to·ral near seashore
sub·lu·nary between moon and earth
sub-machine-gun
sub·mar·gin·al
sub·ma·rine
sub·ma·rin·er
sub·max·il·lary of lower jaw
sub·me·di·ant musical term
sub·men·tal beneath the chin
sub·merge (*or* ·merse)
sub·mers·ibil·ity (*or* ·merg·)
sub·mers·ible (*or* ·merg·)
sub·mer·sion (*or* ·merg·ence)
sub·micro·scop·ic
sub·micro·scopi·cal·ly
sub·miss *Archaic* docile
sub·mis·sion
sub·mis·sive
sub·mis·sive·ly
sub·mis·sive·ness
sub·mit (·mit·ting, ·mit·ted)
sub·mit·table (*or* ·mis·sible)
sub·mit·tal
sub·mit·ter
sub·mit·ting·ly
sub·mon·tane
sub·mu·co·sa (*plural* ·sae)
sub·mul·ti·ple
sub·nor·mal
sub·nor·mal·ity
sub·nor·mal·ly
sub·ocean·ic
sub·or·bi·tal
sub·or·der
sub·or·di·nal
sub·or·di·nary (*plural* ·naries) heraldic term
sub·or·di·nate

sub·or·di·nate·ly
sub·or·di·nate·ness
sub·or·di·na·tion
sub·or·di·na·tive
sub·orn
sub·or·na·tion
sub·or·na·tive
sub·orn·er
sub·ox·ide
sub·phy·lar
sub·phy·lum (*plural* ·la)
sub·plot
sub·poe·na (·nas, ·na·ing, ·naed)
sub·popu·la·tion
sub·prin·ci·pal
sub·re·gion
sub·re·gion·al
sub·rep·tion concealment of facts
sub·rep·ti·tious
sub·ro·gate legal term
sub·ro·ga·tion
sub rosa *Latin* in secret
sub·rou·tine
sub·scapu·lar
sub·scribe
sub·scrib·er
sub·script
sub·scrip·tion
sub·scrip·tive
sub·sec·tion
sub·se·quence
sub·se·quent
sub·serve
sub·ser·vience (*or* ·vi·en·cy)
sub·ser·vi·ent
sub·set
sub·shrub
sub·side
sub·sid·ence
sub·sid·er
sub·sidi·ari·ly
sub·sidi·ari·ness
sub·sidi·ary (*plural* ·aries)
sub·si·diz·able (*or* ·dis·able)
sub·si·di·za·tion (*or* ·sa·tion)
sub·si·dize (*or* ·dise)
sub·si·diz·er (*or* ·dis·er)
sub·si·dy (*plural* ·dies)
sub·sist
sub·sist·ence
sub·sist·ent
sub·sist·er

sub·sist·ing·ly
sub·so·cial
sub·soil
sub·soil·er
sub·so·lar
sub·son·ic
sub·soni·cally
sub·spe·cies (*plural* ·cies)
sub·spe·cif·ic
sub·spe·cifi·cal·ly
sub·stage
sub·stance
sub·stand·ard
sub·stan·tial
sub·stan·tial·ism
sub·stan·tial·ist
sub·stan·ti·al·ity (*or* ·tial·ness)
sub·stan·tial·ly
sub·stan·ti·ate
sub·stan·tia·tion
sub·stan·tia·tive
sub·stan·tia·tor
sub·stan·ti·val grammar term
sub·stan·ti·val·ly
sub·stan·tive
sub·stan·tive·ly
sub·stan·tive·ness
sub·stan·ti·vi·za·tion (*or* ·sa·tion)
sub·stan·tiv·ize (*or* ·ise)
sub·sta·tion
sub·stitu·ent
sub·sti·tuta·bil·ity
sub·sti·tut·able
sub·sti·tute
sub·sti·tu·tion
sub·sti·tu·tive
sub·strate
sub·stra·tive (*or* ·tal)
sub·stra·tum (*plural* ·stra·ta)
sub·struc·tur·al (*or* ·tion·al)
sub·struc·ture (*or* ·tion)
sub·sum·able
sub·sume
sub·sump·tion
sub·sump·tive
sub·tan·gent
sub·tem·per·ate
sub·ten·an·cy (*plural* ·cies)
sub·ten·ant
sub·tend
sub·ter·fuge

sub·ter·ra·nean
sub·ter·res·trial
sub·tili·za·tion (or ·sa·tion)
sub·til·ize (or ·ise) refine
sub·til·iz·er (or ·is·er)
sub·ti·tle
sub·titu·lar
sub·tle
sub·tle·ness
sub·tler more subtle;
   compare sutler
sub·tle·ty (plural ·ties)
sub·tly
sub·ton·ic musical note
sub·tor·rid
sub·to·tal (·tal·ling, ·talled;
   US ·tal·ing, ·taled)
sub·tract
sub·tract·er
sub·trac·tion
sub·trac·tive
sub·tra·hend number
   subtracted
sub·tropi·cal
sub·trop·ics
sub·type
sub·typi·cal
su·bu·late awl-shaped
sub·urb
sub·ur·ban
sub·ur·ban·ite
sub·ur·bani·za·tion (or
   ·sa·tion)
sub·ur·ban·ize (or ·ise)
sub·ur·bia
sub·vene
sub·ven·tion
sub·ven·tion·ary
sub·ver·sion
sub·ver·sive
sub·ver·sive·ly
sub·ver·sive·ness
sub·vert
sub·vert·er
sub·way
sub·zero
suc·ce·da·neous
suc·ce·da·neum (plural
   ·nea) substitute drug
suc·ceed
suc·ceed·able
suc·ceed·er
suc·ceed·ing·ly
suc·cen·tor cathedral cleric
suc·cess

suc·cess·ful
suc·cess·ful·ly
suc·cess·ful·ness
suc·ces·sion
suc·ces·sion·al
suc·ces·sive
suc·ces·sive·ly
suc·ces·sive·ness
suc·ces·sor
suc·ces·sor·al
suc·cin·ate chemical
   compound
suc·cinct
suc·cinct·ness
suc·cin·ic of amber;
   chemistry term
suc·cory (plural ·cories)
   chicory
suc·co·tash US mixed
   vegetables
suc·cour (US ·cor)
suc·cour·able (US ·cor·)
suc·cour·er (US ·cor·)
suc·cu·bus (plural ·bi)
   female demon
suc·cu·lence (or ·len·cy)
suc·cu·lent
suc·cumb
suc·cumb·er
suc·cur·sal subsidiary
suc·cuss
suc·cus·sion
suc·cus·sive
such
such·like
Su·chou variant spelling of
   Soochow
Sü·chow (or Hsü·chou)
   Chinese city
suck
suck·er
sucker·fish (or suck·fish;
   plural ·fish or ·fishes)
suck·le
suck·ler
suck·ling
su·crase enzyme
su·crose sugar
suc·tion
suc·tion·al
suc·to·rial
Su·dan
Su·da·nese (plural
   ·nese)
Su·dan·ic

su·dar·ium (plural ·daria)
   face cloth
su·da·to·rium (or ·tory;
   plural ·to·ria or ·tories)
   steam-bath room
Sud·bury Canadian city
sudd water weed
sud·den
sud·den·ness
Su·deten·land Czech region
Su·detes (or Su·deten)
   European mountains
su·dor sweat
su·dor·al
su·dor·if·er·ous
su·dor·if·ic
suds
sudsy
sue (su·ing, sued)
(sueable) incorrect spelling of
   suable
suede
suer one who sues; compare
   sewer
suet
su·ety
Suez
suf·fer
suf·fer·able
suf·fer·ance
suf·fer·er
suf·fer·ing
suf·fice
suf·fic·er
suf·fi·cien·cy (plural ·cies)
suf·fi·cient
suf·fix
suf·fix·al
suf·fix·ion
suf·fo·cate
suf·fo·cat·ing·ly
suf·fo·ca·tion
suf·fo·ca·tive
Suf·folk
suf·fra·gan assistant bishop
suf·fra·gan·ship
suf·frage
suf·fra·gette
suf·fra·get·tism
suf·fra·gism
suf·fra·gist
suf·fru·ti·cose botany term
suf·fu·mi·gate
suf·fu·mi·ga·tion
suf·fuse

suf·fu·sion
suf·fu·sive
Sufi (*plural* Sufis) Muslim mystic
Su·fic
Su·fism
Su·fis·tic
sug·ar
sug·ari·ness
sugar·plum
sug·ary
sug·gest
sug·gest·er
sug·gest·ibil·ity
sug·gest·ible
sug·gest·ible·ness
sug·gest·ing·ly
sug·ges·tion
sug·ges·tive
sug·ges·tive·ly
sug·ges·tive·ness
sui·cid·al
sui·cid·al·ly
sui·cide
sui gen·eris unique
su·int substance in fleece
suit clothes; set of cards; petition; to be appropriate; *compare* suite
suit·abil·ity (*or* ·able·ness)
suit·able
suit·ably
suit·case
suite set of rooms; furniture; musical piece; *compare* suit
suit·ing
suit·or
Su·khu·mi Georgian port
su·ki·ya·ki Japanese dish
Su·la·we·si Indonesian island
sul·cate
sul·ca·tion
sul·cus (*plural* ·ci) groove
sul·fur US spelling of sulphur; *note all words starting* sulph- *have the US spelling* sulf-
sulk
sulk·er
sulki·ly
sulki·ness
sulky (*adj* sulki·er, sulki·est; *noun, plural* sulkies) sullen; vehicle

sul·lage sewage
sul·len
sul·len·ness
sul·li·able
sul·ly (·lies, ·ly·ing, ·lied)
sul·pha (US ·fa) class of drugs; *compare* sulphur
sul·pha·dia·zine (US ·fa·)
sul·pha·nila·mide (US ·fa·)
sul·phate (US ·fate)
sul·pha·thia·zole (US ·fa·)
sul·pha·tion (US ·fa·)
sul·phide (US ·fide)
sul·phi·soxa·zole (US ·fi·)
sul·phite (US ·fite)
sul·phit·ic (US ·fit·)
sul·phona·mide (US ·fona·) sulpha drug
sul·pho·nate (US ·fo·)
sul·phone (US ·fone)
sul·phon·me·thane (US ·fon·)
sul·phur (US ·fur) chemical element; *compare* sulpha
sul·phur·ate (US ·fur·)
sul·phu·ra·tion (US ·fu·)
sul·phu·reous (US ·fu·)
sul·phu·reous·ness (US ·fu·)
sul·phu·ret (US ·fu·; ·ret·ting, ·ret·ted, US ·ret·ing, ·ret·ed)
sul·phu·ric (US ·fu·)
sul·phu·ri·za·tion (*or* ·sa·tion; US ·fu·ri·za·tion)
sul·phu·rize (*or* ·rise; US ·fu·rize)
sul·phur·ous (US ·fur·)
sul·phur·ous·ness (US ·fur·)
sul·phur·yl (US ·fur·)
sul·tan
sul·tana
sul·tan·ate
sul·tan·ic
sul·tri·ly
sul·tri·ness
sul·try (·tri·er, ·tri·est)
Sulu Philippine archipelago
sum (sum·ming, summed)
su·mach (*or* ·mac) shrub
Su·ma·tra
Su·ma·tran
Su·mer Babylonian region
su·me·rian
sum·ma (*plural* ·mae) medieval compendium

sum·ma cum lau·de highest achievement in examination
sum·mand part of a sum
sum·mari·ly
sum·mari·ness
sum·ma·riz·able (*or* ·ris·able)
sum·ma·ri·za·tion (*or* ·sa·tion)
sum·ma·rize (*or* ·rise)
sum·ma·riz·er (*or* ·ris·er)
sum·mary (*plural* ·maries) brief account; *compare* summery
sum·ma·tion
sum·ma·tion·al
sum·mer
summer·house
sum·meri·ness
sum·mer·sault *variant spelling of* somersault
summer·time
summer·wood
sum·mery like summer; *compare* summary
summing-up (*plural* summings-)
sum·mit
sum·mit·al
sum·mit·ry
sum·mon (*verb*)
sum·mon·able
sum·mons (*noun, plural* ·monses; *verb* ·mons, ·mons·ing, ·monsed)
sum·mum bon·um *Latin* highest good
Sumo wrestling
sump
sump·tua·ry
sump·tu·ous
sump·tu·ous·ness (*or* ·tu·os·ity)
sun (sun·ning, sunned)
sun·bake *Austral* sunbathing
sun·baked
sun·bathe
sun·bather
sun·beam
sun·bird
sun·bonnet
sun·bow
sun·burn

sun·burnt (*or* ·burned)
sun·burst
sun·dae dessert
Sun·da Is·lands
Sun·day
sun·der
sun·der·able
sun·der·ance
sun·der·er
Sun·der·land
sun·dew
sun·dial
sun·dog small rainbow
sun·down
sun·dress
sun·dried
sun·dry (*plural* ·dries)
sun·fast
sun·fish (*plural* ·fish *or* ·fishes)
sun·flower
sung
Sun·ga·ri Chinese river
sun·glass burning glass
sun·glasses spectacles
sun·glow
sun·god
sun·grebe bird
sun·hat
sunk
sunk·en
sun·less
sun·less·ness
sun·light
sun·lit
sunn fibre
Sun·na Islamic law
sunned
Sun·ni (*plural* ·ni) Muslim sect
sun·ni·ly
sun·ni·ness
sun·ning
Sun·nite Muslim
sun·ny (·ni·er, ·ni·est)
sun·ray pleats
sun·rise
sun·roof
sun·set
sun·shade
sun·shine
sun·shiny
sun·spot
sun·spotted
sun·star starfish

sun·stroke
sun·suit
sun·tan
sun·tanned
sun·trap
sun·wards (*or esp. US* ·ward)
sun·wise
sup (sup·ping, supped)
su·per
super·abil·ity (*or* ·able·ness)
super·able
super·ably
super·abound
super·abun·dance
supera·bun·dant
super·add
super·ad·di·tion
super·ad·di·tion·al
super·an·nu·ate
super·an·nu·at·ed
super·an·nua·tion
su·perb
super·ba·zaar Indian store
su·perb·ness
super·cal·en·der
super·car·go (*plural* ·goes)
(supercede) *incorrect spelling of* supersede
super·charge
super·char·ger
super·cili·ary of the eyebrow
super·cili·ous
super·cili·ous·ness
super·class
super·co·lum·nar
super·con·duc·tion
super·con·duc·tive (*or* ·duct·ing)
super·con·duc·tiv·ity
super·con·duc·tor
super·cool (*verb*)
super-duper
super·ego (*plural* ·egos)
super·el·eva·tion
super·emi·nence
super·emi·nent
super·eroga·tory superfluous
super·fami·ly (*plural* ·lies)
super·fe·cun·da·tion
super·fe·tate
super·fe·ta·tion physiology term

super·fi·cial
super·fi·ci·al·ity (*or* ·cial·ness)
super·fi·cial·ly
super·fine
super·fix linguistics term
super·fluid
super·flu·id·ity
super·flu·ity
super·flu·ous
super·flu·ous·ness
super·gi·ant
super·gla·cial
super·heat (*verb*)
super·he·ro (*plural* ·roes)
super·het·ero·dyne radio receiver
super·high·way *US* fast dual carriageway
super·hu·man
super·hu·man·ity (*or* ·man·ness)
super·im·pose
super·im·po·si·tion
super·in·cum·bence (*or* ·ben·cy)
super·in·cum·bent
super·in·duce
super·induce·ment
super·in·duc·tion
super·in·tend
super·in·tend·ence
super·in·tend·en·cy (*plural* ·cies) office of superintendent
super·in·ten·dent
Su·peri·or *US* lake
su·peri·or
su·peri·or·ity
super·ja·cent
super·la·tive
super·la·tive·ly
super·la·tive·ness
super·lun·ar
super·lun·ary
super·man (*plural* ·men)
super·mar·ket
super·nal celestial
super·nal·ly
super·na·tant
super·na·ta·tion
super·natu·ral
super·natu·ral·ism
super·natu·ral·ist
super·natu·ral·is·tic

super·natu·ral·ly
super·natu·ral·ness
super·nor·mal
super·nor·mal·ity (or ·ness)
super·nor·mal·ly
super·no·va (plural ·vae or ·vas)
super·nu·mer·ary (plural ·aries)
super·or·der
super·ordi·nal
super·or·di·nate
super·ox·ide
super·phos·phate
super·physi·cal
super·pos·able
super·pose
super·po·si·tion
super·pow·er
super·satu·rat·ed chemistry term
super·satu·ra·tion
super·scribe
super·script
super·scrip·tion
super·sed·able
super·sede
super·sed·ence
super·sed·er
super·se·dure
super·sen·sible (or ·sory)
super·ses·sion
super·sex genetics term
super·son·ic
super·soni·cal·ly
super·son·ics
super·star
super·sti·tion
super·sti·tious
super·sti·tious·ness
super·store
super·stra·tum (plural ·ta or ·tums)
super·struct build on another structure
super·struc·tur·al
super·struc·ture
super·tank·er
super·tax
super·ton·ic musical note
super·vene
super·veni·ent
super·ven·tion (or ·veni·ence)
super·vise

super·vi·sion
super·vi·sor
super·vi·sory
su·pi·nate
su·pi·na·tion
su·pi·na·tor muscle
su·pine
su·pine·ly
su·pine·ness
su·plex wrestling hold
supped
sup·per
sup·ping
sup·plant
sup·plan·ta·tion
sup·plant·er
sup·ple
supple·jack plant
sup·ple·ly variant spelling of supply
sup·plement
sup·plemen·tal
sup·ple·men·ta·ri·ly (or ·tal·ly)
sup·plemen·ta·ry (plural ·ries)
sup·plemen·ta·tion
sup·plement·er
sup·ple·ness
sup·pletion linguistics term
sup·pletive
sup·pleto·ri·ly
sup·pletory
sup·pli·able
sup·pli·ance (or ·an·cy)
sup·pli·ant
sup·pli·cant (or ·pli·ant)
sup·pli·cate
sup·pli·ca·tion
sup·pli·ca·tory
sup·pli·er
sup·ply (noun, plural ·plies; verb ·plies, ·ply·ing, ·plied)
sup·ply (or sup·ple·ly) in a supple way
sup·port
sup·port·abil·ity (or ·able·ness)
sup·port·ably
sup·port·able
sup·port·er
sup·port·ing
sup·port·ive
sup·pos·able

sup·pose
sup·posed
sup·pos·ed·ly
sup·pos·er
sup·po·si·tion
sup·po·si·tion·al
sup·po·si·tious (or ·posi·ti·tious)
sup·po·si·tious·ness (or ·posi·ti·tious·ness)
sup·posi·tive involving supposition
sup·posi·tory (plural ·tories)
sup·press
sup·press·ible
sup·pres·sion
sup·pres·sive
sup·pres·sor (or ·press·er)
sup·pu·rate
sup·pu·ra·tion
sup·pu·ra·tive
su·pra above
supra·glot·tal
supra·lap·sar·ian theology term
supra·limi·nal
supra·mo·lecu·lar
supra·na·tion·al
supra·na·tion·al·ism
supra·or·bit·al
supra·re·nal
supra·seg·men·tal
su·prema·cist
su·prema·cy
Su·prema·tism cubist art
su·prema·tism
Su·prema·tist
su·preme
su·prême cookery term
su·preme·ly
su·preme·ness
su·prem·ity
su·pre·mo (plural ·mos)
sura Koran chapter
Su·ra·ba·ya (or ·ja, Soe·ra·ba·ja) Indonesian port
su·rah fabric
Su·ra·kar·ta Indonesian town
su·ral anatomy term
Su·rat Indian port
su·rat fabric
sur·base architectural term
sur·base·ment

sur·cease
sur·charge
sur·charg·er
sur·cin·gle horse's girth;
    cassock belt
sur·coat
sur·cu·lose bearing suckers
surd maths term
sure
sure-fire
sure-footed
sure-footed·ly
sure-footed·ness
sure·ly
sure·ness
sure·ty (plural ·ties)
surf breaking waves; compare
    serf
surf·able
sur·face
surface-active
sur·fac·er
sur·fac·tant
surf·bird
surf·board
surf·boat
surf·caster
surf·casting shore-fishing
surf·eit
surf·eit·er
surf·er
surfie Austral surfer
surf·ing
surf·like
surf·perch fish
surf·rider
surfy
surge rush; compare serge
sur·geon
sur·geon·cy (plural ·cies)
surgeon·fish (plural ·fish or
    ·fishes)
surg·er
sur·gery (plural ·geries)
sur·gi·cal
sur·gi·cal·ly
su·ri·cate animal
Su·ri·nam South American
    republic
sur·jec·tion
sur·jec·tive
sur·li·ly
sur·li·ness
sur·ly (·li·er, ·li·est)
sur·mis·able

sur·mise
sur·mis·ed·ly
sur·mis·er
sur·mount
sur·mount·able
sur·mount·able·ness
sur·mount·er
sur·name
sur·pass
sur·pass·able
sur·pas·sing
sur·pass·ing·ly
sur·pass·ing·ness
sur·plice vestment
sur·pliced
sur·plus (plural ·pluses)
    excess
sur·plus·age
sur·print overprint
sur·prise
sur·pris·ed·ly
sur·pris·er
sur·pris·ing
sur·pris·ing·ly
sur·pris·ing·ness
sur·ra animal disease
sur·re·al
sur·re·al·ism
sur·re·al·ist
sur·re·al·is·tic
sur·re·al·is·ti·cal·ly
sur·re·but·tal
sur·re·but·ter
sur·re·join·der
sur·ren·der
sur·ren·der·er
sur·rep·ti·tious
sur·rep·ti·tious·ness
Sur·rey English county
sur·rey carriage
sur·ro·gate
sur·ro·gate·ship
sur·ro·ga·tion
sur·round
sur·round·ing
sur·round·ings
sur·tax
sur·tout overcoat
sur·veil·lance
sur·veil·lant
sur·vey
sur·vey·able
sur·vey·ing
sur·vey·or
sur·vey·or·ship

sur·viv·abil·ity
sur·viv·able
sur·viv·al
sur·vive
sur·vi·vor
Susa ancient Persian city
sus·cep·tance magnetic
    property
sus·cep·tibil·ity (plural
    ·ities)
sus·cep·tible
sus·cep·tibly
sus·cep·tible·ness
sus·cep·tive
sus·cep·tiv·ity (or
    ·tive·ness)
su·shi Japanese food
sus·lik variant spelling of
    souslik
sus·pect
sus·pect·er
sus·pend
sus·pend·er
sus·pend·ibil·ity
sus·pend·ible (or ·pens·)
sus·pense
sus·pense·ful
sus·pen·sion
sus·pen·sive
sus·pen·sive·ness
sus·pen·soid chemistry term
sus·pen·sor
sus·pen·so·ry (plural ·ries)
sus·pi·cion
sus·pi·cion·al
sus·pi·cious
sus·pi·cious·ness
sus·pi·ra·tion
sus·pire sigh
Sus·que·han·na US river
suss
Sus·sex
sus·tain
sus·tain·able
sus·tain·ed·ly
sus·tain·er
sus·tain·ing·ly
sus·tain·ment
sus·te·nance
sus·ten·tacu·lar supporting
sus·ten·ta·tion
    nourishment
sus·ten·tion
su·sur·rant
su·sur·rate

su·sur·ra·tion (*or*
  su·sur·rus)
Suth·er·land former
  Scottish county
Sut·lej Asian river
sut·ler provisioner; *compare*
  subtler
su·tra Sanskrit sayings
sut·tee Hindu custom
Sut·ton London borough
Sut·ton Cold·field English
  town
su·tur·al
su·ture
Suva Fijian capital
Su·wan·nee (*or* Swa·nee)
  US river
su·ze·rain
su·ze·rain·ty (*plural* ·ties)
Sval·bard Norwegian
  archipelago
svelte
Sverd·lovsk *former name of*
  Yekaterinburg
swab (swab·bing, swabbed)
swab·ber
Swa·bia former German
  duchy
Swa·bian
swacked *Slang* intoxicated
swad·dle
swag (swag·ging, swagged)
swage tool
swag·er
swag·ger
swag·ger·er
swag·ger·ing·ly
swag·man (*plural* ·men)
Swa·hi·li (*plural* ·lis *or* ·li)
Swa·hi·lian
swain
swal·low
swal·low·able
swal·low·er
swallow·tail
swallow·wort
swam
swa·mi (*plural* ·mies *or*
  ·mis) Hindu title
swamp
swamp·land
swampy (swampi·er,
  swampi·est)
swan (swan·ning,
  swanned)

Swa·nee *variant spelling of*
  Suwannee
swan·herd
swank
swanki·ly
swanki·ness
swanky (swanki·er,
  swanki·est)
swan·like
swan·nery (*plural*
  ·neries)
swan's-down
Swan·sea
swan·skin
swan-upping
swap (*or* swop; swap·ping,
  swapped *or* swop·ping,
  swopped)
swap·per (*or* swop·)
swa·raj Indian
  self-government
sward (*or* swarth) turf;
  compare sword
swarf metal off-cuttings
swarm
swarthi·ly
swarthi·ness
swarthy (swarthi·er,
  swarthi·est)
swash splash
swash·buck·ler
swash·buck·ling
swash·ing·ly
swas·ti·ka
swat (swat·ting, swat·ted)
  hit; *compare* swot
swatch
swath (*or* swathe; *noun*)
swath·able (*or* swathe·)
swathe (*verb*)
Swa·tow Chinese port
swats *Dialect* beer
swat·ter
sway
sway·able
sway·back
sway·er
sway·ing·ly
Swa·zi (*plural* ·zis *or* ·zi)
Swa·zi·land
swear (swear·ing, swore,
  sworn)
swear·er
swear·ing·ly
swear·word

sweat (sweat·ing, sweat *or*
  sweat·ed)
sweat·band
sweat·box
sweat·er
sweati·ly
sweati·ness
sweat·shop
sweaty (sweati·er,
  sweati·est)
Swede native of Sweden
swede vegetable
Swe·den
Swe·den·bor·gi·an·ism (*or*
  ·bor·gism) religious
  movement
Swe·dish
swee·ny veterinary term
sweep (sweep·ing, swept)
sweep·back
sweep·er
sweep·ing
sweep·ing·ly
sweep·ing·ness
sweep·ings
sweep·stake
sweet
sweet·bread
sweet·brier
sweet·en
sweet·en·er
sweet·en·ing
sweet·heart
sweetie
sweetie·wife (*plural* ·wives)
  Scot talkative woman
sweet·ish
sweet·meal
sweet·meat
sweet·ness
sweet·shop
sweet·sop fruit
swell (swell·ing, swelled,
  swol·len *or* swelled)
swell·fish (*plural* ·fish *or*
  ·fishes)
swell·ing
swel·ter
swel·ter·ing
swel·ter·ing·ly
swept
swept·back
swept·wing
swerv·able
swerve

swerv·er
swerv·ing·ly
swift
swift·er nautical term
swiftie Austral a trick
swift·let bird
swift·ness
swig (swig·ging, swigged)
swig·ger
swill
swill·er
swim (swim·ming, swam, swum)
swim·mable
swim·mer
swim·mer·et zoology term
swim·ming·ly
swim·suit
swin·dle
swin·dler
swin·dling·ly
Swin·don
swine (plural swines)
swine·herd
swine·pox
swing (swing·ing, swung)
swing·boat
swinge (swinge·ing, swinged) punish
swing·er
swing·ing
swin·gle flax-beating instrument
swing·om·eter
swing-wing
swin·ish
swin·ish·ness
swink Dialect toil
swipe
swipes Slang beer
swip·ple (or swi·ple) part of flail
swirl
swirl·ing·ly
swirly
swish
swish·er
swish·ing·ly
swishy
Swiss
switch
switch·back
switch·board
switch·er

switch·eroo US unexpected change
switch·girl Austral switchboard operator
switch-over (noun)
swith·er Scot hesitate
Switz·er a Swiss
Swit·zer·land
swiv·el (·el·ling, ·elled; US ·el·ing, ·eled)
swiv·et Dialect excitement
swizz Slang disappointment
swiz·zle
swol·len
swol·len·ness
swoon
swoon·ing·ly
swoop
swoosh
swop variant spelling of swap
sword weapon; compare sward
sword·bill
sword·craft
sword·fish (plural ·fish or ·fishes)
sword·like
sword·play
swords·man (plural ·men)
swords·man·ship
sword·stick
sword·tail fish
swore
sworn
swot (swot·ting, swot·ted) study; compare swat
swound Dialect swoon
swum
swung
swy Austral gambling game
Syba·ris ancient Greek colony
Syba·rite
syba·rite lover of luxury
syba·rit·ic (or ·riti·cal)
syba·riti·cal·ly
(sybil) incorrect spelling of sibyl
syca·mine mulberry
syca·more
syce (or sice, saice) Indian servant
sy·cee silver ingots
sy·co·nium (plural ·nia) botany term

syco·phan·cy
syco·phant
syco·phan·tic
syco·phan·ti·cal·ly
sy·co·sis skin disease
Syd·ney Australian city; Canadian port
Sy·ene ancient Egyptian town
sy·enite rock
sy·enit·ic
Syk·tyv·kar Russian city
syl·la·bary (plural ·baries)
syl·lab·ic
syl·labi·cal·ly
syl·labi·cate syllabify
syl·labi·fi·ca·tion (or ·labi·ca·tion)
syl·labi·fy (·fies, ·fy·ing, ·fied)
syl·la·bism
syl·la·ble
syl·labo·gram
syl·lab·og·ra·phy
syl·la·bub (or sil·)
syl·la·bus (plural ·buses or ·bi)
syl·lep·sis (plural ·ses) linguistics term
syl·lep·tic
syl·lep·ti·cal·ly
syl·lo·gism
syl·lo·gis·tic
syl·lo·gis·ti·cal
syl·lo·gis·ti·cal·ly
syl·lo·gi·za·tion (or ·sa·tion)
syl·lo·gize (or ·gise)
syl·lo·giz·er (or ·gis·er)
sylph
sylph·ic (or ·id)
sylph·like (or ·ish)
syl·va (or sil·; plural ·vas or ·vae) trees
syl·van (or sil·)
syl·van·ite mineral
Sylvanus variant spelling of Silvanus
syl·vat·ic (or ·ves·tral) occurring in a wood
syl·vite (or ·vine) mineral
sym·bi·ont
sym·bi·on·tic
sym·bio·sis
sym·bi·ot·ic (or ·oti·cal)

sym·bi·oti·cal·ly
sym·bol (·bol·ling, ·bolled;
US ·bol·ing, ·boled) thing
representing something;
compare cymbal
sym·bol·ic (or ·boli·cal)
sym·boli·cal·ly
sym·bol·cal·ness
sym·bol·ism
sym·bol·ist
sym·bol·is·tic (or ·ti·cal)
sym·bol·is·ti·cal·ly
sym·boli·za·tion (or
·sa·tion)
sym·bol·ize (or ·ise)
sym·bo·logi·cal
sym·bol·o·gist
sym·bol·ogy
sym·met·al·lism economic
doctrine
sym·met·ri·cal
sym·met·ri·cal·ly
sym·met·ri·cal·ness
sym·me·tri·za·tion (or
·sa·tion)
sym·me·trize (or ·trise)
sym·me·try (plural ·tries)
sym·pa·thec·to·my (plural
·mies) nerve surgery
sym·pa·thet·ic (or
·theti·cal)
sym·pa·theti·cal·ly
sym·pa·thin hormone
sym·pa·thize (or ·thise)
sym·pa·thiz·er (or
·this·er)
sym·pa·thiz·ing·ly (or
·this·ing·ly)
sym·pa·tho·lyt·ic
pharmacology term
sym·pa·tho·mi·met·ic
pharmacology term
sym·pa·thy (plural ·thies)
sym·pat·ric biology term
sym·pat·ri·cal·ly
sym·pet·al·ous
sym·phile entomology term
sym·phon·ic
sym·phoni·cal·ly
sym·pho·ni·ous
sym·pho·nist
sym·pho·ny (plural ·nies)
sym·phys·ial (or ·eal)
sym·physi·cal·ly (or
·phyti·)

sym·phy·sis (plural ·ses)
anatomy term
sym·phys·tic (or ·phyt·ic)
sym·po·dial
sym·po·dium (plural ·dia)
botany term
sym·po·si·ac
sym·po·sium (plural ·siums
or ·sia)
symp·tom
symp·to·mat·ic (or
·mati·cal)
symp·to·mati·cal·ly
symp·toma·tol·ogy
syn·aer·esis variant spelling
of syneresis
syn·aes·the·sia (US ·es·)
medical term
syn·aes·thet·ic (US ·es·)
syna·gogi·cal (or ·gog·al)
syna·gogue
syna·lepha (or ·loepha)
linguistics term
syn·apse nerve-cell junction
syn·ap·sis (plural ·ses) stage
of meiosis
syn·ap·tic (or ·ti·cal)
syn·ap·ti·cal·ly
syn·ar·chy (plural ·chies)
joint rule
syn·ar·thro·dial
syn·ar·thro·sis (plural ·ses)
anatomy term
sync Slang synchronize;
synchrony
syn·carp botany term
syn·car·pous
syn·car·py
syn·chro (plural ·chros)
electrical device
syn·chro·cy·clo·tron
syn·chro·flash camera
mechanism
syn·chro·mesh
syn·chron·ic
syn·chroni·cal·ly
syn·chro·nism
syn·chro·nis·tic (or ·ti·cal)
syn·chro·nis·ti·cal·ly
syn·chro·ni·za·tion (or
·sa·tion)
syn·chro·nize (or ·nise)
syn·chro·niz·er (or ·nis·er)
syn·chro·nous
syn·chro·nous·ness

syn·chrony
syn·chro·scope (or
·chrono·)
syn·chro·tron
syn·clas·tic maths term
syn·cli·nal
syn·cline geology term
syn·cli·no·rium (plural ·ria)
Syn·com communications
satellite
syn·co·pate
syn·co·pa·tion
syn·co·pa·tor
syn·co·pe
syn·cop·ic (or ·co·pal)
syn·cret·ic (or ·cre·tis·tic)
syn·cre·tism
syn·cre·tist
syn·cre·ti·za·tion (or
·sa·tion)
syn·cre·tize (or ·tise)
combine differing beliefs
syn·cyt·ial
syn·cyt·ium (plural ·cytia)
zoology term
syn·dac·tyl
syn·dac·tyly (or ·tyl·ism)
syn·de·sis linguistics term
syn·des·mo·sis (plural ·ses)
anatomy term
syn·des·mot·ic
syn·det·ic (or ·deti·cal)
syn·deti·cal·ly
syn·de·ton
syn·dic business agent
syn·di·cal
syn·di·cal·ism
syn·di·cal·ist
syn·di·cal·is·tic
syn·di·cate
syn·di·ca·tion
syn·dic·ship
syn·dio·tac·tic chemistry
term
syn·drome
syn·drom·ic
syne Scot since
syn·ec·do·che figure of
speech
syn·ec·doch·ic (or
·dochi·cal)
syn·ec·dochi·cal·ly
syn·eco·log·ic (or ·logi·cal)
syn·eco·logi·cal·ly
syn·ecol·ogy

syn·ec·tics problem solving
syn·er·esis (*or* ·aer·)
    chemistry or phonetics
    term
syn·er·get·ic (*or* ·gis·tic)
syn·er·geti·cal·ly (*or*
    ·gis·ti·)
syn·er·gic
syn·er·gism acting together
syn·er·gist
syn·er·gis·tic
syn·er·gy (*plural* ·gies)
syn·esis linguistics term
syn·es·the·sia US spelling of
    synaesthesia
syn·gam·ic (*or* ·ga·mous)
syn·ga·my (*or* ·gen·esis)
    biology term
syni·zesis phonetics or
    biology term
syn·kary·on biology term
syn·kary·on·ic
syn·od
syn·od·al (*or* ·odi·cal)
syn·od·ic
syn·oecious (*or* syn·ecious,
    synoi·cous) botany term
syn·oekete (*or* ·oecete)
    zoology term
syno·nym
syno·nym·ic (*or*
    ·nymi·cal)
syno·nym·ity
syn·ony·mize (*or* ·mise)
syn·ony·mous
syn·ony·mous·ness
syn·ony·my (*plural* ·mies)
syn·op·sis (*plural* ·ses)
syn·op·tic
syn·op·ti·cal·ly
syn·op·tist
syno·via fluid in joint
syno·vial
syno·vit·ic

syno·vi·tis
syn·sep·al·ous botany term
syn·tac·tic (*or* ·ti·cal)
syn·tac·ti·cal·ly
syn·tac·tics study of
    symbols
syn·tag·ma (*or* syn·tagm;
    plural ·tag·ma·ta *or*
    ·tagms) linguistics term
syn·tax
syn·the·sis (*plural* ·ses)
syn·the·sist
syn·the·si·za·tion (*or*
    ·sa·tion)
syn·the·size (*or* ·sise)
syn·the·siz·er (*or* ·sis·er)
syn·thet·ic
syn·theti·cal
syn·theti·cal·ly
syn·the·tism art term
syn·the·tist
syn·ton·ic psychology
    term
syn·toni·cal·ly
sy·pher woodworking term;
    compare cipher
sy·pher·ing
syphi·lis
syphi·lit·ic
syphi·liti·cal·ly
syphi·loid
syphi·lolo·gist
syphi·lol·ogy
syphi·lo·ma (*plural* ·mas *or*
    ·ma·ta) tumour
sy·phon *variant spelling of*
    siphon
Sy·ra·cuse Italian port; US
    city
Syria
Syri·ac
Syr·ian
sy·rin·ga ornamental shrub;
    compare seringa

sy·ringe
sy·rin·geal
sy·rin·go·my·elia disease
sy·rin·go·my·el·ic
syr·inx (*plural* sy·rin·ges *or*
    syr·inx·es) zoology term
syr·phid fly
syr·up (*US also* sir·)
syr·upy
sys·sar·co·sis (*plural* ·ses)
    anatomy term
sys·sar·cot·ic
sys·tal·tic of heartbeat
sys·tem
sys·tem·at·ic methodical;
    compare systemic
sys·tem·ati·cal·ly
sys·tem·ati·cal·ness
sys·tem·at·ics
sys·tema·tism
sys·tema·tist
sys·tema·ti·za·tion (*or*
    ·sa·tion)
sys·tema·tize (*or* ·tise)
sys·tema·tiz·er (*or* ·tis·er)
sys·tema·tol·ogy
sys·tem·ic affecting whole
    body; *compare* systematic
sys·temi·cal·ly
sys·temi·za·tion (*or*
    ·sa·tion) systematization
sys·tem·iz·er (*or* ·is·er)
sys·to·le
sys·tol·ic
Syz·ran Russian port
syzy·geti·cal·ly
sy·zyg·ial (*or* syzy·get·ic,
    syzy·gal)
syzy·gy (*plural* ·gies)
    astronomy term
Szcze·cin Polish port
Sze·chwan Chinese
    province
Sze·ged Hungarian city

T

ta *Slang* thank you
Taal Philippine volcano
tab (tab·bing, tabbed)
taba·nid fly
tab·ard

taba·ret fabric
Ta·bas·co Mexican state;
    (*Trademark*) sauce
tabbed
tab·bing

tab·by (*plural* ·bies)
tab·er·nac·le
tab·er·nacu·lar
ta·bes wasting
ta·bes·cence

ta·bes·cent
tab·la·ture musical notation
ta·ble
tab·leau (plural ·leaux or ·leaus)
table·cloth
ta·ble d'hôte (plural ta·bles d'hôte)
table·land
table·spoon
table·spoon·ful (plural ·fuls)
tab·let
table-turning
table·ware
tab·loid
ta·boo (or tabu; plural ·boos or ·bus)
ta·bor (or ·bour) drum
tabo·ret (or tabou·) stool
tabo·rin (or tabou·) drum
Ta·briz Iranian city
tabu·lable
tabu·lar
tabu·lar·ize
tabu·late
tabu·la·tion
tabu·la·tor
taca·ma·hac (or tac·ma·hack) gum
ta·cet musical term
tache Archaic buckle; Slang moustache
tach·eom·eter (or ta·chym·) surveying instrument; compare tachometer
tacheo·met·ric (or ·ri·cal, tachy·)
tacheo·met·ri·cal·ly (or tachy·)
tach·eom·etry (or ta·chym·)
tachi·na fly
ta·chis·to·scope
ta·chis·to·scop·ic
ta·chis·to·scopi·cal·ly
tacho·graph speed-recording device
ta·chom·eter speed-measuring device; compare tacheometer
tacho·met·ric (or ·ri·cal)
tacho·met·ri·cal·ly
ta·chom·etry

tachy·car·dia rapid heartbeat
tachy·car·di·ac
ta·chyg·ra·pher (or ·phist)
tachy·graph·ic (or ·graphi·cal)
ta·chyg·ra·phy shorthand
tachy·lyte (or ·lite) basalt
tachy·lyt·ic (or ·lit·)
ta·chym·eter variant of tacheometer
ta·chym·etry variant of tacheometry
tachy·on physics term
tachy·phy·lax·is medical term
tac·it
tac·it·ness
taci·turn
taci·tur·nity
tack
tack·er
tack·et Dialect hobnail
tacki·ly
tacki·ness
tack·le
tack·ler
tacky (tacki·er, tacki·est)
tac·node maths term
taco (plural tacos) Mexican food
Ta·co·ma US port
taco·nite rock
tact
tact·ful
tact·ful·ly
tact·ful·ness
tac·tic
tac·ti·cal
tac·ti·cal·ly
tac·ti·cian
tac·tics
tac·tile
tac·til·ity
tact·less
tact·less·ness
tac·tual
tad US boy
tad·pole
Ta·dzhik (plural ·dzhiks or ·dzhik) Muslim people
Ta·dzhiki·stan Central Asian republic
Tae·gu South Korean city
Tae·jon South Korean city

tae·nia (or esp. US te·; plural ·niae) band; architectural term; compare tinea
tae·nia (US also te·; plural ·niae) tapeworm; compare tinea
tae·nia·cide (US also te·)
tae·nia·fuge (US also te·)
tae·nia·sis (US also te·)
taf·fe·ta
taff·rail ship's rail
Taf·fy (plural ·fies) Slang Welshman
taf·fy (plural ·fies) US sweet
tafia (or taf·fia) rum
Ta·fi·lelt (or Ta·fi·la·let) oasis
tag (tag·ging, tagged)
Ta·ga·log (plural ·logs or ·log) Philippine people
Ta·gan·rog Russian port
tag·gers tin-coated iron sheet
tag·ging
ta·glia·tel·le pasta
tag·meme linguistics term
tag·mem·ic
tag·mem·ics
Ta·gus European river
ta·hi·na sesame paste
Ta·hi·ti
Ta·hi·tian
tahr animal
tah·sil·dar Indian tax collector
Tai·chung (or T'ai-chung) Chinese city
tai·ga subarctic forests
tail appendage; compare tale
tail·back
tail·board
tail-ender
tail·gate
tail·ing
taille (plural tailles) French tax
tail·less
tail·light (or ·lamp)
tail·like
tai·lor
tailor·bird
tailor-made
tail·piece
tail·pipe

tail·plane
tail·race
tails tail coat
tail·skid
tail·spin
tail·stock
tail·wind
tain mirror backing
Tai·nan (or T'ai-nan)
Chinese city
taint
tai·pan snake
Tai·pei (or T'ai-pei)
Taiwanese capital
Tai·wan
Tai·wan·ese
Tai·yuan (or T'ai-yüan)
Chinese city
taj Muslim cap
Taj Ma·hal
taka Bangladeshi currency
tak·able (or take·able)
ta·ka·he bird
Taka·mat·su Japanese port
take (tak·ing, took, tak·en)
take·away
tak·en
take·off
take·over
tak·er
tak·in animal
tak·ing
tak·ing·ness
tak·ings
Ta·ko·ra·di Ghanaian port
tala·poin monkey
ta·laria winged sandals
talc (talck·ing, talcked or
talc·ing, talced)
Tal·ca·hua·no Chilean city
talc·ose (or tal·cous)
tal·cum
tale story; compare tail
tal·ent
tal·ent·ed
ta·les legal term
ta·les·man (plural ·men)
tali·grade zoology term
tali·on legal term
tali·ped
tali·pes club foot
tali·pot palm tree
tal·is·man (plural ·mans)
tal·is·man·ic
talk

talka·bil·ity
talk·able
talka·tive
talka·tive·ly
talka·tive·ness
talk·er
talkie
talking-to (plural -tos)
tall
tal·lage historical tax
Tal·la·has·see US city
tall·boy
tal·li·er
Tal·linn (or ·lin) Estonian
capital
tall·ish
tal·lith (plural ·lai·sim,
·lithes or ·li·toth) prayer
shawl
tall·ness
tal·low
tal·ly (verb ·lies, ·ly·ing,
·lied; noun, plural ·lies)
tally-ho (verb -hos, -hoing,
-hoed; noun, plural -hos)
tally·man (plural ·men)
Tal·mud Jewish literature
Tal·mud·ic (or ·mudi·cal)
Tal·mud·ism
Tal·mud·ist
tal·on
ta·loned
ta·luk (or ·lu·ka, ·loo·ka)
Indian district
ta·lus (plural ·li) anklebone
ta·lus (plural ·luses) scree
tam·abil·ity (or tame·)
tam·able (or tame·)
ta·ma·le Mexican food
ta·man·dua (or ·du) animal
tama·rack tree
ta·ma·rau (or ·rao) cattle
tama·rin monkey
tama·rind (or ·rin·do; plural
·rinds or ·rin·dos) tree,
fruit
tama·risk tree
ta·ma·sha Indian
entertainment
Ta·mau·li·pas Mexican
state
Tam·bo·ra Indonesian
volcano
tam·bour

tam·boura musical
instrument
tam·bou·rin dance
tam·bou·rine musical
instrument
tam·bou·rin·ist
Tam·bov Russian city
tame
tame·able variant spelling of
tamable
tame·ness
tam·er
Tame·side area of Greater
Manchester
Tam·il (plural ·ils or ·il)
Asian people
Tam·il Nadu Indian state
tam·is (plural ·ises) straining
cloth
Tam·ma·ny Hall US
political party
organization
tam·my (plural ·mies)
tam-o'-shanter
tam·ox·i·fen
tamp
Tam·pa Florida resort
tam·per
Tam·pe·re Finnish city
tam·per·er
Tam·pi·co Mexican port
tamp·ing Welsh angry
tam·pi·on (or tom·) gun
plug
tam·pon medical plug
tam·pon·ade
tam-tam gong; compare
tom-tom
tan (tan·ning, tanned)
Tana Ethiopian lake
tana lemur
tana·ger bird
Tana·na Alaskan river
tan·bark
tan·dem
tan·doori
Tang Chinese dynasty
tang
Tan·ga Tanzanian port
Tan·gan·yi·ka African lake
tan·ge·lo (plural ·los) hybrid
fruit
tan·gen·cy
tan·gent
tan·gen·tial

tan·gen·ti·al·ity
tan·gen·tial·ly (or ·tal·ly)
Tan·ge·rine of Tangier
tan·ge·rine fruit
tan·gibil·ity (or ·gible·ness)
tan·gible
Tan·gier Moroccan port
tangi·ness
tan·gle
tan·gle·ment
tan·gler
tan·gly
tan·go (noun, plural ·tos;
   verb ·goes, ·go·ing, ·goed)
tan·go·ist
tan·gram puzzle
Tang·shan Chinese city
tangy (tangi·er, tangi·est)
tanh maths term
Ta·nis ancient Egyptian city
tan·ist heir of Celtic
   chieftain
Tan·jore Indian city
tank
tan·ka (plural ·kas or ·ka)
   Japanese verse
tank·age
tank·ard
tank·er
tank·ful (plural ·fuls)
tan·nage
tan·nate
tanned
tan·ner
tan·nery (plural ·neries)
tan·nic
tan·nin
tan·ning
Tan·noy (Trademark)
tan·sy (plural ·sies) plant
Tan·ta Egyptian city
tan·ta·late
tan·tal·ic
tan·ta·lite mineral
tan·ta·li·za·tion (or
   ·sa·tion)
tan·ta·lize (or ·lise)
tan·ta·liz·er (or ·lis·er)
tan·ta·liz·ing·ly (or
   ·lis·ing·ly)
tan·ta·lous chemistry term;
   compare tantalus
tan·ta·lum chemical
   element
Tantalus mythological king

tan·ta·lus case for bottles;
   compare tantalous
tan·ta·mount
tan·ta·ra fanfare
tan·tivy (plural ·tivies)
   hunting cry
tan·to musical term
Tan·tra Sanskrit books
Tan·tric
Tan·trism
Tan·trist
tan·trum
Tan·za·nia
Tan·za·nian
Tao·ism Chinese
   philosophy
Tao·ist
tap (tap·ping, tapped)
tapa mulberry bark
tap-dance (verb)
tap-dancer
tapa·der·a stirrup covering
tape
ta·per
ta·per·er
ta·per·ing·ly
tap·es·tried
tap·es·try (plural ·tries)
ta·petal
ta·petum (plural ·peta)
   biology term
tape·worm
tap·hole
tapio·ca
ta·pir (plural ·pirs or ·pir)
   animal
tap·is (plural tap·is) carpet
tap·pable
tapped
tap·per
tap·pet
tap·ping
tappit-hen
tap·room
tap·root
tap·ster
tar (tar·ring, tarred)
ta·ra·did·dle variant spelling
   of tarradiddle
ta·ra·ma·sa·la·ta
ta·ran·tass Russian carriage
tar·an·tel·la dance; compare
   tarantula
tar·ant·ism nervous
   disorder

Ta·ran·to Italian port
ta·ran·tu·la (plural ·las or
   ·lae) spider; compare
   tarantella
ta·raxa·cum plant
tar·boosh (or ·bush,
   ·bouche) Muslim cap
Tar·de·noi·sian Mesolithic
   culture
tar·di·grade minute animal
tar·di·ly
tar·di·ness
tardy (·di·er, ·di·est)
tare plant; weight of goods
   container; compare tear
tar·get
tar·iff
Ta·rim Chinese river
tar·la·tan fabric
tar·mac (·mack·ing,
   ·macked)
tarn lake
tar·nal US damned
tar·na·tion
Tarn-et-Garonne French
   department
tar·nish
tar·nish·able
tar·nish·er
taro (plural taros) plant
ta·rot card
tarp Austral tarpaulin
tar·pan extinct horse
tar·pau·lin
Tar·pe·ian Rock
tar·pon (plural ·pons or
   ·pon) fish
tar·ra·did·dle (or ta·ra·)
tar·ra·gon
Tar·ra·sa Spanish city
tarred
tar·ri·ness
tar·ring
tar·ry (verb ·ries, ·ry·ing,
   ·ried; adj ·ri·er, ·ri·est)
tar·sal
tar·si·er animal
tar·so·meta·tar·sal
tar·so·meta·tar·sus (plural
   ·si)
Tar·sus Turkish city
tar·sus (plural ·si) ankle
   bones
tart
tar·tan

Tar·tar *variant spelling of* Tatar

tar·tar deposit on teeth; fearsome person; sauce; chemical substance

tar·tar·ic

tar·tari·za·tion (*or* **·sa·tion**)

tar·tar·ize (*or* **·ise**)

tar·tar·ous of tartar

Tar·ta·rus Hades

Tar·ta·ry *variant spelling of* Tatary

tart·let

tart·ness

tar·trate

tarty

Tar·zan

Tash·kent Uzbek capital

ta·sim·eter temperature-change measurer

tasi·met·ric

ta·sim·etry

task

task·er

task·master (*fem* **·mistress**)

task·work

Tas·ma·nia

Tas·ma·nian

Tas·man Sea

Tass former Soviet news agency

tass *Dialect* cup

tas·sel (**·sel·ling**, **·selled**; *US* **·sel·ing**, **·seled**)

tas·sel·ly

tas·set piece of armour

tast·able

taste

taste·ful

taste·ful·ly

taste·ful·ness

taste·less

taste·less·ness

tast·er

tasti·ly

tasti·ness

tasty (**tasti·er**, **tasti·est**)

tat (**tat·ting**, **tat·ted**)

ta·ta *Slang* goodbye

Ta·tar (*or* **Tar·tar**) Mongoloid people

Ta·tar·ian (*or* **Tar·tar·ian**, **Ta·tar·ic**, **Tar·tar·ic**)

Ta·ta·ry (*or* **Tar·ta·ry**) historical region

ta·ter *Dialect* potato

Tat·ler journal; *compare* tattler

tatou·ay armadillo

Ta·tra mountain range

tat·ted

tat·ter

tat·ter·de·mal·ion

tat·ter·sall fabric

tat·ting

tat·tle

tat·tler one who tattles; *compare* Tatler

tattle·tale

tat·tling·ly

tat·too (*noun, plural* **·toos**; *verb* **toos**, **·too·ing**, **·tooed**)

tat·too·ist (*or* **·er**)

tat·ty (**·ti·er**, **·ti·est**)

tatty-peelin *Scot* pretentious

tau Greek letter; *compare* taw

taught past tense of teach; *compare* taut

taunt

taunt·er

taunt·ing·ly

Taun·ton Somerset town

taupe brownish grey

Tau·ranga New Zealand port

Tau·rean

tau·rine bull-like; biochemical compound

tau·ro·ma·chian

tau·roma·chy bullfighting

Tau·rus constellation; sign of zodiac

taut tight; *compare* taught

taut·en

taut·ness

tau·tog fish

tau·to·logi·cal (*or* **·to·log·ic**, **·tolo·gous**)

tau·to·logi·cal·ly

tau·tolo·gize (*or* **·gise**)

tau·tol·ogy (*plural* **·gies**)

tau·to·mer chemistry term

tau·to·mer·ic

tau·tom·er·ism

tau·to·nym biology term

tau·to·nym·ic (*or* **·tony·mous**)

tau·tony·my

Ta·vel wine

tav·ern

tav·ern·er

taw marble; tanning term; *compare* tau

taw·dri·ly

taw·dri·ness

taw·dry (**·dri·er**, **·dri·est**)

taw·er

taw·ny (*or* **·ney**)

tawse (*or* **taws**) leather strap

tax

tax·abil·ity (*or* **·able·ness**)

tax·able

taxa·ceous botany term

taxa·tion

taxa·tion·al

tax·deduct·ible

tax·eme linguistics term

tax·er

taxi (*noun, plural* **taxis** *or* **taxies**; *verb* **taxies**, **taxi·ing**, **tax·ied**)

taxi·cab

taxi·der·mal (*or* **·mic**)

taxi·der·mist

taxi·der·my

taxi·meter

tax·ing·ly

taxi·plane

tax·is biology term; surgical process

taxis (*or* **taxies**) *plural of* taxi

taxi·way

tax·man (*plural* **·men**)

tax·on (*plural* **taxa**) biology term

taxo·nom·ic (*or* **·nomi·cal**)

taxo·nomi·cal·ly

tax·ono·mist (*or* **·mer**)

tax·ono·my

tax·payer

tax·paying

Tay Scottish river

tay *Irish* tea

tay·ra animal

Tay·side former Scottish region

taz·za wine cup

Tbi·li·si (*or* **Tif·lis**) Georgian capital

te (or ti) musical term;
  compare tea; tee
tea beverage; compare te; tee
tea•berry (plural •berries)
tea•cake
tea•cart
teach (teach•es, teach•ing,
  taught)
teach•able
teach•er
teach•in
teach•ing
tea•cup
tea•cup•ful (plural •fuls)
tea•house
teak
tea•kettle
teal (plural teals or teal)
  duck
team group; compare teem
tea•maker
team•mate
team•ster
team•work
tea•pot
tea•poy table with tripod
  base
tear (tear•ing, tore, torn)
  rip; compare tare
tear drop from eye; compare
  tier
tear•able
tear•er
tear•ful
tear•ful•ly
tear•ful•ness
tear•ing
tear•ing•ly
tear-jerker
tear•less
tea•room
tease
tea•sel (or •zel, •zle;
  •sel•ling, •selled; US
  •sel•ing, •seled)
teas•er
tea•shop
teas•ing•ly
tea•spoon
tea•spoon•ful (plural •fuls)
teat
techi•ly variant spelling of
  tetchily
techi•ness variant spelling of
  tetchiness

tech•ne•tium chemical
  element
tech•nic variant of
  technique
tech•ni•cal
tech•ni•cal•ity (plural •ities)
tech•ni•cal•ly
tech•ni•cian
Tech•ni•col•or (Trademark)
tech•nics study of industry
tech•nique (or •nic)
tech•noc•ra•cy (plural •cies)
tech•no•crat
tech•no•crat•ic
tech•nog•ra•phy
tech•no•logi•cal
tech•no•logi•cal•ly
tech•nolo•gist
tech•nol•ogy (plural •ogies)
tech•no•struc•ture
techy variant spelling of
  tetchy
tec•ton•ic
tec•toni•cal•ly
tec•ton•ics
tec•tri•cial
tec•trix (plural •tri•ces)
  feather
ted (ted•ding, ted•ded)
  shake out hay
ted•der
ted•dy (plural •dies)
Te De•um
te•di•ous
te•di•ous•ness
te•dium
tee (tee•ing, teed) golf term;
  T-shaped part; compare te;
  tea
teem abound; compare team
teem•ing
teen
teen•age
teen•aged
teen•ager
tee•ny (•ni•er, •ni•est)
teeny•bopper
Tees English river
Tees•side
tee•ter
teeth plural of tooth
teethe (verb)
teeth•ing
tee•to•tal
tee•to•tal•ism

tee•to•tal•ler (US •tal•er)
tee•to•tum spinning top
tef (or teff) grass
Tef•lon (Trademark)
teg sheep
teg•men (plural •mi•na)
  zoology term
teg•mi•nal
Te•gu•ci•gal•pa Honduran
  capital
tegu•lar of a tile
tegu•lar•ly
Teh•ran (or Te•he•ran)
Te•huan•tepec Mexican
  region
tek•tite
tela (plural telae) weblike
  structure
tel•aes•the•sia (US •es•)
  paranormal perception
tel•aes•thet•ic (US •es•)
tela•mon (plural •mones)
  supporting pillar
tel•an•gi•ec•ta•sis (or •sia;
  plural •ses) medical term
tel•an•gi•ec•tat•ic
Tel•auto•graph (Trademark)
tel•auto•graph•ic
tel•autog•ra•phy
Tel Aviv
tele•cast (•cast•ing, •cast or
  •cast•ed)
tele•cast•er
tele•com•mu•ni•ca•tion
tele•com•mu•ni•ca•tions
tele•con•fer•ence
tele•con•fer•en•cing
tel•edu badger
te•le•ga cart
tele•gen•ic
tel•eg•no•sis
  parapsychology term
tel•eg•nos•tic
tel•egon•ic
Telegonus son of
  Odysseus
te•lego•ny genetics term
tele•gram
tele•graph
te•leg•ra•pher (or •phist)
tele•graph•ic
tele•graphi•cal•ly
te•leg•ra•phy
tele•ki•ne•sis
tele•ki•net•ic

Tel·e·mach·us son of
  Odysseus
tel·e·mark skiing term
tele·me·di·cine
te·lem·eter
tele·met·ric (or ·ri·cal)
tele·met·ri·cal·ly
te·lem·etry
tel·en·cephal·ic
tel·en·cepha·lon anatomy
  term
teleo·logi·cal (or ·log·ic)
teleo·logi·cal·ly
tele·olo·gism
tele·olo·gist
tel·ol·ogy
tel·eost fish
tele·path·ic
tele·pathi·cal·ly
te·lepa·thist
te·lepa·thize (or ·thise)
te·lepa·thy
tele·phone
tele·phon·er
tele·phon·ic
te·lepho·nist
te·lepho·ny
tele·photo·graph·ic
tele·pho·tog·ra·phy
tele·photo
tele·play
tele·print·er
tele·prompt·er
Tele·ran (*Trademark*)
  navigational aid
tele·scope
tele·scop·ic
tele·scopi·cal·ly
te·les·co·py
tele·script
tele·sis
tele·spec·tro·scope
tele·ste·reo·scope
tel·es·the·sia *US spelling of*
  telaesthesia
te·les·tich poem
tele·thon
tele·tran·scrip·tion
tele·tube *short for* television
  tube
Tele·type (*Trademark*)
Tele·type·set·ter
  (*Trademark*)
tele·type·set·ting
te·leu·to·spore

te·leu·to·spor·ic
tele·vise
tele·vi·sion
tele·vi·sion·al
tele·vi·sion·ary
tele·writ·er
tel·ex
Tel·ford Shropshire town
tel·geni·cal·ly
te·lial
tel·ic purposeful
te·lio·spore
te·lium (*plural* ·lia) fungal
  structure
tell (tell·ing, told)
tell·able
Tell el Amar·na Egyptian
  ruins
tell·er
tell·ing
tell·ing·ly
tell·tale
tel·lu·rate chemistry term
tel·lu·rian of the earth
tel·lu·ric
tel·lu·ride chemical
  compound
tel·lu·ri·on (or ·lu·rian)
  model of earth
tel·lu·rite
tel·lu·rium chemical
  element
tel·lu·rize (or ·rise)
tel·lu·rom·eter surveying
  instrument
tel·lu·rous
tel·ly (*plural* tel·lies)
telo·phase biology term
telo·pha·sic
tel·pher (or ·fer)
tel·pher·age (or ·fer·)
  transport system
tel·pher·ic (or ·fer·)
tel·son zoology term
tel·son·ic
Tel·star satellite
Te·luk·be·tung (or
  Te·loek·be·toeng)
  Indonesian port
Tema Ghanaian port
tem·er·ari·ous
te·mer·ity
temp
tem·per
tem·pera painting medium

tem·per·abil·ity
tem·per·able
tem·pera·ment
tem·pera·men·tal
tem·pera·men·tal·ly
tem·per·ance
tem·per·ate
tem·per·ate·ly
tem·per·ate·ness
tem·pera·ture
tem·per·er
tem·pest
tem·pes·tu·ous
tem·pes·tu·ous·ness
Tem·plar member of
  religious order
tem·plate (or ·plet)
tem·ple
tem·po (*plural* ·pos or ·pi)
tem·po·ral of time or the
  temples
tem·po·ral·ity
tem·po·ral·ly of time
tem·po·rari·ly not
  permanently
tem·po·rari·ness
tem·po·rary (*plural* ·raries)
tem·po·ri·za·tion (or
  ·sa·tion)
tem·po·rize (or ·rise)
tem·po·riz·er (or ·ris·er)
tempt
tempt·able
temp·ta·tion
tempt·er
tempt·ing
tempt·ing·ly
tempt·ress
tem·pu·ra Japanese food
Te·mu·co Chilean city
ten
ten·abil·ity (or ·able·ness)
ten·able
ten·ably
ten·ace bridge term
te·na·cious
te·na·cious·ness
te·nac·ity
te·nacu·lum (*plural* ·la)
  surgical instrument
te·naille fortification
ten·an·cy (*plural* ·cies)
ten·ant
ten·ant·able
ten·ant·ry

tench (*plural* tench)
tend
ten·den·cy (*plural* ·cies)
ten·den·tious (*or* ·cious)
ten·den·tious·ness (*or* ·cious·)
ten·der
ten·der·able
ten·der·er
tender·foot (*plural* ·foots *or* ·feet)
tender·hearted
tender·hearted·ness
ten·deri·za·tion (*or* ·sa·tion)
ten·der·ize (*or* ·ise)
ten·der·iz·er (*or* ·is·er)
ten·der·loin
ten·der·ness
ten·din·itis inflammation of tendon
ten·di·nous of tendons
ten·don
ten·dril
ten·dril·lar (*or* ·ous)
ten·ebrism style of painting
ten·ebrist
ten·ebros·ity
ten·ebrous (*or* te·neb·ri·ous)
Ten·edos Greek island
ten·ement
ten·emen·tal (*or* ·tary)
ten·ement·ed
Ten·erife
te·nes·mic
te·nes·mus medical term
ten·et belief
ten·fold
Ten·gri Nor Chinese lake
te·nia *variant spelling (esp. US) of* taenia
ten·ner
Ten·nes·sean
Ten·nes·see
ten·nis
ten·no (*plural* ·no *or* ·nos) Japanese emperor
ten·on
ten·on·er
ten·or
teno·rite mineral
te·nor·rha·phy (*plural* ·phies) tendon surgery
te·noto·mist

te·noto·my (*plural* ·mies) incision into tendon
ten·pin
ten·pins
ten·rec animal
tense
tense·ly
tense·ness
ten·sibil·ity (*or* ·sible·ness)
ten·sible
ten·sile
ten·sil·ity (*or* ·sile·ness)
ten·sim·eter device measuring vapour pressure
ten·si·om·eter device measuring tensile strength
ten·sion
ten·sion·al
ten·sive
ten·sor
ten·so·rial
tent
ten·ta·cle
ten·ta·cled
ten·tacu·lar
tent·age tents
ten·ta·tion mechanical process
ten·ta·tive
ten·ta·tive·ness
tent·ed
ten·ter
tenter·hook
tenth
tenu·ity
tenu·ous
tenu·ous·ness
ten·ure
tenu·rial
te·nu·to musical term
teo·cal·li (*plural* ·lis) Aztec pyramid
teo·sin·te grass
te·pal botany term
te·pee (*or* tee·) tent
tep·efac·tion
tep·efy (·efies, ·efy·ing, ·efied) make tepid
teph·rite rock
teph·rit·ic
Te·pic Mexican city
tep·id
te·pid·ity (*or* tep·id·ness)
te·qui·la
Te·rai Indian marshland

ter·aph (*plural* ·aphim) biblical god
tera·tism malformed fetus
tera·to·gen
tera·to·gen·ic causing fetal deformity
tera·toid
tera·to·log·ic (*or* ·logi·cal)
tera·tolo·gist
tera·tol·ogy study of fetal abnormalities
tera·to·ma (*plural* ·mas *or* ·ma·ta)
ter·bic
ter·bium chemical element
terce (*or* tierce) canonical hour
ter·cel (*or* tier·cel) male falcon
ter·cen·te·nary (*or* ·cen·ten·nial; *plural* ·naries *or* ·nials)
ter·cet verse
ter·ebene
te·reb·ic acid
ter·ebinth tree
ter·ebin·thine
te·re·do (*plural* ·dos *or* ·di·nes) mollusc
Te·re·si·na Brazilian port
te·rete botany term
ter·gal
ter·gi·ver·sate
ter·gi·ver·sa·tion
ter·gi·ver·sa·tor (*or* ·ver·sant)
ter·gi·ver·sa·tory
ter·gum (*plural* ·ga) zoology term
teri·ya·ki Japanese food
term
ter·ma·gan·cy
ter·ma·gant
ter·mi·nabil·ity (*or* ·nable·ness)
ter·mi·nable
ter·mi·nal
ter·mi·nal·ly
ter·mi·nate
ter·mi·na·tion
ter·mi·na·tion·al
ter·mi·na·tive
ter·mi·na·tor
ter·mi·na·tory
ter·mi·no·logi·cal

ter·mi·nolo·gist
ter·mi·nol·ogy (*plural*
  ·ogies)
ter·mi·nus (*plural* ·ni *or*
  ·nuses)
ter·mi·tar·ium (*plural*
  ·taria) termite nest
ter·mite
ter·mit·ic
term·less
ter·mor (*or* ·mer) legal term
tern bird; *compare* terne;
  turn
ter·na·ry (*plural* ·ries)
ter·nate botany term
terne alloy; *compare* tern;
  turn
Ter·ni Italian city
ter·pene
ter·pe·nic
ter·pin·eol
Terpsichore Greek Muse
Terp·si·cho·rean (*or* ·real)
ter·ra land
ter·race
ter·ra·cot·ta
ter·ra fir·ma
ter·rain surroundings;
  compare terrane
Ter·ra·my·cin (*Trademark*)
ter·rane rock formation;
  compare terrain
ter·ra·pin
ter·rar·ium (*plural* ·rar·iums
  or ·raria) biological
  container
ter·raz·zo
ter·rene earthly; *compare*
  terrine; tureen
terre·plein top of rampart
ter·res·trial
ter·res·tri·al·ly
ter·ret harness ring
terre-verte painting
  pigment
ter·ri·ble
ter·ri·ble·ness
ter·ri·bly
ter·rico·lous living in soil
ter·ri·er
ter·rif·ic
ter·rifi·cal·ly
ter·ri·fi·er
ter·ri·fy (·fies, ·fy·ing, ·fied)
ter·ri·fy·ing·ly

ter·rig·enous of the earth
ter·rine dish; food; *compare*
  terrene; tureen
ter·ri·to·rial
ter·ri·to·ri·al·ism
ter·ri·to·ri·al·ist
ter·ri·to·ri·al·ity
ter·ri·to·ri·ali·za·tion (*or*
  ·sa·tion)
ter·ri·to·ri·al·ize (*or* ·ise)
ter·ri·to·rial·ly
ter·ri·tory (*plural* ·tories)
ter·ror
ter·ror·ful
ter·ror·ism
ter·ror·ist
ter·ror·is·tic
ter·rori·za·tion (*or* ·sa·tion)
ter·ror·ize (*or* ·ise)
ter·ror·iz·er (*or* ·is·er)
terror-stricken (*or* -struck)
ter·ry (*plural* ·ries) towelling
terse
terse·ly
terse·ness
ter·tial ornithology term
ter·tian recurring every
  other day
Ter·tiary geological period
ter·tiary (*plural* ·tiaries)
ter·tium quid a third
  unknown thing
ter·va·lent *variant of*
  trivalent
Tery·lene (*Trademark*)
ter·zet·to (*plural* ·tos *or* ·ti)
  vocal trio
tes·la unit; coil
tes·sel·late
tes·sel·la·tion
tes·sera (*plural* ·serae)
  mosaic tile
tes·ser·act four-dimensional
  figure
tes·ser·al
tes·si·tu·ra musical term
test
tes·ta (*plural* ·tae) seed coat
test-abil·ity
test·able
tes·ta·ceous
tes·ta·cy
tes·ta·ment
tes·ta·men·tal
tes·ta·men·tary

tes·tate
tes·ta·tor (*fem* ·trix)
test-drive (*verb* -driving,
  -drove, -driven)
test·er one who tests
tes·ter canopy; coin
tes·tes *plural of* testis
tes·ti·cle
tes·ticu·lar
tes·ticu·late
tes·ti·fi·ca·tion
tes·ti·fi·er
tes·ti·fy (·fies, ·fy·ing, ·fied)
testi·ly
tes·ti·mo·nial
tes·ti·mo·ny (*plural* ·nies)
testi·ness
test·ing
test·ing·ly
tes·tis (*plural* ·tes)
tes·ton (*or* ·toon) coin
tes·tos·ter·one hormone
tes·tu·di·nal (*or* ·nary) of
  tortoises
tes·tu·do (*plural* ·di·nes)
  Roman military
  manoeuvre
tes·ty (·ti·er, ·ti·est)
te·tan·ic
te·tani·cal·ly
teta·ni·za·tion (*or* ·sa·tion)
teta·nize (*or* ·nise)
teta·nus
teta·ny
te·tar·to·he·dral·ism (*or*
  te·to·he·drism)
te·tar·to·he·dral
tetchi·ly (*or* techi·)
tetchi·ness (*or* techi·)
tetchy (*or* techy; tetchi·er,
  tetchi·est *or* techi·er,
  techi·est)
tête-à-tête (*plural* -têtes *or*
  -tête)
tête-bêche philately term
teth·er
tet·ra (*plural* ·ra *or* ·ras) fish
tetra·ba·sic
tetra·ba·sic·ity
tetra·brach metrical foot
tetra·bran·chi·ate zoology
  term
tetra·chlo·ride
tetra·chord musical term
tetra·chor·dal

te·trac·id chemistry term
tetra·cy·cline
tet·rad
te·trady·mite mineral
tetra·dy·na·mous botany term
tetra·ethyl
te·trago·nal
tetra·gram
tetra·he·dral
tetra·he·drite mineral
tetra·he·dron (plural ·drons or ·dra)
te·tral·ogy (plural ·ogies) set of four
te·tram·er·ism
te·tram·er·ous biology term
tetra·methyl·diar·sine
tetra·ple·gia
tetra·ploid genetics term
tetra·ploidy
tetra·pod
tetra·pod·ic
te·trapo·dy (plural ·dies) metrical unit
te·trap·ter·ous four-winged
te·trarch
te·trarch·ate
te·trar·chic (or ·chi·cal)
te·trar·chy (plural ·chies)
tetra·spore
tetra·spor·ic (or ·ous)
tetra·stich four-line poem
tetra·stich·ic (or tetras·ti·chal)
te·tras·ti·chous botany term
tetra·syl·lab·ic (or ·labi·cal)
tetra·syl·la·ble
tetra·tom·ic
tetra·va·len·cy
tetra·va·lent
tet·rode electronic valve
te·trox·ide
tet·ryl
tet·ter skin eruption
Te·tuán Moroccan city
Teucer mythological character
Teu·ton ancient German
Teu·ton·ic
Teu·ton·ism
Teu·ton·ize (or ·ise)
Tewkes·bury
Tex·an
Tex·as

text
text·book
tex·tile
tex·tu·al of text; compare textural
tex·tu·al·ism
tex·tu·al·ist
tex·tu·al·ly
tex·tu·ary (plural ·aries)
tex·tur·al of texture; compare textual
tex·tur·al·ly
tex·ture
Thai (plural Thais or Thai)
Thai·land
thala·men·cephal·ic
thala·men·cepha·lon (plural ·lons or ·la) anatomy term
tha·lam·ic
tha·lami·cal·ly
thala·mus (plural ·mi) part of brain
tha·las·sic of the sea
thal·as·soc·ra·cy (or ·at·toc·)
tha·ler (or ta·; plural ·ler or ·lers) coin
tha·lido·mide
thal·lic
thal·lium chemical element
thal·loid
thal·lo·phyte
thal·lo·phyt·ic
thal·lous of thallium
thal·lus (plural ·li or ·luses) botany term
thal·weg (or tal·) geography term
Thames
than
thana·top·sis
Thanatos personification of death
thane (or thegn)
Than·et
Than·ja·vur Indian city
thank
thank·ful
thank·ful·ly
thank·ful·ness
thank·less
thank·less·ness
thanks·giving
Thap·sus battle site

Thá·sos Greek island
that
thatch
thatch·er
Thatch·er·ism
Thatch·er·ite supporter of Margaret Thatcher
thatch·ing
thau·ma·tol·ogy study of miracles
thau·ma·trope
thau·ma·tropi·cal
thau·ma·turge miracle performer
thau·ma·tur·gic
thau·ma·tur·gy
thaw
thaw·er
thea·ceous botany term
the·an·throp·ic
the·an·thro·pism
the·an·thro·pist
the·ar·chic
the·ar·chy (plural ·chies) government by gods
thea·tre (US ·ter)
theatre·goer (US theater·)
the·at·ri·cal
the·at·ri·cal·ity (or ·cal·ness)
the·at·ri·cal·ly
the·at·ri·cals dramatic entertainments
the·at·rics exaggerated mannerisms
the·ba·ine drug
The·ban
Thebes
the·ca (plural ·cae) biology term
the·cal (or ·cate)
the·co·dont extinct reptile
thee
theft
thegn variant spelling of thane
the·ine stimulant in tea
their of them; compare there; they're
theirs
the·ism
the·ist
the·is·tic (or ·ti·cal)
the·is·ti·cal·ly
them

the·mat·ic
the·mati·cal·ly
theme
Themis Greek goddess
them·selves
then
the·nar palm of hand
the·nard·ite mineral
thence
thence·forth
thence·forward (or
  ·forwards)
theo·bro·mine
theo·cen·tric theology
  term
theo·cen·tric·ity
theo·cen·trism (or
  ·tri·cism)
the·oc·ra·cy (plural ·cies)
the·oc·ra·sy mingling of
  deities
theo·crat
theo·crat·ic (or ·crati·cal)
theo·crati·cal·ly
the·odi·cy (plural ·cies)
  branch of theology
the·odo·lite
the·odo·lit·ic
the·ogo·ny (plural ·nies)
  origin of the gods
theo·lo·gian
theo·logi·cal
theo·logi·cal·ly
the·olo·gist
the·olo·gi·za·tion (or
  ·sa·tion)
the·olo·gize (or ·gise)
the·olo·giz·er (or ·gis·er)
the·ol·ogy (plural ·ogies)
the·oma·chy (plural ·chies)
  battle among the gods
theo·man·cy
theo·ma·nia
theo·ma·niac
the·ono·my being governed
  by God
the·opa·thy religious
  emotion
the·opha·gy (plural ·gies)
the·opha·ny (plural ·nies)
  manifestation of deity
Theophi·lus moon crater
theo·pho·bia
theo·pho·bi·ac
theo·phyl·line

the·or·bo (plural ·bos)
  musical instrument
theo·rem
theo·remat·ic (or ·rem·ic)
theo·remati·cal·ly
theo·reti·cal (or ·ret·ic)
theo·reti·cal·ly
theo·reti·cian
theo·ret·ics
theo·rist
theo·ri·za·tion (or ·sa·tion)
theo·rize (or ·rise)
theo·riz·er (or r·is·er)
theo·ry (plural ·ries)
theo·soph·ic (or ·sophi·cal)
theo·sophi·cal·ly
the·oso·phism
the·oso·phist
the·oso·phy
thera·peu·tic
thera·peu·ti·cal·ly
thera·peu·tics
thera·pist
the·rap·sid extinct reptile
thera·py (plural ·pies)
there in that place; compare
  their; they're
there·abouts (or ·about)
there·after
there·at
there·by
there·fore
there·from
there·in
there·in·after
there·into
there·of
there·on
there·to
there·to·fore
there·under
there·upon
there·with (or ·with·al)
the·ri·an·throp·ic part
  animal, part human
the·rian·thro·pism
the·rio·morph
the·rio·mor·phic (or
  ·phous) in animal form
therm unit
ther·mae public baths
therm·aes·the·sia (US ·es·)
  sensitivity to temperature
ther·mal
ther·mal·ly

ther·mal·ize (or ·ise)
ther·mic
ther·mi·on
ther·mi·on·ic
ther·mi·on·ics
ther·mis·tor
Ther·mit (or ·mite;
  Trademark)
ther·mite pro·cess
ther·mo·baro·graph
ther·mo·chemi·cal
ther·mo·chemi·cal·ly
ther·mo·chem·ist
ther·mo·chem·is·try
ther·mo·cline
ther·mo·cou·ple
ther·mo·dy·nam·ic (or
  ·nami·cal)
ther·mo·dy·nami·cal·ly
ther·mo·dy·nam·ics
ther·mo·elec·tric (or
  ·tri·cal)
ther·mo·elec·tri·cal·ly
ther·mo·elec·tric·ity
ther·mo·elec·tron
ther·mo·gen·esis
ther·mog·enous (or
  ·mo·genet·ic)
ther·mo·gram
ther·mo·graph
ther·mog·ra·pher
ther·mo·graph·ic
ther·mog·ra·phy
ther·mo·junc·tion
ther·mo·la·bile
ther·mo·lu·mi·nes·cence
ther·mo·lu·mi·nes·cent
ther·moly·sis
ther·mo·lyt·ic
ther·mo·mag·net·ic
ther·mom·eter
ther·mo·met·ric (or ·ri·cal)
ther·mo·met·ri·cal·ly
ther·mom·etry
ther·mo·nu·clear
ther·mo·phile (or ·phil)
  organism thriving in
  warmth
ther·mo·phil·ic (or
  ·phil·ous)
ther·mo·pile radiant-energy
  detector
ther·mo·plas·tic
ther·mo·plas·tic·ity
Ther·mopy·lae battle site

Ther·mos (*Trademark*)
ther·mo·scope
ther·mo·scop·ic (*or*
·**scopi·cal**)
ther·mo·scopi·cal·ly
ther·mo·set·ting
ther·mo·si·phon
ther·mo·sphere
atmospheric layer
ther·mo·sta·bil·ity
ther·mo·stable
ther·mo·stat
ther·mo·stat·ic
ther·mo·stati·cal·ly
ther·mo·stat·ics
ther·mo·tac·tic
ther·mo·tax·is biology term
ther·mo·ten·sile
ther·mo·thera·py
ther·mo·trop·ic
ther·mo·tro·pism botany
term
the·roid beastlike
the·ro·pod dinosaur
the·ropo·dan
the·sau·rus (*plural* ·**ri** *or*
·**ruses**)
these
Theseus mythological
character
the·sis (*plural* ·**ses**)
Thespian
Thes·sa·li·an
Thes·sa·lo·nian
Thes·sa·lo·ni·ca ancient
Thessaloníki
Thes·sa·lo·ní·ki Greek port
Thes·sa·ly Greek region
the·ta
thet·ic of metrical stress
theti·cal·ly
Thetis Greek goddess
the·urg·ic (*or* ·**ur·gi·cal**)
the·ur·gi·cal·ly
the·ur·gist
the·ur·gy (*plural* ·**gies**)
divine intervention
thew muscle
they
they'd they would; they had
they'll they will; they shall
they're they are; *compare*
their; there
they've they have
thia·mine (*or* ·**min**) vitamin

thia·zine
thia·zole (*or* ·**zol**)
thick
thick-and-thin
thick·en
thick·en·er
thick·en·ing
thick·et
thick·head
thick·headed·ness
thick·leaf (*plural* ·**leaves**)
plant
thick·ly
thick·ness
thick·set
thick-skinned
thick-witted
thick-witted·ness
thief (*plural* **thieves**)
thieve
thiev·ery (*plural* ·**eries**)
thiev·ing
thiev·ing·ly
thiev·ish
thiev·ish·ness
thigh
thigh·bone
thig·mo·tac·tic
thig·mo·tax·is biology term
thig·mo·trop·ic
thig·mot·ro·pism botany
term
thim·ble
thim·ble·ful (*plural* ·**fuls**)
thimble·rig game
thimble·weed
thimble·wit *US* dunce
thi·mero·sal antiseptic
thin (*adj* **thin·ner**,
thin·nest; *verb* **thin·ning**,
thinned)
thine
thin-film electronics term
thing
thingu·ma·bob (*or* **thinga·**)
thingu·ma·jig (*or* **thinga·**)
think (**think·ing**, **thought**)
think·able
think·er
think·ing
think-tank
thin·ner
thin·ness
thin·nish
thin-skinned

thio·cya·nate
thio·cy·an·ic acid
thio-ether
thiol
thi·on·ic of sulphur
thio·nine (*or* ·**nin**)
thio·nyl
thio·pen·tone (*US* ·**tal**)
thio·phen (*or* ·**phene**)
thio·sina·mine
thio·sul·phate (*US* ·**fate**)
thio·sul·phur·ic acid (*US*
·**fur·**)
thio·ura·cil
thio·urea
third
third-rate
third·stream jazz
thirl *Dialect* to drill
Thirl·mere Cumbrian lake
thirst
thirst·er
thirsti·ly
thirsti·ness
thirsty (**thirsti·er**,
thirsti·est)
thir·teen
thir·teenth
thir·ti·eth
thir·ty (*plural* ·**ties**)
this
this·tle
thistle·down
this·tly
thith·er (*or* ·**er·ward**)
thither·to
thixo·trop·ic
thix·ot·ro·py chemistry
term
thole (*or* **thole·pin**)
tho·los (*plural* ·**loi**) tomb
Tho·mism doctrine of
Thomas Aquinas
Tho·mist
Thon·bu·ri Thai city
thong
Thor Norse god
tho·rac·ic (*or* ·**ra·cal**)
tho·ra·co·plas·ty (*plural*
·**ties**) surgery
thora·coto·my (*plural*
·**mies**)
thor·ax (*plural* **thor·axes** *or*
tho·ra·ces)
tho·ria chemical compound

tho·ria·nite mineral
tho·ric
tho·rite mineral
tho·rium radioactive element
thorn
thorn·back fish
thorn·bill
thorni·ly
thorni·ness
thorny (thorni·er, thorni·est)
tho·ron radioisotope of radon
thor·ough
Thorough·bred horse
thorough·bred purebred
thorough·fare
thorough·going
thor·ough·ly
thor·ough·ness
thorough·paced
thorough·pin swollen hock
those
Thoth Egyptian god
thou
though
thought
thought·ful
thought·ful·ly
thought·ful·ness
thought·less
thought·less·ness
thought-out
thou·sand
thou·sandth
Thrace Balkan region
thrall
thrall·dom
thrash
thrash·er
thrash·ing
thrawn Dialect crooked
thread
thread·bare
thread·er
thread·fin (plural ·fin or ·fins) fish
threadi·ness
Thread·needle Street
thread·worm
thready (threadi·er, threadi·est)
threap (or threep) Dialect to scold

threat
threat·en
threat·en·er
threat·en·ing
three
three-dimension·al
three·fold
three-legged
three-phase
three-piece
three-ply
three-quarter (adj)
three-quarters
three·score
three·some
three-wheeler
threm·ma·tol·ogy science of breeding
threno·dy (or thre·node; plural ·dies or ·nodes) ode of lamentation
threo·nine amino acid
thresh
thresh·er
thresh·old
threw
thrice
thrift
thrifti·ly
thrifti·ness
thrift·less
thrift·less·ness
thrifty (thrifti·er, thrifti·est)
thrill
thrill·er
thrill·ing
thrips (plural thrips) insect
thrive (thriv·ing, thrived or throve, thrived or thriv·en)
throat
throati·ly
throati·ness
throat·lash (or ·latch) bridle strap
throaty (throati·er, throati·est)
throb (throb·bing, throbbed)
throe violent pang; compare throw
throm·bin enzyme
throm·bo·cyte
throm·bo·cyt·ic

throm·bo·em·bo·lism
throm·bo·gen protein
throm·bo·phle·bi·tis
throm·bo·plas·tic
throm·bo·plas·tin
throm·bose (verb)
throm·bo·sis
throm·bot·ic
throm·bus (plural ·bi) blood clot
throne
throng
thros·tle thrush
throt·tle
throt·tler
through
through·out
through·put
through·way
throw (throw·ing, threw, thrown) cast; compare throe
throw·away (adj, noun)
throw·back
throw·er
thrown
throw·ster yarn spinner
thrum (thrum·ming, thrummed)
thrum·mer
thrush
thrust
thrust·er
thud (thud·ding, thud·ded)
Thug Indian assassin
thug
thug·gee practices of Thugs
thug·gery
thug·gish
thu·ja (or ·ya) tree
Thule ancient northern land; Eskimo settlement
thu·lium chemical element
thumb
thumb·nail
thumb·nut
thumb·print
thumb·screw
thumb·stall
thumb·tack US drawing pin
thump
thump·er
thump·ing
thun·der

thunder·bird
thunder·bolt
thunder·clap
thunder·cloud
thun·der·er
thunder·head cloud
thun·der·ing
thun·der·ous
thunder·shower
thunder·stone
thunder·storm
thunder·struck (or
·stricken)
thun·dery
Thur·gau Swiss canton
thu·ri·ble incense container
thu·ri·fer thurible carrier
Thu·rin·gia German state
Thu·rin·gian
Thur·rock area of Essex
Thurs·day
thus
thwack
thwack·er
thwart
thwart·er
thy
Thyestes mythological
character
thy·la·cine animal
thyme herb
thym·elaea·ceous botany
term
thym·ic
thy·mi·dine
thy·mine
thy·mol
thy·mus (plural ·muses or
·mi)
thymy of thyme
thy·ra·tron
thy·ris·tor
thy·ro·cal·ci·ton·in
hormone
thy·roid
thy·roid·ec·to·my (plural
·mies)
thy·roidi·tis
thy·ro·toxi·co·sis
thy·ro·tro·pin (or ·phin)
hormone
thy·rox·ine (or ·in)
hormone
thyrse (plural therses)
botany term

thyr·soid
thyr·sus (plural ·si) Bacchus'
staff
thysa·nu·ran insect
thy·self
ti plant; variant spelling of te
Tia Ma·ria (Trademark)
ti·ara
ti·ar·aed
Ti·ber
Ti·bes·ti African mountains
Ti·bet
Ti·bet·an
tibia (plural tibiae or tibias)
tib·ial
tic twitch; compare tick
ti·cal (plural ·cals or ·cal)
tic dou·lou·reux neuralgia
Ti·ci·no Swiss canton; river
tick parasite; compare tic
tick·er
tick·et
tick·ing
tick·le
tick·ler
tick·lish
tick·lish·ness
tick·ly
tick·tack
tick-tack-toe US noughts
and crosses
tick·tock
Ti·con·dero·ga US battle
site
tid·al
tid·al·ly
tid·bit US spelling of titbit
tid·dler
tid·dly
tiddly·winks
tide
tide·mark
tide·water
tide·way
ti·di·ly
ti·di·ness
tid·ings
tidy (adj tidi·er, tidi·est;
verb ti·dies, tidy·ing,
ti·died; noun, plural
ti·dies)
tie (ty·ing, tied)
tie·back US curtain
fastening
tie·breaker (or ·break)

tied
tie-dyeing
tie-dyed
tie·man·nite mineral
Tien·tsin (or T'ien-ching)
Chinese city
tie·pin
tier layer; compare tear
tierce fencing position;
variant spelling of terce
tiered
Tier·ra del Fue·go South
American archipelago
tiff
tif·fa·ny (plural ·nies) fabric
tif·fin meal
Tif·lis variant spelling of
Tbilisi
ti·ger
ti·ger·ish
tiger's-eye (or tiger·eye)
gemstone
tight
tight·en
tight·en·er
tight·fisted
tight·knit
tight-lipped
tight·ness
tight·rope
tights
tight·wad
tig·lic acid
ti·gon (or tig·lon) animal
Ti·gré Ethiopian region
ti·gress
Ti·gri·nya Ethiopian
language
Ti·gris Asian river
Ti·jua·na Mexican city
tike variant spelling of tyke
tiki Maori amulet
ti·lapia fish
Til·burg Dutch city
Til·bury Essex region
til·bury (plural ·buries)
carriage
til·de phonetic symbol
tile
tile·fish (plural ·fish or
·fishes)
til·er
tilia·ceous botany term
til·ing
till

till·able

till·age

til·land·sia plant

till·er

til·li·cum *US* friend

Til·sit *former name of*
Sovetsk

tilt

tilt·er

tilth

tilt·yard

Tima·ru New Zealand port

tim·bal (*or* tym·)
kettledrum

tim·bale pie

tim·ber wood; *compare*
timbre

timber·head

tim·ber·ing

timber·land

timber·work

timber·yard

tim·bre tone quality;
compare timber

tim·brel tambourine

Tim·buk·tu Malian town

time

time·able

time·card

time-consum·ing

time-honoured

time·keeper

time·keeping

time-lag

time·less

time·less·ness

time·li·ness

time·ly (·li·er, ·li·est)

time·ous *Scot* timely

time·piece

tim·er

time·saver

time·saving

time·server

time·serving

time·table

time·work

time·worker

time·worn

tim·id

ti·mid·ity (*or* tim·id·ness)

tim·ing

Ti·mi·şoa·ra Romanian city

ti·moc·ra·cy (*plural* ·cies)
political system

Ti·mor Indonesian island

tim·or·ous

tim·or·ous·ness

timo·thy grass

tim·pa·ni (*or* tym·; *sing.*
·no) kettledrums; *compare*
tympanum

tim·pa·nist (*or* tym·)

timps *short for* timpani

tin (tin·ning, tinned)

tina·mou bird

tin·cal borax

tinct tinted

tinc·to·rial of dyeing

tinc·ture

tin·der

tinder·box

tin·dery

tine

tinea ringworm; *compare*
taenia

tin·eal

tin·eid moth

tin·foil

ting

ting-a-ling

tinge (tinge·ing *or* ting·ing,
tinged)

tin·gle

tin·gler

tin·gling·ly

tin·gly

ti·ni·ly

ti·ni·ness

tink·er

tink·er·er

tin·kle

tin·kling

tin·kly

tin liz·zie *Slang* decrepit
car

tinned

tin·ni·ly

tin·ni·ness

tin·ning

tin·ni·tus ringing in ears

tin·ny (·ni·er, ·ni·est)

tin-plate (*verb*)

tin·pot *Slang* inferior

tin·sel (·sel·ling, ·selled; *US*
·sel·ing, ·seled)

tin·smith

tint

Tin·tag·el

tint·ed

tin·tin·nabu·lar (*or* ·lary,
·lous)

tin·tin·nabu·la·tion

tin·tin·nabu·lum (*plural*
·la) bell

tin·type photographic print

tin·ware

tin·work

tiny (tini·er, tini·est)

tip (tip·ping, tipped)

tip·cat game

tip-off (*noun*)

tip·pable

tipped

tip·per

Tip·per·ary

tip·pet cape

tip·ping

tip·ple

tip·pler

tip·si·ly

tip·si·ness

tip·staff

tip·ster

tip·sy (·si·er, ·si·est)

tip·toe (·toe·ing, ·toed)

tip·top

ti·rade

Ti·ra·na (*or* ·në) Albanian
capital

tire exhaust; *US spelling of*
tyre

tire·less

tire·less·ness

tire·some

tire·some·ness

Ti·rich Mir Pakistani
mountain

tir·ing

tiro *variant spelling of* tyro

Ti·rol *variant spelling of*
Tyrol

Ti·ros *US* satellite

Ti·ru·nel·veli Indian city

'tis

ti·sane

tis·sue

tit

Ti·tan Greek god; satellite of
Saturn

ti·tan·ate chemistry term

Ti·tan·esque

Ti·ta·nia satellite of Uranus

ti·tan·ic huge; chemistry
term

ti·tani·cal·ly
ti·tan·if·er·ous
Ti·tan·ism spirit of rebellion
ti·tan·ite mineral
ti·ta·nium chemical
   element
ti·tano·saur
ti·tano·there extinct
   mammal
ti·tan·ous
tit·bit (*US* tid·)
ti·ter *US spelling of* titre
tith·able
tithe
tith·er
tith·ing
Tithonus mythological
   character
titi (*plural* titis) monkey
tit·il·late
tit·il·lat·ing
tit·il·la·tion
tit·il·la·tive
titi·vate (*or* tit·ti·)
titi·va·tion (*or* tit·ti·)
titi·va·tor (*or* tit·ti·)
tit·lark
ti·tle
ti·tled
title·holder
tit·man (*plural* ·men) small
   piglet
tit·mouse (*plural* ·mice)
Ti·to·grad *former name of*
   Podgorica
Ti·to·ism
Ti·to·ist
ti·trant chemistry term
ti·trat·able
ti·trate
ti·tra·tion
ti·tre (*US* ·ter)
tit·ter
tit·ter·er
tit·tle
tittle-tattle
tittle-tattler
tit·tup (·tup·ping, ·tupped)
titu·ba·tion medical term
titu·lar (*or* ·lary; *plural* ·lars
   or ·laries)
Tiv (*plural* Tivs *or* Tiv)
   African people
Tivo·li Italian town
tiz·zy (*plural* ·zies)

Tlax·ca·la Mexican state
Tlin·git (*plural* ·gits *or* ·git)
   American Indian
tme·sis linguistics term
to
toad
toad·fish (*plural* ·fish *or*
   ·fishes)
toad·flax
toad·ish (*or* ·like)
toad·stone
toad·stool
toady (*noun, plural* toadies;
   verb toadies, toady·ing,
   toad·ied)
toady·ism
to-and-fro (*adj*)
toast
toast·er
toast·master (*fem* ·mistress)
to·bac·co (*plural* ·cos *or*
   ·coes)
to·bac·co·nist
To·ba·go West Indian island
to·bog·gan
to·bog·gan·er (*or* ·ist)
To·bruk Libyan port
toby jug
toc·ca·ta
To·char·ian (*or* ·khar·)
   language
to·col·ogy (*or* ·kol·)
   obstetrics
to·coph·er·ol vitamin
toc·sin alarm bell; *compare*
   toxin
tod
to·day
tod·dle
tod·dler
tod·dy (*plural* ·dies)
to-do (*plural* -dos)
tody (*plural* todies) bird
toe (toe·ing, toed)
toea coin
toe·cap
toed
toe·hold
toe-in
toe·ing
toe·nail
toey *Austral* nervous
toff
tof·fee (*or* ·fy; *plural* ·fees *or*
   ·fies)

toft homestead
tog (tog·ging, togged)
toga
to·geth·er
to·geth·er·ness
togged
tog·gery clothes
tog·ging
tog·gle
Tog·li·at·ti Russian city
Togo African republic
To·go·lese
to·he·roa mollusc
toil
toile fabric
toil·er
toi·let lavatory
toi·let·ry (*plural* ·ries)
toi·lette act of dressing
toil·some (*or* ·ful)
toil·some·ness
To·kay wine
to·kay lizard
to·ken
to·ken·ism
toko·loshe mythical
   creature
To·kyo
tola unit of weight
to·lan (*or* ·lane) organic
   compound
tol·bu·ta·mide drug
told
tole metal ware
To·ledo Spanish city; US
   city
tol·er·able
tol·er·able·ness (*or*
   ·abil·ity)
tol·er·ably
tol·er·ance
tol·er·ant
tol·er·ate
tol·era·tion
tol·era·tion·ism
tol·era·tion·ist
tol·era·tive
tol·era·tor
toli·dine
toll
toll·booth (*or* tol·)
toll·gate
toll·house
Tol·pud·dle Dorset town;
   martyrs

Tol·tec (*plural* ·tecs *or* ·tec)
American Indian
tolu·ate chemical
compound
To·lu·ca Mexican city
tolu·ene
to·lu·ic acid
to·lui·dine
tolu·yl
tol·yl
tom male animal
toma·hawk
tom·al·ley lobster liver
to·man coin
to·ma·to (*plural* ·toes)
tomb
tom·bac (*or* tam·) alloy
tomb·like
tom·bo·la lottery
tom·bo·lo (*plural* ·los) sand
bar
tom·boy
tom·boy·ish
tomb·stone
tom·cat
tome book
to·men·tose
to·men·tum (*plural* ·ta)
biology term
tom·fool
tom·fool·ery (*plural* ·eries)
tom·my (*plural* ·mies)
tommy·rot
tomo·gram
to·mog·ra·phy X-ray
technique
to·mor·row
tom·pi·on *variant spelling of*
tampion
Tomsk Russian city
tom·tit
tom-tom drum; *compare*
tam-tam
ton imperial weight; *compare*
tonne; tun
ton·al
to·nal·ity (*plural* ·ities)
ton·al·ly
Ton·bridge Kent town;
compare **Tunbridge Wells**
ton·do (*plural* ·di) circular
painting
tone
tone-deaf
tone·less

tone·less·ness
ton·eme linguistics term
ton·er
to·net·ic linguistics term
tong
Tonga Pacific kingdom
Ton·ga (*plural* ·gas *or* ·ga)
African people
Tong·an
tongs
tongue (tongu·ing,
tongued)
tongue-tied
ton·ic
toni·cal·ly
to·nic·ity
to·night
ton·ing
tonk *Austral* effeminate man
ton·ka tree; bean
Ton·kin (*or* Tong·king)
Chinese gulf
Ton·le Sap Cambodian lake
ton·nage (*or* tun·)
tonne metric weight;
compare ton; tun
ton·neau (*plural* ·neaus *or*
·neaux)
to·nom·eter
tono·met·ric
to·nom·etry
ton·sil
ton·sil·lar (*or* ·lary)
ton·sil·lec·to·my (*plural*
·mies)
ton·sil·lit·ic
ton·sil·li·tis
ton·sil·loto·my (*plural*
·mies)
ton·so·rial
ton·sure
ton·tine annuity scheme
to·nus muscle tone
too
toodle-oo
took
tool
tool·er
tool·ing
tool·less
tool-maker
tool-making
toon tree
toot
toot·er

tooth (*plural* teeth)
tooth·ache
tooth·brush
toothed
toothi·ly
toothi·ness
tooth·less
tooth·paste
tooth·pick
tooth·some
tooth·some·ness
tooth·wort
toothy (tooth·ier,
toothi·est)
too·tle
too·tler
toots (*or* toot·sie) term of
endearment
toot·sy (*or* tootsy-wootsy;
plural ·sies *or* ··wootsies)
Slang foot
top (top·ping, topped)
top·arch ruler
top·ar·chy
to·paz
to·pazo·lite gemstone
top·coat
top-dress (*verb*)
tope
to·pee (*or* topi; *plural* ·pees
or topis) tropical helmet
To·pe·ka US city
top·er
top-flight (*adj*)
top·gal·lant ship's mast
top-heavily
top-heaviness
top-heavy
To·phet (*or* ·pheth) biblical
place
to·phus (*plural* ·phi) gout
stone
topi *variant spelling of* topee
to·pi·ar·ian
to·pia·rist
to·pi·ary
top·ic
topi·cal
topi·cal·ity
topi·cal·ly
top·knot
top·less
top·less·ness
top-level (*adj*)
top·lofty haughty

top·mast
top·min·now (*plural* ·now
    or ·nows) fish
top·most
top·notch
top·notcher
to·pog·ra·pher
topo·graph·ic (*or*
    ·graphi·cal)
topo·graphi·cal·ly
to·pog·ra·phy (*plural*
    ·phies) mapping; *compare*
    topology
topo·logic (*or* ·logi·cal)
topo·logi·cal·ly
to·polo·gist
to·pol·ogy branch of
    geometry; *compare*
    topography
topo·nym
topo·nym·ic (*or* ·nymi·cal)
to·pony·my
top·os (*plural* ·oi) basic
    concept
topo·type
topped
top·per
top·ping
top·ple
top·sail
top-secret (*adj*)
top-shell mollusc
top·side
top·soil
top·spin
topsy-turvy
toque (*or* to·quet) hat
tor hill; *compare* torr
To·rah Jewish writings
Tor·bay Devon town
tor·bern·ite mineral
torch
torch·bearer
tor·chère candelabrum
    stand
tor·chier (*or* ·chiere) lamp
torch·light
torch·lit
tor·chon lace
torch·wood
tore
torea·dor
to·re·ro (*plural* ·ros)
    bullfighter
to·reu·tic

to·reu·tics metalworking
Tor·faen Welsh county
    borough
tori *plural of* torus
tor·ic
to·rii (*plural* ·rii) gateway
tor·ment
tor·ment·ed·ly
tor·men·til plant
tor·ment·ing·ly
tor·men·tor (*or* ·ment·er)
torn
tor·nad·ic
tor·na·do (*plural* ·does or
    ·dos) storm; *compare*
    tournedos
to·roid geometry term
to·roi·dal
to·roi·dal·ly
To·ron·to
To·ron·to·nian
to·rose (*or* ·rous) biology
    term
tor·pe·do (*noun, plural*
    ·does; *verb* ·does, ·do·ing,
    ·doed)
tor·pid
tor·pid·ity (*or* ·ness)
tor·por
tor·por·if·ic
tor·quate
Tor·quay
torque metal collar;
    mechanical force
tor·ques zoology term
torr unit; *compare* tor
Tor·rance US city
tor·re·fac·tion (*or* ·ri·)
tor·re·fy (*or* ·ri·; ·fies,
    ·fy·ing, ·fied) roast
tor·rent
tor·ren·tial
tor·ren·tial·ly
Tor·re·ón Mexican city
Tor·ri·cel·lian physics term
tor·rid
tor·rid·ity (*or* ·ness)
tor·sade ornament on hat
tor·si·bil·ity
tor·sion
tor·sion·al
torsk (*plural* torsks or torsk)
    fish
tor·so (*plural* ·sos or ·si)
tort legal term

torte cake
tor·tel·li·ni pasta
tort·feasor legal term
tor·ti·col·lar
tor·ti·col·lis wryneck
tor·til·la Mexican pancake
tor·tious legal term; *compare*
    tortuous; torturous
tor·toise
tortoise-shell
tor·to·ni ice cream
tor·tri·cid moth
tor·tu·os·ity (*plural* ·ities)
tor·tu·ous twisting; devious;
    compare tortious;
    torturous
tor·tu·ous·ness
tor·ture
tor·tured·ly
tor·tur·er
tor·ture·some
tor·tur·ing·ly
tor·tur·ous causing pain;
    compare tortious; tortuous
To·ruń Polish city
to·rus (*plural* ·ri)
Tory (*plural* Tories)
To·ry·ism
tosh
toss
toss·er
toss·pot *Archaic* drinker
tot (tot·ting, tot·ted)
to·tal (·tal·ling, ·talled; *US*
    ·tal·ing,·taled)
to·tali·tar·ian
to·tali·tar·ian·ism
to·tal·ity (*plural* ·ities)
to·tali·za·tion (*or* ·sa·tion)
to·tali·za·tor (*or* ·sa·tor)
    betting machine
to·tal·ize (*or* ·ise)
to·tal·iz·er (*or* ·is·er)
to·tal·ly
to·ta·quine drug
tote
to·tem
to·tem·ic
to·temi·cal·ly
to·tem·ism
to·tem·ist
to·tem·is·tic
tot·er
to·ti·pal·mate
to·ti·pal·ma·tion

to·tipo·ten·cy
to·tipo·tent zoology term
tot·ted
tot·ter
tot·ter·er
tot·tery
tot·ting
tou·can
touch
touch·able
touch·down
tou·ché acknowledgment
touch·er
touchi·ly
touchi·ness
touch·ing
touch·ing·ly
touch·line
touch·mark
touch·stone
touch·type
touch·typist
touch·wood
touchy (touchi·er, touchi·est)
tough
tough·en
tough·en·er
toughie
tough·ish
tough·ness
Tou·lon French town
Tou·louse French city
tou·pee hairpiece
tour
tou·ra·co (or tu·; plural ·cos) bird
Tou·raine French region
Tou·rane Vietnamese port
tour·bil·lion whirlwind
tour de force (plural tours de force)
tour·er
tour·ism
tour·ist
tour·is·tic
tour·isty
tour·ma·line
tour·ma·lin·ic
tour·na·ment
tour·nedos (plural ·nedos) steak; compare tornado
tour·ney
tour·ni·quet
Tours French town

tou·sle
tous-les-mois plant
tout Slang solicit
tout à fait French completely
tout en·sem·ble French all in all
tout le monde French everyone
to·va·risch (·rich or ·rish) Russian term of address
tow
tow·age
to·ward (adj)
to·wards (prep.)
tow·bar
tow·boat
tow·el (·el·ling, ·elled; US ·el·ing, ·eled)
tow·el·ling (US ·el·ing)
tow·er
Tow·er Ham·lets London borough
tow·er·ing
tow-haired
tow·head
tow·hee bird
tow·line
town
townee
town·hall
town·scape
town·ship
towns·man (plural ·men)
towns·people (or ·folk)
towns·woman (plural ·women)
tow·path
tow·rope
tox·aemia (US ·emia)
tox·aemic (US ·emic)
tox·al·bu·min
toxa·phene
tox·ic
toxi·cal·ly
toxi·cant poison
tox·ic·ity
toxi·co·gen·ic
toxi·co·logi·cal (or ·log·ic)
toxi·co·logi·cal·ly
toxi·colo·gist
toxi·col·ogy
toxi·co·sis
tox·in poison; compare tocsin

tox·oid
tox·ophi·lite archer
tox·ophi·lit·ic
tox·ophi·ly
toxo·plas·mic
toxo·plas·mo·sis
toy
To·ya·ma Japanese city
toy·er
tra·beated (or ·beate) architectural term
tra·bea·tion
tra·becu·la (plural ·lae) anatomy term
tra·becu·lar (or ·late)
Trab·zon Turkish port
trace
trace·abil·ity (or ·able·ness)
trace·able
trace·less
trac·er
trac·ery (plural ·eries)
tra·chea (plural ·cheae)
tra·cheal
tra·cheate
tra·che·id (or ·ide) plant cell
tra·chei·dal
tra·che·itis
tra·cheo·phyte botany term
tra·cheo·osto·my (plural ·mies)
tra·che·oto·mist
tra·che·oto·my (plural ·mies)
tra·cho·ma eye disease
tra·choma·tous
tra·chyte rock
tra·chyt·ic
trachy·toid
trac·ing
track
track·able
track·er
track·less
track·suit
tract
trac·tabil·ity (or ·table·ness)
trac·table
trac·tably
Trac·tar·ian
Trac·tari·an·ism religious movement
trac·tate treatise
trac·tile ductile

trac·til·ity
trac·tion
trac·tion·al
trac·tive
trac·tor
trad *Slang* traditional jazz
trad·able (*or* trade·)
trade
trade-in (*noun*)
trade·mark
trade-off (*noun*)
trad·er
trad·es·can·tia plant
trades·man (*plural* ·men)
trades·people (*or* ·folk)
trades·woman (*plural*
·women)
trade union (*plural* trade
unions) *note* Trades
Union Congress
trad·ing
tra·di·tion
tra·di·tion·al
tra·di·tion·al·ism
tra·di·tion·al·ist
tra·di·tion·al·is·tic
tra·di·tion·al·ly
tra·di·tion·ist
tradi·tor (*plural* ·to·res *or*
·tors) Christian betrayer
tra·duce
tra·duce·ment
tra·duc·er
tra·du·cian·ism theology
term
tra·du·cian·ist (*or* ·du·cian)
tra·du·cian·is·tic
tra·duc·ible
Tra·fal·gar
traf·fic (·fick·ing, ·ficked)
traf·fi·ca·tor car indicator
traf·fick·er
Traf·ford area of Greater
Manchester
traga·canth plant
tra·gal
tra·gedian (*fem* ·gedi·enne)
trag·edy (*plural* ·edies)
trag·ic (*or* tragi·cal)
tragi·cal·ly
tragi·com·edy (*plural*
·edies)
tragi·com·ic (*or* ·comi·cal)
tragi·comi·cal·ly
trago·pan bird

tra·gus (*plural* ·gi) part of
ear
trail
trail·blazer
trail·blazing
trail·er
trail·ing·ly
trail·less
train
train·able
train·band English militia
train·bearer
trainee
train·er
train·ing
traipse
trait characteristic
trai·tor
trai·tor·ous
trai·tor·ous·ness
trai·tress
tra·ject *Archaic* transport
tra·jec·tile
tra·jec·tion
tra·jec·tory (*plural*
·tories)
tra·la
Tra·lee Irish town
tram (tram·ming,
trammed)
tram·car
tram·line
tram·mel (·el·ling, ·elled;
US ·el·ing, ·eled)
tram·mel·ler (*US* ·mel·er)
tram·mie *Austral* tram
driver
tra·mon·tane (*or* trans·)
across mountains
tramp
tramp·er
tramp·ish
tramp·ish·ness
tram·ple
tram·pler
tram·po·line
tram·po·lin·er (*or* ·ist)
tram·way
trance
trance·like
tranche
tran·nie *Slang* transistor
radio
tran·quil
tran·quil·lity

tran·quil·li·za·tion (*or*
·sa·tion; *US* ·quili·za·tion)
tran·quil·lize (*or* ·lise; *US*
·quil·ize)
tran·quil·liz·er (*US*
·quil·iz·er)
tran·quil·ly
tran·quil·ness
trans·act
trans·ac·ti·nide
trans·ac·tion
trans·ac·tion·al
trans·ac·tor
trans·al·pine
trans·at·lan·tic
Trans·cau·ca·sia Central
Asian region
Trans·cau·ca·sian
trans·ceiv·er
trans·cend
tran·scend·ence (*or* ·en·cy)
trans·cend·ent
tran·scen·den·tal
tran·scen·den·tal·ism
tran·scen·den·tal·ist
tran·scen·den·tal·ity
tran·scen·den·tal·ly
tran·scend·ent·ness
trans·con·ti·nen·tal
trans·con·ti·nen·tal·ly
tran·scrib·able
tran·scribe
tran·scrib·er
tran·script
tran·scrip·tion
tran·scrip·tion·al (*or*
·scrip·tive)
trans·cul·tura·tion
trans·cur·rent
trans·duc·er
trans·duc·tion
tran·sect
tran·sec·tion
tran·sept
tran·sep·tal
trans·eunt philosophy term
trans·fer (·fer·ring, ·ferred)
trans·fer·abil·ity
trans·fer·able (*or* ·fer·rable)
trans·fer·ase enzyme
trans·feree
trans·fer·ence
trans·fer·en·tial
trans·fer·rer (*or in legal
contexts* ·fer·or)

trans·fer·rin biochemical
compound
trans·figu·ra·tion
trans·fig·ure
trans·fig·ure·ment
trans·fi·nite
trans·fix (·fix·ing, fixed or
·fixt)
trans·fix·ion
trans·form
trans·form·able
trans·for·ma·tion
trans·for·ma·tion·al
trans·forma·tive
trans·form·er
trans·form·ism
evolutionary theory
trans·form·ist
trans·fuse
trans·fus·er
trans·fus·ible (or ·able)
trans·fu·sion
trans·fu·sive
trans·gress
trans·gress·ible
trans·gress·ing·ly
trans·gres·sion
trans·gres·sive
trans·gres·sor
tran·ship variant spelling of
transship
trans·hu·mance migration
of livestock
trans·hu·mant
tran·si·ence (or ·en·cy,
·ent·ness)
tran·si·ent
trans·il·lu·mi·nate
trans·il·lu·mi·na·tion
trans·il·lu·mi·na·tor
tran·sis·tor
tran·sis·tori·za·tion (or
·sa·tion)
tran·sis·tor·ize (or ·ise)
trans·it
tran·sit·able
tran·si·tion
tran·si·tion·al (or ·ary)
tran·si·tion·al·ly
tran·si·tive
tran·si·tive·ness (or ·tiv·ity)
tran·si·to·ri·ly
tran·si·to·ri·ness
tran·si·tory
Trans-Jordan

Trans-Jordanian
Trans·kei former South
African province
Trans·kei·an
trans·lat·abil·ity (or
·able·ness)
trans·lat·able
trans·late
trans·la·tion
trans·la·tion·al
trans·la·tor
trans·la·to·rial
trans·lit·er·ate
trans·lit·era·tion
trans·lit·era·tor
trans·lo·cate
trans·lo·ca·tion
trans·lu·cence (or ·cen·cy)
trans·lu·cent
trans·lu·nar (or ·nary)
trans·mi·grant
trans·mi·grate
trans·mi·gra·tion
trans·mi·gra·tion·al
trans·mi·gra·tive
trans·mi·gra·tor
trans·mi·gra·tory
trans·mis·sibil·ity
trans·mis·sible
trans·mis·sion
trans·mis·sive
trans·mis·sive·ness
trans·mis·siv·ity
trans·mit (·mit·ting,
·mit·ted)
trans·mit·table (or ·tible)
trans·mit·tal
trans·mit·tance
trans·mit·tan·cy physics
term
trans·mit·ter
trans·mog·ri·fi·ca·tion
trans·mog·ri·fy (·fies,
·fy·ing, ·fied)
trans·mon·tane variant of
tramontane
trans·mun·dane beyond
this world
trans·mut·able
trans·mut·ably
trans·mu·ta·tion
trans·mu·ta·tion·al (or
·ta·tive)
trans·mu·ta·tion·ist
trans·mute

trans·mut·er
trans·ocean·ic
tran·som
tran·son·ic of the sound
barrier
trans·pa·cif·ic
trans·pa·dane
trans·par·en·cy (plural
·cies)
trans·par·ent
trans·par·ent·ness
tran·spicu·ous transparent
trans·pierce
tran·spir·able
tran·spi·ra·tion
tran·spira·tory
tran·spire
trans·plant
trans·plant·able
trans·plan·ta·tion
trans·plant·er
trans·po·lar
tran·spond·er (or
·spon·dor)
trans·pon·tine across a
bridge
trans·port
trans·port·abil·ity
trans·port·able
trans·por·ta·tion
trans·port·ed·ly
trans·port·er
trans·port·ive
trans·pos·abil·ity
trans·pos·able
trans·pos·al
trans·pose
trans·pos·er
trans·po·si·tion
trans·po·si·tion·al (or
·posi·tive)
trans·sexu·al
trans·sex·ual·ism
trans·ship (or tran·ship;
·ship·ping, ·shipped)
trans·ship·ment (or
tran·ship·)
Trans-Siberian Rail·way
tran·sub·stan·tial
tran·sub·stan·ti·ate
tran·sub·stan·tia·tion
tran·sub·stan·tia·tion·al·ist
tran·su·date
tran·su·da·tion
tran·su·da·tory

tran·sude

transu·ran·ic (*or* ra·nian, ·ra·nium) chemistry term

Trans·vaal

Trans·vaal·er

Trans·vaal·ian

trans·valu·ation

trans·value (·valu·ing, ·valued)

trans·valu·er

trans·ver·sal

trans·ver·sal·ly

trans·verse

trans·verse·ly

trans·verse·ness

trans·ves·tism (*or* ·ti·tism)

trans·ves·tite

Transylvania

Transylvanian

trap (trap·ping, trapped)

tra·peze

tra·pezial

tra·pezium (*plural* ·peziums *or* ·pezia)

tra·pezius (*plural* ·peziuses) muscle

tra·pezo·he·dral

tra·pezo·he·dron (*plural* ·drons *or* ·dra)

trap·ezoid

trap·per

trap·pings

Trap·pist monk

trap·rock

traps belongings

trap·shooter

trap·shooting

tra·pun·to (*plural* ·tos) quilting

trash

trashi·ly

trashi·ness

trashy (trashi·er, trashi·est)

trass rock

trat·to·ria

trau·ma (*plural* ·mas, ·ma·ta)

trau·mat·ic

trau·mati·cal·ly

trau·ma·tism

trau·ma·ti·za·tion (*or* ·sa·tion)

trau·ma·tize (*or* ·tise)

trav·ail

trave horse-shoeing cage; crossbeam

trav·el (·el·ling, ·elled; US ·el·ing, ·eled)

trav·el·ler (US ·el·er)

trav·elogue (US also ·elog)

tra·vers·able

tra·vers·al

trav·erse

tra·vers·er

trav·er·tine (*or* ·tin) rock

trav·es·ty (*noun, plural* ·ties; *verb* ·ties, ·ty·ing, ·tied)

tra·vois (*plural* ·vois) sledge

trawl

trawl·er

tray receptacle; *compare* trey

tray·mobile *Austral* trolley

treach·er·ous

treach·er·ous·ness

treach·ery (*plural* ·eries)

trea·cle

trea·cli·ness

trea·cly

tread (tread·ing, trod, trod·den *or* trod)

tread·er

trea·dle

trea·dler

tread·mill

trea·son

trea·son·able (*or* ·ous)

trea·son·able·ness

trea·son·ably

treas·ur·able

treas·ure

treas·ur·er

treas·ur·er·ship

treasure-trove

Treas·ury government department

treas·ury (*plural* ·uries)

treat

treat·able

treat·er

trea·tise

treat·ment

trea·ty (*plural* ·ties)

Trebi·zond *former name of* Trabzon

tre·ble

Tre·blin·ka concentration camp

tre·bly

trebu·chet (*or* tre·buck·et) weapon

tre·cen·tist

tre·cen·to 14th century

tree (tree·ing, treed)

tree·hopper insect

tree·less

tree·less·ness

tre·en wooden

tree·nail (*or* tre·nail, trun·nel) dowel

treen·ware

tre·foil

tre·ha·la sugary substance

tre·ha·lose

treil·lage trellis

trek (trek·king, trekked)

trek·ker

trel·lis

trellis·work

trema·tode parasite

trem·ble

trem·bler

trem·bling·ly

trem·bly

tre·men·dous

tre·men·dous·ness

tremo·lite mineral

tremo·lo (*plural* ·los)

trem·or

trem·or·ous

tremu·lant musical term

tremu·lous

tremu·lous·ness

trench

trench·an·cy

trench·ant

trench·er

trencher·man (*plural* ·men) hearty eater

trend

trendi·ly

trendi·ness

trendy (*adj* trendi·er, trendi·est; *noun, plural* trendies)

Treng·ga·nu Malaysian state

Trent English river

Trentino-Alto Adi·ge Italian region

Tren·ton US city

tre·pan (·pan·ning, panned) surgical instrument

tre·pang sea cucumber
trephi·na·tion
tre·phine surgical
   instrument
trepi·da·tion
trepo·nema (or ·neme;
   plural ·nemas, ·nema·ta,
   or ·nemes) bacterium
trepo·nema·tous
tres·pass
tres·pass·er
tress
tres·sure heraldic term
tressy
tres·tle
trestle·tree
trestle·work
tret commerce term
tre·val·ly fish
trews trousers
trey card or dice thrown;
   compare tray
tri·able
tri·able·ness
tri·ac·id
Tri·ad Chinese secret society
tri·ad
tri·ad·ic
tri·ad·ism
tri·age
tri·al
tri·an·gle
tri·an·gu·lar
tri·an·gu·lar·ity
tri·an·gu·late
tri·an·gu·la·tion
Tri·an·gu·lum constellation
tri·ar·chy (plural ·chies)
Trias geology term
Tri·as·sic
tri·ath·lon
tri·atom·ic
tri·atomi·cal·ly
tri·ax·ial
tria·zine (or ·zin)
tria·zole
tria·zol·ic
trib·ade lesbian
tri·bad·ic
trib·ad·ism
trib·al
trib·al·ism
trib·al·ist
trib·al·ly
tri·ba·sic

tribe
tribes·man (plural ·men)
trib·let spindle
tri·bo·elec·tric
tri·bo·elec·tric·ity
tri·bol·ogy study of friction
tri·bo·lu·mi·nes·cence
tri·bo·lu·mi·nes·cent
tri·brach metrical foot
tri·brach·ic (or ·brach·ial)
tri·bro·mo·etha·nol
tribu·la·tion
tri·bu·nal
tribu·nary
tribu·nate (or
   trib·une·ship)
trib·une
tribu·tari·ly
tribu·tary (plural ·taries)
trib·ute
trice
tri·cen·ten·ary (plural
   ·aries)
tri·cen·ten·nial
tri·ceps (plural ·cepses or
   ·ceps)
tri·cera·tops
tri·chia·sis eye condition
tri·chi·na (plural ·nae)
   parasite
trichi·nia·sis variant of
   trichinosis
trichi·ni·za·tion (or
   ·sa·tion)
trichi·nize (or ·nise)
Trichi·nopo·ly Indian city
trichi·no·sis (or ·nia·)
   parasitic disease
trichi·nous
trich·ite crystal
tri·chit·ic
tri·chlo·ride
tri·chlo·ro·acetic acid
tri·chlo·ro·phenoxy·acetic
   acid
tricho·cyst zoology term
tricho·cys·tic
tricho·gyne botany term
tricho·gyn·ial (or ·ic)
trich·oid
tri·cholo·gist
tri·chol·ogy study of hair
tri·chome plant structure
tri·chom·ic
tricho·mon·ad parasite

tricho·mona·dal (or
   ·mon·al)
tricho·mo·nia·sis
tri·chop·ter·an insect
tri·cho·sis hair disease
tricho·tom·ic (or
   ·choto·mous)
tri·choto·my (plural ·mies)
tri·chro·ic
tri·chro·ism crystallography
   term
tri·chro·mat
tri·chro·mat·ic (or
   ·chro·mic)
tri·chro·ma·tism
trick
trick·er
trick·ery (plural ·eries)
tricki·ly
tricki·ness
trick·ing·ly
trick·le
trick·ling·ly
trick·ly
trick·si·ness
trick·ster
trick·sy (·si·er, ·si·est)
   mischievous
tricky (tricki·er, tricki·est)
tri·clin·ic crystallography
   term
tri·clin·ium (plural ·ia)
   Roman dining room
tri·col·our (US ·or)
tri·col·oured (US ·ored)
tri·corn (or ·corne) hat
tri·cos·tate biology term
tri·cot fabric
tri·co·tine fabric
tri·crot·ic medical term
tri·crot·ism
tric·trac (or trick·track)
   board game
tri·cus·pid
tri·cus·pi·dal
tri·cy·cle
tri·cy·clic chemistry term
tri·cy·clist
tri·dac·tyl (or ·tyl·ous)
tri·dent
tri·den·tate (or ·tal)
Tri·den·tine of Council of
   Trent
tri·di·men·sion·al
tri·di·men·sion·al·ity

trid·uum prayer days
tried
tri·en·nial
tri·en·nial·ly
tri·en·nium (plural ·niums or ·nia)
Trier German city
tri·er one who tries
tri·er·ar·chy (·chies)
Tri·este Italian port
trif·fid fictional plant
tri·fid three-lobed
tri·fle
tri·fler
tri·fling
tri·fo·cal
tri·fo·li·ate (or ·at·ed)
tri·fo·lium plant
tri·fo·rial
tri·fo·rium (plural ·ria) part of church
tri·fur·cate (or ·cat·ed)
tri·fur·ca·tion
trig (trig·ging, trigged) Dialect neat; wedge
tri·gemi·nal anatomy term
trig·ger
trigger·fish (plural ·fish or ·fishes)
tri·glyc·er·ide
tri·glyph architectural term
tri·glyph·ic
tri·gon harp
trigo·nal crystallography term
trigo·no·met·ric (or ·ri·cal)
trigo·no·met·ri·cal·ly
trigo·nom·etry
trigo·nous botany term
tri·graph phonetics term
tri·graph·ic
tri·he·dral
tri·he·dron (plural ·drons or ·dra)
tri·hy·drate
tri·hy·dric (or ·droxy)
tri·io·do·thy·ro·nine
trike Slang tricycle
tri·lat·er·al
tri·lat·er·al·ly
tri·lat·era·tion surveying method
tril·by (plural ·bies)
tri·lem·ma
tri·lin·ear

tri·lin·gual
tri·lin·gual·ism
tri·lin·gual·ly
tri·lit·er·al
tri·lith·ic
tri·lith·on (or tri·lith)
trill
tril·lion
tril·lionth
tril·lium plant
tri·lo·bate three-lobed
tri·lo·bite fossil
tri·locu·lar
tril·ogy (plural ·gies)
trim (adj trim·mer, trim·mest; verb trim·ming, trimmed)
tri·ma·ran
tri·mer chemistry term
trim·er·ous
trim·es·ter
tri·mes·tral (or ·trial)
trim·eter verse line
tri·metha·di·one
tri·met·ric (or ·ri·cal)
tri·met·ro·gon aerial photography
trim·ly
trim·mer
trim·ming
trim·ness
tri·mo·lecu·lar
tri·month·ly
tri·morph
tri·mor·phic (or ·phous)
tri·mor·phism
Tri·mur·ti Hindu gods
tri·nal
tri·na·ry consisting of three
Trin·co·ma·lee Sri Lankan port
trine astrology term
Trini·dad
Trini·dad·ian
Trini·tar·ian believer in the Trinity
Trini·tar·ian·ism
tri·ni·tro·ben·zene
tri·ni·tro·cre·sol
tri·ni·tro·glyc·er·in
tri·ni·tro·phe·nol
tri·ni·tro·tolu·ene (or ·ol)
Trin·ity God
trini·ty (plural ·ities)
trin·ket

trin·ket·ry
tri·nocu·lar
tri·no·mial
trio (plural trios)
tri·ode electronic valve
tri·oecious (or ·ecious) botany term
trio·elein
tri·ol
trio·let verse form
tri·ose
tri·ox·ide
trip (trip·ping, tripped)
tri·pal·mi·tin
tri·par·tite
tri·par·tite·ly
tri·par·ti·tion
tripe
trip·hammer
tri·phe·nyl·me·thane
tri·phibi·ous
triph·thong vowel sound
triph·thong·al
triphy·lite mineral
tri·pin·nate botany term
tri·plane
tri·ple
tri·plet
triple·tail (plural ·tail or ·tails) fish
triple-tongue musical term
Tri·plex (Trademark)
trip·li·cate
trip·li·ca·tion
trip·lic·ity (plural ·ities) group of three
trip·lo·blas·tic
trip·loid biology term
trip·loidy
triply
tri·pod
tripo·dal
tripo·dy (plural ·dies) metrical unit
Tripo·li Libyan capital
tripo·li rock
Tripo·li·ta·nia Libyan region
Tripo·li·ta·nian
tri·pos
trip·per
trip·pet
trip·ping·ly
trip·tane
trip·ter·ous

Triptolemus mythological
  character
trip·tych altarpiece; *compare*
  tryptic
trip·tyque customs permit
Tripu·ra Indian state
trip·wire
tri·que·trous
tri·ra·di·ate
tri·reme
tri·sac·cha·ride
tri·sect
tri·sec·tion
tri·sec·tor
tri·se·rial
tris·kai·deka·pho·bia fear
  of number 13
tris·kai·deka·pho·bic
tris·keli·on (*or* **·kele**)
  symbol
tris·mic
tris·mus lockjaw
tris·oc·ta·he·dral
tris·oc·ta·he·dron (*plural*
  ·drons *or* **·dra**)
tri·some genetics term
tri·so·mic
tri·somy
Tris·tan da Cu·nha South
  Atlantic islands
tris·tich three-line poem
tris·tich·ic
tris·ti·chous
tri·sul·phide
tri·syl·la·ble
tri·syl·lab·ic (*or* **·labi·cal**)
tri·tano·pia blue blindness
tri·tan·op·ic
trite
trite·ly
trite·ness
tri·the·ism belief in Trinity
tri·the·ist
triti·ate chemistry term
tritia·tion
triti·ca·le hybrid cereal
triti·cum cereal grass
trit·ium isotope of
  hydrogen
Tri·ton satellite of Neptune
Triton Greek god
tri·ton mollusc
tri·tone musical term
tritu·rable
tritu·rate grind

tritu·ra·tion
tritu·ra·tor
tri·umph
tri·um·phal
tri·um·phal·ly
tri·um·phant
tri·umph·er
tri·um·vir (*plural* **·virs** *or*
  ·vi·ri)
tri·um·vi·ral
tri·um·vi·rate
tri·une three in one
tri·unity
tri·va·len·cy
tri·va·lent (*or* **ter·**)
Tri·van·drum Indian city
triv·et
trivia (*plural*)
triv·ial
trivi·al·ity (*plural* **·ities**)
trivi·ali·za·tion (*or* **·sa·tion**)
trivi·al·ize (*or* **·ise**)
trivi·al·ly
trivi·al·ness
tri·week·ly (*plural* **·lies**)
Tro·as Trojan region
troat bellow
tro·car surgical instrument
tro·cha·ic of a trochee
tro·chai·cal·ly
tro·chal zoology term
tro·chan·ter anatomy term
troche lozenge
tro·chee metrical foot
trochi·lus hummingbird
troch·lea (*plural* **·leae**)
  anatomy term
troch·le·ar
tro·choid
tro·choi·dal
trocho·phore (*or* **·sphere**)
  zoology term
trod
trod·den
trog (**trog·ging**, **trogged**)
  stroll
trog·lo·dyte
trog·lo·dyt·ic (*or* **·dyti·cal**)
tro·gon bird
troi·ka
Troilus mythological
  character
Tro·jan
troll
trol·ley

trol·lop
trom·bi·dia·sis mite
  infestation
trom·bone
trom·bon·ist
trom·mel
trompe forge apparatus
trompe l'oeil (*plural* **trompe
  l'oeils**) painting illusion
tro·na mineral
Trond·heim Norwegian
  port
troop large group; move in
  group; *compare* **troupe**
troop·er
troops
troop·ship
troost·ite mineral
tro·paeo·lin
tro·paeo·lum (*plural* **·lums**
  or **·la**) plant
trope figure of speech;
  liturgical interpolation
troph·al·lac·tic
troph·al·lax·is
troph·ic of nutrition
trophi·cal·ly
tropho·blast embryonic
  membrane
tropho·blas·tic
tropho·zo·ite zoology term
tro·phy (*plural* **·phies**)
trop·ic line of latitude
tro·pic of a tropism
tropi·cal
tropi·cal·ity
tropi·cali·za·tion (*or*
  ·sa·tion)
tropi·cal·ize (*or* **·ise**)
tropi·cal·ly
tropic·bird
trop·ics
tro·pism biology term
tropo·log·ic (*or* **·logi·cal**)
tro·pol·ogy (*plural* **·ogies**)
  use of tropes
tropo·pause atmospheric
  layer
tro·pophi·lous
tropo·phyte
tropo·phyt·ic
tropo·sphere atmospheric
  layer
tropo·spher·ic
trop·po musical term

Tros·sachs Scottish valley
trot (trot·ting, trot·ted)
troth
trot·line
Trot·sky·ism
Trot·sky·ite (or ·ist)
trot·ter
tro·tyl TNT
trou·ba·dour
trou·ble
trou·bled·ly
trouble·maker
trouble·making
trou·bler
trouble·shooter
trou·ble·some
trou·ble·some·ness
trou·bling·ly
trou·blous
trou-de-loup (*plural* trous-de-loup) pit for defence
trough
trounce
troupe group of performers; *compare* troop
troup·er
trou·pial bird
trouse Irish breeches
trou·sered
trou·sers
trous·seau (*plural* ·seaux or ·seaus)
trout (*plural* trout or trouts)
trou·vère (or ·veur) medieval poet
trove
tro·ver legal term
Trow·bridge Wiltshire town
trow·el (·el·ling, ·elled; *US* ·el·ing, ·eled)
trow·el·ler (*US* ·el·er)
Troy
tru·an·cy
tru·ant
truce
Tru·cial States
truck
truck·age *US* conveyance by lorry
truck·er
truckie *Austral* truck driver
truck·ing
truck·le
truck·ler.

truck·load
trucu·lence (or ·len·cy)
trucu·lent
trudge
trudg·en swimming stroke
trudg·er
true (*adj* tru·er, tru·est; *verb* tru·ing, trued)
true-blue
true-born
true-life (*adj*)
true·love
true·ness
truf·fle
trug
tru·ism
tru·is·tic (or ·ti·cal)
Trujillo Peruvian city
tru·ly
tru·meau (*plural* ·meaux) architectural term
trump
trump·ery (*plural* ·eries)
trum·pet
trum·pet·er
trumpet·weed
trun·cate
trun·cat·ed
trun·ca·tion
trun·cheon
trun·dle
trunk
trunk·fish (*plural* ·fish or ·fishes)
trunk·ful (*plural* ·fuls)
trunks
trun·nion pivot
Tru·ro Cornish town
truss
truss·er
truss·ing
trust
trust·abil·ity
trust·able
trus·tee (·tee·ing, ·teed)
trus·tee·ship
trust·er
trust·ful (or ·ing)
trust·ful·ly (or ·ing·ly)
trust·ful·ness (or ·ing·)
trusti·ly
trusti·ness
trust·worthi·ly
trust·worthi·ness
trust·worthy

trusty (trusti·er, trusti·est)
truth
truth·ful
truth·ful·ly
truth·ful·ness
truth-function logic term
truth-value logic term
try (*verb* tries, try·ing, tried; *noun, plural* tries)
(tryer) *incorrect spelling of* trier
try·ing·ly
try·ing·ness
try·ma (*plural* ·ma·ta) botany term
try-on (*noun*)
try-out (*noun*)
trypa·no·so·mal (or ·som·ic)
trypa·no·some parasite
trypa·no·so·mia·sis sleeping sickness
try·par·sa·mide
tryp·sin enzyme
tryp·sino·gen enzyme
tryp·tic of trypsin; *compare* triptych
tryp·to·phan amino acid
try·sail
tryst
tryst·er
tsar (or czar)
tsar·dom (or czar·)
tsar·evitch (or czar·)
tsa·ri·na (or ·rit·sa, cza·)
tsar·ism (or czar·)
tsar·ist (or czar·)
Tse·li·no·grad *former name* of Astana
tset·se (or tzet·ze)
Tshi·lu·ba African language
Tsi·nan (or Chi·nan, Chi·nan) Chinese city
Tsing·hai (or Ching·hai, Ch'ing-hai) Chinese province
Tsing·tao (or Ching·tao, Ch'ing-tao) Chinese port
Tson·ga (*plural* ·ga or ·gas) African people
tsu·na·mi tidal wave
Tsu·shi·ma Japanese islands
tsu·tsu·ga·mu·shi dis·ease
Tswa·na (*plural* ·na or ·nas) African people

Tua·reg (*plural* ·reg *or* ·regs)
 Berber people
tuart tree
tua·ta·ra reptile
tub (tub·bing, tubbed)
tuba (*plural* tubas *or* tubae)
 musical instrument;
 compare tuber
tu·bal
Tubal-cain biblical
 character
tu·bate
tubbed
tub·bi·ness
tub·bing
tub·by (·bi·er, ·bi·est)
tube
tube·less
tu·ber underground plant
 stem; *compare* tuba
tu·ber·cle
tu·ber·cu·lar
tu·ber·cu·late covered with
 nodules
tu·ber·cu·la·tion
tu·ber·cu·lin
tu·ber·cu·lo·sis
tu·ber·cu·lous
tu·ber·ose plant; *compare*
 tuberous
tu·ber·os·ity (*plural* ·ities)
tu·ber·ous (*or* ·ose) having
 tubers; *compare* tuberose
tu·bi·fex (*plural* ·fex *or*
 ·fexes) worm
tu·bi·form
tub·ing
tub-thumper
tubu·lar
tu·bu·lar·ity
tu·bu·late
tu·bu·la·tion
tu·bu·la·tor
tu·bule
tu·bu·li·flo·rous botany
 term
tu·bu·lous
Tu·ca·na constellation
tu·chun Chinese governor
tuck
tuck·er
tuck·et flourish on trumpet
tu·co·tu·co (*or* tu·cu·tu·cu)
 animal
Tuc·son US city

Tu·cu·mán Argentine city
Tu·dor
Tues·day
tufa soft rock
tuff hard rock
tuffa·ceous
tuf·fet
tuft
tuft·ed
tuft·er
tufty
tug (tug·ging, tugged)
tug·ger
tu·grik (*or* ·ghrik)
 Mongolian currency
tui bird
Tui·ler·ies French palace
tui·tion
tui·tion·al (*or* ·ary)
tu·la·rae·mia (*US* ·re·)
 disease
tu·la·rae·mic (*US* ·remic)
tu·lip
tulip·wood
tulle fabric
Tul·sa US city
tum *Slang* stomach
tum·ble
tumble-down
tumble-drier
tumble·home nautical term
tum·bler
tum·bler·ful (*plural* ·fuls)
tumble·weed
tum·brel (*or* ·bril)
tu·mefa·ci·ent
tu·mefac·tion
tu·mefy (·mefies,
 ·mefy·ing, ·mefied) swell
tu·mes·cence
tu·mes·cent
tu·mid
tu·mid·ity (*or* ·ness)
tum·my (*plural* ·mies)
tu·mor·ous (*or* ·mor·al)
tu·mour (*US* ·mor)
tump *Dialect* small mound
tu·mu·lar
tu·mu·lose (*or* ·lous)
tu·mu·los·ity
tu·mult
tu·mul·tu·ous
tu·mul·tu·ous·ness
tu·mu·lus (*plural* ·li) burial
 mound

tun (tun·ning, tunned)
 cask; *compare* ton; tonne
tuna (*plural* tuna *or* tunas)
tun·able (*or* tune·)
Tun·bridge Wells Kent
 town; *compare* Tonbridge
tun·dra
tune
tune·ful
tune·ful·ly
tune·ful·ness
tune·less
tune·less·ness
tun·er
tune·smith
tung·sten
tung·stic
tung·stite mineral
Tun·gus (*plural* ·guses *or*
 ·gus) Mongoloid people
Tun·gu·sian
Tun·gus·ic language
tu·nic
tu·ni·ca (*plural* ·cae)
 anatomy term
tu·ni·cate marine animal
tu·ni·cle vestment
tun·ing musical term
Tu·nis Tunisian capital
Tu·ni·sia
Tu·ni·sian
tun·nage *variant spelling of*
 tonnage
tun·nel (·nel·ling, ·nelled;
 US ·nel·ing, ·neled)
tun·nel·ler (*US* ·nel·er)
tun·ny (*plural* ·nies *or* ·ny)
 tuna fish
tup (tup·ping, tupped)
tu·pelo (*plural* ·pelos)
 tree
Tupi (*plural* ·pis *or* ·pi)
 South American Indian
tupped
tup·pence *variant spelling of*
 twopence
tup·pen·ny *variant spelling*
 of twopenny
tup·ping
tuque cap
tur·ban
tur·baned
tur·ba·ry (*plural* ·ries)
 peat-cutting area
tur·bel·lar·ian flatworm

tur·bid opaque; muddy; compare turgid
tur·bi·dim·eter
tur·bid·ity (or ·ness)
tur·bi·nate (or ·nal) scroll-shaped
tur·bi·na·tion
tur·bine
tur·bit pigeon
tur·bo·car
tur·bo·charg·er
turbo-electric
tur·bo·fan
tur·bo·gen·era·tor
tur·bo·jet
tur·bo·prop
tur·bo·super·charg·er
tur·bot (plural ·bot or ·bots)
tur·bu·lence (or ·len·cy)
tur·bu·lent
turd
tur·dine of thrushes
tu·reen soup dish; compare terrene; terrine
turf (plural turfs or turves)
turfi·ness
turfy (turfi·er, turfi·est)
tur·ges·cence (or ·cen·cy)
tur·ges·cent
tur·gid swollen; pompous; compare turbid
tur·gid·ity (or ·ness)
tur·gite mineral
tur·gor biology term
Tu·rin Italian city
Turing ma·chine
turi·on plant bud
Turk
Tur·ke·stan variant spelling of Turkistan
Tur·key
tur·key (plural ·keys or ·key)
Tur·ki of Turkic
Tur·kic language
Turk·ish
Tur·ki·stan (or ·ke·) Asian region
Turk·men language
Turk·meni·stan Central Asian country
Turko·man (or Turk·man; plural ·mans or ·men) Asian people
Tur·ku Finnish city
tur·mer·ic

tur·moil
turn move; compare tern; terne
turn·able
turn·about
turn·around
turn·buckle
turn·coat
turn·er
turn·ery (plural ·eries) lathe work
turn·ing
tur·nip
turn·key
turn-off (noun)
turn-on (noun)
turn-out (noun)
turn·over (noun)
turn·pike
turn-round (noun)
turn·sole plant
turn·stile
turn·stone bird
turn·table
turn-up (noun)
tur·pen·tine
tur·peth plant
tur·pi·tude
turps turpentine
tur·quoise
tur·ret
tur·ret·ed
tur·ricu·late (or ·la·ted)
tur·tle
turtle·back part of ship
turtle·dove
turtle·neck
tur·tler
Tus·can
Tus·ca·ny
Tus·ca·ro·ra (plural ·ras or ·ra) American Indian
tusche lithographic substance
Tus·cu·lum ancient city
tush
tusk
tusk·er
tusk·like
tus·sah (or tus·sore) silk
tus·sal
tus·sis cough
tus·sive
tus·sle
tus·sock

tus·socky
tus·sore variant spelling of tussah
tut (tut·ting, tut·ted)
tu·tee
tu·telage
tu·telary (or ·telar; plural ·telaries or ·telars)
tu·ti·or·ism Catholic doctrine
tu·ti·or·ist
tu·tor
tu·tor·age (or ·ship)
tu·to·rial
tu·to·rial·ly
tut·san shrub
tut·ti musical term
tutti-frutti ice cream
tut·ty polishing powder
tutu ballet skirt
Tuvalu Pacific state
tu-whit tu-whoo
tux·edo (plural ·dos)
tu·yère (or twy·er) blast-furnace nozzle
Tver Russian city
twad·dle
twad·dler
twain
twang
twangy
'twas
tway·blade orchid
tweak
twee
Tweed Scottish river
tweed fabric
tweedy (tweedi·er, tweedi·est)
tweeny (plural tweenies) Slang maid
tweet
tweet·er loudspeaker
tweeze
twee·zers
twelfth
Twelfth·tide Epiphany
twelve
twelve·mo (plural ·mos) paper size
twelve·month
twelve-tone musical term
twen·ti·eth
twen·ty (plural ·ties)
'twere

twerp

Twi (*plural* Twi *or* Twis)
language or people

twi·bill (*or* ·bil) tool

twice

twice-laid

Twick·en·ham

twid·dle

twid·dler

twig (twig·ging, twigged)

twig·gy (·gi·er, ·gi·est)

twi·light

twi·lit

twill

twin (twin·ning, twinned)

twine

twin·er

twin-flower

twinge (twinge·ing *or*
twing·ing, twinged)

twink

twin·kle

twin·kler

twin·kling·ly

twirl

twirl·er

twist

twist·abil·ity

twist·able

twist·ed·ly

twist·er

twist·ing·ly

twisty (twisti·er, twisti·est)

twit (twit·ting, twit·ted)

twitch

twitch·er

twitchi·ly

twitchi·ness

twitch·ing·ly

twitchy (twitchi·er,
twitchi·est)

twite bird

twit·ter

twit·ter·er

twit·tery

twixt

two (*plural* twos)

two-by-four

two-dimen·sion·al

two-dimen·sion·al·ity

two-dimen·sion·al·ly

two-edged

two-faced

two-facedly

two-facedness

two·fold

two-handed

two-handed·ly

two·pence (*or* tup·pence)

two·pen·ny (*or*
tup·pen·ny)

two-phase

two-piece

two-ply (*plural* -plies)

two-seater

two-sided

two·some

two-step

two-stroke

two-time

two-timer

two-tone

two-way

Ty·burn

Tyche Greek goddess

tych·ism philosophy term

Ty·cho moon crater

ty·coon

ty·ing

tyke (*or* tike)

ty·lo·pod zoology term

ty·lo·sis botany term

tym·pan printing term

tym·pa·ni *variant spelling of*
timpani

tym·pan·ic

tym·pa·nist *variant spelling
of* timpanist

tym·pa·ni·tes (*or* ·pa·ny)
abdominal distension

tym·pa·nit·ic

tym·pa·ni·tis

tym·pa·num (*plural* ·nums
or ·na) part of ear;
architectural term; *compare*
timpani

tym·pa·ny *variant of*
tympanites

Tyne English river

Tyne and Wear former
English county

Tyne·side

Tyn·wald Manx
Parliament

type

type·bar

type·case

type·cast (·cast·ing, ·cast)

type·cast·er

type·face

type-high

type·script

type·set (·set·ting, ·set)

type·set·ter

type·write (·writ·ing,
·wrote, ·writ·ten)

type·writ·er

typh·li·tic

typh·li·tis intestinal
disorder

typh·lol·ogy study of
blindness

ty·pho·gen·ic causing
typhoid

ty·phoid

ty·phoi·dal

ty·phoi·din

ty·phon·ic

ty·phoon

ty·phous (*adj*)

ty·phus (*noun*)

typi·cal (*or* typ·ic)

typi·cal·ly

typi·cal·ness (*or* ·ity)

typi·fi·ca·tion

typi·fi·er

typi·fy (·fies, ·fy·ing, ·fied)

typ·ing

typ·ist

typo (*plural* typos)

ty·pog·ra·pher

ty·po·graphi·cal (*or*
·graph·ic)

ty·po·graphi·cal·ly

ty·pog·ra·phy

ty·po·logi·cal (*or* ·log·ic)

ty·polo·gist

ty·pol·ogy theology term

ty·poth·etae US printers

ty·ra·mine

ty·ran·ni·cal (*or* ran·nic)

ty·ran·ni·cal·ly

ty·ran·ni·cal·ness

ty·ran·ni·cid·al

ty·ran·ni·cide

ty·ran·nize (*or* ·nise)

ty·ran·niz·er (*or* ·nis·er)

ty·ran·niz·ing·ly (*or*
·nis·ing·ly)

ty·ran·no·saur (*or* ·saur·us)

tyr·an·nous

tyr·an·nous·ness

tyr·an·ny (*plural* ·nies)

tyr·ant

Tyre Lebanese port

tyre (*US* **tire**) wheel ring; *compare* **tire**

Tyr·ian

tyro (*or* **tiro**; *plural* **tyros** *or* **tiros**) novice

ty·ro·ci·dine antibiotic

Ty·rol (*or* **Ti·**) Austrian province

Tyro·lese (*or* **·lean**)

Ty·ro·li·enne dance

Ty·rone Irish county

ty·ron·ic (*or* **ti·**)

ty·ro·si·nase enzyme

ty·ro·sine amino acid

ty·ro·thri·cin antibiotic

Tyr·rhe·nian Sea

Tyu·men Russian port

tzar *less common spelling of* **tsar**

Tzi·gane gipsy

tzet·ze variant spelling of **tsetse**

Tzu·po (*or* **Tze·po**) Chinese city

U

ubi·ety being in particular place

ubiqui·tar·ian Lutheran

ubiqui·tous (*or* **ubiqui·tous·ness**)

ubiquity (*or* **ubiqui·tous·ness**)

ubi su·pra *Latin* where mentioned above

U-boat

Udai·pur Indian city

udal legal term

ud·der

Udi·ne Italian city

udo (*plural* **udos**) plant

Uf·fizi Italian art gallery

UFO (*plural* **UFOs**)

ufol·ogy study of UFOs

Ugan·da

Ugan·dan

Uga·rit·ic language

ugli (*plural* **uglis** *or* **uglies**) fruit

ug·li·fi·ca·tion

ug·li·fi·er

ug·li·fy (**·fies**, **·fy·ing**, **·fied**)

ug·li·ly

ug·li·ness

ugly (**ug·li·er**, **ug·li·est**)

Ugrian Asian people

Ugric language

uh·lan Polish lancer

uhu·ru African national independence

Uigur (*or* **Uighur**; *plural* **Uigur**, **Uigurs** *or* **Uighur**, **Uighurs**) Mongoloid people

Uigu·rian (*or* **·ric**, **Uighu·**)

uin·ta·there extinct mammal

uit·land·er *South African* foreigner

Uj·jain Indian city

ukase tsar's edict

uke·lele *variant spelling of* **ukulele**

uki·yoe (*or* **ukiyo-e**) Japanese art

Ukraine

Ukrain·ian

uku·lele (*or* **uke·**)

Ulan Ba·tor Mongolian capital

Ulan-Ude Russian city

ul·cer

ul·cer·ate

ul·cera·tion

ul·cera·tive

ul·cer·ous

ulema Muslim scholar

ul·lage

ul·laged

Ulls·wa·ter

ul·ma·ceous botany term

ulna (*plural* **ulnae** *or* **ulnas**) arm bone

ul·nar

ulot·ri·chous curly haired

ulot·ri·chy

Ul·ster Northern Ireland

ul·ster overcoat

Ul·ster·man (*plural* **·men**)

ul·te·ri·or

ul·ti·ma final syllable

ul·ti·mate

ul·ti·mate·ly

ul·ti·ma·tum (*plural* **·tums** *or* **·ta**)

ul·ti·mo last month

ul·ti·mo·geni·ture legal term

ul·tra

ultra·cen·trifu·gal

ultra·cen·trifu·ga·tion

ultra·cen·tri·fuge

ultra·con·ser·va·tive

ultra·fiche

ultra·fil·ter

ultra·fil·tra·tion

ultra·high

ultra·ism extreme philosophy

ultra·ist

ultra·is·tic

ultra·ma·rine colour

ultra·mi·crom·eter

ultra·micro·scope

ultra·micro·scop·ic

ultra·mi·cros·co·py

ultra·mod·ern

ultra·mod·ern·ism

ultra·mod·ern·ist

ultra·mod·ern·is·tic

ultra·mon·tane beyond the mountains

ultra·mon·ta·nism religious doctrine

ultra·mon·tan·ist

ultra·mun·dane beyond this world

ultra·na·tion·al

ultra·na·tion·al·chy

ultra·na·tion·al·ism

ultra·na·tion·al·ist

ultra·na·tion·al·is·tic

ultra·short

ultra·son·ic

ultra·soni·cal·ly

ultra·son·ics

ultra·sound

ultra·struc·tur·al

ultra·struc·ture

ultra·vio·let

ul·tra vi·res legal term

ultra·vi·rus

ulu·lant

ulu·late wail

ulu·la·tion
Ul·ya·novsk *former name of* Simbirsk
Umay·yad *variant spelling of* Omayyad
um·bel *botany term*
um·bel·late (*or* ·lar, ·lat·ed)
um·bel·lif·er·ous
um·bel·lu·late
um·bel·lule
um·ber *pigment*
um·bili·cal
um·bili·cate
um·bili·ca·tion
um·bili·cus (*plural* ·ci) navel
um·bili·form
umbo (*plural* um·bo·nes *or* umbos) *small hump*
um·bo·nate (*or* ·bo·nal, ·bon·ic)
um·bra (*plural* ·brae) shadow
um·brage
um·bra·geous *shady*
um·bral
um·brel·la
Um·bria *Italian region*
Um·brian
Um·bri·el *satellite of Uranus*
umi·ak (*or* oomi·) *Eskimo boat*
um·laut
um·pire
um·pire·ship (*or* ·pir·age)
ump·teen
ump·teenth
Um·ta·li *Zimbabwean city*
un·abashed
un·abat·ed
un·able
un·abridged
un·ab·sorbed
un·ac·cent·ed
un·ac·cep·table
un·ac·claimed
un·ac·com·mo·dat·ed
un·ac·com·mo·dat·ing
un·ac·com·pa·nied
un·ac·com·plished
un·ac·count·able
un·ac·count·able·ness (*or* ·abil·ity)
un·ac·count·ably
un·ac·count·ed

un·ac·counted-for
un·ac·cus·tomed
un·ack·nowl·edged
un·ac·quaint·ed
un·ad·mit·ted
un·adopt·ed
un·adorned
un·adul·ter·at·ed
un·ad·ven·tur·ous
un·ad·vised
un·ad·vis·ed·ly
un·ad·vis·ed·ness
un·af·fect·ed
un·afraid
un·aid·ed
un·aimed
un·aired
un·al·loyed *pure*
un·al·ter·able
un·al·ter·ably
un·al·tered
un·am·bigu·ous
un·am·bi·tious
un-Ameri·can
una·nim·ity (*or* unani·mous·ness)
unani·mous
un·an·nounced
un·an·swer·able
un·an·swered
un·ap·peal·able *legal term*
un·ap·peased
un·ap·pre·ciat·ed
un·ap·pre·cia·tive
un·ap·proach·able
un·ap·pro·pri·at·ed
un·apt *inapt*
un·apt·ness
un·argu·able
un·arm
un·armed
unary *consisting of single element*
un·ashamed
un·asham·ed·ly
un·asham·ed·ness
un·asked
un·as·sail·able
un·as·sist·ed
un·as·sumed
un·as·sum·ing
un·atoned
un·at·tached
un·at·tain·able
un·at·tend·ed

un·at·test·ed
un·at·trac·tive
un·authen·ti·cat·ed
un·author·ized
un·avail·able
un·avail·ing
un·avoid·abil·ity (*or* ·able·ness)
un·avoid·able
un·avoid·ably
un·aware
un·aware·ness
un·awares (*adv*)
un·backed
un·bal·ance
un·bal·anced
un·bal·las·ted
un·bar (·bar·ring, ·barred)
un·bear·able
un·bear·able·ness
un·bear·ably
un·beat·able
un·beat·en
un·be·com·ing
un·be·com·ing·ness
un·be·fit·ting
un·be·known (*or* ·knownst)
un·be·lief
un·be·liev·abil·ity (*or* ·able·ness)
un·be·liev·able
un·be·liev·ably
un·be·liev·er
un·be·liev·ing
un·be·liev·ing·ly
un·belt
un·bend (·bend·ing, ·bent)
un·bend·able
un·bend·ing
un·bend·ing·ness
un·bent
un·bi·ased (*or* ·assed)
un·bi·ased·ly (*or* ·assed·)
un·bi·ased·ness (*or* ·assed·)
un·bid·den
un·bind (·bind·ing, ·bound)
un·birth·day
un·blem·ished
un·blessed
un·bless·ed·ness
un·blink·ing
un·block
un·blush·ing

un·bolt
un·bolt·ed
un·boned
un·bon·net remove hat
un·born
un·bos·om relieve by
  disclosing
un·bound released
un·bound·ed unlimited
un·bowed
un·brace relax
un·break·able
un·bred
un·bri·dle
un·bri·dled
un·Brit·ish
un·bro·ken
un·brushed
un·buck·le
un·bur·den
un·bur·ied
un·but·ton
un·caged
uncalled-for
un·can·ni·ly
un·can·ny (·ni·er, ·ni·est)
un·cap (·cap·ping,
  ·capped)
uncared-for
un·car·ing
un·ceas·ing
un·ceas·ing·ness
un·cer·emo·ni·ous
un·cer·emo·ni·ous·ness
un·cer·tain
un·cer·tain·ness
un·cer·tain·ty (plural ·ties)
un·chain
un·chal·lenge·able
un·chal·lenged
un·changed
un·chang·ing
un·chap·er·oned
un·charged
un·chari·table
un·chari·tably
un·chari·table·ness
un·chart·ed not mapped
un·char·tered not
  authorized
un·chaste
un·chaste·ness (or
  ·chas·tity)
un·checked
un·chris·tian

un·church excommunicate
un·cial type of capital letter
un·ci·form hook-shaped
un·ci·na·ria·sis hookworm
  disease
un·ci·nate
un·ci·nus (plural ·ni) small
  hook
un·cir·cum·cised
un·civ·il
un·ci·vil·ity (or ·civ·il·ness)
un·civi·lized (or ·lised)
un·civil·ly
un·clad
un·claimed
un·clasp
un·clas·si·fied
un·cle
un·clean
un·cleaned
un·clean·li·ness
un·clean·ly
un·clean·ness
un·clear
un·clench
un·clip (·clip·ping,
  ·clipped)
un·cloak
un·clog (·clog·ging,
  ·clogged)
un·close
un·clothe (·cloth·ing,
  ·clothed or ·clad)
un·clothed
un·cloud·ed
un·clut·tered
unco Scot strange
un·coil
un·coined
un·com·fort·able
un·com·fort·ably
un·com·mer·cial
un·com·mit·ted
un·com·mon
un·com·mon·ly
un·com·mon·ness
un·com·mu·ni·ca·tive
un·com·pen·sat·ed
un·com·peti·tive
un·com·plain·ing
un·com·plet·ed
un·com·pli·cat·ed
un·com·pli·men·ta·ry
un·com·pro·mis·ing
un·com·pro·mis·ing·ness

un·con·cealed
un·con·cern
un·con·cerned
un·con·cern·ed·ly
un·con·cern·ed·ness
un·con·clud·ed
un·con·di·tion·al
un·con·di·tion·al·ly
un·con·di·tion·al·ness (or
  ·ity)
un·con·di·tioned
un·con·fined
un·con·firmed
un·con·form·abil·ity (or
  ·able·ness)
un·con·form·able
un·con·form·ity (plural
  ·ities)
un·con·gen·ial
un·con·gen·ial·ly
un·con·nect·ed
un·con·nect·ed·ness
un·con·quer·able
un·con·quered
un·con·scion·able
  unscrupulous; excessive
un·con·scious
un·con·scious·ness
un·con·sent·ing
un·con·sti·tu·tion·al
un·con·sti·tu·tion·al·ity
un·con·sti·tu·tion·al·ly
un·con·strained
un·con·sum·mat·ed
un·con·tami·nat·ed
un·con·test·ed
un·con·trol·labil·ity (or
  ·lable·ness)
un·con·trol·lable
un·con·trol·lably
un·con·ven·tion·al
un·con·ven·tion·al·ity
un·con·ven·tion·al·ly
un·con·vert·ed
un·con·vinced
un·con·vinc·ing
un·cooked
un·co·opera·tive
un·co·ordi·nat·ed
un·cork
un·cor·rected
un·cor·robo·rat·ed
un·cor·rupt·ed
un·count·able
un·count·ed

un·cou·ple
un·couth
un·cov·enant·ed
un·cov·er
un·cov·ered
un·criti·cal
un·criti·cal·ly
un·cross
un·crowned
unc·tion
unc·tu·os·ity (or
    ·tu·ous·ness)
unc·tu·ous
un·cul·ti·vat·ed
un·curbed
un·cured
un·curl
un·curt·ained
un·cus (*plural* unci) hooked
    structure
un·cut
un·dam·aged
un·damped
un·dat·ed
un·daunt·ed
un·deca·gon eleven-sided
    polygon
un·de·ceiv·able
un·de·ceive
un·de·ceiv·er
un·de·cid·ed
un·de·cid·ed·ness
un·de·clared
un·de·feat·ed
un·de·fend·ed
un·de·filed
un·de·mand·ing
un·demo·crat·ic
un·demo·crati·cal·ly
un·de·mon·stra·tive
un·de·ni·able
un·de·ni·ably
un·der
under·achieve
under·achieve·ment
under·achiev·er
under·act
under·age
under·arm
under·belly (*plural* ·bellies)
under·bid (·bid·ding, ·bid)
under·bid·der
under·body (*plural* ·bodies)
under·bred
under·breeding

under·brush *US*
    undergrowth
under·buy (·buy·ing,
    ·bought)
under·capi·tal·ize (or ·ise)
under·carriage
under·cart undercarriage
under·charge
under·clay
under·clothes (or
    ·cloth·ing)
under·coat
under·cook
under·cov·er
under·croft underground
    chamber
under·cur·rent
under·cut (·cut·ting, ·cut)
under·de·vel·op
under·de·vel·op·ment
under·do (·does, ·do·ing,
    ·did, ·done)
under·dog
under·done
under·drain
under·drain·age
under·dressed
under·em·ployed
under·em·ploy·ment
under·es·ti·mate
under·es·ti·ma·tion
under·ex·pose
under·ex·po·sure
under·feed (·feed·ing, ·fed)
under·felt
under·floor
under·foot
under·fur
under·gar·ment
under·gird (·gird·ing,
    ·gird·ed or ·girt)
    strengthen from below
under·glaze
under·go (·goes, ·go·ing,
    ·went, ·gone)
under·go·er
under·gone
under·gradu·ate
under·ground
under·grown
under·growth
under·hand
under·hand·ed
under·hand·ed·ly
under·hand·ed·ness

under·hung
under·laid
under·lain
under·lay (·lay·ing, ·laid)
    to place under
under·let (·let·ting, ·let)
under·let·ter
under·lie (·ly·ing, ·lay,
    ·lain) to lie under
under·li·er
under·line
under·ling
under·ly·ing
under·manned
under·men·tioned
under·mine
under·min·er
under·min·ing·ly
under·most
under·named
under·neath
under·nour·ish
under·nour·ished
under·nour·ish·ment
under·paid
under·paint·ing
under·pants
under·pass
under·pay (·pay·ing, ·paid)
under·pay·ment
under·pin (·pin·ning,
    ·pinned)
under·pin·nings
under·play
under·plot subplot
under·price
under·privi·leged
under·pro·duc·tion
under·proof less than proof
    spirit
under·prop (·prop·ping,
    ·propped)
under·quote
under·rate
under·ripe
under·score
under·sea
under·seal
under·sec·re·tary (*plural*
    ·taries)
under·sec·re·tary·ship
under·sell (·sel·ling, ·sold)
under·sell·er
under·set (·set·ting, ·set)
under·sexed

under·sher·iff
under·shirt
under·shoot (·shoot·ing, ·shot)
under·side
under·signed
under·sized
under·skirt
under·slung
under·soil
under·sold
under·spend (·spend·ing, ·spent)
under·staffed
under·stand (·stand·ing, ·stood)
under·stand·able
under·stand·ably
under·stand·ing
under·stand·ing·ly
under·state
under·state·ment
under·stock
under·stood
under·study (*noun, plural* ·studies; *verb* ·studies, ·study·ing, ·stud·ied)
under·sur·face
under·take (·tak·ing, ·took, ·tak·en)
under·tak·er
under·tak·ing
under·thrust geological fault
under·tint
under·tone
under·took
under·tow
under·trick bridge term
under·trump
under·valu·ation
under·value (·valu·ing, ·val·ued)
under·valu·er
under·vest
under·wa·ter
under·wear
under·weight
under·went
under·wing moth
under·world
under·write (·writ·ing, ·wrote, ·writ·ten)
under·writ·er
un·des·cend·ed

un·de·served
un·de·serv·ing
un·de·sign·ing
un·de·sir·abil·ity (*or* ·able·ness)
un·de·sir·able
un·de·sir·ably
un·de·sired
un·de·tect·ed
un·de·ter·mined
un·de·terred
un·de·vel·oped
un·de·vi·at·ing
un·di·ag·nosed
un·did
un·dies
un·dif·fer·en·ti·at·ed
un·di·gest·ed
un·dig·ni·fied
un·di·lut·ed
un·dim·in·ished
un·dimmed
un·dine water spirit
un·di·rect·ed
un·dis·ci·plined
un·dis·closed
un·dis·cov·ered
un·dis·crimi·nat·ing
un·dis·guised
un·dis·put·ed
un·dis·solved
un·dis·tin·guished
un·dis·trib·ut·ed logic term
un·dis·turbed
un·di·vid·ed
undo (un·does, un·do·ing, un·did, un·done)
un·do·er
un·do·ing
un·done
un·doubt·ed
un·doubt·ed·ly
un·dreamed (*or* ·dreamt)
un·dress
un·drink·able
un·due
un·du·lance
un·du·lant
un·du·late
un·du·la·tion
un·du·la·tor
un·du·la·tory
un·du·ly
un·dy·ing
un·earned

un·earth
un·earth·li·ness
un·earth·ly
un·ease
un·easi·ly
un·easi·ness
un·easy
un·eat·able
un·eat·en
un·eco·nom·ic
un·eco·nomi·cal
un·eco·nomi·cal·ly
un·ed·it·ed
un·edu·cat·ed
un·elect·able
un·emo·tion·al
un·emo·tion·al·ly
un·em·ploy·abil·ity
un·em·ploy·able
un·em·ployed
un·em·ploy·ment
un·end·ing
un·en·gaged
un·En·glish
un·en·light·ened
un·en·ter·pris·ing
un·en·thu·si·as·tic
un·en·thu·si·asti·cal·ly
un·en·vi·able
un·equal
un·equalled (*US* ·equaled)
un·equal·ly
un·equivo·cal
un·equivo·cal·ly
un·equivo·cal·ness
un·err·ing
un·err·ing·ly
un·es·sen·tial *less common word for* inessential
un·ethi·cal
un·ethi·cal·ly
un·even
un·even·ness
un·event·ful
un·event·ful·ly
un·ex·am·pled
un·ex·cep·tion·able beyond criticism
un·ex·cep·tion·able·ness (*or* ·abil·ity)
un·ex·cep·tion·al ordinary
un·ex·cit·ing
un·ex·pec·ted
un·ex·pec·ted·ly
un·ex·pect·ed·ness

un·ex·pe·ri·enced
un·ex·pired
un·ex·plain·able *less common word for* inexplicable
un·ex·plained
un·ex·plod·ed
un·ex·plored
un·ex·posed
un·ex·pressed
un·ex·pres·sive
un·ex·pres·sive·ness
un·ex·pur·gat·ed
un·fad·ing
un·fail·ing
un·fair
un·fair·ness
un·faith·ful
un·faith·ful·ly
un·faith·ful·ness
un·fa·mil·iar
un·fa·mili·ar·ity
un·fash·ion·able
un·fash·ion·ably
un·fas·ten
un·fa·thered
un·fath·om·able
un·fath·omed
un·fa·vour·able (US ·vor·)
un·fa·vour·able·ness (US ·vor·)
un·fa·vour·ably (US ·vor·)
un·fed
un·feel·ing
un·feel·ing·ness
un·feigned
un·feigned·ly
un·femi·nine
un·fenced
un·fer·til·ized (or ·ised)
un·fet·ter
un·fil·ial
un·filled
un·fin·ished
un·fit
un·fit·ness
un·fit·ted
un·fit·ting
un·fix
un·flag·ging
un·flap·pabil·ity (or ·pable·ness)
un·flap·pable
un·flat·ter·ing
un·fledged

un·flinch·ing
un·flinch·ing·ness
un·flust·ered
un·fo·cused
un·fold
un·fold·er
un·forced
un·fore·see·able
un·fore·seen
un·for·get·table
un·for·giv·able
un·for·giv·en
un·for·giv·ing
un·for·got·ten
un·formed
un·for·tu·nate
un·for·tu·nate·ly
un·for·tu·nate·ness
un·found·ed
un·found·ed·ness
un·framed
un·freeze (·freez·ing, ·froze, ·fro·zen)
un·fre·quent·ed
un·friend·li·ness
un·friend·ly (·li·er, ·li·est)
un·frock
un·froze
un·fro·zen
un·fruit·ful
un·fruit·ful·ly
un·fruit·ful·ness
un·ful·filled
un·furl
un·fur·nished
un·gain·li·ness
un·gain·ly (·li·er, ·li·est)
Un·ga·va *Canadian region*
un·gen·er·ous
un·gen·tle·man·ly
un·get-at-able
un·glazed
un·god·li·ness
un·god·ly (·li·er, ·li·est)
un·gov·ern·able
un·gov·ern·able·ness
un·gov·ern·ably
un·grace·ful
un·grace·ful·ly
un·gra·cious
un·gram·mati·cal
un·grate·ful
un·grate·ful·ly
un·grate·ful·ness
un·grudg·ing

un·gual (or ·gu·lar) of finger- or toenails
un·guard·ed
un·guard·ed·ness
un·guent *ointment*
un·guen·tary
un·guicu·late *biology term*
un·gui·nous *greasy*
un·guis (*plural* ·gues) *claw or hoof*
un·gu·la (*plural* ·lae) *maths term*
un·gu·lar
un·gu·late *hoofed mammal*
un·gu·li·grade *walking on hooves*
un·hair
un·hal·lowed
un·ham·pered
un·hand
un·hand·some
un·hand·some·ness
un·hap·pi·ly
un·hap·pi·ness
un·hap·py (·pi·er, ·pi·est)
un·harmed
un·har·ness
un·healthi·ly
un·healthi·ness
un·healthy (·healthi·er, ·healthi·est)
un·heard
unheard-of
un·heed·ed
un·heed·ing
un·helm *remove the helmet of*
un·help·ful
un·help·ful·ly
un·her·ald·ed
un·hesi·tat·ing
un·hid·den
un·hinge
un·ho·li·ness
un·ho·ly (·li·er, ·li·est)
un·hon·oured (US ·ored)
un·hook
unhoped-for
un·horse
un·hur·ried
un·hurt
un·hy·gien·ic
un·hy·gieni·cal·ly
un·hy·phen·at·ed
uni *Austral university*

Uni·at (*or* ·ate) Eastern
 Church
Uni·at·ism
uni·ax·ial
uni·cam·er·al
uni·cam·er·al·ism
uni·cam·er·al·ist
uni·cel·lu·lar
uni·cel·lu·lar·ity
uni·col·our (*or* ·oured; *US*
 ·or *or* ·ored)
uni·corn
uni·cos·tate having one rib
uni·cy·cle
uni·cy·clist
un·iden·ti·fi·able
un·iden·ti·fied
uni·di·rec·tion·al
uni·fi·able
uni·fi·ca·tion
uni·fied
uni·fi·er
uni·fo·li·ate botany term
uni·fo·lio·late botany term
uni·form
uni·formi·tar·ian
uni·formi·tari·an·ism
 geological theory
uni·form·ity (*plural* ·ities)
uni·form·ly
uni·form·ness
uni·fy (·fies, ·fy·ing, ·fied)
uni·ju·gate botany term
uni·lat·er·al
uni·lat·er·al·ism (*or* ·ity)
uni·lat·er·al·ly
un·il·lus·trat·ed
uni·locu·lar botany term
un·im·agi·nable
un·im·agi·nably
un·im·agi·na·tive
un·im·ag·ined
un·im·paired
un·im·peach·abil·ity (*or*
 ·able·ness)
un·im·peach·able
un·im·ped·ed
un·im·por·tant
un·im·pos·ing
un·im·pressed
un·im·pres·sive
un·im·proved
un·in·cor·po·ra·ted
un·in·flu·enced
un·in·formed

un·in·hab·it·able
un·in·hab·it·ed
un·in·hib·it·ed
un·in·jured
un·in·spired
un·in·spir·ing
un·in·sur·able
un·in·sured
un·in·tel·li·gence
un·in·tel·li·gent
un·in·tel·li·gible
un·in·tel·li·gibly
un·in·tend·ed
un·in·ten·tion·al
un·in·ten·tion·ally
un·in·ter·est·ed not
 interested; *compare*
 disinterested
un·in·ter·est·ed·ly
un·in·ter·est·ed·ness
un·in·ter·est·ing
un·in·ter·rupt·ed
uni·nu·cleate
un·in·vit·ed
un·in·vit·ing
un·ion
un·ion·ism
un·ion·ist
un·ion·is·tic
un·ioni·za·tion (*or* ·sa·tion)
un·ion·ize (*or* ·ise) join
 trade union
un·ionized not ionized
uni·para *variant of*
 primipara
unip·ar·ous biology term
uni·per·son·al
uni·per·son·al·ity
uni·pla·nar
uni·pod one-legged support
uni·po·lar
uni·po·lar·ity
unique
unique·ly
unique·ness
uni·ra·mous undivided
uni·sep·tate biology term
uni·sex
uni·sexu·al
uni·sexu·al·ity
uni·son
uniso·nous (*or* ·nal, ·nant)
unit
Uni·tar·ian
uni·tar·ian

Uni·tari·an·ism Christian
 belief
uni·tari·an·ism centralized
 government
uni·tary
unite
unit·ed
unit·ed·ly
unit·ed·ness
unit·er
uni·tive
unity (*plural* unities)
uni·va·len·cy
uni·va·lent
uni·valve zoology term
uni·ver·sal
uni·ver·sal·ism
uni·ver·sal·ist
uni·ver·sal·is·tic
uni·ver·sal·ity (*plural* ·ities)
uni·ver·sali·za·tion (*or*
 ·sa·tion)
uni·ver·sal·ize (*or* ·ise)
uni·ver·sal·ly
uni·ver·sal·ness
uni·verse
uni·ver·sity (*plural* ·sities)
uni·vo·cal unambiguous
un·just
un·jus·ti·fi·able
un·jus·ti·fied
un·just·ness
un·kempt
un·kempt·ness
un·kenned *Dialect*
 unknown
un·ken·nel (·nel·ling,
 ·nelled; *US* ·nel·ing,
 ·neled)
un·kind
un·kind·li·ness
un·kind·ness
un·knit (·knit·ting,
 ·knit·ted *or* ·knit)
un·know·able
un·know·able·ness (*or*
 ·abil·ity)
un·know·ing
un·know·ing·ly
un·known
un·known·ness
un·la·belled (*US* ·beled)
un·lace
un·lade unload
un·la·den

un·lady·like
un·laid
un·lam·ent·ed
un·lash
un·latch
un·law·ful
un·law·ful·ly
un·law·ful·ness
un·lay (·lay·ing, ·laid)
  untwist
un·lead printing term
un·lead·ed
un·learn (·learn·ing,
  ·learnt or ·learned)
un·learn·ed ignorant
un·leash
un·leav·ened
un·less
un·let·tered
un·li·censed
un·like
un·like·li·ness (or ·li·hood)
un·like·ly
un·lim·ber prepare for use
un·lim·it·ed
un·lined
un·list·ed
un·lit
un·live
un·lived-in
un·load
un·load·er
un·lock
un·lock·able
unlooked-for
un·loose (or ·loos·en)
un·lov·able
un·loved
un·love·ly
un·lov·ing
un·lucki·ly
un·lucki·ness
un·lucky (·lucki·er,
  ·lucki·est)
un·made
un·make (·mak·ing,
  ·made)
un·mak·er
un·man (·man·ning,
  ·manned)
un·man·age·able
un·man·li·ness
un·man·ly
un·manned
un·man·nered

un·man·ner·li·ness
un·man·ner·ly
un·marked
un·mar·riage·able
un·mar·ried
un·mask
un·mask·er
un·matched
un·mean·ing
un·meant
un·meas·ur·able unable to
  be measured; compare
  immeasurable
un·meas·ured
un·meet unsuitable
un·men·tion·able
un·men·tion·ables
un·mer·ci·ful
un·mer·ci·ful·ly
un·mer·it·ed
un·mind·ful
un·mis·tak·able (or ·take·)
un·mis·tak·ably (or ·take·)
un·miti·gat·ed
un·mixed
un·mo·lest·ed
un·moor
un·mor·al amoral
un·mo·ral·ity
un·mount·ed
un·mourned
un·moved
un·mu·si·cal
un·mu·si·cal·ly
un·mu·si·cal·ness
un·muz·zle
un·name·able
un·named
un·natu·ral
un·natu·ral·ly
un·natu·ral·ness
un·navi·gable
un·nec·es·sari·ly
un·nec·es·sary
un·neigh·bour·ly (US ·bor·)
un·nerve
un·nerv·ing
un·no·ticed
un·num·bered
un·ob·jec·tion·able
un·ob·scured
un·ob·ser·vant
un·ob·served
un·ob·struct·ed
un·ob·tain·able

un·ob·tru·sive
un·ob·tru·sive·ly
un·ob·tru·sive·ness
un·oc·cu·pied
un·of·fend·ing
un·of·fi·cial
un·of·fi·cial·ly
un·opened
un·op·posed
un·or·gan·ized (or ·ised)
un·origi·nal
un·ortho·dox
un·owned
un·pack
un·pack·er
un·paged
un·paid
un·paint·ed
un·pained
un·pal·at·able
un·par·al·leled
un·par·don·able
un·par·lia·men·ta·ry
un·pat·ent·ed
un·pat·ri·ot·ic
un·paved
un·peeled
un·peg (·peg·ging,
  ·pegged)
un·peo·ple (verb)
un·per·ceived
un·per·fo·rat·ed
un·per·son
un·per·turbed
un·pick
un·pin (·pin·ning,
  ·pinned)
un·pity·ing
un·place·able
un·placed
un·planned
un·play·able
un·pleas·ant
un·pleas·ant·ness
un·pleas·ing
un·plug (·plug·ging,
  ·plugged)
un·plumbed
un·poli·tic
un·po·liti·cal
un·polled
un·pol·lut·ed
un·popu·lar
un·popu·lar·ity
un·posed

un·prac·ti·cal impractical
un·prac·ti·cal·ity (or ·ness)
un·prac·tised (US ·ticed)
un·prec·edent·ed
un·pre·dict·abil·ity (or
·able·ness)
un·pre·dict·able
un·pre·dict·ably
un·preju·diced
un·pre·medi·tat·ed
un·pre·medi·ta·tion
un·pre·pared
un·pre·par·ed·ness
un·pre·pos·sess·ing
un·pre·sent·able
un·pre·ten·tious
un·pre·ten·tious·ness
un·pre·vent·able
un·priced
un·prin·ci·pled
un·print·able
un·pro·duc·tive
un·pro·fessed
un·pro·fes·sion·al
un·pro·fes·sion·al·ly
un·prof·it·abil·ity (or
·able·ness)
un·prof·it·able
un·prof·it·ably
un·prom·is·ing
un·prompt·ed
un·pro·nounce·able
un·pro·tect·ed
un·prov·able
un·proved
un·prov·en
un·pro·vid·ed
un·pub·lished
un·punc·tual
un·pun·ished
un·put·down·able
un·quali·fi·able
un·quali·fied
un·quench·able
un·ques·tion·abil·ity (or
·able·ness)
un·ques·tion·able
un·ques·tion·ably
un·ques·tioned
un·ques·tion·ing
un·qui·et
un·quote
un·rav·el (·el·ling, ·elled;
US ·el·ing, ·eled)
un·rav·el·ler (US ·el·er)

un·rav·el·ment
un·reach·able
un·re·ac·tive
un·read
un·read·abil·ity (or
·able·ness)
un·read·able
un·readi·ness
un·ready
un·real
un·re·al·is·tic
un·re·al·isti·cal·ly
un·re·al·ity
un·re·al·ized (or ·ised)
un·rea·son
un·rea·son·able
un·rea·son·able·ness
un·rea·son·ably
un·rea·son·ing
un·reck·on·able
un·rec·og·niz·able (or
·nis·able)
un·rec·og·nized (or ·nised)
un·rec·on·ciled
un·re·con·struct·ed
un·re·cord·ed
un·reeve (·reev·ing, ·rove
or ·reeved) nautical term
un·re·fined
un·re·flect·ed
un·re·flec·tive
un·re·gard·ed
un·re·gen·era·cy
un·re·gen·er·ate
unrepentant
un·reg·is·tered
un·re·hearsed
un·re·lat·ed
un·re·lent·ing
un·re·li·abil·ity (or
·able·ness)
un·re·li·able
un·re·li·ably
un·re·mit·ting
un·re·paired
un·re·peat·able
un·re·pent·ant
un·re·port·ed
un·rep·re·senta·tive
un·rep·re·sent·ed
un·re·quit·ed
un·re·served
un·re·serv·ed·ly
un·re·serv·ed·ness
un·re·sist·ing

un·re·solved
un·re·spon·sive
un·rest
un·re·strained
un·re·strict·ed
un·re·ward·ed
un·re·ward·ing
un·rhymed
un·rid·able
un·rid·dle solve
un·rid·dler
un·ri·fled
un·rig (·rig·ging, ·rigged)
un·right·eous
un·rip (·rip·ping, ·ripped)
un·ripe (or ·rip·ened)
un·ri·valled (US ·valed)
un·roll
un·root
un·round·ed
un·rove nautical term
un·ruf·fled
un·ruf·fled·ness
un·ruled
un·ru·li·ness
un·ru·ly (·li·er, ·li·est)
un·sad·dle
un·safe
un·said
un·sale·able (US ·sal·able)
un·salt·ed
un·sanc·tioned
un·sani·tary
un·sat·is·fac·tori·ly
un·sat·is·fac·tory
un·sat·is·fied
un·sat·is·fy·ing
un·satu·rat·ed
un·satu·ra·tion
un·saved
un·sa·vouri·ly (US ·vori·)
un·sa·vouri·ness (US ·vori·)
un·sa·voury (US ·vory)
un·say (·say·ing, ·said)
un·scal·able
un·scarred
un·scathed
un·scent·ed
un·sched·uled
un·schooled
un·sci·en·tif·ic
un·sci·en·tifi·cal·ly
un·scram·ble
un·scram·bler
un·scratched

un·screened
un·screw
un·script·ed
un·scru·pu·lous
un·scru·pu·lous·ness (or ·los·ity)
un·seal
un·seal·able
un·seam
un·search·able
un·sea·son·able
un·sea·son·ably
un·sea·soned
un·seat
un·sea·worthy
un·secured
un·seed·ed
un·seem·li·ness
un·seem·ly
un·seen
un·seg·re·gat·ed
un·self·con·scious
un·self·ish
un·self·ish·ness
un·sepa·rat·ed
un·ser·vice·able
un·set
un·set·tle
un·set·tled
un·set·tle·ment
un·sex
un·shack·le
un·shad·ed
un·shak·able (or ·shake·)
un·shak·en
un·shap·en
un·shav·en
un·sheathe
un·shed
un·ship (·ship·ping, ·shipped)
un·shock·able
un·sight·ed
un·sight·li·ness
un·sight·ly
un·signed
un·sink·able
un·skil·ful (US ·skill·ful)
un·skilled
un·slaked
un·sling (·sling·ing, ·slung)
un·smil·ing
un·smoked
un·snap (·snap·ping, ·snapped)

un·snarl
un·so·ciabil·ity (or ·ciable·ness)
un·so·ciable
un·so·ciably
un·so·cial
un·sold
un·so·lic·it·ed
un·solv·able
un·solved
un·so·phis·ti·cat·ed
un·so·phis·ti·cat·ed·ness (or ·ca·tion)
un·sort·ed
un·sought
un·sound
un·spar·ing
un·speak·able
un·speak·ably
un·spe·cif·ic
un·speci·fied
un·spent
un·spoiled (or ·spoilt)
un·spo·ken
un·sport·ing
un·spot·ted
un·sta·ble
un·stamped
un·steadi·ly
un·steadi·ness
un·steady (adj ·steadi·er, ·steadi·est; verb ·steadies, ·steady·ing, ·stead·ied)
un·step (·step·ping, ·stepped) nautical term
un·stick (·stick·ing, ·stuck)
un·stint·ing
un·stop (·stop·ping, ·stopped)
un·stop·pable
un·stopped
un·strained
un·strap (·strap·ping, ·strapped)
un·strati·fied
un·stressed
un·stri·at·ed
un·string (·string·ing, ·strung)
un·striped
un·struc·tured
un·strung
un·stuck

un·stud·ied
un·sub·stan·tial
un·sub·stan·ti·al·ity
un·sub·stan·ti·at·ed
un·suc·cess·ful
un·suc·cess·ful·ly
un·sug·ared
un·suit·abil·ity (or ·able·ness)
un·suit·able
un·suit·ably
un·suit·ed
un·sul·ied
un·sung
un·sure
un·sur·passed
un·sus·pect·ed
un·sus·pect·ing
un·swathe
un·swear (·swear·ing, ·swore, ·sworn) retract
un·sweet·ened
un·swept
un·swerv·ing
un·sym·pa·thet·ic
un·sym·pa·theti·cal·ly
un·sys·tem·at·ic
un·taint·ed
un·tame·able
un·tamed
un·tan·gle
un·tapped
un·tast·ed
un·taught
un·teach (·teach·ing, ·taught)
un·teach·able
un·tear·able
un·ten·abil·ity (or ·able·ness)
un·ten·able
un·ten·ant·ed
Un·ter·wal·den Swiss canton
un·test·ed
un·thanked
un·thank·ful
un·thank·ful·ness
un·think (·think·ing, ·thought)
un·think·abil·ity (or ·able·ness)
un·think·able
un·think·ably
un·think·ing

un·thought-of
un·thread
un·ti·di·ly
un·ti·di·ness
un·ti·dy (*adj* ·di·er,
 ·di·est; *verb* ·dies,
 ·dy·ing, ·died)
un·tie (·ty·ing, ·tied)
un·til
un·time·ly
un·tinged
un·tir·ing
un·tit·led
unto
un·told
un·touch·abil·ity
un·touch·able
un·touched
un·to·ward
un·trace·able
un·trained
un·tram·melled (*US*
 ·meled)
un·trans·lat·able
un·trav·elled (*US* ·eled)
un·treat·able
un·treat·ed
un·tried
un·trod·den
un·true
un·truss
un·trust·worthy
un·truth
un·truth·ful
un·truth·ful·ly
un·truth·ful·ness
un·tuck
un·turned
un·tu·tored
un·typi·cal
un·us·able
un·used
un·usual
un·usu·al·ly
un·ut·ter·able
un·ut·tered
un·val·ued
un·var·ied
un·var·nished
un·vary·ing
un·veil
un·veil·ing
un·versed
un·voice phonetics term
un·voiced

un·want·ed
un·war·rant·able
un·war·rant·ed
un·wari·ly
un·wari·ness
un·wary
un·washed
un·watched
un·wat·ered
un·wa·ver·ing
un·wear·able
un·wea·ried
un·weary·ing
un·wed
un·weighed
un·wel·come
un·well
un·wept
un·whole·some
un·whole·some·ly
un·whole·some·ness
un·wieldi·ly (*or*
 ·wield·li·ly)
un·wieldi·ness (*or*
 ·wield·li·ness)
un·wieldy (*or* ·wield·ly)
un·willed
un·will·ing
un·will·ing·ness
un·wind (·wind·ing,
 ·wound)
un·wind·able
un·wind·er
un·wink·ing
un·wise
un·wise·ly
un·wish
un·wished
un·wit·nessed
un·wit·ting
un·wont·ed
un·work·able
un·world·li·ness
un·world·ly
un·worn
un·worthi·ly
un·worthi·ness
un·wor·thy (·thi·er,
 thi·est)
un·wound
un·wrap (·wrap·ping,
 ·wrapped)
un·writ·ten
un·yield·ing
un·yoke

un·zip (·zip·ping,
 ·zipped)
up (up·ping, upped)
up-anchor
up-and-coming
up-and-under
Upani·shad Hindu treatise
upas tree
up·beat
up-bow musical term
up·braid
up·braid·er
up·bring·ing
up·build (·build·ing,
 ·built)
up·build·er
up·cast (·cast·ing, ·cast)
up·country
up·date
up·dat·er
up·draught (*US* ·draft)
up·end
up·grade
up·grad·er
up·growth
up·heav·al
up·heave (·heav·ing,
 ·heaved *or* ·hove)
up·held
up·hill
up·hold (·hold·ing,
 ·held)
up·hold·er
up·hol·ster
up·hol·ster·er
up·hol·stery (*plural* ·steries)
up·hove *variant of*
 upheaved
uphroe *variant spelling of*
 euphroe
up·keep
up·land
up·lift
up·lift·er
up·lift·ing
up·most *variant of*
 uppermost
upon
up·per
upper-case (*adj, verb*)
upper-class (*adj*)
upper·cut (·cut·ting, ·cut)
upper·most (*or* up·most)
up·pish
up·pish·ness

up·pi·ty
Upp·sa·la (or Up·sa·la)
  Swedish city
up·raise
up·rais·er
up·rear
up·right
up·right·ness
up·rise (·ris·ing, ·rose,
  ·ris·en)
up·ris·er
up·ris·ing
up·river
up·roar
up·roari·ous
up·root
up·root·er
up·rose
up·rush
Up·sa·la variant spelling of
  Uppsala
up·set (·set·ting, ·set)
up·set·table
up·set·ter
up·set·ting
up·shot
up·side
upside-down
upside-downness
up·si·lon Greek letter
up·stage
up·stairs
up·stand·ing
up·stand·ing·ness
up·start
up·state
up·stream
up·stretched
up·stroke
up·surge
up·sweep (·sweep·ing,
  ·swept)
up·swing (·swing·ing,
  ·swung)
upsy-daisy
up·take
up·throw
up·thrust
up·tight
up·tilt
up-to-date
up-to-dateness
up·town
up·turn
up·ward (adj)

up·ward·ly
up·ward·ness
up·wards (adv)
up·wind
Ur Sumerian city
ura·cil biochemical
  compound
urae·mia (US ure·)
urae·mic (US ure·)
urae·us (plural ·uses) sacred
  serpent
Ural Russian river
Ural-Altaic language group
Ural·ic (or Ura·lian)
ural·ite mineral
ural·it·ic
Urals Russian mountains
ura·naly·sis variant of
  urinalysis
Ura·nian of Uranus;
  celestial
uran·ic chemistry term
ura·nide chemical element
urani·nite mineral
ura·nite mineral
ura·nit·ic
ura·nium
ura·nog·ra·pher (or ·phist)
ura·no·graph·ic (or
  ·graphi·cal)
ura·nog·ra·phy star
  mapping
ura·nous chemistry term
Ura·nus planet
Uranus Greek god
ura·nyl chemical group
ura·nyl·ic
urate
urat·ic
ur·ban
ur·bane
ur·bane·ly
ur·bane·ness
ur·ban·ite
ur·ban·ity (plural ·ities)
ur·bani·za·tion (or
  ·sa·tion)
ur·ban·ize (or ·ise)
urbi et orbi papal blessing
ur·ceo·late pitcher-shaped
ur·chin
urd bean plant
urdé heraldic term
Urdu
urea

ureal (or ureic)
urease enzyme
ure·dial
uredium (or uredin·ium;
  plural uredia or uredinia)
  fungal structure
uredo (plural uredi·nes)
  urticaria
uredo·so·rus (plural ·so·ri)
  uredium
uredo·spore
ureic variant of ureal
ureide chemical compound
ure·mia US spelling of
  uraemia
ureter
ureter·al (or ·ic)
urethane (or urethan)
  chemistry term
urethra (plural urethrae or
  urethras)
urethral
urethrit·ic
urethri·tis
urethro·scope
urethro·scop·ic
urethros·co·py
uret·ic of urine
urge
ur·gen·cy
ur·gent
urg·er
urg·ing·ly
uric
uri·dine biochemical
  compound
uri·nal
uri·naly·sis (or ura·; plural
  ·ses)
uri·nant heraldic term
uri·nary (plural ·naries)
uri·nate
uri·na·tion
uri·na·tive
urine
uri·nif·er·ous transporting
  urine
uri·no·geni·tal variant of
  urogenital
uri·nous (or ·nose)
Ur·mia Iranian lake
urn
urn·field cemetery
urn·like
uro·chord zoology term

uro·chor·dal

uro·chor·date marine animal

uro·chrome pigment

uro·dele type of amphibian

uro·geni·tal (*or* uri·no·)

urog·enous producing urine

uro·lith stone in urinary tract

uro·lith·ic

uro·log·ic (*or* ·logi·cal)

urolo·gist

urol·ogy branch of medicine

uro·pod crustacean appendage

uropo·dal (*or* ·dous)

uro·pyg·ial

uro·pyg·ium base of bird's tail

uro·scop·ic

uros·co·pist

uros·co·py examination of urine

uro·style zoology term

ur·sine of bears

Ur·su·line nun

Ur·text *German* original text

ur·ti·ca·ceous botany term

ur·ti·caria nettle rash

ur·ti·car·ial (*or* ·cari·ous)

ur·ti·cate medical term

ur·ti·ca·tion

Urua·pan Mexican city

Uru·guay

Uru·guay·an

Urum·chi (*or* Wu-lu-mu-ch'i) Chinese city

uru·shi·ol poisonous liquid

us

us·abil·ity (*or* ·able·ness, use·)

us·able (*or* use·)

us·age

us·ance commerce term

use

use·abil·ity (*or* ·able·ness) *variants of* usability

use·able *variant spelling of* usable

used

use·ful

use·ful·ly

use·ful·ness

use·less

use·less·ness

user

Ush·ant French island

ush·er

ush·er·ette

Usk Welsh river

Üs·kü·dar Turkish town

us·que·baugh Irish liqueur

Usta·shi terrorist organization

Ust-Kameno·gorsk Kazakh city

us·tu·la·tion burning

usu·al

usu·al·ly

usu·al·ness

usu·fruct legal term

usu·fruc·tu·ary (*plural* ·aries)

usu·rer

usu·ri·ous

usu·ri·ous·ness

usurp

usur·pa·tion

usur·pa·tive (*or* ·tory)

usurp·er

usurp·ing·ly

usu·ry (*plural* ·ries)

Utah

Utah·an

Ute (*plural* Utes *or* Ute) American Indian

uten·sil

uter·ine

uter·us (*plural* uteri)

Ut·gard Norse mythological place

Uti·ca ancient African city

utili·tar·ian

utili·tari·an·ism

util·ity (*plural* ·ities)

uti·liz·able (*or* ·lis·able)

uti·li·za·tion (*or* ·sa·tion)

uti·lize (*or* ·lise)

uti·liz·er (*or* ·lis·er)

ut in·fra *Latin* as below

uti pos·si·detis legal term

ut·most (*or* utter·)

Uto-Aztecan language

Uto·pia

Uto·pian (*or* uto·)

Uto·pi·an·ism (*or* uto·)

Utrecht Dutch province

utri·cle (*or* utricu·lus; *plural* utri·cles *or* utricu·li) part of ear

utricu·lar (*or* ·late)

utricu·li·tis

ut su·pra *Latin* as above

Ut·tar Pra·desh Indian state

ut·ter

ut·ter·able

ut·ter·able·ness

ut·ter·ance

ut·ter·er

ut·ter·ly

utter·most *variant of* utmost

U-turn

uva·rov·ite green garnet

uvea part of eye

uveal (*or* uveous)

uveit·ic

uveitis

uvu·la (*plural* ·las *or* ·lae)

uvu·lar

uvu·li·tis

Ux·bridge

uxo·rial wifely

uxo·ri·cid·al

uxo·ri·cide

uxo·ri·ous wife-loving

uxo·ri·ous·ness

Uz·bek (*plural* ·beks *or* ·bek)

Uz·beki·stan Central Asian country

V

Vaal South African river
vac *Slang* vacation
va·can·cy (*plural* ·cies)
va·cant
va·cant·ness
va·cat·able
va·cate
va·ca·tion
va·ca·tion·ist (*or* ·er)
vac·ci·nal
vac·ci·nate
vac·ci·na·tion
vac·ci·na·tor
vac·cine
vac·cinia cowpox
vac·cin·ial
vac·il·lant
vac·il·late
vac·il·lat·ing
vac·il·lat·ing·ly
vac·il·la·tion
vac·il·la·tor
vacua *plural of* vacuum
va·cu·ity (*plural* ·ities)
vacuo·lar
vacuo·late
vacuo·la·tion
vacu·ole cell cavity
vacu·ous
vacu·ous·ness
vacuum (*plural* vacuums *or* vacua)
vacuum-packed
vade me·cum handbook
Va·do·da·ra Indian city
va·dose geology term
Va·duz Liechtenstein capital
vag *Austral* vagrant
vaga·bond
vaga·bond·age
vaga·bond·ism
va·gal of the vagus
va·gary (*plural* ·garies)
va·gi·na (*plural* ·nas *or* ·nae)
vagi·nal
vagi·nate botany term
vagi·nec·tomy (*plural* ·tomies)
vagi·nis·mus vaginal spasm
vagi·ni·tis

va·goto·my (*plural* ·mies) surgery of the vagus
va·go·to·nia overactivity of the vagus
va·go·trop·ic affecting the vagus
va·gran·cy (*plural* ·cies)
va·grant
va·grant·ness
vague
vague·ly
vague·ness
va·gus (*plural* ·gi) nerve
va·hana mythological vehicle
vain conceited; *compare* vane
vain·glo·ri·ous
vain·glo·ry
vain·ly
vain·ness
vair fur trimming
Va·lais Swiss canton
val·ance drapery; *compare* valence
val·anced
Val-de-Marne French department
Val-d'Oise French department
vale *Latin* farewell
vale valley; *compare* veil
val·edic·tion
val·edic·tory (*plural* ·tories)
va·lence (*or* ·len·cy; *plural* ·lences *or* ·cies) chemistry term; *compare* valance
Va·len·cia Spanish port
Va·len·ci·ennes French town; lace
va·len·cy *variant of* valence
val·en·tine
va·lerian plant
va·leria·na·ceous
va·ler·ic
val·et
va·leta *variant spelling of* veleta
Va·let·ta *variant spelling of* Valletta

val·etu·di·nar·ian (*or* ·nary; *plural* ·ians *or* ·naries)
val·etu·di·nar·ian·ism
val·gus medical term
Val·hal·la
val·iance (*or* ·ian·cy, ·iant·ness)
val·iant
val·id
vali·date
vali·da·tion
vali·da·tory
va·lid·ity
val·id·ness
va·line amino acid
va·lise
Valium (*Trademark*)
Val·kyrie (*or* Wal·kyrie, Val·kyr)
Va·lla·do·lid Spanish city
val·la·tion building fortifications
val·lecu·la (*plural* ·lae) biology term
val·lecu·lar (*or* ·late)
Val·le d'Ao·sta Italian region
Val·let·ta (*or* Va·let·ta) Maltese capital
val·ley
va·lo·nia acorns used in tanning
val·ori·za·tion (*or* ·sa·tion)
val·or·ize (*or* ·ise) fix price for
val·or·ous
val·our (*US* ·or)
Val·pa·rai·so Chilean port
valse *French* waltz
valu·able
valu·able·ness
valu·ably
valu·ate
valua·tion
valua·tion·al
valua·tor
value (valu·ing, valued)
value·less
value·less·ness
valu·er

valu·ta currency exchange
rate
val·vate
valve
valve·less
val·vu·lar
val·vule (or valve·let)
val·vu·li·tis heart-valve
inflammation
vam·brace armour
va·moose
vamp
vam·pire
vam·pir·ic (or ·ish)
vam·pir·ism
Van Turkish city
van
vana·date chemical
compound
va·nad·ic
va·nadi·nite mineral
va·na·dium chemical
element
vana·dous
va·na·spa·ti vegetable fat
Van·cou·ver
van·da orchid
Van·dal Germanic invader
van·dal destroyer
van·dal·ism
van·dal·is·tic (or ·dal·ish)
van·dal·ize (or ·ise)
Van·dyke beard; collar
vane flat blade; compare
vain
vang nautical term
van·guard
va·nil·la
va·nil·lic
van·il·lin
van·ish
van·ish·er
van·ish·ing·ly
van·ish·ment
van·ity (plural ·ities)
van·quish
van·quish·able
van·quish·er
van·quish·ment
van·tage
Vanu·atu island republic
van·ward
vap·id
va·pid·ity
vap·id·ness

va·por·es·cence
va·por·es·cent
va·po·ret·to (plural ·ti or
·tos) steamboat
va·por·if·ic
va·por·im·eter
va·por·iz·able (or ·is·able)
va·pori·za·tion (or ·sa·tion)
va·por·ize (or ·ise)
va·por·iz·er (or ·is·er)
va·por·ous
va·por·ous·ness (or ·os·ity)
va·pour (US ·por)
va·pour·abil·ity (US ·por·)
va·pour·able (US ·por·)
va·pour·er (US ·por·)
va·pour·ish (US ·por·)
va·pour·ish·ness (US ·por·)
var unit of power
vara unit of length
va·rac·tor electronic device
Va·ra·na·si Indian city
Va·ran·gian medieval
Scandinavian
var·ec seaweed
varia literary miscellany
vari·abil·ity (or ·able·ness)
vari·able
vari·ably
vari·ance
vari·ant
vari·ate a random variable
vari·ation
vari·ation·al (or ·ative)
vari·cel·la chickenpox
vari·cel·lar
vari·cel·late ridged
vari·cel·loid
vari·ces plural of varix
vari·co·cele medical term
vari·col·oured (US ·ored)
vari·cose
vari·co·sis
vari·cos·ity (plural ·ities)
vari·coto·my (plural ·mies)
varicose-vein surgery
var·ied
var·ied·ness
varie·gate
varie·gat·ed
varie·ga·tion
va·ri·etal
va·ri·ety (plural ·eties)
vari·form
va·rio·la smallpox

va·rio·lar
va·rio·late inoculate
va·rio·la·tion
vari·ole geology term
vari·olite rock
vario·lit·ic
vario·loid mild smallpox
va·rio·lous of smallpox
vari·om·eter
vario·rum annotated text
vari·ous
vari·ous·ly
vari·ous·ness
var·is·cite mineral
var·is·tor electronic
component
vari·type
Vari·typ·er (Trademark)
justifying typewriter
vari·typ·ist
var·ix (plural vari·ces)
varicose vein
var·let
var·mint
Var·na Bulgarian port
var·na Hindu caste
var·nish
var·nish·er
var·sity (plural ·sities) Slang
university
var·us medical term
varve geology term
vary (varies, vary·ing,
var·ied)
vary·ing·ly
vas·al of vas deferens;
compare vassal
vas·cu·lar conducting fluids
vas·cu·lar·ity
vas·cu·lari·za·tion (or
·sa·tion) medical term
vas·cu·lum (plural ·la or
·lums) plant-specimen
container
vas de·fe·rens (plural vasa
de·fe·ren·tia) anatomy
term
vase
vas·ec·to·mize (or ·mise)
vas·ec·to·my (plural ·mies)
Vas·eline (Trademark)
vaso·active affecting blood
vessels
vaso·con·stric·tion
vaso·con·stric·tive

vaso·con·stric·tor

vaso·di·la·tion

vaso·di·la·tor

vaso·in·hibi·tor

vaso·in·hibi·tory

vaso·mo·tor

vaso·pres·sin hormone

vas·sal feudal tenant; *compare* vasal

vas·sal·age

vas·sal·ize (*or* ·ise)

vast

Väs·ter·ås Swedish city

vas·tity

vast·ness

vasty (vasti·er, vasti·est) *Archaic* vast

vat (vat·ting, vat·ted)

vat·ic of a prophet

Vati·can

Vati·can·ism

Vau·cluse French department

Vaud Swiss canton

vau·de·ville

vau·de·vil·lian

vau·de·vil·list

Vau·dois (*plural* ·dois) of Vaud; Waldenses

vault

vault·ed

vault·er

vault·ing

vaunt

vaunt·er

vaunt·ing·ly

vava·sor (*or* ·sour) vassal

veal

veal·er veal calf

vec·tor

vec·to·rial

Veda Hindu scriptures

ve·da·lia ladybird

Ve·dan·ta Hindu school of philosophy

Ve·dan·tic

Ved·da (*or* ·dah; *plural* ·da, ·das *or* ·dah, ·dahs) Sri Lankan people

Ved·doid

ve·dette

Ve·dic of the Veda

veer

veer·ing·ly

veery (*plural* veeries) bird

veg *Slang* vegetables

Vega star

ve·gan

veg·eta·ble

veg·etal of plants; nonsexual

veg·etar·ian

veg·etari·an·ism

veg·etate

veg·eta·tion

veg·eta·tion·al

veg·eta·tive

veg·eta·tive·ness

ve·he·mence

ve·he·ment

ve·hi·cle

ve·hicu·lar

Veii Etruscan city

veil head covering; *compare* vale

veiled

veil·ed·ly

veil·er

veil·ing

vein

vein·ing

vein·let

vein·stone ore material

veiny (veini·er, veini·est)

ve·la·men (*plural* ·lami·na) biology term

ve·lar biology or phonetics term

ve·lar·ium (*plural* ·laria) awning in Roman theatre

ve·lari·za·tion (*or* ·sa·tion)

ve·lar·ize (*or* ·ise) phonetics term

ve·late biology term

Vel·cro (*Trademark*)

veld (*or* veldt)

ve·leta (*or* va·) dance

veli·ger mollusc larva

ve·li·tes Roman troops

vel·le·ity (*plural* ·ities) a wish

Vel·lore Indian town

vel·lum parchment; *compare* velum

ve·lo·ce musical term

ve·loci·pede early bicycle

ve·loc·ity (*plural* ·ities)

ve·lo·drome cycle-racing arena

ve·lours (*or* ·lour) fabric

ve·lou·té sauce

ve·lum (*plural* ·la) biology term; *compare* vellum

ve·lure velvet

ve·lu·ti·nous covered with hairs

vel·vet

vel·vet·een

vel·vety

vena (*plural* venae) vein

vena cava (*plural* venae cavae)

ve·nal open to bribery; *compare* venial

ve·nal·ity

ve·nal·ly

ve·nat·ic (*or* ·nati·cal) of hunting

ve·na·tion arrangement of veins; *compare* vernation

ve·na·tion·al

vend

Ven·da (*plural* ·da *or* ·das) African people

ven·dace (*plural* ·daces *or* ·dace) fish

Ven·dée French department

ven·dee buyer

vend·er *variant spelling of* vendor

ven·det·ta

ven·det·tist

vend·ibil·ity (*or* ·ible·ness)

vend·ible

vend·ing

ven·di·tion

ven·dor (*or* vend·er)

ven·due *US* public sale

ve·neer

ve·neer·er

ve·neer·ing

ven·epunc·ture *variant spelling of* venipuncture

ven·er·abil·ity (*or* ·able·ness)

ven·er·able

ven·er·ably

ven·er·ate

ven·era·tion

ven·era·tion·al (*or* ·era·tive)

ven·era·tor

ve·nereal

ve·nere·olo·gist

ve·nere·ol·ogy

ven·ery hunting; sexual gratification

ven·esec·tion incision into vein

Ve·netia ancient Italian region

Ve·netian

Ve·net·ic language

Ve·neto Italian region

Ven·ezue·la

Ven·ezue·lan

venge·ance

venge·ful

venge·ful·ly

venge·ful·ness

ve·nial easily forgiven; *compare* venal

ve·ni·al·ity (*or* ·al·ness)

ve·nial·ly

Ven·ice

ven·in poison

veni·punc·ture (*or* ven·epunc·ture)

ve·ni·re fa·ci·as legal term

veni·son

Ve·ni·te 95th psalm

Venn dia·gram

ven·om

ven·om·ous

ve·nose

ve·nos·ity

ve·nous

ve·nous·ness

vent

vent·age small hole

ven·tail armour

ven·ter biology or legal term

ven·ti·lable

ven·ti·late

ven·ti·la·tion

ven·ti·la·tive

ven·ti·la·tor

ven·ti·la·tory

ven·tral

ven·tral·ly

ven·tri·cle

ven·tri·cose biology term

ven·tri·cos·ity

ven·tricu·lar

ven·tricu·lus (*plural* ·li) zoology term

ven·tri·lo·quial (*or* ·qual)

ven·trilo·quism (*or* ·quy)

ven·trilo·quist

ven·trilo·quis·tic

ven·trilo·quize (*or* ·quise)

ven·trilo·quy *variant of* ventriloquism

ven·ture

ven·tur·er

ven·ture·some (*or* ·tu·rous)

ven·ture·some·ness

Venturi tube

venue

venu·lar

ven·ule small vein

Ve·nus planet

Venus Roman goddess

Ve·nu·sian

ve·ra·cious truthful; *compare* voracious

ve·ra·cious·ness

ve·rac·ity (*plural* ·ities)

Vera·cruz Mexican state

ve·ran·da (*or* ·dah)

ve·ran·daed (*or* ·dahed)

ve·ra·tri·dine chemical compound

vera·trine (*or* ·trin) former medicine

verb

ver·bal

ver·bal·ism

ver·bal·ist

ver·bali·za·tion (*or* ·sa·tion)

ver·bal·ize (*or* ·ise)

ver·bal·iz·er (*or* ·is·er)

ver·bal·ly

ver·ba·tim

ver·be·na

ver·be·na·ceous botany term

ver·bi·age

ver·bid linguistics term

ver·bi·fi·ca·tion

ver·bi·fy (·fies, ·fy·ing, ·fied)

ver·bose

ver·bose·ly

ver·bos·ity (*or* ·bose·ness)

ver·bo·ten *German* forbidden

ver·dan·cy

ver·dant

ver·der·er

ver·dict

ver·di·gris

ver·din bird

ver·dure

ver·dur·ous

Ve·ree·ni·ging South African city

verge

ver·ger

ver·glas (*plural* ·glases) thin ice

ve·ridi·cal truthful

ve·ridi·cal·ity

veri·fi·able

veri·fi·ca·tion

veri·fi·ca·tive (*or* ·tory)

veri·fi·er

veri·fy (·fies, ·fy·ing, ·fied)

veri·ly

veri·simi·lar likely

veri·si·mili·tude

ver·ism extreme realism

ve·ris·mo type of opera

ver·ist

ve·ris·tic

veri·table

veri·table·ness

veri·tably

ver·ity (*plural* ·ities)

ver·juice

ver·kramp·te Afrikaner nationalist

ver·lig·te South African liberal

ver·meil gilded metal

ver·mi·cel·li

ver·mi·cid·al

ver·mi·cide

ver·micu·lar wormlike

ver·micu·late

ver·micu·la·tion

ver·micu·lite mineral

ver·mi·form

ver·mi·fuge worm-expelling drug

ver·mil·ion (*or* ·mil·lion)

ver·min

ver·mi·na·tion infestation with vermin

ver·mi·nous

ver·min·ous·ness

ver·mis (*plural* ·mes) part of brain

ver·mivo·rous worm-eating

Ver·mont

Ver·mont·er

ver·mouth

ver·nacu·lar

ver·nacu·lar·ism

ver·nal

ver·nali·za·tion (*or* ·**sa·tion**)

ver·nal·ize (*or* ·**ise**) botany term

ver·nal·ly

ver·na·tion leaf arrangement in bud; *compare* **venation**

ver·ni·er measuring scale

ver·nis·sage opening of art exhibition

Ve·ro·na Italian city

Vero·nal (*Trademark*) drug

ve·roni·ca shrub

ver·ru·ca (*plural* ·**cae** *or* ·**cas**)

ver·ru·cose (*or* ·**cous**)

ver·ru·cos·ity

Ver·sailles

ver·sant mountain side

ver·sa·tile

ver·sa·til·ity (*or* ·**tile·ness**)

verse

versed

ver·si·cle

ver·si·col·our (*US* ·**or**)

ver·si·fi·ca·tion

ver·si·fi·er

ver·si·fy (·**fies**, ·**fy·ing**, ·**fied**)

ver·sion

ver·sion·al

vers li·bre *French* free verse

ver·so (*plural* ·**sos**) left-hand page

ver·sus against

vert heraldry term

ver·te·bra (*plural* ·**brae** *or* ·**bras**)

ver·te·bral

ver·te·brate

ver·te·bra·tion

ver·tex (*plural* ·**texes** *or* ·**tices**) apex; *compare* **vortex**

ver·ti·cal

ver·ti·cal·ity (*or* ·**ness**)

ver·ti·cal·ly

ver·ti·ces plural of **vertex**

ver·ti·cil biology term

ver·ti·cil·las·ter botany term

ver·ti·cil·las·trate

ver·tic·il·late

ver·tic·il·la·tion

ver·tigi·nous of vertigo

ver·tigi·nous·ness

ver·ti·go (*plural* ·**ti·goes** *or* ·**tigi·nes**)

ver·tu *variant spelling of* **virtu**

Vertumnus Roman god

(**verucca**) *incorrect spelling of* **verruca**

Veru·la·mium *Latin* St Albans

ver·vain plant

verve

ver·vet monkey

very

Very light

vesi·ca (*plural* ·**cae**) bladder

vesi·cal of the bladder; *compare* **vesicle**

vesi·cant (*or* ·**ca·tory**; *plural* ·**cants** *or* ·**ca·tories**) blistering substance

vesi·cate

vesi·ca·tion

vesi·cle small cavity; *compare* **vesical**

ve·sicu·lar

ve·sicu·late

ve·sicu·la·tion

ves·per evening prayer

ves·per·al prayer book

ves·pers canonical hour

ves·per·tilio·nid zoology term

ves·per·tilio·nine

ves·per·tine occurring in the evening

ves·pi·ary (*plural* ·**aries**) wasps' nest

ves·pid entomology term

ves·pine of wasps

ves·sel

vest

Ves·ta asteroid

Vesta Roman goddess

ves·ta wooden match

ves·tal virgin

vest·ed

ves·ti·ary (*plural* ·**aries**) room for clothes

ves·tibu·lar

ves·ti·bule

ves·tige

ves·tig·ial

vest·ment

vest·ment·al

vest·ment·ed

ves·tral

ves·try (*plural* ·**tries**)

vestry·man (*plural* ·**men**)

ves·tur·al

ves·ture garment

ve·su·vi·an·ite mineral

Ve·su·vi·us

vet (**vet·ting**, **vet·ted**)

vetch

vetch·ling

vet·er·an

vet·eri·nar·ian

vet·eri·nary

veti·ver a grass

veto (*noun, plural* **vetoes**; *verb* **vetoes**, **ve·to·ing**, **ve·toed**)

ve·to·er

vet·ted

vet·ting

vex

vexa·tion

vexa·tious

vexa·tious·ness

vex·ed·ly

vex·ed·ness

vex·er

vex·il·lary (*or* ·**lar**)

vex·il·late

vex·il·lolo·gist

vex·il·lol·ogy study of flags

vex·il·lum (*plural* ·**la**) biology term

vex·ing·ly

via

vi·abil·ity

vi·able

Via Dolo·ro·sa road to Calvary

via·duct

Vi·ag·ra (*Trademark*)

vial *less common spelling of* **phial**

via me·dia *Latin* compromise

vi·and a food

vi·ands provisions

vi·ati·cum (*plural* ·**ca** *or* ·**cums**)

vibes *Slang* vibrations; vibraphone

vib·ist vibraphone player

vi·bracu·lar

vi·bracu·loid
vi·bracu·lum (*plural* ·la)
  zoology term
vi·bra·harp musical
  instrument
vi·bran·cy
vi·brant
vi·bra·phone
vi·bra·phon·ist
vi·brate
vi·bra·tile
vi·bra·til·ity
vi·brat·ing·ly
vi·bra·tion
vi·bra·tion·al
vi·bra·tive
vi·bra·to (*plural* ·tos)
vi·bra·tor
vi·bra·tory
vib·rio (*plural* ·rios)
  bacterium
vib·ri·oid
vi·bris·sa (*plural* ·sae)
  whisker
vi·bris·sal
vi·bron·ic physics term
vi·bur·num
vic·ar
vic·ar·age
vi·car·ial
vi·cari·ate (*or* vic·ar·ship)
vi·cari·ous
vi·cari·ous·ness
vice sin; deputy; in place of
vice (*US* vise) tool
vice ad·mi·ral
vice-admiral·ty
vice-chairman (*plural*
  -chairmen)
vice-chairman·ship
vice chan·cel·lor
vice-chancellor·ship
vice·ge·ral
vice·ge·ren·cy (*plural* ·cies)
vice·ge·rent deputy
vice·like (*US* vise·)
vic·enary of 20
vi·cen·nial 20 years
Vi·cen·za Italian city
vice-presiden·cy (*plural*
  ·cies)
vice presi·dent
vice-presiden·tial
vice-re·gal of viceroy
vice·reine viceroy's wife

vice·roy
vice·roy·al·ty (*plural* ·ties)
vice·roy·ship
vice ver·sa
Vi·chy French town
vi·chy·ssoise soup
vici·nal
vi·cin·ity (*plural* ·ities)
vi·cious
vi·cious·ness
vi·cis·si·tude
vi·cis·si·tu·di·nary (*or*
  ·di·nous)
Vicks·burg US city
vi·comte (*fem* ·com·tesse)
  French noble
vic·tim
vic·timi·za·tion (*or*
  ·sa·tion)
vic·tim·ize (*or* ·ise)
vic·tim·iz·er (*or* ·is·er)
vic·tor
Vic·to·ria place name
vic·to·ria carriage; plum;
  water lily
Vic·to·rian
Vic·to·ri·ana
Vic·to·ri·an·ism
vic·to·ri·ous
vic·to·ri·ous·ness
vic·to·ry (*plural* ·ries)
vict·ual (·ual·ling, ·ualled;
  US ·ual·ing, ·ualed)
vict·ual·ler (*US also* ·ual·er)
vict·uals
vi·cu·ña
vide *Latin* see
vi·deli·cet *Latin* namely
video (*noun, plural* videos;
  verb videos, video·ing,
  videoed)
vid·eo·phone
vid·eo·phon·ic
video-tape (*verb*)
vidi·con small television
  camera tube
vie (vying, vied)
Vi·en·na Austrian capital
Vienne French river;
  department
Vi·en·nese (*plural* ·nese)
Vien·ti·ane Laotian capital
Vi·et·cong (*or* Viet Cong)
Vi·et·minh (*or* Viet Minh)
Vi·et·nam

Vi·et·nam·ese (*plural* ·ese)
view
view·able
view·er
view·finder
view·ing
view·less
view·point
vi·gesi·mal of 20
vig·il
vigi·lance
vigi·lant
vigi·lan·te
vi·gnette
vi·gnet·ting photography
  term
vi·gnet·tist
Vigo Spanish port
vi·go·ro·so musical term
vig·or·ous
vig·or·ous·ness
vig·our (*US* ·or)
Vi·jaya·wa·da Indian town
Vi·king
vi·la·yet Turkish
  administrative division
vile
vile·ly
vile·ness
vili·fi·ca·tion
vili·fi·er
vili·fy (·fies, ·fy·ing, ·fied)
vili·pend treat with
  contempt
vil·la
vil·lage
vil·lag·er
Vil·la·her·mo·sa Mexican
  town
vil·lain (*fem* ·lain·ess)
  wicked person; *compare*
  villein
vil·lain·ous
vil·lain·ous·ness
vil·lainy (*plural* ·lainies)
vil·la·nel·la (*plural* ·las)
  song
vil·la·nelle verse form
Vil·la·no·van archaeology
  term
vil·lat·ic rustic
vil·lein serf; *compare* villain
Ville·ur·banne French town
vil·li *plural of* villus
vil·li·form

vil·los·ity (*plural* ·ities)
vil·lous
vil·lus (*plural* ·li)
Vil·ni·us (*or* ·ny·)
Lithuanian capital
vim *Slang* vigour
vi·men (*plural* vimi·na)
plant shoot
Vimi·nal Roman hill
vi·min·eous
vina musical instrument
vi·na·ceous
Viña del Mar Chilean city
vinai·grette
vi·nasse residue in a still
vin·cible
vin·cu·lum (*plural* ·la)
maths symbol; anatomy
term
vin·di·cabil·ity
vin·di·cable
vin·di·cate
vin·di·ca·tion
vin·di·ca·tor
vin·di·ca·tory
vin·dic·tive
vin·dic·tive·ly
vin·dic·tive·ness
vine
vine·dresser
vin·egar
vin·egar·roon arachnid
vin·egary
vin·ery (*plural* ·eries) place
for growing grapes
vine·yard
vine·yard·ist
vingt-et-un card game
vi·nic of wine
vini·cul·tur·al
vini·cul·ture
vini·cul·tur·ist
vi·nif·er·ous
vi·nifi·ca·tion
vi·nifi·ca·tor wine-making
apparatus
Vin·land *Viking name for* NE
America
Vin·ni·tsa Ukrainian city
vino (*plural* vinos) *Slang*
wine
vin or·di·naire (*plural* vins
or·di·naires)
vi·nos·ity
vi·nous

vin·tage
vin·tag·er grape harvester
vint·ner
viny
(vinyard) *incorrect spelling of*
vineyard
vi·nyl
vi·nyli·dene chemistry term
viol
vio·la
vio·labil·ity (*or* ·lable·ness)
vio·lable
vio·la·ceous botany term
vio·la da gam·ba
vio·la d'amo·re
vio·late
vio·la·tion
vio·la·tive
vio·la·tor (*or* ·lat·er)
vio·lence
vio·lent
vio·let
vio·lin
vio·lin·ist
vi·ol·ist
vio·lon·cel·list
vio·lon·cel·lo (*plural* ·los)
cello
vio·lone musical instrument
vi·per
vi·per·ine
vi·per·ous (*or* ·ish)
vi·ragi·nous
vi·ra·go (*plural* ·goes *or*
·gos)
vi·ral
vir·elay poem
vireo (*plural* vireos) bird
vi·res·cence
vi·res·cent becoming green
vir·ga meteorology term
vir·gate rod-shaped;
obsolete land measure
vir·gin
vir·gin·al
vir·gin·al·ly
Vir·ginia
Vir·gin·ian
vir·gin·ity
virgin's-bower plant
Vir·go constellation; sign of
zodiac
Vir·goan
vir·go in·tac·ta virgin
vir·gu·late rod-shaped

vir·gule printing term
viri·des·cence
viri·des·cent becoming
green
vi·rid·ian green pigment
vi·rid·ity greenness
vir·ile
viri·lism medical term
vi·ril·ity
vi·ro·logi·cal
vi·rolo·gist
vi·rol·ogy
vir·tu (*or* ver·)
connoisseurship
vir·tual
vir·tu·al·ity
vir·tu·al·ly
vir·tue
vir·tu·os·ic
vir·tu·os·ity
vir·tuo·so (*plural* ·sos *or* ·si)
vir·tu·ous
vir·tu·ous·ness
viru·lence
viru·lent
vi·rus (*plural* ·ruses)
visa (vi·sa·ing, vi·saed)
vis·age
Vi·sa·kha·pat·nam *variant*
of Vishakhapatnam
vis-à-vis
Vi·sa·yan (*plural* ·yans *or*
·yan) Philippine people
vis·ca·cha (*or* viz·) animal
vis·cera (*sing.* ·cus) internal
organs
vis·cer·al
vis·ce·ro·mo·tor physiology
term
vis·cid
vis·cid·ity (*or* ·ness)
vis·coid (*or* ·coi·dal)
vis·com·eter (*or*
·co·sim·eter)
vis·co·met·ric (*or* ·ri·cal)
vis·com·etry
vis·cose
vis·cos·ity (*plural* ·ities)
vis·count
vis·count·cy (*or* ·county;
plural ·cies *or* ·counties)
vis·count·ess
vis·cous thick; *compare*
viscus
vis·cous·ness

vis·cus *sing. of* viscera;
  compare viscous
vise *US spelling of* vice
Vi·sha·kha·pat·nam (*or*
  Vi·sa·kha·pat·nam,
  Vi·za·ga·pa·tam) Indian
  port
Vishnu Hindu god
vis·ibil·ity
vis·ible
vis·ible·ness
vis·ibly
Visi·goth
vi·sion
vi·sion·al
vi·sion·ari·ness
vi·sion·ary (*plural* ·aries)
vis·it
vis·it·able
visi·tant
vis·ita·tion
vis·ita·tion·al
vis·ita·to·rial *of official
  visitation*
visi·tor
visi·to·rial
vi·sor (*or* ·zor)
vi·sored (*or* ·zored)
vis·ta
vis·taed
Vis·tu·la Polish river
vis·ual
visu·ali·za·tion (*or* ·sa·tion)
visu·al·ize (*or* ·ise)
visu·al·iz·er (*or* ·is·er)
visu·al·ly
vi·ta·ceous botany term
vi·tal
vi·tal·ism philosophical
  doctrine
vi·tal·ist
vi·tal·is·tic
vi·tal·ity (*plural* ·ities)
vi·tali·za·tion (*or* ·sa·tion)
vi·tal·ize (*or* ·ise)
vi·tal·iz·er (*or* ·is·er)
vi·tal·ly
vi·tals
vita·min
vita·min·ic
Vi·tebsk Belarussian city
vi·tel·lin protein
vi·tel·line *of egg yolk*
vi·ti·able
vi·ti·ate

vi·tia·tion
vi·tia·tor
viti·cul·tur·al
viti·cul·ture grape
  cultivation
viti·cul·tur·er (*or* ·ist)
viti·li·go unpigmented skin
Vi·to·ria Spanish city
Vi·tó·ria Brazilian port
vit·rain coal
vit·re·ous
vit·re·ous·ness (*or* ·os·ity)
vi·tres·cence
vi·tres·cent
vit·ric *of glass*
vit·ri·fi·abil·ity
vit·ri·fi·able
vit·ri·fi·ca·tion
vit·ri·form
vit·ri·fy (·fies, ·fy·ing, ·fied)
vit·rine glass display case
vit·ri·ol (·ol·ing, ·oled *or*
  ·ol·ling, ·olled)
vit·ri·ol·ic
vit·ri·oli·za·tion (*or*
  ·sa·tion)
vit·ri·ol·ize (*or* ·ise)
vit·ta (*plural* ·tae) biology
  term
vit·tate
vi·tu·line *of calves*
vi·tu·per·ate
vi·tu·pera·tion
vi·tu·pera·tive
vi·tu·pera·tor
viva (vi·va·ing, vi·vaed)
  short for viva voce
vi·va·ce musical term
vi·va·cious
vi·va·vious·ly
vi·va·cious·ness
vi·vac·ity (*plural* ·ities)
vi·var·ium (*plural* ·iums *or*
  ·ia)
viva voce oral exam
vi·ver·rine zoology term
viv·id
viv·id·ness
vivi·fi·ca·tion
vivi·fi·er
vivi·fy (·fies, ·fy·ing, ·fied)
vivi·par·ity (*or*
  vi·vipa·rism,
  vi·vipa·rous·ness)
vi·vip·ar·ous

vivi·sect
vivi·sec·tion
vivi·sec·tion·al
vivi·sec·tion·ist
vivi·sec·tor
vix·en
vix·en·ish
vix·en·ish·ness
Vi·yel·la (*Trademark*)
Vi·za·ga·pa·tam *variant
  spelling of*
  Vishakhapatnam
viz·ard mask
viz·ca·cha *variant spelling of*
  viscacha
vi·zier
vi·zier·ate
vi·zor *variant spelling of*
  visor
Vlach (*or* Wa·lach)
  medieval European people
Vla·di·mir Russian port
Vla·di·vos·tok Russian port
vo·cab *short for* vocabulary
vo·cable vocal sound
vo·cabu·lary (*plural* ·laries)
vo·cal
vo·cal·ic
vo·cal·ise vocal exercise;
  variant spelling of vocalize
vo·cal·ism
vo·cal·ist
vo·cal·ity (*or* ·ness)
vo·cali·za·tion (*or* ·sa·tion)
vo·cal·ize (*or* ·ise)
vo·cal·iz·er (*or* ·is·er)
vo·cal·ly
vo·ca·tion
vo·ca·tion·al
voca·tive
vo·cif·er·ance
vo·cif·er·ant
vo·cif·er·ate
vo·cif·era·tion
vo·cif·era·tor
vo·cif·er·ous
vo·cif·er·ous·ness
vod·ka
vogue
voguish
Vo·gul (*plural* ·gul *or* ·guls)
  Siberian people
voice
voiced
voice·ful

voice•less
voice•less•ness
voice-over
voice•print
voic•er
void
void•able
void•able•ness
void•ance annulment
void•ed
void•er
voile fabric
Voio•tia Greek department
voir dire legal term
Voj•vo•di•na (or Voi•)
  Yugoslav region
Vo•lans constellation
vo•lant
Vola•puk artificial language
Vola•puk•ist
vo•lar anatomy term
vola•tile
vola•til•ity
vo•lati•liz•able (or •lis•able)
vo•lati•liza•tion (or
  •lisa•tion)
vo•lati•lize (or •lise)
vol-au-vent
vol•can•ic
vol•cani•cal•ly
vol•can•ic•ity
vol•can•ism (or vul•)
vol•cani•za•tion (or
  •sa•tion)
vol•can•ize (or •ise)
vol•ca•no (plural •noes or
  •nos)
vol•cano•logi•cal (or vul•)
vol•can•olo•gist (or vul•)
vol•can•ol•ogy (or vul•)
vole
Vol•ga Russian river
Vol•go•grad Russian port
voli•tant moving rapidly
vo•li•tion
vo•li•tion•al (or •ary)
voli•tive of the will
vol•ley
volley•ball
vol•ley•er
Vo•log•da Russian city
vo•lost peasant community
vol•plane glide without
  power
Vol•sci Latin people

volt
Vol•ta African river or lake
vol•ta (plural •te) dance
volt•age
vol•ta•ic
vol•ta•ism
vol•tam•eter instrument
  measuring electric charge;
  compare voltmeter
volt•am•meter instrument
  measuring volts or
  amperes; compare
  voltmeter
volt-ampere unit
Vol•ta Re•don•da Brazilian
  city
volte-face (plural volte-face)
  reversal of opinion
volt•me•ter instrument
  measuring volts; compare
  voltameter; voltammeter
vol•ubil•ity (or •uble•ness)
vol•uble
vol•ubly
vol•ume
vol•umed
vo•lu•meter
volu•met•ric
volu•met•ri•cal•ly
vo•lu•metry
vo•lu•mi•nos•ity (or
  •nous•ness)
vo•lu•mi•nous
vol•un•tar•ily
vol•un•tari•ness
vol•un•ta•rism (or •tary•)
vol•un•ta•rist (or •tary•)
vol•un•ta•ris•tic
vol•un•tary (plural •aries)
vol•un•teer
vo•lup•tu•ary (plural •aries)
vo•lup•tu•ous
vo•lup•tu•ous•ness (or
  •os•ity)
vol•ute
vo•lu•tion
vol•va (plural •vae or •vas)
  mushroom sheath;
  compare vulva
vol•vate
Volvo (Trademark)
vol•vox microscopic animal
vol•vu•lus (plural •luses)
  intestinal disorder
vo•mer bone

vo•mer•ine
vom•it
vom•it•er
vomi•tive
vomi•tory (plural •tories)
vomi•tu•ri•tion retching
vomi•tus (plural •tuses)
  vomited matter
voo•doo (noun, plural •doos;
  verb •doos, •doo•ing,
  •dooed)
voo•doo•ism
voo•doo•ist
voo•doo•is•tic
Voor•trek•ker Afrikaner
  settler
vo•ra•cious greedy; compare
  veracious
vo•rac•ity (or
  •ra•cious•ness)
Vor•arl•berg Austrian
  province
vor•la•ge skiing position
Vo•ro•nezh Russian city
Vo•ro•shi•lov•grad former
  name of Lugansk
vor•tex (plural •texes or
  •ti•ces) whirling mass;
  compare vertex
vor•ti•cal
vor•ti•cel•la (plural •lae)
  protozoan
vor•ti•ces plural of vortex
vor•ti•cism art movement
vor•ti•cist
vor•tigi•nous
Vosges French mountain
  range
Vos•tok Soviet spacecraft
vot•able (or vote•)
vo•tar•ess (or vo•tress)
vo•ta•rist
vo•ta•ry (plural •ries)
vote
vote•able variant spelling of
  votable
vot•er
vo•tive
vo•tive•ness
vo•tress variant of votaress
Vo•ty•ak (plural •aks or •ak)
  Finnish people
vouch
vouch•er
vouch•safe

vouch·safe·ment
vouge weapon
vous·soir wedge-shaped
  stone
Vou·vray wine
vow
vow·el
vow·eli·za·tion (or
  ·sa·tion)
vow·el·ize (or ·ise)
vowel·less
vow·er
vox (plural vo·ces) voice
vox organ stop
vox po·pu·li public
  opinion
voy·age
voy·ag·er
vo·ya·geur Canadian
  woodsman
vo·yeur
vo·yeur·ism
vo·yeur·is·tic
vo·yeur·is·ti·cal·ly

vrai·sem·blance
  verisimilitude
vroom exclamation
vug mining term
Vulcan Roman god
vul·ca·nian volcanic
vul·can·ism variant spelling
  of volcanism
vul·can·ite hard rubber
vul·can·iz·able (or ·is·able)
vul·cani·za·tion (or
  ·sa·tion)
vul·can·ize (or ·ise)
vul·can·iz·er (or ·is·er)
vul·can·ol·ogy variant
  spelling of volcanology
vul·gar
vul·gar·ian
vul·gar·ism
vul·gar·ity (plural ·ities)
vul·gari·za·tion (or
  ·sa·tion)
vul·gar·ize (or ·ise)
vul·gar·iz·er (or ·is·er)

vul·gar·ness
Vul·gate Latin Bible
vul·gate commonly
  accepted text
vul·ner·abil·ity (or
  ·able·ness)
vul·ner·able
vul·ner·ably
vul·ner·ary (plural ·aries)
  wound-healing drug
Vul·pecu·la constellation
vul·pine (or ·pecu·lar) of
  foxes
vul·ture
vul·tur·ine
vul·tur·ous
vul·va (plural ·vae or ·vas)
  female external genitals;
  compare volva
vul·val (or ·var, ·vate)
vul·vi·form
vul·vi·tis
vul·vo·vagi·ni·tis
vy·ing

W

Wa·bash US river
wacky (wacki·er,
  wacki·est)
wad (wad·ding,
  wad·ded)
wad·able (or wade·)
wad·ding
wad·dle
wad·dler
wad·dling·ly
wad·dy (noun, plural ·dies;
  verb ·dies, ·dy·ing, ·died)
  Aboriginal club; compare
  wadi
wade
wade·able variant spelling of
  wadable
wad·er
wad·ers
wadi (or wady; plural wadis
  or wa·dies) watercourse;
  compare waddy
Wadi Hal·fa Sudanese
  town
Wad Me·da·ni Sudanese
  town

wad·set (·set·ting, ·set·ted)
  Scot mortgage
wady variant spelling of wadi
wae Dialect woe
wa·fer
wa·fery
waff Dialect gust
waf·fle
waft
waft·age
waft·er
wag (wag·ging, wagged)
wage
wa·ger
wa·ger·er
wages
wag·ga Austral blanket
Wag·ga Wag·ga Australian
  city
wagged
wag·gery
wag·ging
wag·gish
wag·gish·ness
wag·gle
wag·gling·ly

wag·gly
Wag·ne·rian
wag·on (or wag·gon)
wag·on·er (or wag·gon·)
wag·on·ette (or wag·gon·)
wagon-lit (plural
  wagons-lits) sleeping car
wagon·load (or waggon·)
wag·tail
Wah·ha·bi (or Wa·ha·bi;
  plural ·bis) conservative
  Muslim
wa·hi·ne Polynesian
  woman
wa·hoo (plural ·hoos) tree;
  fish
waif
Wai·ka·to New Zealand
  river
Wai·ki·ki Hawaiian resort
wail
wail·er
wail·ful
wail·ing·ly
wain farm wagon; compare
  wane

wain•scot

wain•scot•ed

wain•scot•ing (or •scot•ting)

wain•wright

waist

waist•band

waist•coat

waist•ed

waist•less

waist•line

wait

wait•er

wait•ress

waive relinquish; compare wave

waiv•er relinquishment; compare waver

Wa•kash•an American Indian language

Wa•ka•ya•ma Japanese city

wake (wak•ing, woke, wok•en)

Wake•field

wake•ful

wake•ful•ly

wake•ful•ness

wake•less

wak•en

wak•en•er

wak•er

wake•rife Dialect wakeful

wake-robin plant

wak•ing

Wa•lach variant of Vlach

Wa•la•chia (or Wal•la•chia) former European principality

Wal•brzych Polish city

Wal•che•ren Dutch island

Wal•den•ses Catholic sect

wald•grave medieval German forest officer

Wal•dorf sal•ad

wale weal; ridge

Wa•ler horse; compare whaler

Wales

walk

walk•able

walk•about

walk•er

walkie-talkie (or walky-talky; plural -talkies)

walk-in (adj)

walk•ing

walk-on (noun, adj)

walk•out (noun)

walk•over (noun)

walk•way

Wal•kyrie variant spelling of Valkyrie

walky-talky variant spelling of walkie-talkie

wall

wal•la•by (plural •bies or •by)

Wal•la•chia variant spelling of Walachia

wal•lah (or wal•la) Slang person in charge

wal•la•roo (plural •roos or •roo) large kangaroo

Wal•la•sey Merseyside town

wall•board

walled

wal•let

wall•eye (plural •eyes or •eye)

wall•eyed

wall•flower

wall-like

Wal•loon French-speaking Belgian

wal•lop

wal•lop•er

wal•lop•ing

wal•low

wal•low•er

wall•paper

Walls•end English town

wall-to-wall

wal•ly Slang idiot; Scot made of china

wal•nut

Wal•pur•gis Night

wal•rus (plural •ruses or •rus)

Wal•sall

Wal•tham For•est London borough

waltz

waltz•er

wame Dialect belly; womb

wam•pum shell money

wan (adj wan•ner, wan•nest; verb wan•ning, wanned)

wand

wan•der

wan•der•er

wan•der•ing

wan•der•ing•ly

wan•der•lust

wan•deroo (plural •deroos) monkey

wan•doo (plural •doos) tree

Wands•worth

wane decrease; compare wain

waney (or wany; wani•er, wani•est)

Wan•ga•nui New Zealand port

wan•gle

wan•gler

wank

wan•na Slang want to

wanned

wan•ner

wan•nest

wan•ning

want

want•er

want•ing

wan•ton

wan•ton•ness

wap•en•take former county division

wapi•ti (plural •tis) deer

wap•pen•shaw gathering of clans

war (war•ring, warred)

Wa•ran•gal Indian city

wa•ra•tah shrub

warb Austral dirty person

war•ble

war•bler

ward

ward•ed

war•den

war•den•ry

war•der (fem •dress)

ward•robe

ward•room

ward•ship

ware Archaic beware

ware•house

ware•house•man (plural •men)

wares goods

war•fare

war•fa•rin

war•head

war·horse
wari·ly
wari·ness
wari·son bugle note
War·ley English town
war·like
war·lock
war·lord
warm
warm-blooded
warm-blooded·ness
warm·er
warm-hearted
warm-hearted·ness
warm·ish
warm·ness
war·monger
warmth
warm-up (noun)
warn
warn·er
warn·ing
warp
warp·age
war·path
warp·er
war·plane
war·rant
war·rant·abil·ity
war·rant·able
war·rant·ably
war·rant·ee
war·rant·er one who
warrants
war·ran·tor warranty giver
war·ran·ty (plural ·ties)
warred
war·ren
war·rig·al Austral dingo
war·ring
War·ring·ton Cheshire
town
war·ri·or
War·saw
war·ship
war·sle Dialect wrestle
wart
wart·ed
war·time
warty (warti·er, warti·est)
War·wick
War·wick·shire
wary (wari·er, wari·est)
was
wash

wash·abil·ity
wash·able
wash·basin
wash·board
wash·bowl
wash·day
wash·er
washer·man (plural ·men)
washer·woman (or
wash·woman; plural
·women)
wash·ery (plural ·eries)
wash-house
washi·ly
wash·ing
wash·in aeronautics term
washi·ness
Wash·ing·ton
Wash·ing·to·nian
washing-up
wash·out (noun)
wash·rag US face cloth
wash·room
wash·stand
wash·tub
wash·woman variant of
washerwoman
washy (washi·er, washi·est)
wasn't
wasp
waspi·ly
waspi·ness
wasp·ish
wasp·ish·ness
waspy
was·sail
was·sail·er
wast·able
wast·age
waste
waste·ful
waste·ful·ly
waste·ful·ness
waste·land
waste·paper
wast·er
waste·weir water channel
wast·rel
wat Thai monastery
wa·tap American Indian
thread
watch
watch·case
watch·dog
watch·er

watch·ful
watch·ful·ly
watch·ful·ness
watch-glass
watch·maker
watch·making
watch·man (plural ·men)
watch·strap
watch·tower
watch·word
wa·ter
wa·ter·age transportation
by ship
water·bed
water·borne
water·buck antelope
water·colour (US ·color)
water·colour·ist (US
·color·)
water-cool
water-cooled
water·course
water·craft
water·cress
wa·ter·er
water·fall
Wa·ter·ford
water·fowl
water·front
Water·gate
wa·teri·ness
wa·ter·less
water·logged
Wa·ter·loo
water·man (plural ·men)
water·man·ship
water·mark
water·melon
water·proof
water·proof·ness
water-repellent
water-resistant
water·scape
water·shed
water-sick excessively
irrigated
water·side
water-ski (noun, plural ·skis;
verb ·skis, -skiing, -skied
or ski'd)
water-skier
water·spout
water·tight
water·tightness
water·way

water·weed
water·works
water·worn
wa·tery
Wat·ford
watt unit
watt·age
watt-hour
wat·tle
wattle·bird
watt·meter
Wa·tu·si (or ·tut·; *plural* ·sis
or ·si) African people
waul (or wawl) wail
wave undulation, etc.; move
to and fro; *compare* waive
wave·band
wave·form physics term
wave·guide electronics term
wave·length
wave·let
wave·like
wa·vell·ite mineral
wave·meter
wave·off signal to aircraft
wa·ver hesitate; one who
waves; *compare* waiver
wa·ver·er
wa·ver·ing·ly
wavi·ly
wavi·ness
wavy (wavi·er, wavi·est)
wawl *variant spelling of* waul
wax
wax·berry (*plural* ·berries)
wax·bill bird
wax·en
wax·er
waxi·ly
waxi·ness
wax·like
wax·plant
wax·wing bird
wax·work object
wax·work·er
wax·works exhibition
waxy (waxi·er, waxi·est)
way
way·bill document
way·farer
way·faring
Way·land legendary smith
way·lay (·lay·ing, ·laid)
way·lay·er
way-out

way·side
way·ward
way·ward·ness
wayz·goose printers' annual
outing
Wa·ziri·stan Asian region
we
weak
weak·en
weak·en·er
weak·fish (*plural* ·fish or
·fishes)
weak-kneed
weak·li·ness
weak·ling
weak·ly (·li·er, ·li·est)
weak-minded
weak-minded·ness
weak·ness
weak-willed
weal prosperity
weal (or wheal) mark on
skin
Weald English region
weald open country;
compare wield
wealth
wealthi·ly
wealthi·ness
wealthy (wealthi·er,
wealthi·est)
wean
wean·er
wean·ling
weap·on
weap·oned
weap·on·eer
wea·pon·ry
Wear English river
wear (wear·ing, wore,
worn)
wear·abil·ity
wear·able
wear·er
wea·ri·ful *variant of*
wearisome
wea·ri·less
wea·ri·ly
wea·ri·ness
wear·ing
wear·ing·ly
wea·ri·some (or ·ful)
wea·ri·some·ness (or
·ful·ness)
wear·proof

wea·ry (*adj* ·ri·er, ·ri·est;
verb ·ries, ry·ing, ·ried)
wea·ry·ing·ly
wea·sand *Dialect* windpipe
wea·sel (*plural* ·sel or ·sels)
wea·sel·ly
weath·er climatic
conditions; *compare*
wether; whether
weath·er·abil·ity
weather-beaten
weather·board
weather·boarding
weather-bound
weather·cock
weath·er·er
weather·glass
weath·er·ing
weath·er·ly nautical term
weather·man (*plural* ·men)
weather-proof
weather-wise
weather·worn
weave (weav·ing, wove or
weaved, wo·ven or
weaved)
weav·er one who weaves;
compare weever
weaver·bird
weav·ing
web (web·bing, webbed)
web·bing
web·by (·bi·er, ·bi·est)
we·ber unit
web·foot
web-footed
web·site Internet location
web-toed
wed (wed·ding, wed·ded or
wed)
we'd we had; we would
wed·ding
wed·el·ing skiing turn
wedge
Wedg·wood (*Trademark*)
pottery
wedgy
wed·lock
Wednes·day
wee (wee·ing, wee'd) *Slang*
tiny; to urinate
weed
weed·er
weedi·ly
weedi·ness

weed·killer
weedy (weedi·er,
  weedi·est)
week
week·day
week·end
week·end·er
week·ly (plural ·lies)
week·night
wee·ny (or ween·sy; ·ni·er,
  ·ni·est or ·si·er, ·si·est)
weep (weep·ing, wept)
weep·er
weepi·ness
weep·ing
weep·ing·ly
weepy (adj weepi·er,
  weepi·est; noun, plural
  weepies)
wee·ver fish; compare
  weaver
wee·vil
wee·vily
weft
Wehr·macht German
  armed service
wei·ge·la shrub
weigh
weigh·able
weigh·bridge
weigh·er
weight
weight·er
weighti·ly
weighti·ness
weight·ing
weight·less
weight·less·ness
weight·lifter
weight·lifting
weighty (weighti·er,
  weighti·est)
Wei·hai Chinese port
Wei·mar German city
Wei·mar·an·er dog
(Weir) incorrect spelling of
  Wear
weir
weird
weir·die (or ·do; plural ·dies
  or ·dos)
weird·ness
Weis·mann·ism biological
  theory
weka bird

Welch variant spelling of
  Welsh, now obsolete except
  in regimental names, esp.
  Royal Welch Fusiliers
welch variant spelling of
  welsh
wel·come
wel·come·ly
wel·come·ness
wel·com·er
weld
weld·abil·ity
weld·able
weld·er (or wel·dor)
wel·fare
(welk) incorrect spelling of
  whelk
Wel·kom South African
  town
well
we'll we will; we shall
well-accustomed
well-acquaint·ed
well-acted
well-adapted
well-advised
well-appoint·ed
well-argued
well-assort·ed
well-attend·ed
well-aware
well-balanced
well-behaved
well·being
well·bred
well·built
well-connect·ed
well-construct·ed
well-defined
well-deserved
well-developed
well-disposed
well-document·ed
well-done
well-dressed
well-educat·ed
well-endowed
well-equipped
well-established
well-favoured (US ·favored)
well-fed
well-found
well-founded
well-groomed
well-grounded

well·head
well-heeled
well-hung
wel·lies Slang Wellington
  boots
well-informed
Wel·ling·ton New Zealand
  capital; boot
well-intentioned
well-judged
well-knit
well-known
well-mannered
well-matched
well-meaning
well-nigh
well-off
well-oiled
well-organized (or
  -organised)
well-paid
well-pleased
well-preserved
well-propor·tioned
well-provid·ed
well-qualified
well-read
well-received
well-rounded
Wells Somerset city
well-situat·ed
well-spent
well-spoken
well·spring
well-support·ed
well-tempered
well-thought-of
well-timed
well-to-do
well-tried
well-turned
well-wisher
well-wishing
well-worded
well-worn
Welsh
welsh (or welch) fail in
  obligation
Welsh·man (plural ·men)
Welsh·woman (plural
  ·women)
welt
wel·ter
wel·ter·weight
wel·witschia plant

Wel·wyn Gar·den City
Wem·bley
wen cyst
wench
wench·er
Wend Slavonic people
wend
Wend·ish
Wen·dy house
Wens·ley·dale Yorkshire
   town; cheese
went
wen·tle·trap mollusc
wept
were
we're we are
weren't were not
were·wolf (plural ·wolves)
wer·gild (or were·gild,
   wer·geld) price on life
wer·ner·ite mineral
Wes·ley·an
Wes·ley·an·ism
Wes·sex
west
west·bound
West Brom·wich
west·er to move towards
   west
west·er·ing
west·er·li·ness
west·er·ly (plural ·lies)
west·ern
west·ern·er
west·ern·ism
west·erni·za·tion (or
   ·sa·tion)
west·ern·ize (or ·ise)
west·ern·most
West Ger·many former
   country
West In·dian
West In·dies
west·ing westerly
   movement
West·meath Irish county
West·min·ster
West·mor·land former
   English county
west·northwest
Weston-super-Mare
West·pha·lia
West·pha·lian
west-southwest
west·ward (adj)

west·wards (adv)
wet (adj wet·ter, wet·test;
   verb wet·ting, wet or
   wet·ted) not dry; make
   wet; compare whet
weth·er male sheep; compare
   weather; whether
wet·lands
wet·ness
wet-nurse (verb)
wet·tabil·ity
wet·table
wet·ted
wet·ter
wet·test
wet·ting
wet·tish
we've we have
Wex·ford Irish county
Wey·mouth
whack
whack·er
whack·ing
whacko exclamation
whale (plural whales or
   whale)
whale·boat
whale·bone
whal·er whale catcher;
   whaleboat; compare Waler
whal·ing
wham (wham·ming,
   whammed)
whang
Whan·ga·rei New Zealand
   port
whangee bamboo grass
whare Maori hut
wharf (plural wharves or
   wharfs)
wharf·age
wharf·in·ger
wharve flywheel; pulley
what
what·ev·er
what·not
what·sit
what·so·ev·er
whaup Scot curlew
wheal variant spelling of
   weal
wheat
wheat·ear bird
wheat·en
wheat·worm

whee·dle
whee·dler
whee·dling·ly
wheel
wheel·bar·row
wheel·base
wheel·chair
wheel·er
wheeler-dealer
wheel·house
wheelie skateboarding
   manoeuvre
wheel·less
wheel·work
wheel·wright
wheen Dialect few
wheeze
wheez·er
wheezi·ly
wheezi·ness
wheezi·ing·ly
wheezy (wheezi·er,
   wheezi·est)
whelk
whelp
when
whence
whence·so·ev·er
whene'er
when·ever
when·so·ever
where
where·abouts
where·as
where·at
where·by
where'er
where·fore
where·from
where·in
where·into
where·of
where·on
where·so·ever
where·to
where·upon
wher·ever
where·with
where·with·al
wher·rit worry
wher·ry (plural ·ries) boat
wherry·man (plural ·men)
whet (whet·ting, whet·ted)
   sharpen; stimulate;
   compare wet

wheth·er (*conj.*) *compare*
weather; wether
whet·stone
whet·ter
whey watery liquid
whey·ey (*or* ·ish, ·like)
whey·face
whey·faced
which
which·ever
whick·er whinny; *compare*
wicker
whid·ah *variant spelling of*
whydah
whiff
whiff·er
whif·fle
whif·fler
whif·fle·tree crossbar in
harness
Whig political party
Whig·gery (*or* ·gism)
Whig·gish
Whig·gish·ness
while during; *note* while
away; *compare* wile
whilst
whim
whim·brel bird
whim·per
whim·per·er
whim·per·ing·ly
whim·si·cal
whim·si·cal·ity (*plural*
·ities)
whim·si·cal·ly
whim·si·cal·ness
whim·sy (*or* ·sey; *noun,*
plural ·sies *or* ·seys; *adj*
·si·er, ·si·est)
whin gorse
whin·chat bird
whine
whin·er
whinge
whin·ing·ly
whin·ny (*verb* ·nies,
·ny·ing, ·nied; *noun, plural*
·nies)
whin·stone
whiny (whini·er,
whini·est) peevish;
compare winy
whip (whip·ping,
whipped)

whip·cord
whip·lash
whip·like
whip·per
whipper-in (*plural*
whippers-in)
whip·per·snap·per
whip·pet
whip·ping
whip·poor·will
whippy (whip·pier,
whip·piest)
whip·round (*noun*)
whip·saw
whip·stall aeronautics
term
whip·stitch
whip·stock whip handle
whip·worm
whir (*or* whirr; whir·ring,
whirred)
whirl spin; confusion;
compare whorl
whirl·about
whirl·er
whirli·gig
whirl·ing·ly
whirl·pool
whirl·wind
whirly·bird
whirr *variant spelling of*
whir
whish swish
whisk
whisk·er
whisk·ered
whisk·ers
whisk·ery
whis·key Irish or US whisky
whis·ky (*plural* ·kies)
whis·per
whis·per·er
whist
whis·tle
whis·tler
whis·tling
Whit Christian festival
whit iota
white
white·bait
white·beam tree
white·cap white-crested
wave
White·chapel
white-collar (*adj*)

white·damp mine gas
whit·ed sep·ul·chre
white-eye bird
white·fish (*plural* ·fish *or*
·fishes)
white·fly (*plural* ·flies)
White·hall
white-hot
white-livered
whit·en
whit·en·er
white·ness
whit·en·ing
white·out
whites
white-slaver
white·smith metal polisher
white·throat bird
white·wall tyre
white·wash
white·wash·er
white·wood
whit·ey (*or* wity; *plural* ·eys
or wities)
whith·er
whit·ing (*plural* ·ing *or*
·ings) fish
whit·ing (*or* ·en·ing)
ground chalk
whit·ish
whit·low
Whit·sun
Whit·sun·tide
whit·tle
whit·tler
whit·tlings wood shavings
whity whitish; *variant*
spelling of whitey
whiz (*or* whizz; whiz·zing,
whizzed)
whiz-bang (*or* whizz-)
whiz·zer
who
whoa
who'd who had; who would
who·dun·it (*or* ·dun·nit)
who·ever
whole
whole·food
whole·hearted
whole·hearted·ness
whole·meal
whole·ness
whole·sale
whole·sal·er

whole·some
whole·some·ly
whole·some·ness
who'll who will; who shall
whol·ly
whom
whom·ever
whom·so·ever
whoop
whoo·pee
whoop·er swan
whoop·ing cough
whoops exclamation
whoosh (or woosh)
whop (or wop; whop·ping, whopped or wop·ping, wopped) hit
whop·per
whop·ping
whore
whore·dom
whore·house
whore·monger
whore·son
whor·ish
whorl spiral pattern or arrangement; compare whirl
whorled
whortle·berry (plural ·berries)
who's who is
whose of who
who·so·ever (or who·so)
why (plural whys)
Why·al·la Australian port
whyd·ah (or whid·) bird
Wichi·ta US city
Wick Scottish town
wick
wick·ed
wick·ed·ness
wick·er flexible twig; compare whicker
wicker·work
wick·et
wicket·keeper
wick·ing
wicki·up American Indian hut
Wick·low Irish county
wico·py plant
wid·der·shins variant spelling of withershins
wide

wide-awake
wide-awakeness
wide-eyed
wide·ly
wid·en
wid·en·er
wide·ness
wide-open
wide-ranging
wide-screen (adj)
wide·spread
widg·eon variant spelling of wigeon
widg·et
widgie Austral unruly woman
wid·ish
Wid·nes Cheshire town
wid·ow
wid·ow·er
wid·ow·hood
width
width·wise (or ·ways)
wield manipulate; compare weald
wield·able
wield·er
wieldy (wieldi·er, wieldi·est)
Wie·ner schnit·zel
(wier) incorrect spelling of weir
(wierd) incorrect spelling of weird
Wies·ba·den German city
wife (plural wives)
wife·li·ness
wife·ly
wig (wig·ging, wigged)
Wig·an
wig·eon (or widg·) duck
wigged
wig·ging
wig·gle
wig·gler
wig·gly
Wight (Isle of)
wig·wag (·wag·ging, ·wagged)
wig·wag·ger
wig·wam
wil·co signalling expression
wild
wild·cat (·cat·ting, ·cat·ted)

wild·cat·ter
wil·de·beest (plural ·beests or ·beest)
wil·der·ness
wild-eyed
wild·fire
wild·fowl
wild·fowl·er
wild·fowl·ing
wild-goose chase
wild·ing (or ·ling)
wild·life
wild·ness
wile craftiness; trick; compare while
wil·ful (US will·)
wil·ful·ly (US will·)
wil·ful·ness (US will·)
Wil·helms·ha·ven German port
wili·ly
wili·ness
will
will·able
wil·lem·ite mineral
will·er
wil·let bird
will·ful US spelling of wilful
Wil·liams·burg US city
wil·lies Slang fright
will·ing
will·ing·ness
wil·li·waw US turmoil
will-o'-the-wisp
wil·low
wil·low·herb
wil·lowy
will·power
willy-nilly
wilt
Wil·ton carpet
Wilt·shire
wily (wili·er, wili·est)
wim·ble tool
Wim·ble·don
wimp
wimp·ish
wim·ple
Wim·py (Trademark) hamburger
win (win·ning, won)
wince
winc·er
win·cey fabric
win·cey·ette

winch

winch·er

Win·ches·ter English city; rifle

win·ches·ter large bottle

winc·ing·ly

wind (wind·ing, wound) coil

wind (wind·ing, wind·ed) air current, etc.

wind·able

wind·age

wind·bag

wind·blown

wind·borne

wind·bound

wind·break

wind·broken asthmatic

wind·burn

wind·burnt (or ·burned)

wind·cheater

wind·ed

wind·er

Win·der·mere

wind·fall

wind·flower

wind·gall fetlock swelling

wind·galled

Wind·hoek Namibian capital

wind·hover Dialect kestrel

windi·ly

windi·ness

wind·ing

wind·ing·ly

wind·jam·mer

wind·lass

win·dle·straw Dialect dried grass

wind·mill

win·dow

window-dresser

window-dressing

window·pane

window-shop (-shopping, -shopped)

window-shopper

window·sill

wind·pipe

wind·pollinat·ed

wind·pollina·tion

wind·row line of hay

wind·row·er

wind·sail

wind·screen

wind·shield

wind·sock

Wind·sor

wind·storm

wind·sucker

wind-sucking

wind·swept

wind-up (noun)

wind·ward

windy (windi·er, windi·est)

wine

wine-bibber

wine-bibbing

wine·glass

wine·glass·ful

wine·press

win·ery (plural ·eries)

wine·skin

wing

wing·ding US party

winged

wing·er

wing·less

wing·less·ness

wing·let

wing·like

wing·over aircraft manoeuvre

wing·span (or ·spread)

wink

wink·er

win·kle

win·nable

Win·ne·ba·go (plural ·gos or ·go) US lake; American Indian

win·ner

win·ning

win·ning·ness

win·nings

Win·ni·peg

Win·ni·peg·ger

Win·ni·pego·sis Canadian lake

win·now

win·now·er

wino (plural winos) Slang wine drinker

win·some

win·some·ly

win·some·ness

Winston-Salem US city

win·ter

winter·bourne stream

win·ter·er

winter·feed (·feeding, ·fed)

winter·green shrub

winter·kill

winter·time

win·tri·er

win·tri·est

win·tri·ly

win·tri·ness (or ·teri·ness)

win·try (or ·tery; ·tri·er, ·tri·est)

winy (wini·er, wini·est) like wine; compare whiny

winze mining shaft

wipe

wipe-out (noun)

wip·er

wire

wire·draw (·draw·ing, ·drew, ·drawn)

wire-gauge

wire-haired

wire·less

wire·man (plural ·men) US electrician

wir·er

wire·work

wire·worker

wire·works

wire·worm

wire-wove

wiri·ly

wiri·ness

wir·ing

wir·ra Irish exclamation

Wir·ral English peninsula

wiry (wiri·er, wiri·est)

Wis·con·sin

Wis·con·sin·ite

wis·dom

wise

wisea·cre

wise·crack

wise·crack·er

wise·ly

wise·ness

wi·sent European bison

wish

wish·bone

wish·er

wish·ful

wish·ful·ly

wish·ful·ness

wishy-washy

wisp

wispi·ly
wispi·ness
wispy (wispi·er, wispi·est)
wis·te·ria
wist·ful
wist·ful·ly
wist·ful·ness
wit
wit·an Anglo-Saxon
  council
witch
witch·craft
witch elm *variant spelling of*
  wych elm
witch·ery (*plural* ·eries)
witch·et·ty edible grub
witch ha·zel (*or* wych
  hazel)
witch-hunt
witch-hunter
witch-hunting
witch·ing
witch·like
wite *Scot* blame
wit·ena·gamot witan
with
with·al
with·draw (·draw·ing,
  ·drew, ·drawn)
with·draw·able
with·draw·al
with·draw·er
with·drawn
with·drawn·ness
with·drew
withe (*or* withy; *plural*
  withes *or* withies) flexible
  twig
with·er
with·ered·ness
with·er·er
with·er·ing·ly
with·er·ite mineral
with·ers
with·er·shins (*or*
  wid·der·)
with·hold (·hold·ing,
  ·held)
with·hold·er
with·in
with·out
with·stand (·stand·ing,
  ·stood)
with·stand·er
with·stood

withy (*plural* withies)
  willow tree; *variant spelling*
  of withe
wit·less
wit·less·ness
wit·loof Belgian chicory
wit·ness
wit·ness·able
wit·ness·er
wits
wit·ter
wit·ti·cism
wit·ti·ly
wit·ti·ness
wit·ting·ly intentional
wit·ty (·ti·er, ·ti·est)
Wit·wa·ters·rand South
  African region
wive *Archaic* to marry
wi·vern *variant spelling of*
  wyvern
wives *plural of* wife
wiz·ard
wiz·ard·ry
wiz·en
wiz·ened
woad
woad·ed
wob·be·gong shark
wob·ble
wob·bler
wob·bli·ness
wob·bly (·bli·er, ·bli·est)
Woden (*or* Wodan)
  Anglo-Saxon god
wodge
woe
woe·be·gone
woe·ful
woe·ful·ly
woe·ful·ness
wog·gle
wok
woke
wok·en
Wo·king
wold upland
wolf (*plural* wolves)
wolf·bane (*or* wolfs·bane,
  wolf's-bane) plant
wolf·er *variant of* wolver
wolf·fish (*plural* ·fish *or*
  ·fishes)
wolf·hound
wolf·ish

wolf·ish·ness
wolf·like
wolf·ram tungsten
wolf·ram·ite mineral
wolfs·bane (*or* wolf's-bane)
  variants of wolfbane
wolf-whistle (*verb*)
wol·las·ton·ite mineral
Wol·lon·gong Australian
  city
wol·ly (*plural* ·lies) *Dialect*
  pickled cucumber; *compare*
  wally
Wol·of (*plural* ·of *or* ·ofs)
  African people
wolv·er (*or* wolf·) wolf
  hunter
Wol·ver·hamp·ton
wol·ver·ine animal
wolves *plural of* wolf
wom·an (*plural* ·en)
wom·an·hood
wom·an·ish
wom·an·ish·ness
wom·an·ize (*or* ·ise)
wom·an·iz·er (*or* ·is·er)
wom·an·kind
woman-like
wom·an·li·ness
wom·an·ly
womb
wom·bat
womb·like
wom·en
women·folk
wom·era *variant spelling of*
  woomera
won *past tense of* win
won (*or* hwan; *plural* won
  or hwan) North Korean
  currency
won·der
won·der·er
won·der·ful
won·der·ful·ly
won·der·ful·ness
wonder·land
won·der·ment
wonder-work miracle
wonder-worker
wonder-working
won·drous
won·drous·ness
won·ky (·ki·er, ·ki·est)
Won·san North Korean port

wont accustomed; custom
won't will not
wont·ed
won ton Chinese food
woo (woos, woo·ing, wooed)
wood
wood·bine
wood·borer beetle larva
wood·carver
wood·carving
wood·chat bird
wood·chuck
wood·cock
wood·craft
wood·crafts·man (plural ·men)
wood·cut
wood·cut·ter
wood·cutting
wood·ed
wood·en
wooden·head
wood·en·ness
wood·grouse
woodi·ness
wood·land
wood·lander
wood·lark
wood·louse (plural ·lice)
wood·man (plural ·men)
wood·note natural song
wood·pecker
wood·pile
wood·print
wood·ruff plant
wood·rush
wood·screw
wood·shed
wood·sia fern
woods·man (plural ·men)
wood·wind
wood·work
wood·worker
wood·working
wood·worm
woody (woodi·er, woodi·est)
wooed
woo·er
woof weft; bark of dog
woof·er loudspeaker
woo·ing
wool
wool·gather·er

wool·gather·ing
wool·grower
wool·growing
wool·len (US wool·en)
wool·li·ly
wool·li·ness
wool·ly (US also wooly; adj ·li·er, ·li·est; noun, plural ·lies)
wool·pack
wool·sack
Woom·era Australian town
woom·era (or wom·era) Aboriginal spear thrower
Woop Woop Austral remote town
woosh variant spelling of whoosh
woozi·ly
woozi·ness
woozy (woozi·er, woozi·est)
wop variant spelling of whop; Slang Italian
Worces·ter
Worces·ter·shire former county; note
Worcestershire sauce
word
word·age
word·blind
word·book
word·break
word·deaf
wordi·ly
wordi·ness
word·ing
word·less
word·less·ness
word·perfect
word·play
word·smith
wordy (wordi·er, wordi·est)
wore
work
work·abil·ity (or ·able·ness)
work·able
worka·day
worka·hol·ic
work·bag
work·bench
work·book
work·box
work·day

work·er
worker-priest
work·folk
work-harden
work-harden·ing
work·horse
work·house
work-in (noun)
work·ing
work·load
work·man (plural ·men)
work·man·like
work·man·ly
work·man·ship
work-out (noun)
work·people
work·piece
work·room
works
work·shop
work·shy
Work·sop English town
work·table
work-to-rule (noun)
world
world-beater
world-beating
world·li·ness
world·ling
world·ly (·li·er, ·li·est)
worldly-wise
world-shaking
world-weariness
world-weary
world·wide
worm
worm·cast
worm-eaten
worm·er
worm·hole
worm·like (or ·ish)
worm·seed
worm·wood
wormy (wormi·er, wormi·est)
worn
worn-out
wor·ri·er
wor·ri·ment
wor·ri·some
wor·rit Dialect tease
wor·ry (verb ·ries, ·ry·ing, ·ried; noun, plural ·ries)
wor·ry·wart worrier
worse

wors·en
wor·ship (·ship·ping,
  ·shipped; *US* ·ship·ing,
  ·shiped)
wor·ship·able
wor·ship·ful
wor·ship·ful·ly
wor·ship·ful·ness
wor·ship·per
wor·ship·ping·ly
worst
wor·sted fabric
worst·ed defeated
wort soaked malt
worth
wor·thi·ly
wor·thi·ness
Wor·thing
worth·less
worth·less·ly
worth·less·ness
worth·while
worth·while·ness
wor·thy (*adj* ·thi·er,
  ·thi·est; *noun, plural*
  ·thies)
Wotan Germanic god
would
would-be
wouldn't
wouldst
wound
wound·able
wound·ed
wound·er
wound·ing·ly
wound·wort
wove
wo·ven
wow
wow·ser *Austral* puritanical
  person
wrack seaweed; *variant*
  spelling of rack
wraith
wraith·like
wran·gle
wran·gler
wrap (wrap·ping, wrapped)
wrap·over (*or* ·around,
  ·round)
wrap·per
wrap·ping
wrasse fish; *compare* rasse
wrath anger; *compare* wroth

wrath·ful
wrath·ful·ly
wrath·ful·ness
wreak
wreak·er
wreath (*noun, plural*
  wreaths)
wreathe (*verb*)
wreck
wreck·age
wreck·er
wreck·fish (*plural* ·fish *or*
  ·fishes)
Wre·kin English hill
Wren member of WRNS
wren bird
wrench
wrest
wrest·er
wres·tle
wres·tler
wres·tling
wretch miserable person;
  compare retch
wretch·ed
wretch·ed·ness
Wrex·ham
wried contorted
wri·er *variant spelling of*
  wryer
wri·est *variant spelling of*
  wryest
wrig·gle
wrig·gler
wrig·gling·ly
wrig·gly (·gli·er, ·gli·est)
wright maker or repairer
wring (wring·ing, wrung)
wring·er
wrin·kle
wrin·kly
wrist
wrist·band
wrist·let bracelet
wrist·lock
wrist·watch
writ
writ·able
write (writ·ing, wrote,
  writ·ten)
write-off (*noun*)
writ·er
writhe
writh·er
writh·ing·ly

writ·ing
writ·ten
Wro·cław Polish city
wrong
wrong·doer
wrong·doing
wrong·er
wrong-foot (*verb*)
wrong·ful
wrong·ful·ly
wrong·ful·ness
wrong-headed
wrong-headed·ness
wrong·ly
wrong·ness
wrote
wroth *Archaic* angry;
  compare wrath
wrought
wrought-up
wrung
wry (*adj* wry·er, wry·est *or*
  wri·er, wri·est; *verb* wries,
  wry·ing, wried)
wry·bill bird
wry·ing
wry·ly
wry·neck
wry·ness
Wu Chinese dialect
Wu·han Chinese city
Wu-hsi *variant spelling of*
  Wusih
Wuhu Chinese port
wul·fen·ite mineral
Wu-lu-mu-ch'i *variant of*
  Urumchi
wun·der·kind (*plural* ·kinds
  or ·kind·er) child prodigy
Wup·per·tal German city
wurley (*or* wurlie)
  Aboriginal hut
wurst German sausage
Würt·tem·berg former
  German state
Würz·burg German city
wus Welsh term of address
Wu·sih (*or* Wu-hsi) Chinese
  city
Wy·an·dotte domestic fowl
wych elm (*or* witch elm)
wych hazel *variant spelling
  of* witch hazel
Wyc·lif·fite (*or* Wyc·lif·ite)
Wye British river

Wyke·ham·ist member of Winchester College

wynd *Scot* lane

Wyo·ming

wy·vern (*or* **wi·**) heraldic beast

X

xan·thate chemical compound

xan·tha·tion

xan·the·in plant pigment

xan·thene chemical compound

xan·thic chemistry or botany term

xan·thin plant pigment

xan·thine chemical compound

xan·thoch·ro·ism animal skin condition

xan·tho·ma (*plural* **·mas** *or* **·ma·ta**) skin nodule

xan·tho·phyll plant pigment

xan·tho·phyll·ous

xan·thous having yellowish hair

Xan·thus ancient Asian city

x-axis

X-chromosome

xe·bec (*or* **ze·bec, ze·beck**) ship

xe·nia botany term

xe·nial

xeno·cryst

xe·noga·mous

xe·noga·my cross-fertilization

xeno·gen·esis botany term

xeno·genet·ic (*or* **·gen·ic**)

xeno·glos·sia language ability

xeno·lith geology term

xeno·lith·ic

xeno·mor·phic geology term

xeno·mor·phi·cal·ly

xen·on chemical element

xeno·phile

xeno·phobe

xeno·pho·bia

xeno·pho·bic

xeno·trans·plant surgical procedure

xeno·trans·plan·ta·tion

xer·arch ecology term

xe·ric of dry conditions

xe·ri·cal·ly

xe·ro·der·ma (*or* **·mia**) dry skin

xe·ro·der·mat·ic (*or* **·ma·tous**)

xe·rog·ra·pher

xe·ro·graph·ic

xe·ro·graphi·cal·ly

xe·rog·ra·phy photocopying

xe·ro·mor·phic botany term

xe·ro·phile

xe·rophi·lous living in dry conditions

xe·rophi·ly

xe·roph·thal·mia (*or* **xe·ro·ma**) eye disease

xe·roph·thal·mic

xe·ro·phyte

xe·ro·phyt·ic

xe·ro·phyti·cal·ly

xe·ro·phyt·ism

xe·ro·sere ecology term

xe·ro·sis dryness of tissues

xe·rot·ic

Xer·ox (*Trademark*)

Xho·sa (*plural* **·sa** *or* **·sas**) African people

Xho·san

xi (*plural* **xis**) Greek letter

xiphi·ster·num (*plural* **·na**) part of breastbone

xiph·oid anatomy or biology term

xipho·su·ran zoology term

Xmas

X-radiation

X-ray (*or* **x-ray**)

xy·lan biochemistry term

xy·lem plant tissue

xy·lene chemical compound

xy·li·dine chemical compound

xy·lo·carp botany term

xy·lo·car·pous

xy·lo·graph wood engraving

xy·log·ra·pher

xy·lo·graph·ic (*or* **·graphi·cal**)

xy·log·ra·phy

xy·loid woody

xy·lol chemical compound

xy·lopha·gous wood-eating

xy·lo·phone

xy·lo·phon·ic

xy·lopho·nist

xy·lose sugar

xy·loto·mist

xy·loto·mous wood-boring

xy·loto·my preparing wood for microscopy

xy·lyl chemistry term

xyst (*or* **xys·tus, xys·tos**) portico

xys·ter surgical file

Y

yacht
yacht·ing
yachts·man (*plural* ·men)
yachts·man·ship (*or* yacht·)
yachts·woman (*plural* ·women)
ya·hoo (*plural* ·hoos) coarse person
ya·hoo·ism
yak (yak·king, yakked)
Ya·kut (*plural* ·kuts *or* ·kut) Russian people
Ya·kutsk Russian port
Yale US university; (*Trademark*) lock
Yal·ta Ukrainian port
yam
yam·mer
yam·mer·er
yang Chinese masculine principle; *compare* yin
Yang·tze
yank tug
Yank (*or* Yan·kee) *Slang* American
Yan·kee·ism
Ya·oun·dé (*or* Ya·un·de) Cameroon capital
yap (yap·ping, yapped)
ya·pok animal
ya·pon *variant spelling of* yaupon
yapped
yap·per
yap·ping
yap·py
yar·bor·ough bridge or whist term
yard·age
yard·arm
yard·stick
Yar·mouth
yar·mul·ke skullcap
yarn
yarn-dyed
Ya·ro·slavl Russian city
yar·row
yash·mak (*or* ·mac)
yata·ghan sword
Ya·un·de *variant spelling of* Yaoundé

yau·pon (*or* ya·pon) shrub
yau·tia plant
yaw
yawl
yawn
yawn·er
yawn·ing·ly
yaws disease
y-axis
Y-chromosome
ye
yea
yean·ling goat's or sheep's young
year
year·book
year·ling
year·long
year·ly (*plural* ·lies)
yearn
yearn·er
yearn·ing
yeast
yeasti·ly
yeasti·ness
yeasty (yeasti·er, yeasti·est)
Ye·ka·te·rin·burg Russian city
yell
yell·er
yel·low
yellow·bark
yellow-belly (*plural* -bellies)
yellow·bird
yellow·hammer
yel·low·ish
yellow·legs bird
yel·lows disease
Yellow·stone
yellow·tail (*plural* ·tails *or* ·tail) fish
yellow·weed
yellow·wood
yel·lowy
yelp
yelp·er
Yem·en
Yem·eni
yen (yen·ning, yenned)
yen (*plural* yen) Japanese currency

Ye·ni·sei Russian river
Yen·tai (*or* Yen-t'ai) Chinese port
yeo·man (*plural* ·men)
yeo·man·ry (*plural* ·ries)
Yeo·vil
yer·ba beverage
Ye·re·van Armenian capital
yes
yes-man (*plural* -men)
yes·ter·day
yes·ter·year
yeti
yew
Ygg·dra·sil mythological tree
Yid·dish
yield
yield·able
yield·er
yield·ing·ly
yield·ing·ness
yin Chinese feminine principle; *compare* yang
Ying·kow (*or* Ying-k'ou) Chinese port
yip·pee
ylang-ylang (*or* ilang-ilang) tree
ylem original matter of universe
yob (*or* yob·bo; *plural* yobs *or* yob·bos)
yo·del (·del·ling, ·delled; US ·del·ing, ·deled)
yo·del·ler (US ·del·er)
yoga
yo·ghurt (*or* ·gurt)
yogi (*plural* yo·gis *or* yo·gin) yoga master
yo·gic
yo·gism
yo·gurt *variant spelling of* yoghurt
yo·him·bine medicinal substance
yoicks huntsman's exclamation
yoke frame; burden; link; part of garment; *compare* yolk

yo‑kel
yo‑kel‑ish
Yo‑ko‑ha‑ma Japanese city
Yok‑ya‑kar‑ta (or Jog‑ja‑)
  Indonesian city
yolk part of egg; compare
  yoke
yolky
Yom Kip‑pur
yon (or yond)
yon‑der
yoni female genitalia
Yon‑kers US city
Yonne French department
  and river
yon‑nie Austral stone
yoo‑hoo
yore
York
york‑er cricket term
York‑ist
York‑shire
Yorkshire‑man (plural
  ‑men)
Yo‑ru‑ba (plural ‑bas or ‑ba)
  African people
Yo‑ru‑ban
Yo‑semi‑te US national park

Yoshkar‑Ola Russian city
you
you'd you would; you
  had
you'll you will; you shall
young
young‑berry (plural
  ‑berries)
young‑ish
young‑ster
Youngs‑town US city
your of you
you're you are
yours
your‑self (plural ‑selves)
youth
youth‑ful
youth‑ful‑ly
youth‑ful‑ness
you've you have
yowl
yowl‑er
yo‑yo (plural ‑yos)
Ypres
yt‑ter‑bia chemical
  compound
yt‑ter‑bite mineral

yt‑ter‑bium chemical
  element
yt‑tria chemical compound
yt‑tric
yt‑trif‑er‑ous
yt‑trium chemical element
yuan (plural yuan) Chinese
  currency
Yu‑ca‑tán Mexican state
yuc‑ca
Yuga Hindu age
Yu‑go‑slav (or Ju‑)
Yu‑go‑sla‑via (or Ju‑)
Yu‑go‑sla‑vian (or Ju‑)
yuk
yuk‑ky
Yu‑kon
Yu‑kon‑er
yu‑lan tree
yule
yule‑tide
Yu‑man language group
yum‑my (‑mi‑er, ‑mi‑est)
Yün‑nan Chinese province
yup Slang yes
yup‑pie
Yve‑lines French
  department

Z

za‑ba‑glio‑ne
Za‑brze Polish city
Za‑ca‑te‑cas Mexican state
zaf‑fer (or zaf‑fre) pigment
Zaga‑zig (or Zaqa‑ziq)
  Egyptian city
Za‑greb
zai‑bat‑su Japanese wealthy
  families
Za‑ïre former name of the
  Democratic Republic of
  Congo
Za‑ïr‑ese
Za‑ïr‑ian
Zama ancient African city
Zam‑be‑zi (or ‑se)
Zam‑be‑zian
Zam‑bia
Zam‑bian
Zam‑bo‑an‑ga Philippine
  port
za‑mia plant

za‑min‑dar (or ze‑) Indian
  landowner
za‑min‑dari (or ze‑; plural
  ‑daris) estate
za‑ni‑ly
za‑ni‑ness
Zan‑te Greek island
zan‑thoxy‑lum tree
zany (adj zani‑er, zani‑est;
  noun, plural zanies)
Zan‑zi‑bar
Zan‑zi‑ba‑ri
zap (zap‑ping, zapped)
za‑pa‑dea‑do (plural ‑dos)
  dance
Za‑po‑rozh‑ye Ukrainian
  city
Za‑po‑tec (plural ‑tecs or
  ‑tec) American Indian
Zapo‑tec‑an
Zaqa‑ziq variant of Zagazig
Za‑ra‑go‑za Spanish city

zara‑tite mineral
za‑reba (or ‑ree‑ba) African
  enclosure
zarf coffee‑cup holder
Zar‑ga (or Sar‑ka) Jordanian
  town
Za‑ria Nigerian city
zar‑zue‑la Spanish opera
z‑axis
zeal
Zea‑land Danish island;
  compare Zeeland
zeal‑ot
zeal‑ot‑ry
zeal‑ous
zeal‑ous‑ness
ze‑bec (or ‑beck) variant
  spellings of xebec
Zebedee biblical character
zeb‑ra (plural ‑ras or ‑ra)
zebra‑like (or ze‑bra‑ic)
zebra‑wood

ze·brine (or ·broid)
zebu ox
zec·chi·no (plural ·ni) coin
zed
zedo·ary condiment
zee US zed
Zee·brug·ge
Zee·land Dutch province; compare Zealand
Zee·land·er
zein protein
Zeist Dutch city
Zeit·geist German spirit of the age
ze·min·dar variant spelling of zamindar
ze·min·dari variant spelling of zamindari
Zen
ze·na·na women's part of house
Zen·ic
Zen·ist
zen·ith
zen·ith·al
zeo·lite mineral
zeo·lit·ic
zeph·yr breeze; fabric
Zephyrus Greek god
zep·pe·lin
zero (noun, plural zeros or zeroes; verb zeroes, ze·ro·ing, ze·roed)
zero-rated
zeroth
zest
zest·ful
zest·ful·ly
zest·ful·ness
zesty
zeta Greek letter
zeug·ma figure of speech
zeug·mat·ic
zeug·mati·cal·ly
Zeus
Zhda·nov former name of Mariupol
Zhi·to·mir Ukrainian city
zho variant spelling of zo
zib·el·ine fur
zib·et animal
ziff Austral beard
zig·gu·rat (or zik·ku·rat, ziku·rat) temple tower
zig·zag (·zag·ging, ·zagged)

zig·zag·ged·ness
zig·zag·ger
zila (or zil·la, zil·lah) Indian administrative district
zilch
zil·lion (plural ·lions or ·lion)
Zim·ba·bwe
Zim·ba·bwe·an
zinc
zin·cate
zinc·ic (or ·ous, ·oid)
zinc·if·er·ous
zinc·ite mineral
zinck·en·ite variant spelling of zinkenite
zincky (or zincy, zinky)
zin·co (plural ·cos) short for zincograph
zin·co·graph zinc printing-plate
zin·cog·ra·pher
zin·co·graph·ic (or ·graphi·cal)
zin·cog·ra·phy
zincy variant spelling of zincky
Zin·fan·del wine grape
zing
zin·ga·ro (fem ·ra; plural ·ri or ·re) gipsy
zin·gi·bera·ceous botany term
zingy
zin·jan·thro·pus fossil hominid
zin·ken·ite (or zinck·en·ite) mineral
zinky variant spelling of zincky
zin·nia plant
Zion (or Sion)
Zi·on·ism
Zi·on·ist
Zi·on·is·tic
zip (zip·ping, zipped)
zip·per
zip·py (·pi·er, ·pi·est)
zirc·al·loy
zir·con
zir·co·nia chemical compound
zir·con·ic
zir·co·nium chemical element

zith·er
zith·er·ist
Zla·to·ust Russian town
zlo·ty (plural ·tys or ·ty) Polish currency
zo (or zho, dzo; plural zos, zhos, dzos or zo, zho, dzo) cattle
zo·di·ac
zo·dia·cal
Zo·har Jewish text
zois·ite mineral
Zom·ba Malawian city
zom·bie (or ·bi; plural ·bies or ·bis)
zom·bi·ism
zon·al (or zona·ry)
zon·ate (or zo·nat·ed)
zo·na·tion
Zond Soviet spacecraft
zone
zone·time
zonu·lar
zon·ule
zoo (plural zoos)
zoo·chemi·cal
zoo·chem·is·try
zoo·chore botany term
zoo·geog·ra·pher
zoo·geo·graph·ic (or ·graphi·cal)
zoo·geo·graphi·cal·ly
zoo·geog·ra·phy
zoo·gloea (US ·glea; plural ·gloeas or ·gloeae, US ·gleas or ·gleae) bacterial mass
zoo·gloeal (US ·gleal)
zo·og·ra·pher
zoo·graph·ic (or ·graphi·cal)
zo·og·ra·phy
zo·oid
zo·ol·at·er
zo·ola·trous
zo·ola·try worship of animals
zoo·logi·cal
zo·olo·gist
zo·ol·ogy (plural ·ogies)
zoom
zoo·met·ric (or ·ri·cal)
zo·om·etry
zoo·mor·phic
zoo·mor·phism

zo•ono•sis (*plural* •ses) pathology term

zo•opha•gous feeding on animals

zoo•phile

zo•philia fondness for animals

zo•phil•ic

zo•ophi•lism sexual attraction to animals

zo•ophi•lous pollinated by animals

zoo•pho•bia

zo•opho•bous

zoo•phyte

zoo•phyt•ic (*or* •phyti•cal)

zoo•plank•ton

zoo•plas•tic

zoo•plas•ty surgical transplantation

zoo•sperm

zoo•sper•mat•ic

zoo•spo•ran•gial

zoo•spo•ran•gium (*plural* •gia)

zoo•spore

zoo•spor•ic (*or* zo•os•por•ous)

zo•os•ter•ol biochemical compound

zoo•tech•nics

zoo•tom•ic (*or* •tomi•cal)

zoo•tomi•cal•ly

zo•oto•mist

zo•oto•my animal dissection

zoo•tox•ic

zoo•tox•in

zo•ril•la (*or* zo•rille) animal

Zo•ro•as•trian

Zo•ro•as•tri•an•ism

zos•ter shingles

Zou•ave French infantryman

zounds archaic exclamation

zoy•sia grass

zuc•chet•to (*plural* •tos) skullcap

zuc•chi•ni (*plural* •ni *or* •nis)

zug•zwang chess position

Zui•der Zee (*or* Zuy•)

Zulu (*plural* Zulus *or* Zulu)

Zu•lu•land

Zü•rich

Zwickau German city

zwie•back toasted rusk

Zwing•lian denoting religious movement

zwit•teri•on

zwit•teri•on•ic

zyg•apo•phys•eal (*or* •ial)

zyga•pophy•sis (*plural* •ses) part of vertebra

zy•go•dac•tyl ornithology term

zy•go•dac•tyl•ism

zy•go•dac•ty•lous

zy•go•ma (*plural* •ma•ta) bone

zy•go•mat•ic

zy•go•mor•phic (*or* •phous) botany term

zy•go•mor•phy (*or* •phism)

zy•go•phyl•la•ceous botany term

zy•go•phyte

zy•gose

zy•go•sis (*plural* •ses) biology term

zy•go•spore

zy•go•spor•ic

zy•gote fertilized egg cell

zy•go•tene stage of cell division

zy•got•ic

zy•goti•cal•ly

zy•mase enzyme

zy•mo•gen enzyme precursor

zy•mo•gen•esis

zy•mo•gen•ic

zy•mo•log•ic (*or* •logi•cal)

zy•molo•gist

zy•mol•ogy

zy•moly•sis fermentation

zy•mo•lyt•ic

zy•mom•eter

zy•mo•sis (*plural* •ses) disease

zy•mot•ic

zy•moti•cal•ly

zy•mur•gy branch of chemistry

Zyr•ian language

First Names

Aaron
Abbey (or Abbie, Abby)
Abe
Abel
Abigail
Abner
Abraham
Abram
Absalom
Ada
Adah
Adair
Adam
Adamina
Adamnan
Addie (or Addy)
Adela
Adelaide
Adele
Adelheid
Adelina
Adeline
Adlai
Adolf (or Adolph, Adolphe)
Adolphus
Adrian
Adriana
Adrianne (or Adrienne)
Aeneas
Afra
Agacia
Agatha
Aggie
Agnes
Agneta
Aidan
Aileen
Ailie
Ailis
Ailith
Ailsa
Aimee
Aine
Ainslie (or Ainsley)
Aisling
Aislinn
Aithne
Al
Alain
Alan (or Allan, Allen, Alun)
Alana (or Alanna)

Alaric
Alasdair (or Alastair) *variant spellings of* Alistair
Alban
Albany
Alberic
Albert
Alberta
Albertina
Albertine
Albin
Albina
Albinia
Albreda
Alda
Alden
Aldhelm
Aldis
Aldith
Aldo
Aldous (or Aldus)
Aldred
Aldreda
Aldwyn (or Aldwin)
Alec
Aled
Aledwen
Alethea
Alex
Alexa
Alexander
Alexandra
Alexandria
Alexandrina
Alexia
Alexis
Alf
Alfie
Alfonso *variant spelling of* Alphonso
Alfred
Alfreda
Algar
Alger
Algernon
Algie (or Algy)
Alice (or Alys)
Alicia
Alick
Alina
Aline

Alison (or Allison)
Alistair (or Alasdair, Alastair)
Alix
Allan *variant spelling of* Alan
Allegra
Allen *variant spelling of* Alan
Ally (or Allie)
Alma
Alonso (or Alonzo)
Aloysia (or Aloisia)
Aloysius
Alphonse
Alphonsine
Alphonso (or Alfonso)
Alphonsus
Althea
Alun *variant spelling of* Alan
Alured
Alva (or Alvah)
Alvar
Alvie
Alvin
Alvina
Alvis
Alwyn
Alys *variant spelling of* Alice
Amabel
Amalia
Amalie
Amanda
Amaryllis
Amata
Amber
Ambrose
Ambrosina
Ambrosine
Ambrosius
Amelia
Amias *variant spelling of* Amyas
Amice
Amicia
Aminta
Amos
Amy
Amyas (or Amias)
Anastasia
Ancel
André
Andrea

Andreas
Andrée
Andrew
Andy
Aneira
Aneurin (or Aneirin)
Angel
Angela
Angelica
Angelina
Angeline
Angelique
Angelo
Angharad
Angie
Angus
Anis (or Annis, Annice)
Anita
Ann *variant spelling of* Anne
Anna
Annabel (or Annabelle)
Annabella
Annalisa
Annaple
Anne (or Ann)
Anneliese
Annette
Annice *variant spelling of*
  Anis
Annie
Annika
Annis
Annora
Anona
Anouska
Ansel (or Ansell)
Anselm
Anselma
Anstey
Anstice
Anthea
Anthony (or Antony)
Antoine
Antoinette
Anton
Antonia
Antonina
Antonio
Antony *variant spelling of*
  Anthony
Anwen
Anya
Aphra
Apollonia
Appolina

Appoline
April
Aquila
Arabella
Araminta
Archelaus
Archer
Archibald
Archie (or Archy)
Ariadne
Ariane
Arianna
Arlene (or Arleen) *variant*
  spellings of Arline
Arletta
Arlette
Arline (or Arlene, Arleen)
Armand
Armin
Armina
Armine
Arnaud
Arnold
Art
Artemas (or Artemus)
Artemisia
Arthur
Arthuretta
Arthurina
Arthurine
Artie (or Arty)
Asa
Asher
Ashley
Aspasia
Astra
Astrid
Athelstan
Athene
Athol
Auberon
Aubert
Aubrey
Aud
Audra
Audrey
August
Augusta
Augustina
Augustine (or Augustin)
Augustus
Aulay
Aurea
Aurelia
Aurelian

Aureola
Aureole
Auriel
Auriol
Aurora
Aurore
Austen
Austin
Ava
Aveline
Averil
Avery
Avis (or Avice)
Avril
Axel
Aylmer
Aylwin
Azariah
Bab
Babette
Babs
Baldie
Baldwin
Balthasar (or Balthazar)
Barbara (or Barbra)
Barbary
Barbie
Barclay *variant spelling of*
  Berkeley
Bardolph
Barnabas
Barnaby
Barnard
Barnet
Barney
Baron (or Barron)
Barrett
Barrington
Barry (or Barrie)
Bart
Bartholomew
Bartle
Bartlett (or Bartlet)
Basie
Basil
Basilia
Basilie
Basilla
Bastian
Bathsheba
Baubie
Bea (or Bee)
Beata
Beatrice
Beatrix

Beattie (*or* Beatty)

Beau

Becky

Bedelia

Bedford

Bee *variant spelling of* Bea

Belinda

Bella

Belle (*or* Bell, Bel)

Ben

Benedict (*or* Benedick)

Benedicta

Benet *variant spelling of* Bennet

Benita

Benito

Benjamin

Benjy

Bennet (*or* Bennett, Benet)

Benny

Bentley

Berengaria

Berenger

Berenice

Berkeley (*or* Barclay)

Bernadette

Bernadina

Bernadine

Bernard

Bernardina

Bernardine

Bernhard

Bernice

Bernie (*or* Berny)

Berry

Bert

Berta

Bertha

Berthold

Bertie

Bertram

Bertrand

Beryl

Bess

Bessie (*or* Bessy)

Beta

Beth

Bethan

Bethany

Bethel (*or* Bethell)

Bethia

Betsy

Bette

Bettina

Bettrys

Betty

Beulah

Beverley (*or* Beverly)

Bevis

Bianca

Biddy

Bill

Billy (*or* Billie)

Bina

Bing

Birdie

Birgit

Birgitta

Bjorn

Blaine (*or* Blane)

Blair

Blaise (*or* Blase)

Blake

Blanche (*or* Blanch)

Blane *variant spelling of* Blaine

Blodwen

Blodyn

Blossom

Blythe

Boaz

Bob

Bobby (*or* Bobbie)

Bonamy

Bonar

Boniface

Bonita

Bonnie (*or* Bonny)

Boris

Botolph (*or* Botolf, Botulf)

Boyce

Boyd

Brad

Bradley

Bram

Brandon (*or* Brandan)

Branwen

Brenda

Brendan

Brent

Brett (*or* Bret)

Brian (*or* Bryan)

Brice *variant spelling of* Bryce

Bride

Bridget (*or* Brigit, Brigitte)

Bridie

Brighid (*or* Brigid)

Brigitta

Briony *variant spelling of* Bryony

Brita

Britannia

Britt

Brock

Broderick

Bronwen (*or* Bronwyn)

Bruce

Brunetta

Bruno

Bryan *variant spelling of* Brian

Bryce (*or* Brice)

Bryn

Bryony (*or* Briony)

Bud

Burt

Buster

Byron

Cadel (*or* Cadell)

Caesar

Cai

Caitlin

Caius

Caleb

Calum (*or* Callum)

Calvin

Cameron

Camilla

Camille

Camillus

Campbell

Candace

Candice

Candida

Candy

Canice

Cara (*or* Kara)

Caradoc (*or* Caradog)

Carey *variant spelling of* Cary

Carina (*or* Karina)

Carita

Carl (*or* Karl)

Carla

Carleen (*or* Carlene)

Carlo

Carlos

Carlotta

Carlton (*or* Carleton)

Carly

Carmel

Carmela

Carmelita

Carmen

Carol (*or* Carole)

Carola

Carolina
Caroline
Carolus
Carolyn
Carrie
Carter
Carthach
Carthage
Cary (or Carey)
Caryl
Carys
Casey
Casimir
Caspar
Cass
Cassandra
Cassie
Cath (or Kath)
Catherine (or Katherine, Katharine, Catharine)
Cathleen variant spelling of Kathleen
Cathy (or Kathy)
Catrin
Catriona
Cecil
Cecile
Cecilia
Cecily (or Cecilie)
Cedric (or Cedrych)
Ceinwen
Celeste
Celestina
Celestine
Celia
Celina variant spelling of Selina
Celine
Cerdic
Ceri
Ceridwen
Cerys
Chad
Charis
Charissa
Charity
Charlene
Charles
Charlie (or Charley)
Charlotte
Charlton
Charmaine
Charmian
Chas
Chattie

Chauncey (or Chauncy)
Chay
Cherie (or Sherry, Sherri)
Cherry
Cheryl
Chester
Chloe
Chris
Chrissie (or Chrissy)
Christabel
Christian
Christiana
Christiania
Christie (or Christy)
Christina (or Kristina)
Christine (or Kristine)
Christmas
Christopher
Christy variant spelling of Christie
Chrystal variant spelling of Crystal
Chuck
Cicely
Cilla
Cinderella
Cindy
Cis (or Ciss)
Cissy (or Cissie, Sissy, Sissie)
Claire (or Clare)
Clara
Clarence
Claribel
Clarice
Clarinda
Clarissa
Clark
Clarrie
Claud (or Claude)
Claudette
Claudia
Claudine
Claudius
Clayton
Cledwyn
Clem
Clemence
Clemency
Clement
Clementia
Clementina
Clementine
Cleo
Cleopatra

Cliff
Clifford
Clifton
Clint
Clinton
Clive
Clodagh
Clotilda
Clyde
Colette
Colin
Colina
Colleen
Colley
Colm
Colum
Columba
Columbina
Columbine
Conan
Concepta
Concetta
Conn
Connie
Connor (or Conor)
Conrad
Constance
Constancy
Constant
Constantia
Constantine
Cora
Coral
Coralie
Cordelia
Corinna
Corinne
Cormac
Cornelia
Cornelius
Corney
Cosimo
Cosmo
Courtney (or Courtenay)
Craig
Cressida
Crispian
Crispin
Crystal (or Chrystal)
Cuddy (or Cuddie)
Curt variant spelling of Kurt
Curtis
Cuthbert
Cy
Cynthia

Cyprian
Cyril
Cyrus
Cytherea
Daff *variant spelling of* Daph
Dafydd
Dagmar
Dai
Daisy
Dale
Damaris
Damian (*or* Damien)
Damon
Dan
Dana
Dane
Danette
Daniel
Daniella
Danielle
Danita
Danny
Dante
Danuta
Daph (*or* Daff)
Daphne
Darby (*or* Derby)
Darcy (*or* D'Arcy)
Darlene
Darren
Darryl (*or* Darrell, Daryl, Darrel)
Dave
David
Davida
Davina
Davinia
Davy
Dawn
Dean
Deanna
Deanne
Deb
Debbie
Deborah
Debra
Decima
Decimus
Declan
Dee
Deirdre
Del
Delia
Delilah
Della

Delphine
Delwyn (*or* Delwen)
Delyth
Demelza
Denholm
Denise
Dennie (*or* Denny)
Dennis (*or* Denis, Denys)
Denzil
Derby *variant spelling of* Darby
Derek (*or* Derrick, Deryck, Deryk)
Dermot
Derry
Deryn
Des
Desdemona
Desiree
Desmond
Dewi
Dexter
Diamond
Diana
Diane (*or* Dianne)
Diarmuid (*or* Diarmait)
Dick
Dickie (*or* Dicky)
Dickon
Digby
Diggory
Dillon
Dilys
Dinah
Dion
Dione (*or* Dionne)
Dionysia
Dionysius
Dirk
Dodie
Doll
Dolly
Dolores
Dominic (*or* Dominick)
Dominica
Dominique
Don
Donal
Donald
Donalda
Donaldina
Donna
Donny
Donovan
Dora

Doran
Dorcas
Doreen
Dorette
Doria
Dorian
Dorinda
Doris (*or* Dorice)
Dorita
Dorothea
Dorothy
Dorrie
Dot
Dottie
Doug
Dougal
Dougie (*or* Duggie)
Douglas
Dowsabel
Dreda
Drew
Drogo
Drusilla
Duane (*or* Dwayne)
Dudley
Dugald
Duggie *variant spelling of* Dougie
Duke
Dulce
Dulcibella
Dulcie
Duncan
Dunstan
Durand
Dustin
Dwayne *variant spelling of* Duane
Dwight
Dylan
Dymphna
Dympna
Eamon (*or* Eamonn)
Earl (*or* Erle)
Earnest *variant spelling of* Ernest
Eartha
Easter
Eben
Ebenezer
Ed
Eda
Eddie (*or* Eddy)
Eden
Edgar

Edie
Edith
Edmund (or Edmond)
Edna
Edom
Edward
Edwin (or Edwyn)
Edwina
Effie
Egbert
Egidia
Egidius
Eileen
Eiluned variant spelling of
    Eluned
Eilwen
Eily
Eira
Eirian
Eithne
Elain
Elaine
Eldon
Eldred
Eldreda
Eleanor (or Elinor)
Eleanora
Eleazar
Elena
Eleonora
Elfreda (or Elfrida)
Eli
Elias
Elihu
Elijah
Elined variant spelling of
    Eluned
Elinor variant spelling of
    Eleanor
Eliot variant spelling of
    Elliott
Elisabeth variant spelling of
    Elizabeth
Elise
Elisha
Elissa
Eliza
Elizabeth (or Elisabeth)
Elkanah
Ella
Ellen
Ellery
Ellie
Elliott (or Elliot, Eliot)
Ellis

Elma
Elmer
Eloisa
Eloise
Elroy
Elsa
Elsie
Elspeth
Elspie
Elton
Eluned (or Elined, Eiluned)
Elvie
Elvin
Elvina
Elvira
Elvis
Elwyn
Emanuel (or Emmanuel)
Emanuela (or Emmanuela)
Emblem
Emblyn
Emeline variant spelling of
    Emmeline
Emelyn
Emerald
Emery
Emil (or Emile)
Emilia
Emily
Emlyn
Emma
Emmanuel variant spelling of
    Emanuel
Emmanuela variant spelling
    of Emanuela
Emmeline (or Emeline)
Emmie
Emrys
Ena
Enid
Enoch
Enos
Eoghan
Ephraim
Eppie
Erasmus
Eric (or Erik)
Erica (or Erika)
Erin
Erle variant spelling of Earl
Ermintrude (or
    Ermyntrude)
Ernest (or Earnest)
Ernestine
Ernie

Errol
Erwin variant spelling of
    Irwin
Esau
Esme (or Esmee)
Esmeralda
Esmond
Essie
Estella
Estelle
Esther
Ethan
Ethel
Ethelbert
Etheldreda
Ethelinda
Ethelred
Ethne
Etta
Ettie (or Etty)
Eugene
Eugenia
Eugenie
Eulalia
Eulalie
Eunice
Euphemia
Eustace
Eustacia
Eva
Evadne
Evan
Evangelina
Evangeline
Eve
Eveleen
Evelina
Eveline
Evelyn
Everard
Everild
Evie
Evita
Evonne variant spelling of
    Yvonne
Ewan (or Ewen)
Ezekiel
Ezra
Fabian
Fabiana
Faith
Fanny
Farquhar
Farran (or Farren, Faron)
Faustina

Fay (*or* Faye)
Feargus *variant spelling of*
   Fergus
Fedora
Felice
Felicia
Felicity
Felix
Fenella
Feodora
Ferdinand
Fergie
Fergus (*or* Feargus)
Fern
Fernando
Fidel
Fidelia
Fifi
Finlay
Finola
Fiona
Fionnuala (*or* Fionnghuala)
Fitzroy
Flavia
Fletcher
Fleur
Flora
Florence
Floretta
Florette
Florian
Florinda
Florrie
Floss
Flossie
Flower
Floy
Floyd
Fluellen
Flurry
Fortunatus
Fortune
Foster
Franca
Frances (*fem*)
Francesca
Francesco
Francie
Francine
Francis (*masc*)
Francisca
Francisco
Franco
Frank
Frankie

Franklin
Frannie (*or* Franny)
Fraser (*or* Frazer)
Fred
Freda
Freddie (*or* Freddy)
Frederica (*or* Frederika,
   Fredrica, Fredrika)
Frederick (*or* Frederic,
   Fredrick, Fredric)
Freya
Frieda
Fulbert
Gabby (*or* Gabbie, Gabi,
   Gaby)
Gabriel
Gabriella
Gabrielle
Gaenor *variant spelling of*
   Gaynor
Gail (*or* Gayle, Gale)
Gaius
Gamaliel
Gareth
Garfield
Garnet
Garret (*or* Garrett)
Garrick
Garth
Gary (*or* Garry)
Gaspar
Gavin
Gawain
Gay (*or* Gaye)
Gayle *variant spelling of* Gail
Gaylord
Gaynor (*or* Gaenor)
Gemma (*or* Jemma)
Gene
Genevieve
Genevra *variant spelling of*
   Ginevra
Geoff (*or* Jeff)
Geoffrey (*or* Jeffrey, Jeffery)
Geordie
George
Georgette
Georgia
Georgiana
Georgie
Georgina
Geraint
Gerald
Geraldine
Gerard (*or* Gerrard)

Gerda
Germaine (*or* Germain)
Gerontius
Gerry (*or* Jerry)
Gershom
Gert
Gertie
Gertrude
Gervase (*or* Gervais)
Gerwyn
Gethin
Ghislaine
Gideon
Gil
Gilbert
Gilberta
Gilbertine
Gilda
Giles (*or* Gyles)
Gill (*or* Jill)
Gillian (*or* Jillian, Gillean)
Gilroy
Gina
Ginette
Ginevra (*or* Genevra)
Ginger
Ginny
Gisela
Giselle
Glad
Gladys
Glen (*or* Glenn)
Glenda
Glenna
Glenys (*or* Glenis)
Gloria
Glyn
Glynis (*or* Glinys)
Godfrey
Godwin
Goldie
Goldwin (*or* Goldwyn)
Gordon
Grace
Gracie
Graham (*or* Graeme,
   Grahame)
Grainne
Grania
Grant
Granville
Greg (*or* Gregg)
Gregor
Gregory
Grenville

Greta
Gretchen
Gretel
Griffith
Griselda
Grizel (or Grizzel)
Grover
Guendolen variant spelling of Gwendoline
Guido
Guinevere
Gulielma
Gunter (or Gunther)
Gus
Gussie
Gusta
Gustave (or Gustav, Gustaf)
Gustavus
Guy
Gwen
Gwenda
Gwendoline (or Gwendolyn, Gwendolen, Guendolen)
Gwenllian
Gwilym (or Gwylim)
Gwladys
Gwyn
Gwyneth (or Gwynneth, Gwynedd)
Gwynfor
Gyles variant spelling of Giles
Hadassah
Hadrian
Hagar
Haidee
Hal
Halcyon
Ham
Hamilton
Hamish
Hamlet
Hamlyn
Hammond
Hamnet
Hamo
Hamon
Hank
Hannah
Hannibal
Hans
Hardy
Harley
Harold
Harriet (or Harriette)

Harriot
Harrison
Harry
Hartley
Harvey
Hattie (or Hatty)
Haydn (or Haydon, Hayden)
Hayley
Hazel
Heath
Heather
Hebe
Heber
Hector
Hedda
Hedley
Hedwig
Hedy
Heidi
Helen
Helena
Helene
Helewise
Helga
Héloïse
Hennie (or Henny)
Henri
Henrietta
Henriette
Henry
Hephzibah
Hepsie (or Hepsey, Hepsy)
Hepzibah
Herb
Herbert
Herbie
Hereward
Herman (or Hermann)
Hermia
Hermione
Hervé
Hervey
Hester
Hetty
Heulwen
Hew variant spelling of Hugh
Hezekiah
Hieronymus
Hilary (or Hillary)
Hilda (or Hylda)
Hildebrand
Hildegard (or Hildegarde)
Hillary variant spelling of Hilary

Hippolyta
Hippolytus
Hiram
Hob
Hobart
Holden
Holly
Homer
Honor (or Honour)
Honora
Honoria
Hope
Horace
Horatia
Horatio
Horry
Hortense
Hortensia
Howard
Howell (or Howel) variant spellings of Hywel
Hubert
Hugh (or Huw, Hew)
Hughie (or Huey)
Hugo
Huldah, Hulda
Humbert
Humph
Humphrey
Huw variant spelling of Hugh
Hyacinth
Hyacintha
Hylda variant spelling of Hilda
Hyman
Hymie
Hypatia
Hywel (or Howell, Howel)
Iago
Ian (or Iain)
Ianthe
Ibbie (or Ibby)
Ichabod
Ida
Idonea
Idris
Ifor
Ignatius
Igor
Ike
Ilma
Ilona
Ilse
Immy
Imogen

Ina
Inez
Inga
Inge
Ingeborg
Ingram
Ingrid
Ingvar
Inigo
Iola
Iolanthe
Iolo
Iona
Iorwerth
Ira
Irene
Iris
Irma
Irvin (*or* Irvine)
Irving
Irwin (*or* Erwin)
Isa
Isaac (*or* Izaak)
Isabel (*or* Isabelle)
Isabella
Isadora
Isaiah
Iseult
Ishbel
Isidora
Isidore
Isla
Ismay
Isobel
Isolda
Isolde
Israel
Issy (*or* Izzy)
Ita
Ithel
Ivah
Ivan
Ives
Ivo
Ivor
Ivy
Izaak *variant spelling of* Isaac
Izzy *variant spelling of* Issy
Jabez
Jacinta
Jacinth
Jack
Jackie (*or* Jacky, Jacqui)
Jacob
Jacoba

Jacobina
Jacqueline (*or* Jacquelyn)
Jacques
Jacquetta
Jacqui *variant spelling of*
    Jackie
Jade
Jael
Jago
Jake
James
Jamesina
Jamie
Jan
Jane (*or* Jayne)
Janet
Janetta
Janette
Janice (*or* Janis)
Janie (*or* Janey)
Janine
Japheth
Jarrod (*or* Jarred, Jared)
Jarvis
Jasmine
Jason
Jasper
Jay
Jayne *variant spelling of* Jane
Jean
Jeanette (*or* Jeannette)
Jeanne
Jeannie (*or* Jeanie)
Jeannine
Jed
Jedidiah
Jeff *variant spelling of* Geoff
Jefferson
Jeffrey (*or* Jeffery) *variant*
    spellings of Geoffrey
Jehane
Jem
Jemima
Jemma *variant spelling of*
    Gemma
Jemmy
Jenna
Jennifer (*or* Jenifer)
Jenny (*or* Jennie)
Jephthah
Jeremiah
Jeremias
Jeremy
Jermaine
Jerome

Jerry *variant spelling of* Gerry
Jess
Jessamine (*or* Jessamyn)
Jesse
Jessica
Jessie
Jesus
Jethro
Jewel
Jill *variant spelling of* Gill
Jillian *variant spelling of*
    Gillian
Jim
Jimmy
Jinny
Jo
Joachim
Joan
Joanna
Joanne
Job
Jocasta
Jocelyn (*or* Joscelin)
Jock
Jodie (*or* Jodi, Jody)
Joe
Joel
Joey
Johanna
Johannes
John (*or* Jon)
Johnny (*or* Johnnie)
Jolene (*or* Joleen)
Jolyon
Jonah
Jonas
Jonathan
Jonquil
Jordan
Joscelin *variant spelling of*
    Jocelyn
José
Joseph
Josepha
Josephine
Josette
Josh
Joshua
Josiah
Josias
Josie
Joss
Jotham
Joy
Joyce

Juan
Juanita
Judah
Judas
Judd
Jude
Judith
Judoc
Judy (or Judi)
Jules
Julia
Julian
Juliana
Julianne
Julie
Julienne
Juliet (or Juliette)
Julitta
Julius
June
Junior
Juno
Justin
Justina
Justine
Kane
Kara *variant spelling of* Cara
Karel
Karen
Karin
Karina *variant spelling of* Carina
Karl *variant spelling of* Carl
Karol
Kate
Kath *variant spelling of* Cath
Katherine (or Katharine) *variant spellings of* Catherine
Kathleen (or Cathleen)
Kathryn
Kathy *variant spelling of* Cathy
Katie (or Katy)
Katrina
Katrine
Kay
Keeley
Keir
Keith
Kelda
Kelly (or Kellie)
Kelvin
Ken
Kendal (or Kendall)

Kendra
Kenelm
Kenneth
Kenny
Kenrick
Kent
Kentigern
Kenton
Keren
Kerenhappuch
Kerry (or Kerrie, Kerri, Keri)
Kester
Keturah
Kevin
Keziah (or Kezia)
Kieran
Kim
Kimball
Kimberly (or Kimberley)
Kinborough
King
Kingsley
Kirby
Kirk
Kirsten
Kirsty
Kit
Kitty
Kris
Kristen (or Kristin)
Kristina *variant spelling of* Christina
Kristine *variant spelling of* Christine
Kurt (or Curt)
Kyle
Kylie
Laban
Lachlan
Laetitia (or Letitia)
Lalage
Lambert
Lana
Lance
Lancelot
Lanty
Laraine (or Larraine)
Larissa
Larry
Lars
Launce
Launcelot
Laura (or Lora)
Lauraine
Laureen (or Loreen)

Laurel
Lauren
Laurence (or Lawrence)
Laurencia (or Laurentia)
Lauretta *variant spelling of* Loretta
Laurette (or Lorette)
Laurie (or Lauri, Lori)
Laurina
Laurinda *variant spelling of* Lorinda
Laverne
Lavina (or Lavena)
Lavinia
Lawrence *variant spelling of* Laurence
Lawrie
Layton *variant spelling of* Leighton
Lazarus
Leah
Leander
Leanne (or Lianne)
Lee (or Leigh)
Leighton (or Layton)
Leila (or Leilah, Lela)
Lelia
Lemmy
Lemuel
Lena
Lennox
Lenny (or Lennie)
Lenore
Leo
Leofric
Leoline
Leon
Leona
Leonard
Leonie
Leonora
Leopold
Leroy
Lesley (*fem*)
Leslie (*masc or fem*)
Lester
Leta
Letitia (or Laetitia)
Lettice
Letty (or Lettie)
Levi
Lew
Lewis
Liam
Liana

Lianne *variant spelling of*
  Leanne
Libby
Liddy
Liesl (*or* Liesel)
Lila
Lilac
Lili
Lilian (*or* Lillian)
Lilias (*or* Lillias)
Lilith
Lilla (*or* Lillah)
Lily (*or* Lillie)
Lina
Lincoln
Linda (*or* Lynda)
Lindsay (*masc or fem*)
Lindsey (*fem*)
Lindy
Linette *variant spelling of*
  Lynette
Linnet
Lionel
Lisa
Lisbeth *variant spelling of*
  Lizbeth
Lise
Lisette
Lita
Liz
Liza
Lizanne
Lizbeth (*or* Lisbeth)
Lizzie (*or* Lizzy)
Llewellyn (*or* Llewelyn)
Llinos
Lloyd
Lois
Lola
Lolita
Lolly
Lonnie
Lora *variant spelling of* Laura
Loraine *variant spelling of*
  Lorraine
Loreen *variant spelling of*
  Laureen
Loren (*or* Lorin)
Lorenzo
Loretta (*or* Lauretta)
Lorette *variant spelling of*
  Laurette
Lori *variant spelling of* Laurie
Lorin
Lorinda (*or* Laurinda)

Lorna
Lorne (*or* Lorn)
Lorraine (*or* Loraine)
Lottie (*or* Lotty)
Lou
Louella (*or* Luella)
Louie
Louis
Louisa
Louise
Loveday
Lovell
Lowell
Lucas
Lucasta
Luce
Lucetta
Lucette
Lucia
Lucian (*or* Lucien)
Luciana
Lucie
Lucienne
Lucilla
Lucille
Lucina
Lucinda
Lucius
Lucky
Lucrece
Lucretia
Lucrezia
Lucy
Ludo
Ludovic
Luella *variant spelling of*
  Louella
Luke
Lulu
Luther
Lydia
Lyle
Lyn *variant spelling of* Lynn
Lynda *variant spelling of*
  Linda
Lyndon
Lynette (*or* Lynnette,
  Linette)
Lynn (*or* Lynne, Lyn)
Lynsey
Lyra
Lyulf (*or* Lyulph)
Mabel (*or* Mable)
Mabella
Mabelle

Maddie (*or* Maddy)
Madeleine (*or* Madeline)
Madelina
Madge
Madoc
Madonna
Mae
Maeve (*or* Meave)
Magda
Magdalena
Magdalene (*or* Magdalen)
Maggie
Magnolia
Magnus
Mahala (*or* Mahalah)
Mahalia
Maidie
Mair
Maire
Mairin
Maisie
Malachi (*or* Malachy)
Malcolm
Malise
Mallory (*or* Malory)
Malvin
Malvina
Mamie
Manasseh
Manasses
Mandy
Manfred
Manley
Manny
Mansel (*or* Mansell)
Manuel
Manuela
Manus
Mara (*or* Marah)
Marc
Marcel
Marcella
Marcelle
Marcellus
Marcia
Marcie (*or* Marcy)
Marco
Marcus
Margaret
Margareta (*or* Margaretta)
Margarita (*or* Marguerita)
Marge
Margery *variant spelling of*
  Marjorie
Margie

Margot (or Margo)
Marguerite
Maria
Mariabella
Mariam (or Mariamne)
Marian variant spelling of
 Marion
Marianne
Marie
Mariel
Marietta (or Mariette)
Marigold
Marilyn
Marina
Mario
Marion (or Marian)
Marisa (or Marissa)
Marita
Marius
Marjorie (or Margery)
Mark
Marla
Marlene
Marlin (or Marlyn)
Marmaduke
Marnie (or Marni)
Marsha
Marshall (or Marshal)
Marta
Martha
Marti (or Martie)
Martin (or Martyn)
Martina
Martine
Marty
Marvin (or Marvyn)
Mary
Matilda
Matt (or Mat)
Matthew
Matthias
Mattie (or Matty)
Maud (or Maude)
Maudie
Maura variant spelling of
 Moira
Maureen
Maurice (or Morris)
Mavis
Max
Maximilian
Maxine
Maxwell
May
Maynard

Meave variant spelling of
 Maeve
Meg
Megan (or Meghan)
Meggie (or Meggy)
Mehala (or Mehalah,
 Mehalia)
Mehetabel (or Mehitabel)
Meirion (or Merrion)
Mel
Melania
Melanie (or Melloney)
Melba
Melicent (or Melisent)
Melinda
Meliora
Mélisande
Melissa
Melody (or Melodie)
Melva
Melville
Melvin (or Melvyn)
Melvina
Mercedes
Mercia
Mercy
Meredith
Meriel
Merilyn (or Merrilyn)
Merle
Merlin
Merrion variant spelling of
 Meirion
Merry
Merton
Merv
Mervyn (or Mervin)
Meryl
Meta
Mia
Micah
Michael
Michaela
Michelle (or Michele)
Mick
Mickey (or Micky)
Mignon
Mike
Milborough
Milburn
Mildred
Miles (or Myles)
Millicent
Millie (or Milly)
Milo

Milton
Mima
Mimi
Mina
Minerva
Minna
Minnie
Minty
Mira variant spelling of Myra
Mirabel (or Mirabelle)
Mirabella
Miranda
Miriam
Mitch
Mitchell
Mitzi
Modesty
Moira (or Moyra, Maura)
Moll
Molly
Mona
Monica
Monique
Montague (or Montagu)
Montgomery
Monty (or Monte)
Morag
Moray
Mordecai
Morgan
Morna
Morris variant spelling of
 Maurice
Mort
Mortimer
Morty
Morwenna
Moses
Moshe
Moss
Moyna
Moyra variant spelling of
 Moira
Muir
Mungo
Murdoch
Muriel
Murray
Murtagh
Myfanwy
Myles variant spelling of
 Miles
Myra (or Mira)
Myrna
Myron

Myrtilla
Myrtle
Mysie
Nada
Nadia
Nadine
Nahum
Nan
Nance
Nancy
Nanette
Nanny
Naomi
Napoleon
Narcissus
Nat
Natalia
Natalie
Natasha
Nathan
Nathaniel (*or* Nathanael)
Neal *variant spelling of* Neil
Ned
Neddie (*or* Neddy)
Nehemiah
Neil (*or* Neill, Neal, Niall)
Nell
Nellie (*or* Nelly)
Nelson
Nerina
Nerissa
Nerys
Nessa
Nessie
Nest
Nesta
Netta
Nettie
Neva
Neville (*or* Nevil)
Newton
Niall *variant spelling of* Neil
Nichola *variant spelling of* Nicola
Nicholas (*or* Nicolas)
Nick
Nicky (*or* Nikki)
Nicodemus
Nicol
Nicola (*or* Nichola)
Nicolas *variant spelling of* Nicholas
Nicole
Nicolette
Nigel

Nikki *variant spelling of* Nicky
Nina
Ninette
Ninian
Nita
Noah
Noel (*or* Nowell)
Noeleen (*or* Noeline)
Noelle (*or* Noele)
Nola
Nolan
Nona
Nora (*or* Norah)
Noreen
Norm
Norma
Norman
Norris
Norton
Nova
Nowell *variant spelling of* Noel
Nuala
Nye
Nyree
Obadiah
Oberon
Octavia
Octavian
Octavius
Odette
Odile
Odilia
Odo
Ogden
Olaf
Olave (*or* Olav)
Olga
Oliff
Oliva
Olive
Oliver
Olivet
Olivia
Olivier
Ollie
Olwen (*or* Olwyn)
Olympia
Omar
Ona
Onuphrius
Oonagh (*or* Oona)
Opal

Ophelia
Oriana
Oriel
Orlando
Orrell
Orson
Orval
Orville
Osbert
Osborn (*or* Osborne)
Oscar
Osmond (*or* Osmund)
Ossy (*or* Ossie)
Oswald
Oswin
Otho
Otis
Ottilia
Ottilie
Otto
Owen (*or* Owain)
Owena
Ozzy (*or* Ozzie)
Pablo
Paddy
Padraig
Palmer
Pam
Pamela
Pamelia
Pandora
Pansy
Paolo
Parker
Parnel (*or* Parnell)
Parry
Parthenia
Pascal
Pascale
Pascoe
Pat
Patience
Patricia
Patrick
Patsy
Patti (*or* Patty, Pattie)
Paul
Paula
Paulette
Pauline
Peace
Pearl
Pearlie
Pedro
Peg

Peggy
Pelham
Penelope
Penny
Pepin
Pepita
Perce
Percival (*or* Perceval)
Percy
Perdita
Peregrine
Peronel
Perpetua
Perry
Peta
Pete
Peter
Petra
Petrina
Petronella
Petronilla
Petula
Phebe *variant spelling of*
  Phoebe
Phemie
Phil
Philadelphia
Philemon
Philibert
Philip (*or* Phillip)
Philippa (*or* Phillipa,
  Phillippa)
Phillida *variant spelling of*
  Phyllida
Phillis *variant spelling of*
  Phyllis
Philomena
Phineas (*or* Phinehas)
Phoebe (*or* Phebe)
Phyllida (*or* Phillida)
Phyllis (*or* Phillis)
Pia
Pierre
Piers
Pip
Pippa
Piran
Pleasance
Poldie
Poll
Polly
Pollyanna
Poppy
Portia
Preston

Primrose
Prince
Prisca
Priscilla
Prissy
Pru (*or* Prue)
Prudence
Prunella
Queena
Queenie (*or* Queeny)
Quentin (*or* Quintin)
Quincy
Quinn
Quintin *variant spelling of*
  Quentin
Rab
Rabbie
Rachel (*or* Rachael)
Radcliff (*or* Radcliffe)
Rae
Raelene
Rafael *variant spelling of*
  Raphael
Rafaela *variant spelling of*
  Raphaela
Rafe
Raina
Raine
Rainer *variant spelling of*
  Rayner
Ralph
Ramon
Ramona
Ramsay (*or* Ramsey)
Ranald
Randall (*or* Randal)
Randolph
Randy
Raoul
Raphael (*or* Rafael)
Raphaela (*or* Rafaela)
Ray
Raymond (*or* Raymund)
Raymonde
Rayner (*or* Raynor, Rainer)
Rebecca (*or* Rebekah)
Redvers
Reg
Reggie
Regina
Reginald
Reine
Rena (*or* Rina)
Renata
René (*masc*)

Renée (*fem*)
Renie (*or* Rene)
Reuben
Rex
Reynard
Reynold
Rhea (*or* Ria)
Rhiannon
Rhoda
Rhona
Rhonda
Rhonwen
Rhys
Ria *variant spelling of* Rhea
Rica (*or* Rika)
Ricarda
Ricardo
Rich
Richard
Richenda
Richie
Richmal
Rick
Ricky (*or* Ricki, Rikki)
Rika *variant spelling of* Rica
Rina *variant spelling of* Rena
Rita
Roald
Rob
Robbie
Robert
Roberta
Robin
Robina
Robyn
Rochelle
Rod
Roddy
Roderick
Rodge
Rodger *variant spelling of*
  Roger
Rodney
Rodolph
Rodrigo
Roger (*or* Rodger)
Roisin
Roland (*or* Rowland)
Rolf (*or* Rolph)
Rollo
Rolly
Rolph *variant spelling of* Rolf
Roly
Roma
Romaine

Ron
Rona
Ronald
Ronalda
Ronna
Ronnette
Ronnie
Rory
Ros
Rosa
Rosabel (or Rosabelle)
Rosabella
Rosaleen
Rosalia
Rosalie
Rosalind
Rosalinda
Rosaline (or Rosalyn)
Rosamund (or Rosamond)
Rosanna (or Roseanna)
Rosanne (or Roseann, Roseanne)
Rose
Roseline (or Roselyn)
Rosemary (or Rosemarie)
Rosetta
Rosie
Rosina
Rosita
Roslyn (or Rosslyn)
Ross
Rowan
Rowena
Rowland variant spelling of Roland
Roxana
Roxane (or Roxanne)
Roxanna
Roxy
Roy
Royal
Royston
Rubina
Ruby
Rudolph (or Rudolf)
Rudy (or Rudi)
Rufus
Rupert
Ruperta
Russ
Russell (or Russel)
Ruth
Ruthie
Ryan
Sabina

Sabrina
Sacha
Sacheverell
Sadie
Saffron
Sal
Salamon
Salena (or Salina)
Sally
Salome
Salvador
Salvatore
Sam
Samantha
Sammy
Samson (or Sampson)
Samuel
Sanchia
Sandra
Sandy (or Sandie)
Sapphira
Sapphire
Sarah (or Sara, Sarra)
Sarai
Saranna
Sarina
Sarita
Sarra variant spelling of Sarah
Saul
Saxon
Scarlett (or Scarlet)
Scott
Seamus (or Shamus)
Sean (or Shaun, Shawn)
Seb
Sebastian
Sefton
Selby
Selina (or Selena, Celina)
Selma
Selwyn
Senga
Septima
Septimus
Seraphina
Serena
Serge
Sergei
Sergio
Sergius
Seth
Seumas
Seward
Sextus
Seymour

Shamus variant spelling of Seamus
Shane
Shani
Shannon
Shari
Sharon (or Sharron)
Shaun variant spelling of Sean
Shauna
Shaw
Shawn variant spelling of Sean
Sheba
Sheena (or Shena)
Sheila (or Shelagh, Sheelagh, Sheilah)
Sheldon
Shelley (or Shelly)
Shem
Shena variant spelling of Sheena
Sheridan
Sherry (or Sherri) variant spellings of Cherie
Sheryl
Shirl
Shirley
Sholto
Shona
Shushana (or Shushanna)
Sian
Sibbie (or Sibby)
Sibella
Sibilla
Sibyl
Sibylla
Sid (or Syd)
Sidney (or Sydney)
Sidonia
Sidony (or Sidonie)
Siegfried
Sigismund
Sigmund
Silas
Síle
Silvana
Silvanus (or Sylvanus)
Silvester
Silvia
Sim
Simeon
Simon
Simona
Simone

Sinclair
Sìne
Sinead
Siobhan
Sisley
Sissy (or Sissie) variant
  spellings of Cissy
Solly
Solomon
Sonia (or Sonya, Sonja)
Sophia
Sophie (or Sophy)
Sophronia
Sorcha
Spencer
Stacey (or Stacy)
Stafford
Stan
Stanford
Stanislas (or Stanislaus)
Stanley
Steenie
Stella
Stephanie (or Stefanie)
Stephen (or Steven)
Steve
Stevie
Stewart variant spelling of
  Stuart
Stirling
St John
Stuart (or Stewart)
Sue
Sukey
Susan
Susannah (or Susanna,
  Suzanna)
Susie (or Suzy)
Suzanne (or Susanne)
Suzette
Suzy
Swithin
Sybella
Sybil (or Sibyl)
Sybilla
Syd variant spelling of Sid
Sydney variant spelling of
  Sidney
Sylvanus variant spelling of
  Silvanus
Sylvester (or Silvester)
Sylvia (or Silvia)
Sylvie
Tabitha
Tacey (or Tacy)

Taffy
Talbot
Taliesin
Talitha
Tallulah
Tam
Tamar
Tamara
Tamasine
Tammy
Tamsin
Tancred
Tania variant spelling of
  Tanya
Tanith
Tansy
Tanya (or Tania)
Tara
Tarquin
Tatiana
Taylor
Ted
Teddy (or Teddie)
Tegan
Tegwen
Temperance
Terence (or Terrence)
Teresa (or Theresa)
Terry (or Terri)
Tertius
Tess
Tessa
Tessie
Tetty
Tex
Thaddeus
Thea
Thekla (or Thecla)
Thelma
Theo
Theobald
Theodora
Theodore
Theodoric
Theodosia
Theophania
Theophila
Theophilus
Theresa variant spelling of
  Teresa
Thérèse
Theresia
Thirza (or Thirsa)
Thom
Thomas

Thomasin
Thomasina
Thomasine
Thora
Thorley
Thornton
Thurstan (or Thurston)
Thyra
Tibby
Tiffany
Tilda
Tilly
Tim
Timmy
Timothea
Timothy
Tina
Tirzah
Tisha
Titus
Tobias
Toby
Todd
Tolly
Tom
Tommy
Toni
Tonia (or Tonya)
Tony
Topsy
Torquil
Totty
Tracy (or Tracey)
Travers
Travis
Trevor (or Trefor)
Tricia (or Trisha)
Trina
Trissie
Tristan
Tristram
Trix
Trixie
Troy
Trudy (or Trudie,
  Trudi)
Tryphena
Tudor
Turlough
Tybalt
Tyra
Tyrone
Ulric
Ulrica
Ulysses

Una
Unity
Upton
Urban
Uriah
Ursula
Val
Valda
Valentina
Valentine
Valeria
Valerie
Vanda
Vanessa
Vashti
Vaughan (*or* Vaughn)
Velda
Velma
Venetia
Venus
Vera
Vere
Verena
Verity
Verna
Vernon
Verona
Veronica
Véronique
Vic (*or* Vick)
Vicky (*or* Vicki, Vickie, Vikki)
Victor
Victoria
Victorine
Vida
Vilma
Vin
Vina
Vince
Vincent
Vincentia
Vinnie (*or* Vinny)
Vinny
Viola
Violet
Violetta
Violette

Virgil
Virginia
Vita
Vitus
Viv
Viva
Vivia
Vivian (*or* Vivien, Vyvyan)
Viviana
Vivienne
Wade
Wal
Walburga
Waldo
Wallace (*or* Wallis)
Wally
Walt
Walter
Wanda
Ward
Warner
Warren
Warwick
Washington
Wat
Wayne
Wenda
Wendell
Wendy
Wesley
Wilbert
Wilbur
Wilf
Wilfred (*or* Wilfrid)
Wilfrida (*or* Wilfreda)
Wilhelmina
Will
Willa
Willard
William
Williamina
Willie (*or* Willy)
Willis
Willoughby
Wilma
Wilmer
Wilmot

Win
Windsor
Winfred (*or* Winfrid)
Winifred (*or* Winnifred, Winefred)
Winnie
Winston
Winthrop
Woodrow
Wyatt
Wybert
Wyndham
Wynford
Wynn (*or* Wynne)
Wystan
Xanthe
Xavier
Xenia
Yasmin
Yehudi
Yolanda
Yolande
Yves
Yvette
Yvonne (*or* Evonne)
Zacchaeus
Zachariah
Zacharias
Zachary
Zak (*or* Zack)
Zana
Zandra
Zane
Zara
Zechariah
Zedekiah
Zelda
Zelma
Zena
Zenobia
Zephaniah
Zillah
Zinnia
Zita
Zoë (*or* Zoe)
Zola
Zora (*or* Zorah)
Zuleika

Biographical Names

Aalto, Alvar
Aaltonen, Wäinö
Abbado, Claudio
Abbas
Abbas, Ferhat
Abd Allah (*known as* the
  Khalifa)
'Abd al-Malik ibn Marwan
'Abd ar-Rahman III
  an-Nasir
Abdelkader
Abdulhamid
Abdullah
Abdul Rahman, Tunku
Abel, Sir Frederick
  Augustus
Abel, Niels Henrik
Abelard, Peter
Abercrombie, Sir (Leslie)
  Patrick
Abercromby, Sir Ralph
Aberdeen, George
  Hamilton-Gordon, 4th
  Earl of
Absalom son of King David
Absalon 12th-century
  Danish statesman
Abu al-Wafa
Abu Bakar sultan of Johore
Abu Bakr first caliph
Abu Hanifah
Abu Nuwas
Accius, Lucius
Accoramboni, Vittoria
Achard, Franz Karl
Achebe, Chinua
Acheson, Dean
  (Gooderham)
Acton, John Emerich
  Edward Dalberg-Acton,
  1st Baron
Adalbert
Adam, Adolphe-Charles
Adam, James
Adam, Robert
Adam, William
Adamnan, St
Adamov, Arthur
Adams, Charles Francis
Adams, Gerry
Adams, Henry

Adams, John
Adams, John Couch
Adams, John Quincy
Adams, Richard
Adams, Samuel
Adamson, Robert
Addington, Henry, 1st
  Viscount Sidmouth
Addinsell, Richard
Addison, Joseph
Addison, Thomas
Adenauer, Konrad
Ader, Clément
Adler, Alfred
Adler, Felix
Adler, Larry
Adrian, Edgar Douglas, 1st
  Baron
Aelfric
Aeneas Silvius
Aeschines
Aeschylus
Aesop
Aetius, Flavius
Afghani, Jamal ad-Din al-
Aga Khan
Agassiz, Alexander
Agassiz, Jean Louis
  Rodolphe
Agathocles
Agee, James
Agesilaus
Agha Mohammad Khan
Agnesi, Maria Gaetana
Agnew, Spiro T(heodore)
Agnon, Shmuel Yosef
Agostini, Giacomo
Agricola, Georgius
Agricola, Gnaeus Julius
Agricola, Johann
Agrippa, Marcus
  Vipsanius
Agrippina
Ahad Ha'am
Ahern, Bertie
Ahmad Khan, Sir Sayyid
Ahmad Shah Durrani
Ahmed
Ahmose
Aiken, Howard Hathaway
Ailred of Rievaulx, St

Ainsworth, W(illiam)
  Harrison
Airy, Sir George Biddell
Aistulf
Akbar
Akhenaton (*or* Ikhnaton)
Akhmatova
Akiba ben Joseph
Akihito
Alain-Fournier
Alanbrooke, Alan Francis
  Brooke, 1st Viscount
Alarcón, Pedro Antonio de
Alarcón y Mendoza, Juan
  Ruiz de
Alba, Fernando Alvarez de
  Toledo, Duke of
Albee, Edward
Albéniz, Isaac Manuel
  Francisco
Alberoni, Giulio
Albers, Josef
Alberti, Leon Battista
Alberti, Raphael
Albertus Magnus, St
Albinoni, Tomaso
Alboin
Albuquerque, Alfonso de
Alcaeus
Alcibiades
Alcmaeon
Alcock, Sir John (William)
Alcoforado, Marianna
Alcott, Louisa May
Alcuin
Aldanov, Mark
Aldhelm, St
Aldington, Richard
Aldiss, Brian W(ilson)
Aldrich, Thomas Bailey
Aldridge, Ira Frederick
Alegría, Ciro
Alekhine, Alexander
Alemán, Mateo
Alexander, Sir William, 1st
  Earl of Stirling
Alexander of Tunis,
  Harold, 1st Earl
Alexius Comnenus
al-Farabi, Mohammed ibn
  Tarkhan

Alfieri, Vittorio, Count
Alfonso Spanish king
Alfvén, Hannes Olof Gösta
Algirdas
Algren, Nelson
Ali
Ali, Muhammad
Ali Pasa, Mehmed Emin
Alkan, Charles Henri
  Valentin
al-Khwarizmi, Muhammed
  ibn Musa
Al-Kindi, Abu Yusuf Ya'qub
  ibn Ishaq
Allbutt, Sir Thomas
  Clifford
Allegri, Gregorio
Allen, Ethan
Allen, William, Cardinal
Allen, Woody
Allenby, Edmund Henry
  Hynman, 1st Viscount
Allende (Gossens),
  Salvador
Alleyn, Edward
Allingham, Margery
Allston, Washington
Alma-Tadema, Sir
  Lawrence
Almeida, Francisco de
Almodóvar, Pedro
Alp Arslan
Alphege, St
Altdorfer, Albrecht
Althusius, Johannes
Altichiero
Altman, Robert
Alvarado, Pedro de
Alvarez, Luis Walter
Alvárez Quintero, Joaquin
Alvárez Quintero, Serafin
Alyattes
Alypius
Amadeus the Peaceful
Amalasuntha
Amalia, Anna
Amanollah Khan
Amati, Andrea
Amati, Antonio
Amati, Girolamo
Amati, Nicolò
Ambartsumian, Viktor
  A(mazaspovich)
Ambler, Eric
Amenemhet

Amenhotep
Amherst, Jeffrey, Baron
Amici, Giovanni Battista
Amiel, Henri Frédéric
Amin Dada, Idi
Amis, Sir Kingsley
Amis, Martin
Ammanati, Bartolommeo
Ampère, André Marie
Amr ibn al-As
Amundsen, Roald
Amyot, Jacques
Anacreon
Ananda
Anastasius
Anaxagoras
Anaximander
Anaximenes
Anchieta, José de
Andersen, Hans Christian
Anderson, Carl David
Anderson, Elizabeth
  Garrett
Anderson, John, 1st
  Viscount Waverley
Anderson, Sherwood
Andrássy, Gyula, Count
André, John
Andrea del Sarto
Andrewes, Lancelot
Andrić, Ivo
Andropov, Yuri
  Vladimirovich
Aneirin
Angelico, Fra
Angell, Sir Norman
Angelou, Maya
Anglesey, Henry William
  Paget, 1st Marquess of
Angoulême, Charles de
  Valois, Duc d'
Angoulême, Margaret of
Ångström, Anders Jonas
Ankhesenamen
An Lu Shan
Annan, Kofi
Annigoni, Pietro
Anouilh, Jean
Ansbach, Caroline of
Anselm of Canterbury, St
Ansermet, Ernest
Ansgar, St
Anson, George Anson,
  Baron
Antelami, Benedetto

Antenor
Antheil, George
Anthony, Susan Brownell
Antigonus
Antiochus
Antipas, Herod
Antipater
Antiphon
Antisthenes
Antonello da Messina
Antonescu, Ion
Antoninus Pius
Antonioni, Michelangelo
Anville, Jean-Baptiste
  Bourguignon d'
Anzengruber, Ludwig
Apelles
Aphraates
Apollinaire, Guillaume
Apollonius
Appert, Nicolas
Apuleius, Lucius
Aquaviva, Claudio
Aquinas, St Thomas
Aquino, Cory
Arafat, Yassir
Arago, (Dominique)
  François (Jean)
Aragon, Louis
Arakcheev, Aleksei
  Andreevich, Count
Aram, Eugene
Arany, János
Arbuthnot, John
Arc, St Joan of
Archer, Frederick Scott
Archer, Thomas
Archer, William
Archilochus
Archimedes
Archipenko, Alexander
Archytas
Arcimboldo, Giuseppe
Ardashir
Arduin
Aretino, Pietro
Argyll, Archibald
  Campbell, 1st Marquess
  of
Arimathea, St Joseph of
Ariosto, Ludovico
Aristagoras
Aristarchus
Aristide, Jean Bertrand
Aristides

Aristippus
Aristophanes
Aristotle
Arius
Arkwright, Sir Richard
Arlington, Henry Bennet,
    1st Earl of
Armani, Giorgio
Arminius
Arminius, Jacobus
Armstrong, Edwin Howard
Armstrong, Louis
Armstrong, Neil Alden
Armstrong, William
    George, Baron
Arnauld, Antoine
Arne, Thomas Augustine
Arnold, Benedict
Arnold, Sir Malcolm
Arnold, Matthew
Arnold, Thomas
Arp, Jean (Hans)
Árpád
Arrabal, Fernando
Arrau, Claudio
Arrhenius, Svante August
Arrian
Arrowsmith, Aaron
Arrowsmith, John
Arsinoe
Artaud, Antonin
Artaxerxes
Artevelde, Jacob van
Arthur, Chester A(lan)
Artigas, José Gervasio
Arundel, Thomas
Asch, Sholem
Ascham, Roger
Ashcroft, Dame Peggy
Ashdown, Paddy
Ashe, Arthur (Robert)
Ashkenazy, Vladimir
Ashley Cooper, Anthony
Ashton, Sir Frederick
    (William Mallandaine)
Ashurbanipal
Ashurnasirpal
Asimov, Isaac
Aske, Robert
Asoka
Asquith, Anthony
Asquith, Herbert Henry, 1st
    Earl of Oxford
Asquith, Margot
Assad, Hafiz al-

Asser
Assisi, St Francis of
Astaire, Fred
Astbury, John
Aston, Francis William
Astor, John Jacob
Astor, Nancy Witcher,
    Viscountess
Astor, Waldorf, 2nd
    Viscount
Asturias, Miguel Ángel
Atahuallpa
Atatürk, Kemal
Atget, (Jean) Eugène
    (Auguste)
Athanasius, St
Athelstan
Athenagoras
Athlone, Alexander
    Cambridge, 1st Earl of
Attalus Soter
Attenborough, Sir David
Attenborough, Richard,
    Baron
Atterdag, Valdemar
Attila
Attlee, Clement (Richard),
    1st Earl
Atwood, Margaret
    (Eleanor)
Auber, Daniel François
    Esprit
Aubrey, John
Aubusson, Pierre d'
Auchinleck, Sir Claude
Auckland, George Eden,
    Earl of
Auden, W(ystan) H(ugh)
Audubon, John James
Augereau, Pierre François
    Charles, Duc de
    Castiglione
Aung San
Aung San Suu Kyi
Aurangzeb
Aurelian(us), Lucius
    Domitius
Auric, Georges
Ausonius, Decimus Magnus
Austen, Jane
Austin, Herbert, 1st Baron
Austin, John
Austin, John Langshaw
Averroes
Avery, Oswald Theodore

Avicenna
Ávila, St Teresa of
Avogadro, Amedeo, Conte
    di Quaregna e Ceretto
Avon, (Robert) Anthony
    Eden, 1st Earl of
Awolowo, Obafemi
Ayatollah Ruholla
    Khomeini
Ayckbourn, Alan
Ayer, Sir Alfred (Jules)
Ayesha
Aylward, Gladys
Ayub Khan, Mohammad
Azaña, Manuel
Azikiwe, (Benjamin)
    Nnamdi
Aznavour, Charles
Azorín
Azuela, Mariano
Ba'al Shem Tov
Babbage, Charles
Babbitt, Irving
Babbitt, Milton
Babel, Isaac
    Emmanuilovich
Babeuf, François-Noël
Babington, Anthony
Babur
Bacchylides
Bach, Johann Christian
Bach, Johann Sebastian
Bach, Karl Philipp Emanuel
Bach, Wilhelm Friedemann
Bacon, Francis
Bacon, Francis, 1st Baron
    Verulam, Viscount St
    Albans
Bacon, John
Bacon, Roger
Baden-Powell, Robert
    Stephenson Smyth, 1st
    Baron
Badoglio, Pietro
Baeck, Leo
Baedeker, Karl
Baekeland, Leo Hendrik
Baer, Karl Ernest von
Baeyer, (Johann Friedrich
    Wilhelm) Adolf von
Baez, Joan
Baffin, William
Bagehot, Walter
Baily, Francis
Bain, Alexander

Bainbridge, Beryl
Baird, John Logie
Bairnsfather, (Charles)
  Bruce
Baker, Sir Benjamin
Baker, Dame Janet
  (Abbott)
Baker, Sir Samuel White
Bakewell, Robert
Bakst, Léon
Bakunin, Mikhail
  Aleksandrovich
Balakirev, Mili Alekseevich
Balanchine, George
Balboa, Vasco Núñez de
Balchin, Nigel
Balcon, Sir Michael
Baldwin, James Arthur
Baldwin of Bewdley,
  Stanley, 1st Earl
Balenciaga, Cristóbal
Balfour, Arthur James, 1st
  Earl of
Ball, John
Balla, Giacomo
Ballard, J(ames)
  G(raham)
Ballesteros, Severiano
Balliol, Edward de
Balliol, John de
Balzac, Honoré de
Bana
Banda, Hastings Kamuzu
Bandaranaike, Sirimavo
  Ratwatte Dias
Bandaranaike, S(olomon)
  W(est) R(idgeway)
  D(ias)
Bandeira, Manuel Carneiró
  de Sousa
Bankhead, Tallulah
Banks, Sir Joseph
Bannister, Sir Roger
  (Gilbert)
Banting, Sir Frederick
  Grant
Banville, Théodore Faullain
  de
Barbarossa
Barber, Samuel
Barbirolli, Sir John
Barbour, John
Barbusse, Henri
Barclay de Tolly, Mikhail
  Bogdanovich, Prince

Bardeen, John
Bardot, Brigitte
Barenboim, Daniel
Barents, Willem
Barère, Bertrand
Barham, Richard Harris
Bar Hebraeus
Baring, Evelyn
Barker, George
Barker, Harley Granville
Barkhausen, Heinrich
Bar Kokhba
Barlach, Ernst
Barnard, Christiaan
  Neethling
Barnard, Edward Emerson
Barnardo, Thomas John
Barnave, Antoine Pierre
Barnes, William
Barnum, Phineas Taylor
Baroja, Pío
Barras, Paul François Jean
  Nicolas, Vicomte de
Barrault, Jean-Louis
Barrès, Maurice
Barrie, Sir James (Matthew)
Barry, Sir Charles
Barrymore, Ethel
Barrymore, John
Barrymore, Lionel
Bart, Jean
Bart, Lionel
Barth, Heinrich
Barth, John
Barth, Karl
Bartholdi, Frédéric August
Bartók, Béla
Bartolommeo, Fra
Barton, Clara
Barton, Sir Edmund
Barton, Elizabeth
Baruch, Bernard
Baryshnikov, Mikhail
  (Nikolayevich)
Basie, Count
Baskerville, John
Bassano, Jacopo
Bates, H(erbert) E(rnest)
Bates, Henry Walter
Bateson, William
Báthory, Stephen
Batista y Zaldívar,
  Fulgencio
Battani, al-
Batten, Jean

Battenberg, Prince Louis of
Baudelaire, Charles
Baudouin
Baum, L(yman) Frank
Baumgarten, Alexander
  Gottlieb
Baur, Ferdinand Christian
Bausch, Pina
Bax, Sir Arnold Edward
  Trevor
Baxter, Richard
Bayar, Mahmud Celal
Bayard, Pierre Terrail,
  Seigneur de
Baybars
Bayezid
Bayle, Pierre
Baylis, Lilian
Bayliss, Sir William
  Maddock
Bazaine, Achille François
Beadle, George Wells
Beale, Dorothea
Beardsley, Aubrey Vincent
Beaton, Sir Cecil (Walter
  Hardy)
Beaton, David
Beatty, David, 1st Earl
Beaufort, Henry
Beaufort, Margaret
Beauharnais, Alexandre,
  Vicomte de
Beauharnais, Eugène de
Beauharnais, Hortense de
Beaumarchais,
  Pierre-Augustin Caron de
Beaumont, Francis
Beaumont, William
Beauvais, Vincent of
Beauvoir, Simone de
Beaverbrook, Max(well)
  Aitken, 1st Baron
Bebel, August
Beccaria, Cesare Bonesana,
  Marchese de
Bechet, Sidney
Becket, St Thomas
Beckett, Samuel
Beckford, William
Beckmann, Max
Bequerel, Antoine César
Becquerel, (Antoine) Henri
Beddoes, Thomas Lovell
Bede, St
Bedford, John, Duke of

Birkhoff, George David
Biró, Laszlo
Birtwistle, Sir Harrison
Bishop, Sir Henry Rowley
Bismarck, Otto Eduard
  Leopold, Prince von
Bizet, Georges
Bjerknes, Jakob
Bjerknes, Vilhelm Friman
  Koren
Bjørnson, Bjørnstjerne
  (Martinius)
Black, Joseph
Blackett, Patrick Maynard
  Stuart, Baron
Blackmore, R(ichard)
  D(oddridge)
Blackstone, Sir William
Blackwood, Algernon
  Henry
Blair, Tony
Blake, Peter
Blake, Robert
Blake, William
Blanc, Louis
Blanchard, Jean Pierre
  François
Blanqui, Louis Auguste
Blasco Ibáñez, Vicente
Blasis, Carlo
Blavatsky, Helen Petrovna
Blenkinsop, John
Blériot, Louis
Blessington, Marguerite,
  Countess of
Bligh, William
Bliss, Sir Arthur Edward
  Drummond
Blixen, Karen, Baroness
  Blixen-Finecke (pen name
  Isak Dinesen)
Bloch, Ernest
Bloch, Felix
Blok, Aleksandr
  Aleksandrovich
Blondel, Maurice
Blondin, Charles
Blood, Colonel Thomas
Bloomfield, Leonard
Blow, John
Blücher, Gebhard
  Leberecht von, Prince of
  Wahlstatt
Blum, Léon
Blunden, Edmund Charles

Blunt, Anthony
Blyton, Enid
Boadicea (or Boudicca)
Boas, Franz
Boccaccio, Giovanni
Boccherini, Luigi
Boccioni, Umberto
Bodawpaya
Bodhidharma
Bodin, Jean
Bodoni, Giambattista
Boehm, Theobald
Boehme, Jakob variant
  spelling of Böhme, Jakob
Boethius, Anicius Manlius
  Severinus
Bogarde, Sir Dirk
Bogart, Humphrey
Bohemond
Böhm, Karl
Böhme (or Boehme), Jakob
Bohr, Aage
Bohr, Niels Henrik David
Boiardo, Matteo Maria,
  Conte di Scandiano
Boileau(-Despréaux),
  Nicolas
Boito, Arrigo
Bokassa
Bolden, Buddy
Bolesław
Boleyn, Anne
Bolger, James Brendon
Bolingbroke, Henry St
  John, 1st Viscount
Bolívar, Simón
Böll, Heinrich
Bologna, Giovanni da
Bolt, Robert Oxton
Boltzmann, Ludwig Eduard
Bolyai, János
Bonaparte, Carlo
Bonaparte, Jérôme
Bonaparte, Joseph
Bonaparte, Louis
Bonaparte, Lucien
Bonaparte, Napoleon
Bonaventure, St
Bond, Edward
Bondi, Sir Hermann
Bonham-Carter, Lady
  Violet, Baroness Asquith
Bonhoeffer, Dietrich
Boniface, St
Bonington, Sir Chris

Bonington, Richard Parkes
Bonnard, Pierre
Bonnet, Charles
Boole, George
Boone, Daniel
Booth, Charles
Booth, Edwin
Booth, Evangeline
Booth, John Wilkes
Booth, William
Booth, William Bramwell
Boothroyd, Betty
Borden, Sir Robert Laird
Bordet, Jules Jean Baptiste
  Vincent
Borelli, Giovanni Alfonso
Borg, Bjorn
Borges, Jorge Luis
Borgia, Cesare
Borgia, Lucrezia
Borglum, Gutzon
Borlaug, Norman
Bormann, Martin
Born, Max
Borodin, Aleksandr
  Porfirevich
Borromeo, St Charles
Borromini, Francesco
Borrow, George Henry
Boru, Brian
Bosanquet, Bernard
Bosch, Carl
Bosch, Hieronymus
Bose, Sir Jagadis Chandra
Bose, Subhas Chandra
Bossuet, Jacques Bénigne
Boswell, James
Botha, Louis
Botha, Pieter Willem
Botham, Ian Terence
Bothe, Walther Wilhelm
  Georg Franz
Bothwell, James Hepburn,
  4th Earl of
Botticelli, Sandro
Botvinnik, Mikhail
  Moiseivich
Boucher, François
Boucher de Perthes,
  Jacques
Boudicca variant spelling of
  Boadicea
Boudin, Eugène
Bougainville, Louis
  Antoine de

Bouillon, Godfrey of
Boulanger, Nadia (Juliette)
Boulez, Pierre
Boulle, André Charles
Boult, Sir Adrian (Cedric)
Boulter, Hugh
Boulton, Matthew
Boumédienne, Houari
Bourbaki, Nicolas
Bourdelle, Émile
Bourgeois, Léon
Bourguiba, Habib
Bourmont, Louis Auguste
  Victor de Ghaisnes,
  Comte de
Boutros Ghali, Boutros
Bouts, Dierick
Boveri, Theodor Heinrich
Bovet, Daniel
Bow, Clara
Bowdler, Thomas
Bowen, Elizabeth
Bowen, Norman Levi
Bower, Frederick Orpen
Bowie, David
Boyce, William
Boycott, Charles
  Cunningham
Boyd-Orr of Brechin
  Mearns, John, 1st Baron
Boyer, Charles
Boyle, Robert
Bo Zhu Yi (or Po Chü-i)
Brabham, Jack
Bracegirdle, Anne
Bracton, Henry de
Bradbury, Ray
Bradford, William
Bradlaugh, Charles
Bradley, Andrew Cecil
Bradley, Francis Herbert
Bradley, Omar Nelson
Bradman, Sir Donald
  George
Braganza, Catherine of
Bragg, Sir (William)
  Lawrence
Bragg, Sir William Henry
Brahe, Tycho
Brahms, Johannes
Braille, Louis
Bramah, Joseph
Bramante, Donato
Branagh, Kenneth
Brancusi, Constantin

Brandes, Georg Morris
  Cohen
Brando, Marlon
Brandt, Bill British
  photographer
Brandt, Willy German
  statesman
Branson, Richard
Brant, Joseph
Brant, Sebastian
Branting, Karl Hjalmar
Brantôme, Pierre, Abbé and
  Seigneur de Bourdeille
Braque, Georges
Bratby, John
Brattain, Walter Houser
Brauchitsch, Walther von
Braun, Eva
Brazza, Pierre Paul François
  Camille Savorgnan de
Bream, Julian Alexander
Brébeuf, St Jean de
Brecht, Bertolt
Brendel, Alfred
Brentano, Clemens
Brentano, Franz
Bresson, Robert
Breton, André
Breuer, Josef
Breuer, Marcel Lajos
Breuil, Henri
Brewster, Sir David
Brezhnev, Leonid Ilich
Brian, Havergal
Briand, Aristide
Bridge, Frank
Bridges, Robert Seymour
Bridgman, Percy Williams
Bridie, James
Briggs, Henry
Bright, John
Bright, Richard
Brillat-Savarin, Anthelme
Brindley, James
Brissot, Jacques-Pierre
Britten, (Edward)
  Benjamin, Baron
Broadwood, John
Broch, Hermann
Broglie, Louis Victor, 7th
  Duc de
Bronowski, Jacob
Brontë, Anne
Brontë, Charlotte
Brontë, Emily

Brontë, Patrick Branwell
Bronzino
Brook, Peter
Brooke, Sir James
Brooke, Rupert (Chawner)
Brookeborough, Basil
  Stanlake Brooke, 1st
  Viscount
Broome, David
Brough, Louise
Brouwer, Adriaen
Brouwer, L(uitzen)
  E(gbertus) J(an)
Brown, Sir Arthur
Brown, Capability
Brown, Ford Madox
Brown, George (Alfred),
  Baron George-Brown
Brown, John
Brown, Robert Scottish
  botanist
Browne, Hablot Knight
  (known as Phiz)
Browne, Robert Puritan
  leader
Browne, Sir Thomas
Browning, Elizabeth
  Barrett
Browning, Robert
Brubeck, Dave
Bruce, James
Bruce, Robert the
Bruce of Melbourne,
  Stanley Melbourne, 1st
  Viscount
Bruch, Max
Bruckner, Anton
Brueghel, Jan
Brueghel, Pieter
Brummel, George Bryan
Brunel, Isambard Kingdom
Brunel, Sir Marc Isambard
Brunelleschi, Filippo
Brüning, Heinrich
Brunner, Emil
Bruno, Giordano
Brunswick, Caroline of
Bruton, John Gerard
Brutus, Marcus Junius
Bryant, William Cullen
Bryce, James, 1st Viscount
Buber, Martin
Bucer, Martin
Buchan, John, 1st Baron
  Tweedsmuir

Buchanan, George
Buchanan, James
Büchner, Georg
Buck, Pearl S(ydenstricker)
Buckingham, George
    Villiers, Duke of
Buddha
Buddhaghosa
Budé, Guillaume
Budge, (James) Don(ald)
Bueno, Maria (Esther)
Buffalo Bill see Cody,
    William F(rederick)
Buffet, Bernard
Buffon, Georges Louis
    Leclerc, Comte de
Bugatti, Ettore (Arco
    Isidoro)
Bukhari, al-
Bukharin, Nikolai
    Ivanovich
Bulganin, Nikolai
    Aleksandrovich
Bull, John
Bülow, Bernhard Heinrich,
    Fürst von
Bülow, Hans Guido,
    Freiherr von
Bultmann, Rudolf (Karl)
Bulwer-Lytton, Edward
    George Earle, 1st Baron
    Lytton
Bunche, Ralph
Bunin, Ivan Alekseevich
Bunsen, Robert Wilhelm
Buñuel, Luis
Bunyan, John
Burbage, Richard
Burbank, Luther
Burckhardt, Jacob
    Christoph
Bürge, Joost
Bürger, Gottfried
Burgess, Anthony
Burgess, Guy
Burgh, Hubert de
Burghley, Robert Cecil, 1st
    Earl of Salisbury
Burghley, William Cecil,
    Lord
Burgoyne, John
Buridan, Jean
Burke, Edmund
Burke, Robert O'Hara
Burke, William

Burlington, Richard Boyle,
    3rd Earl of
Burne-Jones, Sir Edward
    Coley
Burnet, Sir Frank
    Macfarlane
Burnet, Gilbert
Burnett, Frances Eliza
    Hodgson
Burney, Charles
Burney, Fanny
Burns, John Elliot
Burns, Robert
Burr, Aaron
Burra, Edward
Burroughs, Edgar Rice
Burroughs, William
Burton, Sir Richard
Burton, Richard
Burton, Robert
Busby, Sir Matt
Bush, Alan Dudley
Bush, George (Herbert
    Walker)
Bushnell, David
Busoni, Ferruccio
Buss, Frances Mary
Bustamante y Sirvén,
    Antonio Sánchez de
Bute, John Stuart, 3rd Earl
    of
Buthelezi, Mangosouthu
    Gatsha
Butler, Benjamin Franklin
Butler, Joseph
Butler, R(ichard) A(usten),
    Baron
Butler, Reg(inald) Cotterell
Butler, Samuel
Butler, Samuel
Butor, Michel
Butt, Dame Clara
Butterfield, William
Buxtehude, Dietrich
Byatt, A(ntonia) S(usan)
Bylot, Robert
Byng, George, Viscount
    Torrington
Byng, John
Byng of Vimy, Julian, 1st
    Viscount
Byrd, Richard E(velyn)
Byrd, William
Byron, George Gordon,
    Lord

Caballé, Montserrat
Cabot, John
Cabot, Sebastian
Cabral, Pedro Álvares
Cabrini, St Frances Xavier
Caccini, Giulio
Cadbury, George
Cadbury, Richard
Cade, Jack
Cadwallader (or
    Cadwaladr)
Caedmon
Caesar, (Gaius) Julius
Cage, John
Cagliostro, Alessandro,
    Conte di
Cagney, James
Caillaux, Joseph
Cain
Calas, Jean
Calder, Alexander
Calderón de la Barca, Pedro
Calhoun, John C(aldwell)
Caligula
Callaghan, (Leonard)
    James, Baron
Callas, Maria
Calles, Plutarco Elías
Callias
Callicrates
Callimachus
Callot, Jacques
Calmette, Albert Léon
    Charles
Calvin, John
Calvin, Melvin
Cambacérès, Jean Jacques
    Régis, Duc de
Cambyses II
Camden, William
Cameron, Julia Margaret
Camões, Luís de
Campanella, Tommaso
Campbell, Colin, Baron
    Clyde
Campbell, Donald Malcolm
Campbell, Gina
Campbell, Sir Malcolm
Campbell, Mrs Patrick
Campbell, Roy
    (Dunnachie)
Campbell, Thomas
Campbell-Bannerman, Sir
    Henry
Campi, Antonio

Campi, Giulio
Campi, Vincenzo
Campion, Edmund
Campion, Thomas
Camus, Albert
Canaletto
Candela, Felix
Canning, Charles John, Earl
Canning, George
Cannizzaro, Stanislao
Cannon, Walter Bradford
Cano, Juan Sebastián del
Canova, Antonio
Cánovas del Castillo, Antonio
Cantor, Georg
Canute
Cao Chan (or Ts'ao Chan, Zao Zhan)
Capablanca y Graupera, José Raúl
Capone, Al
Capote, Truman
Capp, Al
Capra, Frank
Caracalla
Caratacus (or Caractacus)
Caravaggio
Cardano, Girolamo
Cárdenas, Lázaro
Cardigan, James Thomas Brudenell, 7th Earl of
Cardin, Pierre
Carducci, Giosuè
Cardwell, Edward, Viscount
Carew, Thomas
Carey, George Leonard
Carey, William
Carl Gustaf Swedish king
Carlos, Don
Carlyle, Thomas
Carnap, Rudolf
Carné, Marcel
Carnegie, Andrew
Carnera, Primo
Carnot, Lazare Nicolas Marguerite
Carnot, (Nicolas Léonard) Sadi
Caro, Joseph
Carossa, Hans
Carpaccio, Vittore
Carpentier, Georges

Carpini, Giovanni da Pian del
Carr, Robert
Carracci, Agostino
Carracci, Annibale
Carracci, Ludovico
Carranza, Venustiano
Carrel, Alexis
Carrington, Peter Alexander Rupert Carrington, 6th Baron
Carroll, Lewis pen name of Charles Lutwidge Dodgson
Carson, Edward Henry, Baron
Carson, Kit
Carson, Rachel Louise
Carte, Richard D'Oyly
Carter, Elliott (Cook)
Carter, Howard
Carter, Jimmy
Cartier, Jacques
Cartier-Bresson, Henri
Cartwright, Edmund
Caruso, Enrico
Carver, George Washington
Cary, (Arthur) Joyce (Lunel)
Casals, Pablo
Casanova, Giovanni Giacomo, Chevalier de Seingalt
Casement, Sir Roger (David)
Cassander
Cassatt, Mary
Cassiodorus, Flavius Magnus Aurelius
Cassirer, Ernst
Cassius Longinus, Gaius
Cassivelaunus
Casson, Sir Hugh (Maxwell)
Casson, Sir Lewis
Castagno, Andrea del
Castelo Branco, Camilo
Castiglione, Baldassare
Castilho, Antonio Feliciano de
Castlereagh, Robert Stewart, Viscount
Castro (Ruz), Fidel
Catesby, Robert
Catiline
Catlin, George

Cato
Catullus, Valerius
Cauchy, Augustin Louis, Baron
Cavafy, Constantine
Cavalcanti, Guido
Cavalli, Francesco
Cavallini, Pietro
Cavell, Edith
Cavendish, Henry
Cavour, Camillo Benso di, Count
Cawley, Evonne (maiden name Goolagong)
Caxton, William
Cayley, Arthur
Cayley, Sir George
Ceaușescu, Nicolae
Cecil, Lord David
Cecil, Robert Gascoyne-Cecil, 1st Viscount
Cela(y Trulock), Camilo José
Céline, Louis Ferdinand
Cellini, Benvenuto
Celsus, Aulus Cornelius
Cennini, Cennino(di Drea)
Cervantes, Miguel de
Cetshwayo
Cézanne, Paul
Chabrier, Emmanuel
Chabrol, Claude
Chadwick, Sir Edwin
Chadwick, Sir James
Chadwick, Lynn
Chagall, Marc
Chain, Sir Ernst Boris
Chaliapin, Feodor Ivanovich
Challoner, Richard
Chalmers, Thomas
Chamberlain, Sir (Joseph) Austen
Chamberlain, Joseph
Chamberlain, (Arthur) Neville
Chamberlain, Owen
Chambers, Sir William
Champaigne, Philippe de
Champlain, Samuel de
Champollion, Jean-François
Chandler, Raymond
Chandra Gupta

Chandragupta Maurya

Chandrasekhar,
Subrahmanyan

Chanel, Coco

Chaplin, Charlie

Chapman, George

Charcot, Jean-Martin

Chardin,
Jean-Baptiste-Siméon

Charlemagne

Charles, Ray

Charlton, Bobby

Charlton, Jackie

Charpentier, Gustave

Charron, Pierre

Charteris, Leslie

Chartier, Alain

Chateaubriand, Vicomte de

Chatham, William Pitt, 1st
Earl of

Chatterjee, Bankim
Chandra

Chatterton, Thomas

Chaucer, Geoffrey

Chausson, Ernest

Chebishev, Pafnuti Lvovich

Chekhov, Anton Pavlovich

Cheng Ch'eng-kung *variant
spelling of* Zheng Cheng
Gong

Cheng Ho *variant spelling of*
Zheng He

Chénier, André de

Cheops *Greek name of*
Khufu

Chephren *Greek name of*
Khafre

Cherenkov, Pavel
Alekseievich

Cherubini, Maria Luigi

Cheshire, (Geoffrey)
Leonard

Chesterfield, Philip Dormer
Stanhope, 4th Earl of

Chesterton, G(ilbert)
K(eith)

Chevalier, Maurice

Chiang Ch'ing *variant
spelling of* Jiang Qing

Chiang Ching-kuo *variant
spelling of* Jiang Jing Guo

Chiang Kai-shek (*or* Jiang
Jie Shi)

Chicherin, Georgi
Vasilievich

Chichester, Sir Francis
(Charles)

Ch'ien-lung *variant spelling*
of Qian Long

Chifley, Joseph Benedict

Chikamatsu Monzaemon

Childers, Erskine

Childers, Robert Erskine

Chippendale, Thomas

Chirac, Jacques

Chirico, Giorgio de

Chodowiecki, Daniel
Nikolaus

Choiseul, Étienne François,
Duc de

Chomsky, Noam

Chopin, Frédéric
(François)

Chou En-lai (*or* Zhou En
Lai)

Chrétien, (Joseph Jacques)
Jean

Chrétien de Troyes

Christie, Dame Agatha

Christie, Linford

Christoff, Boris

Christophe, Henri

Chrysoloras, Manuel

Chrysostom, St John

Chuang-tzu *variant spelling*
of Zhuangzi

Ch'ü Ch'iu-pai *variant*
spelling of Qu Qiu Bai

Chulalongkorn

Churchill, Charles

Churchill, Lord Randolph
Henry Spencer

Churchill, Sir Winston
(Leonard Spencer)

Churriguera

Chu Teh *variant spelling of*
Zhu De

Chu Xi (*or* Chu Hsi)

Chu Yuan

Ciano, Galeazzo

Cibber, Colley

Cicero, Marcus Tullius

Cimabue, Giovanni

Cimarosa, Domenico

Cimon

Cincinnatus, Lucius
Quinctius

Cinna, Lucius Cornelius

Clair, René

Clare, John

Clarendon, Edward Hyde,
1st Earl of

Clare of Assisi, St

Clark, Jim

Clark, (Charles) Joseph

Clark, Kenneth
(Mackenzie), Baron

Clarke, Jeremiah

Clarke, Marcus (Andrew
Hislop)

Clarkson, Thomas

Claudel, Paul

Claude Lorraine

Claudian *Roman poet*

Claudius *Roman emperor*

Clausewitz, Karl von

Clausius, Rudolf Julius
Emanuel

Clay, Cassius *original name*
of Muhammad Ali

Clay, Henry

Cleanthes

Cleese, John

Cleisthenes

Cleland, John

Clemenceau, Georges

Clementi, Muzio

Cleon

Cleopatra

Cleveland, Stephen Grover

Cleves, Anne of

Clinton, Bill

Clinton, De Witt

Clive of Plassey, Robert,
Baron

Clodion

Clouet, François

Clouet, Jean

Clovis

Coates, Joseph Gordon

Cobbett, William

Cobden, Richard

Cochise

Cochrane, Thomas, 10th
Earl of Dundonald

Cockcroft, Sir John
Douglas

Cockerell, Charles Robert

Cocteau, Jean

Cody, William F(rederick)
(*known as* Buffalo Bill)

Coe, Sebastian

Coen, Jan Pieterszoon

Coeur, Jacques

Cohn, Ferdinand Julius

Coke, Sir Edward
Coke, Thomas William,
  Earl of Leicester of
  Holkham
Colbert, Claudette
Colbert, Jean-Baptiste
Coleridge, Samuel Taylor
Coleridge-Taylor, Samuel
Colet, John
Colette, Sidonie Gabrielle
  Claudine
Coligny, Gaspard de,
  Seigneur de Châtillon
Collier, Jeremy
Collingwood, Cuthbert, 1st
  Baron
Collingwood, Robin George
Collins, Michael
Collins, William
Collins, William Wilkie
Colman, George
Colman, Ronald
Colombo, Matteo Realdo
Colum, Padraic
Columba, St founder of
  Ionian monastery
Columban, St founder of
  monasteries in Gaul and
  Italy
Columbus, Christopher
Comaneci, Nadia
Comenius, John Amos
Commodus, Lucius Aelius
  Aurelius
Commynes, Philippe de
Comnena, Anna
Compton, Arthur Holly
Compton, Denis (Charles
  Scott)
Compton-Burnett, Dame
  Ivy
Comte, Auguste
Condillac, Étienne Bonnot
  de
Condorcet, Marie Jean
  Antoine de Caritat,
  Marquis de
Confucius
Congreve, William
Connery, Sean
Connors, Jimmy
Conrad, Joseph
Conscience, Hendrik
Constable, John
Constant, Benjamin

Constantine, Learie
  Nicholas, Baron
Cook, Captain James
Cook, Sir Joseph
Cook, Thomas
Coolidge, John Calvin
Cooper, Gary
Cooper, James Fenimore
Cooper, Samuel
Copernicus, Nicolaus
Copland, Aaron
Coppola, Francis Ford
Coralli, Jean
Corbusier, Le
Corday, Charlotte
Corelli, Arcangelo
Corelli, Marie
Corneille, Pierre
Cornelius, Peter von
Cornforth, Sir John Warcup
Cornwallis, Charles, 1st
  Marquess
Corot, Jean Baptiste
  Camille
Correggio
Correns, Carl Erich
Cort, Henry
Cortés, Hernán
Cortot, Alfred
Corvo, Baron *pseudonym of*
  Frederick William Rolfe
Cosgrave, Liam
Cosgrave, William
  Thomas
Cosmas, St
Cosway, Richard
Cotman, John Sell
Coulomb, Charles Augustin
  de
Couperin, François
Courbet, Gustave
Courrèges, André
Court, Margaret
Cousin, Jean
Cousin, Victor
Cousteau, Jacques Yves
Coverdale, Miles
Covilhã, Pêro da
Coward, Sir Noel
Cowdrey, Sir (Michael)
  Colin
Cowell, Henry
Cowley, Abraham
Cowper, William
Crabbe, George

Craig, Edward Henry
  Gordon
Craik, Dinah Maria Mulock
Cram, Steve
Cranach the Elder, Lucas
Crane, Hart
Crane, Stephen
Crane, Walter
Cranko, John
Cranmer, Thomas
Crashaw, Richard
Crassus, Marcus Licinius
Crawford, Joan
Creed, Frederick
Creeley, Robert
Cressent, Charles
Crèvecoeur,
  Michel-Guillaume-Jean
  de
Crichton, James
Crick, Francis Harry
  Compton
Crippen, Hawley Harvey
Cripps, Sir (Richard)
  Stafford
Cristofori, Bartolommeo
Crivelli, Carlo
Croce, Benedetto
Crockett, Davy
Crockford, William
Croesus
Crome, John
Crome, John Bernay
Cromer, Evelyn Baring, 1st
  Earl of
Crompton, Richmal
Crompton, Samuel
Cromwell, Oliver
Cromwell, Richard
Cromwell, Thomas, Earl of
  Essex
Cronin, A(rchibald)
  J(oseph)
Cronje, Piet Arnoldus
Crookes, Sir William
Crosby, Bing
Crossman, Richard
  (Howard Stafford)
Cruden, Alexander
Cruft, Charles
Cruikshank, George
Cruyff, Johann
Cruz, Sor Juana Inéz de la
Csokonai Vitéz, Mihaly
Cudworth, Ralph

Culbertson, Ely
Culpeper, Nicholas
Cumberland, Richard
Cumberland, William
  Augustus, Duke of
cummings, e(dward)
  e(stlin)
Cunningham, Merce
Cunobelinus
Curie, Marie
Curie, Pierre
Curry, John (Anthony)
Curtin, John Joseph
Curtiss, Glenn (Hammond)
Curwen, John
Curzon, Sir Clifford
Curzon, George Nathaniel,
  1st Marquess
Cusa, Nicholas of
Cushing, Harvey Williams
Custer, George A(rmstrong)
Cuvier, Georges, Baron
Cuyp, Aelbert Jacobsz
Cuyp, Jacob Gerritsz
Cymbeline
Cynewulf
Cyrano de Bergerac,
  Savinien
Czerny, Karl
Dadd, Richard
Dafydd ap Gwilym
Dagly, Gerhard
Daguerre,
  Louis-Jacques-Mandé
Dahl, Roald
Daigo
Daimler, Gottlieb
  (Wilhelm)
Daladier, Édouard
Dale, Sir Henry Hallett
d'Alembert, Jean le Rond
Dalhousie, James Ramsay,
  1st Marquess of
Dali, Salvador
Dallapiccola, Luigi
Dalton, John
Dam, Carl Peter Henrik
Damian, St 4th-century
  martyr
Damien, Father
  19th-century missionary
Dampier, William
Danby, Francis
Danby, Thomas Osborne,
  1st Earl of

Dance, George
Dandolo, Enrico
Dangerfield, Thomas
Daniel, Samuel
Daniell, John Frederic
D'Annunzio, Gabriele
Dante Alighieri
Danton, Georges Jacques
Da Ponte, Lorenzo
Darío, Rubén
Darius
Darlan, Jean (Louis Xavier)
  François
Darling, Grace
Darnley, Henry Stuart,
  Lord
Darrow, Clarence
Darwin, Charles Robert
Darwin, Erasmus
Datini, Francesco
Daubenton, Louis Jean
  Marie
Daubigny, Charles-
  François
Daudet, Alphonse
Daudet, Léon
Daumier, Honoré
Davenant, Sir William
Davenport, Charles
  Benedict
David, Gerard
David, Jacques Louis
David ap Gruffudd
Davies, Sir Peter Maxwell
Davies, W(illiam) H(enry)
da Vinci, Leonardo
Davis, Bette
Davis, Sir Colin
Davis, Jefferson
Davis, John
Davis, Miles
Davitt, Michael
Davy, Sir Humphry
Dawes, Charles G(ates)
Dayan, Moshe
Day Lewis, C(ecil)
Dazai Osamu
Deák, Ferenc
Deakin, Alfred
Dean, James
Deane, Silas
de Bary, Heinrich Anton
Debray, (Jules) Régis
Debré, Michel
Debrett, John

de Broglie, Louis Victor,
  7th Duc
Debs, Eugene V(ictor)
Deburau, Jean-Gaspard
Debussy, Claude (Achille)
Debye, Peter Joseph
  Wilhelm
Decatur, Stephen
Decius, Gaius Messius
  Quintus Trajanus
Dedekind, (Julius Wilhelm)
  Richard
de Duve, Christian
Dee, John
Defoe, Daniel
De Forest, Lee
Degas, (Hilaire Germain)
  Edgar
De Gasperi, Alcide
de Gaulle, Charles André
  Joseph Marie
De Havilland, Sir
  Geoffrey
Dekker, Thomas
de Klerk, F(rederik)
  W(illem)
de Kooning, Willem
Delacroix, Eugène
De la Mare, Walter
De la Roche, Mazo
Delaroche, (Hippolyte)
  Paul
De La Rue, Warren
Delaunay, Robert
Delcassé, Théophile
Deledda, Grazia
Delescluze, Louis Charles
Delibes, Leo
Delius, Frederick
della Robbia, Andrea
della Robbia, Giovanni
della Robbia, Girolamo
della Robbia, Luca
Delorme, Philibert
Delors, Jacques (Lucien
  Jean)
Delvaux, Paul
de Mille, Agnes
de Mille, Cecil B(lount)
Democritus
De Morgan, Augustus
Demosthenes
Dempsey, Jack
Dench, Dame Judi
  (Olivia)

Deng Xiao Ping *variant*
  spelling of Teng
  Hsiao-p'ing
Denham, Sir John
Denikin, Anton Ivanovich
De Niro, Robert
Denis, Maurice
Denis, St
Denning, Alfred
  Thompson, Baron
d'Éon, Charles de
  Beaumont, Chevalier
Depardieu, Gérard
Depretis, Agostino
De Quincey, Thomas
Derain, André
Derby, Edward (George
  Geoffrey Smith) Stanley,
  4th Earl of
Derrida, Jacques
Desai, (Shri) Morarji
  (Ranchhodji)
Descartes, René
De Sica, Vittorio
Desiderio da Settignano
Desmond, Gerald
  Fitzgerald, 15th Earl of
Desmoulins, Camille
des Prez, Josquin
Dessalines, Jean Jacques
Destutt, Antoine Louis
  Claude, Comte de Tracy
Deus, João de
De Valera, Eamon
de Valois, Dame Ninette
Devine, George
Devonshire, Spencer
  Compton Cavendish, 8th
  Duke of
de Vries, Hugo Marie
Dewar, Donald
de Wet, Christian Rudolf
Dewey, George
Dewey, John
De Wint, Peter
Diaghilev, Sergei
  (Pavlovich)
Dias, Bartolomeu
Díaz, Porfirio
Dibdin, Charles
Dickens, Charles
Dickinson, Emily
Diderot, Denis
Diefenbaker, John G(eorge)
Diels, Otto Paul Hermann

Dieman, Anthony van
Dietrich, Marlene
Digby, Sir Kenelm
Dilthey, Wilhelm
DiMaggio, Joe
Dimitrii Donskoi
Dimitrov, Georgi
D'Indy, Vincent
Dinesen, Isak *pen name of*
  Karen Blixen
D'Inzeo, Piero
D'Inzeo, Raimondo
Dio Cassius
Dio Chrysostom
Diocletian(us), Gaius
  Aurelius Valerius
Diodorus Siculus
Diogenes
Dionysius
Diophantus
Dior, Christian
Dioscorides Pedanius
Dirac, Paul Adrien
  Maurice
Disney, Walt
Disraeli, Benjamin, 1st Earl
  of Beaconsfield
Djilas, Milovan
Djoser (*or* Zoser)
Dobzhansky, Theodosius
Dodgson, Charles
  Lutwidge (*pen name*
  Lewis Carroll)
Dodsley, Robert
Dogen
Dohnányi, Ernö
Dolci, Danilo
D'Oliviera, Basil Lewis
Dollfuss, Engelbert
Dolmetsch, Arnold
Dolmetsch, Carl
Domagk, Gerhard
Domenichino
Domenico Veneziano
Domingo, Placido
Domino, Fats
Domitian(us), Titus Flavius
Donatello
Donatus, Aelius
Dönitz, Karl
Donizetti, Gaetano
Donleavy, J(ames) P(atrick)
Donne, John
Doolittle, Hilda
Doppler, Christian Johann

Doré, (Paul) Gustave (Louis
  Christophe)
Dorgon
Dornier, Claudius
Dos Passos, John
Dostoievski, Fedor
  Mikhailovich
Dou, Gerrit
Doughty, Charles Montagu
Douglas, Gavin
Douglas, (George) Norman
Douglas-Home, Alec, Baron
  Home of the Hirsel
Dowding, Hugh Caswall
  Tremenheere, 1st Baron
Dowland, John
Dowson, Ernest
  (Christopher)
Doyle, Sir Arthur Conan
D'Oyly Carte, Richard
Drabble, Margaret
Draco
Drake, Sir Francis
Drayton, Michael
Dreiser, Theodore
Dreyer, Carl Theodor
Dreyer, Johan Ludvig Emil
Dreyfus, Alfred
Driesch, Hans Adolf Eduard
Drinkwater, John
Droste-Hülshoff, Annette
  von
Drummond of
  Hawthornden, William
Dryden, John
Drysdale, Sir (George)
  Russell
Du Barry, Marie Jeanne
  Bécu, Comtesse
Dubček, Alexander
Dubuffet, Jean (Phillipe
  Arthur)
Du Cange, Charles du
  Fresne, Sieur
Duccio di Buoninsegna
Duchamp, Marcel
Dufay, Guillaume
Du Fu (*or* Tu Fu)
Dufy, Raoul
Duhamel, Georges
Dukas, Paul
Duke, Geoffrey E.
Dulles, John Foster
Dumas, Alexandre
Du Maurier, Dame Daphne

Du Maurier, George (Louis Palmella Busson)
Du Mont, Allen Balcom
Dumont d'Urville, Jules Sébastien César
Dumouriez, Charles François du Périer
Dunant, (Jean-)Henri
Dunbar, William
Duncan, Isadora
Dundee, John Graham of Claverhouse, 1st Viscount
Dunlop, John Boyd
Dunois, Jean d'Orléans, Comte de
Dunsany, Edward John Moreton Drax Plunkett, 18th Baron
Duns Scotus, John
Dunstable, John
Duparc, Henri
du Pré, Jacqueline
Dupré, Marcel
Duras, Marguerite
Dürer, Albrecht
Durham, John George Lambton, 1st Earl of
Durkheim, Emile
Durrell, Gerald Malcolm
Durrell, Lawrence George
Dürrenmatt, Friedrich
Duse, Eleonora
Duval, Claude
Duvalier, François
Duvalier, Jean-Claude
Dvořák, Antonín
Dylan, Bob
Eadred
Eads, John Buchanan
Eadwig (or Edwy)
Eakins, Thomas
Eanes, António dos Santos Ramalho
Earhart, Amelia
Eastman, George
Eastwood, Clint
Ebert, Friedrich
Eccles, Sir John Carew
Ecevit, Bülent
Echegaray y Eizaguirre, José
Eck, Johann Maier von
Eckermann, Johann Peter
Eckert, John Presper

Eckhart, Meister
Eco, Umberto
Eddington, Sir Arthur Stanley
Eddy, Mary Baker
Eden, (Robert) Anthony, 1st Earl of Avon
Edgar the Aetheling
Edgeworth, Maria
Edison, Thomas Alva
Edwards, Jonathan
Edwy variant of Eadwig
Egmont, Lamoraal, Graaf van
Ehrenberg, Iliya Grigorievich
Ehrlich, Paul
Eichendorff, Josef, Freiherr von
Eichler, August Wilhelm
Eichmann, Adolf
Eijkman, Christiaan
Einhard
Einstein, Albert
Einthoven, Willem
Eisenhower, Dwight D(avid)
Eisenstein, Sergei
El Cid (or Rodrigo Diáz de Vivar)
Elgar, Sir Edward
El Greco
Eliot, George
Eliot, Sir John
Eliot, T(homas) S(tearns)
Ellenborough, Edward Law, Earl of
Ellington, Duke
Ellis, (Henry) Havelock
Elton, Charles
Éluard, Paul
Elyot, Sir Thomas
Emerson, Ralph Waldo
Emin Paşa, Mehmed
Emmet, Robert
Empedocles
Empson, Sir William
Enders, John Franklin
Endlicher, Stephan Ladislaus
Enesco, Georges
Engels, Friedrich
Engler, Gustav Heinrich Adolf
Ennius, Quintus

Ensor, James Sydney, Baron
Enver Pasha
Epaminondas
Epictetus
Epicurus
Epstein, Sir Jacob
Erasistratus of Ceos
Erasmus, Desiderius
Eratosthenes of Cyrene
Erceldoune, Thomas of
Ercilla, Alonso de
Erhard, Ludwig
Ericsson, John
Erigena, John Scotus
Erik Swedish king
Erlanger, Joseph
Ernst, Max
Erskine, Thomas Erskine, 1st Baron
Erté
Esarhaddon
Eschenbach, Wolfram von
Escoffier, Auguste
Essex, Robert Devereux, Earl of
Estienne, Henri
Estienne, Robert
Ethelwulf
Etherege, Sir George
Etty, William
Eucken, Rudolf Christoph
Euclid
Eudoxus of Cnidus
Eugène of Savoy, Prince
Eugénie empress of France
Euler, Leonhard
Euphronios
Eupolis
Euripides
Eusebius of Caesarea
Eustachio, Bartolommeo
Evans, Sir Arthur John
Evans, Dame Edith
Evans, Sir Geraint
Evans, Oliver
Evelyn, John
Evert, Chris(tine)
Ewald, Johannes
Exekias
Eyre, Edward John
Eysenck, Hans Jürgen
Fabergé, Peter Carl
Fabius Maximus, Quintus

Fabre, Jean Henri
Fabricius ab Aquapendente, Hieronymus
Fabritius, Carel
Fabry, Charles
Fadden, Sir Arthur William
Fahd Ibn Abdul Aziz
Fa-hsien *variant spelling of* Fa Xian
Faidherbe, Louis (Léon César)
Fairbanks, Douglas
Fairfax, Thomas, 3rd Baron
Faisal
Faisal Ibn Abdul Aziz
Fakhr ad-Din II
Falla, Manuel de
Fallopius, Gabriel
Fangio, Juan Manuel
Fa Ngum
Fantin-Latour, (Ignace) Henri (Joseph Théodore)
Faraday, Michael
Farel, Guillaume
Fargo, William
Farnaby, Giles
Farnese, Alessandro, Duke of Parma
Farouk
Farquhar, George
Fassbinder, Rainer Werner
Fateh Singh, Sant
Fatimah
Faulkner, William
Fauré, Gabriel (Urbain)
Fawcett, Henry
Fawcett, Dame Millicent Garrett
Fawkes, Guy
Fa Xian (*or* Fa-hsien)
Fechner, Gustav Theodor
Feininger, Lyonel (Charles Adrian)
Fellini, Federico
Fénelon, François de Salignac de la Mothe
Ferlinghetti, Lawrence
Fermat, Pierre de
Fermi, Enrico
Fernandel
Ferrar, Nicholas
Ferrier, Kathleen
Ferrier, Susan Edmonstone
Feuchtwanger, Lion
Feuerbach, Ludwig Andreas

Feuillère, Edwige
Feydeau, Georges
Feynman, Richard Phillips
Fibonacci, Leonardo
Fichte, Johann Gottlieb
Ficino, Marsilio
Field, Cyrus West
Field, John
Fielding, Henry
Fields, Gracie
Fields, W. C.
Fife, Duncan *variant spelling of* Phyfe, Duncan
Filarete
Fillmore, Millard
Finlay, Carlos Juan
Finney, Albert
Finsen, Niels Ryberg
Firbank, (Arthur Annesley) Ronald
Firdausi
Firth, J(ohn) R(upert)
Fischer, Bobby
Fischer, Emil Hermann
Fischer-Dieskau, Dietrich
Fischer von Erlach, Johann Bernhard
Fisher, Andrew
Fisher, John Arbuthnot, 1st Baron
Fisher, St John
Fitzgerald, Edward
Fitzgerald, Ella
Fitzgerald, F(rancis) Scott (Key)
Fitzgerald, George Francis
Fitzsimmons, Bob
Flagstad, Kirsten Malfrid
Flaherty, Robert (Joseph)
Flamininus, Titus Quinctius
Flaminius, Gaius
Flamsteed, John
Flaubert, Gustave
Flaxman, John Henry
Flecker, (Herman) James Elroy
Flémalle, Master of
Fleming, Sir Alexander
Fleming, Ian (Lancaster)
Fleming, Sir John Ambrose
Fleming, Paul
Fletcher, John
Fleury, André Hercule de, Cardinal

Flinders, Matthew
Flood, Henry
Florey, Howard Walter, Baron
Florio, John
Floris, Cornelis
Floris, Frans
Flotow, Friedrich von
Fludd, Robert
Flynn, Errol
Fo, Dario
Foch, Ferdinand
Fokine, Michel
Fokker, Anthony Hermann Gerard
Foley, John Henry
Fonda, Henry
Fonda, Jane
Fonda, Peter
Fontana, Domenico
Fontane, Theodor
Fontanne, Lyn
Fontenelle, Bernard le Bovier de
Fonteyn, Dame Margot
Foot, Michael (Mackintosh)
Forbes, George William
Ford, Ford Madox
Ford, Gerald R(udolph)
Ford, Harrison
Ford, Henry
Ford, John
Foreman, George
Forester, C(ecil) S(cott)
Forman, Miloš
Forster, E(dward) M(organ)
Fortescue, Sir John
Foscolo, Ugo
Foster, Jodie
Foster, Sir Norman
Foster, Stephen Collins
Fothergill, John
Foucault, Jean Bernard Léon
Fouché, Joseph, Duc d'Otrante
Fouqué, Friedrich Heinrich Karl, Baron de la Motte
Fouquet, Jean
Fouquet, Nicolas
Fourier, (François Marie) Charles
Fourier, Jean Baptiste Joseph, Baron
Fourneyron, Benoît

Fowler, Francis
Fowler, H(enry) W(atson)
Fowles, John
Fox, Charles James
Fox, George
Foxe, John
Fragonard, Jean Honoré
Frampton, Sir George James
France, Anatole
Francis, Sir Philip
Franck, César Auguste
Franck, James
Franco, Francisco
Frank, Anne
Frankfurter, Felix
Franklin, Benjamin
Franklin, Sir John
Fraser, (John) Malcolm
Fraser, Peter
Fraunhofer, Joseph von
Frazer, Sir James George
Frazier, Joe
Frederick Barbarossa
Frege, Gottlob
Frei (Montalva), Eduardo
Frémont, John C(harles)
French, John, Earl of Ypres
Freneau, Philip
Fresnel, Augustin Jean
Freud, Anna
Freud, Clement
Freud, Lucian
Freud, Sigmund
Friedman, Milton
Friedman, Rose
Friedrich, Caspar David
Friml, Rudolph
Frisch, Karl von
Frisch, Max
Frisch, Otto Robert
Frisch, Ragnar
Frobisher, Sir Martin
Fröding, Gustaf
Froebel, Friedrich Wilhelm
    August
Froissart, Jean
Fromm, Erich
Frontenac, Louis de Buade,
    Comte de Palluau et de
Frost, Robert Lee
Froude, James Anthony
Fry, Christopher
Fry, Elizabeth
Fry, Roger (Eliot)
Fu'ad

Fuchs, (Emil Julius) Klaus
Fuchs, Sir Vivian (Ernest)
Fugard, Athol
Fujimori, Alberto
Fuller, J(ohn) F(rederick)
    C(harles)
Fuller, Richard
    Buckminster
Fuller, Roy (Broadbent)
Fuller, Thomas
Fulton, Robert
Furtwängler, Wilhelm
Fuseli, Henry
Fust, Johann
Gabin, Jean
Gable, Clark
Gabo, Naum
Gabor, Dennis
Gabrieli, Andrea
Gabrieli, Giovanni
Gaddafi, Moammar al-
Gaddi, Agnolo
Gaddi, Taddeo
Gagarin, Yuri Alekseevich
Gage, Thomas
Gainsborough, Thomas
Gaitskell, Hugh (Todd
    Naylor)
Galbraith, John Kenneth
Galen
Galerius
Galileo Galilei
Gall, Franz Joseph
Galle, Johann Gottfried
Galli-Curci, Amelita
Gallup, George Horace
Galois, Évariste
Galsworthy, John
Galt, John
Galton, Sir Francis
Galuppi, Baldassare
Galvani, Luigi
Galway, James
Gama, Vasco da
Gambetta, Léon
Gamliel
Gandhi, Indira
Gandhi, Mohandas
    Karamchand
Gandhi, Rajiv
Gandhi, Sanjay
Garbo, Greta
García Lorca, Federico
García Márquez, Gabriel
Gardiner, Stephen

Garibaldi, Giuseppe
Garland, Judy
Garrick, David
Gaskell, Elizabeth
    Cleghorn
Gassendi, Pierre
Gasser, Herbert Spencer
Gates, Bill
Gates, Horatio
Gaudier-Brzeska, Henri
Gaudí y Cornet, Antonio
Gauguin, Paul
Gaultier, Jean-Paul
Gaunt, John of, Duke of
    Lancaster
Gauss, Karl Friedrich
Gautama Siddhartha
    original name of Buddha
Gautier, Théophile
Gay, John
Gay-Lussac, Joseph Louis
Geber
Gediminas
Geiger, Hans
Geldof, Bob
Gell-Mann, Murray
Genet, Jean
Genghis Khan
Genseric
Gentile, Giovanni
Gentile da Fabriano
Geoffroy Saint-Hilaire,
    Étienne
George, Stefan
Gérard, François (Pascal
    Simon), Baron
Géricault, (Jean Louis
    André) Théodore
Germanicus Julius Caesar
Geronimo
Gershwin, George
Gershwin, Ira
Gerson, Jean de
Gesner, Conrad
Gesualdo, Carlo, Prince of
    Venosa
Getty, J(ean) Paul
Geulincx, Arnold
Ghazna, Mahmud of
Ghiberti, Lorenzo
Ghirlandaio, Domenico
Giacometti, Alberto
Giambologna
Gibbon, Edward
Gibbons, Grinling

Gibbons, Orlando
Gibbs, James
Gibbs, Josiah Willard
Gibran, Khalil
Gibson, Mel
Gide, André
Gielgud, Sir (Arthur) John
Gierek, Edward
Gigli, Beniamino
Gilbert, Sir Humphrey
Gilbert, William
Gilbert, Sir William
Schwenk
Giles, Carl Ronald
Gill, (Arthur) Eric (Rowton)
Gillespie, Dizzy
Gillray, James
Ginkel, Godert de, 1st Earl
of Athlone
Ginsberg, Allen
Giordano, Luca
Giorgione
Giotto
Giraldus Cambrensis
Giraudoux, Jean
Girtin, Thomas
Giscard d'Estaing, Valéry
Gish, Dorothy
Gish, Lillian
Gislebertus
Gissing, George Robert
Giulini, Carlo Maria
Giulio Romano
Gladstone, W(illiam)
E(wart)
Glanville, Ranulf de
Glaser, Donald Arthur
Glass, Philip
Glazunov, Aleksandr
Konstantinovich
Glendower, Owen
Glinka, Mikhail Ivanovich
Gluck, Christoph Willibald
Gneisenau, August
(Wilhelm Anton), Graf
Neithardt von
Gobbi, Tito
Gobind Singh (or Govind
Singh)
Gobineau, Joseph Arthur,
Comte de
Godard, Jean-Luc
Goddard, Robert
Hutchings
Gödel, Kurt

Goderich, George Frederick
Samuel Robinson,
Viscount
Godiva, Lady
Godolphin, Sidney, Earl of
Godoy, Manuel de
Godunov, Boris
(Fedorovich)
Godwin, William
Goebbels, (Paul) Joseph
Goes, Hugo van der
Goethe, Johann Wolfgang
von
Gogol, Nikolai Vasilievich
Gold, Thomas
Golding, Sir William
Goldoni, Carlo
Goldschmidt, Richard
Benedict
Goldsmith, Oliver
Goldwyn, Samuel
Golgi, Camillo
Gollancz, Victor
Golovkin, Gavril
Ivanovich, Count
Gómez, Juan Vicente
Gomułka, Władysław
Goncharov, Ivan
Aleksandrovich
Goncourt, Edmond de
Goncourt, Jules de
Gondomar, Diego
Sarmiento de Acuña,
Conde de
Góngora y Argote, Luis de
González de Mendoza,
Pedro
Goodman, Benny
Goodyear, Charles
Goolagong, Evonne maiden
name of Evonne Cawley
Goossens, Sir Eugene
Goossens, Leon
Gorbachov, Mikhail
Sergeevich
Gordon, Charles George
Gore, Al(bert)
Górecki, Henryk
Göring, Hermann Wilhelm
Gorki, Maksim
Gorky, Arshile
Gorton, Sir John Grey
Gossaert, Jan (known as
Mabuse)
Gosse, Sir Edmund

Gottfried von Strassburg
Gottsched, Johann
Christoph
Goujon, Jean
Gounod, Charles François
Govind Singh variant
spelling of Gobind Singh
Gower, John
Gowon, Yakubu
Goya(y Lucientes),
Francesco (Jose) de
Goyen, Jan Josephszoon
van
Gozzi, Carlo
Gozzoli, Benozzo
Gracchus, Gaius
Sempronius
Gracchus, Tiberius
Sempronius
Grace, W(illiam) G(ilbert)
Graf, Steffi
Graham, Billy
Graham, Martha
Graham, Thomas
Grahame, Kenneth
Grainger, Percy Aldridge
Gramsci, Antonio
Granados, Enrique
Granby, John Manners,
Marquess of
Grant, Cary
Grant, Duncan James
Corrowr
Grant, Ulysses S(impson)
Granville, Granville George
Leveson-Gower, 2nd Earl
Granville, John Carteret,
1st Earl
Granville-Barker, Harley
Grappelli, Stephane
Grass, Günter
Gratian(us), Flavius
Grattan, Henry
Graves, Robert (Ranke)
Gray, Asa
Gray, Thomas
Greeley, Horace
Green, Henry
Greenaway, Kate
Greenaway, Peter
Greene, (Henry) Graham
Greene, Nathaneal
Greene, Robert
Greenough, Horatio
Greenwood, Walter

Harlow, Jean

Harmsworth, Alfred, 1st
   Viscount Northcliffe

Harmsworth, Harold, 1st
   Viscount Rothermere

Harnack, Adolf von

Harriman, W(illiam)
   Averell

Harrington, James

Harris, Joel Chandler

Harris, Roy

Harrison, Benjamin

Harrison, George

Harrison, William Henry

Harsa (or Harsha)

Hart, Moss

Harte, (Francis) Bret(t)

Hartley, L(esley) P(oles)

Hartmann, (Karl Robert)
   Eduard von

Hartmann, Nicolai

Hartnell, Sir Norman

Harun ar-Rashid

Harvey, William

Hasan al-Basri, al-

Hasdrubal (Barca)

Hašek, Jaroslav

Haselrig, Sir Arthur variant
   spelling of Hesilrig, Sir
   Arthur

Hassall, John

Hassan

Hastings, Francis
   Rawdon-Hastings, 1st
   Marquess of

Hastings, Warren

Hathaway, Anne

Hatshepsut

Hauptmann, Gerhart

Haussmann,
   Georges-Eugène, Baron

Havel, Václav

Haw-Haw, Lord see Joyce,
   William

Hawke, Edward, 1st Baron

Hawke, Robert (James Lee)

Hawking, Stephen
   (William)

Hawkins, Sir John

Hawkins, Sir Richard

Hawks, Howard

Hawksmoor, Nicholas

Haworth, Sir Walter
   Norman

Hawthorn, Mike

Hawthorne, Nathaniel

Hay, Will

Haya de la Torre, Victor
   Raúl

Haydn, Franz Joseph

Hayes, Rutherford
   B(irchard)

Hazlitt, William

Healey, Denis (Winston),
   Baron

Heaney, Seamus (Justin)

Hearst, William Randolph

Heath, Sir Edward (Richard
   George)

Heaviside, Oliver

Hebbel, (Christian)
   Friedrich

Hébert, Jacques-René

Heenan, John Carmel,
   Cardinal

Hegel, Georg Wilhelm
   Friedrich

Heidegger, Martin

Heifetz, Jascha

Heine, Heinrich

Heisenberg, Werner Karl

Heller, Joseph

Hellman, Lillian

Helmholtz, Hermann
   Ludwig Ferdinand von

Helmont, Jan Baptist van

Helpmann, Sir Robert

Helvétius, Claude Adrien

Hemingway, Ernest

Henderson, Arthur

Hendrix, Jimi

Henry, Joseph

Henry, O.

Henry, Patrick

Henryson, Robert

Henze, Hans Werner

Hepburn, Katharine

Hepplewhite, George

Hepworth, Dame Barbara

Heraclitus Greek
   philosopher

Heraclius Byzantine
   emperor

Herbart, Johann Friedrich

Herbert, George

Herder, Johann Gottfried

Hereward the Wake

Hermann von Reichenau

Hermite, Charles

Herod

Herodotus

Hero of Alexandria

Herophilus

Herrera, Francisco de

Herrera, Juan de

Herrick, Robert

Herriot, Édouard

Herschel, Caroline

Herschel, Sir John

Herschel, Sir William

Hertz, Heinrich Rudolf

Hertzog, James Barry
   Munnik

Herzen, Aleksandr
   (Ivanovich)

Herzl, Theodor

Herzog, Werner

Hesilrige (or Haselrig), Sir
   Arthur

Hesiod

Hess, Dame Myra

Hess, Rudolf

Hess, Victor Francis

Hesse, Hermann

Hevesy, George Charles
   von

Heyerdahl, Thor

Heywood, Thomas

Hezekiah

Hickok, James Butler

Hideyoshi

Highsmith, Patricia

Hilbert, David

Hill, Archibald Vivian

Hill, Damon

Hill, David Octavius

Hill, Graham

Hill, Octavia

Hill, Sir Rowland

Hillary, Sir Edmund
   (Percival)

Hillel

Hillery, Patrick (John)

Hilliard, Nicholas

Hilton, James

Himmler, Heinrich

Hincmar of Reims

Hindemith, Paul

Hindenburg, Paul von
   Beneckendorff und von

Hines, Earl (Fatha)

Hinkler, Herbert John
   Lewis

Hinshelwood, Sir Cyril
   Norman

Hipparchus
Hippocrates
Hirohito
Hiroshige
Hirst, Damien
Hitchcock, Sir Alfred
Hitler, Adolf
Hoad, Lew(is Alan)
Hobbema, Meindert
Hobbes, Thomas
Hobbs, Jack
Hochhuth, Rolf
Ho Chi Minh
Hockney, David
Hoddinott, Alun
Hodgkin, Sir Alan Lloyd
Hodgkin, Dorothy Mary
 Crowfoot
Hodgkin, Thomas
Hoffman, Dustin
Hofmann, Joseph Casimir
Hofmannsthal, Hugo von
Hofmeister, Wilhelm
 Friedrich Benedict
Hogan, Ben
Hogarth, William
Hogg, James
Hohenlohe-Schillingsfürst,
 Chlodwig Karl Viktor,
 Fürst zu
Hokusai
Holbein, Hans
Holberg, Ludvig, Baron
Hölderlin, (Johann
 Christian) Friedrich
Holiday, Billie
Holinshed, Raphael
Holland, Henry
Holland, Sir Sidney
 (George)
Hollar, Wenceslaus
Holles, Denzil, Baron
Holliger, Heinz
Holmes, Oliver Wendell
Holst, Gustav (Theodore)
Holt, Harold (Edward)
Holyoake, Sir Keith Jacka
Home, Daniel Douglas
Home of the Hirsel, Alec
 Douglas-Home, Baron
Homer
Homer, Winslow
Honecker, Erich
Honegger, Arthur
Hong-wu (or Hung-wu)

Hong Xiu Quan (or Hung
 Hsiu-ch'uan)
Honorius
Honthorst, Gerrit von
Hooch, Pieter de
Hood, Samuel, 1st Viscount
Hood, Thomas
Hooft, Pieter Corneliszoon
Hooke, Robert
Hooker, Sir Joseph Dalton
Hooker, Richard
Hooker, Sir William
 Jackson
Hoover, Herbert (Clark)
Hoover, J(ohn) Edgar
Hope, Anthony
Hope, Bob
Hopkins, Sir Anthony
Hopkins, Sir Frederick
 Gowland
Hopkins, Gerard Manley
Hopkins, Harry (Lloyd)
Hopkinson, John
Hoppner, John
Hore-Belisha, (Isaac) Leslie,
 1st Baron
Horn, Filips van
 Montmorency, Graaf van
Horowitz, Vladimir
Horta, Victor
Horthy de Nagybánya,
 Miklós
Hotspur see Percy, Sir
 Henry
Hotter, Hans
Houdini, Harry
Houdon, Jean Antoine
Houphouët-Boigny, Félix
Housman, A(lfred)
 E(dward)
Hovell, William Hilton
Howard, Catherine
Howard, Sir Ebenezer
Howard, Henry, Earl of
 Surrey
Howard, John
Howard, John (Winston)
Howard, Leslie
Howard, Trevor
Howard of Effingham,
 Charles, 2nd Baron
Howe, Elias
Howe, (Richard Edward)
 Geoffrey, Baron
Howe, Richard, Earl

Howe, William, 5th
 Viscount
Hoxha, Enver
Hoyle, Edmond
Hoyle, Sir Fred
Hsia Kuei variant spelling of
 Xia Gui
Hsuan-tsang variant spelling
 of Xuan Cang
Hua Guo Feng (or Hua
 Kuo-feng)
Huascar
Hubble, Edwin Powell
Huddleston, Trevor
Hudson, Henry
Hudson, W(illiam) H(enry)
Huggins, Sir William
Hughes, Howard (Robard)
Hughes, Richard
Hughes, Ted
Hughes, Thomas
Hughes, William M(orris)
Hugo, Victor (Marie)
Huizinga, Johan
Hull, Cordell
Humbolt, (Friedrich
 Wilhelm Karl Heinrich)
 Alexander von
Humboldt, (Karl) Wilhelm
 von
Hume, Basil George,
 Cardinal
Hume, David
Hume, Hamilton
Hume, John
Hume, Joseph
Hummel, Johann Nepomuk
Humperdinck, Engelbert
Humphrey, Hubert Horatio
Hung Hsiu-ch'uan variant
 spelling of Hong Xiu Quan
Hung-wu variant spelling of
 Hong-wu
Hunt, Henry
Hunt, James
Hunt, (Henry Cecil) John,
 Baron
Hunt, (James Henry) Leigh
Hunt, William Holman
Hunter, John
Hunter, William
Huntingdon, Selina
 Hastings, Countess of
Hunyadi, János
Hus, Jan

Jongkind, Johan Barthold
Jonson, Ben
Joplin, Scott
Jordaens, Jakob
Jordan, Dorothy
Jordan, Michael
Joselito
Joseph, Sir Keith (Sinjohn)
Josephson, Brian David
Josephus, Flavius
Josquin des Prez
Joubert, Piet
Joule, James Prescott
Jouvet, Louis
Jovian, Flavius
Jowett, Benjamin
Joyce, James
Joyce, William (known as
    Lord Haw-Haw)
Juan Carlos
Juantorena, Alberto
Juárez, Benito (Pablo)
Judah ha-Levi
Jugurtha
Jung, Carl Gustav
Jussieu, Antoine de
Jussieu, Antoine-Laurent de
Jussieu, Bernard de
Jussieu, Joseph de
Justinian
Juvenal
Kádár, János
Kafka, Franz
Kahn, Louis I(sadore)
Kaiser, Georg
Kakinomoto Hitomaro
Kalidasa
Kalinin, Mikhail Ivanovich
Kamehameha
Kamenev, Lev Borisovich
Kandinsky, Wassily
Kang Xi (or K'ang-hsi)
Kang You Wei
Kant, Immanuel
Kapil Dev
Kapitza, Peter Leonidovich
Karageorge
Karajan, Herbert von
Karamanlis, Constantine
Karan, Donna
Karloff, Boris
Károlyi, Mihály, Count
Karpov, Anatoly
Kasavubu, Joseph
Kassem, Abdul Karim

Kästner, Erich
Katsura Taro
Kauffmann, Angelica
Kaufman, George S(imon)
Kaunda, Kenneth (David)
Kaunitz, Wenzel Anton,
    Count von
Kawabata Yasunari
Kay, John
Kazan, Elia
Kazantzakis, Nikos
Kean, Edmund
Keating, Paul
Keaton, Buster
Keats, John
Keble, John
Keegan, Kevin
Keene, Charles Samuel
Keitel, Wilhelm
Kekulé von Stradonitz,
    (Friedrich) August
Keller, Gottfried
Keller, Helen Adams
Kelly, Grace
Kelly, Ned
Kelvin, William Thomson,
    1st Baron
Kemal, (Mehmed) Namik
Kemble, Charles
Kemble, Frances Ann
Kemble, John Philip
Kemble, Roger
Kempe, Margery
Kempe, Rudolf
Kempis, Thomas à
Kendall, Edward Calvin
Kendall, Henry
Kendrew, Sir John Cowdery
Keneally, Thomas Michael
Kennedy, Edward Moore
Kennedy, John Fitzgerald
Kennedy, Joseph Patrick
Kennedy, Robert Francis
Kennelly, Arthur Edwin
Kent, William
Kenyatta, Jomo
Kenyon, Dame Kathleen
Kepler, Johannes
Kerenski, Aleksandr
    Feodorovich
Kern, Jerome (David)
Kerouac, Jack
Kertanagara
Kesey, Ken
Kesselring, Albert

Ketch, Jack
Kettering, Charles Franklin
Keynes, John Maynard, 1st
    Baron
Khachaturian, Aram Ilich
Khafre
Khalid Ibn Abdul Aziz
Khalifa see Abd Allah
Khama, Sir Seretse
Khlebnikov, Velimir
Khomeini, Ayatollah
    Ruholla
Khorana, Har Gobind
Khosrow
Khrushchev, Nikita
    S(ergeevich)
Khufu
Kidd, William
Kidinnu
Kierkegaard, Søren
Kilvert, Francis
Kim Il Sung
King, Billie Jean
King, Martin Luther
King, William Lyon
    Mackenzie
Kingsley, Charles
Kingsley, Mary Henriette
Kinsey, Alfred
Kipling, (Joseph) Rudyard
Kirchhoff, Gustav Robert
Kirchner, Ernst Ludwig
Kirk, Norman (Eric)
Kirov, Sergei Mironovich
Kissinger, Henry (Alfred)
Kitagawa Utamaro
Kitasato, Shibasaburo
Kitchener of Khartoum,
    Horatio Herbert, 1st Earl
Kivi, Alexis
Klaproth, Martin Heinrich
Kléber, Jean Baptiste
Klebs, Edwin
Klee, Paul
Klein, Melanie
Kleist, Heinrich von
Klemperer, Otto
Klimt, Gustav
Klinger, Friedrich
    Maximilian von
Klint, Kaare
Klopstock, Friedrich
    Gottlieb
Kneller, Sir Godfrey
Knight, Harold

Knight, Dame Laura
Knox, John
Knox, Ronald (Arbuthnott)
Kobayashi Masaki
Koch, Robert
Köchel, Ludwig von
Kodály, Zoltan
Koestler, Arthur
Koffka, Kurt
Kohl, Helmut
Köhler, Wolfgang
Kokoschka, Oskar
Kolbe, (Adolf Wilhelm) Hermann
Kolchak, Alexander Vasilievich
Koldewey, Robert
Kolmogorov, Andrei Nikolaevich
Koniecpolski, Stanisław
Koniev, Ivan Stepanovich
Konoe Fumimaro, Prince
Korchnoi, Victor
Korda, Sir Alexander
Kornberg, Arthur
Kornilov, Lavrentia Georgievich
Koroliov, Sergei Pavlovich
Kosciuszko, Tadeusz Andrezei Bonawentura
Kossuth, Lajos
Kosygin, Aleksei Nikolaevich
Kotzebue, August von
Koussevitsky, Sergei
Koxinga see Zheng Cheng Gong
Kozirev, Nikolai Aleksandrovich
Krafft-Ebing, Richard von
Krebs, Sir Hans Adolf
Kreisky, Bruno
Kreisler, Fritz
Křenek, Ernst
Kreutzer, Rodolphe
Krishna Menon
Krochmal, Nachman
Kropotkin, Peter, Prince
Kroto, Sir Harold
Kruger, (Stephanus Johannes) Paul(us)
Krum
Krupp, Alfred
Krupp, Alfried
Krupp, Arndt

Krupp, Bertha
Krupp, Friedrich
Krupp, Gustav von Bohlen und Halbach
Kuang-hsü variant spelling of Guang Xu
Kubelik, Jan
Kubelik, Rafael
Kublai Khan
Kubrick, Stanley
Kukai
Kun, Béla
Kundera, Milan
Kuo Mo-jo
Kurchatov, Igor Vasilievich
Kurosawa, Akira
Kusunoki Masashige
Kutuzov, Mikhail Ilarionovich, Prince of Smolensk
Kuznets, Simon
Kyd, Thomas
Kyprianou, Spyros
Labiche, Eugène
La Bruyère, Jean de
Laclos, Pierre Choderlos de
La Condamine, Charles Marie de
Lacroix, Christian
Laënnec, René Théophile Hyacinth
Lafayette, Marie Joseph Gilbert Motier, Marquis de
La Fayette, Mme de
Lafontaine, Henri-Marie
La Fontaine, Jean de
Laforgue, Jules
Lagerkvist, Pär (Fabian)
Lagerlöf, Selma Ottiliana Lovisa
Lagrange, Joseph Louis, Comte de
La Guardia, Fiorello Henry
Laing, R(onald) D(avid)
Laird, Macgregor
Lalande, Joseph-Jérôme Le Français de
Lalique, René
Lally, Thomas, Comte de
Lalo, (Victor Antoine) Édouard
Lalor, Peter
Lamarck, Jean-Baptiste de Monet, Chevalier de

Lamartine, Alphonse de
Lamb, Lady Caroline
Lamb, Charles
Lamb, Henry
Lamb, Sir Horace
Lambert, Constant
Lambert, Johann Heinrich
Lambert, John
Lamerie, Paul de
Lampedusa, Giuseppe Tomasi di
Lancaster, Sir Osbert
Lanchester, Frederick William
Land, Edwin Herbert
Landau, Lev Davidovich
Landor, Walter Savage
Landowska, Wanda
Landseer, Sir Edwin Henry
Landsteiner, Karl
Lane, Sir Allen
Lanfranc
Lang, Andrew
Lang, Fritz
Lange, David Russell
Langland, William
Langley, Samuel Pierpont
Langmuir, Irving
Langton, Stephen
Langtry, Lillie
Lanier, Sidney
Lankester, Sir Edwin Ray
Lansbury, George
Lansdowne, Henry Charles Keith Petty-Fitzmaurice, 5th Marquess of
Lao Zi (or Lao Tzu)
Laplace, Pierre Simon, Marquis de
Lara, Brian
Lardner, Ring
Larkin, Philip
La Rochefoucauld, François, Duc de
Larousse, Pierre
Lars Porsena
Lartet, Édouard Armand Isidore Hippolyte
La Salle, Robert Cavelier, Sieur de
Lascaris, Theodore
Las Casas, Bartolomé de
Las Cases, Emmanuel, Comte de
Lasdun, Sir Denys

Lasker, Emanuel
Laski, Harold Joseph
Laski, Marghanita
Lassalle, Ferdinand
Lassus, Roland de
László
Latimer, Hugh
Latini, Brunetto
La Tour, Georges de
La Tour, Maurice-Quentin de
Laud, William
Lauda, Niki
Lauder, Sir Harry
Lauderdale, John Maitland, Duke of
Laue, Max Theodor Felix von
Laughton, Charles
Laurel, Stan
Laurier, Sir Wilfrid
Lautréamont, Comte de
Laval, Pierre
La Vallière, Louise de Françoise de la Baume le Blanc, Duchesse de
Laver, Rod(ney George)
Laveran, Charles Louis Alphonse
Lavoisier, Antoine Laurent
Law, (Andrew) Bonar
Law, William
Lawes, Sir John Bennet
Lawler, Ray
Lawrence, St
Lawrence, D(avid) H(erbert)
Lawrence, Ernest Orlando
Lawrence, Gertrude
Lawrence, John Laird Mair, 1st Baron
Lawrence, T(homas) E(dward)
Lawrence, Sir Thomas
Laxness, Halldór (Kiljan)
Layamon
Layard, Sir Austen Henry
Leach, Bernard (Howell)
Leacock, Stephen (Butler)
Leadbelly
Leakey, Louis Seymour Bazett
Leakey, Mary
Leakey, Richard
Lean, Sir David

Lear, Edward
Leavis, F(rank) R(aymond)
Le Brun, Charles
Le Carré, John
Le Châtelier, Henri-Louis
Leconte de Lisle, Charles Marie René
Lecoq de Boisbaudran, Paul-Émile
Le Corbusier
Lederberg, Joshua
Le Duc Tho
Lee, Bruce
Lee, Gypsy Rose
Lee, Jenny, Baroness
Lee, Laurie
Lee, Robert E(dward)
Lee, Spike
Lee, Tsung-Dao
Leech, John
Lee Kuan Yew
Leeuwenhoek, Antonie van
Le Fanu, (Joseph) Sheridan
Legendre, Adrien Marie
Léger, Fernand
Lehár, Franz
Lehmann, Lilli
Lehmann, Lotte
Leibniz, Gottfried Wilhelm
Leicester, Robert Dudley, Earl of
Leichardt, (Friedrich Wilhelm) Ludwig
Leif Eriksson
Leigh, Vivien
Leighton of Stretton, Frederic, Baron
Leland, John
Lely, Sir Peter
Lemaître, Georges Édouard, Abbé
Le Nain, Antoine
Le Nain, Louis
Le Nain, Mathieu
Lenclos, Ninon de
L'Enfant, Pierre-Charles
Lenglen, Suzanne
Lenin, Vladimir Ilich
Lennon, John
Le Nôtre, André
Lenya, Lotte
Leonardo da Vinci
Leoncavallo, Ruggiero
Leonidas
Leonov, Leonid

Leopardi, Giacomo
Leopold
Lepidus, Marcus Aemilius
Lermontov, Mikhail
Lerner, Alan Jay
Lesage, Alain-René
Leschetizky, Theodor
Lescot, Pierre
Lesseps, Ferdinand de
Lessing, Doris
Lessing, Gotthold Ephraim
Leszczyński, Stanisław
Le Tellier, Michel
Leucippus
Leuckart, Karl Georg Friedrich Rudolph
Le Vau, Louis
Leven, Alexander Leslie, 1st Earl of
Leverhulme, William Hesketh Lever, 1st Viscount
Leverrier, Urbain Jean Joseph
Lévesque, René
Lévi-Strauss, Claude
Lewes, George Henry
Lewis, Carl
Lewis, C. Day
Lewis, C(live) S(taples)
Lewis, Matthew Gregory
Lewis, (Harry) Sinclair
Lewis, (Percy) Wyndham
Libby, Willard Frank
Lichtenstein, Roy
Liddell Hart, Sir Basil Henry
Lie, Trygve (Halvdan)
Liebig, Justus, Baron von
Liebknecht, Karl
Liebknecht, Wilhelm
Lifar, Serge
Ligeti, György
Li Hong Zhang (or Li Hung-chang)
Lilburne, John
Lilienthal, Otto
Liliuokalani
Lillie, Beatrice
Limburg, de
Limosin, Léonard
Linacre, Thomas
Lin Biao (or Lin Piao)
Lincoln, Abraham

Lind, Jenny
Lindbergh, Charles
  A(ugustus)
Lindsay, (Nicholas) Vachel
Lindwall, Raymond Russell
Linklater, Eric
Linnaeus, Carolus
Lin Ze Xu (or Lin Tse-hsü)
Liouville, Joseph
Lipchitz, Jacques
Li Bo (or Li Po)
Lippershey, Hans
Lippi, Filippino
Lippi, Fra Filippo
Lipscomb, William Nunn
Lissitzky, El
List, Friedrich
Lister, Joseph, 1st Baron
Liszt, Franz
Littlewood, Joan
Litvinov, Maksim
  Maksimovich
Liu Shao Qi (or Liu
  Shao-sh'i)
Liverpool, Robert Banks
  Jenkinson, 2nd Earl of
Livia Drusilla
Livingstone, David
Livy
Llewellyn, Harry
Llewellyn, Richard
Lloyd, Harold
Lloyd, Marie
Lloyd George, David, 1st
  Earl
Lloyd George, Dame
  Margaret
Lloyd Webber, Andrew,
  Baron
Lloyd Webber, Julian
Llywelyn ap Gruffudd
Llywelyn ap Iorwerth
Lobachevski, Nikolai
  Ivanovich
Lobengula
Lochner, Stefan
Locke, John
Locke, Matthew
Lockhart, Sir (Robert
  Hamilton) Bruce
Lockhart, John Gibson
Lockyer, Sir Joseph
  Norman
Lodge, Henry Cabot
Lodge, Sir Oliver Joseph

Lodge, Thomas
Loeb, Jacques
Loeffler, Friedrich August
  Johannes
Loewe, Frederick
Loewi, Otto
Lomax, Alan
Lomax, John Avery
Lombard, Peter
Lombardo, Antonio
Lombardo, Pietro
Lombardo, Tullio
Lombroso, Cesare
Lomonosov, Mikhail
  Vasilievich
London, Jack
Longfellow, Henry
  Wadsworth
Longhi, Alessandro
Longhi, Pietro
Longinus
Lonsdale, Gordon Arnold
Lonsdale, Dame Kathleen
Loos, Adolph
Lope de Vega
López, Carlos Antonio
López, Francisco Solano
López de Ayala, Pero
Lorca, Federico Garcia
Loren, Sophia
Lorentz, Hendrick
  Antoon
Lorenz, Konrad
Lorenzetti, Ambrogio
Lorenzetti, Pietro
Lorenzo Monaco
Lorrain, Claude
Lorraine, Charles, Cardinal
  de
Los Angeles, Victoria de
Losey, Joseph
Lothair
Loti, Pierre
Lotto, Lorenzo
Louis, Joe
Louis Philippe
Louvois, Michel Le Tellier,
  Marquis de
Lovecraft, H(oward)
  P(hilips)
Lovelace, Richard
Lovell, Sir Bernard
Lovett, William
Low, Sir David (Alexander
  Cecil)

Lowell, Amy
Lowell, James Russell
Lowell, Percival
Lowell, Robert
Lowry, L(awrence)
  S(tephen)
Lowry, (Clarence)
  Malcolm
Lubitsch, Ernst
Lucan
Lucas van Leyden
Luce, Clare Booth
Luce, Henry R(obinson)
Lucretius
Lucullus, Lucius Licinius
Ludendorff, Erich
Lugard, Frederick Dealtry,
  1st Baron
Lu Hsün
Lukacs, Giorgi
Lull, Ramón
Lully, Jean Baptiste
Lumière, Auguste
Lumière, Louis
Lumumba, Patrice
  (Hemery)
Lunt, Alfred
Lynne Fontanne
Lurçat, Jean
Luria, Isaac
Luther, Martin
Lutoslawski, Witold
Lutuli, Albert (John
  Mvumbi)
Lutyens, Sir Edwin
  Landseer
Lutyens, Elisabeth
Luxemburg, Rosa
Lvov, Georgi Yevgenievich,
  Prince
Lyautey, Louis Hubert
  Gonzalve
Lydgate, John
Lyell, Sir Charles
Lyly, John
Lynch, Jack
Lynd, Helen
Lynd, Robert Staughton
Lyons, Joseph Aloysius
Lysander
Lysenko, Trofim
  Denisovich
Lysias
Lysippus
Lyttelton, Humphrey

Lytton, Edward George Earle Bulwer-Lytton, 1st Baron
Maazel, Lorin
Mabuse *see* Gossaert, Jan
McAdam, John Loudon
MacAlpine, Kenneth
MacArthur, Douglas
Macarthur, John
Macaulay, Dame Rose
Macaulay, Thomas Babington, 1st Baron
Macbeth
MacBride, Seán
McBride, Willie John
McCarthy, Joseph R(aymond)
McCarthy, Mary
McCartney, Linda
McCartney, Paul
McClellan, George B(rinton)
McClure, Sir Robert John Le Mesurier
McCullers, Carson
MacDiarmid, Hugh
MacDonald, Flora
Macdonald, Sir John (Alexander)
MacDonald, (James) Ramsay
McEnroe, John (Patrick)
McEwan, Ian (Russell)
McGonagall, William
Mach, Ernst
Machaut, Guillaume de
Machel, Samora Moïses
Machen, Arthur (Llewellyn)
Machiavelli, Niccolò
McIndoe, Sir Archibald Hector
Macintosh, Charles
Macke, August
McKellen, Sir Ian
McKenna, Siobhán
Mackenzie, Sir (Edward Montague) Compton
Mackerras, Sir Charles
Mackinder, Sir Halford John
McKinley, William
Mackintosh, Charles Rennie
Maclean, Donald
Macleish, Archibald

Macleod, Iain (Norman)
Macleod, John James Rickard
Mac Liammóir, Micheál
Maclise, Daniel
McLuhan, (Herbert) Marshall
MacMahon, Marie Edme Patrice Maurice, Comte de
McMahon, William
Macmillan, Alexander
Macmillan, Daniel
McMillan, Edwin Mattison
Macmillan, (Maurice) Harold, 1st Earl of Stockton
MacMillan, Sir Kenneth
Macmillan, Kirkpatrick
MacMurrough, Dermot
MacNeice, Louis
Maconchy, Elizabeth
Macquarie, Lachlan
McQueen, Steve
Macready, William Charles
Madariaga y Rojo, Salvador de
Maderna, Carlo
Madison, James
Maecenas, Gaius
Maes, Nicolas
Maeterlinck, Maurice
Magellan, Ferdinand
Magendie, François
Magnani, Anna
Magritte, René
Mahavira *title of* Vardhamana
Mahdi, al-
Mahfouz, Naguib
Mahler, Gustav
Mahmud
Mailer, Norman
Maillol, Aristide
Maimonides, Moses
Maintenon, Mme de
Maistre, Joseph de
Major, John
Makarios
Malachy, St
Malamud, Bernard
Malan, Daniel F(rançois)
Malaparte, Curzio
Malcolm, George (John)
Malebranche, Nicolas

Malenkov, Georgi Maksimilianovich
Malesherbes, Chrétien Guillaume de Lamoignon de
Malevich, Kazimir
Malherbe, François de
Malik-Shah
Malinowski, Bronisław
Malipiero, Gian Francesco
Mallarmé, Stéphane
Malle, Louis
Malmesbury, William of
Malory, Sir Thomas
Malpighi, Marcello
Malraux, André
Malthus, Thomas Robert
Ma'mun, al-
Manasseh ben Israel
Mandela, Nelson (Rolihlahla)
Mandela, Winnie
Mandelstam, Osip
Mandeville, Sir John
Manet, Edouard
Manin, Daniele
Manley, Michael
Mann, Heinrich
Mann, Thomas
Mannerheim, Carl Gustaf Emil, Baron von
Manning, Henry Edward, Cardinal
Mansart, François
Mansell, Nigel
Mansfield, Katherine
Mansfield, William Murray, 1st Earl of
Mansholt, Sicco
Mansholt Plan
Mansur, Abu Ja'far al-
Mantegna, Andrea
Manutius, Aldus
Manutius, Paulus
Manzoni, Alessandro
Mao Tse-tung (*or* Mao Ze Dong)
Maradona, Diego
Marat, Jean Paul
Marc, Franz
Marceau, Marcel
Marcellus, Marcus Claudius
Marchand, Jean Baptiste
Marconi, Guglielmo

Marcos, Ferdinand
  E(dralin)
Marcus Aurelius
Marcuse, Herbert
Marenzio, Luca
Margrethe Danish queen
Mariette, Auguste
  Ferdinand François
Marinetti, Filippo
  Tommaso
Marini, Marino
Maritain, Jacques
Marius, Gaius
Marivaux, Pierre Carlet de
  Chamblain de
Mark Antony
Markiewicz, Constance,
  Countess of
Markov, Andrei Andreevich
Markova, Dame Alicia
Marks, Michael
Marks, Simon, 1st Baron
Marlborough, John
  Churchill, 1st Duke of
Marlborough, Sarah
  Churchill, Duchess of
Marlowe, Christopher
Marot, Clément
Marquand, J(ohn) P(hillips)
Marquette, Jacques
Marryat, Captain Frederick
Marsh, Dame Ngaio
Marshall, George C(atlett)
Marshall, John
Marsilius of Padua
Marston, John
Martel, Charles
Martel, Geoffrey
Martí, José Julián
Martial
Martin, Archer John Porter
Martin, John
Martin, Pierre-Émile
Martin, Richard
Martin du Gard, Roger
Martineau, Harriet
Martini, Simone
Martinů, Bohuslav
Marvell, Andrew
Marx, Chico
Marx, Groucho
Marx, Gummo
Marx, Harpo
Marx, Karl (Heinrich)
Marx, Zeppo

Masaccio
Masaryk, Jan (Garrigue)
Masaryk, Tomáš (Garrigue)
Mascagni, Pietro
Masefield, John
Masinissa
Masolino
Mason, A(lfred) E(dward)
  W(oodley)
Masséna, André
Massenet, Jules
Massey, Anna
Massey, Daniel
Massey, Raymond
Massey, William Ferguson
Massine, Léonide
Massinger, Philip
Massys, Quentin
Masters, Edgar Lee
Masters, William Howell
Mastroianni, Marcello
Mata Hari
Matisse, Henri
Matsuo Basho
Matteotti, Giacomo
Matthews, Sir Stanley
Mauchly, John W.
Maudslay, Henry
Maugham, Robin
Maugham, W(illiam)
  Somerset
Maupassant, Guy de
Maupertuis, Pierre Louis
  Moreau de
Mauriac, François
Maurois, André
Maurras, Charles
Maxim, Sir Hiram Stevens
Maxwell, James Clerk
Mayakovskii, Vladimir
Mayer, Julius Robert von
Mayer, Louis B.
Mayer, Sir Robert
Mayhew, Henry
Mayo, Charles Horace
Mayo, Charles William
Mayo, William James
Mayo, William Worrall
Mazarin, Jules, Cardinal
Mazzini, Giuseppe
Mbeki, Thabo
Mboya, Tom
Mead, Margaret
Meade, Richard
Meads, Colin Earl

Mechnikov, Ilya *variant*
  spelling of Metchnikov,
  Ilya
Medawar, Sir Peter Brian
Medici, Catherine de'
Medici, Cosimo de'
Medici, Lorenzo de'
Medici, Piero de'
Médicis, Marie de
Meegeren, Hans van
Mehemet Ali
Mehta, Zubin
Meiji *title of* Mutsuhito
Meir, Golda
Meissonier,
  Jean-Louis-Ernest
Meitner, Lise
Melanchthon, Philip
Melba, Dame Nellie
Melbourne, William Lamb,
  2nd Viscount
Melchett, Alfred Mond, 1st
  Baron
Melchior, Lauritz
Mellon, Andrew William
Melville, Herman
Memling, Hans
Menander
Mencius
Mencken, H(enry) L(ouis)
Mendel, Gregor Johann
Mendeleyev, Dimitrii
  Ivanovich
Mendelssohn, Felix
Mendelssohn, Moses
Menderes, Adnan
Mendès-France, Pierre
Mendoza, Antonio de
Menelik
Menem, Carlos (Saúl)
Menes
Mengelberg, William
Mengs, Anton Raphael
Menno Simons
Menon, Krishna
Menotti, Gian Carlo
Menuhin, Hephzibah
Menuhin, Jeremy
Menuhin, Yaltah
Menuhin, Yehudi, Baron
Menzies, Sir Robert Gordon
Mercator, Gerardus
Mercer, David
Merchant, Ismael
Mercouri, Melina

Meredith, George
Meredith, Owen *pen name*
  of Robert Bulmer-Lytton,
  1st Earl of Lytton
Mérimée, Prosper
Merleau-Ponty, Maurice
Merneptah
Mesmer, Franz Anton
Messager, André (Charles
  Prosper)
Messalina, Valeria
Messerschmitt, Willy
Messiaen, Olivier
Messier, Charles
Meštrović, Ivan
Metastasio, Pietro
Metaxas, Ioannis
Metchnikov (*or*
  Mechnikov), Ilya Ilich
Methodius, St
Metsu, Gabriel
Metternich, Klemens
  Wenzel Nepomuk Lothar,
  Fürst von
Meyerbeer, Giacomo
Meyerhof, Otto Fritz
Meyerhold, Vsevolod
  Emilievich
Michelangelo Buonarroti
Michelet, Jules
Michelin, André
Michelin, Édouard
Michelozzo di
  Bartolommeo
Michelson, Albert Abraham
Mickiewicz, Adam
Middleton, Thomas
Mies van der Rohe, Ludwig
Mihajlović, Draža
Miles, Bernard, Baron
Milhaud, Darius
Mill, James
Mill, John Stuart
Millais, Sir John Everett
Millay, Edna St Vincent
Miller, Arthur
Miller, Glenn
Miller, Henry
Millet, Jean François
Millikan, Robert Andrews
Mills, Hayley
Mills, Sir John
Mills, Juliet
Milne, A(lan) A(lexander)
Milner, Alfred, Viscount

Miloš
Milošević, Slobodan
Milstein, Nathan
Miltiades
Milton, John
Minamoto Yoritomo
Minamoto Yoshitsune
Mindszenty, József,
  Cardinal
Mingus, Charlie
Minnelli, Liza
Mintoff, Dom(inic)
Mirabeau, Honoré Gabriel
  Riquetti, Comte de
Miró, Joan
Mishima, Yukio
Mistinguett
Mistral, Frédéric
Mistral, Gabriela
Mitchell, Margaret
Mitchell, R(eginald)
  J(oseph)
Mithridates
Mitterrand, François
  (Maurice)
Mizoguchi Kenji
Mobutu, Sese Seko
Mocenigo, Andrea
Mocenigo, Giovanni
Mocenigo, Pietro
Mocenigo, Tommaso
Modigliani, Amedeo
Mohamad, Mahathir bin
Mohammed (*or*
  Muhammad)
Mohammed Askia
Moholy-Nagy, László
Moi, Daniel arap
Molière
Molina, Luis de
Molinos, Miguel de
Molnár, Ferenc
Molotov, Vyacheslav
  Mikhailovich
Moltke, Helmuth, Graf von
Moltke, Helmuth Johannes
  Ludwig von
Mommsen, Theodor
Mond, Alfred, 1st Baron
  Melchett
Mond, Ludwig
Mondrian, Piet
Monet, Claude
Monge, Gaspard
Moniz, Antonio Egas

Monk, Thelonius (Sphere)
Monmouth, James Scott,
  Duke of
Monnet, Jean
Monod, Jacques-Lucien
Monroe, James
Monroe, Marilyn
Monsarrat, Nicholas
Montagu, Lady Mary
  Wortley
Montaigne, Michel de
Montale, Eugenio
Montcalm, Louis Joseph de
  Montcalm-Grozon,
  Marquis de
Montefeltro, Federigo,
  Duke of Urbino
Montefiore, Sir Moses
Montespan, Françoise
  Athénaïs de
  Rochechouart, Marquise
  de
Montesquieu, Charles Louis
  de Secondat, Baron de
Monteux, Pierre
Monteverdi, Claudio
Montez, Lola
Montezuma
Montfort, Simon de, Earl of
  Leicester
Montgolfier,
  Jacques-Étienne
Montgolfier, Joseph-Michel
Montgomery of Alamein,
  Bernard Law, 1st
  Viscount
Montherlant, Henry de
Montrose, James Graham,
  1st Marquess of
Moody, Dwight Lyman
Moore, Bobby
Moore, G(eorge) E(dward)
Moore, Gerald
Moore, Henry
Moore, Sir John
Moore, Marianne
Moore, Thomas
Morandi, Giorgio
Moravia, Alberto
Moray, James Stuart, Earl
  of
More, Henry
More, Sir Thomas
Moreau, Gustave
Moreau, Jean Victor

Morgagni, Giovanni Battista

Morgan, Charles

Morgan, Sir Henry

Morgan, John Pierpont

Morgan, Thomas Hunt

Mörike, Eduard Friedrich

Morison, Stanley

Morisot, Berthe

Morland, George

Morley, Edward Williams

Morley, Robert

Morley, Thomas

Mornay, Philippe de, Seigneur du Plessis-Marly

Moro, Aldo

Moroni, Giovanni Battista

Morphy, Paul Charles

Morris, Desmond John

Morris, William

Morrison, Herbert Stanley, Baron

Morrison, Toni

Morse, Samuel Finley Breese

Mortier, Édouard Adolphe Casimir Joseph, Duc de Trévise

Mortimer, Roger de, 1st Earl of March

Morton, James Douglas, 4th Earl of

Morton, Jelly Roll

Morton, John

Moseley, Henry Gwyn Jeffries

Mosley, Sir Oswald Ernald

Moss, Stirling

Motherwell, Robert

Mo-tzu variant spelling of Mo-Zi

Mountbatten of Burma, Louis, 1st Earl

Mozart, Wolfgang Amadeus

Mo-Zi (or Mo-tzu)

Mu'awiyah

Mubarak, (Mohammed) Hosni (Said)

Mugabe, Robert (Gabriel)

Muhammad variant spelling of Mohammed

Muhammad Ahmad original name of al-Mahdi

Muir, Edwin

Mujibur Rahman, Sheik

Muller, Hermann Joseph

Müller, Paul Hermann

Mulliken, Robert Sanderson

Mulready, William

Mumford, Lewis

Munch, Charles

Munch, Edvard

Münchhausen, Karl Friedrich, Freiherr von

Munnings, Sir Alfred

Munro, H(ector) H(ugh) (pen name Saki)

Munthe, Axel

Müntzer, Thomas

Murasaki Shikibu

Murat, Joachim

Murdoch, Dame Iris

Murdock, William

Murillo, Bartolomé Esteban

Murray, Gilbert

Murray, Sir James (Augustus Henry)

Murray, Len

Murrow, Edward R(oscoe)

Murry, John Middleton

Musgrave, Thea

Musil, Robert

Musset, Alfred de

Mussolini, Benito (Amilcare Andrea)

Mussorgski, Modest Petrovich

Mutanabbi, Abu At-Tayyib Ahmad Ibn Husayn al-

Mutesa

Mutsuhito

Muybridge, Eadweard

Muzorewa, Bishop Abel (Tendekayi)

Myers, F(rederic) W(illiam) H(enry)

Myrdal, Alva

Myrdal, Gunnar

Mzilikazi

Nabokov, Vladimir

Nadar

Nader, Ralph

Nader Shah

Naevius, Gnaeus

Nagarjuna

Nagy, Imre

Naipaul, Sir V(idiadhur) S(urajprasad)

Namier, Sir Lewis Bernstein

Nanak

Nana Sahib

Nansen, Fridtjof

Napier, Sir Charles James

Napier, John

Napier of Magdala, Robert Cornelis, 1st Baron

Narayan, R(asipuram) K(rishnaswamy)

Narses

Nash, John

Nash, Ogden

Nash, Paul

Nash, Richard

Nash, Sir Walter

Nashe, Thomas

Nasser, Gamal Abdel

Navratilova, Martina

Nazianus, St Gregory of

Nebuchadnezzar

Necker, Jacques

Neer, Aert van der

Nefertiti

Negrín, Juan

Nehru, Jawaharlal

Neill, A(lexander) S(utherland)

Nekrasov, Nikolai Alekseevich

Nelson, Horatio, Viscount

Nemery, Jaafar Mohammed al

Nennius

Neri, St Philip

Nernst, Walther Hermann

Nero (Claudius Caesar)

Neruda, Pablo

Nerva, Marcus Cocceius

Nerval, Gérard de

Nervi, Pier Luigi

Nesbit, Edith

Nesselrode, Karl Robert, Count

Netanyahu, Benjamin

Neto, Agostinho

Neumann, (Johann) Balthasar

Neumann, John von

Nevsky, Alexander

Newcastle, Thomas Pelham-Holles, 1st Duke of

Newcastle, William Cavendish, Duke of

Newcombe, John

Newcomen, Thomas
Ne Win
Newman, John Henry,
  Cardinal
Newman, Paul
Newton, Sir Isaac
Nexø, Martin Andersen
Ney, Michel, Prince of
  Moscow
Ngo Dinh Diem
Niarchos, Stavros Spyros
Nicholson, Ben
Nicholson, Jack
Nicholson, William
Nicias
Nicklaus, Jack William
Nicolai, Otto Ehrenfried
Nicolson, Sir Harold
  (George)
Niebuhr, Barthold Georg
Nielsen, Carl (August)
Niemeyer, Oscar
Niemöller, Martin
Nietzsche, Friedrich
Nightingale, Florence
Nijinsky, Vaslav
Nikisch, Arthur
Nilsson, Birgit Marta
Nimitz, Chester W(illiam)
Nirenberg, Marshall
  Warren
Nithsdale, William
  Maxwell, 5th Earl of
Niven, David
Nixon, Richard Milhous
Nizam al-Mulk
Nkomo, Joshua
Nkrumah, Kwame
Nobel, Alfred Bernhard
Nobile, Umberto
Noble, Sir Andrew
Nobunaga Oda
Noel-Baker, Philip John
Noguchi, Hideyo
Nolan, Sir Sidney
Nolde, Emil
Nollekens, Joseph
Nono, Luigi
Nordenskjöld, Nils Adolf
  Erik, Baron
Norfolk, Thomas Howard,
  Duke of
Noriega, Manuel
North, Frederick, Lord
North, Sir Thomas

Northcliffe, Alfred Charles
  William Harmsworth, 1st
  Viscount
Northrop, John Howard
Northumberland, John
  Dudley, Duke of
Nostradamus
Novalis
Novello, Ivor
Novotný Antonín
Noyes, Alfred
Nu, U
Nuffield, William Richard
  Morris, 1st Viscount
Nureyev, Rudolf
Nurhachi
Nurmi, Paavo Johannes
Nyerere, Julius
  (Kambarage)
Nyssa, St Gregory of
Oakley, Annie
Oastler, Richard
Oates, Lawrence Edward
  Grace
Oates, Titus
Obote, (Apollo) Milton
O'Brien, Conor Cruise
O'Brien, Flann
O'Brien, William
O'Brien, William Smith
O'Casey, Sean
Ockham, William of
O'Connell, Daniel
O'Connor, Feargus
O'Connor, Frank
Oda Nobunaga
Odets, Clifford
Odoacer
Oë, Kenzaburo
Oehlenschläger, Adam
  (Gottlob)
Oersted, Hans Christian
Offa
Offenbach, Jacques
O'Flaherty, Liam
Ogden, C(harles) K(ay)
Ogdon, John
Oglethorpe, James
  Edward
O'Hara, John (Henry)
O'Higgins, Bernardo
Ohm, Georg Simon
Oistrakh, David
Oistrakh, Igor
O'Keeffe, Georgia

Okeghem, Jean d'
Olbers, Heinrich Wilhelm
  Matthäus
Oldcastle, Sir John
Oldenbarneveldt, Johan
  van
Oldenburg, Claes (Thure)
Oliphant, Sir Mark
  Laurence Elwin
Olivares, Gaspar de
  Guzmán, Conde-Duque
  de
Oliver, Isaac
Olivier, Laurence (Kerr),
  Baron
Omar Khayyam
Onassis, Aristotle Socrates
Oñate, Juan de
O'Neill, Eugene
O'Neill, Terence, Baron
Onsager, Lars
Ophüls, Max
Opie, John
Opitz (von Boberfeld),
  Martin
Oppenheimer, J. Robert
Orcagna, Andrea
Orczy, Baroness Emmusca
Oresme, Nicole d'
Orff, Carl
Origen
Orlando, Vittorio
  Emanuele
Orléans, Charles, Duc d'
Orléans, Louis Philippe
  Joseph, Duc d'
Orlov, Aleksei Grigorievich
Orlov, Grigori Grigorievich,
  Count
Ormandy, Eugene
Ormonde, James Butler, 1st
  Duke of
Orozco, José
Ortega (Saavedra), Daniel
Ortega y Gasset, José
Ortelius, Abraham
Ortoli, François Xavier
Orwell, George
Osborne, Dorothy
Osborne, John
O'Shea, Katherine Page
Osler, Sir William
Osman
Ossian
Ossietsky, Carl von

Petrie, Sir (William
    Matthew) Flinders
Petronius Arbiter
Petrosian, Tigran
    Vartanovich
Pevsner, Antoine
Pevsner, Sir Nikolaus
    (Bernhard Leon)
Phaedrus
Phalaris
Phidias
Phidippides
Philadelphus, Ptolomy
Philby, Harold Adrian
    Russell
Philby, H(arry) St John
    (Bridge)
Philemon
Philidor, André Danican
Philidor, François André
    Danican
Phillip, Arthur
Philo Judaeus
Phiz see Browne, Hablot
    Knight
Phryne
Phyfe (or Fife), Duncan
Piaf, Edith
Piaget, Jean
Picabia, Francis
Picasso, Pablo
Piccard, Auguste
Piccard, Jacques
Piccard, Jean-Félix
Pickford, Mary
Pico della Mirandola,
    Giovanni, Conte
Pieck, Wilhelm
Piero della Francesca
Piero di Cosimo
Piggott, Lester Keith
Pilate, Pontius
Piłsudski, Józef Klemens
Pinckney, Charles
Pinckney, Charles
    Cotesworth
Pinckney, Thomas
Pindar
Pinero, Sir Arthur Wing
Pinkerton, Allan
Pinochet, Augusto
Pinter, Harold
Pinturicchio
Piozzi, Hester Lynch
    (married name Thrale)

Piper, John
Pirandello, Luigi
Piranesi, Giambattista
Pisanello
Pisano, Andrea
Pisano, Giovanni
Pisano, Nicola
Pisistratus
Pissarro, Camille
Pissarro, Lucien
Pitman, Sir Isaac
Pitt, William
Pitt-Rivers, Augustus Henry
    Lane Fox
Pius pope
Pizarro, Francisco
Place, Francis
Planck, Erwin
Planck, Max Karl Ernst
    Ludwig
Plantagenet surname of
    English kings 1154–1485
Plath, Sylvia
Plato
Plautus, Titus Maccius
Pleasence, Donald
Plekhanov, Georgi
    Valentinovich
Pliny
Plomer, William
Plotinus
Plowright, Joan
Plunket, St Oliver
Plutarch
Pocahontas
Po Chü-i variant spelling of
    Bo Zhu Yi
Podgorny, N(ikolai)
    V(iktorovich)
Poe, Edgar Allan
Poggio Bracciolini,
    Giovanni Francesco
Poincaré, Jules Henri
Poincaré, Raymond
Poisson, Siméon Dénis
Poitiers, Diane de,
    Duchesse de Valentinois
Polanski, Roman
Pole, Reginald, Cardinal
Polignac, Auguste Jules
    Armand Marie, Prince de
Poliziano
Polk, James K(nox)
Pollaiuolo, Antonio
Pollaiuolo, Piero

Pollock, Jackson
Polo, Marco
Polybius
Polycarp, St
Polyclitus
Polycrates
Pombal, Sebastião José de
    Carvalho e Mello,
    Marquês de
Pompadour, Mme de
Pompey
Pompidou, Georges (Jean
    Raymond)
Ponce de Leon, Juan
Poniatowski, Józef
Poniatowski, Stanisław
Pontiac
Pontormo, Jacopo da
Pope, Alexander
Popov, Aleksandr
    Stepanovich
Popov, Oleg
    Konstantinovich
Popper, Sir Karl Raimund
Porphyriogenitus,
    Constantine
Porphyry
Porter, Cole (Albert)
Porter, Katherine Anne
Porter, Peter
Portland, William Henry
    Cavendish Bentinck, 3rd
    Duke of
Potemkin, Grigori
    Aleksandrovich
Potter, Beatrix
Potter, Paul
Potter, Stephen
Poulenc, Francis
Pound, Ezra
Poussin, Nicolas
Powell, Anthony
Powell, Cecil Frank
Powell, (John) Enoch
Powys, John Cowper
Powys, Theodore Francis
Praetorius, Michael
Prandtl, Ludwig
Prasad, Rajendra
Praxiteles
Preminger, Otto (Ludwig)
Prescott, John (Leslie)
Prescott, William
    Hickling
Presley, Elvis (Aaron)

Prester John
Pretorius, Andries
  (Wilhelmus Jacobus)
Pretorius, Marthinus
  Wessel
Prévert, Jacques
Previn, André
Prévost d'Exiles, Antoine
  François, Abbé
Pride, Thomas
Priestley, J(ohn) B(oynton)
Priestley, Joseph
Primo de Rivera, José
  Antonio
Primo de Rivera, Miguel
Prior, Matthew
Priscian
Pritchett, Sir V(ictor)
  S(awdon)
Proclus
Procopius
Prokofiev, Sergei
Prokop
Propertius, Sextus
Protagoras
Proudhon, Pierre Joseph
Proust, Joseph-Louis
Proust, Marcel
Prout, William
Prud'hon, Pierre Paul
Prynne, William
Psamtik
Pseudo-Dionysius the
  Areopagite
Ptolemy
Puccini, Giacomo
Pucelle, Jean
Pudovkin, Vsevolod
Pufendorf, Samuel von
Pugachov, Yemelyan
  Ivanovich
Pugin, Augustus Welby
  Northmore
Pulci, Luigi
Pullman, George Mortimer
Purcell, Edward Mills
Purcell, Henry
Purchas, Samuel
Pusey, Edward Bouverie
Pushkin, Aleksandr
Puttnam, Sir David
  (Terence)
Puvis de Chavannes, Pierre
  (Cécile)
Pu Yi, Henry

Pym, John
Pynchon, Thomas
Pyrrhon
Pyrrhus
Pythagoras
Pytheas
Qaboos ibn Sa'id
Qaddafi, Moammar al-
Qian Long (or Ch'ien-lung)
Quant, Mary
Quasimodo, Salvatore
Queneau, Raymond
Quercia, Jacopo della
Quesnay, François
Quesnel, Pasquier
Quiller-Couch, Sir Arthur
  Thomas
Quine, Willard van Orman
Quintilian
Quisling, Vidkun (Abraham
  Lauritz Jonsson)
Qu Qiu Bai (or Ch'ü
  Ch'iu-pai)
Rabelais, François
Rabi, Isidor Isaac
Rachmaninov, Sergei
Racine, Jean
Rackham, Arthur
Radcliffe, Ann (Ward)
Radcliffe-Brown, Alfred
  Reginald
Radek, Karl
Radić, Stjepan
Radiguet, Raymond
Raeburn, Sir Henry
Raeder, Erich
Raffles, Sir Thomas
  Stamford
Rafsanjani, Hojatoleslam
  Ali Akbar Hashemi
Raglan, FitzRoy James
  Henry Somerset, 1st
  Baron
Raikes, Robert
Raine, Kathleen
Rainier, Prince
Rais, Gilles de
Rákóczy, Ferenc
Raleigh, Sir Walter
Ramakrishna
Raman, Sir
  Chandrasekhara Venkata
Ramanuja
Rambert, Dame Marie
Rameau, Jean Philippe

Ramón y Cajal, Santiago
Ramsay, Allan
Ramsay, Sir William
Ramses
Ramsey, Sir Alf
Ram Singh
Ramus, Petrus
Ranjit Singh, Maharaja
Ranjitsinhji Vibhaji, Kumar
  Shri, Maharajah Jam
  Sahib of Nawanagar
Rank, J(oseph) Arthur, 1st
  Baron
Rank, Otto
Ranke, Leopold von
Ransom, John Crowe
Ransome, Arthur Mitchell
Raphael
Rashi
Rasmussen, Knud Johan
  Victor
Rasputin, Grigori
  Yefimovich
Rathenau, Walther
Rattigan, Sir Terence
Rattle, Sir Simon
Ratushinskaya, Irina
Rauschenberg, Robert
Ravel, Maurice
Rawlinson, Sir Henry
  Creswicke
Rawsthorne, Alan
Ray, John
Ray, Man
Ray, Satyajit
Rayleigh, John William
  Strutt, 3rd Baron
Rayleigh, Robert John
  Strutt, 4th Baron
Razi, ar-
Razin, Stenka
Read, Sir Herbert
Reade, Charles
Reading, Rufus Daniel
  Isaacs, 1st Marquess of
Reagan, Ronald
Réaumur, René-Antoine
  Ferchault de
Reber, Grote
Recamier, Jeanne Françoise
  Julie Adelaide
Redford, Robert
Redgrave, Corin
Redgrave, Lynn
Redgrave, Sir Michael

Redgrave, Vanessa
Redmond, John Edward
Redon, Odilon
Redouté, Pierre Joseph
Reed, Sir Carol
Reed, John
Reed, Lou
Reed, Walter
Reeves, William Pember
Reger, Max
Regiomontanus
Regnier, Henri François
   Joseph de
Regulus, Marcus Attilus
Rehoboam
Reich, Wilhelm
Reid, Sir George Houston
Reid, Thomas
Reinhardt, Django
Reinhardt, Max
Reith, John Charles
   Walsham, 1st Baron
Remarque, Erich Maria
Rembrandt (Harmenszoon)
   van Rijn
Remington, Eliphalet
Renan, (Joseph) Ernest
Rendell, Ruth (Barbara),
   Baroness
Reni, Guido
Rennie, John
Renoir, Jean
Renoir, Pierre Auguste
Resnais, Alain
Respighi, Ottorino
Retz, Jean François Paul de
   Gondi, Cardinal de
Reuter, Paul Julius, Baron
   von
Revere, Paul
Reynaud, Paul
Reynolds, Albert
Reynolds, Sir Joshua
Rhee, Syngman
Rheticus
Rhine, Joseph Banks
Rhodes, Cecil (John)
Rhodes, Wilfred
Rhys, Jean
Ribbentrop, Joachim von
Ribera, José de
Ricardo, David
Ricci, Marco
Ricci, Matteo
Ricci, Sebastiano

Riccio, David
Rich, Richard, 1st Baron
Richard, Sir Cliff
Richards, Frank
Richards, Sir Gordon
Richards, I(vor)
   A(rmstrong)
Richardson, Henry Handel
Richardson, Henry Hobson
Richardson, Sir Ralph
Richardson, Samuel
Richelieu, Armand Jean du
   Plessis, Cardinal de
Richler, Mordecai
Richter, Hans
Richter, Johann Paul
   Friedrich.
Richter, Sviatoslav
   (Teofilovitch)
Richthofen, Manfred,
   Freiherr von
Ridley, Nicholas
Ridolfi, Roberto
Riebeeck, Jan van
Riefensthal, Leni
Riel, Louis
Riemann, Georg Friedrich
   Bernhard
Rienzo, Cola di
Riesman, David
Riley, Bridget Louise
Rilke, Rainer Maria
Rimbaud, Arthur
Rimsky-Korsakov, Nikolai
Rivera, Diego
Rizzio, David
Roach, Hal
Robbe-Grillet, Alain
Robbins, Frederick
   Chapman
Robbins, Jerome
Roberts, Frederick Sleigh,
   1st Earl
Roberts, Tom
Robeson, Paul
Robespierre, Maximilien
   François Marie Isidore de
Robey, Sir George
Robinson, Edward G.
Robinson, Edwin Arlington
Robinson, John (Arthur
   Thomas)
Robinson, Mary
Robinson, Sir Robert
Robinson, Sugar Ray

Robinson, William Heath
Robson, Dame Flora
Rochester, John Wilmot,
   2nd Earl of
Rockefeller, John D(avison)
Rockefeller, Nelson
   A(ldrich)
Rockingham, Charles
   Watson-Wentworth, 2nd
   Marquess of
Roderic Irish king
Rodgers, Richard Charles
Rodin, Auguste
Rodney, George Brydges,
   1st Baron
Rodrigo, Joaquín
Roebling, John Augustus
Roebling, Washington
   Augustus
Roentgen, Wilhelm Konrad
Rogers, Ginger
Rogers, John
Rogers, Sir Richard
Roget, Peter Mark
Röhm, Ernst
Rokitansky, Karl, Freiherr
   von
Rolfe, Frederick William
Rolland, Romain
Rolls, Charles Stewart
Romains, Jules
Rommel, Erwin
Romney, George
Romulus Augustulus
Ronsard, Pierre de
Roon, Albrecht, Graf von
Roosevelt, Eleanor
Roosevelt, Franklin
   D(elano)
Roosevelt, Theodore
Root, Elihu
Rory O'Connor
Rosa, Salvator
Roscelin
Roscius, Quintus
Rosebery, Archibald Philip
   Primrose, 5th Earl of
Rosenberg, Ethel
Rosenberg, Julius
Rosewall, Ken(neth
   Ronald)
Ross, Sir James Clark
Ross, Sir Ronald
Rosse, William Parsons, 3rd
   Earl of

Rossellini, Roberto
Rossetti, Christina
  Georgina
Rossetti, Dante Gabriel
Rossini, Gioacchino
  Antonio
Rostand, Edmond
Rostropovich, Mstislav
Roth, Philip
Rothermere, Harold Sydney
  Harmsworth, 1st
  Viscount
Rothko, Mark
Rothschild, James
Rothschild, Karl Mayer
Rothschild, Lionel Nathan
Rothschild, Mayer Amschel
Rothschild, Nathan Mayer
Rothschild, Nathaniel
  Mayer Victor, 3rd Baron
Rothschild, Salomon Mayer
Rouault, Georges (Henri)
Roubillac, Louis François
Rouget de l'Isle, Claude
  Joseph
Rousseau, Henri
Rousseau, Jean Jacques
Rousseau, (Pierre Étienne)
  Théodore
Roussel, Albert
Roussel, Raymond
Roux, Pierre Paul Emile
Rowe, Nicholas
Rowlandson, Thomas
Rowley, Thomas
Rowse, A(lfred) L(eslie)
Royce, Sir (Frederick)
  Henry
Royce, Josiah
Rubbra, Edmund
Rubens, Peter Paul
Rubinstein, Anton
Rubinstein, Artur
Rublyov, Andrey
Ruggles, Carl
Ruisdael, Jacob van
Ruysdael, Salomon van
Ruiz, Juan
Rumford, Benjamin
  Thompson, Count
Runcie, Robert Alexander
  Kennedy, Baron
Rundstedt, (Karl Rudolf)
  Gerd von
Runeberg, Johan Ludvig

Runyon, Damon
Rurik
Rushdie, Salman
Rusk, (David) Dean
Ruskin, John
Russell, Bertrand Arthur
  William, 3rd Earl
Russell, John, 1st Earl
Russell, Ken
Russell, Lord William
Russell, Sir William
  Howard
Rutherford, Ernest, 1st
  Baron
Rutherford, Dame Margaret
Rutherford, Mark
Ruyter, Michiel
  Adriaanszoon de
Ryder, Sue, Baroness
Rykov, Aleksei Ivanovich
Ryle, Gilbert
Ryle, Sir Martin
Saarinen, Eero
Sabatier, Paul
Sachs, Hans
Sachs, Nelly (Leonie)
Sackville, Thomas, 1st Earl
  of Dorset
Sadat, Anwar
Sade, Donatien Alphonse
  François, Marquis de
Sa'di
Sagan, Françoise
Saigo Takamori
Sainte-Beuve,
  Charles-Augustin
Saint-Exupéry, Antoine de
Saint-Just, Louis (Antoine
  Léon) de
Saint-Laurent, Yves
Saint-Saëns, Camille
Saint-Simon, Claude Henri
  de Rouvroy, Comte de
Saint-Simon, Louis de
  Rouvroy, Duc de
Sakharov, Andrei
  Dimitrievich
Saki pen name of H(ector)
  H(ugh) Munro
Saladin
Salam, Abdus
Salazar, António de
  Oliveira
Sales, St Francis of
Salieri, Antonio

Salinger, J(erome) D(avid)
Salisbury, Robert Arthur
  Talbot Gascoyne-Cecil,
  3rd Marquess of
Salisbury, Robert Cecil, 1st
  Earl of
Sallust
Sampras, Pete
Samudra Gupta
Samuel, Herbert Louis, 1st
  Viscount
Sand, George
Sandage, Allan Rex
Sandburg, Carl
Sandwich, John Montagu,
  4th Earl of
Sanger, Frederick
Sankara
San Martin, José de
Santa Anna, Antonio López
  de
Santayana, George
Santer, Jacques
Sapir, Edward
Sapper pen name of
  H(erman) C(yril) McNeile
Sappho
Sardou, Victorien
Sargent, John Singer
Sargent, Sir Malcolm
Sargon
Saroyan, William
Sarraute, Nathalie
Sarto, Andrea del
Sartre, Jean-Paul
Sassetta
Sassoon, Siegfried
Satie, Erik
Sato Eisaku
Saud
Saussure, Ferdinand de
Savage, Michael Joseph
Savage, Richard
Savery, Thomas
Savonarola, Girolamo
Saxe, Maurice, Comte de
Saxe-Weimar, Duke
  Bernhard of
Saxo Grammaticus
Sayers, Dorothy L(eigh)
Scaliger, Joseph Justus
Scaliger, Julius Caesar
Scarfe, Gerald
Scargill, Arthur
Scarlatti, Alessandro

Scarlatti, Domenico
Scarron, Paul
Schacht, Hjalmar
Scheel, Walter
Scheele, Carl Wilhelm
Schelling, Friedrich
Schiaparelli, Elsa
Schiele, Egon
Schiller, (Johann
  Christoph) Friedrich(von)
Schlegel, August Wilhelm
  von
Schegel, (Carl Wilhelm)
  Friedrich von
Schleiden, Matthias Jakob
Schlesinger, John
Schlick, Moritz
Schlieffen, Alfred, Graf von
Schliemann, Heinrich
Schmeling, Max
Schmidt, Helmut
Schnabel, Artur
Schnitzler, Arthur
Schoenberg, Arnold
Schopenhauer, Arthur
Schreiner, Olive
Schrödinger, Erwin
Schubert, Franz (Peter)
Schumacher, Michael
Schuman, Robert French
  statesman; compare
  Schumann, Robert
Schuman, William
  (Howard)
Schumann, Clara
Schumann, Elisabeth
Schumann, Robert
  (Alexander) German
  composer; compare
  Schuman, Robert
Schuschnigg, Kurt von
Schütz, Heinrich
Schwann, Theodor
Schwarzenberg, Felix, Fürst
  zu
Schwarzkopf, Dame
  Elisabeth
Schweitzer, Albert
Schwitters, Kurt
Scipio Aemilianus
  Africanus grandson of
  Scipio Africanus
Scipio Africanus
Scofield, (David) Paul
Scorsese, Martin

Scott, Sir George Gilbert
Scott, Sir Giles Gilbert
Scott, Sir Peter Markham
Scott, Robert Falcon
Scott, Ronnie
Scott, Sir Walter
Scriabin, Alexander
Scullin, James Henry
Seaborg, Glenn Theodore
Searle, Ronald William
  Fordham
Seddon, Richard John
Seeger, Pete
Seferis, George
Seghers, Hercules
  Pieterzoon
Segovia, Andrés
Segrè, Emilio
Selden, John
Seleucus I Nicator
Selkirk, Alexander
Sellers, Peter
Selwyn Lloyd, John, Baron
Selznick, David O(liver)
Semiramis
Sempringham, St Gilbert
  of
Senanayake, D(on)
  S(tephen)
Senanayake, Dudley
Seneca
Senefelder, Aloys
Senghor, Léopold Sédar
Sennacherib
Sennett, Mack
Sergius of Radonezh, St
Servetus, Michael
Sesostris
Sesshu
Sessions, Roger
Seth, Vikram
Seton, Ernest Thompson
Seurat, Georges
Severini, Gino
Severus, Lucius Septimius
Severus Alexander
Sévigné, Marie de
  Rabutin-Chantal,
  Marquise de
Seymour, Jane
Shackleton, Sir Ernest
  Henry
Shadwell, Thomas
Shaffer, Anthony
Shaffer, Peter

Shaftesbury, Anthony
  Ashley Cooper, Earl of
Shah Jahan
Shahn, Ben
Shaka
Shakespeare, William
Shamir, Yitzhak
Shankar, Ravi
Shapur
Sharp, Cecil (James)
Shastri, Shri Lal Bahadur
Shaw, Artie
Shaw, George Bernard
Shaw, (Richard) Norman
Sheene, Barry
Shelburne, William Petty
  Fitzmaurice, 2nd Earl of
Shelley, Mary
  Wollstonecraft
Shelley, Percy Bysshe
Shenstone, William
Shepard, Ernest Howard
Shepard, Allan Bartlett
Sheppard, Jack
Sheraton, Thomas
Sheridan, Philip H(enry)
Sheridan, Richard Brinsley
Sherman, John
Sherman, William
  Tecumseh
Sherrington, Sir Charles
  Scott
Shevardnadze, Eduard
Shockley, William
  Bradfield
Sholes, Christopher
  Latham
Sholokhov, Mikhail
Shostakovich, Dmitri
Shostakovich, Maxim
Shovell, Sir Cloudesley
Shrapnel, Henry
Shute, Nevil
Sibelius, Jean
Sica, Vittoria De
Sickert, Walter Richard
Siddons, Sarah
Sidgwick, Henry
Sidmouth, Henry
  Addington, 1st Viscount
Sidney, Algernon
Sidney, Sir Philip
Siemens, Ernst Werner von
Siemens, Friedrich
Siemens, Karl

Siemens, Sir William
Sienkiewicz, Henryk
Sieyès, Emmanuel Joseph
Siger of Brabant
Signac, Paul
Signorelli, Luca
Sigurdsson *variant spelling of*
 Sverrir
Sihanouk, Norodim, Prince
Sikorski, Władysław Polish
 statesman
Sikorsky, Igor Ivan US
 engineer
Sillitoe, Alan
Silone, Ignazio
Si-ma Qian (*or* Ssu-ma
 Ch'ien)
Simenon, Georges
Simeon Stylites, St
Simms, William Gilmore
Simnel, Lambert
Simon, John Allsebrook, 1st
 Viscount
Simon, (Marvin) Neil
Simon, Paul
Simonov, Konstantin
Simpson, George Gaylord
Simpson, N(orman)
 F(rederick)
Sinatra, Frank
Sinclair, Upton
Singer, Isaac Bashevis
Singer, Isaac Merrit
Siqueiros, David Alfaro
Sisley, Alfred
Sitwell, Edith
Sitwell, Sir Osbert
Sitwell, Sacheverell
Sivaji
Sixtus pope
Skalkottas, Nikos
Skanderbeg
Skelton, John
Skinner, Burrhus Frederic
Slade, Felix
SlánskýRudolf
Slim, William Joseph, 1st
 Viscount
Sloane, Sir Hans
Sluter, Claus
Smart, Christopher
Smetana, Bedřich
Smiles, Samuel
Smith, Adam
Smith, Bessie

Smith, Harvey
Smith, Ian (Douglas)
Smith, John
Smith, Joseph
Smith, Sir Keith
 Macpherson
Smith, Dame Maggie
Smith, Sir Ross Macpherson
Smith, Stevie
Smithson, Alison
Smithson, Peter
Smollett, Tobias (George)
Smuts, Jan (Christiaan)
Smythe, Pat
Snefru
Snow, C(harles) P(ercy),
 Baron
Snowdon, Antony
 Armstrong-Jones, Earl of
Snyders, Frans
Soames, (Arthur)
 Christopher (John),
 Baron
Soane, Sir John
Soares, Mario
Sobers, Sir Garry
Sobieski, John
Socinus, Faustus
Socinus, Laelius
Socrates
Soddy, Frederick
Söderblom, Nathan
Solon
Soloviov, Vladimir
 Sergevich
Solti, Sir Georg
Solzhenitsyn, Aleksandr
Somers, John, Baron
Somerset, Edward
 Seymour, 1st Duke of
Somerset, Robert Carr, Earl
 of
Sommerfeld, Arnold
 Johannes Wilhelm
Sondheim, Stephen
 (Joshua)
Song (*or* Sung), T. V.
Song Qing-ling (*or* Sung
 Ch'ing-ling)
Song Mei-ling (*or* Sung
 Mei-ling)
Sophocles
Sopwith, Sir Thomas
 Octave Murdoch
Soranus of Ephesus

Sorel, Georges
Sosigenes of Alexandria
Soter, Ptolomy
Soto, Hernando de
Soufflot, Jacques Germain
Soult, Nicolas Jean de Dieu,
 Duc de Dalmatie
Souphanouvong, Prince
Sousa, John Philip
Soustelle, Jacques (Émile)
Southampton, Henry
 Wriothesley, 3rd Earl of
Southcott, Joanna
Southey, Robert
Soutine, Chaim
Soyinka, Wole
Spaak, Paul Henri
Spallanzani, Lazzaro
Spark, Dame Muriel
Spartacus
Spassky, Boris
Spearman, Charles Edward
Speke, John Hanning
Spence, Sir Basil
Spencer, Herbert
Spencer, Sir Stanley
Spencer, Thomas
Spender, Sir Stephen
Spengler, Oswald
Spenser, Edmund
Speranski, Mikhail
 Mikhailovich
Spielberg, Steven
Spillane, Mickey
Spinoza, Benedict
Spitz, Mark (Andrew)
Spock, Benjamin McLane
Spohr, Louis
Spooner, William
 Archibald
Ssu-ma Ch'ien *variant*
 spelling of Si-ma Qian
Staël, Anne Louise
 Germaine Necker,
 Madame de
Stahl, Georg Ernst
Stainer, Sir John
Stalin, Joseph
Stamitz, Johann
Standish, Myles
Stanford, Sir Charles
 (Villiers)
Stanhope, Charles, 3rd Earl
Stanhope, James, 1st Earl
Stanislavsky, Konstantin

Stanisław, St
Stanley, Sir Henry Morton
Stanton, Elizabeth Cady
Stark, Dame Freya
  (Madeline)
Starr, Ringo
Staudinger, Hermann
Stauffenberg, Claus, Graf
  von
Steel, Sir David (Martin
  Scott)
Steele, Sir Richard
Steen, Jan
Stefan Dušan
Stein, Sir (Marc) Aurel
Stein, Gertrude
Stein, Karl, Freiherr vom
Steinbeck, John
Steiner, Rudolf
Steinmetz, Charles Proteus
Steinway, Henry
  (Engelhard)
Stendhal
Steno, Nicolaus
Stephen, Sir Leslie
Stephenson, George
Stephenson, Robert British
  civil engineer; compare
  Stevenson, Robert Louis
Stern, Isaac
Sternberg, Josef von
Sterne, Laurence
Stevens, Wallace
Stevenson, Adlai E(wing)
Stevenson, Frances
Stevenson, Robert Louis
  Scottish novelist; compare
  Stephenson, Robert
Stewart, Jackie
Stewart, James (Maitland)
Stewart, Rod
Stieglitz, Alfred
Stiernhielm, Georg
  Olofson
Stilicho, Flavius
Stilwell, Joseph W(arren)
Stirling, Sir James
Stockhausen, Karlheinz
Stoker, Bram
Stokes, Sir George Gabriel
Stokowski, Leopold
Stolypin, Petr Arkadievich
Stopes, Marie Charlotte
  Carmichael
Stoppard, Miriam

Stoppard, Tom
Storey, David
Storm, (Hans) Theodor
  Woldsen
Stoss, Veit
Stowe, Harriet Beecher
Strabo
Strachey, (Giles) Lytton
Stradivari, Antonio
Strafford, Thomas
  Wentworth, 1st Earl of
Stratton, Charles (known as
  Tom Thumb)
Strauss, Johann
Strauss, Richard
Stravinsky, Igor
Strawson, Sir Peter
  Frederick
Streep, Meryl
Streicher, Julius
Streisand, Barbra
Stresemann, Gustav
Strindberg, August
Stroheim, Erich von
Strong, Sir Roy (Colin)
Struve, Otto
Stuart surname of Scottish
  and English monarchs
Stuart, John McDouall
Stubbs, George
Stubbs, William
Sturluson, Snorri
Sturt, Charles
Stuyvesant, Peter
Suárez (Gonzalez), Adolfo,
  Duke of
Suarez, Francisco de
Suckling, Sir John
Sucre, Antonio José de
Su Dong Po (or Su
  Tung-p'o)
Sue, Eugène
Suetonius
Suger of Saint-Denis
Suharto
Sukarno
Suleiman
Sulla, Lucius Cornelius
Sullivan, Sir Arthur
Sullivan, John Lawrence
Sullivan, Louis Henry
Sully, Maximilien de
  Béthune, Duc de
Sully-Prudhomme, René
  François Armand

Sunderland, Robert
  Spencer, 2nd Earl of
Sun Yat-sen (or Sun Zhong
  Shan)
Suppiluliumas
Surrey, Henry Howard, Earl
  of
Surtees, John
Surtees, Robert Smith
Suslov, Mikhail
Sutcliffe, Herbert
Sutherland, Graham Vivian
Sutherland, Dame Joan
Sutton, Walter
  Stanborough
Suvorov, Aleksandr
  Vasilievich, Count
Sverrir (or Sigurdsson)
Svevo, Italo
Swammerdam, Jan
Swan, Sir Joseph Wilson
Swedenborg, Emanuel
Sweyn Forkbeard
Swift, Jonathan
Swinburne, Algernon
  Charles
Swithin, St
Symonds, John Addington
Symons, Arthur (William)
Synge, John Millington
Szabó, Istvan
Szell, George
Szent-Györgyi, Albert(von
  Nagyrapolt)
Szewinska, Irena
Szilard, Leo
Szymanowski, Karol
Tabari, Muhammad ibn
  Jarir al-
Tacitus, Cornelius
Taft, Robert Alphonso
Taft, William Howard
Tagore, Debendranath
Tagore, Rabindranath
Taine, Hippolyte Adolphe
Talbot, William Henry Fox
Taliesin
Talleyrand
Tallien, Jean Lambert
Tallis, Thomas
Tamerlane variant of Timur
Tancred
Tange Kenzo
Tanguy, Yves
Tanizaki Jun-ichiro

Tannhäuser
Tasman, Abel Janszoon
Tasso, Torquato
Tate, Allen
Tate, Harry
Tate, Nahum
Tati, Jacques
Tattersall, Richard
Tatum, Art(hur)
Tatum, Edward Lawrie
Tavener, John 20th-century
  British composer
Taverner, John
  16th-century English
  composer
Tawney, R(ichard) H(enry)
Taylor, A(lan) J(ohn)
  P(ercivale)
Taylor, Brook
Taylor, Elizabeth
Taylor, Frederick Winslow
Taylor, Jeremy
Taylor, Zachary
Tchaikovsky, Peter Ilich
Teach, Edward
Tebaldi, Renata
Teck, Mary of
Tecumseh
Tedder, Arthur William, 1st
  Baron
Teilhard de Chardin, Pierre
Te Kanawa, Dame Kiri
Telemann, Georg Philipp
Telesio, Bernardino
Telford, Thomas
Teller, Edward
Temple, Frederick
Temple, Shirley
Temple, William
Teng Hsiao-p'ing *variant*
  spelling of Deng Xiao Ping
Teniers, David
Tenniel, Sir John
Tennyson, Alfred, Lord
Tenzing Norgay
Terborch, Gerard
Terbrugghen, Hendrik
Terman, Lewis Madison
Terry, Dame Ellen (Alice)
Tertullian(us), Quintus
  Septimius Florens
Tesla, Nikola
Tetrazzini, Luisa
Tetzel, Johann
Teyte, Dame Maggie

Thackeray, William
  Makepeace
Thais
Thales
Thatcher, Margaret (Hilda),
  Baroness
Themistocles
Thenard, Louis-Jacques
Theocritus
Theodorakis, Mikis
Theodoric
Theodosius
Theophrastus
Thespis
Thibaud, Jacques
Thiers, Louis Adolphe
Thistlewood, Arthur
Thomas, Dylan
Thomas, Edward
Thompson, Emma
Thompson, Francis
Thomson, Sir George Paget
Thomson, James
Thomson, Sir Joseph John
Thomson, Kenneth Roy,
  2nd Baron
Thomson, Virgil
Thomson, William, 1st
  Baron Kelvin
Thomson of Fleet, Roy
  Herbert, 1st Baron
Thoreau, Henry David
Thorndike, Dame Sybil
Thornhill, Sir James
Thorpe, (John) Jeremy
Thorvaldsen, Bertel
Thrale, Hester Lynch
  (*maiden name* Piozzi)
Throckmorton, Francis
Throckmorton, Sir
  Nicholas
Thucydides
Thurber, James
Thutmose
Tibaldi, Pellegrino
Tiberius
Tibullus, Albius
Tieck, (Johann) Ludwig
Tiepolo, Giovanni Battista
Tiepolo, Giovanni
  Domenico
Tiglath-pileser
Tilak, Bal Gangadhar
Tillett, Benjamin
Tilley, Vesta

Tillich, Paul (Johannes)
Tilly, Johan Tserclaes, Graf
  von
Timoshenko, Semyon
  Konstantinovich
Timur (*or* Tamerlane)
Tinbergen, Jan
Tinbergen, Niko(laas)
Tintoretto
Tippett, Sir Michael
Tipu Sahib
Tirpitz, Alfred von
Tirso de Molina
Tissot, James Joseph
  Jacques
Titian
Tito
Titus (Flavius Vespasianus)
Tobey, Mark
Tocqueville, Alexis de
Todd, Alexander Robertus,
  Baron
Toghril Beg
Togliatti, Palmiro
Togo Heihachiro
Tojo Hideki
Tokugawa Ieyasu
Tolkien, J(ohn) R(onald)
  R(euel)
Toller, Ernst
Tolstoy, Leo (Nikolaevich),
  Count
Tom Thumb *see* Stratton,
  Charles
Tone, (Theobald) Wolfe
Tong Zhi (*or* T'ung-chih)
Tooke, John Horne
Torquemada, Tomás de
Torricelli, Evangelista
Tortelier, Paul
Toscanini, Arturo
Tostig
Totila
Toulouse-Lautrec, Henri
  (Marie Raymond) de
Touré, (Ahmed) Sékou
Tournefort, Joseph Pitton
  de
Tourneur, Cyril
Tours, St Gregory of
Toussaint-L'Ouverture,
  François Dominique
Townes, Charles Hard
Townshend, Charles, 2nd
  Viscount

Townshend, Pete
Toynbee, Arnold (Joseph)
Toynbee, (Theodore)
   Philip
Tracy, Spencer
Traherne, Thomas
Trajan(us), Marcus Ulpius
Traven, B(en) US novelist
Travers, Ben(jamin) British
   dramatist
Tree, Sir Herbert (Draper)
   Beerbohm
Trenchard, Hugh
   Montague, 1st Viscount
Trevelyan, George
   Macaulay
Trevelyan, Sir George Otto
Trevino, Lee
Trevithick, Richard
Trevor-Roper, Hugh
   Redwald, Baron Dacre
Trilling, Lionel
Trimble, David
Trollope, Anthony
Tromp, Cornelis
   (Martenszoon)
Tromp, Maarten
   (Harpertszoon)
Trotsky, Leon
Trudeau, Pierre Elliott
Trueman, Freddy
Truffaut, François
Trujillo (Molina), Rafael
   (Leónidas)
Truman, Harry S.
Truth, Sojourner
Tryggvason, Olaf
Ts'ao Chan *variant spelling*
   of Cao Chan
Tshombe, Moise (Kapenda)
Tsiolkovski, Konstantin
   Eduardovich
Tsvetaeva, Marina
Tubman, Harriet
Tubman, William
   V(acanarat) S(hadrach)
Tudjman, Franjo
Tu Fu *variant spelling of* Du
   Fu
Tull, Jethro
Tulsidas
T'ung-chih *variant spelling of*
   Tong Zhi
Tunney, Gene
Tupac Amarú

Tupolev, Andrei
   Niklaievich
Turenne, Henri de la Tour
   d'Auvergne, Vicomte de
Turgenev, Ivan
Turgot, Anne Robert
   Jacques, Baron de l'Aulne
Turishcheva, Ludmilla
Turner, Joseph Mallord
   William
Turner, Nat
Turpin, Dick
Tussaud, Marie
Tutankhamen
Tutu, Desmond
Tutuola, Amos
Twain, Mark
Tyler, John
Tyler, Wat
Tylor, Sir Edward Burnett
Tyndale, William
Tyndall, John
Tzimisces, John
Tz'u-hsi *variant spelling of* Zi
   Xi
Uccello, Paolo
Udall, Nicholas
Uhland, (Johann) Ludwig
Ulanova, Galina
Ulbricht, Walter
Umberto
Unamuno y Jugo, Miguel
   de
Undset, Sigrid
Ungaretti, Giuseppe
Updike, John (Hoyer)
Urban *pope*
Urey, Harold Clayton
Urfé, Honoré d'
Ussher, James
Ustinov, Sir Peter
   (Alexander)
Utagawa Kuniyoshi
Utamaro, Kitagawa
Utrillo, Maurice
Valdemar (*or* Waldemar)
Valens
Valentinian
Valentino, Rudolf
Valera, Eamon De
Valéry, Paul
Valla, Lorenzo
Valois, Dame Ninette de
Valois, Margaret of
Van Allen, James Alfred

Vanbrugh, Sir John
Van Buren, Martin
Vance, Cyrus
Vancouver, George
Vanderbilt, Cornelius
Van der Post, Sir Laurens
Van der Waals, Johannes
   Diderik
van de Velde, Adriaen
van de Velde, Esaias
van de Velde, Henry
van de Velde, Willem
van Dieman, Anthony
Van Dyck, Sir Anthony
Vane, Sir Henry
van Eyck, Hubert
van Eyck, Jan
Van Gogh, Vincent
Vansittart, Robert Gilbert,
   1st Baron
Van't Hoff, Jacobus
   Henricus
Vardhamana *see* Mahavira
Varèse, Edgard
Vargas, Getúlio
Vargas Llosa, (Jorge) Mario
   (Pedro)
Varro, Marcus Terentius
Vasarely, Victor
Vasari, Giorgio
Vauban, Sébastien Le
   Prestre de
Vaughan, Henry
Vaughan Williams, Ralph
Vavilov, Nikolai Ivanovich
Vega (Carpio), Lope Félix
   de
Velázquez, Diego Rodriguez
   de Silva
Vendôme, Louis Joseph,
   Duc de
Venizélos, Eleuthérios
Ventris, Michael
Vercingetorix
Verdi, Giuseppe
Verhaeren, Émile
Verlaine, Paul
Vermeer, Jan
Verne, Jules
Vernon, Edward
Veronese, Paolo
Verrocchio, Andrea del
Versace, Gianni
Verwoerd, Hendrik Frensch
Vesalius, Andreas

Vespasian
Vespucci, Amerigo
Vicente, Gil
Vicky *pen name of* Victor Weisz
Vico, Giambattista
Victor Emmanuel Italian king
Victoria, Tomás Luis de
Vidal, Gore
Vidal de la Blache, Paul
Vignola, Giacomo da
Vigny, Alfred de
Villa, Pancho
Villa-Lobos, Heitor
Villars, Claude Louis Hector, Duc de
Villehardouin, Geoffroi de
Villeneuve, Pierre
Villiers de l'Isle-Adam, Philippe Auguste, Comte de
Villon, François
Vincent de Paul, St
Viollet-le-Duc, Eugène Emmanuel
Virchow, Rudolf
Viren, Lasse Artturi
Visconti, Luchino
Vitruvius
Vittorini, Elio
Vittorino da Feltre
Vivaldi, Antonio
Vivekananda, Swami
Vivès, Juan Luis
Vladimir, St
Vlaminck, Maurice de
Volta, Alessandro Giuseppe Antonio Anastasio, Count
Voltaire
Vondel, Joost van den
Vonnegut, Kurt
Voroshilov, Kliment Yefremovich
Vorster, Balthazar Johannes
Voysey, Charles Francis Annesley
Voznesenskii, Andrei
Vuillard, (Jean) Édouard
Vyshinskii, Andrei Yanuareevich
Wace
Wade, Virginia
Wagner, (Wilhelm) Richard

Wagner, Siegfried
Wagner, Wieland
Wagner von Jauregg, Julius
Wain, John British novelist; *compare* Wayne, John
Wajda, Andrzej
Wakefield, Edward Gibbon
Waksman, Selman Abraham
Walafrid Strabo
Walburga, St
Walcott, Derek
Waldemar *variant spelling of* Valdemar
Waldheim, Kurt
Wałęsa, Lech
Waley, Arthur
Walker, Alice
Wallace, Alfred Russel
Wallace, Edgar
Wallace, Lew(is)
Wallace, Sir William
Wallenstein, Albrecht Wenzel von
Waller, Edmund
Waller, (Thomas) Fats
Wallis, Sir Barnes (Neville)
Walpole, Horace 4th Earl of Orford
Walpole, Sir Hugh (Seymour)
Walpole, Sir Robert, 1st Earl of Orford
Walsingham, Sir Francis
Walter, Bruno
Walter, Hubert
Walter, John
Walther von der Vogelweide
Walton, Ernest Thomas Sinton
Walton, Izaak
Walton, Sir William (Turner)
Wang An Shi (*or* Wang An-shih)
Wang Jing Wei (*or* Wang Ching-wei)
Warbeck, Perkin
Ward, Artemus
Ward, Barbara, Baroness Jackson
Ward, Mrs Humphry
Ward, Sir Joseph George
Ward, Sir Leslie

Warhol, Andy
Warlock, Peter
Warren, Earl
Warton, Joseph
Warton, Thomas
Warwick, Richard Neville, Earl of
Washington, Booker T(aliaferro)
Washington, George
Wasserman, August von
Waterhouse, Alfred
Watson, James Dewey
Watson, John Broadus
Watson, John Christian
Watson-Watt, Sir Robert Alexander
Watt, James
Watteau, (Jean) Antoine
Watts, George Frederick
Waugh, Alec (Raban)
Waugh, Auberon
Waugh, Evelyn (Arthur St John)
Wavell, Archibald Percival, 1st Earl
Wayne, John US actor; *compare* Wain, John
Webb, Beatrice (Potter)
Webb, Mary
Webb, Sidney (James), Baron Passfield
Weber, Carl Maria von
Weber, Ernst Heinrich
Weber, Max
Weber, Wilhelm Eduard
Webern, Anton von
Webster, John
Webster, Noah
Wedekind, Frank
Wedgwood, Dame Cicely Veronica
Wedgwood, Josiah
Weelkes, Thomas
Wegener, Alfred Lothar
Weil, Simone
Weill, Kurt
Weir, Peter (Lindsay)
Weismann, August Friedrich Leopold
Weiss, Peter
Weissmuller, Johnny
Weisz, Victor (*pen name* Vicky)
Weizmann, Chaim (Azriel)

Weldon, Fay
Welensky, Sir Roy
Welles, (George) Orson
Wellesley, Richard Colley, Marquess
Wellesz, Egon
Wellington, Arthur Wellesley, 1st Duke of
Wells, Henry
Wells, H(erbert) G(eorge)
Wenceslas
Wentworth, Thomas, 1st Earl of Strafford
Wentworth, William Charles
Werfel, Franz
Wergeland, Henrik Arnold
Wesker, Arnold
Wesley, Charles
Wesley, John
Wesley, Samuel
Wesley, Samuel Sebastian
West, Benjamin
West, Mae
West, Nathanael
West, Dame Rebecca
Westwood, Vivienne
Weyden, Rogier van der
Wharton, Edith (Newbold)
Wheatstone, Sir Charles
Wheeler, Sir (Robert Eric) Mortimer
Whistler, James (Abbott) McNeill
Whistler, Laurence
Whistler, Rex
White, Gilbert
White, Patrick
White, T(erence) H(anbury)
Whitefield, George
Whitehead, A(lfred) N(orth)
Whitelaw, William (Stephen Ian), 1st Viscount
Whitgift, John
Whitlam, (Edward) Gough
Whitman, Walt
Whitney, Eli
Whittier, John Greenleaf
Whittington, Dick
Whittle, Sir Frank
Whorf, Benjamin Lee
Whymper, Edward
Widor, Charles Marie

Wieland, Christoph Martin
Wiener, Norbert
Wiesenthal, Simon
Wigner, Eugene Paul
Wilberforce, William
Wilde, Oscar
Wilder, Billy
Wilder, Thornton
Wilkes, John
Wilkie, Sir David
Wilkins, Sir George Hubert
Wilkins, Maurice Hugh Frederick
Williams, John
Williams, J(ohn) P(eter) R(hys)
Williams, Roger
Williams, Shirley (Vivien Teresa Brittain)
Williams, Tennessee
Williams, William Carlos
Williams-Ellis, Sir Clough
Williamson, Henry
Williamson, Malcolm
Willis, Ted
Wills (Moody), Helen
Wilson, Sir Angus
Wilson, Charles Thomson Rees
Wilson, Colin
Wilson, Edmund US critic
Wilson, Edmund Beecher US biologist
Wilson, (James) Harold, Baron
Wilson, Sir Henry Hughes
Wilson, Henry Maitland, 1st Baron
Wilson, Richard
Wilson, (Thomas) Woodrow
Winckelmann, Johann Joachim
Wingate, Orde Charles
Winkler, Hans Günter
Winstanley, Gerrard
Winterhalter, Franz Xavier
Winthrop, John
Wise, Thomas James
Wiseman, Nicholas Patrick Stephen
Wishart, George
Wissler, Clark
Witt, Johan de

Witte, Sergei Yulievich
Wittgenstein, Ludwig
Wodehouse, Sir P(elham) G(renville)
Woffington, Peg
Wöhler, Friedrich
Wolf, Hugo
Wolfe, Charles
Wolfe, James
Wolfe, Thomas
Wolfenden, John Frederick, Baron
Wolf-Ferrari, Ermanno
Wölfflin, Heinrich
Wolfit, Sir Donald
Wolfram von Eschenbach
Wolfson, Sir Isaac
Wollstonecraft, Mary
Wolseley, Garnet Joseph, 1st Viscount
Wolsey, Thomas, Cardinal
Wood, Aaron
Wood, Enoch
Wood, Sir Henry (Joseph)
Wood, John
Wood, Ralph
Woodville, Elizabeth
Woodward, Robert Burns
Woolf, Leonard (Sidney)
Woolf, (Adeline) Virginia
Woollett, William
Woolley, Sir Leonard
Woolworth, F(rank) W(infield)
Wootton, Barbara, Baroness
Wordsworth, William
Wotton, Sir Henry
Wouwerman, Jan
Wouwerman, Philips
Wouwerman, Pieter
Wrangel, Ferdinand Petrovich, Baron von
Wrangel, Peter Nikolaievich, Baron
Wren, Sir Christopher
Wren, P(ercival) C(hristopher)
Wright, Frank Lloyd
Wright, Judith
Wright, Orville
Wright, Richard
Wright, Wilbur
Wu Hou
Wundt, Wilhelm

READ MORE IN PENGUIN

In every corner of the world, on every subject under the sun, Penguin represents quality and variety – the very best in publishing today.

For complete information about books available from Penguin – including Puffins, Penguin Classics and Arkana – and how to order them, write to us at the appropriate address below. Please note that for copyright reasons the selection of books varies from country to country.

In the United Kingdom: Please write to *Dept. EP, Penguin Books Ltd, Bath Road, Harmondsworth, West Drayton, Middlesex UB7 0DA*

In the United States: Please write to *Consumer Services, Penguin Putnam Inc., 405 Murray Hill Parkway, East Rutherford, New Jersey 07073-2136*. VISA and MasterCard holders call 1-800-631-8571 to order Penguin titles

In Canada: Please write to *Penguin Books Canada Ltd, 10 Alcorn Avenue, Suite 300, Toronto, Ontario M4V 3B2*

In Australia: Please write to *Penguin Books Australia Ltd, 487 Maroondah Highway, Ringwood, Victoria 3134*

In New Zealand: Please write to *Penguin Books (NZ) Ltd, Private Bag 102902, North Shore Mail Centre, Auckland 10*

In India: Please write to *Penguin Books India Pvt Ltd, 11 Community Centre, Panchsheel Park, New Delhi 110017*

In the Netherlands: Please write to *Penguin Books Netherlands bv, Postbus 3507, NL-1001 AH Amsterdam*

In Germany: Please write to *Penguin Books Deutschland GmbH, Metzlerstrasse 26, 60594 Frankfurt am Main*

In Spain: Please write to *Penguin Books S. A., Bravo Murillo 19, 1°B, 28015 Madrid*

In Italy: Please write to *Penguin Italia s.r.l., Via Vittorio Emanuele 45/a, 20094 Corsico, Milano*

In France: Please write to *Penguin France, 12, Rue Prosper Ferradou, 31700 Blagnac*

In Japan: Please write to *Penguin Books Japan Ltd, Iidabashi KM-Bldg, 2-23-9 Koraku, Bunkyo-Ku, Tokyo 112-0004*

In South Africa: Please write to *Penguin Books South Africa (Pty) Ltd, P.O. Box 751093, Gardenview, 2047 Johannesburg*

READ MORE IN PENGUIN

PENGUIN POPULAR REFERENCE

The **Penguin Popular Reference** series provides top quality reference titles at the keenest possible prices.

Pocket Dictionary of English Idioms – a close look at a vast range of idioms, providing clear definitions and explaining how they should be used.

Pocket Dictionary of Quotations – an immense array of quotations, including the literary, the biblical, the humorous, the serious and the momentous.

Pocket English Dictionary – contains more entries than any other popularly priced dictionary.

Pocket French Dictionary – an indispensable passport to the French language, containing over 75,000 entries.

Pocket Guide to English Usage – points out common errors in the way we write and shows us how to correct them.

Pocket Spanish Dictionary – modern, comprehensive, handy and convenient to use.

Pocket Spelling Dictionary – with over 100,000 spellings, a must for students and writers of English.

Pocket Students' Dictionary – a pioneering dictionary that defines phrases and expressions as well as individual words.

Pocket Thesaurus – ideal for everyone who wishes to extend their vocabulary, broaden their verbal range and spice up their linguistic dexterity.